D0742514

Music Industry Directory
formerly The Musician's Guide

Reference books published by Marquis Professional Publications

Annual Register of Grant Support
Biographical Directory of the Computer Graphics Industry
Biographical Directory of Online Professionals
Consumer Protection Directory
Directory of Certified Psychiatrists and Neurologists
Directory of Medical Specialists
Directory of Publishing Opportunities
Directory of Registered Lobbyists and Lobbyist Legislation
Environmental Protection Directory
Family Factbook
Grantsmanship: Money and How to Get It
Mental Health in America: The Years of Crisis
Music Industry Directory
NASA Factbook
NIH Factbook
NSF Factbook
Sourcebook of Equal Educational Opportunity
Sourcebook on Aging
Sourcebook on Death and Dying
Sourcebook on Food and Nutrition
Sourcebook on Mental Health
Standard Education Almanac
Standard Medical Almanac
Yearbook of Adult and Continuing Education
Yearbook of Higher Education
Yearbook of Special Education
Worldwide Directory of Computer Companies
Worldwide Directory of Federal Libraries

Music Industry Directory

formerly The Musician's Guide

Seventh Edition
1983

Marquis Professional Publications
Marquis Who's Who, Inc.
200 East Ohio Street
Chicago, Illinois 60611

International Standard Book Number: 0-8379-5602-1
Product Code Number: 031124

Manufactured in the United States of America
1 2 3 4 5 6 7 8 9 10

Preface

The Seventh Edition of *Music Industry Directory* (formerly *The Musician's Guide*) provides comprehensive coverage of the music industry. It contains descriptive listings for service and professional organizations, schools and colleges, competitions, periodicals, festivals, libraries, and foundations, as well as addresses and phone numbers for hundreds of music businesses.

Divided into seven parts for easy reference, *Music Industry Directory* is a practical source of current information for anyone who has an interest in music and the music business—students, teachers, performers, music publishers and songwriters, radio and television personnel. Information for this edition has been obtained primarily through responses to questionnaires, original sources, or staff research.

Part I: Organizations and Councils includes service and professional music associations in the United States and Canada; directories of state arts agencies and advocacy organizations; and locals of the American Federation of Musicians of the United States and Canada. **Part II: Competitions, Awards, and Grants** covers national and international music competitions; awards and scholarships sponsored by or listed with the National Federation of Music Clubs; and foundations and grant-making organizations whose support includes the field of music. In **Part III: Education** are listings for United States and Canadian two-year and four-year institutions offering at least an Associate degree in music; non-degree granting music schools and conservatories; and a chart covering ten career areas and over fifty specialties in the music field.

Descriptive listings of music libraries in the United States and Canada begin **Part IV: Resources.** This is followed by national and international music periodicals; and publishers of reference works, trade books, textbooks, and monographs in the field of music or the performing arts. **Part V: Performance** includes United States and Canadian symphony orchestras and opera companies, musical theatre companies, and workshops, coded by annual operating budget or classification. Also listed are national and international music festivals. **Part VI: Profession** covers music editors and critics for United States and Canadian newspapers; affiliated chapters of Volunteer Lawyers for the Arts; and booking agents, theatrical agents, and personal managers in the United States and Canada. The last section, **Part VII: Trade and Industry,** lists record companies; independent record producers; and music publishers affiliated with ASCAP, BMI, and SESAC.

Each section is arranged alphabetically by country. In those sections where the entries are listed by state or province and, in some cases, by city, an alphabetical cross-index immediately follows the section. A general index completes the volume.

We are grateful to the many individuals and organizations whose generous cooperation and assistance made the compilation of this directory possible; and in particular to National Assembly of State Arts Agencies; American Federation of Musicians; National Federation of Music Clubs; National Association of Schools of Music; National Guild of Community Schools of the Arts; Music Educators National Conference; Music Teachers National Association; Music Library Association; International Association of Music Libraries; National Library of Canada; American Symphony Orchestra League; Central Opera Service; Music Critics Association; Volunteer Lawyers for the Arts; International Theatrical Agencies Association; ASCAP; BMI; SESAC; and the many individuals who answered our questionnaires.

Marquis Professional Publications, a division of Marquis Who's Who, Inc., strives to provide the reader with comprehensive, up-to-date information in the field of music. The staff of Marquis Professional Publications urges the users of this edition to inform us of corrections or additions to existing entries and to suggest future improvements.

Contents

I. ORGANIZATIONS AND COUNCILS

Music Associations/Societies
State Arts Agency Directory
State Arts Advocacy Organizations
American Federation of Musicians Locals

Music Associations/Societies

U.S. and Canadian associations and societies are listed alphabetically within each country. Phone number, officers, purpose and activities, and publications are given for most organizations. The number 1 following an organization's name indicates that they did not respond to our questionnaire. The symbols *, †, and ‡ following an organization's name indicate membership.

- * Member organization of National Music Council (NMC)
- † Affiliate organization of National Federation of Music Clubs (NFMC)
- ‡ Organization associated with Music Educators National Conference (MENC)

A

ACADEMY OF COUNTRY MUSIC
PO Box 508
Hollywood, CA 90028
(213) 462-2351
Officers: Johnny Mosley, President; Fran Boyd, Executive Secretary
Purpose and Activities: Dedicated to the promotion and enhancement of country music worldwide. The Academy holds a quarterly membership meeting, with members entertaining, and sponsors special events. The annual awards presentation is aired over national television.
Publication: *ACM Newsletter* (monthly; free to members)

ACADEMY OF WIND AND PERCUSSION ARTS[1]
PO Box 6
Ada, OH 45810
(419) 634-7600
Officer: Alan H. Drake, Executive Secretary-Treasurer
Purpose and Activities: This division of the National Band Association recognizes individuals who make outstanding contributions of musical and educational significance to bands and band music. Annual convention is linked to NBA in December.

ACCORDION FEDERATION OF NORTH AMERICA, INC.
11438 Elmcrest St.
El Monte, CA 91732
(213) 686-1769
Officers: Larry Pino, President; Peggy Milne, Executive Secretary
Purpose and Activities: To encourage wider public interest in the accordion. To elevate moral, ethical and cultural standards of those interested in the accordion as teachers, studio or school operators, artists, composers, arrangers, instrument wholesalers, students, etc., thereby standardizing and coordinating the different phases of the accordion industry. To promote and elevate the accordion, with special effort to acquaint the public with its possibilities and advantages, and to improve teaching methods, and therefore, teaching standards. Holds four-day series of contests for students at all levels of study on an annual basis.
Publication: *Newsletter*

ACCORDION TEACHERS' GUILD, INC.[1]
18 Sibley Pl.
Rochester, NY 14607
(716) 271-7044
Officers: Mrs. Joan Cochran Sommers, President; Mrs. Betty Walker, Executive Secretary
Purpose and Activities: To raise the standard of the accordion, of accordion teachers, and of accordion teaching material. Sponsors annual accordion competitions, teachers' workshops, concert.
Publication: *Accordion Teachers' Guild Bulletin* (10 issues/year; members only)

ACTORS EQUITY ASSOCIATION
165 West 46th St.
New York, NY 10036
(212) 869-8530
Officers: Ellen Burstyn, President; Alan Eisenberg, Executive Secretary
Purpose and Activities: Theatrical union to protect actors' rights and welfare.
Publication: *Equity News* (monthly; free to members,$.25 to nonmembers)

AFFILIATE ARTISTS INC.[1]
155 West 68th St., Ste. 35F
New York, NY 10023
(212) 580-2000
Officers: Richard C. Clark, President; Anderson D. Clark, Senior Vice President; Nicholas J. Poliseno, Vice President
Purpose and Activities: This national not-for-profit organization, founded in 1966, is the leading producer of residencies for solo performing artists of all disciplines in the U.S. Residencies vary from one to seven weeks and are sponsored by corporations, foundations, and government agencies.

Special programs include (1) the Exxon/Arts Endowment Conductors Program, which places gifted young conductors in full-time residencies with America's major symphony orchestras and opera companies, and (2) the San Francisco/Affiliate Artists-Opera Program, which combines a full year of advanced training and performance opportunities at the San Francisco Opera with an Affiliate Artists Residency in a West Coast Community.
Publication: *Affiliate Artists News* (quarterly; free)

AFRO-AMERICAN MUSIC OPPORTUNITIES ASSOCIATION[1]
2801 Wazata Blvd.
Minneapolis, MN 55405
(612) 377-3730
Officer: C. Edward Thomas, President and Executive Director
Purpose and Activities: A non-profit organization founded in 1969, AAMOA hopes to contribute to the enrichment of the total musical life of America, by finding a way to cut through the social and economic obstacles preventing black musicians from participating in that musical life.
Publication: *AAMOA Reports*

AMATEUR CHAMBER MUSIC PLAYERS, INC.*
633 E. St., N.W.
Washington, DC 20004
(202) 628-0099
Officers: Donald R. Spuehler, Chairman; Mrs. Ruth McGregor, Honorary Secretary
Purpose and Activities: Publishes *Directory of Members* (North America and Overseas editions) to enable strangers to write or call each other for the purpose of playing chamber music.
Publication: *Newsletter* (1-2 /year; with membership)

AMATEUR ORGANIST ASSOCIATION INTERNATIONAL
7720 Morgan Ave. S.
Minneapolis, MN 55423
(612) 866-3421
Officers: Crane J. Bodine, President; Ernest J. Sampson, Executive Vice President
Purpose and Activities: To help beginners, intermediates and advanced organ players play better. This national club holds national and regional organ shows with all the stars of the pop organ world.
Publication: *Hurdy Gurdy* (bimonthly; $16.50/year)

AMERICAN ACADEMY AND INSTITUTE OF ARTS AND LETTERS
633 West 155th St.
New York, NY 10032
(212) 368-5900
Officers: Arthur Schlesinger, Jr., President; Margaret M. Mills, Executive Director
Purpose and Activities: To further the interest of literature and fine arts in the U.S., the Academy-Institute confers a series of awards.
Publication: *Yearbook; Annual Proceedings;* catalogues of arts and manuscript exhibitions.

AMERICAN ACADEMY OF TEACHERS OF SINGING[1]*
c/o William Gephart
75 Bank St.
New York, NY 10014
(212) 242-1836
Officers: Williard Young, Chairman; William Gephart, Secretary
Purposes and Activities: Dedicated to the improvement of the vocal profession, this organization's aim is to establish a professional code of ethics and to promote knowledge, culture, cooperation and good fellowship. Membership is limited to 40.
Publication: *Pronouncements* (song lists, etc) from time to time.

AMERICAN ACCORDIONISTS' ASSOCIATION*
580 Kearny Avenue
Kearny, NJ 07032
(201) 991-5010
Officer: Maddalena Belfiore Greco, President
Purpose and Activities: To encourage wider public interest in the accordion; to recognize outstanding ability and conspicuous service to the accordion industry.
Publication: *American Accordionists' Association Newsletter* (quarterly)

AMERICAN ACCORDION MUSICOLOGICAL SOCIETY
334 South Broadway
Pitman, NY 08071
(609) 589-8308
Officers: Sherrie Darrow, President; Joanne Arnold, Secretary
Purpose and Activities: Formed in 1969 to promote the accordion as a serious instrument, the Society sponsors an annual symposium and maintains a library of tapes, manuscripts and scores.
Publication: *Compendium*

AMERICAN ASSOCIATION FOR MUSIC THERAPY[1]*
35 West Fourth St.
New York, NY 10003
(212) 598-3491 or 598-3492
Officer: Dr. Kenneth Bruscia, President
Purpose and Activities: Fosters communications between and disseminates information about music therapy to its members. The organization also approves programs in music therapy and certifies music therapists.
Publications: *AAMT Newsletter* (quarterly; free to members); *Music Therapy* (annual; free to members)

AMERICAN BACH FOUNDATION
1211 Potomac St., Northwest
Washington, DC 20007
(202) 338-1111
Officer: Mrs. Raissa Tselentis Chadwell, Founder-President
Purpose and Activities: Founded "For the education and cultural development of students, teachers and the general public who may desire to avail themselves of such facilities as seminars, lectures, concerts and, in time, the facilities of a library of recordings and books on the music of J.S. Bach." The Foundation sponsors the J.S. Bach International Competitions.

THE AMERICAN BANDMASTERS ASSOCIATION
2019 Bradford Dr.
Arlington, TX 76010
(817) 261-8629
Officers: Frederick C. Ebbs, President; Jack H. Mahan, Secretary-Treasurer
Publication: *Journal of Band Research* (industry & institutions, $5)

AMERICAN BANJO FRATERNITY
2665 Woodstock Rd.
Columbus, OH 43221
(614) 451-3462
Officer: W.C. Kentner, Executive Secretary
Purpose and Activities: To promote the interests of the Classic Banjo: its history, instruments, music, and performers. The Classic Banjo is a 5-String Banjo, fitted with gut strings and played with bare fingers of the right hand; as played in concert and stage between 1870-1915.
Publication: *5-Stringer* (quarterly; $5 with membership)

AMERICAN CHORAL DIRECTORS ASSOCIATION‡
PO Box 5310
Lawton, OK 73504
(405) 355-8161
Officers: Maurice Casey, President; Dr. Gene Brooks, Executive Secretary
Purpose and Activities: Promulgation of choral ideas and techniques; cooperation with similar choral and vocal associations throughout the world. The organization holds a national convention and seven division conventions.
Publication: *The Choral Journal* (9 issues/year; $25 for members and nonmembers)

AMERICAN CHORAL FOUNDATION, INC.[1]
130 West 56th St.
New York, NY 10019
(212) 246-3361
Officer: Sheldon Soffer, President
Purpose and Activities: The organization publishes a research memorandum series and has a lending library for the use of its members, who are mostly choral directors.
Publication: *American Choral Review* ($22.50 for members and nonmembers)

AMERICAN COLLEGE OF MUSICIANS*
PO Box 1807
Austin, TX 78767
Officers: Irl Allison, Jr., President; Walter Merchant, Vice President
Purpose and Activities: To encourage artistic piano playing. Group sponsors Spring Private Auditions, Annual Composition Test, International Piano Competition and Van Cliburn International Quadrennial Piano Competition.
Publication: *Piano Guild Notes*

AMERICAN COMPOSERS ALLIANCE*
170 West 74th St.
New York, NY 10023
(212) 362-8900
Officers: Frank Wigglesworth, President; Francis Thorne, Executive Director
Purpose and Activities: Membership composers' works, subsidizes recordings, promotes radio broadcasts, prints catalogues of members' compositions, contracts, etc. Grants annual Laurel Leaf Award to

individuals and organizations "for distinguished achievement in fostering and encouraging American music."

The American Composers Alliance was instrumental in the founding of Composers Recordings, Inc. (1954) and the American Composers Orchestra (1976).

AMERICAN COUNCIL FOR THE ARTS
570 Seventh Ave.
New York, NY 10018
(212) 354-6655
Officer: Milton Rhodes, President; W. Grant Brownrigg, Executive Director
Purpose and Activities: To promote and strengthen the national's cultural activities by providing national leadership in innovative programs and services that have substantial impact on all the arts. Programs include a full range of publications including surveys, directories, financial management for the arts, and landmark books on such topics as the arts and local government; conferences and seminars; united arts fund raising; arts advocacy; cultural integration; management training; community development and information delivery.
Publication: *American Arts* (bimonthly; $15/year, $24/2 years)

AMERICAN DANCE THERAPY ASSOCIATION[1]
2000 Century Plaza, Ste. 230
Columbia, MD 21044
(301) 997-4040
Officer: Erma Alperson, President
Purpose and Activities: To develop and promote professional standards of education and clinical competence in the field and to facilitate communication among dance therapists through publications, conferences and regional groups.
Publication: *American Journal of Dance Therapy* (semi-annual; $11/year to members, $15/year to nonmembers, $20/year to libraries)

AMERICAN FEDERATION OF MUSICIANS*
1500 Broadway
New York, NY 10036
(212) 869-1330
Officer: Victor W. Fuentealba, President
Purpose and Activities: The Federation unites its local unions into a single influential organization that can speak with authority on behalf of professional musicians; enforces fair dealing; encourages good faith.
Publication: *International Musician* (monthly;$.60/year to members, $15 nonmembers in U.S.; $20 nonmembers in Canada; $25 foreign

AMERICAN FEDERATION OF TELEVISION & RADIO ARTISTS (AFTRA)
1350 Avenue of the Americas
New York, NY 10019
(212) 265-7700
Officers: Bill Hillman, President; Sanford I. Wolff, National Executive Secretary
Purpose and Activities: Labor organization covering performers in radio, television, commercials, phonograph recordings, slide film, and cassettes.
Publication: *AFTRA* (quarterly; free)

AMERICAN FOLKLORE SOCIETY, INC.[1]
Milton S. Hershey Medical Center
Pennsylvania State University
Hershey, PA 17033
(202) 232-8800
Officer: Charles Camp, Executive Secretary-Treasurer
Purpose and Activities: Founded in 1888 for individuals and institutes interested in collecting and publishing folklore.
Publication: *American Folklore Newsletter* (quarterly) and *Journal of American Folklore* (quarterly)

AMERICAN FRIENDS OF SCOTTISH OPERA, INC.
281 Park Ave. S.
New York, NY 10010
(212) 674-7491
Officers: Wallace S. Jones, Esq., President; Miss Duncan MacDonald, Executive Vice President
Purpose and Activities: To build support for Scottish Opera (Glasgow) in America.
Publication: *NEWS from Theatre Royal and Scottish Opera* (quarterly; $15/year)

AGAC/THE SONGWRITERS GUILD*
40 West 57th St.
New York, NY 10019
(212) 757-8833
Officers: George David Weiss, President; Lewis M. Bachman, Executive Director
Purpose and Activities: The Guild represents writers in their dealings with publishers; audits on their behalf; notifies them of copyrights coming up for renewal; sponsors fair, uniform contracts.
Publication: *AGAC News* (semi-annual; free to members)

THE AMERICAN GUILD OF ENGLISH HANDBELL RINGERS, INC.
601 W. Riverview Ave.
Dayton, OH 45406
(513) 223-5065
Officers: David R. Davidson, President; Andrew L. Flanagan, Executive Director
Purpose and Activities: Nonprofit organization established in 1954 to promote the art of English handbell ringing. Strives to stimulate the exchange of ideas related to techniques of ringing, composing and arranging handbell music, conducting, and other pertinent information through national and area festivals.
Publication: *Overtones* (6/year; free with membership)

AMERICAN GUILD OF MUSIC
PO Box 3
Downers Grove, IL 60515
(312) 968-0173
Officers: Leonard Mostek, President; Elmer Herrick, Executive Secretary
Purpose and Activities: To encourage music of all types; to educate and train better teachers; to improve educational materials.
Publication: *American Guild Associate News* (every 2-3 months; free with membership only)

AMERICAN GUILD OF MUSICAL ARTISTS*
1841 Broadway
New York, NY 10019
(212) 265-3687
Officers: Don Yule, President; Gene Boucher, National Executive Secretary
Purpose and Activities: A national labor union having jurisdiction over the professional entertainment fields of opera, ballet, dance, concert, recital, and oratorio. Its purpose is to secure for its members greater economic security, better employment conditions, protection from unfair practices, and fairer standards of compensation.
Publication: *Agmazine*

AMERICAN GUILD OF ORGANISTS*
815 Second Ave., Ste. 318
New York, NY 10017
(212) 687-9188
Officers: Edward Hansen, AAGO, President; Daniel N. Colburn II, Executive Director
Purpose and Activities: To advance the cause of organ and choral music, to increase their contributions to aesthetic and religious experiences, and to promote their understanding, appreciation and enjoyment. To improve the proficiency of organists and conductors, and evaluate attainments by examination and granting certificates. There are 310 local chapters nationwide.
Publication: *The American Organist* (monthly; free to members, $20/year to nonmembers)

AMERICAN GUILD OF VARIETY ARTISTS[1]
184 Fifth Ave.
New York, NY 10010
(212) 675-1003
Officer: Alan Jan Nelson, Executive President
Purpose and Activities: Represents performers in the night club, variety, circus, fair and allied fields in the U.S. and Canada.
Publication: *AGVA News* (sporadic; free)

AMERICAN HARP SOCIETY, INC.*
6331 Quebec Dr.
Hollywood, CA 90068
(213) 463-0716
Officer: Dorothy Remsen, Office Manager
Purpose and Activities: For further appreciation of the harp as an instrument; to raise the quality of harp performance, composition and manufacture. The organization sponsors competitions, student recitals, scholarships and grants (in performance and composition), and holds a national conference with workshops.
Publication: *American Harp Journal* (2 issues/year; $15 for members and nonmembers)

AMERICAN INSTITUTE FOR VERDI STUDIES
Department of Music
New York University
Faculty of Arts and Sciences
24 Waverly Pl.
Room 268
New York, NY 10003
Officer: Dr. Martin Chusid, Director
Purpose and Activities: For people interested in the works of Giuseppe Verdi.
Publication: *Verdi Newsletter* (annually; free to members; $7.50 others)

AMERICAN INTERNATIONAL MUSIC FUND[1]
415 Madison Ave.
New York, NY 10017
(212) 752-5300
Purpose and Activities: To bring attention to the new symphonic repertoire and to promote wider performance and appreciation of works of composers during their lifetime, through Tape Recording Project and the Koussevitsky International Recording Award.

THE AMERICAN LISZT SOCIETY, INC.[1]*
One E. Mt. Vernon Pl.
Peabody Institute
Johns Hopkins University
Baltimore, MD 21202
(301) 935-5655
Officer: Prof. Fernando Laires, President
Purpose and Activities: To promote scholarship and general understanding of the full creative and historical significance of Franz Liszt in the development of 19th and 20th century western culture. Annual festivals are held, as well as regular conferences.
Publication: *Journal of the American Liszt Society*

AMERICAN MATTHAY ASSOCIATION*
2142 Chinook Trail
Maitland, FL 32751
(305) 645-4628
Officers: Dr. Gary Wolf, President
Purpose and Activities: To foster the principles of Tobias Matthay in teaching and playing the piano; to encourage a high standard of performance and teaching.
Publication: *The Matthay News* (3 issues/year; sent only to members and friends)

AMERICAN MUSICAL INSTRUMENT SOCIETY[1]
Shrine to Music Museum
PO Box 194
University of South Dakota
Vermillion, SD 57069
(605) 677-5306
Officer: Andre Larson, President
Purpose and Activities: International organization that promotes the study of the history, design and use of musical instruments in all cultures and from all periods.
Publication: *The Journal of the American Musical Instrument Society* (annual; $18/year; *Newsletter* (3 issues/year)

AMERICAN MUSIC CENTER, INC.*
250 West 54th St., Room 300
New York, NY 10019
(212) 247-3121
Officers: Donald Erb, President; Margaret F. Jory, Executive Director
Purpose and Activities: A non-profit service organization formed to foster and encourage the composition of contemporary music and to promote its production, distribution and performance in every possible way.

The Center is the official U.S. Music Information Center. It has a library of 18,000 unpublished and published scores, sound recordings, composer biographical files, informational files on performing ensembles, music organizations and publishers of American music.
Publication: *American Music Center Newsletter* (quarterly; free to members; $7.50/year nonmembers)

AMERICAN MUSIC CONFERENCE*
1000 Skokie Blvd.
Wilmette, IL 60091
(312) 251-1600
Officers: J. Roman Babiak, Executive Director
Purpose and Activities: Noncommercial, not-for-profit service organization supported by the music industry to advance music participation in the U.S.

AMERICAN MUSICOLOGICAL SOCIETY
201 S. 34th St.
Philadelphia, PA 19104
Officers: Richard Crawford, President; Alvin H. Johnson, Executive Director
Purpose and Activities: The advancement of research in the various fields of music as a branch of learning and scholarship. The Society publishes matter pertinent to its interest. It meets annually; its 15 chapters meet more often.
Publication: *Journal of the American Musicological Society* (3 issues/year; $25 for members and nonmembers)

AMERICAN ORFF-SCHULWERK ASSOCIATION*
Department of Music
Cleveland State University
Cleveland, OH 44115
(216) 543-5366
Officers: Janice Rapley, President; Cindi Wobig, Executive Secretary
Purpose and Activities: To demonstrate Orff-Schulwerk's vitality and relevance to American music education; to disseminate news and ideas in regard to Schulwerk's philosophies and activities. The Association has 64 regional chapters and holds an annual national conference.
Publication: *The Orff Echo* (quarterly; free with membership only)

AMERICAN SCHOOL BAND DIRECTORS ASSOCIATION[1]
c/o Ernest M. Boling, Jr.
Box 349
Merigold, MS 38759
Officer: Ernest M. Boling, Jr., President

AMERICAN SOCIETY OF MUSIC ARRANGERS
P.O. Box 11
Hollywood, CA 90028
Officer: Billy May, President
Purpose and Activities: To represent arrangers and orchestrators within the AFM. To educate the public as to the function of arrangers and orchestrators. To promote interaction between members by organizing social functions. To educate through workshops and teaching clinics. To recognize outstanding achievement in the field with the presentation of the Golden Score award.

AMERICAN SOCIETY FOR AESTHETICS
C.W. Post Center of Long Island University
Greenvale, NY 11548
(516) 299-2341
Officers: John Hospers, President; Arnold Berleant, Secretary-Treasurer
Purpose and Activities: To promote study, research, discussion and publication in aesthetics. The term "aesthetics" is understood to include all studies of the arts (visual arts, literature, music, and theater arts) and related types of experience from a philosophic, scientific or other theoretical standpoint, including those of psychology, sociology, anthropology, cultural history, art criticism, and education.
Publication: *Journal of Aesthetics and Art Criticism* (quarterly; $20/year)

AMERICAN SOCIETY OF ANCIENT INSTRUMENTS
1205 Blythe Ave.
Drexel Hill, PA 19026
(215) 789-1205
Officer: Fred J. Stad
Purpose and Activities: An ensemble of five instrumentalists (four viols and a harpsichord) that presents "musical treasures"—great, but seldom heard, pre-18th century music played on the authentic instruments for which it was written. Annual Festival of several concerts, usually with guest artists, lecturers, symposia and other concerts.

AMERICAN STRING TEACHERS ASSOCIATION, INC.*†‡
UGA Station Box 2066
Athens, GA 30602
(404) 542-5254, x48
Officers: Prof. Lucas Drew, President; J. Kimball Harriman, Executive Director
Purpose and Activities: A musical and educational organization serving string, guitar, orchestra teachers, and players and students. It promotes and encourages professional and amateur string and orchestra study, performance, teacher education, research, and pedagogy.
Publication: *American String Teacher* (quarterly; free to members)

AMERICAN SYMPHONY ORCHESTRA LEAGUE*
633 E St., NW
Washington, DC 20004
(202) 628-0099
Officer: Catherine French, Chief Executive Officer
Purpose and Activities: A national service organization, chartered by Congress, for North America's symphony orchestras. The purpose of the League is to ensure the artistic excellence and administrative effectiveness of its constituents.
Publication: *Symphony Magazine* (bimonthly; $25 with membership; $15 library subscription)

AMERICAN THEATRE ASSOCIATION[1]
1000 Vermont Ave., NW, Ste. 902
Washington, DC 20005
(202) 628-4634
Officers: David Gooder, President; Dr. Jack Morrison, Executive Director
Purpose and Activities: A national, nonprofit theatre association comprised of divisions concerned with community, senior adult and children's theatre, as well as the spectrum of educational theatre. It publishes three journals, two newsletters and various special reports. Major activities include nine regional and one national convention, a placement service and national festivals of university and community theatres.
Publication: *Theatre News* (nine times annually, $7.50 per year)

AMERICAN THEATRE ORGAN SOCIETY, INC.
National Headquarters
PO Box 43
Olivenhain, CA 92024
(619) 727-6534
Officer: Lois F. Segur, President
Purpose and Activities: To preserve and further the use and understanding of the theatre pipe organ and its music.
Publication: *Theatre Organ* (bimonthly; $20 with membership)

AMERICAN UNION OF SWEDISH SINGING[1]
c/o Nelson World Travel Bureau, Inc.
333 N. Michigan Ave.
Chicago, IL 60601
(312) 236-0577
Officer: Martin Ahlm, Secretary
Purpose and Activities: To promote Swedish songs, male choruses and quartets.
Publication: *Misiktidning* (ten issues annually)

AMERICAN VIOLA SOCIETY/AMERICAN CHAPTER OF THE INTERNATIONAL VIOLA RESEARCH SOCIETY
512 Roosevelt Blvd.
Ypsilanti, MI 48197
(313) 482-6288
Officer: Dr. Maurine W. Riley, President
Purpose and Activities: To promote and further the history, musical literature, performance, and all research activities related to the viola.
Publication: *Newsletter* (2 issues/year); *Yearbook* (annual)

AMERICA'S BOYCHOIR FEDERATION
Div. of International Federation of Children's Choirs
PO Box 677
125 S. Fourth St.
Connellsville, PA 15425
(412) 696-3636
Officer: Rodolfo Torres, President
Publication: *America's Boychoir Federation Newsletter* (quarterly; $8/year)

AMUSEMENT AND MUSIC OPERATORS ASSOCIATION
2000 Spring Rd.
Oak Brook, IL 60521
(312) 654-2662
Officers: Wesley S. Lawson, President; Leo A. Droste, Executive Vice President
Purpose and Activities: National trade association of operators, distributors and manufacturers of coin-operated games and music (jukeboxes) equipment. Sponsor National Jukebox Awards (annual) and International Exposition of Games and Music; publish special reports; and represent the industry to Congress and Federal agencies.
Publication: *The Location* (newsletter; monthly; members only)

ASCAP (AMERICAN SOCIETY OF COMPOSERS, AUTHORS AND PUBLISHERS)*
One Lincoln Plaza
New York, NY 10023
(212) 595-3050
Officer: Hal David, President
Purpose and Activities: Performing rights society whose members include more than 17,500 men and women who write our nation's music and their 6,500 publishers.
Publication: *ASCAP in Action* (3 issues/year; free)

ASSOCIATED ACTORS & ARTISTES OF AMERICA
165 West 46th St.
New York, NY 10036
(212) 869-0358
Officer: Frederick O'Neal, President
Purpose and Activities: An international union of entertainment unions, including the American Guild of Music Artists.

ASSOCIATED MALE CHORUSES OF AMERICA, INC.
106 Maplefield
Pleasant Ridge, MI 48069
(313) 544-1995
Officers: Robert Anderson, Sr., President; Russell R. Fleharty, Executive Secretary
Purpose and Activities: To help extend male chorus singing among the men of North America and to promote fellowship, good will and cooperation.
Publication: *The Chorister* (nine issues annually, $7.50 per year for associate members)

ASSOCIATION FOR THE ADVANCEMENT OF CREATIVE MUSICIANS, INC.
PO Box 5757
Chicago, IL 60680
(312) 752-2212
Officers: Douglas R. Ewart, President; Janis C. Lane, Administrator
Purpose and Activities: Cultivation of musicians in order to create music of a high artistic level; conducting a music training program for inner-city young people; encouraging sources of employment for worthy, creative musicians; contributing financially to charitable organizations; stimulating spiritual growth in creative artists through participation in concerts, recitals; and to uphold the tradition of elevated, cultured musicians handed down from the past.

ASSOCIATION FOR RECORDED SOUND COLLECTIONS
PO Box 1643
Manassas, VA 22110
(703) 361-3901
Officers: Tim Brooks, President; Les Waffen, Executive Secretary

Purpose and Activities: An organization of collectors, private and institutional, dedicated to the exchange and dissemination of information on all aspects of the gathering and preservation of recorded sound.
Publications: *ARSC Journal* (3 issues/year; with membership); *Newsletter* (quarterly; with membership); *Bulletin* (annual; with membership)

ASSOCIATION OF CHORAL CONDUCTORS[1]
130 West 56th St.
New York, NY 10019
(212) 246-3361
Officer: Sheldon Soffer, Administrative Director
Purpose and Activities: Nonprofit organization sponsored by The American Choral Foundation, Inc. and devoted to furthering the choral art by providing services for conductors of community, church, school, college and professional choral groups. Publishes Research Memorandum Series, supplements to articles and reports in the *American Choral Review.*
Publication: *American Choral Review* (quarterly; free with membership; $17.50 to nonmembers)

ASSOCIATION OF COLLEGE, UNIVERSITY AND COMMUNITY ARTS ADMINISTRATORS, INC.[1]
6225 University Ave.
Madison, WI 53705
(608) 233-7400
Officer: William M. Dawson, Executive Director
Purpose and Activities: An organization of educational institutions and community arts organizations whose representatives share information on the selection, presentation and promotion of the performing arts, and who are devoted to improving the quality and extent of such programming.
Publication: *ACUCAA Bulletin* (monthly; free with membership only)

ASSOCIATION OF CONCERT BANDS, INC.
19 Benton Circle
Utica, NY 13501
(315) 732-2737
Officers: Herbert L. Schultz, President; J. Edward Hacker, Executive Secretary
Purpose and Activities: To assist the adult band musician; to promote the growth and development of concert and community bands in America and abroad.
Publication: *Woodwind • Brass • Percussion* (8/year; $5 members; $9 nonmembers)

ASSOCIATION OF COUNTRY ENTERTAINERS[1]
PO Box 110208
Nashville, TN 37211
(615) 248-2809
Officer: Jean Shepard, Administrative Officer
Purpose and Activities: Improvement of working conditions and career opportunities and to help deserving performers in times of emergency. The organization also strives to contribute toward expansion of the country music industry.

ASSOCIATION OF PROFESSIONAL VOCAL ENSEMBLES (APVE)
1830 Spruce St.
Philadelphia, PA 19103
(215) 545-4444
Officers: Michael Korn, President; Janice F. Kestler, National Executive Secretary
Purpose and Activities: APVE is a national non-profit service organization created to promote the growth and quality of professional vocal ensembles and to encourage greater appreciation and enjoyment of vocal music by all segments of American society. The Association provides: advocacy,data, conferences/workshops, media projects, newsletter, researching, consultation, internship program, health insurance. Dues categories for membership in APVE range form $10 to $250.
Publication: *VOICE* (bimonthly; free to all members)

AUDIO ENGINEERING SOCIETY, INC.[1]
60 East 42nd St., Room 449
New York, NY 10017
(212) 661-8528
Officer: Donald J. Plunkett, Executive Director
Purpose and Activities: Promotes interests of audio engineers, holds three meetings annually.
Publication: *Journal of the Audio Engineering Society* (ten issues annually)

AUSTRIAN FORUM, INC.
11 East 52nd St.
New York, NY 10022
(212) 873-0672
Officers: Margaret Bush, President; Eva Dworecki, Executive Vice President, General Secretary
Purpose and Activities: Cultural exchange between Austria and the U.S.

AUTOMATIC MUSIC INSTRUMENT COLLECTORS' ASSOCIATION[1]
PO Box 387
LaHabra, CA 90631
Officer: D. Bromage, Publisher
Purpose and Activities: This forum for collectors of instruments using perforated music rolls encourages public education on the historical and cultural significance of these instruments and the need for their preservation and restoration.
Publication: *The AMICA* (10 issues/year; $15 to members)

B

BEYOND BAROQUE FOUNDATION[1]
Old Venice City Hall
681 Venice Blvd.
Venice, CA 90291
(213) 822-3006
Officer: Jocelyn Fisher, President
Purpose and Activities: To sponsor performances of music, dance and drama and to assist with festivals.
Publication: *Beyond Baroque Magazine*

BIG BANDS COLLECTOR'S CLUB
PO Box 3171
Pismo Beach, CA 93449
(805) 543-2952
Officers: Hank Jensen, President; Jeanne Scaief, Secretary
Purpose and Activities: To promote and preserve the music of the Big Band era and sponsor dances featuring the sounds of the Big Bands
Publication: *RATE News* (quarterly); $5 with membership

BLUEGRASS CLUB OF NEW YORK
380 Lexington Ave., Ste. 1119
New York, NY 10017
(212) 860-0865
Officer: Douglas Tuchman, President
Purpose and Activities: To promote Bluegrass and traditional country music in the metropolitan area. A year-round series of concerts is produced commercially by Douglas Tuchman.
Publication: *The Bluegrass Club of New York Newsletter* (monthly; $5 individual, $7 household)

BLACK MUSIC ASSOCIATION[1]
1500 Locust, Ste. 1905
Philadelphia, PA 19105
(215) 545-8600
Officers: Kenneth Gamble, Founder-President; Jules Mulamud, Vice President
Purpose and Activities: To further black music nationally and internationally.
Publication: *Inner Visions* (newsletter)

THE ERNEST BLOCH SOCIETY
Star Route 2
Gualala, CA 95445
(707) 884-3473
Officer: Colin Hampton, President; Lucienne Bloch Dimitroff, Secretary-Treasurer
Purpose and Activities: To develop a greater appreciation of the music of Ernest Bloch by encouraging more concerts, recordings, and performances of his works; to establish an archive of Bloch's recordings, scores, articles and letters.
Publication: *The Ernest Bloch Society Bulletin* (annually, $15.00)

BMI[1]*
320 West 57th St.
New York, NY 10019
(212) 586-2000

Officers: Edward M. Cramer, President; Russ Sanjek, Vice President-Public Relations
Purpose and Activities: The world's largest licensing organization represents over 55,000 affiliated writers and publishers in the U.S. and, by reciprocal agreements with foreign societies, around the world.
Publications: *BMI: The Many Worlds of Music* (quarterly; free to members, educational institutions, libraries)

THE BOHEMIANS - (NEW YORK MUSICIANS CLUB)
200 West 55th St.
New York, NY 10019
(212) 247-5332
Officers: Jascha Zayde, President; Brent Williams, Secretary
Purpose and Activities: Sponsors the Musicians Foundation, Inc., that helps needy musicians. Members are professional musicians and music teachers; nonprofessionals may become associate members.

LOUIS BRAILLE FOUNDATION FOR BLIND MUSICIANS
215 Park Ave., S.
New York, NY 10003
(212) 982-7290
Officer: Sheldon Freund, Executive Director
Purpose and Activities: Auditions, evaluates and counsels blind musicians and composers. Sponsors showcase concerts; musical instructions; training scholarships aid and special equipment, based on financial need.

BROADCASTING FOUNDATION OF AMERICA
404 Park Ave., S., Ste 1209
New York, NY 10016
(212) 679-3388
Officer: George E. Probst, Chairman
Purpose and Activities: Distributes tapes of the major music festivals of Europe, East Europe, Israel, Japan, U.S.S.R. and elsewhere for radio and other use; this includes the great classical festivals as well as jazz and occasional folk gatherings.

BRUCKNER SOCIETY OF AMERICA, INC.
PO Box 2570
Iowa City, IA 52244
(319) 338-0313
Officer: Charles I. Eble, President
Purpose and Activities: To promote interest in the works of Bruckner and Mahler.
Publication: *Chord and Discord*

THE BUSINESS COMMITTEE FOR THE ARTS[1]
1700 Broadway
New York, NY 10019
(212) 921-0700
Officer: Edward M. Strauss, Jr., President
Purpose and Activities: Promotes corporate aid to the arts; co-sponsors "Business in the Arts" awards.
Publications: *Arts-Business* (newsletter), *News* (quarterly), other books, monographs and pamphlets

C

CAMEO - CREATIVE AUDIO & MUSIC ELECTRONICS ORGANIZATION
10 Delmar Ave.
Framingham, MA 01701
(617) 877-4651
Officer: Larry Blakely, President
Purpose and Activities: CAMEO is a nonprofit organization made up of professional audio and music electronics equipment manufacturers. It is dedicated to the development and progress of this rapidly expanding market.

CANTORS ASSEMBLY
150 Fifth Ave.
New York, NY 10011
(212) 691-8020
Officers: Abraham B. Shapiro, President; Samuel Rosenbaum, Executive Vice President
Purpose and Activities: To promote and advance the traditions of Jewish religious worship and Conservative Judaism; to maintain high standards among Hazzanim as clergyman and to provide for their commissioning as Ministers of Religion; to preserve and enlarge the religious, liturgical, and sacred musical heritage of the Jewish People.
Publication: *Journal of Synagogue Music* (semiannual; $7.50 members; $12.50 nonmembers)

CATGUT ACOUSTICAL SOCIETY, INC.†
112 Essex Ave.
Montclair, NJ 07042
(201) 744-3051
Officers: Dr. Robert H. Scanlan, President; Dr. Carleen M. Hutchins, Permanent Secretary
Purpose and Activities: The Society sponsors research, development and construction of musical instruments, particularly of the violin family. A membership of interested laymen and professionals—performing musicians and musicologists, instrument makers, composers, scientists, engineers, educators.
Publications: *Catgut Acoustical Society Newsletter* (semiannual; members only, $15 individual, $25 library, $20 foreign)

CENTRAL OPERA SERVICE*
Metropolitan Opera, Lincoln Center
New York, NY 10023
(212) 799-3467
Officers: Robert L. B. Tobin, Honorary National Chairman; Elihu M. Hyndman, National Chairman; Martha F. Rich, Executive Director
Purpose and Activities: National organization for information on all aspects of opera, serving opera companies, workshops, educational organizations, national arts organizations, state and federal agencies, and foundations, as well as individuals active in the field. The organization holds annual national conferences and publishes special directories.
Publications: *Central Opera Service Bulletin* (quarterly; free to members, $15 to individuals, $30 to groups, $50 to institutions)

CHAMBER MUSIC AMERICA*
215 Park Ave., S.
New York, NY 10003
(212) 460-9030
Officers: Michael Jaffee, President; David Klein, Chairman
Purpose and Activities: National membership service organization created in 1977 to advance the interests of chamber music in all its forms. It serves as an advocate and coordinator for major initiatives in the field. Voting members include professional chamber ensembles, presenters of chamber music concerts, and chamber music training institutions.
Publication: *American Ensemble* (quarterly; $10/year)

CHINESE MUSICAL AND THEATRICAL ASSOCIATION[1]
181 Canal St.
New York, NY 10013
(212) 226-8744
Officer: Stanley S. Chiu, Executive Director
Purpose and Activities: Members perform Chinese classical music for charitable purposes.

CHINESE MUSIC SOCIETY OF NORTH AMERICA
National Headquarters
2329 Charmingfare
Woodridge, IL 60517
(312) 985-1606
Officers: Sinyan Shen, Ph.D., President; Yuan-Yuan Lee, Ph.D., Vice President
Purpose and Activities: To increase and diffuse the knowledge of theoretical and applied Chinese music. Many lectures and concerts are sponsored which heighten the understanding and appreciation of Chinese music among the music community and the public.
Publication: *Chinese Music* (quarterly; members free; $18, insitutions; $10 individuals.)

CHORISTERS GUILD
PO Box 38188
Dallas, TX 75238
Officers: Leonard Lilyers, President; John T. Burke, Executive Director
Purpose and Activities: To make the children's choir an effective force in the development of Christian character and worthy of musical respect; to train leaders; and to maintain a central office to which directors may turn for help and information.
Publication: *Choristers Guild Letters* (10 issues/year; $20/year)

CHURCH MUSIC ASSOCIATION OF AMERICA
548 Lafond Ave.
St. Paul, MN 55103
(612) 293-1710
Officer: Msgr. Richard J. Schuler, President
Purpose and Activities: The advancement of Roman Catholic liturgical music and providing members with professional help.
Publication: *Sacred Music* (quarterly; $10/year)

CHURCH MUSIC PUBLISHERS ASSOCIATION[1]
PO Box 4239
Washington DC, 20012
(616) 459-6900
Officer: Peter Kladder, Jr., President
Purpose and Activities: Promotes interests of Protestant Churches music publishers. Holds annual spring meeting.

CHUSEI KOTO SOCIETY OF IOWA
Music Department
Cornell College
Mt. Vernon, IA 52314
(319) 895-8811
Officer: Jesse G. Evans. President and Musical Director
Purpose and Activities: To stimulate, cultivate and propigate the study and enjoyment of the koto. The society also hopes to promote better understanding of the Japanese culture by giving concerts of koto music to acquaint the people of Iowa and surrounding states with Japanese music.

COLEMAN CHAMBER MUSIC ASSOCIATION
202 S. Lake Ave., Ste. 201
Pasadena, CA 91101
(213) 793-4191
Officers: Mrs. John Laufer, President; George Heussenstamm, Manager
Purpose and Activities: Presents chamber music concerts, children's concerts and youth concerts; sponsors a national competition for chamber ensembles; supports the music department of the Pasadena Public Library with books, records and building fund money.

COLLEGE BAND DIRECTORS' NATIONAL ASSOCIATION‡
Baylor University, School of Music
Waco, TX 76798
(817) 755-3571
Officers: H. Robert Reynolds, President; Richard L. Floyd, Secretary-Treasurer
Purpose and Activities: CBDNA is the MENC association for college band directors. It has six national divisions, geographically divided. Each year, the organization's roughly 900 members assemble for a conference, either at the divisional or at the national level.
Publications: *CBDNA Newsletter* (11/year; free with membership); *CBDNA Journal* (3/year; free with membership)

COLLEGE MUSIC SOCIETY*
University of Colorado
Regent Box 44
Boulder, CO 80309
(303) 492-5049
Officer: Craig Short, Executive Secretary
Purpose and Activities: A broadly based forum of communication within the academic music profession; devoted to the philosophy, content and practice of music teaching in higher education. Meets annually and publishes a variety of materials of use to the profession, including the *Directory of Music Faculties in Colleges and Universities.* Offers Faculty Placement services and a mailing labels service.
Publications: *College Music Symposium* (semi-annual; $14 to nonmembers); *Bibliographies in American Music.*

THE COMPANY OF FIFERS AND DRUMMERS
PO Box 318
Westbrook, CT 06498
Officers: Eldrick Arsenault, President; William Alexander, Secretary
Purpose and Activities: To perpetuate early American martial music. Committees for archives, muster aid, ancients fund, for building, education, jaybirds, music, travel, publications, membership, junior activities, company store.
Publication: *The Ancient Times* (quarterly; $4/year; $7/2 years; $9/3 years)

COMPOSERS' FORUM, INC.
One Fifth Ave.
New York, NY 10003
(212) 673-8794
Officers: Joel Chadabe, President; Hollis Headrick, Managing Director
Purpose and Activities: Composers' Forum was founded in 1935 for the purpose of helping composers gain recognition. Programs include six concerts annually, services to composers, and publications.
Publications: *The Directory* (annually; free to members); *New Music* (quarterly; free to members)

COMPOSERS RECORDINGS, INC. (CRI)
170 West 74th St.
New York, NY 10023
(212) 873-1250
Officers: David Olan, President; Carter Harman, Executive Director
Purpose and Activities: A nonprofit recording company dedicated to the promotion and preservation of 20th century serious music. Releases new disks of music by contemporary American composers and reissues records of historical importance deleted by commercial record companies at the rate of about 20 per year; all disks are permanently available.

COMPOSERS THEATRE
Div. of Composers & Choreographers Theatre, Inc.
225 Lafayette Street, Room 906
New York, NY 10012
(212) 925-3721
Officer: John Watts, President and Artistic Director
Purpose and Activities: Nonprofit, tax-exempt educational and cultural organization concerned with a better performance environment for contemporary American music (and modern dance), services to the field, and music (dance) programs in affiliation with the New School for Social Research.

CONCERT ARTISTS GUILD, INC.
154 West 57th Street
New York, NY 10019
(212) 757-8344
Officer: Dr. Jerome Bunke, Director
Purpose and Activities: A nonprofit organization devoted to the career development of young classical artists. Musicians are chosen to make recital debuts through annual auditions and are eligible for other professional engagements. Auditions are open to soloists (instrumentalists and vocalists) and ensembles. For audition application write to CAG; deadline is mid-January.

CONCERT MUSIC BROADCASTERS ASSOCIATION[1]
c/o WCLV
Terminal Tower
Cleveland, OH 44113
Officer: Robert Conrad, President
Purpose and Activities: To foster and promote the development of the arts of concert music broadcasting in all its forms, and to encourage and promote customs and practices that will strengthen and maintain the concert music broadcasting industry to the end that it may best serve the public.

CONNECTICUT TRADITIONAL JAZZ CLUB
44 Mead Street, Apt. 1
Stamford, CT 06907
Officer: R.Z. Najarian, President

CONTINUUM (PERFORMERS' COMMITTEE INC.)
333 West End Avenue, #16C
New York, NY 10023
(212) 873-3258
Officers: Cheryl Seltzer, President and Co-Director; Joel Sachs, Co-Director
Purpose and Activities: Performance of 20th Century music through concerts, workshops, lecture-recitals, etc.; other ancilliary activities in 20th century music.

COUNCIL FOR RESEARCH IN MUSIC EDUCATION
University of Illinois
1205 W. California
Urbana, IL 61801
(217) 333-1027
Officers: Robert Bays, President; Richard Colwell, Editor
Purpose and Activities: Disseminate results of research, compile data on graduate and research programs, publish a bulletin, monographs, and occasional paper.
Publication: *Council for Research in Music Education, Bulletin (quarterly; $10/year)*

COUNTRY DANCE AND SONG SOCIETY OF AMERICA
505 8th Avenue
New York, NY 10018
(212) 594-8833
Officers: J.F. Warner, President; Sue A. Salmons, Acting Chief Executive Officer
Purpose and Activities: Sponsors concerts, dances, weekend and week-long workshops. Maintains a library and a sales department. Publishes books and records.
Publication: *Country Dance and Song* (annual; free with membership); *CDSS News* (bimonthly; free with membership)

COUNTRY MUSIC ASSOCIATION, INC.*
PO Box 22299
Nashville, TN 37202
(615) 244-2840
Officers: Joe Galante, President; Mrs. Jo Walker, Executive Director
Purpose and Activities: A trade association that promotes the use and sale of country music worldwide through presentations, seminars, printed aids, surveys, awards, kits, newsletter and films.
Publication: *CMA Close-Up* (monthly; free with membership)

COUNTRY MUSIC FOUNDATION[1]
4 Music Square East
Nashville, TN 37203
(615) 256-1639
Officer: William Ivey, Director
Purpose and Activities: A nonprofit educational foundation dedicated to the preservation of country music. Owns and operates a museum, hall of fame, research library, audio lab, Studio B, a press, and country store; admission is charged for the museum hall of fame and studio.
Publication: *The Journal of Country Music* (3 issues/year; $10/year in the U.S., $13/year foreign)

COUNTRY MUSIC FOUNDATION OF COLORADO
PO Box 19435
Denver, CO 80219
(303) 936-7762
Officer: Gladys Hart, President
Purpose and Activities: Nonprofit Foundation to promote all facets of the country music industry, to provide new artists with information on the basic fundamentals essential for career advancement, and to groom up-and-coming talent. The organization holds an Annual Colorado Country Music Festival and a trade convention.
Publication: *Country Music Foundation of Colorado News Release* (6 issues/year; free with membership)

CREATIVE MUSIC FOUNDATION[1]
PO Box 671
Woodstock, NY 12498
(914) 338-7640
Officer: Karl Berger, Co-director
Purpose and Activities: To sponsor and develop musical expression in all forms. The concept for the Foundation grew from a desire to provide opportunities for musicians, composer/performers, students and audiences to pursue the highest levels of personal achievement in the creation, study and enjoyment of music and the allied arts regardless of styles or forms of expression favored by existing commercial or academic structures. Activities include colloquia, workshops, seminars, residency programs, performances and artist management services.
Publication: *OUTLOOK: the Creative Music Quarterly* (quarterly; free)

CULTURAL EXCHANGE SOCIETY OF AMERICA, INC. (CESA)
1410 York Ave., Ste. 2D
New York, NY 10021
(212) 628-6315
Officer: Bruno George Ronty, President
Purpose and Activities: To further the exchange of musical programs between the U.S. and other countries. The Society conducts lectures on the musical history of musicians' countries

D

DANCE FILMS ASSOCIATION
241 E. 34th St., Rm 301
New York, NY 10018
(212) 686-7019
Officer: Susan Braun, President
Purpose and Activities: Nonprofit organization that acts as an intermediary among the user, producer and distributor of audiovisual material. The Association maintains a film rental library; sponsors programs and an annual film and videotape festival on dance and the related arts; and has published the *Dance and Mime Film and Videotape Catalog.*
Publication: *Newsletter* (12 issues/year; with membership)

DELTA OMICRON INTERNATIONAL MUSIC FRATERNITY[1]*†‡
1352 Redwood Ct.
Columbus, OH 43229
(614) 888-2640
Officers: Jo Swindall Holt, President; Mrs. John Kuckuk, Executive Secretary
Purpose and Activities: To foster fellowship among musicians; to promote performance and appreciation of good music; and to encourage women musicians. Gives aid to worthy music students.
Publication: *The WHEEL of Delta Omicron* (4 issues/year; $3/year)

DETROIT WALDHORN SOCIETY[1]
1014 Marshfield
Ferndale, MI 48220
(313) 547-2751
Officer: Lowell Greer, Executive Officer
Purpose and Activities: To perform authentic instruments; to restore them or to construct replicas; and to discover neglected music for the valveless horn or waldhorn.

THE DUKE ELLINGTON SOCIETY, NEW YORK CHAPTER[1]
PO Box 31
Church Street Station
New York, NY 10008
(212) 469-4464
Officer: Charles L. Russell, President
Purpose and Activities: Meets monthly to listen to Ellington's music on records and tapes, with guest speaker who is, or has been, in some way related to the musical world of Ellington. Sponsors annual concerts devoted to Ellington's compositions.

F

FEDERATION OF WORKERS' SINGING SOCIETIES OF THE U.S.A.[1]
4085 Klepinger
Dayton, OH 45416
(513) 276-3322
Officer: Kurt J. Pfeil, President
Purpose and Activities: A federation of German-American choral groups.
Publication: *Saenger Zeitung* (ten issues annually)

FELLOWSHIP OF CHRISTIAN MUSICIANS
PO Box 55151
Tulsa, OK 74155
(918) 252-3862
Officer: Bill Anderson, Executive Secretary
Purpose and Activities: To provide encouragement for Christian musicians through fellowship meetings at music professional meetings; to prompt the formation of high school and college student chapters of FCM; to work together to be a positive influence in our profession, both on an individual and on an organizational level.
Publication: *FCM Newsletter* (3/year; free)

FELLOWSHIP OF UNITED METHODISTS IN WORSHIP, MUSIC & OTHER ARTS[1]
PO Box 840
Nashville, TN 37202
(214) 361-9386
Officer: Mrs. Patti Evans, Executive Secretary
Purpose and Activities: The Fellowship exists "to be a sharing and enabling fellowship that affirms the sacramental life embracing preaching, music, drama, dance, architecture, and all the visual arts appropriate for the inclusive life of the Church."
Publication: *News Notes* (monthly; $10)

FESTIVAL PLAYERS OF CALIFORNIA†
2449 Glendale Blvd.
Los Angeles, CA 90039
(213) 665-6444 or 666-4174
Officers: Dr. Dorye Roettger, Founder-Director; Marion E. Rutger, President
Purpose and Activities: Nonprofit educational fine arts organization providing school children and adults with arts experiences including fine music. Other services include concert and lecture series, classes, seminars and residencies for schools and community groups.

FINLANDIA FOUNDATION, INC.
1433 San Vicente Blvd.
Santa Monica, CA 90402
(213) 451-5147
Officer: Vaino A. Hoover, Ph.D., President
Purpose and Activities: Devoted to the cultural interchange of the U.S. and Finland and to bring to the attention of the people of the U.S. the music, art and literature of Finland. Gives scholarships in the field of music.
Publication: *Finlandia Foundation Newsletter* (bi-annually or annually; with membership)

FIRST CHAIR OF AMERICA, INC.
PO Box 125
Greenwood, MS 38930
(601) 453-1880
Officer: Roy M. Martin, President and Chairman
Purpose and Activities: A national honor recognition organization for music directors in the secondary schools of American and special recognition for the section leaders in the high school band in the 50 states.
Publication: *First Chair of America* (annual; $10 members; $25 nonmembers)

FOUNDATION FOR THE EXTENSION & DEVELOPMENT OF THE AMERICAN PROFESSIONAL THEATRE (FEDAPT)
165 West 46th Street, Suite 310
New York, NY 10036
(212) 869-9690
Officers: Vincent Beck, President of the Board; Frederic B. Vogel, Executive Director
Purpose and Activities: National not-for-profit service agency offering a process of Management Technical Assistance to professionally oriented theatre projects and dance companies in funding development, audience development, fiscal management, board structure and development, and any and all other areas of day-to-day management of a dance or theatre company.

FOUNDATION FOR RESEARCH IN THE AFRO-AMERICAN CREATIVE ARTS,INC.
PO Drawer I
Cambria Heights, NY 11411
Officer: Joseph Southern, President
Purpose and Activities: Disseminate information about black-American musicians and other musicians of African descent in Europe and Africa. Small grants are given when funds are available; in the past, such grants have been given to commission works from black composers, to college students engaged in relevant research, to an integrated symphony orchestra.
Publication: *The Black Perspective in Music* (semiannual; $7/year individuals; $8/year institutions; $10/year foreign)

FRETTED INSTRUMENT GUILD OF AMERICA
2344 South Oakley Avenue
Chicago, IL 60608
(312) 376-1143
Officers: Horis A. Warde, President; Ann Pertoney, Secretary-Treasurer
Purpose and Activities: Nonprofit organization founded to promote the fretted instruments banjo, mandolin, guitar and their kindred instruments and to preserve their out-of-print and current music. Conventions are held annually where workshops and concerts are given for the benefit of the membership.
Publication: *FIGA Magazine* (bimonthly; $12.50 U.S., $20 foreign)

G

GOSPEL MUSIC ASSOCIATION
PO Box 23201
Nashville, TN 37202
(615) 242-0303
Officers: Frances Preston, President; Donald W. Butler, Sr., Executive Director
Purpose and Activities: Promotion of Gospel music, service to industry. Publishes an annual directory.
Publication: *Good News* (monthly; members only)

GUILD OF AMERICAN LUTHIERS
8222 South Park Ave.
Tacoma, WA 98408
(206) 472-7853
Officer: Debra G. Olsen, Executive Director
Purpose and Activities: Nonprofit membership organization acts as a clearinghouse for information on the construction and repair of string musical instruments (guitars, lutes, banjos, harpsichords, etc) through quarterly journal and data sheets and biennial convention/exhibition.
Publication: *Guild of American Luthiers Quarterly* (quarterly; with membership)

THE GUILD OF CARILLONNEURS IN NORTH AMERICA (GCNA)
3718 Settle Rd.
Cincinnati, OH 45227
(513) 271-8519
Officers: William De Turk, President; Richard D. Gegner, Secretary
Purpose and Activities: The purpose of the Guild is to carry on such educational activities as may be appropriate (1) to promote the development of proficient carillonneurs by dissemination information useful to carillonneurs and by giving them the opportunity to discuss their common problems and to hear different styles of playing; (2) to improve the quality of carillon music by encouraging composition, assisting with arranging, issuing music for the carillon, and developing a standard of musical notation most helpful to the carillonneur; (3) to encourage the improvement of carillon installations by making available advice concerning desirable location, tower design and construction, and standards of keyboard construction and of bell tuning; and, in general, (4) to advance the art, the literature, and the science of the carillon in North America.
Publication: *Bulletin* (1 issue/year); *Carillon News* (2 issues/year)

GUILD OF TEMPLE MUSICIANS
6636 N. Talman
Chicago, IL 60645
(312) 761-1382
Officer: Judith H. Karzen, President
Purpose and Activities: Educational

organization of organists, music directors, soloists, teachers working in field of Jewish music (U.S. and Canada); yearly convention, seminars, newsletter; publications keep members abreast of latest developments and sources in Jewish music.
Publication: *GTM Newsletter* (biannual; $30)

GUITAR & ACCESSORY MANUFACTURERS ASSOCIATION OF AMERICA[1]
150 E. Huron
Chicago, IL 60611
(312) 266-7200

GUITAR FOUNDATION OF AMERICA‡
Box 5311
Garden Grove, CA 92645
Officers: John Schneider, President; Jim Forrest, General Manager
Purpose and Activities: Offers its members the combined advantages of a guitar society, a library, a publisher, a continuing education resource, and an arts council.
Publication: *Soundboard* (quarterly; $15 per year)

H

HARP RENAISSANCE SOCIETY[1]
1036 Beechwood Blvd.
Pittsburgh, PA 15206
(412) 661-6161
Officers: Dr. Samuel M. Hirshbein, President; Diana Salvi, Executive Secretary
Purpose and Activities: Research in the history of the harp as a solo instrument. To furnish up-to-date information useful in the writing of program notes and other studies.
Publications: *Harp Review* (annual); *Harp Bulletin* (monthly)

THE HYMN SOCIETY OF AMERICA, INC.[1]
Wittenberg University
Springfield, OH 45501
(513) 327-6308
Officers: W. Thomas Smith, Executive Director
Purpose and Activities: A national voluntary organization of 3,500 founded in 1922 to promote new hymns and tunes; to increase interest in writing texts and tunes; and to encourage the use of hymns by congregations of all faiths.
Publications: *The Hymn* (quarterly); *The Stanza* (semi-annually)

I

INSTITUTE FOR STUDIES IN AMERICAN MUSIC
Brooklyn College
Brooklyn, NY 11210
(212) 852-1270
Officer: H. Wiley Hitchcock, Director
Purpose and Activities: Contributes to American music studies by publishing monographs, bibliographies, discographies, and newsletter.
Publication: *I.S.A.M. Newsletter* (2/year; free)

THE INSTITUTE OF THE AMERICAN MUSICAL, INC.
121 N. Detroit St.
Los Angeles, CA 90036
(213) WE 4-1221
Officers: Miles Kreuger, President; Jonathan Paul Dyer, Associate Director
Purpose and Activities: Not-for-profit corporation that houses the world's largest archival collection of materials expressly on the American musical theatre and motion pictures—includes 35,000 disc, cylinder and tape recordings back to the 1890's; roughly 200,000 stills from films back to 1914; piano vocal scores and sheet music from musicals and operettas back to 1844; theatre playbills (mostly Broadway) and periodicals back to the 1880's; books on theatre, film, music, biography, broadcasting, world's fairs, New York City; phonograph record catalogues to the 1890's; specialized research files on theatre, film, personalities, etc. The collection is available by appointment to scholars and professional researchers. The Institute also produces public events, including film retrospectives and exhibitions, and engages in ongoing preservation activities. It plans to publish a quarterly periodical on the history of musical theatre and motion pictures, beginning in 1984.

INTER-AMERICAN MUSIC COUNCIL[1]
Technical Unit on the Performing Arts
Organization of American States
1889 F St., NW
Washington, DC 20006
Officer: Efraine Paesky, Secretary General

INTERCOLLEGIATE MUSICAL COUNCIL, INC.
Loyola Marymount University
West 80th & Loyola Blvd.
Los Angeles, CA 90045
(213) 642-2780
Officers: Thomas Sokol, President; Richard Trame, Executive Secretary
Purpose and Activities: To encourage and to improve male choruses and group male singing of the highest caliber in the universities, colleges, and preparatory schools of the U.S. and other parts of the world. To work for greater recognition of male musical activities on the campus and in the curricula.
Publication: *QUODLIBET* (3/year; $30/year with associate membership)

INTERLOCHEN CENTER FOR THE ARTS
Interlochen, MI 49643
(616) 276-9221
Officer: Roger E. Jacobi, President
Purpose and Activities: The purpose of the Center is to provide education in the arts and sciences for youth. The summer division National Music Camp (established in 1928) is an 8-week season offering intensive study in the arts (dance, drama, music, visual arts) to students from 8 years through college graduates at all levels from exploratory to pre-professional, along with a recreational and camping program. Over 1,500 students attend from 48 states and 21 foreign countries. The winter division Interlochen Arts Academy is a college preparatory boarding school offering intensive study in dance, drama, creative writing, music and the visual arts in addition to an enriched academic program. Established in 1962 it serves students in grades 9 through 12 from approximately 40 states and 12 foreign countries. Over 600 programs are presented annually. The Center owns and operates a 115,000-watt radio station, WIAA-FM, which is a charter member of NPR.
Publications: annual catalogs

INTERNATIONAL ALBAN BERG SOCIETY, LTD.
Ph.D. Program in Music
City University of New York
33 West 42nd St.
New York, NY 10036
Officer: Barbara Jazwinski, Secretary-Treasurer
Purpose and Activities: To promote the artistic heritage of Alban Berg, and facilitate performance and publication of his works, by fostering public interest, enlisting material support and encouraging relevant research.
Publication: *International Alban Berg Society Newsletter* (annually; $10 individuals; $15 institutions; $6 students)

INTERNATIONAL ASSOCIATION OF MUSIC LIBRARIES - UNITED STATES BRANCH
Northwestern University Music Library
Evanston, IL 60201
(312) 492-3434
Officers: Geraldine Ostrove, President; Don L. Roberts, Secretary-Treasurer
Purpose and Activities: Promote international activities relating to music librarianship and music bibliography.
Publication: *Fontes Artis Musicae* (quarterly; members only)

INTERNATIONAL ASSOCIATION OF ORGAN TEACHERS*
48 Maple Dr.
Bedford, NH 03102

(617) 472-5566
Officers: Paul Bordeleau, President; Emmitte Miller, Vice President; Bernard J. Wickenheiser, Secretary/Treasurer
Purpose and Activities: Foster improvement of organ teaching, materials and methods; measurement of student and teacher progress through annual organ playing evaluations and composition tests; foster all music/all stages/all organs/-all ages teaching workshops; provide communication and liaison among teacher-training and other professional and business elements; provide incentives and scholarships.
Publication: *The Organ Teacher* (5/year; free with membership)

THE INTERNATIONAL CLARINET SOCIETY
4611 Mounds Rd.
Anderson, IN 46013
(317) 643-2914
Officer: Jerry D. Pierce, President
Purpose and Activities: Nonprofit organization of performers, teachers, students, industry personnel and all others interested in focusing attention on the importance of the clarinet. Dedicated to supporting projects that will benefit clarinet performance. Provides an opportunity for the exchange of ideas, materials and information among members. Fosters the composition, publication, recording and distribution of music for the clarinet. The extensive I.C.S. Research Library is housed at the University of Maryland, College Park, MD 20742
Publication: *The Clarinet* (quarterly; free with membership)

INTERNATIONAL CONFERENCE OF SYMPHONY AND OPERA MUSICIANS[1]
RD No. 3
Export, PA 15632
(412) 327-0969
Officer: Stanley Dombrowski, Vice Chairman
Purpose and Activities: Affiliated with the American Federation of Musicians. Disseminates inter-orchestral information.
Publication: *Senza Sordino* (bimonthly)

INTERNATIONAL CONGRESS ON WOMEN IN MUSIC
PO Box 366
Loyola Blvd. at W. 80th St.
Los Angeles, CA 90045
(213) 248-1249
Officers: Jeannie G. Pool, President; Gertrude Rivers Robinson, Membership Chair
Purpose and Activities: Promotion and development of scholarship for women in music and for music composed by women; an international membership association which holds an annual conference/music festival.
Publication: *The International Congress on Women in Music Newsletter* (quarterly; $20/year)

INTERNATIONAL CONTEMPORARY MUSIC EXCHANGE[1]
58 West 58th St., Ste. 29B
New York, NY 10019
(212) 371-1858
Officer: Igor Buketoff, Director
Purpose and Activities: Dedicated to the enrichment of cultural life through the recognition and promotion of the best orchestral music of our time. Founded on the premise that the masterworks of tomorrow are being composed today, the Exchange is committed to the search for these masterworks, with the aim of making them easily accessible to the general public.

Currently expanding its activities, the organization plans to move its home office to Houston, TX, in the near future; this office will serve as the International Division. The New York office will continue to function as the American Division, concentrating on American contemporary music for American audiences, in addition to some international work.

INTERNATIONAL COUNCIL FOR TRADITIONAL MUSIC
(Formerly, International Folk Music Council)
Department of Music
Columbia University
New York, NY 10027
(212) 678-0332
Officers: Dr. Erich Stockmann, President; Prof. Dieter Christensen, Secretary General
Purpose and Activities: The Council assists in the study, practice, documentation, preservation and dissemination of traditional music, including folk, popular, classical and urban music and dance of all countries.
Publication: *Yearbook for Traditional Music; Bulletin of the ICTM* (Yearbook, annually; Bulletins, semiannually; individual membes $20.00, institutions $22.00)

INTERNATIONAL DOUBLE REED SOCIETY
Department of Music
Michigan State University
East Lansing, MI 48824
(517) 355-7727
Officer: Sol Schoenbach, President
Purpose and Activities: To give double reed players (oboists and bassoonists) a means and body through which communication can be fostered on a world-wide basis. This is done through four yearly publications and an annual meeting, featuring performances by the world's leading artists.
Publications: *The Double Reed* and the *Journal of the International Double Reed Society (The Double Reed,* 3/year; the *Journal,* once a year; $20; $10 students)

INTERNATIONAL FAN CLUB ORGANIZATION
PO Box 177
Wild Horse, CO 80862
(303) 962-3543 or 962-3506
Officers: Loudilla, Loretta and Kay Johnson, Co-Presidents
Purpose and Activities: Clearinghouse for fan clubs that assists in the planning stages, set-up and actual operational stages of a fan club; individual fan clubs, however, are maintained by presidents in offices other than the Organization's. The Organization sponsors fan-artists tours overseas and stages showcases for up-and-coming artists in various locales.
Publication: *International Fan Club Organization* (3/year; $10/year with membership)

INTERNATIONAL FEDERATION OF CHILDREN'S CHOIRS
PO Box 677
125 South Fourth St.
Connellsville, PA 15425
(412) 628-3939
Officer: Francis Delvin, President
Publication: *Newsletter* (quarterly; $8/year)

INTERNATIONAL HORN SOCIETY
1213 Sweet Briar Rd.
Madison, WI 53705
(608) 233-6336
Officers: Paul Anderson, President; Ruth Hokanson, Executive Secretary
Purpose and Activities: To establish contact between horn players of the world for the exchange and publication of ideas and research in all fields pertaining to the horn.
Publication: *The Horn Call* (2 /year; $15/year, $20/year overseas)

INTERNATIONAL LEAGUE OF WOMEN COMPOSERS*
PO Box 42
3 Mile Bay, NY 13693
(315) 649-5086
Officer: Elizabeth Hayden Pizer, President and Administrative Officer
Purpose and Activities: A nonprofit organization devoted to expanding opportunities for women composers of serious music in areas insufficiently accessible to them; promotes members' music through a quarterly newsletter, chamber music concerts, a radio series and advocacy activities; sponsors an annual Search for New Music by women student composers, with monetary awards and possible performance.
Publications: *Newsletter* $20/year professional musicians; $15/year institutions; $10/year seniors and composition students)

INTERNATIONAL PIANO GUILD
PO Box 1807
808 Rio Grande
Austin, TX 78767
Officer: Walter Merchant, Vice President
Purpose and Activities: The organization is a working part of the American College of Musicians.

INTERNATIONAL POLKA ASSOCIATION
4145 S. Kedzie Ave.
Chicago, IL 60632
(312) 254-7771
Officer: Richard F. Berkowicz, President
Purpose and Activities: An educational and social organization for the preservation and advancement of polka music; to promote, maintain and advance interest in polka music, dancing, and traditional folklore; to sponsor and present the annual international polka festival, and to honor personalities who have made outstanding contributions to the advancement of polka music.
Publication: *IPA News* (monthly; free to members)

INTERNATIONAL RHYTHM & BLUES ASSOCIATION
11616 South Lafayette
Chicago, IL 60628
Officer: William C. Tyson, President

THE INTERNATIONAL ROCK N' ROLL MUSIC ASSOCIATION, INC.
PO Box 50111
Nashville, TN 37205
(615) 297-9072
Officers: Bernard Walters, President; Deborah Hickman, Administrative Director
Purpose and Activities: To create a complete reference service for all aspects of rock 'n roll music; to organize the first complete rock 'n roll museum and library housing recorded sound and periodicals for research and reference, to hold slide shows, and exhibits on the history of rock 'n roll.
Publication: *The Communique* (6/year; $10 enthusiast; $9 student; $25 professional)

INTERNATIONAL SOCIETY OF BASSISTS[1]*
University of Cincinnati, College-Conservatory of Music
Cincinnati, OH 45221
(513) 475-5674
Officer: Barry Green, Executive Director
Purpose and Activities: The ISB has approximately 1800 members and publishes newsletters with current information on record reviews, recitals, new music, education news, symphony news, repair news, etc.
Publications: *ISB Newsletter* (3 issues/year); *Journal* (annual)

INTERNATIONAL SOCIETY OF PERFORMING ARTS ADMINISTRATORS[1]
James W. Miller Auditorium
Western Michigan University
Kalamazoo, MI 49008
(616) 383-0925
Officer: Gordon D. Smith, Secretary

INTERNATIONAL STEEL GUITAR CONVENTION
9535 Midland Boulevard
Overland, MO 63114
(314) 427-7794
Officers: DeWitt Scott, Sr., President; Mary Scott, Administrative Officer
Purpose and Activities: Promote the steel guitar and the people that play the instrument.
Publications: *Steel Guitar International* (quarterly newsletter; $15/year)

INTERNATIONAL TROMBONE ASSOCIATION[1]
University of Arizona
School of Music
c/o Stan Adams
Tucson, AZ 85721
(602) 792-1877 or 626-1655
Officer: Tom Garvin, Acting Secretary/Treasurer
Purpose and Activities: Dedicated to the artistic advancement of trombone teaching, performance and literature.
Publications: *Newsletter* (3 issues/year); *Journal* (annual)

INTERNATIONAL TRUMPET GUILD
Bryan Goff School of Music
Florida State University
Tallahassee, FL 32306
Officers: Charles Gorham, President; Bryan Goff, Treasurer
Purpose and Activities: To promote communications among trumpet players around the world and to improve the artistic level of performance, teaching, and literature associated with the trumpet.
Publication: *ITG Journal* (quarterly; $20/year)

J

JAZZ COMPOSERS ORCHESTRA ASSOCIATION
500 Broadway
New York, NY 10012
(212) 925-2121
Officers: Timothy Marquand, President; Michael Mantler, Executive Director
Purpose and Activities: The New Music Distribution Service, a division of JCOA, distributes artist-made and independently-produced recordings of new music to record retailers and individuals and promotes the recordings to press and radio.
Publication: *New Music Distribution Service Catalog* (annual)

JAZZ INTERACTIONS, INC.
PO Box 268
Glen Oaks, NY 11004
(212) 423-0488 (89)
Officers: Joe Newman, President; Arthur R. Hill, Treasurer
Purpose and Activities: Nonprofit educational organization dedicated to the furtherance of jazz. Concerts, workshops, trips. Maintains JAZZLINE (212) 423-0488/9), a 24-hour taped telephone message reporting jazz activities in and around New York City.
Publication: *Jazz Interactions* (weekly; $30/year, $25 renewals)

JAZZMOBILE[1]
159 West 127th Street
New York, NY 10027
(212) 866-4900
Officer: S. David Bailey, Director
Purpose and Activities: To equip mobile units to bring jazz in the District of Columbia, Maryland, New Jersey, New York and Pennsylvania during the summer. Also sponsors free, regular jazz concerts.

JAZZ WORLD SOCIETY
(Formerly International Jazz Federation, Inc.)
PO Box 777
Times Square Station
New York, NY 10108-0777
(201) 939-0836
Officer: Jan A. Byrczek, Executive Director
Purpose and Activities: The Jazz World Society is an offspring of the European Jazz Federation. It is a non-profit organization bringing together some 6,000 members including leading jazz personalities, artists, producers, critics, booking agents, festivals, collectors, journalists, and jazz enthusiasts.
Publications: *Jazz World Index* and *Reference: Jazz Business USA* (bimonthly; $25 with membership)

JEWISH MUSIC ALLIANCE[1]
One Union Square W., Rm 711
New York, NY 10003
(212) 924-8311
Officers: Mazim Brodyn, National Secretary
Purpose and Activities: Represents 22 choral groups in the United States and Canada; provides repertory of music and folklore.

JEWISH MUSIC COUNCIL OF JWB[1]
15 East 26th Street
New York, NY 10010
(212) 532-4949
Officers: Ruth S. Frank, Coordinator
Purpose and Activities: (1) To promote fine performances of Jewish music of high quality in concerts, radio-TV and recordings. (2) To encourage the composition of new musical works, additional publications, and academic research in the field of Jewish music.

(3) To offer information on Jewish music to individuals and groups in the United States and abroad. (4) To serve the music cultural needs of the Jewish Community Centers and the national Jewish organizations, and to broaden the scope of general community participation in Jewish music activities, program events, and special projects.

Founded in 1944, the Council annually sponsors and promotes the Jewish Music Festival and publishes a variety of publications designed as aids for planning Jewish music programs.

K

KAPPA KAPPA PSI NATIONAL HONORARY BAND FRATERNITY*‡
122 Seretean Center
Oklahoma State University
Stillwater, OK 74078
(405) 372-2333
Officers: David Oakley, National President; Thomas F. Sirridge, Executive Secretary
Purpose and Activities: A national honorary fraternity for college and university band members, recognizing superior performance, interest and leadership.
Publications: *The Podium* (2 issues/year; free to members, $5 for nonmembers)

THE KITCHEN CENTER FOR VIDEO, MUSIC AND DANCE
59 Wooster St.
New York, NY 10012
(212) 925-3615
Officers: Mary MacArthur, Director; Anne deMarinis, Music Director
Purpose and Activities: The Kitchen is a center for experimental art, with programs in music, video, dance and performance art. The Contemporary Music Series, now operating for almost 12 years, features the music of living composers as performed by the composers and their ensembles. The series offers about 40 concerts per season (September-June).

KOUSSEVITZKY MUSIC FOUNDATION, INC.
415 Madison Ave.
New York, NY 10017
(212) PL 2-5300
Officers: Jacob Druckman, President; Ellis J. Freedman, Secretary
Purpose and Activities: Commissions composers of demonstrated merit and engages in other activities in support of contemporary music.

L

LEAGUE OF COMPOSERS INTERNATIONAL SOCIETY FOR CONTEMPORARY MUSIC (ISCM)*
c/o American Music Center
250 West 54th St., Room 300
New York, NY 10019
(212) 247-3121
Officer: Louis Karchin, President
Purpose and Activities: The League promotes contemporary music performances, sponsors six concert series in the Carnegie Recital hall, and a National Composer's Competition.

THE LESCHETIZKY ASSOCIATION*
105 West 72nd St.
New York, NY 10023
(212) EN 2-3912
Officer: Genia Robinor, President
Purpose and Activities: To perpetuate the principles of Theodore Leschetizky in playing and teaching, and to honor his memory. The organization sponsors a triennual New York debut and recital award.
Publication: *Leschetizky Association News Bulletin* (annual; free to members)

LIEDERKRANZ FOUNDATION
6 East 87th St.
New York, NY 10028
(212) 534-0880
Officer: Edward Weiss, Vice President
Purpose and Activities: Encourages amateur, professional participation in choral groups; stages plays; sponsors variety of concerts; and fosters close ties to U.S. and German-speaking countries, as well as funding scholarships.
Publication: *Lieder Kranz News* (bi-monthly)

LOS ANGELES MASTER CHORALE ASSOCIATION
The Music Center
135 North Grand Ave.
Los Angeles, CA 90012
(213) 972-7282
Officers: Anne Shaw Price, President; Robert Willoughby Jones, Executive Director
Purpose and Activities: Sponsors a yearly series of concerts of choral-orchestral music from all periods in the Dorothy Chandler Pavilion of the Music Center.

THE LUTE SOCIETY OF AMERICA[1]
1930 Cameron Court
Concord, CA 94518
(415) 686-1828
Officer: Nancy S. Carlin, Administrator
Purpose and Activities: Founded in 1966 to promote study of the lute and related instruments, to stimulate interest in lute music on the part of the general public, and to sponsor a central source of assistance and information available to lutenists worldwide.

The Society maintains a microfilm library of over 500 lute manuscripts and academic publications, organizes annual seminars dealing with lute technique and performance, and sustains an active publishing program.
Publication: *Journal of the Lute Society of America* (annually; with memberhship); *The LSA Newsletter* (quarterly; with membership)

M

MEMPHIS RECORDING PRODUCERS ASSOCIATION
One Comerce Sq., Ste. 1590
Memphis, TN 38103
(901) 523-0533
Officers: John Fry, President; Harold C. Steibich, Secretary/Treasurer
Purpose and Activities: Trade association for recording producers headquartered in the mid-south area surrounding Memphis and outside recording producers who come in and use Memphis recording facilities.

WILLEM MENGELBERG SOCIETY
PO Box 232
Greendale, WI 53129
Purpose and Activities: Spread interest in and increase knowledge of the Dutch orchestral conductor Willem Mengelberg (1871-1951) and to encourage the publication of his phonograph recordings.
Publication: *Newsletter* (3/year; $4/year, U.S. and Canada; $5 elsewhere)

METROPOLITAN OPERA ASSOCIATION, INC.[1]
Lincoln Center
New York, NY 10023
(212) 799-3100
Officers: William Rockefeller, Board Chairman
Purpose and Activities: Parent organization of the Metropolitan Opera Company.

THE METROPOLITAN OPERA GUILD, INC.
1865 Broadway
New York, NY 10023
(212) 582-7500
Officers: Katharine T. O'Neil, President; Geoff Peterson, Managing Director
Purpose and Activities: To develop and cultivate a wider public interest in opera and its allied arts and to contribute to their support in general and to the Metropolitan Opera in particular.
Publications: *Opera News* (17/year; $29.95/year, including National Opera Membership in the Guild); *Ballet News* (monthly; $18/year, including National Ballet Membership in the Guild)

MID-WEST NATIONAL BAND & ORCHESTRA CLINIC[1]
1607 North Channel Drive
Round Lake, IL 60073
(312) 546-8851

Officers: Richard Madden, President; Barbara Buehlman, Executive Administrator
Purpose and Activities: To raise the standards of music education; to improve the methods employed in music education; to develop new teaching techniques; to disseminate information to school music teachers, directors, supervisors and others interested in music education to assist in their professional work.

MODERN MUSIC MASTERS[1]
PO Box 347
Park Ridge, IL 60068
(312) 825-1451
Officer: Linda Darlington, Executive Secretary
Purpose and Activities: International nonprofit educational society chartering chapters in junior and senior high schools, serving music educators and honor students, emphasizing "Service Through Music."
Publication: *Tri-M Notes Newsletter* (4 issues/year; free)

THE MORAVIAN MUSIC FOUNDATION, INC.[1*]
Drawer Z, Salem Station
Winston-Salem, NC 27108
(919) 725-0651
Officers: James Boeringer, Director
Purpose and Activities: The Foundation is custodian of thousands of rare music manuscripts of the German-American Moravian tradition and of the library of colonial New England and Pennsylvania tunebooks in the Irving Lowens Musical American collection. It carries on a continuing program of editing modern editions of music from the manuscript collections and of sponsoring recordings by leading record companies. The Foundation's resources are accessible to qualified scholars and students for research. General information is provided upon request.
Publications: *The Moravian Music Foundation Bulletin* (semiannual; free upon request)

MU BETA PSI NATIONAL HONORARY MUSICAL FRATERNITY
3401 Hickory Crest Drive
Marietta, GA 30064
(404) 428-1748
Officer: Ralph W. Daniel, Executive Secretary
Purpose and Activities: To advance music and fellowship among musicians. Encourages participation in collegiate musical activities; holds lectures; and helps arrange concerts.
Publication: *The Clef*

MU PHI EPSILON*†‡
(International Professional Music Fraternity)
25824 Sugar Pine Dr.
Pioneer, CA 95666
(209) 295-4787
Officers: Ruth Dean Morris, President; Roberta White O'Connell, Executive Secretary
Purpose and Activities: The recognition and promotion of scholarship and musicianship; the promotion of friendship within its membership; and the advancement of music in America and throughout the world.
Publications: *The Triangle* (4 issues/year; $2/issue, $40 life subscription)

MUSIC NOSTRA ET VOSTRA
National Corporation of America (MNEV)
1410 York Ave., Ste. 2D
New York, NY 10021
(212) 628-6315
Officer: Bruno George Ronty, President
Purpose and Activities: Dedicated to furthering the exchange of musical programs in the U.S. and between the U.S. and other countries. For the general public, including youths, senior citizens, minority groups, the armed forces and others not usually served by formal music organizations.

MUSICAL BOX SOCIETY, INTERNATIONAL[1]
Rt. 3, Box 202
Morgantown, IN 46160
(812) 983-7545
Officer: Marguerite K. Fabel, Secretary/Treasurer
Purpose and Activities: To foster an interest in the history and the preservation of all types of musical boxes (including Swiss Cylinder boxes, disc music boxes, player pianos, reproducing pianos, band organs, orchestrions, and all related instruments).
Publication: *The Bulletin* (monthly; $12/year)

MUSICAL THEATRES ASSOCIATION
5 Westland Road
Hamden, CT 06517
(203) 281-0322
Officer: Robert Hall, President
Purpose and Activities: Acts as individual bargaining agent with unions for theatres with seating of 1,000 or more, concentrating on musical shows and acts.

MUSIC CRITICS ASSOCIATION, INC./ MCA EDUCATIONAL ACTIVITIES, INC.*
6201 Tuckerman Lane
Rockville, MD 20852
(301) 530-9527
Officers: Robert Commanday, President; Richard D. Freed, Executive Director
Purpose and Activities: (1) To act as an educational medium for the promotion of high standards of music criticism in the press of the Americas; (2) to hold meetings in which self-criticism and exchange of ideas will promote educational opportunities; (3) to increase general interest in music in the growing culture of the Americas.
Publications: *Newsletter of the Music Critics Association, Inc.* (3 issues/year; free)

MUSIC DISTRIBUTORS ASSOCIATION
(formerly National Association of Musical Merchandise Wholesalers)
135 W. 29th St.
New York, NY 10001
(212) 564-0251
Officers: Alvin Cohen, President; Jerome Hershman, Executive Vice President
Purpose and Activities: To promote the growth of the music industry and the wholesalers' function as an important segment in the distribution of music industry products.

MUSIC EDUCATION RESEARCH COUNCIL‡
Florida State University
School of Music
Tallahassee, FL 32306
Officers: Clifford K. Madsen, Chairman
Purposes and Activities: Encourage and advance research in areas pertinent to music education. The Council sponsors, through MENC, research training activities and disseminates music education research findings.
Publication: *Journal of Research in Music Education* (quarterly; $8 members, $10 institutions)

MUSIC EDUCATORS NATIONAL CONFERENCE*‡
1902 Association Drive
Reston, VA 22091
(703) 860-4000
Officers: Dr. Russell P. Getz, President; Dr. Donald W. Dillon, Executive Director
Purpose and Activities: The Conference's purpose is the achievement of music education. Its activities include conferences, commissions, conventions, in-service training, numerous publications, and an historical research center for music education.
Division Presidents:
Eastern (1981-83) Paul L. Gayzagian, College of Music, University of Lowell, Lowell, MA 01854
North Central (1982-84)—Harry R. Mamlin
Indianapolis Public Schools
120 E. Walnut St., Rm. 506
Indianapolis, IN 46204
Northwest (1981-83)—Bert A. Burda
Idaho State Department of Education, Len B. Jordan Office Bldg.
Boise, ID 93720
Southern (1982-84)—Robert W. Surplus
Music Department
Eastern Kentucky University

Richmond, KY 40475
Southwestern (1981-83)—Alex B. Campbell
Jefferson County School District R-1
1209 Quail,
Lakewood, CO 80215
Western (1982-84)—William S. English
Division of Music Education
Arizona State University
Tempe, AZ 85281
President of Auxiliary Organization (1982-1984): *Music Industry Council*—Richard J. Richardson, Slingerland/Degan,
6633 N. Milwaukee Ave.
Niles, IL 60648
Publications: *Music Educators Journal* (9/year, free to membership); *Journal of Research in Music Education* (quarterly, free to membership)

MUSIC INDUSTRIES MARKETING ASSOCIATION
600 S. Dearborn St.
Chicago, IL 60605
(312) 922-2433
Officer: Charles Suber, President
Purpose and Activities: To promote the common business interests of its members by encouraging the worldwide purchase and use of their goods and services. Membership is open to any individual, firm, partnership, or corporation engaged in the manufacture of music instruments and equipment, parts and accessories, music related products, publishing of music, or wholesalers and distributors of musical goods.
Publication: *MIMA Newsletter* (monthly; free to members; $24 nonmembers; $35 foreign)

MUSICIANS EMERGENCY FUND
35 W. 4th St., Room 778
New York, NY 10003
(212) 598-7782 or 477-6341
Officers: Mrs. Walter Wilds, President
Purpose and Activities: Provides paid employment through musical performances in hospitals and nursing homes; sponsors music therapy programs and research; gives financial assistance to needy musicians.

THE MUSICIANS FOUNDATION, INC.
200 West 55th Street
New York, NY 10019
(212) 247-5332
Officers: Brent Williams, Executive Director; Mrs. Carl Stern, President
Purpose and Activities: Established as the philanthropic arm of "The Bohemians" in 1914 to foster the interests and advance the condition and social welfare of professional musicians, and to provide voluntary aid and assistance to musicians and their families in case of need.

MUSICIANS NATIONAL HOT LINE ASSOCIATION
277 E. 6100 S.
Salt Lake City, UT 84107
(801) 268-2000
Officer: Marvin C. Zitting, Executive Director
Purpose and Activities: To increase the employment of musicians in our society, operates a telephone hot line, computer search file, and newsletter to help musicians find bands and help bands find musicians. Also helps music educators and music-related occupations.
Publication: *Hot Line New* ($20 members only)

MUSIC INDUSTRY COUNCIL[1]
Magnamusic-Baton, Inc.
10370 Page Industrial Blvd.
St. Louis, MO 63132
Officer: Norman A. Goldberg, President
Purpose and Activities: An organization that represents the interests of music equipment suppliers.

MUSIC INDUSTRY EDUCATORS ASSOCIATION
Music Department
Elmhurst College
Elmhurst, IL 60126
(312) 279-4100, x357
Officers: David B. Leonard, President; Paul R. Kelly, Secretary
Purpose and Activities: To promote interaction among professionals active in music industry education in the U.S. and Canada; to promote communication between music industry education and the music industry; to encourage quality research in music industry studies at colleges and universities; and to establish and maintain standards of quality in music industry education.
Publication: *MIEA Notes* (3-4 times per year; $24/year)

MUSIC LIBRARY ASSOCIATION
2017 Walnut Street
Philadelphia, PA 19103
(215) 569-3948
Officers: Mary Wallance Davidson, President; John Shiffert, Admissions Secretary
Purpose and Activities: Promotes development of music libraries, establishes and improves standards. Publishes library and bibliographic materials. Affords opportunity for music and general librarians to obtain and exchange advice in solving mutual problems. Assists general librarians in the area of music.
Publication: *Notes* (quarterly; $24 members, $21 nonmembers, $31 institutions)

MUSIC PUBLISHERS' ASSOCIATION[1]*
130 W. 57th St.
New York, NY 10019
(212) 582-1122
Officer: Howard Wattenberg, General Counsel
Purpose and Activities: To safeguard the welfare and further the interests of its members through legal action; to disseminate information; and to protect the copyrights of MPA members. The association also publishes pamphlets.

MUSIC TEACHERS NATIONAL ASSOCIATION (MTNA)*†
2113 Carew Tower
Cincinnati, OH 45202
(513) 421-1420
Officers: Joseph Brye, President; Mariann H. Clinton, Executive Director
Purpose and Activities: A nonprofit organization representing music teachers in all work situations. Membership is open to all music teachers and all individuals, organizations and businesses interested in music teaching. The Association has commenced a teacher certifying program.
Publications: *American Music Teacher* (6/year; free to membership $7.50 to nonmembers)

N

NASHVILLE ASSOCIATION OF TALENT DIRECTORS
803 18th Ave. So.
Nashville, TN 37203
(615) 321-5003
Officer: Don Light, President; Maggie Cavender, Executive Director
Purpose and Activities: Association of talent directors and managers in the Nashville area whose purpose is to promote the artists and the locale.

NASHVILLE SONGWRITERS ASSOCIATION INTERNATIONAL
803 18th Ave., So
Nashville, TN 37203
(615) 321-5004
Officer: Ann Stuckey, President; Maggie Cavender, Executive Director

NATIONAL ACADEMY OF POPULAR MUSIC*[1]
1 Times Square
New York, NY 10036
(212) 221-1252
Officers: Jack H. Bergman, Executive Director
Purpose and Activities: Organized to honor America's great songwriters, long ignored by the public in favor of the singers of their songs. The Academy sponsors The Songwriters Hall of Fame Awards (three per year) and the Songwriters Hall of Fame Museum, which features an extensive collection of memorabilia on American popular song.

NATIONAL ACADEMY OF RECORDING ARTS & SCIENCES
4444 Riverside Drive, Suite 202

Burbank, CA 91505
(213) 843-8233
Officer: Christine M. Farnon, Executive Director
Purpose and Activities: NARAS presents the annual Grammy Awards for outstanding achievements in the arts and sciences of phonograph recording. It is a nonprofit association headquartered in Burbank, CA, whose members belong to any one of the seven chapters: Los Angeles, New York, Nashville, Chicago, Atlanta, San Francisco, Memphis. Members are vocalists, musicians, recording producers, engineers, composers and other creative persons in the recording field. Chapters give seminars, panel discussions and scholarships.

NATIONAL ACADEMY OF TELEVISION ARTS AND SCIENCES [1]
110 W. Fifty-seventh St.
New York, NY 10019
(212) 586-8424
Officer: John Cannon, President
Purpose and Activities: A non-profit organization that is open to anyone connected with television, including students, the academy organizes and produces the annual Emmy Awards.

NATIONAL ASSOCIATION FOR HUMANITIES EDUCATION
School of Humanities and Sciences
University of South Carolina -Spartanburg
Spartanburg, SC 29303
Officer: Vasant Merchant, President; Bryan Lindsay, Executive Secretary
Publication: *Humanities Journal* (2/year; $8/year)

NATIONAL ASSOCIATION FOR MUSIC THERAPY†
1001 Connecticut Ave., NW, Ste. 800
Washington, DC 20036
(202) 331-7792
Officers: Frederick Tims, RMT, President; C. Gail Simmons, Executive Director
Purpose and Activities: Advancement of research, distribution of pertinent information, establishment of qualifications and standards of training for music therapists, and improvement of techniques involving therapeutic uses of music.
Publications: *Journal of Music Therapy* (quarterly; $12 domestic, $14 foreign)

NATIONAL ASSOCIATION OF BROADCAST EMPLOYEES AND TECHNICIANS[1]
7101 Wisconsin Avenue
Suite 1303
Washington, DC 20014
(202) 265-3601
Officer: Edward Lynch, President
Purpose and Activities: A trade union affiliated with AFL-CIO.
Publication: monthly news

NATIONAL ASSOCIATION OF BROADCASTERS
1771 N St., NW
Washington, DC 20036
(202) 293-3516
Officer: Edward Fritts, President
Purpose and Activities: To represent local radio and television stations and national radio and television networks.
Publications: *Highlights* (weekly); *RadioActive* (monthly); *I.F.* (quarterly)

NATIONAL ASSOCIATION FOR CAMPUS ACTIVITIES
(Formerly the National Entertainment and Campus Activities Association)
PO Box 11489
Columbia, SC 29211
(803) 799-0768
Officer: Rich Mais, Marketing Services Coordinator
Purpose and Activities: An association of higher education institutions that provide co-curricular activities for the educational enrichment of their campus communities, as well as persons or businesses selling, marketing or promoting services and products necessary for such activities. NACA exists to provide assistance for member institutions; to establish and produce quality campus activities programming by providing education, information and resources for students and administrators; and to facilitate cooperative consumer efficiency and marketplace effectiveness.
Publication: *Student Activities Programming* (monthly; free to members)

NATIONAL ASSOCIATION OF COLLEGE WIND AND PERCUSSION INSTRUCTORS‡
308 Hillcrest Dr.
Kirksville, MO 63501
(816) 785-4442
Officers: William De Jong, President; Dr. Richard Weerts, Executive Secretary-Treasurer
Purpose and Activities: The Association is a forum for communication within the profession of applied music on college and university campuses. Projects of the association include a placement service, a research library, a composition project, and a quarterly publication.
Publications: *NACWPI Journal* (quarterly; $15/year)

NATIONAL ASSOCIATION OF COMPOSERS/USA*
PO Box 49652
Barrington Station
Los Angeles, CA 90049
(213) 541-8213
Officers: Marshall H. Bialosky, President
Purpose and Activities: The promotion, performance, publication and broadcasting of new music by the organization's members in all areas of the country.
Publications: *Composer/USA* (quarterly, $8/year)

NATIONAL ASSOCIATION OF ELECTRONIC ORGAN MANUFACTURERS
1801 Gilbert Ave.
Cincinnati, OH 45202
(513) 852-7899
Officers: Jack Flon, President; Glenn Derringer, Secretary/Treasurer
Purpose and Activities: To prepare industry figures on the sale of electronic organs and to consider means to improve industry sales.

NATIONAL ASSOCIATION OF JAZZ EDUCATORS‡
PO Box 724
Manhattan, KS 66502
(913) 539-3752
Officers: Dr. Warrick Carter, President; Matt Betton, Executive Director
Purpose and Activities: To cooperate with all organizations dedicated to the development of musical culture in America; to foster and promote the understanding and appreciation of jazz and popular music and its artistic performance.
Publication: *Jazz Educators Journal* (4/year; free to members)

NATIONAL ASSOCIATION OF MUSIC MERCHANTS (NAMM)
500 N. Michigan Ave.
Chicago, IL 60611
(312) 527-3200
Officers: Charles K. Hale, President; Larry R. Linkin, Executive Vice President
Purpose and Activities: A trade association serving the music products industry.
Publication: *Music Retailer News* (6/year; free with membership); *Business Barometer* (24/year; free with membership)

NATIONAL ASSOCIATION OF PASTORAL MUSICIANS[1]
225 Sheridan St., NW
Washington, DC 20011
Officer: Rev. Virgil C. Funk, Executive Director
Purpose and Activities: National membership organization for parish clergy and musicians whose purpose is to foster and celebrate the art of liturgical music. Services include a job referral service, a central referring service for the purchase of all records directed towards liturgical worship, and a ministry formation program, which includes training for a certificate in music workshops, summer institutes and a diocesan development program. The Association holds an annual national meeting and has a wide range

of resource publications.
Publication: *Pastoral Music* bimonthly; with membership $15;) *Pastoral Music Notebook* (bimonthly newsletter; with membership)

THE NATIONAL ASSOCIATION OF PROFESSIONAL BAND INSTRUMENT REPAIR TECHNICIANS (NAPBIRT)
PO Box 51
Normal, IL 61761
(309) 452-4257
Officers: Walter P. Stryszyk, President; Chuck Hagler, Executive Secretary
Purpose and Activities: A non-profit, international organization dedicated to technical integrity and professionalism in the craft of repair, maintenance, and restoration of band instruments.
Publication: *TECHNI-COM* (bimonthly; members only)

NATIONAL ASSOCIATION OF RECORDING MERCHANDISERS
1008-F Astoria Blvd.
Cherry Hill, NJ 08034
(609) 424-7404
Officer: Ms. Mickey Granberg, Executive Director; Joseph A. Cohen, Executive Vice President
Publication: *Sounding Board* (monthly; free to members)

NATIONAL ASSOCIATION OF SCHOOL MUSIC DEALERS[1]
642 Wabash Ave.
Terre Haute, IN 47808
Officer: Warner H. Paige, President

NATIONAL ASSOCIATION OF SCHOOLS OF MUSIC*
11250 Roger Beacon Dr., No. 5
Reston, VA 22090
(703) 437-0700
Officers: Thomas Miller, President; Samuel Hope, Executive Director
Purpose and Activities: The accrediting agency for educational programs in music.
Publications: *Directory* (annual; $6). *Handbook* (biennial; $5); *Proceedings* (annual; $6); *Music in Higher Education* (annual; $6)

NATIONAL ASSOCIATION OF TEACHERS OF SINGING*
250 W. 57th St.
New York, NY 10019
(212) 582-4043
Officers: John Burgin, President; James Browning, Executive Secretary
Purpose and Activities: Organized for the purposes of establishing and maintaining the highest ethical principles and standards of practice in the profession of teaching singing and vocal art; to encourage and conduct vocal research and to disseminate any and all resultant information to the profession at large; to encourage effective cooperation among vocal teachers for their welfare and advancement.
Publications: *The NTAS Bulletin* (5/year; $11/year to nonmembers); *Inter Nos* (newsletter)

NATIONAL BAND ASSOCIATION‡
PO Box 3228
Augusta, GA 30904
(404) 736-4798
Officers: James Neilson, President; Alan H. Drake, Executive Secretary-Treasurer
Purpose and Activities: A nonprofit organization whose purpose is to promote a national voice fostering the continuous development of bands and band music, and to promote the musical and educational significance of bands.
Publications: *NBA Journal*

NATIONAL CATHOLIC BANDMASTERS ASSOCIATION
Box 523
Notre Dame, IN 46556
(219) 239-7136
Officers: Joseph Cardinale, President; Rev. George Wiskirchen, C.S.C., Executive Secretary
Purpose and Activities: To assist in the promotion and development of instrumental music in the Catholic school.
Publication: *The NCBA Newsletter* (monthly; free with membership)

NATIONAL CHORAL COUNCIL/NATIONAL CHORALE
20 West 40th St.
New York, NY 10018
(212) 869-0970
Officer: Barry H. Garfinkel, Chairman Board of Directors; Martin D. Josman, Executive Director
Purpose and Activities: Nonprofit organization dedicated to the support and extension of choral activities professional, educational, and community—nationwide. National Chorale is the professional choral repertory company sponsored by the Council; it presents concert series at Lincoln Center, national tours and residencies, American Musical Theatre series, and Young People's Concert.

NATIONAL CONSORTIUM FOR COMPUTER-BASED MUSIC INSTRUCTION
School of Music
University of Illinois
1114 W. Nevada
Urbana, IL 61801
(217) 333-0675
Officer: G. David Peters, President
Purpose and Activities: Consortium was organized to share information on the development of computer-based music instruction between members. Serving as a clearing-house for information and computer programs, the organization has meetings twice a year to present research and developmental projects.
Publication: *The NCCBMI Newsletter/ADCIS Newsletter* (bimonthly; free to members; $5 nonmembers)

NATIONAL COUNCIL FOR THE TRADITIONAL ARTS, INC[1]
1346 Connecticut Ave., NW, Ste 1118
Washington, DC 20036
(202) 296-0068
Officer: Joseph T. Wilson, Executive Director
Purpose and Activities: Private, nonprofit, honorary membership organization, founded in 1933, dedicated to the study, presentation and advocacy of authentic tribal and folk arts of U.S. groups.

NATIONAL COUNCIL OF MUSIC IMPORTERS AND EXPORTERS
135 W. 29th St.
New York, NY 10001
(212) 564-0251
Officers: Herbert Hagel, President; Jerome Hershman, Secretary-Treasurer
Purpose and Activities: Trade association of U.S. importers and exporters of musical merchandise to foster international trade in musical merchandise.
Publication: *Newsletter* (10/year; free with membership)

NATIONAL FEDERATION OF MUSIC CLUBS*
1336 North Delaware Street
Indianapolis, IN 46202
(317) 638-4003
Officers: Mrs. Jack C. Ward, President; Mrs. Barbara T. Bryant, Executive Secretary
Purpose and Activities: Aids and encourages advancement of musical arts through creative artists, organizations and composition; stimulates knowledge and appreciation of music; promotes musical activities in the armed forces; aids veterans in musical careers; uses the power of music to promote good will among nations.
Publications: *Music Clubs Magazine* (quarterly, $5/year)

NATIONAL FLUTE ASSOCIATION, INC.*
805 Laguna Drive
Denton, TX 76201
(817) 387-9472
Officers: Ronald L. Waln, President; Myrna Brown, Financial Coordinator
Purpose and Activities: To further the cause of the flute: in encouraging new publications for the instrument, exchanging information on technological advancements, making repertoire known and available, providing performance and competition opportunities, interchanging ideas and inspiration at conventions and through

organization's newsletter, and supporting projects of common interest.
Publications: *Newsletter of the National Flute Association, Inc.* (quarterly; with membership only)

NATIONAL FORUM FOR GREEK ORTHODOX CHURCH MUSICIANS
1700 N. Walnut, Apt. 314
Bloomington, IN 47401
(812) 339-3142
Officer: Dr. Vicki Pappas, National Chairman
Purpose and Activities: To promote establishment of music education programs in the Greek Orthodox Church; to provide a platform for national discussion and exchange of ideas; to provide avenues for greater development, publication, and availability of music, and to provide assistance to regional choir federations and local church choirs.
Publication: *LIturgical Guidebook* (annually $7)

NATIONAL FRATERNITY OF STUDENT MUSICIANS
Box 1807
Austin, TX 78767
(512) 478-5775
Officer: Walter M. Merchant, Vice President
Purpose and Activities: Student division of the American College of Musicians offers worthwhile goals for teachers and their students through standardized piano curriculum embodying the best in piano literature, with particular stress on the works of American composers. Provides a sensible classification for piano students through 17 years and beyond of study, with suitable rewards for the attainment of each goal in certificates, fraternity pins, diplomas, medals and scholarships.
Publication: *Piano Guild Notes* (bimonthly; $10/year)

NATIONAL GUILD OF COMMUNITY SCHOOLS OF THE ARTS, INC.*
PO Box 583
Teaneck, NJ 07666
(201) 836-5594
Officers: Henry Bridges, President; Lolita Mayadas, Executive Director
Purpose and Activities: Association of nonprofit, non-degree granting, community schools of the arts offering music, dance, drama, and visual arts instruction to students of all ages and backgrounds. Programs include technical assistance, consultancy and referral services; communications, research, advocacy and professional training and development programs for Trustees, administrators and faculty in the field of community arts. Annual conference and regional workshops.
Publications: *Guildletter* (quarterly; free); *Guildnotes* (monthly; members only); *Guildpeople* (quarterly); *Employment Opportunities* (monthly; members only)

NATIONAL GUILD OF PIANO TEACHERS*
PO Box 1807
Austin, TX 78767
(512) 478-5775
Officers: Irl Allison, Jr., President; Walter M. Merchant, Vice President and Administrative Officer
Purpose and Activities: Promotes educational opportunities for piano students through auditions with qualified teacher-judges; offers incentives (certificates, cash awards, and scholarships) to encourage students to study music longer. Also seeks to improve business conditions and training for piano teachers through a standardized program of materials and curriculum.
Publications: *Piano Guild Notes* (bimonthly; $10/year)

NATIONAL LEAGUE OF AMERICAN PEN WOMEN, INC.[1]
1300 Seventeenth Street, Northwest
Washington, DC 20036
(202) 785-1997
Officer: Maxine Lampshire, National President
Purpose and Activities: Organized in 1897 to promote and conduct creative and educational activities in the arts, letters and music. Membership includes more than 125 composers.
Publication: *The Pen Woman* (nine issues annually)

NATIONAL MUSIC COUNCIL*
250 W. 54th St., Ste. 300
New York, NY 10019
(212) 265-8132
Officers: Victor Fuentealba, President; Doris O'Connell, Executive Secretary
Purpose and Activities: The main purpose of the council, which is composed of more than 60 national music organizations, is to speak with one voice whenever an authoritative expression of opinion is desirable.

NATIONAL MUSIC PUBLISHERS' ASSOCIATION, INC.*
110 East 59th Street
New York, NY 10022
(212) PL 1-1930
Officers: Salvatore T. Chiantia, Chairman; Leonard Feist, President
Purpose and Activities: The Association, founded in 1917, is the trade association of the popular music publishing business.
Publications: *NMPA Bulletin* (quarterly; free with membership)

NATIONAL OLD-TIME FIDDLERS ASSOCIATION[1]
PO Box 544
Mesilla Park, NM 88047
(602) 586-2675
Officer: John Wilson, President
Purpose and Activities: Dedicated to reviving and preserving old-time fiddle music.
Publication: *Newsletter* (quarterly)

NATIONAL OPERA INSTITUTE
John F. Kennedy Center for the Performing Arts
Washington, DC 20566
(202) 254-3694
Officers: Harold Prince, Chairman; Lee Day Gillespie, President; John M. Ludwig, Executive Director
Purpose and Activities: To encourage the growth and development of music theater in the U.S. through: individual grants to singers; apprenticeships in administration and production; singer contract support; Music Theater Workshop for previews and rewrites of new works; Colloquia on topics of current interest to the profession.
Publication: *The National Opera Institute Newsletter* (quarterly; free)

NATIONAL ORATORIO SOCIETY*
6686 Brook Way
Paradise, CA 95969
(916) 877-8360
Officers: Thomas E. Wilson, President
Purpose and Activities: To promote the performance of oratorios by master American composers and to encourage such compositions.

NATIONAL ORCHESTRAL ASSOCIATION
111 West 57th Street
New York, NY 10019
(212) CI 7-1228
Officer: Carol P. Madeira, Administrative Director; Alvaro Cassuto, Music Director; Roger Nierenberg, Associate Conductor
Purpose and Activities: To give professional orchestral training to highly competent instrumentalists.

NATIONAL PIANO FOUNDATION
230 North Michigan Avenue
Chicago, IL 60601
(312) 372-9800
Officer: George M. Otto, Executive Director

NATIONAL PIANO MANUFACTURERS ASSOCIATION OF AMERICA, INC.[1]*
c/o George M. Otto Associates
230 N. Michigan Ave.
Chicago, IL 60611
(312) 372-9800
Officer: George M. Otto, President

NATIONAL PIANO TRAVELERS ASSOCIATION[1]
c/o Charles Ramsey Corporation
15 Gage Street
Kingston, NY 12401
(914) 338-1464
Officer: Harry C. Kapreilan, Treasurer

NATIONAL RECREATION AND PARKS ASSOCIATION[1]
1601 North Kent Street
Arlington, VA 22209
(703) 525-0606
Officer: John H. Davis, Executive Director
Purpose and Activities: Association that covers park facilities who team up with the American Music Conference for staging and encouraging amateur music concerts.

NATIONAL SCHOOL ORCHESTRA ASSOCIATION*†‡
330 Bellevue Drive
Bowling Green, KY 42101
(502) 842-7121
Officers: G. Jean Smith, President
Purposes and Activities: Founded to promote and improve school orchestras at all levels of instruction and to act as a national voice for orchestra directors. Activities include an orchestra composition contest, listing of available positions, a continual evaluation of newly published music, a summer workshop, awards for both students and adults interested in orchestra, and sponsorship of youth orchestras.
Publications: *NSOA Bulletin* (quarterly; free with membership, $8 to libraries)

NATIONAL SHEET MUSIC SOCIETY, INC.
PO Box 2901
Pasadena, CA 91105
Officer: Dr. David Friedman, President; Marilyn Brees, Corresponding and Newsletter Secretary
Purpose and Activities: To save from oblivion the published music of the people, which is rapidly disappearing in a mechanized age. "The Story of a Nation is told in its song."
Publication: *National Sheet Music Newsletter* (monthly except July and August; $10/year)

NATIONAL SOCIETY OF STUDENT ORGANISTS
7938 Bertram Avenue
Hammond, IN 46324
Officer: Dorothy S. Greig, President
Purpose and Activities: Student fraternity sponsored by the International Association of Organ Teachers USA.

NBTA-INTERNATIONAL, INC.
(Formerly National Baton Twirling Association, Inc.)
PO Box 266
Janesville, WI 53545
(608) 754-2238
Officers: Don Sartell, President
Purpose and Activities: NBTA is the oldest, largest and most active twirling organization in the world. A nonprofit organization, it has played a vital role in developing the twirling field.
Publication: *Drum Major Magazine* (11/year; $7.50/year)

NEW MUSIC ENSEMBLE
School of Music
University of Houston
4800 Calhoun Street
Houston, TX 77004
(713) 749-1116
Officer: Michael Horvit, Director
Purpose and Activities: The performance of contemporary chamber music, with an emphasis on works composed since 1970.

NEW ORLEANS JAZZ CLUB
PO Box 52084
New Orleans, LA 70152
(504) 242-0468
Officer: Ed Morgan, President
Purpose and Activities: To research, preserve, stimulate and encourage, advertise and promote New Orleans jazz and all the ramifications and forms thereof. Membership meetings of varying programs, featuring live jazz, lectures, etc.

The Club operated the New Orleans Jazz Museum; the material has since been donated to the Louisiana State Museum and is known as the New Orleans Jazz Club Collections.
Publication: *The Second Line* (quarterly; $15 to active members, $10 to students)

NEW ORLEANS JAZZ CLUB OF CALIFORNIA
Box 1225
Kerrville, TX 78028
(512) 896-2285
Officer: William F. Bacin, President and Administrative Director
Purpose and Activities: To preserve the traditional New Orleans Dixieland jazz; to aid, educate and encourage those members of the music community who have been, are, or will be part of this heritage.
Publication: *The Jazzologist* (5 issues/year; $7.50 domestic, $9.50 foreign)

THE NEW YORK BARTOK ARCHIVE
2 Tulip Street
Cedarhurst, NY 11516
(516) 569-1468
Officer: Dr. Benjamin Suchoff, Director
Purpose and Activities: To collect documents and memorabilia by and about Bela Bartok, to treat and preserve them so as to aid in the study of Bartok's life, compositions, and ethnomusicological works.
Publication: *The Bela Bartok Archives: History and Catalogue* (1963); *Rumanian Folk Music - I Instrumental Melodies, II Vocal Melodies, III Texts* (1967), *IV Carols and Christmas Songs, V Maramures County* (1975); *Turkish Folk Music from Asia Minor* (1976); *Bela Bartok Essays* (1976); *Yugoslav Folk Music - I Serbo-Croatian Folk Songs, II Tabulation of Material, III Source Melodies: Part One, IV Source Melodies: Part Two* (1978); *The Hungarian Folk Song* (1981); *The Bartok Archive Edition* (piano works), Vols. I and II), 1981.

NEW YORK CHORAL SOCIETY
165 West 57th Street
New York, NY 10019
(212) 972-0113
Officer: P. Reich, President; Robert DeCormier, Music Director
Purpose and Activities: Avocational chorus that presents concerts of music of all centuries. Sponsors 28 Summer Sings, which are open readings of choral literature, from June to September. Run entirely by volunteers, except for paid professional orchestra and soloists. Depends on public support to meet its extensive financial obligations.

NEW YORK PINEWOODS FOLK MUSIC CLUB
c/o Country Dance & Song Society
505 8th Avenue, Room 2500
New York, NY 10018
(212) 594-8833
Officer: Maddy DeLeon, President
Purpose and Activities: Part of the Country Dance & Song Society, a nonprofit, educational corporation. Sponsors folk singing and concerts in the New York area and a folk music camp and workshop at Camp Freedman, Falls Village, CT. Individual members dues at $12/year.
Publication: *NY Pinewoods Folk Music Club Newsletter* (monthly, except August; free to members)

NEW YORK STATE SCHOOL MUSIC ASSOCIATION
Onondaga Community College
Music Department
Syracuse, NY 13215
(315) 469-7741, x 256
Officer: Andreas Paloumpis, President; Donald B. Miller, Chairman
Purpose and Activities: Two-year education in performance.

NORTH AMERICAN GUILD OF CHANGE RINGERS
47-G Forst Acres Dr.
Bradford, MA 01830
(617) 372-4553
Officer: Beryl E. Morrison, General Secretary
Purpose and Activities: To improve communication among change ringers in the U.S. and to improve their standard of ringing (tower bells). The Guild prints a newsletter, runs a book service which sells books and tapes, distributes a pamphlet, and has meetings and courses here and in England. There are about 250 members in the U.S. and Canada, and 200 members overseas.

Publication: *The Clapper* (quarterly; $12 members, including dues; $8 nonmembers)

NORTH CAROLINA FOLKLORE SOCIETY
Department of English
Appalachian State University
Boone, NC 28608
(704) 262-3098 or 262-4072
Officers: Robert Byington, President; Thomas McGowan, Secretary-Treasurer
Purpose and Activities: To promote study of North Carolina folklife and folklore.
Publication: *North Carolina Folklore Journal* (2/year); *Newsletter of the North Carolina Folklore Society* (quarterly; subscriptions for both are included with Society membership; $4/year individuals, $6/year institutions)

NORTHEASTERN SAENGERBIEND OF AMERICA[1]
21 A Independence Parkway
Crestwood Village
Whiting, NJ 08759
Officer: John Becker, President
Purpose and Activities: Male singers from the eastern states sing German songs, speak the language, present the customs and sociability of that people.

NORWEGIAN SINGER'S ASSOCIATION OF AMERICA
3316 Xenwood Avenue South
Minneapolis, MN 55416
(612) 925-4658
Officer: Erling Stone, Executive Vice President
Purpose and Activities: To promote love for Scandinavian male chorus music; to create friendship among its members and to assist and encourage Scandinavian musicians; and to arrange the International Singers Convention every other year to publicize Scandinavian music.
Publication: *Sanger-Hilsen (Singers Greetings)* (bimonthly; $5/year)

O

OPERA AMERICA, INC.
633 E St., NW
Washington, DC 20004
(202) 347-9262
Officer: David DiChiera, President; Martin I. Kagan, Executive Director
Purpose and Activities: To promote growth of operatic form by fostering and improving education, training and development of operatic composers, singers, and allied talents; assisting in developing residential professional opera companies through cooperative artistic and management services; and encouraging greater appreciation and enjoyment of opera by all segments of society.
Publication: *Intercompany Announcements* (monthly; free to members); *Profile: OPERA America and the Professional Opera Companies* (annually; $7.50)

OPPORTUNITY RESOURCES FOR THE ARTS
1501 Broadway
New York, NY 10036
(212) 575-1688
Officer: Marian Pardo, President; Freda Mindlin, Executive Director
Purpose and Activities: The primary purpose is to match the management-personnel needs of cultural organizations nationally with the most qualified individuals available. For a modest fee, the group provides professional personnel search services for cultural groups.

THE ORGAN HISTORICAL SOCIETY, INC.
PO Box 26811
Richmond, VA 23261
(804) 264-2126
(717) 872-5190
Officer: William T. Van Pelt, Executive Director
Purpose and Activities: A non-profit educational organization of 1,500 members concerned with the history and study of American organs and organbuilding, particularly 17th, 18th, 19th and early 20th century organs. Also engage in preservation activities.
Publications: *The Tracker* (quarterly); and the *Annual Organ Handbook* (annually; $22/year for both publications)

ORGANIZATION OF AMERICAN KODALY EDUCATORS
(Formerly the National Kodaly Educators Association)
University of Wisconsin-Whitewater
Continuing Education
Whitewater, WI 53190
(414) 472-3165
Officers: Jean Sinov, President; Robert Perinchief, Executive Secretary
Purpose and Activities: To open lines of communication and to perpetuate the spirit of cooperation among all Kodaly educators. To encourage the continuing development of the child through music at all stages of school life.
Publication: *Kodaly Envoy* (quarterly; $20/year)

THE ORGAN LITERATURE FOUNDATION‡
45 Norfolk Road
Braintree, MA 02184
(617) 848-1388
Officers: Henry Karl Baker, President; Karl Henry Baker, Vice President
Purpose and Activities: Largest distributor of organ books and recordings in the world. Have published numerous books on organ history and construction; main function is publishing and reprinting historic materials on the organ.
Publications: *Organ Books and Records Catalogue* (annual; $1/year)

P

THE PEDAL STEEL GUITAR ASS'N, INC.
PO Box 248
Floral Park, NY 11001
Officer: Bob Maickel, President
Purpose and Activities: Nonprofit organization of steel guitarists established to help one another improve playing abilities and make others aware of the potential of the instrument. Conducts seminars and clinics.
Publication: *The Pedal Steel Newsletter* (10 issues/year; with membership)

PEOPLE-TO-PEOPLE MUSIC COMMITTEE*
712 Auburn Ave.
Takoma Park, MD 20912
(202) 254-3654
Officers: Ann Schein, President; Mrs. Ruth Sickafus, Executive Director
Purpose and Activities: To assist schools and music organizations in developing countries in various ways, including gifts of music materials; to encourage awareness and performance of American music in more musically advanced countries; to assist foreign musicians visiting the U.S.

PERCUSSIVE ARTS SOCIETY, INC.
214 W. Main
Box 697
Urbana, IL 61801-0697
(217) 367-4098
Officer: Larry Vanlandingham, President; Dennis Wiziecki, Administrative Manager
Purpose and Activities: The Percussive Arts Society is a worldwide organization founded in 1961 and incorporated in 1969 as a not-for-profit corporation under the laws of the State of Indiana and the State of Illinois. Its purpose is educational, promoting through its activities a wide range of musical knowledge, encompassing the young percussion student, the teacher, and the performer. Its mission is to facilitate communication between all areas of the percussive arts. PAS accomplishes its goals through six annual issues of *Percussive Notes*, its worldwide network of chapters, and its annual International Convention (PASIC).
Publication: *Percussive Notes* (6/year; $15/year U.S.; $18/year Canada and Mexico; $20/year overseas)

PERFORMING AND VISUAL ARTS SOCIETY (PAVAS)
PO Box 102
Kinnelon, NJ 07405
(201) 838-5360
Officer: Paul De Francis, President and Executive Director
Purpose and Activities: To honor and recognize the productively talented secondary school juniors and seniors in all areas of the performing and visual arts. Activities include seminars, original induction ceremonies, and programs imported to the schools by the chapter.
Publication: *PAVASTUFF* (1/year; free)

PHI BETA CREATIVE AND PERFORMING ARTS FRATERNITY*
4364 Graduate Circle
Houston, TX 77004
Officers: Dr. Martha Haun, National President; Karen A. Odegard, Central Office
Purpose and Activities: To promote the best in music, speech, drama, dance and art. Chapters are located in U.S. colleges and universities; scholarships are awarded to members at collegiate and recent graduate levels. Philanthropic contributions are given to the MacDoweel Colony, Peterborough, NH.
Publications: *The Baton* (3/year; $4.50/year members; $5/year nonmembers)

PHI BETA MU*
c/o Richard Crain
1111 Belaya St.
Houston, TX 77090
Officers: Richard Crain, Executive Secretary
Purpose and Activities: A non-profit fraternity to encourage the building of better bands and the development of better musicians in American schools and to foster deeper appreciation of good music.
Publications: *School Musician* (column)

PHI MU ALPHA SINFONIA FRATERNITY
"Lyrecrest"
10600 Old State Road
Evansville, IN 47711
(812) 867-2433
Officer: Maurice Laney, President
Purpose and Activities: To encourage and actively promote the highest standards of creativity, performance, education, and research in music in America; to foster the mutual welfare and brotherhood of students of music; and to instill in all people an awareness of music's important role in the enrichment of the human spirit.
Publication: *Sinfonian Newsletter* (4 issues/year; with membership)

PIANIST FOUNDATION OF AMERICA
4001 E. Blacklidge Dr., #1
Tucson, AZ 85712
(602) 326-7340
Officer: Ozan Marsh, President; Phyllis Stender, Executive Secretary
Purpose and Activities: Assists, guides young artists, especially pianists, in education, studies and careers in performing arts. Has concert tours, special study programs.

PIANO TECHNICIANS GUILD, INC.[1]*
113 Dexter Avenue, North
Seattle, WA 98109
(206) 283-7440
Officer: Don L. Santy, Executive Director
Purpose and Activities: Promotes high technical and ethical standards of piano service by maintaining registry of qualified members; constituting subordinate bodies; sponsoring technical institutes; publishing a technical journal; conducting an advanced training program; and cooperating with manufacturers, dealers and teachers in educating the public to the importance of adequate piano service.
Publications: *The Piano Technicians Journal*

PI KAPPA LAMBDA[1]
National Music Honor Society
PO Box 6222
University, AL 35486
(205) 348-6741
Officers: Wilbur H. Rowand, Executive Secretary/Treasurer
Purpose and Activities: The furtherance of music in education and institutions of higher learning. Selects and recognizes those juniors, seniors and graduate students who have demonstrated superior achievement in a program of instruction offered by the institution in which the chapter is established.
Publications: *Newsletter*

POLISH SINGERS ALLIANCE OF AMERICA
1217 78th Street
Brooklyn, NY 11228
(212) 748-3817
Officer: Eugene Pilis, President; Walter Falencki, General Secretary
Publication: *Singers Bulletin* (5 issues/year; free)

R

RADIO & TV REGISTRY
314 W. 53rd,
2nd Floor
New York, NY 10019
(212) 246-7676
Officer: Rockwood Lynn, President
Purpose and Activities: To locate and direct some 800 recording musicians to musical dates. Work directly with musical contractors. Membership is limited.

RECORDING INDUSTRY ASSOCIATION OF AMERICA, INC.*
888 Seventh Ave., 9th Flr.
New York, NY 10106
(212) 765-4330
Officers: Stanley Gortikov, President; Stephen Traiman, Executive Director
Purpose and Activities: Non-profit trade association for U.S. audio and video recording companies whose purpose is to promote their interests and the betterment of the industry.
Publications: *Activity Report* (annual); *Newsletter* (quarterly; free); *News from RIAA* (periodic; free)

RELIGIOUS ARTS GUILD
25 Beacon Street
Boston, MA 02108
(617) 742-2100
Officer: Barbara M. Hutchins, Executive Secretary
Purpose and Activities: Conducts music Anthem Award workshops; has choral music library. Office open mid-September to mid-June.
Publication: *Newsletter* (3/year; $10/year individuals; $20/year church)

RENAISSANCE ARTISTS AND WRITERS ASSOCIATION[1]
854 Pearl St.
Denver, CO 80203
(303) 832-6465
Officer: Kirk Cuthbert, Coordinating Secretary
Purpose and Activities: Projects include music supply co-operatives for financially-restricted artists and visitation programs for institutionalized people, as well as sponsorship of concerts, festivals.
Publication: *quarterly news*

RHYTHM AND BLUES ROCK'N ROLL SOCIETY, INC.[1]
PO Box 1949
New Haven, CT 06510
(203) 735-2736
Officer: William J. Nolan, Director
Purpose and Activities: To sustain rhythm and blues music. The Society sponsors benefit concerts, and sponsors music concerts and festivals to help amateur talent. It seeks to encourage the employment of minorities in music-related jobs in the production of educational radio and TV shows and films. Workshops on rhythm and blues culture are given.
Publication: *The Big Beat* (biannual; $5/year)

THE RUTGERS INSTITUTE OF JAZZ STUDIES
Rutgers, The State University of New Jersey
Bradley Hall
Newark, NJ 07102
(201) 648-5595
Officer: Dan Morganstern, Director
Purpose and Activities: To collect,

preserve and make available for research and study materials pertaining to jazz and related musics. Archives include 70,000 records; thousands of books, and periodicals; tapes, piano rolls, cylinder records, photographs, sheet music, catalogues, research files, art works, memorabilia, oral history tapes and transcripts.
Publication: *Annual Review of Jazz Studies* (1 issues/year; $12)

S

SCHUMANN MEMORIAL FOUNDATION INC.
2904 East Lake Road
Livonia, NY 14487
(716) 346-2745
Officer: June M. Dickinson, President
Purpose and Activities: To make material of scholarly value accessible to serious students of the lives and works of Robert and Clara Schumann and their associations. The Foundation has the largest collection of its kind in the U.S. in private hands.

SCREEN ACTORS GUILD, INC.
7750 Sunset Boulevard
Hollywood, CA 90046
(213) 876-3030
Officers: Edward Asner, President; Ken Orsatti, Executive Director
Purpose and Activities: Develops wages and working conditions for professional screen performers (including singers and voice-overs) Union representation for screen actors.
Publication: *Screen Actor News* (6/year; $4/year U.S.; $7/year foreign)

SESAC, INC.*
10 Columbus Circle
New York, NY 10019
(212) 586-3450
Officers: Alice H. Prager, Chairman and President
Purpose and Activities: A composers/publisher performing rights organization. Administers performing rights for its members.

SIGMA ALPHA IOTA[1]
4119 Rollins Avenue
Des Moines, IA 50312
(515) 255-3079
Officers: Mrs. J.C. Whinery, National Executive Secretary
Purpose and Activities: To form chapters of musicians and music students who uphold the highest ideals of a music education; to expand the musical life of the U.S.; to develop international musical exchange and understanding.
Publications: *Pan Pipes of Sigma Alpha Iota* (quarterly, $10.00 per year)

THE SIR THOMAS BEECHAM SOCIETY[1]
664 South Irena Avenue
Redondo Beach, CA 90277
(213) 374-0865
Officers: Stanley H. Mayes, Executive Secretary
Purpose and Activities: To support the memory of Sir Thomas Beecham and other "Giants of the past:" to act as a pressure group to seek the release of new commercial recordings and to prevent deletions from the catalog of currently-available recordings.
Publications: *Le Grand Baton* (quarterly); *newsletter* (bimonthly); *Bulletin* (semi-annually)

SOCIETY FOR ASIAN MUSIC[1]
Center for Near Eastern Studies
50 Washington Sq. S.
New York University
New York, NY 10003
(212) 769-1900
Officer: Pat Kennedy, Secretary
Purpose and Activities: Mid- to Far-Eastern Asian music appreciation and performance.
Publication: *Asian Music* (semi-annually)

SOCIETY FOR ETHNOMUSICOLOGY INC.
201 South Main Street, Room 513
Ann Arbor, MI 48104
(313) 761-7787
Officer: Gerard Behague, President; Don Roberts, Treasurer
Purpose and Activities: Members are primarily educators and graduate students interested in research in ethnomusicology, the study of music in its cultural context, particularly non-Western and folk music. The Society holds an annual meeting and publishes special monographs.
Publication: *Ethnomusicology* and *Newsletter* (3 /year; $35 regular, $20/year student members, $30/year institutions)

SOCIETY FOR FOLK HARPERS AND CRAFTSMEN
PO Box 29521
Los Angeles, CA 90029
(213) 247-4177
Officer: Sylvia Woods, President
Purpose and Activities: To strengthen the foundation of folk harp activities around the world, to stimulate and encourage regional activities, to advance research into the past of the folk harp and its music, and to identify the people who have meant so much to the continued survival of this instrument.
Publication: *Folk Harp Journal* (quarterly; $12 U.S.; $14 outside U.S.)

SOCIETY FOR STRINGS
170 West Seventy-third Street
Apartment 10A
New York, NY 10023
(212) 877-8378
Officer: Mrs. Ivan Galamion, President
Purpose and Activities: Promotes string playing in America and operates Meadowmount School of Music in Westport, NY.

SOCIETY FOR THE PRESERVATION AND ADVANCEMENT OF THE HARMONICA[1]
PO Box 865
Troy, MI 48099
(313) 647-2706
Officer: Gordon M. Mitchell, President
Purpose and Activities: To advance and preserve good harmonica music. Members perform regularly for service organizations.
Publication: *Harmonica Happenings* (quarterly)

SOCIETY FOR THE PRESERVATION AND ENCOURAGEMENT OF BARBER SHOP QUARTET SINGING IN AMERICA, INC. (SPEBSQSA)*
6315 Third Avenue
PO Box 575
Kenosha, WI 53141
(414) 654-9111
Officers: Hank Vomacka, President; Hugh Ingraham, Executive Director
Purpose and Activities: To perpetuate barbershop harmony through the singing of quartets and choruses.
Publications: *The Harmonizer* (6 issues/year; free to members, $6/year to nonmembers)

SOCIETY FOR TRADITIONAL MUSIC[1]
c/o Folklore Center
321 Sixth Avenue
New York, NY 10014
(212) 243-9714
Officer: Ralph Wrinzler, Executive Officer
Purpose and Activities: To present traditional music performers who might not be discovered by other promoters. Has occasional workshops. Formerly known as *Friends of Old-Time Music.*

SOCIETY OF STAGE DIRECTORS AND CHOREOGRAPHERS[1]
1501 Broadway
New York, NY 10019
(212) 391-1070
Officer: A. Harrison Cromer, Executive Secretary
Purpose and Activities: To represent the interests of directors and choreographers.

SOCIETY OF THE CLASSIC GUITAR
PO Box 566
Lenox Hill Station
New York, NY 10021
(212) 807-7709
Officer: Andres Segovia, Honorary President; Vladimir Bobri, President
Purpose and Activities: A nonprofit organization, the society meets monthly to hear guitar performances.
Publication: *SCG Newsletter* (6/year)

SONGWRITERS RESOURCES AND SERVICES*
6318 Hollywood Boulevard
Hollywood, CA 90028
(213) 463-7178 or 463-5691
Officers: Pat Luboff, President; Billy James, Vice President
Purpose and Activities: To protect and educate songwriters; to provide access to music publishing and recording; to provide guidelines for developing the song writing craft.
Publications: *Newsletter* (6/year; free to members)

SONNECK SOCIETY[1]
c/o Kate Keller
8102 Thoreau Dr.
Bethesda, MD 20817
(301) 229-9488
Officer: Kate Keller, Treasurer
Purpose and Activities: To encourage the study of music in America--all of its facets.
Publication: newsletter, thrice annually; membership directory, annually

SOUTHEASTERN COMPOSERS' LEAGUE
Music Deaprtment
PO Box 5261
Mississippi State University
Mississippi State, MS 39762
Officer: Fred Geissley, President
Purpose and Activities: To encourage the writing and performance of original contemporary music in the fourteen states and the District of Columbia. Co-sponsors Symposium for New Woodwind Quintet and Electronic Music Plus. Sponsors Salop-Slates Student Composition Contest, SCL Forum Festival of members' composition performances and general Annual Meeting.
Publication: *Music Now* (three times annually, free to members; $3.00 annually for libraries)

SOUTHERN APPALACHIAN DULCIMER ASSOCIATION
Rt. 1, Box 473
Helena, AL 35080
(205) 988-3350
Officer: Charles Ellis, Festival Chairman
Purposes and Activities: The organization has quarterly meetings and annual festival (the first Sunday afternoon in May).
Publication: A quarterly newsletter ($2/year, dues)

SOUTHERN CALIFORNIA VOCAL ASSOCIATION
PO Box 6048
El Monte, CA 91743-2048
(213) 445-0311
Officers: Lawrence R. Warden, President and Executive Director
Purpose and Activities: To upgrade the professional quality of choral and solo voice teaching. Serves secondary and college choral and vocal teachers in the 11 counties of Southern California. Choral festival program serves 35,000 students in 75 festivals. Sponsors solo and ensemble festival; solo scholarships; two workshop institutes per year.
Publications: *SCVA Newsletter/Bulletin* (5-6/year; $20/year with active membership; $10/year student/retired; $20/year association)

SUZUKI ASSOCIATION OF THE AMERICAS, INC.‡
319 E. Second St., Ste. 302
Muscatine, IA 52761
(319) 263-3071
Officers: Doris B. Preucil, President; Robert Klein Reinsager, Executive Officer
Purpose and Activities: A nonprofit professional association of teachers and parents in the Americas dedicated to meeting the needs of all those interested in talent education, or the "mother tongue" approach to music education. The association provides an opportunity for music educators and parents to join together in an exciting adventure of nurturing and realizing the potential of each child.
Publication: *American Suzuki Journal* (6/year, including Institute Issue and Membership Director; active members $32)

SWEET ADELINES, INC.‡
PO Box 45168
Tulsa, OK 74145
(918) 622-1444
Officer: Marsha O'Neill, President; Peggy Chambers, CAE, Executive Director
Purpose and Activities: An international nonprofit organization of women whose purpose is to teach the American folk art of singing four-part harmony, barbershop style, without instrumental accompaniment; and, through performances, to encourage a universal appreciation of the tradition of that music.
Publication: *The Pitch Pipe* (quarterly-January, April July, October); *The Rechorder* (February, May, August, November; joint subscription only; $2/year members; $4/year nonmembers)

T

TAU BETA SIGMA NATIONAL HONORARY BAND SORORITY*‡
122 Seretean Center
Oklahoma State University
Stillwater, OK 74078
(405) 372-2333
Officer: Julie Kuhns, National President; Thomas F. Sirridge, Executive Secretary
Purpose and Activities: A national honorary sorority for college and university band members, recognizing superior performance, interest and leadership.
Publication: *The PODIUM Magazine* (2/year; $5 for nonmembers)

TENNESSEE FOLKLORE SOCIETY
Middle Tennessee State University
Box 201
Murfreesboro, TN 37132
Officer: Charles Wolfe, Secretary
Purpose and Activities: Seeks to document and promote traditional folk culture and music of the mid-South; we publish a quarterly journal, issue phonograph records, sponsor television documentaries and other research projects.
Publication: *Tennessee Folklore Society Bulletin* (quarterly; $5/year with membership)

THEATRE COMMUNICATIONS GROUP, INC.[1]
355 Lexington Avenue
New York, NY 10017
(212) 697-5230
Officer: Alan Schneider, President; Peter Zeisler, Director
Purpose and Activities: A national arts organization combining the activities of both service organization and national professional association by addressing artistic and management concerns, serving artists and institutions, and acting as advocate and provider of services or a field diverse in its aesthetic aims and located in every part of this country.
Publication: *Theatre Communications* (monthly; $18/year individuals; $24/year institutions)

ARTURO TOSCANINI SOCIETY[1]
PO Box 7312
Burbank, CA 91505
Officer: Clyde J. Key, Founder-President
Purpose and Activities: To preserve the memory of Arturo Toscanini by maintaining a library of books and recordings, transcripts and tapes of rehearsals and concerts.
Publications: quarterly bulletin, *The Maestro* (annual)

TUBISTS UNIVERSAL BROTHERHOOD ASSOCIATION[1]
School of Music
North Texas State University
Denton, TX 76203
(817) 788-2791
Officer: Donald C. Little, Secretary-Treasurer
Purpose and Activities: To expand performance and jobs; redefine image and role of euphonists, tubists and their instruments; and encourage new designs and new music. Has competitions and awards.
Publication: *T.U.B.A. Journal* (quarterly) brochures; membership roster

THE TURECK BACH INSTITUTE, INC.*
(Formerly the International Bach Society)
c/o The Manhattan School of Music
120 Claremont Ave.
New York, NY 10027
(212) 744-8882
Officer: Rosalyn Tureck, Director
Purpose and Activities: To integrate at the highest levels the art of performance with scholarly studies in all media. Annual International Bach Symposium. Awards scholarships.
Publication: *Report to Members* (2/year)

U

UNITED IN GROUP HARMONY ASSOCIATION
PO Box 185
Clifton, NY 07011
(201) 365-0049
Officer: Ronnie Italiano, President & Board Chairman
Purpose and Activities: To preserve and expose the local group harmony music of the 50's and 60's as a music culture.
Publication: *Harmony Tymes* (quarterly; $6/year)

V

VIDEO ALLIANCE FOR THE PERFORMING ARTS[1]
150 West Fifty-fifth Street
New York, NY 10019
(212) 246-7820
Officer: Homer Poupart, Executive Director
Purpose and Activities: To make music, along with other arts, the topic of educational tapes, films and multi-media presentations for educational television, Public Television System, colleges, libraries and other civic groups.

VIOLA DA GAMBA SOCIETY OF AMERICA, INC.
1536 Third St., Apt. 6
Charleston, IL 61920
(217) 345-3995
Officer: Phyllis Olson, President; John A. Whisler, Executive Secretary
Purpose and Activities: To foster interest in viol playing. The Society sponsors an annual conclave and maintains a microfilm library.
Publication: *Journal of the Viola da Gamba Society of America* (annual); *VdGSA News* (quarterly); *Music Series*

VIOLA D'AMORE SOCIETY OF AMERICA
39-23 47th Street
Sunnyside, NY 11104
(212) 786-1467

10917 Pickford Way
Culver City, CA 90230
(213) 837-7596
Officer: Dr. Myron Rosenblum and Dr. Daniel Thomason, Co-Directors
Purpose and Activities: To promote and further the study, research, history, musical literature, and performance of the viola d'amore.
Publication: *Newsletter* (2/year; $9/year with membership)

VIOLIN SOCIETY OF AMERICA
23 Culver Hill
Southampton, NY 11968
(516) 283-8573
Officer: Norman C. Pickering, President
Purpose and Activities: The Society sponsors annual conventions and regional meetings offering lectures, demonstrations and discussions pertaining to all aspects of stringed bowed instruments and bows. International competitions are held biennially, and awards given to outstanding instruments and bows. The Society has a world-wide membership of approximately 1200.
Publication: *Journal of the Violin Society* (quarterly; with membership - $35 domestic; $50 overseas; $25 domestic student; $30 overseas student)

VIOLONCELLO SOCIETY, INC.
101 W. 57th St./2-D
New York, NY, 10019
(212) 246-3267
Officer: Claus Adam, President; Arthur Aaron, Secretary; Esther Prince, Administrator
Purpose and Activities: To promote and further the art of cello playing in this country; to provide a common meeting ground for professional and amateur cellists; to promote interest in the cello as a solo instrument; to provide opportunity of performances for artist and composer.
Publication: *Violoncello Society Newsletter* (3/year; with membership)

VOICE OF AMERICA - MUSIC BRANCH[1]
330 Independence Avenue, Southwest
Washington, DC 20547
(202) 755-4799
Officers: Michael H. Gray, Librarian
Purpose and Activities: Responsible for the selection, acquisition and evaluation of music and musical events for subsequent broadcast abroad by the Voice of America and its overseas facilities.

W

WOLF TRAP FARM PARK FOR THE PERFORMING ARTS[1]
1624 Trap Road
Vienna, VA 22180
(703) 938-3810
Officer: Carol V. Harford, President
Purpose and Activities: Nonprofit organization that finances the productions on its Filene Center Stage. Wolf Trap, a national park donated by Mrs. Jouett Shouse, offers concerts in symphony, opera, musicals, jazz, pop, chamber music, and dance.

THE WOMEN BAND DIRECTORS NATIONAL ASSOCIATION‡
3580 Rothschild Dr.
Pensacola, FL 32503
(904) 432-2887
Officers: Laurie Neeb, President; Marie Cotaya, Secretary
Purpose and Activities: To include any woman who is or has been a band director; to be represented at the national level, regardless of the length of her experience, or the level at which she works; to develop a comprehensive program that will be of musical and educational benefit to women band directors and their students; and to provide encouragement for young women entering the instrumental field.
Publications: *School Musician Magazine* (monthly; free to members) *Newsletter* (quarterly; free to members—$15/year active members and affiliate members; $25/year institutions; $8/year students)

WOMEN'S ASSOCIATION FOR SYMPHONY ORCHESTRAS[1]
2119 Bellmeade
Houston, TX 77019
(713) 529-4053
Officer: Mrs. Edward W. Kelley, Jr., President
Purpose and Activities: Education and dissemination of information among volunteers for major orchestras of the U.S. and Canada. The association strengthens and furthers the support of major orchestras and helps insure their continued existence. WASO also holds bi-annual conferences.
Publication: *Symphony News* (quarterly, members only)

Y

YOUNG AUDIENCES, INC.
115 East 92nd Street
New York, NY 10028
(212) 831-8110
Officer: J. McLain Stewart, Chairman; Warren H. Yost, National Executive Director
Purpose and Activities: Sends ensemble groups to schools for demonstrations, lectures and dialogue with students.
Publications: *Annual Report* (annually); *Newsletter* (quarterly); *Program Booklet* (irregular)

YOUNG CONCERT ARTISTS, INC.
250 West 57th St.
New York, NY 10019
(212) 307-6655
Officer: Susan Wadsworth, Director;

Nancy Wellman, Associate Director, Treasurer
Purpose and Activities: A nonprofit, concert management that discovers and launches the careers of today's extraordinary young solo musicians. YCA alumni include Emanuel Ax, Steven De Groote, Pinchas Zukerman, Paula Robison and the Tokyo String Quartet. Artists are selected through annual auditions by a jury of distinguished artists.
Publication: *YCA's Audition Announcement, YCA Series* brochures for Washington and New York

YOUNG MUSICIANS FOUNDATION
914 South Robertson Boulevard
Los Angeles, CA 90035
(213) 659-3766
Officer: Daniel Lewis, President; Erich Vollmer, Executive Director
Purpose and Activities: To encourage and assist exceptionally gifted young musicians by offering them significant performance opportunities and financial assistance. Programs currently offered are: the Debut Orchestra and Conductor-in-Training and Manager-in-Training; Debut Competition; Musical Encounter; Scholarship; and Chamber Music Workshops.

CANADA

A

THE ACADEMY OF COUNTRY MUSIC ENTERTAINMENT
PO Box 574
Thornhill, ON L3T 4A2
(416) 883-9294
Officers: Gordon Burnett, President; Gordon Ambrose, Secretary/Treasurer
Purpose and Activities: The Academy is a non-profit trade organization created to foster and promote the development of the Canadian Country Music Industry and to contribute towards higher artistic standards.
Publication: *Country Music News* (quarterly; free)

ALLIANCE CHORALE NOVEAU-BRUNSWICK[1]
120, rue Victoria
Moncton, NB E1C 1P9
(506) 382-5641
Officers: Aline O'Brien, Directrice Generale
Purpose and Activities: Integrating the choral activities of New Brunswick with other Provinces' concerts. Staging to perfection such activities as musicals, rhythms and vocal culture. Coordinating the province's national and international activities.

ALLIANCE FOR CANADIAN NEW MUSIC PROJECTS[1]
1263 Bay Street
Toronto, ON M5R 2C1
(416) 239-5195
Officer: Mary Gardiner, President; Eva Michalak, Executive Secretary
Purpose and Activities: To promote the teaching and performance of new music, in particular new Canadian music through such projects as a biennial festival of adjudications; workshops; concerts; commissioning of "paedogogical" works.
Publication: *Contemporary Showcase Syllabus* (biennial; free)

AMERICAN FEDERATION OF MUSICIANS OF THE UNITED STATES AND CANADA
86 Overlea Boulevard, Suite 404
Toronto, ON M4H 1C6
(416) 425-1831
Officer: J. Alan Wood, Vice President from Canada

ASSOCIATED MANITOBA FESTIVALS INC.
177 Lombard Ave.
Winnipeg, MB R3B 0W5
(204) 944-4578 or 944-2214
Officer: Grace Schellenber, President; Elizabeth Lupton Enns, Executive Director
Purpose and Activities: To promote and encourage higher standards in music and related arts through the medium of annual festivals, competitions, concerts and workshops throughout the Province of Manitoba.
Publication: *Associated Manitoba Arts Festivals Annual* (1/year; $.50 to members)

ASSOCIATION OF CANADIAN ORCHESTRAS
56 The Esplanade
Ste. 311
Toronto, ON M5E 1A7
(416) 366-8834
Officers: Michael Allerton, President; Betty Webster, Executive Director
Purpose and Activities: An arts service organization.

ASSOCIATION OF CANADIAN TELEVISION AND RADIO ARTISTS (ACTRA)[1]
105 Carlton Street
Toronto, ON M5B 1M2
(416) 977-6335
Officer: Jack Gray, President; Paul Siren, General Secretary
Purpose and Activities: Negotiation of collective agreements for performers and writers in television, radio and film.
Publication: *ACTRAScope* (eight issues annually)

ASSOCIATION OF CULTURAL EXECUTIVES
120 South Dr.
Toronto, ON M4W 1R8
Officer: Shirley Gibson, President
Purpose and Activities: Dedicated to the establishment of professional standards and to the improvement of working conditions for all members.

B

BRITISH COLUMBIA REGISTERED MUSIC TEACHERS' ASSOCIATION
10956 Swan Crescent
Surrey, BC V3R 5B6
(604) 581-3041
Officers: Mrs. Meryl Shether, President; Mrs. Beryl F. Wiebe, Secretary/Treasurer
Purpose and Activities: To raise the standard of the interest of music teachers in British Columbia and to promote the activities of the association, which include sponsoring Canada Music Week. Branches of the association hold recitals for students; Provincial Association subsidizes a workshop program available to all branches. Branches offer scholarships; Provincial association holds a Young Artists' Competition biennially, with students from each branch competing. The winner receives a scholarship.
Publications: *Provincial Newsletter* (quarterly, members only)

BRITISH COLUMBIA REGISTERED MUSIC TEACHERS ASSOCIATION—VANCOUVER BRANCH[1]
PO Box 76855, Station S
3366 Kingsway
Vancouver, BC, U5R 5S7
(604) 321-1994
Officer: Mrs. S.J. Mackie, President
Purpose and Activities: To hold workshops to upgrade teaching, festivals and recitals for the students of teachers who are members. The association also provides guidelines to standardize teaching and rates charged.
Publication: *Newsletter* (membership only)

BRITISH COLUMBIA TOURING COUNCIL[1]
572 Beatty Street
Vancouver, BC, Canada V6B 2L3
(604) 669-2800
Officer: Stephen Chetly, General Manager
Purpose and Activities: Provides information and assistance for artists touring British Columbia and for sponsors of performing artists.

C

THE CANADA COUNCIL
Le Conseil des Arts du Canada
PO Box 1047

Ottawa, ON K1P 5V8
(613) 237-3400
Officers: Timothy Porteous, Director; Franz Kraemer, Head of Music Section; Barry Cole, Officer; Rex Trotter, Officer; Yvonne Goudreau, Officer (Music)
Purpose and Activities: The major grant-giving organization in Canada.

CANADA OPERA PICOLA
3737 Oak St.
Vancouver, BC V6H 2M4
(604) 736-1916
Officers: David L. Vaughn, Q.C., President; J.J. Johannesen, General Manager; Leopold Simoneau, Director
Purpose and Activities: Dedicated to production of chamber operas, old and new; specifically created for touring purposes. Average strength of company, 25, including 6-9 singers, orchestral ensemble of 12-14 musicians with conductor and stage personnel.

CANADIAN AMATEUR MUSICIANS
PO Box 353
Westmount, PQ H3Z 2T5
(514) 932-8755
Officer: Jan Simons, Director General
Purpose and Activities: CAMMAC is a nonprofit organization established to encourage music learning and participation for people of all ages and levels of musical experience. CAMMAC runs an eight week music camp every summer.
Publications: *The Amateur Musician/Le Musicien Amatuer, Journal de CAMMAC/CAMMAC Journal* (3-4/year; free to members)

CANADIAN ASSOCIATION FOR MUSIC THERAPY[1]
PO Box 1208
Woodstock, ON N4S 8T6
Officer: Susan Munro, President
Purpose and Activities: To promote the use and development of music therapy and remedial music in the treatment, education and training, and rehabilitation of children and adults suffering from emotional, physical or mental handicaps. To serve as an organizational agency for its members.
Publication: *The Journal* (annual or biannual; free with membership); *Annual Conference Proceedings*

CANADIAN ASSOCIATION OF MUSIC LIBRARIES (CAML)
c/o Music Division
National Library of Canada
395 Wellington Street
Ottawa, ON K1A 0N4
(613) 996-3530
Officer: Alison Hall, President
Purpose and Activities: (1) To encourage the development of music libraries and collections. (2) To encourage cooperation among libraries; to share information about and to promote access to music. (3) To initiate and participate in projects and publications dealing with music resources. (4) To cooperate with other organizations concerned with music. (5) To act as the Canadian branch of the International Association of Music Libraries.
Publication: *CAML Newsletter* (quarterly; $20 to members, $10 to nonmembers)

THE CANADIAN BAND DIRECTORS ASSOCIATION
21 Tecumseh Street
Brantford, ON N3S 2B3
(519) 753-1858
Officer: Morley Calvert President; Frank McKinnon, Secretary
Purpose and Activities: To assist school, community and reserve militia bands and their leaders through clinics and workshops.
Publications: *C.B.D.A. Newsletter* (bimonthly; with membership)

CANADIAN BUREAU FOR THE ADVANCEMENT OF MUSIC
Exhibition Place
Toronto, Ontario, Canada M6K 3C3
(416) 598-2798
Officer: Lt. Col. C.O. Hunt, C.D., Managing Director
Purpose and Activities: Bring music education to elementary schools at an extremely low rate. Train qualified musicians to teach.
Publication: *CBAM Newsletter* (bimonthly; $40/year CBAM teachers; $15/year associate members)

THE CANADIAN COMPOSER[1]
Le Compositeur Canadien
1240 Bay Street, Suite 401
Toronto, ON M5R 2A7
(416) 925-5138
Officer: Richard Flohil, Editor
Publication: *The Canadian Composer* (10 issues/year; $2/year to nonmembers)

CANADIAN CONFERENCE OF THE ARTS
Conference canadienne des arts
141 Laurier Avenue West, Suite 707
Ottawa, ON K1P 5J3
(613) 238-3561
Officer: Lister Sinclair, President; Jeffrey Holmes, National Director
Purpose and Activities: Arts-based advocate for the arts in Canada.
Publication: *ARTS Bulletin* (bimonthly; with membership)

CANADIAN FEDERATION OF MUSIC TEACHERS' ASSOCIATIONS
Federation Canadienne des Associations de Professeurs
5 Weldon Street
Sackville, NB E0A 3C0
(506) 536-0143
Officer: Ernst Schneider, President; Shirley McCreedy, Business Manager
Purpose and Activities: An association of all Provincial registered music teachers in Canada, incorporated in 1935. Group has biennial, national convention.
Publication: *Canadian Federation of Music Teachers' Associations Newsletter* (3-4/year, membership)

CANADIAN FOLK MUSIC SOCIETY
Societe Canadienne de Musique Folklorique
1314 Shelbourne St., SW
Calgary, AB T3C 2K8
(403) 244-2804
Officer: Tim Rogers, President; Ian Robb, Treasurer
Purpose and Activities: Encouragement of the publication, performance, research and popularization of the folk music of Canada.
Publications: *Canadian Folk Music Journal* (annual); *Canadian Folk Music Society Bulletin* (quarterly)

CANADIAN INDEPENDENT RECORD PRODUCTION ASSOCIATION
144 Front St., W., Ste. 330
Toronto, ON M5J 2L7
(416) 593-4545
Officers: Vic Wilson, President; Earl Rosen, Executive Director
Purpose and Activities: A non-profit trade organization that represents independently owned companies in the recording industry. Over 100 producers, labels, studios and managers from across Canada have given CIRPA their support in an effort to build a stronger, independent recording industry.
Publication: *CIRPA Newsletter* (8 times per year; free to members; $50 Canada; $75 outside Canada)

CANADIAN LEAGUE OF COMPOSERS
Ligue Canadienne de Compositeurs
1263 Bay St.
Toronto, ON M5R 2C1
(416) 964-1364
Officers: Dr. Paul McIntyre, President; Josette Fitch, Executive Secretary
Purpose and Activities: The voice of the Canadian composer, seeking to influence government policy as it affects Canadian music. The CLC also seeks to encourage the performance of the music of its members, and to inform the members regularly on matters of professional concern.

CANADIAN MUSIC CENTRE
Centre de Musique Canadienne
1263 Bay St.
Toronto, ON M5R 2C1
(416) 961-6601
Officers: John A. Miller, Executive Director; J. Eric Ford, President
Purpose and Activities: Houses 7,000 scores of Canadian works both published and unpublished—orchestral works, operas, chamber music, choral, vocal and keyboard works and music especially useful for teaching, extensive collection of recordings of

Canadian works on disc, tape and cassette, performance material of orchestral and chamber music. Producers of Canadian concert record lable, *Centrediscs.*

CANADIAN MUSIC COMPETITIONS INC.
1600 Berri, Suite 267
Montreal, PQ 4E4
(514) 844-8836
Officer: Guy Lavigueur, President; Claude Deschamps, General Director; Helene M. Stevens, Co-General Director
Purpose and Activities: Nationwide, nonprofit organization that encourages young Canadians having significant talent and substantial promise by giving outstanding young musicians—selected through a rigorous national competition—the opportunity to perform before audiences.

THE CANADIAN MUSIC COUNCIL
Conseil Canadien de la Musique
36 Elgin
Ottawa, ON K1P 5K5
(613) 238-5893
Officer: Mme. Micheline Tessier, President; Guy Huot, Secretary General
Publication: *Musicanada* (quarterly; free to members, $7.50/year otherwise)

CANADIAN MUSIC EDUCATORS' ASSOCIATION
CMEA - National Resource Center
PO Box 1461
St. Catharines, ON L2R 7J8
(416) 684-4664
Officer: Dennis Humenick, President; Pat Jones, Membership Secretary
Publication: *Canadian Music Educator* (3/year; $15/year members/libraries, $20/year to corporations); *CMEA Newsletter* (quarterly)

CANADIAN MUSIC PUBLISHERS ASSOCIATION (CMPA)
Association Canadienne des Editeurs de Musique
111 Avenue Road, Suite 302
Toronto, ON M5R 3J8
(416) 922-4170
Officer: Brian Chater; President; Paul M. Berry, Secretary
Purpose and Activities: (1) To safeguard and advance the interests of the composer and publisher in accordance with the provisions of the Canadian Copyright Act. (2) To encourage fair trade practices and maintain high professional standards of workmanship and service in the publishing business.

CANADIAN RECORDING INDUSTRY ASSOCIATION
89 Bloor Street East
Toronto, ON M4W 1A9
Officer: Brian Robertson, President

CANADIAN STRING TEACHERS' ASSOCIATION[1]
506 St. James Street
London, Ontario, Canada N5Y 3P3
(519) 438-6285
Officers: Dr. Robert Skelton, President; Marion McDougall, Secretary
Purpose and Activities: To improve both the quality and quantity of string performances and instruction throughout Canada.
Publications: *Notes* (3 issues/year; $8 individual, $4 student, $15 institutional)

CANADIAN UNIVERSITY MUSIC SOCIETY/SOCIETE DE MUSIQUE DES UNIVERSITES CANADIENNES
Department of Music
University of Alberta
Edmonton, AB T6G 2F1
(403) 432-3263
Officers: Dr. Robert A. Stangeland, President; Dr. Michael Roeder, Secretary
Purpose and Activities: For the general membership: Stimulate research, performance creative activities, and the improvement of instructional methods through scholarly papers, concerts, symposia and publications; and to provide a forum for the exchange of views, discussion of common problems, and other matters of professional concern. For the council of Member Schools: Strengthen and maintain the position of music study in Canadian universities; consult and advise on new university music programs and monitor existing programs as is appropriate; and provide a forum for the exchange of views, discussion of common problems and other matters of professional concern.
Publication: *Canadian University Music Review/Revue de musique des universites canadiennes* (annually; $10)

COMPOSERS, AUTHORS AND PUBLISHERS ASSOCIATION OF CANADA LIMITED (CAPAC)
Association des Compositeurs, Auteurs et Editeurs du Canada Limitee
1240 Bay Street, 9th Floor
Toronto, ON M5R 2C2
Officer: John V. Mills, OC, QC, General Manager
Publication: *Canadian Composer* (monthly, except July and August; $2/year)

D

DEEP RIVER INSTRUMENTAL MUSIC ASSOCIATION[1]
PO Box 740
Deep River, ON
Officers: H.W. Tracey, President; Charles Van Wagner, Administrative Officer
Purpose and Activities: To bring good music to the community through live performances by both members and other musical organizations.

E

EDMONTON OPERA
1012-101 St., Ste. 503
Edmonton, AB T5J 0S5
(403) 442-4919
Officers: James A. Boyles, General Manager; Irving Guttman, Artistic Director
Purpose and Activities: To produce opera and expand the audience for opera by touring to schools and communities beyond Edmonton. There is a winter season of grand opera, a summer session of light opera, and a 30-week touring program which trains young singers and educates young audiences. This season we are developing a second stage for presentation of light works and recitals during the winter season.

F

FEDERATION OF CANADIAN MUSIC FESTIVALS[1]
304-310 Donald Street
Winnipeg, MB R3B 2H4
(204) 943-6098
Officers: G. Murray Campbell, Executive Director
Publications: *Digest Report* (annual; with membership)

THE FEDERATION OF MUSIC FESTIVALS OF NOVA SCOTIA
21 Oakburn Court
Halifax, NS B3M 2W5
(902) 443-2471
Officer: Marjorey Walters, President; Shirley Baker, Secretary-Treasurer

FESTIVAL CONCERT SOCIETY
3737 Oak St., Ste. 103
Vancouver, BC V6H 2M4
(604) 736-7661
Officers: Clive D.G. Roberts, President; J.J. Johannesen, Executive Director & Chief Executive Officer
Purpose and Activities: To tour professional artists in BC in the schools and small communities of the Interior as well as assist artists and schools for residency programs. The Society also showcases local talent in a weekly Sunday coffee concert series at the Q.E. Playhouse.

G

GUITAR SOCIETY OF TORONTO
19 Belmont Street
Toronto, ON M4N 1K6
(416) 922-8002

Officers: Peter Teeson, President
Purpose and Activities: A non-profit foundation dedicated to regular monthly meetings, creation of scholarship facilities, publication of news and information relating to the guitar. Liaison with classical guitar organizations.
Publications: *The Bulletin* (monthly, September-May; free to members)

H

HARMONY, INC.[1]
1496 Woodward Avenue
Ottawa, ON K1Z 7W6
(613) 722-5050
Officers: Dianne Pethick, President; Reta D. Brown, Executive Secretary
Purpose and Activities: 55 organized chapters for women who love to sing barbershop harmony and perfect the barbershop craft throughout the U.S. and Canada. Competitions are held each spring, with an annual convention and competition in November.
Publications: *The Key Note* (quarterly; $2.50)

I

INTERNATIONAL FOLK MUSIC COUNCIL[1]
Queen's University, Department of Music
Kingston, ON K7L 3N6
(613) 544-6226
Officers: Poul Rovsing Olsen, President; Graham George, Secretary-General
Publications: *Yearbook* (annual; free to members, $15/year nonmembers); *Bulletin* (2/year; free to members)

INTERNATIONAL SOCIETY FOR MUSIC EDUCATION
c/o MENC
10 Gorsey Square
Scarborough, ON M1B 1A7

J

JEUNESSES MUSICALES DU CANADA/YOUTH AND MUSIC CANADA
1250, Sanguinet
Montreal, PQ H2X 3E7
(514) 845-4108
Officers: Mario Duschenes, President; Jean-Claude Picard, General Director
Purpose and Activities: Promote music and help young musicians.

K

KODALY INSTITUTE OF CANADA[1]
PO Box 20, Station A
Ottawa, ON K1N 8V1
(613) 235-6886
Officers: Professor Kenneth Bray, President; Mae Daly, Executive Director
Publications: *Notes* (quarterly, $5 to nonmembers)

L

LADIES' MORNING MUSICAL CLUB[1]
1410 Guy Street, Ste. 32
Montreal, PQ H3H 2L7
(514) 932-6796
Officers: Constance V. Pathy, President; Mme S. Gamache, Secretary-Treasurer
Purpose and Activities: Founded in 1892, the organization presents a series of concerts of chamber music. All disciplines are represented—piano, strings, winds, voice and small ensembles in different combinations.

LETHBRIDGE SYMPHONY ASSOCIATION
PO Box 1101
Lethbridge, AB T1J 0W5
(403) 328-8168
Officers: Steve Wild, President; Peter Sametz, Business Manager
Purpose and Activities: To perform live symphonic concerts; to operate a string training program; and to educate the public towards symphony music.

M

MANITOBA CHORAL DIRECTORS ASSOCIATION[1]
32 Garnet Bay
Winnepeg, Manitoba, Canada R3T 0L5
(204) 284-0865
Officers: John Standing, Coordinator
Purpose and Activities: To promote choral singing in Manitoba and to encourage high standards of performance.
Publications: *MCDA Newsletter* (quarterly, $5.00)

MUSIC GALLERY
30 St. Patrick St.
Toronto, ON M5T 1V1
(416) 598-2400
Officers: Al Mattes, President; Bob Wilcox, Manager
Purpose and Activities: A center for contemporary music including performance space, 8-track recording studio/record company with a catalogue of 25 records, and a music publication.
Publication: *Musicworks* (quarterly)

MUSIC INDUSTRIES ASSOCIATION OF CANADA (MIAC)
130 Bloor St., W., Ste. 1101
Toronto, ON M5S 2X7
(416) 964-2875
Officers: William E. Locke, President; Al Kowalenko, Executive Secretary
Purpose and Activities: A Canadian association for manufacturers, wholesalers, and distributors of musical instruments and accessories, published music and sound reinforcement products. Music retail dealers are not members of MIAC.
Publication: *MIAC Newsletter* (bimonthly; free to members)

N

NATIONAL PROFESSIONAL MUSIC TEACHERS' ASSOCIATION[1]
2285 E. 61st Ave.
Vancouver, BC, Canada V5P 2K5
(604) 324-3415

NATIONAL YOUTH ORCHESTRA ASSOCIATION OF CANADA[1]
76 Charles Street, West
Toronto, Ontario, Canada M5S 1K8
(416) 922-5031
Officer: Dr. Stanley Saunders, President; John Brown, General Director
Publication: *Who We Are and What We Do* (annual; free)

NEW BRUNSWICK FEDERATION OF MUSIC FESTIVALS, INC.[1]
PO Box 415
190 Blvd. J.D. Gauthier
Shippagan, NB E0B 2P0
(506) 336-4323
Officer: Mrs. Margaret Grant, President; Mrs. Hectorine Lauzier, Executive Secretary

NIAGARA SYMPHONY ASSOCIATION
85 Church St.
St. Catharines, ON L2R 3C7
(416) 685-7358
Officers: Josephine Henderson, President; Ian Spraggon, General Manager
Purpose and Activities: Professional symphony orchestra employing 65 musicians and one resident composer. Eighteen concerts per season divided among three series. Also operates Niagara Symphony Chorus, 65 members.

NOVA SCOTIA CHORAL FEDERATION
5516 Spring Garden Rd., Ste. 305
Halifax, NS B3J 1G6
(902) 423-4688
Officer: William A. Perrot, President; Rachel DeWolf-Swetnam, Executive Director
Publication: *Chorus* (bimonthly; free with membership)

O

OKANAGAN SYMPHONY SOCIETY
PO Box 1120
Kelowna, BC V1Y 7P8
(604) 763-7544
Officers: William L. Arthur, President; Karen Patterson, General Manager
Purpose and Activities: To cultivate an appreciation of music and foster an

interest in music; and to present musical concerts and other entertainments for the general public.

OLD TIME MUSIC CLUB OF CANADA
1421 Gohier St.
St. Laurent, PQ H4L 3K2
(514) 748-7251
Officers: Bob Fuller, Secretary
Publications: *Underground* (2-3/year; free to members, $.50 nonmembers)

ONTARIO CHORAL FEDERATION
208 Bloor St., W., Ste. 303
Toronto, ON M5S 1T8
(416) 925-5525
Officer: Mrs. Bobbi Cain, President; Mrs. Norah Bolton, Executive Administrator
Publications: *Newsletter* (bimonthly; $20/year individuals; $30/year choir; $45/year corporate)

ONTARIO DRUM CORPS ASSOCIATION
466 Lake Dr. South
Keswick, ON L4P 1R1
(415) 476-5472
Officers: John Jones, President; Allen J. Tierney, Executive Director
Purpose and Activities: A non-profit organization formed to promote and develop drum and bugle corps in the province of Ontario.
Publication: *Information Drum Corps* (monthly; free to members)

ONTARIO FEDERATION OF SYMPHONY ORCHESTRAS
56 The Esplanade, Suite 311
Toronto, ON M5E 1A7
(416) 366-8834
Officer: Paul Robinson, President; Betty Webster, Executive Director
Purpose and Activities: Service organization for member orchestras.
Publication: *Orchestra Canada/Orchestres Canada* (10/year; $5/year)

ONTARIO REGISTERED MUSIC TEACHERS' ASSOCIATION
PO Box 712
Barrie, ON L4M 4Y5
(705) 456-2101
Officer: Margaret E. Dailey, Provincial Treasurer/Registrar
Publication: *ORMTA Newsletter* (3/year; free with membership)

P

PERFORMING RIGHTS ORGANIZATION OF CANADA, LTD.
41 Valleybrook Dr.
Toronto, ON M3B 2S6
(416) 445-8700
Officers: Dr. Jan Matejcek, Managing Director
Purpose and Activities: P.R.O. Canada is a performing rights society, representing more than 14,000 Canadian authors, composers, and music publishers. It collects license fees from the users of music and distributes these in the form of performance royalties to copyright owners, based on the performance of their music.
Publication: *The Music Scene/La Scene Musicale* (6/year; free)

PRO MUSICA SOCIETY OF CANADA, INC.
1270 Sherbrooke St., W.
Montreal, PQ M36 1H7
(514) 845-0532
Officers: Maurice Corbeil, President; Mercedes Charland, Secretary-Treasurer
Purpose and Activities: A non-profit organization presenting a season of 9 concerts of chamber music to the public.

R

THE RAGTIME SOCIETY, INC.[1]
PO Box 520, Station A
Weston, ON M9N 3N3
(416) 244-9761
Officers: John Arpin, President; John Fairhead, Treasurer and Chairman of the Board
Purpose and Activities: To preserve classical ragtime music and to pursue such other activities as shall serve to maintain and develop interest in classical ragtime music and music related thereto.
Publication: *The Ragtimer* (bimonthly; $8/year)

ROYAL CANADIAN COLLEGE OF ORGANISTS
212 King Street West, Suite 300A
Toronto, ON M5H 1K5
(416) 593-4025
Officer: Margaret Drynan, President; T.J. Hillier, General Secretary

S

SASKATCHEWAN MUSIC FESTIVAL ASSOCIATION
2205 Victoria Ave.
Regina, SK S4P 0S4
(306) 522-3651
Officers: Mrs. Janet Wendland, President; Doris Covey Lazecki, Executive Director
Publications: *Saskatchewan Music Festival Association Official Syllabus* (annual)

SASKATCHEWAN REGISTERED MUSIC TEACHERS ASSOCIATION[1]
(Regina Branch)
4121 Princess Street
Regina, SK S4T 3A5
(403) 586-1365
Officer: Mrs. Shirley Lummerding, President

SASKATOON SYMPHONY SOCIETY
Box 1361
Saskatoon, SK S7K 3N9
(306) 665-6414
Officers: Mrs. Shirley McKercher, President; Mr. John Holland, General Manager
Purpose and Activities: Presentation of concerts throughout the year involving the Saskatoon Symphony Orchestra.

V

VANCOUVER OPERA ASSOCIATION
548 Cambie St.
Vancouver, BC V6N 2B7
(604) 682-2871
Officers: Colin Warner, President; Cathrine M.L. Miciak, Administrator
Purpose and Activities: Presents professional opera productions, performances of opera in schools, and professional development of young singers (master classes).
Publication: *Vancouver Opera Journal* (quarterly)

VICTORIA SYMPHONY SOCIETY
631 Superior St.
Victoria, BC V8V 1V1
(604) 385-9771
Officers: Warren Wolmuth, President; Edgar Hemingway, Operations Manager
Purpose and Activities: To provide symphonic music for Victoria and the Province of British Columbia.

State Arts Agency Directory

Agencies are listed alphabetically by state. Listings of Community Arts Agencies in each state may be obtained by contacting the state agency. A listing of Regional Organizations follows the state listings. Both lists were made available through the courtesy of the National Assembly of State Arts Agencies (NASAA), Washington, DC.

ALABAMA STATE COUNCIL ON THE ARTS & HUMANITIES
Lamar Rainer, Chair
PO Box 340
Elba, AL 36323
(205) 897-2252

M.J. Zakrzewski, Executive Director
114 N. Hull St.
Montgomery, AL 36130
(205) 832-6758

ALASKA STATE COUNCIL ON THE ARTS
Robert Miller, Chair
8240 Resurrection Dr.
Anchorage, AK 99504
(907) 337-8876

Chris D'Arcy, Acting Executive Director
619 Warehouse Ave., Ste. 220
Anchorage, AK 99501
(907) 279-1558

AMERICAN SAMOA ARTS COUNCIL
Palauni Tuiasosopo, Chair
Office of the Governor
Pago Pago, AS 96799
633-4115

Matilda Lolotai, Executive Director
PO Box 1540
Office of the Governor
Pago Pago, AS 96799
633-4347

ARIZONA COMMISSION ON THE ARTS
Richard Whitney, Chair
201 N. Central, #3300
Phoenix, AZ 85073
(602) 257-7422

Adrienne Hirsch, Executive Director
2024 N. Seventh St., Ste. 201
Phoenix, AZ 85006
&502) 255-5882

ARKANSAS ARTS COUNCIL
Candace Burton, Chair
912 S. 22nd
Arkadelphia, AR 71923
(501) 246-4531, x142

Carolyn Staley, Executive Director
Continental Bldg., Ste. 500
Little Rock, AR 72201
(501) 371-2539

CALIFORNIA ARTS COUNCIL
Consuelo Santos Killans, Chair
2064 Alameda Way
San Jose, CA 95726
(408) 984-5340

Marilyn Ryan, Executive Director
1901 Broadway, Ste. A
Sacramento, CA 95818
(916) 445-1530

COLORADO COUNCIL ON THE ARTS & HUMANITIES
Lucien Wulsin, Chair
1380 Lawrence St., Ste. 880
Denver, CO 80202
(303) 573-7181

Ellen Pierce, Executive Director
770 Pennsylvania Ave.
Denver, CO 80203
(303) 866-2617

CONNECTICUT COMMISSION ON THE ARTS
Susan Kelly, Chair
86 Bloomfield Ave.
Hartford, CT 06105
(203) 233-4885

Gary Young, Executive Director
340 Capitol Ave.
Hartford, CT 06106
(203) 566-4770

DELAWARE STATE ARTS COUNCIL
Judy Hoopes, Chair
104 Brookmeadow Rd., West Farm
Wilmington, DE 19807
(302) 652-5618

Ann Houseman, Executive Director
State Office Bldg.
Wilmington, DE 19801
(302) 571-3540

DISTRICT OF COLUMBIA (DC) COMMISSION ON THE ARTS & HUMANITIES
Peggy Cooper-Cafritz, Chair
2900 44th St., NW
Washington, DC 20016
(202) 244-1966

Mildred Bautista, Executive Director
420 7th St., NW, 2nd Flr.
Washington, DC 20004
(202) 724-5613

ARTS COUNCIL OF FLORIDA
Jack Clark, Chair,
PO Box 190
Ocala, FL 32678
(904) 732-3121

Chris Doolin, Executive Director
Department of State, The Capitol
Tallahassee, FL 32304
(904) 487-2980

GEORGIA COUNCIL FOR THE ARTS & HUMANITIES
Rosemary Stiefel, Chair
880 Clifton Rd., NE
Atlanta, GA 30307
(404) 373-3582

Frank Ratka, Executive Director
2082 E. Exchange Pl., Ste. 100
Tucker, GA 30084
(404) 656-3967

INSULAR ARTS COUNCIL
Marilyn Abalos, Chair
4 Chichirica
Dededo, GU 96912
632-9615

Annie Benavente Stone, Executive Director

PO Box 2950
Agana, GU 96910
477-7413

STATE FOUNDATION ON CULTURE AND THE ARTS (HAWAII)
Naomi Morita, Chair
PO Box 4160
82-Makalani St.
Hilo, HI 96720
(808) 961-7351

Sarah Richards, Executive Director
335 Merchant St., Ste. 202
Honolulu, HI 96813
(808) 548-4145

IDAHO COMMISSION ON THE ARTS
Annette Park, Chair
901 Balsam
Boise, ID 83706
(208) 345-9921

Joan Lolmaugh, Executive Director
304 W. State St.
Boise, ID 83720
(208) 334-2119

ILLINOIS ARTS COUNCIL
David Connor, Chair
301 SW Adams
Peoria, IL 61631
(309) 674-7781

Carl Petrick, Executive Director
111 N. Wabash Ave., Ste. 700
Chicago, IL 60602
(312) 793-6750

INDIANA ARTS COMMISSION
Stuart L. Main, Chair
Lafayette National Bank
PO Box 780
Lafayette, IN 47902
(317) 423-8397

Susan Zurbuchen, Acting Executive Director
155 E. Market St.
Indianapolis, IN 46204
(317) 232-1268

IOWA ARTS COUNCIL
Don Singer, Chair
320 Lillian Ln.
Waterloo, IA 50701
(319) 234-6891

Sam Grabarski, Executive Director
State Capitol Bldg.
Des Moines, IA 50319
(515) 281-4451

KANSAS ARTS COMMISSION
Ruth Browne, Chair
1603 5th St.
Clay City, KS 67432
(913) 632-2618

John Reed, Executive Director
112 W 6th St.
Topeka, KS 66603
(913) 296-3335

KENTUCKY ARTS COUNCIL
Albert P. Smith, Chair
Editor & Publisher
The Sentinel-Echo
115 W. 5th St.
London, KY 40701
(606) 878-7400

Nash Cox, Executive Director
Berry Hill
Frankfort, KY 40601
(502) 564-3757

LOUISIANA STATE ARTS COUNCIL
Naomi Marshall, Chair
21 Maryland Dr.
New Orleans, LA 70124
(504) 522-9884

Al Head, Executive Director
PO Box 44247
Baton Rouge, LA 70804
(504) 925-3934

MAINE STATE COMMISSION ON THE ARTS & HUMANITIES
John Scarcelli, Chair
64 High St.
Farmington, ME
(207) 778-3501, x478

Alden C. Wilson, Executive Director
55 Capitol St.
State House Station 25
Augusta, ME 04333
(207) 289-2724

MARYLAND STATE ARTS COUNCIL
Dr. Gerald W. Johnson, Chair
1221 Coulborne Mill Rd., Rustic Acres
Salisbury, MD 21801
(301) 651-2200, x267

Hank Johnson, Acting Executive Director
15 W. Mulberry St.
Baltimore, MD 21201
(301) 685-6740

MASSACHUSETTS COUNCIL ON THE ARTS & HUMANITIES
Vernon Alden, Chair
J. Hancock TWR-49th Flr.
200 Clarendon St.
Boston, MA 02116
(617) 727-0767

Anne Hawley, Executive Director
One Ashburton Pl.
Boston, MA 02108
(617) 727-3668

MICHIGAN COUNCIL FOR THE ARTS
Dr. Oscar Remick, Acting Chair
President Alma College
Alma, MI 48801

E. Ray Scott, Executive Director
1200 6th Ave., Executive Plaza
Detroit, MI 48226
(313) 256-3735

MINNESOTA STATE ARTS BOARD
Katherine Murphy, Chair
3139 S. Rivershore Dr.
Moorhead, MN 56560
(218) 233-4504

G. James Olsen, Executive Director
432 Summit Ave.
St. Paul, MN 55102
(612) 297-2603

MISSISSIPPI ARTS COMMISSION
Dr. Aubrey K. Lucas, Chair
Southern Station, Box 5001
Hattiesburg, MS 39406-5001
(601) 266-5001

Lida Rogers, Executive Director
301 N. Lamar St.
PO Box 1341
Jackson, MS 39205
(601) 354-7336

MISSOURI ARTS COUNCIL
Mrs. Talbot MacCarthy, Chair
6 Robin Hill Ln.
St. Louis, MO 63124
(314) 994-7971

Rick Simoncelli, Executive Director
111 N. 7th St., Ste. 105
St. Louis, MO 63101
(314) 444-6845

MONTANA ARTS COUNCIL
Jessica Stickney, Chair
2206 Main St.
Miles City, MT 59301
(406) 232-1100

David Nelson, Executive Director
1280 S. 3rd St., W.
Missoula, MT 59801
(406) 543-8286

NEBRASKA ARTS COUNCIL
Lavon Crosby, Chair
3720 S. 40th St.
Lincoln, NE 68506
(402) 488-1700

Robin Tryloff, Executive Director
1313 Farnam-on-the-Mall
Omaha, NE 68102
(402) 554-2122

NEVADA STATE COUNCIL ON THE ARTS
Royal Orser, Chair
1917 View Dr.
Elko, NV 89801
(702) 738-5530

Jacqueline Belmont, Executive Director
329 Flint St.
Reno, NV 89501
(702) 784-6231

NEW HAMPSHIRE COMMISSION ON THE ARTS
Barbara J. Dunfey, Chair
14 Wood Knoll Dr.
North Hampton, NH 03862
(603) 964-9821

Robb Hankins, Executive Director
Phenix Hall
40 N. Main St.
Concord, NH 03301
(603) 271-2789

NEW JERSEY STATE COUNCIL ON THE ARTS
Clement A. Price, Chair
82 Fairmont Terr.

East Orange, NJ 07018
(201) 648-5414 or 5410

Wendy McNeil, Acting Executive Director
109 W. State St.
Trenton, NJ 08608
(609) 292-6130

NEW MEXICO ARTS DIVISION
Consuelo Thompson, Chair
Drawer JJ
Espanola, NM 87532
(505) 753-3076

Bernard Lopez, Executive Director
113 Lincoln
Santa Fe, NM 87501
(505) 827-6490

NEW YORK STATE COUNCIL ON THE ARTS
Kitty Hart, Chair
80 Centre St.
New York, NY 10013
(212) 587-4595

Mary Hays, Executive Director
80 Centre St.
New York, NY 10013
(212) 587-4597

NORTH CAROLINA ARTS COUNCIL
Michael Newman, Chair
Newman, Calloway, Johnson & Winfree
635 W. 4th St., Box 2475
Winston-Salem, NC 27102
(919) 724-1503

Mary Regan, Executive Director
Department of Cultural Resources
Raleigh, NC 27611
(919) 733-2821

NORTH DAKOTA COUNCIL ON THE ARTS
Susan Freeman, Chair
1215 S. 8th St.
Fargo, ND 58103
(701) 235-4384

Donna Evenson, Executive Director
Black Building, Ste. 811
Fargo, ND 58102
(701) 237-8962

COMMONWEALTH ARTS COUNCIL OF THE NORTHERN MARIANAS
Jose Rios, Chair
Mayor of Saipan
Saipan, CM 96950
677-7230

Ana Teregeyo, Executive Director
Department of Community & Cultural Affairs
Saipan, CM 96950
677-7230

OHIO ARTS COUNCIL
John Henle, Chair
5704 Olentangy Blvd.
Worthington, OH 43085
(614) 885-7810

Wayne Lawson, Executive Director
727 E. Main St.
Columbus, OH 43205
(614) 466-2613

STATE ARTS COUNCIL OF OKLAHOMA
William Horton, Chair
PO Box 1603
Shawnee, OK 74801
(405) 521-2931

Betty Price, Executive Director
Jim Thorpe Bldg. #640
Oklahoma City, OK 73105
(405) 521-2931

OREGON ARTS COMMISSION
Marythea Grebner, Chair
Southern Oregon State College
1250 Siskiyou Blvd.
Ashland, OR 97520
(503) 482-6361

Peter deC. Hero, Executive Director
835 Summer St., NE
Salem, OR 97301
(503) 378-3625

PENNSYLVANIA COUNCIL ON THE ARTS
Diana Rose, Chair
1035 Devon Rd.
Pittsburgh, PA 15213
(412) 682-1708

June Arey, Executive Director
Finance Bldg, Room 216
Harrisburg, PA 17120
(717) 787-6883

INSTITUTE OF PUERTO RICAN CULTURE
Carlos Sanz, Chair
Apartado Postal 4184
San Juan, PR 00905
(809) 723-2115

Leticia del Rosario, Executive Director
Apartado Postal 4184
San Juan, PR 00905
(809) 723-2115

RHODE ISLAND STATE COUNCIL ON THE ARTS
Daniel Lecht, Chair
Rhode Island Lithograph Corporation
PO Box 1267
Pawtucket, RI 02862
(401) 725-0500

Christina A. White, Executive Director
312 Wickenden St.
Providence, RI 02903-4494
(401) 277-3880

SOUTH CAROLINA ARTS COMMISSION
Thomas M. Creech, Chair
First Federal Savings & Loan
PO Box 408
Greenville, SC 29602
(803) 271-7222

Scott Sanders, Executive Director
1800 Gervais St.
Columbia, SC 29201
(803) 758-3442

SOUTH DAKOTA ARTS COUNCIL
Margaret Quintal, Chair
1520 N. Ridge Rd.
Mitchell, SD 57301
(605) 996-6592

Charlotte Carver, Executive Director
108 W. 11th St.
Sioux Falls, SD 57102
(605) 339-6646

TENNESSEE ARTS COMMISSION
Nellie McNeill, Chair
3632 Orebank Rd.
Kingsport, TN 37664
(615) 926-4242

Arthur Keeble, Executive Director
505 Deaderick St., Ste. 1700
Nashville, TN 37219
(615) 741-1701

TEXAS COMMISSION ON THE ARTS
Hugo V. Neuhaus, Jr., Chair
13406 1st International Plaza
Houston, TX 77002
(713) 757-7312

Richard Huff, Executive Director
PO Box 13404, Capitol Station
Austin, TX 78711
(512) 475-6593

UTAH ARTS COUNCIL
JoAnn Freed, Chair
846 E. Capitol
Salt Lake City, UT 84103
(801) 363-8474

Ruth Draper, Executive Director
617 E. South Temple St.
Salt Lake City, UT 84102
(801) 533-5895

VERMONT COUNCIL ON THE ARTS
Michael A. Weinberger, Chair
39 Central St.
Woodstock, VT 05091
(802) 828-3291

Ellen McCulloch-Lovell, Executive Director
136 State St.
Montpelier, VT 05602
(802) 828-3291

VIRGINIA COMMISSION FOR THE ARTS
Carla Gay, Chair
6802 University Dr.
Richmond, VA 23229
(804) 282-4603

Peggy Baggett, Executive Director
400 E. Grace St., 1st Flr.
Richmond, VA 23219
(804) 786-4492

VIRGIN ISLANDS COUNCIL ON THE ARTS
Mary Holter, Chair
PO Box 91
Cruz Bay, St. John, VI 00830
(809) 776-6342

Stephen Bostic, Executive Director
Caravelle Arcade

Christiansted, St. Croix, VI 00820
(809) 773-3075

WASHINGTON STATE ARTS COMMISSION
Wallie Funk, Chair
212 1st Ave., S.
Seattle, WA 98104
(206) 622-4791

Michael Croman, Executive Director
Mail Stop GH-11
Olympia, WA 98504
(206) 753-3860

WEST VIRGINIA ARTS & HUMANITIES DIVISION
Kay Goodwin, Chair
One Vail Dr.
Ripley, WV 25271
(304) 372-8737

James Andrews, Executive Director
Department of Culture & History
Capitol Complex
Charleston, WV 25305
(304) 348-0240

WISCONSIN ARTS BOARD
Father J. Thomas Finucan, Chair
St. Stanislaus Church
838 Fremont St.
Stevens Point, WI 54481
(715) 344-3970

Marvin Weaver, Executive Director
123 W. Washington Ave.
Madison, WI 53702
(608) 266-0190

WYOMING COUNCIL ON THE ARTS
John Freeman, Chair
1703 S. Seventeenth St.
Laramie, WY 82070
(307) 766-5496

David Fraher, Executive Director
Equality State Bank Bldg., 2nd Flr.
Cheyenne, WY 82002
(307) 777-7742

Regional Organizations

AFFILIATED STATE ARTS AGENCIES OF THE UPPER MIDWEST (ND, SD, MN, IA, WI)
David Haugland, Executive Director
Hennepin Center for the Arts
528 Hennepin Ave., Ste. 302
Minneapolis, MN 55403
(612) 341-0755

CONSORTIUM FOR PACIFIC ARTS & CULTURES (AK, HI, GUAM, CA, AS, CM)
Richard Cornwell, Executive Director
PO Box 4204
Honolulu, HI 96813
(808)524-6128

GREAT LAKES ARTS ALLIANCE (OH, MI, IN, IL)
Gregory G. Gibson, Executive Director
11424 Bellflower Rd.
Cleveland, OH 44106
(216) 229-1098

MID-AMERICA ARTS ALLIANCE (NE, KS, OK, MO, AR)
Henry Moran, Executive Director
20 West 9th St., Ste. 550
Kansas City, MO 64105
(816) 421-1388

MID ATLANTIC STATES ARTS CONSORTIUM (MD, D.C., NY, WV, NJ, DE, PA, VA)
Sandra Lorentzen, Executive Director
11 E. Chase St., Ste. 7-B
Baltimore, MD 21202
(301) 685-1400

NEW ENGLAND FOUNDATION FOR THE ARTS (CT, ME, VT MA, NH, RI)
Thomas Wolf, Executive Director
25 Mount Auburn St.
Cambridge, MA 02138
(617) 492-2914

SOUTHERN ARTS FEDERATION (AL, FL, GA, KY, MS, NC, SC, LA, VA, TN)
Jim Backas, Executive Director
1401 Peachtree St., NE, Ste. 122
Atlanta, GA 30309
(404) 874-7244

WESTERN STATES ARTS FOUNDATION (WA, OR, UT, MT, ID, WY, NV, CO, AZ, NM)
Bill Jamison, Executive Director
141 E. Palace Ave.
Santa Fe, NM 87501
(505) 988-1166

NATIONAL ASSEMBLY OF STATE ARTS AGENCIES STAFF
Geoffrey Plate Jr., Executive Director
Gloria Cohen, Assistant Director
Ronya McMillen, Information Services Coordinator
Elizabeth J. Michel, Membership Services Coordinator
Connie Vohs, Administrative and Fiscal Assistant
Naomi Hurley, Secretary/Receptionist
Tom Birch, Legislative Counsel

State Arts Advocacy Organizations

Organizations are listed alphabetically by state. A listing of National Organizations follows the state listings. Both lists were made available through the courtesy of the National Assembly of State Arts Agencies (NASAA), Washington, DC.

ALABAMA FEDERATION FOR THE ARTS
Van Braun Civic Center
700 Monroe St.
Huntsville, AL 35801
Officer: Ramona Baker, President

ALASKA ARTS ALLIANCE
PO Box 3102
Anchorage, AK 99510
(907) 276-8161
Officer: Gordon A. Smith, President

ARIZONANS FOR CULTURAL DEVELOPMENT
4235 N. Scottsdale Rd., Ste. 204
Scottsdale, AZ 85251
(602) 990-1664
Officer: Carol Kenan, Executive Director

ARKANSANS FOR THE ARTS
309 Center St.
Little Rock, AR 72201
(501) 372-1116
Officer: Gordon Holl

CALIFORNIA CONFEDERATION OF THE ARTS
849 S. Broadway, Ste. 611
Los Angeles, CA 90014
(213) 627-9273
Officer: June Gutfleisch, Executive Director

CONNECTICUT ADVOCATES FOR THE ARTS
110 Audubon St.
New Haven, CT 06511
(203) 278-6035
Officer: Marleen Sansone, Executive Director

CULTURAL ALLIANCE OF GREATER WASHINGTON
633 E St., N.W.
Washington, DC 20004
(202) 638-2406

FLORIDA CULTURAL ACTION ALLIANCE
PO Box 10589
Tallahassee, FL 32301
Officer: G. David Black, Acting President

GEORGIA CITIZENS FOR THE ARTS
1404 Spring St., N.W.
Atlanta, GA 30309
(404) 873-4356
Officer: Donna Izlar, President

ARTS COUNCIL OF HAWAII
PO Box 50225
Honolulu, HI 96850
(808) 524-7120
Officer: Karl Ichida, Executive Director

ARTS ADVOCACY LEAGUE
804 Resigne
Boise, ID 83702
(208) 384-9121
Officer: Sally Ahlstedt

ILLINOIS ARTS ALLIANCE/ARTS ACTION COALITION
22 W. Monroe, Ste. 801
Chicago, IL 60603
(312) 977-1730
Officer: Mort Kaplan, President; Diane Gallert, Treasurer

INDIANA ADVOCATES FOR THE ARTS
5219 Old Mill Rd.
Fort Wayne, IN 46807
(219) 745-0133
Officer: Colleen Benninghoff, President

FOUNDATION FOR THE ARTS IN IOWA
647 Polk Ave.
Des Moines, IA 50312
(515) 255-8121
Officer: Jan Sholwell, Executive Director

KANSAS CONCERNED CITIZENS FOR THE ARTS
110 N. Market St.
Wichita, KS 67202
Officer: Harry Litwin

KENTUCKY CITIZENS FOR THE ARTS
PO Box 152
Frankfort, KY 40602
Officer: Louis deLuca, Executive Director

ASSOCIATION OF LOUISIANA ARTS AND ARTISTS
Baton Rouge Arts and Humanities Council
427 Laurel St.
Baton Rouge, LA 70801
Officer: Kyle Walls, President

MARYLAND CITIZENS FOR THE ARTS
Sue Hess, President
401 Bering Rd.
Ocean City, MD 21842
(301) 532-2787

MASSACHUSETTS ARTS ADVOCACY COMMITTEE
Barbara Garvey, Director of Development
Elms College
291 Springfield St.
Chicopee, MA 01013
(413) 598-8351
Officer: Barbara Garvey, Director of Development

MINNESOTA CITIZENS FOR THE ARTS
Landmark Center
75 W. Fifth St.
St. Paul, MN 55102
(612) 227-5963
Officer: Megan Jones, Executive Director

FRIENDS OF THE ARTS IN MISSISSIPPI
PO Box 1531
Jackson, MS 39205
(601) 354-7336
Officer: Linda Stratford, Executive Secretary

MISSOURI CITIZENS FOR THE ARTS
PO Box 15119
St. Louis, MO 63110
(314) 721-0049
Officer: Chris Vincent, Director

MONTANA ARTS ADVOCACY
Box 5731
Helena, MT 59604
(406) 449-2417
Officer: Claudette Johnson, Chair

NEBRASKANS FOR THE ARTS
PO Box 674 DTS
Omaha, NE 68101
(402) 341-6698
Officer: Judi Huzlett, Advocacy Coordinator

NEVADA ALLIANCE FOR THE ARTS
624 S. 9th St.
Las Vegas, NV 89101
Officer: Pat Marchese, President; Cynthia Cunningham, Executive Director

AD HOC ARTS ALLIANCE OF NEW MEXICO
New Mexico Symphony Orchestra
PO Box 769
Albuquerque, NM 87103
(505) 842-8586
Officer: William Weinrod

ALLIANCE OF NEW YORK STATE ARTS COUNCIL
18 W. Carver St.
Huntington, NY 11743
(516) 423-1818
Officer: Elizabeth H. Howard, Executive Director

NORTH CAROLINA ASSOCIATION OF ARTS COUNCIL
120 Morris St.
Durban, NC 27201
(919) 682-5519
Officer: Jan Ellis Kohl

OHIO CITIZENS' COMMITTEE FOR THE ARTS
636 Citizens Building
Canton, OH 44702
(216) 455-4409 or 452-6129
Officer: William Blair, Director

OKLAHOMA ADVOCATES FOR THE ARTS
1520 E. 26th Pl.
Tulsa, OK 74114
(918) 747-7895
Officer: Erma Henson

OREGON ADVOCATES FOR THE ARTS
310 Reed Opera House
189 Liberty NE
Salem, OR 97301
(503) 588-2787
Officer: John Evey, Executive Director

CITIZENS FOR THE ARTS IN PENNSYLVANIA
1121 Myrtle St.
Harrisburg, PA 18510
(717) 347-2903
Officer: Sondra Myers, President

RHODE ISLAND ARTS ALLIANCE
Trinity Square Repertory Company
201 Washington St.
Providence, RI 02903
(401) 521-1100
Officer: Simone Joyaux

FOUNDATION FOR THE ARTS IN SOUTH DAKOTA
Box 642
Sioux Falls, SD 57101
(605) 334-7561
Officer: Orrin Juel, Advocacy Chair

TENNESSEANS FOR THE ARTS
PO Box 2756
Nashville, TN 37219
(615) 329-3033
Officer: George Carpenter

TEXAS ARTS ALLIANCE
Box 5513
Austin, TX 78763
(512) 474-2263
Officer: Susan Morehead, Executive Director

UTAH CITIZENS FOR THE ARTS
524 B Street
Salt Lake City, UT 84103
(801) 359-5908
Officer: Beverly Whitney, President

ALLIANCE FOR ARTS EDUCATION
PO Box 217
Kingshill, St. Croix, VI 00850
Officer: Paul Youngblood, Chair

WASHINGTON STATE ARTS ALLIANCE
PO Box 9407
Seattle, WA 98109
(206) 447-4700
Officer: LeAnn Davis, President; Casey Johnston, Executive Director

WEST VIRGINIA ARTS ADVISORY COMMITTEE
2033 McCoy Rd.
Huntington, WV 25701
(304) 529-2701
Officer: Roberta Shinn Emerson, Chair

WISCONSIN CITIZENS FOR THE ARTS
22 N. Carroll St., Ste. 303
Madison, WI 53703
(608) 251-0471
Officer: Lucinda Brodgen, Executive Director

WYOMING CITIZENS FOR THE ARTS
PO Box 1204
Saratoga, WY 82331
Officer: Betty Ferguson

National Organizations

AMERICAN ARTS ALLIANCE
424 C. St., NE
Washington, D.C.
(202) 544-3900
Officer: Anne Murphy, Executive Director

AMERICAN ARTS COUNCIL
570 Seventh Ave.
New York, NY
(212) 354-6655
Officer: Jack Duncan, Special Counsel on National Policy

NATIONAL ASSEMBLY OF STATE ARTS AGENCIES
1010 Vermont Ave., NW; Ste. 316
Washington, D.C. 20005
(202) 347-6352
Officer: Tom Birch

American Federation of Musicians Locals

All member locals in the U.S. and Canada are listed alphabetically by state or province and city. Phone number, local number, and officers are given for each local. An alphabetical cross-index appears at the end of this section.

ALABAMA

BIRMINGHAM
BIRMINGHAM MUSICIANS' PROTECTIVE ASSOCIATION (256-733)
715 6th Street, S.W.
Birmingham, AL 35211
(205) 786-1201
Officers: Frank B. Carpenter, President; Robert L. (Bob) Summers, Secretary

MOBILE
MOBILE FEDERATION OF MUSICIANS (407-613)
951 Government St., Ste. 522
Mobile, AL 36604
(205) 432-2934
Officers: Melzar Williams, President; Arthur E. Henry, Jr., Secretary

MONTGOMERY
MONTGOMERY FEDERATION OF MUSICIANS (479-718)
P.O. Box 11385
Green Lantern Station
Montgomery, AL 36111
(205) 288-1064
Officers: William R. Norwood, President; V.H. Humphries, Secretary

TUSCALOOSA
THE TUSCALOOSA MUSICIANS PROTECTIVE ASSOCIATION (435)
P.O. Box 19
Tuscaloosa, AL 35404
(205) 553-8288
(205) 752-7176
Officers: Bernard Rosenbush, President; Marcia Winter, Secretary.

ALASKA

ANCHORAGE
ANCHORAGE MUSICIANS' ASSOCIATION (650)
109 West Sixth Ave.,
Anchorage, AK 99501
(907) 279-3415
Officers: Richard T. Schopf, President; H.E. "Bud" Quimby, Secretary

FAIRBANKS
MUSICIANS' PROTECTIVE UNION (481)
P.O. Box 99701
Fairbanks, AK 97701
(907) 456-3199
Officers: Bruce Shileika, President; Harlon C. Walrath, Secretary

JUNEAU
MUSICIANS' PROTECTIVE UNION (672)
107 West First St.
Juneau, AK 99801
(907) JU 6-1003
(907) 789-9419
Officers: James R. Gregg, President; Anita Garnick Kodzoff, Secretary

ARIZONA

PHOENIX
PHOENIX FEDERATION OF MUSICIANS (586)
1202 East Oak St.
Phoenix, AZ 85006
(602) 254-8838
Officers: Hal C. Sunday, President; JoAnne Drum, Secretary

TUCSON
TUCSON MUSICIANS' ASSOCIATION (771)
620 South Sixth Ave.
Tucson, AZ 85701
(602) 624-3688
Officers: Al Saunders, President; Marty Barnett, Secretary.

ARKANSAS

FAYETTEVILLE
MUSICIANS' PROTECTIVE UNION (273)
P.O. Box 321
Jasper, AR 72641
(501) 446-2300
Officers: Kenneth E. Murphy, President; Arlene Murphy, Secretary

FORT SMITH
PROFESSIONAL MUSICIANS' ASSOCIATION (385)
PO Box 4064
Fort Smith, AR 72901
(501) 474-3330
Officers: Lucien Sabin, President; Wesley Fisher, Secretary.

LITTLE ROCK
MUSICIANS' PROTECTIVE UNION (266)
1517 South Taylor
Little Rock, AR 72204
(501) 663-5420
Officers: C.W. Newth, President; Ben F. Thompson, Secretary

CALIFORNIA

BAKERSFIELD
MUSICIANS' MUTUAL PROTECTIVE ASSOCIATION (263)
802 Union Ave.
Bakersfield, CA 93307
(805) 325-1650
Officers: Harry S. Passehl, President; Lucia K. Evans, Acting Secretary

EUREKA
MUSICIANS' ASSOCIATION (333)
Box 758
Eureka, CA 95501
(707) 443-3366
Officers: Say Nygard, President; Robert H. Armstrong, Secretary

FRESNO
MUSICIANS' PROTECTIVE ASSOCIATION (210)
139 West Olive
Fresno, CA 93728
(209) 485-3600
Officers: Ralph Manfredo, President; Mrs. Margaret Bettencourt, Secretary

IMPERIAL VALLEY
THE IMPERIAL VALLEY FEDERATION OF MUSICIANS (347)
534 Main St.
El Centro, CA 92243
(714) 353-4224
Officers: Jimmie Cannon, President; Creon Thomas, Secretary

LONG BEACH
MUSICIANS' ASSOCIATION (353)
5215 Arbor Rd
Long Beach, CA 90808
(213) 421-4747
Officers: Fred Peters, President; Therese R. Wilkinson, Secretary

LOS ANGELES
MUSICIANS' UNION (47)
P.O. Box 38928
817 N. Vine St.
Hollywood, CA 90038
(213) 462-2161
Officers: Max Herman, President; Marl Young, Secretary

MERCED
MUSICIANS' PROTECTIVE UNION (454)
111 West 20th St.
Merced, CA 95340
(209) 722-6033
Officers: Verner H. Taylor, Jr., President; William M. Wivell, Secretary

MODESTO
MUSICIANS' ASSOCIATION (652)
1410 Carver Road
Modesto, CA 95350
(209) 522-8015
(209) 523-1524
Officers: Lynn Russell, President; Mrs. Blanche A. Matthews, Secretary.

MONTEREY
MUSICIANS' ASSOCIATION OF MONTEREY COUNTY (616)
591 Lighthouse Ave.
Monterey, CA 93940
(408) 375-6166
Officers: Millard M. Hawkins, President

NAPA
MUSICIANS' PROTECTIVE UNION (541)
3175 Solano Ave.
Napa, CA 94558
(707) 255-7533
Officers: Donald Meehan, President; Elmer A. Bradley, Secretary

RICHMOND
MUSICIANS' PROTECTIVE UION (424)
4 Marina Way
Richmond, CA 94801
(415) BE 2-0465
Officers: Al DelSimone, President; Joe Pallotta, Jr., Secretary

SACRAMENTO
MUSICIANS' PROTECTIVE UNION (12)
2623½ J Street
Sacramento, CA 95816
(916) 444-6660
Officers: Thomas P. Kenny, President; Frank Giordano, Secretary.

SAN BERNARDINO
ORANGE BELT MUSICIANS' ASSOCIATION (167)
1265 LaCadena Dr., Ste. 9
Colton, CA 92324
(714) 824-1450
Officers: Roger G. Myers, President; James Mackintosh, Secretary

SAN DIEGO
MUSICIANS' ASSOCIATION OF SAN DIEGO COUNTY (325)
1717 Morena Blvd.
San Diego, CA 92110
(714) 276-4324
Officers: Jack Maynard, President; C. Patrick Oakley, Secretary

SAN FRANCISCO
MUSICIANS' UNION (6)
230 Jones St.
San Francisco, CA 94102
(415) 775-8118
Officers: J.J. Spain, President; William J. Catalano, Sr., Vice President; Don Menary, Secretary

SAN JOSE
SAN JOSE FEDERATION OF MUSICIANS (153)
915 Almaden Ave.
San Jose, CA 95110
(408) 286-8602
Officers: Orrin Blattner, President; Don Hoque, Secretary

SAN LEANDRO
MUSICIANS' PROTECTIVE UNION (510)
P.O. Box 547
San Leandro, CA 94577
(415) 483-5470/5478
Officers: Tony Cervone, President; Irene Acosta, Secretary.

SAN LUIS OBISPO
MUSICIANS' PROTECTIVE UNION (305)
660 Majestic Dr.
Santa Maria, CA 93454
(805) 937-2333
Officers: Joseph Bardelli, President/Acting Secretary

SANTA ANA
MUSICIANS' ASSOCIATION (7)
2050 South Main St.
Santa Ana, CA 92707
(714) 546-8166
Officers: B. Douglas Sawtelle, President; Robert W. Stava, Secretary

SANTA BARBARA
MUSICIANS' MUTUAL PROTECTIVE ASSOCIATION (308)
2904½ De La Vina St.
Santa Barbara, CA 93105
(805) 687-3519
Officers: Harry Chanson, President; Earl Smith, Secretary

SANTA CRUZ
MUSICIANS' ASSOCIATION (346)
125 Walnut Ave.
Santa Cruz, CA 95060
(408) 426-1776
Officers: William H. Newman, President; Mrs. Frances Doherty, Secretary

SANTA ROSA
MUSICIANS' MUTUAL PROTECTIVE ASSOCIATION (292)
Labor Center
1718 Corby Ave.
Santa Rosa, CA 95401
(707) 545-1434
Officers: Richard W. Norcross, President; Nick Bardes, Secretary

STOCKTON
STOCKTON MUSICIANS' ASSOCIATION (189)
2626 N. California St., Room 9
Stockton, CA 95204
(209) 464-4016
Officers: Buddy L. Walter, President; James L. Urbani, Secretary

VALLEJO
MUSICIANS' PROTECTIVE UNION (367)
600 Nebraska St.
Vallejo, CA 94590
(707) 642-6152
Officers: Alton G. Robinson, President; Wilfred Yeaman, Secretary

VENTURA
MUSICIANS' MUTUAL PROTECTIVE ASSOCIATION (581)
P.O. Box 622
Ventura, CA 93002
(805) 643-9953
Officers: Darrell E. Larsen, President; James C. Hallowell, Secretary

COLORADO

BOULDER
UNIVERSITY MUSICIANS' ASSOCIATION (275)
1445 Balsam Ave.
Boulder, CO 80302

(303) 442-6518
Officers: Stephen C. Christopher, President; William K. Matthiesen, Secretary

COLORADO SPRINGS
PIKE'S PEAK MUSICIANS' ASSOCIATION (154)
1210 N. Tejon St.
Colorado Springs, CO 80903
(303) 632-5033
Officers: Allen E. Uhles, President; Charles Gilbert, Secretary

DENVER
DENVER MUSICIANS' ASSOCIATION (20-623)
6850 E. Evans Ave.
Denver, CO 80224
(303) 753-1914
Officers: Tasso Harris, President; James Griggsmiller, Secretary

GRAND JUNCTION
MUSICIANS' PROTECTIVE UNION (164)
919 Mesa Ave.
Grand Junction, CO 81501
(303) 242-0722
Officers: Clyde Jorgensen, President; Roy Weaver, Secretary

GREELEY
GREELEY MUSICIANS' ASSOCIATION (396)
2020 18th Ave.
Greeley, CO 80631
(303) 352-8566
Officers: Clay Taylor, President; Fred H. Werner, Secretary

PUEBLO
PUEBLO MUSICIANS' ASSOCIATION (69)
331 Colorado Building
Peublo, CO 81003
(303) 544-4725
Officers: Charles Quaranta, President; Constance M. Bregar, Secretary

CONNECTICUT

BRIDGEPORT
BRIDGEPORT MUSICIANS' ASSOCIATION (63-549)
337 William St.
Bridgeport, CT 06608
(203) 333-2017
(203) 334-8972
Officers: Anthony Carella, President; Lawrence M. Sutay, Secretary

BRISTOL
MUSICIANS' PROTECTIVE ASSOCIATION (432)
43 Tuttle St.
Bristol, CT 06010
(203) 583-3890
Officers: Hugo A. Grignoli, President; Walter Osenkowski, Secretary

DANBURY
DANBURY MUSICIANS' ASSOCIATION (87)
5 Oak Lane
Danbury, CT 06810
(203) 748-3058
Officers: Kenneth M. Lee, Jr., President; Evelyn Dewan, Secretary

HARTFORD
HARTFORD MUSICIANS' ASSOCIATION (400)
Suite 5, Great Meadow Towers
1800 Silas Deane Highway
Rocky Hill, CT 06067
(203) 563-1606
Officers: Louis J. Zebedo, President; Ralph S. Mixer, Secretary

MERIDEN
MERIDEN FEDERATION OF MUSICIANS (55)
35 Pomeroy Ave.
Wallingford, CT 06492
(203) 269-7508
Officers: Nicholas Azzolina, President; Robert E. Erdos, Secretary

MIDDLETOWN
MIDDLETOWN MUSICIANS' PROTECTIVE ASSOCIATION (499)
PO Box 955
Middletown, CT 06457
(203) 347-7805
Officers: Michael D. Moroni, President; Clifford E. Hamlin, Secretary

NEW BRITAIN
NEW BRITAIN MUSICIANS' ASSOCIATION (440)
19 Basset St.
New Britain, CT 06053
(203) 223-7334
Officers: Joseph De Fazio, President

NEW HAVEN
NEW HAVEN FEDERATION OF MUSICIANS (234-486)
45 Water St.
New Haven, CT 06511
(203) 562-4197
Officers: John F. Beesmer, President; R. George D'Alessio, Secretary

NEW LONDON
MUSICIANS' PROTECTIVE ASSOCATION (285)
113 Oneco St.
Norwich, CT 06360
(203) 887-7388
Officers: Francis R. Fain, President; Edward Brennan, Secretary

NORWALK
NORWALK MUSICIANS' ASSOCIATION (52)
64 Wall St.
Suite 400
Norwalk, CT 06851
(203) 853-9598
Officers: Anthony Santella President; Marie A. Bossert, Secretary

STAMFORD
STAMFORD MUSICIANS' ASSOCIATION (626)
65 Ogden Rd.
Stamford, CT 06905
(203) 325-1651
Officers: E. Richard Zaffino, President; Anthony J. Matteis, Secretary

TORRINGTON
TORRINGTON MUSICIANS' ASSOCIATION (514)
662 Main St.
Torrington, CT 06790
(203) 482-6439
Officers: Edward Henniquin, President; Joseph Languell, Secretary

WATERBURY
MUSICIANS' ASSOCIATION OF GREATER WATERBURY (186)
PO Box 4573
Waterbury, CT 06704
(203) 753-1354
Officers: Peter A. Ciavarella, President; Robert Mobilio, Secretary

WILLIMANTIC
MUSICIANS' UNION (403)
96 Northwood Rd.
Storrs, CT 06268
(203) 487-1887
Officers: Brian Klitz, President; Sandra Haines, Secretary

DELAWARE

WILMINGTON
DELAWARE MUSICAL SOCIETY (311-641)
6 West 30 St.
Wilmington, DE 19802
(302) 762-4993
Officers: Manny Klein, President; Helen T. Rairigh, Secretary

DISTRICT OF COLUMBIA

DISTRICT OF COLUMBIA FEDERATION OF MUSICIANS (161-710)
5020 Wisconsin Ave, N.W.
Washington, DC 20016
(202) 244-8833
Officers: Sam Jack Kaufman, President; Robert D'Arcy, Secretary

FLORIDA

CLEARWATER
MUSICIANS' PROTECTIVE UNION (729)
609 Court St.
Clearwater, FL 33516

(813) 441-9447
Officers: Joseph P. Verdi, President; Jeanne Pisano, Secretary

DAYTONA
DAYTONA BEACH FEDERATION OF MUSICIANS (601)
Suite 107
115 Seabreeze Blvd.
Daytona Beach, FL 32018
(904) 252-6333
Officers: Joe Pace, President; William Benton, Secretary

FORT MYERS
FORT MYERS FEDERATION OF MUSICIANS (730)
2222 Liberty St.
Fort Myers, FL 33901
(813) 334-3423
Officers: Donovan F. McLean, President; Phil Lester, Secretary

JACKSONVILLE
MUSICIANS' ASSOCIATION OF JACKSONVILLE (444)
2030 Schumacher Ave.
Jacksonville, FL 32207
(904) 398-9735
Officers: John William Arnold, President; J.P. Buddy Pitts, Secretary

KEY WEST
KEY WEST FEDERATION OF MUSICIANS (202)
1508 19th St.
Key West, FL 33040
(305) 296-2276
Officers: Orlando Caraballo, President, Jim Vagnini, Secretary

MIAMI
MIAMI FEDERATION OF MUSICIANS (655)
1779 Northwest 28th St.
Miami, FL 33142
(305) NE 3-3235
Officers: Frank Casciola, President; Porter Thomas, Secretary

ORLANDO
ORLANDO MUSICIANS' ASSOCIATION (389)
3020 E. Robinson
Orlando, FL 32803
(305) 894-8666
Officers: John R. Giattino, President; Max E. Miller, Secretary

PENSACOLA
PENSACOLA FEDERATION OF MUSICIANS (283)
923 W. Michigan Ave.
Pensacola, FL 32505
(904) 434-5113
Officers: Frank S. Horne, President; Arthur Symington, Secretary

ST. PETERSBURG
GREATER ST. PETERSBURG MUSICIAN'S ASSOCIATION (427)
P.O. Box 12333
St. Petersburg, FL 33733
(813) 894-5059
Officers: Robert E. Burklew, President; Dick Crockett, Secretary

TAMPA
MUSICIANS' ASSOCIATION (721)
208 S. Howard Ave.
Tampa, FL 33606
(813) 254-0191/0231
Officers: Carlisle Hutchinson, President; Joseph Riesgo, Secretary

WEST PALM BEACH
MUSICIANS' ASSOCIATION OF THE PALM BEACHES (806)
3361-S Belvedere Rd.
West Palm Beach, FL 33406
(305) 684-6832
Officers: Henry Chernin, President; Glenn Young, Secretary

GEORGIA

ATLANTA
FEDERATION OF MUSICIANS (148-462)
551 Dutch Valley Rd., N.E.
Atlanta, GA 30324
(404) 873-2033
Officers: Karl A. Bevins, President; James A. Taylor,Sr., Secretary

AUGUSTA
AUGUSTA FEDERATION OF MUSICIANS (488)
125 Georgia Ave., N.
Augusta, GA 29841
(803) 279-4066
Officers: Robert E. Maxwell, Jr., President; James A. Kitchings, Secretary

COLUMBUS
COLUMBUS MUSICIANS' PROTECTIVE ASSOCIATION (331)
1001 Turner Rd.
Columbus, GA 31904
(404) 323-2481
Officers: Robert C. Money, President; Lewis B. Carver, Secretary

MACON
MACON FEDERATION OF MUSICIANS (359)
2 McCowen Plaza
2110 Ingleside Ave.
Macon, GA 31204
(912) 746-6035
Officers: Roger Dennison, President; Charles E. Steeley, Jr., Secretary

SAVANNAH
SAVANNAH FEDERATION OF MUSICIANS (447-704)
P.O. Box 1942
Savannah, GA 31402
(912) 352-9470
Officers: Russell Sena, President; Henry B. Hill, Secretary

HAWAII

HONOLULU
MUSICIANS' ASSOCIATION OF HAWAII (677)
949 Kapiolani Blvd.
Honolulu, HI 96814
(808) 521-1881
Officers: I.B. (Buddy) Peterson, President; Ray N. Tanaka, Secretary

IDAHO

BOISE
MUSICIANS' PROTECTIVE ASSOCIATION (537)
1611 Pomander Rd.
Boise, ID 83705
(208) 345-0537
Officers: James C. Johnson, President; Gail W. Green, Secretary

COEUR D'ALENE
MUSICIANS' PROTECTIVE UNION (225)
P.O. Box 188
Coeur D'Alene, ID 83814
(208) 773-1350
Officers: Richard B. Kuck, President; Jon H. Harwood, Secretary

LEWISTON
MUSICIANS' PROTECTIVE UNION (664)
Box 85
Spalding, ID 83551
(208) 843-2486
Officers: James W. Albright, President; Mrs. Bonnie Albright, Secretary

NAMPA
MUSICIANS' PROTECTIVE UNION (423)
P.O. Box 216
Nampa, ID 83651
(208) 466-9057
Officers: Loris W. Stewart, President; Carolyn Patterson, Secretary

POCATELLO
MUSICIANS' PROTECTIVE ASSOCIATION (295)
Rt. 4, Box 62
Blackfoot, ID 83221
(208) 785-2509
Officers: Eddie Ashcraft, President; John Miller, Secretary

REXBURG
MUSICIANS' PROTECTIVE UNION (371)
37 S. Third East
Rexburg, ID 83440
(208) 356-5797
Officers: Ross E. Dunn, President; Garr Gibson, Secretary

SUN VALLEY
SUN VALLEY MUSICIANS' ASSOCIATION (474)

Box 274
Hailey, ID 83333
(208) 726-9681
Officers: Reed Coulam, President; Joe Maccarillo, Jr., Secretary

ILLINOIS

ALTON
MUSICIANS' PROTECTIVE ASSOCIATION (282)
2609 Mariana Dr.
Godfrey, IL 62035
(618) 466-7385
Officers: Henry Lenhardt, President; Phillip H. Youngberg, Secretary

AURORA
MUSICIANS' PROTECTIVE UNION (181)
1159 Rathbone Ave.
Aurora, IL 60506
(312) 897-6894
Officers: Ralph B. Hesselbaum, President, Richard Bates, Sr., Secretary

BELLEVILLE
BELLEVILLE MUSICAL UNION (29)
1801 McClintok
Belleville, IL 62221
(618) 233-0525
Officers: Donald L. James, President; Elmer R. Humphries, Secretary

BENLD
TRI-COUNTY MUSICIANS' UNION (88)
211 S. Illinois St.
Benld, IL 62009
(217) 835-4539
Officers: Richard Sies, President; Ferdinand Girardi, Secretary

BLOOMINGTON
FEDERATION OF MUSICIANS (102)
104 East Monroe
508 N. East St.
Bloomington, IL 61701
(309) 828-6814
Officers: W.J. Donovan, President; Hazel J. Cambron, Secretary

CANTON
FULTON COUNTY MUSICIANS' PROTECTIVE UNION (304)
525 Royal Ct.
Canton, IL61520
(309) 647-7535
Officers: William Hughes, President; Marvin Robinson, Secretary

CENTRALIA
MUSICIANS' PROTECTIVE ASSOCIATION (681)
427 S. Lincoln
Centralia, IL 62801
(618) 532-6867
Officers: Robert J. Brown, President; King D. Lambird, Secretary

CHAMPAIGN
CHAMPAIGN FEDERATION OF MUSICIANS (196)
PO Box 534
506 West Clark St.
Champaign, IL 61820
(217) 356-4151
Officers: Marion Gulick, President; Paul E. Karlstrom, Secretary

CHICAGO
CHICAGO FEDERATION OF MUSICIANS (10-208)
175 West Washington St.
Chicago, IL 60602
(312) 782-0063
Officers: Nicholas G. Bliss, President; Emil Podsada, Secretary

CHICAGO HEIGHTS
THE CHICAGO HEIGHTS FEDERATION OF MUSICIANS (386)
1510 Otto Blvd.,C.
Chicago Heights, IL 60411
(312) 755-5580
Officers: Edward L. Skowronski, President; Henri Buttell, Secretary

COAL CITY
MUSICIANS' PROTECTIVE UNION (323)
429 West Ave.
Morris, IL 60450
(815) 942-3566
Officers: Robert Peterson, President; Gerald R. Belt, Secretary

COLLINSVILLE
MUSICIANS' PROTECTIVE UNION (350)
146 W. Washington Ave.
Collinsville, IL 62234
(618) 345-0504
Officers: Robert W. Sale, President; Tom Hopper, Secretary

DANVILLE
MUSICIANS' ASSOCIATION (90)
R.R. No. 5, Brewer Rd.
Box 105
Danville, IL 61832
(217) 446-1944
Officers: Ernest Strain, President; Carolyn Tooker, Secretary

DECATUR
DECATUR ASSOCIATION OF MUSICIANS (89)
3142 Kent Court
Decatur, IL 62526
(217) 877-8158
Officers: Hallie Bafford, President; Stan Kupish, Secretary

DE KALB
MUSICIANS' PROTECTIVE ASSOCIATION (572)
2972 E. Pleasant
DeKalb, IL 60115
(815) 756-9036
Officers: Dee Palmer, President; Edwin W. Harding, Secretary

DIXON
DIXON MUSICIANS' UNION (525)
503 S. Dixon Ave.
Dixon, IL 61021
(815) 288-1660
Officers: Gerald Schnake, President; Robert J. McConnaughay, Secretary

EAST ST. LOUIS
MUSICIANS' PROTECTIVE UNION (717)
3160 Aubrey St.
Granite City, IL 62040
(618) 876-2442
Officers: Arthur A. Zeiss, President; Howard W. Bolton, Secretary

EDWARDSVILLE
MUSICIANS' PROTECTIVE UNION (98)
614 Bollman
Edwardsville, IL 62025
(618) 656-2803
Officers: Ervin Mouish, President; Robert Wehling, Secretary

ELGIN
MUSICIANS' UNION (48)
169 E. Chicago St.
Elgin, IL 60120
(312) 742-3757
Officers: Charles O. Brinckley, President; Lucille Kerber, Secretary

FREEPORT
FREEPORT MUSICAL ASSOCIATION (340)
1239 S. Oak
Freeport, IL 61032
(815) 232-2976
Officers: W. "Curly" Robbins, President; Richard Moore, Secretary

GALESBURG
MUSICIANS' PROTECTIVE UNION (178)
439 N. Henderson St.
Galesburg, IL 61401
(309) 342-3007
Officers: Gene Fanning, President; Dick Higbee, Secretary

HERRIN
HERRIN FEDERATION OF MUSICIANS (280)
390 Mulberry
Carterville, IL 62918
(618) 985-4704
Officers: Robert Ledbetter, President; Bruce Groll, Secretary

HILLSBORO
MUSICIANS' PROTECTIVE UNION (516)
1439 Vandalia Rd.
Hillsboro, IL 62049
(217) KE 2-3862
Officers: Hermon Guile, President/Secretary

JACKSONVILLE
MUSICIANS' PROTECTIVE UNION (128)
605 Caldwell St.
Jacksonville, IL 62650
(217) 245-5562

Officers: Larry Brennan, President; Earl Rabjohns, Secretary

JOLIET

JOLIET FEDERATION OF MUSICIANS (37)
1318 Caton Ave.
Joliet, IL 60435
(815) 725-7692
(815) 727-4011
Officers: Dominic Paone, President; Roy Carloss, Secretary

KANKAKEE

KANKAKEE MUSICIANS' ASSOCIATION (288)
Glen Rd., Box 516
RR 2
Bourbonnais, IL 60914
(815) 933-2733
Officers: Mel Blanchette, President; Mrs. Josephine Leone, Secretary

KEWANEE

MUSICIANS' PROTECTIVE ASSOCIATION (100)
935 Cambridge St.
Kewanee, IL 61443
(309) 852-3252
Officers: Dennis Kubiak, President; Julian Heene, Secretary

LA SALLE

MUSICIANS' PROTECTIVE UNION (307)
117 East Erie St.
Spring Valley, IL 61362
(815) 644-4252
Officers: Ralph F. Schmoeger, President; Joseph M. DeZutti, Secretary

LINCOLN

MUSICIANS' PROTECTIVE UNION (268)
1015 Delavan St.
Lincoln, IL 62656
(217) 732-6483
Officers: Dan Hardin, President; Don W. Smith, Secretary

MACOMB

MUSICIANS' PROTECTIVE UNION (330)
Box 363
Macomb, IL 61455
(217) 322-6428
Officers: Robert L. Boyd, President; William D. DeJong, Secretary

MATTOON

MUSICIANS' PROTECTIVE UNION (224)
1 Trimble Lane
Newman, IL 61942
(217) 837-2077
Officers: Chuck White, President; Gene Trimble, Secretary

MT. VERNON

MUSICIANS' PROTECTIVE ASSOCIATION (465)
1809 Briarwood Dr.
Mt. Vernon, IL 62864
(618) 224-1024
Officers: Rolland Mays, President; Wilma Chambers, Secretary

MURPHYSBORO

MUSICIANS' PROTECTIVE UNION (697)
Route No. 5
Murphysboro, IL 62966
(618) 687-1183
Officers: Thomas Hardy, President; Joseph F. Stanes, Secretary

OTTAWA

MUSICIANS' PROTECTIVE UNION (391)
325 Erickson St.
Ottawa, IL 61350
(815) 433-2403
Officers: Donald Brooks, President; Ernest Brevik, Secretary

PEKIN

MUSICIANS' PROTECTIVE UNION (301)
P.O. Box 46A
Tremont, IL 61568
(309) 925-3519
Officers: Lyle Hauser, President; Kim L. Streenz, Secretary

PEORIA

PEORIA FEDERATION OF MUSICIANS (26)
405 William Kumpf Blvd.
Peoria, IL 61605
(309) 674-0507
Officers: Svata Ciza, President; Walter B. Coughlin, Secretary

PONTIAC

MUSICIANS' PROTECTIVE UNION (759)
1116 Prairie View Lane
Pontiac, IL 61764
(815) 844-3333
Officers: John P. Rhode, President; John A. Rhode, Secretary

PRINCETON

MUSICIANS' PROTECTIVE UNION (431)
P.O. Box 41
Buda, IL
(309) 895-2544
Officers: Glenn C. Russell, President; Marvin Stone, Secretary

QUINCY

MUSICIANS' PROTECTIVE UNION (265)
828 Maine St.
Quincy, IL 62301
(217) 222-0941
Officers: James Delabar, President; Carl Landrum, Secretary

ROCKFORD

MUSICAL UNION (240)
119 N. Church St., Ste. 308 No. State Bldg.
Rockford, IL 61101
(815) 965-2132
Officers: Vincent F. LaLoggia, President; Morry Hill, Secretary

SPRINGFIELD

SPRINGFIELD MUSICIANS' ASSOCIATION (19-675)
2003 S. 11th St.
Springfield, IL 62703
(217) 546-7546
(217) 528-0786
Officers: Howard E. Wikoff, President; Horace Sweet, Secretary

STERLING

MUSICIANS' PROTECTIVE UNION (329)
108½ W. 3rd St.
Sterling, IL 61081
(815) 625-5623
Officers: Philip Stein, President; Lorrie Lee, Secretary

STREATOR

MUSICIANS' PROTECTIVE UNION (131)
211 N. Fourth St.
Streator, IL 61364
(815) 672-8661
Officers: Ray Shull, President; Robert Yedinak, Secretary

TAYLORVILLE

MUSICIANS' PROTECTIVE UNION(798)
111 S. Houston St.
Taylorville, IL 62568
(217) 824-6520
Officers: Joe Calandro, President; Robert V. Jeisy, Secretary

TRENTON

MUSICIANS' PROTECTIVE UNION(175)
2104 Easy St.
Highland, IL 62249
(618) 654-8135
Officers: Wilson Dorries, President; Darlene Frank, Secretary

VIRDEN

MUSICIANS' PROTECTIVE UNION(354)
428 N. Springfield
Virden, IL 62690
(217) 965-3933
Officers: William F. Keirs, President; W.W. Manning, Secretary

WAUKEGAN

WAUKEGAN FEDERATION OF MUSICIANS (284)
915 Greenwood Ave.
Waukegan, IL 60087
(312) 623-6430
Officers: Leonard Yotko, President; Lorraine Maynard, Secretary

INDIANA

ANDERSON

MUSICIANS' PROTECTIVE ASSOCIATION (32)
1028 Kingsmill Rd.
Anderson, IN 46012

(317) 642-3628
Officers: James C. Clark, Acting President; Chet Carter, Secretary

DECATUR
MUSICIANS' PROTECTIVE UNION (607)
RR 5
Decatur, IN 46733
(219) 724-7670
Officers: Vernon Hebble, President; Robert J. Rice, Secretary

ELKHART
ELKHART MUSICIANS' ASSOCIATION (192)
320 W. Dinehart
Elkhart, IN 46514
(219) 522-5453
Officers: Fred D. Corbin, President; Richard Miller, Secretary

EVANSVILLE
MUSICIANS' ASSOCIATION (35)
301 N. Weinbach Ave.
Evansville, IN 47711
(812) 479-0866
Officers: David Holzman, President; Rudy Hillenbrand, Secretary

FORT WAYNE
MUSICIANS' PROTECTIVE ASSOCIATION (58)
Station D
PO Box 8149
2223 Goshen Road
Fort Wayne, IN 46898
(219) 484-3931
Officers: Louis Pooler, President; Harold Stout, Secretary

FRANKFORT
MUSICIANS' PROTECTIVE UNION (352)
505 N. Main St.
Frankfort, IN 46041
(317) 654-8291
Officers: Ray E. Nease, President; Charles V. Benge, Secretary

HAMMOND
MUSICIANS' GUILD (203)
7414 Indianapolis Blvd.
Hammond, IN 46324
(219) 845-0666
Officers: George R. Adams, President; Red Arbuckle, Secretary

INDIANAPOLIS
INDIANAPOLIS MUSICIANS' ASSOCIATION (3)
325 N. Delaware St.
Indianapolis, IN 46204
(317) 636-3595
Officers: Thomas C. Berry, President; Hal Bailey, Secretary

KOKOMO
KOKOMO FEDERATION OF MUSICIANS (141)
2413 Balmoral Blvd.
Kokomo, IN 46902
(317) 453-0271
Officers: James L. Porter, President; Larry Kirkman, Secretary

LAFAYETTE
LAFAYETTE FEDERATION OF MUSICIANS (162)
60 Carolyn Ct.
Lafayette, IN 47905
(317) 474-3013
Officers: James D. Rardon, President; Mr. Ardith Huff, Acting Secretary

LA PORTE
LA PORTE FEDERATION OF MUSICIANS (421)
810 Second St.
La Porte, IN 46350
(219) 362-6636
Officers: John Diedrich, President; Altus Salzwedel, Secretary

LOGANSPORT
MUSICIANS' PROTECTIVE ASSOCIATION (53)
1515 E. Broadway
Logansport, IN 46947
(219) 753-6781
Officers: Robert J. Parente, President; Stewart Gordon, Secretary

MARION
MUSICIANS' PROTECTIVE ASSOCIATION (45)
711 Tippy Dr.
Marion, IN 46952
(317) 662-2561
Officers: Russell L. Felton, President; Calvin Snapp, Secretary

MICHIGAN CITY
MICHIGAN CITY FEDERATION OF MUSICIANS (578)
405 Hendricks St.
Michigan City, IN 46360
(219) 874-6171
(219) 872-2533
Officers: George Ludtke, President; Richard L. Anderson, Secretary

MUNCIE
MUSICIANS' PROTECTIVE UNION (245)
2905 N. Virginia Ave.
Muncie, IN 47303
(317) 288-5487
Officers: Roland Eastman, President; Don Tuttle, Secretary

RICHMOND
MUSICIANS' PROTECTIVE UNION (388)
427 Kinsey St.
Richmond, IN 47374
(317) 962-6917
Officers: Kirby Bales, President; J. Michael Jordan, Secretary

SOUTH BEND
MUSICIANS' PROTECTIVE UNION (278)
Ste. 702
Hazlitt Building
120 West LaSalle Ave.
South Bend, IN 46601
(219) 233-8111
Officers: Eddie Jarrett, President; Craig Heitger, Secretary

TERRE HAUTE
TERRE HAUTE FEDERATION OF MUSICIANS (25)
517 Wabash Ave.
Terre Haute, IN 47807
(812) 235-9414
Officers: Virgil E. Dean, President; Bryan Seward, Secretary

VALPARAISO
MUSICIANS' PROTECTIVE UNION (732)
352 Harrison Blvd.
Valparaiso, IN 46383
(219) 462-6136
Officers: Henry Hallberg, President; Duane E. Hamacher, Secretary.

IOWA

BOONE
MUSICIANS' PROTECTIVE UNION (574)
821 22nd St.
Boone, IA 50036
(515) GE 2-2383
Officers: Leonard Sternquist, President; Herbert Forbell, Secretary

BURLINGTON
MUSICIANS' PROTECTIVE UNION (646)
3004 Ave. K
Fort Madison, IA 52627
(319) 372-8252
Officers: Richard Poindexter, President; George D. Biggs, Secretary

CEDAR RAPIDS
MUSICIANS' PROTECTIVE UNION (137)
220 Guaranty Bank Building
Cedar Rapids, IA 52401
(319) EM 3-1693
Officers: Vern Josifek, President; Miles Adams, Secretary

CLINTON
CLINTON MUSICIANS' PROTECTIVE ASSOCIATION (79)
140 Fourth Ave.
South Clinton, IA 52732
(319) CH 2-1604/1613
Officers: Emerson Sweesy, President; Warren Wiggins, Secretary

DAVENPORT
TRI-CITY MUSICAL SOCIETY (67)
304 East Third St.
Davenport, IA 52801
(319) 324-7088
Officers: Peter H. Schumaker,

President; Vincent A. Petersen, Secretary

DES MOINES
MUSICIANS' ASSOCIATION (75)
640 19th St.
Des Moines, IA 50314
(515) 244-2058
Officers: Francis M. Hrubetz, President; Roger Chrysler, Secretary

DUBUQUE
DUBUQUE MUSICIANS' ASSOCIATION (289)
210 Cody St.
Cuba City, WI 53807
(608) 744-2833
Officers: Paul E. Hemmer, President; Roger Svoboda, Secretary

FORT DODGE
FORT DODGE MUSICIANS' ASSOCIATION (504)
2016 North 24th Place
Fort Dodge, IA 50501
(515) 576-3452
Officers: Arch Thorson, President; Russell Thorson, Secretary

IOWA CITY
MUSICIANS' PROTECTIVE UNION (450)
Box 1067
Iowa City, IA 52240
(319) 338-8202
Officers: Richard Watson, President; Julia Munson, Acting Secretary

MASON CITY
MUSICIANS' PROTECTIVE UNION (230)
314 N. 11th
Clear Lake, IA 50428
(515) 357-4421
Officers: Dale W. Huebner, President; G.F. Barney Reynolds, Secretary

MUSCATINE
MUSICIANS' PROTECTIVE UNION (551)
1010 Grandview Ave.
Muscatine, IA 52761
(319) 263-1702
Officers: Donald Olson, President; Albert Knapp, Secretary

OELWEIN
MUSICIANS' PROTECTIVE UNION (483)
Hawkeye, IA 52147
(319) 427-3485

SIOUX CITY
MUSICIANS' PROTECTIVE UNION (254)
267 Insurance Exchange Building
Sioux City, IA 51101
(712) 258-4266
Officers: Clyde Wagner, President; Rockley W. Beck, Secretary

WATERLOO
WATERLOO FEDERATION OF MUSICIANS (334)
Suite 011
425 Washington
Waterloo, IA 50701
(319) 232-6924
Officers: David Kennedy, President; Jack Dunlevy, Secretary

KANSAS

COFFEYVILLE
MUSICIANS' PROTECTIVE UNION (449)
Box 166
205 N. Ohio
Coffeyville, KS 67337
(316) 251-4274
Officers: Mike Mason, President; Milford A. Unruh, Secretary

FORT SCOTT
MUSICIANS' PROTECTIVE UNION (755)
406 Circle Dr.
Fort Scott, KS 66701
(316) 223-4424
Officers: W. Marion Shrimplin, Jr., President; Beth King, Secretary

HUTCHINSON
MUSICIANS' PROTECTIVE ASSOCIATION (110)
322 N. Main St.
Hutchinson, KS 67501
(316) 663-9881
Officers: Stephen Ambler, President; Roland S. Gunn, Secretary

LAWRENCE
MUSICIANS' PROTECTIVE UNION (512)
2912 Rimrock Dr.
Lawrence, KS 66044
(913) 843-4966
Officers: William L. Kelly, President; J. Rober Stoner, Secretary

MANHATTAN
MANHATTAN MUSICIANS' ASSOCIATION (169)
1720 Colorado St.
Manhattan, KS 66502
(913) 537-7178
Officers: J. Vaughn Bolton, President; Ferrol K. Oberhelman, Secretary

PITTSBURG
MUSICIANS' PROTECTIVE UNION (452)
204 E. Elm
Girard, KS 66743
(316) 724-6541
Officers: Mike Loy, President; J. Phil Kurtz, Secretary

SALINA
SALINA MUSICIANS' ASSOCIATION (207)
2055 S. Ohio
Salina, KS 67401
(913) 827-9975
Officers: Steven Freed, President; Ken Fowler, Secretary

TOPEKA
TOPEKA MUSICAL ASSOCIATOIN (36-665)
1737 Randolph
Topeka, KS 66604
(913) 233-9264
Officers: Fred L. Evans, President; Gilbert Anderson, Secretary

WICHITA
WICHITA MUSICIANS' ASSOCIATION (297)
4323 East Kellogg
Wichita, KS 67218
(316) 684-1311
Officers: Dennis Danders, President; Vernon K. Nydegger, Secretary

KENTUCKY

ASHLAND
ASHLAND FEDERATION OF MUSICIANS (691)
Box 905
Ashland, KY 41101

967 Greenup St.
Catlettsburg, KY 41129
(606) 324-4300
(606) 739-6403
Officers: Richard A. Hawkins, President/Secretary

LEXINGTON
LEXINGTON MUSICIANS' ASSOCIATION (554-635)
426 Andover Dr.
Lexington, KY 40502
(606) 266-5384
Officers: Fredrick F. Moore, President; William M. McGinnis, Secretary

LOUISVILLE
LOUISVILLE FEDERATION OF MUSICIANS (11-637)
1436 Bardstown Rd.
Louisville, KY 40204
(502) 451-7509
Officers: Herbert E. Hale, President; Don R. Shumate, Secretary

PADUCAH
PADUCAH FEDERATION OF MUSICIANS (200)
45 Black Oaks Apartments
Paducah, KY 42001
(502) 443-2057
Officers: Gary D. Moore, President; James E. Windsor, Secretary

LOUISIANA

BATON ROUGE
BATON ROUGE MUSICIANS' ASSOCIATION (538)
8367 Airline Highway
Baton Rouge, LA 70815

(504) 926-5088/5039
Officers: Cleo Yarbrough, President; Matt Omari, Secretary

MONROE
MUSICIANS' PROTECTIVE UNION (425)
1205 North 5th
West Monroe, LA 71291
(318) 387-5030
Officers: Robert McGill, President; Les Winslow, Secretary

NEW ORLEANS
MUSICIANS' MUTUAL PROTECTIVE UNION (174-496)
2401 Esplanade Ave.
New Orleans, LA 70119
(504) 947-1700
Officers: David Winstein, President; John Scheuermann, Jr., Secretary

SHREVEPORT
SHREVEPORT FEDERATION OF MUSICIANS (116)
517 Creswell
Shreveport, LA 71101
(318) 222-5183
(318) 424-3513
Officers: Gilbert Phillips, President/Secretary

MAINE

BANGOR
MUSICIANS' PROTECTIVE UNION (768)
PO Box 663
Bangor, ME 04401
(207) 989-4057
(207) 945-6582
Officers: Lester J. Nadeau, President; Harold S. Burrill, Jr., Secretary

BIDDEFORD
BIDDEFORD MUSICIANS' ASSOCIATION (408)
13 Oxford St.
Sanford, ME 04073
(207) 324-4128
Officers: Donald R. Guillerault, President; Norman I. Stansfield, Sr., Secretary

PORTLAND-LEWISTON
PORTLAND-LEWISTON MUSICIANS' ASSOCIATION (364-409)
500 Forest Ave.
Portland, ME 04101
(207) 775-1342
Officers: Gloria J. McCullough, President; Jerry Der Boghosian, Secretary

MARYLAND

BALTIMORE
MUSICIANS' ASSOCIATION OF METROPOLITAN BALTIMORE (40-543)
1055 Taylor Ave., Ste. 203
Baltimore, MD 21204
(301) 337-7277
Officers: Albert Sigismondi, President; Jack Hook, Secretary

CUMBERLAND
MUSICIANS' PROTECTIVE UNION (787)
315 Valley View Ave.
Keyser, WV 26726
(304) 788-1178
Officers: Jack Means, President; Arthur E. Shafer, Secretary

HAGERSTOWN
MUSICIANS' UNION (770)
114 N. Potomac St.
Hagerstown, MD 21740
(301) 791-1551
Officers: James F. Strine, President; Edwin M. Kemp, Secretary

SALISBURY
SALISBURY FEDERATION OF MUSICIANS (44)
PO Box S
Salisbury, MD 21801
(301) 742-1644
(301) 742-4357
Officers: Kendall A. Martin, President; Russell M. Miles, Secretary

MASSACHUSETTS

BOSTON
BOSTON MUSICIANS' ASSOCIATION (9-535)
56 St. Botolph St.
Boston, MA 02116
(617) 536-2486
Officers: Joseph MacDonald, President; Howard Garniss, Secretary

BROCKTON
BROCKTON FEDERATION OF MUSICIANS (138)
22 Nilsson St.
Brockton, MA 02401
(617) 588-4944
Officers: Abraham Dumanis, President; James R. Dowling, Secretary

FALL RIVER
FALL RIVER FEDERATION OF MUSICIANS (216)
176 Bedford St.
Fall River, MA 02722
(617) 678-5321
Officers: James M. Considine, President; David Nadien, Secretary

FITCHBURG
MUSICIANS' MUTUAL ASSOCIATION (173)
115 Warren St.
Fitchburg, MA 01420
(617) 345-7191
Officers: John R. Pacetti, President; Charles F. Miller, Secretary

FRAMINGHAM-MARLBORO
FRAMINGHAM-MARLBORO MUSICIANS' ASSOCIATION (393)
173 Winter St.
Ashland, MA 01721
(617) 881-1254
Officers: John R. Lynch, Secretary

GREENFIELD
FRANKLIN COUNTY MUSICIANS' ASSOCIATION (621)
259 Main St.
Deerfield, MA 01373
(413) 665-2549
Officers: James J. Gallagher, President; Mrs. Mary G. Scoville, Secretary

HAVERHILL
HAVERHILL MUSICIANS' ASSOCIATION (302)
Meeting House Hill Road
West Newbury, MA 01985
(617) 363-2682
Officers: William Fasulo, President; Emery Hollerer, Secretary

HOLYOKE
HOLYOKE MUSICIANS' UNION (144)
5 Lakeview Ave.
South Hadley, MA 01075
(413) 532-6535
Officers: Charles L. Wall, President; Donald J. Baptiste, Secretary

HYANNIS
CAPE COD MUSICIANS' ASSOCIATION (155)
PO Box 713
713 Occum Lane
Falmouth, MA 02541
(617) 548-6366
Officers: Russell Kelsey, President; Jane Ross, Secretary

LAWRENCE
MUSICIANS' PROTECTIVE UNION (372)
343 Gile St.
Haverhill, MA 01830
(617) 372-9500
Officers: Raymond E. DiFiore, President; Irene Mazzaglia, Secretary

LOWELL
GREATER LOWELL MUSICIANS' ASSOCIATION (83)
64 Broadway St.
Westford, MA 01886
(617) 692-3169
Officers: William J. Notini, President; Angelo L. Bergamini, Secretary

LYNN
NORTH SHORE MUSICIANS' ASSOCIATION (126)
5 Summit Ave.
Salem, MA 01970
(617) 744-3512
Officers: Louis Amico, President; Arthur Axelrod, Secretary

MILFORD
MUSICIANS' PROTECTIVE

UNION (319)
17 Woodland Ave.
Milford, MA 01757
(617) 473-7614
Officers: John Ghiringhelli, President; Peter A. Paradiso, Secretary

NEW BEDFORD
GREATER NEW BEDFORD ASSOCIATION OF MUSICIANS (214)
403 Rivet St.
New Bedford, MA 02740
(617) 999-3443
Officers: Frank C. Monteiro, President; John A. Couto, Secretary

NEWBURYPORT
NEWBURYPORT FEDERATION OF MUSICIANS (378)
377 Elm St.
Salisbury, MA 01952
(617) 462-6291
Officers: Norman Roy, President; William R. Dickie, Secretary

NORTH ADAMS
MUSICIANS' PROTECTIVE ASSOCIATION (96)
254 Walker St.
North Adams, MA 01247
(413) 664-2416
Officers: Gregory S. Mitchell, President; Ronald Lively, Secretary

NORTHAMPTON
NORTHAMPTON FEDERATION OF MUSICIANS (220)
25 Madison Ave.
Northampton, MA 01060
(413) 584-0352
Officers: Edmund J. Schott, President; Raymond B. Black, Secretary

NORWOOD
MUSICIANS' PROTECTIVE UNION (343)
76 Allen St.
Walpole, MA 02081
(617) 769-1933
(617) 762-1596
Officers: Robert Seixas, President; Robert G. Schuller, Secretary

PITTSFIELD
PITTSFIELD FEDERATION OF MUSICIANS (109)
261 Pecks Rd.
Pittsfield, MA 01201
(413) 442-5796
Officers: William O'Donnell, President; Joseph Andrews, Secretary

PLYMOUTH
MUSICIANS' PROTECTIVE UNION (281)
14 Riverview Ave.
Kingston, MA 02364
(617) 585-6870
Officers: John Pacheco, Pesident; Donald C. Besegai, Secretary

SOUTHBRIDGE
SOUTHBRIDGE MUSICIANS' ASSOCIATION (494)
151 Mechanic St.
Southbridge, MA 01550
(617) 764-4652
Officers: Bernard J. Baldyga, President; Richard J. Bergeron, Sr., Secretary

SPRINGFIELD
GREATER SPRINGFIELD MUSICIANS' ASSOCIATION (171)
Room 205
134 Chestnut St.
Springfield, MA 01103
(413) 736-5187
Officers: John J. Brogan, Jr., President; George T. Lull, Secretary

TAUNTON
MUSICIANS' PROTECTIVE UNION (231)
25 Marvel St.
Taunton, MA 02780
(617) 822-3355
Officers: Louis E. Perry, President; Richard J. Furtado, Secretary

WORCESTER
WORCESTER MUSICIANS' ASSOCIATION (143)
130 Barnard Rd.
Worcester, MA 01605
(617) 852-3244
Officers: George Cohen, President; Rudolph J. Forge, Secretary

MICHIGAN

ANN ARBOR
ANN ARBOR FEDERATION OF MUSICIANS (625)
Suite 310
Wolverine Building
202 East Washington St.
Ann Arbor, MI 48108
(313) 668-8041
Officers: Max W. Crosman, President; Reade S. Pierce, Secretary

BATTLE CREEK
BATTLE CREEK FEDERATION OF MUSICIANS (594)
PO Box 1701
Battle Creek, MI 49016
(616) 962-3063
Officers: John D. Anglin, President; George H. Pendill, Secretary

BAY CITY
FEDERATION OF MUSICIANS (127)
1301 Airfield
Midland, MI 48640
(517) 832-7713
Officers: Robert Williams, President; Donald Brink, Secretary

BENTON HARBOR
THE TWIN CITY FEDERATION OF MUSICIANS (232)
1336 Lupine Dr.
St. Joseph, MI 49805
(616) 429-8777
Officers: Al Davino, Jr., President; Joe Ferris, Secretary

DETROIT
FEDERATION OF MUSICIANS (5)
19161 Schaefer Highway
Detroit, MI 48235
(313) 345-6200
Officers: Merle M. Alvey, President; Fred Netting, Secretary

ESCANABA
MUSICIANS' PROTECTIVE UNION (663)
2616 Lake Shore Dr.
Escanaba, MI 49829
(906) 786-0271
Officers: Robert Shepich, President; Ray Richards, Secretary

FLINT
FLINT FEDERATION OF MUSICIANS (542)
215 S. Averill Ave.
PO Box 6071
Flint, MI 48506
(313) 742-6802
Officers: Russell G. Berryman, President; Earl L. Durkee, Secretary

GRAND RAPIDS
GRAND RAPIDS FEDERATION OF MUSICIANS (56)
3234 Wildridge, N.E.
Grand Rapids, MI 49505
(616) 361-1178
Officers: Robert Gold, President; Clyde Falk, Secretary

IRON MOUNTAIN
IRON COUNTY MUSICIANS' ASSOCIATION (249)
Box 566
601 Margaret St.
Iron Mt., MI 49801
(906) 774-1533
Oficers: Anthony J. Giovannini, President; Carolo Calo, Secretary

JACKSON
MUSICIANS' PROTECTIVE UNION (387)
1931 Horton Rd., Bldg. No. 1
Jackson, MI 49203
(517) 784-2724
Officers: Roy A. Saari, President; Michael J. Austin, Secretary

KALAMAZOO
KALAMAZOO FEDERATION OF MUSICIANS (228)
1415 Portage St.
Kalamazoo, MI 49001
(616) 343-4123
Officers: William Morris, President; Don Brocato, Secretary

LANSING
LANSING FEDERATION OF MUSICIANS (303)
2703 N. Turner St.
Lansing, MI 48906
(517) 484-4461
Officers: Darwin D. Hart, President; Otto H. Van Sickle, Secretary

MARQUETTE
MUSICIANS' FEDERATION (218)
111 Elm Ave.
Munising, MI 49862
(906) 387-2123
Officers: John G. Major, President; Mark H. French, Secretary

MENOMINEE, MI/MARINETTE, WI
TWIN CITY MUSICIANS' ASSOCIATION OF MARINETTE, WISCONSIN, AND MENOMINEE, MICHIGAN (39)
1409 16th Ave.
Menominee, MI 49858
(906) 863-2548
Officers: William Plemel, President; Elmer Vojcihoski, Secretary

MUSKEGON
MUSKEGON MUSICIANS' ASSOCIATION (252)
169 E. Broadway
Muskegon Heights, MI 49444
(616) 733-2227
Officers: Raymond J. Stralko, President; Jack Lupien, Secretary

PONTIAC
PONTIAC FEDERATION OF MUSICIANS (784)
2101 S. Telegraph
Bloomfield Hills, MI 48013
(313) 333-7177
Officers: Frank Merwin, President; Peter G. Flore, Secretary

PORT HURON
PORT HURON FEDERATION OF MUSICIANS (33)
1219 Scott Ave.
Port Huron, MI 48060
(313) 984-1841
Officers: Charles Nelson, President; Donald C. Vincent, Secretary

SAGINAW
SAGINAW MUSICAL ASSOCIATION (57)
3725 Towerline Rd.
Bridgeport, MI 48722
(517) 777-1191
Officers: Leroy E. Brandimore, President; Paul W. Daines, Secretary

SAULT STE. MARIE
MUSICIANS' MUTUAL PROTECTIVE UNION (593)
1700 Ashmun
Sault Ste. Marie, MI 49783
(906) 635-5371
Officers: Americo Metro, President; John Quigley, Secretary

STAMBAUGH
IRON COUNTY MUSICIANS' ASSOCIATION (523)
Box 386, 300 Baltic
Caspian, MI 49915
(906) 265-2646
Officers: Joseph Shepich, President; Joseph E. DeAmicis, Secretary

MINNESOTA

ALBERT LEA
MUSICIANS' PROTECTIVE UNION (567)
PO Box 68
Albert Lea, MN 56007
(507) 373-3329
Officers: Steve Oman, President; Harlan S. Erickson, Secretary

AUSTIN
AUSTIN MUSICIANS' ASSOCIATION (766)
1108 W. Oakland Ave.
Austin, MN 55912
(507) 437-7217
(507) 433-4507
Officers: Duane Kime, President; William F. Apold, Secretary

BRAINERD
MUSICIANS' PROTECTIVE ASSOCIATION (487)
Route 4
Box 64
Brainerd, MN 56401
(218) 764-2438
Officers: Clinton Wheeler, President; Mrs. Carolyn Kassulker, Secretary

DULUTH
DULUTH MUSICIANS' ASSOCIATION (18)
302 Board of Trade Building
Duluth, MN 55802
(218) 722-1961
Officers: Sigurd Erickson, President; Jean Moore, Secretary

FARIBAULT
MUSICIANS' PROTECTIVE ASSOCIATION (565)
620 Prairie Ave.
Faribault, MN 55021
(507) 334-4934
Officers: Terry T. Trinka, President; Dan Moline, Secretary

HIBBING
MUSICIANS' PROTECTIVE UNION (612)
16 4th St., S.W.
Chisholm, MN 55719
(218) 254-3127
Officers: Ben A. Martella, President; Ronald P. Gazelka, Secretary

INTERNATIONAL FALLS
BORDER MUSICIANS' ASSOCIATION (156)
P.O. Box 347
International Falls, MN 56649
(218) 283-2251
Officers: Art DeBenedet, President; Werner Schuschke, Secretary

MANKATO
MUSICIANS' PROTECTIVE UNION (477)
Route 5
Box 139A
Mankato, MN 56001
(507) 625-3339
Officers: Cletus Frederick, President; Roy Perry, Secretary

NEW PRAGUE
MUSICIANS' PROTECTIVE UNION (602)
311 4th Ave., N.W.
New Prague, MN 56071
(612) 758-2310
Officers: Harold Picha, President; George Maxa, Secretary

NEW ULM
MUSICIANS' PROTECTIVE ASSOCIATION (513)
PO Box 201
New Ulm, MN 56073
(507) 354-6807
Officers: Arley Rolloff, President; LeRoy Dewanz, Secretary

OWATONNA
MUSICIANS' PROTECTIVE UNION (490)
Rt. 2, Box 200
New Richland, MN 56072
(507) 465-8284
Officers: Werner Halvorson, President; Ron Brey, Secretary

ROCHESTER
MUSICIANS' PROTECTIVE UNION
609 First Ave., SW
Rochester, MN 55901
(507) 288-1519
Officers: Duane Johnson, President; Kendall Heins, Secretary

ST. CLOUD
MUSICIANS' PROTECTIVE UNION (536)
Rt. 2
St. Cloud, MN 56374
(612) 363-8896
Officers: William Bach, President; Norman Scherer, Secretary

ST. PAUL-MINNEAPOLIS
TWIN CITIES MUSICIANS UNION (30-73)
2147 University Ave., No. 205
St. Paul, MN 55114
(612) 646-7829
Officers: Patrick J. Rian, President; Russell J. Moore, Secretary

VIRGINIA
MUSICIANS' PROTECTIVE ASSOCIATION (459)

P.O. Box 166
Virginia, MN 55792
(218) 741-8488
Officers: Gus Josephson, President; Emily M. Huppert, Secretary

WINONA
WINONA MUSICIANS' ASSOCIATION (453)
622 Main
Winona, MN 55987
(507) 452-4236
Officers: Richard Ahrens, President; Catherine Ingvalson, Secretary

MISSISSIPPI

HATTIESBURG
HATTIESBURG FEDERATION OF MUSICIANS (568)
PO Box 1103
Hattiesburg, MS 39401
(601) 582-7451
Officers: Gerald Johnston, President; Frank S. Uher, Secretary

JACKSON
JACKSON FEDERATION OF MUSICIANS (579)
PO Box 9923
Jackson, MS 39206
(601) 982-8500
Officers: Jimmy E. Mullen, Jr., President; W.C. Van Devender, Secretary

MISSOURI

JEFFERSON CITY
MUSICIANS' PROTECTIVE UNION (217)
1709 Swifts Highway
Jefferson City, MO 65101
(314) 636-3730
Officers: Archie Stegemen, President; Frank E. Ovaitt, Secretary

JOPLIN
JOPLIN MUSICIANS' ASSOCIATION (620)
P.O. Box 1523, 1932 Empire
Joplin, MO 64801
(417) 624-1892
Officers: Robert T. Estes, President; Charles B. Konkol, Secretary

KANSAS CITY
KANSAS CITY FEDERATION OF MUSICIANS (34-627)
1017 Washington
Kansas City, MO 64105
(816) 221-6934
Officers: Ruel L. Joyce, President; John W. Kost, Secretary

ST. JOSEPH
MUSICIANS' ASSOCIATION (50)
1212 Faraon Street
St. Joseph, MO 64501
(816) 232-9348
Officers: G. Deon Jensen, President; Robert Speer, Secretary

ST. LOUIS
MUSICIANS' ASSOCIATION OF ST. LOUIS (2-197)
2103 59th Street
St. Louis, MO 63110
(314) 781-6612
Officers: Dick Renna, President; Harry A. Gosling, Secretary

SEDALIA
SEDALIA MUSICIANS' ASSOCIATION (22)
618 West Sixth St.
Sedalia, MO 65301
(816) 826-3807
Officers: Lloyd H. Knox, President; James L. Eschbacher, Secretary

SPRINGFIELD
ASSOCIATION OF MUSICIANS (150)
1468 East Portland
Springfield, MO 65804
(417) TU 1-7475
Officers: David J. William, President; Willard Shunk, Secretary

MONTANA

ANACONDA
MUSICAL SOCIETY (81)
Box 706
Anaconda, MT 59711
(406) 563-7952
Officers: Donald Loranger, President; Louis C. Mertzig, Jr., Secretary

BILLINGS
BILLINGS PROFESSIONAL MUSICIANS' UNION (439)
210 Behner Building
2822 3rd Ave., North
Billings, MT 59101
(406) 245-3360
Officers: Roderick R. Wright, President; Frank N. Holzer, Secretary

BOZEMAN
MUSICIANS' PROTECTIVE ASSOCIATION (709)
820 South Tracy Ave.
Bozeman, MT 59715
(406) 586-9158
Officers: Ralph C. Challender, President; E. P. Sedivy, Secretary

BUTTE
MUTUAL PROTECTIVE UNION (241)
22 North Dakota St.
Butte, MT 59701
(406) 792-3272
Officers: Joseph E. Hughes, President; Ms. Louise Zanchi, Secretary

GREAT FALLS
MUSICIANS' PROTECTIVE UNION (365)
PO Box 1454
Great Falls, MT 59403
(406) 452-3962
Officers: Frank C. McKenna, President; Jack D. Harper, Secretary

HELENA
MUSICIANS' PROTECTIVE UNION (642)
1547 Beaverhead Rd.
Helena, MT 59601
(406) 933-5985
Officers: Harry Harlen, President; N.C. Slead, Secretary

KALISPELL
MUSICIANS' PROTECTIVE UNION
P.O. Box 126, 1125 Bierey Creed Rd.
Lakeside, MT 59922
(406) 844-3635
Officers: Herb White, President; Robert McCandless, Secretary

LIVINGSTON
MUSICIANS' PROTECTIVE ASSOCIATION (358)
624 North Yellowstone St.
Livingston, MT 59047
(406) 222-1274
Officers: Edward Tecca, President; Louis J. Armentaro, Secretary

MILES CITY
MUSICIANS' ASSOCIATION (429)
1101 South Lake
Miles City, MT 59301
(406) 232-2005
Officers: Eugene Forsyth, President; Keith W. Keller, Secretary

MISSOULA
MUSICIANS' PROTECTIVE UNION (498)
207 East Main
Missoula, MT 59801
(406) 251-3868
Officers: Joe R. Duham, President; Mrs. Mardell J. Lockwood, Secretary

NEBRASKA

GRAND ISLAND
CENTRAL NEBRASKA MUSICIANS' ASSOCIATION (777)
PO Box 874
Grand Island, NE 68801
(308) 382-7932
(308) 384-2955
Officers: Orie Kerwood, President; Harvey O. Larsen, Secretary.

LINCOLN
LINCOLN MUSICIANS' ASSOCIATION (463)
508 South 13th St.
Lincoln, NE 68508
(402) 474-3868
Officers: Ruben Haun, President; Keith W. Heckman, Secretary

NORTH PLATTE
MUSICIANS' ASSOCIATION (609)
Box 53
East Tyron Route
North Platte, NE 69101
(308) 532-5037
Officers: Larry Romeiser, President; Hadley Barrett, Secretary

OMAHA
MUSICIANS' ASSOCIATION (70-558)
1615 Howard St.
445 Aquila Court Bldg.
Omaha, NE 68102
(402) 341-7352
Officers: Ron Ellis, President; Shorty Vest, Secretary

NEVADA

LAS VEGAS
MUSICIANS' UNION OF LAS VEGAS (369)
PO Box 7467
Las Vegas, NV 89101
(702) 739-9369
Officers: Mark Tully Massagli, President; Bob Pierson, Secretary

RENO
RENO MUSICIANS' UNION (368)
PO Box 208
Reno, NV 89504
(702) 323-2116
Officers: Stan Rutherford, President; Merle L. Snider, Secretary.

NEW HAMPSHIRE

CONCORD
CONCORD FEDERATION OF MUSICIANS (374)
112 School St.
Concord, NH 03301
(603) 225-3515
Officers: Paul T. Giles, President; Frank Doyle, Jr., Secretary

KEENE
ASSOCIATED MUSICIANS OF KEENE, NEW HAMPSHIRE (634)
54 Vine St.
Keene, NH 03431
(603) 352-9398/0964
Officers: Richard Hutchins, President; James F. Fletcher, Jr., Secretary

MANCHESTER
MANCHESTER FEDERATION OF MUSICIANS (349)
89 Pennacook St.
Manchester, NH 03104
(603) 622-9084
Officers: Albert L'Heureux, President; Raymond T. Pare, Secretary

PORTSMOUTH
MUSICIANS' PROTECTIVE UNION (376)
Rt. 1, Box 635, Idelwood Lane
Kittery, ME 03904
(207) 439-1113
Officers: Howard Dearborn, President; Richard Draper, Secretary

NEW JERSEY

ASBURY PARK
MUSICIANS' PROTECTIVE ASSOCIATION (399)
511 5th Ave.
Belmar, NJ 07719
(201) 681-3315
Officers: Thomas R. Flanagan, President: Frank Rummler, Secretary

ATLANTIC CITY
ATLANTIC CITY MUSICIANS' ASSOCIATION (661-708)
418 N. Main St.
Pleasantville, NJ 08232
(609) 641-9275
(609) 645-7740
Officers: Victor J. Marrandino, President; George A. Fognano, Secretary

BURLINGTON
BURLINGTON MUSICAL SOCIETY (336)
48 West 2nd Street
Florence, NJ 08518
(609) 499-0569
Officers: Robert J. Bell, President; William Parker, Secretary

DOVER
MUSICIANS' PROTECTIVE UNION (237)
54 Windsor Ave.
Dover, NJ 07801
(201) 366-7640
Officers: Thomas J. Casapulla, President; Arthur Weiner, Secretary

ELIZABETH
MUSICIANS' ASSOCIATION (151)
906 Laurita Street
Linden, NJ 07036
(201) 925-4151
Officers: Nick Sabbatelli, President; James Drake, Secretary

JERSEY CITY
MUSICIANS' PROTECTIVE UNION (526)
130 Central Ave.
Jersey City, NJ 07306
(201) 653-0750/0751
Officers: Wilson Bonito, President; George T. Triano, Secretary

MORRISTOWN
MUSICIANS' PROTECTIVE UNION (177)
P.O. Box 1213 R
Morristown, NJ 07960
(201) 766-6177
Officers: Rudolph Spagnola, President; Edward Dorman, Secretary

NEWARK
MUSICIANS' GUILD OF ESSEX COUNTY (16)
Suburban Office Plaza
141 S. Harrison St.
East Orange, NJ 07018
(201) 675-1333
Officers: Lew Mallett, President; Philip J. Failla, Secretary

NEW BRUNSWICK
ASSOCIATION OF PROFESSIONAL MUSICIANS (204)
146 U.S. Hwy. No. 1, Ste. 25
Edison, NJ 08817
(201) 572-2832
Officers: Louis Melia, President; Eddie Shanholtz, Secretary

PATERSON
MUSICIANS' MUTUAL PROTECTIVE AND BENEVOLENT UNION (248)
77 Prospect St.
Paterson, NJ 07505
(201) 278-8418/8420
Officers: Isadore Freeman, President; Al Cimiluca, Secretary

PERTH AMBOY
MUSICIANS' PROTECTIVE UNION (373)
P.O. Box 373
Perth Amboy, NJ 08862
(201) 826-5615
Officers: Frank J. Kreisel, President; Andy Kucktyak, Secretary

PLAINFIELD
MUSICIANS' PROTECTIVE UNION (746)
194 Hoover Pl.
Union, NJ 07083
Officers: Andres Mingione, President; John E. Tallman, Secretary

TRENTON
TRENTON MUSICAL ASSOCIATION (62)
28 Assunpink Blvd.
Trenton, NJ 08619
(609) 586-0022
Officers: Lawrence (Stan) Kennedy, President; Frank Herrera, Secretary

VINELAND
MUSICIANS' PROTECTIVE UNION (595)
1070 Chestnut Ave.
Vineland, NJ 08360
(609) 691-1039
Officers: Frank Testa, President; Enrico Serra, Secretary

NEW MEXICO

ALBUQUERQUE
MUSICIANS' PROTECTIVE UNION (618)
5301 Central Ave. N.E. Room 807
Albuquerque, NM 87108
(505) 255-2069
Officers: Orlie Wagner, President; Vern Swingle, Secretary

NEW YORK

ALBANY
ALBANY MUSICIANS' ASSOCIATION (14)

Knights of Columbus Bldg.
218 Osborn Rd.
Albany, NY 12205
(518) 489-5122
Officers: Vincent Catalano, President; Joseph A. Lauria, Secretary

AMSTERDAM
MUSICIANS' PROTECTIVE UNION (133)
247 Church St.
Amsterdam, NY 12010
(518) 842-5865
Officers: Stanley Czelusniak, President; David J. Dybas, Secretary

AUBURN
MUSICAL UNION (239)
24 Drummond St.
Aburn, NY 13021
(315) 252-2503
Officers: James Mamuscia, President; Walter Light, Secretary

BATAVIA
MUSICIANS' PROTECTIVE UNION (575)
P.O. Box 766
115 Ross St.
Batavia, NY 14020
(716) 343-1812
Officers: Daniel Martino, President; John J. Stone, Secretary

BINGHAMTON
MUSICIANS' PROTECTIVE UNION (380)
PO Box 12
Vestal, NY 13850
(607) 729-1377
Officers: David Agard, President; Stephen Stafford, Secretary

BUFFALO
BUFFALO MUSICIANS' ASSOCIATION (92)
452 Franklin St.
Buffalo, NY 14202
(716) 882-6466/6467
Officers: Vincent Impellitter, President; Angelo J. Callea, Secretary

CORTLAND
CORTLAND MUSICIANS' ASSOCIATION (528)
799 Stupke Rd.
Cortland, NY 13045
(607) 753-3327
(607) 749-4619
Officers: Sam Forcucci, President; Patricia Stout, Secretary

DUNKIRK
MUSICIANS' PROTECTIVE ASSOCIATION (108)
Old Main Rd.
Silver Creek, NY 14136
(716) 366-1773
Officers: Richard Kalfas, President; Paul S. Butryn, Secretary

EAST AURORA
MUSICIANS' ASSSOCIATION OF EAST AURORA (366)
1935 Union Rd.
West Seneca, NY 14224
(716) 674-5054
Officers: Allen Schwartz, President; Clarence H. Hopper, Secretary

ELMIRA
ELMIRA-CORNING MUSICIANS' ASSOCIATION (314)
901 Pennsylvania Ave.
Elmira, NY 14904
(607) 739-3928
Officers: Vincent Stepules, President; Kenneth Stone, Secretary

FULTON
MUSICIANS' PROTECTIVE UNION (267)
9 Pershing Dr.
Fulton, NY 13069
(315) 592-4347
Officers: Joseph Cortini, President; Allen Boyce, Secretary

GENEVA
GENEVA MUSICIANS' ASSOCIATION (570)
187 Genessee St.
Geneva, NY 14456
(315) 789-5441
Officers: George J. Telarico, President/Secretary

GLEN FALLS
ADIRONDACK ASSOCIATION OF MUSICIANS (129)
11 Mechanic St.
Hudson Falls, NY 12839
(518) 747-3128
Officers: John Marine, Jr. President; Theodore C. Firth, Secretary

GLOVERSVILLE
MUSICIANS' PROTECTIVE ASSOCIATION (163)
2 Pearl St.
Johnstown, NY 12095
(518) 762-3632/9823
Officers: Milton G. Brookins, President; Ralph J. Gardner, Secretary

HAMBURG
MUSICIANS' PROTECTIVE UNION (649)
4256 North St.
Blasdell, NY 14219
(716) 826-7887
Officers: Eugene Zugger, President; Ronald A. Norris, Secretary

HORNELL
MUSICIANS' PROTECTIVE UNION (416)
8 Union St.
Canisteo, NY 14823
(607) 698-4566
Officers: John Koskie, President; Clifford Dennis, Secretary

HUDSON
MUSICIANS' PROTECTIVE UNION (676)
RD 3, Box B-5
Hudson, NY 12534
(518) 828-3140
Officers: Fred Stark, President; Raymond H. Ringer, Secretary

ITHACA
MUSICIANS' PROTECTIVE UNION (132)
204 Lake Ave.
Ithaca, NY 14850
(607) 273-4313/2682
Officers: Amandus "Mike" Teeter, President; Edward J. Moore, Jr., Secretary

JAMESTOWN
JAMESTOWN MUSICAL ASSOCIATION (134)
Room 42
Gokey Building
Jamestown, NY 14701
(716) 484-5951
(716) 488-6893
Officers: Allan K. Swanson, President; Vincent F. Mallare, Secretary

KINGSTON
MUSICIANS' UNION (215)
508-510 Albany Ave.
Kingston, NY 12401
(914) 331-4408
(914) 339-3762
Officers: Harry Castiglione, President; William F. Paulus, Secretary

LARCHMONT
MUSICIANS' ASSOCIATION OF WESTCHESTER COUNTY, NEW YORK (38)
132 Larchmont Ave.
Larchmont, NY 10538
(914) 834-0823/0826
Officers: Al Guarino, President; Peter Pugliese, Secretary

LOCKPORT
LOCKPORT FEDERATION OF MUSICIANS (97)
6279 Hamm Rd.
Lockport, NY 14094
(716) 434-2229
Officers: Frank R. Loiars, President; Robert J. Ciszewski, Secretary

MEDINA
MUSICIANS' PROTECTIVE UNION (312)
111 Chamberlain St.
Albion, NY 14411
(716) LT 9-6758
Officers: Luther Burroughs, President; Charles L. Piazza, Secretary

MIDDLETOWN
MUSICIANS' PROTECTIVE UNION (809)

Box 89
Swan Lake, NY 12783
(914) 292-7589/5260
Officers: Joseph Stellato, Sr., President; Meyer E. Rubenstein, Secretary

NEWBURGH
MUSICIANS' UNION (291)
26 Cross St.
New Windsor, NY 12550
(914) 562-7375
Officers: Thomas V. Wilson, President; Anthony J. Martini, Secretary

NEW YORK CITY
ASSOCIATED MUSICIANS OF GREATER NEW YORK (802)
261 West 52nd St.
New York, NY 10019
(212) 757-7722
Officers: Max L. Arons, President; Lou (Russ) Russo, Secretary

NIAGRA FALLS
MUSICIANS' ASSOCIATION OF NIAGARA FALLS, NEW YORK (106)
2526 Park View Dr.
Niagara Falls, NY 14305
(716) 297-6301
Officers: Sam Cassano, President; Salvatore L. Paonessa, Secretary

OLEAN-SALAMANCA
OLEAN-SALMANCA MUSICIANS' UNION (115-614)
R.D. No. 1, Blakeslee Hollow Rd.
Olean, NY 14760
(716) 372-5504
Officers: Angelo Melaro, President; Walter L. Hedlund, Secretary

ONEONTA
MUSICIANS' PROTECTIVE ASSOCIATION (443)
2 Bugbee Rd.
Oneonta, NY 13820
Officers: Charles Schneider, President; Linus Houck, Secretary

OSSINING
OSSINING MUSICIANS' ASSOCIATION (398)
569 Bedford Rd.
North Tarrytown, NY 10591
(914) 631-8860
Officers: Andy Clores, President; John C. Sundholm, Secretary

OSWEGO
MUSICIANS' PROTECTIVE UNION (441)
180 East 11th St.
Oswego, NY 13126
Officers: Kenneth E. Goodness, President; David B. Brown, Secretary

PORT JERVIS
PORT JERVIS MUSICIANS' PROTECTIVE ASSOCIATION (667)
RD 4
Box 31
Port Jervis, NY 12771
(914) 856-1322
Officers: Douglas R. Bachelder, President; G. Earl Cummings, Secretary

POUGHKEEPSIE
PROFESSIONAL MUSICIANS' ASSOCIATION (238)
199 Roosevelt Rd.
Hyde Park, NY 12538
(914) 229-7634
Officers: George F. Cacchione, President; Retta Gelormino, Secretary

ROCHESTER
ROCHESTER MUSICIANS' ASSOCIATION (66)
857 E. Main St.
Rochester, NY 14605
(716) 442-2220
Officers: Al Bruno, President; Norbert Klem, Secretary

ROME
MUSICIANS' PROTECTIVE ASSOCIATION (313)
1829 N. James St.
Rome, NY 13440
(315) 337-3944
Officers: Joseph J. Trophia, President; Vincent D. Petrucci, Secretary

SARATOGA SPRINGS
SARATOGA MUSICAL UNION (506)
Box 81
Saratoga Springs, NY 12866
(518) 518-4223
Officers: Ronald H. Partch, President; Henry L. Gagne, Secretary

SCHENECTADY
MUSICAL UNION (85)
2198 Robinwood Ave.
Schenectady, NY 12306
(518) 372-1496
Officers: Abe Rapp, President; Eugene J. Sennes, Secretary

SYRACUSE
SYRACUSE MUSICIANS PROTECTIVE ASSOCIATION (78)
718-720 Wilson Building
Syracuse, NY 13202
(315) 422-3820
Officers: Phillip R. MacArthur, President; Herbert LaHood, Secretary

TONAWANDA
THE TONAWANDAS MUSICIANS' ASSOCIATION (209)
1408 Forbes St.
North Tonawanda, NY 14120
(716) 692-7109
Officers: Herm J. Janus, President; Gerald Ryan, Secretary

TROY
TROY MUSICIANS, INC. (13)
Troy Building Trades Building
1700 6th Ave.
Troy, NY 12180
(518) 274-4661
Officers: Romeo Mitri, President; Frank Vadala, Secretary

UTICA
MOHAWK VALLEY MUSICIANS' ASSOCIATION (51)
RD 1, Box 382
Sauquoit, NY 13456
(315) 737-8180
Officers: Stewart J. Wagner, President; Thomas M. Notman, Secretary

WATERTOWN
MUSICIANS' ASSOCIATION (734)
235 Woolworth Building
Watertown, NY 13601
(315) 782-5470
Officers: Morris Trahan, President; Leland Tallman, Secretary

YONKERS
MUSICIANS' ASSOCIATION (402)
1 North St.
Hastings-on-Hudson, NY 10706
(914) 478-0402
Officers: Antonio Lombardo, President; Vito T. Raimondi, Secretary

NORTH CAROLINA

CHARLOTTE
CHARLOTTE MUSICIANS' ASSOCIATION (342)
2122 Eastway Dr.
Charlotte, NC 28205
(704) 568-3465
Officers: Joseph P. Little, President; Bennie R. Jones, Secretary

GREENSBORO
MUSICIANS' PROTECITVE UNION (332)
1812 Efland Dr.
Greensboro, NC 27408
(919) 288-1093
Officers: Richard L. Wells, President; M. Howard Waynick, Jr., Secretary

RALEIGH
MUSICIANS' ASSOCIATION (500)
PO Box 2931
West Durham, NC 27705
(919) 286-4806
Officers: Richard Southwick, President; Russell Olson, Secretary

NORTH DAKOTA

BISMARCK
MUSICIANS' PROTECTIVE ASSOCIATION (229)
201 Missouri River Rd.
Mandan, ND 58554
(701) 667-1077
Officers: Gerry Serhienko, President; Vern Cermak, Secretary

FARGO
MUSICIANS' ASSOCIATION (382)
Suite L-139
112 N. University Dr.
Fargo, ND 58102
(701) 235-4279
Officers: Edward Christianson, President; David Sether, Secretary

GRAND FORKS
MUSICIANS' PROTECTIVE UNION (485)
2308 7th Ave.
North Grand Forks, ND 58201
(701) 775-9290
Officers: Hartley Brown, President; Bill Henderson, Secretary

MINOT
MINOT MUSICIANS' ASSOCIATION (656)
P.O. Box 521
5 Labor Temple
Minot, ND 58701
(701) 838-0845
Officers: Jeff Lesmeister, President; Marliss Hanson, Secretary

OHIO

AKRON
AKRON FEDERATION OF MUSICIANS (24)
Room 315
Metropolitan Building
Akron, OH 44308
(216) 376-8174
Officers: Eldon "Pete" Motz, President; Jack Faller, Secretary

ALLIANCE
ALLIANCE FEDERATION OF MUSICIANS (68)
119 E. State St.
Alliance, OH 44601
(216) 823-3388
Officers: Wilbur T. Fites, President; Charles Moushey, Secretary

ASHTABULA
MUSICIANS PROTECTIVE ASSOCIATION (107)
6431 Murray Ave.
Ashtabula, OH 44004
(216) 993-5451
Officers: William F. Giannel, President; Francis J. Montanaro, Secretary

CAMBRIDGE
MUSICIANS' PROTECTIVE UNION (415)
PO Box 934
Cambridge, OH 43725
(614) 432-3636
Officers: Leonard Patterson, President; Sara Ann Vergari, Secretary

CANTON-MASSILLON
CANTON FEDERATION OF MUSICIANS (111)
1914 W. Tuscarawas St.
Canton, OH 44708
(216) 454-7430
Officers: Frank L. Corbi, President; John C. Smith, Secretary

CINCINNATI
CINCINNATI MUSICIANS ASSOCIATION (1)
19 West Ct.
Cincinnati, OH 45202
(513) 241-0900
Officers: Eugene V. Frey, President; Kenneth S. McLaughlin, Secretary

CLEVELAND
THE CLEVELAND FEDERATION OF MUSICIANS (4)
2200 Carnegie Ave.
Cleveland, OH 44115
(216) 771-1802
Officers: Michael Scigliano, President; Michael Scigliano, Secretary

COLUMBUS
FEDERATION OF MUSICIANS (103)
2829 Cleveland Ave.
Columbus, OH 43224
(614) 261-9826/9827
Officers: Lucian Tiberi, President; Tommy Dale, Secretary

COSHOCTON
COSHOCTON FEDERATION OF MUSICIANS (478)
112 E. 6th St.
West Lafayette, OH 43845
(614) 545-6121
Officers: Randy Pierce, President; Michael Williams, Secretary

DAYTON
DAYTON MUSICIANS' ASSOCIATION (101-473)
415 Troy St.
Dayton, OH 45404
(513) 223-6962
Officers: Paul W. Rogers, President; Mrs. Mae W. Jean, Secretary

EAST LIVERPOOL
MUSICIANS' MUTUAL PROTECTIVE ASSOCIATION (172)
PO Box 322
East Liverpool, OH 43920
(216) 385-0637/5082
Officers: Robert L. Hall, President; Frank R. Craven, Secretary

FOSTORIA
FOSTORIA FEDERATION OF MUSICIANS (121)
118 W. Center St.
Fostoria, OH 44830
(419) 435-8748
Officers: Ernest Duffield, President; John L. Peck, Secretary

GREENVILLE
GREENVILLE MUSICIANS' ASSOCIATION (599)
PO Box 279
Greenville, OH 45331
(513) 548-6714
Officers: Richard Locke, President; Ralph T. Plessinger, Secretary

HAMILTON
HAMILTON MUSICIANS' ASSOCIATION (31)
1619 Brookcrest Dr.
Hamilton, OH 45013
(513) 863-6024
Officers: Dominic Roberts, President; Rita Line, Secretary

LANCASTER
LANCASTER FEDERATION OF MUSICIANS (683)
123 Cleveland Ave.
Lancaster, OH 43130
Officers: Richard Hammond, President; Greg Dickson, Secretary

LIMA
THE LIMA FEDERATION OF MUSICIANS (320)
954 East High St.
Lima, OH 45801
(419) 227-1372
Officers: Donald Hurless, President; Ed McElderry, Secretary

LORAIN AND ELYRIA
MUSICIANS' UNION (146)
4642 Oberlin Ave.
Lorain, OH 44053
(216) 282-3707
Officers: Ed Litchtenberg, President; Pete Galanic, Secretary

MANSFIELD
MUSICIANS' PROTECTIVE ASSOCIATION (159)
606 Sunset Blvd.
Mansfield, OH 44907
(419) 756-4857
Officers: Luis A. Mendez, Jr., President; "Eddie" Chiudioni, Secretary

MARIETTA
MUSICIANS' PROTECTIVE UNION (179)
102 Nelson
Marietta, OH 45750
(614) 373-6322
Officers: Donald Shafer, President; Dick Goddard, Secretary

MARION
MARION MUSICIANS' ASSOCIATION (531)
PO Box 681
Marion, OH 43302
Officers: Harold L. Ebert, President; Richard Meyers, Secretary

MENTOR
LAKE AND GEAUGA COUNTY FEDERATION OF MUSICIANS (657)
Box 75
8528 Mentor Blvd.
Mentor, OH 44060

(216) 255-2501
Officers: Ken Fleckenstein, President; Roger K, Kraft, Secretary

MIDDLETOWN
MUSICIANS' PROTECTIVE UNION (321)
1109 Ellen Dr.
Middletown, OH 45042
(513) 423-6854
Officers: Robert C. Farmer, President; Garwood Wells, Secretary

MT. VERNON
MT. VERNON MUSICIANS' ASSOCIATION (338)
P.O. Box 367
Mt. Vernon, OH 43050
(614) 397-8187
Officers: F. William Fetters, President; Doris F. Moran, Secretary

NEWARK
NEWARK FEDERATION OF MUSICIANS (122)
1763 Evergreen Court
Newark, OH 43055
(614) 323-1556
Officers: Lawrence Griffin, President; Mrs. Nora Mae Huffman, Secretary

NEW PHILADELPHIA-DOVER
TUSCAWARAS-CARROLL COUNTIES FEDERATION OF MUSICIANS (404)
1304 N. Walnut
Dover, OH 44622
(216) 343-4557
Officers: Robert Z. Randolph, President; Donald L. Angel, Secretary

PIQUA
PIQUA MUSICIANS' ASSOCIATION (576)
1626 Beck Dr.
Sidney, OH 45365
(513) 492-4259
Officers: Kenneth K. McMaken, President; Frank W. Neville, Jr., Secretary

PORTSMOUTH
MUSICIANS' PROTECTIVE UNION (482)
2555 Ritchie St.
Portsmouth, OH 45662
(614) 354-6419
Officers: Gary Billups, President; Bob Taylor, Secretary

SALEM
SALEM FEDERATION OF MUSICIANS (222)
Box 155
Hanoverton, OH 44423
(216) 337-9275
Officers: Nick Buta, President; Michael Kupinski, Secretary

SANDUSKY
SANDUSKY MUSICIANS' ASSOCIATION (573)
Box 1084
Sandusky, OH 44870
(419) 626-0578
Officers: Frank Fosco, President; Robert E. Frank, Secretary

SPRINGFIELD
SPRINGFIELD MUSICIANS' ASSOCIATION (160)
1500 Malden Ave.
Springfield, OH 45504
(513) 390-0618/2351
Officers: Robert A. Ware, President; John R. Dessinger, Secretary

STEUBENVILLE
STEUBENVILLE MUSICIANS' ASSOCIATION (223)
507 First National Bank Building
Steubenville, OH 43952
(614) 282-5212
Officers: Paul Paolisso, President; W.C. Powelson, Secretary

TOLEDO
TOLEDO FEDERATION OF MUSICIANS (15-286)
308 Hillcrest Hotel
Madison & 16th St.
Toledo, OH 43699
(419) 243-2017
Officers: Steve Chromik, President; Randall J. Richie, Secretary

WARREN
WARREN FEDERATION OF MUSICIANS (118)
3207 Youngstown Rd., S.E.
Warren, OH 44484
(216) 369-6745
Officers: Roy C. Billion, President; Rudy Sulek, Secretary

YOUNGSTOWN
YOUNGSTOWN FEDERATION OF MUSICIANS (86-242)
2520 South Ave.
Youngstown, OH 44502
(216) 788-8451
Officers: Herbert MacPherson, President; Danny Barber, Acting Secretary

ZANESVILLE
MUSICIANS' PROTECTIVE ASSOCIATION (54)
612 Merrick Ave.
Zanesville, OH 43701
(614) 452-5691
Officers: Clarence E. Shirer, President; Paul Mitter, Secretary

OKLAHOMA

BARTLESVILLE
MUSICIANS' UNION (316)
157 S.E. Rockwood Dr.
Bartlesville, OK 74003
Officers: Don Berger, President; C.H. Van Sant, Secretary

OKLAHOMA CITY
OKLAHOMA CITY FEDERATION OF MUSICIANS (375)
Civic Center Music Hall
Room 208
Oklahoma City, OK 73102
(405) 235-5079
Officers: John B. Williams, President; Baird Jones, Secretary

TULSA
TULSA MUSICIANS' PROTECTIVE ASSOCIATION (94)
5237 South Peoria, Ste. 116
Tulsa, OK 74105
(918) 743-0515
Officers: Jamie McIntosh, President; Weymouth B. Young, Secretary

OREGON

EUGENE
MUSICIANS' MUTUAL ASSOCIATION (689)
2489 Portland St.
Eugene, OR 97405
(503) 484-0951
Officers: Scott Linden, President; F. Dennis Lynch, Secretary

PENDLETON
MUSICIANS' PROTECTIVE UNION (560)
609 N.W. Despain
Pendleton, OR 97801
(503) 276-7586
Officers: Buford Kinnison, President; W.J. (Bryan) Branstetter, Secretary

PORTLAND
MUSICIANS' MUTUAL ASSOCIATION (99)
325 N.E. 20th Ave.
Portland, OR 97232
(503) 235-8791
Officers: Joe Dardis, President; Robert L. Findley, Secretary

PENNSYLVANIA

ALLENTOWN
MUSICIANS' PROTECTIVE ASSOCATION (561)
Suite BBB
44 S. Fulton St.
Allentown, PA 18102
(215) 433-0156
Officers: William Laubach, President; Matthew R. Cascioli, Secretary

ALTOONA
MUSICAL ASSOCIATION (564)
109 West 11th Ave.
Altoona, PA 16601
(814) 943-9936
Officers: Richard Potter, President; Loy W. Appleman, Secretary

BANGOR-STROUDSBURG
MUSICIANS' PROTECTIVE UNION (577)
631 N. Falcone Ave.
Roseto, PA 18013
(215) 588-2586

Officers: Duane Walck, President; Philip A. DeMilio, Jr., Secretary

BEAVER FALLS
MUSICIANS' PROTECTIVE UNION (82)
102 Clover Dr.
Monaca, PA 15061
(412) 774-8829
Officers: Andrew A. Mignanelli, President; Steve E. Blanda, Secretary

BERWICK
MUSICIANS' PROTECTIVE UNION (727)
203 S. Mercer St.
Berwick, PA 18603
(717) 752-4438
Officers: Joseph Malatesta, President; Robert W. Romberger, Secretary

BETHLEHEM
MUSICIANS' ASSOCIATION (411)
1212 Shelbourne Dr.
Bethlehem, PA 18018
(215) 691-0302
Officers: George J. Kanuck, President; Stephen P. Reisteter, Secretary

BRADFORD
MUSICAL UNION (84)
34 Maplewood Ave.
Bradford, PA 16701
(814) 368-8031
Officers: Michael Figula, President; Raymond A. Arnold, Secretary

BUTLER
BUTLER FEDERATION OF MUSICIANS (188)
Valley View Estates
Lot 10
530 Pillow St.
Butler, PA 16001
Officers: John J. Chiprean, Jr., President; Norman E. Gour, Secretary

CANONSBURG
CANONSBURG FEDERATION OF MUSICIANS (509)
Box 255
RD No. 1
Canonsburg, PA 15317
(412) 746-1017
Officers: Lee Barrett, President; Val Kerin, Secretary

CARBONDALE
MUSICIANS' PROTECTIVE UNION (130)
505 Main St.
Peckville, PA 18452
(717) 383-0301
(717) 876-2164
Officers: Bernard Cerra, President; Egidio S. Lemoncelli, Secretary

CHARLEROI
CHARLEROI MUSICAL SOCIETY (592)
78 Scenery Blvd.
Monessen, PA 15062
(412) 684-3300
Officers: William D. Fries, President; Joseph G. Yadrick, Secretary

MUSICIANS' PROTECTIVE UNION (484)
Plaza 352 Shopping Center
Middletown Rd.
Brookhaven, PA 19015
(215) TR 2-4421
(215) TR 1-9015
Officers: Vincent Caruso, President; Edward Grueninger, Secretary

COLUMBIA
MUSICIANS' PROTECTIVE UNION (296)
RD 3
Norwood Heights
Columbia, PA 17512
(717) 684-7138
Officers: James M. Smith, Jr., President; John P. Metzger, Secretary

CONNELLSVILLE
MUSICAL SOCIETY (417)
212 South Tenth St.
Connellsville, PA 15425
(412) 628-2772
Officers: Amedeo Molinaro, President; Charles E. Gross, Secretary

EASTON
MUSICIANS' PROTECTIVE UNION (379)
351 Ferry St.
Easton, PA 18042
(215) 252-0430
Officers: Roger F. Miller, President; Pam Brader, Secretary

ELWOOD CITY
MUSICIANS' PROTECTIVE UNION (545)
505 Pershing St.
Ellwood City, PA 16117
(412) 758-5354 after 5:30 p.m.
Officers: Charles Navolio, President; E.W. Moncreif, Secretary

ERIE
MUSICIANS' PROTECTIVE ASSOCIATION (17)
504 Masonic Building
Erie, PA 16501
(814) 454-0868
Officers: Bernard F. Pacy, President; William M. Fairgraves, Secretary

FREELAND
MUSICIANS' PROTECTIVE UNION (557)
125 Church St.
White Haven, PA 18861
(717) 443-8805
(717) 455-7325
Officers: Francis Carr, President; Emil E. Harakal, Secretary

GLEN LYON
MUSICIANS' PROTECTIVE UNION (696)
60 West Union St.
Nanticoke, PA 18634
(717) 735-4730
Officers: Michael Yalch, President; Sylvester Czyzyk, Secretary

GREENSBURG
GREENSBURG MUSICAL SOCIETY (339)
527 Sewickley St.
Greensburg, PA 15601
(412) 834-5596
Officers: John Faulk, President; Julius Falcon, Secretary

GREENVILLE
MUSICIANS' PROTECTIVE UNION (460)
69 Goetsch Rd.
Greenville, PA 16125
(412) 588-7604
Officers: John Baird, President; Ronald C. Rohland, Secretary

HANOVER
HANOVER MUSICIANS' ASSOCIATION (49)
Box 395
20 York St.
Hanover, PA 17331
(717) 637-4900
Officers: Gary L. Urick, President; William A. Sanders, Secretary

HARRISBURG
MUSICAL ASSOCIATION (269)
1927 Paxton St.
Harrisburg, PA 17104
(717) 234-8400
Officers: Harold W. Sanders, President; Charles R. Morrison, Secretary

HAZLETON
MUSICIANS' PROTECTIVE UNION (139)
38 James St.
Kelayres, PA 18231
(717) 929-1307
Officers: Joseph Buglio, President; Peter M. Notaro, Secretary

INDIANA
INDIANA MUSICIANS' ASSOCIATION (251)
63 North Third St.
Indiana, PA 15701
(412) 465-6895
Officers: Kenneth F. Maurey, President; Enrico Vincent Colonna, Secretary

JOHNSTOWN
MUSICAL SOCIETY (41)
381 Maple Ave.
Johnstown, PA 15902
(814) 536-0751
Officers: Sam S. Signorino, President; Harry W. Anderson, Secretary

KITTANNING
MUSICIANS' UNION (603)
Box 102

Cowansville, PA 16218
(412) 543-4359
Officers: Joseph A. Alese, President; Ethel Fahlor, Secretary

LANCASTER
THE GREATER LANCASTER FEDERATION OF MUSICIANS (294)
812 Pointview Ave.
Ephrata, PA 17522
(717) 733-3410
Officers: Gerald S. Wingenroth, President; Jo Wingenroth, Secretary

LANSFORD
MUSICIANS' ASSOCIATION (436)
118 Center St.
Tamaqua, PA 18252
(717) 668-0584
Officers: Wash King, President; John F. Davis, Secretary

LEBANON
LEBANON MUSICAL SOCIETY (750)
227 Chestnut St.
Lebanon, PA 17042
(717) 273-5251
Officers: Charles H. Harper, President; George W. Swanger, Jr., Secretary

LEIGHTON
CARBON MUSICAL SOCIETY (659)
215 N. 4th St.
Leighton, PA 18235
(215) 377-3240
Officers: Paul David, President; Donald F. Mantz, Secretary

MAHANOY CITY
MUSICIANS' PROTECTIVE UNION (170)
6 Weston Pl.
Shenandoah, PA 17976
(717) 462-1677
Officers: John F. Dempsey, President; Anthony Liscusky, Secretary

MEADVILLE
THE MEADVILLE MUSICAL SOCIETY (344)
Box 58
Meadville, PA 16335
(814) 333-1104
Officers: James Reid, President; Samuel Marks, Secretary

NEW CASTLE
MUSICAL UNION (27)
809 Dushane St.
New Castle, PA 16101
(412) 652-3354
Officers: Mike Isabella, President; Michael Phillips, Secretary

NEW KENSINGTON
NEW KENSINGTON MUSICAL SOCIETY (630)
Sons of Italy Bldg.
1010 5th Ave.
New Kensington, PA 15068
(412) 335-6651
Officers: Joseph S. DeSimone, President; Edmond P. Manganelli, Secretary

NORRISTOWN
THE NORRISTOWN MUSICIANS' ASSOCIATION (341)
Hamilton Hall
Norristown, PA 19401
(215) 272-6210
Officers: William S. March, President; Thomas Middleton, Secretary

OIL CITY
MUSICAL ASSOCIATION (61)
RD 1
Box 209
Pone Lane
Franklin, PA 16323
(814) 432-5518
Officers: William Snyder, President; Fran Fry, Jr., Secretary

PHILADELPHIA
THE PHILADELPHIA MUSICAL SOCIETY (77)
120 North 18th St.
Philadelphia, PA 19103
(215) 567-2428
Officers: Don Diogenia, President; Tibby Tiberini, Secretary

PITTSBURGH
PITTSBURGH MUSICAL SOCIETY (60-471)
709 Forbes Ave.
Pittsburgh, PA 15219
(412) 281-1822
Officers: Herbert I. Osgood, President; Joseph E. Schafer, Secretary

POTTSTOWN
MUSICIANS' PROTECTIVE ASSOCIATION (221)
113 East Third St.
Pottstown, PA 19464
(215) 323-6929
Officers: Frank Buttaro, President; Daniel Lutz, Secretary

POTTSVILLE
POTTSVILLE MUSICAL SOCIETY (515)
1645 W. Norwegian St.
Pottsville, PA 17901
(717) 622-8784
Officers: John J. Direnzo, President; F. John Tucci, Secretary

PUNXSUTAWNEY
MUSICIANS' PROTECTIVE UNION (624)
326 Sutton St.
Punxsutawney, PA 15767
(814) 938-6089
Officers: John Parise, President; Michael A. Catanzarito, Secretary

QUAKERTOWN
MUSICIANS' PROTECTIVE UNION (569)
PO Box 548
Provident National Bank Bldg.
224 W. Broad St.
Quakertown, PA 18951
(215) 536-8717
Officers: A. Richard Allem, President; Everett Afflerbach, Secretary

READING
READING MUSICAL SOCIETY (135)
Riverdale Rd.
Reading, PA 19605
(215) 926-2826
Officers: Vernon A. Deysher, Jr., President; Daniel W. Youse, Secretary

REINERTON
MUSICIANS' PROTECTIVE UNION (401)
322 South Fourth St.
Tower City, PA 17980
(717) 647-4851
Officers: Francis Rickenbach, President; David C. Minnich, Secretary

RIDGWAY
RIDGWAY MUSICIANS' ASSOCIATION (317)
217 Irwin Ave.
Ridgway, PA 15853
(814) 772-4195
Officers: Richard G. Butterfuss, President; Frank S. Frederico, Secretary

SAYRE
MUSICIANS' PROTECTIVE ASSOCIATION (645)
Box 263
Sayre, PA 18840
(717) 888-0569
Officers: Robert D. Gauss, Jr., President; Charles A. Hammond, Secretary

SCRANTON
MUSICIANS' PROTECTIVE ASSOCIATION (120)
Hotel Casey Inn
100 Adams Ave.
Scranton, PA 18503
(717) 344-5656
Officers: Irving T. Miller, President; James Parette, Secretary

SHAMOKIN
MUSICIANS' PROTECTIVE ASSOCIATION (456)
1036 West Arch St.
Shamokin, PA 17872
(717) 648-0883
Officers: Charles L. Verano, President; William Porto, Secretary

SHARON
THE SHARON MUSICIANS' ASSOCIATION (187)
945 Fruit Ave.
Farrell, PA 16121
(412) 342-5283

Officers: Joseph Cantelupe, President; Tony Antonino, Secretary

STATE COLLEGE
STATE COLLEGE AREA MUSICIANS' ASSOCIATION (660)
335 W. Arbor Way
State College, PA 16801
(814) 237-2695
Officers: Elmer C. Wareham, Jr., President; Hubert H. Haugh, Secretary

SUNBURY
SUNBURY FEDERATION OF MUSICIANS (605)
RD 1
Box 353
Middleburg, PA 17842
(717) 837-0127
Officers: August F. Korten, President; Ray M. Fulmer, Secretary

UNIONTOWN
UNIONTOWN MUSICAL SOCIETY (596)
150 Eicher St.
Uniontown, PA 15401
(412) 439-4114
Officers: George Salay, President; Pete P. Porreca, Secretary

VANDERGRIFT
THE VANDERGRIFT MUSICAL SOCIETY (476)
617 First St.
Leechburg, PA 15656
(412) 845-7273
Officers: Carl Spaniel, President; Leo Allera, Secretary

WASHINGTON
WASHINGTON MUSICAL SOCIETY (277)
800 Washington Trust Building
Washington, PA 15301
(412) 225-6600
Officers: James Hill, President; John W. McCreight, Secretary

WILKES-BARRE
MUSICIANS' PROTECTIVE UNION (140)
720 Main St.
Sugar Notch, PA 18706
(717) 829-3978
Officers: Alfred R. Seidel, President; Anthony F. Kane, Jr., Secretary

WILLIAMSPORT
WILLIAMSPORT FEDERATION OF MUSICIANS (761)
Rear 57 N. Main St.
PO Box 190
Hughesville, PA 17737
(717) 584-4341
Officers: Bernard P. Henrichs, President; James T. Lundy, Secretary

YORK
MUSICIANS' PROTECTIVE UNION (472)
P.O. Box 424
York, PA 17405
(717) 848-2272
Officers: Donald R. Miller, President; Clair H. Brenner, Secretary

RHODE ISLAND

NEWPORT
NEWPORT FEDERATION OF MUSICIANS (529)
235 Eustis Ave.
Newport, RI 02840
(401) 849-2360
Officers: Sylvia Stoun, President/ Secretary

PROVIDENCE
PROVIDENCE FEDERATION OF MUSICIANS (198-457)
179 Broadway
Providence, RI 02903
(401) 751-2036/2717
Officers: Joseph Conte, President; Aime Triangolo, Secretary

WOONSOCKET
MUSICIANS' PROTECTIVE UNION (262)
21 Avenue B
Woonsocket, RI 02895
(401) 769-9657/3400
Officers: Chester J. Krajewski, President; Paul Kazanowski, Secretary

SOUTH CAROLINA

CHARLESTON
CHARLESTON FEDERATION OF MUSICIANS (502)
1519 Burclair
Charleston, SC 29412
(803) 795-6232
Officers: John D. Droze, President; Willard Bolchoz, Secretary

GREENVILLE
GREENVILLE FEDERATION OF MUSICIANS (694)
PO Box 8127
Greenville, SC 29604
(803) 246-1289
Officers: Dan A. Ellis, President; J. Furman Neal, Secretary.

SOUTH DAKOTA

HURON
MUSICIANS' PROTECTIVE UNION (693)
PO Box 255
Huron, SD 57350
(605) 883-4235
Officers: Randall Lampe, President; Luverne Better, Secretary

MITCHELL
MUSICIANS' PROTECTIVE AND BENEFIT ASSOCIATION OF MITCHELL (773)
1509 Bridle Dr.
Mitchell, SD 57301
(605) 996-5467
Officers: Arnold Braught, President; Joseph F. Pekas, Secretary

RAPID CITY
WEST RIVER MUSICIANS' UNION (686)
6511 Janet Dr.
Rapid City, SD 55701
(605) 342-2062
Officers: Derek Kinzler, Secretary.

SIOUX FALLS
MUSICIANS' UNION (114)
1723 South Minnesota
Sioux Falls, SD 57105
(605) 336-8508
Officers: Robert Niblick, President; Leonard E. Martinek, Secretary

YANKTON
MUSICIANS' ASSOCIATION (255)
601 E. 16th St.
Yankton, SD 57078
(605) 665-2488
Officers: Harry C. Turen, President; Rex Hays, Secretary

TENNESSEE

BRISTOL, TN/BRISTOL, VA
MUSICIANS' ASSOCIATION (556)
132 Tyler Dr.
Bristol, TN 37620
(615) 968-3102
Officers: Charles Goodwin, President; Rudolph Brinkley, Secretary

CHATTANOOGA
CHATTANOOGA MUSICIANS' UNION (80)
Memorial Auditorium
Chattanooga, TN 37402
(615) 266-5912
Officers: Jimmy Tawater, President; James Petty, Secretary

JACKSON
JACKSON FEDERATION OF MUSICIANS (639)
64 Glen Eden Dr.
Jackson, TN 38101
(901) 668-5176
Officers: James Allen, President; James Petty, Secretary

KNOXVILLE
MUSICIANS' PROTECTIVE ASSOCIATION (546)
406½ West Church Ave.
Knoxville, TN 37902
(615) 524-1897
Officers: W.G. Collins, President; Al Smith, Secretary

MEMPHIS
MEMPHIS FEDERATION OF

MUSICIANS (71)
2282 Young Ave.
Memphis, TN 38104
(901) 272-1746
Officers: Bob Taylor, President; Russ Spotswood, Secretary

NASHVILLE
ASSOCIATION OF MUSICIANS (257)
PO Box 120399
11 Music Circle No.
Nashville, TN 37212
(615) 244-9514
Officers: Johnny DeGeorge, President; Vic Willis, Secretary

TEXAS

AMARILLO
AMARILLO FEDERATION OF MUSICIANS (532)
PO Box 990
Amarillo, TX 79105
(806) 374-2532
(806) 352-0332
Officers: Richard McMillen, President; John D. Roberts, Secretary

AUSTIN
AUSTIN FEDERATION OF MUSICIANS (433)
302 West 15th
Suite 204
Austin, TX 78701
(512) 476-6798
Officers: Leon Grizzard, President; Randy McCall, Secretary

BEAUMONT-PORT ARTHUR
PROFESSIONAL MUSICIANS' ASSOCIATION (464-615)
1135 Boston Ave.
Nederland, TX 77627
(713) 727-1872
Officers: R.T. DeLoache, President; Max Bishop, Secretary

CORPUS CHRISTI
CORPUS CHRISTI MUSICIANS' ASSOCIATION, INC. (644)
530 Indiana
Corpus Christi, TX 78404
(512) 851-0612
Officers: Edward Galvan, President; Mrs. Billie Ferrell, Secretary

DALLAS
DALLAS FEDERATION OF MUSICIANS (147)
2829 West North West Highway 235
Dallas, TX 75220
(214) 358-4447
Officers: Richard B. Cole, President/Secretary

EL PASO
EL PASO FEDERATION OF MUSICIANS (466)
2100 East Yandell
El Paso, TX 79903
(915) 532-5851
Officers: John T. Bracey, President; Robert H.W. Booth, Secretary

FORT WORTH
FORT WORTH PROFESSIONAL MUSICIANS ASSOCIATION (72)
3458 Blue Bonnet Circle
Fort Worth, TX 76109
(817) 927-8478
Officers: Ken Foeller, President/Secretary

GALVESTON
MUSICIANS' PROTECTIVE ASSOCIATION (74)
716 25th
Galveston, TX 77550
(713) 763-4329
Officers: R.S. Graugnard, President; Carlos Pena, Secretary

HOUSTON
HOUSTON PROFESSIONAL MUSICIANS' ASSSOCIATION (65)
609 Chenevert
Houston, TX 77003
(713) 236-8676
Officers: E.C. Holland, President; Don Cannon, Secretary

SAN ANGELO
MUSICIANS' PROTECTIVE UNION (361)
PO Box 463
San Angelo, TX 76901
(915) 653-2690
Officers: Calvin Bell, President; Bill Aylor, Secretary

SAN ANTONIO
MUSICIANS' SOCIETY (23)
Suite 203
611 N. Flores St.
San Antonio, TX 78205
(512) 227-3582
Officers: Don Kraft, President; Ishmael Gonzalez, Secretary

WACO
WACO MUSICIANS' ASSOCIATION (306)
197 S. 18th St.
Mid City, Waco, TX 76701
(817) 544-8127
Officers: Shep Barrier, President/Secretary

WICHITA FALLS
WICHITA FALLS MUSICIANS' ASSOCIATION (688)
340 Hilltop St.
Wichita Falls, TX 76303
(817) 766-0859
Officers: W.G. (Billy) Peeler, President/Secretary

UTAH

OGDEN
MUSICIANS' PROTECTIVE UNION (356)
2046 Adams Ave.
Ogden, UT 84403
(801) 393-9558
Officers: Herbert M. Hillier, President; Jeff W. Benson, Secretary

PROVO
MUSICIANS' PROTECTIVE UNION (272)
1662 West 820 North
Provo, UT 84601
(801) 377-8080
Officers: Don L. Earl, President; Robert H. Bird, Secretary

SALT LAKE CITY
FEDERATED MUSICIANS (104)
1931 South 1100 East, No. 205
Salt Lake City, UT 84105
(801) 486-0713
Officers: William D. Sullivan, President; David J. Wilkins, Secretary

VERMONT

BURLINGTON
BURLINGTON MUSICIANS' ASSOCIATION (351)
111 N. Winooski Ave.
Burlington, VT 05401
(802) 863-2287
Officers: Edwin Arey, President; Robert J. Mario, Secretary

VIRGINIA

BRISTOL, VA/BRISTOL, TN
(*See* **BRISTOL, TN**)

COVINGTON
MUSICIANS' PROTECTIVE UNION (674)
158 Wake Robin Trail
Rolling Hills
Lewisburg, WV 24901
(304) 645-1870
Officers: Roy U. Arritt, President; Gary Williams, Secretary

LYNCHBURG
MUSICIANS' PROTECTIVE UNION (157)
PO Box 2181
500 Stuart St.
Lynchburg, VA 24501
(804) 845-8794/2383
Officers: Richard Reed, President; Ted Simopoulos, Secretary

NEWPORT NEWS
MUSICIANS' PROTECTIVE UNION (199)
700 New Market Square
Suite 327
Newport News, VA 23605
(804) 380-1022
Officers: Clarence F. Curry, President; W.H. Smith, Secretary

NORFOLK
NORFOLK MUSICIANS' ASSOCIATION (125)
PO Box 201
Norfolk, VA 23501
(804) 622-8095
Officers: Bob Sawyer, President; Herb Sebren, Secretary

RICHMOND
MUSICAL PROTECTIVE ASSOCIATION (123)
113 North Mall
Willow Lawn Shopping Center
Richmond, VA 23230
(804) 285-0114
Officers: Robert C. Barker, President; James A. Whitely, Secretary

ROANOKE
MUSICIANS' PROTECTIVE UNION (165)
PO Box 5471
Roanoke, VA 24012
(703) 563-4533
Officers: E.E. Wiggins, President; Adrian Willis, Secretary

WASHINGTON

ABERDEEN
MUSICIANS' PROTECTIVE UNION (236)
619 Boone St.
Aberdeen, WA 98520
(206) 532-1848
Officers: Myron Hinkle, President; R.J. Brawley, Secretary

ANACORTES
MUSICIANS' ASSOCIATION OF SKAGIT COUNTY, WASHINGTON (461)
1572 Dunbar Rd.
Mount Vernon, WA 98273
(206) 424-4995
Officers: Wilbur Wigner, President; Lawrence M. Seitz, Secretary

BELLINGHAM
MUSICIANS' PROTECTIVE UNION (451)
Ste. No. 1, 1509 Broadway
Bellingham, WA 98225
(206) 733-2670
Officers: Lew Nordby, President; Robert J. Wood, Secretary

EVERETT
MUSICIANS' ASSOCIATION (184)
2602 Grand Ave.
Everett, WA 98201
(206) 258-3519
Officers: R.E. Draper, President; Mrs. Janis C. Fifield, Secretary.

KELSO-LONGVIEW
MUSICIANS' MUTUAL PROTECTIVE UNION (668)
PO Box 1852
Longview, WA 98632
(206) 423-5010
Officers: Toi Niemi, President; Gerald E. Philbrook, Secretary

OLYMPIA
MUSICIANS' ASSOCIATION (124)
119½ Capitol Way
Labor Temple
Room 9
Olympia, WA 98501
(206) 357-5220
Officers: Derek Basham, President; Deena Tveden, Secretary

PASCO
TRI-CITY MUSICIANS ASSOCIATION (524)
Suite 105
507 North Fourth Ave.
Pasco, WA 93301
(509) 547-6622
Officers: Wayne E. McGuffin, President; Ted O. Myrick, Secretary

PORT ANGELES
MUSICIANS' PROTECTIVE UNION (395)
515 West 13th St.
Port Angeles, WA 98362
(206) 457-6958
Officers: Carla Umbehocker, President; Ruth Hanson, Secretary

RENTON-AUBURN
MUSICIANS' PROTECTIVE UNION (360)
126 Logan Ave., South
Renton, WA 98055
(206) BA 6-5360
Officers: A.H. Scotty Kelly, President; Mrs. Evelyn Allyn, Secretary

SEATTLE
MUSICIANS' ASSOCIATION (76)
2620 Third Ave.
Seattle, WA 98121
(206) 623-0025
Officers: Chet Ramage, President; Carl H. Challstedt, Secretary

SPOKANE
MUSICIANS' ASSOCIATION (105)
W. 418½ Sprague Ave.
Spokane, WA 99204
(509) 624-3102
Officers: Joseph T. Baker, President; John F. Baker, Secretary

TACOMA
MUSICIANS' ASSOCIATION OF TACOMA (117)
1518 Pacific Ave., S.
Tacoma, WA 98402
(206) 627-8706
Officers: George A. Doll, President; Robert L. Colombini, Jr., Secretary

YAKIMA
MUSICIANS' PROTECTIVE ASSOCIATION (442)
Room 314
Larson Building
6 South 2nd St.
Yakima, WA 98901
(509) 452-0802
Officers: John R. Schactler, President; Bill Davison, Secretary

WEST VIRGINIA

BLUEFIELD
BLUEFIELD FEDERATION OF MUSICIANS (419)
1115 Augusta
Bluefield, WV 24701
(304) 325-6026
Officers: E.G. Watkins, President; John R. Palmer, Secretary

CHARLESTON
CHARLESTON MUSICIANS' UNION (136)
1562 Kanawha Blvd., East
Charleston, WV 25311
(304) 346-9693
Officers: Ned H. Guthrie, President; Frank C. Thompson, Secretary

CLARKSBURG
CLARKSBURG FEDERATION OF MUSICIANS (580)
407 Austin Ave.
Clarksburg, WV 26301
(304) 622-5642
Officers: Sam B. Folio, President; William T. Kirkpatrick, Secretary

FAIRMONT
FAIRMONT FEDERATION OF MUSICIANS (507)
PO Box 941
Fairmont, WV 26555
(304) 363-0927
Officers: Joseph F. Eates, President; Mrs. Edna D. Kopp, Secretary

GRAFTON
TYGART VALLEY FEDERATION OF MUSICIANS (684)
Route 1
Box 349
Shinnston, WV 26431
(304) 592-2639
Officers: Lloyd W. Spring, III, President; Guy E. Ward, Secretary

HUNTINGTON
MUSICIANS' PROTECTIVE UNION (362)
900 Pine St.
Kenova, WV 25530
Officers: Philip B. Stone, President; Carol J. Stone, Secretary

MORGANTOWN
MUSICIANS' PROTECTIVE ASSOCIATION (562)
K of C Bldg., Room 8
227 Chestnut St.
Morgantown, WV 26507-0400
(304) 292-3756
Officers: Richard E. Powell, President; Kenneth Vance, Secretary

MOUNDSVILLE
MUSICIANS' PROTECTIVE UNION (492)
1306 Third St.
Moundsville, WV 26041
(304) 845-3796
Officers: J. Ryland Cox, President; Harold Kirby, Secretary

PARKERSBURG
MUSICIANS' MUTUAL PROTECTIVE UNION (259)
Box 1842
Parkersburg, WV 26101
(304) 422-1331
Officers: Richard Leonhart, President; Miss Margaret A. Alexander, Secretary

WHEELING
WHEELING MUSICAL SOCIETY (142)
17th and Jacobs Sts.
Wheeling, WV 26003
(304) 233-0620
Officers: Logan C. Daugherty, President; Joe Cesario, Secretary

WISCONSIN

ABBOTSFORD
MUSICIANS' PROTECTIVE UNION (194)
Box 57
Curtiss, WI 54422
(715) 223-4071
Officers: Dean Strobach, President; Paul Kramas, Secretary

BARABOO
ASSOCIATED MUSICIANS (327)
835 12th St.
Baraboo, WI 53913
(608) 356-6125
Officers: Charles Pfaff, President; Ira E. Perry, Secretary

BELOIT
BELOIT MUSICIANS' ASSOCIATION (183)
2003 Burton St.
Beloit, WI 53511
(608) 362-5165
Officers: James Giacalone, President; Vernard Sanborn, Secretary

EAU CLAIRE
CHIPPEWA VALLEY MUSICIANS' ASSOCIATION (345)
Labor Temple
2233 Birch St.
Eau Claire, WI 54701
(715) 832-1937
Officers: Roy Rankin, President; Mrs. Marion Peplau, Secretary

ELKHORN
ELKHORN FEDERATION OF MUSICIANS (680)
Route 66
Elkhorn, WI 53121
(414) 728-9523
Officers: Frank Bleser, President; Edd Hennerley, Secretary

FOND DU LAC
FOND DU LAC MUSICIANS' ASSOCIATION (309)
44 E. 12th St.
Fond Du Lac, WI 54935
(414) 923-1610
Officers: Al Buerger, President; James Sabel, Secretary

GREEN BAY
GREEN BAY FEDERATION OF MUSICIANS (205)
325 St. George St.
Green Bay, WI 54302
(414) 432-1340
Officers: Fred J. Orland, President; Richard J. Conley, Secretary

JANESVILLE
JANESVILLE MUSICIANS' ASSOCIATION (328)
27 S. Randall Ave.
Janesville, WI 53545
(608) 754-7474
Officers: John Kerr, President; Ilene Kerr, Secretary

KENOSHA
KENOSHA FEDERATION OF MUSICIANS (59)
711 Washington Rd.
Kenosha, WI 53140
(414) 652-1465
Officers: Joe Perry, President; Ben Strobl, Secretary

KEWAUNEE
KEWAUNEE FEDERATION OF MUSICIANS (604)
Route 1
Luxemburg, WI 54217
(414) 845-5021
Officers: Gene LeBotte, President; Melvin A. Gaedtke, Secretary

LA CROSSE
MUSICIANS' ASSOCIATION (201)
1619 Weston St.
LaCrosse, WI 54601
(608) 788-4145
Officers: Kenneth G. Bye, President; Edgar Wuensch, Secretary

MADISON
MADISON MUSICIANS' ASSOCIATION (166)
222 North Midvale Blvd.
Madison, WI 53705
(608) 238-3421
Officers: Robert Ramsdell, President; Robert Johnson, Secretary

MANITOWOC
MANITOWOC MUSICIANS' ASSOCIATION (195)
2706 33rd St.
Two Rivers, WI 54241
(414) 793-1235
Officers: Arthur Nickels, President; Clarence F. Doleysh, Secretary

MARINETTE, WI/MENOMINEE, MI
See **MENOMINEE, MI**

MARSHFIELD
MUSICIANS' PROTECTIVE UNION (270)
1227 East 15th St.
Box 143
Marshfield, WI 54449
(715) 384-5911
Officers: Ray Kraemer, President; Lynn Winch, Jr., Secretary

MILWAUKEE
MUSICIANS' ASSOCIATION (8)
2200 North 45th St.
Milwaukee, WI 53208
(414) 444-5234
Officers: James Higgins, President; Robert Couey, Secretary

MONROE
MUSICIANS' PROTECTIVE UNION (243)
1723 21st St.
Monroe, WI 53566
(608) 325-5764
Officers: Leo C. Peterson, President; Stanley Neuberger, Secretary

NEENAH AND MENASHA
MUSICIANS' PROTECTIVE UNION (182)
983 Bridgewood Dr.
Neenah, WI 54956
(414) 722-3690
Officers: Richard Remmel, President; Mildred Yost, Secretary

OCONTO FALLS
MUSICIANS' PROTECTIVE ASSOCIATION (648)
526 Sunrise Lane
Green Bay, WI 54301
(414) 336-0702
Officers: Joe Valenta, President; Joe Melton, Secretary

OSHKOSH
OSHKOSH MUSICIANS' ASSOCIATION (46)
Box 2765
1763 Southland Ave.
Oshkosh, WI 54903
(414) 231-7004
Officers: Frank Novotny, President; Milton H. Galow, Secretary

RACINE
MUSICIANS' UNION (42)
PO Box 404
Racine, WI 53401
(414) 634-4712
Officers: Norman Sill, President; John Shelby, Secretary

RHINELANDER
MUSICIANS' PROTECTIVE ASSOCIATION (489)

503 Lennox St.
Rhinelander, WI 54501
(715) 362-4865
Officers: Howard Olsen, President; Elmer R. Luebcke, Secretary

SHAWANO
SHAWANO FEDERATION OF MUSICIANS (227)
205 East Zingler Ave.
Shawano, WI 54166
(715) 526-5346
Officers: Willard Kumm, President; Frank Cheyka, Secretary

SHEBOYGAN
MUSICIANS' ASSOCIATION (95)
2617 Saemann Ave.
Sheboygan, WI 53081
(414) 457-5937
Officers: Michael Brendze, President; Mrs. Gloria Witte, Secretary

STEVENS POINT
MUSICIANS' PROTECTIVE UNION (213)
3854 Bluebird Dr.
Stevens Point, WI 54481
(715) 344-7550
Officers: Herman Bella, President; Anton C. Kunst, Secretary

STURGEON BAY
STURGEON BAY FEDERATION OF MUSICIANS (654)
4764 North Bay Shore Dr.
Sturgeon Bay, WI 54235
(414) 743-5116
Officers: Gerald Mickelson, President; John W. Schack, Secretary

SUPERIOR
MUSICIANS' PROTECTIVE UNION (260)
Labor Temple Building
Superior, WI 54880
(715) 394-5173
Officers: Robert Skudstad, President; Henry A. Koski, Secretary

WATERTOWN
WATERTOWN MUSICIANS' ASSOCIATION (469)
Box 13
Watertown, WI 53094
(414) 261-5839
Officers: Will Eske, President; Eugene Kelm, Secretary

WAUKESHA
MUSICIANS' ASSOCIATION (193)
1726 S. West Ave.
Waukesha, WI 53186
(414) 547-7031
Officers: Laurel I. Houlihan, President; Ray Von Gunten, Jr.

WAUSAU
MUSICIANS PROTECTIVE ASSOCIATION (480)
3118 Seymour Laune
Wausau, WI 54401
(715) 842-7835
Officers: Garen Reich, President; Brian Seehafer, Secretary

WISCONSIN RAPIDS
CENTRAL WISCONSIN MUSICIANS' ASSOCIATION (480)
351 5th St., North
Wisconsin Rapids, WI 54494
(715) 421-0066
Officers: George Middlecamp, President; Wally Ives, Secretary

WYOMING

CASPER
CASPER MUSICIANS' ASSOCIATION (381)
PO Box 1566
Casper, WY 82601
(307) 237-8616
Officers: Tom Kinser, President; Terence Gunderson, Secretary

CHEYENNE
MUSICIANS' PROTECTIVE UNION (590)
4023 Dillon Ave.
Cheyenne, WY 82001
(307) 632-0178
Officers: Johnnie W. Grant, President; Harry J. Cushing, Secretary

PUERTO RICO

SAN JUAN
FEDERACION DE MUSICOS DE PUERTO RICO (468)
255 Canals St.
Stop 20
Santurce, PR 00907
(809) 724-2396/2380/2381
Officers: Abraham Pena, President; Jose A. Montenegro, Secretary

U.S. VIRGIN ISLANDS

VIRGIN ISLANDS
MUSICIANS' PROTECTIVE UNION (491)
PO Box 714
St. Thomas, VI 00801
(809) 774-2359
Officers: Alfred Lockhart, President; Aubrey Haynes, Secretary

CANADA

ALBERTA

CALGARY
CALGARY MUSICIANS' ASSOCIATION (547)
Suite 703
630 Eighth Ave., S.W.
Calgary, AB T2P 1G6
(403) 264-6610
Officers: John Mackie, President; Ray Petch, Secretary

EDMONTON
EDMONTON MUSICIANS' ASSOCIATION
Room 202
10026 105th St.
Edmonton, AB T5J 1C3
(403) 422-2449
(403) 424-9924
Officers: Hank Smith, President; E. Eddy Bayens, Secretary

BRITISH COLUMBIA

VANCOUVER
MUSICIANS' ASSOCIATION (145)
The Dominion Bank Building
510-207 West Hastings St.
Vancouver, BC V6B 1J6
(604) 684-1564
Officers: Robert Reid, President

VICTORIA
VICTORIA MUSICIANS' ASSOCIATION (247)
8-819 Fort St.
Victoria, BC V8W 1H6
(604) 385-3954
Officers: Thomas Tucker, President; Patrick G. Hughes, Secretary

MANITOBA

BRANDON
BRANDON MUSICIANS' ASSOCIATION (475)
220 Russell St.
Brandon, MB
(204) 727-8506
Officers: W.F. Dinsdale, President; R.A. Patterson, Secretary

WINNIPEG
WINNIPEG MUSICIANS' ASSOCIATION (190)
409 Royal Tower
504 Main St.
Winnipeg, MB R3B 1B8
Officers: David J. Jandrisch, President; Joseph H. Karr, Secretary

NEW BRUNSWICK

SAINT JOHN
NEW BRUNSWICK MUSICIANS' ASSOCIATION (815)
PO Box 913
Saint John, N.B., Canada E2L 4C3
(506) 652-6620
Officers: Ronald H. Cooke, President; Charles M. Williams, Secretary

NEWFOUNDLAND

ST. JOHN'S
NEWFOUNDLAND AND LABRADOR

MUSICIANS' ASSOCIATION (820)
P.O. Box 1876, Station C.
St. John's, NF A1C 5R4
Officers: Peter Gardner, President; Wayne Hynes, Secretary

NOVA SCOTIA

CAPE BRETON
CAPE BENTON MUSICIANS' ASSOCIATION (355)
65 Hankard St.
Sydney, NS B1N 1Y4
(902) 539-0968
Officers: Steve Hasiuk, President; Eddie Parris, Secretary

HALIFAX
ATLANTIC FEDERATION OF MUSICIANS (571)
6307 Chebucto Rd.
Halifax, NS B3L 1K9
(902) 422-6492
Officers: Peter J. Power, President; Ervin F. Street, Secretary

ONTARIO

BELLEVILLE
BELLEVILLE FEDERATION OF MUSICIANS (357)
233 John St.
Belleville, ON K8N 3G2
(613) 962-5880
Officers: Charles Tilbrook, President; J.R. Burchill, Secretary

BRANTFORD
BRANTFORD MUSICIANS' ASSOCIATION (467)
182 Elgin St.
Brantford, ON
(519) 752-7973
Officers: Albert Chowhan, President; Howard G. Johnson, Secretary

BROCKVILLE
BROCKVILLE MUSICIANS' ASSOCIATION (384)
PO Box 398
Brockville, ON K6V 5V6
(613) 342-5181
Officers: Richard Crotty, President; C. Stuart Paterson, Secretary

CHATHAM
CHATHAM FEDERATION OF MUSICIANS (582)
6 Cardinal Crescent
Chatham, ON N7L 3V3
(519) 354-6307
Officers: Bill Neff, President; Bill Mankiss, Secretary

CORNWALL
THE CORNWALL MUSICIANS' GUILD (800)
PO Box 11
2004 Pitt St.
Cornwall, ON
(613) 933-2377
Officers: Michael Heenan, President; H. Bradley Lewis, Secretary

HAMILTON
HAMILTON MUSICIANS' GUILD (293)
Suite 408
20 Jackson St., West
Hamilton, ON L8P 1L2
(416) 525-4040
Officers: Samuel Taylor, President; James H. Begg, Secretary

HUNTSVILLE
HUNTSVILLE MUSICIANS' ASSOCIATION (682)
Box 1977
Brunel Rd.
Huntsville, ON POA 1K0
(705) 789-8108
Officers: William Urban, President; Steve Michell, Secretary

KINGSTON
KINGSTON MUSICIANS' UNION (518)
181½ Division St.
Kingston, ON K7K 3Y9
(613) 542-3732
Officers: Rick Fondell, President; Richard Baldwin, Secretary

KITCHENER
CENTRAL ONTARIO MUSICIANS' ASSOCIATON (226)
125 Union St., East
Waterloo, ON N2J 4E5
(519) 744-4891
Officers: John T. Conrad, President; Douglas Janke, Secretary

LONDON
LONDON MUSICIANS' ASSOCIATION (279)
149 Wortley Rd.
London, ON N6C 3P4
(519) 438-3870
Officers: George Ross, President; Ron Shadbolt, Secretary

NIAGARA FALLS
NIAGARA FALLS MUSICIANS' ASSOCIATION (298)
5848 Main St.
Niagara Falls, ON L2G 5Z5
(416) 357-4642
Officers: Robert D. Keppy, President'; Leah Ann Kinghorn, Secretary

NORTH BAY
NORTH BAY MUSICIANS' ASSOCIATION (458)
187 Morland Blvd.
North Bay, ON
(705) 474-8485
Officers: L.D. Barham, President; Norm Mauro, Secretary

OTTAWA
OTTAWA-HULL DISTRICT FEDERATION OF MUSICIANS (180)
485 Bank St.
Ottawa, ON K2P 1Z2
(613) 233-9481/9451
Officers: Edward Hall, President; Robert Langley, Secretary

PETERBOROUGH
THE PETERBOROUGH FEDERATION OF MUSICIANS (191)
300 Aylmer St., North
Peterborough, ON K9J 3K7
(705) 743-3309
Officers: Clifford Endicott, President; Gary W. Warriner, Secretary

SARNIA
SARNIA MUSICIANS' ASSOCIATION (628)
1151 Confederation St.
Sarnia, ON N7S 3Y5
(519) 336-1790
Officers: John Chevalier, President; Ivan Vanstone, Secretary

SAULT STE. MARIE
MUSICIANS' PROTECTIVE UNION (276)
719 Queen St., East
Sault Ste. Marie, ON
(705) 254-2210
Officers: O. Sicoly, President; Ned Ciaschini, Secretary

ST. CATHARINES
ST. CATHARINES MUSICIANS' ASSOCIATION (299)
187½ Church St.
St. Catharines, ON L2R 3E8
(416) 688-0273
Officers: Ron Simpson, President; Stephen Boyuk, Secretary

ST. THOMAS
FEDERATION OF MUSICIANS (633)
6 Sinclair Ave.
St. Thomas, ON N5R 3A8
(519) 633-3730
Officers: Eber J. Rice, President; Richard Butterwick, Secretary

STRATFORD
STRATFORD MUSICIANS' ASSOCIATION (418)
Box 329
St. Marys, ON
(519) 284-1288
Officers: Norman M. Carnegie, President; Ronald Coulthard, Secretary

SUDBURY
SUDBURY FEDERATION OF MUSICIANS (290)
194 Elm St., West
Sudbury, ON P3C 1V3
(705) 674-4241
Officers: Con Di Salle, President; Carole Ann Lefebvre, Secretary

THUNDER BAY
MUSICIANS' PROTECTIVE ASSOCIATION (591)
P.O. Box 1053 "F"

Thunder Bay, ON P7C 4X8
(807) 622-1062
Officers: Roy Coran, President; James Watts, Secretary

TIMMINS

TIMMINS MUSICIANS' ASSOCIATION (817)
P.O. Box 1044
Timmins, ON P4N 7W7
Officers: Jiggs Basso, President; Edward Sheculski, Secretary

TORONTO

TORONTO MUSICIANS' ASSOCIATION (149)
Thorncliffe Park Dr.
Toronto, ON M4H 1M1
(416) 421-1020
Officers: Sam Levine, President; Victor Bridgewater, Secretary

WINDSOR

WINDSOR FEDERATION OF MUSICIANS (566)
Suite 202
744 Ouellette Ave.
Windsor, ON N9A 1C3
(519) 258-2288
Officers: Carm Adams, President; Stanley Grose, Secretary

QUEBEC

MONTREAL

MUSICIANS' GUILD OF MONTREAL (406)
1500 bl de Maisonneuve est
Montreal, PQ H2L 2B1
(514) 527-3401
Officers: Emil Subirana, President; Claude Landry, Secretary

QUEBEC

QUEBEC MUSICIANS' ASSOCIATION (119)
1406 W. St. Cyrille Blvd.
Quebec, PQ G1S 1X2
(418) 688-1722
Officers: Robert Vocelle, President; Jean Pierre Gagnon, Secretary

SAGUENAY

SAGUENAY MUSICIANS' ASSOCIATION (816)
132 Morin St.
Janquiere, PQ G7X 6T7
(418) 547-0545
Officers: Lucien Lepage, President; Celine Guerin, Secretary

SASKATCHEWAN

REGINA

REGINA MUSICIANS' ASSOCIATION (446)
321 Elphinstone St.
Regina, SK S4R 3W7
(306) 543-8545
Officers: William A. Winters, President; N. Mosienko, Secretary

SASKATOON

SASKATOON MUSICIANS' ASSOCIATION (553)
2014 Cumberland Ave., South
Saskatoon, SK S7J 1Z1
Officers: Tom Cuthill, President; Harry Smith, Secretary

American Federation of Musicians Locals Index

A

B

C

D

E

F

G

H

I

J

K

L

M

T

U

V

W

Y

Z

II. COMPETITIONS, AWARDS, AND GRANTS

Music Competitions
NFMC Scholarships and Awards Chart
Foundations and Funding Organizations

Music Competitions

U.S., Canadian, and International competitions are listed alphabetically within each country. Phone number, type, eligibility requirements, deadlines, date of competition/audition, frequency, award, and person to contact for additional information or applications are given for most competitions, when supplied by the director.

A

ABA-NABIM BAND COMPOSITION CONTEST
2019 Bradford Dr.
Arlington, TX 76010
Type: Composition for band
Eligibility: No restrictions; full score and tape recording required
When: Deadline is December 31, with competition the first week in January; annually
Award: Monetary
Contact: Dr. Charles A. Wiley, Chairman of ABA Contest Committee

THE ACADEMY OF VOCAL ARTS AUDITIONS
(*See* Competitive Auditions for Admission to The Academy of Vocal Arts)

AFFILIATE ARTISTS INC.
155 W. 68th St.
New York, NY 10023
(212) 580-2000
Type: Voice, instruments, drama, mime, dance/choreography, and conducting
Eligibility: Applicants should generally have at least three but no more than ten years of professional performing experience; guidelines vary by discipline
When: Auditions held throughout the year
Award: Appointed performers participate in Affiliate Artists Residencies, Affiliate Artists' Xerox Pianists Program, and the Exxon/Arts Endowment Conductors Program
Contact: Carol Wolff, Director of Artist Recruitment and Qualification

AMERICA-ISRAEL CULTURAL FOUNDATION
(*See* Scholarship-Fellowship Program in Israel)

AMERICAN ACADEMY IN ROME FELLOWSHIPS
(*See* Rome Prize Fellowships of the American Academy in Rome)

AMERICAN ACCORDIONISTS' ASSOCIATION UNITED STATES VIRTUOSO SOLO COMPETITIONS
580 Kearny Ave.
Kearny, NJ 07032
(201) 991-5010
Type: Accordion solos
Eligibility: Open to winners of the U.S. Accordion Cup Competitions
When: Annually
Award: Study Scholarships
Contact: Maddalena Belfiore, Executive Secretary

AMERICAN ACCORDION MUSICOLOGICAL SOCIETY ACCORDION COMPOSITION CONTEST
334 S. Broadway
Pitman, NJ 08071
(609) 589-8308
Type: Composition for classical accordion
Eligibility: No restrictions
When: Deadline is September 30; annually
Award: Monetary
Contact: Sherrie Darrow, President

AMERICAN COLLEGE THEATRE FESTIVAL ASCAP COLLEGE MUSICAL THEATRE AWARD
John F. Kennedy Center for the Performing Arts
Washington, DC 20566
(202) 254-3437
Type: Musical theatre
Eligibility: Open to full-time undergraduate or graduate students of accredited institutions of higher learning; musical play must be fully produced by a college or university to be considered for the award
When: National prizewinner selected no later than March 1; annually
Award: Monetary
Contact: Producing Director, American College Theatre Festival

AMERICAN FEDERATION OF MUSICIANS CONGRESS OF STRINGS
1500 Broadway
New York, NY 10036
(212) 869-1330
Type: Strings
Eligibility: Open to string players 16-23 years of age. Applicants must compete in a local level contest conducted in the U.S. or Canada
When: Annually
Award: Scholarship for eight-week summer program
Contact: J. Martin Emerson, Secretary-Treasurer

AMERICAN FRIENDS OF THE ALDEBURGH COMPETITION
(*See* Benjamin Britten Memorial Fund/American Friends of the Aldeburgh)

AMERICAN GUILD OF ORGANISTS NATIONAL OPEN COMPETITION IN ORGAN PLAYING
815 Second Ave., Ste. 318
New York, NY 10017
(212) 687-9188
Type: Organ
Eligibility: Applicants must be under 25 years of age by July 1 of competition year. Participants must first compete in chapter and regional events
When: Chapter competitions are held from September to mid-March, with Finals in June; biennially (1984)
Award: Monetary
Contact: Philip E. Baker, National Director

AMERICAN HARP SOCIETY NATIONAL PLAYING COMPETITION
6331 Quebec Dr.

Hollywood, CA 90068
(213) 463-0716
Type: Harp
Eligibility: Open to harpists of the U.S. and AHS members; three levels of competition
When: June; triennially (1984)
Award: Monetary
Contact: JoAnn Turovsky, Competition Chairman

AMERICAN MUSIC SCHOLARSHIP ASSOCIATION INTERNATIONAL PIANO COMPETITION
1826 Carew Tower
Cincinnati, OH 45202
(513) 421-5342
Type: Piano
Eligibility: Two divisions: Young Artist, ages 5-18; and Artist, ages 18-30. Further eligibility requirements available on request
When: Regional evaluations are in March and April, with International Finals and Semi-Finals and the last full week in June; annually
Award: Monetary and performances
Contact: Gloria Ackerman, Executive Director

AMERICAN NATIONAL CHOPIN COMPETITION
c/o Chopin Foundation of the United States
1440 79th St. Causeway
Miami, FL 33141
(305) 868-0624
Type: Piano
Eligibility: Open to American citizens 17-30 years of age
When: Quinquennially (1985)
Award: Monetary, plus transportation to the Frederic Chopin Concours International de Piano in Poland; some scholarships and professional engagements
Contact: Dr. F. Warren O'Reilly, President and Director

AMERICAN WIND SYMPHONY ORCHESTRA INTERNATIONAL COMPETITION FOR WOODWINDS, PERCUSSION & BRASS
P.O. Box 1824
Pittsburgh, PA 15230
(412) 281-8866
Type: Woodwind quintets, percussion quartets, and brass trios
Eligibility: Open to instrumentalists 18-35 years of age
When: June; biennially (1984)
Award: Monetary
Contact: Virginia Steiger, Coordinator

ARTISTS INTERNATIONAL'S DISTINGUISHED ARTISTS AUDITIONS
663 Fifth Ave.
New York, NY 10022
(212) 757-6454
Type: Piano, strings, winds, voice, and chamber ensembles
Eligibility: Open to classical artists and ensembles who have received at least one review from a major New York publication for a solo recital performance and are not under management; no age limit
Eligibility: Application deadline is late January, with auditions from late February to the first week in March; annually
Award: Solo recital at Carnegie Recital Hall or The Merkin Concert Hall in New York City
Contact: Leo B. Ruiz, Director

ARTISTS INTERNATIONAL'S YOUNG MUSICIANS AUDITIONS
663 Fifth Ave.
New York, NY 10022
(212) 757-6454
Type: Piano, strings, winds, voice, and chamber ensembles
Eligibility: Open to classical musicians who have not given a New York recital debut or have not received a New York review for a solo recital performance; instrumentalists and chamber ensembles must be under 32 years of age, singers under 35 years of age by date of auditions
When: Application deadline is late January, with auditions from late February to the first week in March; annually
Award: Solo recital at Carnegie Recital Hall in New York City
Contact: Leo B. Ruiz, Director

ASCAP COLLEGE MUSICAL THEATRE AWARD
(*See* American College Theatre Festival ASCAP College Musical Theatre Award)

ASUC-SESAC STUDENT COMPOSITION CONTEST
250 W. 54th St., Room 300
New York, NY 10019
(212) 247-3122
Composition
Eligibility: Open to student composers no older than 28 years of age; must be students of ASUC members, or student members of ASUC
When: Annually
Award: Monetary
Contact: Paul Marcontell, Executive Committee Chairman

"AUDITIONS OF THE AIR"
(*See* WGN-Illinois Opera Guild "Auditions of the Air")

B

JOHANN SEBASTIAN BACH INTERNATIONAL COMPETITIONS FOR PIANISTS
1211 Potomac St. NW
Washington, DC 20007
(202) 338-1111
Type: Piano
Eligibility: Open to pianists 20-40 years of age; contestants are visible during performance to the audience, but are hidden behind a screen for judges
When: Deadline is July 1, with competition in late September; annually
Award: Monetary, plus concert appearances
Contact: Raissa Tselentis, Founder and President

GINA BACHAUER INTERNATIONAL PIANO COMPETITION
c/o Utah Symphony
P.O. Box 11664
Salt Lake City, UT 84121
(801) 533-5626
Type: Piano
Eligibility: Open to pianists 19-33 years of age; any nationality
When: Deadline is March 10, with competition the last two weeks in June; biennially (1984)
Award: Steinway Grand Piano, New York debut, monetary prizes, for six finalists and many concert and recital appearances
Contact: Dr. Paul C. Pollei, Chairman

NATIONAL VOCAL COMPETITION FOR OPERATIC ARTISTS BALTIMORE OPERA COMPANY
40 W. Chase St.
Baltimore, MD 21201
(301) 727-0592
Type: Voice
Eligibility: Applicants must be 20-32 years of age on the commencement date of competition; all auditions must be made in person
When: Deadline is in April, with competition form mid- to late May; annually
Award: Monetary
Contact: Jay C. Holbrook, General Manager

BALTIMORE SYMPHONY ORCHESTRA YOUNG CONDUCTOR'S COMPETITION
Joseph Meyerhoff Symphony Hall
1212 Cathedral St.
Baltimore, MD 21201
(301) 727-7300
Type: Conducting
Eligibility: Open to U.S. citizens or permanent residents 35 years of age or under; must have symphonic conducting experience
When: Late spring; biennially
Award: Monetary
Contact: Ann Goldberg, Music Adminstrator and Coordinator, Young Conductor's Competition

THE JOSEPH H. BEARNS PRIZE IN MUSIC
Bearns Prize Committee
703 Dodge Hall
Columbia University
New York, NY 10027
(212) 280-3825
Type: Composition (two categories: Composition in one of the larger forms

and Composition in one of the smaller forms)
Eligibility: Open to U.S. citizens who are at least 18 years of age and no more than 25 years of age on January 1 of the award year
When: Manuscripts must be received on or before February 1 to be considered for the awards the following May, annually
Award: Monetary
Contact: Secretary, Department of Music

FRANK HUNTINGTON BEEBE FUND FOR MUSICIANS
290 Huntington Ave.
Boston, MA 02115
(617) 262-1120 x201
Type: Music study
Eligibility: Open to post-graduate students of music in America who wish to study abroad
When: Deadline is January 10; annually
Award: Scholarships
Contact: Beebe Fund Secretary

BMI AWARDS TO STUDENT COMPOSERS
Broadcast Music Inc.
320 W. 57th St.
New York, NY 10019
(212) 586-2000
Type: Composition
Eligibility: Open to students who are citizens or permanent residents of the Western Hemisphere and who are enrolled in accredited secondary schools, colleges or conservatories or are engaged in private study with recognized and established teachers anywhere in the world. Contestants must be under 26 years of age on December 31. There are no limitations as to instrumentation, stylistic consideration, or length of work submitted
When: Deadline is February 15; annually
Award: Monetary
Contact: James G. Roy, Jr., Director

BOOKLAND PIANO COMPETITION
(*See* Portland Symphony Orchestra/Bookland Piano Competition)

WILLIAM S. BOYD PIANO COMPETITION
c/o Augusta Symphony
P.O. Box 3684
Augusta, GA 30904
(404) 733-9739
Type: Piano
Eligibility: Open to pianists 18-30 years of age on April 18 of contest year; required repertoire available on request
When: Deadline is mid-April, with competition in early June; biennially (1985)
Award: Monetary and appearance with the Augusta Symphony
Contact: Dorothy R. Stoddard, Executive Secretary

BRANDEIS UNIVERSITY CREATIVE ARTS AWARDS
12 E. 77th St.
New York, NY 10021
(212) 472-1501
Type: Fine arts, dance, composition, literature, and theater
Eligibility: Open to established artists active in their careers. Winners are selected by professional juries and no applications are accepted
When: March or April; annually
Award: Monetary
Contact: Israel Nash, Director

BENJAMIN BRITTEN MEMORIAL FUND/AMERICAN FRIENDS OF THE ALDEBURGH
135 E. 83rd St.
New York, Ny 10028
(212) 861-1107
Type: Strings and voice
Eligibility: Open to American students who wish to study at the Britten-Pears School for Advanced Musical Studies in Aldeburg, Suffolk, England. Auditions are held in New York for string players and vocalists
When: Deadline is January 15 for singers, March 1 for strings; annually
Award: Scholarship for summer sessions at the Britten-Pears School
Contact: Betty Randolph Bean, Chairman

BROADCAST MUSIC INC. AWARDS TO STUDENT COMPOSERS
(*See* BMI Awards to Student Composers)

KATHLEEN AND JOSEPH M. BRYAN YOUNG ARTISTS COMPETITION
North Carolina Symphony
P.O. Box 28026
Raleigh, NC 27611
(919) 733-2750
Type: Strings (annually); voice (1984) and piano (1985), alternating years
Eligibility: Open to instrumentlists 30 years of age or younger and singers 35 years of age or younger by date of auditions; must be U.S. citizen or foreign student studying in the U.S.
When: Deadline is November 15, with competition the first week in January; annually
Award: Monetary, plus performance with 1st prize
Contact: Jackson Parkhurst, Competition Director

C

ROBERT CASADESUS INTERNATIONAL PIANO COMPETITION
Cleveland Institute of Music
11021 East Blvd.
Cleveland, OH 44106
(216) 791-5165
Type: Piano
Eligibility: Open to pianists 17-32 years of age
When: Deadline is July 1, with competition in August; biennially (1985)
Award: Monetary, plus appearance with the Cleveland Orchestra; other solo appearances and recitals
Contact: Grant Johannesen, President, Cleveland Institute of Music

CHAUTAUQUA INSTITUTION SCHOOL OF MUSIC AUDITIONS
(*See* National Scholarship Auditions for Summer Study, Chautauqua Institution School of Music)

CHOPIN FOUNDATION OF THE UNITED STATES
(*See* American National Chopin Competion)

CHOPIN PIANO COMPETITION
The Kosciuszko Foundation
15 E. 65th St.
New York, NY 10021
(212) 734-2130
Type: Piano
Eligibility: Open to highly talented Americans or permanent residents of the U.S., regardless of ethnic, religious, or racial background, who are studying for a concert career. Applicants must be 15-21 years of age by opening date of competition
When: Application deadline is March 31, with competition commencing the first Monday in June; annually
Award: Monetary (scholarships)
Contact: Music Competitions

CINCINNATI OPERA AUDITIONS
(*See* Young American Artists Program of Cincinnati Opera)

CIVIC ORCHESTRA OF CHICAGO
220 S. Michigan Ave.
Chicago, IL 60604
(312) 435-8159
Type: Orchestral and keyboard instruments
Eligibility: Soloist auditions are open to instrumentalists who will have reached their 17th but not their 26th birthday by October 1 of year of audition
When: Auditions for all positions are held each September and May; annually
Award: Tuition, scholarships
Contact: Secretary, Civic Orchestra of Chicago

CLEVELAND INSTITUTE OF MUSIC AWARD
(*See* Robert Casadesus International Piano Competition)

CLEVELAND QUARTET COMPETITION
Eastman School of Music of the University of Rochester
26 Gibbs St.
Rochester, NY 14604
(716) 275-3050
Type: String quartets or individuals

Eligibility: Open to existing quartets (preferred) or to individuals
When: Applicants must be heard by the Cleveland Quartet no later than April 1; biennially (1985)
Award: Tuition remission and stipends for coaching with the Cleveland Quartet and other Eastman string faculty
Contact: Jon Engberg, Associate Director for Academic Affairs

VAN CLIBURN INTERNATIONAL PIANO COMPETITION
3505 W. Lancaster
Fort Worth, TX 76107
(817) 738-6536
Type: Piano
Eligibility: Open to pianists of all nationalities; Grand Prize Winners of previous Van Cliburn Competitions are not eligible to compete. Applicants must have been born after June 1, 1955 and before May 18, 1967
When: Auditions in January 1985 with competition May 18—June 2, 1985; quadrennially
Award: Monetary, engagements, management services for two years following the Competition
Contact: Andrew Raeburn, Executive Director

COLEMAN CHAMBER ENSEMBLE COMPETITION
202 S. Lake Ave., Ste 201
Pasadena, CA 91101
(213) 793-4191
Type: Chamber ensembles
Eligibility: Open to chamber ensembles of from three to eight players, prepared under the direction of a fully qualified, professional coach. Three divisions: Seniors, under age 26; Intermediates, under age 20; Juniors, under age 16
When: Deadline is in March, with Competition the last week in April; annually
Award: Monetary
Contact: George Heussenstamm, Manager, Coleman Chamber Music Association

COLLEGIATE ARTIST COMPETITION
(*See* Music Teachers National Association Collegiate Artist Competition)

COLUMBIA UNIVERSITY AWARD
(*See* The Joseph H. Bearns Prize in Music)

COMPETITIVE AUDITIONS FOR ADMISSION TO THE ACADEMY OF VOCAL ARTS
Admissions Office
1920 Spruce St.
Philadelphia, PA 19103
(215) 735-1685
Type: Voice
Eligibility: Open to operatic singers who have outstanding vocal quality and maturity, plus an obvious flair for the operatic stage; musicality; performing experience; desire for a professional career. Women should be generally no older than 28; men 30. Applicants should have at least two years, preferably four, of college training or its equivalent in private study. Catalogue and application forms available upon request
When: Last week in March, first week in April; annually
Award: Full tuition scholarship
Contact: Mareen Bixler, Assistant Director

CONCERT ARTISTS GUILD ANNUAL AUDITIONS
154 W. 57th St., Studio 136
New York, NY 10019
(212) 757-8344
Type: Instrumental (piano, strings, winds, brass, harp); voice; and ensembles
Eligibility: Applicants should be ready for a formal New York debut; applicants are judged in performance
When: Application deadline is mid-January with auditions the last two weeks in April; annually
Award: Monetary and New York debut at Carnegie Recital Hall
Contact: Dr. Jerome Bunke, Director

CONCERTO COMPETITION OF THE ROME FESTIVAL ORCHESTRA
170 Broadway, Ste. 201
New York, NY 10038
(212) 349-1980
Type: Instrumental (violin, viola, violoncello, string bass, oboe, and french horn)
Eligibility: Two letters of recommendation, application to Summer Institute of Rome Festival (Italy), application fee, and tape of one movement of standard concerto required; equal opportunity, all ages
When: Deadline is January 15; annually
Award: Performance in Rome, scholarship to Summer Institute
Contact: Janet Poland, Personnel Manager

CONGRESS OF STRINGS
(*See* American Federation of Musicians Congress of Strings)

CONTEMPORARY MUSIC FESTIVAL COMPOSITION CONTEST
Music Department
Indiana State University
Terre Haute, IN 47809
(812) 232-4736 x2367
Type: Orchestral composition
Eligibility: No restrictions
When: Deadline is mid-March, with competition in late September; annually
Award: Performance by Indianapolis Symphony Orchestra, plus honorarium to cover expenses of attending the festival
Contact: James Dailey, Chairman, Contemporary Music Festival

THE AARON COPLAND CONTEST FOR YOUNG COMPOSERS
c/o Purchase Music Ensemble and School
P.O. Box 477
Purchase, NY 10577
(914) 949-8308
Type: Composition
Eligibility: "Serious" music submitted must have been written by composers 5-12 years of age; minimum duration for each piece is 3 minutes; any instrumentation
When: Entry deadline is April 9, with winners announced May 14
Award: Premiere with the Purchase Music Ensemble and publication; TV talk show and radio interviews
Contact: Elide M. Solomon, Music Director

CREATIVE ARTS AWARDS
(*See* Brandeis University Creative Arts Awards)

D

DALLAS MORNING NEWS G.B. DEALEY AWARDS
Communications Center
Dallas, TX 75265
(214) 745-8141
Type: Instrumental (1984) and voice (1985), alternating years
Eligibility: Open to instrumentalists and singers not older than 32 years of age by date of auditions
When: Deadline is January 31, with auditions in May; annually
Award: Monetary
Contact: Diana Clark, Coordinator

D'ANGELO YOUNG ARTIST COMPETITION
c/o Mercyhurst College
501 E. 38th St.
Erie, PA 16546
(814) 825-0362
Type: Voice (1984), strings (1985), and piano (1986), rotating annually
Eligibility: Open to performers 30 years of age or under
When: Deadline is March 31, with competition in mid-July; annually
Award: Monetary, plus performance with Erie Philharmonic
Contact: Dr. Louis A. Mennini, Director, D'Angelo School of Music

G.B. DEALEY AWARDS
(*See* Dallas Morning News G.B. Dealey Awards)

DELIUS COMPOSITION CONTEST
c/o Jacksonville University
College of Fine Arts
Jacksonville, FL 32211

(904) 744-3950
Type: Composition (three categories: vocal, keyboard, instrumental)
Eligibility: Open to composers who have not reached their 35th birthday by deadline; contest rules available on request
When: Deadline is October 15; annually
Award: Monetary, plus performance during the Delius Festival in Jacksonville, Florida, in March
Contact: Prof. William McNeiland, College of Fine Arts

DELTA OMICRON INTERNATIONAL MUSIC FRATERNITY COMPOSITION COMPETITION
115 Lawrence
Prattville, AL 36067
(205) 365-4335
Type: Composition
Eligibility: Open to women composers of college age and older; work must not have been previously published or publically performed
When: Deadline is August 1 of year preceding competition; triennially (1984)
Award: Monetary, plus premiere of composition at Triennial Conference of Delta Omicron
Contact: Jo S. Holt, President

DETROIT GRAND OPERA ASSOCIATION SCHOLARSHIPS
500 Temple Ave.
Detroit, MI 48201
(313) 832-5200
Type: Voice
Eligibility: Open to operatic singers in the Detroit District of the Metropolitan Opera National Council or to students during the past six months in the district. Applicants must be in the following age brackets: sopranos, 20-30; mezzos and contraltos, 20-30; tenors, 20-32; baritones, 20-32; basses, 20-33; additional requirements available on request
When: Application deadline is mid-October, with auditions in late October or early November; annually
Award: Samuel J. Lang Scholarship, Elizabeth Hodges Donovan Award, Henry E. Wenger Award
Contact: Mrs. Sam B. Williams, Scholarship Chairman

DIABLO SYMPHONY ASSOCIATION YOUNG ARTIST AWARD
P.O. Box 2222
Walnut Creek, CA 94595
(415) 939-7121
Type: Oboe (1984), cello (1985), harp (1986), other instruments (clarinet, horn, viola, bassoon, trumpet), rotating annually
Eligibility: Open to instrumentalists 16-25 years of age
When: Deadline is February 15, with auditions the first Saturday in March; annually
Award: Contract to perform auditioned concerto with The Diablo Symphony Orchestra at its regular June concert, plus honorarium
Contact: William M. Donaldson, Auditions Coordinator, 3248 Tice Creed Dr., #2, Walnut Creek, CA 94595

DISTINGUISHED ARTISTS AUDITIONS
(*See* Artists International's Distinguished Artists Auditions)

E

EAST & WEST ARTISTS ANNUAL AUDITIONS
310 Riverside Dr. #313
New York, NY 10025
Type: Instrumental, ensembles, and voice
Eligibility: First category: Open to instrumentalists, ensembles, and singers 18-35 years of age who have not given a New York debut recital, or those who have given their New York City debuts but were not reviewed. Second category: No age restrictions to instrumentalists, ensembles, and singers who have given at least one solo recital in a major hall in New York City and received a review; performers must not be under any kind of management
When: First category: application deadline is mid-February, with auditions in March; Second category: application deadline is April 1, with auditions in May, annually
Award: Solo debut or recital in Carnegie Recital Hall
Contact: Ms. Adolovni Acosta, Director-Founder

EASTMAN SCHOOL OF MUSIC OF THE UNIVERSITY OF ROCHESTER
(*See* Cleveland Quartet Competition)

ECCO! (ENSEMBLE COMPANY OF CINCINNATI OPERA)
1241 Elm St.
Cincinnati, OH 45210
(513) 621-1919
Type: Voice
Eligibility: Applicants must have professional operatic and musical theater experience; related classroom/teaching experience helpful
When: Application deadline is March 1, with auditions by invitation in New York at the end of March and in Cincinnati in April; annually
Award: Contract with Cincinnati Opera from October through July, round-trip air fare from point of origin to Cincinnati, and performance of roles in Music Hall and on tour
Contact: Betty Schulte, Executive Assistant

F

FARGO-MOORHEAD SYMPHONY ORCHESTRAL ASSOCIATION
(*See* Sigvald Thompson Composition Competition)

FISCHOFF NATIONAL CHAMBER MUSIC COMPETITION
Century Center
120 S. St. Joseph St.
South Bend, IN 46601
(219) 284-9711
Type: Chamber ensembles
Eligibility: Open to ensembles of three to five members, with not more than one vocal member. Senior division—maximum average age of 30 at time of competition; Junior division—no individual member may be older than 18 at time of competition. Required repertoire available on request
When: Deadline is February 1, with competition the third week in March; annually
Award: Monetary
Contact: Mary Gause, Competition Coordinator

AVERY FISHER ARTIST PROGRAM
Lincoln Center for the Performing Arts, Inc.
140 W. 65th St.
New York, NY 10023
(212) 877-1800
Type: Instrumental
Eligibility: Awards are made to young solo instrumentalists who are U.S. citizens; no specific age limit; by nomination only
When: Annually
Award: Monetary and appearances; career grants
Contact: Paula Kahn, Administrative Associate

FORT COLLINS SYMPHONY SOCIETY YOUNG ARTISTS COMPETITION
P.O. Box 1963
Fort Collins, CO 80522
(303) 482-4823
Type: Piano (annually); strings (1984) and woodwinds, brass, and percussion (1985), rotating annually
Eligibility: As of March 1, contestants must be 18 years of age or younger to enter the junior level, or 23 years of age or younger to enter the senior level. Students of any age below 23 who wish to compete at the senior level may do so
When: Deadline is February 1, with competition the second weekend in March; annually
Award: Monetary at junior level; monetary, plus performance at senior level
Contact: Mildred Unfug, Competition Chairman, 927 Pioneer Ave., Fort Collins, Co 80521

THE FRIDAY MORNING MUSIC CLUB FOUNDATION, INC.
(*See* Washington International Competition)

FRIEDHEIM AWARDS
(*See* Kennedy Center Friedheim Awards)

G

HARVEY GAUL COMPOSITION CONTEST
Pittsburgh New Music Ensemble, Inc.
6538 Darlington Rd.
Pittsburgh, PA 15217
(412) 421-5281
Type: Composition
Eligibility: Must be composition for specific instrumentation; applications and rules available September 1983
When: Begins September 1983, with a deadline in spring 1984; biennially
Award: N/A
Contact: David Stock, Conductor

H

HEMPHILL-WELLS SORANTIN YOUNG ARTISTS AWARD
(*See* San Angelo Symphony Hemphill-Wells Sorantin Young Artists Award)

IMA HOGG NATIONAL YOUNG ARTIST AUDITION
c/o Houston Symphony
615 Louisiana
Houston, TX 77002
(713) 224-4240
Type: Instrumental and piano
Eligibility: Open to musicians 19-27 years of age
When: Deadline is March 1, with competition in May; annually
Award: Monetary, plus appearance with Houston Symphony
Contact: Geraldine Priest, Chairman

HUDSON VALLEY PHILHARMONIC YOUNG ARTISTS' COMPETITION
P.O. Box 191
Poughkeepsie, NY 12602
(914) 454-1222
Type: Violin, viola, and cello
Eligibility: Applicants must be at least 18 but not 25 years of age by competition weekend
When: Deadline is mid-January, with competition in mid-March; annually
Award: Monetary and solo performance
Contact: Mrs. Dean Landriau, Chairman

I

ILLINOIS OPERA GUILD AWARD
(*See* WGN-Illinois Opera Guild "Auditions of the Air")

INTERNATIONAL AMERICAN MUSIC COMPETITIONS
Carnegie Hall/The Rockefeller Foundation
c/o Carnegie Hall
881 Seventh Ave.
New York, NY 10019
(212) 397-2800
Type: Piano (1984), voice (1985), and violin (1986), rotating annually
Eligibility: No restrictions
When: Application deadline is February 15 with auditions in June and Semi-Finals and Finals in September; annually
Award: Monetary, plus limited recording contract and concert management
Contact: Willa Rouder, Competition Coordinator

INTERNATIONAL COMPETITION FOR WOODWINDS, PERCUSSION & BRASS
(*See* American Wind Symphony Orchestra International Competition for Woodwinds, Percussion & Brass)

INTERNATIONAL PIANO COMPETITION
(*See* American Music Scholarship Association International Piano Competition)

INTERNATIONAL PIANO FESTIVAL AND COMPETITION
(*See* University of Maryland International Piano Festival and Competition)

INTERNATIONAL PIANO RECORDING COMPETITION
(*See* National Guild of Piano Teachers' International Pianl Recording Competition)

K

KENNEDY CENTER FRIEDHEIM AWARDS
John F. Kennedy Center for the Performing Arts
Washington, DC 20566
(202) 254-5241
Type: Composition: orchestral works (1984) and chamber works (1985), alternating years
Eligibility: A work must receive its American premiere between July 1st of the two previous calendar years and June 30th of the award year. Orchestral works must be at least 15 minutes in length, and chamber works 15 minutes and scored for from one to thirteen instruments. Anyone, including the composer, may make a nomination
When: Deadline for nominations is July 15, with awards announced at the conclusion of a free concert at the Kennedy Center in October; annually
Award: Monetary
Contact: Clytie M. Salisbury, Coordinator

ARAM KHACHATURIAN COMPETITION AND AWARD
c/o Armenian General Benevolent Union of America
585 Saddle River Rd.
Saddle Brook,NJ 07662
(201) 797-7600
Type: Composition for piano
Eligibility: Open to amateur composers under 35 years of age who are of Armenian descent
When: Deadline is in February, with competition in the spring; biennially (1984)
Award: Monetary
Contact: Terry Chisholm

KINGSPORT SYMPHONY ORCHESTRA CONCERTO COMPETITION
509 Watauga St.
Kingsport, TN 37660
(615) 246-9036
Type: Orchestral instruments (including piano and saxophone)
Eligibility: Open to instrumentalists 26 years of age or younger; by recommendation of private instructor
When: Tape deadline is October 1, with Finals in mid-November; annually
Award: Performance and monetary
Contact: John Gordon Ross, Music Director and Conductor

KATE NEAL KINLEY MEMORIAL FELLOWSHIP
608 Lorado-Taft Dr.
Champaign, IL 61820
(217) 333-1661
Type: Music, art, and architecture
Eligibility: Open to graduates of 4-year institutions (B.S. degree) in any of the above areas
When: Auditions are held the last weekend in March or the first weekend in April; annually
Award: Monetary
Contact: Jack H. McKenzie, Dean of College of Fine and Applied Arts

ZOLTAN KODALY ACADEMY & INSTITUTE
53 W. Jackson, Ste. 1664
Chicago, IL 60604
Type: Composition
Eligibility: Open to professional composers 35 years of age or under in year of entry
When: Deadlines are December 31, April 30, and August 31; annually
Award: N/A
Contact: Dr. Francois D'Albert, President

THE KOSCIUSZKO FOUNDATION
(*See* Chopin Piano Competition; The Marcella Sembrich Scholarship in Voice; The Michael Twarowski Scholarship)

L

LIEDERKRANZ FOUNDATION
SCHOLARSHIP AWARDS FOR PIANO
6 E. 87th St.
New York, NY 10028
(212) 245-8769 or 757-7876
Type: Piano
Eligibility: Open to pianists of proven training and experience. Applicants must be 17-30 years of age as of date of Scholarship Awards Concert
When: Application deadline is January 15 with auditions from November through February; Scholarship Awards Concert in April at Alice Tully Hall; annually
Award: Monetary and/or tuition payments
Contact: Prof. Edward Weiss, Scholarship Committee Chairman

LIEDERKRANZ FOUNDATION
SCHOLARSHIP AWARDS FOR VOICE
6 E. 87th St.
New York, NY 10028
(212) 245-8769 or 757-7876
Type: Voice
Eligibility: Open to singers of proven training and experience. Applicants must be 17-30 years of age as of date of Scholarship Awards Concert
When: Application deadline is January 15, with auditions from October through February; Scholarship Awards Concert in April at Alice Tully Hall; annually
Award: Monetary and/or tuition payments
Contact: Prof. Edward Weiss, Scholarship Committee Chairman

LIEDERKRANZ FOUNDATION
WAGNERIAN COMPETITION
6 E. 87th St.
New York, NY 10028
(212) 245-8769 or 757-7876
Type: Wagnerian singers
Eligibility: Open to singers of proven vocal training and experience. There is no age limit; however, an applicant's age may be taken into consideration in evaluating his/her audition
When: Application deadline is January 15, with auditions from October through February; Scholarship Awards Concert in April at Alice Tully Hall; annually
Award: Monetary and/or tuition payments
Contact: Prof. Edward Weiss, Scholarship Committee Chairman

LIMA SYMPHONY ORCHESTRA WOMEN'S GUILD YOUNG MUSICIANS COMPETITION
3472 Woodhaven Ln.
Lima, OH 45806
(419) 991-6928
Type: Strings and voice (1984), piano and winds (1985), rotating annually
Eligibility: Open to high school and college students in two separate divisions
When: Annually
Award: Monetary, plus appearances with Lima Symphony Orchestra
Contact: Mrs. Robert S. Cheney, Chairman

M

MACDOWELL COLONY INC.
680 Park Ave.
New York, NY 10021
(212) 535-9690 or (603) 924-3866 (NH)
Type: Professional composers, other artists
Eligibility: To recognize outstanding contribution to the fine arts, the colony awards a studio, room and board during spring, summer, winter, and fall at the MacDowell Colony in Peterborough, NH
When: Deadlines are January 15 for summer, April 15 for fall, July 15 for winter, and October 15 for spring; annually
Award: Residency fellowships
Contact: Christopher Barnes, Director

MEROLA OPERA PROGRAM
(*See* San Francisco Opera Center Auditions)

METROPOLITAN OPERA NATIONAL COUNCIL'S REGIONAL AUDITIONS PROGRAM
Lincoln Center
New York, NY 10023
(212) 974-0238
Type: Opera singing
Eligibility: Open to sopranos 19-33 years of age; mezzos and contraltos 20-33 years of age; and tenors, baritones, and basses 20-35 years of age
When: N/A
Award: Possible job with the Met
Contact: R. Stevens, Auditions Executive Director

MINNESOTA SYMPHONY ORCHESTRA WOMEN'S ASSOCIATION AWARD
(*See* Women's Association of Minnesota Symphony Orchestra Young Artist Competition)

MOZART FESTIVAL YOUNG ARTIST COMPETITION
c/o Pueblo Symphony Association Inc.
431 E. Pitkin
Pueblo, CO 81004
(303) 546-0333
Type: Violin (1984) and piano (1985), alternating annually
Eligibility: Two levels of competition: one for musicians under 18 years of age, and one for musicians under 26 years of age
When: Deadline is December 1, with competition in January; annually
Award: Monetary, plus appearance with Youth Symphony or solo performance with Pueblo Symphony Orchestra
Contact: Rita Horvat, Manager

MU PHI EPSILON COMPETITION
(*See* Sterling Staff International Competition of Mu Phi Epsilon)

OUTSTANDING PERFORMERS' AWARDS
MUSIC & ARTS INSTITUTE
2622 Jackson St.
San Francisco, CA 94115
(415) 567-1445
Type: Vocal or instrumental solo
Eligibility: Applicants must present annual solo recital at Music and Arts Institute and maintain grade average of B+
When: Scheduled upon application (3 Awards per year)
Award: Partial scholarship for advanced studies at Music and Arts Institute leading to Bachelor or Master of Music Degrees
Contact: Ross McKee, Director

MUSIC TEACHERS NATIONAL ASSOCIATION COLLEGIATE ARTIST COMPETITION
c/o Odessa College
Department of Music
Odessa, TX 79762
(915) 335-6626
Type: Piano, strings, woodwinds, percussion, brass, guitar, organ, and voice
Eligibility: Open to high school graduates under 26 years of age by date of the national audition; applicants must be studying under an MTNA member and must win state and division competitions
When: March; annually
Award: Monetary
Contact: Jack Hendrix, National Chairman

MUSIC TEACHERS NATIONAL ASSOCIATION STUDENT COMPOSITION CONTEST
16628 62nd Ave. W
Lynnwood, WA 98036
(206) 743-1660
Type: Composition
Eligibility: Applicants must be studying with an MTNA member who supervises composing and must win state and division competitions
When: December; annually
Award: Monetary
Contact: Carolyn B. Malnes, Chairman

N

NAFTZGER YOUNG ARTISTS AUDITIONS AND MUSIC AWARDS
Century II Concert Hall, Ste. 207
225 W. Douglas
Wichita, KS 67202
(316) 267-5259
Type: Piano, strings, and voice
Eligibility: Open to residents of Kansas,Oklahoma, or Missouri or students who are working toward a music degree. Instrumentalists must be

18-26 years of age, singers 20-28 years of age of date of competition
When: Deadline is in March, with competition in late April or early May; annually
Award: Monetary, plus possible appearance with the Wichita Symphony Orchestra
Contact: Mitchell A. Berman, General Manager

NATIONAL ASSOCIATION OF COMPOSERS/USA YOUNG COMPOSERS COMPETITION
Box 49652 Barrington Station
Los Angeles, CA 90049
(213) 541-8213
Type: New music composition
Eligibility: Open to members of NACUSA, 18-30 years of age
When: Deadline is October 15; annually
Award: Monetary, plus publication and performance
Contact: Marshall Bialosky, President

NATIONAL ASSOCIATION OF COMPOSERS/USA YOUNG PERFORMERS COMPETITION
Box 49652 Barrington Station
Los Angeles, CA 90049
(213) 541-8213
Type: Performance of new American music
Eligibility: Open to performers 18-30 years of age
When: Tape deadline is March 15, with final auditions in mid-May; annually
Award: Monetary, plus possible performance
Contact: Marshall Bialosky, President

NATIONAL ASSOCIATION OF TEACHERS OF SINGING ARTIST AWARD
250 W. 57th St., Ste. 2129
New York, NY 10107
(212) 582-4043
Type: Voice
Eligibility: Applicants must be at least 21 years of age but not more than 35 years of age on deadline entry date; applicant's most recent teacher must be a NATS member in good standing, and applicant must have studied with a NATS teacher continuously for at least one academic year; NATS members in good standing for at least one year prior to the deadline date are eligible
When: Every 18 months (July 1983)
Award: Monetary, plus performance
Contact: Vernon Yenne, National Coordinator, NATSAA, 6020 E. Murdock, Wichita, KS 67208, (316) 684-9704 or 689-3103

NATIONAL CHAMBER MUSIC COMPETITION
(*See* Fischoff National Chamber Music Competition)

NATIONAL CONDUCTING COMPETITION
P.O. Box 2554
La Crosse, WI 54601
(608) 788-3796
Type: Conducting
Eligibility: Candidates must be at least 30 years of age
When: Deadline is end of May, with competition from late July to early August; annually
Award: Monetary
Contact: Francesco Italiano, Director

NATIONAL FEDERATION OF MUSIC CLUBS
1336 N. Delaware St.
Indianapolis, IN 46202
(317) 638-4003
Type: Voice, instrumental, performance, dance, and composition
Eligibility: Applicants must be members of the National Federation of Music Clubs; chart explaining categories and requirements available on request
When: Annually or biennially, depending on category
Award: Various scholarships and awards
Contact: Barbara Bryant, Executive Secretary

NATIONAL FLUTE ASSOCIATION YOUNG ARTIST COMPETITION
805 Laguna Dr.
Denton, TX 76201
(817) 387-9472
Type: Flute
Eligibility: Applicants must be under 27 years of age
When: Third week in August; annually
Award: Monetary
Contact: Myrna Brown, Executive Director

NATIONAL GUILD OF PIANO TEACHERS' INTERNATIONAL PIANO RECORDING COMPETITION
c/o American College of Musicians
P.O. Box 1807
808 Rio Grande
Austin, TX 78767
Type: Piano
Eligibility: Open to member teachers and their students; competition is judged on submitted tapes
When: Deadline is December 1; annually
Award: Monetary
Contact: Irl Allison, Jr., President

NATIONAL OPEN COMPETITION IN ORGAN PLAYING
(*See* American Guild of Organists National Open Competition in Organ Playing)

NATIONAL OPERA INSTITUTE CAREER AWARDS FOR PERFORMERS
John F. Kennedy Center
Washington, DC 20566
(202) 254-3695
Type: Voice
Eligibility: Open to operatic singers with professional solo experience with a recognized professional opera company; by recommendation of company director
When: Deadline is August 1, with Regionals in the fall and Finals in January; annually
Award: Monetary
Contact: John M. Ludwig, Executive Director

NATIONAL PIANO CONCERTO COMPETITION
(*See* Youngstown Symphony Society National Piano Concerto Competition)

NATIONAL SCHOLARSHIP AUDITIONS FOR SUMMER STUDY, CHAUTAUQUA INSTITUTION SCHOOL OF MUSIC
Schools Office, Box 1098
Chautauqua, NY 14722
(716) 357-4411
Type: Orchestral, piano, voice and organ
Eligibility: Proficiency in performance in the following categories: Orchestral (college age), Youth Orchestra (high school age), piano (age 16 and over), voice (age 16 and over), and organ
When: February and March; annually
Award: Scholarships in varying amounts
Contact: Mr. Richard Redington, Director, Education, Youth, and Recreation

NATIONAL VOCAL COMPETITION FOR OPERATIC ARTISTS
(*See* Baltimore Opera Company National Vocal Competition for Operatic Artists)

NEBRASKA SINFONIA COMPETITION
(*See* Omaha Symphony Guild New Music Competition)

NEW JERSEY SYMPHONY ORCHESTRA YOUNG ARTISTS AUDITIONS
213 Washington St.
Newark, NJ 07101
(201) 624-3713
Type: Piano, strings, and brass or woodwinds (in alternate years)
Eligibility: Applicants must be legal residents of the State of New Jersey and under 20 years of age; they must adhere to repertoire requirements
When: Deadline is in March, with auditions in early spring; annually
Award: Monetary
Contact: Judith Nachison, Auditions Coordinators

NEW MUSIC FOR YOUNG ENSEMBLES INTERMEDIATE ENSEMBLE COMPOSITION COMPETITION
490 West End Ave.
New York, NY 10024
(212) 595-2298
Type: Composition for chamber

ensembles
Eligibility: Open to resident American composers; no age limit
When: Deadline is March 15, with competition in March; annually
Award: New York City debut, monetary
Contact: Claire Rosengarten, Founder and Executive Director

NORTH CAROLINA SYMPHONY
(*See* Kathleen and Joseph M. Bryan Young Artists Competition)

O

OHIO VALLEY YOUNG MUSICIANS' CONCERTO COMPETITION FOR STRINGS
Wheeling Symphony Society
Hawley Building, Ste. 307
Wheeling, WV 26003
(304) 323-6191
Type: Violin, viola, and cello
Eligibility: Open to residents of or students in West Virginia, Pennsylvania, Ohio, Kentucky, Illinois, and Indiana; applicants must be 17-28 years of age
When: Application deadline is late January, with competition in early to mid-April; annually
Award: Monetary and solo appearance
Contact: Susan C. Nelson, General Manager

OKLAHOMA SYMPHONY ORCHESTRA WOMEN'S COMMITTEE YOUNG ARTIST AUDITIONS
512 Civic Center Music Hall
Oklahoma City, OK 73102
(405) 232-4292
Type: Piano, strings, and voice
Eligibility: Open to residents of or students in Okalahoma, Kansas, Missouri, Nebraska, Arkansas, and Texas; applicants must be no more than 30 years of age
When: Application deadline is January 31, with auditions in early March; annually
Award: Monetary and performance with the Oklahoma Symphony Orchestra
Contact: Mrs. John Hanes, Audition Chairman, 12401 Blue Sage Rd., Oklahoma City, OK 73120

OMAHA SYMPHONY GUILD NEW MUSIC COMPETITION
c/o Omaha Symphony Association
310 Aquila Ct.
Omaha, NE 68102
(402) 342-3560
Type: Composition
Eligibility: Open to all composers; no age limit
When: Deadline is March 15; annually
Award: Monetary, plus possible performance by the Nebraska Sinfonia
Contact: Janet Mardis, New Music Chairman, 9465 Pauline, Omaha, NE 68124, (402) 393-0667

OPERA COMPANY OF PHILADELPHIA/LUCIANO PAVAROTTI INTERNATIONAL VOICE COMPETITION
Opera Company of Philadelphia
1500 Walnut St., Ste. 1300
Philadelphia, PA 19102
(215) 732-5811
Type: Voice
Eligibility: Open to all voice categories from any country in the world. Candidates must be under the ages of 35 (men) and 33 (women); cannot have made a major debut with a major opera company; and must be recommended to the Competition or may write for an audition
When: Spring; biennially (1985)
Award: Debut with Luciano Pavarotti in an Opera Company of Philadelphia production or in an OCP production without Mr. Pavarotti
Contact: Jane Grey Nemeth, Competition Director

ORATORIO SOCIETY OF NEW YORK SOLO COMPETITION FOR SINGERS
Carnegie Hall, Ste. 504
881 Seventh Ave.
New York, NY 10019
(212) 247-4199
Type: Voice
Eligibility: Open to singers of all nationalities 35 years of age or under by January 1. Applicants may not have made a formal New York Oratorio debut in a reviewed performance in a major New York City concert hall
When: Application deadline is April 15, with competition in May; annually
Award: Monetary, plus possible contracts for performance
Contact: Janet Plucknett, Competition Chairman

P

PAGANINI COMPETITION FOR CLASSICAL GUITAR AND COMPETITION FOR STRINGS
c/o Augusta Symphony
P.O. Box 3684
Augusta, GA 30904
(404) 733-9739
Type: Classical guitar and strings
Eligibility: Open to instrumentalists 18-30 years of age on April 18 of contest year; required repertoire available on request
When: Early June; biennially (1984)
Award: Monetary and appearance with the August Symphony (strings) or solo recital in Augusta (classical guitar)
Contact: Dorothy R. Stoddard, Executive Secretary

LUCIANO PAVAROTTI INTERNATIONAL VOICE COMPETITION
(*See* Opera Company of Philadelphia/Luciano Pavarotti International Voice Competition)

PEABODY MASON MUSIC FOUNDATION SPONSORSHIP FOR PIANISTS
192 Commonwealth Ave., Ste. 4
Boston, MA 02116
(617) 266-3314
Type: Piano
Eligibility: Open to U.S. citizens 25-35 years of age; tapes of live performances in solo repertoire and chamber music required
When: Deadline is October 1; annually
Award: Two-year stipend, plus New York, and Boston recitals
Contact: Paul Doguereau, President

PERFORMERS OF CONNECTICUT YOUNG ARTISTS COMPETITION
c/o Heida Hermanns, Coordinator
2-C Cross Hwy.
Westport, CT 06880
(203) 227-6770
Type: Vocal and instrumental ensembles (1983) and soloists (1984), alternating annually
Eligibility: Open to instrumentalists 29 years of age and under; vocalists 32 years of age and under (female), 35 (male); ensembles average 29 years of age. Applicants must meet one of the following: (1) born or (2) residing in Connecticut; (3) studying now or formerly in New England.
When: Deadline is October 31, with Competition the first weekend in December; annually
Award: Monetary and performance
Contact: Heida Hermanns, Coordinator

PITTSBURGH NEW MUSIC ENSEMBLE, INC.
(*See* Harvey Gaul Composition Contest)

PORTLAND SYMPHONY ORCHESTRA/ BOOKLAND PIANO COMPETITION
30 Myrtle St.
Portland, ME 04101
(207) 773-8191
Type: Piano
Eligibility: Open to pianists 20-28 years of age
When: Deadline is February 1, with competition the last weekend in March; biennially (1984)
Award: Monetary
Contact: Russell I. Burleigh, Manager

PRO MUSICIS FOUNDATION INC
140 W. 79th St.
New York, NY 10024
(212) 787-0993
Type: Concert solo
Eligibility: Open to concert soloists with proven exceptional talent
When: Deadline is May 1; annually
Award: Recitals, appearances
Contact: Rev. Eugene Merlet, President

PULITZER PRIZE IN MUSIC
702 Journalism Building
Columbia University
New York, NY 10027

(212) 280-3841/3842
Type: Composition
Eligibility: For distinguished musical composition by an American in any of the larger forms including chamber, orchestral, choral, opera, song, dance, or other forms of musical theatre, which has had its first performance in the United States during the year. Works which receive their American premiere during the twelve months from March 15 through March 14 are considered
When: Nomination deadline is March 1; annually
Award: Monetary, plus certificate
Contact: Robin Kuzen, Assistant Administrator

PURCHASE MUSIC ENSEMBLE AND SCHOOL
(*See* The Aaron Copland Contest for Young Composers)

R

ROME FESTIVAL ORCHESTRA COMPETITION
(*See* Concerto Competition of the Rome Festival Orchestra)

ROME PRIZE FELLOWSHIPS OF THE AMERICAN ACADEMY IN ROME (AAR)
41 E. 65th St.
New York, NY 10021
(212) 535-4250
Type: Composition
Eligibility: Applicants must be U.S. citizens and hold a Bachelor's degree, or its equivalent, in musical composition from an accredited institution
When: Application deadline is November 15; annually
Award: One year of residence at the AAR with room, studio, and partial board; monthly stipend and travel allowance
Contact: Robin Herstand

ROTARY YOUNG ARTIST AWARDS
c/o Fresno Philharmonic Orchestra
1362 N. Fresno St.
Fresno, CA 93703
(209) 485-3020
Type: Voice (1984), instrumental (1985), and piano (1986), rotating annually
Eligibility: Open to residents of or students in Washington, Oregon, California, Idaho, Nevada, Utah, Arizona, Montana, Wyoming, Colorado, New Mexico, Alaska, or Hawaii; must be 18-35 years of age, depending on category
When: Last weekend in January or first weekend in February; annually
Award: Monetary, plus performance with Fresno Philharmonic Orchestra
Contact: Stewart Comer, General Manager, Fresno Philharmonic Orchestra

S

SAN ANGELO SYMPHONY HEMPHILL-WELLS SORANTIN YOUNG ARTISTS AWARD
P.O. Box 5922
San Angelo, TX 76902
(915) 658-5877
Type: Orchestral instruments, voice, and keyboard instruments
Eligibility: Open to instrumentalists/pianists 25 years of age or under, and vocalists 29 years of age or under
When: Application deadline is November 1, with competition the weekend before Thanksgiving; annually
Award: Monetary, plus performance with the San Angelo Symphony Orchestra
Contact: Gene C. Smith, Competition Manager

SAN FRANCISCO OPERA CENTER AUDITIONS
War Memorial Opera House
San Francisco, CA 94102
(415) 861-4008
Type: Voice
Eligibility: Open to sopranos 20-30 years of age; all other voices 20-34 years of age. Singers must compete in regional auditions to be eligible.
When: Deadlines vary by region; annually
Award: Determined by sponsoring organizations, possible opportunity to participate in Merola Opera Program
Contact: Elaine Snyder

SANTA BARBARA SYMPHONY YOUNG ARTIST AWARD
3 W. Carrillo St., Ste. 9
Santa Barbara, CA 93101
(805) 965-6596
Type: Piano (1984), instrumental (1985), rotating annually
Eligibility: Open to California residents or students 18-25 years of age
When: Fall, annually
Award: Monetary, plus solo appearance with Santa Barbara Symphony
Contact: Genevieve Fisher, Managing Director

SAVANNAH SYMPHONY YOUNG ARTIST COMPETITION
P.O. Box 9505
Savannah, GA 31412
(912) 236-9536
Type: Voice, piano, strings, woodwinds, and brass, rotating annually. 1984 competition is for strings
Eligibility: Open to performers 18-26 years of age
When: Preliminary deadline for tapes is late October, with competition in January; annually
Award: Monetary and performance
Contact: Chairman

SCHOLARSHIP-FELLOWSHIP PROGRAM IN ISRAEL
America-Israel Cultural Foundation
485 Madison Ave.
New York, NY 10022
(212) 751-2700
Type: Composition and performance (voice, piano, strings, harp, guitar, percussion, brass, woodwinds)
Eligibility: Awards based on age, years of study, and proficiency in instrument
Award: Late fall, early spring; annually
Award: Monetary
Contact: Morton Weissman, Executive Director

THE MARCELLA SEMBRICH SCHOLARSHIP IN VOICE
The Kosciuszko Foundation
15 E. 65th St.
New York, NY 10021
(212) 734-2130
Type: Voice
Eligibility: Open to citizens or legal residents of the U.S. regardless of ethnic background, who have demonstrated unusual musical ability but have not yet made extensive professional appearances; must be 19-25 years of age. Application and tape of at least 20 minutes in length, including at least one song or aria by a Polish composer, must be submitted
When: Application deadline is March 1; annually
Award: Scholarship
Contact: Grants Office

ELEANOR STEBER MUSIC FOUNDATION VOCAL COMPETITION
2109 Broadway
New York, NY 10023
(212) 362-2938
Type: Voice
Eligibility: Open to young professional singers affiliated with opera apprentice programs
When: Every 18 months; early October 1983
Award: Monetary, plus New York recital
Contact: Martha Moore Smith, Executive Secretary

STERLING STAFF INTERNATIONAL COMPETITION OF MU PHI EPSILON
6208 86th Ave.
New Carrollton, MD 20784
Type: Flute, piano, organ, violin, viola, and cello
Eligibility: Open to members of Mu Phi Epsilon 18-30 years of age by April 1 of contest year. Applicants must not be under contract with professional management
When: Deadline is in January, with competition in August; triennially (1983)
Award: Contracts, plus concert appearances
Contact: Ann Gibbens Davis, Coordinator

THE JULIUS STULBERG AUDITIONS, INC.
P.O. Box 107
Kalamazoo, MI 49005

(616) 342-9371
Type: Violin, viola, cello, and string bass
Eligibility: Open to performers 19 years of age or younger
When: Deadline is late January, with competition in February or March; annually
Award: Monetary and performance
Contact: Mrs. Esther Stulberg, President

WILLIAM MATHEUS SULLIVAN MUSIC FOUNDATION, INC.
410 E. 57th St.
New York, NY 10022
(212) 755-8158
Type: Voice
Eligibility: Open to gifted young singers who have finished school and are on their way to professional careers.
When: Application deadline is October 10; annually
Award: Engagements
Contact: Hugh Ross, Vice-President and Executive Director

T

SIGVALD THOMPSON COMPOSITION COMPETITION
Fargo-Moorhead Symphony Orchestral Association
P.O. Box 1753
Fargo, ND 58107
(218) 233-8397
Type: Composition
Eligibility: Open to composers of the Upper Midwest Area
When: Deadline is January 31; annually
Award: Monetary and performance by the Fargo-Moorhead Symphony Orchestra during its concert season
Contact: Evelyn Nelson, Manager

THREE RIVERS PIANO COMPETITION
c/o WQED-FM
4802 Fifth Ave.
Pittsburgh, PA 15213
(412) 622-1435
Type: Piano
Eligibility: Open to pianists under 30 years of age. Contestants compete in preliminary auditions in seven cities, followed by semi-finals and finals in Pittsburgh
When: Annually
Award: Monetary; Vesuvius Gold Award John J. Sommers Award; performance with Pittsburgh Symphony Orchestra
Contact: N/A

MICHAEL TWAROWSKI SCHOLARSHIP
The Kosciuszko Foundation
15 E. 65th St.
New York, NY 10021
(212) 734-2130
Type: Piano or violin study
Eligibility: Open to Americans of Polish extraction
When: Application deadline is January 15, with awards announced on or about May 15; annually
Award: Scholarship for full-time graduate study
Contact: Grants Office

U

UNITED STATES VIRTUOSO SOLO COMPETITIONS
(*See* American Accordionists' Association United States Virtuoso Solo Competitions)

UNIVERSITY OF MARYLAND INTERNATIONAL PIANO FESTIVAL AND COMPETITION
Summer Programs
University of Maryland
College Park, MD 20742
(301) 454-5276
Type: Piano
Eligibility: Open to pianists 16-32 years of age as of April 1
When: Application and tape deadline is April 1; annually
Award: Monetary, plus engagements
Contact: Laura Fletcher, Festival and Competition Coordinator

W

WASHINGTON INTERNATIONAL COMPETITION
The Friday Morning Music Club Foundation, Inc
3310 35th St. NW
Washington, DC 20016
(202) 966-8811
Type: Piano (1984), strings (1985), and voice (1986), rotating annually
Eligibility: Open to pianists and string players 18-28 years of age, and to singers 20-30 years of age. Applicants must not be under personal professional management
When: Deadline is mid-February, with competition in April; annually
Award: Monetary, plus one or more concert appearances in Washington, DC
Contact: Jane Goetz Lea, Competition Chairman

WGN-ILLINOIS OPERA GUILD "AUDITIONS OF THE AIR"
2501 Bradley Pl.
Chicago, IL 60618
(312) 528-2311
Type: Voice
Eligibility: Open to U.S. citizens 20-33 years of age who have not made an operatic debut with a major opera company
When: Annually
Award: Monetary, plus appearance
Contact: Dick Jones, Executive Director

WHEELING SYMPHONY SOCIETY COMPETITION
(*See* Ohion Valley Young Musicians' Concerto Competition)

WOMEN'S ASSOCIATION OF MINNESOTA SYMPHONY ORCHESTRA YOUNG ARTIST COMPETITION
1111 Nicollet Ave.
Minneapolis, MN 55403
(612) 371-5654
Type: Orchestral instruments
Eligibility: Open to residents of or students in Minnesota, North Dakota, South Dakota, Iowa, Nebraska, Missouri, Wisconsin, Manitoba, or Western Ontario. Applicants must be no older than 26 years of age on December 1 of contest year
When: Deadline is August 15, with competition in early fall; annually
Award: Monetary, plus possible performance with Minnesota Symphony Orchestra; scholarships and recitals
Contact: Lola May Thompson, Chairman

Y

YM-YWHA OF METROPOLITAN NEW JERSEY YOUNG ARTISTS COMPETITION
760 Northfield Ave.
West Orange, NJ 070752
(201) 736-3200
Type: Classical instruments and voice
Eligibility: Open to instrumentalists 16-30 years of age, and singers 16-35 years of age; must be residents of New Jersey
When: Deadline is March 1, with competition the first week in April; annually
Award: Monetary, plus performance; possible recital opportunities
Contact: Stanley Weinstein, Director of Arts & Education

YOUNG AMERICAN ARTISTS PROGRAM OF CINCINNATI OPERA
1241 Elm St.
Cincinnati, OH 45210
(513) 621-1919
Type: Voice
Eligibility: Open to singers 22-35 years of age. Applicants must have professional operatic experience beyond the college level
When: Application deadline is end of October, with auditions by invitation in New York in early January and in Cincinnati in February; annually
Award: Eight-week contract with Cincinnati Opera in June and July; role coachings, master classes from visiting artists, and more
Contact: Betty Schulte, Executive Assistant

YOUNG CONCERT ARTISTS INTERNATIONAL AUDITIONS
250 W. 57th St.
New York, NY 10019
(212) 307-6655
Type: Instrumental and voice
Eligibility: Applicants who offer

repertoire within the categories required, appropriate letters of recommendation, are not under management, and are ready to begin professional concert careers are eligible to be accepted for the Preliminary Auditions
When: Application deadline is mid-February, with auditions from late February through early May; annually
Award: New York and Washington, DC, recitals; management services; and special prizes
Contact: Amy Roberts Frawley, Auditions Coordinator

YOUNG CONDUCTOR'S COMPETITION
(*See* Baltimore Symphony Orchestra Young Conductor's Competition)

YOUNG MUSICIANS AUDITIONS
(*See* Artists International's Young Musicians Auditions)

YOUNG MUSICIANS FOUNDATION SCHOLARSHIP PROGRAM
914 S. Robertson Blvd.
Los Angeles, CA 90035
(213) 659-3766
Type: Instrumental and voice
Eligibility: Open to residents within a 200-mile radius of Los Angeles. Instrumentalists must be no older than 17; vocalists no older than 23
Award: Scholarship
Contact: Erich Vollmer, Executive Director

YOUNGSTOWN SYMPHONY SOCIETY NATIONAL PIANO CONCERTO COMPETITION
260 Federal Plaza West
Youngstown, OH 44503
(216) 744-4269
Type: Piano
Eligibility: Pianists must not be more than 25 years of age on January 1st; and must perform specified concerto
When: Deadline is March 1, with competition in May; annually
Award: Monetary, plus appearance with the Youngstown Symphony Orchestra
Contact: Mrs. A.B. Greene, Competition Chairman

Z

THE LOREN L. ZACHARY SOCIETY FOR THE PERFORMING ARTS OPERA AWARDS AUDITIONS
2250 Gloaming Way
Beverly Hills, CA 90210
(213) 276-2731
Type: Voice
Eligibility: Open to operatic singers 21-35 years of age; must be thoroughly trained and ready to pursue a professional operatic career. Applications sent only upon receipt of a self-addressed stamped envelope
When: April-May; annually
Award: Round-trip flight to Europe for auditioning purposes, plus monetary prizes
Contact: Nedra Zachary, Coordinator of Auditions

CANADA

BANFF INTERNATIONAL STRING QUARTET COMPETITION
Banff Centre School of Fine Arts
Box 1020
Banff, AB T0L 0C0
(403) 762-6100
Type: String quartet
Eligibility: Open to quartets whose members are under 35 years of age at time of competition
When: Last week of April; biennially (1985)
Award: Monetary, tour, and residency at Banff Centre
Contact: Kenneth S. Murphy, Assistant Director of Music

LESLIE BELL SCHOLARSHIP
Ontario Choral Federation
51 Linwood Ave.
Agincourt, ON M1S 1H3
(416) 293-5338
Type: Choral conducting
Eligibility: Open to Ontario residents actively practicing choral leadership
When: Late spring; annually
Award: Scholarship
Contact: Mrs. J. Pyper, Chairman of Leslie Bell Scholarship Committee

BRANDON UNIVERSITY COMPETITION
(*See* Eckhardt-Gramatte National Competition for the Performance of Canadian Music)

CANADIAN MUSIC COUNCIL AWARD
(*See* Jules Leger Prize for New Chamber Music)

CBC NATIONAL RADIO COMPETITION FOR YOUNG COMPOSERS
P.O. Box 500, Station "A"
Toronto, ON M5W 1E6
(416) 925-3311, local 2083
Type: Composition (three categories: electronic music, compositions requiring up to 12 performers, and lyric theatre)
Eligibility: Open to all composers who are Canadian citizens or landed immigrants and who are 29 years of age or younger
When: Deadline is June 1, with concert of finalists in October; biennially (1984)
Award: Monetary, plus performance broadcast
Contact: Jana Gonda or David Jaeger, Radio Music, Canadian Broadcasting Corporation

COMPOSERS, AUTHORS AND PUBLISHERS ASSOCIATION OF CANADA, LTD (CAPAC)
(*See* The Hugh Le Caine Award; The William St. Clair Low Awards; The Sir Ernest Macmillan Awards)

CONCOURS OSM
200 West, Blvd. de Mainsonneuve
Montreal, PQ H2X 1Y9
(514) 842-3402
Type: Strings, winds (1984) and piano, voice (1985), rotating annually
Eligibility: Open to Canadian citizens or landed immigrants in the following age groups: strings, 18-25 years of age (Class A) and 17 years of age and under (Class B); winds, 16-25 years of age; voice, 18-30 years of age; piano, 18-25 years of age (Class A) and 17 years of age and under (Class B)
When: Deadline is mid-October, with competition the first two weeks in November; annually
Award: Monetary (scholarship) and performance
Contact: Denyse Beique, Chairman

ECKHARDT-GRAMATTE NATIONAL COMPETITION FOR THE PERFORMANCE OF CANADIAN MUSIC
c/o School of Music, Brandon University
Brandon, Manitoba R7A 6A9
(204) 727-9631
Type: Piano (1984), strings (1985), and voice (1986), rotating annually
Eligibility: Open to Canadian citizens 35 years of age or under
When: Tape deadline is November 1, with Semi-Finals and Finals the first weekend in May; annually
Award: Monetary and concert tour
Contact: Dr. Lorne Watson, Artistic Director

THE HUGH LE CAINE AWARD (CAPAC)
1240 Bay St.
Toronto, ON M5R 2C2
(416) 924-4427
Type: Composition realized on tape with electronic means
Eligibility: Open to Canadian citizens under 30 years of age on closing date of competition. Candidate must not be a member of any performing rights society other than CAPAC, but need not be a member of CAPAC
When: Deadline is September 30, with winners announced on or before October 31; annually
Award: Monetary
Contact: Paul Spurgeon, Executive Assistant, Legal Affairs

JULES LEGER PRIZE FOR NEW CHAMBER MUSIC
c/o Canadian Music Council
36 Elgin St.
Ottawa, ON K1P 5K5
(613) 238-5893
Type: Composition for chamber groups
Eligibility: Open to composers who are Canadian citizens or landed immigrants. Works must have received a premier performance of professional

quality within the three years preceding the closing date of competition
When: Entry deadline is March 31; annually
Award: Monetary, plus performance and broadcast
Contact: Guy Huot, Secretary General, Canadian Music Council

THE WILLIAM ST. CLAIR LOW AWARDS (CAPAC)
1240 Bay St.
Toronto, ON M5R 2C2
(416) 924-4427
Type: Composition for chamber ensemble
Eligibility: Open to Canadian citizens under 30 years of age on closing date of competition. Candidate must not be a member of any performing rights society other than CAPAC, but need not be a member of CAPAC
When: Deadline is September 30, with winners announced on or before October 31; annually
Award: Monetary
Contact: Paul Spurgeon, Executive Assistant, Legal Affairs

THE SIR ERNEST MACMILLAN AWARDS (CAPAC)
1240 Bay St.
Toronto, ON M5R 2C2
(416) 924-4427
Type: Composition for orchestra
Eligibility: Open to Canadian citizens under 30 years of age on closing date of competiton. Candidate must not be a member of any performing rights society other than CAPAC, but need not be a member of CAPAC
When: Deadline is September 30, with winners announced on or before October 31; annually
Award: Monetary
Contact: Paul Spurgeon, Executive Assistant, Legal Affairs

MONTREAL INTERNATIONAL MUSIC COMPETITION
Place des Arts
1501, Jeanne-Mance St.
Montreal, PQ H2X 1Z9
(514) 285-4380
Type: Piano (1984), voice (1985), recess (1986), and violin (1987), rotating annually
Eligibility: Open to musicians of all nationalities 16-35 years of age
When: Deadline is March 1, with competition the last week in May or first week in June: annually (with recess every fourth year)
Award: Monetary
Contact: Genevieve Touchette, Secretary

ONTARIO ARTS COUNCIL SCHOLARSHIP
(*See* Heinz Unger Scholarship)

ONTARIO CHORAL FEDERATION AWARD
(*See* Leslie Bell Scholarship)

HEINZ UNGER SCHOLARSHIP
c/o Ontario Arts Council
151 Bloor St. W
Toronto, ON M5S 1T6
(416) 961-1660
Type: Conducting (orchestral)
Eligibility: Applicant must be participants in Conductors Workshop, Royal Conservatory of Music
When: Spring; annually
Award: Scholarship prize
Contact: B. Sheffield, Information Officer

ARGENTINA

INTERNATIONAL COMPETITION FOR YOUNG PIANISTS
Asociation Filharmonica de Mendoza
Catamarca 31, Local A-24
Mendoza, Argentina
Contact: Competition coordinator
Type: Piano
When: Annually
Eligibility: Pianists must be 30 years old or younger and born or residing in the Mendoza region
Award: Monetary, plus concert performances

LATIN AMERICAN CENTER FOR ADVANCED MUSICAL STUDIES COMPETITION
Torcuato di Tella Institute
Supero 1502, Belgrano R.
Buenos Aires, Argentina
Contact: Competition coordinator
Type: Composition and music teaching
When: Annually
Eligibility: Candidates must be residents of Canada, U.S., or Latin America.
Award: Scholarship

AUSTRALIA

A.B.C. VOCAL AND INSTRUMENTAL COMPETITION
Australian Broadcasting Commission
164 William St.
Sydney, N.S.W. 2000, Australia
Contact: Competition coordinator
Type: Voice and all instruments
When: Annually
Eligibility: All musicians may participate
Award: Prizes vary

AUSTRALIAN MUSIC EXAMINATIONS BOARD COMPETITION
University of Melbourne
Parkville, Victoria 3052, Australia
Contact: Competition coordinator
Type: Voice and all instruments
When: Biennially
Eligibility: Instrumentalists must be 16-21 years old; vocalists must be 16-24 years old
Award: Scholarship

AUSTRALIAN OPERA AUDITIONS
"Fairwater"
560 New S. Head Rd.
Double Bay, N.S.W. 2028, Australia
Contact: N/A
Type: Opera
When: Annually
Eligibility: Opera performers may audition
Award: Scholarship

GWEN ROBINSON AWARD
Music Teachers' Association of South Australia
4 Toronto Ave.
Clapham, S. Australia 5062, Australia
Contact: N/A
Type: Piano
When: Biennially
Eligibility: Pianists must be students between 13 and 15 years old
Award: Monetary

NORMAN SELLICK MEMORIAL SCHOLARSHIP
Music Teachers' Association of South Australia
4 Toronto Ave.
Clapham, S. Australia 5062, Australia
Contact: N/A
Type: All instruments
When: Annually
Eligibility: Instrumentalists must be students of age 12 or younger
Award: Scholarship

SUN ARIA COMPETITION
Sun Newspaper
235 Jones St.
Broadway, N.S.W. 2007, Australia
Contact: N/A
Type: Opera
When: Annually
Eligibility: Opera performers must be born or residing in Australia, New Zealand, United Kingdom, or the Commonwealth
Award: Monetary, plus scholarship

SYDNEY INTERNATIONAL PIANO COMPETITION
Conservatorium of Music
Macquarie St.
Sydney, N.S.W. 2000, Australia
(02) 27-42-06
Contact: Rex Hobcroft, Vice-President; Virginia Braden, Competition Coordinator
Type: Piano
When: Quadrennially (1985)
Eligibility: Pianists must be 30 years old or younger and may be any nationality
Award: Monetary, plus engagements

AUSTRIA

LUDWIG VAN BEETHOVEN INTERNATIONAL PIANO

COMPETITION
Lothringerstr. 18
A-1037 Vienna, Austria
(0222) 56-16-85
Contact: Elga Ponzer, Secretary General
Type: Piano
When: Quadrennially (1985)
Eligibility: Pianists must have been born between January 1, 1949, and December 31, 1964
Award: Monetary, plus piano and U.S. recitals

CONCOURS INTERNATIONAL DE COMPOSITION
Oesterreichischer Komponistenbund
Baumannstr. 8-10
A-1030 Vienna, Austria
(0222) 75-72-33
Contact: N/A
Type: Symphonic composition
When: Quadrennially (1985)
Eligibility: Composers may apply

INTERNATIONAL ANTON BRUCKNER ORGAN COMPETITION
Untere Donaulande 7
A-4010 Linz, Austria
(0732) 75-2-25
Contact: Dr. Margareta Woss, Music Director
Type: Organ
When: Quadrennially (1986)
Eligibility: Organists of all nations and all ages may apply
Award: Monetary

INTERNATIONAL CHORAL COMPETITION
Kulturreferat der Stadgemeinde
9800 Spittal, Austria
Contact: N/A
Type: Choir
When: Annually
Eligibility: Choirs performing artistic or folk songs may participate
Award: Prizes vary from year to year

INTERNATIONAL FRITZ KREISLER COMPETITION
Rabengasse 3
A-1034 Vienna, Austria
(0222) 75-12-01
Contact: Professor Fritz Haendschke
Type: Violin
When: Quadrennially (1983)
Eligibility: Violinists must be under 25 years old
Award: Monetary, plus engagements

INTERNATIONAL ORGAN IMPROVISATION COMPETITION
P.O. Box 959
1011 Vienna, Austria
Contact: N/A
Type: Organ
When: Annually
Eligibility: Organists must be 30 years old or younger
Award: Prizes vary

INTERNATIONAL HANS SWAROWSKY CONDUCTING COMPETITION
Hanuschgasse 3
3. Stock
A-1010 Vienna, Austria
(0222) 52-28-85
Contact: N/A
Type: Conducting
When: Quadrennially (1984)
Eligibility: Students and professional conductors who are 35 years old or younger may participate
Award: Monetary

TELEVISION OPERA PRIZE OF THE CITY OF SALZBURG
Argentinierstrasse 22
1041 Vienna, Austria
Contact: N/A
Type: Opera composition
When: Triennially
Eligibility: All broadcasting organizations belonging to the European Broadcasting Union may participate
Award: Monetary

UNIVERSITY OF VIENNA COMPETITION
1010 Vienna 1, Austria
Contact: Dr. Karl-Lueger, Ring 1
Type: Music history
When: Annually
Eligibility: Applicants must have spent at least 1 year at a European university or 2 years at a European college and may be residing in any country
Award: Scholarship

"YOUTH MAKES MUSIC" INSTRUMENTAL COMPETITION FOR YOUNG PEOPLE OF AUSTRIA
Hauptplatz 16
8700 Leoben, Austria
Contact: N/A
Type: Each competition features a different instrument
When: Biennially
Eligibility: Instrumentalists may participate

BELGIUM

BELGIAN INTERNATIONAL SONG COMPETITION
39 rue Fritz-Toussaint
1050 Brussels, Belgium
Contact: N/A
Type: Voice
When: Annually
Eligibility: Vocalists must be 35 years old or younger

EUROPEAN CUP FOR MIXED CHOIRS
W. Churchillaan 18
B-8300 Knokke-Heist, Belgium
(050) 60-12-32
Contact: Jacques Maertens, Director
Type: Mixed choir
When: Triennially (1983)
Eligibility: Mixed choirs, excluding professionals, that have at least 25 members, may participate

INTERNATIONAL FORTNIGHT OF MUSIC
c/o Festival of Flanders
C. Mansionstr. 30
B-8000 Bruges, Belgium
(50) 33-22-83
Contact: R. Dewitte, Director
Type: Emphasis changes; 1982 contest was for organ, 1983 for harpsichord, and 1984 for music antiqua
When: Annually
Eligibility: Soloists must have been born after December 31, 1948; ensembles and consorts must have an average age no greater than 30 years
Award: Monetary

INTERNATIONAL SINGING CONTEST
rue de Chene 10
1000 Brussels, Belgium
Contact: N/A
Type: Voice
When: Annually
Eligibility: Vocalists must be 33 years old or younger

QUEEN ELISABETH INTERNATIONAL MUSIC COMPETITION
Rue Baron Horta 11
B-1000 Brussels, Belgium
512-10-02
Contact: Count J.P. de Launoit, Executive Committee President
Type: Emphasis changes; among piano, violin, and composition
When: Irregularly (piano 1983; violin, 1985; composition, 1986)
Eligibility: Composers must be 40 years old or younger; all others must be 17-31 years old
Award: Monetary

TELEVISED INTERNATIONAL OPERA & BEL CANTO COMPETITION/CASION-KURSAAL OSTEND
A. Reyerslaan 52
B-1040 Brussels, Belgium
736-26-40
Contact: Eddy Steylaerts, Manager
Type: Opera
When: Annually
Eligibility: Vocalists must be 21-33 years old and delegated by a radio or television organization, an opera house or studio, or an official music institution
Award: Monetary

BRAZIL

INTERNATIONAL PIANO COMPETITION
c/o Museum Villa-Lobos
Rua da Imprensa 16
Ste. 913
Rio de Janeiro, Brazil
236-2022
Contact: N/A

Type: Piano; mainly works by Villa-Lobos, but also other Brazilian composers
Eligibility: Pianists of all nationalities may participate
Award: Monetary, medals, and diplomas

INTERNATIONAL SINGING CONTEST OF RIO DE JANEIRO
Av. Franklin Roosevelt 23
Ste. 310
Rio de Janeiro, Brazil
(021) 275-6456, 392-0681
Contact: Helena A. Oliveira, President
Type: Voice
When: Biennially (1983)
Eligibility: Vocalists must be 32 years old or younger
Award: Monetary, medals, diplomas, engagements

ALDO PARISOT INTERNATIONAL CELLO COMPETITION
Av. Casper Libero 58
Sala 503
Sao Paulo, S.P. 01033, Brazil
(203) 453-4233
Contact: Michael Kelly, Administrator
Type: Cello
When: Annually
Eligibility: Cellists must be 17-35 years old
Award: Monetary, plus medals

BULGARIA

INTERNATIONAL COMPETITION FOR YOUNG OPERA SINGERS
56 Rue Alabine
1040 Sofia, Bulgaria
87-17-72
Contact: Gancho Georgiev, Secretary
Type: Voice
When: Quadrennially (1984)
Eligibility: Vocalists must have been born after January 1, 1950
Award: Medals and diplomas, other awards

CZECHOSLOVAKIA

ACADEMY OF ARTS COMPETITION
Smetanova Nabr. 2
Prague 1, Czechoslovakia
Contact: N/A
Type: Music study
When: Annually
Eligibility: Applicants must be music graduates
Award: Scholarship (music tuition and expenses)

CONCERTINO PRAGA INTERNATIONAL RADIO COMPETITION FOR YOUNG MUSICIANS
Czechoslovak Radio
Vinohradska 12
120 99
Prague 2, Czechoslovakia
Contact: N/A
Type: Clarinet, flute, French horn, oboe, trumpet
When: Annually
Eligibility: Musicians must be 16 years old or younger and nominated by a member of the International Radio and Television Organization or the European Broadcasting Union
Award: Monetary

DUSEK'S COMPETITION OF MUSICAL YOUTH
ul. Pohranicni straze 1
160 00
Prague 6, Czechoslovakia
Contact: N/A
Type: Chamber music, piano, string instruments, voice, wind instruments
When: Annually
Eligibility: Instrumentalists must be 13-21 years old; vocalists must be 17-25 years old
Award: Monetary

INTERPRETATION COMPETITION OF THE CZECHOSLOVAKIAN SOCIALIST REPUBLIC
Valdstejnska 10
110 00
Prague 1, Czechoslovakia
Contact: N/A
Type: Brass, chamber ensemble, wind
When: Annually
Eligibility: Musicians must be students or graduates of musical schools in Czechoslovakia and be 35 years old or younger (chamber ensembles) or 18-30 years old (brass and wind)
Award: Monetary

LYRE OF BRATISLAVA COMPETITION
Leningradska 5
890 36 Bratislava, Czechoslovakia
Contact: N/A
Type: Compostiion
When: Annually
Eligibility: Composers from Czechoslovakia and other socialist countries may participate
Award: Monetary

MUSICAL PRIZE OF RADIO BRNO
Czechoslovak Radio
Beethovenova 4
Brno, Czechslovakia
Contact: N/A
Type: Radio musical program
When: Annually
Eligibility: Radio organizations throughout the world may participate
Award: Monetary

ORIGINAL COMPOSITION COMPETITION
Piestany International Music Festival
Postova St. 1
92134 Piestany, Czechoslovakia
Contact: N/A
Type: Vocal, chamber, or orchestral compostion
When: Annually
Eligibility: Composers of Czech nationality may participate
Award: Monetary, plus festival performance

PRAGUE SPRING INTERNATIONAL MUSIC COMPETITION
Alsovo nabrezi 12
CS-110 00 Prague 1, Czechoslovakia
63582
Contact: N/A
Type: Emphasis changes each year; past categories have included horn, trumpet and posaune.
When: Annually
Eligibility: Candidates must be 30 years old or younger
Award: Monetary

SMETANA PIANO CONTEST
Park of Rest and Culture
Armady 300
Hradec Kralore, Czechoslovakia
Contact: N/A
Type: Piano
When: Annually
Eligibility: Pianists must be 28 years old or younger
Award: Monetary

DENMARK

INTERNATIONAL CARL NIELSEN VIOLIN COMPETITION
Kongensgade 68
DK-5000 Odense C, Denmark
Contact: N/A
Type: Violin
When: June 1984
Eligibility: Violinists must be under 30 years old and may be of any nationality
Award: Monetary, plaques, and diplomas

NICOLAI MALKO INTERNATIONAL COMPETITION FOR YOUNG CONDUCTORS
Radio Denmark
Rosenoerns Alle 22
DK-1999 Copenhagen V, Denmark
(01) 350647, local 6011
Contact: Sven Tregart, General Secretary
Type: Conducting
When: Triennially (1983)
Eligibility: Conductors must be 21-30 years old
Award: Monetary

ENGLAND

EMILY ANDERSON PRIZE FOR VIOLIN PLAYING
Royal Philharmonic Society
124 Wigmore St.
London W1H OAX, England
Contact: N/A
Type: Violin
When: Every 4-5 years
Eligibility: Participants must be 18-30 years old and may be any nationality
Award: Monetary

ANTHONY ASQUITH MEMORIAL FUND
2 Soho Square
London W.1, England
Contact: N/A
Type: Composition
When: Annually
Eligibility: Composers may submit works that are "imaginative uses of music in a film or televison feature."
Award: Wedgwood plaque

ASSOCIATED BOARD OF THE ROYAL SCHOOL OF MUSIC SCHOLARSHIPS
14, Bedford Square
London WC1B, 3JG, England
Contact: N/A
Type: Instrumental and vocal
When: Annually
Eligibility: Instrumentalists must be 16-20 years old; vocalists must be 18-25 years old
Award: Scholarship

ASSOCIATED BOARD OF THE ROYAL SCHOOLS OF MUSIC SCHOLARSHIPS FOR OVERSEAS SCHOLARS
14, Bedford Square
London WC1B 3JG, England
Contact: N/A
Type: Instrumental and voice
When: Annually
Eligibility: Instrumentalists must reside outside the United Kingdom and must be 16-20 years old; vocalists must live outside the United Kingdom and be 18-25 years old
Award: Scholarship

ASSOCIATION OF MUSICAL INSTRUMENT INDUSTRIES COMPETITION
8 Hollywood Way
Woodford Green
Essex, England
Contact: N/A
Type: Violin construction
When: Annually
Eligibility: Candidates must be students of music trades at the London College of Furniture
Award: Monetary

AUDIO RECORD REVIEW COMPETITION
Heathcock Press Ltd.
Heathcock Court
London WC2, England
Contact: N/A
Type: Recording
When: Annually
Eligibility: Long-playing recordings may be submitted
Award: Statuettes (given to individuals on behalf of their companies)

BACH CHOIR CAROL COMPETITION
5 Park Village W.
London NW1 4AE, England
Contact: N/A
Type: Composition
When: Annually
Eligibility: Composers may apply

BBC PIANO COMPETITION
Kensington House, Richmond Way
London W14 OAX, England
Contact: Room 104, P.O. Box 27, Manchester M6O 1SJ, England
Type: Piano
When: Irregularly
Eligibility: Pianists must be 30 years old or younger
Award: Monetary

SIR THOMAS BEECHAM SCHOLARSHIP
The Leche Trust
7 Relton Mews
London SW7 1ET, England
Contact: Secretaries to the Trust, Gartmore Investment Ltd., Cayzer House, 2 St. Mary Axe, London EC3A 8DP, England
Type: Opera
When: Annually
Eligibility: Opera singers between 25 and 35 years old may apply
Award: Scholarship for opera training abroad

BENSON & HEDGES GOLD AWARD FOR CONCERT SINGERS
5 Dryden St.
London WC2E 9NW, England
(01) 240-2430
Contact: Sir Peter Pears, Chairman; Jacob de Vries, Director; Betty Randolph Bean, U.S. Administrator, 135 E. 83rd ST., New York, NY 10028, (212) 861-1107
Type: Voice (excluding opera and oratorio arias)
When: Annually
Eligibility: Vocalists must be 35 years old or younger. Songs must be sung in their original language
Award: Monetary, plus performances

W.T. BEST MEMORIAL SCHOLARSHIP
Worshipful Company of Musicians
4 St. Paul's Churchyard
London EC4M 8AY, England
Contact: N/A
Type: Organ
When: Annually
Eligibility: Organists may apply
Award: Scholarship

BIO-STRATH INTERNATIONAL VIOLIN SCHOLARSHIP
24 Cadogan Sq.
London SW1, England
Contact: N/A
Type: Violin
When: Irregularly
Eligibility: Violinists may apply
Award: Scholarship

BOISE FOUNDATION COMPETITION
14 Bedford Sq.
London WC1B 3JG, England
Contact: N/A
Type: Performance
When: Annually
Eligibility: Musical performers must be 30 years old or younger
Award: Monetary

BONWICK BEQUEST
Royal College of Organists
Kensington Gore
London SW7 2QS, England
Contact: N/A
Type: Organ
When: Annually
Eligibility: Organists must be 20 years old or younger
Award: Monetary

BRITISH ACADEMY COMPETITION
Burlington House, Piccadilly
London W1V ONS, England
Contact: N/A
Type: Music theory or history
When: Annually
Eligibility: Researchers may apply
Award: Research grant

GEORGE BUTTERWORTH MEMORIAL TRUST COMPETITION
Clarendon Laborator
Oxford, England
Contact: N/A
Type: Composition
When: Annually
Eligibility: Composers may apply
Award: Grants

CHOWN MUSIC SCHOLARSHIP FUND
Toynbee Hall
28 Commercial St.
London E1 6LS, England
Contact: N/A
Type: Music study
When: Annually
Eligibility: Musicians living in the East End of London who are 17 years old or older may apply
Award: Scholarship

COUNT CINZANO OPERA SCHOLARSHIP
Cinzano (U.K.)Ltd.
c/o International News Service
INS House
W. Central St.
London, W.C.1., England
Contact: N/A
Type: Opera
When: Annually
Eligibility: Opera singers must be 20-30 years old
Award: Scholarship, plus cash

CITY OF PORTSMOUTH INTERNATIONAL STRING QUARTET COMPETITION
Civic Offices
Guildhall Square
Portsmouth, Hants. PO1 2AL, England
(0705) 834-106
Contact: Yehudi Menuhin, Artistic Director; Yfrah Neaman, Artistic Consultant
Type: String quartet
When: Trienially (1985)
Eligibility: Ensemble members' ages

may not total more than 120 years
Award: Monetary, plus prize

CLEMENTS MEMORIAL PRIZE
St. Margaret's
Broomfield Ave.
London N13 4JJ, England
Contact: N/A
Type: Composition
When: Biennially
Eligibility: Chamber music compositions must be for 3-6 instruments and of 15-30 minutes' duration. Composers may be of any age
Award: Monetary

JOHN CLEMENTI COLLARD FELLOWSHIP
Worshipful Company of Musicians
4 St. Paul's Churchyard
London EC4M 8AY, England
Contact: N/A
Type: Composition, research, performance, conducting
When: Triennially
Eligibility: Professional musicians may apply
Award: Fellowship

CROYDON SYMPHONY ORCHESTRA SOLOIST AWARD
18 Temple Rd.
Croydon CRO 1HT, England
Contact: N/A
Type: Voice and solo instruments
When: Annually
Eligibility: Musicians must be residing in Surrey, Sussex, Kent, or a Greater London borough south of the Thames and must be 28 years old or younger
Award: Monetary, plus solo concert performance

CUNNINGHAM SCHOLARSHIP IN MUSIC
Barber Institute of Fine Arts
University of Birmingham
Birmingham B15 2TS, England
Contact: N/A
Type: General music
When: Annually
Eligibility: Musicians may apply
Award: Scholarship

HENRY AND LILY DAVIS FUND
Arts Council of Great Britain
105 Piccadilly
London W1V OAU, England
Contact: N/A
Type: Peformers' music study
When: Biannually
Eligibility: British or Commonwealth postgraduate musical performers between 21 and 30 years old may apply
Award: Scholarship

DIO FUND
Arts Council of Great Britain
105 Piccadilly
London W1V OAU, England
Contact: N/A
Type: Composition
When: Annually
Eligibility: British or Commonwealth students may submit an instrumental and/or vocal work
Award: Monetary (commission fee)

KATHLEEN FERRIER MEMORIAL SCHOLARSHIP
Royal Philharmonic Society
124 Wigmore St.
London W1H OAX, England
Contact: N/A
Type: Voice
When: Annually
Eligibility: British vocalists between 21 and 26 years old may apply
Award: Scholarship

ISRAEL FIEFF VIOLIN SCHOLARSHIP
International Festival of Youth Orchestras
24 Cadogan Sq.
London SW1X OJP, England
Contact: N/A
Type: Violin
When: Annually
Eligibility: Young violinists attending the festival may participate
Award: Scholarship

CARL FLESCH INTERNATIONAL VIOLIN COMPETITION
c/o City Arts Trust
P.O. Box 270, Guildhall
London EC2P 2EJ, England
Contact: Yfrah Neaman, Artistic Director; Virginia Harding, Administrator
Type: Violin
When: Biennially (1984)
Eligibility: Violinists must be under 28 years old and may be of any nationality
Award: Monetary

FRIENDS OF COVENT GARDEN SCHOLARSHIPS
Royal Opera House
Covent Garden
London WC2, England
Contact: N/A
Type: Voice/opera
When: Annually
Eligibility: Opera singers may apply
Award: Scholarship

HELENA MONICA HAYTON SCHOLARSHIP
City of Nottingham Education Committee
Exchange Building
Nottingham NG1 2DG, England
Contact: N/A
Type: Voice
When: Annually
Eligibility: Singers who are at least 17 years old, live in the Nottingham area, and wish to become professionals may apply
Award: Scholarship

IMPERIAL TOBACCO CELLO AWARDS
c/o Kallaway Arts Sponsorship Management
William Blake House
Marshall St.
London W1V 2AJ, England
Contact: N/A
Type: Cello
When: Biennially
Eligibility: Cellists of any nationality may participate
Award: Monetary, plus concert performances

IMPERIAL TOBACCO CELLO AWARDS
Western Orchestral Society
13, Gervis Place
Bournemouth BH1 2AW, England
Contact: N/A
Type: Cello
When: Annually
Eligibility: Young cellists may apply

INCORPORATED SOCIETY OF MUSICIANS AWARDS
48 Gloucester Pl.
London W1A 4LN, England
Contact: N/A
Type: Voice and instrumental
When: Annually
Eligibility: Young professional musicians who are members of the society may participate; vocalists must be under 30 years old. Instrumentalists must be under 27 years old
Award: Recital

INTERPRETATION COMPETITION
International Organ Festival Society
The Abbey
St. Albans AL1 1BY, England
Contact: N/A
Type: Organ
When: Biennially
Eligibility: Organists must be 31 years old or younger
Award: Monetary, plus recitals

ITALIAN INSTITUTE SCHOLARSHIPS
39 Belgrave Square
London SW1X 8NX, England
Contact: N/A
Type: Voice and instrumental
When: Annually
Eligibility: Musicians and vocalists may be apply
Award: Scholarship to Italian music academy or conservatory

LEEDS INTERNATIONAL PIANOFORTE COMPETITION
Education Dept.
Great George St.
Leeds, Yorkshire LS1 3AE, England
46-27-00
Contact: R.S. Johnson, Honorary Administrator
Type: Piano
When: Triennially
Eligibility: Candidates must be professional pianists born on or after September 1, 1951

Award: Piano; monetary, plus performances, recording contracts, and medal

LEEDS NATIONAL MUSIC PLATFORM COMPETITION
c/o Bursar's Department
University of Leeds
Leeds LS2 9JT, England
Contact: N/A
Type: Performance (excuding solo piano)
When: Triennially
Eligibility: Musicians must be British or British residents, must have been bona fide students in the United Kingdom, and must be 30 years old or younger
Award: Monetary, plus concert performances

MAISIE LEWIS YOUNG ARTISTS' FUND
Worshipful Company of Musicians
4 St. Paul's Churchyard
London EC4M 8AY, England
Contact: N/A
Type: General
When: Annually
Eligibility: Musicians must be 28 years old or younger
Award: Monetary (to allow young musicians to take part in concerts)

MIRIAM LICETTE SCHOLARSHIP
Arts Council of Great Britain
105 Piccadilly
London W1V OAU, England
Contact: N/A
Type: Female voice
When: Annually
Eligibility: Female singers may apply
Award: Scholarship for study in Paris

LIGHT MUSIC SOCIETY COMPETITION
10 Heddon St.
Regent St.
London W1R 8QB, England
Contact: N/A
Type: Light orchestral composition
When: Annually
Eligibility: Compositions must be no longer than 9 minutes

MARTIN MUSICAL SCHOLARSHIP FUND
61 Carey St.
London WC2A, 2JG, England
Contact: N/A
Type: Instrumental
When: Annually
Eligibility: Musicians must be 30 years old or younger
Award: Monetary

MECHANICAL-COPYRIGHT PROTECTION SOCIETY LTD. COMPETITION
Elgar House
380 Streatham High Road
London SW16 6HR, England
Contact: N/A
Type: Composition
When: Annually
Eligibility: Students of music at the University of Surrey may participate
Award: Monetary

MENDELSSOHN SCHOLARSHIP
14 Bedford Sq.
London WC1B, 3JG, England
Contact: N/A
Type: Composition
When: Biennially
Eligibility: Composers must be 30 years old or younger
Award: Scholarship

MENUHIN COMPETITION FOR YOUNG COMPOSERS
Westminster Arts Council
Marylebone Library
Marylebone Rd.
London NW1 5PS, England
Contact: Menuhin Prize Management Committee
Type: Composition
When: Triennially
Eligibility: Composers must be residents of the United Kingdom and must be 30 years old or younger
Award: Monetary, plus performance and possible publication, broadcasting, and recording of the composition

MERCHANT TAYLORS' COMPANY COMPETITION
Bursary
Merchant Taylors' Hall
30 Threadneedle St.
London EC2R 8AY, England
Contact: N/A
Type: Voice or instrumental
When: Annually
Eligibility: Vocalists or instrumentalists must be attending the Merchant Taylor's School
Award: Scholarship to Guildhall School of Music and Drama

MOZART MEMORIAL PRIZE
London Mozart Players
70 Leopold Rd.
Wimbledon, London SW19, England
Contact: N/A
Type: Mozart interpretation—piano or violin; flute, oboe, bassoon, or horn; voice
When: Biennially
Eligibility: Musicians must be 30 years old or younger
Award: Monetary, plus concert performances

COUNTESS OF MUNSTER MUSICAL TRUST COMPETITION
Wormley Hill
Godalming GU8 5SG, England
Contact: N/A
Type: Voice, instrumental, conducting, composition
When: Annually
Eligibility: Candidates must be British or Commonwealth vocalists, musicians, conductors, or composers between 11 and 30 years old
Award: Scholarship

STELLA MURRAY MEMORIAL PRIZE
Royal Over-Seas League
Over-Seas House
London SW1A 1LR, England
Contact: N/A
Type: Any branch of music
When: Annually
Eligibility: New Zealanders who are 30 years old or younger may apply
Award: Monetary

MUSIC SCHOLARSHIP
Sir Thomas White's Education Foundation
c/o General Charities Office
Old Bablake
Hill St.
Coventry CV1 4AN, England
Contact: N/A
Type: Instrumental or voice
When: Annually
Eligibility: Music students born or residing in Coventry may apply
Award: Scholarship

NATIONAL FEDERATION OF MUSIC SOCIETIES' AWARD
29 Exhibition Rd.
London SW7, England
Contact: N/A
Type: Performance (competition is different each year)
When: Annually
Eligibility: Intrumentalists must be 25 years old or younger; vocalists must be 28 years old or younger
Award: Monetary, plus concert performances

NATIONAL ORGAN COMPETITION
Holy Trinity Church
Southport, England
Contact: N/A
Type: Organ
When: Biennially
Eligibility: Organists may participate
Award: Monetary

PERFORMING RIGHT SOCIETY IVOR NOVELLO AWARDS
Song Writers' Guild of Great Britain
Ascot House
52/53 Dean St.
London W1V 5HJ, England
Contact: N/A
Type: Lyrics, composition, music publishing and record manufacturing; all types of music
When: Annually
Eligibility: Lyricists, composers, publishers, and record manufacturers may apply.
Award: Statuettes and certificates

POLISH CULTURAL INSTITUTE COMPETITION
16 Devonshire St.
London W1N 2BS, England
Contact: N/A
Type: Composition
When: Annually
Eligibility: Graduates of British music

colleges may apply
Award: Scholarship to one of the Polish Academies of Music at Cracow, Warsaw or Katowice

RADCLIFFE MUSIC AWARD
11 Coulson St.
London SW3, England
Contact: N/A
Type: Chamber music composition
When: Biennially
Eligibility: United Kingdom or Commonwealth citizens and residents who are 40 years old or younger may participate
Award: Monetary

ERIC RICE MEMORIAL PRIZE FOR ACCOMPANISTS
Royal Over-Seas League
Over-Seas House
London SW1A 1LR, England
Contact: N/A
Type: Accompanying
When: Annually
Eligibility: United Kingdom and Commonwealth accompanists at the Royal Over-Seas League Music Festival may participate
Award: Monetary

ROYAL ACADEMY OF MUSIC COMPETITIONS
Marylebone Rd.
London NW1 5HT, England
Contact: N/A
Type: Voice and all instruments
When: Annually
Eligibility: Candidates in most competitions must be 18-21 years old
Award: Scholarships, monetary prizes, bursaries, etc

ROYAL AMATEUR ORCHESTRAL SOCIETY SILVER MEDAL AWARD
19 Nireh Ct.
Haywards Heath, Sussex, England
Contact: N/A
Type: Solo instrument or voice
When: Annually
Eligibility: Musicians must be under 28 years old
Award: Monetary and medal

ROYAL COLLEGE OF MUSIC SCHOLARSHIPS
Prince Consort Rd.
London SW7, England
Contact: N/A
Type: Voice, instrumental, and composition
When: Annually
Eligibility: Candidates must be 16-25 years old
Award: Scholarship

ROYAL OVER-SEAS MUSIC FESTIVAL COMPETITION
Royal Over-Seas League
Over-Seas House
London SW1A 1LR, England
Contact: N/A
Type: Voice, instrumental
When: Annually
Eligibility: United Kingdom and Commonwealth students may participate. Instrumentalists must be 25 years old or younger; vocalists must be 30 years old or younger
Award: Monetary

ROYAL PHILHARMONIC SOCIETY COMPOSITION PRIZE
124 Wigmore St.
London W1H OAX, England
Contact: N/A
Type: Composition
When: Annually
Eligibility: Candidates must be 26 years old or younger and must be past or present students of Guildhall School of Music and Drama, Royal Academy of Music, Royal College of Music, Royal Northern College of Music, Royal Scottish Academy of Music and Drama, or Trinity College of Music
Award: Monetary

RUPERT FOUNDATION INTERNATIONAL YOUNG CONDUCTORS AWARDS
P.O. Box 120
Aylesbury, Buckinghamshire HP21 8SZ, England
(0296) 21214
Contact: Ivan Piercy, General Administrator; Jean Smith, Administrative Secretary
Type: Conducting
When: Every 18 months (approx.)
Eligibility: Conductors must be 28 years old or younger
Award: Monetary, plus possible work with BBC symphony orchestras

AMY STOCKWIN MUSIC SCHOLARSHIP
City of Nottingham Education Committee
Exchange Building
Nottingham NG1 2DF, England
Contact: N/A
Type: Instrumental
When: Annually
Eligibility: Instrumentalists who are at least 17 years old, live in the Nottingham area, and wish to become professionals may apply
Award: Scholarship

STROUD FESTIVAL INTERNATIONAL COMPOSERS COMPETITION
Lenton, Houdscroft
Stroud, Gloucestershire GL5 5DG, England
Contact: A.M.C. Shaw, Secretary
Type: Flute and piano duet competition
When: Annually
Eligibility: Composers must be under 40 years old. Compositions may have one or more movements
Award: Monetary, plus festival performance

PETER STUYVESANT FOUNDATION SCHOLARSHIPS
27 Baker St.
London W1M 1AE, England
Contact: N/A
Type: Opera
When: Annually
Eligibility: Opera singers must be 28 years old or younger
Award: Scholarship

GUILHERMINA SUGGIA GIFT FOR THE CELLO
9 Long Acre
London WC2E 9LH, England
(01) 379-7717
Contact: Eric Thompson, Associate Music Director
Type: Cello
When: Annually
Eligibility: Cellists must be under 21 years old
Award: Monetary

MRS. SUNDERLAND MUSICAL COMPETITION
J.W. Pearce Music Trust
Pearce Fund Trustees
The Polytechnic
Queensgage, Huddersfield HD1 3DH, England
Contact: N/A
Type: Performance
When: Annually
Eligibility: Musicians born or living in the Huddersfield area and 15-25 years old may participate. Performance must be 15 minutes long or shorter
Award: Monetary

RICHARD TAUBER MEMORIAL SCHOLARSHIP
Anglo-Austrian Society
139 Kensington High St.
London W.8, England
Contact: N/A
Type: Voice
When: Annually
Eligibility: British and Austrian vocalists may participate
Award: Scholarship (travel bursary, study grant, and recital in London)

MAGGIE TEYTE PRIZE
75 Woodland Rise
London N10 3UN, England
Contact: N/A
Type: Female voice
When: Biennially
Eligibility: Female vocalists must be 30 years old or younger
Award: Monetary

H.A. THEW FUND
Arts Council of Great Britain
105 Piccadilly
London W1V OAU, England
Contact: N/A
Type: Musicians and musical organizations
When: Annually
Eligibility: Musicians and musical

organizations in the Liverpool and Merseyside area may apply
Award: Monetary

TOURNEMIRE PRIZE
International Organ Festival Society
The Abbey
St. Albans AL1 1BY, England
Contact: N/A
Type: Organ improvisation
When: Biennially
Eligibility: Organists must be 31 years old or younger
Award: Monetary, plus recital

DONALD TOVEY MEMORIAL PRIZE
University of Oxford
University Registry
Clarendon Building
Broad St.
Oxford OX1 3BD, England
Contact: N/A
Type: Music history
When: Triennally
Eligibility: Candidates must be interested in furthering or publishing research in the understanding or history of music and may be any nationality
Award: Monetary/grant

TRINITY COLLEGE OF MUSIC COMPETITION
Mandeville Place
London W1M 6AQ, England
Contact: N/A
Type: General music
When: Annually
Eligibility: Candidates must be 16-23 years old and may be any nationality
Award: Scholarship

YOUNG COMPOSER COMPETITION
Greater London Arts Association
25-31 Tavistock Place
London WC1H 9SG, England
Contact: N/A
Type: Composition
When: Annually
Eligibility: Composers must be 26 years old or younger and reside in London. Compositions may be for an instrument or unaccompanied solo voice
Award: Monetary, plus concert performance

YOUNG COMPOSERS' COMPETITION
International Festival of Youth Orchestras
24 Cadogan Square
London SW1X OJP, England
Contact: N/A
Type: Composition
When: Annually
Eligibility: Composers who are 25 years old or younger and were born or are residing in Scotland may participate
Award: Monetary

FINLAND

FOUNDATION FOR THE PROMOTION OF MUSIC IN FINLAND COMPETITION
Pilvettatenpolku 1
02100 Tapiola, Finland
Contact: N/A
Type: Music teaching, music study, performance, and composition
When: Annually
Eligibility: Teachers, students, performers, and composers may participate
Award: Varies in value

INTERNATIONAL JEAN SIBELIUS VIOLIN COMPETITION
P. Rautatiekatu 9
SF-00100 Helsinki 10, Finland
44 87 77
Contact: N/A
Type: Violin
When: Quinquennially (1985)
Eligibility: For 1985, violinists must have been born between 1952 and 1969
Award: Monetary

FRANCE

COMPETITION OF CHORAL SINGING
Recontres Internationales de Chant Choral
Hotel de Ville
37000 Tours, France
Contact: N/A
Type: Female and children's voice; male and female voice
When: Annually
Eligibility: Nonprofessional choruses of 25-35 members may participate
Award: Monetary

COMPOSITION COMPETITION
Recontres Internationales de Chant Choral
Hotel de Ville
37000 Tours, France
Contact: N/A
Type: Composition of mixed chorus and chorus containing and equal number of women's and children's voices
When: Annually
Eligibility: Composers from any country may participate
Award: Monetary

CONCOURS INTERNATIONAL DE CHANT DE LA VILLE DE TOULOUSE
Theatre du Capitole
F-31000 Toulouse, France
(61) 23-21-35
Contact: Gerald Van Ham, Secretary General
Type: Voice
When: Annually
Eligibility: Vocalists must be 18-33 years old
Award: Monetary

CONCOURS INTERNATIONAL DE CHANT DE PARIS
14 bis Av. du President Wilson
F-75116 Paris, France
(01) 723-6223
Contact: Raymonde J. Roullet, President
Type: Voice
When: Biennially (1984)
Eligibility: Female vocalists must be 32 years old or younger; male vocalists must be 34 years old or younger
Award: Monetary, plus performances

CONCOURS INTERNATIONAL DE CLAVECIN
c/o Festival Estival de Paris
5, place des Ternes
F-75017 Paris, France
(01) 227-1268
Contact: Bernard Bonaldi, Director
Type: Harpsichord
When: Binenially (1983)
Eligibility: Harpsichordists must be 20-32 years old
Award: Monetary

CONCOURS INTERNATIONAL DE GUITARE
116 av. du President Kennedy
F-75786 Paris, France
(01) 224-3485, 2585
Contact: Robert J. Vidal, Founder-Producer
Type: Classical guitar
When: Annually (1983)
Eligibility: Guitarists must have been born afterJanuary 1, 1951
Award: Monetary, medals, performances

CONCOURS INTERNATIONAL DE JEUNES CHEFS D'ORCHESTRE
2 D, rue Isenbart
F-25000 Besancon, France
(81) 80-73-26
Contact: Pierre Lagrange
Type: Conducting
When: Annually
Eligibility: Conductors must be under 30 years old
Award: Emile Vuillermoz and other prizes

CONCOURS INTERNATIONAL DE MUSIQUE ELECTRO-ACOUSTIQUE
Maitre Miny
1, rue Coursarlon
F-18000 Bourges, France
(48) 20-41-87
Contact: Christian Clozier, Head
Type: Electro-acoustic music
When: Annually
Eligibility: Composers may be any age and nationality
Award: Monetary

CONCOURS INTERNATIONAL D'ENSEMBLES DE MUSIQUE DE CHAMBRE
4, rue d'Unterlinden
F-68000 Colmar, France
(89) 41 02 29
Contact: N/A
Type: Emphasis changes annually; 1982 was wind quintet
When: Annually

Eligibility: Candidate must be 32 years old or younger.
Award: Monetary

CONCOURS INTERNATIONAL DE PIANO
4, quai des Bons-Enfants
F-88000 Epinal, France
82-21-68
Contact: N/A
Type: Piano
Eligibility: Pianists must be 30 years old or younger
Award: Monetary

CONCOURS INTERNATIONAL D'ORGUE "GRAND PRIX DE CHARTRES"
75, rue de Grenelle
F-75007 Paris, France
(01) 548-3174
Contact: Pierre Firmin-Didot, President-Founder
Type: Organ improvisation and interpretation
When: Biennially (1984)
Eligibility: Organists must have been born after January 1, 1947
Award: Monetary

CONCOURS INTERNATIONAL DU FESTIVAL DE MUSIQUE DE TOULON
Palais de la Bourse
Av. Jean-Moulin
F-83000 Toulon, France
93-52-84
Contact: Henri Tiscornia, President
Type: Emphasis changes annually; 1982 competition was for bassoon
When: Annually
Eligibility: Candidates must be 18-30 years old
Award: Monetary

CONCOURS INTERNATIONAL MARGUERITE LONG-JACQUES THIBAUD
32, avenue Matignon
F-75008 Paris, France
(01) 266-66180
Contact: Secretariat du Concours International
Type: Piano and violin
When: Annually (piano, 1983; violin, 1984)
Eligibility: Pianists and violinists must be 16-32 years old
Award: Monetary

CONCOURS MESSIAEN: CONCOURS INTERNATIONAL DE PIANO POUR LA MUSIQUE CONTEMPORAINE
32, rue Washington
F-75008 Paris, France
(01) 563-6151
Contact: Claude Samuel, Artistic Director
Type: Piano; contemporary music
When: Annually
Eligibility: Pianists must be 33 years old or younger

FONDATION DES ETATS-UNIS HARRIET HALE WOOLEY SCHOLARSHPS
15, blvd. Jourdan
F-75690 Paris, France
(01) 589-3579
Contact: N/A
Type: Music study
When: Annually
Eligibility: Candidates must be American citizens, 21-34 years old, and prepared for graduate study
Award: Scholarship for study in Paris

FRIENDS OF THE ORGAN COMPETITION
52, rue Boileau
75016 Paris, France
Contact: N/A
Type: Composition and performance
When: Sporadically
Eligibility: Varies
Award: Varies

INTERNATIONAL IMPROVISATION PRIZE
Hotel de Ville
69 Lyon, France
Contact: N/A
Type: Classical piano, jazz piano, organ
When: Annually
Eligibility: Musicians must be 45 years old or younger
Award: Monetary

INTERNATIONAL MUSIC CRITICS' COMPETITION
Festival Estival
5, place des Ternes
75017 Paris, France
Contact: N/A
Type: Written criticism of compositions
When: Annually
Eligibility: Candidates must be prepared to perform the works they are criticizing

INTERNATIONAL PERCUSSION COMPETITION FOR CONTEMPORARY MUSIC
La Recherche Artistique
104, rue de la Tour
75016 Paris, France
Contact: N/A
Type: Percussion
When: Annually
Eligibility: Musicians must be 33 years old or younger
Award: Monetary, plus concert performances

INTERNATIONAL PIANO COMPETITION
85, rue d'Hauteville
Paris 10e, France
Contact: N/A
Type: Performance
When: Annually
Eligibility: Musicians must be 32 years old or younger

INTERNATIONAL STRING QUARTET CONTEST
Chateau de Blonay
F-745000 Evian, France
75-03-78
Contact: Serge Zehnacker, Festival d'Evian Director
Type: String Quartet
When: Annually
Eligibility: Quartets' average age must be no greater than 30
Award: Monetary

OLIVER MESSIAEN COMPETITION
La Recherche Artistique
104, rue de la Tour
75016 Paris, France
Contact: N/A
Type: Piano; contemporary music
When: Annually
Eligibility: Pianists must be 33 years old or younger and may reside in any country
Award: Monetary, plus solo engagements on television, at concerts and recordings

PRIX INTERNATIONAL DE COMPOSITION ANDRE CHEVILLION
45, rue la Boetie
F-75008 Paris, France
(01) 561-0455
Contact: Marcel Fournet, Secretary General
Type: Composition
When: Biennially
Eligibility: Candidates must be 32 years old or younger and must be winners of the Concours International Marguerite Long
Award: Monetary

GERMAN DEMOCRATIC REPUBLIC

INTERNATIONAL JOHANN SEBASTIAN BACH COMPETITION
Grassistr. 8
DDR-7010 Leipzig, German Democratic Republic
311-209
Contact: Professor Rudolf Fischer, President; Christine Piech, Secretary
Type: Piano, voice, organ, violin, and harpsichord
When: Annually
Eligibility: Musicians must be 32 years old or younger
Award: Monetary

INTERNATIONAL ROBERT SCHUMANN CONTEST
Muenzstrasse
DDR-95 Zwickau, German Democratic Republic
2636
Contact: N/A
Type: Voice and piano
When: Annually
Eligibility: Vocalists must have been born after 1951; pianists must have been born after 1956
Award: Monetary, plus medals or diplomas

GERMAN FEDERAL REPUBLIC

CONDUCTORS' COMPETITION
Berlin Philharmonic Orchestra
Matthaikirehstrasse 1
1 Berlin 30, German Federal Republic
Contact: N/A
Type: Conducting
When: Annually
Eligibility: Conductors must be 20-30 years old
Award: Monetary

INTERNATIONAL CONDUCTORS' COMPETITION
Bundesallee 1-12
D-1000 Berlin 15, German Federal Republic
Contact: N/A
Type: Conducting
Eligibility: Conductors must be 30 years old or younger and may be any nationality

INTERNATIONALER WETTBEWERB FUER STELCHQUARTETT (KARL KLINGER-PRELS)
Emmichplatz 1
D-3000 Hanover, German Federal Republic
Contact: Roland Scholl, Chancellor
Type: String quartet
When: Biennially (1983)
Eligibility: String quartets may enter
Award: Monetary

INTERNATIONAL MUSIC COMPETITION FOR THE BROADCASTING CORPORATIONS OF THE FEDERAL REPUBLIC OF GERMAN
Bayerischer Rundfunk
Rundfunkplatz 1
D-8000 Munich, German Federal Republic
5900-2471
Contact: Jurgen Meyer-Josten,Director; Renate Ronnefeld, Secretary General
Type: Voice, violoncello, clarinet, guitar, string quartet, and others (emphases change annually)
When: Annually
Eligibility: Solo instrumentalists must have been born between 1952 and 1965; string quartets must have been born between 1947 and 1965; with the average total of the four musicians' ages not to exceed 120
Award: Monetary

KRANICHSTEINER MUSIKPREIS
Darmstadt International Music Institute
Nieder-Ramstaedter Strasse 190
6100 Darmstadt, German Federal Republic
Contact: N/A
Type: Composition and interpretation
When: Annually
Eligibility: Participants must be 30 years old or younger
Award: Monetary, plus diploma

MUSICAL YOUTH OF GERMANY SCHOLARSHIPS
Hirschgartenallee 19
8 Munich 19, German Federal Republic
Contact: N/A
Type: General
When: Annually
Eligibility: Candidates must be 16-30 years old
Award: Scholarship

GIBRALTAR

GIBRALTAR SONG FESTIVAL COMPETITION
c/o Gibraltar Tourist Office
Cathedral Square
Gibraltar
Contact: N/A
Type: Composition, lyrics, and voice
When: Annually
Eligibility: Singers, composers, and lyricists may participate

GREECE

ATHENAEUM INTERNATIONAL CULTURAL CENTER MUSIC COMPETITIONS: OPERA/ORATORIA—LIED "MARIA CALLAS" AND PIANO COMPETITION
Kefallinias St. 36A
Athens 802, Greece
823-8827, 822-2193
Contact: Louli Psichoulis and Anna Koukouraki, Founders
Type: Voice and piano
When: Biennially (1983)
Eligibility: Female vocalists must be 30 years old or younger; male vocalists must be 32 years old or younger; pianists must be 30 years old or younger
Award: Monetary

GREEK SONG FESTIVAL OF THESSALONIKI COMPETITION
Thessaloniki 36, Greece
Contact: N/A
Type: Composition, lyrics, voice, and orchestral directing
When: Annually
Eligibility: Composers, lyricists, vocalists, and orchestral directors may participate
Award: Monetary

HUNGARY

BELA BARTOK INTERNATIONAL CHOIR CONTEST
Voros Hadsereg utja 26/a
4001 Debrecen, Hungary
Contact: N/A
Type: Choir
When: Biennially
Eligibility: Children's, female, male, and mixed choirs may participate
Award: Monetary

BUDAPEST MUSIC WEEKS COMPETITION
Vorosmarty ter 1
Budapest 5, Hungary
Contact: N/A
Type: Competition changes each year
When: Annually
Eligibility: Musicians must be 32 years old or younger
Award: Monetary

CASALS CELLO COMPETITION
International Music Competition
Vorosmarty ter 1
1366 P.O. Box 80
Budapest 5, Hungary
Contact: N/A
Type: Cello
When: Irregularly
Eligibility: Cellists must be 32 years old or younger and may be any nationality
Award: Monetary

INTERNATIONAL CONDUCTORS COMPETITION OF THE HUNGARIAN TELEVISION
c/o Hungarian Television
Music Department
H-1810 Budapest, Hungary
Contact: Andrea Fellner, Music Editor
Type: Conducting
When: Triennially (1983)
Eligibility: Conductors must be 35 years old or younger
Award: Monetary, plus television engagement

LIZST-BARTOK PIANO COMPETITION
International Music Competition, Vorosmarty ter 1
1366 P.O. Box 80
Budapest 5, Hungary
Contact: N/A
Type: Piano
When: Irregularly
Eligibility: Pianists must be 32 years old or younger and may be any nationality
Award: Value varies

JOZSEF SZIGETI VIOLIN COMPETITION
International Music Competition
Vorosmarty ter 1
1366 P.O. Box 80
Budapest 5, Hungary
Contact: N/A
Type: Violin
When: Irregularly
Eligibility: Violinists must be 32 years old or younger and may reside in any country
Award: Monetary, plus medal

VOICE AND VIOLIN COMPETITION
International Music Competition
Vorosmarty ter 1
1366 P.O. Box 80
Budapest 5, Hungary
Contact: N/A
Type: Voice and violin
When: Irregularly
Eligibility: Vocalists and violinists must be 32 years old or younger
Award: Monetary

WEINER CHAMBER MUSIC COMPETITION
International Music Competition
Vorosmarty ter 1
1366 P.O. Box 80
Budapest 5, Hungary
Contact: N/A
Type: Chamber music
When: Irregularly
Eligibility: Musicians must be 32 years old or younger and may reside in any country
Award: Monetary

WEINER STRING-QUARTET COMPETITION
c/o Budapest Office of Music Competitions
P.O. Box 80
1366 Budapest 5, Hungary
Contact: N/A
Type: String quartet
When: Annually
Eligibility: String quartets may participate
Award: Monetary

INDIA

KESARBAI KERKAR SCHOLARSHIP
National Centre for the Performing Arts
89 Bhulabhai Desai Rd.
Bombay 400 036, India
Contact: N/A
Type: Indian classical music
When: Annually
Eligibility: Young professional musicians trained in Indian classical music may participate
Award: Monetary

IRELAND

CASTLEBAR SONG CONTEST
Castlebar, Eire
Contact: N/A
Type: Voice
When: Annually
Eligibility: Vocalists may enter various sections of the contest
Award: Prizes vary

FEMALE CHOIRS CONTEST
Cork International Choral and Folk Dance Festival
15 Bridge St.
Cork, Eire
Contact: N/A
Type: Choir
When: Annually
Eligibility: Choir members must be amateurs
Award: Monetary

MALE CHOIRS CONTEST
Cork International Choral and Folk Dance Festival
15 Bridge St.
Cork, Eire
Contact: N/A
Type: Choir
When: Annually
Eligibility: Choir members must be amateurs
Award: Monetary

MIXED CHOIRS CONTEST
Cork International Choral and Folk Dance Festival
15 Bridge St.
Cork, Eire
Contact: N/A
Type: Choir
When: Annually
Eligibility: Choir members must be amateurs
Award: Monetary

SCHOOLS CHOIRS CONTEST
Cork International Choral and Folk Dance Festival
15 Bridge St.
Cork, Eire
Contact: N/A
Type: Choir
When: Annually
Eligibility: Choir members must be amateurs
Award: Monetary

ISRAEL

INTERNATIONAL HARP CONTEST
4 Aharonowitz St.
Tel Aviv 63 566, Israel
(03) 280-233
Contact: Yerach M. Aharon, Director
Type: Harp
When: Triennially (1985)
Eligibility: Harpists must be under 35 years old
Award: Harp; monetary

LIEBERSON PRIZE CONTEST
League of Composers of Israel
P.O. Box 11180
73, Nordau Blvd.
Tel-Aviv, Israel
Contact: N/A
Type: Instrumental composition
When: Annually
Eligibility: Composers may participate
Award: Prizes vary

ARTHUR RUBINSTEIN INTERNATIONAL PIANO MASTER COMPETITION
P.O. Box 29404
Shalom Tower, 5th Floor
Tel Aviv, Israel
(03) 65-16-04
Contact: N/A
Type: Piano
When: Triennially (1983)
Eligibility: Pianists must be 18-32 years old
Award: Gold medals plus monetary prize; silver medals plus monetary prize; concert and recording engagements

ITALY

ASSOCIZIONE CONCORSI & RASSEGNE MUSICALI CITTA DI FIRENZE/"PREMIO VITTORIO GUL"
c/o Assessorato alla Cultura
Via S. Egidio 21
I-50100 Florence, Italy
(055) 283-713
Contact: Sergio Mealli, President
Type: Chamber music
When: Annually
Eligibility: Musicians must be 35 years old or younger
Award: Monetary

F. BUSONI INTERNATIONAL PIANO COMPETITION
c/o Mayor of Bolzano
Piazza Domenicani 19
I-39100 Bolzano, Italy
(0471) 23.579
Contact: N/A
Type: Piano
When: Annually
Eligibility: Pianists must be 15-32 years old
Award: Monetary plus concert engagements

ALESSANDRO CASAGRANDE CONCORSO PIANISTICO INTERNAZIONALE
Comune di Terni
I-05100 Terni, Italiy
(0744) 401.173
Contact: N/A
Type: Piano
When: Biennially (1984)
Eligibility: Pianists must be 32 years old or younger
Award: Monetary, plus diplomas

DINO CIANI-TEATRO ALLA SCALA INTERNATIONAL COMPETITION FOR YOUNG PIANISTS
Teatro alla Scala
Via Filodrammatici 2
I-20121 Milan, Italy
88.79
Contact: Sergio Barzotto, Director
Type: Piano
When: Triennially
Eligibility: Pianists must be under 30 years old
Award: Monetary, plus concert engagements and recording

CONCORSO INTERNAZIONALE DE CHITARRA CLASSICA 'CITTA DI ALESSANDRIA"
Presso il Conservatorio di Musica "A. Vivaldi"
Via Parma
I-15100 Alessandria, Italy
(0131) 53.363
Contact: N/A
Type: Classical guitar
When: Annually
Eligibility: Guitarists may apply
Award: Monetary

CONCORSO INTERNAZIONALE DI VIOLINO "ALBERTO CURCI"
Nia Nardones 8

I-80132 Naples, Italy
417.244
Contact: Dario Biancogiglio, Secretary
Type: Violin
When: Biennially (1983)
Eligibility: Violinists may be up to 32 years old
Award: Monetary

CONCORSO INTERNAZIONALE PER FOCI VERDIANE COMUNE DI BUSSETO (PARMA)
c/o Famiglia Artistica Milanese
Corso Porta Vittoria 16
1-20122 Milan, Italy
702.119
Contact: Dr. Alberto Monti, Secretary General
Type: Voice
When: Annually
Eligibility: Sopranos and tenors must be under 32 years old; mezzos, contraltos, baritones, and basses must be under 35
Award: Monetary

CONCORSO INTERNAZIONALE PIANISTICO LISZT "PREMIO MARIO ZANFI"
Conservatorio di Musica "A. Boito"
I-43100 Parma, Italy
Contact: N/A
Type: Piano
When: Quadrenially (1984)
Eligibility: Pianists must be 16-32 years old and may be any nationality
Award: Monetary

CONCORSO INTERNAZIONALE PIANISTICO "ETTORE POZZOLI"
Palazzo Municipale
I-20038 Seregno, Italy
Contact: Cav. Carlo Galli, Secretary
Type: Piano
When: Biennially (1983)
Eligibility: Pianists must be 35 years old or younger

CONCORSO PIANISTICO INTERNAZIONALE "ALFREDO CASELLA"
Accademia Musicale Napoletana
Circolo della Stampa
Villa Comunale
I-80121 Naples, Italy
Contact: N/A
Type: Piano and composition
When: Annually
Eligibility: Pianists must be 18-32 years old; composers may be any age
Award: Monetary, plus cup or medal

"CONQUEST OF THE CLASSIC GUITAR" INTERNATIONAL COMPETITION
c/o Comitato Organizzatore Accademia della Chitarra Classica
Viale Marche 31
Milan, Italy
(02) 680.076
Contact: Vincenzo Degni, Artistic Director
Type: Classical guitar
When: Annually
Eligibility: Guitarists of any age may participate
Award: Monetary, plus medals and guitars

INTERNATIONAL CENTRE FOR STUDIES FOR THE DIFFUSION OF ITALIAN MUSIC SCHOLARSHIPS
Via dei Greci 18
Rome, Italy
Contact: N/A
Type: Music study
When: Annually
Eligibility: Students with a degree or diploma from a musical academy or conservatory must be 35 years old or younger
Award: Scholarship

INTERNATIONAL COMPETITION FOR CHAMBER ORCHESTRA COMPOSTION
piazza S. Angelo
20121 Milan, Italy
Contact: N/A
Type: Orchestral composition
When: Annually
Eligibility: Compositions must be 15-25 minutes in duration
Award: Monetary

INTERNATIONAL "RICARDO ZANDONAI" COMPOSITION COMPETITION
c/o Tourist Office
Rovereto, Italy
Contact: N/A
Type: Composition for two pianos
When: Annually
Eligibility: Composers must be 35 years old or younger; compositions must be 5-10 minutes long

DANIELE NAPOLITANO COMPOSITION PRIZE
c/o Accademia Musical Napoletana
Via S. Pasquale a Chiara 62
80121 Naples, Italy
Contact: N/A
Type: Composition
When: Biennially
Eligibility: Composition must be for trio, quartet, or quintet with optional piano

"NICOLO PAGANINI" PREMIO INTERNAZIONALE DI VIOLINO
Palazzo Tursi
Via Garibaldi 9
I-16100 Genoa, Italy
20.98
Contact: Avv. Prof. L. de Bernardis, President; Alberto Erede, Artistic Director
Type: Violin
When: Annually
Eligibility: Violinists must be 35 years old or younger
Award: Monetary

PREMIO MUSICALE GUIDA VALCARENGHI
Italian Society of Authors and Editors
Foro Bonaparte 18
Milan, Italy
Contact: N/A
Type: Composition
When: Annually
Eligibility: Compositions must be musical, operatic, or theatrical

"G.B. VIOTTI" CONCORSO INTERNAZIONALE DI MUSICA
Casella Postale 127
I-13100 Vercelli, Italy
65264
Contact: Dr. Joseph Robbone, Chief Officer
Type: Voice, instrumental, and composition
When: Annually
Eligibility: Vocalists and instrumentalists must be under age 35; composers may be any age
Award: Monetary

JAPAN

INTERNATIONAL CONTEST
Tokyo Broadcasting System
5-3-6 Akasaka
Minato-ku
Tokyo, Japan
Contact: N/A
Type: Vocal composition
When: Annually
Eligibility: Composers may participate
Award: Monetary, plus trophies

WORLDWIDE "MADAME BUTTERFLY" COMPETITION
4-4, 1-chome, Akasaka
Minato-ku
Tokyo, Japan
Contact: N/A
Type: Voice
When: Annually
Eligibility: Sopranos and tenors under age 35 may participate
Award: Monetary

MALTA

GOLDEN CROSS FESTIVAL COMPETITION
Malta
Contact: N/A
Type: Vocal composition
When: Annually
Eligibility: Composers from any country may participate. Vocal compositions must be 3½ minutes long or shorter
Award: Golden cross, trophy

MONACO

PRIX DE COMPOSITION MUSICALE PRINCE PIERRE DE MONACO
Ministere d'Etat
Monaco
30.19.21
Contact: Rene Novella, Secretary-General

Type: Composition; emphasis changes annually
When: Annually
Eligibility: All musicians and composers may compete
Award: Monetary

THE NETHERLANDS

'S-HERTOGENBOSCH INTERNATIONAL SINGING COMPETITION
P.O. Box 1225
5200 BG 's-Hertogenbosch, Netherlands
(073) 155-404
Contact: A. de Laat, Secretary
Type: Voice
When: Annually
Eligibility: Vocalists must have been born after December 31, 1949
Award: Monetary

INTERNATIONAL CHOIR FESTIVAL
Postbus 496
The Hague, Netherlands
Contact: N/A
Type: Children's, female, male, mixed, and youth choirs
When: Biennially
Award: Children's choir members must be 16 years old or younger; youth choir members must be 16-25 years old

INTERNATIONAL CHORAL FESTIVAL
Federation of Dutch Singers' Association
P.O. Box 496
The Hague, Netherlands
Contact: N/A
Type: Voice
When: Biennially
Eligibility: Vocalists may participate
Award: Value varies

INTERNATIONAL GAUDEAMUS COMPETITION
P.O. Box 30
Bilthoven, Netherlands
(030) 787-033
Contact: Chris Walraven, Director
Type: Contemporary music for instruments, voice, composition
When: Annually
Eligibility: Solo musicians must be 35 years old or younger; ensemble members must be an average age of 35
Award: Monetary

INTERNATIONAL JUBILEE COMPETITION FOR DUTCH CHAMBER MUSIC
c/o B.U.M.A.
Marius Bauerstraat 30
Amsterdam 1017, Netherlands
Contact: N/A
Type: Chamber music
When: Annually
Eligibility: Chamber music ensembles of 3-6 players may participate
Award: Monetary

INTERNATIONAL ORGAN COMPOSITION COMPETITION
Emmawijk 2
Zwolle, Netherlands
Contact: N/A
Type: Organ composition
When: Annually
Eligibility: Composers may apply
Award: Prizes vary

WORLD MUSIC CONTEST
Netherlands
Contact: N/A
Type: Bands, conducting, instrumental, orchestras, voice
When: Quadrennially
Eligibility: Candidates must be 30 years old or younger and may be from any country

NEW ZEALAND

MOZART FELLOWSHIP
University of Otago
Dunedin, New Zealand
Contact: N/A
Type: Performance
When: Annually
Eligibility: Candidates must be under 27 years old and born or residing in New Zealand
Award: Monetary

NORTHERN IRELAND

ULSTER ORCHESTRA COMPOSERS' COMPETITION
26-34 Antrim Rd.
Belfast BT15 2AA, Northern Ireland
Contact: N/A
Type: Composition for strings or orchestra
When: Irregularly
Eligibility: Composers must be residents of Northern Ireland and must be 25 years old or younger
Compositions must be 5-15 minutes long

NORWAY

EDMUND RUDD AND KATE AND ALICE WALLENBERG'S SCHOLARSHIPS
Tollbodgaten 27
Oslo, Norway
Contact: N/A
Type: Female voice
When: Annually
Eligibility: Female vocalists may participate.
Award: Scholarship

PERU

C. HARSHMANINI KEYBOARD AND HARP AWARD
Fundacion Codesa
P.O. Box 5715
Lima, Peru
Contact: N/A
Type: Piano and harp
When: Annually
Eligibility: Pianists and harpists may be any age
Award: Value varies

THE PHILIPPINES

MANILA SYMPHONY ORCHESTRA SCHOLARSHIPS
Manila Symphony Society
P.O. Box 664
Manila, Philippines
Contact: N/A
Type: Instrumental music
When: Annually
Eligibility: Instrumental music students may apply
Award: Scholarship

MANILA SYMPHONY ORCHESTRA YOUNG ARTISTS COMPETITION
Manila Symphony Society
P.O. Box 664
Manila, Philippines
Contact: N/A
Type: Performance
When: Annually
Eligibility: Young musical performers may participate

POLAND

MARIA ANDRZEJEWSKA PRIZE
Association of Polish Musicians
Krucza 24-26
00-526 Warsaw, Poland
Contact: N/A
Type: Development of Polish music
When: Annually

ASSOCIATION OF POLISH MUSICIANS MUSIC CRITICS' PRIZES
Krucza 24-26
00-526 Warsaw, Poland
Contact: N/A
Type: Writing (best article in periodicals, radio and television)
When: Annually
Eligibility: Music critics may apply
Award: Monetary

"FREDERIC CHOPIN" INTERNATIONAL PIANO COMPETITION
ul. Okolnik 1
PL-00-368 Warsaw, Poland
27-95-89
Contact: Wiktor Weinbaum, Director General
Type: Piano
When: Quinquennially (1985)
Eligibility: Pianists may apply
Award: Monetary, plus medals

COMPETITION FOR YOUNG COMPOSERS
Rynek Starego Miasta 27
00-272 Warsaw, Poland
Contact: N/A
Type: Composition
When: Annually

Eligibility: Musical compositions of any kind may be submitted

GRZEGORZ FITELBERG INTERNATIONAL COMPETITION FOR CONDUCTORS
ul. Zawadzkiego 2
40-048 Katowice, Poland
58-98-85
Contact: N/A
Type: Conducting
When: Quadrennially (1983)
Eligibility: Conductors must be 35 years old or younger
Award: Medals

GOLD AWARD
Association of Polish Musicians
Krucza 24-26
00-526 Warsaw, Poland
Contact: N/A
Type: Service
When: Annually
Eligibility: Awards made to the most meritorious members of the association

INTERNATIONAL HENRYK WIENIAWSKI COMPETITIONS—FOR COMPOSITION, VIOLINMAKERS & VIOLIN
Swietoslowsk St. 7
PL-61-840 Poznan, Poland
526-42, 589-91
Contact: Edmund Grabowski, Director
Type: Emphasis changes among composition, violin and violin makers
When: Quadrennially (composers 1985; violin and violin makers, 1986)
Eligibility: Violinists must be professionals and must be 30 years old or younger

ARTHUR MALAWSKI COMPETITION FOR COMPOSERS
Bohaterow Stalingradu 3
31-038 Cracow, Poland
Contact: N/A
Type: Composition
When: Annually
Eligibility: Composers may apply

PORTUGAL

VIANNA DA MOTTA PIANO COMPETITION
Rua Castilho 35
11-H Lisbon, Portugal
65 38 08
Contact: Sequeira Costa, President
Type: Piano
When: Quadrennially
Eligibility: Pianists must be 16-30 years old

SCOTLAND

SIR JAMES CAIRD'S TRAVELLING SCHOLARSHIPS IN MUSIC
Sir James Caird Trust
136 Nethergate
Dundee DD1 4PA, Scotland
Contact: N/A
Type: Voice, instrumental, or composition
When: Annually
Eligibility: Scottish singers, instrumentalists, or composers may apply
Award: Scholarship

INTERNATIONAL COMPETITION FOR JUNIOR VIOLINISTS
Glasgow Arts Centre
Washington Building for the Arts
12 Washington St.
Glasgow G3 9AZ, Scotland
Contact: N/A
Type: Violin
When: Annually
Eligibility: Violinists must be 12-18 years old
Award: Monetary

IAN WHYTE AWARD
Scottish National Orchestra
150 Hope St.
Glasgow G2 2TH, Scotland
Contact: N/A
Type: Orchestral composition
When: Triennially
Eligibility: Composers must be 35 years old or younger. Compositions must be unpublished and unperformed

WISEMAN PRIZE
Sir James Caird Trust
136 Nethergate
Dundee DD1 4PA, Scotland
Contact: N/A
Type: Performance
When: Annually
Eligibility: Scottish musical performers may audition
Award: Monetary

SOUTH AFRICA

ELLIE MARX MEMORIAL SCHOLARSHIP
Ladywood, Hillwood Ave., Claremont 7700
Cape, South Africa
Contact: N/A
Type: Stringed instrument
When: Annually
Eligibility: Musicians who play stringed instruments may apply
Award: Scholarship

SCHOLARSHIP FOR SOUTH AFRICAN COMPOSERS
South African Music Rights Organization
SAMRO house
De Beer and Juta Sts.
Braamfontein, Johannesburg, South Africa
Contact: N/A
Type: Composition
When: Biennially
Eligibility: Composers residing in South Africa, Southwest Africa, Botswana, Lesotho, Rhodesia, or Swaziland may participate
Award: Scholarship

SCHOLARSHIP FOR SOUTH AFRICAN PERFORMING ARTISTS
South African Music Rights Organization
SAMRO House
De Beer and Juta Sts.
Braamfontein, Johannesburg, South Africa
Contact: N/A
Type: Performance
When: Biennially
Eligibility: Musicians residing in South Africa, Southwest Africa, Botswana, Lesotho, Rhodesia, or Swaziland may participate
Award: Scholarship

SOUTH AFRICA BROADCASTING CORPORATION MUSIC PRIZE
Broadcast House Commissioner St.
P.O. Box 8686
Johannesburg, South Africa
Contact: N/A
Type: Piano and sometimes other instruments
When: Annually
Eligibility: Musicians must be 18-30 years old
Award: Monetary

SPAIN

ACCORDION PRIZE OF THE CITY OF SAN SEBASTIAN
Theatre
San Sebastian, Spain
Contact: N/A
Type: Accordion
When: Annually
Eligibility: Accordionists may participate

COMPETITION FOR NEW ARTISTS
La Voz de Espana
San Sebastian, Spain
Contact: N/A
Type: Instrumental, voice, vocal duet, vocal group
When: Annually
Eligibility: Musicians from any country may participate

CONCURSO DE COMPOSICION DE CANCION FOLCLORICA VASCA & POLIFONIA A CAPELLA
Centro de Iniciativas Turisticas
Calle San Juan
s/n Tolosa, Spain
(943) 65-15-70
Contact: N/A
Type: Composition
When: Annually
Eligibility: Composers may apply
Award: Monetary, plus publication

CONCURSO INTERNACIONAL DE EJECUCION MUSICAL MARIA CANALS DE BARCELONA
Gran Via 654

Barcelona 10, Spain
318-7731
Contact: Maria Canals, Ars Nova Music Academy Director; Elisabeth Martinez, General Secretary
Type: Emphasis changes annually
When: Annually
Eligibility: Instrumentalists must be 18-32 years old
Award: Monetary

CONSERVATORY OF MUSIC INTERNATIONAL COMPETITION
plaza Mayor 2
Orense, Spain
Contact: N/A
Type: Piano
When: Annually
Eligibility: Pianists may participate

GUIPUZCOA CHORAL FESTIVAL
Bajos del Teatro Victoria Eugenia
San Sebastian, Spain
Contact: N/A
Type: Voice
When: Annually
Eligibility: Vocalists of any age may participate

INTERNATIONAL OSCAR ESPLA PRIZE
Town Hall
Alicante, Spain
Contact: N/A
Type: Composition
When: Annually
Eligibility: Symphonic compositions must be 15-25 minutes long.
Award: Monetary

INTERNATIONAL MUSIC COMPETITION "MARIA CANALIS"
Ave. Jose Antonio 654
Barcelona 10, Spain
Contact: N/A
Type: Instrumental and voice; sections change each year
When: Annually
Eligibility: Vocalists must be 18-35 years old; instrumentalists must be 18-32 years old
Award: Monetary

INTERNATIONAL PIANO COMPETITION PRIZE "JAEN"
Secretaria del Instituto de Estudios Giennenses
Palacio Provincial
Jaen, Spain
Contact: N/A
Type: Piano
When: Annually
Eligibility: Pianists of any nationality may apply; no previous Jaen Prize winners may participate
Award: Monetary, plus medal and concert performances

PALOMA O'SHEA INTERNATIONAL PIANO COMPETITION
Hernan Cortes 3
Santander, Spain
21-4801
Contact: Paloma O'Shea, President, Founder, and Director; Edel Teja, Secretary
Type: Piano
When: Annually
Eligibility: Pianists must be 15-32 years old
Award: Monetary, plus medals and concert performances

"FRANCISCO VINAS" INTERNATIONAL SINGING CONTEST
Bruch 125
Barcelona 37, Spain
215-4227, 257-8646
Contact: Maria Vilardell, President
Type: Voice
When: Annually
Eligibility: Female vocalists must be 18-32 years old; male vocalists must be 20-35 years old. Singers may compete in opera, oratorio-lied, or special opera contest
Award: Monetary, plus medals, concert tours, and scholarships

SWITZERLAND

CONCOURS GEZA ANDA
Tonhalle-Gesellschaft Zurich
Gottharstr. 1
CH-8002 Zurich, Switzerland
(01) 201-15-57
Contact: N/A
Type: Piano
When: Triennally (1985)
Eligibility: Pianists must be 32 years old or younger
Award: Concert engagements

CONCOURS INTERNATIONAL DE COMPOSITION MUSICAL OPERA ET BALLET
Case Postale 233
Maison de la Radio
66, Blvd. Carl-Vogt
CH-1211 Geneva 8, Switzerland
(022) 29-23-33
Contact: N/A
Type: Musical theater composition; emphasis alternates between opera and ballet
When: Biennially (1983)
Eligibility: All composers may apply
Award: Monetary

FESTIVAL TIBOR VARGA INTERNATIONAL COMPETITION FOR VIOLINISTS
Bureau du Festival
P.O. Box 3374
Ch-1951 Sion, Switzerland
(027) 22-66-52
Contact: N/A
Type: Violin
When: Annually
Eligibility: Violinists must be 15-35 years old
Award: Monetary

GOLDEN ROSE TELEVISION FESTIVAL
c/o Tourist Office
42, Grand-Rue
1820 Montreux, Switzerland
Contact: N/A
Type: Musical television programs
When: Annually
Eligibility: Musical television programs may be submitted

CLARA HASKIL PIANO COMPETITION
P.O. Box 124
Av. des Alpes 14
CH-1820 Montreux, Switzerland
(021) 61-3384
Contact: Rene Klopfenstein, Director
Type: Piano
When: Biennially (1983)
Eligibility: Pianists must be 32 years old or younger
Award: Monetary

INTERNATIONAL COMPETITION FOR MUSICAL PERFORMERS
12, rue de l'Hotel-de-Ville
Ch-1204 Geneva, Switzerland
(022) 28-62-08
Contact: Claude Viala, President; Franco Fisch, Secretary General
Type: Emphasis changes annually among voice, piano, instrument, and conducting
When: Annually
Eligibility: For 1983, female opera singers must be 20-32 years old; other vocalists must be 22-34 years old; saxophonists, double bass players, and flutists must be 15-30 years old
Award: Monetary

MUSICAL PRIZE CONTEST QUEEN MARIE-JOSE
Merlinge By
CH-1249 Geneva, Switzlernad
Contact: N/A
Type: Composition
When: Biennially(1984)
Eligibility: All composers may participate
Award: Monetary

URUGUAY

CONCURSO INTERNACIONAL DE PIANO "CIUDAD DE MONTEVIDEO"
Enrique Munoz 815
Montevideo, Uruguay
70-70-09
Contact: Aurora Alvarez de Silva Ledesma, President; Antaram Aharonia, Secretary General
Type: Piano
When: Quadrennially (1986)
Eligibility: Pianists must be 32 years old or younger
Award: Monetary, plus medals and concert engagements

U.S.S.R.

INTERNATIONAL P.I. TCHAIKOVSKY COMPETITION
15 Neglinnaya St.
Moscow, U.S.S.R.
Contact: Yuri Gostevsky, Chairman
Type: Piano, violin, cello, voice
When: Quadrennially (1986)

Eligibility: Instrumentalists must be 16-30 years old; vocalists must be 18-32 years old
Award: Monetary, medals, badges

WALES

FEMALE CHOIRS CONTEST
Llangollen International Musical Eisteddfod
International Eisteddfod Office
Llangollen LL20 8NG, Clwyd, N. Wales
Contact: N/A
Type: Female choir
When: Annually
Eligibility: Female choirs may have up to 60 voices; members must be 16 years old or older
Award: Monetary, plus trophy

CATHERINE AND LADY GRACE JAMES FOUNDATION GRANTS
9 Market St.
Aberystwyth, Dyfed, Wales
Contact: N/A
Type: Music study
When: Annually
Eligiblity: Welsh male students may apply
Award: Education grant

MALE CHOIRS CONTEST
Llangollen International Musical Eisteddfod
International Eisteddfod Office
Llangollen LL20 8NG, Clwyd, N. Wales
Contact: N/A
Type: Male choir
When: Annually
Eligibility: Male choirs may have up to 60 voices; members must be 16 years old or older
Award: Monetary, plus trophy

MIXED CHOIRS CONTEST
Llangollen International Musical Eisteddfod
International Eisteddfod Office
Llangollen LL20 8NG, Clwyd, N. Wales
Contact: N/A
Type: Mixed choir
When: Annually
Eligibility: Mixed choirs may have up to 80 voices; members must be 16 years old or older
Award: Monetary, plus trophy

ROYAL NATIONAL EISTEDDFOD OF WALES COMPETITION
Pen-y-Garreg
Porthaethwy
Ynys Mon
Gwynedd, Wales
Contact: N/A
Type: Instrumental, choir, brass band, composition
When: Annually
Eligibility: Instrumentalists, choirs, brass bands, and composers may participate
Award: Monetary

YUGOSLAVIA

ENCOUNTER OF OCTETS AT SENTJERNEJ
c/o Drustvo Srecanje Oktetov
68310 Sentjernej, Yugoslavia
Contact: Marjan Mocivnik, President
Type: Vocal octet
When: Annually
Eligibility: Octets must be amateur
Award: None

VACLAV HUMI INTERNATIONAL VIOLIN COMPETITION
c/o Hrvatski Glazbeni Zavod
Gunduliceva 6
41000 Zagreb, Yugoslavia
(041) 440-635
Contact: Zlatko Stahuljak, Secretary General
Type: Violin
When: Quadrennially (1985)
Eligibility: As of January 1, 1985, violinists must be 16-30 years old
Award: 7 prizes

INTERNATIONAL JEUNESSES MUSICALES COMPETITION
Terazije 26/II
11000 Belgrade, Yugoslavia
(011) 322-796
Contact: Miodrag Pavlovic, Director
Type: Viola and string orchestra with continuo; emphasis changes annually.
When: Annually
Eligibility: Musicians must be under 30 years old. Each unsemble must have no more than 17 musicians, excluding conductor
Award: Prizes, plus concert tour

SARAJEVO SONG FESTIVAL COMPETITION
Danijela Ozme-7
71000 Sarajevo, Yugoslavia
Contact: N/A
Type: Voice, lyrics, composition
When: Annually
Eligibility: Vocalists, lyricists, and composers may participate

SLOVENIAN SONG FESTIVAL
c/o Tavcarjeva - 17
61000 Ljubljana, Yugoslavia
Contact: N/A
Type: Voice, lyrics, and composition
When: Annually
Eligibility: Vocalists, lyricists, and composers may participate

SONG FESTIVAL ZAGREB
Udruzenje Kompositora SRH
41000 Zagreb, Yugoslavia
Contact: N/A
Type: Voice, lyrics, and composition
When: Annually
Eligibility: Vocalists, lyricists, and composers may participate

SPLIT SUMMER COMPETITION
c/o Dalmacijakoncert
Trg. Republike 1
58000 Split, Yugoslavia
Contact: N/A
Type: Music and song
When: Annually
Eligibility: All musicians may apply

YOUTH FESTIVAL
Dom Kulture
Gradska Kuca
2400 Subotica, Yugoslavia
Contact: N/A
Type: All branches of music
When: Annually
Eligibility: All musicians may apply

YUGOSLAV TV SONG FESTIVAL
c/o Dezmanov Prolaz 10
41000 Zagreb, Yugoslavia
Contact: N/A
Type: Voice, lyrics, and composition
When: Annually
Eligibility: Vocalists, lyricists, and composers may apply

National Federation of Music Clubs Scholarships and Awards Chart

This chart was made available through the courtesy of the National Federation of Music Clubs, Indianapolis, IN. Chairman of the Scholarship Department and Scholarship Board is Mrs. Arthur M. Emmerling, 1311 Starfield Rd., North Little Rock, AR 72116.

The Chart is in seven sections. Opportunities offered in sections 4, 6, and 7 include both Junior and Student Divisions. Junior age—must not have reached the 19th birthday by March 1; Student age—must have reached the 16th but not the 26th birthday by March 1. Entrants of 16, 17, and 18 years may enter either Junior or Student competitions but not both at the same time.

1. BIENNIAL AWARDS
ODD NUMBERED YEARS

Name	Category	Age Limit	Entry Fee	Amount of Award	Deadline for Application	NFMC Chairman
Young Artist Auditions. (Held at state, district and national levels)	Piano, Strings, Man's Voice, Woman's Voice, Oratorio (Louis Sudler Award)	**Instrumentalists:** Must have reached the 18th birthday but not the 30th by March 1 of the year of audition **Vocalists:** Must have reached the 23rd birthday but not the 35th by March 1 of the year of auditions	$10.00 for each category	$5000 in each category (NFMC and Louis Sudler Awards plus Agnes Fowler Supplement for each.) See Young Artist BULLETIN for Supplemental Awards.	Dec. 1 prior to year of Auditions	Mrs. Glen M. Weakley, 42 Waterway Road, Ocean City, N.J. 08226
The NFMC Opera Award honoring Dr. Merle Montgomery. A Past National President Award.	Opera Voice	Must have reached the 23rd birthday but not the 35th by year of audition.	Included in the Young Artist Entrance Fee	$1,000 biennially to an opera voice from among those participating in NFMC semi-finals Young Artist Auditions.	Young Artist Audition Deadline	Mrs. J. Knox Byrum, 1702 N. Broadway Shawnee, Oklahoma 74801
Biennial Student Awards (Auditions through state, district and national levels)	Piano, Organ, Harp, Man's Voice, Woman's Voice, Violin, Viola, Violoncello, Double Bass and Classical guitar, Orchestral Winds.	**Instrumentalists:** Must have reached the 16th birthday but not the 26th by March 1 of the year of audition. **Vocalists:** Must have reached the 18th birthday but not the 26th.	$5.00 (Student Auditions fee)	$550 in each category (NFMC award plus Muir and Agnes Fowler supplements) and performance at Biennial Convention when feasible. See Student Auditions BULLETIN for Supplemental Awards	Dec. 1 prior to year of Auditions	Mrs. Robert Casey R.R. #3 Box 435 Walkerton, Indiana 46574
Edwin B. Ellis Award in Piano	Piano entrants, Student Auditions	Must have reached the 16th birthday but not the 26th by March 1 of year of audition	Included in Student Auditions fee	$750 funded from the Edwin B. Ellis Endowment	Dec. 1 prior to year of Auditions	Mrs. Robert Casey R.R. #3 Box 435 Walkerton, Indiana 46574
Josef Kaspar Award in Violin	Violin entrants, Student Auditions	Must have reached the 16th birthday but not the 26th by March 1 of year of audition	Included in Student Auditions fee	$750 funded by Endowment. Gift by Miss Mary Park Clements.	Dec. 1 prior to year of Auditions	Mrs. Robert Casey R.R. #3 Box 435 Walkerton, Indiana 46574

Name	Category	Age Limit	Entry Fee	Amount of Award	Deadline for Application	NFMC Chairman
Irene S. Muir Scholarship in Voice (through auditions at state, district and national levels) Funded from Muir gift.	Man's Voice and Woman's Voice entrants. Student Auditions	Must have reached the 18th birthday but not the 26th by March 1 of year of audition	Included in Student Auditions fee	$1000 each and performance at Biennial Convention when feasible to voice major, toward a music degree in an accepted university or college music department, a music school, or a conservatory	Dec 1 prior to year of Auditions	Mrs. Frank A. Vought 2865 Hundred Oaks Avenue Baton Rouge, Louisiana 70808
Louise Oberne Award Funded by the Oberne Bequest	Entrants in Student Auditions in Strings (Violin, Viola, Violoncello)	Must have reached the 16th birthday but not the 26th by March 1 of year of audition	Included in Student Auditions fee	$600 First Place $400 Second Place	Dec 1 prior to year of Auditions	Mrs. Robert Casey R.R. #3 Box 435 Walkerton, Indiana 46574
Berkshire Music Center Lenox, Massachusetts 01240 (Ada Holding Miller Fellowship) A Past National President Endowment Fund for Ada Holding Miller	Composition Instrumental Choral Opera	18-25 as of March 1 Top Student	None	$1,000 Partial awarded Biennially	April 1	Miss Irene L. Mulick 15 Concord Avenue Cranston, Rhode Island 02910

EVEN NUMBERED YEARS

Name	Category	Age Limit	Entry Fee	Amount of Award	Deadline for Application	NFMC Chairman
Adult Composers Contest	Works for vocal solo, chorus, 3 minutes duration; for instrumental solos, 4 minutes duration	none	$2.00	$50	December 1	Mrs. L.W. Kranert 1119 Locust Avenue, S.E. Huntsville, Alabama 35801

2. ANNUAL-ARTIST AND ADVANCED MUSICIAN

Name	Category	Age Limit	Entry Fee	Amount of Award	Deadline for Application	NFMC Chairman
Vera Wardner Dougan Artist Award. A Past National President Award	NFMC Young Artist winner who has attained professional excellence.	None	None	$500 presented to an NFMC Artist Winner selected to perform during Peninsula Music Festival, Fish Creek, Wisconsin	By invitation	Committee: Music Director of Festival, Dr. Vera Wardner Dougan; and the NFMC President
Anne M. Gannett Award for Vetarans A Past National President Award	Veteran whose musical career has been interrupted by service in the Armed Forces.	None	None	$500 Award Funded by the Gannett Endowment	March 15	Mrs. J. Knox Byrum 1702 N. Broadway Shawnee, Oklahoma 74801
NFMC Koussevitzky Award	A composer who has attained recognition in his own country	24-37	None	Free housing for September and October in Koussevitzky Composer's Studio, Lenox, Massachusetts.	February 1	Dr. Merle Montgomery 400 East 71st Street New York, N.Y. 10021
Apprentice Artists Program, Santa Fe Opera (Ruth Freehoff Memorial) Sante Fe, New Mexico	Voice	20-30	None	$200 partially funded by the Freehoff legacy.	November 15	Mrs. Bert Kempers 600 Ridgecrest Dr. S.E. Albuquerque, N.M. 87108

3. ANNUAL STUDENT**

Members of the Student Division should also carefully check Section 7, NFMC Summer Scholarships, as various age levels are included in Summer Music Center and camp opportunities.

Name	Category	Age Limit	Entry Fee	Amount of Award	Deadline for Application	NFMC Chairman
Dance Awards	Ballet, Modern Dance	Must have reached the 16th birthday but not the 26th by March 1 of year of audition.	$5.00 (Student Auditions fee)	One $200 scholarship for either Ballet or Modern Dance.	Dec. 1 Prior to year of Audition	Mrs. Susan C. McLean 1101 Government St. Apt. E-1 Mobile, Alabama 36604
Dorothy Dann Bullock Award in Music Therapy, A Past National President Award	Music Therapy at a school offering M.T. degree, approved by National Association of Music Therapists	Offered to Music Therapy majors (college sophomores, juniors, seniors) already enrolled in accredited schools offering M.T. degree, approved by NAMT	Write National Chairman	$500 towards further study (paid to approved school of recipient's choice) Funded by the Bullock Endowment	April 1	Mrs. James M. Challener 1404 California Avenue McKeesport, Penn. 15131
Music Therapy Awards 2 NFMC Awards 1 Ruth Robertson Award	Same as above	Same as above	Same as above	Three awards of $250 each towards further study (as above)	April 1	Mrs. C. Thomas Hammond 108 Christy Road Battle Creek, Michigan 49015
Hinda Honigman Scholarship for the Blind A Past National President Award	Instrumentalist or Vocalist	Must have reached the 16th birthday but not the 26th by March 1 of year of audition	Write National Chairman	$500 for continued study. Funded by the Hinda Honigman Endowment	March 15	Mrs. Glenn W. Morrison 116 E. Maxwell Dr., Lakeland, Florida 33803

Name	Category	Age Limit	Entry Fee	Amount of Award	Deadline for Application	NFMC Chairman
Music for the Blind* (See Below)	Composition	Must have reached the 19th birthday but not the 31st by March 1 of year of competition	$2.00	$200	March 20	Mrs. Edward P. Nelson 55 Janssen Place Kansas City, Missouri 64109
Victor Herbert ASCAP Young Composers Awards	Composition: Class I Sonata for solo Wind or String Instrument with Piano or 3 to 5 Orchestral Instruments; Class II Choral; Class III Piano Solo	Must have reached the 18th birthday but not the 26th by March 1 of the year of competition	$1.25 per manuscript	First Prize $1,000 Second $500 Third $500	March 1	Mrs. Russell C. Hatz First and Pine Aves. Mt. Gretna, Pennsylvania 17064
Devora Nadworney Award	Class IV Composition for Solo Voice with Piano, Organ or Orchestral Accompaniment. English Text. Minimum duration, 4 minutes	Must have reached the 18th birthday but not the 26th by March 1 of the year of competition	$1.25 per manuscript	First Prize $150 Second prize $75 From funds given by Devora Nadworney	March 1	Mrs. Russell C. Hatz First and Pine Aves. Mt. Gretna, Pennsylvania 17064
Marie Morrisey Keith Award 1982 Western 1983 Northeastern 1984 Southeastern 1985 Central Past National President Award	Piano, Voice, Strings Orchestral Winds	Must have reached the 16th birthday but not the 26th by March 1 of year of audition	$5.00 (Student Auditions fee)	$250, renewable for second year Funded from Marie Morrisey Keith Endowment	Dec. 1 prior to year of Auditions	Mrs. Robert Casey R.R. #3 Box 435 Walkerton, Indiana 46574
Ruby Simmons Vought Scholarship in Organ A Past National President Award	Organ	18-25 as of March 1 the year of the auditions	$5.00 paid by December 1 preceding the year of the auditions	$1,000 Funded by the Vought Endowment	Dec. 1 Preceding the year of the audition	Mrs. Robert Henderson 733 Santander Ave. Coral Gables, Florida 33134
Thor Johnson Chamber Music Award	Chamber Music Group of not more than six members, submitting a proposed performance project and a taped sample of a performance by the group	Must have reached the 16th birthday but not the 26th by March 1 of the year of audition	None	$350 Funded by the Thor Johnson Bequest	Dec. 1	Mr. Archer Summerson, 47 N. Princeton Circle Lynchburg, Virginia 24503

**Entrance Rule except for Young Artist Auditions: Applicants must be members or become members of the National Federation of Music Clubs, either by individual or group affiliation before the applications are accepted.

Bulletins for Young Artist Auditions, Student Auditions, Junior Festivals, Stillman-Kelley Rules and Procedures and Scholarship and Awards Charts may be ordered from NFMC Headquarters. Request a Publications List which indicates the cost of the above bulletins from: National Federation of Music Clubs, 1336 North Delaware Street, Indianapolis, Indiana 46202.

*REGIONAL CHAIRMEN FOR MUSIC FOR THE BLIND

Central: Mrs. Dean Wilson
1914 Seven Hills Rd.
Jefferson City, Missouri 65101

Northeastern: Mrs. Chris L. Nelson
365 Clinton Avenue
Bridgeport, Connecticut 06605

Southeastern: Mrs. James W. Milne, Sr.
429 Allison Road S.W.
Roanoke, Virginia 24016

Western: Mrs. W. Paul Benzinger
4814 South Birch Street
Tempe, Arizona 85282

See Section 6 for states included in each Region.

4. ANNUAL SPECIAL

Orchestra Composition Award offered by Lancaster (Pennsylvania) Summer Arts Festival	Composition: Symphonic Work	Must have reached the 15th birthday but not the 26th by March 1 of the year of competition	$2.50	$1,000 and public performance by Lancaster Symphony Orchestra Funded by Lancaster Summer Arts Festival	March 1	Mrs. Glen Weakley 42 Waterway Road Ocean city, N.J. 08226

5. ANNUAL JUNIOR

Members of the Junior Division should also carefully check Section 7, NFMC Summer Scholarships, as various age levels are included in Summer Music Center and camp opportunities.

Stillman-Kelley Scholarship rotating by Regions: 1982—Southeastern 1983—Central 1984—Western 1985—Northeastern Funded by Stillman-Kelley Endowment	Instrumentalists	Must not have reached the 17th birthday by March 1 of the year of audition	Write National Chairman	First Place—$1,000 (towards further study) payable $500 annually for 2 consecutive years, provided highest standards of accomplishment are maintained. Second Place—$500. $250 for each of two consecutive years.	February 1	Mrs. Willis Harris 101 Argyle Circle Gadsden, Alabama 35901

Name	Category	Age Limit	Entry Fee	Amount of Award	Deadline for Application	NFMC Chairman
Thelma Byrum Piano Award rotating by Regions, same as Stillman-Kelley. From earnings of funds in honor of Thelma Byrum.	Pianists only	Must not have reached the 17th birthday by March 1 of year of audition	Write National Chairman	$200 toward further study in year of audition. This award will be given to the best pianist in the Stillman-Kelley Competition. If the Stillman-Kelley winner is a pianist, the Thelma Byrum Piano Award will go to the second best pianist.	February 1	Mrs. Willis Harris 101 Argyle Circle Gadsden, Alabama 35901
Wendell Irish Viola Award	Violists	Must have reached the 12th birthday but not the 19th by March 1 the year of audition.	Write National Chairman	Four awards per year. One in each of the four NFMC Regions. Amount of each award is $700 given in two payments, $350 in year of audition and $350 in following year.	March 1	Mrs. L.M. Hall, Jr. 4137 Whitfield, Fort Worth, Texas 76109
Music for the Blind Performance Awards	Instrumentalists and Vocalists	Must not have reached the 19th birthday by March 1 of year of audition	Write National Chairman	Eight $100 (two in each of the four Regions of NFMC)	March 20 to Regional Chairmen (see listing above)	Mrs. Edward P. Nelson 55 Janssen Place Kansas City, Missouri 64109
Florence Wilkinson National Award. Gift of Florence Wilkinson	Given to the best of the Eight Regional Winners in the classification above			$100 Funded by Florence Wilkinson	March 20	Regional Chairman Winners to National Chairman
W. Paul Benzinger Memorial Award. Music for the Blind Performance Award. Gift of Mrs. W. Paul Benzinger	Instrumentalists and Vocalists	Must not have reached the 14th birthday by March 1 of the year of audition		One $100 award in each of the four NFMC Regions Funded by Mrs. W. Paul Benzinger	March 20	Regional Chairman
Music for the Blind	Composition	Must have reached the 10th birthday but not the 19th by March 1 of the year of audition.	$2.00 per manuscript	$100	March 20	Mrs. Edward P. Nelson 55 Janssen Place Kansas City, Missouri 64109
Junior Festival Awards for Performers	Instrumentalists and Vocalists	Must not have reached the 19th birthday by March 1 of year of audition	See Junior Festivals Bulletin	See Junior Festivals Bulletin	See Junior Festivals Bulletin	Mrs. Crawford Jent Rt. 2 Box 124 Madisonville, Kentucky 42431
Dance Awards	Ballet, Modern Dance	Must have reached the 12th birthday but not the 19th by March 1 of the year of audition	See Junior Festivals Bulletin	One $200 scholarship for either Ballet or Modern Dance.	See Junior Festivals Bulletin	Mrs. Susan C. McLean 1101 Government St. Apt. E-1 Mobile, Alabama 36604
Junior Composers Awards "Calvalcade for Creative Youth"	Composition	Must not have reached the 19th birthday by March 1 of the year of competition	$1.25 per manuscript	$35, $25, $30, $20, $25, $10 plus incentive awards for non-winners showing special talent	April 1	Mrs. Ben K. Wright 382 Parkside Dr., Palo Alto, California 94306
Fred Waring Award	Composition Vocal Solo or Ensemble preferred but instrumental will be considered	Must not have reached the 19th birthday by March 1 of the year of competition	See Junior Festivals Bulletin	$50	April 1	same as above
John and Margaret Pierson Award in Composition Funded from a gift by Mrs. Malcolm Denise	Composition	Must have reached the 12th birthday but not the 16th by March 1 of the year of competition	Included in "Calvalcade for Creative Youth" Fee	$125 to assist in attending summer music camp or for study with a teacher of the recipient's choice.	April 1	same as above
Junior Composers String Award	Composition for Strings, Solo or Ensemble	Must have reached the 16th birthday but not the 19th by March 1 of the year of competition	See Junior Festivals Bulletin	$50	April 1	same as above
Laura K. Wilson Memorial Award honoring Dorothy Dann Bullock. Grant from Pittsburgh (Pa.) Piano Teachers Association	Composition, Piano	Must have reached the 16th but not the 19th birthday by March 1 of the year of competition	See Junior Festivals Bulletin	$50	April 1	same as above

6. COLLEGE AND UNIVERSITY SCHOLARSHIPS LISTED WITH THE NATIONAL FEDERATION OF MUSIC CLUBS

Chairman of Music in Schools and Colleges for NFMC
Mrs. Norman Hamre, 1709 North Jay, Aberdeen, South Dakota 57401

Deadline—for receiving tapes: February 1, annually

Requirement: Tapes are to be sent directly to colleges and universities accompanied by application form provided by NFMC and obtained from Regional chairman. (See listing next page.) A copy of each application form MUST be sent to the Regional Chairman representing the institution where student is applying. Unless otherwise indicated, these scholarships are planned for students enrolling in colleges as freshmen.

Name of School	Category	Amount of Award	Send Application Form and Tapes to
Abilene Christian University Department of Music Abilene, Texas 79601	Piano, Voice, Orchestra, Band and Chorus	Piano and Voice, $300-$500 awards over two years. Other awards vary from $50 to $200 per semester	Dr. Sarah Reid Dept of Music. ACU Station, Box 8274 Abilene, Texas 79699
Alabama, University of Department of Music Tuscaloosa, Alabama 35486	Piano, Voice, Organ, Strings, Orchestral & Band Instruments	No set number of Scholarships. Renewable through baccalaureate if progress maintained. Amount varies to full tuition as determined by Scholarship Committee of Dept.	Dr. Wayne M. Sheley Department of Music University of Alabama Tuscaloosa, Alabama 35486
The American University Washington, D.C. 20016	Undergraduate Scholarships for Strings, String Quartet. Graduate Assistantships	The program offers undergraduate String Quartet Scholarships (full tuition for four students) and the Wainhouse String Scholarship each year. Approximately $1,200.00 Graduate assistantships are available as Studio Accompanist, Theory Assistant, Orchestra/Band Assistant, Music Library Assistant and Concert Manager. 24 hours remitted tuition, and $4,000 stipend.	George C. Schuetze, Jr. Director, Music Program Department of Performing Arts The American University Washington, D.C. 20016
Arizona, University of Southwest Pianists' Foundation Tucson, Arizona 85719	Piano study with Ozan Marsh, concert pianist	One scholarship of $250 per semester.	Ozan Marsh School of Music U. of Arizona Tucson, Arizona 85719
Ball State University School of Music Muncie, Indiana 47306	All wind and string instruments, keyboard, voice, electronic music, music theatre, opera, ballet, jazz, marching band; Graduate assistantships and doctoral fellowships available in performance, conducting, musicology, composition.	Awards vary depending upon talent and/or financial need of applicant	Dr. Eugene Karjala Coordinator of Undergraduate Programs School of Music Ball State University Muncie, In 47306 Dr. Kirby Koriath Coordinator of Graduate Programs School of Music Ball State University Muncie, IN 47306
Boston University The School of Music 855 Commonwealth Ave. Boston, MA 02215	Voice, Strings, Harp, Keyboard, Wind, Brass, Percussion, Music History, Theory/Composition, Music Education	Limited number of full four-year performance awards; financial-need assistance through PCS, renewable possible. Some competitive performance awards for full-time students. Graduate assistance available by application only.	Dr. Wilbur D. Fullbright Director School of Music Boston University 855 Commonwealth Ave. Boston, MA 02215
Bradley University Division of Music Peoria, Illinois 61625	Piano, Voice, Organ, Strings, Orchestral & Band Instruments, Composition	A number of scholarships worth $650 a year for 4 years ($2600 total) based upon musical talent without regard to financial need are available. Additional financial aid also available based on need. H.S. seniors high in their class who have received high ACT or SAT scores may receive additional financial aid. Assistantships and scholarships are available for graduate students also.	Allen Cannon, Director Division of Music Bradley University Peoria, Illinois 61625
Catholic University of America School of Music Washington, D.C. 20064	Electronic music, musicology, strings, theory, piano, winds, vocal coaching, vocal accompaniment, and general graduate and undergraduate scholarships and contributed assistantships in music education, and graduate assistantships.	VARIABLE: up to four years tuition scholarship	Dr. Thomas Mastroianni Dean, School of Music Catholic University of America Washington, D.C. 20064
Cincinnati, University of College-Conservatory of Music Cincinnati, Ohio 45221	All undergraduate music majors plus dance; all performing instruments, non-performance majors, Musical Theater & Theater Production	Variable, up to 4 years full tuition; $10,000 out-of-state, $4200 in state. Satisfactory progress must be maintained. Awards are based solely on talent and merit.	David Patterson Admissions Officer College-Conservatory of Music University of Cincinnati Cincinnati, Ohio 45221
Converse College School of Music Spartanburg, S.C. 29301	Orchestral and Band Instruments, Voice	Two scholarships, $100 to $1000 per annum, to be determined by Scholarship Committee of College according to need, renewable if satisfactory progress maintained.	Dr. Henry Janiec, Dean School of Music Converse College Spartanburg, S.C. 29301
Eastman School of Music 26 Gibbs Street Rochester, N.Y. 14604	All Orchestral instruments; piano, organ and voice; all academic programs.	Each award may vary from $500 to full tuition depending upon the talent and/or financial need of applicant	Mr. Charles Krusenstjerna Director of Admissions Eastman School of Music 26 Gibbs Street Rochester, N.Y. 14604
Hartford, University of Hartt College of Music West Hartford, Connecticut 06117	Opera Voice, or Orchestral Instrument	$1500 scholarship, renewable	Mr. Roger G. Murtha, Chm. Student Aid Committee Hartt College of Music West Hartford, Connecticut 06117

Name of School	Category	Amount of Award	Send Application Form and Tapes to
Illinois State University Department of Music Normal, Illinois 61761	Keyboard, Voice, Orchestral and Band Instruments	Amount varies from $150 to full tuition plus $150 as determined by the Scholarship Committee of the Department of Music	Dr David L Shrader, Chm Department of Music Illinois State University Normal, Illinois 61761
Indiana University School of Music Bloomington, Indiana 47401	All areas, performance and academic	275 undergraduate scholarships from $100 to $1000 per year renewable if progress is maintained 250 Associate Instructorships in all areas from $1200 to $2000 plus fee remission	Dr. Charles H. Webb, Dean School of Music Indiana University Bloomington, Indiana 47401
Jacksonville University College of Fine Arts Jacksonville, Florida 32211	All instruments and voice for full-time Music Major	Each award may vary from $500 to $1000 depending upon the talent and/or financial need of applicant Also Symphony salary possible	Dr. David Sikes, Acting Dean College of Fine Arts Jacksonville University Jacksonville, Florida 32211
Lakeland College Sheboygan, Wisconsin 53081	1 Flute 2 Organ/Piano	One four-year scholarship in each, $100 up to full tuition	Mr Roy Carroll Department of Music Lakeland College Box 520 Sheboygan, Wisconsin 53081
Manhattan School of Music 120 Claremont Avenue New York, N.Y. 10027	All instruments, voice and composition	Scholarships based on merit, financial aid based on need Renewable Audition required	John O Crosby, President Manhattan School of Music 120 Claremont Avenue New York, N Y 10027
Midwestern State University Department of Music Wichita Falls, Texas 76308	Voice, Strings, Keyboard, Band Instruments	40 four-year scholarships ranging from $50 to $500 per semester. One graduate assistantship in voice $3600.	Dr Don Maxwell, Chm Department of Music Midwestern State University Wichita Falls, Texas 76308
Millikin University Music Department Decatur, Illinois 62522	Piano, Voice, Strings, Orchestral Winds	Four 4-year scholarships of $1500 each	Dr Ronald Gregory, Dean Music Department Millikin University Decatur, Illinois 62522
Mississippi University for Women Columbus, Mississippi 39701	All performing areas	Awards of $100-$500, renewable if progress maintained as determined by Music Department Waiver of out-of-state tuition available in some areas if applicable	James V Cobb, Jr, Head Department of Music Mississippi University for Women Columbus, Mississippi 39701
Mississippi, University of Department of Music University, Mississippi 38677	All performing areas	$300 scholarships, renewable for three years plus waiver of out-of-state tuition when applicable	Dr. James Coleman, Chm. Department of Music University of Mississippi University, Mississippi 38677
New School of Music 301 S. 21st Street Philadelphia, Pa 19103	All symphony orchestra instruments and piano	Approximately forty awards ranging up to full tuition Renewable for four years	Financial Aid Officer New School of Music 301 S 21st Street Philadelphia, Pa 19103
North Texas State University School of Music Denton, Texas 76203	All performing areas and composition	Approximately 200 service awards from $100-$400 per academic year Limited scholarships from $200-$1000 per academic year 100 graduate teaching assistantships in all areas (performance and academic) up to $4000 per year	Dr. Marceau Myers, Dean School of Music North Texas State University Denton, Texas 76203
Oklahoma College of Liberal Arts Chickasha, Oklahoma 73018	Organ, Piano, Violin, Viola, Voice or Music Education	$250 scholarship, $125 per semester, renewable for second year	Mr Robert Garwell, Chm Oklahoma College of Liberal Arts Chickasha, Oklahoma 73018
Palm Beach Atlantic College Department of Music 1101 South Olive Ave. West Palm Beach, Florida 33401	Applied (Voice, Keyboard, Orchestral Instruments), Music Education, Theory	No set number of scholarships, Grants-in-aid Renewable through baccalaureate if progress and academic standing maintained Awards based on ability, potential, need Audition required (Tape acceptable if distance warrants)	Stan Doyle, Chairman Department of Music Palm Beach Atlantic College 1101 S. Olive Ave. West Palm Beach, Florida 33401
Presbyterian College Department of Fine Arts Music Clinton, South Carolina 29325	Piano, Voice, Organ and Band Instruments	Five scholarships, each renewable: two $1,500 scholarships per year and three $1,000 scholarships per year. Other service awards from $100 to $300 per year	Dr. Charles T. Gaines Chairman, Department of Fine Arts Presbyterian College Clinton, South Carolina 29325
Rollins College Winter Park, Florida 32789	Piano, Voice, Organ, Strings Instruments	No set number of scholarships, Scholarly ability, musicality, need basis for grants Renewable	Ross Rosazza Department of Music Rollins College Winter Park, Florida 32789
San Francisco Conservatory of Music 1201 Ortega Street San Francisco, California 94122	Violin, Viola, or Violoncello	$3700 scholarship covers tuition, renewable annually if satisfactory progress and scholastic standing maintained	Mr Richard Howe, Dean San Francisco Conservatory of Music 1201 Ortega Street San Francisco, Calif 94122
Shenandoah College and Conservatory of Music Winchester, Virginia 22601	All instruments, voice, composition, music theatre	Awards may vary from $100 to full tuition depending on the talent and/or financial need of applicant	Mr Dana C Parker Director of Financial Aid Shenandoah College and Conservatory of Music Winchester, VA 22601
Shreveport Symphony Shreveport, LA 71104 (for Centenary College)	Violin, Viola, Violoncello, Double Bass, Piano	No set number of scholarships, renewable to BA degree at Centenary College, Shreveport, Louisiana Amount varies from $1500 to $2450	Mr. John Shenaut Director, Shreveport Symphony Symphony House 2803 Woolawn Avenue Shreveport, Louisiana 71104
Southwest Texas State University Department of Music San Marcos, Texas 78666	Piano, Voice, Instruments	Private lesson fees to full tuition costs No set number of awards Renewable Graduate teaching assistantships also available	Dr. Arlis Hiebert, Chm. Department of Music Southwest Texas State University San Marcos, Texas 78666

Name of School	Category	Amount of Award	Send Application Form and Tapes to
Texas Woman's University Department of Music Denton, Texas 76204	All performing areas and composition	Undergraduate awards $100-$300 renewable annually Graduate Assistantships available on request	Dr Barbara Noel Acting Chairman Department of Music and Drama Texas Woman's University Denton, Texas 76204

REGIONAL CHAIRMEN FOR MUSIC IN SCHOOLS AND COLLEGES

Central Region: Mrs. Leo H. Whinery, Route 2, Box 29, Nobel, Oklahoma 73068

For schools in: Arkansas, Illinois, Iowa, Kansas, Minnesota, Missouri, Nebraska, North Dakota, Oklahoma, South Dakota, Texas, Wisconsin

Southeastern Region: Mrs. Enos M. Burt, 2 Elizabeth Lane, Natchez, Mississippi 36120.

For schools in: Alabama, District of Columbia, Delaware, Florida, Georgia, Kentucky, Louisiana, Maryland, Mississippi, North Carolina, South Carolina, Tennessee, Virginia, West Virginia

Northeastern Region: Mrs. Ralph Curtis, 2020 Noble Rd., Oxford, Michigan 48051.

For schools in: Connecticut, Indiana, Maine, Massachusetts, Michigan, New Hampshire, New Jersey, New York, Ohio, Pennsylvania, Rhode Island, Vermont

Western Region: Mrs. Samuel B. Hitt, 5453 Valley Ridge Avenue, Los Angeles, California 90043.

For schools in: Alaska, Arizona, California, Colorado, Hawaii, Idaho, Montana, New Mexico, Oregon, Utah, Washington, Wyoming

7. NFMC SUMMER MUSIC SCHOLARSHIPS

Chairman of Summer Scholarships, Mrs. George Jordan, 740 Chestnut St., Camden, Arkansas 71701

ANNUAL

School	Category	Age Group	Amount of Scholarship	Camp Date	Write for Information to	Deadline for Application	NFMC Representative
Alaska Fine Arts Camp Alaska Festival of Music Wasilla, Alaska Mrs. John A. Farmer, Dir.	Instrumental or Voice	Grades 6-12	$150 partial tuition private lessons, board, room, transportation Anchorage to King's Lake	July	NFMC Representative	April 1	Mrs. John A. Farmer Box 24 Anchorage, Alaska 99510
Aspen School of Music Dr. Gordon Hardy, Director Exce. Vice President and Dean, Music Associates of Aspen, Inc., Aspen, Colorado	Strings	Up to 25 as of March 1	$500 Partial	9 weeks June August	School	April 1	Dr. Isabelle Terrill 2423 Meadow Lark Lane Glenwood Springs, Colorado 81601
Boston University Tanglewood Institute 855 Commonwealth Ave Boston, Mass 02215	Vocal and all standard Orchestral Instruments	Sophomore through Senior HS 15-19	Given by Institute Varies, depending on financial need of student and needs of orchestra or chorus	Depends on Program in which student participates	Gary L. Zeller 855 Commonwealth Ave. Boston, Mass 02215	April 1	Miss Irene L. Mulick 15 Concord Avenue Cranston, Rhode Island 02910
Brevard Music Center Brevard, North Carolina 28712 Dr. Henry Janiec, Director P.O. Box 349 Converse Station Spartanburg, S.C. 29301 Hinda Honigman Scholarship	Instrumentalist (Band or Orchestra)	12-20	$550 Partial	6½ weeks June August	NFMC Representative	March 15	Mrs. Harold G. Deal 375-4th St. N.W. Hickory, N.C. 28601
The Center for Chamber Music Apple Hill Farm Nelson, N.H. 03445 Eugene A. Rosov, Executive Director 18 Lanark Road Wellesley, Mass. 02181	Strings	12-15	$825 Funded by the Center	5 weeks July-August	Executive Director	May 31	
Chautauqua Music School Chautauqua, New York 14722 Mrs. Jean Quinette, Coordinator for Schools	Piano, Strings, Organ, Dance	Violin, no minimum; Dance and Others 14 through 25	4 from $350 to $400 Funded by Conn., N.Y. Ohio, Penn	7 weeks July August	School	March 1 Audition by tape only	Mrs. William B. Millard Devon Tower Apt. 701 4920 Centre Avenue Pittsburgh, Pa. 15213
NFMC Eleanor Pasco Scholarship in Voice at Chautauqua Funded by family Endowment	Voice	16-25	NFMC $350 Matched by Chautauqua	7 weeks July August	School	June 1 Auditions held at Chautauqua near end of June	Mrs. William B. Millard Devon Tower Apt. 701 4920 Centre Avenue Pittsburgh, Pa. 15213
Eastern Music Festival Greensboro North Carolina 27405 Mr. Clare Humphrey Executive Director	Orchestral Instruments, Piano	12-18	$290 Partial Matched by Festival	6 weeks June July	School Director	April 1	Mrs. Stewart Cass 5712 Friendswood Dr. Greensboro, N.C. 27409
Foster, Stephen Collins, Music Camp Eastern Kentucky University Richmond, Kentucky 40475 Robert W. Hartwell, Director (Irene Muir Scholarships) Past National President Award	Instruments and Voice	Junior and Senior High	$500 to be awarded. 2 scholarships of $200 each, 1 of $100 (Funded by Muir Gift)	4 weeks	School Director c/o Eastern Kentucky University	May 1	Mrs. John Vickers 708 Hycliffe Drive Richmond, Kentucky 40475
Hummingbird Summer Music Camp Jemez Mountains, N. Mexico K. Lloyd Higgins, Director 1109 Dartmouth Dr. N.E. Albuquerque, N.M. 87106	Orchestra, Band	8-14	$87.50 1 week (½ session)	July-August	Director	April 1	Mrs. L.C. Rosenbaum 1813 Girard N.E. Apt. 4 Albuquerque, N.M. 87106
Idaho Federation of Music Clubs Gwladys Comstock Award for Music Camp of recipient's choice	Instrumental, Voice	12-18	$500 Funded by Idaho Federation		NFMC Representative	March 1 Audition by tape only	Mrs. Charles L. Wilson 511 Eighth Avenue, South Nampa, Idaho 83651

School	Category	Age Group	Amount of Scholarship	Camp Date	Write for Information to	Deadline for Application	NFMC Representative
Inspiration Point Fine Arts Colony Eureka Springs, Ark. 72632 Roger Cantrell, Executive Director Rt. 2, Box 348 AA (Hazel Post Gillette Scholarship)	Opera Study	High School or College	$500 Partial toward tuition, room, board	6 weeks June-July	NFMC Representative	April 15	Mrs. David C. Hobart 4035 Bluebonnet Houston, Texas 77025
International Music Camp Peace Gardens, North Dakota 58318 Dr. Merton Utgaard, Director Bottineau, North Dakota 58318 (Agnes Jardine Scholarships) A National Past President Award	Band, Orchestra, Twirling, Music, Drama, Dance	Senior in High School and Adult	$500 in Partials; One week each winner Funded by Jardine Endowment	8 weeks June-July	NFMC Representative	April 1	Mrs. Charles M. Pollock Park East Apt. 5-301 One South Second St. Fargo, North Dakota 58103
Kneisel Hall, Blue Hill, Maine 04614 Mr. Leslie Parnas, Director 6 Brentwood Avenue Newton Centre, Mass. 02159 NFMC Scholarship honoring Marianne Kneisel	Strings and Piano	15-28	$450 NFMC Matched by Center	7 weeks June-August	Mrs. Frank Kneisel Dean of Students Box 251 Castine, Maine 04421	April 1	Mrs. Ruth Simonds 104 West State Portland, Maine 04102
Marrowstone Music Festival 400 Boren Ave., North Seattle, Washington 98109 Vilem Sokol, Conductor and Director	Orchestral Instruments (except Percussion)	13-21	$220 Partial	3 weeks August	Seattle Youth Symphony 523 Pine Street Seattle, Wa. 98101	April 1	Mrs. Ralph Peel Rt. 1, Box 1522 Bremerton, Wa. 98310
Meadowmount Camp Westport, New York Mr. Ivan Galamian, Director c/o Society for Strings 170 West 73rd Street New York, N.Y. 10023	Strings	10-25	3 Partial; $100 each; matched by camp	8 weeks from last of June	School Director	April 1	Ms. Martha Beck Box 261 Rt. 3 Troy, New York 12180
Music Academy of the West Santa Barbara, California Miss Susanne L. Byars 1070 Fairway Road Santa Barbara, California 93103	Opera Study, Voice Technique	Open	$275 Partial Funded by California	July August	School Director	Feb. 1	Mrs. George Heimrich 29500 Heathercliff 128 Malibu, California 90265
National Music Camp Interlochen, Michigan 49643 Mr. Edward J. Downing Director	Piano, Voice Orchestral Instruments	Must be in High School	2 Partials; $600 each Funded by NFMC Lodge Income	8 weeks July August	NFMC Representative	Feb. 1	Mrs. Erwin E. Johnson 1424 Sherwood Ave. S.E. East Grand Rapids Michigan 49506
Oglebay Institute Opera Workshop Wheeling, West Virginia 26003 Boris Goldovsky, Director	Opera Coach Training for a Pianist Accompanist	18-25	$275 (tuition, room, board) Partial	4 weeks	NFMC Representative who is Director of Performing Arts	June 1	Mrs. Chase Greer 383 Oglebay Drive Wheeling, W. Va. 26003
Philadelphia College for the Performing Arts Schubert Theatre Bldg. 250 South Broad St. Philadelphia, Pa. 19102 Dr. Joseph Castaldo, Director	String Quartet	14-21	$1,000 Funded by the College	8 weeks July-August	School Director	March 1	Mr. Francis Welsh 992 Pratt St. Philadelphia Pa. 19124
Rocky Ridge Music Center Estes Park, Colorado 80517 Mrs. Beth Miller Harrod, Director	String Quartet	Junior or Senior High School	$350 NFMC (Partial) $150 Josephine Trott Memorial from state, matched by camp for quartet	7 weeks	NFMC Representative	April 1	Mrs. Dewey J. Ratcliff 507 Plumb Place Atwood, Kansas 67730
Santa Fe Opera Apprentice Artists Program P.O. Box 2408 Santa Fe, New Mexico 87501 John O. Crosby, Director (Ruth Freehoff Memorial)	Voice	20-30	$200 Partially funded by Ruth Freehoff bequest	Approx. June 15-August 30	Santa Fe Opera P.O. Box 2408 Santa Fe, N.M. 87501	Nov. 15	Mrs. Bert Kempers 600 Ridgecrest Dr. S.E. Albuquerque, N.M. 87108
Sewanee Music Center University of the South Sewanee, Tennessee 37375 Mrs. Martha McCrory, Director	Instrumentalist or Voice	High School or College	$500	5 weeks	School Director	April 1	Mrs. Charles S. Cuyler 4505 Princeton Road Memphis, Tennessee 38117
University of Wyoming Summer Music Camp Laramie, Wyoming 82070 Mr. Robert Mayes, Director Dept. of Music, University Station Box 3037 Laramie, Wyoming 82071	Orchestra, Band, Chorus, Piano, Theory	12-17 Grades 7-12	$100 for tuition, room, board	2 weeks June	School Director	May 15	Mrs. Bruce Howar 2904 Central Avenue Cheyenne, Wyoming 82001
Upper Midwest Music Camp University of South Dakota Vermillion, South Dakota 57069 Ray T. DeVilbiss, Director	Voice and Instrumental	Grades 8-12	$67 Partial	Second week of June	Director	April 15	Mrs. Clark Y. Gunderson 205 Lewis Vermillion, S.D. 57069
The Waldon School LTD Mountain School in Vershire Center, Vermont P.O. Box 5630 Baltimore, Maryland 21210 NFMC Scholarship in memory of Grace Newsom Cushman	Composition and Theoretical Skills	9-18	$400 Partial	5 weeks	Walden School LTD P.O. Box 5630 Baltimore, Md. 21210	April 1	Mrs. Henry Tiemeyer, Jr. 638 Aldershot Rd. Baltimore, Maryland 21229

BIENNIAL

School	Category	Age Group	Amount of Scholarship	Camp Date	Write for Information to	Deadline for Application	NFMC Representative
Berkshire Music Center Lenox, Mass. 01240 (Ada Holding Miller Fellowship) A Past National President Endowment Fund for Ada Holding Miller	Composition, Instrumental, Choral, Opera	18-25 as of March 1 Top Student	$1,000 partial School Awarded Biennially	8 weeks July August	Daniel Gustin Symphony Hall Boston, Mass. 02115	April 1 year of audition	Miss Irene L. Mulick 15 Concord Avenue Cranston, Rhode Island 02910

**Entrance Rule except for Young Artist Auditions: Applicants must be members or become members of the National Federation of Music Clubs, either by individual or group affiliation before the applications are accepted.

Bulletins for Young Artist Auditions, Student Auditions, Junior Festivals, Stillman-Kelley Rules and Procedures and Scholarship and Awards Charts may be ordered from NFMC Headquarters. Request a Publications List which indicates the cost of the above bulletins from: National Federation of Music Clubs, 1336 North Delaware Street, Indianapolis, Indiana 46202.

Foundations and Funding Organizations

U.S. foundations and grant-making organizations are listed alphabetically by state. The listing for Canada follows those for the U.S. Phone number, officers, areas of interest and support embracing the field of music, eligibility requirements, and person to contact for further information are given for most organizations. The number 1 following an organization's name indicates that they did not respond to our questionnaire. An alphabetical cross-index appears at the end of this section.

ALABAMA

ALABAMA STATE COUNCIL ON THE ARTS AND HUMANITIES
114 N. Hull St.
Montgomery, AL 36130
(205) 832-6758
Officers: Lamar S. Rainer, Jr., Council Chairman
Interests/Support: Music, creative and performing arts are among the Council's interests. Technical and financial assistance are given within communities thoughout Alabama to qualified organizations sponsoring arts events or programs; qualified organizations include local arts councils, arts associations, museums, literary associations, colleges and universities, dance and theatre groups with nonprofit status. The Council from time to time offers fellowships to Individual Alabama Artists who create art works: e.g., composers rather than performing musicians.
Contact for Further Information: Barbara George, Programs Coordinator

M.W. SMITH, JR., FOUNDATION
P.O. Box 691
Daphne, AL 36526
(205) 626-5436
Officers: Mrs. Eugene Pearson, Chairman; Ms. Margaret Huey, Advisor; Mrs. Mary Riser, Secretary; Mr. Ken Niemeyer, Trustee
Interests/Support: Music/performing arts will be of major interest to this Foundation in the next four years; however, the distribution committee has pledged most of the available funds for the next four years for a performing arts building at Huntington College in Montgomery, AL.
Eligibility: Applicants must be citizens of the State of Alabama, preferably southweat Alabama. No grants to individuals.
Contact for Further Information: Mrs. Mary Riser, Secretary; or Ms. Margaret Huey, Advisor, 25 Edgefield Rd., Mobile, AL 36608

ARKANSAS

ARKANSAS ARTS COUNCIL
Office of Arkansas State Arts and Humanities
Continental Bldg., Ste. 500
Markham at Main Sts.
Little Rock, AR 72201
(501) 371-2539
Officer: Mrs. Carolyn Staley, Executive Director
Interests/Support: Music, creative and performing arts are among the Council's interests. Grants are given on a matching fund requirements basis to supplement arts projects in the state. Grants may not be used for capital expenditures, entertaining, or deficit removal.
Eligibility: Matching-fund requirement; must be nonprofit organization located in Arkansas.
Contact for Further Information: Mrs. Carolyn Staley, Executive Director.

CALIFORNIA

ATLANTIC RICHFIELD FOUNDATION[1]
515 S. Flower St.
Los Angeles, CA 90071
(213) 486-3342
Officers: Walter D. Eichner, Executive Director; Fred A. Nelson, Associate Director; W.M. Marcussen, President
Interests/Support: Approximately 21% of the Foundation's giving is in the area of music/performing arts. Support is available for operating needs, projects that improve financial self-sufficiency, or for specific programs that promise specific impact.
Eligibility: Grants are limited to a few distinguished national cultural institutions and to organizations of regional significance that are located in geographic areas where the Foundations focuses its interest. No grants to individuals.
Contact for Further Information: Program Officer/Humanities & Arts

BANKAMERICA FOUNDATION
P.O. Box 37000 #3246
San Francisco, CA 94137
(415) 953-3175
Officers: Edward Truschke, Executive Director; Rosemary Mans, Associate Director; Victoria Wood, Program Officer, Cultural Affairs
Interests/Support: Music/performing arts is major interest within the Cultural Program. Support is limited primarily to orchestras located throughout California and major California performing arts organizations. The Foundation does not fund fellowships, scholarships, individual project grants, field study support, or curriculum development in this category.
Eligibility: Guidelines available on request.
Contact for Further Information: Victoria Wood, Program Officer, Cultural Affairs

LITTLE EMO
4105 Via Nivel
Palos Verdes Estates, CA 90274
(213) 375-3569

Officers: James Sitterly, Director and President; Claire Guillemin, Assistant Director
Interests/Support: Music/performing arts is a major interest. Little Emo seeks ways for musicians and other artists to complete their specific plans, including composition, performance, recording, publishing, and production of artistic projects that fall within the realms of positive reaffirmation of the greater good to humanity. Support is provided in the form of direct grants and technical assistance. Eligibility: Musicians should provide information about themselves and their projects in highly original and thought-provoking ways Applicants should show primary goals of humanitarian concern and artistic professionalism.
Contact for Further Information: James Sitterly, Director

MUSIC & ARTS INSTITUTE
2622 Jackson St.
San Francisco, CA 94115
(415) 567-1445
Officers: Ross McKee, Director and Trustee; LeRoy G. von Schottenstein, Paul L. Andrieu, John A. Cron, Mrs. Phyllis Mendoza, Mrs. Betty Lin, Mr. Lawrence R. Sherrill, Trustees
Interests/Support: Regular full-time tuition is based on a a subsidy of $2,000 per year in addition to the following: Outstanding Performers Award (3 per year) - $600 partial scholarship assistance for outstanding performers in programs leading to Bachelor and Master of Music Degrees; based on outstanding performance (one solo recital each year in school) and B+ grade average. Student Financial Assistance - $250 each school year based on need and satisfactory academic progress.
Contact for Further Information: Ross McKee, Director

DAVID & LUCILE PACKARD FOUNDATION
P.O. Box 1330
Los Altos, CA 94022
(415) 948-7658
Officers: David Packard, President; Lucile Packard, Vice-President and Treasurer; Nathan Finch, Secretary
Interests/Support: Music/performing arts is major among the Foundation's interests. Support is primarily for music in the schools; grants are available to regional orchestras and choirs, symphony orchestras, and music festivals.
Eligibility: Must be tax deductible organization serving the people of San Mateo, Santa Clara, Santa Cruz, and Monterey Counties.
Contact for Further Information: Cole Wilbur, Executive Director

PILLSBURY FOUNDATION
Santa Barbara Foundation, Trustee
11 E. Carrillo St.
Santa Barbara, CA 93101
(805) 963-1873
Officers: Arthur L. Brown, President; Edward R. Spaulding, Executive Director; Isable H. Bartolome, Scholarship Director.
Interests/Support: Music/performing arts is a major interest. Scholarship grants are available.
Eligibility: Must be a U.S. citizen and a rsident of Santa Barbara County.
Contact for Further Information: Isabel H. Bartolome, Scholarship Director

THE L.J. SKAGGS AND MARY C. SKAGGS FOUNDATION
1330 Broadway, Ste. 1730
Oakland, CA 94612
(415) 451-3300
Officers: Jillian Steiner Sandrock, Program Officer; Laura J. Lederer, Program Officer; Philip M. Jelley, Foundation Manager, Secretary
Interests/Support: Music/performing arts is major interest. Support is available for project grants.
Eligibility: Must have 510 (c) 3 tax-exempt status. No grants to individuals.
Contact for Further Information: David Knight, Administrative Assistant

YOUNG MUSICIANS FOUNDATION
914 S. Robertson Blvd.
Los Angeles, CA 90035
(213) 659-3766
Officers: Daniel Lewis, President; Erich Vollmer, Executive Director
Interests/Support: The Foundation offers exceptionally gifted young musicians significant peformance opportunities and financial assistance. Programs currently offered are: the Debut Orchestra and Conductor-in-Training and Manager-in-Training; Debut Competition; Musical Encounter; Scholarship; and Chamber Music Workshops.
Contact for Further Information: Erich Vollmer, Executive Director

THE LOREN L. ZACHARY SOCIETY FOR THE PERFORMING ARTS
2250 Gloaming Way
Beverly Hills, CA 90210
(213) 276-2731
Officers: Loren L. Zachary, M.D., President; Richard L. Wilkerson, Vice-President; Nedra Zachary, Secretary
Interests/Support: Music/performing arts is major interest. Support is available through an annual audition program for singers who are thoroughly trained and ready to pursue a professional operatic career.
Eligibility: Open to operatic singers between the ages of 21 and 35. Applications sent only upon receipt of self-addressed stamped envelope; apply in January each year.
Contact for Further Information: Nedra Zachary, Secretary

COLORADO

BOETTCHER FOUNDATION
800 Boston Bldg.
Denver, CO 80202
(303) 571-5510
Officers: John C. Mitchell, President and Executive Director; Mrs. Charles Boettcher, II, Chairman of the Board.
Interests/Support: Music/performing arts in a minor interest. Operating support is available for musical/performing arts organizations in the State of Colorado.
Eligibility: Must have 501 (c) (3) organization located in Colorado. No grants to individuals.
Contact for Further Information: John C. Mitchell, President and Executive Director

COLORADO COUNCIL ON THE ARTS & HUMANITIES
770 Pennsylvania St.
Denver, CO 80203
(303) 866-2617
Officers: Ellen Pierce, Executive Director; Lucien Wulsin, Chairman
Interests/Support: Music/performing arts is a major interest. Grants are available for nonprofit, tax-exempt, music organizations; fellowships to composers are planned.
Eligibility: Must be nonprofit tax-exempt organization located in Colorado.
Contact for Further Information: Lee Betton, Director of Arts Organizations Programs

THE DENVER FOUNDATION[1]
1880 Gaylord St.
Denver, CO 80206
(303) 322-5680
Officer: Patricia J. Harrington, Director
Interests/Support: Music/performing arts is a minor interest. The Denver Symphony Orchestra is supported with annual grants designated by the donor of one of the Denver Foundation Funds.
Eligibility: Giving is primarily local. The
Contact for Further Information: Patricia J. Harrington, Director.

THE FROST FOUNDATION, LTD.
650 S. Cherry St., Ste. 940
Denver, CO 80222
(303) 388-1687
Officers: Edwin F. Whited, President; Theodore Kauss, Vice-President and Executive Director; Greg Bradley, Secretary-Treasurer
Interests/Support: Music/performing arts is a minor interest. Grants are directed to the Shreveport Symphony and the Shreveport Regional Arts Council.
Eligibility: Must be tax-exempt organization. No grants to individuals.

Giving is local and regional.
Contact for Further Information: Theodore Kauss, Vice-President and Executive Director

GATES FOUNDATION
155 S. Madison St., Ste. 332
Denver, CO 80209
(303) 388-0871
Officers: Charles C. Gates, President; Robert G. Bonham, Vice-President; Jace E. McCandless, Treasurer
Interests/Support: Music/performing arts is a minor interest. Grants are available for capital construction and equipment for music and the performing arts.
Eligibility: Must have 501(c)(3) classification letter from the Internal Revenue Service; must have headquarters in Colorado, and project must also take place in Colorado.
Contact for Further Information: F. Charles Forelicher, Executive Director

CONNECTICUT

CONNECTICUT COMMISSION ON THE ARTS
340 Capitol Ave.
Hartford, CT 06106
(203) 566-7076
Officers: Susan Roach Kelly, Chairperson; Gary M. Young, Executive Director
Interests/Support: Grants are available to Connecticut artists, arts institutions, arts organizations and arts-sponsoring organizations for project support, technical assistance, and operational aid. Operational support is awarded to a selected group of professional arts organizations; a limited number of artists' fellowships are awarded each year.
Eligibility: Giving is limited to Connecticut.
Contact for Further Information: Gary M. Young, Executive Director.

DELAWARE

DELAWARE STATE ARTS COUNCIL
820 N. French St.
Wilmington, DE 19801
(302) 571-3540
Officers: Dr. Ann Houseman, Administrator; Mrs. Robert R. Hoopes, Chairman
Interests/Support: The Arts Council serves all arts disciplines equally. Support is available for the following: Individual Artist Fellowships; matching-fund Project Grants for organizations; Mini Grants; Artist-in-Education (residencies for artists or artistic groups in educational settings); and Ticket Sharing Grants (subsidy from the Arts Council for a portion of students' tickets to performing arts events, including musical presentations).
Eligibility: In general, and for most programs, Delaware residency and nonprofit, tax-exempt status are required. Specific requirements available on request.
Contact for Further Information: Dr. Ann Houseman, Administrator.

DISTRICT OF COLUMBIA

AMERICAN COLLEGE THEATER FESTIVAL
John F. Kennedy Center for the Performing Arts
Washington, DC 20566
(202) 254-3437
Officers: David Young, Producing Director; Evelyn Dewey, Administrator; Rick Graves, National Chairman
Interests/Support: Music/performing arts is major interest. The ASCAP College Musical Theatre Award is presented for outstanding achievement in the creation of a work for the musical theatre by college and university students.
Eligibility: Open only to full-time undergraduate or graduate students of accredited institutions of higher learning. Specific eligibility requirements available on request.
Contact for Further Information: Susan Henry, ACTF Staff Assistant

DISTRICT OF COLUMBIA COMMISSION ON THE ARTS AND HUMANITIES
420 Seventh St., 2nd Flr.
Washing, DC 20004
(202) 724-5613
Officers: Peggy Cooper Cafritz, Chairperson; Mildred E. Bautista, Executive Director
Interests/Support: Music/performing arts is major interest. Project and individual grants are available.
Eligibility: Must be residents of the District of Columbia.
Contact for Further Information: Staff Liaison, Music

THE KIPLINGER FOUNDATION, INC.
1729 H St., NW
Washington, DC 20006
(202) 887-6400
Officers: Austin H. Kiplinger, President; Arnold B. Barach, Secretary; Norman B. Mumaw, Treasurer; Rozella O. Flick, Assistant Secretary
Interests/Support: Music/performing arts is among the Foundation's interests. General support is available.
Eligibility: Giving is primarily local. No grants to individuals.
Contact for Further Information: Arnold B. Barach, Secretary

NATIONAL ENDOWMENT FOR THE ARTS
Columbia Plaza
2401 E St., NW
Washington, DC 20506
(202) 634-6369
Interests/Support: Grants to support excellence in music performance and creativity and to develop informed audiences for music throughout the country include: 1) nonmatching fellowships for composers to encourage the creation of new compositions, the completion of works in progress, and to generally assist their professional development; 2) assistance to artistic and educational programs that involve individuals and groups; 3) matching grants for postsecondary institutions whose programs provide outstanding training for professional careers in the field of music; 4) matching grants for symphony and chamber orchestras and national service organizations; 5) matching grants for ensembles, presenting organizations, and national service organizations to encourage the performance of new music, improve the quality of new music performances, and make new music performances more widely available; 6) matching grants for ensembles, presenting organizations, and national service organizations to encourage the performance of chamber music, improve the quality of chamber music performances, and make chamber music performance more widely available; 7) matching grants for choruses that pay all their singers, choruses affiliated with orchestras that are eligible for grants from the Endowment's Orchestra Program, independent choruses that pay some or none of their singers, and organizations that provide services to choruses in a major region or throughout the country to support high-qualifty choral activity and enhance the professional status fo the choral singer; 8) matching grants for music festivals whose programs involve two or more music program categories; 9) matching grants for nonprofit organizations for the recording and distribution of American music; 10) nonmatching fellowships for professional jazz performers for support of rehearsals, performances, and the preparation of audio and video demonstration tapes, professional jazz composers to encourage the creation of new works, the completion of works in progress, and the reproduction of scores or parts of completed works; and jazz performers and composers to study with recognized jazz masters of their choice in noninstitutional settings. In Fiscal Year 1984, the following grants are planned: 1) nonmatching fellowships for solo recitalists (vocalists and keyboard recitalists) to encourage their professional development; 2) matching grants for presenting organizations to present solo recitalists and residencies by solo recitalists; 3) matching grants for career development organizations which are devoted primarily to the professional career development of

American solo recitalists.
Eligibility: Requirements vary. Guidelines available on request.
Contact for Further Information: Music Program, National Endowment for the Arts.

NATIONAL OPERA INSTITUTE
John F. Kennedy Center
Washington, DC 20566
(202) 254-3694
Officers: Hal Prince, Chairman; Mrs. Lee D. Gillespie, President; Ann Getty, Dr. James Semans, Vice-Presidents; R.W. Driscoll, Secretary; H.E. Muller, Treasurer; John M. Ludwig, Executive Director; C.B. Ruttenberg, General Counsel.
Interests/Support: Support is available for all forms of music theater, including opera and musical theater. Also available are internships in production, administration, and composition; career grants for performers; and a workshop for works-in-progress
Eligibility: Organizations must have tax-exempt status under IRS Code 501(c)(3). Requirements vary.
Contact for Further Information: John M. Ludwig, Executive Director.

SMITHSONIAN INSTITUTION
Division of Performing ARts
2100 L'Enfant Plaza
Washington, DC 20560
(202) 287-3410
Officers: James R. Morris, Director; James M. Weaver, Director, Chamber Music Programs; Jewell S. Dulaney, Administrative Officer
Eligibility: Music/performing arts is a major interest. Fellowships and volunteer internships are available.
Eligibility: Requirements vary.
Contact for Further Information: James R. Morris, Director

FLORIDA

EDYTH BUSH CHARITABLE FOUNDATION, INC.
199 E. Welbourne Ave., P.O. Box 1967
Winter Park, FL 32790
(305) 647-4322
Officers: Charlotte B. Heuser, Chairman; David B. Roberts, President and CEO; H. Clifford Lee, Secretary/General Counsel
Interests/Support: Music/performing arts is minor interest for grantmaking. Project grants or grants through the United Fund for the Arts are limited to a five-county Central Florida area, with certain exceptions for special interests of Board Directors resident elsewhere.
Eligibility: Must be more than 51% privately funded and not controlled by tax-supported institute or government entity. Must have IRS 501(c)(3)—509(a) IRS exemption and "publicly supported" status.
Contact for Further Information: David R. Roberts, President (initial telephone contact preferred)

FLORIDA DEPARTMENT OF STATE
Division of Cultural Affairs
The Capitol
Tallahassee, FL 32301
(904) 487-2980
Officers: Phillip A. Werndli, Director
Interests/Support: Support is available for the following: Organizational/Institutional Grants-in-Aid; Individual Artists Fellowships; Technical Assistance Grants; and many other programs.
Eligibility: Organizations must be not-for-profit and incorporated in Florida. Individuals must be over 18 years of age resident in Florida. *Guidelines* for specific requirements available on request.
Contact for Further Information: Dr. Margaret Grauer, Arts Coordinator

GEORGIA

GEORGIA COUNCIL FOR THE ARTS AND HUMANITIES
2082 E. Exchange Pl., Ste. 100
Tucker, GA 30084
Officers: Frank Ratka, Director; Mrs. Rosemary C. Stiefel, Chairman
Interests/Support: Support is available for techinical assistance and grants for the arts, including music throughout Georgia.
Eligibility: Must be nonprofit, tax-exempt organization.

HAWAII

ATHERTON FAMILY FOUNDATION[1]
c/o Hawaiian Trust Company, Ltd.
P.O. Box 3170
Honolulu, HI 96802
(808) 525-8511
Officers: Alexander S. Atherton, President; Jane R. Giddings, Secretary
Interests/Support: Music/performing arts is a minor interest. Short term project grants are available.
Eligibility: Giving is primarily local. No grants to individuals.
Contact for Further Information: Jane R. Giddings, Secretary

SAMUEL N. & MARY CASTLE FOUNDATION[1]
c/o Hawaiian Trust Company, Ltd.
P.O. Box 3170
Honolulu, HI 96802
(808) 525-8511
Officers: W. Donald Castle, President; Jane R. Giddings, Secretary; James C. Castle, Vice-President
Interests/Support: Music is a minor interest. Short term project grants are available.
Eligibility: Giving is primarily local. No grants to individuals.
Contact for Further Information: Jane R. Giddings, Secretary

COOKE FOUNDATION, LIMITED[1]
c/o Hawaiian Trust Company, Ltd.
P.O. Box 3170
Honolulu, HI 96802
(808) 525-8511
Officers: Richard A. Cooke, Jr., President; Charles C. Spalding, Vice-President; Mrs. E. Lewers Paris, Secretary
Interests/Support: Music/performing arts is a minor interest. Short term project grants are available.
Eligibility: Giving is primarily local. No grants to individuals.
Contact for Further Information: Jane R. Giddings, Assistant Secretary

HAWAII STATE FOUNDATION ON CULTURE AND THE ARTS
335 Merchant St., Room 202
Honolulu, HI 96813
(808) 548-4145
Officers: Naomi Morita, Chairman; Sarah M. Richards, Executive Director
Interests/Support: Music/performing arts is major interest. Support is available for project grants to organizations.
Eligibility: Specific requirements available on request.
Contact for Further Information: Sarah M. Richards, Executive Director

MCINERNY FOUNDATION
P.O. Box 2390
Honolulu, HI 96804
(808) 523-2111
Interests/Support: Music/performing arts is a minor interest. Project and program grants are available.
Eligibility: Giving is limited to Hawaii. No grants to individuals.
Contact for Further Information: Lois C. Loomis, Vice-President and Charitable Foundations Officer, Bishop Trust Co., Ltd., Trustee

IDAHO

IDAHO COMMISSION ON THE ARTS
304 W. State St.
Boise, ID 83720
(208) 334-2119
Officers: Annette Park, Chairman; Joan Lolmaugh, Executive Director; George E. Michel, Community Arts Coordinator
Interests/Support: Music/performing arts is major interest. Support is available for project grants.
Eligibility: Must be nonprofit, tax-exempt organization or individual artist in Idaho.
Contact for Further Information: George E. Michel, Community Arts Coordinator.

ILLINOIS

ALSDORF FOUNDATION
4300 W. Peterson Ave.
Chicago, IL 60646
(312) 685-2001
Officers: James W. Alsdorf, President;

Marilynn B. Alsdorf, Vice-President; Belle Richard, Secretary
Interests/Support: Support is available for project grants, field study, and curriculum development; unrestricted grants are also available.
Eligibility: Must be tax-exempt organizations. No grants or awards to individuals.
Contact for Further Information: James W. Alsdorf, President

AMOCO FOUNDATION, INC.[1]
200 E. Randolph
Chicago, IL 60601
(312) 856-6306
Officers: Donald G. Schroeter, Executive Director
Interests/Support: Music/peforming arts is a minor interest. Support is available for operating, capital, and projects.
Eligibility: Giving is primarily local. No grants to individuals.
Contact for Further Information: D.G. Schroeter, Executive Director

BORG-WARNER FOUNDATION, INC.
200 S. Michigan Ave.
Chicago, IL 60604
(312) 322-8657
Officers: R.O. Bass, President
Interests/Support: Music/peforming arts is among the Foundation's interests. Support is given in the form of project grants.
Eligibility: Giving is primarily local. No grants to individuals.
Contact for Further Information: Ellen J. Benjamin, Grant Coordinator

THE CHICAGO COMMUNITY TRUST[1]
208 S. LaSalle St., Ste. 850
Chicago, IL 60604
(312) 372-3356
Officers: Mrs. Robert L. Foote, Chairman, Executive Committee; Robert W. Reneker, Vice-Chairman, Executive Committee; Bruce L. Newman, Executive Director
Interests/Support: Music/performing arts is a minor interest. Project grants, operating grants, and capital grants are available.
Eligibility: Giving in primarily local. No grants to individuals.
Contact for Further Information: Judy Southwich, Communications Officer

CIVIC ORCHESTRA OF CHICAGO
220 S. Michigan Ave.
Chicago, IL 60604
(312) 435-8159
Officers: Sir Georg Solti, Music Director; John S. Edwards, General Manager; Gordon B. Peters. Principal Conductor and Administrator
Interests/Support: All students accepted into the Civic Orchestra receive full tuition scholarships. Scholarships are also available to Civic Orchestra members to help defray the cost of private lessons.
Eligibility: Auditions for all positions ar held each September and May, and are judged by Chicago Symphony members.

THE CONSOLIDATED FOODS FOUNDATION
The First National Plaza
Chicago, IL 60602
(312) 726-2600
Officers: Robert L. Lauer, President; Barbara A. Quinn, Vice-President and Executive Director; Gordon H. Newman, Vice-President and Secretary
Interests/Support: Music/performing arts is among the Foundation's interests. Support is available for the following: matching grants program for employee gifts (include cultural organizations); direct grants to major Chicago cultural institutions; and special projects grants.
Eligibility: Must qualify as a tax-exempt charity under IRS Code 501 (c) 3.
Contact for Further Information: Barbara A. Quinn, Vice-President and Executive Director

DR. SCHOLL FOUNDATION[1]
111 W. Washington St.
Chicago, IL 60602
(312) 782-5515
Officers: William H. Scholl, President; Robert L. Milligan, Vice-President; James P. Economos, Secretary
Interests/Support: Music/performing arts is a minor interest. Project grants are available, primarily on a local basis.
Contact for Further Information: Charles F. Scholl, Associate Director

HARRIS BANK FOUNDATION
111 W. Monroe St.
Chicago, IL 60606
(312) 461-2121
Officers: John L. Stephens, President; Philip A. Delaney, Vice-President; H. Kris Ronnow, Secretary-Treasurer
Interests/Support: Education and cultural programs are among the Foundation's interests.
Eligibility: Giving is limited to the Chicago metropolitan area. No grants to individuals.
Contact for Further Information: H. Kris Ronnow, Secretary

INLAND STEEL-RYERSON FOUNDATION, INC.
30 W. Monroe St.
Chicago, IL 60603
(312) 346-0300
Officers: O. Robert Nottelmann, President; Raymond N. Carlen, Vice-President; Robert T. Carter, Secretary; Jay E. Dittus, Treasurer
Interests/Support: Music/performing arts is a minor interest. Suport is available to selected orchestras and opera companies.
Eligibility: Giving is in geographic areas of primary company concern. No grants to individuals.
Contact for Further Information: Robert T. Carter, Secretary

KATE NEAL KINLEY MEMORIAL FELLOWSHIP
University of Illinois at Urbana-Champaign
College of Fine and Applied Arts
110 Architecture Bldg.
608 E. Lorado Taft Dr.
Champaign, IL 61820
(217) 333-1661
Officers: Jack H. McKenzie, Dean, College of Fine & Applied Arts; Prof. Eugene Wicks, Director, School of Art & Design; Dr. Robert Bays, Director, School of Music
Interests/Support: Music/performing arts is major interest. One fellowship of $4,500 for advanced study in the fine arts is given annually.
Eligibility: Open to graduates of the College of Fine and Applied Arts of the University of Illinois and to graduates of similar institutions of equal educational standing whose principal or major studies have been in one of the following: Architecture, Art, or Music.
Contact for Further Information: Jack H. McKenzie, Dean

ROBERT R. MCCORMICK FOUNDATION
435 N. Michigan Ave., Ste. 1231
Chicago, IL 60611
(312) 222-3512
Officers: Charles T. Brumback, Chairman; William N. Clark, Executive Director and Secretary; George D. Hoffmann, Controller
Interests/Support: Music/performing arts is minor interest. Support is available for project grants and curriculum development.
Eligibility: Must be 501 (c) 3 organization in metropolitan Chicago.
Contact for Further Information: William N. Clark, Executive Director

THE NALCO FOUNDATION
2901 Butterfield Rd.
Oak Brook, IL 60521
(312) 887-7500
Officers: Charles A. LaToza, President & Director; Rita J. Secor, Vice-President, Executive Director & Director; Lloyd J. Palmer, Director; Clifford J. Carpenter, Treasurer; Pauline A. Russ, Secretary; Theresa A. Ryan, Assistant Secretary
Interests/Support: Music/performing arts is among the Foundation's interests. Grants are available for general operating expenses.
Eligibility: One- to two-page letter required. Must have 501 (c) (3) tax-exempt status. Giving is limited to the following geographic locations: Illinois, mainly the Chicago metropolitan area including DuPage County; Carson, CA; Garyville, LA; Jonesboro, GA; Paulsboro, NJ; and Sugar Land and

Freeport, TX. Deadline is October 1.
Contact for Further Information: Rita J. Secor, Vice-President and Executive Director

THE NORTHERN TRUST COMPANY CHARITABLE TRUST
50 S. LaSalle St.
Chicago, IL 60675
(312) 630-6000, x3538
Officers: Lawrence W. Gougler, Executive Vice-President, Corporate Secretary, and Chairman of the Contributions Committee; Marjorie W. Lundy, Community Affairs Officer and Secretary of the Contributions Committee
Interests/Support: Music/performing arts is a major interest. General support, capital support, project grants, and matching gifts are available.
Eligibility: Giving is primarily local. Must have nonprofit, tax-exempt status. No grants to individuals.
Contact for Further Information: Marjorie W. Lundy, Community Affairs Officer

THE QUAKER OATS FOUNDATION
345 Merchandise Mart Plaza
Chicago, IL 60654
(312) 222-6981
Officers: Robert D. Stuart, Jr., President; Luther C. McKinney, Vice-President; Richard D. Jacquith, Treasurer; W. Thomas Phillips, Secretary
Interests/Support: The Foundation has a Matching Gift Program for music/performing arts.
Eligibility: No grants to individuals
Contact for Further Information: W. Thomas Phillips, Secretary

UNITED AIRLINES FOUNDATION[1]
P.O. Box 66100
Chicago, IL 60666
(312) 952-5714
Officers: Monte Lazarus, President; Eileen M. Younglove, Vice-President and Secretary; D.O. Danis, Treasurer
Interests/Support: Music/performing arts is a major interest. Project grants and general operating funds are available for music/performing arts.
Eligibility: No grants to individuals. Grants and funds are restricted to citites serviced by United Airlines.
Contact for Further Information: Eileen M. Younglove, Vice-President and Secretary

INDIANA

CUMMINS ENGINE FOUNDATION
Box 3005-91052
Columbus, IN 47201
(812) 379-8617
Officers: Diana C. Leslie, Executive Director
Interests/Support: Performing arts is a minor interest. General support is given to local arts councils/groups where the Foundation maintains facilities (Columbus, IN; Jamestown, NY; Charleston, SC; Fostoria, OH; Memphis and Cookeville, TN).
Eligibility: Must have 501 (c) 3 status. Preference is given to plant community groups.
Contact for Further Information: David Dodson, Program Officer

LILLY ENDOWMENT INC.
2801 N. Meridian St.
P.O. Box 88068
Indianapolis, IN 46208
Officers: James T. Morris, Executive Vice-President
Interests/Support: Grants for music/performing arts are restricted to Indianapolis and Indiana.
Eligibility: Must be tax-exempt organization or institution. No grants to individuals.
Contact for Further Information: James T. Morris, Executive Vice-President

NATIONAL FEDERATION OF MUSIC CLUBS
1336 N. Delaware St.
Indianapolis, IN 46202
(317) 638-4003
Officers: Mrs. Jack C. Ward, President
Interests/Support: Scholarships and awards are available for students and adults who show proficiency in the fields of voice, instrumental peformance, dance, and composition. In most cases, applicants must be members of the National Federation of Music Clubs. Prizes are given for the performance and promotion of American music at summer music festivals; this program is open to summer music festivals, centers, and camps in the U.S. and its territories.
Contact for Further Information: Barbara Bryant, Executive Secretary; or Mrs. George Jordan, Chairman, Summer Scholarship, 740 Chestnut St., Camden, AR 71701

SINFONIA FOUNDATION
10600 Old State Rd.
Evansville, IN 47711
(812) 867-2433
Officer: Emile Serposs
Interests/Support: Research Assistance Grants are awarded to individuals for work in American music or music education.
Eligibility: Individuals must show evidence of previous successful writing and research or unusual knowledge or competence in the field. Candidate must hold a Masters degree or equivalent. Amount of grants vary, depending on need and nature of request.
Contact for Further Information: Daniel Beeman, Secretary-Treasurer

IOWA

IOWA ARTS COUNCIL
State Capital Complex
Des Moines, IA 50319
(515) 281-4451
Officers: Dr. Sam W. Grabarski, Executive Director; J.D. "Don" Singer, Chairman; Mary Hutchinson Tone, Vice-Chair
Interests/Support: Music/performing arts is part of the Council's multidisciplinary support of the arts. Funding is available for touring suport, project grants, and completion grants for some creative artists.
Eligibility: Cash match; must be nonprofit, tax-exempt organization in Iowa or Iowa resident.
Contact for Further Information: Marilyn Parks, Grants Officer

KANSAS

KANSAS ARTS COMMISSION
112 W. 6th, Ste. 401
Topeka, KS 66603
(913) 296-3335
Officers: Ruth Browne, President, Louise Brock-Lawson, Vice-President; Karen Rogers, Secretary/Treasurer
Interests/Support: Project grants are available for the coordination and development of the visual performing and literary arts in Kansas.
Eligibility: Institutions, individuals, associations, and corporations sponsoring arts projects in Kansas are eligible.
Contact for Further Information: Hannes Zacharias, Assistant Director and Grantsman

KENTUCKY

KENTUCKY ARTS COUNCIL
Berry Hill
Frankfort, KY 40601
(502) 564-3757
Officers: Al Smith, Chairman; Nash Cox, Director
Interests/Support: Music/performing arts is major interest. Project grants, technical assistance, and challenge grants are available. A pilot program is being developed for fellowships.
Eligibility: Must be nonprofit arts or community organization in Kentucky.
Contact for Further Information: Anne Ogden, Director, Arts Program

MASSACHUSETTS

BERKSHIRE MUSIC CENTER
Boston Symphony Orchestra, Inc.
Symphony Hall
Boston, MA 02115
(617) 266-5241
Officers: Richard Ortner, Administrator
Interests/Support: The Fellowship Program aids young musicians (composers, conductors, singers, and instrumentalists) who have completed formal training and are interested in

undertaking intensive work on performance. Fellowships are tenable at the Berkshire Music Center, Tanglewood, Lenox, MA, for a period of eight weeks in July and August.
Eligibility: Admission is by audition only.
Contact for Further Information: Richard Ortner, Administrator

CUMMINGTON COMMUNITY OF THE ARTS
Cummington, MA 01026
(413) 634-2172
Officer: Carol Morgan, Director
Interests/Support: Summer and winter residencies at the Community are available to writers, musicians, visual artists and other artists.
Eligibility: Must be 18 years of age or older.
Contact for Further Information: Carol Morgan, Director

THE EASTERN ASSOCIATED FOUNDATION
One Beacon St.
Boston, MA 02108
(617) 742-9200
Officers: Jesse R. Mohorovic, Secretary; Eleanor A. Tishler, Contributions Representative
Interests/Support: Approximately 22% of the Foundation's budget is allocated to civic and cultural organizations.
Eligibility: Giving is primarily in the greater Boston area, Appalachia, and the Mississippi River Valley. Must be nonprofit, tax-exempt organization. No grants to individuals.
Contact for Further Information: Eleanor A. Tishler, Contributions Representative

FROMM MUSIC FOUNDATION AT HARVARD UNIVERSITY
Music Building
Cambridge, MA 02138
(617) 495-2791
Officers: Christoph Wolff, Chairman; Paul Fromm, Gunther Schulier, Directors
Interests/Support: Performance, publication, and recording of contemporary music are the Foundation's interests. Prizes for existing works are also awarded.

PEABODY MASON MUSIC FOUNDATION SPONSORSHIP FOR PIANISTS[1]
192 Commonwealth Ave., Ste. 4
Boston, MA 02116
(617) 266-3314
Officer: Paul Doguereau, President
Officers: An annual cash stipend for two years, plus a New York and Boston recital; is awarded to one qualified pianist with financial means to concentrate on repertoire development for two full year.
Eligibility: Must send application and tapes of repertoire, five performances.

PERMANENT CHARITY FUND OF BOSTON
One Boston Pl
Boston, MA 02106
(617) 723-7415
Officers: Dwight L. Allison, President; William W. Wolbach, Vice-President; Geno A. Ballotti, Director
Interests/Support: Music/performing arts is among the Fund's interests. Project grants are available.
Eligibility: Giving is primarily local. Must be tax-exempt organization. No grants to individuals.
Contact for Further Information: Geno A. Ballotti, Director

POLAROID FOUNDATION, INC.
750 Main St.
Cambridge, MA 02139
(617) 577-4035
Officers: Marcia Schiff, Executive Director; Donna Ferrovia, Administrator
Interests/Support: Contributions are based on review and decisions made by an Operating Committee that meets monthly. Four subcommittees regularly review and evaluate proposals—Community, Cultural, Education, and New Bedford. Fine arts organizations and community-based groups with an interest in grass roots cultural activities are assisted through the Cultural Matching Gifts Program for Polaroid Corporation employees and directors and through direct grants.
Eligibility: Giving is primarily local. No grants to individuals.
Contact for Further Information: Marcia Schiff, Executive Director; Donna Ferrovia, Administrator

TRUSTEES UNDER THE WILL OF LOTTA M. CRABTREE
Lotta Educational Fund
73 Tremont St.
Boston, MA 02108
Officers: Thomas F. Donohue, Michael J. Harney, and Edward C. Hamaty, Trustees
Interests/Support: Support is available through a scholarship grant to the New England Conservatory of Music for the benefit of four students.
Eligibility: Students must apply at the conservatory and be recommended by the Conservatory to the Trustees.

MICHIGAN

ASSOCIATED MALE CHORUSES OF AMERICA, INC. SCHOLARSHIP FUND
106 Maplefield Rd.
Pleasant Ridge, MI 48069
Officers: William June, Chairman; Russell R. Fleharty, Executive Secretary
Interests/Support: Four scholarships of $300 per year are given to deserving male vocal students to further vocal training while in college.
Contact for Further Information: William June, Chairman, P.O. Box 218, Munising, MI 49862

DETROIT GRAND OPERA ASSOCIATION
500 Temple Ave.
Detroit, MI 48201
(313) 832-5200
Officers: Melodee A. DuBois, Vice-President and Managing Director
Interests/Support: The following opera scholarships and awards are available to musical performers in the Detroit District of the Metropolitan Opera National Council or to students during the past six months in the district: Samuel J. Lang Scholarship; Elizabeth Hodges Donovan Award; Henry E. Wenger Award. Auditions are held In the fall, generally in late October or early November.
Eligibility: Open to residents of Michigan and Lucas, Fulton, and Ottawa Counties in Ohio. Applicants must be in following age brackets: sopranos, 20-30; mezzos and contraltos, 20-30; tenors, 20-32; baritones, 20-32; basso, 20-33. Additional requirements available on request.
Contact for Further Information: Mrs. Sam B. Williams, Scholarship Chairman

THE KRESGE FOUNDATION
P.O. Box 3151
2401 W. Big Beaver Rd.
Troy, MI 48084
(313) 643-9630
Officers: William H. Baldwin, Chairman; Alfred H. Taylor, Jr., President; John E. Marshall, III, Executive Vice-President
Interests/Support: Music/performing arts is among the seven categories of interest. Grants are made only toward construction of facilities, renovation of facilities, purchase of major movable equipment (unit cost of at least $75,000), or purchase of real estate.
Eligibility: Must be tax-exempt institution. No grants to individuals. Brochure describing policies and application procedures available on request.
Contact for Further Information: Alfred H. Taylor, Jr., President

MCGREGOR FUND
333 W. Fort Bldg., Ste. 1380
Detroit, MI 48226
(313) 963-3495
Officers: Elliott H. Phillips, President; Lem Bowen, Vice-President; W. Warren Shelden, Secretary; Jack L. Otto,Executive Director
Interests/Support: Music/performing arts is a minor interst. Support is available for project grants to nonprofit organizations.
Eligibility: Must be nonprofit organization located in Michigan, preferably southeastern Michigan.
Contact for Further Information: Sylvia L. McNarney, Program Director

MICHIGAN COUNCIL FOR THE ARTS
1200 Sixth Ave.
Detroit, MI 48226
(313) 256-3732
Officers: Governor appointed board
Interests/Support: Music/performing arts is major interest. Project grants for musical organizations, commissions, and series; and Fellowship/Creative Artist grants for composers are available. Services and publications are available free of charge.
Eligibility: Must be a Michigan-based nonprofit organization or artist resideing in Michigan.
Contact for Further Information: Jack Olds, Director, Office of Grants Programs; or Craig Carver, Artist Grants Coordinator

THE MIDLAND FOUNDATION
117 McDonald St.,
P.O. Box 289
Midland, MI 48640
(517) 839-9661
Officers: Mrs. Esther S. Gerstacker, President; Mrs. Mary Neely, Vice-President; Mr. E. Ned Brandt, Vice-President; Mr. Julius Grosberg, Treasurer; Dr. Roy Goethe, Vice-President; Mr. James Kendall, Secretary
Interests/Support: One scholarship to the Interlochen Arts Academy is available.
Contact for Further Information: Mr. Firmin A. Paulus, Executive Director

MINNESOTA

BURLINGTON NORTHERN FOUNDATION[1]
176 E. Fifth St.
St. Paul, MN 55101
(612) 298-3191
Officers: R.W. Bernard, Executive Director
Interests/Support: Music/performing arts is a minor interest. Primarily local giving in the form of oeprating and capital to symphony orchestras in cities local to operations of Burlington Northern, Inc.
Contact for Further Information: R.W. Bernard, Executive Director

DAYTON HUDSON FOUNDATION
777 Nicollet Mall
Minneapolis, MN 55402
(612) 370-6553
Officers: Peter C. Hutchinson, Chairman; Margaret V.B. Wurtele, Manager; Terri D. Barreiro, Manager
Interests/Support: Music/performing arts is a major interest. Support available includes general, capital, program, project, exhibition underwriting, equipment and staff development to full-time professional arts organizations in communities where Dayton Hudson Corporation has retail operations (primarily Minneapolis-St. Paul area).
Eligibility: No grants to individuals. Must have 501 (c) (3) status.
Contact for Further Information: Margaret Wurtele, Manager.

HONEYWELL FUND[1]
Honeywell Plaza (MN12-5259)
Minneapolis, MN 55408
(612) 870-6822
Officers: Edward C. Lund, President; Wayne E. Petersen, Vice-President; Lou E. Navin, Treasurer
Interests/Support: Music/performing arts is a minor interest—less than 20% of total budget. Boston Symphony Orchestra receives operating funds; Guild of Performing Arts (Minneapolis) receives funds for community concerts.
Eligibility: Support is generally restricted to citites where Honeywell has major manufacturing facilities. No grants to individuals.
Contact for Further Information: John N. Mitchell, Director

MINNEAPOLIS STAR AND TRIBUNE COMPANY CONTRIBUTIONS PROGRAM[1]
IDS Tower, 6th Flr.
Minneapolis, MN 55402
(612) 375-7000
Officers: Elizabeth F. Stevenson, Director of Public Affairs
Interests/Support: About 66% of total grants are to arts organizations; grants to the arts total about 20% of the Company's grants. Support is generally for operating expenses for several area theaters, orchestras, and an opera company.
Eligibility: Giving is primarily local. No grants to individuals.
Contact for Further Information: Elizabeth F. Stevenson, Director of Public Affiars

MINNEAPOLIS STAR AND TRIBUNE FOUNDATION[1]
IDS Tower, 6th Flr.
Minneapolis, MN 55402
(612) 375-7000
Officers: Elizabeth F. Stevenson, Executive Vice-President
Interests/Support: About 40% of total grants are to arts organizations; grants to the arts total about 36% of all Foundation grants. Grants are made over several years to performing arts organizations for capital improvements and endowment funds.
Eligibility: Giving is primarily local. No grants to individuals.
Contact for Further Information: Elizabeth F. Stevenson, Executive Vice-President

MINNESOTA STATE ARTS BOARD
432 Summit Ave.
St. Paul, MN 55102
(612) 297-2603
Interests/Support: Support is available for the following programs: direct grants to producing organizations in the disciplines of performing arts and literary arts; project grants to individuals in the disciplines of music, theater, and dance; arts in education support in all disciplines; and local art development support in all disciplines.
Eligibility: Must be individual artist or nonprofit, tax-exempt organization in Minnesota.

NORTHWEST AREA FOUNDATION
W975 First National Bank Bldg.
St. Paul, MN 55101
(612) 224-9635
Officers: W. John Driscoll, Chairman of the Board and Treasurer; Irving Clark, First Vice-Chairman of the Board; John D. Taylor, President, Secretary and Assistant Treasurer
Interests/Support: The Foundation sends out a Request for Proposal in the Arts annually. It is distributed to arts agencies in the Saint Paul/Minneapolis area. It changes annually.
Eligibility: Must be nonprofit, tax-exempt organization.
Contact for Further Information: John D. Taylor

MISSOURI

MISSOURI ARTS COUNCIL
Wainwright State Office Complex
111 N. 7th St., Ste. 105
St. Louis, MO 63101
(314) 444-6845
Officers: Rick Simoncelli, Executive Director
Interests/Support: Financial Matching Assistance is available to the limit of appropriated funds for worthwhile arts related projects by qualifying arts organizations on a competitive basis. An appointed council makes decisions on all projects annually.
Eligibility: Criteria available on request.
Contact for Further Information: Information Officer

SPENCER T. AND ANN W. OLIN FOUNDATION
7701 Forsyth Blvd., Ste. 1239
St. Louis, MO 63105
(314) 727-6202
Officers: Rolla J. Mottaz, President; J. Lester Willemetz, Treasurer
Interests/Support: Music/performing arts is a minor interest. Support is local and has been limited to the St. Louis Symphony
Contact for Further Information: Rolla J. Mottaz, President

MONTANA

MONTANA ARTS COUNCIL
1280 S. Third St. West
Missoula, MT 59801
(406) 543-8286
Officers: David E. Nelson, Executive Director; Jessica Stickney,

Chairperson; Jo-Anne Mussulman, Grants Officer
Interests/Support: Music/performing arts is major interest, along with dance, drama, visual arts, and special projects. Support is available for project grants.
Eligibility: 501 (c) (3) status.
Contact for Further Information: David E. Nelson, Executive Director

NEBRASKA

NEBRASKA ARTS COUNCIL
1313 Farnam-on-the-Mall
Omaha, NE 68102-1873
(402) 554-2122
Officers: LaVon K. Crosby, Chairman; Dick C.E. Davis, Vice-Chairman
Interests/Support: Music/performing arts is major interest. Available support includes project grants; general operating support to arts organizations; and artist residencies through the Artists-in-Schools/Communities program.
Eligibility: Must have articles of Incorporation on file with the State of Nebraska as a not-for-profit organization. Additional requirements are listed in the "Nebraska Arts Council Guidelines", available on rquest.
Contact for Further Information: Robin Tryloff, Executive Director

NEVADA

NEVADA STATE COUNCIL ON THE ARTS
329 Flint St.
Reno, NV 89501
(702) 784-6231
Officers: Royal Orser, Chairman; Nancy Houssels, Vice-Chairman; Toni Lowden, Secretary-Treasurer
Interests/Support: Music/performing arts is major interest. Grants are awarded to individuals and arts organizations; technical assistance and information services are available. The Agency also offers a statewide Artists-in-Residence program.
Eligibility: Individual grant applicants must have been a resident of Nevada for at least one year. Organizational applicants must be nonprofit, tax-exempt organizations incorporated in Nevada.
Contact for Further Information: Jacqueline Belmont, Executive Director

NEW JERSEY

ALLIED FOUNDATION
Box 2245-R
Morristown, NJ 07960
(201) 455-2671
Officers: E.L. Hennessy, Jr., Chairman; D.G. Powell, President; A.S. Painter, VP and Executive Director
Interests/Support: Music/performing arts is minor interest. Operating grants to symphonies, orchestras, and dance companies are available.
Eligibility: As a policy, program must be located near a principal facility.
Contact for Further Information: Mrs. M. Peter, Administrator

NEW JERSEY STATE COUNCIL ON THE ARTS
109 W. State St.
Trenton, NJ 08608
(609) 292-6130
Officer: Wendy McNeil, Acting Assistant Executive Director
Interests/Support: Fellowships and matching grants are available for artists who are residents of New Jersey. Disciplines include music, dance, music composition, crafts, prose, poetry, film, video, photography, playwriting, sculpture, painting and mixed media graphics.
Eligibility: Must be New Jersey resident or nonprofit organization located in New Jersey.
Contact for Further Information: Wendy McNeil, Acting Assistant Executive Director

NEW MEXICO

HELENE WURLITZER FOUNDATION OF NEW MEXICO
P.O. Box 545
Taos, NM 87571
(505) 758-2413
Officer: Henry A. Sauerwein, Jr., President
Interests/Support: Residence grants are provided to stimulate creativity in music and other fields of the humanities.
Contact for Further Information: Henry A. Sauerwein, Jr., President

NEW YORK

AFFILIATE ARTISTS INC.
155 W. 68th St.
New York, NY 10023
(212) 580-2000
Officers: Richard C. Clark, President; Jesse Rosen, Vice-President, Program Development and Suport; Nicholas J. Poliseno, Vice-President, Finance and Treasurer
Interests/Support: Music/performing arts is major interests. Appointed performers participate in Affiliate Artists Residencies, Affiliate Artists' Xerox Pianists Programs, and the Exxon/Arts Endowment Conductors Program.
Contact for Further Information: Open to classical singers, instrumentalists, actors, mimes, dancer/choreographers, and conductors. Applicants should generally have at least 3 but no more than 10 years of professional performing experience; guidelines vary by discipline.
Contact for Further Information: Carol Wolff, Director of Artist Recruitment and Qualification

AMERICAN ACADEMY AND INSTITUTE OF ARTS AND LETTERS
633 W. 155th St.
New York, NY 10032
(212) 368-5900
Interests/Support: The Richard Rodgers Production Award is given to subsidize a production in the City of New York of a musical play by authors and composers whose works have not been commercially performed. Goddard Lieberson Fellowships are given to a young composer(s) of extraordinary gifts. Marc Bitzstein Award for Musical Theatre is given periodically to a composer, lyricist, or librettist to encourage the creation of works of merit for the musical theater. Charles Ives Scholarships are given to young composers for continued study in composition. Academy-Institute Awards are given to honor and encourage distinguished artists, composers and writers who are not members of the Institute to help them to continue their creative work. The Marjorie Peabody Waite Award is conferred on an older artist, writer or composer, in rotation, for continuing achievement and integrity in his art. The Gold Medal is an annual award for distinguished achievement in two of eleven categories of the arts, including music, and is based on the entire work of the recipient, who must be a U.S. citizen.
Eligibility: Fellowships, awards and scholarships are by nomination only.

AMERICAN EXPRESS FOUNDATION[1]
American Express Plaza
New York, NY 10004
(212) 323-3475
Officers: Stephen S. Halsey, President; Juliet F.J. Zygmunt, Secretary; M. Beth Salerno, Assistant Secretary
Interests/Support: A small percent of the budget goes to music/performng arts. Contributions are made to a few of the national performing arts centers. A limited number of modest grants are made to some of the major music organizations in headquarters community and major operations centers in Phoenix, AZ; Ft. Lauderdale, FL; and Denver, CO.
Eligibility: No grants to individuals.
Contact for Further Information: Leenie Eisenberg, Contributions Assistant

AMERICAN SOCIETY OF COMPOSERS, AUTHORS AND PUBLISHERS[1]
One Lincoln Plaza
New York, NY 10023
(212) 595-3050
Interests/Support: ASCAP-Deems Taylor Awards are given for the best nonfiction books and for the best articles about music and/or its

creators. Book awards are $500 each; article awards are $250 each.
Contact for Further Information: Michael A. Kerker

ASIAN CULTURAL COUNCIL
280 Madison Ave.
New York, NY 10016
(212) 684-5450
Officers: Richard S. Lanier, President; Elizabeth J. McCormack, Vice-President and Secretary; Isaac Shapiro, Treasurer
Interests/Support: Music/performing arts is major interests. Fellowships are available for individual artists, students, and scholars from Asia for observation, training, study, and research in the United States. Very limited support is available for Americans going to Asia.
Contact for Further Information: Richard S. Lanier, Director

CHARLES ULRICK AND JOSEPHINE BAY FOUNDATION, INC.
14 Wall St., 16th Flr.
New York, NY 10005
(212) 227-8746
Officers: Synnova Hayes, President and Director; Frederick Bay, Secretary and Director; Robert W. Ashton, Executive Director; Raymond I. Paul, Vice-President and Director
Interests/Support: Music/performing arts is minor interest. Support for performing arts groups is available only indirectly for educational programming for pre-college children, which is part of the educational grants category of the Foundation.
Eligibility: Must be publicly supported, tax-exempt organization.
Contact for Further Information: Robert W. Ashton, Executive Director

THE MARY DUKE BIDDLE FOUNDATION
30 Rockefeller Plaza, Room 4304/5
New York, NY 10020
(212) 247-3400
Officers: James H. Semans, Chairman; Mary D.B.T. Semans, Vice-Chairman; F.R. Pemberton, Secretary-Treasurer
Interests/Support: Music/performing arts is a major interest.
Eligibility: Must be tax-exempt organization in the states of New York and North Carolina.
Contact for Further Information: F.R. Pemberton, Secretary-Treasurer

BOOTH FERRIS FOUNDATION
30 Broad St.
New York, NY 10004
(212) 269-3850
Officers: Robert J. Murtagh, Trustee; Morgan Guaranty Trust Co., Trustee
Interests/Support: Music/performing arts is a minor interest. General fund, program, and Capital support is available.
Eligibility: Must be legal not-for-profit agency or institution. No grants to individuals.
Contact for Further Information: Robert Murtagh, Trustee

CARRIER CORPORATION FOUNDATION, INC.[1]
Carrier Tower
P.O. Box 4800
Syracuse, NY 13221
(315) 424-4787
Officers: Richard Morris, President; Patricia W. Gonzalez, Vice-President and Secretary
Interests/Support: Capital development support is available for music/perpforming arts.
Eligibility: Giving is primarily in headquarters and plant cities. No grants to individuals.
Contact for Further Information: Patricia W. Gonzalez, Vice-President and Secretary

MARY FLAGLER CARY CHARITABLE TRUST
16 E. 34th St.
New York, NY 10016
Interests/Support: Support is available for professional performing organizations, the training of orchestral musicians, new music, and the teaching of music in several community music schools.
Eligibility: Must be tax-exempt organization. No grants to individuals. Giving is limited to New York City.
Contact for Further Information: Edward A. Ames, Trustee

THE CHASE MANHATTAN BANK, N.A.[1]
1 Chase Manhattan Plaza
New York, NY 10081
(212) 552-4411/13
Officers: John R. Meekin, VP and Director of Philanthropic Activities; Daniel F. Bonner, Contributions Officer; Alice Sachs Zimet, Contributions Officers
Interests/Support: Music/performing arts is a minor interest. Support is usually given for general operating purposes; occasionally, support is given for special projects.
Eligibility: Giving is primarily in the metropolitan New York area. No grants to individuals.
Contact for Further Information: Alice S. Zimet, Contributions Officer

THE CLARK FOUNDATION
30 Wall St.
New York, NY 10005
Officers: Stephen C. Clark, Jr., President, Michael A. Nicolais, Vice-President; Edward W. Stack, Secretary
Interests/Support: Music/performing arts is a minor interest.
Eligibility: Giving is primarily local. No grants to individuals.
Contact for Further Information: Edward W. Stack, Secretary

CORNING GLASS WORKS FOUNDATION[1]
Corning, NY 14831
(607) 974-8489
Officers: Thomas S. Buechner, President; Richard B. Bessey, Vice-President and Executive Director; George H. Southworth, Program Director
Interests/Support: Music/performing arts is a minor interest. Program support is usually restricted to communities where Corning Glass Works has manufacturing plants.
Eligibility: No grants to individuals.
Contact for Further Information: George H. Southworth, Program Director

THE CORPORATION OF YADDO
Box 395
Saratoga Springs, NY 12866
(518) 584-0746
Officers: Curtis Harnack, Executive Director; Carol Bullard, Director for Development; Newman E. Wait, Jr., President
Interests/Support: Music/performing arts is a major interest. The Corporation provides room, board, and studio space for composers generally from two weeks to two months.
Eligibility: Composers must have had work of high artistic merit performed and have other projects underway.
Contact for Further Information: Curtis Harnack, Executive Director (written inquiries only).

CREATIVE ARTISTS PROGRAM SERVICE, INC. (CAPS)
250 W. 57th St.
New York, NY 10019
(212) 247-6303
Interests/Support: Music composition is among the fields of interest. Fellowships are available to individual New York artists to create new work or complete work in progress. All recipients participate in short-term community-related and/or residencies in community organizations or institutions, public and private in New York state.
Eligibility: Must be residents of New York state.
Contact for Further Information: Hildy Tow, Applications Coordinator

ALICE M. DITSON FUND OF COLUMBIA UNIVERSITY
703 Dodge
Columbia University
New York, NY 10027
(212) 280-3825
Officers: Jack Beeson, Secretary; Douglas Hunt, Otto Leuning, J. Kellum Smith, Jr., Vladimir Ussachevsky, and Robert Ward, Officers of the Advisory Committee
Interests/Support: Music/performing arts is a minor interest. Aid is available to living American composers who are not

yet widely known, specifically to those of later years who have undeservedly received little notice. Aid is given primarily for performance, recording or publication.
Eligibility: Letter to Secretary required.
Contact for Further Information: Jack Beeson, Secretary, Advisory Committee

FORD FOUNDATION[1]
320 E. 43rd St.
New York, NY 10017
(212) 537-5000
Officers: Richard Sheldon and Marcia T. Thompson, Program Officers; Laurice H. Sarraf, Administrative Officer
Interests/Support: Music creative and performing arts are special interests of the Ford Foundation. Grants are aimed at various types of music, from opera to jazz, and various types of musical skills, writing music, lyrics, librettos, etc. Grants are given locally and nationally to associations, colleges and universities, conservatories, small touring productions, foundations, and training institutes.
Contact for Further Information: Richard Sheldon, Program Officer

GANNETT FOUNDATION, INC.
Lincoln Tower-26th Flr.
Rochester, NY 14604
(716) 262-3315
Officers: Eugene C. Dorsey, President; John A. Scott, Chairman
Interests/Support: Music/performing arts is a minor interest. Support is available primarily for one-time project grants: capital and operating support in the areas of dance, drama, and music. No fellowships, scholarships, field study support, or curriculum development are available.
Eligibility: Must be nonprofit, tax-exempt organization located in an area served by Gannett Co., Inc.; on newspapers, broadcast stations, and outdoor advertising companies who have the recommendation of that Gannett chief executive officer.
Contact for Further Information: Calvin Mayne, Vice-President/Grants Administration

JOHN SIMON GUGGENHEIM MEMORIAL FOUNDATION
90 Park Ave.
New York, NY 10016
(212) 687-4470
Officers: Gordon N. Ray, President; G. Thomas Tanselle, Vice-President; Stephen L. Schlesinger, Secretary
Interests/Support: Music fellowships are awarded to composers of music or to scholars who propose research into the history or theory of music.
Eligibility: Fellows are usually between 30 and 45 years of age; the Committee of Selection is empowered, however, to nominate persons older than 45 and younger than 30.
Contact for Further Information: Stephen L. Schlesinger, Secretary.

HEINEMAN FOUNDATION FOR RESEARCH, EDUCATIONAL, CHARITABLE & SCIENTIFIC PURPOSES, INC.
c/o Fox & Co.
1211 Ave. of the Americas
New York, NY 10036
(212) 688-2028
Officers: James H. Heineman, President; Marion Rose, Vice-President; Robert Fehr, Treasurer
Interests/Support: Music/performing arts is a minor interest. General purpose support is available.
Contact for Further Information: James H. Heineman, President

INSTITUTE OF INTERNATIONAL EDUCATION
809 United Nations Plaza
New York, NY 10017
(212) 883-8454
Interests/Support: Partial travel grants for participation in selected international music competitions abroad are available. Competitions to be included in each year's program are selected by the Institute's Music Committee
Contact for Further Information: Robert F. Morris, Secretary, Music Committee

INTERNATIONAL PAPER COMPANY FOUNDATION
International Paper Plaza
77 W. 45th St.
New York, NY 10036
(212) 536-5986
Officers: James W. Guedry, President; Gladys F. Waltemade, Vice-President
Interests/Support: Music/perpforming arts is a minor interest. Project support is available to organizations in International Paper Company communities.
Eligibility: Must be tax-exempt organization. No grants to individuals.
Contact for Further Information: Gladys F. Waltemade, Vice-President

THE CHRISTIAN A. JOHNSON ENDEAVOR FOUNDATION
1060 Park Ave.
New York, NY 10028
(212) 534-6752
Officers: Mrs. Wilmot H. Kidd, President
Interests/Support: Music/performing arts is a minor interest. Scholarship grants are available to institutions. Some limited sustaining support of musical organizations is known to the Foundation.
Eligibility: No grants to individuals. Giving is limited to Eastern U.S. Proposals must be received from October 1 to February 1.
Contact for Further Information: Mrs. Wilmot H. Kidd, President

THE KOSCIUSZKO FOUNDATION
15 E. 65th St.
New York, NY 10021
(212) 734-2130
Interests/Support: Music and performing arts are a major interest. Support includes the following: The Chopin Piano Scholarships and the Marcella Sembrich Scholarship in Voice for further study at recognized music schools or with a private teacher; and The Michael Twarowski Scholarship for piano or violin graduate study for an American of Polish extraction.
Eligibility: Requirements vary depending on specific scholarship.
Contact for Further Information: Grants Office (address above)

ALBERT KUNSTADTER FAMILY FOUNDATION
1035 Fifth Ave.
New York, NY 10028
(212) 249-1733 or (212) 593-0274
Officers: P. Kunstadter, Chairman; J.W. Kunstadter, President; G.S. Kunstadter, Vice-President and Secretary
Interests/Support: Music/performing arts is a minor interest. General support is available.
Eligibility: Must have 501 (c) 3 status.
Contact for Further Information: John W. Kunstadter, President

LIEDERKRANZ FOUNDATION
6 E. 87th St.
New York, NY 10028
(212) 534-0880, 245-8769
Interests/Support: Scholarships are given to encourage and provide financial assistance to deserving musical talents.
Contact for Further Information: Professor Edward Weiss, Vice-President, Music and Arts

THE MACMILLAN FOUNDATION
866 Third Ave.
New York, NY 10022
(212) 935-2017
Officers: Paul Chenet, Assistant Treasurer
Interests/Support: Music/performing arts is a minor interest. Support is available for grants.
Eligibility: Written proposal required; Must have tax-exempt status.
Contact for Further Information: Paul Chenet, Assistant Treasurer

MANUFACTURERS HANOVER FOUNDATION[1]
350 Park Ave.
New York, NY 10022
Interests/Support: Music/performing arts is among the Foundation's interests. Giving is primarily local.

MEET THE COMPOSER, INC.
250 W. 57th St., Ste. 2532
New York, NY 10107
(212) 247-4082

Officers: John Duffy, President and Director; Cornell Wright, Treasurer; Richard Mittenthal, Chairman, Finance Committee
Interests/Support: Living composers of new music is the sole interest of Meet the Composer, Inc. MTC offers grants to nonprofit presenting organizations toward payment of the composer's fee for public events that feature the music and personal participation of the composer. Support covers the entire musical spectrum: concert, choral, orchestral, chamber, folk/ethnic, jazz, dance, theatre, opera, film multi-media, experimental. MTC promotes the music of our time, develops wider audiences for the works of living composers, and generates career opportunities and commissions.
Eligibility: All 501 (c) (3) nonprofit presenting organizations may apply, including: arts centers, opera companies, community centers, civic groups, service organizations, orchestras, schools and colleges, arts councils, conservatories, museums, libraries, educational radio & TV stations, dance companies, churches, etc.
Contact for Further Information: Andrea Rockower, Program Manager

THE MEMTON FUND, INC.
1 E. 75th St.
New York, NY 10021
(212) 570-4814
Officers: Samuel R. Milbank, President; Francis H. Musselman, Vice-President/Treasurer; Lillian Daniels, Secretary
Interests/Support: Music/performing arts is a minor interest. General support is available.
Eligibility: Giving is primarily local. No grants to individuals.
Contact for Further Information: Lilian Daniels, Secretary

METROPOLITAN OPERA NATIONAL COUNCIL[1]
Lincoln Center
New York, NY 10023
Officers: Alexander Saunderson, President; Kenyon Bolton, Honorary Vice-President; James P. Gillis, Vice-President and Chairman, Executive Committee; Mrs. Gilbert W. Humphrey, Vice-President
Interests/Support: A variety of awards and scholarships are available at the national and regional level to young singers interested in furthering their musical studies toward an ultimate operatic career.
Contact for Further Information: Regional Auditions, Metropolitan Opera National Council

MILLAY COLONY FOR THE ARTS
Steepletop
Austerlitz, NY 12017
(518) 392-3103
Officers: Ann-Ellen Lesser, Executive Director; Gail Giles, Assistant Director
Interests/Support: Composing is a major interest. Support is available to composers for one-month residencies a the Colony to enable pursuit of artistic achievement.
Eligibility: Application required.
Contact for Further Information: Gail Giles, Assistant Director

MORGAN GUARANTY TRUST COMPANY OF NEW YORK CHARITABLE TRUST
23 Wall St.
New York, NY 10015
(212) 483-2090
Officers: Robert F. Longley, Senior Vice-President; Jeanne Erwin, Vice-President
Interests/Support: Arts organizations receive 13% of the Trust's budget. Unrestricted operating grants are made to organizations located in New York City.
Eligibility: No grants to individuals.
Contact for Further Information: Write to Jeanne Erwin, Vice-President, for application form

NATIONAL ASSOCIATION OF TEACHERS OF SINGING FOUNDATION
250 W. 57th St. (2129)
New York, NY 10107
(212) 582-4043
Officers: Bruce Lunkley, President; James Browning, Executive Secretary/Treasurer
Interests/Support: Music/performing arts is a major interest. Small grants are given to selected participants in the Foundation's workshop programs. An annual voice scholarship to a voice student at the summer Aspen program is also available.
Eligibility: Requirements vary.
Contact for Further Information: Bruce Lunkley, President, Box 1602, Austin College, Sherman, TX 75090

THE NATIONAL ORCHESTRAL ASSOCIATION
111 W. 57th St., Ste. 1400
New York, NY 10019
(212) 247-1228
Officers: Alvaro Cassuto, Music Director; Roger Nierenberg, Associate Conductor; Carol P. Madeira, Administrative Director; Kate Wheeler, Development Administrator
Interests/Support: Fellowships are available for graduate orchestral training with The National Orchestra of New York.
Eligibility: Excellent proficiency on an orchestral instrument required. Fellowship granted on audition only.
Contact for Further Information: Carol P. Madeira, Administrative Director

JOSEPHINE BAY PAUL & C. MICHAEL PAUL FOUNDATION INC.
14 Wall St.
New York, NY 10005
(212) 227-8200
Officers: Robert W. Ashton, Executive Director; Raymonde I. Paul, President
Interests/Support: Music/performing arts is a major interest. The Foundation is currently suporting C. Michael Paul Chamber Music Residencies for professional ensembles, administered and awarded through a panel chosen by Chamber Music America.
Eligibility: No grants to individuals.
Contact for Further Information: B.J. Bucker, Executive Director, Chamber Music America, 215 Park Ave. South, New York, NY 10003

PEPSICO FOUNDATION, INC.[1]
Purchase, NY 10577
(914) 253-3153
Officers: D.M. Kendall, Chairman; C.D. DeLoach, President; J.R. Millan, Vice-President, Contributions
Interests/Support: Music/performing arts is a major interest. Project grants and curriculum development support are available.
Eligibility: Giving is in all localities. No grants to individuals.
Contact for Further Information: Mrs. Jacqueline R. Millan, Coordinator, Corporation Contributions

PRO MUSICIS FOUNDATION, INC.
140 W. 79th St.
New York, NY 10024
(212) 787-0993
Officer: Rev. Eugene Merlet, President
Interests/Support: Young solo concert artists who perform for the aged, handicapped, infirm, etc., will be sponsored in national recitals and appearances with orchestras.
Eligibility: The solo artist must be of exceptional skill and talent and capable of striving for high international standards.

THE FREDERICK W. RICHMOND FOUNDATION
743 Fifth Ave.
New York, NY 10022
(212) 752-1668
Officers: Timothy E. Wyman, President; Beatriz Mirich, Treasurer; William J Butler, Secretary
Interests/Support: Music/performing arts is a major interest. Support is available for project grants to organizations.
Eligibility: Must have tax-exempt status. No grants to individuals.
Contact for Further Information: Pauline Nunen, Executive Director

THE ROCKEFELLER FOUNDATION
1133 Ave. of the Americas
New York, NY 10036
(212) 869-8500

Officers: Alberta Arthurs, Director, Arts and Humanities; Howard Klein, Deputy Director, Arts and Humanities; Steven Lavine, Assistant Director, Arts and Humanities
Interests/Support: Music/performing arts is a major interest. The Foundatin has two major programs of support in the field of music. One is a composers-in-residence program, which is administered by Meet the Composer in New York City, and involves seven American symphony orchestras. The objective of this program, which is not open for direct application, is to establish a working relationship between American composers and the orchestras and to infuse American music into the symphony repertory. The second program, sponsored in conjunction with Carnegie Hall, is the series of International American Music Competitions, which are intended to stimulate greater interest on the part of performers, teachers, and students in the large body of recital music written by Americans since 1900. The competitive awards rotate annually among pianists, vocalists, and violinists.
Contact for Further Information: Ellen Buchwalter, Program Associate, Arts and Humanities

STANLEY DRAMA AWARD
Wagner College
Staten Island, NY 10301
(212) 390-3256
Officers: J.J. Boies, Director
Interests/Support: Music/performing arts is a minor interest. $1,000 is awarded annually as a prize for best play or musical not yet commercially produced or with trade book publication.
Eligibility: Recommendation of a professional sponsor required; former winners are not eligible.
Contact for Further Information: J.J. Boies, Director

THE ELEANOR STEBER MUSIC FOUNDATION
2109 Broadway
New York, NY 10023
(212) 362-2938
Officers: Eleanor Steber, President; Martha Moore Smith, Executive Secretary
Interests/Support: Through competition, a minimum of four winners receive cash awards of $2,500 each to be used for whatever paramount needs the winners may have to futher their career development. Winners are also presented in New York recital.
Eligibility: Applicants must be young professional singers affiliated with an apprentice/intern program offered by a professional opera company in the U.S. during the year of the competition entered. Preliminary screening via tape and resume sent to Foundation. Those singers chosen from the preliminary evaluation then audition in New York before a panel of distinguished judges.
Contact for Further Information: Martha Moore Smith, Executive Secretary

WILLIAM MATHEUS SULLIVAN MUSIC FOUNDATION, INC.
410 E. 57th St.
New York, NY 10022
Officers: Hugh Ross, Vice-President and Executive Director
Interests/Support: The Foundation assists gifted young singers who have finished school and are on their way to professional careers by arranging engagements with orchestras, musical groups, operatic societies and other performing companies.
Eligibility: Applicants must write no later than October 10th when applying for New York auditions and must have at least one future engagement with full orchestra that comes after November. A copy of the contract or contracts and resume must be included with letter. The Foundation is hoping to re-establish its West Coast Auditions.
Contact for Further Information: Hugh Ross, Vice-President and Executive Director

LUDWIG VOGELSTEIN FOUNDATION, INC.
P.O. Box 537
New York, NY 10013
Officers: Robert Braunschweig, President; Douglas Blair Turnbaugh, Treasurer
Interests/Support: Music/performing arts is a major interest. Grants are given to individuals of mature achievement in the arts and humanities, including peforming artists and composers. No student aid or faculty assistance is given.
Eligibility: Anyone may apply. Applications are accepted for projects representing turning points in the individual's career for which funds from other sources are not available.
Contact for Further Information: Douglas Blair Turnbaugh, Treasurer (by letter only; no phone calls)

THE WESTERN NEW YORK FOUNDATION
Ste. 1402, Main-Seneca Bldg.
Buffalo, NY 14203
(716) 847-6440
Officers: Welles V. Moot, Jr., President; Richard E. Moot, Treasurer; Mrs. Cecily M. Johnson, Vice-President; Mr. Robert S. Scheu, Vice-President; John R. Moot, Secretary
Interests/Support: Support is available for capital grants and "seed money" project grants.
Eligibility: IRS exemption letter required; no religioius affiliation. No grants to individuals.
Contact for Further Information: Welles V. Moot, Jr.
President

YOUNG CONCERT ARTISTS, INC.
250 W. 57th St.
New York, NY 10019
(212) 307-6655
Officers: Susan Wadsworth, Director; Nancy Wellman, Associate Director
Interests/Support: Music/performing arts is the sole interest. Young Concert Artists provides management services to the young solo musicians who win the annual Young Concert Artists auditions. The nonprofit management organization provides professional concert opportunitities for its artists, thereby providing income, and also presents the winners in recital in the Young Concert Artists Series at the 92nd St. Y in New York and at the Kennedy Center in Washington, DC
Eligibility: Artists must have the repertoire required and be at the start of their careers.
Contact for Further Information: Susan Wadsworth, Director

NORTH CAROLINA

A.J. FLETCHER EDUCATIONAL AND OPERA FOUNDATION, INC.
P.O. Box 12800
Raleigh, NC 27605
(919) 821-8782
Officers: James F. Goodmon, President; Louise H. Stephenson, Secretary; A.H. Moore, Jr., Treasurer
Interests/Support: Music/performing arts is a major interest. Grants are given to North Carolina institutions of higher learning from music scholarships. Scholarship contracts are also available for ten persons for the roster fo the National Opera Company (season of eight months, peforming four productions).
Contact for Further Information: David H. Witherspoon, Vice-President

SIGMUND STERNBERGER FOUNDATION, INC.[1]
P.O. Box 3111
Greensboro, NC 27402
(919) 378-1791
Officers: Leah Louise B. Tannenbaum, Chairman; Sidney J. Stern, Jr., Secretary-Treasurer
Interests/Support: Music/performing arts is a minor interest. limited local scholarships are offered in Guilford County, NC. Seed money grants are available. Support is given to the local arts council and to the Eastern Music Festival.
Contact for Further Information: Robert O. Klepfer, Jr., Executive Director

NORTH DAKOTA

THE FARGO-MOORHEAD SYMPHONY ORCHESTRAL ASSOCIATION[1]

Box 1753
Fargo, ND 58107
(218) 233-8397
Interests/Support: The Sigvald Thompson Composition Award is given annually to a composer of the Upper Midwest Area. The Award consists of $1,000 plus copying costs and a premier performance of a composition of medium length (8-15 minutes) by the Fargo-Moorhead Symphony Orchestra during its concert season.
Eligibility: No grants to individuals.
Contact for Further Information: L.M.Buckingham, Trustee

NORTHERN PLAINS INTERNATIONAL FESTIVAL OF MUSIC

Dickinson State College
Dickinson, ND 58601
(701) 227-2305
Officers: Dr. Frank C. Pearson, Chairman, Department of Music
Interests/Support: Musical performance is a major interest. The Festival, L.M. Buckingham, Trustee
fees and music department funds, is open to high school students from states in the area surrounding western North Dakota and the adjacent provinces of Canada.
Eligibility: HIgh school students selected from audition tapes for participation in honor choir and honor band.
Contact for Further Information: Dr. Frank C. Pearson, Chairman, Department of Music.

OHIO

THE WILLIAM BINGHAM FOUNDATION

1250 Leader Bldg.
Cleveland, OH 44114
(216) 781-3270
Officers: Laurel Blossom, President; C. Bingham Blossom, Treasurer; Mary E. Gale, Assistant Treasurer; Thomas H. Gale, Vice-President; Thomas F. Allen, Secretary
Interests/Support: Grants are made in education, fine arts, health, and welfare nationwide.
Eligibility: No grants to individuals. Must be tax-exempt organization within the U.S.
Contact for Further Information: Mary Ann Gera, Executive Director

THE GAR FOUNDATION

1 Cascade Plaza, 15th Flr.
Akron, OH 44308
(216) 376-5300
Officer: L.M. Buckingham, Trustee
Interests/Support: Music/performing arts is a minor interest. The Foundation supports the Cleveland Orchestra, Akron Symphony Orchestra, Ohio Ballet, Blossom Center, and a Bach Festival at Baldwin-Wallace University.

IDDINGS FOUNDATION

Ste. 1620, Winters Bank Tower
Dayton, OH 45423
(513) 224-1773
Interests/Support: Music/performing arts is a minor interest. The performing arts fund offers general support annually.
Eligibility: Must be 501 (c) (3) organization in Ohio. No grants to individuals. Giving is primarily local.
Contact for Further Information: Maribeth Eiken, Administrative Assistant

MARTHA HOLDEN JENNINGS FOUNDATION

1040 Union Commerce Bldg.
Cleveland, OH 44114
(216) 589-5700
Officers: George B. Chapman, Jr., Chairman, Advisory Committee; Arthur S. Holden, Jr., President; Joan Johnson, Program Officer
Interests/Support: Music/performing arts is a minor interest. Grants are made to school or educational institutions in Ohio.
Eligibility: Must have 501 (c) (3) tax-exempt status. No grants to individuals.
Contact for Further Information: Joan Johnson, Program Director

THE ANDREW JERGENS FOUNDATION

700 Gynne Bldg.
602 Main St.
Cincinnati, OIH 45202
(513) 651-3966
Officers: The Reverend Andrew N. Jergens, Jr., President; Thomas C. Hays, Vice-President; Leonard S. Meranus, Secretary-Treasurer
Interests/Support: Suport is available for organizations and special projects that benefit young children.
Eligibility: Must have 501 (c) (3) status. No grants to individuals. Giving is limited primarily to the greater Cincinnati area.
Contact for Further Information: The Reverend Andrew N. Jergens, Jr., President

KNIGHT FOUNDATION

One Cascade Plaza
Akron, OH 44308
(216) 253-9301
Officers: C.C. Gibson, President; David Catrow, Treasurer
Interests/Support: Grants are available primarily for education, arts, and culture
Eligibility: Must be 501 (c) (3) organization; not private foundation. No grants outside geographic preference area.
Contact for Further Information: C.C. Gibson, President

S. LIVINGSTON MATHER CHARITABLE TRUST

1460 Union Commerce Bldg.
Cleveland, OH 44115
(216) 942-6484
Officer: S. Sterling McMillan, Secretary
Interests/Support: Music/performing arts is a minor interest. General support is available.
Eligibility: Giving is limited to the Cleveland area. Must be charitable and civic organization with IRS exempt status. No grants to individuals.
Contact for Further Information: S. Sterling McMillan, Secretary

FRANK M. TAIT FOUNDATION

1840 Winters Bank Tower
Dayton, OH 45423
(513) 222-2401
Officers: Irvin G. Bieser, Sr., President; Susan T. Rankin, Secretary, Treasurer, and Executive Director
Interests/Support: Projects and program grants are available. Music/performing arts is a minor interest.
Eligibility: Must have 501 (c) (3) tax-exempt status. No grants to individuals. Giving is local (Montgomer County).
Contact for Further Information: Susan T. Rankin, Executive Director

TREUHAFT FOUNDATION

10701 Shaker Blvd.
Cleveland, OH 44104
(216) 229-3000
Officers: Elizabeth M. Treuhaft, Eugene H. Freedheim and Arthur W. Treuhaft, Trustees
Interests/Support: Music/performing arts is a minor interest. The Foundation has no special interests, but requests are considered as they are received.
Eligibility: No grants to individuals. Giving is primarily local.
Contact for Further Information: Mrs. Wm. C. Treuhaft, Trustee

OKLAHOMA

OKLAHOMA SYMPHONY ORCHESTRA WOMEN'S COMMITTEE

512 Civic Center Music Hall
Oklahoma City, OK 73102
(405) 232-4292
Officers: Awards of $6,000 and performance with the Oklahoma Symphony Orchestra are given. Auditions are held for piano, strings, and voice.
Eligibility: Open to residents or students in Oklahoma, Kansas, Missouri, Nebraska, Arkansas, or Texas, Must be no more than 30 years old.
Contact for Further Information: Mrs. John Hanes, Audition Chairman, 12409 Blue Sage Rd., Oklahoma City, OK 73120

OREGON

OREGON ARTS COMMISSION
835 Summer St.
Salem, OR 97301
(503) 378-3625
Officers: Dr. Marythea Grebner, Chairperson; Peter Hero, Executive Director; Jalaine Madura, Assistant Director
Interests/Support: Music/performing arts is a major interest. Project grants, performing arts touring resource director, and artists fellowships are available.
Eligibility: Individuals may apply for fellowships; nonprofit, tax-exempt groups may apply for grants.
Contact for Further Information: Jalaine Madura, Assistant Director

PENNSYLVANIA

THE ACADEMY OF VOCAL ARTS
1920 Spruce St.
Philadelphia, PA 19103
(215) 735-1685
Officers: Dino Yannopoulos, Director; Mareen Bixler, Assistant Director
Interests/Support: Opera and vocal music are the only interests. All students accepted into the Academy of Vocal Arts receive full tuition scholarships. There is no other financial aid available directly through the school.
Eligibility: Two years, preferably four, of college music training or the equivalent in private study required. Women must be no older than 28; men no older than 30. Audition requirements; five arias. preferably representing two or more languages.
Contact for Further Information: Send request for catalog/application to address above.

AMERICAN MUSICOLOGICAL SOCIETY, INC.
University of Pennsylvania
201 S. 34th St.
Philadelphia, PA 19104
Interests/Support: Travel grants, administered by the American Council of Learned Societies are given to enable American Scholars to participate in international meetings abroad. Each grant covers round-trip tourist class plane fare.
Eligibility: Individuals must have Ph.D. or equivalent. Meeting must be international and outside the U.S., Canada, and Mexico.
Contact for Further Information: Prof. Frank Traficante, Liaison Officer for Travel Grants, Dept. of Music, Claremont Graduate School, Claremont, CA 91711

MAY LOUISE CURTIS BOK FOUNDATION[1]
1726 Locust St.
Philadelphia, PA 19103
(205) 893-5252
Interests/Support: Music and music education are primary interests. The Foundation supports the Curtis Institute of Music, a scholarship education program.

THE BUHL FOUNDATION
Four Gateway Center, Room 1522
Pittsburgh, PA 15222
(412) 566-2711
Officers: John G. Frazer, Jr., President; William H. Rea, Vice-President; Francis B. Nimick, Jr., Vice-Presient; John M. Arthur, Treasurer
Interests/Support: Music/performing arts is a minor interest. Project grants and field study support are available for encouragement of music education and appreciation of music in the young people of Pittsburgh and vicinity.
Eligibility: Must be nonprofit, tax-exempt institution in the Pittsburgh metropolitan area. No grants to individuals.
Contact for Further Information: Doreen E. Boyce, Director

DELTA OMICRON FOUNDATION, INC.
400 Walnut Pl.
Havertown, PA 19083
(215) 449-8891
Officers: Adelaide L. Collyer, President; Anna Marie Gantner, Treasurer
Interests/Support: Scholarship for study in the areas of music performance, music education, composition, and conducting are available to qualified members of Delta Omicron International Music Fraternity. Occasionally, scholarships are awarded to outstanding musicians not affiliated with the Fraternity.
Eligibility: Scholarships are awarded on an individual basis.
Contact for Further Information: Adelaide L. Collyer, President

THE ERIE COMMUNITY FOUNDATION
419 G. Daniel Baldwin Bldg.
P.O. Box 1818
Erie, PA 16507
(814) 454-0843
Officers: Edward C. Doll, President; Charles H. Bracken, Secretary-Treasurer; William F. Grant, Vice-President
Interests/Support: Music/performing arts is a minor interest. An annual grant is given to the Erie Arts Council, which is a combination organization of most of the performing arts in the community. One grant is given annually to a local art student.
Contact for Further Information: Edward C. Doll, President

HOWARD HEINZ ENDOWMENT[1]
301 Fifth Ave., Ste 1417
Pittsburgh, PA 15222
Interests/Support: Music and the arts are among the Endowment's interest. Grants are limited to organizations in Pennsylvania and generally to Pittsburgh.

INA FOUNDATION[1]
1600 Arch St.
Philadelphia, PA 19101
(215) 241-2858
Officers: Charles K. Cox, Chairman; Andrew M. Rouse, President; Jeffrey P. Lindtner, Executive Director
Interests/Support: Music/performing arts is a minor interest. Support is available for continuing and annual campaigns.
Eligibility: Giving is primarily local. No grants to individuals.
Contact for Further Information: Jeffrey P. Lindtner, Executive Director

MELLON BANK FOUNDATION
Mellon Bank
Mellon Square
Pittsburgh, PA 15230
(412) 234-6266
Officers: J. David Barnes, President; Charles H. Fletcher, Vice-President; Sylvia Clark, Secretary
Interests/Support: Music/performing arts is a minor interest. Operating, endowment, and capital support are available.
Eligibility: Giving is limited to Allegheny, Armstrong, Beaver, Butler, Washington, and Westmoreland Counties in Pennsylvania. No grants to individuals.
Contact for Further Information: Sylvia Clark, Secretary

WILLIAM PENN FOUNDATION
1617 John F. Kennedy Blvd.
Philadelphia, PA 19103
(215) LO8-2870
Officers: John C. Haas, Chairman; Bernard C. Watson, President
Interests/Support: Approximately 10% of total grants are in the area of music/performing arts. Support is in the form of project grants.
Eligibility: Giving is primarily in the Philadelphia area. Must be 501 (c) (3) tax-exempt organization. No grants to individuals.
Contact for Further Information: Harry E. Cerino, Vice President

PEW MEMORIAL TRUST
c/o Glenmede Trust Company
229 S. 18th St.
Philadelphia, PA 19103
(215) 875-3200
Officers: Robert I. Smith, President; F.H. Billups, Vice-President/Charitable Trusts; Ruth K. Parker, Trust Officer
Interests/Support: Music/performing arts is a minor interest. Project grants and program support are available.
Eligibility: Giving is primarily local. No grants to individuals.
Contact for Further Information: F.H. Billups, Vice President/Charitable Trusts

PITTSBURGH NEW MUSIC ENSEMBLE, INC.
6538 Darlington Rd.
Pittsburgh, PA 15217
(412) 421-5281
Officers: Barbara Laswell, Ph.D., President; Bruce Wilder, M.D., Secretary; Kathleen Donnelly, Treasurer
Interests/Support: Music/performing arts is the exclusive interest. The Harvey Gaul Composition Contest is held biennally (next contest is scheduled to begin September 1983, with a deadline in spring 1984).
Eligibility: Must be composition for specific instrumentation. Applications and rules available September 1983.
Contact for Further Information: David Stock, Conductor

MINNA KAUFMANN RUUD FUND
Chatham College
Woodland Rd.
Pittsburgh, PA 15232
(412) 441-8200
Interests/Support: Music/performing arts is a minor interest. The Fund provides scholarships for students with outstanding ability in voice. Special priority is given to those students who plan to follow a career in the concert, operatic, or teaching fields.
Eligibility: Applicant must be a student attending Chatham College.
Contact for Further Information: Kim L. Moreland, Director of Financial Aid

ADAM AND MARIA SARAH SEYBERT INSTITUTION FOR POOR BOYS & GIRLS
1500 Walnut St., 15th Flr.
Philadelphia, PA 19102
(215) 893-8228
Officers: H. Gates Lloyd, III, President; William C. Bullitt, Esq., Secretary; Steven R. Garfinkel, Treasurer
Interests/Support: Seybert is limited under the terms of the Will setting up the fund to poor boys and girls of the City of Philadelphia. Music/performing arts is a minor interest. Modest project grants are available for cultural, artistic, and craft programs through agencies, including services to children, with a special concern for counseling in the area of child abuse, drugs, drop-outs, and runaways. The Seybert Scholarship Grant Program supports the education of needy children through participating schools.
Eligibility: Must be 501 (c) (3)—509 (a) charitable organization in Philadelphis, PA.
Contact for Further Information: Mrs. Helen R. Green, Executive Secretary

ETHEL SERGEANT CLARK SMITH MEMORIAL FUND
c/o Charles A. Fritz, III, Senior Trust Officer
P.O. Box 7618
Philadelphia National Bank
Philadelphia, PA 19101
Interests/Support: Music/performing arts is a minor interest. Funding for musical performances and education in Delaware County, PA is available.
Eligibility: Must be charitable 501 (c) 3 organization located in or near Delaware County, PA.
Contact for Further Information: Charles A. Fritz, III, Senior Trust Officer

THE WYOMISSING FOUNDATION, INC.
1015 Penn Ave.
Wyomissing, PA 19610
(215) 376-7496
Interests/Support: Music/performing arts is a minor interest. No individual fellowships, scholarships, field study support, or curriculum development are available. Support is mainly for current operations of existing selected public performing classical groups.
Eligibility: Must be 501 (c) (3) organization. No grants to individuals. Support limited to local area only.
Contact for Further Information: Lawrence A. Walsky, Assistant Secretary-Treasurer

RHODE ISLAND

CHAMPLIN FOUNDATION
P.O. Box 637
Providence, RI 02901
(401) 421-3719
Interests/Support: Music/performing arts is a minor interest. The foundations make direct grants for capital needs to tax-exempt organizations in Rhode Island. Grants are not awarded for program or eating expenses, or to individuals.
Eligibility: Must be tax-exempt organization. No grants to individuals. Giving is limtied to Rhode Island.
Contact for Further Information: David A. King, Secretary

GEORGE A. AND ELIZA GARDNER HOWARD FOUNDATION
Brown University Graduate School
Box 1867
Providence, RI 02912
(401) 863-2640
Officers: Howard Swearer, Chiarman; Ernest S. Frerichs, Secretary
Interests/Support: Fellowships for independent projects are offered in the following areas on a three-year rotational basis: 1) Literary criticism and scholarship, linguistics, foreign language studies, art history, art criticism, musicology, and theatre and film criticism; 2) History, philosophy, sociology, psychology, anthropology, archaeology, political science, religion; 3) Fine, applied, and performing arts, including the plastic and graphic arts, music, theatre, filmmaking, media-related projects, creative writing. Fellowships for 1984-85 are offered in the second category.
Contact for Further Information: Mark Schupack

RHODE ISLAND STATE COUNCIL ON THE ARTS
312 Wickenden St.
Providence, RI 02903
(401) 277-3880
Officers: Christina White, Executive Director; Janice E. Irwin, Grants Coordinator; Robert Demers, Arts Services Coordinator
Interests/Support: The Council supports all arts disciplines. Grants are made for general operating support and project support; grants-in-aid, to individual artists are available.
Eligibility: Requirements vary by program; guidelines available on request.
Contact for Further Information: Janice E. Irwin, Grants Coordinator (re: general operating and project support); Robert Demers, Arts Services Coordinator (re: grants-in-aid to individual artists)

SOUTH CAROLINA

SOUTH CAROLINA ARTS COMMISSION
1800 Gervais St.
Columbia, SC 29201
(803) 758-3442
Officers: Tom Creech, Commission Member
Interests/Support: The Commission supports arts programming for all arts forms reaching all strata of the South Carolina population, and provides financial and moral support to promising artists of exceptional talent. Programs are individual artist grants, requiring a 50% match; nonmatching artist fellowships in four categories: visual arts (2 fellowships); crafts (1 fellowship); literature (1 fellowship); and performing arts (1 fellowship). Awards are given in film/video and music composion on alternate years.
Eligibility: Must be resident of South Carolina.
Contact for Further Information: Elizabeth Strom, Grants in Aid

TEXAS

AMERICAN PETROFINA FOUNDATION[1]
P.O. Box 2159
Dallas, TX 75221
(214) 750-2838
Officers: Verne H. Maxwell, President; J.F. Stizell, Vice-President/Treasurer; T.G. Chambers, Vice-President/ Secretary; Gwen Murray, Assistant Secretary
Interests/Support: Music/performing arts is among the Foundation's interest. General support is available for operations.
Eligibility: Giving is primarily local. No grants to individuals.
Contact for Further Information: Gwen Murray, Assistant Secretary

THE CULLEN FOUNDATION
601 Jefferson
Houston, TX 77252
(712) 651-8837
Interests/Support: Music/performing arts is among the Foundation's interest.
Eligibility: Grants are limited to Texas.
Contact for Further Information: Joseph C. Graf, Executive Secretary, The Cullen Foundation, P.O. Box 1600, Houston, TX 77251

HOBLITZELLE FOUNDATION
2522 RepublicBank Bldg.
Dallas, TX 75201
(214) 744-0163
Officers: James W. Aston, Chairman and Chief Executive Officer; James W. Keay, President; Robert Lynn Harris, Executive Vice-President and Grant Coordinator
Interests/Support: Music/performing arts is a minor interest. Support is available for project grants and capital.
Eligibility: No grants to individuals. No grants outside Texas.
Contact for Further Information: Robert Lynn Harris, Executive Vice-President

MEADOWS FOUNDATION, INC.
310 Meadows Bldg.
Dallas, TX 75206
(214) 691-8954
Officers: Curtis W. Meadows, Jr., President; Sally R. Lancaster, Executive Vice-Presient and Grants Administrator; Nancy Nelson, Associate Grants Administrator; B.T. Crenshaw, Treasurer
Interests/Support: Music/performing arts is interest. Support is available for program, project, capital, and more.
Eligibility: No grants to individuals.
Contact for Further Information: Sally R. Lancaster, Executive Vice-President and Grants Administrator

SID W. RICHARDSON FOUNDATION
309 Main St.
Fort Wth, TX 76102
(817) 336-0494
Officers: Perry R. Bass, President; Nancy Lee Bass, Vice-President; M.E. Chappell, Vice-President/Treasurer; H.B. Fuqua, Vice-President; Sid R. Bass, Vice-President
Interests/Support: Music/performing arts is a major interest. General support is available.
Eligibility: Must have IRS 501 (c) (3) tax-exempt status. Giving is primarily local. No grants to individuals.
Contact for Further Information: Valleau Wilkie, Jr., Executive Vice-President

THE TYLER FOUNDATION
3100 Southland Center
Dallas, TX 75201
(214) 747-8251
Officer: Ben R. Murphy, President
Interests/Support: Music/performing arts is a minor interest. General funds are available for music/performing arts.
Eligibility: No grants to individuals. Giving is exclusively local.
Contact for Further Information: Lowell A. Murphy, Director of Corporation Communications

WORTHAM FOUNDATION
2777 Allen Pkwy., Ste. 984
Houston, TX 77109
(713) 526-8849
Officers: Allen H. Carruth, President; H.C. Boxwell, E.A. Stumpf III, R.W. Wortham III, Vice-Presidents
Interests/Support: Music/performing arts is a minor interest. Support is limited to local symphony, opera, and ballet.
Eligibility: No grants to individuals. Giving is primarily local.
Contact for Further Information: Allen H. Carruth, President

VERMONT

VERMONT COUNCIL ON THE ARTS[1]
136 State St.
Montpelier, VT 05602
(802) 828-3291
Officers: Dorothy Olson, President; Violet Coffin, Vice-President; Gerald Keneally, Treasurer; T. Hunter Wilson, Secretary
Interests/Support: Music/performing arts is one of many interests that include painting, design, crafts, theatre, and dance. Available are: organization and individual awards, subsidy of touring artists' fees, placement of artists in residence, and employment in public service capacities.
Eligibility: Must be nonprofit organization; town, county, or government agency; or individual artist of demonstrated ability who are Vermont residents. Support varies according to each program. Applicants should request the VCA handbook which contains an application form.
Contact for Further Information: Public Information Officer

VIRGINIA

VIRGINIA CENTER FOR THE CREATIVE ARTS
Sweet Briar, VA 24595
(804) 946-7236
Officers: William Smart, Director; Stephen Humphrey, Assistant Director; Randee Humphrey, Administrative Assistant
Interests/Support: Music/performing arts is a major interest. The Center provides residencies of one to three months at the Mt. San Angelo Estate for artists to work without distraction. Room, board, and individual studio space is available year round for 2 composers, 9 visual artists, and 13 writers at one time. Financial assistance is also available.
Eligibility: Apply at least three months in advance. References, curriculum vita, and work samples required at the time of application. Main criterion for selection is professional achievement or promise of achievement.
Contact for Further Information: William Smart, Director

VIRGINIA COMMISSION FOR THE ARTS
400 E. Grace St.
Richmond, VA 23219
(804) 786-4492
Officers: Peggy J. Baggett, Executive Director
Interests/Support: Music/performing arts is a major interest. Project and general operating support grants for nonprofit music organizations and touring support for nonprofit sponsors of groups listed in Commission Tour Director are available.
Eligibility: Must be nonprofit Virginia organization.
Contact for Further Information: Peggy J. Baggett, Executive Director

WISCONSIN

MILWAUKEE FOUNDATION
161 W. Wisconsin Ave., Ste. 5146
Milwaukee, WI 53203
(414) 272-5805
Officers: David M.G. Huntington, Executive Director
Interests/Support: Music/performing arts is one of many interests of this community foundation.
Eligibility: Giving is primarily local. Must be nonprofit agency serving the people of the greater Milwaukee community. No grants to individuals.
Contact for Further Information: David M.G. Huntington, Executive Director

THE WALTER & OLIVE STIEMKE FOUNDATION
161 W. Wisconsin Ave., Ste 5146
Milwaukee, WI 53202
(414) 272-5805
Officers: The Rev. Frederick A. Stiemke, Chairman; Herbert J. Mueller, Secretary
Interests/Support: Grants are made to meet the capital fund requirements of cultural agencies serving the greater Milwaukee community, among other program fields. Grants may be made to organizations in other parts of the State of Wisonsin if they benefit the people of Milwaukee community. Grants may not be used to operate a charity or to add to or establish endowment funds. Grants have been given in the past to music theaters, ballet foundations, symphony orchestras, and repertory theaters.
Eligibility: Giving is primarily local. No grants to individuals. A brief statement describing the agency, the specific project for which funds are needed,

and the anticipated costs is required.
Contact for Further Information:
Herbert J. Mueller, Secretary

VIRGIN ISLANDS

VIRGIN ISLANDS COUNCIL OF THE ARTS
Caravelle Arcade
Christiansted
St. Croix, VI 00820
(809) 773-3075

Interests/Support: Grants, general organizational support, and technical assistance are available to individual artists, arts organizations, and education institutions in the Virgin Islands. Funds are not grants for capital improvements, erasing deficits, or building, renovation, or maintenance of facilities.

Eligibility: Considered on an individual need basis. Giving is limited to the Virgin Islands.

Contact for Further Information:
Stephen J. Bostic, Executive Director

CANADA

THE CANADA COUNCIL
255 Albert St.
P.O. Box 1047
Ottawa, ON K1P 5V8
(613) 237-3400
Officers: Timothy Porteous, Director
Interests/Support: Grants are available for artists who have completed basic training and are recognized as professionals in the fields of music, theatre, dance, performance, etc.
Eligibility: Applicants must be Canadian citizens or landed immigrants five years resident in Canada.

Foundations and Funding Organizations Index

A

B

C

D

E

F

G

T

U

V

W

Y

Z

III. EDUCATION

Colleges and Conservatories
Community Colleges
Music Schools
Careers in Music

Colleges and Conservatories

U.S. and Canadian colleges and conservatories that offer at least a four-year course of study leading to a Bachelor's degree in Music are listed alphabetically by state or province; non-degree granting institutions are not included. The name of the head of the music department, institution's affiliation, accrediting agency, areas of study, degrees offered, and scholarships available are given for most schools. The number 1 following the name of the institution indicates that they did not respond to our questionnaire. An alphabetical cross-index appears at the end of this section.

The following abbreviations have been used for accrediting agencies:

AABC - American Association of Bible Colleges
ATS - Association of Theological Schools
AUCC - Association of Universities and Colleges of Canada
CUMS - Canadian University Music Society
MSA - Middle States Association of Colleges and Schools
NAMT - National Association for Music Therapy
NASC - Northwest Association of Schools and Colleges
NASM - National Association of Schools of Music
NCA - North Central Association of Colleges and Schools
NCATE - National Council for Accreditation of Teacher Education
NEA - New England Association of Schools and Colleges
SACS - Southern Association of Colleges and Schools
WASC - Western Association of Schools and Colleges

The following abbreviations have been used for areas of study:

App Mus - Applied Music
Hist & Lit - Music History & Literature
Th & An - Theory & Analysis
Comp - Composition
Cond - conducting
Orch - Orchestration
Opera - Opera
Hist Musicol - Historical Musicology
Ethnomusicol - Ethnomusicology
Church Mus - Church Music
Mus Ed (Elem & HS) - Music Education (Elementary & High School)
Mus Therapy - Music Therapy
Theater Mus - Theater Music
Piano Tech - Piano Technology (Tuning)
Instr Rep - Instrument Repair
Electr Mus - Electronic Music
Perf - Performance
Ped - Pedagogy
Intro - Introductory
Accomp - Accompanying
Aesth - Aesthetics
Arrang - Arranging
Arts Mgmt - Arts Management
Commer Mus - Commercial Music
Counterpt - Counterpoint
Ens - Ensembles
Gen Mus - General Music
Hist Jazz - History of Jazz
Ind Study - Independent Study
Mus Apprec - Music Appreciation
Mus Bus - Music Business
Mus Lib - Music Librarianship
Mus Merch - Music Merchandising
Mus Mgmt - Music Management
Vocal Dict - Vocal Diction

The following abbreviations have been used for degrees offered:

BA - Bachelor of Arts (music major)
BFA - Bachelor of Fine Arts
BM - Bachelor of Music
BS - Bachelor of Science
BCM - Bachelor of Church Music
BSM - Bachelor of Sacred Music
BRE - Bachelor of Religious Education
BS, Mus Ed - Bachelor of Science in Music Education
MA - Master of Arts (in music or some area of music)
MM - Master of Music
MSM - Master of Sacred Music
MA, Ed - Master of Arats in Education (music concentration)
MAIS - Master of Arts in Interdisciplinary Studies
MCM - Master of Church Music
MLM - Master of Liturgical Music
MMT - Master of Music Training
MS, Ed - Master of Science in Education (music concentration)
MME - Master of Music Education
MEd - Master of Education
MS, Mus Ed - Master of Science in Music Education
MAT - Master of Arts in Teaching
MST - Master of Science in Teaching
MT - Master of Teaching
DA - Doctor of Arts
DFA - Doctor of Fine Arts
DMA - Doctor of Music Arts
EdD - Doctor of Education
PhD - Doctor of Philosophy (in music or some area of music)

ALABAMA

ALABAMA STATE UNIVERSITY
School of Music
P.O. Box 271
Montgomery, AL 36195-0301
(205) 293-4341
Staff: Dr. Thomas E. Lyle, Acting Dean
Affiliation: State-supported university
Accreditation: NASM; SACS
Areas: App Mus; Hist & Lit; Th & An; Comp; Cond; Orch; Opera; Intro; Mus Ed (Elem & HS); Perf
Degrees: BFA, BME, MME

ATHENS STATE COLLEGE[1]
Department of Music
Athens, AL 35611
(205) 232-1802
Staff: Annette Trent, Chairman
Affiliation: State
Accreditation: SACS
Areas: Cond; Mus Ed (Elem & HS); Th & An; Orch; Comp; Hist & Lit
Degrees: BA; BS; BS, Mus Ed

AUBURN UNIVERSITY[1]
Department of Music
Auburn University, AL 36849
(205) 826-4164
Staff: Wilbur Hinton, Head
Affiliation: State
Accreditation: SACS; NASM
Areas: Orch; Intro; Th & An: Hist & Lit; Comp; Opera
Degrees: BA; BM; BS, Mus Ed; MM; MS, Mus Ed

BIRMINGHAM-SOUTHERN COLLEGE[1]
Division of Fine and Performing Arts
800 8th Ave. W.
Birmingham, AL 35204
(205) 328-5250, ext. 346
Staff: Thomas Gibbs, Chairman
Affiliation: Church-related liberal arts college (United Methodist)
Accreditation: NASM; SACS
Areas: App Mus; Hist & Lit; Th & An; Cond; Orch; Opera; Church Mus; Mus Ed (Elem & HS)
Degrees: BA; BM; BME

HUNTINGDON COLLEGE
Department of Visual and Performing Arts
1500 E. Fairview Ave.
Montgomery, AL 36106
(205) 265-0511
Staff: Dr. Jeanne E. Shaffer, Head
Affiliation: Private church-related liberal arts college (United Methodist)
Accreditation: SACS; NASM
Areas: App Mus; Hist & Lit; Th & An; Comp; Cond; Orch; Church Mus; Mus Ed (Elem & HS)
Degrees: BA; BME
Scholarships: Scholarships available

JACKSONVILLE STATE UNIVERSITY
Music Department
Jacksonville, AL 36265
(205) 435-9820
Staff: James P. Fairleigh, Head
Affiliation: State-supported university
Accreditation: SACS; NCATE
Areas: App Mus; Hist & Lit; Th & An; Cond; Orch; Opera; Hist Musicol; Mus Ed (Elem & HS); Theater Mus
Degrees: BA; BS, Mus Ed; MA; MS, Mus Ed
Scholarships: Talent scholarships awarded in recognition of outstanding proficiency in major area of performance; faculty scholarships given in recognition of outstanding academic achievement in music curriculum

JUDSON COLLEGE
Music Department
Marion, AL 36756
(205) 683-6161
Staff: L. Bracey Campbell, Coordinator
Affiliation: Church-related liberal arts college (Southern Baptist)
Accreditation: NASM; SACS
Areas: App Mus; Hist & Lit; Th & An; Comp; Cond; Mus Ed (Elem & HS); Mus Apprec
Degrees: BA; BS, Mus Ed
Scholarships: Lockhart Competitive Scholarships (performance) of $1000 each, renewable

LIVINGSTON UNIVERSITY
Division of Fine Arts
Livingston, AL 35470
(205) 652-9661
Staff: Dr. Dennis P. Kudlawiec, Chairman
Affiliation: State-supported university
Accreditation: SACS
Areas: App Mus; Hist & Lit; Th & An; Comp; Cond; Orch; Mus Ed (Elem & HS)
Degrees: BA; BME; BS; MAT; MSEd; MEd
Scholarships: Band and choral scholarships available

MILES COLLEGE[1]
PO Box 3800
Birmingham, AL 35208
(205) 923-2771
Staff: James L. Bright, Chairman
Affiliation: Church-related (Christian Methodist Episcopal)
Accreditation: SACS
Areas: Th & An; Hist & Lit; Orch; Cond; Intro; Mus Ed (Elem & HS)
Degrees: BA

MOBILE COLLEGE
Music Department
PO Box 13220
Mobile, AL 36613
(205) 675-5990
Staff: Kenneth Bergdolt, Chairman
Affiliation: Church-related liberal arts college (Southern Baptist)
Accreditation: SACS

Areas: App Mus; Hist & Lit; Th & An; Comp; Cond; Orch; Church Mus; Intro; Mus Ed (Elem & HS)
Degrees: BA; BS, Mus Ed; BSM
Scholarships: Some awards based on ability, some on need

SAMFORD UNIVERSITY
School of Music
800 Lakeshore Dr.
Birmingham, AL 35229
(205) 870-2851
Staff: Dr. L. Gene Black, Dean
Affiliation: Private church-related university (Baptist)
Accreditation: NASM; SACS
Areas: App Mus; Hist & Lit; Th & An; Comp; Cond; Orch; Opera; Hist Musicol; Church Mus; Mus Ed (Elem & HS); Perf
Degrees: BA; BM; BME; MM; MME
Scholarships: Talent scholarships awarded by audition before examination board

STILLMAN COLLEGE[1]
Department of Music
3601 15th St.
Tuscaloosa, AL 35403
(205) 752-2548
Staff: James A. Williams, Chairman
Affiliation: Church-related (Presbyterian, U.S.)
Accreditation: SACS
Areas: Th & An; Hist & Lit; Cond; Mus Ed (Elem & HS)
Degrees: BA

TALLADEGA COLLEGE
Music Department
Talladega, AL 35160
(205) 362-0206, x293
Staff: Dr. Horace R. Carney, Jr., Acting Head
Affiliation: Church-related liberal arts college (United Church of Christ-Congregational)
Accreditation: SACS
Areas: App Mus; Hist & Lit; Th & An; Comp; Cond; Ethnomusicol; Intro; Mus Ed (Elem & HS); Mus Therapy; Perf
Degrees: BA
Scholarships: Performance scholarships available for students with a 3.0 (B) GPA

TROY STATE UNIVERSITY
Music Department
Troy, AL 36082
(205) 566-3000
Staff: John M. Long, Chairman, Music Department; Dean, College of Arts & Sciences; Dean, School of Fine Arts
Affiliation: State-supported university
Accreditation: SACS; NCATE
Areas: App Mus; Hist & Lit; Th & An; Comp; Cond; Orch; Opera; Church Mus; Mus Ed (Elem & HS); Theater Mus
Degrees: BA; BME; MM; MS; Mus Ed
Scholarships: All types of scholarships awarded by audition

UNIVERSITY OF ALABAMA
Department of Music
P.O. Box 2876
University, AL 35486
(205) 348-7110
Staff: Dr. Dennis C. Monk, Head
Affiliation: State-supported university
Accreditation: SACS; NASM
Areas: Perf; Hist & Lit; Th & An; Comp; Cond; Orch; Opera; Hist Musicol; Mus Ed (Elem & HS); Instr Rep; Electr Mus
Degrees: BA; BM; EdD
Scholarships: Awarded to music majors

UNIVERSITY OF ALABAMA, BIRMINGHAM
Department of Music, School of Humanities
321 Bldg. #3, UAB
Birmingham, AL 35294
(205) 934-7375
Staff: Dr. Ronald Clemmons, Chairman
Affiliation: State-supported university
Accreditation: SACS
Areas: Hist & Lit; Th & An; Comp; Cond; Orch; Mus Ed (Elem); Electr Mus; Intro; App Mus (limited); Chorus; Band; Mus Therapy; Jazz; Choir; Commer Mus
Degrees: BA

UNIVERSITY OF ALABAMA, HUNTSVILLE
Department of Music
Huntsville, AL 35899
(205) 895-6436
Staff: Dr. D. Royce Boyer, Chairman
Affiliation: State-supported university
Accreditation: SACS
Areas: App Mus; Hist & Lit; Cond; Intro; Mus Ed (Elem & HS); Piano Tech; Perf
Degrees: BA; BA, Mus Ed
Scholarships: Scholarships of partial and full tuition available

UNIVERSITY OF MONTEVALLO
Music Department
Montevallo, AL 35115
(205) 665-2521, x202
Staff: Theodore M. Pritchett, Chairman
Affiliation: State-supported university
Accreditation: NASM; NCATE; SACS
Areas: App Mus; Hist & Lit; Th & An; Comp; Cond; Orch; Opera; Church Mus; Mus Ed (Elem & HS); Perf
Degrees: BA; BM; BME; BS, Mus; MM; MME
Scholarships: Band and music scholarships awarded on the basis of audition and 1.5 GPA (on 3.0 scale)

UNIVERSITY OF NORTH ALABAMA[1]
Music Department
Florence, AL 35632
(205) 766-4100, ext. 361
Staff: Dr. James K. Simpson, Chairman
Affiliation: State-supported university
Accreditation: SACS; NCATE
Areas: App Mus; Commer Mus
Degrees: BA; BA, Commer Mus; BS, Commer Mus; MA, Ed
Scholarships: Small Scholarships available to select members of band and choir

UNIVERSITY OF SOUTH ALABAMA
Department of Music
9 Faculty Court E.
Mobile, AL 36688
(205) 460-6136
Staff: Dr. Andrew Harper, Chairman
Affiliation: State-supported university
Accreditation: NASM; NCATE; SACS
Areas: App Mus; Hist & Lit; Th & An; Comp; Cond; Orch; Opera; Church Mus; Mus Ed (Elem & HS); Perf
Degrees: BA; BM; MS, Mus Ed
Scholarships: Awarded on the basis of competitive auditions

ALASKA

UNIVERSITY OF ALASKA[1]
Department of Music
Fairbanks, AK 99701
(907) 479-7555
Staff: Theodore DeCorso, Head
Affiliation: State-supported university
Accreditation: NASM; NASC
Areas: Hist & Lit; Ethnomusicol; Mus Ed (Elem & HS); Perf
Degrees: BA; BM; MA

ARIZONA

ARIZONA STATE UNIVERSITY[1]
School of Music
Tempe, AZ 85281
(602) 965-3371
Staff: George E. Umberson, Director
Affiliation: State-supported university
Accreditation: NASM; NCA
Areas: App Mus; Hist & Lit; Th & An; Comp; Mus Ed (Elem & HS); Mus Therapy; Theater Mus; Perf
Degrees: BA; BM; MA; MM; EdD; PhD
Scholarships: Scholarships in all areas awarded by audition

GRAND CANYON COLLEGE
Music Department, Performing Arts
3300 W. Camelback Rd.
Phoenix, AZ 85017
(602) 249-3300
Staff: Dr. Louis L. Sherman, Chairman, Performing Arts
Affiliation: Christian liberal arts college (Southern Baptist)
Accreditation: NCA
Areas: App Mus; Hist & Lit; Th & An; Comp; Cond; Opera; Church Mus; Intro; Mus Ed (Elem & HS); Perf; Theater Mus; Perf Arts
Degrees: BA; BS, Mus Ed
Scholarships: Vocal, instrumental, piano, and organ scholarships awarded by audition (in person or on tape) and application

NORTHERN ARIZONA UNIVERSITY
College of Creative Arts
Music Department

Flagstaff, AZ 86011
(602) 523-9011, 3731
Staff: Dr. Pat B. Curry, Chairman, Music Department
Affiliation: State-supported university
Accreditation: NASM; NCATE: NCA
Areas: App. Mus; Hist & Lit; Th & An; Comp; Cond; Orch; Opera; Mus Ed (Elem & HS); Piano Tech; Perf
Degrees: BA; BM; BME; BS; MM; MA, Mus Ed
Scholarships: Band, choral, orchestra, opera, piano, accompanying scholarships available

THE UNIVERSITY OF ARIZONA
School of Music
Tucson, AZ 85721
(602) 884-1655
Staff: Dr. Robert J. Werner, Director
Affiliation: State-supported university
Accreditation: NASM; NCA
Areas: App Mus; Hist & Lit; Th & An; Comp; Orch; Opera; Hist Musicol; Intro; Mus Ed (Elem & HS); Theater Mus; Electr Mus; Perf; Cond
Degrees: BA; BM; MM; DMA; PhD
Scholarships: Full-tuition waivers and cash awards based on application and audition

ARKANSAS

ARKANSAS COLLEGE[1]
Humanities Division
Batesville, AR 72501
(501) 793-9813
Staff: Dr. Terrell Tebbetts, Program Director
Affiliation: Church-related liberal arts college (Presbyterian)
Accreditation: NCA
Areas: App Mus; Hist & Lit; Th & An; Cond; Mus Ed (HS)
Degrees: BA
Scholarships: Few scholarships available

ARKANSAS STATE UNIVERSITY
Division of Music
State University, AR 72467
(501) 972-2094
Staff: Ervin J. Dunham, Interim Chairman
Affiliation: State
Accreditation: NASM; NCATE; NCA
Areas: App Mus; Hist & Lit; Th & An; Comp; Cond; Orch; Mus Ed (Elem & HS); Opera; Church Mus; Perf
Degrees: BM; BME; MM; MME
Scholarships: Scholarships available through audition in keyboard, band, choir

ARKANSAS TECH UNIVERSITY
Music Department, School of Liberal and Fine Arts
Russellville, AR 72801
(501) 968-0368
Staff: Robert L. Casey, Head
Affiliation: State-supported university
Accreditation: NASM; NCATE: NCA
Areas: App Mus; Hist & Lit; Th & An; Comp; Cond; Orch; Mus Ed (Elem & HS)
Degrees: BA; BA, Mus Ed; MEd
Scholarships: Performance scholarships awarded by audition

THE COLLEGE OF THE OZARKS
Department of Music, Division of Humanities and Fine Arts
Clarksville, AR 72830
(501) 754-3642
Staff: William E. Borland, Instructor in Music
Affiliation: Private church-related liberal arts college (Presbyterian)
Accreditation: NCA
Areas: App Mus; Hist & Lit; Th & An; Cond; Orch; Mus Ed (Elem & HS)
Degrees: BA; BME
Scholarships: Awards based on declaration of music major and performance in one or more ensembles

HARDING UNIVERSITY
Music Department
Box 772
Searcy, AR 72143
(501) 268-6161, x343
Staff: Dr. Kenneth Davis, Jr., Chairman
Affiliation: Private liberal arts Christian university (Church of Christ)
Accreditation: NCATE, NCA
Areas: App Mus; Hist & Lit; Th & An; Comp; Cond; Orch; Church Mus; Mus Ed (Elem & HS)
Degrees: BA; BM; BME
Scholarships: Scholarships available for orchestra, band, choral, and various instruments; based on personal audition or letter and audition tape

HENDERSON STATE UNIVERSITY[1]
Department of Music
Arkadelphia, AR 71923
(501) 246-4627
Staff: Wendell O. Evanson, Chairman
Affiliation: State
Accreditation: NASM; NCA
Areas: App Mus; Cond; Th & An; Mus Ed (Elem & HS); Opera; Orch; Cond; Hist & Lit
Degrees: BA, BM, BME, MME

HENDRIX COLLEGE
Music Department
1525 Washington
Conway, AR 72032
(501) 450-1245
Staff: Harold Thompson, Chairman
Affiliation: Church-related (United Methodist)
Accreditation: NASM; NCA
Areas: App Mus; Hist & Lit; Th & An; Cond; Orch; Mus Ed (Elem & HS)
Degrees: BA

JOHN BROWN UNIVERSITY
Music Department
Siloam Springs, AR 72761
(501) 524-3131, x154
Staff: Joe Zimmerman, Head
Affiliation: Interdenominational
Accreditation: NCA; NCATE
Areas: App Mus; Hist & Lit; Th & An; Cond; Church Mus; Mus Ed (Elem & HS)
Degrees: BA, BM, BME
Scholarships: Music scholarships awarded on basis of ability shown at an audition for admissions.

OUACHITA BAPTIST UNIVERSITY
School of Music
Arkadelphia, AR 71923
(501) 246-4531
Staff: Dr. Charles N. Wright, Dean
Affiliation: Church-related liberal arts university (Baptist)
Accreditation: NASM; NCATE: NCA
Areas: App Mus; Hist & Lit; Th & An; Comp; Cond; Orch; Opera; Church Mus; Mus Ed (Elem & HS); Electr Mus; Perf; Hist Musicol; Intro
Degrees: BA; BM; BME; MME
Scholarships: Music scholarships in voice, piano, organ, woodwinds, strings, brass, percussion awarded through application and audition

PHILANDER SMITH COLLEGE[1]
PO Box 2500
812 W. 13th St.
Little Rock, AR 72203
(501) 375-9845
Staff: Grace G. Eubanks, Assistant Professor
Affiliation: Church-related (United Methodist)
Accreditation: NCA
Areas: Th & An; Mus Ed (Elem & HS); Hist & Lit
Degrees: BA

SOUTHERN ARKANSAS UNIVERSITY
Music Department
Magnolia, AR 71753
(501) 234-5120
Staff: David L. Crouse, Head
Affiliation: State-supported university
Accreditation: NASM; NCA
Areas: App Mus; Hist & Lit; Th & An; Cond; Orch; Church Mus; Mus Ed (Elem & HS)
Degrees: BA; BME
Scholarships: Voice, keyboard, choral, band, instrumental scholarships awarded through audition

UNIVERSITY OF ARKANSAS AT FAYETTEVILLE
Music Department
FAA 201A
Fayetteville, AR 72701
(501) 575-4701
Staff: Arthur Tollefson, Chairman
Affiliation: State-supported university
Accreditation: NASM; NCA
Areas: App Mus; Hist & Lit; Th & An; Comp; Cond; Orch; Opera; Hist Musicol; Intro; Mus Ed (Elem & HS);

Electr Mus; Perf
Degrees: BA; BM; BS, Mus Ed; MM; MA, Mus Ed
Scholarships: Applied music scholarships up to full tuition awarded by audition

UNIVERSITY OF ARKANSAS AT LITTLE ROCK
Department of Music, College of Fine Arts
33rd and University
Little Rock, AR 72204
(501) 569-3294
Staff: Dr. Richard Sieber, Chairman
Affiliation: State-supported university
Accreditation: NASM; NCA; NCATE
Areas: App Mus; Hist & Lit; Th & An; Mus Ed (Elem & HS); Perf; Comp; Cond; Orch; Intro; Hist Jazz
Degrees: BA; BM; BME
Scholarships: Approximately 25 $100–$800 annual awards based on audition

UNIVERSITY OF ARKANSAS AT MONTICELLO
Department of Fine Arts
P.O. Box 3607-UAM
Monticello, AR 71655
(501) 367-6811
Staff: Annette Hall, Acting Head,
Affiliation: State-supported university
Accreditation: NASM; NCA
Areas: App Mus; Hist & Lit; Th & An; Comp; Cond; Orch; Opera; Church Mus; Intro; Mus Ed (Elem & HS)
Degrees: BA
Scholarships: Choir and band scholarships awarded by audition

UNIVERSITY OF CENTRAL ARKANSAS[1]
Music Department
Box 1726-UCA
Conway, AR 72032
(501) 450-3163
Staff: Dr. Sam Driggers, Chairman
Affiliation: State-supported liberal arts and teachers college
Accreditation: NASM; NCA
Areas: App Mus; Mus Hist & Lit; Th & An; Comp; Cond; Orch; Opera; Hist Musicol; Intro; Mus Ed (Elem & HS); Instr Rep; Perf
Degrees: BM; BME; MME
Scholarships: Performance scholarships (full tuition and applied fee waivers) awarded in all areas of applied music, band, and choir

CALIFORNIA

AZUSA PACIFIC COLLEGE[1]
Division of Fine Arts
Citrus and Alosta
Azusa, CA 91702
(213) 969-3434
Staff: Dr. Gary Bonner, Chairman
Affiliation: Church-related liberal arts college (Christian)
Accreditation: WASC
Areas: App Mus; Hist & Lit; Th & An; Comp; Cond; Orch; Opera; Church Mus; Intro; Mus Ed (Elem & HS); Perf
Degrees: BA
Scholarships: Scholarships of up to $1,200 awarded on the basis of audition and participation in performance group(s)

BETHANY BIBLE COLLEGE
Music Division
800 Bethany Dr.
Santa Cruz, CA 95066
(408) 438-3800
Staff: Kathryn Wilson, Chairperson
Affiliation: Church-related college (Assembly of God)
Accreditation: AABC; WASC
Areas: App Mus; Hist & Lit; Th & An; Comp; Cond; Orch; Church Mus; Mus Ed (Elem & Hs); Perf
Degrees: BA
Scholarships: Available by audition

BIOLA UNIVERSITY[1]
Department of Music
13800 Biola Ave.
La Mirada, CA 90639
(213) 944-0351, x3230
Staff: Dr. Jack W. Schwarz, Chairman
Affiliation: Private Christian liberal arts college
Accreditation: NASM; WASC
Areas: App Mus; Hist & Lit; Th & An; Comp; Cond; Orch; Opera; Church Mus; Intro; Mus Ed (Elem & HS); Electr Mus; Perf
Degrees: BA; BM
Scholarships: Performance scholarships awarded through application and audition; major awards given annually in composition and organ

CALIFORNIA BAPTIST COLLEGE
Riverside, CA 92504
(714) 689-5771
Staff: Donald Shannon, Chairman
Affiliation: Church-related (Southern Baptist)
Accreditation: WASC
Areas: App Mus; Hist & Lit; Church Mus; Th & An; Mus Ed (Elem)
Degrees: BA; BM
Scholarships: Performing ensemble scholarships, 50% tuition per semester; merit scholarships, $250 per semester

CALIFORNIA INSTITUTE OF THE ARTS[1]
School of Music
24700 McBean Pkwy
Valencia, CA 91355
(805) 255-1050
Staff: Dr. Nicholas M. England, Dean
Affiliation: College of performing and visual arts
Accreditation: NASM; WASC
Areas: Comp; Perf; Gen Mus
Degrees: BFA; MFA; Cert
Scholarships: Scholarships, work-study programs, NDSL, and FISL awarded on the basis of financial need and musical accomplishment; special scholarships for Twentieth-Century Players (ensemble) and String Quartets

CALIFORNIA LUTHERAN COLLEGE
Music Department
60 Olsen Rd.
Thousand Oaks, CA 91360
(805) 492-2411
Staff: Prof. Carl B. Swanson, Chairman
Affiliation: Church-related liberal arts college (Lutheran)
Accreditation: WASC
Areas: App Mus; Hist & Lit; Th & An; Comp; Cond; Orch; Opera; Church Mus; Mus Ed (Elem)
Degrees: BA

CALIFORNIA STATE COLLEGE, SAN BERNARDINO[1]
Music Department
5500 State College Pkwy.
San Bernardino, CA 92407
(714) 887-7454
Staff: Loren Filbeck, Chairman
Affiliation: State
Accreditation: WASC
Areas: App Mus; Hist & Lit; Th & An; Comp; Mus Ed (Elem & HS); Cond; Orch; Opera; Hist Musicol; Ethnomusicol; Perf
Degrees: BA

CALIFORNIA STATE COLLEGE, STANISLAUS
800 Monte Vista Ave.
Turlock, CA 95380
(209) 667-3421
Staff: Dr. Donald Williams, Chairman
Affiliation: State-supported liberal arts college
Accreditation: WASC, NASM
Areas: App Mus; Th & An; Comp; Hist & Lit; Orch; Cond; Intro; Mus Ed (Elem & HS); Electr Mus; Perf
Degrees: BA
Scholarships: Scholarships from $100 to $400 available on the basis of performance ability, scholastic achievement, recommendations

CALIFORNIA POLYTECHNIC STATE UNIVERSITY
Music Department, School of Communication Arts & Humanities
San Luis Obispo, CA 93407
(805) 546-2406
Staff: Prof. Bessie R. Swanson, Head
Affiliation: State-supported university
Accreditation: WASC
Areas: App Mus; Hist & Lit; Th & An; Comp; Cond; Intro; Mus Ed (Elem); Perf; Orch; Hist Musicol
Degrees: Intro courses only; no music major offered; strong music minor with upper division courses

CALIFORNIA POLYTECHNIC STATE UNIVERSITY, POMONA
Music Department
3801 W. Temple Ave.
Pomona, CA 91768
(714) 598-4587
Staff: Dr. Donald Ambroson, Chairman
Affiliation: State university
Accreditation: WASC
Areas: App Mus; Hist & Lit; Th & An; Comp; Cond; Orch; Opera; Ethnomusicol; Mus Ed (Elem & HS); Theater Mus; Jazz Studies; Intro; Electr Mus
Degrees: BA
Scholarships: Hemmick Award in voice; Patricia J. Richards Piano Scholarship; music department scholarships

CALIFORNIA STATE UNIVERSITY, CHICO
Department of Music
Chico, CA 95929
(916) 345-5152
Staff: Raymond Barker, Chairman
Affiliation: State-supported university
Accreditation: NASM; WASC
Areas: App Mus; Hist & Lit; Th & An; Comp; Cond; Orch; Opera; Church Mus; Intro; Mus Ed (Elem & HS); Instr Rep; Electr Mus; Perf
Degrees: BA; MA
Scholarships: Scholarships of $100 to $500 available; most require recipients to play in a performing group

CALIFORNIA STATE UNIVERSITY, DOMINGUEZ HILLS
Department of Music
Carson, CA 90747
(213) 516-3543
Staff: Frances Steiner, Chairman
Affiliation: State-supported university; part of 19-campus state university and college system
Accreditation: NASM; WASC
Areas: App Mus; Hist & Lit; Th & An; Comp; Cond; Orch; Intro; Mus Ed (Elem); Electr Mus; Perf; Ethno Musicol; Recording; Telecommunications
Degrees: BA
Scholarships: Several scholarships offered each year; auditions held in April; large grants available for orchestral players

CALIFORNIA STATE UNIVERSITY, FRESNO
Fresno, CA 93740
(209) 294-2654
Staff: Phyllis A. Irwin, Professor
Affiliation: State
Accreditation: NASM; WASC
Areas: Comp; Perf; Hist Musicol; Th & An; App Mus; Hist & Lit; Orch; Intro; Cond; Opera; Mus Ed (Elem & HS); Theater Mus; Electr Mus
Degrees: BA; MA

CALIFORNIA STATE UNIVERSITY, FULLERTON
Department of Music
800 N. State College Blvd.
Fullerton, CA 92634
(714) 773-3511
Staff: David Thorsen, Chairman
Affiliation: State-supported university
Accreditation: NASM; WASC
Areas: App Mus; Hist & Lit; Th & An; Comp; Cond; Orch; Opera; Hist Musicol; Mus Ed (Elem & HS); Perf; Electr Mus
Degrees: BA; BM; MA; MM
Scholarships: Limited funds available to cover fees only; audition required

CALIFORNIA STATE UNIVERSITY, HAYWARD
Music Department
Hayward, CA 94542
(415) 881-3135
Staff: Allen Gove, Chairman
Affiliation: State-supported university
Accreditation: NASM; WASC
Areas: App Mus; Hist & Lit; Th & An; Comp; Cond; Orch; Opera; Mus Ed (Elem & HS)
Degrees: BA; MA
Scholarships: Scholarships available

CALIFORNIA STATE UNIVERSITY, LONG BEACH
Department of Music
1250 Bellflower Blvd.
Long Beach, CA 90840
(213) 498-4781
Staff: Dr. David Kuehn, Chairman
Affiliation: State-supported university
Accreditation: NASM; WASC
Areas: App Mus; Hist & Lit; Comp; Opera; Mus Ed (Elem & HS); Mus Therapy; Theater Mus; Perf; Commer Mus
Degrees: BA; BM; MA
Scholarships: Various scholarships available

CALIFORNIA STATE UNIVERSITY, LOS ANGELES
Department of Music, School of Fine and Applied Arts
5151 State University Dr.
Los Angeles, CA 90032
(213) 224-3448
Staff: Dr. J. Zebulon King, Chairman
Affiliation: State university
Accreditation: NASM; WASC
Areas: App Mus; Hist & Lit; Th & An; Comp; Cond; Orch; Opera; Hist Musicol; Ethnomusicol; Intro; Mus Ed (Elem & HS); Perf
Degrees: BA; BM; MA; MA, Mus Ed
Scholarships: 300 scholarships per year awarded by audition or faculty recognition of talent

CALIFORNIA STATE UNIVERSITY, NORTHRIDGE
Department of Music
18111 Nordhoff St.
Northridge, CA 91330
(213) 885-3184
Staff: Clarence Wiggins, Chairman
Affiliation: State-supported university
Accreditation: NASM; WASC
Areas: App Mus; Hist & Lit; Th & An; Comp; Cond; Orch; Opera; Hist Musicol; Church Mus; Mus Ed (Elem & HS); Mus Therapy; Piano Tech; Instr Rep; Jazz; Commer Mus
Degrees: BA; BM; MA; MA, Mus Ed
Scholarships: Music achievement awards granted by audition

CALIFORNIA STATE UNIVERSITY, SACRAMENTO
Music Department
6000 Jay St.
Sacramento, CA 95819
(916) 454-6514
Staff: Louis O. Clayson, Chairman
Affiliation: State-supported university
Accreditation: NASM; WASC
Areas: App Mus; Hist & Lit; Th & An; Comp; Cond; Orch; Opera; Hist Musicol; Ethnomusicol; Mus Ed (Elem & HS); Theater Mus; Jazz Studies
Degrees: BA; BM; MA
Scholarships: Applied music scholarships awarded by audition

CHAPMAN COLLEGE
Department of Music
333 N. Glassell St.
Orange, CA 92666
(714) 997-6871
Staff: Thomas G. Hall, Chairman
Affiliation: Private liberal arts college
Accreditation: WASC
Areas: App Mus; Hist & Lit; Th & An; Comp; Cond; Orch; Opera; Hist Musicol; Mus Ed (Elem & HS); Intro; Electr Mus; Perf
Degrees: BA; BM; BME
Scholarships: Tuition awards granted on the basis of scholastic achievement and performance excellence (some awards not based on need)

CLAREMONT GRADUATE SCHOOL[1]
Music Department
Claremont, CA 91711
(714) 621-8081
Staff: Dr. Frank Traficante, Chairman
Affiliation: School of Music in a privately endowed university
Accreditation: WASC
Areas: App Mus; Hist & Lit; Th & An; Comp; Cond; Orch; Opera; Hist Musicol, Ethnomusicol, Church Mus (incorporated into other courses); Mus Ed (Elem & HS)
Degrees: MA; DMA; PhD

COLLEGE OF NOTRE DAME
Music Department
Ralston Ave.
Belmont, CA 94002
(415) 593-1601, x425
Staff: Birgitte Moyer, Chairman
Affiliation: Private church-related liberal arts college (Catholic)
Accreditation: NASM; WASC

Areas: App Mus; Hist & Lit; Th & An; Comp; Cond; Orch; Opera; Mus Ed (Elem & HS)
Degrees: BA; BM; MM; MAT
Scholarships: Sr. Anthony Marie Memorial Scholarship; John S. Brooks Scholarship; music assistance grants, based on performance and/or need; College of Notre Dame scholarships, based on need and GPA; Regents Merit Scholarships, based on GPA only, available to transfer students

DOMINICAN COLLEGE OF SAN RAFAEL
Music Department
San Rafael, CA 94901
(415) 457-4440
Staff: Ted M. Blair, Chairman
Affiliation: Church-related liberal arts college (Catholic)
Accreditation: WASC
Areas: App Mus; Hist & Lit; Th & An; Comp; Cond; Orch; Opera; Hist Musicol; Intro; Perf
Degrees: BA; BM; MA; MM
Scholarships: Scholarships for lessons available to music majors only; music scholarships awarded on a competitive basis for performers, composers, scholars; internships with the Marin Opera; may be aplied toward music fees, accompanists/coaches, tuition

FRESNO PACIFIC COLLEGE
Music Department
1717 S. Chestnut
Fresno, CA 93702
(209) 251-2194
Staff: Dr. Larry Warkentin, Chairman
Affiliation: Private church-related liberal arts college (Mennonite Brethren)
Accreditation: WASC
Areas: App Mus; Hist & Lit; Th & An; Comp; Cond; Church Mus; Intro; Mus Ed (Elem & HS); Perf
Degrees: BA
Scholarships: Music performance scholarships awarded by audition

GOLDEN GATE BAPTIST THEOLOGICAL SEMINARY
Church Music Division
Strawberry Point
Mill Valley, CA 94941
(415) 388-8080
Staff: Dr. Craig Singleton, Chairman
Affiliation: One of 6 seminaries supported by Southern Baptist Convention
Accreditation: ATS; WASC; NASM
Areas: App Mus; Hist & Lit; Th & An; Comp; Cond; Orch; Church Mus; Mus Ed (Elem & HS)
Degrees: Assoc. of Church Music; Church Mus
Scholarships: Organ scholarship awarded on the basis of need; several fellowships and assistantships available

HOLY NAMES COLLEGE
Music Department
3500 Mountain Blvd.
Oakland, CA 94619
(415) 436-1052, 1031
Staff: Sr. Mary Alice Hein, Chairman
Affiliation: Private church-related liberal arts college (Catholic order—Sisters of the Holy Names)
Accreditation: NASM; WASC
Areas: App Mus; Hist & Lit; Th & An; Comp; Cond; Orch; Hist Musicol; Mus Ed (Elem & HS); Piano Tech
Degrees: BA; BM; MA; MM, Mus Ed; MS, Mus Ed; Cert in Kodaly Method of Education
Scholarships: 11 full and partial scholarships awarded to music majors on the basis of financial need, scholarship, and musical ability

HUMBOLDT STATE UNIVERSITY[1]
Department of Music
Arcata, CA 95521
(707) 826-3531
Staff: Janet Spinas, Chairman
Affiliation: State
Accreditation: NASM; WASC
Areas: App Mus; Hist & Lit; Th & An; Comp; Cond; Orch; Opera; Mus Ed (Elem & HS); Instr Rep
Degrees: BA, MA

LOMA LINDA UNIVERSITY
Department of Music
La Sierra Campus
Riverside, CA 92515
(714) 785-2036
Staff: Donald Thurber, Chairman
Affiliation: Church-related (Seventh-Day Adventist)
Accreditation: WASC
Areas: App Mus; Hist & Lit; Th & An; Comp; Cond; Orch; Church Mus; Mus Ed (Elem & HS); Hist Musicol; Intro; Perf
Degrees: BA, BM; BME
Scholarships: Several scholarships, $600, available for incoming freshmen on the basis of performing excellence and GPA 3.0 or better

LOS ANGELES BAPTIST COLLEGE
Music Department
21726 W. Placerita Canyon Rd.
Box 878
Newhall, CA 91321
(805) 259-3540; (213) 367-6193
Staff: Paul T. Plew, Chairman
Affiliation: Private church-related liberal arts college (General Association of Regular Baptist Churches)
Accreditation: NASM; WASC
Areas: App Mus; Hist & Lit; Th & An; Comp; Cond; Orch; Church Mus; Mus Ed (Elem & HS); Instr Techniques; Accomp; Voice/Piano Lit & Ped; Intro; Organ Lit & Ped
Degrees: BA
Scholarships: Memorial scholarships and college (departmental) scholarships awarded on the basis of need, GPA, attitude, and excellence in music

LOYOLA MARYMOUNT UNIVERSITY[1]
Music Department
Loyola Blvd. at W. 80th St.
Los Angeles, CA 90045
(213) 642-2700
Staff: Leroy W. Southers, Jr., Chairman
Affiliation: Church-related liberal arts college (Roman Catholic)
Accreditation: WASC; NCATE
Areas: App Mus; Hist & Lit; Th & An; Comp; Cond; Orch; Ethnomusicol; Mus Ed (Elem & HS)
Degrees: BA

MILLS COLLEGE[1]
Music Department
Oakland, CA 94613
(415) 430-2100
Staff: Dr. Susan Summerfield, Head
Affiliation: Private liberal arts college
Accreditation: WASC
Areas: App Mus; Hist & Lit; Th & An; Comp; Cond; Ethnomusicol; Intro; Electr Mus; Perf
Degrees: BA; MA; MFA
Scholarships: Awarded on the basis of performance/composition ability

MOUNT ST. MARY'S COLLEGE[1]
Department of Music
12001 Chalon Road
Los Angeles, CA 90049
(213) 476-2237 x263
Staff: Sr. Teresita Espinosa, Chairman
Affiliation: Church-related (Roman Catholic)
Accreditation: NASM; WASC
Areas: App Mus; Hist & Lit; Th & An; Comp; Church Mus; Mus Ed (Elem & HS)
Degrees: BA, BM

MUSIC AND ARTS INSTITUTE OF SAN FRANCISCO
2622 Jackson St.
San Francisco, CA 94115
(415) 567-1445
Staff: Ross McKee, Director
Affiliation: College preparatory training for high school students; junior division for children
Accreditation: California State
Areas: Comp; Cond; Perf; Voice; Opera; Choral; Instruments; Ped; Harmony; Counterpoint, Form & Analysis; Ensembles; Intensive English and Speech Program
Degrees: BA; MA (music degrees)
Scholarships: Outsanding performer scholarships, $600 per year, require 1 full solo recital each year of study and maintained scholarship standing; partial scholarships, $250 per year, must maintain satisfactory grades and demonstrate financial need

OCCIDENTAL COLLEGE
Department of Music
1600 Campus Rd.
Los Angeles, CA 90041
(213) 259-2785
Staff: Dr. Richard Grayson, Chairman
Affiliation: Private
Accreditation: WASC
Areas: App Mus; Hist & Lit; Th & An; Comp; Cond; Orch; Hist Musicol
Degrees: BA

PACIFIC UNION COLLEGE
Department of Music
Angwin, CA 94508
(707) 965-6201
Staff: James McGee, Chairman
Affiliation: Church-related liberal arts college (Seventh-day Adventist)
Accreditation: NASM; WASC
Areas: App Mus; Hist & Lit; Th & An; Comp; Cond; Orch; Hist Musicol; Church Mus; Intro; Mus Ed (Elem & HS); Perf; Piano Ped
Degrees: BA; BM

PEPPERDINE UNIVERSITY AT MALIBU
Seaver College
Humanities-Fine Arts Division
Malibu, CA 90265
(213) 456-4225
Staff: James E. Smythe, Chairman
Affiliation: Church-related liberal arts university (Church of Christ)
Accreditation: NASM; WASC
Areas: App Mus; Hist & Lit; Th & An; Comp; Opera; Mus Ed (Elem & HS); Perf
Degrees: BA
Scholarships: Performance scholarships available

POINT LOMA COLLEGE
Music Department
3900 Lomaland Dr.
San Diego, CA 92106
(714) 222-6474, x210
Staff: Dr. Reuben Rodeheaver, Chairman
Affiliation: Private church-related liberal arts college (Church of the Nazarene)
Accreditation: WASC
Areas: App Mus; Hist & Lit; Th & An; Comp; Cond; Orch; Opera; Ethnomusicol; Church Mus; Mus Ed (Elem & HS); Perf; Intro; Mus Bus
Degrees: BA
Scholarships: Music grants for full-time music majors awarded by audition

POMONA COLLEGE[1]
Department of Music
Thatcher Music Building
Claremont, CA 91711
(714) 621-8155
Staff: William F. Russell, Chairman
Affiliation: Privately supported liberal arts college
Accreditation: WASC
Areas: App Mus; Hist & Lit; Th & An; Comp; Cond; Orch; Hist Musicol; Perf
Degrees: BA
Scholarships: All scholarships in general pool; none specifically in music

SAN DIEGO STATE UNIVERSITY[1]
Department of Music
5402 College Ave.
San Diego, CA 92182
(714) 265-6031
Staff: Robert E. Brown, Chairman
Affiliation: State-supported university
Accreditation: NASM; WASC
Calendar: Semester
Areas: App Mus; Hist & Lit; Th & An; Comp; Cond; Opera; Hist Musicol; Ethnomusicol; Mus Ed (Elem & HS); Theater Mus; Electr Mus; Harry Partch Ens; Jazz
Degrees: BA; BM; MA
Scholarships: Band and orchestra performance scholarships of tuition and cash awarded on the basis of audition system

SAN FRANCISCO CONSERVATORY OF MUSIC
1201 Ortega St.
San Francisco, CA 94122
(412) 564-8086
Staff: Richard Howe, Dean
Affiliation: Privately supported independent conservatory
Accreditation: NASM; WASC
Areas: App Mus; Hist & Lit; Th & An; Comp; Cond; Orch; Opera; Perf
Degrees: BM; MM
Scholarships: Awarded on the basis of audition

SAN FRANCISCO STATE UNIVERSITY[1]
Department of Music
1600 Holloway Ave.
San Francisco, CA 94132
(415) 469-1431
Staff: Richard Webb, Chair
Affiliation: State-supported university
Accreditation: NASM; WASC
Areas: App Mus; Hist & Lit; Th & An; Comp; Orch; Opera; Hist Musicol; Mus Ed (Elem & HS)
Degrees: BA; BM; MA
Scholarships: Performance and scholastic scholarships available for full-time students

SAN JOSE BIBLE COLLEGE
Music Department
PO Box 1090
San Jose, CA 95108
(Street Address: 790 S. 12th St., San Jose, CA 95112)
(408) 295-5053
Staff: Eileen McDaniel, Professor and Chairman
Affiliation: Private church-related college (Christian Churches & Churches of Christ)
Accreditation: AABC
Areas: App Mus; Hist & Lit; Th & An; Cond; Church Mus; Choral Methods; Arrang
Degrees: BS, Mus minor
Scholarships: 10 tuition scholarships for students involved in traveling music ensemble; 1 full scholarship for a selected student involved in local music ministry in a church

SAN JOSE STATE UNIVERSITY
Music Department
125 S. Seventh
San Jose, CA 95192
(408) 277-2905
Staff: Dr. Gus C. Lease, Interim Chairman
Affiliation: State-supported liberal arts university
Accreditation: NASM; WASC
Areas: App Mus; Hist & Lit; Th & An; Comp; Cond; Orch; Opera; Hist Musicol; Ethnomusicol; Church Mus; Intro; Mus Ed (Elem & HS); Theater Mus; Instr Rep; Electr Mus; Perf; Jazz
Degrees: BA; BM; MA; MA, Mus Ed
Scholarships: More than 40 scholarships granted on level of performance ability

SCRIPPS COLLEGE
Music Department
10th St., Columbia Ave.
Claremont, CA 91711
(714) 621-8000, ext. 3266
Staff: Preethi de Silva, Executive Officer, Music Faculty
Affiliation: Private liberal arts college
Accreditation: WASC
Areas: App Mus; Hist & Lit; Th & An; Comp; Cond; Orch; Intro; Perf
Degrees: BA

SIMPSON COLLEGE
Music Department
801 Silver Ave.
San Francisco, CA 94134
(415) 334-7400
Affiliation: Church-related liberal arts college (Christian and Missionary Alliance)
Accreditation: WASC; AABC
Areas: App Mus; Hist & Lit; Th & An; Cond; Church Mus; Mus Ed (Elem)
Degrees: BA
Scholarships: Tuition scholarships awarded on the basis of need, audition, and GPA

SONOMA STATE UNIVERSITY
Department of Music
1801 E. Cotati Ave.
Rohnert Park, CA 94928
(707) 664-2324
Staff: Larry A. Snyder, Associate Dean of Performing Arts; Gardner Rust, Chairman, Music Department
Affiliation: State-supported university, California State College and University system
Accreditation: NASM; WASC
Areas: App Mus; Hist & Lit; Th & An; Comp; cond; Orch; Opera; Hist Musicol; Ethnomusicol; Mus Ed (Elem & HS); Rec; Electr Mus Comp

Degrees: BA, (degree options in Jazz, Commer Mus, Perf)
Scholarships: Tuition scholarships of approximately $100 per semester awarded on the basis of audition or submission of compositions or papers; consult Department of Music for details

SOUTHERN CALIFORNIA COLLEGE
Music Department, Humanities Division
55 Fair Dr.
Costa Mesa, CA 92626
(714) 556-3610
Staff: John M. Leverett, Chairman
Affiliation: Church-related liberal arts college (Assemblies of God)
Accreditation: WASC
Areas: App Mus; Hist & Lit; Th & An; Comp; Cond; Church Mus; Intro; Mus Ed (Elem & HS)
Degrees: BA
Scholarships: Music scholarships available to deserving and needy music majors

STANFORD UNIVERSITY
Department of Music
Stanford, CA 94305
(415) 497-3811
Staff: Albert Cohen, Chairman
Affiliation: Private university
Accreditation: WASC
Areas: App Mus; Hist & Lit; Th & An; Comp; Cond; Orch; Opera; Hist Musicol; Church Mus; Hist Perf Prac; Computer Comp
Degrees: BA; MA; DMA; PhD
Scholarships: Contact the Department of Music for information

UNIVERSITY OF CALIFORNIA, BERKELEY
Music Department
Berkeley, CA 94720
(415) 642-2678
Staff: Lawrence H. Moe, Chairman
Affiliation: State-supported university
Accreditation: WASC
Areas: App Mus; Hist & Lit; Th & An; Comp; Cond; Orch; Hist Musicol; Ethnomusicol; Electr Mus
Degrees: BA; MA; PhD
Scholarships: Numerous types of scholarships awarded on the basis of scholastic standing and financial need

UNIVERSITY OF CALIFORNIA, DAVIS
Department of Music
Davis, CA 95616
(916) 752-0666
Staff: D. Kern Holoman, Chairman
Affiliation: State-supported university
Accreditation: WASC
Areas: App Mus; Hist & Lit; Th & An; Comp; Cond; Orch; Opera; Hist Musicol; Mus Ed (Elem & HS); Electr Mus
Degrees: BA; MA; MAT

UNIVERSITY OF CALIFORNIA, IRVINE
Music Department
Irvine, CA 92717
(714) 833-6615
Staff: Prof. Peter S. Odegard, Chairman
Affiliation: State-supported university
Accreditation: NASM; WASC
Areas: App Mus; Hist & Lit; Th & An; Comp; Cond; Orch; Opera; Hist Musicol; Theater Mus; Perf;Intro; Ethnomusicol
Degrees: BA; BM; MFA
Scholarships: Scholarships available in performance, composition, and history based on auditions

UNIVERSITY OF CALIFORNIA, LOS ANGELES
Department of Music
405 Hilgard Ave.
Los Angeles, CA 90024
(213) 825-4761
Staff: Dr. Abraham A. Schwadron, Chairman
Affiliation: State-supported university
Accreditation: WASC
Areas: App Mus; Hist & Lit; Th & An; Comp; Cond; Opera; Hist Musicol; Ethnomusicol; Intro; Mus Ed (Elem & HS); Electr Mus; Perf
Degrees: BA; MA; MFA; PhD
Scholarships: Numerous scholarships available—for new students by audition, and for continuing students by competition

UNIVERSITY OF CALIFORNIA, RIVERSIDE
Department of Music
Riverside, CA 92502
(714) 787-3138/5491
Staff: Prof. John C. Crawford, Chair
Affiliation: State-supported university
Accreditation: WASC
Areas: App Mus; Hist & Lit; Th & An; Comp; Hist Musicol; Perf; Electr Mus
Degrees: BA; MA
Scholarships: Chancellor's performance awards; graduate fellowships and teaching assistants

UNIVERSITY OF CALIFORNIA, SANTA BARBARA
Department of Music
Santa Barbara, CA 93106
(805) 961-2066
Staff: Dr. Dolores M. Hsu, Chairman
Affiliation: State-supported university
Accreditation: WASC
Areas: App Mus; Hist & Lit; Th & An; Comp; Cond; Orch; Opera; Hist Musicol; Electr Mus; Ethnomusicol; Perf
Degrees: BA; BM; MA; PhD

UNIVERSITY OF CALIFORNIA, SANTA CRUZ
Board of Studies in Music
Santa Cruz, CA 95064
(408) 429-2292, 2809
Staff: Linda Burman-Hall, Chair
Affiliation: State-supported university
Accreditation: WASC
Areas: App Mus; Hist & Lit; Th & An; Comp; Orch; Hist Musicol; Ethnomusicol; Early Mus Perf
Degrees: BA
Scholarships: Performance scholarships awarded by audition

UNIVERSITY OF REDLANDS
School of Music
1200 E. Colton Ave.
Redlands, CA 92373
(714) 793-2121
Staff: Philip J. Swanson, Director
Affiliation: Private selective liberal arts university
Accreditation: NASM; WASC
Areas: Hist & Lit; Th & An; Comp; Cond; Orch; Church Mus; Electr Mus; Black Mus; Mus Ed (Elem & HS); Intro; Theater Mus; Piano Tech; Perf
Degrees: BA; BFA; BM; MA; MM
Scholarships: 25 talent scholarships awarded annually—value between $300 and $3,000; extensive financial aid programs

UNIVERSITY OF SAN DIEGO
San Diego, CA 92110
(714) 291-6480 x4426
Staff: Marjorie Hart, Chairman
Affiliation: Church-related (Roman Catholic)
Accreditation: WASC
Areas: Opera; Intro; Hist & Lit; Th & An; Orch; App Mus
Degrees: BA

UNIVERSITY OF SANTA CLARA
Music Department
Santa Clara, CA 95053
(408) 984-4428
Staff: Lynn Shurtleff, Chairman
Affiliation: Privately endowed church-related university (Jesuit)
Accreditation: NASM; WASC
Areas: App Mus; Hist & Lit; Th; Comp; Cond; Church Mus
Degrees: BA
Scholarships: Awarded on the basis of admission to the university, maintenance of a C average, and audition in area of interest

UNIVERSITY OF SOUTHERN CALIFORNIA
School of Music
University Park
Los Angeles, CA 90089
(213) 743-6935
Staff: Dr. William Thomson, Director
Affiliation: Privately endowed university
Accreditation: NASM; WASC
Areas: App Mus; Hist & Lit; Th & An; Comp; Cond; Orch; Opera; Hist Musicol; Church Mus; Intro; Mus Ed (Elem & HS); Theater Mus; Electr Mus; Perf
Degrees: BA; BM; MA; MM; MME; DMA; PhD
Scholarships: Various scholarships awarded on the basis of performance

ability, academic achievement and financial need

UNIVERSITY OF THE PACIFIC
Conservatory of Music
3601 Pacific Ave.
Stockton, CA 95211
(209) 946-2415
Staff: Dr. Carl Nosse, Dean
Affiliation: Privately endowed university
Accreditation: NASM; NAMT; WASC
Areas: App Mus; Hist & Lit; Th & An; Com; Orch; Opera; Mus Ed (Elem & HS); Mus Therapy; Mus Mgmt-Bus
Degrees: BA; BM; MA; MM; EdD; BME; MAT
Scholarships: Scholarships available to outstanding students; financial aid available to qualified students

WESTMONT COLLEGE
955 La Paz Rd.
Santa Barbara, CA 93103
(805) 969-5051 x507
Staff: John Rapson, Chairman
Affiliation: Interdenominational Christian liberal arts college
Accreditation: WASC
Areas: App Mus; Hist & Lit; Th & An; Comp; Cond; Intro; Perf; Church Mus;
Degrees: BA

WHITTIER COLLEGE
Music Department
13406 E. Philadelphia
Whittier, CA 90608
(213) 693-0771, x319
Staff: Dr. Stephen A. Gothold, Chairman
Affiliation: Private liberal arts college
Accreditation: WASC
Areas: App Mus; Hist & Lit; Th & An; Comp; Cond; Orch; Mus Ed (Elem & HS)
Degrees: BA
Scholarships: Scholarships available

COLORADO

ADAMS STATE COLLEGE[1]
Music Department, Division of Arts and Letters
Alamosa, CO 81102
(303) 589-7703
Staff: Dr. Gordon Childs, Head
Affiliation: State-supported college
Accreditation: NCA
Areas: App Mus; Hist & Lit; Th & An; Cond; Orch; Intro; Mus Ed (Elem & HS); Theater Mus; Perf
Degrees: BA; MA, Mus Ed
Scholarships: Out-of-state scholarships very limited; application and audition required for activity grants

COLORADO COLLEGE
Music Department
Colorado Springs, CO 80903
(303) 473-2233 x545
Staff: Dr. Michael D. Grace, Chairman
Affiliation: Private liberal arts college
Accreditation: NASM; NCA
Areas: App Mus; Hist & Lit; Th & An; Comp; Cond; Orch; Opera; Hist Musicol; Ethnomusicol; Mus Ed (Elem & HS)
Degrees: BA; MAT

COLORADO STATE UNIVERSITY
Music Department
Fort Collins, CO 80521
(303) 491-5528
Staff: James McCray, Chairman
Affiliation: State-supported university
Accreditation: NASM; NCA
Areas: App Mus; Hist & Lit; Th & An; Comp; Cond; Church Mus; Intro; Mus Ed (Elem & HS); Mus Therapy; Perf
Degrees: BA; BM; BM, Mus Ed; MM
Scholarships: Performance awards and graduate teaching assistantships

FORT LEWIS COLLEGE
Music Department
Durango, CO 81301
(303) 247-7329
Staff: Dr. Ralph A. Downey, Chairman
Affiliation: State-supported liberal arts college
Accreditation: NCA; NCATE; candidate NASM
Areas: App Mus; Hist & Lit; Th & An; Comp; Cond; Orch; Intro; Mus Ed (Elem & HS); Perf
Degrees: BA
Scholarships: Presidential scholarships on the basis of GPA; Al Rose Scholarships awarded on the basis of musical talent and need; fine arts scholarships

LORETTO HEIGHTS COLLEGE
Music Department
3001 S. Federal Blvd.
Denver, CO 80236
(303) 936-8441, x337
Staff: Max Dijulio, Chairman
Affiliation: Private
Accreditation: NCA
Areas: App Mus; Hist & Lit; Th & An; Comp; Cond; Orch; Ethnomusicol; Church Mus; Mus Therapy; Theater Mus; Mus Ed (Elem & HS)
Degrees: BA

MESA COLLEGE[1]
Music Department
Grand Junction, CO 81501
(303) 248-1427
Staff: Darrell Blackburn, Chairman
Affiliation: State-supported college
Accreditation: NCA
Areas: App Mus; Hist & Lit; Th & An; Comp; Cond; Orch; Opera; Intro; Theater Mus; Perf
Degrees: BA; AA
Scholarships: Scholarship of $300 a year awarded to member of performing group

METROPOLITAN STATE COLLEGE[1]
Department of Music
1006 11th St.
Denver, CO 80204
(303) 629-3180
Staff: Dr. Hal Tamblyn, Chairman
Affiliation: State-supported urban-oriented college
Accreditation: NASM; NCA
Areas: App Mus; Hist & Lit; Th & An; Comp; Cond; Orch; Opera; Intro; Mus Ed (Elem & HS); Theater Mus; Perf
Degrees: BA
Scholarships: Colorado Scholars Awards of full tuition available

NAROPA INSTITUTE
Music Department
2130 Arapahoe Ave.
Boulder, CO 80302
(303) 444-0202
Staff: William Douglas, Administrator
Affiliation: Private liberal arts college; upper divisional
Accreditation: Candidate NCA
Areas: App Mus; Hist & Lit; Th & An; Comp; Mus Therapy; Jazz; World Mus
Degrees: BA
Scholarships: Scholarships available to outstanding applicants demonstrating financial need

UNIVERSITY OF COLORADO
College of Music
Boulder, CO 80309
(303) 492-6352
Staff: Robert R. Fink, Dean
Affiliation: State-supported university
Accreditation: NCA; NASM
Areas: App Mus; Hist & Lit; Th & An; Comp; Cond; Orch; Opera; Hist Musicol; Church Mus; Mus Ed (Elem & HS); Hist of Jazz; Aesth; Electr Mus Lab; Perf Prac of Early Mus
Degrees: BA; BM; BME; MM; MME; DMA; PhD
Scholarships: Various scholarships available

UNIVERSITY OF COLORADO AT DENVER[1]
College of Music
1100 14th St.
Denver, CO 80202
(303) 629-2727
Staff: Franz L. Roehmann, Resident Dean
Affiliation: Public state-supported university
Accreditation: NCA; NASM
Areas: App Mus; Hist & Lit; Th & An; Comp; Orch; Sound Synth; Rec Tech; Mus Bus
Degrees: BS, Mus
Scholarships: Channel 9 (ABC affiliate) offers 5 scholarships in media (music degree)

UNIVERSITY OF DENVER[1]
Lamont School of Music
2370 E. Evans Ave.
Denver, CO 80208
(303) 753-2197

Staff: Vincent C. LaGuardia, Jr., Director
Affiliation: Privately endowed university
Accreditation: NASM; NCA
Areas: App Mus; Hist & Lit; Th & An; Comp; Cond; Orch; Opera; Hist Musicol; Church Mus; Mus Ed (Elem & HS)
Degrees: BA; BFA; BM; BME; MA; MA, Mus Ed
Scholarships: Academic scholarships; music activity grants for members of instrumental and choral ensembles; Lamont teacher's scholarships in applied music awarded by audition; Dorthea C. Seeman Memorial Scholarship/Vivian Scholarship for students majoring in piano; Theodore Presser Foundation Scholarship of $400 per year for undergraduate music education majors awarded on the basis of merit and financial need; Lorena McDuff Scholarship of $1,000 per year for voice students; Jean Stewart Erdmann String Award of $1,000 awarded by audition; Lamont Competition Award of $1,000 cash and $8,000 in activity awards to cover 4 years of study awarded solely on the basis of competition

UNIVERSITY OF NORTHERN COLORADO
School of Music
Greeley, CO 80639
(303) 351-2678
Staff: James E. Miller, Director
Affiliation: State-supported university
Accreditation: NASM; NCA
Areas: App Mus; Hist & Lit; Th & An; Comp; Ethnolmusicol; Intro; Perf; Cond; Orch; Opera; Hist Musicol; Church Mus; Mus Ed (Elem & HS); Theater Mus; Instr Rep; Electr Mus
Degrees: BA; BM; BME; MM; MME; DME; DA
Scholarships: Performing scholarships in strings and talentships in all areas available

UNIVERSITY OF SOUTHERN COLORADO[1]
Department of Music
2200 N. Bonforte Blvd.
Pueblo, CO 81001
(303) 549-2552
Staff: Doyle K. Muller, Chairman
Affiliation: State-supported university
Accreditation: NASM; NCA
Areas: App Mus; Hist & Lit; Th & An; Cond; Orch; Mus Ed (Elem & HS)
Degrees: BA; BS, Mus Th; BS, Mus Perf
Scholarships: Presidential Achievement Award and limited private scholarships awarded on the basis of successful performance audition and appropriate GPA

WESTERN STATE COLLEGE OF COLORADO
Division of Music
Gunnison, CO 81230
(303) 943-3093
Staff: Dr. David Sweetkind, Chairman
Affiliation: State-supported liberal arts college
Accreditation: NASM; NCA
Areas: App Mus; Hist & Lit; Th & An; Comp; Cond; Orch; Opera; Intro; Mus Ed (Elem & HS); Electr Mus; Perf
Degrees: BA; MA
Scholarships: Scholarships available for in-state students; limited funds available for outstanding out-of-state students through foundations

CONNECTICUT

CENTRAL CONNECTICUT STATE COLLEGE
Music Department
1615 Stanley St.
New Britain, CT 06050
(203) 827-7251
Staff: B. Glenn Chandler, Chairman
Affiliation: State-supported liberal arts and teachers college
Accreditation: NEA; NCATE
Areas: App Mus; Hist & Lit; Th & An; Comp; Cond; Orch; Opera; Intro; Mus Ed (Elem & HS); Electr Mus
Degrees: BS, Mus Ed; MS in Ed (Mus Concentration)

CONNECTICUT COLLEGE
Department of Music
Mohegan Ave.
New London, CT 06320
(203) 447-1911
Staff: Thomas Stoner, Chairman
Affiliation: Private liberal arts college
Accreditation: NEA
Areas: App Mus; Hist & Lit; Th & An; Comp; Cond; Opera; Hist Musicol; Ethnomusicol; Electr Mus; Perf
Degrees: BA; MA
Scholarships: Contact Office of Financial Aid for information

EASTERN CONNECTICUT STATE UNIVERSITY
Music Department
83 Windham St.
Willimantic, CT 06226
(203) 456-2231
Staff: Edward J. Drew, Chairman
Affiliation: State-supported university
Accreditation: NEA
Degrees: BA (fine arts major, no music major)

HARTT SCHOOL OF MUSIC
University of Hartford
200 Bloomfield Ave.
West Hartford, CT 06117
(203) 243-4467
Staff: Donald Harris, Dean; Elizabeth Warner, Dean for Academic Affairs
Affiliation: One of the founding schools of the University of Hartford, an independent urban university. Hartt facilities are housed in the three-building Alfred C. Fuller Music Center.
Accreditation: NASM; NEA
Areas: App Mus; Hist & Lit; Th & An; Comp; Cond; Opera; Church Mus; Mus Ed (Elem & HS); Electr Mus; Perf
Degrees: BM; MM; DMA; MME; BS, Engineering, with major in Acoustics and Music
Scholarships: General scholarships, academic scholarships, talent awards, grants-in-aid, supplemental grants (Connecticut residents); assistantship and tuition abatement awards at the graduate level

SAINT JOSEPH COLLEGE
Music Department
1678 Asylum Ave.
West Hartford, CT 06117
(203) 232-4571
Staff: Prof. John M. Doney, Chairman
Affiliation: Church-related liberal arts college (Roman Catholic)
Accreditation: NEA
Areas: App Mus; Hist & Lit; Th & An; Church Mus; Intro; Electr Mus
Degrees: BA
Scholarships: General scholarships only

TRINITY COLLEGE[1]
300 Summit St.
Hartford, CT 06106
(203) 527-3151 x258
Staff: Gerald Moshell, Chairman
Affiliation: Private
Accreditation: NEA
Areas: Cond; Comp; Hist & Lit; Th & An; Mus Ed (Elem & HS)
Degrees: BA; BM; BS, Mus Ed; MS, Mus Ed

UNIVERSITY OF BRIDGEPORT[1]
Department of Music
380 University Ave.
Bridgeport, CT 06602
(203) 576-4404
Staff: Robert S.C. Myers, Chairman
Affiliation: Independent university
Accreditation: NASM: NEA
Areas: App Mus; Comp; Cond; Mus Ed; Jazz Studies
Degrees: BS, Mus Ed; BA; BM; MS, Mus Ed

UNIVERSITY OF CONNECTICUT[1]
Department of Music
Storrs, CT 06268
(203) 486-3728
Staff: Daniel J. Patrylak, Head
Affiliation: State-supported university
Accreditation: NASM; NEA
Areas: App Mus; Hist & Lit; Th & An; Comp; Cond; Orch; Opera; Church Mus; Mus Ed (Elem & HS)
Degrees: BA; MA; PhD, Ed

UNIVERSITY OF NEW HAVEN
Department of Humanities

300 Orange Ave.
West Haven, CT 06516
(203) 934-6321
Staff: Michael Kaloyanides, Coordinator of Music
Affiliation: Private independent urban university
Accreditation: NEA
Areas: Hist & Lit; Th & An; Ethnomusicol
Degrees: BA, World Mus

WESLEYAN UNIVERSITY[1]
Music Department
High St.
Middletown, CT 06457
(203) 347-9411, x235
Staff: Mark Slobin (I) and David McAllester (II), Chairmen
Affiliation: Private liberal arts college
Accreditation: NEA
Areas: App Mus; Hist & Lit; Th & An; Comp; Cond; Orch; Opera; Hist Musicol; Ethnomusicol; Instr Rep; Intro
Degrees: BA; MA; PhD
Scholarships: Awarded to graduate students working toward MA or PhD degree

WESTERN CONNECTICUT STATE UNIVERSITY
181 White St.
Danbury, CT 06810
(203) 797-4320
Staff: Howard Tuvelle, Chairman
Affiliation: State
Accreditation: NEA
Areas: Cond; Comp; Hist & Lit; Th & An; Mus Ed (Elem & HS); App Mus; Orch; Opera; His Musicol; Intro; Electr; Perf; Jazz
Degrees: BA; BM; BS, Mus Ed

YALE INSTITUTE OF SACRED MUSIC
409 Prospect St.
New Haven, CT 06510
(203) 436-2915
Staff: Aidan Kavanagh, O.S.B., Acting Director
Affiliation: Graduate center within Yale University
Accreditation: NASM
Areas: Cond; Church Mus
Degrees: MM; MMA; DMA; MDiv; MAReligion; MST, through Yale Divinity School
Scholarships: Financial aid is awarded by the Institute primarily on the basis of need (according to GAPSFAS analysis)

YALE UNIVERSITY
School of Music
96 Wall St.
New Haven, CT 06520
(203) 436-8740
Staff: Frank Tirro, Dean
Affiliation: Private
Accreditation: NASM; NEA
Areas: App Mus; Hist & Lit; Thn & An; Comp; Cond; Orch; Church Mus; Electr Mus; Perf
Degrees: MM; MMA; DMA

DELAWARE

DELAWARE STATE COLLEGE[1]
Department of Music Education
Dover, DE 19901
(302) 678-4901
Staff: Howard B. Brockington, Chairman
Affiliation: State-supported liberal arts college
Accreditation: MSA
Areas: Mus Ed (Elem & HS)
Degrees: BS, Mus Ed
Scholarships: Awarded to members of band, concert choir, gospel choir

UNIVERSITY OF DELAWARE
Music Department
Newark, DE 19711
(302) 738-2850
Staff: Dr. Larry Peterson, Chairman
Affiliation: State-supported private university
Accreditation: NASM; MSA
Areas: App Mus; Hist & Lit; Th & An; Comp; Cond; Orch; Opera; Intro; Mus Ed (Elem & HS); Electr Mus; Perf
Degrees: BA; BM; BME
Scholarships: Amount of awards determined by need; audition required

DISTRICT OF COLUMBIA

THE AMERICAN UNIVERSITY
Division of Music, Department of Performing Arts
Massachusetts and Nebraska Aves.
Washington, DC 20016
(202) 686-2162
Staff: Dr. Lynn M. Trowbridge, Director
Affiliation: Church-related university (United Methodist)
Accreditation: NASM; NCATE; MSA
Areas: App Mus; Th & An; Comp; Hist Musicol; Church Mus; Intro; Mus Ed (Elem & HS); Perf; Theater Mus; Hist & Lit
Degrees: BA; BM; BME; MA
Scholarships: String scholarships (all levels) available through audition; graduate assistantships (orchestral management, theory, studio accompaniment, choral accompaniment, concert management)

THE CATHOLIC UNIVERSITY OF AMERICA
School of Music
Washington, DC 20064
(202) 635-5414
Staff: Elain R. Walter, Dean
Affiliation: Church-related university (Roman Catholic)
Accreditation: NASM; NCATE; NAMT
Areas: App Mus; Hist; Th; Comp; Cond; Orch; Hist Musicol; Mus Ed (Elem & HS); Mus Therapy; Liturgical Mus
Degrees: BA; BM; MA; MM; DMA; PhD; MLM
Scholarships: Scholarships of from full tuition, room, and board to partial tuition awarded on the basis of GRE scores and audition

THE GEORGE WASHINGTON UNIVERSITY
Music Department
Washington, DC 20006
(202) 676-6245
Staff: Prof. George Steiner, Chairman
Affiliation: Private university
Accreditation: NASM; MSA
Areas: App Mus; Hist & Lit; Th & An; Comp; Cond; Orch; Opera; Hist Musicol; Mus Ed (HS)
Degrees: BA; BM; MA; MM

HOWARD UNIVERSITY
Department of Music
Washington, DC 20059
(202) 636-7082, 7083
Staff: Dr. Doris E. McGinty, Chairman
Affiliation: Private university supported by federal funds
Accreditation: NASM; MSA
Areas: App Mus; Hist & Lit; Th & An; Comp; Cond; Orch; Hist Musicol; Intro; Mus Ed (Elem & HS); Mus Therapy; Piano Tech; Instr Rep; Perf; Ethnomusicol; Jazz
Degrees: BM; BME; MM; MME
Scholarships: Trustee, full tuition for students with 3.00 and above GPA (competitive); special talent, partial or full tuition for students with outstanding talent and a minimum of 2.00 GPA

TRINITY COLLEGE
Music Department
Michigan and Franklin NE
Washington, DC 20017
(202) 269-2270/2275
Staff: Dr. Sharon G. Shafer, Chairman
Affiliation: Church-related liberal arts college (Roman Catholic)
Accreditation: MSA
Areas: App Mus; Hist & Lit; Th & An; Cond; Orch; Opera; Hist Musicol; Intro; Mus Ed (Elem & HS); Mus Therapy; Perf
Degrees: BA

FLORIDA

BARRY UNIVERSITY
11300 NE 2nd Ave.
Miami Shores, FL 33161
(305) 758-3392 x223
Staff: Richard Lanshe, Chairman
Affiliation: Church-related (Roman Catholic)
Accreditation: SACS
Areas: App Mus; Hist & Lit; Th & An; Cond
Degrees: BM

BETHUNE-COOKMAN COLLEGE[1]
640 Second Ave.
Daytona Beach, FL 32015
(904) 255-1401 x268
Staff: Robert Williams, Chairman

Affiliation: Church-related (United Methodist)
Accreditation: SACS
Areas: App Mus; Th & An; Intro; Cond; Orch; Hist & Lit
Degrees: BA

ECKERD COLLEGE
Creative Arts Collegium
PO Box 12560
St. Petersburg, FL 33733
(813) 867-1166
Staff: Prof. William E. Waters, Coordinator.
Affiliation: Private church-related liberal arts college (Presbyterian)
Accreditation: SACS
Areas: App Mus; Hist & Lit; Th & An; Comp; Cond; Orch; Opera; Church Mus; Mus Ed (Elem & HS)
Degrees: BA
Scholarships: 2 keyboard scholarships (1 in piano, 1 in organ); voice scholarship; achievement scholarships; financial aid for private study

FLORIDA AGRICULTURAL AND MECHANICAL UNIVERSITY[1]
Department of Music
Tallahassee, FL 32307
(904) 222-8030
Staff: Dr. William P. Foster, Chairman
Affiliation: State
Accreditation: SACS
Areas: App Mus; Mus Ed (Elem & HS); Cond; Th & An; Orch; Hist & Lit
Degrees: BA; BS, Mus Ed

FLORIDA ATLANTIC UNIVERSITY
Department of Music
Boca Raton, FL 33431
(305) 393-3820
Staff: Marysue Barnes, Chairperson
Affiliation: State-supported university
Accreditation: NASM; SACS
Areas: App Mus; Hist & Lit; Th & An; Comp; Cond; Orch; Mus Ed (Elem & HS); Electr Mus; Perf
Degrees: BA; BFA; BAE, Mus Ed; BFA, Mus Ed; MA, Mus Ed; EdD
Scholarships: Scholarships in all fields awarded by audition in February

FLORIDA SOUTHERN COLLEGE
Lakeland, FL 33802
(813) 683-5521, x288
Staff: Robert MacDonald, Chairman
Affiliation: Private church-related liberal arts college (United Methodist)
Accreditation: SACS
Areas: App Mus; Hist & Lit; Th & An; Cond; Opera; Church Mus; Intro; Mus Ed (Elem & HS); Instr Rep; Perf
Degrees: BA; BM; BME; BSM; BS, Mus Mgmt
Scholarships: Several scholarships ranging from performance scholarships to work-study program

FLORIDA STATE UNIVERSITY
School of Music
Tallahassee, FL 32306
(904) 644-3424
Staff: Dr. Robert Glidden, Dean
Affiliation: State-supported university
Accreditation: SACS; NASM; NCATE
Areas: App Mus; Hist & Lit; Th & An; Comp; Opera; Musicol; Mus Ed (Elem & HS); Mus Therapy; Theater Mus; Piano Tech; Perf
Degrees: BA; BM; BME; MM; MA, Mus Ed; DM; EdD; PhD
Scholarships: Out-of-state waivers; undergraduate service awards; private organization funds

JACKSONVILLE UNIVERSITY
College of Fine Arts, Division of Music
Jacksonville, FL 32211
(904) 744-3950
Staff: William Vessels, Chairman
Affiliation: Privately endowed university
Accreditation: NASM; SACS
Areas: App Mus; Hist & Lit; Th & An; Comp; Cond; Orch; Opera; Church Mus; Mus Ed (Elem & HS); Electr Mus; Mus Bus
Degrees: BA; BFA; BM; BME
Scholarships: Awarded on the basis of tape submission

MIAMI CHRISTIAN COLLEGE
Sacred Music Department
2300 Northwest 135th St.
Miami, FL 33167
(305) 685-7431
Staff: Thomas E. Goetz, Chairperson
Affiliation: Private church-related Bible college (interdenominational)
Accreditation: AABC
Areas: App Mus; Hist & Lit; Th & An; Cond; Church Mus; Choral Meth & Lit; Mus Ed (Elem & HS)
Degrees: BA; BS, Sacred Mus
Scholarships: Honor scholarship for outstanding ability in music and academics; IFCA scholarship for music students; ensemble scholarships based on audition

NEW COLLEGE OF THE UNIVERSITY OF SOUTH FLORIDA
Division of Humanities
Sarasota, FL 33580
(813) 355-7671
Staff: James G. Moseley, Chairman, Division of Humanities; Ronald Riddle, Director of Music
Affiliation: Liberal arts college; honors college of Florida State University
Accreditation: SACS
Areas: App Mus; Hist & Lit; Th & An; Comp; Cond; Orch; Opera; Hist Musicol; Ethnomusicol; Church Mus; Mus Therapy; Chamber Mus Rehearsal & Perf
Degrees: BA
Scholarships: Scholarships funded by the New College Foundation (private corporation that helps support college) vary from year to year

PALM BEACH ATLANTIC COLLEGE
Department of Music
1101 S. Olive Ave.
West Palm Beach, FL 33401
(305) 833-8592
Staff: Dr. Ronnie L. Smith, Chairman
Affiliation: Private church-related liberal arts college (Baptist)
Accreditation: SACS
Areas: App Mus; Hist & Lit; Th & An; Comp; Cond; Orch; Opera; Church Mus; Mus Ed (Elem & HS); Ancient Instr; Cl Guitar
Degrees: BA; BS, Mus Ed
Scholarships: Vocal and instrumental scholarships awarded on the basis of audition, retained through maintenance of specific academic averages (music and overall)

ROLLINS COLLEGE[1]
Department of Music
Winter Park, FL 32789
(305) 646-2233
Staff: William K. Gallo, Chairman
Affiliation: Private liberal arts college
Accreditation: NASM; SACS
Areas: App Mus; Hist & Lit; Th & An; Comp; Hist Musicol
Degrees: BA; MAT

SAINT LEO COLLEGE
PO Box 2127
St. Leo, FL 33574
(904) 588-8200 x294
Staff: Dr. Larry Sledge, Area Coordinator of Music
Affiliation: Church-related (Roman Catholic)
Accreditation: SACS
Areas: App Mus; Mus Ed (Elem & HS); Theater Mus; Arts Mgmt
Degrees: BA
Scholarships: Honor scholarship, music awards; work-study available based on talent, academic record and need

STETSON UNIVERSITY
School of Music
Deland, FL 32720
(904) 734-4121
Staff: Paul Langston, Dean
Affiliation: Privately endowed university (Baptist)
Accreditation: NASM; SACS
Areas: App Mus; Hist & Lit; Th & An; Comp; Cond; Orch; Opera; Church Mus; Intro; Mus Ed (Elem & HS); Perf
Degrees: BA; BM; BME
Scholarships: Performance scholarships awarded by audition

UNIVERSITY OF CENTRAL FLORIDA[1]
Music Department
Orlando, FL 32816
(305) 275-2867
Staff: Dr. J. Gary Wolf, Chairman
Affiliation: State-supported university
Accreditation: NASM; SACS
Areas: App Mus; Hist & Lit; Th & An; Comp; Cond; Orch; Opera; Hist

Musicol; Intro; Mus Ed (Elem & HS); Perf
Degrees: BA; BA, Mus Ed; MA, Mus Ed
Scholarships: Awarded on the basis of maintaining 2.5 GPA, 3.0 GPA in music, applied music and ensemble grades of B and above, and other music grades of C and above

UNIVERSITY OF FLORIDA
Department of Music
Gainesville, FL 32611
(904) 392-0223
Staff: Budd A. Udell, Chairman
Affiliation: State-supported university
Accreditation: NASM; NCATE; SACS
Areas: App Mus; Hist & Lit; Comp; Cond; Church Mus; Mus Ed (Elem & HS); Th & An; Electr Mus; Perf
Degrees: BA; BM; BME; BSM; MFA; MME
Scholarships: Music performance scholarships awarded by audition

UNIVERSITY OF MIAMI
School of Music
Coral Gables, FL 33124
(305) 284-2433
Staff: Dr. Ted J. Crager, Dean
Affiliation: Privately endowed university
Accreditation: NASM; NCATE: NAMT: SACS
Areas: App Mus; Hist & Lit; Th & Comp; Cond; Mus Ed (Elem & HS); Mus Therapy; Mus Theatre; Perf; Mus Engineering Tech; Mus Merch; Studio Mus and Jazz; Accomp; Jazz Ped; Jazz Perf; Multiple Woodwinds; Mus Lib; Musicol; Studio Writing & Prod; Arts Admin
Degrees: BM; BFA, Dance; MM; DMA; PhD
Scholarships: Awarded by audition

UNIVERSITY OF NORTH FLORIDA[1]
Department of Fine Arts
4567 St. Johns Bluff Rd.
Jacksonville, FL 32216
(904) 646-2960
Staff: M.J. Palmer, Chairman
Affiliation: State-supported upper level university
Accreditation: SACS
Areas: App Mus; Hist & Lit; Th & An; Cond; Opera; Church Mus; Mus Ed (Elem & HS); Chorus; Orch; Band
Degrees: BA; MA Ed (mus)
Scholarships: Awarded on the basis of academic standing

UNIVERSITY OF SOUTH FLORIDA[1]
Department of Music
4202 Fowler Ave.
Tampa, FL 33620
(813) 974-2311
Staff: L. Cullison, Chairman
Affiliation: State-supported university
Accreditation: SACS
Areas: App Mus; Hist & Lit; Th & An; Comp; Cond; Orch; Opera; Hist Musicol; Intro; Mus Ed (Elem & HS); Electr Mus; Perf
Degrees: BA; MM; MA, Mus Ed
Scholarships: Scholarships of up to full tuition awarded for performance

UNIVERSITY OF TAMPA[1]
Department of Music
401 W. Kennedy Blvd.
Tampa, FL 33606
(813) 253-8861
Staff: Judith Edberg, Music Coordinator
Affiliation: Private liberal arts university
Accreditation: NASM; SACS
Areas: App Mus; Hist & Lit; Th & An; Comp; Cond; Orch; Mus Ed (Elem & HS); Arts Mgmt
Degrees: BM; BS; Arts Mgmt
Scholarships: Talent scholarships awarded by audition

UNIVERSITY OF WEST FLORIDA
Department of Music/Theatre
Pensacola, FL 32504
(904) 476-9500, x317
Staff: Grier M. Williams, Chairman
Affiliation: State-supported university
Accreditation: NASM; SACS
Areas: App Mus; Hist & Lit; Th & An; Cond; Orch; Mus Ed (Elem & HS)
Degrees: BA
Scholarships: Scholarships of $75 to $300 per quarter awarded on the basis of high level of music performance and an overall B average; out-of-state waivers also available

GEORGIA

AGNES SCOTT COLLEGE[1]
East College Ave.
Decatur, GA 30030
(404) 373-2571
Staff: Ronald Byrnside, Chairman
Affiliation: Private
Accreditation: SACS
Areas: Th & An; Cond; Hist & Lit
Degrees: BA

ALBANY STATE COLLEGE[1]
Music Department
504 College Dr.
Albany, GA 31705
(912) 439-4027
Staff: T. Marshall Jones, Chairman
Affiliation: State
Accreditation: SACS
Areas: Intro; Hist & Lit; Th & An; Orch; Comp; Cond; Mus Ed (Elem & HS)
Degrees: BA; BS, Mus Ed; MME

ARMSTRONG STATE COLLEGE
Department of Fine Arts
11935 Abercorn St.
Savannah, GA 31406
(912) 927-5325
Staff: Stephen P. Brandon, Head
Affiliation: State-supported university
Accreditation: SACS
Areas: App Mus; Hist & Lit; Th & An; Comp; Cond; Orch; Opera; Hist Musicol; Mus Ed (Elem & HS)
Degrees: BA; BME; BS, Mus Ed
Scholarships: General scholarships awarded by audition

AUGUSTA COLLEGE
Department of Fine Arts
Augusta, GA 30910
(404) 838-3211
Staff: Alan H. Drake, Chairman
Affiliation: State-supported college
Accreditation: NASM; SACS
Areas: App Mus; Hist & Lit; Th & An; Comp; Cond; Orch; Opera; Intro; Mus Ed (Elem & HS); Perf
Degrees: BA; BM; BME
Scholarships: Applied music and partial tuition scholarships normally awarded on the basis of talent

BERRY COLLEGE
Department of Music
Mt. Berry, GA 30149
(404) 232-5374, x2289
Staff: Dr. Darwin G. White, Head
Affiliation: Privately endowed college
Accreditation: NASM; NCATE; SACS
Areas: App Mus; Hist & Lit; Th & An; Comp; Cond; Orch; Opera; Church Mus; Mus Ed (Elem & HS); Intro; Perf
Degrees: BA; BM
Scholarships: Awarded by audition

CLARK COLLEGE[1]
Music Department
240 Chestnut St., SW
Atlanta, GA 30314
(404) 681-3080, x285
Staff: Dr. Florence Crim Robinson, Chairperson
Affiliation: Private liberal arts college (United Methodist)
Accreditation: SACS
Areas: App Mus; Hist & Lit; Th & An; Comp; Cond; Orch; Church Mus; Intro; Mus Ed (Elem & HS); Perf
Degrees: BA
Scholarships: Choir, marching and symphonic band, string orchestra, and jazz orchestra grants available

COLUMBUS COLLEGE
Department of Music
Algonquin Dr.
Columbus, GA 31993
(404) 568-2049
Staff: L. Rexford Whiddon, Head
Affiliation: Senior college in the university system of Georgia (state-supported)
Accreditation: NASM; SACS; NCATE
Areas: App Mus; Hist & Lit; Th & An; Comp; Cond; Orch; Opera; Hist Musicol; Ethnomusicol; Church Mus; Mus Ed (Elem & HS); Piano Ped
Degrees: MEd, Mus Ed; BM; BME
Scholarships: Awards range from cost of applied lessons to full tuition and fees

EMORY UNIVERSITY
Department of Music
Atlanta, GA 30322
(404) 329-6445
Staff: Dr. Frank Hoogerwerf, Chairman
Affiliation: Private liberal arts institution
Accreditation: SACS
Areas: App Mus; Hist & Lit; Th & An; Comp; Cond; Hist Musicol; Church Mus; Intro; Mus Ed (Elem); Perf
Degrees: BA

GEORGIA COLLEGE
Music Department
Milledgeville, GA 31061
(912) 453-4226
Staff: Dr. Robert F. Wolfersteig, Chairman
Affiliation: State-supported college
Accreditation: NASM; NAMT; SACS
Areas: App Mus; Mus Ed (Elem & HS); Mus Therapy; Perf; Church Mus; Piano Ped
Degrees: BM; BME; B Mus Therapy
Scholarships: Theodore Presser Scholarship for rising senior; Max Noah Music Scholarship for rising juniors and seniors; Milledgeville Music Club Award for rising sophomore; alternating awards from Alumni Association

GEORGIA SOUTHERN COLLEGE
Music Department, School of Arts and Sciences
Box 8052, Landrum Center
Statesboro, GA 30460-8052
(912) 681-5396
Staff: Dr. Raymond Marchionni, Head
Affiliation: State-supported college
Accreditation: SACS; NASM
Areas: App Mus; Hist & Lit; Th & An; Comp; Cond; Orch; Opera; Hist Musicol; Church Mus; Intro; Mus Ed (Elem & HS); Electr Mus; Perf
Degrees: BA; BM; EdS
Scholarships: Performance scholarships awarded by live audition or tape

GEORGIA STATE UNIVERSITY
Department of Music
University Plaza
Atlanta, GA 30303
(404) 658-2349
Staff: Dr. Steven D. Winick, Chairman
Affiliation: State-supported university
Accreditation: NASM; NCATE; SACS
Areas: App Mus; Hist & Lit; Th & An; Comp; Cond; Orch; Opera; Hist Musicol; Ethnomusicol; Church Mus; Mus Ed (Elem & HS); Mus Therapy; Theater Mus; Instr Rep; Piano Ped; Jazz Studies; Intro
Degrees: BM; MM; TS-6 degree
Scholarships: Scholarships of $50 to $750 a year awarded on the basis of need, talent, and departmental needs

MERCER UNIVERSITY
Music Department
1500 Coleman Ave.
Macon, GA 31207
(912) 744-2748
Staff: Dr. H. Lowen Marshall, Chairman
Affiliation: Private church-related liberal arts university (Baptist)
Accreditation: NASM; SACS
Areas: App Mus; Hist & Lit; Th & An; Comp; Cond; Orch; Hist Musicol; Church Mus; Intro; Mus Ed (Elem & HS); Perf
Degrees: BA; BM; BME
Scholarships: Awarded through annual auditions

MERCER UNIVERSITY IN ATLANTA
Music Department, Fine Arts Division
3000 Flowers Rd. So.
Atlanta, GA 30341
(404) 451-0331
Staff: Michael O'Neal, Chairman, Fine Arts Division
Affiliation: Church-related liberal arts college (Baptist)
Accreditation: SACS; NASM
Areas: App Mus; Hist & Lit; Th & An; Comp; Cond; Orch; Opera; Church Mus; Intro; Mus Ed (Elem & HS); Electr Mus; Perf
Degrees: BA; BM
Scholarships: 4-year music scholarships awarded on the basis of talent, financial need, and scholastic ability

MOREHOUSE COLLEGE[1]
Music Department
Atlanta, GA 30314
(404) 681-2800 x257
Staff: Wendell P. Whalum, Chairman
Affiliation: Private
Accreditation: SACS
Areas: Th & An; Comp; Hist & Lit
Degrees: BA

MORRIS BROWN COLLEGE[1]
Music Department
643 M. L. King Jr. Dr., NW
Atlanta, GA 30314
(404) 525-7831
Staff: Dr. G. Johnson Hubert, Chairman
Affiliation: Private church-related liberal arts college (African Methodist Episcopal)
Accreditation: SACS
Areas: App Mus; Hist & Lit; Th & An; Cond; Orch; Opera; Mus Ed (Elem & HS); Instr Rep
Degrees: BA; BS, Mus Ed
Scholarships: Scholarships available for participation in band, choir, and brass ensemble

NORTH GEORGIA COLLEGE[1]
Department of Fine Arts
Dahlonega, GA 30597
(404) 864-3391 x82
Staff: Robert L. Owens, Chairman
Affiliation: State
Accreditation: SACS
Areas: Mus Ed (Elem & HS); Cond; Th & An; Hist & Lit
Degrees: BS, Mus Ed

OGLETHORPE UNIVERSITY
Music Department
4484 Peachtree Rd. NE
Atlanta, GA 30319
(404) 261-1441
Staff: James A. Bohart, Chairman
Affiliation: Private liberal arts university
Accreditation: SACS
Areas: App Mus; Hist & Lit; Th & An; Mus Ed (Elem & HS); Intro
Degrees: No music major offered
Scholarships: Applied lessons scholarships available

PIEDMONT COLLEGE
Demorest, GA 30535
(404) 778-8033
Staff: Ralph Boggess, Chairman
Affiliation: Private
Accreditation: SACS
Areas: App Mus; Hist & Lit; Th & An; Cond; Intro; Mus Ed (Elem & HS)
Degrees: BFA, music minor
Scholarships: Music scholarships based on audition

SAVANNAH STATE COLLEGE[1]
Department of Fine Arts
Savannah, GA 31404
(912) 356-2208
Staff: Dr. O. F. Becker, Head
Affiliation: State-supported college
Accreditation: SACS
Areas: App Mus; Hist & Lit; Th & An; Comp; Cond; Church Mus; Intro; Electr Mus
Degrees: BA

SHORTER COLLEGE
Music Department
Rome, GA 30161
(404) 291-2121 x45
Staff: John Ramsaur, Chairman
Affiliation: Church-related (Georgia Baptist Convention)
Accreditation: NASM; SACS
Areas: App Mus; Hist & Lit; Th & An; Comp; Cond; Orch; Opera; Church Mus; Mus Ed (Elem & HS); Theater Mus; Perf
Degrees: BA; BM; BME; B Sacr Mus
Scholarships; Full to ¼ tuition

SPELMAN COLLEGE
Department of Music
350 Spelman Ln., SW
Atlanta, GA 30314
(404) 681-3643, x260, 261
Staff: Dr. Roland L. Allison, Chairman
Affiliation: Private liberal arts college
Accreditation: NASM; NCATE; SACS
Areas: App Mus; Hist & Lit; Th & An; Comp; Cond; Orch; Opera; Hist Musicol; Mus Ed (Elem & HS); Ethnomusicol
Degrees: BA
Scholarships: Special music scholarships, college honors program, and general financial aid available

TOCCOA FALLS COLLEGE
School of Music
Toccoa Falls, GA 30598
(404) 886-6831
Staff: Frederick Steffen, Director
Affiliation: Private Bible college (unaffiliated)
Accreditation: AABC; SACS (pending)
Areas: App Mus; Hist & Lit; Th & An; Comp; Cond; Orch; Church Mus; Mus Ed (Elem & HS); Intro
Degrees: BA; BS, Mus Ed; B Sacr Mus

UNIVERSITY OF GEORGIA
School of Music
Athens, GA 30601
(404) 542-1526
Staff: Dr. Ralph E. Verrastro, Head
Affiliation: State-supported university
Accreditation: SACS; NASM
Areas: App Mus; Hist & Lit; Th & An; Comp; Cond; Orch; Opera; Hist Musicol; Church Mus; Mus Ed (Elem & HS); Mus Therapy
Degrees: BA; BFA; BM; BME; BSM; BA, Mus Therapy; MA; MFA; MM, Mus Ed; EdD; DMA

VALDOSTA STATE COLLEGE
Department of Music
Valdosta, GA 31601
(912) 247-3323
Staff: Dr. John C. Huxford, Chairman
Affiliation: Four-year unit of state university system
Accreditation: NASM; SACS; NCATE
Areas: App Mus; Hist & Lit; Th & An; Comp; Cond; Orch; Opera; Church Mus; Intro; Mus Ed (Elem & HS); Theater Mus; Electr Mus; Perf
Degrees: BA; BM; MME
Scholarships: Various scholarships awarded for musicianship, performance, and academic excellence

WESLEYAN COLLEGE
Music Department
4760 Forsyth Rd.
Macon, GA 31297
(912) 477-1110
Staff: Fletcher Anderson, Chairman
Affiliation: Church-related liberal arts college (United Methodist)
Accreditation: NASM; SACS
Areas: App Mus; Hist & Lit; Th & An; Comp; Cond; Opera; Church Mus; Intro; Mus Ed (Elem & HS); Perf; Piano Ped
Degrees: BA; BM
Scholarships: Talent awards based on audition

WEST GEORGIA COLLEGE
Department of Fine Arts
Carrollton, GA 30118
(404) 834-1224
Staff: Dr. Robert M. Coe, Head
Affiliation: State-supported liberal arts and teachers college
Accreditation: NASM; NCATE; SACS
Areas: App Mus; Hist & Lit; Th & An; Comp; Cond; Orch; Opera; Mus Ed (Elem & HS); Class Piano; Class Voice; Piano Ped
Degrees: BM; MM
Scholarships: Various scholarships awarded by audition

HAWAII

BRIGHAM YOUNG UNIVERSITY
Hawaii Campus
Music Department
55-220 Kulanui St.
Laie, HI 96762
(808) 293-3900
Staff: James Brague, Coordinator
Affiliation: Church-related private liberal arts college (Latter-day Saints)
Accreditation: WASC
Areas: App Mus; Hist & Lit; Th & An; Cond; Orch; Intro; Mus Ed (Elem & HS); Theater Mus; Perf
Degrees: BA; BS, Mus Ed
Scholarships: Full tuition for exceptional talent, 3.0 GPA; up to half tuition for ensemble students with recommendation, 2.0 GPA

UNIVERSITY OF HAWAII
Music Department
2411 Dole St.
Honolulu, HI 96822
(808) 948-7756
Staff: Robert S. Hines, Chairman
Affiliation: State-supported university
Accreditation: NASM; WASC
Areas: App Mus; Hist & Lit; Th & An; Comp; Cond; Orch; Opera; Hist Musicol; Ethnomusicol; Intro; Mus Ed (Elem & HS); Perf
Degrees: BA; BM; BME; MA; MA, Mus Ed; MM
Scholarships: Applied music, marching band, orchestra, music education, and ethnomusicology scholarships

UNIVERSITY OF HAWAII AT HILO
Performing Arts Department
1400 Kapiolani St.
Hilo, HI 96720
(808) 961-9352
Staff: Kenneth W. Staton, Chairperson
Affiliation: State-supported university
Accreditation: WASC
Areas: App Mus; Hist & Lit; Th & An; Cond; Orch; Mus Ed (Elem & HS); Theater Mus; Intro; Comp; Hist Musicol; Perf
Degrees: BA
Scholarships: Tuition waivers and memorial scholarships awarded on the basis of participation in performing ensemble

IDAHO

BOISE STATE UNIVERSITY[1]
Department of Music
1910 University Dr.
Boise, ID 83725
(208) 385-1771
Staff: Wilber D. Elliott, Chairman
Affiliation: State-supported liberal arts university
Accreditation: NASM; NASC
Areas: App Mus; Hist & Lit; Th & An; Comp; Cond; Intro; Mus Ed (Elem & HS); Perf
Degrees: BA; BM; MA, Mus Ed
Scholarships: Awarded on the basis of application, audition, and scholarship

THE COLLEGE OF IDAHO
Music Department
Cleveland Blvd.
Caldwell, ID 83605
(208) 459-5011
Staff: Dr. James Gabbard, Chairman
Affiliation: Church-related liberal arts college (Presbyterian)
Accreditation: NASC
Areas: App Mus; Hist & Lit; Th & An; Cond; Orch; Intro; Mus Ed (Elem & HS)
Degrees: BA
Scholarships: Performing scholarships awarded by tape or live audition submitted by May 1

IDAHO STATE UNIVERSITY
Department of Music
PO Box 8099
Pocatello, ID 83209
(208) 236-3636
Staff: Dr. Alan E. Stanek, Chairman
Affiliation: State-supported university
Accreditation: NASM; NCATE; NASC
Areas: App Mus; Hist & Lit; Th & An; Cond; Orch; Opera; Mus Ed (Elem & HS); Theater Mus
Degrees: BA; BM; BME
Scholarships: Scholarships for participation in band, choir, orchestra, or marching band, and for piano accompanying awarded by audition

NORTHWEST NAZARENE COLLEGE[1]
Music Department
Nampa, ID 83651
(208) 467-8011
Staff: Dr. James Willis, Chairman
Affiliation: Church-related liberal arts college (Nazarene)
Accreditation: NASC
Areas: App Mus; Hist & Lit; Th & An; Comp; Cond; Orch; Church Mus; Mus Ed (Elem & HS)
Degrees: BA
Scholarships: Activity scholarships available

UNIVERSITY OF IDAHO
School of Music
Moscow, ID 83843
(208) 885-6231
Staff: Thomas E. Richardson, Director
Affiliation: State-supported university
Accreditation: NASM; NASC
Areas: App Mus; Hist & Lit; Th & An; Comp; Mus Ed (Elem & HS)
Degrees: BA; BM; MA; MM; MAT
Scholarships: Contact School of Music for information

ILLINOIS

AMERICAN CONSERVATORY OF MUSIC
116 S. Michigan Ave.
Chicago, IL 60603
(312) 263-4161
Staff: Charles Moore, President
Affiliation: Private college-conservatory
Accreditation: NASM
Areas: App Mus; Hist & Lit; Th & An; Comp; Cond; Orch; Opera; Hist Musicol; Church Mus; Mus Ed (Elem & HS)
Degrees: BM; BME; MM; MME; DMA
Scholarships: Collins Memorial Scholarships in applied music and composition

AUGUSTANA COLLEGE
Department of Music
Rock Island, IL 61201
(309) 794-7233
Staff: Alan Hersh, Chairman
Affiliation: Church-related liberal arts college (Lutheran—LCA)
Accreditation: NASM; NCA
Areas: App Mus; Church Mus; Mus Ed (Elem & HS); Perf
Degrees: BA; BM; BME
Scholarships: Endowed, music, and academic scholarships awarded on the basis of application and acceptance to college, plus music audition

BLACKBURN COLLEGE
Music Department
Carlinville, IL 62626
(217) 854-3231
Staff: Roger M. Hatlestad, Chairman
Affiliation: Private church-related liberal arts college (Presbyterian)
Accreditation: NCA
Areas: App Mus; Hist & Lit; Th & An; Comp; Cond; Mus Ed (Elem & HS); Choirs and Ens; Orch; Hist Musicol; Intro; Perf; Band
Degrees: BA
Scholarships: Tuition scholarships awarded on the basis of need and merit; Agnes Webster Scholarships, up to full tuition, based on music accomplishment and financial need

BRADLEY UNIVERSITY
Division of Music
Peoria, IL 61625
(309) 676-7611
Staff: Dr. Allen Cannon, Director
Affiliation: Privately endowed university
Accreditation: NASM; NCA
Areas: App Mus; Hist & Lit; Th & An; Comp; Cond; Orch; Intro; Mus Ed (Elem & HS); Electr Mus; Perf
Degrees: BM; BME; BS, Mus Ed; BS, Mus Bus; MM; MME
Scholarships: Talent scholarships available; separate need awards available; graduate assistantships in all fields

CHICAGO MUSICAL COLLEGE OF ROOSEVELT UNIVERSITY
430 S. Michigan Ave.
Chicago, IL 60605
(312) 341-3780
Staff: Dr. George H. Wilson, Dean
Affiliation: College of music in a private university
Accreditation: NASM; NCA
Areas: App Mus; Hist & Lit; Th & An; Comp; Cond; Orch; Opera; Hist Musicol; Ped; Mus Ed (vocal/choral, instr, gen, jazz, special ed); Mus Theater; Electr Mus; Perf; Ped; Vocal; Jazz
Degrees: BM; MM
Scholarships: Scholarships at all levels awarded by competition; deadline for applications is March 1

CHICAGO STATE UNIVERSITY
Music Department
95th St. at King Dr.
Chicago, IL 60628
(312) 995-2155
Staff: Leonard J. Simutis, Chairman
Affiliation: State
Accreditation: NCATE; NCA
Areas: App Mus; Hist & Lit; Th & An; Comp; Mus Ed; Intro; Perf
Degrees: BA
Scholarships: Talent scholarships available, require better than a C average and participation in a performing group

COLLEGE OF ST. FRANCIS
Creative Arts Department
500 N. Wilcox
Joliet, IL 60435
(815) 740-3360
Staff: Sr. Rosaire Schlueb
Affiliation: Church-related (Roman Catholic)
Accreditation: NCA
Areas: Creative arts with music emphasis
Degrees: BA

COLUMBIA COLLEGE
Contemporary American Music Program
72 E. 11th St.
Chicago, IL 60605
(312) 663-9462
Staff: William Russo, Director
Affiliation: Private liberal arts college
Accreditation: NCATE; NCA
Areas: App Mus; Hist & Lit; Comp; Cond; Orch; Opera; Theater Mus; Perf; Film composition; Blues Perf; Ensemble; Jazz Ensemble; Rec Prod; Pop Arr
Degrees: BA
Scholarships: Work aid available

CONCORDIA COLLEGE[1]
Music Department
7400 Augusta St.
River Forest, IL 60305
(312) 771-8300
Staff: Herbert M. Gotsch, Chairman
Affiliation: Church-related college
Accreditation: NCA; NCATE
Areas: App Mus; Hist & Lit; Th & An; Comp; Cond; Orch; Church Mus; Mus Ed (Elem & HS)
Degrees: BA; BM; BME; MCM
Scholarships: Performance scholarships for undergraduates awarded by audition; assistantship stipends available to graduates

DE PAUL UNIVERSITY
School of Music
804 W. Belden Ave.
Chicago, IL 60614
(312) 321-7760
Staff: Dr. Frederick Miller, Dean
Affiliation: School of Music in a church-related university
Accreditation: NCA; NASM; NCATE
Areas: App Mus; Comp; Mus Ed (Elem & HS); Mus Therapy
Degrees: BM; MM
Scholarships: Scholarships awarded on the basis of performance ability and audition

EASTERN ILLINOIS UNIVERSITY
Music Department
Fine Arts Center
Charleston, IL 61920
(217) 581-2917
Staff: DuWayne Hansen, Chairman
Affiliation: State-supported university
Accreditation: NASM; NCA
Areas: App Mus; Hist & Lit; Th & An; Comp; Cond; Orch; Hist Musicol; Intro; Mus Ed (Elem & HS); Theater Mus; Electr Mus; Perf
Degrees: BM; BS, Mus Ed; MA
Scholarships: Tuition waivers and cash stipends awarded by audition

ELMHURST COLLEGE
Music Department
190 Prospect
Elmhurst, IL 60126
(312) 279-4100
Staff: Paul Westermeyer, Chairman
Affiliation: Church-related liberal arts college (United Church of Christ)
Accreditation: NCA
Areas: App Mus; Hist & Lit; Th & An; Comp; Cond; Orch; Church Mus; Intro; Mus Ed (Elem & HS); Mus Bus
Degrees: BA; BM; BS, Mus Bus
Scholarships: Several scholarships of $100 per year awarded through recommendations; one scholarship of $120 per year awarded through recommendations and audition for pianist

EUREKA COLLEGE
Music Department
300 E. College Ave.
Eureka, IL 61530
(309) 467-3721
Staff: Greg Upton, Associate Professor of Music

Affiliation: Church-related liberal arts college (Disciples of Christ)
Accreditation: NCA
Areas: App Mus; Hist & Lit; Th & An; Comp; Cond; Opera; Church Mus; Intro; Perf
Degrees: BA
Scholarships: Presidential (academic) scholarships available

GOVERNORS STATE UNIVERSITY[1]
Division of Fine and Performing Arts
Park Forest South, IL 60466
(312) 534-5000, x2447
Staff: Warrick L. Carter, Chairman
Affiliation: State-supported university
Accreditation: NCA
Areas: App Mus; Hist & Lit; Th & An; Comp; Cond; Orch; Mus Ed (Elem & HS); Electr Mus; Rec Techniques; Steel Drum Constr
Degrees: BA; MA
Scholarships: Talent scholarship for tuition awarded on the basis of portfolio and tape of performance or compositions plus letters of recommendation

GREENVILLE COLLEGE[1]
Music Department
Greenville, IL 62246
(618) 664-1840
Staff: Dr. James E. Wilson, Chairman
Affiliation: Church-related liberal arts college (Free Methodist)
Accreditation: NCATE; NCA
Areas: App Mus; Hist & Lit; Th & An; Cond; Mus Ed (Elem & HS)
Degrees: BA; BME
Scholarships: Scholarships of ½ applied music tuition awarded by audition

ILLINOIS COLLEGE
Department of Music
1101 W. College Ave.
Jacksonville, IL 62650
(217) 245-7126, x284
Staff: Rudolf Zuiderveld, Chairman
Affiliation: Church-related private liberal arts college (Presbyterian Church and United Church of Christ)
Accreditation: NCA
Areas: App Mus; Hist & Lit; Th & An; Cond; Church Mus; Mus Ed (Elem); Perf; Intro
Degrees: BA (music major)
Scholarships: Awarded for applied music study

ILLINOIS STATE UNIVERSITY
Music Department
Normal, IL 61761
(309) 436-7631
Staff: Arthur Corra, Chairman
Affiliation: State
Accreditation: NASM; NCA
Areas: App Mus; Hist & Lit; Th & An; Comp; Cond; Orch; Mus Ed (Elem & HS); Hist Musicol; Intro; Mus Therapy; Theater Mus; Piano Tech; Electr Mus; Perf
Degrees: BA; BM; BS, Mus Ed; BME; MA; MM; MS, Mus Ed; MME
Scholarships: Talent grants, grants-in-aid, tuition waivers, graduate assistantships available based on talent audition

ILLINOIS WESLEYAN UNIVERSITY
School of Music
PO Box 2900
Bloomington, IL 61701
(309) 556-3061
Staff: Charles G. Goyer, Director
Affiliation: Church-related (United Methodist)
Accreditation: NASM; NCA
Areas: App Mus; Hist & Lit; Th & An; Comp; Cond; Orch; Opera; Church Mus; Mus Ed (Elem & HS); Intro; Theater Mus
Degrees: BA; BFA; BM; BME; BSM
Scholarships: Grants, talent awards, loans, work-study avaiable to all students accepted for admission

JUDSON COLLEGE[1]
Department of Fine Arts
1151 N. State St.
Elgin, IL 60120
(312) 695-2500
Staff: David Larson, Head
Affiliation: Church-related (American Baptist)
Accreditation: NCA
Areas: App Mus; Hist & Lit; Th & An; Comp; Cond; Church Mus
Degrees: BA

KNOX COLLEGE
Music Department
Galesburg, IL 61401
(309) 343-0112
Staff: Charles Farley, Chairman
Affiliation: Privately endowed liberal arts college
Accreditation: NCA; NCATE
Areas: App Mus; Hist & Lit; Th & An; Comp; Cond; Orch; Ethnomusicol; Intro; Mus Ed (Elem & HS)
Degrees: BA

LAKE FOREST COLLEGE
Music Department
Sheridan Rd.
Lake Forest, IL 60045
(312) 234-3100
Staff: Prof. Ann D. Bowen, Chairman
Affiliation: Private liberal arts college
Accreditation: NCA
Areas: App Mus; Hist & Lit; Th & An; Opera
Degrees: BA

LEWIS UNIVERSITY
Department of Music
Route 53
Lockport, IL 60441
(815) 838-0500, x415, 416
Staff: Prof. Daniel Binder, Chairman
Affiliation: Private church-related liberal arts university (Catholic)
Accreditation: NCA
Areas: App Mus; Hist & Lit; Th & An; Comp; Cond; Orch; Hist Musicol; Mus Ed (Elem & HS); Mus Merch
Degrees: BA
Scholarships: Music scholarships awarded on the basis of audition and ACT score of 20+

LINCOLN CHRISTIAN COLLEGE[1]
Music Department
Box 178, Keokuk at Limit
Lincoln, IL 62656
(217) 732-3168
Staff: Thomas O. Myers, Chairman
Affiliation: Christian ministerial training college and seminary (Church of Christ)
Accreditation: AABC
Areas: App Mus; Hist & Lit; Th & An; Comp; Cond; Church Mus
Degrees: BA; B Sacr Mus
Scholarships: Private scholarships of tuition for sophomores and above awarded on the basis of academic achievement, proven musical ability, and financial need

MACMURRAY COLLEGE
Department of Music
Jacksonville, IL 62650
(217) 245-6151
Staff: Dr. Richard Hanson, Chairman
Affiliation: Private liberal arts college
Accreditation: NASM; NCA
Areas: App Mus; Hist & Lit; Th & An; Comp; Cond; Opera; Ethnomusicol; Church Mus; Intro; Mus Ed (Elem & HS); Theater Mus
Degrees: BA; BM; BS
Scholarships: Fine arts and name scholarships awarded for talent, training, and academic standing

MCKENDREE COLLEGE[1]
Division of Fine Arts
701 College Rd.
Lebanon, IL 62254
(618) 537-4481, x153
Staff: Glenn H. Freiner, Chairman
Affiliation: Church-related (United Methodist)
Accreditation: NCA
Areas: App Mus; Hist & Lit; Th & An; Cond; Mus Ed (Elem & HS)
Degrees: BA, BME

MILLIKIN UNIVERSITY
School of Music
1184 W. Main St.
Decatur, IL 62522
(217) 424-6300
Staff: Dr. A. Wesley Tower, Dean
Affiliation: An endowed institution
Accreditation: NASM; NCA
Areas: App Mus; Hist & Lit; Th & An; Comp; Cond; Orch; Opera; Church Mus; Intro; Mus Ed (Elem & HS); Theater Mus; Perf; Commer Mus; Mus Bus

Degrees: BA; BFA; BM; BS, Mus Ed; BS, Mus (with minor in Bus Admin)
Scholarships: Talent awards granted on the basis of performing ability

MONMOUTH COLLEGE
Music Department
Monmouth, IL 61462
(309) 457-2382
Staff: John E. Luebke, Chairman
Affiliation: Church-related liberal arts college (United Presbyterian Church)
Accreditation: NCA
Areas: App Mus; Hist & Lit; Th & An; Cond; Orch; Mus Ed (Elem & HS); Intro; Perf; Mus Bus; Jazz
Degrees: BA
Scholarships: Performance scholarships awarded by audition; Monmouth College music scholarships, $2000 award, for participation in one of college's ensembles, awarded by audition

MUNDELEIN COLLEGE
Music Department
6363 Sheridan Rd.
Chicago, IL 60660
(312) 262-8100
Staff: Sr. Eliza Kenney, Chairwomen
Affiliation: Church-related liberal arts college (Roman Catholic)
Accreditation: NCATE; NCA
Areas: App Mus; Hist & Lit; Th & An; Orch; Church Mus; Intro; Mus Ed (Elem & HS)
Degrees: BA
Scholarships: Applied and music study grants awarded by applied audition

NORTH CENTRAL COLLEGE
Music Department
Naperville, IL 60540
(312) 355-5500
Staff: Prof. Bernard Izzo, Chairman
Affiliation: Church-related liberal arts college (Evangelical United Brethren Church)
Accreditation: NCA
Areas: Th & An; Cond; Intro; Mus Hist & Lit; Opera
Degrees: BA

NORTHEASTERN ILLINOIS UNIVERSITY[1]
Department of Music
5500 N. St. Louis Ave.
Chicago, IL 60625
(312) 583-4050, x560, 561
Staff: Harold E. Berlinger, Chairman
Affiliation: State-supported university
Accreditation: NCA; NCATE
Areas: App Mus; Hist & Lit; Th & An; Comp; Cond; Orch; Opera; Intro; Mus Ed (Elem & HS); Perf
Degrees: BA
Scholarships: Music talent scholarships available

NORTHERN ILLINOIS UNIVERSITY
Department of Music,
College of Visual and Performing Arts
DeKalb, IL 60115
(815) 753-1551
Staff: Donald J. Funes, Chairman
Affiliation: State-supported university
Accreditation: NCA; NASM; NCATE; NCA
Areas: App Mus; Hist & Lit; Th & An; Comp; Cond; Orch; Opera; Ethnomusicol; Intro; Mus Ed (Elem & HS); Electr Mus; Perf; Electr Mus
Degrees: BA; BM; BME; MM; Post Master Performer's Certificate
Scholarships: Tuition waivers for undergraduates; graduate assistantships

NORTH PARK COLLEGE
Division of Fine Arts,
Music Department
5125 N. Spaulding Ave.
Chicago, IL 60625
(312) 583-2700
Staff Monroe Olson, Chairman, Division of Fine Arts
Affiliation: Church-related liberal arts college (Evangelical Covenant Church)
Accreditation: NASM; NCA
Areas: App Mus; Mus Ed (Elem & HS); Perf
Degrees: BA; BM
Scholarships: Performance scholarships awarded according to need

NORTHWESTERN UNIVERSITY
School of Music
Evanston, IL 60201
(312) 492-7575
Staff: Thomas W. Miller, Dean
Affiliation: Privately endowed university
Accreditation: NASM; NCA
Areas: App Mus; Hist & Lit; Th & An; Comp; Cond; Orch; Opera; Hist Musicol; Ethnomusicol; Church Mus; Mus Ed (Elem & HS); Jazz Wkshp
Degrees: BM; BME; MM; DM; PhD

OLIVET NAZARENE COLLEGE
Music Department, Division of Fine Arts
Kankakee, IL 60901
(815) 939-5306
Staff: Harlow Hopkins, Chairman
Affiliation: Private church-related liberal arts college (Church of the Nazarene)
Accreditation: NCA; NASM; NCATE
Areas: App Mus; Hist & Lit; Th & An; Cond; Orch; Church Mus; Mus Ed (Elem & HS); Instr Rep
Degrees: BA; BS, Mus
Scholarships: Scholarships available to incoming freshmen; scholarships awarded to selected upperclassmen on the basis of GPA and competitive audition

PRINCIPIA COLLEGE
Music Department
Elsah, IL 62028
(618) 374-2131
Staff: David Sussman, Instructor in Music
Affiliation: Private liberal arts college; students and faculty are Christian Scientists
Accreditation: NCA
Areas: App Mus; Hist & Lit; Th & An; Comp; Cond; Hist Musicol; Mus Ed (Elem); Instr Tech; Hist Jazz; Electr Mus; Opera; Intro
Degrees: BA
Scholarships: Funds provided for applied music lessons on the basis of need

QUINCY COLLEGE
Music Department
Quincy, IL 62301
(217) 222-8020
Staff: Dr. Lavern Wagner, Chairman
Affiliation: Private liberal arts college
Accreditation: NASM; NCA
Areas: App Mus; Hist & Lit; Th & An; Comp; Cond; Orch; Church Mus; Intro; Mus Ed (Elem & HS); Perf
Degrees: BA; BS, Mus Ed; BS, Mus Bus
Scholarships: Awarded on the basis of performing ability

ROCKFORD COLLEGE
Music Department
5050 E. State St.
Rockford, IL 61101
(815) 226-4000
Staff: Walter Whipple, Chairman
Affiliation: Private liberal arts college
Accreditation: NCA
Areas: App Mus; Hist & Lit; Th & An
Degrees: BA; BFA

ROSARY COLLEGE
Music Department
7900 W. Division
River Forest, IL 60305
(312) 366-2490
Staff: Sr. Baptist Stohrer, Chairperson
Affiliation: Church-related liberal arts college (Roman Catholic)
Accreditation: NCA; NASM
Areas: App Mus; Hist & Lit; Th & An; Cond; Orch; Opera; Intro; Mus Ed (Elem & HS)
Degrees: BA; BME
Scholarships: Applied music scholarships awarded on the basis of audition and need

SAINT XAVIER COLLEGE
Department of Music
3700 W. 103rd St.
Chicago, IL 60655
(312) 779-3300
Staff: Sr. Mary V. Obertin, Chairman
Affiliation: Private church-related liberal arts college
(Roman Catholic)
Accreditation: NCA

Areas: App Mus; Hist & Lit; Th & An; Cond; Mus Ed (Elem & HS); Comp; Orch; Intro; Perf
Degrees: BA
Scholarships: Applied Music Awards, one or two semester hours' tuition per semester

SHERWOOD MUSIC SCHOOL
1014 S. Michigan Ave.
Chicago, IL 60605
(312) 427-6267
Staff: Ralph Sunden, Music Director
Affiliation: Private
Accreditation: NASM
Areas: App Mus; Hist & Lit; Th & An; Comp; Cond; Orch; Opera; Perf
Degrees: BM
Scholarships: Sherwood Scholarship, full or partial tuition, available based on talent and financial need

SOUTHERN ILLINOIS UNIVERSITY AT CARBONDALE[1]
School of Music
Carbondale, IL 62901
(618) 453-2263
Staff: C.B. Hunt, Jr., Dean; Robert Roubos, Director
Affiliation: State-supported university
Accreditation: NASM; NCA
Areas: App Mus; Hist & Lit; Th & An; Comp; Cond; Orch; Opera; Mus Ed (Elem & HS)

SOUTHERN ILLINOIS UNIVERSITY AT EDWARDSVILLE
Department of Music
Edwardsville, IL 62026
(618) 692-3900
Staff: Dr. Donald G. Loucks, Chairman
Affiliation: State-supported university
Accreditation: NASM; NCA
Areas: App Mus; Hist & Lit; Th & An; Comp; Cond; Orch; Opera; Mus Ed (Elem & HS); Instr Rep; Perf; Intro; Jazz
Degrees: BA; BM; MM
Scholarships: Tuition waivers and talent awards awarded on the basis of competitive auditions

TRINITY CHRISTIAN COLLEGE
Music Department
6601 W. College Dr.
Palos Heights, IL 60463
(312) 597-3000
Staff: Karen De Mol, Principal Faculty Member
Affiliation: Private liberal arts college
Accreditation: NCA
Areas: App Mus; Hist & Lit; Th & An; Cond; Orch; Church Mus; Intro; Mus Ed (Elem & HS)
Degrees: BA

TRINITY COLLEGE
Music Department
2045 Half Day Rd.
Deerfield, IL 60015
(312) 945-6700
Staff: Dr. Morris Faugerstrom, Chairman
Affiliation: Independent Christian liberal arts college
Accreditation: NCA
Areas: App Mus; Hist & Lit; Th & An; Comp; Cond; Orch; Church Mus; Mus Ed (Elem & HS)
Degrees: BA
Scholarships: Special ability grants based on talent and/or need

UNIVERSITY OF CHICAGO
Department of Music
5845 S. Ellis Ave.
Chicago, IL 60637
(312) 962-8484
Staff: Philip Gossett, Chairman
Affiliation: Private university
Accreditation: NCA
Areas: Hist & Lit; Th & An; Comp; Cond; Hist Musicol
Degrees: BA; MA; PhD

UNIVERSITY OF ILLINOIS AT CHICAGO
Department of Music
Box 4348
Chicago, IL 60680
(312) 996-2977
Staff: William Kaplan, Department Head
Affiliation: Chicago campus of the state university
Accreditation: NCA
Areas: App Mus; Hist & Lit; Th & An; Comp; Cond; Orch; Opera; Electr Mus
Degrees: BA
Scholarships: Approximately fifteen tuition waivers are granted each year to performers chosen by audition

UNIVERSITY OF ILLINOIS, URBANA/CHAMPAIGN
School of Music
2136 Music Building
Urbana, IL 61801
(217) 333-2620
Staff: Robert Bays, Director
Affiliation: State-supported university
Accreditation: NASM; NCA; NCATE
Areas: App Mus; Hist & Lit; Th & An; Comp; Cond; Orch; Opera; Hist Musicol; Ethnomusicol; Intro; Mus Ed (Elem & HS); Electr Mus; Perf
Degrees: BA; BM; BS, Mus Ed; MM; MS, Mus Ed; EdD; DMA; PhD
Scholarships: Undergraduate scholarships and tuition waivers; graduate tuition waivers; fellowships and assistantships

VANDERCOOK COLLEGE OF MUSIC
3209 S. Michigan Ave.
Chicago, IL 60616
(312) 225-6288
Staff: Anthony G. Gunia, Director of Admissions
Affiliation: Private
Accreditation: NASM; NCA
Areas: Mus Ed (Elem & HS)
Degrees: BME, MME
Scholarships: Tuition waivers, awards, other financial aid available in several instrumental areas

WESTERN ILLINOIS UNIVERSITY[1]
Department of Music
900 W. Adams
Macomb, IL 61455
(309) 298-1544
Staff: James A. Keene, Chairman
Affiliation: State-supported university
Accreditation: NASM; NCA
Areas: App Mus; Hist & Lit; Th & An; Comp; Cond; Orch; Opera; Hist Musicol; Mus Ed (Elem & HS); Theater Mus
Degrees: BA; BME; MA; MS, Ed

WHEATON COLLEGE
Conservatory of Music
Wheaton, IL 60187
(312) 260-5098
Staff: Dr. Harold M. Best, Dean
Affiliation: Privately endowed liberal arts college
Accreditation: NASM; NCATE; NCA
Areas: App Mus; Hist & Lit; Th & An; Comp; Cond; Church Mus; Mus Ed (Elem & HS); Ethnomusicol; Perf
Degrees: BA; BM; BME

INDIANA

BALL STATE UNIVERSITY
School of Music
Muncie, IN 47306
(317) 285-4433
Staff: Dr. Emanuel Rubin, Director
Affiliation: State-supported university
Accreditation: NASM; NCA
Areas: App Mus; Hist & Lit; Th & An; Comp; Cond; Orch; Opera; Hist Musicol; Ethnomusicol; Church Mus; Intro; Mus Ed (Elem & HS); Mus Therapy; Theater Mus; Piano Tech; Instr Rep; Electr Mus; Perf
Degrees: BA; BM; BS, Mus Ed; MA; MM; MA, Mus Ed; EdD; DA
Scholarships: Full and half tuition merit scholarships available

BETHEL COLLEGE
1001 W. McKinley
Mishawaka, IN 46544
(219) 259-8511, x66
Staff: Dr. Elliott A. Nordgren, Chairman
Affiliation: Church-related (Missionary Church)
Accreditation: NCA
Areas: App Mus; Hist & Lit; Th & An; Comp; Cond; Orch; Opera; Church Mus; Mus Ed (Elem & HS); Theater Mus
Degrees: BA
Scholarships: Grants in aid from $500 to full tuition for accompanying and ensembled based on audition

DE PAUW UNIVERSITY[1]
School of Music

Greencastle, IN 46135
(317) 658-4816
Staff: Cassel W. Grubb, Director
Affiliation: Privately endowed liberal arts university
Accreditation: NASM; NCA
Areas: App Mus; Hist & Lit; Th & An; Comp; Cond; Orch; Opera; Mus Ed (Elem & HS); Perf
Degrees: BA; BM
Scholarships: Awarded by audition

EARLHAM COLLEGE
Music Department
National Rd. W.
Richmond, IN 47374
(317) 962-6561
Staff: Leonard C. Holvik, Chairman
Affiliation: Private liberal arts college (Society of Friends)
Accreditation: NCA; ATS
Areas: App Mus; Hist & Lit; Th & An; Comp; Intro; Mus Ed (Elem); Perf
Degrees: BA
Scholarships: Presser Scholarship for outstanding senior; scholarships to several students for applied music fees; freshman string quartet scholarship; freshman applied music scholarship

FORT WAYNE BIBLE COLLEGE
Department of Music
1025 W. Rudisill
Fort Wayne, IN 46807
(219) 456-2111
Staff: Jay D. Platte, Chairman
Affiliation: Church-related Bible college
Accreditation: AABC; candidate NCA
Areas: App Mus; Hist & Lit; Th & An; Comp; Cond; Orch; Church Mus; Mus Ed (Elem & HS); Piano Tech; Instr Rep; Phil/Aesth
Degrees: BM; BME; BS, Church Mus

GOSHEN COLLEGE
Music Department
1700 S. Main
Goshen, IN 46526
(219) 533-3161
Staff: Philip K. Clemens, Chairman
Affiliation: Church-related liberal arts college (Mennonite)
Accreditation: NCA
Areas: App Mus; Hist & Lit; Th & An; Cond; Church Mus; Mus Ed (Elem & HS); Piano Ped; Intro; Perf; Electr Mus
Degrees: BA
Scholarships: Awarded on the basis of financial need and audition or tape

GRACE COLLEGE
Music Department
Winona Lake, IN 46590
(219) 267-8191
Staff: Donald E. Ogden, Chairman
Affiliation: Church-related college (Fellowship of Grace Brethren Churches)
Accreditation: NCA
Areas: App Mus; Hist & Lit; Th & An; Cond; Church Mus; Mus Ed (Elem & HS); Instr Rep; Mus Mgmt
Degrees: BA; BS, Mus Ed; BS, Mus Perf; BS, Mus Mgmt
Scholarships: Tuition aid of $115 to ¼ tuition per semester available; application form available on request

HANOVER COLLEGE[1]
Department of Music
Hanover, IN 47243
(812) 866-2151
Staff: J. David Wagner, Chairman
Affiliation: Church-related liberal arts college (Presbyterian)
Accreditation: NCA
Areas: App Mus; Hist & Lit; Th & An; Cond; Orch; Church Mus; Intro; Mus Ed (Elem & HS)
Degrees: BA
Scholarships: Available only through college program, not departmentally

HUNTINGTON COLLEGE[1]
2303 College Ave.
Huntington, IN 46750
(219) 356-6000, x55
Staff: Marlene J. Langosch, Chairman
Affiliation: Church-related (United Brethren)
Accreditation: NCA
Areas: App Mus; Hist & Lit; Th & An; Comp; Cond; Mus Ed (Elem & HS)
Degrees: BA; BS, Mus Ed

INDIANA CENTRAL UNIVERSITY[1]
Department of Music
1400 E. Hanna Ave.
Indianapolis, IN 46227
(317) 788-3255
Staff: James P. Lamberson, Chairman
Affiliation: Privately endowed church-related liberal arts college (United Methodist)
Accreditation: NASM; NCA
Areas: App Mus; Hist & Lit; Th & An; Cond; Orch; Opera; Intro; Mus Ed (Elem & HS); Perf
Degrees: BA; BS, Mus Ed; MA
Scholarships: Scholarships ranging from $400 to full tuition awarded according to performance ability

INDIANA STATE UNIVERSITY
Music Department
Terre Haute, IN 47809
(812) 232-6311, x2213
Staff: Robert L. Cowden, Chairman
Affiliation: State
Accreditation: NASM; NCA
Areas: App Mus; Hist & Lit; Th & An; Comp; Mus Ed (Elem & HS)
Degrees: BA; BS, Mus Ed; MA; MS, Mus Ed

INDIANA UNIVERSITY
School of Music
Bloomington, IN 47401
(812) 337-1582
Staff: Charles H. Webb, Dean
Affiliation: State-supported university
Accreditation: NASM; NCA
Areas: App Mus; Hist & Lit; Th & An; Comp; Cond; Orch; Opera; Hist Musicol; Ethnomusicol; Church Mus; Mus Ed (Elem & HS); Mus Therapy; Theater Mus; Piano Tech; Instr Rep
Degrees: BA; BM; BME; BS, Mus Ed; MA; MM; MA, Mus Ed; DMA; EdD; PhD
Scholarships: Awarded for music merit

INDIANA UNIVERSITY-PURDUE UNIVERSITY AT FORT WAYNE
Division of Music
2101 Coliseum Blvd. E
Fort Wayne, IN 46805
(219) 482-5746
Staff: Dr. John Roberts, Chairman
Affiliation: State-supported university
Accreditation: NASM; NCA
Areas: App Mus; Hist & Lit; Th & An; Comp; Cond; Orch; Opera; Hist Musicol; Church Mus; Intro; Mus Ed (Elem & HS); Mus Therapy; Theater Mus; Perf
Degrees: BM; BME; BS, Mus Therapy; BS, Mus and outside field
Scholarships: Music scholarships awarded by audition

INDIANA UNIVERSITY, SOUTH BEND
Division of Music
1825 Northside Blvd.
South Bend, IN 46615
(219) 237-4101
Staff: Robert William Demaree, Jr., Chairman
Affiliation: State-supported university
Accreditation: NCA
Areas: App Mus; Hist & Lit; Th & An; Comp; Cond; Orch; Opera; Mus Ed (Elem & HS); Theater Mus
Degrees: AA, Jazz, Commer Mus; BM; BME; BS (in music and outside field); MM; MS, Mus Ed

INDIANA UNIVERSITY SOUTHEAST
Music Department
4201 Grant Line Rd.
New Albany, IN 47150
(812) 945-2731
Staff; Dr. W.C. Greckel, Professor of Music
Affiliation: State-supported university, regional campus of I.U. Bloomington
Accreditation: NCA
Areas: App Mus; Th & An; Mus Ed (Elem); Mus Therapy; Theater Mus; Electr Mus; Perf
Degrees: Music minor only
Scholarships: Chamber orchestra scholarships offered

JORDAN COLLEGE OF FINE ARTS OF BUTLER UNIVERSITY
Department of Music
4600 Clarendon Road
Indianapolis, IN 46208
(317) 283-9231
Staff: Dr. Louis F. Chenette, Dean
Affiliation: School of performing arts in a privately endowed university
Accreditation: NASM; NCATE; NCA

Areas: App Mus; Hist & Lit; Th & An; Comp; Cond; Orch; Opera; Hist Musicol; Church Mus; Intro; Mus Ed (Elem & HS); Instr Rep; Electr Mus; Perf
Degrees: BA; BM; MM
Scholarships: One-quarter, one-half, three-fourths, or full tuition by audition

MANCHESTER COLLEGE
Music Department
North Manchester, IN 46962
(219) 982-2141
Staff: Dr. John H. Planer, Chairman
Affiliation: Church-related liberal arts college (Church of the Brethren)
Accreditation: NASM; NCATE; NCA
Areas: App Mus; Hist & Lit; Th & An; Comp; Cond; Church Mus; Intro; Mus Ed (Elem & HS)
Degrees: BA; BS, Mus Ed
Scholarships: Endowed scholarships based on need and ability

MARIAN COLLEGE
Music Department
3200 Cold Spring Rd.
Indianapolis, IN 46222
(317) 924-3291
Staff: Sr. Vivian Rose Morshauser, Chairman
Affiliation: Private college
Accreditation: NCA; NCATE
Areas: App Mus; Hist & Lit; Th & An; Cond; Orch; Church Mus; Mus Ed (Elem & HS)
Degrees: BA
Scholarships: Performance scholarships awarded by audition

OAKLAND CITY COLLEGE[1]
Oakland City, IN 47660
(812) 749-4781, x59
Staff: Gloria Heyde, Assistant Professor
Affiliation: Church-related (General Baptist)
Accreditation: NCA
Areas: Hist & Lit; Mus Ed (Elem & HS)
Degrees: BA; BS, Mus Ed

SAINT JOSEPH'S COLLEGE[1]
Department of Music
Rensselaer, IN 47978
(219) 866-7111
Staff: John B. Egan, Chairman
Affiliation: Church-related liberal arts college (Roman Catholic)
Accreditation: NCA
Areas: App Mus; Hist & Lit; Th & An; Comp; Cond; Orch; Church Mus; Intro; Mus Ed (Elem & HS); Perf
Degrees: BA; BS; MA
Scholarships: Grants awarded for ensemble participation

SAINT MARY-OF-THE-WOODS COLLEGE
Music Department
St. Mary-of-the-Woods, IN 47876
(812) 535-4141
Staff: Sr. Laurette Bellamy, Chairman
Affiliation: Liberal arts college
Accreditation: NASM; NCA
Areas: App Mus; Hist & Lit; Th & An; Comp; Cond; Orch; Hist Musicol; Church Mus; Intro; Mus Ed (Elem & HS); Perf; Music Therapy; Voice & Drama
Degrees: BA; BS, Mus Ed
Scholarships: Performing arts scholarship of $1,000 a year, renewable annually, awarded on the basis of audition or taped performance of three representative memorized compositions; other scholarships available

SAINT MARY'S COLLEGE
Music Department
Notre Dame, IN 46556
(219) 284-4632
Staff: Prof. Clayton Henderson, Chairman
Affiliation: Church-related college of arts and sciences (Roman Catholic)
Accreditation: NASM; NCATE; NCA
Areas: App Mus; Th & An; Comp; Cond; Opera; Intro; Mus Ed (Elem & HS); Perf
Degrees: BA; BM; BM, Mus Ed
Scholarships: Scholarships available; contact Financial Aid Office for information

TAYLOR UNIVERSITY
Music Department
Upland, IN 46989
(317) 998-2751
Staff: Dr. Timothy W. Sharp, Chairman
Affiliation: Private university (interdenominational)
Accreditation: NASM; NCA
Areas: App Mus; Hist & Lit; Comp; Mus Ed (Elem & HS); Perf; Church Mus; Piano Ped
Degrees: BA; BS, Mus Ed; BM, Church Mus
Scholarships: Various scholarships awarded on the basis of audition

UNIVERSITY OF EVANSVILLE
Department of Music
1800 Lincoln Ave., PO Box 329
Evansville, IN 47702
(812) 479-2742
Staff: Dr. Edwin Lacy, Head
Affiliation: Private liberal arts university
Accreditation: NCA; NASM; NCATE
Areas: App Mus; Hist & Lit; Th & An; Comp; Cond; Orch; Opera; Mus Ed (Elem & HS); Mus Therapy; Piano Tech; Instr Rep; Perf; Church Mus
Degrees: BA; BM; BME; BM, Mus Therapy' BS, Mus Mgmt; BS, Mus & Assoc Studies; MA; MM
Scholarships: Scholarships awarded on the basis of need and merit

UNIVERSITY OF NOTRE DAME[1]
Department of Music
Notre Dame, IN 46556
(219) 283-6211
Staff: Calvin M. Bower, Chairman
Affiliation: Privately endowed university
Accreditation: NASM; NCA
Areas: App Mus; Hist & Lit; Th & An; Comp; Cond; Orch; Hist Musicol; Church Mus; Intro
Degrees: BA; BM; MA; MM
Scholarships: Assistantships and tuition scholarships available only on the graduate level

VALPARAISO UNIVERSITY
Music Department
University Place
Valparaiso, IN 46383
(219) 464-5454
Staff: Frederick H. Telschow, Chairman
Affiliation: Independent private church-related institution (Lutheran)
Accreditation: NASM; NCATE; NCA
Areas: App Mus; Hist & Lit; Th & An; Comp; Cond; Orch; Opera; Hist Musicol; Church Mus; Intro; Mus Ed (Elem & HS); Electr Mus
Degrees: BA; BM; BME; MA; MM
Scholarships: Music Activity Awards granted on the basis of audition and need for instrument

WABASH COLLEGE
Music Department
Crawfordsville, IN 47933
(317) 362-1400
Staff: Fredric Enenbach, Chairman
Affiliation: Private liberal arts college
Accreditation: NCA
Areas: Hist & Lit; Th & An; Comp
Degrees: BA

IOWA

BRIAR CLIFF COLLEGE
Division of Fine Arts, Department of Music
3303 Rebecca St.
Sioux City, IA 51104
(712) 279-5567
Staff: Sr. Mary Day, Chairperson, Department of Music
Affiliation: Private church-related liberal arts college (Roman Catholic)
Accreditation: NCA
Areas: App Mus; Hist & Lit; Th & An; Comp; Cond; Opera; Church Mus; Mus Ed (Elem & HS); Theater Mus; Choral and Instr Ens
Degrees: BA
Scholarships: Academic scholarships awarded on the basis of talent; audition required

BUENA VISTA COLLEGE[1]
Music Department
Storm Lake, IA 50588
(712) 749-2351
Staff: Frances Heusinkveld, Chairman
Affiliation: Church-related liberal arts college (United Presbyterian)
Accreditation: NCA; NCATE
Areas: App Mus; Hist & Lit; Th & An; Comp; Cond; Intro; Mus Ed (Elem & HS); Perf
Degrees: BA

Scholarships: Scholarships for music majors awarded on the basis of audition, performance in groups, and 2.0 GPA in nonmusic subjects, 2.5 GPA in music subjects; participation scholarships awarded for participation in groups and 2.0 GPA

CENTRAL UNIVERSITY OF IOWA
Music Department
Pella, IA 50219
(515) 628-4151
Staff: Davis L. Folkerts, Chairman
Affiliation: Church-related liberal arts college (Reformed Church in America)
Accreditation: NCA; NASM
Areas: App Mus; Hist & Lit; Th & An; Comp; Cond; Orch; Mus Ed (Elem & HS); Church Mus; Intro; Perf
Degrees: BA
Scholarships: Gift aid available to students successfully auditioning by tape or on campus; must be in upper 50 percent of high school graduating class

CLARKE COLLEGE
Music Department
1550 Clarke Dr.
Dubuque, IA 52001
(319) 588-6412
Staff: John A. Lease, Chairman
Affiliation: Church-related liberal arts college (Catholic)
Accreditation: NASM; NCATE; NCA
Areas: App Mus; Mus Ed (Elem & HS)
Degrees: BA
Scholarships: Scholarships awarded by audition

COE COLLEGE
Music Department
1220 First Avenue, N.E.
Cedar Rapids, IA 52402
(319) 399-8521
Staff: Dean M. Karns, Chairman
Affiliation: Private
Accreditation: NASM; NCA
Areas: App Mus; Hist & Lit; Th & An; Comp; Cond; Orch; Opera; Mus Ed (Elem & HS); Jazz
Degrees: BA, BM

CORNELL COLLEGE
Music Department
Mount Vernon, IA 52314
(319) 895-8911
Staff: Dr. Jesse G. Evans, Chairman
Affiliation: Church-related liberal arts college (Methodist)
Accreditation: NASM; NCA
Areas: App Mus; Hist & Lit; Th & An; Cond; Orch; Mus Ed (Elem & HS); Nonwestern Mus; Comp; Ethnomusicol; Intro; Theater Mus; Perf
Degrees: BA; BM; BME; BSS, Mus
Scholarships: Awarded on the basis of musicianship and school record in music

DORDT COLLEGE
Music Department
Sioux Center, IA 51250
(712) 722-3771
Staff: Gerald Bouma, Chairman
Affiliation: Private church-related liberal arts college (Christian Reformed Church)
Accreditation: NCA
Areas: Hist & Lit; Th & An; Comp; Cond; Church Mus; Mus Ed (Elem & HS); App Mus; Orch; Intro; Perf
Degrees: BA
Scholarships: Freshmen music grants available; 3 scholarships for upperclassmen; 1 organ scholarship

DRAKE UNIVERSITY
Music Department, College of Fine Arts
25th and University
Des Moines, IA 50311
(515) 271-3879
Staff: Marion A. Hall, Chairman
Affiliation: Private university
Accreditation: NASM; NCA
Areas: App Mus; Hist & Lit; Th & An; Comp; Cond; Orch; Opera; Hist Musicol; Church Mus; Mus Ed (Elem & HS)
Degrees: BM; BME; BM, Church; MM; MME
Scholarships: Talent scholarships awarded by audition

GRACELAND COLLEGE[1]
Division of Fine Arts
Lamoni, IA 50140
(515) 784-5000
Staff: Oliver C. Houston, Chairman
Affiliation: Church-related college (Reorganized Church of Jesus Christ of Latter Day Saints)
Accreditation: NCA
Areas: App Mus; Hist & Lit; Th & An; Comp; Cond; Orch; Mus Ed (Elem & HS)
Degrees: BA; BA, Mus Ed
Scholarships: Ensemble scholarships awarded according to openings in sections

GRINNELL COLLEGE[1]
Music Department
Grinnell, IA 50112
(515) 236-6181
Staff: John Jensen, Chairman
Affiliation: Privately endowed liberal arts college
Accreditation: NCA
Areas: App Mus; Hist & Lit; Th & An; Comp; Hist Musicol; Ethnomusicol; Intro; Electr Mus; Perf
Degrees: BA
Scholarships: Applied music scholarships available; contact Financial Aid Office

IOWA STATE UNIVERSITY
Department of Music
Ames, IA 50011
(515) 294-5364
Staff: Dr. Arthur G. Swift, Head.
Affiliation: State-supported university
Accreditation: NASM; NCATE; NCA
Areas: App Mus; Hist & Lit; Th & An; Comp; Cond; Orch; Opera; Hist Musicol; Intro; Mus Ed (Elem & HS); Electr Mus; Perf
Degrees: BA; BM
Scholarships: Scholarships of $170 to $1100 awarded on the basis of audition, recommendations, and achievement

IOWA WESLEYAN COLLEGE
Music Department
Mount Pleasant, IA 52641
(319) 385-8021
Staff: Prof. Burton P. Mahle, Chairman
Affiliation: Church-related liberal arts college (United Methodist)
Accreditation: NCA
Areas: App Mus; Hist & Lit; Th & An; Mus Ed; Church Mus
Degrees: BA; BME
Scholarships: Scholarships of $1000 to $2000 available through taped or live audition

LORAS COLLEGE
Music Department
1450 Alta Vista
Dubuque, IA 52001
(319) 588-7153
Staff: Joseph C. Colaluca, Chairman
Affiliation: Church-related liberal arts college (Catholic)
Accreditation: NCATE; NCA
Areas: Mus Ed (Elem & HS)
Degrees: BA; BME
Scholarships: Financial scholarships awarded by audition

LUTHER COLLEGE[1]
Department of Music
Decorah, IA 52101
(319) 387-1208
Staff: Dr. Maurice E. Monhardt, Chairman
Affiliation: Church-related liberal arts college (Lutheran)
Accreditation: NASM; NCA
Calendar: Semester
Areas: App Mus; Hist & Lit; Th & An; Comp; Cond; Opera; Church Mus; Mus Ed (Elem & HS); Piano Tech
Degrees: BA

MARYCREST COLLEGE[1]
Music Department
1607 W. 12th St.
Davenport, IA 52804
(319) 326-9512
Staff: Elizabeth Schneider, Head
Affiliation: Private liberal arts college
Accreditation: NCA; NCATE
Calendar: Semester
Areas: App Mus; Hist & Lit; Th & An; Cond; Mus Ed (Elem & HS)
Degrees: BA, Mus Ed; BA, Mus
Scholarships: Fine arts grants awarded on the basis of GPA and audition

MORNINGSIDE COLLEGE
Music Department
Sioux City, IA 51106
(712) 274-5210
Staff: Harlan H. Buss, Chairman
Affiliation: Church-related liberal arts college (Methodist)
Accreditation: NASM; NCATE; NCA
Areas: App Mus; Hist & Lit; Th & An; Comp; Cond; Orch; Mus Ed (Elem & HS)
Degrees: BA; BM; BME
Scholarships: Music grants-in-aid awarded on the basis of talent and audition

MOUNT MERCY COLLEGE[1]
Music Department
1330 Elmhurst Dr. NE
Cedar Rapids, IA 52402
(319) 363-8213
Staff: William R. Medley, Chairman
Affiliation: Church-related liberal arts college (Roman Catholic)
Accreditation: NCA
Areas: App Mus; Hist & Lit; Th & An; Cond; Mus Ed (Elem & HS); Theater Mus; Intro; Piano Ped
Degrees: BA
Scholarships: Applied music scholarships awarded by audition

NORTHWESTERN COLLEGE
Music Department
Orange City, IA 51041
(712) 737-4821
Staff: Charles Canaan, Chairman
Affiliation: Church-related (Reformed Church in America)
Accreditation: NCA
Areas: App Mus; Hist & Lit; Th & An; Cond; Orch; Church Mus; Mus Ed (Elem & HS); Intro; Perf
Degrees: BA; BA, Mus Ed
Scolarship: Performance scholarships available in keyboard, vocal, instrumental; activity grants for students involved in performance ensembles

ST. AMBROSE COLLEGE
Music Department
518 W. Locust
Davenport, IA 52803
(319) 383-8800
Staff: Dr. Joan T. Fish, Chairman
Affiliation: Church-related liberal arts college (Roman Catholic)
Accreditation: NCA
Areas: App Mus; Hist & Lit; Th & An; Cond; Church Mus; Intro; Mus Ed (Elem & HS); Perf
Degrees: BA; BM; BME
Scholarships: Scholarship grants of up to one-half of tuition

SIMPSON COLLEGE[1]
Department of Music
Indianola, IA 50125
(515) 961-6251, x637
Staff: Dr. Robert L. Larsen, Chairman
Affiliation: Church-related liberal arts college (United Methodist)
Accreditation: NASM; NCA
Areas: App Mus; Hist & Lit; Th & An; Comp; Cond; Orch; Opera; Church Mus; Intro; Mus Ed (Elem & HS); Theater Mus; Piano Tech; Perf
Degrees: BA; BM; BME
Scholarships: Vocal, instrumental, and keyboard scholarships awarded by audition

UNIVERSITY OF DUBUQUE[1]
Music Department
2050 University
Dubuque, IA 52001
(319) 589-3247
Staff: Dennis Williams, Chairman
Affiliation: Church-related liberal arts college (Presbyterian)
Accreditation: NCA; NCATE
Areas: App Mus; Hist & Lit; Th & An; Cond; Orch; Hist Musicol; Intro; Mus Ed (Elem & HS); Perf
Degrees: BA; BM
Scholarships: Music awards based on audition and academic standing

UNIVERSITY OF IOWA[1]
School of Music
Iowa City, IA 52242
(319) 353-3445
Staff: Prof. Marilyn F. Somville, Director
Affiliation: State-supported university
Accreditation: NASM; NCATE; NCA
Areas: App Mus; Hist & Lit; Th & An; Comp; Cond; Orch; Opera; Hist Musicol; Intro; Mus Ed (Elem & HS); Mus Therapy; Electr Mus; Perf
Degrees: BA; BM; MA; MFA
Scholarships: Tuition scholarships awarded by audition

UNIVERSITY OF NORTHERN IOWA
School of Music
Cedar Falls, IA 50613
(319) 273-2024
Staff: Dr. Ronald D. Ross, Director
Affiliation: State-supported university
Accreditation: NASM; NCA
Areas: App Mus; Hist & Lit; Th & An; Comp; Cond; Mus Ed (Elem & HS); Theater Mus; Perf
Degrees: BA; BFA; BM; BME; MA; MM; MA, Mus Ed
Scholarships: Performance scholarships awarded by audition

UPPER IOWA UNIVERSITY
Music Department
Fayette, IA 52142
(319) 425-3311
Staff: Larry Keig, Head
Affiliation: Private liberal arts college
Accreditation: NCA
Areas: App Mus; Hist & Lit; Th & An; Comp; Cond; Orch; Mus Ed (Elem & HS); Instr Rep; Mus Mgmt; Intro
Degrees: BA
Scholarships: Performance scholarships of $300 to $1,500 a year available

WARTBURG COLLEGE
Music Department
Waverly, IA 50677
(319) 352-1200
Staff: Dr. Franklin E. Williams, Chairman
Affiliation: Private church-related liberal arts college (American Lutheran)
Accreditation: NASM; NCA
Areas: App Mus; Hist & Lit; Th & An; Comp; Cond; Church Mus; Mus Ed (Elem & HS); Mus Therapy; Instr Rep; Perf
Degrees: BA; BM; BME; BME, Mus Therapy
Scholarships: Meistersinger scholarships and scholarships for all applied areas awarded on the basis of audition

WESTMAR COLLEGE[1]
Music Department
LeMars, IA 51031
(712) 546-7081
Staff: Frank N. Summerside, Chairman
Affiliation: Private church-related college (United Methodist)
Accreditation: NCA
Areas: App Mus; Hist & Lit; Th & An; Cond; Intro; Mus Ed (Elem & Hs); Perf
Degrees: BA; BME
Scholarships: Performance grants available in all areas

WILLIAM PENN COLLEGE[1]
Fine Arts Department
Oskaloosa, IA 52577
(515) 673-8311
Staff: David Evans, Chairman
Affiliation: Church-related liberal arts college (Quaker)
Accreditation: NCATE; NCA
Areas: App Mus; Hist & Lit; Th & An; Comp; Cond; Orch; Mus Ed (Elem & HS); Theater Mus; Instr Rep
Degrees: BA
Scholarships: Activity scholarships awarded on the basis of talent, need, and contribution to department; academic scholarships awarded on the basis of GPA

KANSAS

BAKER UNIVERSITY
Music Department
Baldwin City, KS 66006
(913) 594-6451, x478
Staff: Dr. Alfred Service, Chairman
Affiliation: Church-related senior college (United Methodist)
Accreditation: NCA
Areas: App Mus; Hist & Lit; Th & An; Comp; Cond; Orch; Opera; Church Mus; Intro; Mus Ed (Elem & HS); Mus Therapy
Degrees: BA; BME; MA (in conjunction with Southern Methodist University)
Scholarships: Annually renewable achievement awards in music granted

by audition; size of award depends on music achievement (not tied to financial need); one Fine Arts Day Scholarship annually based on achievement and personal audition

BENEDICTINE COLLEGE
Music Department
South Campus
Atchison, KS 66002
(913) 367-6110
Staff: Dr. Russell T. Waite, Chairman
Affiliation: Church-related liberal arts college (Roman Catholic—Benedictine Order)
Accreditation: NASM; NCA
Areas: App Mus; Hist & Lit; Th & An; Comp; Cond; Orch; Opera; Church Mus; Mus Ed (Elem & HS); Mus Marketing
Degrees: BA; BM; BME; BM, Mus Ed
Scholarships: Named music scholarships are available, as well as ample opportunity for tuition scholarships, honor awards, achievement awards, etc.

BETHANY COLLEGE
Music Department
Lindsborg, KS 67456
(913) 227-3312
Staff: Eugene I. Holdsworth, Chairman
Affiliation: Church-related liberal arts college (Lutheran-LCA)
Accreditation: NASM; NCATE; NCA
Areas: App Mus; Hist & Lit; Th & An; Comp; Cond; Orch; Church Mus; Intro; Mus Ed (Elem & HS)
Degrees: BA
Scholarships: Departmental and divisional scholarships available; audition required

BETHEL COLLEGE
Music Department
North Newton, KS 67117
(316) 283-2500
Staff: Donald Kehrberg, Head
Affiliation: Church-related liberal arts college (Mennonite)
Accreditation: NCA
Areas: App Mus; Hist & Lit; Th & An; Comp; Cond; Opera; Church Mus; Mus Ed (Elem & HS); Jazz Studies
Degrees: BA
Scholarships: Awarded on the basis of audition or tape recording

EMPORIA STATE UNIVERSITY
Department of Music
1200 Commercial St.
Emporia, KS 66801
(316) 343-1200, x431
Staff: Dr. Kenneth W. Hart, Chairperson
Affiliation: State-supported Regent's Institution
Accreditation: NASM; NCATE; NCA
Areas: App Mus; Hist & Lit; Th & An; Comp; Cond; Orch; Opera; Hist Musicol; Mus Ed (Elem & HS); Piano Tech; Instru Rep; Electr Mus; Perf
Degrees: BA; BM; BME; MM; BSMM (Music Merchandising)
Scholarships: Talent scholarships based on audition are given; automatic $300 for high academic standing in HS; general aid based on need

FORT HAYS STATE UNIVERSITY
Music Department
600 Park St.
Hays, KS 67601
(913) 628-4226
Staff: John E. Huber, Chairman
Affiliation: State-supported
Accreditation: NASM; NCA
Areas: App Mus; Hist & Lit; Th & An; Comp; Mus Ed (Elem & HS)
Degrees: BA, BM, MM
Scholarships: Scholarships range from $100 to $500 per year based on audition (musical performance level and scholarship)

FRIENDS BIBLE COLLEGE
Box 288
Haviland, KS 67059
(316) 862-5891
Staff: Robert Ham, Chairman
Affiliation: Church-related (Friends Church)
Accreditation: AABC
Areas: App Mus; Hist & Lit; Th & An; Cond; Church Mus; Intro
Degrees: BA
Scholarships: Music scholarships up to $800

FRIENDS UNIVERSITY[1]
Division of Fine Arts
2100 University Ave.
Wichita, KS 67213
(316) 261-5800
Staff: Dr. Cecil J. Riney, Chairman
Affiliation: Church-related liberal arts college (Quaker)
Accreditation: NASM; NCA; NCATE
Areas: App Mus; Church Mus; Mus Ed (Elem & HS)
Degrees: BA; BM
Scholarships: Scholarships available

KANSAS NEWMAN COLLEGE[1]
3100 McCormick Ave.
Wichita, KS 67213
(316) 942-4291, x41
Staff: Sr. Betty Adams, Instructor
Affiliation: Church-related (Roman Catholic)
Accreditation: NCA
Areas: Th & An; Intro; Hist & Lit
Degrees: BA

KANSAS STATE UNIVERSITY
Music Department
Manhattan, KS 66506
(913) 532-5740
Staff: Dr. Robert A. Steinbauer, Head
Affiliation: State-supported university
Accreditation: NASM; NCA
Areas: App Mus; Hist & Lit; Th & An; Comp; Opera; Hist Musicol; Church Mus; Intro; Mus Ed (Elem & HS); Electr Mus; Perf
Degrees: BA; BM; BME; MM
Scholarships: Music Service Guild awards based on performance excellence

KANSAS WESLEYAN[1]
Music Department
100 E. Claflin
Salina, KS 67401
(913) 827-5541, x257
Staff: Donald Donaldson, Chairman
Affiliation: Church-related (United Methodist)
Accreditation: NCA
Areas: App Mus; Hist & Lit; Th & An; Cond; Church Mus; Mus Ed (Elem & HS)
Degrees: BA

MANHATTAN CHRISTIAN COLLEGE
Music Department
1407 Anderson
Manhattan, KS 66502
(913) 539-7582
Staff: Dr. Donn Leach, Vice-President for Academic Affairs
Affiliation: Bible college for ministers, church educators, missionaries, and church musicians; unusual programs of studies in cooperation with Kansas State University (adjacent to the college) also offer students the opportunity to combine Biblical studies with other types of professional education (Christian Churches/Churches of Christ)
Accreditation: AABC
Areas: App Mus; Hist & Lit; Th & An; Cond; Orch; Church Mus; Mus Ed (Elem & HS, at KSU); Comp; Intro
Degrees: BS, Bible/Church Mus
Scholarships: Limited scholarships of $250 maximum per semester awarded by audition

MARYMOUNT COLLEGE OF KANSAS[1]
Department of Music
Salina, KS 67401
(913) 825-2101, x203
Staff: David C. Rayl, Chairman
Affiliation: Church-related liberal arts college (Roman Catholic)
Accreditation: NASM; NCA; NCATE
Areas: App Mus; Hist & Lit; Th & An; Comp; Cond; Orch; Church Mus; Intro; Mus Ed (Elem & HS); Theater Mus; Perf
Degrees: BA; BM; BME
Scholarships: Performance scholarships available through faculty audition

MCPHERSON COLLEGE
Music Department
McPherson, KS 67460
(316) 241-0731
Staff: Prof Stephanie B. Graber, Chairman
Affiliation: Church-related liberal arts college (Church of the Brethren)
Accreditation: NCA

Areas: App Mus; Hist & Lit; Th & An; Comp; Cond; Orch; Church Mus; Mus Ed (Elem & HS); Perf
Degrees: BA; BS, Mus Ed
Scholarships: Performance award for high level of musicianship awarded by audition; activity award for active participation in musical groups

OTTAWA UNIVERSITY
Music Department
Ottawa, KS 66067
(913) 242-5200
Staff: Dr. Stanley L. DeFries, Chairman
Affiliation: Church-related liberal arts university (American Baptist Convention)
Accreditation: NCA
Areas: App Mus; Hist & Lit; Th & An; Comp; Cond; Hist Musicol; Church Mus; Intro; Mus Ed (Elem & HS); Mus Therapy; Theater Mus; Instr Rep; Perf
Degrees: BA
Scholarships: Awarded by audition of two pieces from standard classical repertoire

PITTSBURG STATE UNIVERSITY
Music Department
Pittsburg, KS 66762
(316) 231-7000, x273
Staff: Gene E. Vollen, Chairman
Affiliation: State
Accreditation: NASM; NCA
Areas: App Mus; Hist & Lit; Th & An; Comp; Cond; Orch; Opera; Mus Ed (Elem & HS)
Degrees: BA; BM; BME; MM
Scholarships: General music scholarships available based on audition

SAINT MARY COLLEGE
Music Department
Leavenworth, KS 66048
(913) 682-5151
Staff: Sr. Anne Callahan, Chairman
Affiliation: Liberal arts college (Roman Catholic)
Accreditation: NASM; NCA
Areas: App Mus; Hist & Lit; Th & An; Comp; Cond; Orch; Opera; Hist Musicol; Church Mus; Intro; Mus Ed (Elem & HS); Perf
Degrees: BA; BM; BME
Scholarships: Music scholarships awarded on the basis of audition and GPA

ST. MARY OF THE PLAINS COLLEGE
Music Department
Dodge City, KS 67801
(316) 225-4171, x66
Staff: John D. Lauer, Director of Fine Arts
Affiliation: Private Christian liberal arts college
Accreditation: NASM; NCATE; NCA
Areas: App Mus; Mus Ed (Elem & HS); Mus Bus
Degrees: BA; BME

Scholarships: Scholarships of up to ½ tuition awarded by audition

SOUTHWESTERN COLLEGE
Division of Fine Arts
Winfield, KS 67156
(316) 221-4150
Staff: Richard Bobo, Chairman
Affiliation: Church-related (Methodist)
Accreditation: NCA; NASM
Areas: App Mus; Hist & Lit; Th & An; Comp; Cond; Orch; Church Mus; Mus Ed (Elem & HS)
Degrees: BA, BM, BME

STERLING COLLEGE
Music Department, Humanities Division
Sterling, KS 67579
(316) 278-2173
Staff: Robert W. Gordon, Chairman
Affiliation: Church-related liberal arts college (United Presbyterian)
Accreditation: NCATE; NCA
Areas: App Mus; Hist & Lit; Th & An; Cond; Orch; Church Mus; Intro; Mus Ed (Elem & HS); Instr Rep; Perf; Marching Band Techiniques
Degrees: BA
Scholarships: Awarded on the basis of talent, GPA, and need

TABOR COLLEGE
Music Department
400 S. Jefferson
Hillsboro, KS 67063
(316) 947-3121
Staff: Jonah C. Kliewer, Chairman
Affiliation: Church-related (Mennonite Brethren)
Accreditation: NASM; NCA
Areas: App Mus; Hist & Lit; Th & An; Cond; Church Mus; Mus Ed (Elem & HS)
Degrees: BA

UNIVERSITY OF KANSAS
School of Fine Arts
Lawrence, KS 66045
(913) 864-3421
Staff: James Moeser, Dean
Affiliation: State-supported university
Accreditation: NASM; NCA
Areas: App Mus; Hist & Lit; Th & An; Comp; Cond; Orch; Hist Musicol; Church Mus; Mus Ed (Elem & HS); Mus Therapy; Theater Mus; Electr Mus; Perf
Degrees: BA; BFA; BM; BME; MM; MME; DMA; EdD; PhD
Scholarships: Scholarships available

WASHBURN UNIVERSITY OF TOPEKA
Music Department, Division of Creative and Performing Arts
1700 College
Topeka, KS 66621
(913) 295-6511
Staff: Dr. Floyd Hedberg, Chairman
Affiliation: Municipal liberal arts university
Accreditation: NASM; NCA
Areas: App Mus; Mus Ed (Elem & HS); Hist & Lit; Th & An; Cond; Opera Instr Rep; Electr Mus
Degrees: BA; BM
Scholarships: Several scholarships available; audition required in spring term prior to grant

WICHITA STATE UNIVERSITY[1]
School of Music
1845 Fiarmount
Wichita, KS 67208
(316) 689-3502
Staff: Gordon B. Terwilliger, Dean, College of Fine Arts
Affiliation: State-supported univelrsity
Accreditation: NASM; NCA
Areas: App Mus; Hist & Lit; Th & An; Comp; Cond; Orch; Opera; Hist Musicol; Ethnomusicol; Intro; Mus Ed (Elem & HS); Mus Therapy; Electr Mus; Perf
Degrees: BA; BM; BME; MM; MME
Scholarships: Awarded on the basis of 3.0 GPA, need, and performance

KENTUCKY

ASBURY COLLEGE
Department of Fine Arts
201 N. Lexington Ave.
Wilmore, KY 40390
(606) 858-3511
Staff: Gilbert H. Roller, Chairman
Affiliation: Private church-related liberal arts college (Christian)
Accreditation: NASM; SACS
Areas: N/A
Degrees: BA; BS, Mus Ed

BELLARMINE COLLEGE
Humanities Division
2000 Norris Pl.
Louisville, KY 40205
(502) 452-8224
Staff: Gus Coin, Chairman
Affiliation: Church-related liberal arts college (Roman Catholic)
Accreditation: SACS
Areas: App Mus; Hist & Lit; Cond; Orch; Intro; Mus Ed (Elem & HS)
Degrees: BA
Scholarships: Partial scholarship in instrumental music

BEREA COLLEGE
Music Department
CPO 2352
Berea, KY 40404
(606) 986-9341, x359
Staff: Robert J. Lewis, Chairman
Affiliation: Private liberal arts college with teacher education program
Accreditation: SACS; NCATE
Areas: App Mus; Hist & Lit; Th & An; Cond; Orch; Ethnomusicol; Intro; Mus Ed (Elem & HS); Perf
Degrees: BA

Scholarships: All students receive scholarship assistance and participate in student labor program; Presser Scholarship awarded through performance competition; applied music scholarships awarded on the basis of need

BRESCIA COLLEGE[1]
Division of Fine Arts
120 W. Seventh St.
Owensboro, KY 42301
(502) 685-3131
Staff: James D. White, Chairman
Affiliation: Church-related liberal arts college (Roman Catholic)
Accreditation: SACS
Areas: App Mus; Th & An; Cond; Intro; Hist & Lit; Mus Ed (Elem)
Degrees: BM; BME

CAMPBELLSVILLE COLLEGE
Division of Fine Arts
Campbellsville, KY 42718
(502) 465-8158
Staff: James W. Moore, Acting Chairman
Affiliation: College of liberal arts and sciences privately supported by and affiliated with the Kentucky Baptist Convention
Accreditation: SACS
Areas: App Mus; Hist & Lit; Th & An; Cond; Orch; Church Mus; Mus Ed (Elem & HS)
Degrees: BA; BM; BS, Mus Ed
Scholarships: Awarded on the basis of ACT scores and talent

CENTRE COLLEGE OF KENTUCKY
Music Program, Humanities Division
Danville, KY 40422
(606) 236-5211
Staff: John Paul Brantley, Chair
Affiliation: Private church-affiliated liberal arts college (United Presbyterian Church, USA)
Accreditation: SACS
Areas: App Mus; Hist & Lit; Th & An; Comp; Cond; Orch; Hist Musicol; Mus Ed (Elem & HS); Intro
Degrees: BA

CUMBERLAND COLLEGE
Music Department
Williamsburg, KY 40769
(606) 549-2200, x332
Staff: Dr. Harold R. Wortman, Head
Affiliation: Church-related liberal arts college (Baptist)
Accreditation: NASM; SACS
Areas: App Mus; Comp; Cond; Church Mus; Mus Ed (Elem & HS)
Degrees: BA; BM (Mus Ed, Church Mus); BS, Mus Merch
Scholarships: Performance and accompanying scholarships awarded through audition

EASTERN KENTUCKY UNIVERSITY
Department of Music
Richmond, KY 40475
(606) 623-3266
Staff: George E. Muns, Chairman
Affiliation: State-supported university
Accreditation: NASM; SACS
Areas: App Mus; Hist & Lit; Th & An; Comp; Cond; Orch; Opera Workshop; Church Mus; Mus Ed (Elem & HS)
Degrees: BA; BM; BME; MA (teaching major); MME; MM
Scholarships: Varying amounts; audition or tape necessary

GEORGETOWN COLLEGE
Music Department
Georgetown, KY 40324
(502) 863-8011
Staff: Prof. W. Wayne Johnson, Chairman
Affiliation: Church-related liberal arts college (Southern Baptist)
Accreditation: SACS
Areas: App Mus; Hist & Lit; Th & An; Cond; Orch; Opera; Hist Musicol; Intro; Mus Ed (Elem & HS); Perf; Church Mus; Electr Mus
Degrees: BA; BME
Scholarships: Performance scholarships awarded on the basis of ability in applied music

KENTUCKY STATE UNIVERSITY[1]
Department of Music
East Main St.
Frankfort, KY 40601
(502) 564-6496
Staff: Carl H. Smith, Coordinator
Affiliation: State-supported liberal arts college
Accreditation: NASM; SACS; NCATE
Areas: Th & An; Orch; Cond; Comp; Intro; Mus Ed (Elem & HS); Opera
Degrees: BA; BS, Mus Ed

KENTUCKY WESLEYAN COLLEGE[1]
Department of Music
Owensboro, KY 43201
(502) 926-3111
Staff: Jerome Redfearn, Chairman
Affiliation: Church-related liberal arts college (United Methodist)
Accreditation: SACS
Areas: Th & An; Cond; Comp; Hist & Lit; Mus Ed (Elem & HS); Church Mus
Degrees: BA; BM; BME

MOREHEAD STATE UNIVERSITY
Department of Music, School of Humanities
Morehead, KY 40351
(606) 783-2473
Staff: Dr. William M. Bigham, Head
Affiliation: State-supported university
Accreditation: NASM; SACS
Areas: App Mus; Hist & Lit; Th & An; Comp; Cond; Orch; Church Mus; Mus Ed (Elem & HS); Theater Mus; Instr Rep; Jazz and Studio Mus
Degrees: BA; BM; BME; MM; MA, Ed
Scholarships: Awarded by audition

MURRAY STATE UNIVERSITY
Department of Music
Box 2022, University Station
Murray, KY 42071
(502) 762-4288
Staff: Dr. Roger E. Reichmuth, Chairman
Affiliation: Public tax-supported university
Accreditation: NASM; SACS
Areas: App Mus; Hist & Lit; Th & An; Comp; Cond; Orch; Intro; Perf; Mus Ed (Elem & HS)
Degrees: BA; BM (Perf); BME; MME
Scholarships: Departmental scholarships, Dean's Scholarship, Chairman's Scholarships, Walker Scholarships for Bass Singers, marching band stipends, orchestra scholarships; awarded on varying bases

NORTHERN KENTUCKY UNIVERSITY[1]
Division of Fine Arts
Nunn Dr.
Highland Heights, KY 41076
(606) 572-5100
Staff: Rosemary Stauss, Acting Chairman
Affiliation: State-supported university
Accreditation: SACS
Areas: App Mus; Hist & Lit; Th & An; Comp; Cond; Orch; Opera; Hist Musicol; Mus Ed (Elem & HS); Theater Mus; Instr Rep; Mus Apprec; Choir; Concert Band; Funds & Skills for Classroom Teacher
Degrees: BA; BM; BME; MA, Ed (music emphasis)
Scholarships: Institutional scholarships and scholarships funded by state money awarded by audition

PIKEVILLE COLLEGE
Department of Music
Pikeville, KY 41501
(606) 432-9300
Staff: Asst. Prof. Jeffrey R. Sandborg, Chairman
Affiliation: Church-related college (United Presbyterian)
Accreditation: SACS
Areas: App Mus; Hist & Lit; Th & An' Cond; Orch; Intro; Mus Ed (Elem & HS); Perf
Degrees: BA; BME
Scholarships: General music (instrumental and vocal) scholarships awarded on the basis of performance, the college's need, and the student's financial need

SOUTHERN BAPTIST THEOLOGICAL SEMINARY
School of Church Music
Louisville, KY 40280
(502) 897-4115

Staff: Dr. Milburn Price, Dean
Affiliation: Theological seminary supported by the Southern Baptist Convention
Accreditaion: NASM; SACS; ATS
Areas: App Mus; Hist & Lit; Th & An; Comp; Cond; Orch; Opera; Hist Musicol; Church Mus; Perf
Degrees: MCM; DMA
Scholarships: Several scholarships available from seminary; none offered specifically for music

TRANSYLVANIA UNIVERSITY[1]
Program in Music, Fine Arts Division
300 N. Broadway
Lexington, KY 40508
(606) 233-8141
Staff: Dr. Gary L. Anderson, Chairman
Affiliation: Private church-related liberal arts institution (Disciples of Christ)
Accreditation: SACS
Areas: App Mus; Hist & Lit; Th & An; Comp; Cond; Orch; Opera; Church Mus; Intro; Mus Ed (Elem & HS); Electr Mus; Perf
Degrees: BA
Scholarships: Activity grants available for students showing promise in an applied area

UNION COLLEGE[1]
School of Music
College Street
Barbourville, KY 40906
(606) 546-4151, x132
Staff: Leo Dontchos, Chairman
Affiliation: Church-related liberal arts college (Methodist)
Accreditation: SACS
Areas: Th & An; Hist & Lit; Mus Ed (Elem & HS)
Degrees: BM; BM, Mus Ed

UNIVERSITY OF KENTUCKY
School of Music
Fine Arts Building
Lexington, KY 40506
(606) 258-4936
Staff: Dr. Joe B. Buttram, Director
Affiliation: State-supported university
Accreditation: NASM; NCATE; SACS
Areas: App Mus; Hist & Lit; Th & An; Comp; Cond; Orch; Opera; Hist Musicol; Mus Ed (Elem & HS); Intro; Perf
Degrees: BA; BM; BME; MA; MM; MA, Mus Ed; DMA; PhD
Scholarships: Scholarships in all areas awarded by audition; departmental and marching band scholarships up to full tuition

UNIVERSITY OF LOUISVILLE[1]
School of Music
Louisville, KY 40292
(502) 588-6907
Staff: Jerry W. Ball, Dean
Affiliation: State-supported university
Accreditation: NASM; SACS; NCATE
Areas: App Mus; Hist & Lit; Th & An; Comp; Cond; Orch; Opera; Hist Musicol; Ethnomusicol; Church Mus; Intro; Mus Ed (Elem & HS); Piano Tech; Instr Rep; Electr Mus; Perf
Degrees: BM; BME; MM; MAT
Scholarships: Awarded on the basis of performance and need

WESTERN KENTUCKY UNIVERSITY
Department of Music
Bowling Green, KY 42101
(502) 745-3751
Staff: Dr. Wayne Hobbs, Head
Affiliation: State-supported university
Accreditation: NASM; SACS; NCATE
Areas: App Mus; Hist & Lit; Th & An; Comp; Cond; Orch; Opera; Hist Musicol; Church Mus; Intro; Mus Ed (Elem & HS); Theater Mus; Perf
Degrees: BA; BFA; BM; BME; MA; MM
Scholarships: Tuition grants awarded by audition

LOUISIANA

CENTENARY COLLEGE OF LOUISIANA
School of Music
Shreveport, LA 71104
(318) 869-5235
Staff: Dr. Frank M. Carroll, Dean
Affiliation: Church-related liberal arts college (United Methodist)
Accreditation: NASM; SACS
Areas: App Mus; Hist & Lit; Th & An; Comp; Cond; Orch; Opera; Church Mus; Mus Ed (Elem & HS)
Degrees: BA; BM
Scholarships: Academic scholarships awarded on basis of ACT and HS GPA; talent scholarships on basis of audition

DILLARD UNIVERSITY[1]
Department of Music
2601 Gentilly Blvd.
New Orleans, LA 70122
(504) 949-2123, x276
Staff: Violet G. Bowers, Coordinator
Affiliation: Private liberal arts university
Accreditation: NASM: SACS
Areas: Mus Ed
Degrees: BA

GRAMBLING STATE UNIVERSITY[1]
Department of Music
Grambling, LA 71245
(318) 247-6941, x254
Staff: Dr. Theodore M. Jennings, Jr., Chairman
Affiliation: State-supported university
Accreditation: NASM; SACS
Areas: App Mus; Th & An; Mus Ed (Elem & HS)
Degrees: BA; BS, Mus Ed
Scholarships: Choir, band, and orchestra scholarships awarded through auditions

LOUISIANA COLLEGE
Department of Music
Pineville, LA 71360
(318) 487-7336
Staff: Dr. James N. Anderson, Chairperson
Affiliation: Church-related liberal arts college (Southern Baptist)
Accreditation: NASM; SACS
Areas: App Mus; Hist & Lit; Th & An; Cond; Orch; Opera; Church Mus; Intro; Mus Ed (Elem & HS); Perf
Degrees: BM
Scholarships: Substantial scholarships available for performing, academic excellence, and accompanying

LOUISIANA STATE UNIVERSITY, BATON ROUGE
School of Music
Baton Rouge, LA 70803
(504) 388-3261
Staff: Dr. Lyle Merriman, Director
Affiliation: State-supported university
Accreditation: NASM; SACS
Areas: App Mus; Hist & Lit; Th & An; Comp; Cond; Orch; Opera; Hist Musicol; Church Mus; Mus Ed (Elem & HS); Mus Therapy; Theater Mus; Instr Rep
Degrees: BA; BM; BME; MA; MM; MME; DMA; PhD
Scholarships: Tuition scholarships available for music majors

LOUISIANA TECH UNIVERSITY
Music Department, College of Arts and Sciences
Ruston, LA 71272
(318) 257-4233
Staff: Raymond G. Young, Head
Affiliation: State-supported university
Accreditation: NASM; NCATE; SACS
Areas: App Mus; Th & An; Comp; Mus Ed (Elem & HS); Perf; Church Mus
Degrees: BA; BFA; BME; MA, Mus Ed
Scholarships: Scholarships for piano, voice, strings, wind and percussion awarded on the basis of major ensemble participation and performance ability

LOYOLA UNIVERSITY
College of Music
6363 St. Charles Ave.
New Orleans, LA 70118
(504) 865-3037
Staff: David Swanzy, Dean
Affiliation: Church-related university (Roman Catholic)
Accreditation: NASM; SACS
Areas: App Mus; Th & An; Comp; Mus Ed (Elem & HS); Mus Therapy; Perf; Church Mus; Mus Bus; Piano Ped; Jazz Studies
Degrees: BM; BME; BM, Mus Therapy; MM; MM, Mus Therapy; MME
Scholarships: Scholarships available by audition

McNEESE STATE UNIVERSITY[1]
Department of Music
Lake Charles, LA 70609
(318) 477-2520, x419
Staff: William C. Groves, Head
Affiliation: State-supported liberal arts university
Accreditation: NASM; SACS
Areas: App Mus; Hist & Lit; Th & An; Comp; Intro; Mus Ed (Elem & HS); Perf
Degrees: BA; BM; BME; MM; MMEd
Scholarships: Fee waivers available through audition

NEW ORLEANS BAPTIST THEOLOGICAL SEMINARY
Division of Church Music Ministries
3939 Gentilly Blvd.
New Orleans, LA 70126
(318) 282-4455
Staff: Dr. Al Washburn, Chairman
Affiliation: Theological seminary of the Southern Baptist Convention
Accreditation: NASM; SACS; ATS
Areas: App Mus; Hist & Lit; Th & An; Comp; Cond; Orch; Hist Hymnology; Church Mus; Intro; Mus Ed (Elem & HS); Perf
Degrees: AA (Church Mus minor); MCM; DMA
Scholarships: Performance awards based on audition

NICHOLLS STATE UNIVERSITY
Department of Music
University Station
Thibodaux, LA 70310
(504) 446-8111, x255
Staff: Dr. John Croom, Head
Affiliation: State-supported university
Accreditation: SACS; NASM; NCATE
Areas: App Mus; Hist & Lit; Th & An; Comp; Cond; Orch; Opera; Hist Musicol; Mus Ed (Elem & HS); Theater Mus; Counterpt (16th, 18th, and 20th cent); Jazz Improv
Degrees: BM; BME
Scholarships: Band and choral scholarships available to participants; piano scholarships awarded by audition

NORTHEAST LOUISIANA UNIVERSITY
School of Music
Monroe, LA 71201
(318) 372-2120
Staff: Richard A. Worthington, Director
Affiliation: State-supported university
Accreditation: NASM; SACS; NCATE
Areas: App Mus; Hist & Lit; Th & An; Comp; Cond; Orch; Opera; Hist Musicol; Mus Ed (Elem & HS); Instr Rep
Degrees: BA; BM; BME; MM; MME
Scholarships: Tuition talent grants

NORTHWESTERN STATE UNIVERSITY OF LOUISIANA
Music Department
Natchitoches, LA 71457
(318) 357-4436
Staff: Richard Jennings, Chairman
Affiliation: State-supported university
Accreditation: NASM; NCATE; SACS
Areas: App Mus; Th & An; Comp; Intro; Mus Ed (Elem & HS); Perf; Theater Mus; Instr Rep; Sound Recording
Degrees: BA; BM; BME; MM; MME
Scholarships: Piano, band, orchestra, and choir scholarships awarded by personal performance audition

SAINT JOSEPH SEMINARY COLLEGE
Music Department
Saint Benedict, LA 70457
(504) 892-1800
Staff: Assoc. Prof. Rev. Dominic Braud, Director of Music
Affiliation: Church-related liberal arts college (Roman Catholic)
Accreditation: SACS
Areas: App Mus; Intro; Mus Apprec; Chorus; Organ
Degrees: No music major offered

SOUTHEASTERN LOUISIANA UNIVERSITY[1]
Department of Music
Hammond, LA 70402
(504) 549-2184
Staff: Robert Weatherly and David McCormick, Co-Chairmen
Affiliation: State-supported university
Accreditation: NASM; NCATE; SACS
Areas: App Mus; Hist & Lit; Th & An; Cond; Orch; Opera; Hist Musicol; Intro; Mus Ed (Elem & HS); Theater Mus; Instr Rep; Electr Mus; Perf; Marching Band; Symph Band; Chorus; Concert Choir; Jazz Ens; Small Ens; Collegium Musicum
Degrees: BA; BM; BME; MM
Scholarships: Performance grants awarded for participation in ensembles; stipends paid at the end of each semester; marching band budget, $60,000; other music budget, $20,000

SOUTHERN UNIVERSITY[1]
Division of Music
Baton Rouge, LA 70813
(504) 771-3440, 3441, 3442
Staff: Dr. Aldrich W. Adkins, Chairman
Affiliation: State-supported university
Accreditation: NASM; SACS
Areas: App Mus; Hist & Lit; Th & An; Cond; Orch; Opera; Intro; Mus Ed (Elem & HS); Instr Rep; Perf
Degrees: BA; BM; BME
Scholarships: Performance scholarships available in all areas

TULANE UNIVERSITY[1]
Newcomb College
Department of Music
6823 Saint Charles Ave.
New Orleans, LA 70118
(504) 865-5267
Staff: Francis L. Monachino, Head
Affiliation: Privately endowed university
Accreditation: NASM; SACS
Areas: Th & An; Cond; Comp; Intro; Hist & Lit; Musicol; Mus Ed (Elem & HS)
Degrees: BA; BFA; MA; MFA; MAT

UNIVERSITY OF NEW ORLEANS
Music Department
Lakefront
New Orleans, LA 70148
(504) 286-6381
Staff: Prof. Mary Ann Bulla, Chairman
Affiliation: State-supported university
Accreditation: NASM; SACS
Areas: App Mus; Hist & Lit; Th & An; Comp; Cond; Orch; Opera; Hist Musicol; Mus Ed (Elem & HS)
Degrees: BA
Scholarships: Outstanding performer scholarships granted by audition only

UNIVERSITY OF SOUTHWESTERN LOUISIANA
School of Music
USL Box 41207
Lafayette, LA 70504
(318) 231-6016
Staff: Prof. Nolan Sahuc, Director
Affiliation: State-supported university
Accreditation: NASM; SACS
Areas: App Mus; Hist & Lit; Th & An; Comp; Cond; Orch; Opera; Hist Musicol; Mus Ed (Elem & HS); Theater Mus; Perf; Intro
Degrees: BA; BM; BME; MM; MME
Scholarships: Awarded by audition, interview and/or application

XAVIER UNIVERSITY OF LOUISIANA
Music Department
7325 Palmetto St.
New Orleans, LA 70125
(504) 486-7411
Staff: Malcolm J. Breda, Chairman
Affiliation: Church-related liberal arts college (Roman Catholic)
Accreditation: NASM; SACS
Areas: App Mus; Hist & Lit; Th & An; Comp; Cond; Orch; Opera; Mus Ed (Elem & HS); Perf
Degrees: BA; BM; BME
Scholarships: Talent scholarships and financial aid packets awarded on the basis of serious talent, audition and music aptitude test

MAINE

BATES COLLEGE
Music Department
Lewiston, ME 04240
(207) 783-3323
Staff: Prof. Ann B. Scott, Chairman
Affiliation: Private liberal arts college
Accreditation: NEA
Areas: App Mus; Hist & Lit; Th & An; Comp; Cond; Orch; Opera; Hist Musicol
Degrees: BA
Scholarships: Presser Scholarship of $1,000 awarded to a promising senior

BOWDOIN COLLEGE
Music Department
Brunswick, ME 04011
(207) 725-8731
Staff: Prof. Elliott Schwartz, Chairman
Affiliation: Private liberal arts college
Accreditation: NEA
Areas: App Mus; Hist & Lit; Th & An; Comp; Orch; various apprec (opera, symphony, jazz, etc.); Electr Mus
Degrees: BA

COLBY COLLEGE
Music Department
Waterville, ME 04901
(207) 873-1131
Staff: Prof. James Armstrong, Chairman
Affiliation: Private liberal arts college
Accreditation: NEA
Areas: App Mus; Hist & Lit; Th & An; Comp; Cond; Electr Mus
Degrees: BA
Scholarships: Scholarships available

NASSON COLLEGE[1]
Humanities Division
Main St.
Springvale, ME 04083
(207) 324-5340
Staff: Dr. Morton Gold, Professor of Music
Affiliation: Privately endowed liberal arts college
Accreditation: NEA
Areas: Hist & Lit; Th & An; Comp; Cond; Orch; Intro
Degrees: Music minor only
Scholarships: Awarded according to talent

UNIVERSITY OF MAINE AT ORONO
Music Department
Orono, ME 04469
(207) 581-1240
Staff: Richard M. Jacobs, Chairman
Affiliation: State-supported university
Accreditation: NASM; NEA; NCATE
Areas: Th & An; Cond; Comp; Intro; Hist & Lit; Musicol; Mus Ed (Elem & HS); Opera; App Mus; Orch; Perf
Degrees: BA; BM; BME; MM; MME
Scholarships: Financial aid and musical talent scholarships; graduate assistantships

UNIVERSITY OF SOUTHERN MAINE
Music Department
100 Corthell Hall, College Ave.
Gorham, ME 04038
(207) 780-5265
Staff: Dr. Jerry L. Bowder, Chairman
Affiliation: State-supported university
Accreditation: NCATE; NASM; NEA
Areas: App Mus; Hist & Lit; Th & An; Cond; Orch; Mus Ed (Elem & HS); Comp; Opera; Intro; Theater Mus; Electr Mus; Perf
Degrees: BA; BM, Perf; BS, Mus Ed; MEd (Mus concentration)

MARYLAND

BOWIE STATE COLLEGE
Department of Fine and Performing Arts, Music Component
Bowie, MD 20715
(301) 464-3441, 3442
Staff: Dr. H. D. Flowers II, Chairman
Affiliation: State-supported liberal arts and teachers college
Accreditation: MSA
Calendar: Semester; two summer sessions
Areas: App Mus; Hist & Lit; Church Mus; Intro; Mus Ed (Elem & HS); Theater Mus; Perf
Degrees: BA; BS, Mus Ed
Scholarships: Awarded on the basis of auditions

COLUMBIA UNION COLLEGE[1]
Department of Music
7600 Flower Ave.
Takoma Park, MD 20012
(301) 270-9200, x258
Staff: Van Knauss, Chairman
Affiliation: Church-related liberal arts college (Seventh-day Adventist)
Accreditation: MSA; NASM
Areas: App Mus; Th & An; Cond; Comp; Hist & Lit; Mus Ed (Elem & HS); Church Mus
Degrees: BA; BS, Mus; BS, Mus Ed

FROSTBURG STATE COLLEGE
Music Department
East College Ave.
Frostburg, MD 21532
(301) 689-4381
Staff: Thomas H. Yeager, Head
Affiliation: State-supported liberal arts and teacher education college
Accreditation: MSA
Areas: App Mus; Hist & Lit; Th & An; Comp; Cond; Orch; Opera; Intro; Mus Ed (Elem & HS)
Degrees: BA; BS, Mus Ed; BA, Perf; BS, Perf
Scholarships: $500 scholarships by audition only

GOUCHER COLLEGE[1]
Music Department
1021 Dulaney Valley Rd.
Towson, MD 21204
(301) 337-6000
Staff: George R. Woodhead, Chairman
Affiliation: Privately endowed liberal arts college
Accreditation: MSA
Areas: Th & An; Orch; Cond; Comp; Intro; Hist & Lit; Musicol
Degrees: BA; MA, Ed

HOOD COLLEGE[1]
Department of Music
Rosemont Ave.
Frederick, MD 21701
(301) 663-3131, x250
Staff: William Sprigg, Chairman
Affiliation: Private liberal arts college
Accreditation: MSA
Areas: Th & An; Intro
Degrees: BA

MORGAN STATE UNIVERSITY
Music Department
Cold Spring and Hillen Rds.
Baltimore, MD 21239
(301) 444-3286, 3287
Staff: Dr. Kenneth A. Keeling, Chairman
Affiliation: State-supported university
Accreditation: NASM; MSA
Areas: App Mus; Hist & Lit; Th & An; Comp; Cond; Orch; Mus Ed (Elem & HS)
Degrees: BA; BS, Mus Ed; MA; MS, Mus Ed
Scholarships: Scholarships available

PEABODY INSTITUTE OF THE JOHNS HOPKINS UNIVERSITY
(Peabody Conservatory of Music)
1 E. Mount Vernon Pl.
Baltimore, MD 21202
(301) 659-8100
Staff: Robert Pierce, Acting Director and Dean
Affiliation: Conservatory of music
Accreditation: NASM; MSA
Areas: App Mus; Hist & Lit; Th & An; Comp; Cond; Orch; Opera; Mus Ed (Elem & HS); Electr Mus
Degrees: BM; MM; DMA
Scholarships: Numerous scholarships available; awards based on superior musical talent and financial need

ST. MARY'S COLLEGE OF MARYLAND
Music Department, Division of Arts and Letters
St. Mary's City, MD 20686
(301) 863-7100
Staff: Dr. Eleanor Miller, Chairperson
Affiliation: State-supported liberal arts college
Accreditation: MSA; NASM
Areas: App Mus; Hist & Lit; Th & An; Comp; Intro; Mus Ed (Elem & HS); Perf
Degrees: BA
Scholarships: Varied scholarships available

SALISBURY STATE COLLEGE OF MARYLAND
Music Department, Musical Arts Center
Salisbury, MD 21801
(301) 543-6385
Staff: Dr. Arthur L. Delpaz, Chairman
Affiliation: State-supported liberal arts college
Accreditation: NCATE; MSA
Areas: App Mus; Hist & Lit; Th & An; Comp; Cond; Orch; Opera; Hist Musicol; Ethnomusicol; Church Mus; Mus Ed (Elem & HS); Theater Mus; Perf
Degrees: BS, Liberal Studies (Music Education concentration); BA, Liberal Studies (Music Major)

TOWSON STATE UNIVERSITY[1]
Department of Music
Baltimore, MD 21204

(301) 321-2143
Staff: Dr. David Marchand, Chairperson
Affiliation: State-supported liberal arts and teachers college
Accreditation: NASM; MSA
Areas: App Mus; Hist & Lit; Th & An; Comp; Cond; Orch; Opera; Hist Musicol; Ethnomusicol; Intro; Mus Ed (Elem & HS); Perf
Degrees: BA; BS, Mus Ed; BS, Mus; MME; music minor
Scholarships: Scholarships available for marching band, strings, piano, voice, and wind instruments

UNIVERSITY OF MARYLAND
Department of Music
College Park, MD 20742
(301) 454-2501
Staff: Stewart Gordon, Chairman
Affiliation: State-supported university
Accreditation: NASM; MSA
Areas: App Mus; Hist & Lit; Th & An; Comp; Cond; Orch; Opera; Hist Musicol; Ethnomusicol; Intro; Mus Ed (Elem & HS); Theater Mus; Electr Mus; Perf
Degrees: BA; BM; BS, Mus Ed; MM; MA, Mus Ed; DMA; EdD; PhD
Scholarships: Scholarships available; contact Department of Music for information

UNIVERSITY OF MARYLAND, BALTIMORE COUNTY
Department of Music
5401 Wilkens Ave.
Baltimore, MD 21228
(301) 455-2942
Staff: Dr. Felix L. Powell, Chairman
Affiliation: State-supported university
Accreditation: MSA
Areas: App Mus; Hist & Lit; Th & An; Comp; Cond; Orch; Opera; Hist Musicol; Ethnomusicol
Degrees: BA; MA; PhD

UNIVERSITY OF MARYLAND, EASTERN SHORE
Department of Music
Princess Anne, MD 21853
(301) 651-2200, x267
Staff: Gerald W. Johnston, Chairman
Affiliation: State-supported university
Accreditation: MSA
Areas: Th & An; Cond; Intro; Hist & Lit; Mus Ed (Elem & HS)
Degrees: BA, Mus Ed

WASHINGTON COLLEGE
Music Department
Chestertown, MD 21620
(301) 778-2800, x203
Staff: Kathleen J. Mills, Chairman
Affiliation: Privately endowed liberal arts college
Accreditation: MSA
Areas: App Mus; Hist & Lit; Th & An; Comp; Cond; Orch; Opera
Degrees: BA

WESTERN MARYLAND COLLEGE
Music Department
Westminster, MD 21157
(301) 848-7000
Staff: Carl L. Dietrich, Chairman
Affiliation: Private liberal arts college
Accreditation: NASM; MSA
Areas: App Mus; Intro; Mus Ed (Elem & HS); Perf
Degrees: BA

MASSACHUSETTS

AMHERST COLLEGE
Music Department
Amherst, MA 01002
(413) 542-2364
Staff: Bruce G. McInnes, Chairman
Affiliation: Privately endowed liberal arts college
Accreditation: NEA
Areas: App Mus; Hist & Lit; Th & An; Comp; Ethnomusicol
Degrees: BA
Scholarships: General college scholarships awarded according to need; none specifically for music

ANNA MARIA COLLEGE
Music Department
Sunset Ln.
Paxton, MA 01612
(617) 757-4586
Staff: Robert H. Goepfert, Chairman
Affiliation: Church-related liberal arts college (Catholic)
Accreditation: NASM; NAMT: NEA
Areas: App Mus; Hist & Lit; Th & An; Cond; Orch; Church Mus; Mus Ed (Elem & HS); Mus Therapy; Perf
Degrees: BA; BM

ASSUMPTION COLLEGE
Department of Music and Fine Arts
500 Salisbury St.
Worcester, MA 01609
(617) 752-5615
Staff: Dr. Donat Lamothe, A.B., Chairman
Affiliation: Church-related liberal arts college (Roman Catholic)
Accreditation: NEA
Areas: App Mus; Hist & Lit; Th & An; Hist Musicol; Church Mus; Intro
Degrees: BA

ATLANTIC UNION COLLEGE
Thayer Conservatory of Music
Main St.
South Lancaster, MA 01561
(617) 365-4561, x359
Staff: Dr. Margarita Merriman, Chairman
Affiliation: Church-related college (Seventh-day Adventist)
Accreditation: NCATE; NEA
Areas: App Mus; Hist & Lit; Th & An; Comp; Cond; Orch; Church Mus; Mus Ed (Elem & HS); Electr Mus; Perf
Degrees: BA; BM

BERKLEE COLLEGE OF MUSIC
1140 Boylston St.
Boston, MA 02215
(617) 266-1400
Staff: Lee Eliot Berk, President
Affiliation: Private college of music
Accreditation: NEA
Areas: App Mus; Hist & Lit; Th & An; Comp; Cond; Orch; Mus Ed (Elem & HS); Theater Mus; Piano Tech; Instr Rep; Electr Mus; Perf; Film Sc; Arrang; Jazz Comp & Arrang; Mus Prod & Eng
Degrees: BM; Professional Diploma
Scholarships: Variable scholarships available for instrumentalists and vocalists based on merit and need

BERKSHIRE CHRISTIAN COLLEGE[1]
Music Department
200 Stockbridge Rd.
Lenox, MA 01240
(413) 637-0838
Staff: Wesley Ross, Chairman
Affiliation: Church-related college (Advent Christian Church)
Accreditation: AABC
Areas: App Mus; Th & An; Voice; Church Mus
Degrees: BA, Church Mus

BOSTON COLLEGE
Music Department, College of Arts & Sciences
St. Mary's House, Newton Campus
Chestnut Hill, MA 02167
(617) 969-0100, x4438
Staff: Dr. Olga Stone, Musician-in-Residence and Director, Music Program
Affiliation: University with several colleges—arts and sciences, law, social work, school of management, education, nursing, etc.
Accreditation: NEA
Areas: App Mus; Hist & Lit; Th & An; Orch; Hist Musicol; Perf
Degrees: BA
Scholarships: Partial scholarships and Boston College grants available through office of financial aid

BOSTON CONSERVATORY
8 The Fenway
Boston, MA 02215
(617) 536-6340
Staff: William A. Seymour, President
Affiliation: Private conservatory; a college of music, dance, and theatre
Accreditation: NASM; NEA
Areas: Cond; Mus Ed (Elem & HS); Opera; Perf; Theater Mus; Comp
Degrees: BFA; BM; MM
Scholarships: Performance scholarships available to those who display outstanding ability and show promise for a successful career in music

BOSTON UNIVERSITY
School of Music, School for the Arts
855 Commonwealth Ave.
Boston, MA 02215

(617) 353-3341
Staff: Dr. Peter Schoenbach, Executive Administrator
Affiliation: Privately endowed university
Accreditation: NASM; NEA
Areas: Hist & Lit; Th & Comp; Mus Ed (Elem & HS); Perf
Degrees: BM; MM; DMA
Scholarships: Various scholarships available

BRANDEIS UNIVERSITY
Department of Music
415 South St.
Waltham, MA 02254
(617) 647-2557
Staff: Allan Keiler, Chairman
Affiliation: Private liberal arts university
Accreditation: NEA
Areas: App Mus; Hist & Lit; Th & An; Comp; Orch; Opera; Hist Musicol; Ethnomusicol; Electr Mus; Cond; Intro; Theater Mus; Perf
Degrees: BA; MFA; PhD
Scholarships: Grants to finance private lessons, by competitive audition; awards to support summer projects between junior and senior years, by competitive application; graduate fellowships for dissertation research abroad, by competitive application and interview

CLARK UNIVERSITY
Music Program, Department of Visual and Performing Arts
Worcester, MA 01610
(617) 793-7349
Staff: Gerald Castonguay, Director
Affiliation: Privately endowed university
Accreditation: NEA
Areas: App Mus; Hist & Lit; Th & An; Comp; Hist Musicol; Electr Mus; Perf
Degrees: BA

EASTERN NAZARENE COLLEGE
Music Department
23 E. Elm Ave.
Quincy, MA 02170
(617) 773-6350
Staff: Robert J. Howard, Head
Affiliation: Church-related college (Church of the Nazarene)
Accreditation: NEA
Areas: App Mus; Hist & Lit; Th & An; Cond; Orch; Church Mus; Mus Ed (Elem & HS)
Degrees: BA; BS, Mus Ed
Scholarships: Upper-division piano and several alumnae scholarships awarded on the basis of quality of academic work

EMERSON COLLEGE[1]
Music Department
100 Beacon St.
Boston, MA 02115
(617) 262-2010, x250
Staff: Asst. Prof. Anthony Tommasini, Chairman
Affiliation: Independent specialized college offering degrees in communication arts and sciences
Accreditation: NEA
Areas: App Mus; Hist & Lit; Th & An; Comp; Opera; Theater Mus; Hist Jazz; Mus Programming (for media)
Degrees: BFA
Scholarships: General scholarships only

EMMANUEL COLLEGE
Music Department
400 The Fenway
Boston, MA 02115
(617) 277-9340
Staff: Donna M. Chadwick, Chairman
Affiliation: Private liberal arts college
Accreditation: NEA
Areas: App Mus; Hist & Lit; Mus Ed (Elem & HS); Th & An; Comp; Mus Therapy
Degrees: BA

GORDON COLLEGE
Music Department
255 Grapevine Rd.
Wenham, MA 01984
(617) 927-2300
Staff: Fred Broer, Chairman
Affiliation: Private liberal arts college (interdenominational)
Accreditation: NASM; NEA
Areas: App Mus; Hist & Lit; Th & An; Cond; Orch; Intro; Mus Ed (Elem & HS); Perf
Degrees: BA; BM; BME
Scholarships: Scholarships for music majors only awarded by competition

HAMPSHIRE COLLEGE[1]
Department of Music
Amherst, MA 01002
(413) 549-4600
Affiliation: Private liberal arts college
Accreditation: NEA
Areas: App Mus; Th & An; Comp; Ethnomusicol
Degrees: BA

HARVARD UNIVERSITY
Music Department
Music Building
Cambridge, MA 02138
(617) 495-2791
Staff: Ms. Marjorie Swindell, Administrator
Affiliation: Private liberal arts college
Accreditation: NASM; NEA
Areas: App Mus; Hist & Lit; Th & An; Comp; Cond; Orch; Opera; Hist Musicol; Ethnomusicol; Piano Tech; Electr Mus
Degrees: BA; BM; MA; PhD
Scholarships: Fellowships and scholarships (money and tuition)

LONGY SCHOOL OF MUSIC
1 Follen St.
Cambridge, MA 02128
(617) 876-0956
Staff: Roman Totenberg, Director
Affiliation: Private conservatory affiliated with Emerson College and Lesley College
Accreditation: NASM
Areas: App Mus; Hist & Lit; Th & An; Comp; Cond; Orch; Intro; Perf; Dalcroze eurhythmics
Degrees: BM; MM; Diploma; Dalcroze License and Cert
Scholarships: Scholarships for full-time students awarded by audition; application required

MASSACHUSETTS INSTITUTE OF TECHNOLOGY
School of Humanities and Social Science, Music Section
Cambridge, MA 02139
(617) 253-3210
Staff: Prof. David Epstein, Chairman
Affiliation: Private technological institute
Accreditation: NEA
Areas: App Mus; Hist & Lit; Th & An; Comp; Orch; Opera; Hist Musicol; Ethnomusicol; Intro; Electr Mus; Perf
Degrees: BA
Scholarships: Limited funds available; Ragnar D. Naess Scholarships for private instrumental or voice study, awarded by nomination and panel decision

MOUNT HOLYOKE COLLEGE[1]
Department of Music
South Hadley, MA 01075
(413) 538-2306
Staff: Jacqueline H. Melnick, Chairman
Affiliation: Private college
Accreditation: NEA
Areas: App Mus; Th & An; Cond; Comp; Intro; Hist & Lit; Hist Musicol
Degrees: BA; MA

NEW ENGLAND CONSERVATORY OF MUSIC
290 Huntington Ave.
Boston, MA 02115
(617) 262-1120
Staff: Andrew J. Falender, Administrative Vice President
Affiliation: Private college-conservatory
Accreditation: NASM; NEA
Areas: Perf (26 instruments, voice, Jazz Studies, Third Stream, Early Music); Comp; Vocal Accomp; Vocal Ped; Cond (Choral, Orchestral, Wind Ensemble); App Mus; Hist & Lit; Th & An; Orch; Opera; Ethnomusicol; Church Mus; Theater Mus; Intro; Mus Ed (Elem & HS); Piano Tech; Mus Therapy; Instr Rep; Electr Mus; Perf; Jazz Comp
Degrees: BM; MM; Artist Diploma
Scholarships: Contact Financial Aid Office for information

NORTHEASTERN UNIVERSITY
Music Department
307 Ell-Huntington Ave.
Boston, MA 02115
(617) 437-4128

Staff: Prof. Herbert H. Silverman, Acting Chairman
Affiliation: Private
Accreditation: NEA
Areas: Hist & Lit; Th & An; Opera; Ethnomusicol; Mus Ed (Elem & HS); Mus Therapy; Theater Mus; Perf
Degrees: LA major (and minor), Music Literature

REGIS COLLEGE
Music Department
235 Wellesley Street
Weston, MA 02193
(617) 893-1820
Staff: Sr. Margaret W. McCarthy, Chairman
Affiliation: Church-related liberal arts college
Accreditation: NEA
Areas: App Mus; Hist & Lit; Th & An; Comp; Cond; Opera; Church Mus; Intro; Perf
Degrees: BA
Scholarships: General scholarships available to music students

SIMMONS COLLEGE
Music Department
300 The Fenway
Boston, MA 02115
(617) 738-2000
Staff: Prof. Robert Gronquist, Director of Musical Activities
Affiliation: Private liberal arts college for women; Music Department operated in association with New England Conservatory of Music
Accreditation: NEA
Areas: App Mus; Hist & Lit; Th & An; Comp; Cond; Orch; Opera; Hist Musicol; Ethnomusicol; Church Mus; Mus Ed (Elem & HS); Piano Tech; Instr Rep
Degrees: BA
Scholarships: Scholarships available

SMITH COLLEGE
Music Department
Sage Hall
Northampton, MA 01063
(413) 584-2700, x2261
Staff: Peter A. Bloom, Chairman
Affiliation: Private liberal arts college
Accreditation: NEA
Areas: App Mus; Hist & Lit; Th & An; Comp; Cond; Hist Musicol; Intro; Mus Ed (Elem & HS); Electr Mus; Perf; Early Mus
Degrees: BA; MA; MAT

SOUTHEASTERN MASSACHUSETTS UNIVERSITY
Music Department, College of Visual and Performing Arts
Old Westport Rd.
North Dartmouth, MA 02747
(617) 999-8568
Staff: Dr. Eleanor Carlson, Chairperson
Affiliation: State-supported university
Accreditation: NEA
Areas: App Mus; Hist & Lit; Th & An; Comp; Orch; Opera; Ethnomusicol; Intro; Mus Ed (Elem); Electr Mus; Perf
Degrees: BM

TUFTS UNIVERSITY
Music Department
Medford, MA 02155
(617) 628-5000
Staff: Prof. Mark DeVoto, Chairman
Affiliation: Endowed university
Accreditation: NEA
Areas: App Mus; Hist & Lit; Th & An; Comp; Ethnomusicol
Degrees: BA; MA

UNIVERSITY OF LOWELL[1]
College of Music
Lowell, MA 01854
(617) 452-5000
Staff: Paul Gayzagian, Acting Dean
Affiliation: State-supported university
Accreditation: NASM; NEA
Areas: Hist & Lit; Th & An; Mus Ed (Elem & HS); Perf
Degrees: BA; BM; MM
Scholarships: For information, contact Walter Costello, Director, Financial Aid Office

UNIVERSITY OF MASSACHUSETTS
Department of Music and Dance
Amherst, MA 01003
(413) 545-0642
Staff: Dr. Charles Bestor, Professor and Head
Affiliation: State-supported university
Accreditation: NASM; NCATE; NEA
Areas: App Mus; Hist & Lit; Th & An; Comp; Cond; Orch; Opera Wkshp; Intro; Mus Ed (Elem & HS); Piano Tech; Electr Mus; Perf
Degrees: BA; BM; MM
Scholarships: Many scholarships available for performance and need

WELLESLEY COLLEGE
Music Department
Wellesley, MA 02181
(617) 235-0320, x401
Staff: Arlene Zallman, Chairman
Affiliation: Private college
Accreditation: NEA
Areas: App Mus; Th & An; Comp; Intro; Hist & Lit; Hist Musicol; Ethnomusicol (African and Afro-Amer); Perf
Degrees: BA

WESTFIELD STATE COLLEGE
Department of Music
Western Ave.
Westfield, MA 01086
(413) 568-3311, x356
Staff: Arthur Jannery, Chairman
Affiliation: State-supported liberal arts college
Accreditation: NEA; NCATE
Areas: App Mus; Th & An; Orch; Cond; Comp; Intro; Hist & Lit; Mus Ed (Elem & HS); Hist Musicol; Theater Mus; Perf; Mus Merch
Degrees: BA, BA, Mus Ed; MS, Ed
Scholarships: Scholarships available for performers on double reed and string instruments

WHEATON COLLEGE
Department of Music
Norton, MA 02766
(617) 285-7722
Staff: Charles K. Fassett, Chairman
Affiliation: Private college
Accreditation: NEA
Areas: App Mus; Th & An; Cond; Comp; Intro; Hist & Lit
Degrees: BA

WILLIAMS COLLEGE
Department of Music
Bernhard Music Center
Williamstown, MA 01267
(413) 597-2127
Staff: Douglas B. Moore, Chairman
Affiliation: Private college
Accreditation: NEA
Areas: App Mus; Th & An; Comp; Intro; Hist & Lit; Hist Musicol
Degrees: BA

MICHIGAN

ADRIAN COLLEGE[1]
Music Department
110 S. Madison St.
Adrian, MI 49221
(517) 265-5161
Staff: Richard A. Goolian, Chairman
Affiliation: Church-related liberal arts college (Methodist)
Accreditation: NCA; NCATE
Areas: App Mus; Hist & Lit; Th & An; Comp; Cond; Orch; Hist Musicol; Mus Ed (Elem & HS)
Degrees: BA; BM; BME
Scholarships: Performance scholarships awarded by audition

ALBION COLLEGE
Music Department
Albion, MI 49224
(517) 629-5511, x251
Staff: Melvin Larimer, Chairman
Affiliation: Church-related liberal arts college (Methodist)
Accreditation: NASM; NCATE; NCA
Areas: App Mus; Hist & Lit; Th & An; Comp; Cond; Opera; Church Mus; Intro; Mus Ed (Elem & HS); Perf
Degrees: BA
Scholarships: Scholarships for voice, keyboard, and all orchestral and band instruments available; personal audition preferred, but taped performance acceptable

ALMA COLLEGE[1]
Department of Music
Alma, MI 48801
(517) 463-7167
Staff: Dr. P. Cameron Russell, Chairman

Affiliation: Church-related liberal arts college (Presbyterian)
Accreditation: NASM; NCA
Areas: App Mus; Hist & Lit; Th & An; Cond; Orch; Church Mus; Mus Ed (Elem & HS); Electr Mus
Degrees: BA; BM
Scholarships: Awarded on the basis of achievement and need

ANDREWS UNIVERSITY
Department of Music
Berrien Springs, MI 49104
(616) 471-7771
Staff: Dr. Charles Hall, Chairman
Affiliation: Church-related university (Seventh-day Adventist)
Accreditation: NASM; NCA; NCATE; ATS
Areas: Th & An; Comp; Intro; Hist & Lit; Perf; Mus Ed (Elem & HS)
Degrees: BA; BM, Mus Ed; MA; MM, Mus Ed; MM
Scholarships: Assistantships and fellowships available for undergraduate and graduate levels

AQUINAS COLLEGE
Music Department
1607 Robinson Rd.
Grand Rapids, MI 49506
(616) 459-8281
Staff: Dr. R. Bruce Early, Chairman
Affiliation: Private church-related liberal arts college (Roman Catholic)
Accreditation: NCA
Areas: App Mus; Hist & Lit; Th & An; Comp; Cond; Orch; Opera; Hist Musicol; Church Mus; Mus Ed (Elem & HS); Jazz; Mus Mgmt; Liturgy & Mus
Degrees: BA; BM; BME; BS, Mus Ed; AA, Liturgy & Mus
Scholarships: Individualized scholarships available

CALVIN COLLEGE
Music Department
1801 E. Beltline SE
Grand Rapids, MI 49506
(616) 949-4000
Staff: Dr. Howard Slenk, Chairman
Affiliation: Church-related liberal arts college (Christian Reformed)
Accreditation: NCATE; NCA
Areas: App Mus; Hist & Lit; Th & An; Comp; Cond; Orch; Church Mus; Mus Ed (Elem & HS); Intro; Perf; Keyboard Ped
Degrees: BA
Scholarships: Performance awards of $500 granted by audition tapes

CENTRAL MICHIGAN UNIVERSITY
Department of Music
Mt. Pleasant, MI 48859
(517) 774-3281
Staff: Robert Barris, Chairman,
Affiliation: State-supported university
Accreditation: NASM; NCA; NCATE
Areas: Th & An; Orch; Cond; Comp; Hist & Lit; Mus Ed (Elem & HS); Opera; Perf
Degrees: BA; BM; BME; BS, Mus Ed; MM, Mus Ed; MA; MM

EASTERN MICHIGAN UNIVERSITY
Music Department
Ypsilanti, MI 48197
(313) 487-0244
Staff: James B. Hause, Head
Affiliation: State-supported university
Accreditation: NASM; NCATE; NCA
Areas: App Mus; Hist & Lit; Th & An; Comp; Cond; Opera; Intro; Mus Ed (Elem & HS); Mus Therapy; Perf
Degrees: BA; BM; BME; BS; MA, Mus; MA, Mus Ed
Scholarships: Merit, service, and need scholarships awarded on the basis of 3.0 GPA and talent

GRACE BIBLE COLLEGE[1]
Music Department
1011 Aldon St., SW
Grand Rapids, MI 49509
(616) 538-2330
Staff: Ronald F. Denison, Professor of Music
Affiliation: Church-related college (Grace Gospel Fellowship)
Accreditation: AABC
Areas: App Mus; Hist & Lit; Th & An; Cond; Church Mus
Degrees: BREd (mus major)
Scholarships: Awarded on the basis of scholastic standing

GRAND VALLEY STATE COLLEGES
Music Department
Allendale, MI 49401
(616) 895-6611, x484
Staff: Prof. Larry W. Edwards, Chairman
Affiliation: State-supported liberal arts college
Accreditation: NASM; NCA
Areas: App Mus; Hist & Lit; Th & An; Comp; Cond; Orch; Intro; Mus Ed (Elem & HS); Perf
Degrees: BA; BM; BME; BS
Scholarships: Awarded on the basis of performance ability

HOPE COLLEGE[1]
Department of Music
Holland, MI 49423
(616) 392-5111
Staff: Dr. Stuart W. Sharp, Chairman
Affiliation: Church-related liberal arts college (Reformed Church in America)
Accreditation: NASM; NCA; NCATE
Areas: App Mus; Hist & Lit; Th & An; Comp; Cond; Orch; Opera; Church Mus; Intro; Mus Ed (Elem & HS); Theater Mus; Perf
Degrees: BA; BM; BME
Scholarships: Academic recognition awards based on excellent scholarship and performing ability; freshman music prize based on performing ability

KALAMAZOO COLLEGE
Music Department
1200 Academy St.
Kalamazoo, MI 49007
(616) 383-8511
Staff: Lawrence R. Smith, Chairman
Affiliation: Private college
Accreditation: NCA
Areas: App Mus; Th & An; Cond; Comp; Intro; Hist & Lit; Ethnomusicol; Mus Ed (Elem & HS)
Degrees: BA; BA, Mus Ed
Scholarships: Four performance scholarships, competitive

MADONNA COLLEGE
Music Department
36600 Schoolcraft
Livonia, MI 48150
(313) 591-5000
Staff: Sr. Edith Agdanowski, Chairperson
Affiliation: Independent private church-related college sponsored by the Felician Sisters (Roman Catholic)
Accreditation: NCA; NCATE
Areas: App Mus; Hist & Lit; Th & An; Cond; Mus Ed (Elem & HS); Mus Mgmt
Degrees: BA
Scholarships: 2 $500 music merit scholarships awarded on the basis of 3.0 GPA in high school academic subjects and full-time status as Madonna student

MARYGROVE COLLEGE[1]
Music Department
8425 W. McNichols Rd.
Detroit, MI 48221
(313) 862-8000, x64
Staff: Herbert L. Riggins, Chairman
Affiliation: Church-related liberal arts college (Catholic). A consortium with 5 other colleges offers students music courses at Marygrove and the University of Detroit (1 mile distant).
Accreditation: NCA; NCATE
Areas: App Mus; Hist & Lit; Th & An; Comp; Cond; Orch; Opera; Hist Musicol; Church Mus; Intro; Mus Ed (Elem & HS); Mus Therapy; Perf
Degrees: BA; BM; BME; B Sacr Mus

MICHIGAN STATE UNIVERSITY
Department of Music
East Lansing, MI 48824
(517) 455-4583
Staff: Kenneth Bloomquist, Chairman
Affiliation: State-supported university
Accreditation: NASM; NCA
Areas: App Mus; Hist & Lit; Th & An; Comp; Cond; Orch; Hist Musicol; Church Mus; Mus Ed (Elem & HS); Mus Therapy; Piano Tech; Electr Mus; Perf
Degrees: BA; BM; MA; MM; DMA; PhD
Scholarships: Performance-oriented

NORTHERN MICHIGAN UNIVERSITY
Department of Music
Marquette, MI 49855
(906) 227-2563
Staff: Dr. Elda Tate, Head
Affiliation: State-supported university

Accreditation: NASM; NCA
Areas: App Mus; Hist & Lit; Th & An; Cond; Mus Ed (Elem & HS); Perf
Degrees: BA; BM; BS, Mus Ed; MA; MA, Mus Ed
Scholarships: Applied music scholarships of $200 to $1,000 available

OAKLAND UNIVERSITY
Department of Music
Rochester, MI 48063
(313) 377-2030
Staff: David Daniels, Chairman
Affiliation: State-supported liberal arts university
Accreditation: NCA
Areas: App Mus; Hist & Lit; Th & An; Comp; Cond; Orch; Ethnomusicol; Church Mus; Intro; Mus Ed (Elem & HS); Theater Mus; Piano Tech; Perf; Jazz; Commer Mus
Degrees: BA; BM; BS, Mus Ed; MM
Scholarships: Academic, performance, service scholarships available

OLIVET COLLEGE[1]
Department of Music and Performing Arts
Olivet, MI 49076
(616) 749-7694
Staff: Danford Byrens, Chairman
Affiliation: Church-related liberal arts college (Congregational Church and the United Church of Christ)
Accreditation: NCA
Areas: App Mus; Hist & Lit; Th & An; Comp; Cond; Orch; Opera; Hist Musicol; Church Mus; Mus Ed (Elem & HS)
Degrees: BA; BM; BME
Scholarships: General scholarships awarded on the basis of scholarship and need

SIENA HEIGHTS COLLEGE
Music Department
1247 E. Siena Hgts. Dr.
Adrian, MI 49221
(517) 263-0731
Staff: Susan Matych-Hager, Chairperson
Affiliation: Church-related liberal arts college (Roman Catholic)
Accreditation: NCA
Areas: App Mus; Hist & Lit; Th & An; Comp; Cond; Orch; Intro; Mus Ed (Elem & HS); Perf
Degrees: BA
Scholarships: Departmental scholarships awarded on the basis of audition, teacher recommendation, and high school transcript

SPRING ARBOR COLLEGE[1]
Division of Humanities
106 Main St.
Spring Arbor, MI 49283
(517) 750-1200
Staff: Kennistan P. Bauman, Chairman
Affiliation: Private church-related liberal arts college (Free Methodist)
Accreditation: NCA
Areas: App Mus; Hist & Lit; Th & An; Comp; Cond; Church Mus; Mus Ed (Elem & HS); Piano Tech; Vocal Ped; Dict; Contrapuntal Styles; Piano Ped; Brass, Perc, Woodw, and String Meth
Degrees: BA
Scholarships: Performance scholarships awarded on the basis of participation in performance group of area; departmental scholarships awarded for outstanding achievement; scholastic scholarships awarded on the basis of GPA of 3.5 and higher

UNIVERSITY OF MICHIGAN
School of Music
Ann Arbor, MI 48109
(313) 764-0584
Staff: Paul C. Boylan, Dean
Affiliation: State-supported university
Accreditation: NASM; NCA
Areas: App Mus; Hist & Lit; Th & An; Comp; Cond; Orch; Opera; Hist Musicol; Ethnomusicol; Church Mus; Mus Ed (Elem & HS); Piano Tech; Mus Theater
Degrees: BA; BM; MA; MM; DMA; EdD; PhD

THE UNIVERSITY OF MICHIGAN[1]**-FLINT**
Music Department
303 E. Kearsley
Flint, MI 48503
(313) 762-3377
Staff: Dr. Johannes Tall, Associate Professor and Chairman
Affiliation: State-supported university
Accreditation: NCA; NASM
Areas: App Mus; Hist & Lit; Th & An; Comp; Cond; Orch; Ethnomusicol; Church Mus; Mus Ed (Elem & HS); Theater Mus; Instr Rep; Mus Bus; Perf
Degrees: BA; BME; music major with business minor
Scholarships: Scholarships of up to full tuition awarded by audition; performance stipend awarded by audition

WAYNE STATE UNIVERSITY
Music Department
Detroit, MI 48202
(313) 577-1795
Staff: Prof. Robert Lawson, Chairman
Affiliation: State-supported university
Accreditation: NASM; NCA
Areas: Hist & Lit; Th & An; Comp; Cond; Church Mus; Mus Ed (Elem & HS); Mus Therapy; Perf; Jazz Studies; Mus Ind Mgmt; App Mus; Orch
Degrees: BA; BM; MA; MM
Scholarships: Awards for full-time students

WESTERN MICHIGAN UNIVERSITY[1]
School of Music
Kalamazoo, MI 49008
(616) 383-0910
Staff: Donald Bullock, Director
Affiliation: State-supported university
Accreditation: NASM; NCA
Areas: App Mus; Hist & Lit; Th & An; Comp; Cond; Orch; Opera; Hist Musicol; Intro; Mus Ed (Elem & HS); Mus Therapy; Theater Mus; Electr Mus; Perf; Jazz Studies
Degrees: BA; BM; BME; BS, Mus Ed; MM; MA, Mus Ed
Scholarships: Music talent awards based on auditions

WILLIAM TYNDALE COLLEGE
Music Department
35700 W. Twelve Mile Rd.
Farmington Hills, MI 48018
(313) 553-7200
Staff: Thomas E. Zimmerman, Chairman
Affiliation: Private nondenominational liberal arts college
Accreditation: AABC
Areas: App Mus; Hist & Lit; Th & An; Comp; Cond; Orch; Church Mus; Perf
Degrees: BM

MINNESOTA

AUGSBURG COLLEGE[1]
Department of Music
731 21st Ave. S
Minneapolis, MN 55454
(612) 330-1000
Staff: Dr. L. L. Fleming, Chairman
Affiliation: Church-related liberal arts college (American Lutheran)
Accreditation: NCA; NCATE
Areas: App Mus; Hist & Lit; Cond; Mus Ed (Elem & HS); Mus Therapy
Degrees: BA; BM

BEMIDJI STATE UNIVERSITY
Department of Music
Bemidji, MN 56601
(218) 755-2915
Staff: Dr. Thomas L. Swanson, Chairman
Affiliation: State-supported university
Accreditation: NCA; NCATE
Areas: App Mus; Hist & Lit; Th & An; Comp; Cond; Orch; Opera; Hist Musicol; Mus Ed (Elem & HS)
Degrees: BA; BS, Mus Ed; MS
Scholarships: Scholarships of about $200 each awarded to approximately 15 students

BETHEL COLLEGE
Department of Music
3900 Bethel Dr.
St. Paul, MN 55112
(612) 638-6400
Staff: John Nordquist, Chairman
Affiliation: Church-affiliated liberal arts college (Baptist)
Accreditation: NCA
Areas: App Mus; Hist & Lit; Th & An;

Cond; Orch; Church Mus; Intro; Mus Ed (Elem & HS); Perf
Degrees: BA
Scholarships: Participation grants for students who participate in performance organizations awarded on the basis of director's recommendations and student need

CARLETON COLLEGE
Department of Music
Northfield, MN 55057
(507) 663-4347
Staff: Stephen Kelly and Anne Mayer, Co-chairmen
Affiliation: Private college
Accreditation: NCA
Areas: App Mus; Hist & Lit; Th & An; Comp; Cond; Orch; Opera; Perf
Degrees: BA

COLLEGE OF SAINT BENEDICT
Music Department
Saint Joseph, MN 56374
(612) 363-5717
Staff: Robert Koopmann, Chairperson
Affiliation: Private church-related liberal arts college (Catholic—Benedictine)
Accreditation: NCA
Areas: App Mus; Hist & Lit; Th & An; Comp; Cond; Orch; Opera; Church Mus; Mus Ed (Elem & HS); Electr Mus
Degrees: BA; BM
Scholarships: Scholarships to cover lesson fees and/or partial tuition awarded by audition in performance areas

THE COLLEGE OF ST. CATHERINE
Music Department
2004 Randolph
St. Paul, MN 55105
(612) 690-6000
Staff: Helen Bambenek, Chairperson
Affiliation: Church-related college administered by the Sisters of St. Joseph of Corondelet (Roman Catholic)
Accreditation: NASM; NCATE; NCA
Areas: App Mus; Hist & Lit; Th & An; Cond; Orch; Opera; Hist Musicol; Church Mus; Mus Ed (Elem & HS); Theater Mus; Perf
Degrees: BA
Scholarships: Applied music scholarships awarded on the basis of talent and need

COLLEGE OF ST. SCHOLASTICA
Department of Music
1200 Kenwood Ave.
Duluth, MN 55811
(218) 723-6194
Staff: D. LeAnn House, Chairperson
Affiliation: Private church-related liberal arts college (Roman Catholic)
Accreditation: NCA
Areas: App Mus; Hist & Lit; Th & An; Cond; Orch; Mus Ed (Elem & HS); Chamber Mus (Early Mus, Piano, Voice, Strings); Intro
Degrees: BA
Scholarships: Applied music scholarships offered to promising students to cover cost of applied music lessons; Tobin scholarship for female vocalist(s); Herz scholarship; 2 Matinee Musicale scholarships of varying amounts for music majors

COLLEGE OF SAINT TERESA[1]
Department of Music
Winona, MN 55987
(507) 452-9302
Staff: Dr. Paul Rusterholz, Music Program Director
Affiliation: Church-related liberal arts college (Roman Catholic)
Accreditation: NASM; NCA
Areas: App Mus; Hist & Lit; Th & An; Cond; Church Mus; Intro; Mus Ed (Elem & HS); Mus Therapy; Perf
Degrees: BA
Scholarships: All tuition awards figured into total financial aid package; students may audition as high school seniors

COLLEGE OF ST. THOMAS
Music Department
2115 Summit Avenue
St. Paul, MN 55105
(612) 647-5285
Staff: Merritt C. Nequette, Chairman
Affiliation: Church-related liberal arts college (Roman Catholic)
Accreditation: NCA; NCATE; NCA
Areas: App Mus; Hist & Lit; Th & An; Cond; Orch; Mus Ed (Elem & HS); Church Mus; Perf; Mus Bus; Arts Administration (pending)
Degrees: BA; MA
Scholarships: Available for performance studies for majors; must audition, given through financial aid office

CONCORDIA COLLEGE
Music Department
Moorhead, MN 56560
(218) 299-4414
Staff: Roy E. Stahl, Chairman
Affiliation: Private church-related liberal arts college (American Lutheran)
Accreditation: NASM; NCATE; NCA
Areas: App Mus; Hist & Lit; Th & An; Comp; Cond; Orch; Mus Ed (Elem & HS); Perf
Degrees: BA; BM; BA, Mus Ed
Scholarships: Ranging from $100-$300, applied music scholarships, all class levels; awarded by faculty during the 2nd semester of each year, based on performance and scholarship

CONCORDIA COLLEGE
Music Department
Division of Fine Arts
Hamline and Marshall
St. Paul, MN 55104
(612) 641-8248
Staff: Assoc. Prof. Friedrich E. Brauer, Chairman, Division of Fine Arts
Affiliation: Private church-related liberal arts college with emphasis on teacher education and church music (Lutheran Church, Missouri Synod)
Accreditation: NCATE; NCA
Areas: App Mus; Hist & Lit; Th & An; Comp; Cond; Orch; Church Mus; Intro; Mus Ed (Elem & HS); Perf
Degrees: BA
Scholarships: 1 general music scholarship per year awarded on the basis of written application and tape of approximately 10 to 15 minutes of instrumental or vocal capabilities; choral scholarship under consideration

DR. MARTIN LUTHER COLLEGE[1]
Music Division
College Heights
New Ulm, MN 56073
(507) 354-8221
Staff: Edward H. Meyer, Chairman
Affiliation: Church-related college offering elementary education major only (Lutheran)
Accreditation: NCA
Areas: App Mus; Hist & Lit; Th & An; Cond; Church Mus; Mus Ed (Elem); Intro
Degrees: BS, Mus Ed

GUSTAVUS ADOLPHUS COLLEGE
Department of Music
St. Peter, MN 56082
(507) 931-7364
Staff: Mark E. Lammers, Chairman
Affiliation: Private liberal arts college affiliated with the Lutheran Church in America (LCA)
Accreditation: NASM; NCATE; NCA
Areas: App Mus; Church Mus; Mus Ed (Elem & HS); Gen Mus
Degrees: BA
Scholarships: Awarded on the basis of need

HAMLINE UNIVERSITY[1]
Department of Music
St. Paul, MN 55104
(612) 641-2281
Staff: Dr. George S. T. Chu, Chairman
Affiliation: Church-related liberal arts college (Methodist)
Accreditation: NASM; NCA
Areas: App Mus; Hist & Lit; Th & An; Cond; Intro; Mus Ed (Elem & HS); Perf
Degrees: BA
Scholarships: Cullen Scholarship for strings

MACALESTER COLLEGE[1]
Department of Music
1600 Grand Ave.
St. Paul, MN 55105
(612) 696-6383
Staff: Prof. Donald Betts, Chairman
Affiliation: Private liberal arts college
Accreditation: NASM; NCA
Areas: App Mus; Th & An; Orch; Cond; Comp; Intro; Hist & Lit; Church Mus
Degrees: BA; BA, Mus Ed

MANKATO STATE UNIVERSITY
Music Department
Mankato, MN 56001
(507) 389-2119
Staff: Dr. William R. Lecklider, Chairman
Affiliation: State-supported university
Accreditation: NASM; NCATE; NCA
Areas: App Mus; Hist & Lit; Th & An; Comp; Orch; Mus Ed (Elem & HS); Theater Mus; Perf
Degrees: BA; BM; BS, Mus Ed; MM; MS, Mus Ed
Scholarships: Scholarships available for full-time (12 credit hours per quarter) music majors and minors, awarded on merit basis

MINNESOTA BIBLE COLLEGE
Music Department
920 Mayowood Rd. SW
Rochester, MN 55901
(507) 288-4563
Staff: Dr. Dennis R. Martin, Chairman
Affiliation: Bible college supported by Churches of Christ
Accreditation: AABC
Areas: App Mus; Hist & Lit; Th & An; Comp; Cond; Church Mus; Intro; Perf
Degrees: BA; BS
Scholarships: Ruby Graham Memorial Scholarships, up to $1000/yr., based on ability and need, audition and formal application required; Christian Service Grants for incoming students, based on potential; music students also eligible to apply for more general college grants and scholarships

MOORHEAD STATE UNIVERSITY
Department of Music
Moorhead, MN 56560
(218) 236-2101
Staff: Dr. Robert Pattengale, Chairman
Affiliation: State-supported liberal arts and teachers university
Accreditation: NASM; NCA; NCATE
Areas: App Mus; Hist & Lit; Th & An; Comp; Cond; Orch; Opera; Hist Musicol; Mus Ed (Elem & HS); Electr Mus; Intro; Perf
Degrees: BA; BM; BS, Mus Ed; MS, Mus Ed
Scholarships: Music performance scholarships and graduate assistantships available

NORTH CENTRAL BIBLE COLLEGE
Music Department
910 Elliot Ave. S.
Minneapolis, MN 55404
(612) 332-3491, x232
Staff: Larry Bach, Acting Chairman
Affiliation: Church-related Bible college (Assemblies of God)
Accreditation: AABC; candidate NCATE
Areas: Th & An; Intro; Hist & Lit; App Mus; Cond; Orch; Ethnomusicol; Church Mus; Perf; Mus Drama; Mus Mvmt
Degrees: B Sacr Mus
Scholarships: Joe Jorris Music Scholarship for upperclassmen music major; Teen Talent available to all students who place in Assembly of God Talent Division

NORTHWESTERN COLLEGE
Division of Music
3003 N. Snelling
Roseville, MN 55113
(612) 636-4840
Staff: Dr. David C. Osterlund, Chairman
Affiliation: Private liberal arts college
Accreditation: NCA
Areas: App Mus; Hist & Lit; Th & An; Comp; Cond; Orch; Church Mus; Mus Ed (Elem & HS); Intro; Perf
Degrees: BA; BS, Mus Ed

ST. CLOUD STATE UNIVERSITY
Department of Music
St. Cloud, MN 56301
(612) 255-0121
Staff: Dr. James H. Flom, Chairman
Affiliation: State-supported university
Accreditation: NASM; NCA; NCATE
Areas: Th & An; Orch; Cond; Comp; Intro; Hist & Lit; Mus Ed (Elem & HS); App Mus
Degrees: BA; BM; BS, Mus Ed; Ms, Mus Ed

ST. JOHN'S UNIVERSITY
Music Department
Collegeville, MN 56321
(612) 363-3371
Staff: Robert Koopmann, Chairman
Affiliation: Private church-related liberal arts university
Accreditation: NCA
Areas: App Mus; Hist & Lit; Th & An; Comp; Cond; Orch; Opera; Church Mus; Mus Ed (Elem & HS)
Degrees: BA; MA, Liturgical Studies, Church Mus
Scholarships: Need and ability scholarships awarded by audition

ST. MARY'S COLLEGE
Music Department
Winona, MN 55987
(507) 452-4430
Staff: Dr. William H. Steven, Chairman
Affiliation: Private church-related liberal arts college (Roman Catholic)
Accreditation: NASM (pending); NCA
Areas: App Mus; Hist & Lit; Th & An; Cond; Orch; Church Mus; Mus Ed (HS); Perf
Degrees: BA; BM
Scholarships: About 10 $100 scholarships awarded by music faculty each year, sponsored by Winona Music Guild; Phi Mu Alpha chapter provides $300 scholarship, awarded by committee

ST. OLAF COLLEGE
Music Department
Northfield, MN 55057
(507) 663-3180
Staff: Dr. Charles Forsberg, Chairman
Affiliation: Church-related liberal arts college (Lutheran)
Accreditation: NASM; NCATE; NCA
Areas: App Mus; Hist & Lit; Th & An; Comp; Cond; Orch; Church Mus; Mus Ed (Elem & HS); Intro; Electr Mus
Degrees: BA; BM

ST. PAUL BIBLE COLLEGE
Music Department
Bible College, MN 55375
(612) 446-1411
Staff: Leland Flickinger, Chairman
Affiliation: Church-related college (Christian and Missionary Alliance)
Accreditation: NCA; AABC
Areas: App Mus; Hist & Lit; Th & An; Comp; Cond; Church Mus; Mus Ed (Elem & HS)
Degrees: BM; BME; BM, Church Music; BM, Church Music and Ministries
Scholarships: Available to all students regardless of major

SOUTHWEST STATE UNIVERSITY
Music Department
Marshall, MN 56258
(507) 537-7234
Staff: Rollin R. Potter, Chairman
Affiliation: State-supported liberal arts university
Accreditation: NCA
Areas: App Mus; Hist & Lit; Th & An; Comp; Cond; Orch; Mus Ed (Elem & HS)
Degrees: BA; BS, Mus Ed
Scholarships: Presidential scholarships for outstanding incoming freshmen; Munkhof scholarships for outstanding upperclassmen

UNIVERSITY OF MINNESOTA
School of Music
104 Scott Hall
Minneapolis, MN 55455
(612) 373-3546
Staff: Dr. Lloyd Ultan, Director
Affiliation: State-supported university
Accreditation: NASM; NCA
Areas: App Mus; Hist & Lit; Th & An; Comp; Cond; Orch; Opera; Hist Musicol; Ethnomusicol; Church Mus; Intro; Mus Ed (Elem & HS); Mus Therapy; Electr Mus; Perf
Degrees: BA; BM; BS, Mus Ed; MA; MM; MA, Mus Ed; DMA; PhD
Scholarships: Many scholarships available; contact School of Music for information

UNIVERSITY OF MINNESOTA, DULUTH
Music Department
Duluth, MN 55812
(218) 726-8207
Staff: Dr. Frank P. Comella, Head
Affiliation: State-supported university
Accreditation: NASM; NCATE; NCA
Areas: App Mus; Hist & Lit; Th & An; Comp; Cond; Orch; Opera; Intro; Mus Ed (Elem & HS); Perf; Piano Ped
Degrees: BM; MA

Scholarships: Talent awards and teaching assistantships available

UNIVERSITY OF MINNESOTA, MORRIS
Humanities Division
Morris, MN 56267
(612) 589-2211
Staff: Dr. Clyde E. Johnson, Coordinator of Music
Affiliation: Public liberal arts university
Accreditation: NCA
Areas: App Mus; Hist & Lit; Th & An; Comp; Cond; Opera; Intro; Mus Ed (Elem & HS); Perf
Degrees: BA
Scholarships: Scholarships of $180 a year cover applied music fee

WINONA STATE UNIVERSITY[1]
Department of Music
Winona, MN 55987
(507) 457-2109
Staff: Richard H. McCluer, Chairman
Affiliation: State-supported liberal arts and teachers university
Accreditation: NASM; NCA
Areas: App Mus; Hist & Lit; Th & An; Comp; Cond; Orch; Intro; Mus Ed (Elem & HS); Perf
Degrees: BA; BS, Mus Ed
Scholarships: Awarded on the basis of ensemble participation

MISSISSIPPI

ALCORN STATE UNIVERSITY[1]
Department of Fine Arts
P.O. Box 29
Alcorn State University, MS 39096
(601) 877-3711, x255
Staff: Joyce J. Bolden, Chairperson
Affiliation: State-supported university
Accreditation: SACS; NASM
Areas: App Mus; Th & An; Orch; Cond; Intro; Hist & Lit; Mus Ed (Elem & HS)
Degrees: BME

BELHAVEN COLLEGE
Music Department
Jackson, MS 39202
(601) 948-3818
Staff: Prof. Virginia Hoogenakker, Chairman
Affiliation: Church-related liberal arts college (Presbyterian)
Accreditation: NASM: SACS
Areas: App Mus; Hist & Lit; Th & An; Comp; Cond; Orch; Hist Musicol; Mus Ed (Elem); Perf
Degrees: BM
Scholarships: Piano, voice, and strings scholarships available through audition

BLUE MOUNTAIN COLLEGE
Music Department, Division of Fine Arts
Blue Mountain, MS 38610
(601) 685-5761
Staff: Dr. Philip C. Meyer, Chairman
Affiliation: Church-related liberal arts college (Southern Baptist)
Accreditation: SACS
Areas: App Mus; Hist & Lit; Th & An; Comp; Cond; Orch; Church Mus; Intro; Mus Ed (Elem & HS); Perf
Degrees: BA; BM; BS, Mus Ed
Scholarships: 6 scholarships for freshmen awarded on the basis of tape and letter of recommendation

DELTA STATE UNIVERSITY
Music Department
Cleveland, MS 38733
(601) 843-3701
Staff: Dr. W. James Craig, Chairman
Affiliation: State-supported liberal arts and teachers university
Accreditation: NASM; SACS; NCATE
Areas: App Mus; Hist & Lit; Th & An; Comp; Cond; Opera; Church Mus; Mus Ed (Elem & HS)
Degrees: BA; BM; BME; MEd; EdS
Scholarships: Talent awards and service grants

JACKSON STATE UNIVERSITY[1]
Department of Music, Division of Fine Arts
1400 J. R. Lynch St.
Jackson, MS 39217
(601) 968-2141
Staff: Dr. Dollye M. E. Robinson, Head and Division Chairman
Affiliation: State-supported institution designated the Urban University in the State of Mississippi
Accreditation: NCATE; SACS; NASM
Areas: App Mus; Hist & Lit; Th & An; Comp; Cond; Orch; Opera; Ethnomusicol; Church Mus; Mus Ed (Elem & HS)
Degrees: BM; BME; MME
Scholarships: Scholarships of tuition, half-expense and full-expense awarded on the basis of auditions and academic scholarships based on ACT/SAT scores

MISSISSIPPI COLLEGE[1]
Department of Music
PO Box 4186
Clinton, MS 39058
(601) 924-5131, x230
Staff: Dr. J. Lawrence Lyall, Head
Affiliation: Church-related college (Southern Baptist)
Accreditation: NASM; SACS
Areas: Th & An; Cond; Hist & Lit; Mus Ed (Elem & HS); Church Mus; Perf
Degrees: BA; BM; BME; MM; MM, Mus Ed

MISSISSIPPI INDUSTRIAL COLLEGE[1]
Department of Music
Washington Hall
Holly Springs, MS 38635
(601) 252-3411
Staff: Lady S. Tucker, Chairman
Affiliation: Church-related college (Christian Methodist Episcopal Church)
Accreditation: SACS
Areas: Cond; Intro; Mus Ed (Elem & HS)
Degrees: BS, Mus Ed

MISSISSIPPI STATE UNIVERSITY
Department of Music Education
Drawer F
State University, MS 39762
(601) 325-3070
Staff: W. Thomas West, Head
Affiliation: State-supported university
Accreditation: SACS; NCATE
Areas: App Mus; Hist & Lit; Th & An; Comp; Cond; Orch; Opera; Hist Musicol; Church Mus; Mus Ed (Elem & HS)
Degrees: BA; BME; MME
Scholarships: Piano, voice, instrumental, band, choral scholarships awarded by audition

MISSISSIPPI UNIVERSITY FOR WOMEN
Music/Fine & Performing Arts Division
PO Box 250—MUW
Columbus, MS 39701
(601) 328-6202
Staff: Dr. Marilyn Swingle, Music Coordinator, Department of Music
Affiliation: State-supported college
Accreditation: NASM; SACS
Areas: App Mus; Hist & Lit; Th & An; Comp; Cond; Opera; Church Mus; Intro; Mus Ed (Elem & HS); Perf
Degrees: BA; BM; BME
Scholarships: Performance awards to incoming students; audition required

RUST COLLEGE[1]
Department of Music
Holly Springs, MS 38635
(601) 252-4661, x271
Staff: Norman Chapman, Chairman
Affiliation: Church-related college (United Methodist)
Accreditation: SACS
Areas: App Mus; Th & An; Hist & Lit; Mus Ed (Elem & HS)
Degrees: BA; BA, Mus Ed

TOUGALOO COLLEGE[1]
Music Department
Tougaloo, MS 39174
(601) 956-4941, x19
Staff: Dr. Ben E. Bailey, Chairman and Professor of Music
Affiliation: Church-related liberal arts college (Disciples of Christ)
Accreditation: SACS
Areas: App Mus
Degrees: BA

UNIVERSITY OF MISSISSIPPI[1]
Department of Music
University, MS 38677
(601) 232-7268
Staff: Andrew Fox, Acting Chairman
Affiliation: State-supported university
Accreditation: NASM; SACS
Areas: App Mus; Hist & Lit; Th & An; Comp; Opera; Hist Musicol; Intro; Mus Ed (Elem & HS); Theater Mus; Perf
Degrees: BA; BM; MFA; MM; DA
Scholarships: Band, orchestra, and music merit scholarships awarded on the basis of performance auditions and GPA

UNIVERSITY OF SOUTHERN MISSISSIPPI
Music Department, College of Fine Arts
Hattiesburg, MS 39406-5081
(601) 266-5363
Staff: Ronald McCreery, Chairman, Music Department
Affiliation: State-supported university
Accreditation: NASM; SACS
Areas: App Mus; Hist & Lit; Th & An; Comp; Cond; Church Mus; Mus Ed (Elem & HS); Perf; Mus Bus
Degrees: BM; BME; MM; DMA; EdD; PhD
Scholarships: Orchestra, choral & piano, and band scholarships available to in-state and out-of-state students; students do not have to major in music to receive scholarships

WESLEY COLLEGE
Music Program
Florence, MS 39073
(601) 845-2265
Staff: Patsy Gilmore, Chairman
Affiliation: Church-related Bible college with general education program (Congregational Methodist)
Accreditation: AABC
Areas: App Mus; Hist & Lit; Th & An; Comp; Cond; Church Mus; Mus Ed (Elem & HS)
Degrees: BS, Church Mus; BS, Christian Ministries
Scholarships: Public relations and music scholarships awarded on the basis of good character, 2.0 GPA, and performance

WILLIAM CAREY COLLEGE
School of Music
Tuscan Ave.
Hattiesburg, MS 39401
(601) 582-5051, x29
Staff: Dr. James H. Fry, Dean
Affiliation: Church-related liberal arts college (Southern Baptist)
Accreditation: NASM; SACS; NAMT
Areas: Th & An; Orch; Cond; Comp; Intro; Mus Ed (Elem & HS); Church Mus; Mus Therapy; App Mus; Hist & Lit; Hist Musicol; Intro
Degrees: BA; BM; MM
Scholarships: Music grants available for undergraduates, assistantships for graduates

MISSOURI

AVILA COLLEGE[1]
Music Division, Performing and Visual Arts Department
11901 Wornall Rd.
Kansas City, MO 64145
(816) 942-8400, x251
Staff: Sr. de La Salle McKeon, Coordinator
Affiliation: Private church-related liberal arts college sponsored by Sisters of St. Joseph of Carondolet (Roman Catholic)
Accreditation: NCA
Areas: App Mus; Hist & Lit; Th & An; Hist Musicol; Church Mus; Mus Ed (Elem & HS); Piano Tech
Degrees: BA; BM
Scholarships: Scholarships of up to $500 awarded by application to Music Coordinator; President Scholarships of from $500 to $2,000 awarded automatically to accepted students with high ACT or SAT score (no application procedure necessary)

CENTRAL BIBLE COLLEGE[1]
Music Division
3000 N. Grant Ave.
Springfield, MO 65803
(417) 833-2551, x52
Staff: Paul Cope, Admin.-Chairman
Affiliation: Church-related ministry training college (Assembly of God)
Accreditation: AABC
Areas: App Mus; Hist & Lit; Th & An; Comp; Cond; Orch; Church Mus; Instr Tech
Degrees: BA, Sacr Mus

CENTRAL METHODIST COLLEGE
Swinney Conservatory of Music
Fayette, MO 65248
(816) 248-3391, x217
Staff: Dr. Donald Alan Pyle, Dean
Affiliation: Church-related liberal arts college (United Methodist)
Accreditation: NASM; NCA
Areas: App Mus; Hist & Lit; Th & An; Comp; Cond; Orch; Mus Ed (Elem & HS); Perf
Degrees: BA; BM; BME
Scholarships: Freshman talent awards based on scholarship auditions; scholarships renewable for 4 years if BPA of 3.0 is maintained

CENTRAL MISSOURI STATE UNIVERSITY
Department of Music
Warrensburg, MO 64093
(816) 747-4530
Staff: Dr. Russell Coleman, Chair
Affiliation: State-supported university
Accreditation: NASM; NCATE; NCA
Areas: App Mus; Hist & Lit; Th & An; Comp; Cond; Orch; Opera; Hist Musicol; Intro; Mus Ed (Elem & HS); Electr Mus; Perf
Degrees: BA; BM; BME; MA· MS, Mus Ed
Scholarships: Scholarships in applied (performance) studies for freshmen awarded on the basis of audition with the faculty committee and standing in upper 50 percent of high school graduating class

CULVER-STOCKTON COLLEGE
Department of Music
Canton, MO 63435
(314) 288-5221, x39
Staff: John H. Gerber, Chairman
Affiliation: Church-related college (Disciples of Christ)
Accreditation: NCA
Areas: Th & An; Orch; Comp; Intro; Hist & Lit; Mus Ed (Elem & HS); Church Mus
Degrees: BA; BS, Mus; BM; BA, Mus Ed; BS, Mus Ed; BME
Scholarships: Performance and academic scholarships available

DRURY COLLEGE
Department of Music
Springfield, MO 65802
(417) 865-8731
Staff: Sidney R. Vise, Chairman
Affiliation: Private liberal arts college
Accreditation: NCA
Areas: App Mus; Hist & Lit; Th & An; Comp; Cond; Orch; Hist Musicol; Mus Ed (Elem & HS); Mus Apprec
Degrees: BA; BM; BME

EVANGEL COLLEGE[1]
Department of Music
1111 N. Glenstone
Springfield, MO 65802
(417) 865-2811, x211
Staff: John S. Shows, Chairman
Affiliation: Church-related college (Assemblies of God)
Accreditation: NASM; NCA
Areas: App Mus; Hist & Lit; Th & An; Comp; Cond; Orch; Church Mus; Mus Ed (Elem & HS); Piano Tech; Instr Rep
Degrees: BME
Scholarships: Scholarships available in applied music areas, for music majors only

FONTBONNE COLLEGE
Department of Music
Wydown & Big Bend Blvds.
St. Louis, MO 63105
(314) 862-3456
Staff: Dr. Mary Ann Mulligan, Chairman
Affiliation: Private liberal arts college (Roman Catholic)
Accreditation: NASM; NCATE; NCA
Areas: App Mus; Mus Ed (Elem & HS); Theater Mus; Perf; Piano Ped; Mus Bus; Perf; Music, Early Childhood
Degrees: BA; BM
Scholarships: $400 to $1,500 awards based on audition and need; piano accompaniment assistantships available

HANNIBAL-LAGRANGE COLLEGE
Music Department
Humanities Division
Hannibal, MO 63401
(314) 221-3675
Staff: Dr. Floyd D. McCoy, Chairman
Affiliation: Church-related college (Southern Baptist)
Accreditation: NCA
Areas: App Mus; Hist & Lit; Th & An; Cond; Orch; Church Mus; Mus Ed (Elem & HS); Perf; Survey of Church Mus
Degrees: BS, Mus Ed; Church Music
Scholarships: Scholarships available for music accompanists, band and choir

LINCOLN UNIVERSITY
Department of Fine Arts
820 Chestnut
Jefferson City, MO 65101
(314) 751-2325, x333
Staff: John A. Taylor, Head
Affiliation: State-supported liberal arts university
Accreditation: NASM; NCATE; NCA
Areas: Mus Ed (Elem & HS)
Degrees: BME
Scholarships: Awarded on the basis of participation in music performance organizations and academic success

THE LINDENWOOD COLLEGES
Music Department
St. Charles, MO 63301
(314) 723-7152
Staff: Dr. Kenneth G. Greenlaw, Chairman
Affiliation: Private liberal arts college
Accreditation: NCA; NCATE
Areas: App Mus; Hist & Lit; Th & An; Cond; Orch; Opera; Hist Musicol; Church Mus; Intro; Mus Ed (Elem & HS); Theater Mus; Perf
Degrees: BA; BM; BME; BS
Scholarships: Awarded on the basis of performance audition and academic honors

MARYVILLE COLLEGE[1]
Department of Music
13550 Conway Rd.
St. Louis, MO 63141
(314) 576-9300
Staff: Sr. H. A. Padberg, Professor of Music
Affiliation: Independent community-focused college committed to the Judeo-Christian tradition, offering a diversity of quality programs in career-oriented liberal arts study
Accreditation: NCA
Areas: App Mus; Hist & Lit; Th & An; Comp; Cond; Orch; Church Mus; Intro; Mus Ed (Elem & HS); Mus Therapy
Degrees: BA; BS, Mus Ed
Scholarships: Leo C. Miller Music Therapy Scholarship awarded on the basis of academic standing, audition, interview, and recommendations

MISSOURI SOUTHERN STATE COLLEGE
Music Department, Department of Fine Arts
Newman and Duquesne Rds.
Joplin, MO 64801
(417) 624-8100
Staff: Dr. F. Joe Sims, Head, Department of Fine Arts
Affiliation: State-supported college
Accreditation: NCATE; NCA
Areas: App Mus; Hist & Lit; Th & An; Cond; Orch; Mus Ed (Elem & HS); Theater Mus; Mus Apprec
Degrees: BA; BS, Mus Ed
Scholarships: Marching band scholarships awarded for band performance; scholarships for music majors awarded on the basis of talent

MISSOURI WESTERN STATE COLLEGE
Department of Music
4525 Downs Dr.
St. Joseph, MO 64507
(816) 271-4420
Staff: F.M. Gilmour, Chairman
Affiliation: State-supported university
Accreditation: NCATE; NASM; NCA
Areas: App Mus; Hist & Lit; Th & An; Comp; Cond; Mus Ed (Elem & HS)
Degrees: BA; BS, Mus Ed; Intro
Scholarships: Solo performance, ensemble performance, accompanying, marching band, and harmony college scholarships awarded on the basis of grade point average and audition

NORTHEAST MISSOURI STATE UNIVERSITY
Division of Fine Arts
Kirksville, MO 63501
(816) 665-5121
Staff: Dale A. Jorgenson, Head
Affiliation: State-supported university
Accreditation: NASM; NCATE; NCA
Areas: App Mus; Hist & Lit; Th & An; Comp; Cond; Orch; Opera; Intro; Mus Ed (Elem & HS); Theater Mus; Instr Rep; Mus Bus
Degrees: BA; BM; BME; MA, Mus Ed
Scholarships: Tuition scholarships awarded by audition; graduate and teaching assistantships

NORTHWEST MISSOURI STATE UNIVERSITY[1]
Division of Fine Arts
Music Department
Maryville, MO 64468
(816) 582-7141, x1325
Staff: Robert Sunkel, Head
Affiliation: State-supported university
Accreditation: NASM; NCA; NCATE
Areas: Th & An; Orch; Cond; Intro; Hist & Lit; Mus Ed (Elem & HS)
Degrees: BS, Mus Ed; MS, Mus Ed

PARK COLLEGE
Music Department
Kansas City, MO 64152
(816) 741-2000
Staff: Dr. Theodore Albrecht, Chairman
Affiliation: Privately endowed college associated with RLDS Church
Accreditation: NASM; NCA
Areas: App Mus; Hist & Lit; Th & An; Comp; Cond; Orch; Mus Ed (Elem & HS); Ind Studies; Special Topics (TBA)
Degrees: BA; BA, Mus Ed
Scholarships: Awarded on the basis of audition and reference; 3.0 GPA required

ST. LOUIS CONSERVATORY OF MUSIC
560 Trinity
St. Louis, MO 63130
(314) 863-3033
Staff: Joel Revzen, Dean
Affiliation: Private independent conservatory
Accreditation: NASM
Areas: App Mus; Hist & Lit; Th & An; Comp; Orch; Opera
Degrees: BM; MM; Diploma in Mus Perf for graduates and undergraduates
Scholarships: Merit scholarships awarded to students who demonstrate a high level of artistic and scholastic achievement

ST. LOUIS UNIVERSITY
Music Department
221 N. Grand Blvd.
St. Louis, MO 63103
(314) 658-2410
Staff: Francis J. Guentner, S.J, Chairman
Affiliation: Church-related liberal arts college (Roman Catholic)
Accreditation: NCA
Areas: App Mus; Hist & Lit; Th & An; Mus Ed (Elem & HS)
Degrees: BA
Scholarships: Talent awards based on audition

THE SCHOOL OF THE OZARKS
Music Department
Point Lookout, MO 65726
(417) 334-6411
Staff: Dr. John Mizell, Chairman
Affiliation: Private liberal arts college
Accreditation: NASM; NCATE; NCA
Areas: App Mus; Mus Ed (Elem & HS); Hist & Lit; Th & An; Comp; Cond; Orch; Theater Mus; Perf
Degrees: BA; BS, Mus Ed
Scholarships: Full work scholarships for all resident students (covering tuition, room, and board) based primarily on demonstrated financial need and ACT score

SOUTHEAST MISSOURI STATE UNIVERSITY
Music Department
Cape Girardeau, MO 63701
(314) 651-2141
Staff: Dr. Doyle A. Dumas, Chairman
Affiliation: State-supported university
Accreditation: NASM; NCATE; NCA
Areas: App Mus; Hist & Lit; Th & An; Comp; Cond; Orch; Church Mus; Mus Ed (Elem & HS); Instr Rep
Degrees: BA; BM; BME; MME; MAT
Scholarships: Applied music scholarships available in all areas

SOUTHWEST BAPTIST UNIVERSITY[1]
Department of Music
1601 S. Springfield
Bolivar, MO 65613
(417) 326-5281, x328
Staff: Susan Baker, Chairman
Affiliation: Church-related liberal arts college (Southern Baptist)
Accreditation: NASM; NCA
Areas: App Mus; Hist & Lit; Th & An; Comp; Cond; Orch; Opera; Church Mus;

Intro; Mus Ed (Elem & HS)
Degrees: BA; BM; BME
Scholarships: Performance scholarships awarded through audition

SOUTHWEST MISSOURI STATE UNIVERSITY[1]
Department of Music
901 S. National Ave.
Springfield, MO 65802
(417) 836-5648
Staff: Robert Scott, Acting Head
Affiliation: State-supported university
Accreditation: NASM; NCA
Areas: App Mus; Hist & Lit; Th & An; Comp; Cond; Orch; Opera; Mus Ed (Elem & HS); Instr Rep; Instr Materials and Ped; Perf
Degrees: BA; BM; BS, Mus Ed
Scholarships: Grants, awards, and fee waivers awarded through application

STEPHENS COLLEGE
Music Department
Columbia, MO 65215
(314) 442-2211
Staff: Eula Simmons, Chairman
Affiliation: Privately endowed liberal arts college
Accreditation: NASM; NCA
Areas: App Mus; Hist & Lit; Th & An; Cond; Opera; Intro; Theater Mus; Perf
Degrees: BA; BFA
Scholarships: Small scholarships for female students in piano and voice; large work scholarships for a few male performers in voice

UNIVERSITY OF MISSOURI, COLUMBIA
Music Department
Columbia, MO 65201
(314) 882-2604
Staff: Donald E. McGlothlin, Chairman
Affiliation: State-supported university
Accreditation: NASM; NCA
Areas: App Mus; Hist & Lit; Th & An; Comp; Cond; Orch; Opera; Hist Musicol; Intro; Mus Ed (Elem & HS); Theater Mus; Electr Mus; Perf
Degrees: BA, BM; BS, Mus Ed; MA; MM; MS, Mus Ed; EdD; PhD
Scholarships: Performance scholarships available

UNIVERSITY OF MISSOURI, KANSAS CITY
Conservatory of Music
4949 Cherry
Kansas City, MO 64110
(816) 363-4300
Staff: Dr. Lindsey Merrill, Dean
Affiliation: State-supported university
Accreditation: NASM; NCATE; NCA
Areas: App Mus; Hist & Lit; Th & An; Comp; Cond; Orch; Opera; Hist Musicol; Church Mus; Intro; Mus Ed (Elem & HS); Mus Therapy; Piano Tech; Instr Rep; Electr Mus; Perf
Degrees: BA; BM; BME; MA; MM; MME; DMA
Scholarships: Scholarships of up to full tuition awarded on the basis of need and talent

UNIVERSITY OF MISSOURI, ST. LOUIS
Department of Music
8001 Natural Bridge Rd.
St. Louis, MO 63121
(314) 553-5890
Staff: Leonard Ott, Chairman
Affiliation: State-supported university
Accreditation: NCA
Areas: App Mus; Th & An; Orch; Cond; Comp; Intro; Hist & Lit; Ethnomusicol; Mus Ed (Elem & HS); Mus Mgmt
Degrees: BA; BM; BME
Scholarships: Scholarships available in all performance areas, based on audition

WASHINGTON UNIVERSITY
Music Department
St. Louis, MO 63130
(314) 863-0100
Staff: Dr. Tilford Brooks, Chairman
Affiliation: Privately endowed university
Accreditation: NASM; NCA
Areas: App Mus; Hist & Lit; Th & An; Comp; Cond; Orch; Opera; Hist Musicol; Mus Ed (Elem & HS); Mus Therapy
Degrees: BA; MA; MM; MA, Mus Ed; EdD; PhD

WEBSTER COLLEGE
Department of Music
470 E. Lockwood
St. Louis, MO 63119
(314) 968-7032
Staff: Dr. Eloise Jarvis, Chairman
Affiliation: Private college-conservatory
Accreditation: NASM; NCA
Areas: App Mus; Hist & Lit; Th & An; Comp; Cond; Orch; Intro; Mus Ed (Elem & HS); Theater Mus; Electr Mus; Perf; Jazz Studies
Degrees: BA; BM; BME; MM
Scholarships: Scholarships of $200 to $1,500 a year awarded on the basis of audition and grade record; graduate assistantships in piano, voice, accompanying, $3000—$3,300 per year

WILLIAM JEWELL COLLEGE
Department of Music
Liberty, MO 64068
(816) 781-3806
Staff: Dr. Donald C. Brown, Chairman
Affiliation: Church-related liberal arts college (Baptist)
Accreditation: NCA; NASM
Areas: App Mus; Hist & Lit; Th & An; Comp; Cond; Opera; Church Mus; Mus Ed (Elem & HS); Mus Bus
Degrees: BA; BS, Mus Ed
Scholarships: Academic, financial need and special skills scholarships available

WILLIAM WOODS COLLEGE
Music Department, Area of Fine Arts
Fulton, MO 65251
(314) 642-2251
Staff: Mary Jane Shipp, Assoc. Prof. of Music and Chairman
Affiliation: Independent church-affiliated college
Accreditation: NCA
Areas: App Mus; Hist & Lit; Th & An; Comp; Cond; Hist Musicol
Degrees: BA; BS
Scholarships: Young Artist in Music Scholarship awarded to music major by audition

MONTANA

BIG SKY BIBLE COLLEGE
Music Department
Lewistown, MT 59457
(406) 538-3452
Staff: Gary Munson, Chairman
Affiliation: Independent Bible college (Conservative Evangelical)
Accreditation: AABC (pending)
Areas: App Mus; Hist & Lit; Th & An; Comp; Cond; Orch; Church Mus; Perf
Degrees: BSM

EASTERN MONTANA COLLEGE
Music Department
Billings, MT 59101
(406) 657-2350
Staff: Gary Behm, Chairman
Affiliation: Liberal arts college
Accreditation: NASM; NAMT; NASC
Areas: App Mus; Hist & Lit; Th & An; Comp; Cond; Orch; Opera; Mus Ed (Elem & HS); Mus Therapy; Piano Tech; Instr Rep; Perf
Degrees: BA; BS, Mus Ed; BA, Mus Therapy; BA, Mus Merch
Scholarships: Music waiver fee (2/3 tuition) awarded on the basis of 3 letters of recommendation and audition in person or on tape

MONTANA STATE UNIVERSITY
Music Department
Bozeman, MT 59717
(406) 994-3561
Staff: Prof. H. Creech Reynolds, Head
Affiliation: State-supported university
Accreditation: NCATE; NASM; NASC
Areas: App Mus; Hist & Lit; Th & An; Comp; Cond; Opera; Intro; Mus Ed (Elem & HS); Instr Rep; Electr Mus; Perf; Orch; Mus Bus
Degrees: BME
Scholarships: Cash and fee-reduction scholarships awarded on the basis of performance audition

ROCKY MOUNTAIN COLLEGE[1]
Music Department
1511 Poly Dr.
Billings, MT 59102
(406) 245-6151

Staff: Prof. Donald F. Pihlaja, Director
Affiliation: Church-related liberal arts college (United Church of Christ; Methodist, Presbyterian)
Accreditation: NASC
Areas: App Mus; Hist & Lit; Th & An; Comp; Cond; Opera; Intro; Mus Ed (Elem & HS)
Degrees: BA; BS, Mus Ed
Scholarships: Activity grants (band, choir, etc.) awarded by audition in person or on tape

UNIVERSITY OF MONTANA
Department of Music
Missoula, MT 59801
(406) 243-6880
Staff: Dr. Donald Simmons, Chairman
Affiliation: State-supported university
Accreditation: NASM; NASC
Areas: App Mus; Hist & Lit; Th & An; Comp; Cond; Orch; Opera; Hist Musicol; Mus Ed (Elem & HS); Perf
Degrees: BA; BM; BME; MA; MM; MME (Elem or HS)
Scholarships: Talent scholarships and fee waivers based on musical talent and potential for academic success

NEBRASKA

CHADRON STATE COLLEGE
Division of Fine Arts
Chadron, NE 69337
(308) 432-5571
Staff: Dr. Charles H. Harrington, Chairman
Division of Fine Arts
Affiliation: State-supported college
Accreditation: NCA
Areas: App Mus; Hist & Lit; Th & An; Comp; Cond; Orch; Hist Musicol; Mus Ed (Elem & HS); Instr Rep
Degrees: BS, Mus Ed

COLLEGE OF SAINT MARY
Music Department
1901 S. 72nd St.
Omaha, NE 68124
(402) 399-2400
Staff: Dr. Michon Rozmajzl, R.S.M., Chairman
Affiliation: Women's liberal arts college (Catholic)
Accreditation: NCA
Areas: App Mus; Hist & Lit; Th & An; Cond; Church Mus; Mus Ed (Elem & HS); Perf
Degrees: BA
Scholarships: At least three $4,000 scholarships ($1,000 per year) awarded on the basis of audition and scholastic ability to maintain an overall C average (B average in music classes)

CONCORDIA TEACHERS COLLEGE
Music Division
800 N. Columbia
Seward, NE 68434
(402) 643-3651
Staff: David Held, Chairman
Affiliation: Church-related college (Lutheran—Missouri Synod)
Accreditation: NCATE; NCA
Areas: App Mus; Hist & Lit; Th & An; Comp; Cond; Orch; Church Mus; Mus Ed (Elem & HS)
Degrees: BA; BM; BME; BSM
Scholarships: 4 scholarships awarded to outstanding new music students; 8 scholarships awarded to outstanding current students

DANA COLLEGE
Music Department
Blair, NE 68008
(402) 426-4101
Staff: Dr. Thomas Williams, Chairman
Affiliation: Church-related liberal arts college (American Lutheran)
Accreditation: NCA; NCATE
Areas: App Mus; Hist & Lit; Th & An; Comp; Cond; Orch; Mus Ed (Elem & HS)
Degrees: BA; BS, Mus
Scholarships: Awarded by audition

DOANE COLLEGE[1]
Department of Music
Crete, NE 68333
(402) 826-2161
Staff: James Bastian, Chairman
Affiliation: Church-related college (United Church of Christ)
Accreditation: NCA
Areas: Th & An; Intro; Hist & Lit; Mus Ed (Elem & HS)
Degrees: BA; BA, Mus Ed

HASTINGS COLLEGE[1]
Department of Music
800 N. Turner Ave.
Hastings, NE 68901
(402) 463-2402
Staff: Prof. Duane E. Johnson, Chairman
Affiliation: Church-affiliated liberal arts college (United Presbyterian)
Accreditation: NASM; NCA
Areas: App Mus; Hist & Lit; Th & An; Comp; Cond; Orch; Opera; Intro; Mus Ed (Elem & HS); Perf
Degrees: BA; BM; BME
Scholarships: Special skills scholarships awarded on the basis of application and maintenance of 2.5 GPA

KEARNEY STATE COLLEGE
Music Department
Kearney, NE 68847
(308) 236-4446
Staff: Dr. Gary Thomas, Head
Affiliation: State-supported college
Accreditation: NASM; NCA
Areas: App Mus; Mus Ed (Elem & HS); Perf; Mus Merch
Degrees: BA; BFA; MA; BS
Scholarships: Tuition waivers and cash grants awarded by audition

MIDLAND LUTHERAN COLLEGE
Department of Music
720 E. Ninth St.
Fremont, NE 68025
(402) 721-5480
Staff: Prof. Charles S. Wilhite, Department of Music
Affiliation: Church-related college (Lutheran Church in America)
Accreditation: NCA
Areas: App Mus; Th & An; Hist & Lit; Mus Ed (Elem & HS); Opera; Church Mus
Degrees: BA

NEBRASKA WESLEYAN UNIVERSITY
Department of Music
50th and Huntington
Lincoln, NE 68504
(402) 466-2371
Staff: Paul R. Swanson, Chairman
Affiliation: Private liberal arts college (Methodist)
Accreditation: NASM; NCA
Areas: App Mus; Hist & Lit; Th & An; Comp; Cond; Orch; Opera; Hist Musicol; Church Mus; Mus Ed (Elem & HS); Theater Mus
Degrees: BA; BM
Scholarships: Awards based on performance

PERU STATE COLLEGE
Department of Music
Peru, NE 68421
(402) 872-3815
Staff: Dr. David M. Edris, Director of Music Activities
Affiliation: State-supported college
Accreditation: NCA; NCATE
Areas: App Mus; Hist & Lit; Th & An; Comp; Cond; Orch; Intro; Mus Ed (Elem & HS)
Degrees: BA; BFA
Scholarships: Menc Alumni Scholarship, awarded to a music major through performance competition; Victor Jindra Scholarship, awarded to a music major through scholastic ability; tuition waivers in music for music majors and non-music majors who participate in music organizations; G. Holt "Pop" Steck Scholarship, awarded to music major through scholastic ability

UNION COLLEGE
Division of Musical Arts
3800 S. 48th St.
Lincoln, NE 68506
(402) 488-2331
Staff: Dr. Robert Walters, Chairman
Affiliation: Church-related liberal arts college (Seventh-day Adventist)
Accreditation: NASM; NCATE; NCA
Areas: App Mus; Hist & Lit; Th & An; Comp; Cond; Mus Ed (Elem & HS); Perf; Orch, Church Mus; Intr
Degrees: BA; BME; AS, Ped
Scholarships: Applied music scholarships available

UNIVERSITY OF NEBRASKA, LINCOLN
School of Music
Lincoln, NE 68588
(402) 472-2503
Staff: Raymond Haggh, Director
Affiliation: State-supported university
Accreditation: NASM; NCA
Areas: App Mus; Hist & Lit; Th & An; Comp; Cond; Orch; Opera; Hist Musicol; Ethnomusicol; Church Mus; Intro; Mus Ed (Elem & HS); Piano Tech; Electr Mus; Perf
Degrees: BA; BM; BME; BS, Mus Ed; MM
Scholarships: Awards of $200 and up available to music majors in various areas; full-tuition and half-tuition waivers available to string players

UNIVERSITY OF NEBRASKA, OMAHA
Music Department
Omaha, NE 68182
(402) 554-2251
Staff: Roger Foltz, Chairman
Affiliation: State-supported university
Accreditation: NCA
Areas: App Mus; Hist & Lit; Th & An; Comp; Cond; Orch; Mus Ed (Elem & HS)
Degrees: BM
Scholarships: Various vocal and instrumental scholarships available

WAYNE STATE COLLEGE
Music Department, Division of Fine Arts
Wayne, NE 68787
(402) 375-2200, x359
Staff: Jay O'Leary, Chairman
Affiliation: State-supported college
Accreditation: NCA; NCATE
Areas: Th & An; Cond; Intro; Hist & Lit; Instr Rep; App Mus; Orch; Mus Ed (Elem & HS)
Degrees: BFA; BA, Mus Ed
Scholarships: Up to full tuition scholarships available based on performance standards and scholarship

NEVADA

SIERRA NEVADA COLLEGE
Music Department
800 Campbell Rd., P.O. Box 4269
Incline Village, NV 89450
(702) 831-1314
Staff: Thomas A. Delaney, Chairman
Affiliation: Private 4-year college of arts and sciences
Accreditation: NASC
Areas: App Mus; Hist & Lit; Th & An; Comp; Cond; Orch; Piano Tech; Electr Mus; Perf; Ear Training; Voice; Woodwinds; Guitar
Degrees: BA
Scholarships: General scholarships

UNIVERSITY OF NEVADA, LAS VEGAS[1]
Department of Music
4505 Maryland Pkwy.
Las Vegas, NV 89154
(702) 739-3332
Staff: Kenneth M. Hanlon, Chairman,
Affiliation: State-supported university
Accreditation: NASM; NASC
Areas: App Mus; Hist & Lit; Th & An; Comp; Cond; Orch; Opera; Intro; Mus Ed (Elem & HS); Perf
Degrees: BA; MM
Scholarships: Scholarships for music majors from $300 to $2,500 per year; grants-in-aid available for non-music majors

UNIVERSITY OF NEVADA, RENO
Music Department
Reno, VN 89557
(702) 784-6145
Staff: Dr. Perry Jones, Chairman
Affiliation: State-supported university
Accreditation: NASM; NASC
Areas: App Mus; Mus Ed (Elem & HS)
Degrees: BA; BM; MA; MM
Scholarships: Full waivers and scholarships (service in music ensembles)

NEW HAMPSHIRE

DARTMOUTH COLLEGE
Department of Music
Hopkins Center
Hanover, NH 03755
(603) 646-2520
Affiliation: Privately endowed liberal arts college
Accreditation: NEA
Areas: App Mus; Hist & Lit; Th & An; Comp; Cond; Orch; Hist Musicol; Ethnomusicol; Intro; Electr Mus; Perf
Degrees: BA

KEENE STATE COLLEGE
Department of Music
229 Main St.
Keene, NH 03431
(603) 352-1909, x327
Staff: Douglas A. Nelson, Coordinator
Affiliation: State-supported college
Accreditation: NEA; NCATE
Areas: App Mus; Th & An; Orch; Comp; Hist & Lit; Cond; Opera; Hist Musicol, Intro; Mus Ed (Elem & HS); Perf
Degrees: BA; BM; BM, Mus Ed
Scholarships: Four full tuition 4-yr. talent scholarships; various other forms of financial aid

NOTRE DAME COLLEGE[1]
Music Department
2321 Elm St.
Manchester, NH 03104
(603) 669-4298
Staff: Sr. Anita Marchesseault, Music Department Coordinator
Affiliation: Private liberal arts college, self-supported
Accreditation: NEA
Areas: App Mus; Hist & Lit; Th & An; Cond; Sacred Mus; Mus Ed (Elem & HS); Perf; Intro; Cond; Orch; Comp
Degrees: BM; MA; AA

PLYMOUTH STATE COLLEGE
Department of Music and Theatre
Main St.
Plymouth, NH 03264
(603) 536-1550
Staff: Prof. Robert F. Swift, Chairman
Affiliation: State-supported liberal arts and teachers preparation institution
Accreditation: NCATE; NEA
Areas: App Mus; Hist & Lit; Th & An; Comp; Cond; Orch; Opera; Intro; Mus Ed (Elem & HS); Theater Mus; Perf
Degrees: BA; BS, Mus Ed
Scholarships: Academic scholarships, loans, work-study, federal and state grants, departmental scholarships and awards are available

RIVIER COLLEGE
Music Department
429 Main St.
Nashua, NH 03060
(603) 888-1311
Staff: Sr. Gabrielle Hebert, Chairman
Affiliation: Privately owned liberal arts college
Accreditation: NEA
Areas: App Mus; Hist & Lit; Th & An; Cond; Orch; Intro; Mus Ed (Elem & HS); Perf
Degrees: BA

UNIVERSITY OF NEW HAMPSHIRE
Department of Music
Paul Creative Arts Center
Durham, NH 03824
(603) 862-1234
Staff: Asso. Prof. Cleveland L. Howard, Chairman
Affiliation: State-supported university
Accreditation: NASM; NEA; NCATE
Areas: Th & An; Comp; Intro; Hist & Lit; Mus Ed (Elem & HS); App Mus; Electr Mus; Perf
Degrees: BA; BM; BME; MA, MS, Mus Ed
Scholarships: No-need university scholarships; endowed scholarships; undergraduate fellowships

NEW JERSEY

CALDWELL COLLEGE
Music Department
Division of Fine Arts
Ryerson Ave.
Caldwell, NJ 07006
(201) 228-4424, x255
Staff: Sr. Mary Ann O'Connor, O.P., Chairperson
Affiliation: Private church-related liberal arts college (Roman Catholic); formerly a woman's college, now accepting men in Continuing Education sections of programs
Accreditation: MSA
Areas: App Mus; Hist & Lit; Th & An;

Comp; Cond; Orch; Opera; Church Mus; Mus Ed (Elem & HS); Theater Mus; Piano Tech; Perf
Degrees: BA
Scholarships: Two 4-year scholarships are offered on a rotational scale (as each one is completed it is offered again for another 4-year period); scholarships cover tuition and are based on scholastic standing and musical performance

COLLEGE OF SAINT ELIZABETH[1]
Music Department
Convent Station, NJ 07961
(201) 539-1600
Staff: Sr. Eileen Dolan, Chairman
Affiliation: Church-related liberal arts college (Roman Catholic)
Accreditation: MSA
Areas: App Mus; Hist & Lit; Th & An; Comp; Cond; Orch; Opera; Intro; Mus Ed (Elem & HS); Perf
Degrees: BA
Scholarships: Full or partial scholarships in voice or instrument available

DOUGLASS COLLEGE OF RUTGERS UNIVERSITY[1]
Music Department
New Brunswick, NJ 08903
(201) 932-1766
Staff: George M. Jones, Chairman, Music Department
Affiliation: Liberal arts college in a state-supported university
Accreditation: NASM; MSA
Areas: App Mus; Hist & Lit; Th & An; Comp; Cond; Orch; Opera; Hist Musicol; Mus Ed (Elem & HS); Perf
Degrees: BS, Mus Ed
Scholarships: Awarded on the basis of merit and scholastic standing

DREW UNIVERSITY[1]
Music Department
36 Madison Ave.
Madison, NJ 07940
(201) 377-3000
Staff: Norman Lowrey, Chairman
Affiliation: Privately endowed liberal arts college
Accreditation: MSA
Areas: App Mus; Hist & Lit; Th & An; Comp; Hist Musicol; Intro; Electr Mus; Perf
Degrees: BA; MA

FAIRLEIGH DICKINSON UNIVERSITY, TEANECK
Department of Fine Arts
1000 River Rd.
Teaneck, NJ 07666
(201) 692-2254
Staff: Prof. Mary Ann Farese, Fine Arts Chairperson
Affiliation: Privately-endowed university
Accreditation: MSA
Areas: App Mus; Hist & Lit; Th & An; Comp; Cond; Orch; Opera; Mus Ed (Elem & HS); Intro; Hist Musicol; Theater Mus; Electr Mus; Jazz
Degrees: BA

GLASSBORO STATE COLLEGE
Department of Music
Glassboro, NJ 08028
(609) 445-6041
Staff: Veda Zuponcic, Chairman
Affiliation: State-supported multi-purpose institution
Accreditation: NASM; NCATE; MSA
Areas: App Mus; Hist & Lit; Th & An; Comp; Cond; Orch; Opera; Hist Musicol; Intro; Mus Ed (Elem & HS); Theater Mus; Piano Tech; Instr Rep; Electr Mus; Perf
Degrees: BA; BME; MA; MA, Mus Ed
Scholarships: Scholarships available; applicants must be accepted by the college and department; awards based on talent, GPA, departmental need, and financial need

JERSEY CITY STATE COLLEGE[1]
Department of Music, School of Arts and Sciences
2039 Kennedy Blvd.
Jersey City, NJ 07305
(201) 547-3151
Staff: Dick Scott, Chairman
Affiliation: State-supported college
Accreditation: NASM; MSA
Areas: App Mus; Hist & Lit; Th & An; Comp; Cond; Orch; Opera; Ethnomusicol; Church Mus; Mus Ed (Elem & HS); Theater Mus; Instr Rep; Mus-Bus Admin; Jazz Studies
Degrees: BA; MA; MA, Mus Ed
Scholarships: Awarded on the basis of performance before a jury

KEAN COLLEGE OF NEW JERSEY[1]
Department of Music
Union, NJ 07083
(201) 527-2108
Staff: Joseph B. Volpe, Chairman
Affiliation: State-supported college
Accreditation: NASM; MSA
Areas: Orch; Cond; Comp; Intro; Hist & Lit; Opera
Degrees: BA; BA, Mus Ed

LIVINGSTON COLLEGE IN RUTGERS, THE STATE UNIVERSITY[1]
Department of Music
New Brunswick, NJ 08903
(201) 932-4150
Staff: Larry Ridley, Chairman
Affiliation: College in the state university of New Jersey
Accreditation: MSA
Areas: Th & An; Comp; Hist & Lit; Musicol; Ethnomusicol
Degrees: BA

MONTCLAIR STATE COLLEGE[1]
Department of Music, School of Fine & Performing Arts
Upper Montclair, NJ 07043
(201) 893-5103
Staff: Donald Mintz, Dean
Affiliation: State-supported college
Accreditation: NASM; MSA
Areas: App Mus; Th & An; Orch; Comp; Intro; Hist & Lit; Musicol; Mus Therapy; Mus Ed (Elem & HS)
Degrees: BM; BA, Mus Therapy; BA, Mus Ed; MA, App Mus; MA, Mus Ed; MA, Th

NORTHEASTERN BIBLE COLLEGE
Department of Music
12 Oak Ln.
Essex Falls, NJ 07021
(201) 226-1074

Staff: Mr. Gerard L. DeMatteo, Chairman
Affiliation: Independent evangelical college
Accreditation: MSA; AABC
Areas: App Mus; Hist & Lit; Th & An; Comp; cond; Orch; Church Mus; Mus Ed (Elem & HS)
Degrees: BABL, Mus Ed. (Bachelor of Biblical Lit-Mus Ed); BSM
Scholarships: Five first-year half tuition scholarships available for new or transfer students; one-half tuition scholarship for an incoming freshman that lasts for the student's entire program; eligibility based on exceptional musical ability judged by entrance and placement tests and audition

PRINCETON UNIVERSITY
Music Department
Princeton, NJ 08540
(609) 921-7012
Staff: Harold S. Powers, Chairman
Affiliation: Private university
Accreditation: MSA
Areas: Hist & Lit; Th & An; Comp; Hist Musicol; Ethnomusicol
Degrees: BA; MFA; PhD

RAMAPO COLLEGE OF NEW JERSEY
School of Contemporary Arts
505 Ramapo Valley Road
Mahwah, NJ 07430
(201) 825-2800
Staff: Harold Lieberman, Professor of Music
Affiliation: State-supported college
Accreditation: NCATE; MSA
Areas: App Mus; Th & An; Comp; Intro; Hist & Lit; Ethnomusicol; Opera; Theater Mus; Electr Mus; Perf
Degrees: BA

RIDER COLLEGE[1]
Department of Fine Arts
Lawrenceville Rd.
Lawrenceville, NJ 08648
(609) 896-5000
Staff: Patrick J. Chmel, Chairman
Affiliation: Private college
Accreditation: MSA
Areas: Th & An; Intro; Hist & Lit
Degrees: BFA

RUTGERS, THE STATE UNIVERSITY OF NEW JERSEY
Music Department
73 Easton Ave.
New Brunswick, NJ 08903
(201) 932-7020, 7976
Staff: Robert D. Lincoln, Chairman (New Brunswick campus); Robert Moevs, Graduate Director
Affiliation: State-supported university
Accreditation: NASM; MSA
Areas: App Mus; Hist & Lit; Th & An; Comp; Cond; Orch; Opera; Hist Musicol; Ethnomusicol; Mus Ed (Elem & HS)
Degrees: BA; MA; MM; MAT; PhD
Scholarships: Undergraduate scholarships of diverse amounts awarded on the basis of merit (Department of Music, Douglass College); graduate teaching assistantships also available

RUTGERS UNIVERSITY, NEWARK CAMPUS[1]
Department of Music
Newark, NJ 07102
(201) 648-1766
Staff: Kenneth Wilson, Chairman
Affiliation: State-supported university
Accreditation: MSA
Areas: App Mus; Th & An; Orch; Cond; Hist & Lit; Musicol; Ethnomusicol; Mus Ed (Elem & HS)
Degrees: BA; BA, Mus Ed

TRENTON STATE COLLEGE
Music Department
Hillwood Lakes
CN 550
Trenton, NJ 08625
(609) 771-2551
Staff: Dr. Robert J. Rittenhouse, Chairman
Affiliation: State-supported college
Accreditation: NASM; MSA
Areas: App Mus; Th & An; Orch; Cond; Comp; Intro; Hist & Lit; Musicol; Mus Ed (Elem & HS)
Degrees: BA; BA, Mus Ed; MA; MEd, Mus Ed

UPSALA COLLEGE[1]
Fine Arts Department
East Orange, NJ 07019
(201) 875-7187
Staff: David Milgrome, Chairman
Affiliation: Private church-related liberal arts college (Lutheran Church in America)
Accreditation: MSA
Areas: Th & An; Cond; Intro; Hist & Lit; Theater Mus
Degrees: BA

WESTMINSTER CHOIR COLLEGE
Princeton, NJ 08540
(609) 921-7100
Staff: Dr. Ray E. Robinson, President
Affiliation: Private independent college of music
Accreditation: NASM; MSA
Areas: App Mus; Cond; Church Mus; Mus Ed (Elem & HS); Perf; Accomp & Coaching; Ped
Degrees: BM; MM
Scholarships: Scholarships available

WILLIAM PATERSON COLLEGE[1]
Department of Music, School of Fine & Performing Arts
300 Pompton Rd.
Wayne, NJ 07470
(201) 595-2314
Staff: Robert L. Latherow, Chairperson
Affiliation: State-supported college
Accreditation: NASM; MSA; NCATE
Areas: App Mus; Th & An; Orch; Cond; Comp; Intro; Hist & Lit; Mus Ed (Elem & HS)
Degrees: BA, BS, Mus Ed
Comp; Intro; Hist & Lit; Mus Ed (Elem & HS)
Degrees: BA, BS, Mus Ed

NEW MEXICO

COLLEGE OF SANTA FE[1]
Department of Performing Arts
Santa Fe, NM 87501
(505) 473-6011
Staff: John Weckesser, Chairman
Affiliation: Independent church-related college (Christian Brothers)
Accreditation: NCA
Areas: Th & An; Cond; Intro; Hist & Lit; Ethnomusicol
Degrees: BA

EASTERN NEW MEXICO UNIVERSITY
School of Music
Portales, NM 88130
(505) 562-2376
Staff: Paul K. Formo, Director
Affiliation: State-supported university
Accreditation: NASM; NCATE; NCA
Areas: Th & An; Orch; Cond; Comp; Intro; Hist & Lit; Mus Ed (Elem & HS); Theater Mus; Perf; App Mus; Opera; Mus Therapy; Instr Rep; Mus Bus
Degrees: BM; BME
Scholarship: Scholarships available through audition

NEW MEXICO HIGHLANDS UNIVERSITY
Discipline of Music, Division of Fine Arts
National Avenue
Las Vegas, NM 87701
(505) 425-7511, x359
Staff: Dr. Loren E. Wise, Chairman
Affiliation: State-supported university
Accreditation: NCA
Areas: App Mus; Hist & Lit; Th & An; Comp; Cond; Orch; Intro; Mus Ed (Elem & HS); Perf
Degrees: BA; MA
Scholarships: Activity awards for tuition based on audition in wind, percussion, voice, or classical guitar

NEW MEXICO STATE UNIVERSITY
Department of Music
Box 3F, NMSU
Las Cruces, NM 88003
(505) 646-2421
Staff: Warner Hutchison, Head
Affiliation: State-supported university
Accreditation: NASM; NCA
Areas: App Mus; Hist & Lit; Th & An; Comp; Cond; Orch; Opera; Hist Musicol; Intro; Mus Ed (Elem & HS); Electr Mus; Perf
Degrees: BA; BM; BME; MM; MAT
Scholarships: Band grants, choral/vocal scholarships, string scholarships, and keyboard scholarships awarded on the basis of audition and academic standing

UNIVERSITY OF ALBUQUERQUE[1]
Department of Music
St. Joseph Pl., NW
Albuquerque, NM 87140
(505) 831-1111
Staff: Grier Davis, Chairman
Affiliation: Church-related university (Roman Catholic)
Accreditation: NCA
Areas: Th & An; Cond; Intro; Hist & Lit; Mus Ed (Elem)
Degrees: BA; BS, Mus Ed

UNIVERSITY OF NEW MEXICO
Department of Music
Albuquerque, NM 87131
(505) 277-2126
Staff: Dr. Peter L. Ciurczak, Chairman
Affiliation: State-supported university
Accreditation: NASM; NCATE; NCA
Areas: App Mus; Hist & Lit; Th & An; Comp; Cond; Orch; Opera; Hist Musicol; Intro; Mus Ed (Elem & HS); Perf
Degrees: BM; BME; MM; MME
Scholarships: Awards based on live or taped audition plus admission to the university; also on academic achievement, high school graduating rank, or need

WESTERN NEW MEXICO UNIVERSITY
Department of Music
Silver City, NM 88061
(505) 538-6226
Staff: Roger Brandt, Coordinator of Music
Affiliation: State-supported university
Accreditation: NCATE; NCA
Areas: App Mus; Hist & Lit; Th & An; Comp; Cond; Orch; Mus Ed (Elem & HS); Perf
Degrees: BA; BS, Mus Ed
Scholarships: Performance grants for instrumental and vocal, work-study grants, graduate assistantships

NEW YORK

ADELPHI UNIVERSITY[1]
Department of Music

Garden City, NY 11530
(516) 294-8700, x7371
Staff: John Maerhofer, Chairman
Affiliation: Private university
Accreditation: MSA
Areas: Th & An; Cond; Intro; Opera
Degrees: BA

ALFRED UNIVERSITY
Division of Performing Arts
Alfred, NY 14802
(607) 871-2251
Staff: James W. Chapman, Chairperson
Affiliation: Privately endowed university
Accreditation: MSA
Areas: App Mus; Hist & Lit; Th & An; Intro; Theater Mus
Degrees: BA, Perf Arts (concentration in music)
Scholarships: $500 awarded each year to winner of Performing Arts Competition Scholarship, open to high school juniors and seniors if they maintain a 3.0 average in College of Liberal Arts

BARD COLLEGE[1]
Music Department
Annandale-on-Hudson, NY 12504
(914) 758-6169
Staff: B. A. Boretz, Chairperson
Affiliation: Private liberal-arts college
Accreditation: MSA
Areas: Perf; Comp; Improv; Descrip; Aud; Contemplation; Acquaint
Degrees: BA

BARNARD COLLEGE, COLUMBIA UNIVERSITY[1]
Music Department
606 W. 120th St.
New York, NY 10027
(212) 280-2346
Staff: Hubert Doris, Chairman
Affiliation: Private liberal arts college
Accreditation: MSA
Areas: Hist & Lit; Th & An; Comp; Orch; Hist Musicol; Ethnomusicol
Degrees: BA

BROOKLYN COLLEGE OF THE CITY UNIVERSITY OF NEW YORK
Conservatory of Music
Bedford Avenue and Avenue H
Brooklyn, NY 11210
(212) 780-5286
Staff: Prof. Dorothy A. Klotzman, Director
Affiliation: Liberal arts college in a public university system
Accreditation: MSA
Areas: App Mus; Hist & Lit; Th & An; Comp; Cond; Orch; Opera; Hist Musicol; Mus Ed (Elem & HS); Electr Mus Studio
Degrees: BA (Mus or Mus Ed); MA; PhD (through CUNY); BS (Mus Perf or Comp)
Scholarships: Limited scholarships available

THE CITY COLLEGE OF THE CITY UNIVERSITY OF NEW YORK
Music Department
Convent Ave. and W. 138th St.
New York, NY 10031
(212) 690-5411, x5412
Staff: John Graziano, Chairman
Affiliation: Liberal-arts college and school of education in a public university system
Accreditation: MSA
Areas: App Mus; Hist & Lit; Th & An; Comp; Hist Musicol; Ethnomusicol; Mus Ed (Elem & HS); Perf; Cond; Orch; Intro; Jazz & Popular Mus
Degrees: BA; BFA; BS, Mus Ed; MA
Scholarships: Awarded to graduate students and some performance majors

COLGATE UNIVERSITY
Music Department
Hamilton, NY 13346
(315) 824-1000, x645
Staff: Marietta Cheng, Chairman
Affiliation: Privately-endowed, liberal-arts college
Accreditation: MSA
Areas: App Mus; Hist & Lit; Th & An; Comp; Ethnomusicol; Intro; Cond
Degrees: BA

COLLEGE OF ST. ROSE
Music Division
432 Western Avenue
Albany, NY 12203
(518) 454-5178
Staff: J. Robert Sheehan, Chairman
Affiliation: Independent liberal arts college
Accreditation: MSA
Areas: App Mus; Hist & Lit; Th & An; Cond; Orch; Opera; Intro; Mus Ed (Elem & HS); Instr Rep; Electr Mus; Perf; Mus in Special Ed; Studio Mus; Mus Bus
Degrees: BS, Mus Ed; BS, Mus; MA; MS, Mus Ed
Scholarships: Academic scholarships awarded on the basis of performance and scholastic record

THE COLLEGE OF STATEN ISLAND OF THE CITY UNIVERSITY OF NEW YORK
Music Section, Performing & Creative Arts
120 Stuyvesant Pl.
Staten Island, NY 10301
(212) 390-7992
Staff: Prof. Victor H. Mattfeld, Music Section
Affiliation: Comprehensive college within City University of New York
Accreditation: MSA
Areas: Hist & Lit; Th & An; Comp
Degrees: BA; BS, Mus

COLUMBIA UNIVERSITY
Music Department
Broadway and W. 116th St., Dodge Hall
New York, NY 10027
(212) 280-3825
Staff: Prof. Ernest H. Sanders, Chairman
Affiliation: Endowed university
Accreditation: MSA
Areas: App Mus; Hist & Lit; Th & An; Comp; Cond; Orch; Opera; Hist Musicol; Ethnomusicol; Intro; Electr Mus; Perf
Degrees: BA; MA; DMA; PhD
Scholarships: Awarded on the basis of need

CONCORDIA COLLEGE
Division of Literature & Music
171 White Plains Rd.
Bronxville, NY 10708
(914) 337-9300
Staff: James Brauer, Chairman
Affiliation: Private church-related liberal arts college (Lutheran Church, Missouri Synod)
Accreditation: MSA
Areas: App Mus; Hist & Lit; Th & An; Comp; Cond; Hist Musicol; Church Mus; Mus Ed (Elem & HS)
Degrees: BA; BS, Mus Ed
Scholarships: Achievement scholarships available

CORNELL UNIVERSITY[1]
Music Department
Lincoln Hall
Ithaca, NY 14853
(607) 256-4097
Staff: James Webster, Chairman
Affiliation: Privately endowed university
Accreditation: MSA
Areas: App Mus; Hist & Lit; Th & An; Comp; Cond; Orch; Hist Musicol
Degrees: BA; MA; MFA; DMA; PhD

DAEMEN COLLEGE[1]
Department of Music
4380 Main St.
Amherst, NY 14226
(716) 839-3600, x265
Staff: Arthur J. Ness, Chairman
Affiliation: Liberal arts college
Accreditation: MSA
Areas: App Mus; Hist & Lit; Th & An; Comp; Cond; Orch; Opera; Hist Musicol; Mus Ed (Elem & HS); Mus Therapy; Piano Tech; Instr Rep
Degrees: BA; BM; BS, Mus Ed; BA or BS, Mus Therapy minor
Scholarships: Scholarships available

DOWLING COLLEGE[1]
Arts Division, Music Discipline
Oakdale, NY 11769
(516) 589-6100
Staff: Prof. Carlo Lombardi, Coordinator
Affiliation: Private liberal arts college
Accreditation: MSA
Areas: Hist & Lit; Th & An; Opera; Mus Ed (Cert); Perf
Degrees: BA

EASTMAN SCHOOL OF MUSIC
University of Rochester

26 Gibbs St.
Rochester, NY 14604
(716) 275-3040
Staff: Robert Freeman, Director
Affiliation: School of Music in a privately endowed university
Accreditation: NASM; MSA
Areas: App Mus; Hist & Lit; Th & An; Comp; Cond; Orch; Opera; Hist Musicol; Mus Ed (Elem & HS); Electr Mus; Perf; Jazz
Degrees: BA; BM; MA; MM; DMA; PhD
Scholarships: Direct grants, work scholarships, and loans available

EISENHOWER COLLEGE OF ROCHESTER INSTITUTE OF TECHNOLOGY[1]
Music Department, Humanities Program
Seneca Falls, NY 13148
(315) 568-7173
Staff: Charles Warren, Associate Professor of Music
Affiliation: Private college
Accreditation: MSA
Areas: Intro; Hist & Lit; Musicol
Degrees: BA

ELMIRA COLLEGE[1]
Division of Creative Arts
Elmira, NY 14901
(607) 734-3911
Staff: Dr. Roger Held, Director
Affiliation: Private liberal arts college
Accreditation: MSA
Areas: App Mus; Hist & Lit; Th & An; Opera; Theater Mus
Degrees: BA
Scholarships: Roberta Peters Scholarship awarded on the basis of need and ability

THE GRADUATE SCHOOL AND UNIVERSITY CENTER OF THE CITY UNIVERSITY OF NEW YORK
PhD Program in Music
33 W. 42nd St.
New York, NY 10036
(212) 790-4554
Staff: Prof. Barry S. Brook, Executive Officer
Affiliation: City- and state-supported university
Accreditation: NASM; MSA
Areas: Hist & Lit; Th & An; Comp; Hist Musicol; Enthnomusicol
Degrees: PhD
Scholarships: Scholarships available

HAMILTON COLLEGE
Music Department
Clinton, NY 13323
(315) 859-7331
Staff: Prof. Stephen Bonta, Chairman
Affiliation: Private liberal arts college
Accreditation: MSA
Areas: App Mus; Hist & Lit; Th & An; Comp; Cond; Orch; Intro; Electr Mus
Degrees: BA

HARTWICK COLLEGE
Music Department
Oneonta, NY 13820
(607) 432-4200
Staff: Dr. George A. Cavanagh, Chairman
Affiliation: Private liberal-arts college
Accreditation: MSA
Areas: App Mus; Mus Ed (Elem & HS); Perf
Degrees: BA; BS, Mus Ed
Scholarships: Music performance scholarships

HERBERT H. LEHMAN COLLEGE OF THE CITY UNIVERSITY OF NEW YORK
Music Department
Bedford Park Blvd. W
Bronx, NY 10468
(212) 960-8247
Staff: Jack Hyatt, Chairman
Affiliation: State-supported city university
Accreditation: MSA
Areas: App Mus; Hist & Lit; Th & An; Comp; Cond; Orch; Hist Musicol; Mus Ed (Elem & HS)
Degrees: BA; BM
Scholarships: State TAP and BOG grants available

HOBART & WILLIAM SMITH COLLEGES[1]
Music Department
Geneva, NY 14456
(315) 789-5500
Staff: Prof. Nicholas V. D'Angelo, Chairman
Affiliation: Hobart—Church-related liberal arts college (Episcopalian); William Smith—nonsectarian liberal arts college
Accreditation: MSA
Areas: App Mus; Hist & Lit; Th & An; Comp; Cond; Orch; Opera; Hist Musicol; Ethnomusicol; Church Mus; Mus Ed (Elem & HS)
Degrees: BA
Scholarships: Tuition scholarships awarded on the basis of audition and scholarship

HOFSTRA UNIVERSITY
Music Department
1000 Fulton Ave.
Hempstead, NY 11550
(516) 560-5490
Staff: Prof. Edgar Dittemoie, Chairman
Affiliation: Private university
Accreditation: NCATE; MSA
Areas: App Mus; Hist & Lit; Th & An; Comp; Cond; Orch; Opera; Theater Mus; Mus Ed (Elem & HS); Electr Mus; Perf; Mus Merch; Intro; Instr Rep
Degrees: BS, Perf; BS, Comp; BS, Mus Merch; BS, Mus Ed
Scholarships: Grants-in-aid awarded on the basis of performance proficiency and financial need

HOUGHTON COLLEGE
School of Music
Houghton, NY 14744
(716) 567-2211
Staff: Dr. Donald Bailey, Director
Affiliation: Church-related liberal arts college (Wesleyan)
Accreditation: NASM; MSA
Areas: App Mus; Hist & Lit; Th & An; Comp; Cond; Orch; Church Mus; Intro; Mus Ed (Elem & HS); Opera
Degrees: BA; BM
Scholarships: Talent scholarships available to freshmen; achievement scholarships available to seniors

HUNTER COLLEGE OF THE CITY UNIVERSITY OF NEW YORK
Music Department
695 Park Ave.
New York, NY 10021
(212) 570-5736
Staff: Prof. L. Michael Griffel, Chairman
Affiliation: City- and state-supported liberal-arts and teachers college
Accreditation: MSA
Areas: App Mus; Hist & Lit; Th & An; Comp; Cond; Orch; Opera; Hist Musicol; Ethnomusicol; Intro; Mus Ed (Elem & HS); Electr Mus; Perf
Degrees: BA; BM; BS, Mus Ed; Ma
Scholarships: Performance scholarships by audition

ITHACA COLLEGE
School of Music
Ithaca, NY 14850
(607) 274-3171
Staff: Dr. Joel R. Stegall, Dean
Affiliation: Private college
Accreditation: NASM; MSA
Areas: App Mus; Hist & Lit; Th & An; Comp; Cond; Orch; Opera; Mus Ed (Elem & HS); Instr Rep; Intro; Theater Mus; Piano Tech; Electr Mus; Jazz
Degrees: BA; BFA; BM; MM; MS, Mus Ed
Scholarships: Scholarship awards based on need and ability; audition required

THE JUILLIARD SCHOOL
Lincoln Center
New York, NY 10023
(212) 799-5000
Staff: Peter Mennin, President
Affiliation: Privately endowed professional school of music, dance, and drama
Accreditation: MSA
Areas: Th & An; Cond; Comp; Hist & Lit; Opera; Perf
Degrees: BM; MM; DMA; Diploma

KEUKA COLLEGE[1]
Division of Fine Arts
Keuka Park, NY 14478
(315) 536-4411
Staff: Gary Jurysta, Chairman
Affiliation: Private church-related liberal arts college (American Baptist Church)
Accreditation: MSA

Areas: App Mus; Hist & Lit; Th & An; Cond; Mus Ed (Elem & HS)
Degrees: BA; BS, Mus Ed
Scholarships: Awarded to students who qualify for financial aid on the basis of audition

THE KING'S COLLEGE[1]
Music Department
Briarcliff Manor, NY 10510
(914) 941-7200
Staff: James W. Terry, Chairman
Affiliation: Christian liberal arts college (nondenominational)
Accreditation: MSA
Areas: App Mus; Hist & Lit; Th & An; Comp; Cond; Orch; Mus Ed (Elem & HS)
Degrees: BS, Mus Ed; BS, App Mus
Scholarships: Partial tuition scholarships awarded by audition

LONG ISLAND UNIVERSITY, BROOKLYN CENTER
Music Department
University Plaza
Brooklyn, NY 11201
(212) 403-1051
Staff: Jack W. Chaikin, Chairman
Affilication: Private liberal arts college
Accreditation: MSA
Areas: App Mus; Hist & Lit; Th & An; Comp; Opera; Perf; Ensembles; Jazz Studies
Degrees: BA; Performance Certificate
Scholarships: Half and full scholarships in performance; audition required

LONG ISLAND UNIVERSITY, C.W. POST CENTER[1]
Music Department
Greenvale, NY 11548
(516) 299-2474
Staff: Prof. Raoul Pleskow, Chairman
Affiliation: Liberal arts campus of a private university
Accreditation: MSA
Areas: App Mus; Hist & Lit; Th & An; Comp; Cond; Orch; Opera; Intro; Mus Ed (Elem & HS); Mus Therapy; Arts Mgmt; Perf
Degrees: BFA; BS, Mus Ed; MA; MS, Mus Ed
Scholarships: Scholarships related to department ensemble performance awarded by audition

MANHATTAN COLLEGE
Fine Arts Department
Manhattan College Pkwy
Bronx, NY 10471
(212) 920-0372
Staff: Prof. George L. McGeary, Head
Affiliation: Church-related liberal arts college (Catholic)
Accreditation: MSA
Areas: Hist & Lit; Th & An; Intro
Degrees: BA

MANHATTAN SCHOOL OF MUSIC
120 Claremont Ave.
New York, NY 10027
(212) 749-2802
Staff: John O. Crosby, President
Affiliation: Private college-conservatory
Accreditation: NASM; MSA
Areas: App Mus; Hist & Lit; Th & An; Comp; Orch; Opera; Mus Ed (Elem & HS); Electr Mus; Perf
Degrees: BM; MM; DMA
Scholarships: Scholarships applicable to tuition awarded on the basis of talent and performing ability

MANHATTANVILLE COLLEGE
Department of Music
Purchase, NY 10577
(914) 694-2200
Staff: Dr. Anthony La Magra, Director of Music
Affiliation: Private liberal arts college
Accreditation: NASM; MSA
Areas: App Mus; Hist & Lit; Th & An; Comp; Cond; Orch; Opera; Church Mus; Intro; Mus Ed (Elem & HS); Electr Mus; Perf; Jazz
Degrees: BA; BM; B Sacr Mus; MAT

THE MANNES COLLEGE OF MUSIC
157 East 74th St.
New York, NY 10021
(212) 737-0700
Staff: Charles Kaufman, President, Robert Cuckson, Dean
Affiliation: Private college-conservatory
Accreditation: MSA
Areas: App Mus; Hist & Lit; Th & An; Comp; Cond; Orch; Opera; Electr Mus; Perf
Degrees: BM; MM; Diploma, Post-graduate
Scholarships: Full and partial scholarships available to all majors by audition; George Szell Fellowships, full tuition awards for complete degree programs

MERCY COLLEGE[1]
Department of Music and Fine Arts
555 Broadway
Dobbs Ferry, NY 10522
(914) 693-4500
Staff: Joshua Berrett, Chairman
Affiliation: Independent liberal arts college
Accreditation: MSA
Areas: App Mus; Hist & Lit; Th & An; Opera; Church Mus; Mus Ed (Elem)
Degrees: Music offered in cooperation with the Westchester Conservatory of Music

NAZARETH COLLEGE OF ROCHESTER
Music Department
4245 East Ave.
Rochester, NY 14610
(716) 586-2525, x620
Staff: Dr. Thomas J. McGary, Chairman
Affiliation: Independent college
Accreditation: NASM; MSA
Areas: App Mus; Th & An; Orch; Cond; Comp; Intro; Hist & Lit; Musicol; Ethnomusicol; Mus Ed (Elem & HS); Opera; Mus Therapy
Degrees: BS, Mus; BS, Mus Therapy; BS, Mus Ed

NEW YORK UNIVERSITY
Music Department
Washington Square
268 Waverly Building
New York, NY 10003
(212) 598-3431
Staff: David Burrows, Chairman
Affiliation: Private liberal arts college
Accreditation: NASM; MSA
Areas: Hist & Lit; Th & An; Comp; Orch; Hist Musicol; Ethnomusicol
Degrees: BA; MA; PhD
Scholarships: Scholarships available; apply through Office of Financial Aid

NEW YORK UNIVERSITY
School of Education
Room 777 Education Building
35 W. 4th St.
New York, NY 10003
(212) 598-3494
Staff: Roger P. Phelps, Chairman, Department of Music and Music Education
Affiliation: Private Urban university
Accreditation: NASM; NCATE; NAMT; MSA
Areas: App Mus; Th & An; Comp; Cond; Orch; Opera; Mus Ed (Elem & HS); Mus Therapy; Theater Mus; Electr Mus; Perf; Computer Mus; Jazz; Mus Bus & Tech
Degrees: BS, Mus Ed; MA; EdD; PhD; DA
Scholarships: A limited number of scholarships are available through audition

NYACK COLLEGE
Division of Music
Nyack, NY 10960
(914) 358-1710
Staff: Paul F. Liljestrand, Chairman
Affiliation: Church-related Bible college
Accreditation: NASM; MSA
Areas: App Mus; Hist & Lit; Th & An; Comp; Cond; Orch; Church Mus; Mus Ed (Elem & HS)
Degrees: BM; B Sacr Mus
Scholarships: 1 scholarship awarded yearly for student with 2.5 and above GPA; one scholarship awarded every other year to student with 2.5 and above GPA; achievement grants available to new freshmen with outstanding high school achievements

QUEENS COLLEGE OF THE CITY UNIVERSITY OF NEW YORK
Music Department
65-30 Kissena Blvd.
Flushing, NY 11367
(212) 520-7340
Staff: Joel Mandelbaum, Chairman
Affiliation: College in a municipal university sponsored by city and state
Accreditation: MSA
Areas: App Mus; Hist & Lit; Th & An;

Comp; Cond; Orch; Opera; Hist Musicol; Ethnomusicol; Mus Ed (Elem & HS); Theater Mus; Intro; Electr Mus; Perf; Microtonal Mus
Degrees: BA; BM; MA; MS, Mus Ed
Scholarships: Awarded on the basis of academic and outstanding performing abilities

ROBERTS WESLEYAN COLLEGE
Music Department, Division of Fine Arts
2301 Buffalo Rd.
Rochester, NY 14624
(716) 549-9471
Staff: Prof. Robert Shewan, Chairman
Affiliation: liberal-arts college (Free Methodist)
Accreditation: NASM; MSA
Areas: App Mus; Hist & Lit; Th & An; Comp; Cond; Orch; Mus Ed (Elem & HS); Piano Ped; Intro
Degrees: BA; BS, Mus Ed
Scholarships: String scholarships available

ST. LAWRENCE UNIVERSITY
Music Department
Canton, NY 13617
(315) 379-5186
Staff: Dr. Norman Hessert, Chairman
Affiliation: Privately-endowed university
Accreditation: MSA
Areas: App Mus; Hist & Lit; Th & An; Comp; Cond; Ethnomusicol; Perf
Degrees: BA

SARAH LAWRENCE COLLEGE
Music Department
Bronxville, NY 10708
(914) 337-0700
Staff: Prof. Harold Akj, Chairman
Affiliation: Private, liberal-arts college
Accreditation: MSA
Areas: App Mus; Hist & Lit; Th & An; Comp; Cond; Orch; Opera; Intro; Theater Mus; Electr Mus; Perf
Degrees: BA; MFA

SKIDMORE COLLEGE
Department of Music
Saratoga Springs, NY 12866
(518) 584-5000, x604
Staff: Isabelle Williams, Chair
Affiliation: Private college
Accreditation: MSA
Areas: Th & An; Comp; Intro; Hist & Lit; Mus Ed (Elem & HS); App Mus; Orch; Opera; Hist Musicol; Electr Mus; Perf
Degrees: BA; BS, Mus; BS, Mus Ed

STATE UNIVERSITY COLLEGE AT BROCKPORT
Theater Department
Brockport, NY 14420
(716) 395-2319
Staff: Susan E. Edmunds, Chairperson
Affiliation: State university college; liberal arts college
Accreditation: MSA
Areas: Gen Mus; Band; Chorus
Degrees: BA

STATE UNIVERSITY COLLEGE AT BUFFALO
Music Department, Performing Arts Department
1300 Elmwood Ave.
Buffalo, NY 14222
(716) 878-6401
Staff: James F. Mabry III, Chairman
Affiliation: State-supported liberal arts college in the state university system
Accreditation: MSA
Areas: App Mus; Hist & Lit; Th & An; Comp; Cond; Orch; Hist Musicol; Ethnomusicol; Mus Ed (Elem); Jazz Improv; Perf; Intro
Degrees: BA

STATE UNIVERSITY COLLEGE AT CORTLAND
Music Department
Cortland, NY 13045
(607) 753-2811
Staff: Samuel L. Forcucci, Chairman
Affiliation: State-supported university college of liberal arts
Accreditation: MSA; NCATE
Areas: Th & An; Comp; Intro; Hist & Lit; Musicol; Mus Ed (Elem & HS); Church Mus; App Mus
Degrees: BA

STATE UNIVERSITY COLLEGE AT FREDONIA
Department of Music
Fredonia, NY 14063
(716) 673-3151
Staff: Dr. Thomas H. Carpenter, Chairman
Affiliation: College of the State University of New York
Accreditation: NASM; MSA
Areas: App Mus; Hist & Lit; Comp; Cond; Orch; Opera; Hist Musicol; Intro; Mus Ed (Elem & HS); Mus Therapy; Theater Mus; Instr Rep; Electr Mus; Perf
Degrees: BA; BFA; BM; BS, Sound Recording Tech; MM
Scholarships: Small scholarships available to students who show financial need

STATE UNIVERSITY COLLEGE AT GENESEO
Music Department
Geneseo, NY 14454
(716) 245-5824
Staff: Dr. James H. Willey, Chairman
Affiliation: State-supported liberal arts and science college
Accreditation: MSA
Areas: App Mus; Th & An; Orch; Cond; Comp; Hist & Lit; Ethnomusicol; Mus Theater
Degrees: BA

STATE UNIVERSITY COLLEGE AT NEW PALTZ
Music Department
New Paltz, NY 12561
(914) 257-2404
Staff: Martin Sperber, Chairperson
Affiliation: State-supported public college
Accreditation: NASM; NAMT; MSA
Areas: App Mus; Hist & Lit; Mus Therapy; Th & Comp; Intro; Perf
Degrees: BA; BS; BS, Mus Therapy

STATE UNIVERSITY COLLEGE AT ONEONTA
Department of Music
Oneonta, NY 13820
(607) 431-3415
Staff: John P. Mazarak, Chairman
Affiliation: Liberal arts college within the State University of New York
Accreditation: MSA
Areas: App Mus; Hist & Lit; Th & An; Comp; Cond; Orch; Opera; Nonwestern Mus (Intro & Perf)
Degrees: BA
Scholarships: Only general academic scholarships based on federal and state guidelines for need

STATE UNIVERSITY COLLEGE AT OSWEGO[1]
Department of Music
Oswego, NY 13126
(315) 341-2130
Staff: George Cuppernull, Chairperson
Affiliation: State-supported university
Accreditation: MSA; NASM
Areas: App Mus; Hist & Lit; Th & An; Comp; Cond; Orch; Opera; Hist Musicol; Church Mus; Mus Ed (Elem); Theater Mus; Jazz Studies; Counterpt; Ped; Repertoire; Bus and Mus
Degrees: BA; BS (mus in elem educ)
Scholarships: Applied music or composition scholarships for talented students and strings scholarship awarded on the basis of admittance to the college, application, and tape

STATE UNIVERSITY COLLEGE AT POTSDAM
Crane School of Music
Potsdam, NY 13676
(315) 267-2413
Staff: Robert Washburn, Dean of Music
Affiliation: College of a state university
Accreditation: NASM
Areas: App Mus; Hist & Lit; Th & An; Comp; Cond; Orch; Opera; Hist Musicol; Ethnomusicol; Church Mus; Intro; Mus Ed (Elem & Hs); Theater Mus; Instr Rep; Electr Mus; Perf
Degrees: BA; BM; MM
Scholarships: Contact Office of Associate Dean, Crane School of Music, for information

STATE UNIVERSITY COLLEGE AT PURCHASE
School of the Arts, Music Division
Purchase, NY 10577
(914) 253-5000

Staff: Alvin Brehn, Dean of Music
Affiliation: State-supported university campus, comprising a College of Letters and Science and a professional School of the Arts (dance, film, music, television, theater, and the visual arts)
Accreditation: MSA
Areas: App Mus; Hist & Lit; Th & An; Opera; Perf; Comp
Degrees: BFA
Scholarships: Limited scholarships available

STATE UNIVERSITY OF NEW YORK AT ALBANY
Department of Music
1400 Washington Ave.
Albany, NY 12222
(518) 457-3300
Staff: Laurence Farrell, Chairman
Affiliation: State-supported university
Accreditation: MSA
Areas: App Mus; Th & An; Orch; Cond; Comp; Intro; Hist & Lit; Musicol; Instr Rep
Degrees: BA

STATE UNIVERSITY OF NEW YORK AT BINGHAMTON
Music Department
Binghamton, NY 13901
(607) 798-2592
Staff: Albert Hamme, Chairperson
Affiliation: State-supported university
Accreditation: MSA
Areas: App Mus; Hist & Lit; Th & An; Comp; Cond; Orch; Opera; Hist Musicol; Ethnomusical; Perf
Degrees: BA; MA; MM
Scholarships: Assistantships for graduate students

STATE UNIVERSITY OF NEW YORK AT BUFFALO[1]
Department of Music
Buffalo, NY 14260
(716) 831-4116
Staff: Jan Williams, Chairman
Affiliation: State-supported university
Accreditation: NASM; MSA
Areas: Hist & Lit; Th & An; Comp; Mus Ed; Perf
Degrees: BA; BFA; MA; MFA; PhD

STATE UNIVERSITY OF NEW YORK AT STONY BROOK[1]
Music Department
Long Island, NY 11794
(516) 246-5672, 5673
Staff: Billy Jim Layton, Chairman
Affiliation: State-supported university
Accreditation: MSA
Areas: App Mus; Hist & Lit; Th & An; Comp; Cond; Orch; Hist Musicol
Degrees: BA; MA; MM; PhD; DMA

SYRACUSE UNIVERSITY
School of Music
215 Crouse College
Syracuse, NY 13210
(315) 423-2191
Staff: Donald A. Mattran, Director
Affiliation: Privately endowed university
Accreditation: NASM; MSA
Areas: App Mus; Hist & Lit; Th & An; Comp; Cond; Orch; Opera; Mus Ed (Elem & HS); Theater Mus; Electr Mus; Mus Industry; Perf
Degrees: BA; BM; BME; MM; MS, Mus Ed; EdD; PhD
Scholarships: Scholarships available

UNIVERSITY OF ROCHESTER, RIVER CAMPUS COLLEGES[1]
River Campus Station
Rochester, NY 14627
(716) 275-2828
Staff: Dr. Roger Wilhelm, Director of Music, River Campus; Associate Professor, Eastman School of Music
Affiliation: Privately-endowed university. (The School of Music is the Eastman School of Music. The College of Arts & Sciences offers a BA program at the River Campus with the collaboration of the Eastman School.)
Accreditation: MSA
Areas: Hist & Lit; Th & An; (offered by Eastman at the River Campus). All Eastman courses are also open to qualified students.
Degrees: BA

VASSAR COLLEGE
Music Department
Poughkeepsie, NY 12601
(914) 452-7000
Staff: Todd Crow, Chairman
Affiliation: Independent liberal arts college
Accreditation: MSA
Areas: App Mus; Hist & Lit; Th & An; Comp; Hist Musicol; Intro; Electr Mus; Perf
Degrees: BA

WELLS COLLEGE
Division of the Arts
Aurora, NY 13026
(315) 364-3281
Staff: Crawford R. Thoburn, Chairman
Affiliation: Private liberal arts college
Accreditation: MSA
Areas: Th & An; Cond; Hist & Lit; App Mus; Intro; Mus Ed (HS)
Degrees: BA

YORK COLLEGE OF THE CITY UNIVERSITY OF NEW YORK
Music Department
150-14 Jamaica Ave.
Jamaica, NY 11451
(212) 969-4114
Staff: David Ernst, Chairman
Affiliation: College in a city- and state-supported university system
Accreditation: MSA
Areas: App Mus; Th & An; Comp; Intro; Hist & Lit; Mus Ed (Elem & HS); Electr Mus
Degrees: BA; BS, Mus Ed

NORTH CAROLINA

APPALACHIAN STATE UNIVERSITY[1]
Department of Music
Boone, NC 28608
(704) 262-3020
Staff: B.G. McCloud, Chairman
Affiliation: State-supported university
Accreditation: NASM; SACS
Areas: App Mus; Comp; Church Mus; Mus Ed (Elem & HS); Piano Ped; Mus Merch
Degrees: BM; MA, Mus Ed
Scholarships: Applied music scholarships awarded by audition

ATLANTIC CHRISTIAN COLLEGE[1]
W. Lee St.
Department of Music
Wilson, NC 27893
(919) 237-3161
Staff: J. Ross Albert, Chairman
Affiliation: Private church-related liberal arts college (Disciples of Christ)
Accreditation: NASM; SACS
Areas: App Mus; Hist & Lit; Th & An; Comp; Cond; Orch; Opera; Ethnomusicol; Church Mus; Mus Ed (Elem & HS); Piano Tech; Vocal Dict & Ped; Black Gospel; Instr Ped
Degrees: BA; BS, Mus Ed
Scholarships: 8 $4,000 honor scholarships awarded on the basis of performance and GPA; 10 fee waiver scholarships awarded on the basis of performance competition

CAMPBELL UNIVERSITY
Division of Music, Art and Drama
Buie's Creek, NC 27506
(919) 893-4111
Staff: Dr. Paul M. Yoder, Chairman
Affiliation: Church-related liberal arts college (North Carolina Baptist Convention)
Accreditation: SACS
Areas: Th & An; Orch; Cond; Comp; Hist & Lit; Musicol; Mus Ed (Elem & HS)
Degree: BA

CATAWBA COLLEGE
School of Performing Arts
Salisbury, NC 28144
(704) 637-4476
Staff: Hoyt McCachren, Head
Affiliation: Church-related liberal arts college (United Church of Christ)
Accreditation: SACS
Areas: App Mus; Hist & Lit; Th & An; Comp; Cond; Orch; Mus Ed (Elem & HS); Intro
Degrees: BA
Scholarships: Scholarships available through college and School of Performing Arts, awarded by audition and need

DUKE UNIVERSITY
Music Department
Box 6695, College Station

Durham, NC 27708
(919) 684-2534
Staff: Fenner Douglass, Chairman
Affiliation: Privately-endowed university
Accreditation: SACS
Areas: App Mus; Hist & Lit; Th & An; Comp; Cond; Orch; Opera; Hist Musicol; Ethnomusicol; Mus Ed (Elem & HS)
Degrees: BA; MA, Comp; PhD, Musicol
Scholarships: Performance scholarships awarded on the basis of leadership and outstanding musical talent; composition scholarships awarded on the basis of outstanding abilities in student composing; graduate awards

EAST CAROLINA UNIVERSITY
School of Music
Greenville, NC 27834
(919) 757-6851
Staff: Dr. Charles F. Schwartz, Dean
Affiliation: State-supported university
Accreditation: NASM; SACS; NCATE
Areas: App Mus; Th & An; Comp; Church Mus; Mus Ed (Elem & HS); Mus Therapy; Electr Mus; Perf; Piano Ped; Voice Ped; Accomp
Degrees: BA; BM; MM; Certificate, Advanced Study, Mus Ed
Scholarships: Academic scholarships awarded on the basis of performance

ELIZABETH CITY STATE UNIVERSITY
Music Department
Parkview Dr.
Elizabeth City, NC 27909
(919) 335-3359
Staff: Dr. Edna L. Davis, Chairman
Affiliation: State-supported university
Accreditation: SACS
Areas: App Mus; Hist & Lit; Th & An; Comp; Cond; Church Mus; Mus Ed (Elem); Mus Merchandising; Mus Publishing; Arts Mgmt
Degrees: BA
Scholarships: Limited number for talented students, especially recruited for choir, band and music major; out-of-state tuition reduction scholarships available

ELON COLLEGE
Department of Fine Arts
Elon College, NC 27244
(919) 584-9711, x440
Staff: Cardon V. Burnham, Chairman
Affiliation: Church-related college (United Church of Christ)
Accreditation: SACS
Areas: Th & An; Cond; Intro; Hist & Lit; Mus Ed (Elem & HS); Opera; App Mus; Comp; Orch; Theater Mus; Perf
Degrees: BA; BS, Mus Ed
Scholarships: Performance and academic scholarships and awards based on musical and academic performance

GARDNER-WEBB COLLEGE
Department of Fine Arts
Boiling Springs, NC 28017
(704) 434-2361
Staff: Dr. George Robert Cribb, Chairman
Affiliation: Church-related liberal arts college (Baptist)
Accreditation: NASM; SACS
Areas: App Mus; Hist & Lit; Th & An; Cond; Orch; Opera; Church Mus; Intro; Mus Ed (Elem & HS); Perf
Degrees: BA
Scholarships: Talent scholarships awarded by audition

GREENSBORO COLLEGE[1]
Division of Fine Arts
815 W. Market St.
Greensboro, NC 27420
(919) 272-7102
Staff: Frederick Beyer, Chairperson
Affiliation: Church-related liberal arts college (Methodist)
Accreditation: NASM; SACS
Areas: App Mus; Th & An; Orch; Cond; Comp; Intro; Hist & Lit; Mus Ed (Elem & HS); Opera; Church Mus
Degrees: BA; BM; BME

LENOIR-RHYNE COLLEGE
Music Department
Hickory, NC 28601
(704) 328-1741
Staff: E. Ray McNeely, Jr., Chairman
Affiliation: Private liberal arts college (Lutheran—LCA)
Accreditation: NCATE; SACS
Areas: App Mus; Hist & Lit; Th & An; Cond; Orch; Opera; Mus Ed (Elem & HS)
Degrees: BA; BME
Scholarships: Awarded on the basis of personal interview, audition 2-3 recommendations, and school records

MARS HILL COLLEGE
Music Department
Mars Hills, NC 28754
(704) 689-1209
Staff: Wayne Pressley, Chairman
Affiliation: Church-related liberal arts college (Baptist)
Accreditation: NASM; SACS
Areas: App Mus; Hist & Lit; Th & An; Comp; Cond; Church Mus; Mus Ed (Elem & HS); Theater Mus
Degrees: BA; BM
Scholarships: Performance scholarships awarded by audition

MEREDITH COLLEGE
Department of Music and the Performing Arts
Raleigh, NC 27611
(919) 833-6461
Staff: Dr. W. David Lynch, Chairman
Affiliation: Church-related liberal arts college (Baptist)
Accreditation: NASM; SACS
Areas: App Mus; Mus Ed (Elem & HS); Church Mus
Degrees: BA; BM
Scholarships: 5 music talent scholarships awarded each year to incoming freshmen; admission to college, application, and audition required; program stresses talent, previous musical accomplishments, and potential artistic achievement

METHODIST COLLEGE
Music Department
Raleigh Rd.
Fayetteville, NC 28301
(919) 488-7110, x256
Staff: Jean Ishee, Chairman
Affiliation: Church-related liberal arts college (United Methodist)
Accreditation: SACS
Areas: Th & An; Cond; Intro; Hist & Lit; Mus Ed (Elem & HS)
Degrees: BA; BM, Perf; BM, Mus Ed
Scholarships: Music scholarships available

NORTH CAROLINA A & T STATE UNIVERSITY
Department of Music
312 N. Dudley St.
Greensboro, NC 27411
(919) 379-7926
Staff: Clifford E. Watkins, Chairman
Affiliation: State-supported university
Accreditation: SACS
Areas: Th & An; Orch; Cond; Comp; Intro; Hist & Lit; Ethnomusicol; Mus Ed (Elem & HS); Opera; Electr Mus
Degrees: BA; BS, Mus Ed

NORTH CAROLINA CENTRAL UNIVERSITY
Department of Music
1805 Fayetteville St.
Durham, NC 27707
(919) 683-6319
Staff: Prof. Paul Gene Strassler, Chairman
Affiliation: State-supported university
Accreditation: SACS
Areas: App Mus; Hist & Lit; Th & An; Hist Musicol; Church Mus; Jazz; Mus Ed (Elem & HS)
Degrees: BA; BM; MA

NORTH CAROLINA SCHOOL OF THE ARTS
School of Music
PO Box 12189
200 Waughtown St.
Winston-Salem, NC 27117-2189
(919) 784-7170
Staff: Robert Hickok, Dean of Music
Affiliation: State-sponsored institution providing education on the professional level in music, dance, and drama. NCSA includes a Secondary School Division (HS diploma program, grades 7 through 12) as well as a College Division
Accreditation: SACS
Areas: App Mus; Hist & Lit; Th & An; Comp; Cond; Orch; Opera; Perf; Bas Musicianship; Chorus; Perc In; Jazz
Degrees: BM

NORTH CAROLINA STATE UNIVERSITY
Music Department
Box 5937
University Station
Raleigh, NC 27650
(919) 737-2981
Staff: J. Perry Watson, Director of Music
Affiliation: A predominantly scientific and technological state supported university
Accreditation: SACS
Areas: Performing organizations coupled with elective academic courses

NORTH CAROLINA WESLEYAN COLLEGE
Department of Music
Rocky Mount, NC 27801
(919) 442-7121
Staff: Dr. William G. Sasser, Chairman
Affiliation: Church-related liberal arts college (United Methodist)
Accreditation: SACS
Areas: App Mus; Hist & Lit; Th & An; Comp; Cond; Orch; Opera; Church Mus; Intro; Mus Ed (Elem & HS)
Degrees: BA
Scholarships: Tuition and outright grants awarded on the basis of scholarship, talent, and need

PEMBROKE STATE UNIVERSITY
Music Department
Pembroke, NC 28372
(919) 521-4214
Staff: Dr. Robert L. Romine, Chairman
Affiliation: State-supported regional university
Accreditation: NASM; SACS
Areas: App Mus; Hist & Lit; Th & An; Comp; Cond; Orch; Church Mus; Mus Ed (Elem & HS); Electr Mus; Perf
Degrees: BA; BS, Mus Ed
Scholarships: Full-tuition scholarships available for music majors; half-tuition scholarships available for non-music majors; audition required

PFEIFFER COLLEGE
Department of Music
Misenheimer, NC 28109
(704) 463-7343
Staff: Stanley R. Scheer, Head
Affiliation: Church-related liberal arts college (Methodist)
Accreditation: NASM; SACS
Areas: App Mus; Hist & Lit; Th & An; Comp; Cond; Orch; Church Mus; Intro; Mus Ed (Elem & HS); Electr Mus; Perf
Degrees: BA
Scholarships: Awarded on the basis of performance audition

PIEDMONT BIBLE COLLEGE
Department of Music
716 Franklin St.
Winston-Salem, NC 27101
(919) 725-8344, x65
Staff: Gordon A. Smith, Chairman
Affiliation: Private Bible college
Accreditation: AABC
Areas: App Mus; Th & An; Cond; Hist & Lit; Church Mus
Degrees: BM, Church Mus

QUEENS COLLEGE[1]
Department of Fine Arts
1900 Selwyn Ave.
Charlotte, NC 28274
(704) 332-7121
Staff: Dr. George A. Stegner, Chairman
Affiliation: Church-related liberal arts college (Presbyterian)
Accreditation: NASM; SACS; NAMT
Areas: App Mus; Hist & Lit; Th & An; Comp; Cond; Orch; Church Mus; Mus Ed (Elem & HS)
Degrees: BA; BM

ST. ANDREWS PRESBYTERIAN COLLEGE
Music Program
Laurinburg, NC 28352
(919) 276-3652
Staff: Robert Engelson, Chairman
Affiliation: Church-related liberal arts college (Presbyterian)
Accreditation: NASM; SACS
Areas: App Mus; Hist & Lit; Th & An; Cond; Intro; Mus Ed (Elem)
Degrees: BA

ST. AUGUSTINE'S COLLEGE
Department of Music
Oakwood and Tarboro
Raleigh, NC 27611
(919) 828-4451, x313
Staff: Dr. Addison W. Reed, Chairman
Affiliation: Church-related liberal arts college (Episcopal)
Accreditation: SACS
Areas: App Mus; Hist & Lit; Th & An; Cond; Orch; Hist Musicol; Church Mus; Mus Ed (Elem & HS)
Degrees: BA
Scholarships: Awarded by audition

SALEM COLLEGE
School of Music
Winston-Salem, NC 27108
(919) 721-2600
Staff: Clemens Sandresky, Dean
Affiliation: Church-related liberal arts college (Moravian)
Accreditation: NASM; SACS
Areas: App Mus; Hist & Lit; Th & An; Comp; Cond; Orch; Church Mus; Intro; Mus Ed (Elem & HS); Perf
Degrees: BA; BM
Scholarships: Talent scholarships based on competition; B.C. Dunford, renewable scholarships, audition required; Nell Folger Glenn, renewable scholarships; audition required; Vardell scholarships, audition required; H.A. Shirley string scholarships, renewable, audition required; Fogle organ scholarships, audition required

SHAW UNIVERSITY
Department of Music
118 E. South St.
Raleigh, NC 27611
(919) 755-4907
Staff: Dr. Nancy R. Ping-Robbins, Coordinator of Music
Affiliation: Private university
Accreditation: SACS
Areas: App Mus; Hist & Lit; Th & An; Cond; Orch; Intro; Perf; Jazz; Commer Mus; American Mus
Degrees: BA
Scholarships: A.J. Fletcher Foundation Scholarships in Music Performance, based on performance audition and satisfactory academic standing

SOUTHEASTERN BAPTIST THEOLOGICAL SEMINARY
Music Department
Wake Forest, NC 27587
(919) 556-3101
Staff: Prof. Ben Johnson, Director of Music
Affiliation: Church-related seminary
Accreditation: ATS; SACS
Areas: App Mus; Hist & Lit; Cond; Church Mus; Mus Ed (Church); Liturgies; Aesth
Degrees: For music and religious ed majors—MDiv; MRE; D Min
Scholarships: Voice and organ scholarships awarded on the basis of audition; candidates must have bachelor's degree with music major

UNIVERSITY OF NORTH CAROLINA AT CHAPEL HILL
Department of Music
Chapel Hill, NC 27514
(919) 933-1039, 3720
Staff: James W. Pruett, Chairman
Affiliation: State-supported university
Accreditation: SACS
Areas: App Mus; Hist & Lit; Th & An; Comp; Cond; Hist Musicol; Mus Ed
Degrees: BA; BM; BME; MA; MM; PhD
Scholarships: Performance scholarships awarded by audition

UNIVERSITY OF NORTH CAROLINA AT CHARLOTTE[1]
Department of Creative Arts
UNCC Station
Charlotte, NC 28223
(704) 597-2387
Staff: John E. Wrigley, Acting Chairman
Affiliation: State-supported university
Accreditation: SACS
Areas: Th & An; Cond; Comp; Intro; Hist & Lit; Mus Ed (Elem & HS); Opera; Church Mus
Degrees: B Creative Arts

UNIVERSITY OF NORTH CAROLINA AT GREENSBORO
School of Music
Greensboro, NC 27412
(919) 379-5560
Staff: Dr. Robert L. Blocker, Dean
Affiliation: State-supported university
Accreditation: NASM; NCATE; SACS

Areas: App Mus; Hist & Lit; Comp; Cond; Th & An; Orch; Opera; Hist Musicol; Intro; Mus Ed (Elem & HS); Instr Rep; Perf
Degrees: BA; BM; BME; MM; MME; EdD
Scholarships: Annual talent awards of $100 to $1000 for undergraduate students; $900 to $3000 for masters candidates; $4000 for doctorate

UNIVERSITY OF NORTH CAROLINA AT WILMINGTON
Music Division, Department of Creative Arts
PO Box 3725
Wilmington, NC 28401
(919) 791-4330, x70
Staff: Dennis Sporre, Chairman, Department of Creative Arts
Affiliation: State-supported university for liberal and fine arts, sciences, and teaching
Accreditation: SACS
Areas: App Mus; Hist & Lit; Th & An; Comp; Cond; Orch; Intro; Electr Mus
Degrees: BA
Scholarships: Grants-in-aid (full in-state tuition) awarded on the basis of application to Music Division

WAKE FOREST UNIVERSITY
Department of Music
P.O. Box 7345
Winston-Salem, NC 27109
(919) 761-5364
Staff: Susan Borwick, Chairman
Affiliation: Church-related liberal arts university (Baptist)
Accreditation: SACS; NCATE
Areas: Th & An; Cond; Comp; Intro; Hist & Lit; Hist Musicol; App Mus; Church Mus; Mus Ed (Elem & HS); Perf
Degrees: BA
Scholarships: Marie Thornton Willis and Miriam Carlyle Willis Scholarship: music achievement and need; Thane Edward McDonald and Marie Dayton McDonald Memorial Scholarship: music achievement and need

WARREN WILSON COLLEGE[1]
Music Department
Swannanoa, NC 28778
(704) 298-3325
Staff: Dr. Schuyler Robinson, Chairman
Affiliation: Church-related liberal arts college (Presbyterian, USA)
Accreditation: SACS
Areas: App Mus; Hist & Lit; Th & An; Cond; Church Mus; Intro; Mus Ed (Elem & HS); Piano Tech; Perf
Degrees: BA

WESTERN CAROLINA UNIVERSITY
Music Department
Cullowhee, NC 28723
(704) 227-7242
Staff: Dr. Thomas Tyra, Head
Affiliation: State-supported university
Accreditation: SACS; NCATE
Areas: App Mus; Hist & Lit; Th & An; Cond; Orch; Intro; Mus Ed (Elem & HS)
Degrees: BA; BS, Mus Ed; MME
Scholarships: Various scholarships available

WINGATE COLLEGE
Music Department, Division of Fine Arts
Wingate, NC 28174
(704) 233-4061
Staff: Dr. Ron Bostic, Chairman, Division of Fine Arts
Affiliation: Private liberal arts college (Baptist)
Accreditation: NASM; SACS
Areas: App Mus; Hist & Lit; Th & An; Cond; Orch; Church Mus; Intro; Mus Ed (Elem & HS); Instr Rep; Perf
Degrees: AM; BA; BM; BME; BS, Mus-Bus
Scholarships: Scholarships awarded to superior performers

WINSTON-SALEM STATE UNIVERSITY[1]
Department of Music
Winston-Salem, NC 27102
(919) 761-2046
Staff: Dr. Winston A. Bell, Chairman
Affiliation: State-supported university
Accreditation: SACS; NASM
Areas: App Mus; Hist & Lit; Th & An; Comp; Cond; Orch; Church Mus; Mus Ed (Elem & HS); Commer Mus; Studio Rec; Electr Mus
Degrees: BS, Mus Ed
Scholarships: Scholarships available to sophomores and juniors on the basis of performance and academic average

NORTH DAKOTA

DICKINSON STATE COLLEGE
Department of Music
Dickinson, ND 58601
(701) 227-2305
Staff: Dr. Frank C. Pearson, Chairman
Affiliation: State-supported liberal arts and teachers college
Accreditation: NCA: NCATE
Areas: App Mus; Hist & Lit; Th & An; Comp; Cond; Orch; Mus Ed (Elem & HS); Instr Rep; Electr Mus; Intro; Perf
Degrees: BA; BS, Mus Ed
Scholarships: Need and merit scholarships awarded by performance audition

JAMESTOWN COLLEGE[1]
Music Department
Jamestown, ND 58401
(701) 253-2522
Staff: Dr. Richard Smith, Chairman
Affiliation: Church-related liberal arts college (Presbyterian)
Accreditation: NCA
Areas: App Mus; Hist & Lit; Th & An; Cond; Orch; Church Mus; Mus Ed (Elem & HS); Piano Tech; Instr Rep
Degrees: BA
Scholarships: Performance scholarships awarded by auditions on tape or at the campus

MARY COLLEGE
Music Department
Bismarck, ND 58501
(701) 255-4681, x335
Staff: Loran L. Eckroth, Chairman
Affiliation: Private church-related liberal arts college (Roman Catholic)
Accreditation: NCA
Areas: App Mus; Hist & Lit; Th & An; Comp; Cond; Orch; Mus Ed (Elem & HS); Instr Rep
Degrees: BA; BS, Mus Ed
Scholarships: Scholarships ranging from $100 to $2,000 awarded on the basis of music skills and academic potential

MAYVILLE STATE COLLEGE
Music Department
Mayville, ND 58257
(701) 786-2301, x284
Staff: Dr. Anthony Thein, Chairman, Division of Humanities and Social Science
Affiliation: State-supported college
Accreditation: NCA; NCATE
Areas: Th & An; Intro; Hist & Lit; Mus Ed (Elem & HS); App Mus; Perf
Degrees: BA; BS, Mus

MINOT STATE COLLEGE
Division of Music
Minot, ND 58701
(701) 857-3185
Staff: John A. Strohm, Chairman
Affiliation: State-supported college
Accreditation: NASM; NCA; NCATE
Areas: App Mus; Hist & Lit; Th & An; Comp; Cond; Orch; Opera; Hist Musicol; Intro; Mus Ed (Elem & HS); Theater Mus; Piano Tech; Instr Rep; Electr Mus; Perf; Rec Arts
Degrees: BA (music major or mus ed)
Scholarships: Tuition scholarships awarded on the basis of audition, talent, and academic standing

NORTH DAKOTA STATE UNIVERSITY
Music Department
Music Education Center
PO Box 5521
Fargo, ND 58105
(701) 237-7932
Staff: Edwin R. Fissinger, Chairman
Affiliation: State-supported university
Accreditation: NASM; NCA
Areas: App Mus; Hist & Lit; Th & An; Comp; Cond; Orch; Opera; Mus Ed (Elem & HS)
Degrees: BA; BS, Mus Ed
Scholarships: Awarded on the basis of ability and need

UNIVERSITY OF NORTH DAKOTA
Music Department
Grand Forks, ND 58201
(701) 777-2644
Staff: Dr. Reynold J. Krueger, Chairman
Affiliation: State-supported university

Accreditation: NASM; NCA
Areas: App Mus; Hist & Lit; Th & An; Comp; Intro; Mus Ed (Elem & HS); Perf
Degrees: BA; BFA; BM (Perf & Mus Ed); BS, Mus Ed; MA; MEd
Scholarships: Numerous scholarships are available; contact Music Department Chairman

VALLEY CITY STATE COLLEGE
Music Department, Division of Fine Arts
Valley City, ND 58072
(701) 845-7272
Staff: Stuart Glazer, Chairman, Division of Fine Arts
Affiliation: State-supported college
Accreditation: NCA; NCATE
Areas: App Mus; Hist & Lit; Th & An; Comp; Cond; Orch; Church Mus; Mus Ed (Elem & HS); Intro; Electr Mus; Perf
Degrees: BA; BS, Mus Ed
Scholarships: Awarded on the basis of scholarship, performance ability, and need

OHIO

ANTIOCH COLLEGE
Music Department
Yellow Springs, OH 45387
(513) 767-7331, x434
Staff: John Ronsheim, Chairperson
Affiliation: Private liberal arts college
Accreditation: NCA
Areas: App Mus; Hist & Lit; Th & An; Comp; Amer Mus (including Hist Jazz)
Degrees: BA
Scholarships: Scholarships available

ASHLAND COLLEGE
Music Department
Ashland, OH 44805
(419) 289-4085
Staff: Anthony DiBartolomeo, Chairman
Affiliation: Church-related liberal arts college (Brethren)
Accreditation: NASM; NCA
Areas: App Mus; Hist & Lit; Th & An; Comp; Cond; Orch; Opera; Church Mus; Mus Ed (Elem & HS)
Degrees: BA; BM
Scholarships: Scholarships and grants are available to capable and needy students

BALDWIN-WALLACE COLLEGE
Conservatory of Music
96 Front St.
Berea, OH 44017
(216) 826-2375
Staff: Warren A. Scharf, Director, Conservatory of Music
Affiliation: Private liberal arts college (Methodist)
Accreditation: NASM; NCA; NCATE
Areas: App Mus; Hist & Lit; Th & An; Comp; Cond; Orch; Opera; Mus Ed (Elem & HS); Mus Therapy
Degrees: BA; BM; BME

BLUFFTON COLLEGE
Music Department
Bluffton, OH 45817
(419) 358-2461
Staff: Earl W. Lehman, Chairman
Affiliation: Church-related liberal arts college (Mennonite)
Accreditation: NASM; NCA
Areas: App Mus; Hist & Lit; Th & An; Comp; Cond; Orch; Church Mus; Mus Ed (Elem & HS)
Degrees: BA
Scholarships: Awarded on the basis of talent and academic performance

BOWLING GREEN STATE UNIVERSITY[1]
College of Music Arts
Bowling Green, OH 43403
(419) 372-2181
Staff: Kenneth A. Wendrich, Dean
Affiliation: State-supported university
Accreditation: NASM; NCA
Areas: App Mus; Hist & Lit; Th & An; Comp; Cond; Orch; Opera; Hist Musicol; Ethnomusicol; Piano Tech
Degrees: BA; BM; MM

CAPITAL UNIVERSITY
Conservatory of Music
2199 E. Main St.
Columbus, OH 43209
(614) 236-6474
Staff: Larry L. Christopherson, Dean
Affiliation: Church-related, private conservatory-college (American Lutheran)
Accreditation: NASM; NCA
Areas: App Mus; Th & An; Comp; Mus Ed (Elem & HS); Jazz Ens; Church Mus; Intro; Perf
Degrees: BM
Scholarships: Entry music scholarship, up to $2000 per year; 10 endowed scholarships, $200 to $3500 per year

CASE WESTERN RESERVE UNIVERSITY[1]
Department of Music
Haydn Hall
Cleveland, OH 44106
(216) 368-2400
Staff: Dr. John G. Suess, Chairman
Affiliation: Privately endowed university
Accreditation: NASM; NCA
Areas: App Mus; Hist & Lit; Th & An; Hist Musicol; Intro; Mus Ed (Elem & HS); Mus Therapy; Perf; Early Mus Perf Prac
Degrees: BA; BS, Mus Ed; MA; DMA; PhD
Scholarships: Undergraduate university scholarships; graduate fellowships and assistantships

CEDARVILLE COLLEGE
Department of Music
Cedarville, OH 45314
(513) 766-2211
Staff: Dr. David L. Matson, Chairman
Affiliation: Private church-related liberal arts college (Baptist/GARBC)
Accreditation: NCA
Areas: App Mus; Hist & Lit; Th & An; Comp; Cond; Orch; Church Mus; Mus Ed (Elem & HS)
Degrees: BA; BME; BA, Mus Ed
Scholarships: Limited work-study scholarships available to returning students only

CENTRAL STATE UNIVERSITY[1]
Department of Music
Wilberforce, OH 45384
(513) 376-6403
Staff: Dr. William Komla Amoaku, Chairman
Affiliation: State-supported university
Accreditation: NASM; NCA
Areas: App Mus; Hist & Lit; Th & An; Comp; Cond; Orch; Mus Ed; Perf
Degrees: BA; BS, Mus Ed; BM
Scholarships: Scholarship for band and music education majors awarded on the basis of academic achievement

THE CINCINNATI BIBLE SEMINARY
Music Department
2700 Glenway Ave.
Cincinnati, OH 45204
(513) 244-8165
Staff: Byron Cartwright, Field Chairman
Affiliation: Church-related college (nondenominational Christian)
Accreditation: AABC; ATS
Areas: App Mus; Hist & Lit; Th & An; Cond; Church Mus; Mus Ed (Elem); Accomp Tech; Piano Ped; Vocal Ped; Philosophy of the Music Ministry; Hymnology; Basic Keyboard Skills; Church Mus Intership; Mus in Worship & Evangelism; Seminar in Church Mus
Degrees: BM; BS; AS; MMin

THE CLEVELAND INSTITUTE OF MUSIC[1]
11021 East Blvd.
Cleveland, OH 44106
(216) 791-5165
Staff: Grant Johannesen, President; Frank Caputo, Dean
Affiliation: Independent privately supported conservatory of music
Accreditation: NASM; NCA
Areas: App Mus; Hist & Lit; Th & An; Comp; Cond; Orch; Opera; Hist Musicol; Mus Ed (Elem & HS); Electr Mus; Perf
Degrees: BA; BM; BS, Mus Ed; MA; MM; MA, Mus Ed; DMA; PhD

CLEVELAND STATE UNIVERSITY
Music Department
Cleveland, OH 44115
(216) 687-2000
Staff: Dr. Edwin London, Chairman, Music Department
Affiliation: State-supported university
Accreditation: NASM; NCA
Areas: App Mus; Hist & Lit; Th & An; Comp; Cond; Orch; Opera; Hist Musicol; Ethnomusicol; Mus Ed (Elem

& HS); Mus Therapy; Perf
Degrees: BA; BM; MM
Scholarships: Performance scholarships available

COLLEGE OF MOUNT ST. JOSEPH-ON-THE-OHIO
Delhi Pike and Neeb Rd.
Mount St. Joseph, OH 45051
(513) 244-4863
Staff: Dr. Jo Ann Domb, Chairperson
Affiliation: Church-related private college (Roman Catholic)
Accreditation: NASM; NAMT; NCATE; NCA
Areas: Th & An; Orch; Cond; Comp; Mus Therapy; App Mus; Hist & Lit; Intro; Perf; Mus Merch
Degrees: BA, Mus Ed; BA, Mus Therapy; BA, Mus Merch
Scholarships: Orlando Music Scholarship, partial tuition, renewable yearly, based on talent

COLLEGE OF WOOSTER
Music Department
Wooster, OH 44691
(216) 264-1234
Staff: Prof. D. W. Winter, Chairman
Affiliation: Church-related liberal arts college (Presbyterian)
Accreditation: NCA; NASM
Areas: App Mus; Hist & Lit; Th & An; Comp; Mus Ed (Elem & HS); Mus Therapy
Degrees: BA; BM; BME
Scholarships: Scholarships available through competition, based on talent alone; separate scholarships available for financial need

DEFIANCE COLLEGE[1]
Music Department
Defiance, OH 43512
(419) 784-4010
Staff: Richard W. Stroede, Chairman
Affiliation: Church-related liberal arts and teacher education college (United Church of Christ)
Accreditation: NCA
Areas: Th & An; Comp; Intro; Hist & Lit; Mus Ed (Elem & HS); Church Mus
Degrees: BS, Mus; BS, Mus Ed

DENISON UNIVERSITY
Department of Music
Granville, 0H 43023
(614) 587-6220
Staff: Dr. William Osborne, Chairman
Affiliation: Privately endowed college
Accreditation: NASM; NCA
Areas: App Mus; Hist & Lit; Th & An; Comp; Cond; Orch; Opera; Mus Ed (Elem & HS); Intro; Perf
Degrees: BA; BM; BME
Scholarships: 10 scholarships, ranging from $100 to full tuition available

EDGECLIFFE COLLEGE OF XAVIER UNIVERSITY[1]
2220 Victory Pkwy.
Cincinnati, OH 45206
(513) 961-3770
Staff: Helmut J. Roehrig, Chairman
Affiliation: Church-related, liberal arts college (Roman Catholic)
Accreditation: NCA
Areas: Th & An; Cond; Opera
Degrees: BA

FINDLAY COLLEGE[1]
Division of Fine Arts
Findlay, OH 45840
(419) 422-8313, x277
Staff: Barry Alexander, Chairman
Affiliation: Church-related liberal arts college (Churches of God)
Accreditation: NCA
Areas: App Mus; Hist & Lit; Th & An; Comp; Cond; Orch; Mus Ed (Elem & HS)
Degrees: BA; BS, Mus Ed

HEIDELBERG COLLEGE
Department of Music
Tiffin, OH 44883
(419) 448-2505
Staff: Dr. Ferris E. Ohl, Chairman
Affiliation: Endowed liberal arts college affiliated with United Church of Christ
Accreditation: NASM; NCA
Areas: App Mus; Hist & Lit; Th & An; Comp; Cond; Orch; Opera; Church Mus; Intro; Mus Ed (Elem & HS); Theater Mus; Piano Tech; Instr Rep; Electr Mus; Perf; Mus Merch
Degrees: BA; BM; BME
Scholarships: Awarded on the basis of talent, scholarship, and need

HIRAM COLLEGE
Music Department
Hiram, OH 44234
(216) 569-5294
Staff: David F. Atwater, Chairman
Affiliation: Private, liberal-arts college
Accreditation: NASM; NCA
Areas: App Mus; Hist & Lit; Th & An; Mus Ed (Elem & HS); Intro
Degrees: BA
Scholarships: Scholarships available to cover cost of applied music lessons; audition required

JOHN CARROLL UNIVERSITY[1]
Department of Fine Arts
University Heights, OH 44118
(216) 491-4387
Staff: Roger A. Welchans, Chairman
Affiliation: Private church-related liberal arts university operated by the Society of Jesus (Jesuits—Catholic)
Accreditation: NCA; NCATE
Areas: Hist & Lit; Th & An; Opera; Hist Musicol; Church Mus
Degrees: BA

KENT STATE UNIVERSITY
School of Music
Kent, OH 44242
(216) 672-2172
Staff: Dr. Walter Watson, Director
Affiliation: State-supported university
Accreditation: NASM; NCA
Areas: App Mus; Hist & Lit; Th & An; Comp; Cond; Orch; Opera; Hist Musicol; Ethnomusicol; Intro; Mus Ed (Elem & HS); Theater Mus; Electr Mus; Perf
Degrees: BA; BM; MA; MM; PhD
Scholarships: Undergraduate awards based on talent and need; graduate assistantships, teaching fellowships, and other graduate awards based on talent

KENYON COLLEGE
Department of Music
Gambier, OH 43022
(614) 427-2244, x2200
Staff: Dr. Daniel V. Robinson, Chairman
Affiliation: Private liberal arts college
Accreditation: NCA
Areas: App Mus; Hist & Lit; Th & An; Comp; Intro; Perf; Opera; Theater Mus
Degrees: BA
Scholarships: Some scholarships available in applied music, based on financial need

MALONE COLLEGE
Division of Fine Arts
515 25th St., NW
Canton, OH 44709
(216) 489-0800
Staff: Richard D. Mountford, Chairman
Affiliation: Private church-related liberal arts college (Friends Church)
Accreditation: NASM: NCA
Areas: App Mus; Hist & Lit; Th & An; Cond; Orch; Church Mus; Mus Ed (Elem & HS)
Degrees: BA; BS, Mus Ed
Scholarships: Division scholarships available; other scholarships awarded on the basis of GPA

MARIETTA COLLEGE[1]
Edward E. MacTaggart Department of Music
Marietta, OH 45750
(614) 373-4643
Staff: Dr. H. Dean Cummings, Chairman
Affiliation: Privately-supported, liberal-arts college
Accreditation: NCA
Areas: App Mus; Hist & Lit; Th & An; Cond; Orch; Opera; Intro; Mus Ed (Elem & HS)
Degrees: BA

MIAMI UNIVERSITY
Department of Music, School of Fine Arts
Oxford, OH 45056
(513) 529-6010 (Dean)
Staff: Dr. Lawrence DeWitt, Chairman
Affiliation: State-assisted university
Accreditation: NASM; NCA
Areas: App Mus; Hist & Lit; Th & An; Comp; Cond; Orch; Hist Musicol; Intro; Mus Ed (Elem & HS); Electr Mus; Perf
Degrees: BM; MM; AB

Scholarships: Scholarships of full tuition and private lessons awarded by audition

MOUNT UNION COLLEGE
Department of Music
Alliance, OH 44601
(216) 823-3206
Staff: Dr. Lewis A. Phelps, Chairman
Affiliation: Church-related liberal arts college (United Methodist)
Accreditation: NCA; NASM
Areas: App Mus; Hist & Lit; Th & An; Comp; Cond; Orch; Opera; Hist Musicol; Church Mus; Mus Ed (Elem & HS); Perf
Degrees: BA; BM; BME
Scholarships: Proficiency-achievement scholarships awarded on the basis of need and/or ability

MOUNT VERNON NAZARENE COLLEGE
Music Department
Martinsburg Road
Mount Vernon, OH 43050
(614) 397-1244
Staff: Stephen Self, Chairman
Affiliation: Church-related college (Nazarene)
Accreditation: NCA
Areas: App Mus; Hist & Lit; Th & An; Cond; Orch; Opera; Church Mus; Mus Ed (Elem & HS); Instr Rep; Choral Arrang; Vocal & Piano Ped; Intro
Degrees: BA; BA (Mus Ed, Church Mus, Ped)
Scholarships: Activity scholarships awarded to music majors by audition

MUSKINGUM COLLEGE
Department of Creative and Performing Arts
New Concord, OH 43762
(614) 826-8315
Staff: Richard Probert, Chair
Affiliation: Church-related liberal arts college (Presbyterian)
Accreditation: NASM; NCA
Areas: App Mus; Hist & Lit; Th & An; Comp; Cond; Orch; Mus Ed (Elem & HS)
Degrees: BSM; BS, Mus Ed

NOTRE DAME COLLEGE
Music Department
4545 College Rd.
Cleveland, OH 44121
(216) 381-1680
Staff: Madeline Columbro, PhD, Chairman
Affiliation: Church-related liberal arts college (Roman Catholic)
Accreditation: NCA
Areas: App Mus; Hist & Lit; Th & An; Cond; Church Mus; Mus Ed (Elem & HS); Hist Musicol; Intro
Degrees: BA

OBERLIN COLLEGE CONSERVATORY OF MUSIC
Oberlin, OH 44074
(216) 775-8200
Staff: David Boe, Dean
Affiliation: Conservatory; part of a privately-endowed college
Accreditation: NASM; NCA
Areas: App Mus; Hist & Lit; Th & An; Comp; Cond; Orch; Opera; Hist Musicol; Ethnomusicol; Intro; Mus Ed (Elem & HS); Mus Therapy; Electr Mus; Perf
Degrees: BA; BFA; BM; MM; MMT; MME
Scholarships: Awarded on the basis of parents' confidential financial statement

OHIO DOMINICAN COLLEGE
Music Department
1216 Sunbury Rd.
Columbus, OH 43219
(614) 253-7522
Staff: Prof. Michael Pavone, Chairman
Affiliation: Church-related liberal arts college (Roman Catholic)
Accreditation: NCA
Areas: Intro; App Mus; Mus Ed (Elem)
Degrees: No music major offered

OHIO NORTHERN UNIVERSITY
Music Department
525 S. Main St.
Ada, OH 45810
(419) 772-2150
Staff: Dr. Edwin L. Williams, Chairman
Affiliation: Private university
Accreditation: NASM; NCA
Areas: App Mus; Hist & Lit; Th & An; Comp; Cond; Orch; Mus Ed (Elem & HS); Electr Mus; Perf
Degrees: BA; BM; BME
Scholarships: Performance scholarships, high level of performance required; academic scholarships also offered

OHIO STATE UNIVERSITY
School of Music
1899 N. College
Columbus, OH 43210
(614) 422-6571
Staff: Dr. David Meeker, Director
Affiliation: State-supported university
Accreditation: NASM; NCA
Areas: App Mus; Hist & Lit; Th & An; Comp; Cond; Orch; Opera; Hist Musicol; Church Mus; Intro; Mus Ed (Elem & HS); Electr Mus; Perf; Audio Recording
Degrees: BA; BM; BME; MA; MM; MA, Mus Ed; DMA; PhD; BSAR
Scholarships: Talent scholarships available

OHIO UNIVERSITY
School of Music
Athens, OH 45701
(614) 594-5587
Staff: Dr. Gerald J. Lloyd, Director
Affiliation: State-supported university
Accreditation: NASM; NCA
Areas: App Mus; Hist & Lit; Comp; Mus Ed (Elem & HS); Mus Therapy; Perf
Degrees: BA; BM
Scholarships: Fee waivers and endowed scholarships of $100 to full tuition awarded on the basis of talent and scholastic achievement; almost all scholarships awarded without regard to financial need

OHIO WESLEYAN UNIVERSITY
Music Department
Delaware, OH 43015
(614) 369-4431, x700
Staff: Robert A. Griffith, Chairman
Affiliation: Privately controlled, church-related liberal arts college (Methodist)
Accreditation: NASM; NCA
Areas: App Mus; Hist & Lit; Th & An; Cond; Orch; Intro; Mus Ed (Elem & HS); Perf
Degrees: BA; BM
Scholarships: Merit scholarships awarded to music education majors on the basis of audition, interview, and recommendations

OTTERBEIN COLLEGE
Department of Music
Westerville, OH 43081
(614) 890-3000
Staff: Dr. Morton Achter, Chairman
Affiliation: Church-related liberal-arts college (United Methodist)
Accreditation: NASM; NCA; NCATE
Areas: App Mus; Hist & Lit; Th & An; Comp; Cond; Orch; Opera; Church Mus; Mus Ed (Elem & HS); Perf
Degrees: BA; BME
Scholarships: Four-year scholarships of $400 to $2,000 awarded through audition

UNIVERSITY OF AKRON
Music Department
Akron, OH 44325
(216) 375-7590
Staff: Frank Bradshaw, Head
Affiliation: State-supported university
Accreditation: NASM; NCA
Areas: App Mus; Hist & Lit; Th & An; Comp; Cond; Orch; Opera; Hist Musicol; Church Mus; Intro; Mus Ed (Elem & HS); Electr Mus; Perf; Accomp
Degrees: BA; BM; BS, Mus Ed; MM; MME
Scholarships: Scholarships available

UNIVERSITY OF CINCINNATI
College-Conservatory of Music
Cincinnati, OH 45221
(513) 475-3737
Staff: Norman Dinerstein, Dean
Affiliation: Component college of the University of Cincinnati, a state-affiliated university
Accreditation: NASM; NCA
Areas: App Mus; Hist & Lit; Th & An; Comp; Cond; Opera; Hist Musicol; Intro; Mus Ed (Elem & HS); Mus Theater; Electr Mus; Perf; Jazz/Studio Mus; Ballet; Tech Theater; Accomp (grad); Broadcasting; Arts Admin

Degrees: BA; BFA; BM; MA; MM; DMA; PhD; DME
Scholarships: Scholarships awarded through audition, academic strength, needs of the school, etc.

UNIVERSITY OF DAYTON
Music Division
Dayton, OH 45469
(513) 229-3936
Staff: Dr. Richard Benedum, Chairman
Affiliation: Church-related university (Roman Catholic)
Accreditation: NASM; NAMT; NCA
Areas: App Mus; Hist & Lit; Th & An; Comp; Cond; Orch; Intro; Mus Ed (Elem & HS); Mus Therapy; Perf
Degrees: BA; BM; BME
Scholarships: Scholarships available through Music Division and Financial Aid Office

UNIVERSITY OF TOLEDO
Music Department
2801 W. Bancroft St.t
Toledo, OH 43606
(419) 537-2447
Staff: Prof. Bernard Sanchez, Chairman
Affiliation: State-supported university
Accreditation: NASM; NCATE; NCA
Areas: App Mus; Hist & Lit; Th & An; Comp; Cond; Orch; Opera; Intro; Mus Ed (Elem & HS); Electr Mus; Perf
Degrees: BA; BM; BME

URSULINE COLLEGE[1]
Department of Music
2550 Lander Rd.
Pepper Pike, OH 44124
(216) 449-4200
Staff: Sr. Rosemary Hozdic, Chairperson
Affiliation: Church-related liberal-arts college (Roman Catholic)
Accreditation: NCA
Areas: App Mus; Hist & Lit; Th & An; Cond; Orch; Mus Ed (Elem & HS)
Degrees: BA
Scholarships: Renewable scholarship of $500 a year awarded for proficiency in applied instrument—piano, organ, voice, flute

WILBERFORCE UNIVERSITY[1]
Music Department
Wilberforce, OH 45384
(513) 376-2911
Staff: James Argent, Chairman
Affiliation: Private church-related college (African Methodist Episcopal)
Accreditation: NCA
Areas: App Mus; Hist & Lit; Th & An; Comp; Cond; Orch; Mus Ed (Elem & HS); Piano Tech
Degrees: BA; BS, Mus Ed

WITTENBERG UNIVERSITY[1]
School of Music
Springfield, OH 45501
(513) 327-7212
Staff: Dr. Frederick Jackisch, Dean
Affiliation: Church-related liberal arts university (Lutheran Church in America)
Accreditation: NASM; NCA
Areas: App Mus; Hist & Lit; Th & An; Comp; Cond; Opera; Church Mus; Intro; Mus Ed (Elem & HS); Theater Mus; Instr Rep; Perf
Degrees: BA; BM; BME
Scholarships: Scholarships available

WRIGHT STATE UNIVERSITY
Music Department
Dayton, OH 45435
(513) 873-2346
Staff: Sarah O. Johnson, Chairman, Music Department
Affiliation: State-supported university
Accreditation: NASM
Areas: App Mus; Hist & Lit; Th & An; Comp; Cond; Orch; Opera; Hist Musicol; Mus Ed (Elem & HS); Theater Mus; Electr Mus
Degrees: BA; BM; MM
Scholarships: 4-year academic and performance scholarships; graduate assistantships

YOUNGSTOWN STATE UNIVERSITY
Dana School of Music
Youngstown, OH 44555
(216) 742-3636
Staff: Donald W. Byo, Director
Affiliation: State-supported university
Accreditation: NASM; NCATE; NCA
Areas: App Mus; Hist & Lit; Th & An; Comp; Cond; Orch; Opera; Hist Musicol; Intro; Mus Ed (Elem & HS); Theater Mus; Electr Mus; Perf
Degrees: BA; BM; MM
Scholarships: Performance awards up to full tuition, based on auditions; academic awards up to full tuition, based on ACT/SAT scores and academic record

OKLAHOMA

BETHANY NAZARENE COLLEGE
6729 NW 39th Expressway
Bethany, OK 73008
(403) 789-6400, x2212
Staff: Howard G. Oliver, Chairman
Affiliation: Church-related, private college (Church of the Nazarene)
Accreditation: NCA; NCATE
Areas: App Mus; Th & An; Orch; Cond; Intro; Hist & Lit; Mus Ed (Elem & HS); Church Mus
Degrees: BA; BS; BME

CAMERON UNIVERSITY
Department of Performing Arts
2800 W. Gore Blvd.
Lawton, OK 73505
(405) 248-2200, x440
Staff: Dr. Jack Bowman, Chairman
Affiliation: State-supported college
Accreditation: NASM; NCA
Areas: App Mus; Hist & Lit; Th & An; Comp; Cond; Orch; Mus Ed (Elem & HS); Theater Mus
Degrees: BA
Scholarships: Performance scholarships awarded by audition

CENTRAL STATE UNIVERSITY
Music Department
Edmond, OK 73034
(405) 341-2980
Staff: Dr. Clarence E. Garder, Chairman
Affiliation: State-supported college
Accreditation: NCA; NCATE
Areas: App Mus; Hist & Lit; Th & An; Comp; Cond; Orch; Mus Ed (Elem & HS); Hist Musicol; Intro; Perf
Degrees: BM; BME; MME
Scholarships: Scholarships available in the undergraduate performance area; tuition scholarships in voice, piano, instrumental, based on musical ability and financial need

EAST CENTRAL OKLAHOMA STATE UNIVERSITY
Department of Music
Ada, OK 74820
(405) 332-8000
Staff: Douglas Nelson, Chairman
Affiliation: State-supported liberal arts university
Accreditation: NCA; NCATE
Areas: App Mus; Hist & Lit; Th & An; Cond; Orch; Opera; Intro; Mus Ed (Elem & HS); Perf
Degrees: BME
Scholarships: Academic, choral/vocal, and band scholarships available

LANGSTON UNIVERSITY
Music Department
Langston, OK 73050
(405) 466-2231
Staff: Prof. Lemuel Berry, Jr., Chairman
Affiliation: State-supported university
Accreditation: NCA; NCATE
Areas: App Mus; Hist & Lit; Th & An; Cond; Orch; Hist Musicol; Ethnomusicol; Intro; Mus Ed (Elem & HS); Perf
Degrees: BA; BS
Scholarships: Awards of $125 to $400 per semester available for music majors

NORTHEASTERN OKLAHOMA STATE UNIVERSITY[1]
Division of Arts and Letters
Tahlequah, OK 74464
(918) 456-5511, x2503
Staff: Tom Contrill, Chairman
Affiliation: State-supported, liberal arts and teachers college
Accreditation: NCA; NCATE
Areas: App Mus; Hist & Lit; Th & An; Cond; Orch; Mus Ed (Elem & HS)
Degrees: BA; MM, Mus Ed

NORTHWESTERN OKLAHOMA STATE UNIVERSITY
Music Department
Alva, OK 73717
(405) 327-1700

Staff: Ed Huckeby, Chairman
Affiliation: State-supported liberal arts and teacher training university
Accreditation: NCA; NCATE
Areas: App Mus; Hist & Lit; Th & An; Comp; Cond; Orch; Intro; Mus Ed (Elem & HS); Perf
Degrees: BA; BA, Mus Ed; MEd
Scholarships: Scholarships for instrumental music, vocal music, accompanying, and performance awarded on the basis of auditions, recommendations, and need

OKLAHOMA BAPTIST UNIVERSITY[1]
College of Arts
Shawnee, OK 74801
(405) 275-2850, x2306
Staff: James D. Woodward, Dean
Affiliation: Church-related fine- and liberal-arts college (Southern Baptist)
Accreditation: NASM; NCATE
Areas: App Mus; Hist & Lit; Th & An; Comp; Cond; Orch; Opera; Church Mus; Intro; Mus Ed (Elem & HS); Piano Tech; Perf
Degrees: BA; BM; BME; B Sacr Mus
Scholarships: Talentships for voice, piano, and instruments awarded on the basis of talent, ACT, and audition by tape or in person

OKLAHOMA CHRISTIAN COLLEGE
Oklahoma City; OK 73111
(401) 478-1661
Staff: Ken Adams, Director
Affiliation: Private, Christian college
Accreditation: NCA; NCATE
Areas: Th & An; Cond; Intro; Hist & Lit; Mus Ed (Elem & HS); Opera; App Mus; Orch; Intro
Degrees: BME
Scholarships: Full Tuition schoalrships available based on audition

OKLAHOMA CITY UNIVERSITY
School of Music and Performing Arts
2501 N. Blackwelder
Oklahoma City, OK 73106
(405) 521-5315
Staff: Richard E. Thurston, Dean
Affiliation: Privately-endowed university (United Methodist)
Accreditation: NASM; NCA
Areas: App Mus; Hist & Lit; Comp; Cond; Orch; Opera; Mus Ed (Elem & HS); Perf; Th & An; Intro; Church Mus; Theater Mus; Dance
Degrees: BA; BM; BPA; MM; MPA
Scholarships: Music merit scholarships, endowed scholarships, graduate assistantships

OKLAHOMA STATE UNIVERSITY
Department of Music
121 Seretean Center for the Performing Arts
Stillwater, OK 74078
(405) 624-6133
Staff: Dr. James Woodward, Chairman
Affiliation: State-supported land grant university
Accreditation: NASM; NCA
Areas: App Mus; Hist & Lit; Th & An; Comp; Cond; Orch; Opera; Mus Ed (Elem & HS)
Degrees: BA; BM; BME
Scholarships: Service scholarships available to students performing in organizations, to librarians, etc.

ORAL ROBERTS UNIVERSITY[1]
Department of Musc
7777 Lewis Ave.
Tulsa, OK 74171
(918) 495-6161
Staff; E. Macon Delavan, Acting Chairman
Affiliation: Private church-related university (nondenominational)
Accreditation: NCA; NASM
Areas: App Mus; Hist & Lit; Th & An; Comp; Cond; Orch; Opera; Church Mus; Mus Ed (Elem & HS); Piano Tech
Degrees: BA; BM; BME
Scholarships: Talent awards granted by audition

PHILLIPS UNIVERSITY
Fine Arts Division
University Station
Enid, OK 73701
(405) 237-4433, x200, 221
Staff: Dr. Wesley L. McCoy, Chairman
Affiliation: Church-related liberal arts college (Disciples of Christ)
Accreditation: NASM; NCA
Areas: App Mus; Hist & Lit; Th & An; Comp; Cond; Orch; Hist Musicol; Mus Ed (Elem & HS); Mus Therapy; Instr Rep
Degrees: BM; BME
Scholarships: Talent-service scholarships awarded on the basis of skill; academic scholarships awarded on the basis of GPA, ACT

SOUTHEASTERN OKLAHOMA STATE UNIVERSITY
Department of Music
Durant, OK 74701
(405) 924-0121
Staff: Dr. Paul M. Mansur, Chairman
Affiliation: State-supported liberal arts and teachers university
Accreditation: NASM; NCA; NCATE
Areas: App Mus; Th & An; Comp; Church Mus; Mus Ed (Elem & HS)
Degrees: BA; BME; MA, Mus Ed
Scholarships: Service scholarships available for students who have a 2.5 minimum GPA; audition required

SOUTHWESTERN OKLAHOMA STATE UNIVERSITY[1]
Department of Music
Weatherford, OK 73096
(405) 772-6611, x4305
Staff: Dr. James W. Jurrens, Chairman
Affiliation: State-supported teachers college
Accreditation: NASM; NCA
Areas: App Mus; Hist & Lit; Th & An; Comp; Cond; Orch; Opera; Church Mus; Mus Ed (Elem & HS)
Degrees: BA; BME; MM, Mus Ed

UNIVERSITY OF OKLAHOMA
School of Music
560 Parrington Oval
Norman, OK 73019
(405) 325-2081
Staff: Allan Ross, Director
Affiliation: State-supported university
Accreditation: NASM; NCA
Areas: App Mus; Hist & Lit; Th & An; Comp; Cond; Hist Musicol; Intro; Mus Ed (Elem & HS); Perf
Degrees: BFA; BM; BME; MM; MA, Mus Ed; DMA; PhD
Scholarships: Performance, graduate, and undergraduate scholarships awarded by audition

UNIVERSITY OF SCIENCE AND ARTS OF OKLAHOMA
Music Department
Box 3388
Chickasha, OK 73018
(405) 224-3140, x396
Staff: Dr. E. Harvey Jewell, Chairman
Affiliation: State liberal arts university
Accreditation: NASM; NCATE; NCA
Areas: App Mus; Hist & Lit; Th & An; Comp; Cond; Orch; Opera; Intro; Mus Ed (Elem & HS); Theater Mus; Electr Mus
Degrees: BA, Mus; BA, Mus Ed
Scholarships: Awarded annually on the basis of talent, academic and musical achievement, and financial need; audition before the Music Scholarship Committee required

UNIVERSITY OF TULSA
School of Music
600 S. College
Tulsa, OK 74104
(918) 592-6000
Staff: Stephen H. Barnes, Director
Affiliation: Privately endowed university
Accreditation: NCATE; NASM; NCA
Areas: App Mus; Th & An; Comp; Cond; Orch; Opera; Hist Musicol; Mus Ed (Elem & HS); Intro; Electr Mus
Degrees: BA; BM; BME; MM; MME

OREGON

COLUMBIA CHRISTIAN COLLEGE[1]
Fine Arts Department
200 NE 91st Ave.
Portland, OR 97220
(503) 255-7060
Staff: James Bean, Chairman
Affiliation: Private church-related liberal arts college (Church of Christ)
Accreditation: NASC
Areas: App Mus; Hist & Lit; Th & An; Comp; Cond; Orch; Church Mus; Mus Ed (Elem & HS)
Degrees: BA; BA, Mus Ed
Scholarships: Scholarships awarded on the basis of vocal and instrumental audition and GPA

EASTERN OREGON STATE COLLEGE
Humanities Division

8th and K Aves.
La Grande, OR 97850
(503) 963-2171
Staff: John Cobb, Chairman
Affiliation: State-supported liberal arts college
Accreditation: NCATE; NASC
Areas: App Mus; Hist & Lit; Th & An; Comp; Cond; Orch; Opera; Mus Ed (Elem & HS); Theater Mus; Instr Rep
Degrees: BA; BS, Mus Ed

EUGENE BIBLE COLLEGE
Music Department
2155 Bailey Hill Rd.
Eugene, OR 97405
(503) 485-1780
Staff: Darrell Dahlman, Director
Affiliation: Church-related college (Open Bible)
Accreditation: Candidate AABC
Areas: App Mus; Hist & Lit; Th & An; Comp; Cond; Church Mus; Music Internship (Church)
Degrees: BA
Scholarships: Various scholarships available

GEORGE FOX COLLEGE
Division of Fine and Applied Arts
Newberg, OR 97132
(503) 538-8383
Staff: Dr. Dennis B. Hagen, Chairman
Affiliation: Church-related liberal arts college (Friends)
Accreditation: NASM; NASC
Areas: App Mus; Hist & Lit; Th & An; Comp; Cond; Orch; Church Mus; Intro; Mus Ed (Elem & HS); Theater Mus; Perf
Degrees: BA; BS, Mus Ed
Scholarships: Grants-in-aid of $1,200 over a 4-year period awarded by audition; 1 $500 award given to an incoming freshman by audition each year; applied music scholarships covering cost of lessons awarded by audition

LEWIS AND CLARK COLLEGE
School of Music
Portland, OR 97219
(503) 244-6161
Staff: Jerry D. Luedders, Director
Affiliation: Private, liberal-arts college
Accreditation: NASM: NCATE; NASC
Areas: App Mus; Th & An; Comp; Cond; Opera; Ethnomusicol; Church Music; Intro; Mus Ed (Elem & HS); Electr Mus; Perf
Degrees: BA; BM; BME; MM; MME
Scholarships: Auditions required, based on need and/or talent

LINFIELD COLLEGE
Music Department
McMinnville, OR 97128
(503) 472-4121, x275
Staff: Dr. Greg Steinke, Chairman
Affiliation: Church-related liberal arts college (Baptist)
Accreditation: NASM; NASC
Areas: App Mus; Hist & Lit; Th & An; Comp; Mus Ed (Elem & HS); Perf
Degrees: BA
Scholarships: Some awards based on need and talent; others based on talent alone

MARYLHURST COLLEGE FOR LIFELONG LEARNING
Music Division
Marylhurst, OR 97036
(503) 636-8141
Staff: Sr. Lucie Hutchinson, Chairman
Affiliation: Church-related liberal arts college (Catholic)
Accreditation: NASM; NASC
Areas: Hist & Lit; Th & Comp; Perf; Ped; Jazz Studies
Degrees: BA; BM
Scholarships: Federal and state college grants (BEOG); work/study programs

MULTNOMAH SCHOOL OF THE BIBLE
Music Department
8435 NE Glisan
Portland, OR 97220
(503) 255-0332
Staff: Frank A. Eaton, Chairman
Affiliation: Private Bible institute (nondenominational)
Accreditation: AABC
Areas: App Mus; Hist & Lit; Th & An; Comp; Cond; Church Mus; Sight Singing; Mus Internship; Perf
Degrees: B Sacr Mus

OREGON STATE UNIVERSITY[1]
Department of Music
Corvallis, OR 97331
(503) 754-4061
Staff: David Eiseman, Chairman
Affiliation: State-supported land/sea grant university
Accreditation: NASM; NASC
Areas: App Mus; Hist & Lit; Th & An; Comp; Cond; Orch; Hist Musicol; Ethnomusicol; Intro; Mus Ed (Elem & HS); Theater Mus; Electr Mus; Perf
Degrees: BA; BS, Mus Ed; MAIS
Scholarships: Awarded on the basis of audition, academic record, and interview

PACIFIC UNIVERSITY
Music Department
Forest Grove, OR 97116
(503) 357-6151, x251
Staff: Donald Schwejda, Chairman
Affiliation: Privately endowed university
Accreditation: NASM; NASC
Areas: App Mus; Hist & Lit; Th & An; Comp; Cond; Orch; Mus Ed (Elem & HS); Intro; Perf; Theater Mus; Opera
Degrees: BA; BM; BME
Scholarships: Scholarships available to music majors; awards based on academic record and performance ability

PORTLAND STATE UNIVERSITY
Department of Music
PO Box 751
Portland, OR 97207
(503) 229-3011
Staff: Wilma F. Sheridan, Head
Affiliation: State-supported university
Accreditation: NASM; NCATE; NASC
Areas: App Mus; Hist & Lit; Th & An; Comp; Cond; Orch; Opera; Mus Ed (Elem & HS)
Degrees: BA/BS; BA/BS, Mus Ed; MAT/MST
Scholarships: Scholarships for entering undergraduates awarded on the basis of performance; scholarships for continuing undergraduates awarded on the basis of performance and scholarship; scholarships for graduates awarded on the basis of performance and scholarship

REED COLLEGE[1]
Division of the Arts, Department of Music
3203 SE Woodstock Blvd.
Portland, OR 97202
(503) 771-1112
Staff: Judy Massee, Chair, Division of the Arts; Leila Falk, Chair, Dept. of Music
Affiliation: Private liberal arts college
Accreditation: NASC
Areas: App Mus; Hist & Lit; Th & An; Comp; Opera; Hist Musicol
Degrees: BA
Scholarships: 2 scholarships awarded to students in the top 10 percent of the class who demonstrate financial need

SOUTHERN OREGON STATE COLLEGE
Music Department
1250 Siskiyou Blvd.
Ashland, OR 97520
(503) 482-6101
Staff: Stuart Turner, Chairman
Affiliation: State college; part of the Oregon State system of higher education
Accreditation: NASM; NASC
Areas: App Mus; Hist & Lit; Th & An; Comp; Cond; Orch; Opera; Mus Ed (Elem & HS)
Degrees: BA; BS, Mus Ed; BS, Perf; BA, Mus-Bus
Scholarships: Performance scholarships awarded by scholarship committee on the basis of audition on tape and/or in person

UNIVERSITY OF OREGON
School of Music
Eugene, OR 97403
(503) 686-5661
Staff: Dr. Morrette L. Rider, Dean
Affiliation: State-supported university
Accreditation: NASM; NCATE; NASC
Areas: App Mus; Hist & Lit; Th & An; Comp; Cond; Orch; Opera; Hist Musicol; Church Mus; Intro; Mus Ed (Elem & HS); Piano Tech; Electr Mus; Perf; Piano Ped; Mus Bus
Degrees: BA; BM; MM; MA, Mus Ed; DMA; EdD; PhD

Scholarships: Close Competition scholarship of about $75,000 annually awarded by competition in March; Stauffer scholarship of about $25,000 annually awarded by competition in April

UNIVERSITY OF PORTLAND
Department of Performing and Fine Arts
5000 N. Williamette Blvd.
Portland, OR 97203
(503) 283-7228
Staff: Dr. Margaret A. Vance, Chairman
Affiliation: Church-related, privately-endowed university (Roman Catholic)
Accreditation: NASC
Areas: App Mus; Hist & Lit; Th & An; Comp; Cond; Orch; Mus Ed (Elem & HS);
Theater Mus; Intro; Electr Mus; Mus Merch; Mus Mgmt
Degrees: BM; BME; MM; MME

WESTERN BAPTIST COLLEGE[1]
Music Department
5000 Deer Park Dr., SE
Salem, OR 97301
(503) 581-8600, x26
Staff: Robert E. Whittaker, Chairman
Affiliation: Church-related, liberal arts college (Baptist)
Accreditation: AABC; NASC
Areas: App Mus; Hist & Lit; Th & An; Comp; Cond; Orch; Hist Musicol; Church Mus; Mus Ed (Elem & HS)
Degrees: BS, Mus Ed

WESTERN OREGON STATE COLLEGE
Creative Arts Department
Monmouth, OR 97361
(503) 838-1220, x461
Staff: Dr. Ronald L. Wynn, Chairman
Affiliation: State-supported liberal arts college
Accreditation: NASM; NCATE; NASC
Areas: App Mus; Hist & Lit; Th & An; Comp; Cond; Orch; Opera; Hist Musicol; Intro; Mus Ed (Elem & HS); Theater Mus; Electr Mus; Perf
Degrees: BA; BS, Mus Ed; MME

WILLAMETTE UNIVERSITY[1]
Department of Music
Salem, OR 97301
(503) 370-6325
Staff: James Cook, Chairman
Affiliation: Endowed university
Accreditation: NASM; NASC
Areas: App Mus; Hist & Lit; Th & An; Comp; Cond; Orch; Opera; Church Mus; Intro; Mus Ed (Elem & HS); Mus Therapy; Perf
Degrees: BA; BM; BME; BS, Mus Ed
Scholarships: Talent awards based on audition

PENNSYLVANIA

ALLEGHENY COLLEGE
Department of Music
N. Main St.
Meadville, PA 16335
(814) 724-3356
Staff: Robert Bond, Chairperson
Affiliation: Liberal arts college
Accreditation: NASM; MSA
Areas: App Mus; Hist & Lit; Th & An; Cond; Opera; Piano Tech
Degrees: BA

ALVERNIA COLLEGE
Music Department
Reading, PA 19607
(215) 777-5411
Staff: Sr. Mercylle, Director, Music Studies
Affiliation: Private liberal arts college (Roman Catholic)
Accreditation: MSA
Areas: App Mus; Hist & Lit; Th & An; Comp; Cond; Orch; Church Mus; Mus Marketing
Degrees: BA
Scholarships: Scholarships available in piano and voice; piano applicant must prove eligibility and proficiency

BAPTIST BIBLE COLLEGE OF PENNSYLVANIA
Department of Music Ministries
538 Venard Rd.
Clarks Summit, PA 18411
(717) 587-1172
Staff: Dr. Donald P. Ellsworth, Chairman
Affiliation: Church-related private Bible college (Regular Baptist)
Accreditation: AABC; candidate MSA
Areas: App Mus; Hist & Lit; Th & An; Comp; Cond; Church Mus; Mus Ed (Elem & HS)
Degrees: B Sacr Mus

BEAVER COLLEGE[1]
Music Department
Glenside, PA 19038
(215) 884-3500, x364
Staff: William V. Frabizio, Chairman
Affiliation: Church-related, liberal arts college (Presbyterian)
Accreditation: MSA
Areas: App Mus; Hist & Lit; Th & An; Comp; Cond; Orch; Opera; Mus Ed (Elem)
Degrees: BA

BLOOMSBURG STATE COLLEGE
Department of Music
Bloomsburg, PA 17815
(717) 389-4284
Staff: Dr. Stephen Wallace, Chairman
Affiliation: State-supported liberal arts and teachers college
Accreditation: MSA; NCATE
Areas: App Mus; Hist & Lit; Th & An; Cond; Orch; Opera; Intro; Mus Ed (Elem); Theater Mus; Perf
Degrees: BA
Scholarships: Application required

BRYN MAWR COLLEGE
Music Department
Bryn Mawr, PA 19010
(215) 645-6235
Staff: Isabell Cazeaux, Chairman
Affiliation: Private liberal arts college with graduate School of Arts and Sciences and graduate School of Social Work
Accreditation: MSA
Areas: Hist & Lit; Hist Musicol
Degrees: BA (Music major offered at Haverford College, with advanced courses in Hist and Musicol offered at Bryn Mawr); PhD (no new candidates accepted)
Scholarships: Scholarships awarded for senior year, graduate studies, or traveling on the basis of excellent academic work

BUCKNELL UNIVERSITY
Music Department
Lewisburg, PA 17837
(717) 524-1216
Staff: Dr. Jackson Hill, Head
Affiliation: Privately supported university
Accreditation: NASM; MSA
Areas: App Mus; Hist & Lit; Th & An; Comp; Cond; Orch; Hist Musicol; Ethnomusicol; Mus Ed (Elem & HS)
Degrees: BA; BM
Scholarships: Vocal and instrumental performance scholarships awarded on the basis of academic standing and musical ability; music scholarships for majors; talent grants irrespective of major

CARNEGIE MELLON UNIVERSITY
Department of Music
Schenley Park
Pittsburgh, PA 15213
(412) 678-2372
Staff: Harry Franklin, Head
Affiliation: Privately-endowed university
Accreditation: NASM; MSA
Areas: App Mus; Hist & Lit; Th & An; Comp; Cond; Orch; Opera; Hist Musicol; Mus Ed (Elem & HS); Theater Mus
Degrees: BFA; MFA; MFA, Mus Ed

CHESTNUT HILL COLLEGE
Department of Music
Philadelphia, PA 19118
(215) 248-7000
Staff: Sr. Marie Therese Cogan, Chairman
Affiliation: Church-related liberal-arts college (Roman Catholic)
Accreditation: NASM; MSA
Areas: App Mus; Hist & Lit; Th & An; Comp; Cond; Orch; Opera; Intro; Mus Ed (Elem & HS); Perf
Degrees: BA; BS, Mus Ed

CLARION STATE COLLEGE[1]
Department of Music
Clarion, PA 16214
(814) 226-2287, 2288
Staff: Milutin Lazich, Chairman
Affiliation: State-supported liberal arts,

business, communication, library media, and professional education studies college
Accreditation: MSA; NCA
Areas: App Mus; Hist & Lit; Th & An; Comp; Cond; Orch; Opera; Intro; Mus Ed (Elem & HS); Perf
Degrees: BM; BS, Mus Ed
Scholarships: Frank Lesser Scholarship; Presidents Award for Talented Youth; Music Department Scholarship; String Scholarship; Music Activity Fund Scholarship

COLLEGE MISERICORDIA
Music Department
Dallas, PA 18612
(717) 675-2181
Staff: Ms. Betty W. Porzuczek, Chairman
Affiliation: Private liberal arts college (Sisters of Mercy)
Accreditation: NAMT; NASM; MSA
Areas: App Mus; Hist & Lit; Th & An; Comp; Cond; Orch; Mus Ed (Elem & HS); Mus Therapy
Degrees: BA; BM
Scholarships: Performance scholarships available

THE CURTIS INSTITUTE OF MUSIC[1]
1726 Locust St.
Philadelphia, PA 19103
(215) 893-5252
Staff: John de Lancie, Director
Affiliation: Private college-conservatory
Accreditation: NASM
Areas: App Mus; Hist & Lit; Th & An; Comp; Orch; Opera; Perf
Degrees: BM
Scholarships: All students are on full scholarship

DICKINSON COLLEGE
Music Department
Carlisle, PA 17013
(717) 245-1568
Staff: Truman Bullard, Chairman
Affiliation: Private liberal arts college
Accreditation: MSA
Areas: App Mus; Hist & Lit; Th & An; Comp; Opera; Hist Jazz; Biog Studies; Early Mus Perf Prac
Degrees: BA
Scholarships: Alfred Swan applied music scholarship awarded on the basis of need and outstanding promise

DUQUESNE UNIVERSITY
School of Music
Pittsburgh, PA 15282
(412) 434-6080
Staff: Michael Kumer, Acting Dean
Affiliation: Church-affiliated university (Roman Catholic)
Accreditation: NASM; MSA
Areas: App Mus; Hist & Lit; Th & An; Comp; Cond; Orch; Opera; Ethnomusicol; Mus Ed (Elem & HS); Church Mus; Intro; Mus Therapy; Theater Mus; Piano Tech; Perf
Degrees: BM; BS, Mus Ed; MM; MME
Scholarships: Sixty music awards per year, based on academic and musical excellence

EDINBORO UNIVERSITY OF PENNSYLVANIA
Music Department
Edinboro, PA 16444
(814) 732-2555
Staff: Dr. William Alexander, Chairman
Affiliation: State-supported university
Accreditation: NASM; MSA
Areas: App Mus; Hist & Lit; Th & An; Comp; Cond; Orch; Opera; Hist Musicol; Ethnomusicol; Mus Ed (Elem & HS)
Degrees: BA; BS, Mus Ed

ELIZABETHTOWN COLLEGE
Music Department
Elizabethtown, PA 17022
(717) 367-1151
Staff: Carl N. Shull, Chairman
Affiliation: Church-related college (Church of the Brethren)
Accreditation: NASM; MSA; NAMT
Areas: App Mus; Hist & Lit; Th & An; Cond; Hist Musicol; Mus Ed (Elem & HS); Mus Therapy; Orch; Intro
Degrees: BA; BS, Mus Ed; BS, Mus Therapy
Scholarships: Scholarships available upon audition

GENEVA COLLEGE
Department of Music
Beaver Falls, PA 15010
(412) 846-5100, x247
Staff: Robert M. Copeland, Chairman
Affiliation: Church-related college (Reformed Presbyterian)
Accreditation: MSA
Areas: App Mus; Th & An; Orch; Cond; Comp; Hist & Lit; Mus Ed (Elem & HS); Intro; Mus Bus; Gen Mus
Degrees: BA; BS, Mus Ed
Scholarships: Five per year, half-tuition, renewable for four years to music majors in good standing

GETTYSBURG COLLEGE
Music Department
Gettysburg, PA 17325
Staff: Robert F. Zellner, Chairman
Affiliation: Church-related liberal arts college (Baptist)
Accreditation: MSA
Areas: App Mus; Hist & Lit; Th & An; Comp; Cond; Orch; Opera; Mus Ed (Elem & HS); Intro; Perf
Degrees: BA; BS, Mus Ed

GROVE CITY COLLEGE
Department of Music and Fine Arts
Grove City, PA 16127
(412) 458-6600
Staff: Oscar A. Cooper, Chairman
Affiliation: Church-related liberal-arts college (Presbyterian)
Accreditation: App Mus; Hist & Lit; Th & An; Cond; Orch; Church Mus; Mus Ed (Elem & HS)
Areas: BM

HAVERFORD COLLEGE
Music Department
Haverford, PA 19041
(215) 896-1008
Staff: John Davison, Chairman
Affiliation: Private liberal arts college established by the Religious Society of Friends but no longer formally affiliated; a strong Quaker tradition still exists
Accreditation: MSA
Areas: App Mus; Hist & Lt; Th & An; Comp; Hist Musicol; Ethnomusicol (Jazz); Intro
Degrees: BA

IMMACULATA COLLEGE
Music Department
Immaculata, PA 19345
(215) 647-4400
Staff: Sr. Jean Anthony, Chairman
Affiliation: Church-related liberal arts college (Roman Catholic)
Accreditation: NASM; NAMT; MSA
Areas: App Mus; Hist & Lit; Th & An; Comp; Cond; Orch; Hist Musicol; Church Mus; Mus Ed (Elem & HS); Mus Therapy
Degrees: BA; BME
Degrees: Full-tuition scholarship available

INDIANA UNIVERSITY OF PENNSYLVANIA
Music Department
Indiana, PA 15701
(412) 357-2390
Staff: Dr. Richard S. Knab, Chairman
Affiliation: State-owned university
Accreditation: NASM; MSA
Areas: App Mus; Hist & Lit; Th & An; Comp; Cond; Orch; Opera; Hist Musicol; Mus Ed (Elem & HS); Theater Mus; Perf; Intro
Degrees: BA; BFA; BS, Mus Ed; MA; MA, Mus Ed
Scholarships: Several scholarships available, awarded on varying bases

JUNIATA COLLEGE[1]
Department of Music
Huntingdon, PA 16652
(814) 643-4310
Staff: Mary Ruth Linton, Chairperson
Affiliation: Private independent liberal arts college
Accreditation: MSA
Areas: App Mus; Hist & Lit; Th & An; Cond; Orch; Opera; Church Mus; Theater Mus
Degrees: BA
Scholarships: Rebecca S. Funk Scholarship of $500, Barbara A. Linton Scholarship of $200, John W. Linton Scholarship of $350, Ruth W. Philips Memorial Music Scholarship Fund of $800, and Eva W. Swigart Scholarship of $1,000 all based on need

KUTZTOWN STATE COLLEGE
Music Department
Kutztown, PA 19530

(215) 683-4475
Staff: Dr. Edwin Schatkowsky, Chairperson
Affiliation: State-owned institution
Accreditation: MSA
Areas: App Mus; Hist & Lit; Th & An; Comp; Cond; Hist Musicol; Mus Ed (Elem)
Degrees: BA; BFA

LAFAYETTE COLLEGE
Department of Music
Williams Center for the Arts
Easton, PA 18042
(215) 250-5000
Staff: William E. Melin, Associate Professor and Head
Affiliation: Church-related liberal arts college (Presbyterian)
Accreditation: MSA
Areas: App Mus; Hist & Lit; Th & An; Comp; Orch; Hist Musicol; Ethnomusicol; Intro
Degrees: BA

LANCASTER BIBLE COLLEGE[1]
Church Music Department
901 Eden Rd.
Lancaster, PA 17601
(717) 569-7071
Staff: Warren W. Whitney, Chairman
Affiliation: Church-related college (nondenominational)
Accreditation: AABC; MSA
Areas: App Mus; Hist & Lit; Th & An; Cond; Ethnomusicol; Church Mus; Intro
Degrees: BS, Bible (emphasis in Church Mus)

LA SALLE COLLEGE
Division of Fine Arts
Philadelphia, PA 19141
(215) 951-1000
Staff: George K. Diehl, Chairman
Affiliation: Private liberal arts college
Accreditation: MSA
Areas: Hist & Lit; Th & An; Comp; Orch; Opera
Areas: BA

LEBANON VALLEY COLLEGE
Music Department
Annville, PA 17003
(717) 867-4411
Staff: Dr. Robert C. Lau, Chairman
Affiliation: Church-related liberal arts college (United Methodist)
Accreditation: NASM; MSA
Areas: App Mus; Hist & Lit; Th & An; Comp; Cond; Orch; Mus Ed (Elem & HS)
Degrees: BA; BS, Mus Ed; BM
Scholarships: Only institutional scholarships are available; awarded on the basis of on-campus testing, status in the upper 1/5 of high school class, and satisfactory SAT scores

LEHIGH UNIVERSITY[1]
Department of Music
Lamberton Hall, Number 34
Bethlehem, PA 18015
(215) 861-3835
Staff: Prof. Jerry T. Bidlack, Chairman
Affiliation: Independent university
Accreditation: MSA
Areas: Hist & Lit; Th & An; Comp; Hist Musicol; Electr Mus Studio/Comp
Degrees: BA

LOCK HAVEN STATE COLLEGE[1]
Music Department
Lock Haven, PA 17745
(717) 893-2137
Staff: Dr. Faith H. NcNitt, Chairman
Affiliation: State-supported college
Accreditation: MSA
Areas: App Mus; Hist & Lit; Th & An; Cond; Ethnomusicol; Intro; Mus Ed (Elem); Theater Mus; Perf
Degrees: BA
Scholarships: Scholarships for band and for music majors awarded on the basis of application and audition (for entering students)

LYCOMING COLLEGE
Music Department
Williamsport, PA 17701
(717) 326-1951, x265
Staff: Fred Thayer, Chairman
Affiliation: Church-related college (United Methodist)
Accreditation: MSA
Areas: Th & An; Cond; Intro; Hist & Lit; App Mus; Comp; Orch; Electr Mus; Perf
Degrees: BA
Scholarships: Music fellowships; choral and keyboard recipients do not have to be music majors, auditions required

MANSFIELD STATE COLLEGE
Music Department
Mansfield, PA 16933
(717) 662-4080
Staff: Donald A. Stanley, Chairman
Affiliation: State-supported liberal arts and teachers college
Accreditation: NASM; MSA; NCATE
Areas: App Mus; Hist & Lit; Th & An; Comp; Cond; Orch; Opera; Hist Musicol; Mus Ed (Elem & HS); Mus Therapy
Degrees: BA; BS, Mus Ed; BM

MARYWOOD COLLEGE
Music Department
2300 Adams Ave.
Scranton, PA 18509
(717) 348-6268
Staff: Sr. M. Jeremy Hornung, Chairperson
Affiliation: Church-related liberal arts college (Roman Catholic)
Accreditation: NSAM; MSA; NAMT; NCATE
Areas: App Mus; Hist & Lit; Th & An; Cond; Orch; Hist Musicol; Church Mus; Intro; Mus Ed (Elem & HS); Mus Therapy; Perf
Degrees: BA; BM; MA; BA Perf Arts
Scholarships: Talent scholarships awarded by audition on major instrument or voice

MERCYHURST COLLEGE
d'Angelo School of Music
501 E. 38th St.
Erie, PA 16546
(814) 825-0362
Staff: Dr. Louis A. Mennini, Director
Affiliation: Private liberal arts college
Accreditation: NASM; MSA
Areas: App Mus; Hist & Lit; Th & An; Comp; Cond; Orch; Opera; Hist Musicol; Mus Ed (Elem & HS)
Degrees: BA; BM
Scholarships: Merit, financial aid, and competitive scholarships available

MESSIAH COLLEGE
Music Department
Grantham, PA 17027
(717) 766-2511
Staff: Dr. Ronald L. Miller, Chairman
Affiliation: Church-related, liberal-arts college (Brethren)
Accreditation: MSA
Areas: App Mus; Mus Ed (Elem & HS)
Degrees: BA; BS, Mus Ed
Scholarships: Awards made through all-college President's Scholarships

MILLERSVILLE STATE COLLEGE
Music Department
Millersville, PA 17551
(717) 872-3357
Staff: Dr. Paul G. Fisher, Chairman
Affiliation: State-supported liberal arts and teachers college
Accreditation: NASM; NCATE; MSA
Areas: App Mus; Church Mus; Hist & Lit; Th & An; Comp; Cond; Orch; Intro; Mus Ed (Elem & HS)
Degrees: BA; BS, Mus Ed
Scholarships: Scholarships available to freshmen only; audition required

MORAVIAN COLLEGE
Music Department
Bethlehem, PA 18018
(215) 861-1459
Staff: Monica Schantz, Chairman
Affiliation: Church-related liberal arts college (Moravian)
Accreditation: MSA; ATS
Areas: App Mus; Hist & Lit; Th & An; Comp; Cond; Orch; Opera; Church Mus; Mus Ed (Elem & HS); Electr Mus; Intro; Perf
Degrees: BA; BM
Scholarships: General scholarships awarded on the basis of audition, ability, and need

MUHLENBERG COLLEGE[1]
Music Department
Allentown, PA 18104
(215) 433-3191
Staff: Dr. Charles McClain, Music Head
Affiliation: Church-related, liberal arts college (Lutheran Church in America)
Accreditation: MSA; NCATE
Areas: App Mus; Hist & Lit; Th & An; Comp; Opera; Church Mus
Degrees: BA

THE NEW SCHOOL OF MUSIC
301 S. 21st St.
Philadelphia, PA 19103
(215) 732-3966
Staff: Tamara Brooks, President
Affiliation: Private college-conservatory
Accreditation: MSA
Areas: App Mus; Hist & Lit; Th & An; Comp; Cond; Perf
Degrees: BM
Scholarships: Scholarships of partial to full tuition based on potential for professional musical development

THE PENNSYLVANIA STATE UNIVERSITY
School of Music
232 Music Building
University Park, PA 16802
(814) 865-0431
Staff: Prof. Maureen A. Carr, Director
Affiliation: State-supported university
Accreditation: NASM; MSA
Areas: App Mus; Hist & Lit; Th & An; Comp; Cond; Orch; Hist Musicol; Intro; Mus Ed (Elem & HS); Electr Mus; Perf
Degrees: BA; BM; BS, Mus Ed; MA; MM; MA, Mus Ed; EdD
Scholarships: Available in music

PHILADELPHIA COLLEGE OF BIBLE
Music Department
Langhorne Manor
Langhorne, PA 19047
(215) 752-5800, x329
Staff: Dr. Ronald Alan Matthews, Chairman
Affiliation: Bible college (Protestant-Interdenominational)
Accreditation: NASM; MSA; AABC
Areas: App Mus; Hist & Lit; Th & An; Comp; Cond; Orch; Hist Musicol; Church Mus; Intro; Perf; Electr Mus
Degrees: BM; BS, Bible
Scholarships: Freshman scholarships awarded by audition to outstanding entering freshmen; award scholarships granted to outstanding performers already in course given on recommendation of faculty

PHILADELPHIA COLLEGE OF THE PERFORMING ARTS[1]
250 S. Broad St.
Philadelphia, PA 19102
(215) 875-2202
Staff: Joseph Castaldo, President
Affiliation: Private, independent college of performing arts
Accreditation: NASM; MSA
Areas: App Mus; Th; Comp; Opera; Mus Ed (Elem & HS); Dance; Dance Ed; Perf
Degrees: BM; BM-BME; MM; BFA, Dance/Dance Ed; MFA, Dance
Scholarships: Awards based on audition, GPA of 3.00, and financial need

ST. VINCENT COLLEGE[1]
Music Department
Latrobe, PA 15650
(412) 539-9761
Staff: Joseph P. Bronder, Chairman
Affiliation: Church-related, liberal arts college (Roman Catholic)
Accreditation: MSA
Areas: Coop with Seton Hill College; App Mus; Hist & Lit; Th & An; Comp; Cond; Orch; Opera; Church Mus; Mus Ed (Elem & HS)
Degrees: BM

SETON HILL COLLEGE[1]
Department of Music
Greensburg, PA 15601
(412) 834-2200
Staff: George L. Dadisman, Chairman
Affiliation: Church-related, liberal arts college (Roman Catholic)
Accreditation: NASM; MSA
Areas: App Mus; Hist & Lit; Th & An; Cond; Orch; Intro; Mus Ed (Elem & HS); Comp
Degrees: BM

SLIPPERY ROCK STATE COLLEGE
Music Department
Slippery Rock, PA 16057
(412) 794-7276
Staff: Mr. Dwight B. Baker, Chairman
Affiliation: State-supported college
Accreditation: NASM; MSA; NCATE; NAMT
Areas: App Mus; Hist & Lit; Th & An; Comp; Cond; Orch; Hist Musicol; Intro; Mus Ed (Elem); Mus Therapy; Theater Mus; Perf
Degrees: BA; BM; BS, Mus Therapy
Scholarships: College-sponsored scholarships available through audition and individual endowments

SUSQUEHANNA UNIVERSITY[1]
Department of Music
Selinsgrove, PA 17870
(717) 374-0101
Staff: Galen Deibler, Chairman
Affiliation: Church-related liberal arts college (Luthern Church in America)
Accreditation: NASM; MSA
Areas: App Mus; Hist & Lit; Th & An; Comp; Cond; Orch; Opera; Church Mus; Intro; Mus Ed (Elem & HS)
Degrees: BA; BM; B Sacr Mus
Scholarships: Scholarships available

SWARTHMORE COLLEGE
Music Department
Swarthmore, PA 19081
(215) 447-7233
Staff: James Freeman, Chairman
Affiliation: Private liberal arts college
Accreditation: MSA
Areas: App Mus; Hist & Lit; Th & An; Comp; Cond; Opera; Hist Musicol; Ethnomusicol; Intro; Perf
Degrees: BA
Scholarships: Available to qualified performers

TEMPLE UNIVERSITY
College of Music
Philadelphia, PA 19122
(215) 787-8301
Staff: Helen Laird, Dean
Affiliation: Privately endowed and state-affiliated university
Accreditation: NASM; MSA
Areas: App Mus; Hist & Lit; Th & An; Comp; Cond; Opera; Hist Musicol; Intro; Mus Ed (Elem & HS); Mus Therapy; Electr Mus; Perf; Piano Tech
Degrees: BA; BM; BME; MM; MA, Mus Ed; DMA; PhD
Scholarships: Full and partial scholarships available

THIEL COLLEGE[1]
Department of Music
Greenville, PA 16125
(412) 588-7700
Staff: Marlowe W. Johnson, Chairman
Affiliation: Church-related, liberal arts college (Lutheran Church in America)
Accreditation: MSA
Areas: App Mus; Hist & Lit; Th & An; Comp; Cond; Orch; Opera; Church Mus; Mus Therapy; Mus Ed (Elem & HS)
Degrees: BA

UNITED WESLEYAN COLLEGE
Music Department
1414 E. Cedar St.
Allentown, PA 18103
(215) 439-8709
Staff: Faith Ingles, Chairman
Affiliation: Church-related college (Wesleyan)
Accreditation: AABC; Candidate MSA
Areas: App Mus; Hist & Lit; Th & An; Comp; Cond; Church Mus; Perf
Degrees: BS, Mus Ed; BSM
Scholarships: Scholarships available

UNIVERSITY OF PENNSYLVANIA[1]
Music Department
201 S. 34th St.
Philadelphia, PA 19104
(215) 243-7544
Staff: Eugene Narmour, Chairman
Affiliation: Private university
Accreditation: MSA
Areas: Hist & Lit; Th & An; Comp; Cond; Hist Musicol
Degrees: BA; MA; PhD

UNIVERSITY OF PITTSBURGH
Music Department
Bigelow and Fifth
Pittsburgh, PA 15260
(412) 621-4126
Staff: Dr. Don O. Franklin, Chairman
Affiliation: State-related university
Accreditation: MSA
Areas: App Mus; Hist & Lit; Th & An; Comp; Cond; Orch; Hist Musicol; Ethnomusicol; Electr Mus; Jazz; Opera
Degrees: BA; MA; PhD
Scholarships: 1 scholarship awarded to outstanding senior

VALLEY FORGE CHRISTIAN COLLEGE[1]
Music Department
Charlestown Rd.

Phoenixville, PA 19460
(215) 935-0450
Staff: Lena Mae Leach, Chairman
Affiliation: Northeastern regional college of the Assemblies of God
Accreditation: AABC
Areas: App Mus; Hist & Lit; Th & An; Comp; Cond; Orch; Church Mus
Degrees: B Sacr Mus
Scholarships: Peter Natoli Music Scholarship; keyboard scholarship, usually divided between a male student and a female student

WEST CHESTER STATE COLLEGE[1]
School of Music
West Chester, PA 19380
(215) 436-2628
Staff: Irving H. Cohen, Acting Director
Affiliation: State-supported college
Accreditation: NASM; NCATE; MSA
Areas: App Mus; Hist & Lit; Th & An; Comp; Cond; Opera; Mus Ed (Elem & HS); Hist Musicol; Perf; Intro; Theater Mus; Electr Mus
Degrees: BA; BM; BS, Mus Ed; MA; MM
Scholarships: Instrumental and vocal scholarships; awards in performance and conducting

WESTMINSTER COLLEGE[1]
Department of Music
New Wilmington, PA 16142
(412) 946-8761, x301
Staff: Dr. Clarence J. Martin, Chairman
Affiliation: Church-related liberal arts college (Presbyterian)
Accreditation: MSA; NASM
Areas: App Mus; Hist & Lit; Th & An; Comp; Cond; Orch; Church Mus; Intro; Mus Ed (Elem & HS); Perf
Degrees: BA; BM
Scholarships: Awarded on the basis of talent and need

WILKES COLLEGE
Department of Music
170 S. Franklin St.
Wilkes-Barre, PA 18703
(717) 824-4651
Staff: Terrance Anderson, Chairman
Affiliation: Independent liberal arts college
Accreditation: MSA
Areas: App Mus; Hist & Lit; Th & An; Comp; Mus Ed (Elem & HS); Perf
Degrees: BA; BM; BS
Scholarships: Music scholarships up to full tuition based on academic and musical proficiency, personal audition

WILSON COLLEGE[1]
Division of Visual & Performing Arts
Chambersburg, PA 17201
(717) 264-4141
Affiliation: Church-related liberal arts college (Presbyterian)
Accreditation: MSA
Areas: App Mus; Hist & Lit; Th & An; Comp (Ind Study); Cond; Hist Musicol; Intro
Degrees: BA

YORK COLLEGE OF PENNSYLVANIA[1]
Department of Humanities and Fine Arts
Country Club Road
York, PA 17405
(717) 846-7788
Staff: Dr. Paul Diener, Chairman
Affiliation: Private, liberal-arts college
Accreditation: MSA
Areas: App Mus; Hist & Lit; Th & An; Orch; Mus Ed (Elem)
Degrees: BA
Scholarships: Awarded on the basis of need; application required

RHODE ISLAND

BARRINGTON COLLEGE
Division of Fine Arts, School of Music
Middle Highway
Barrington, RI 02806
(401) 246-1200
Staff: Dr. Douglas E. Schoen, Chairman
Affiliation: Private Christian liberal arts college
Accreditation: NASM; NEA
Areas: App Mus; Th & An; Cond; Intro; Hist & Lit; Mus Ed (Elem & HS); Opera; Church Mus; Comp; Orch; Theater Mus; Perf; Hist Jazz
Degrees: BA; BM

BROWN UNIVERSITY[1]
Music Department
1 Young Orchard St.
Providence, RI 02912
(401) 863-3234
Staff: Prof. David Josephson, Chairman
Affiliation: Privately endowed university
Accreditation: NEA
Areas: App Mus; Hist & Lit; Th & An; Comp; Hist Musicol; Ethnomusicol
Degrees: BA; MA; PhD

PROVIDENCE COLLEGE
Academic Program in Music
Providence, RI 02918
(401) 865-1000
Staff: Rosaline Y. Chua, Music Program Director
Affiliation: Private church-related liberal arts college
Accreditation: NEA
Areas: App Mus; Hist & Lit; Th & An; Comp; Orch; Church Mus; Intro; Theater Mus; Perf
Degrees: BA

RHODE ISLAND COLLEGE
Music Department
Providence, RI 02908
(401) 831-6600
Staff: Dr. Robert W. Elam, Chairman
Affiliation: State-supported liberal-arts and teachers college
Accreditation: NASM; NCATE; NEA
Areas: App Mus; Hist & Lit; Th & An; Comp; Cond; Orch; Opera; Intro; Mus Ed (Elem & HS); Mus Therapy; Theater Mus; Perf
Degrees: BA; BM; BS, Mus Ed; MAT
Scholarships: Audition required for special talent awards, Bicho Scholarship, and string scholarships

UNIVERSITY OF RHODE ISLAND
Department of Music
Kingston, RI 02881
(401) 792-2431
Staff: John R. Heard, Chairman
Affiliation: State-supported university
Accreditation: NASM; NEA
Areas: App Mus; Hist & Lit; Th & An; Comp; Mus Ed (Elem & HS); Perf
Degrees: BA; BM; MM
Scholarships: Various scholarships awarded through audition

SOUTH CAROLINA

BAPTIST COLLEGE AT CHARLESTON[1]
Department of Music
P.O. Box 10087
Charleston, SC 29411
(803) 797-4107
Staff: David W. Cuttino, Jr., Chairman
Affiliation: Church-related liberal arts college (Southern Baptist)
Accreditation: NASM; SACS
Areas: App Mus; Hist & Lit; Th & An; Comp; Cond; Orch; Church Mus; Mus Ed (Elem & HS); Mus Therapy
Degrees: BA
Scholarships: Scholarships of full and half tuition available for voice, piano, and orchestra

BENEDICT COLLEGE[1]
Division of Fine Arts
Blanding and Harding Sts.
Columbia, SC 29204
(803) 256-4220
Staff: Dr. Walter Yeh, Chairman
Affiliation: Private liberal arts college
Accreditation: SACS
Areas: Th & An; Intro; Mus Ed (HS)
Degrees: BA

BOB JONES UNIVERSITY
Division of Music, School of Fine Arts
Greenville, SC 29614
(803) 242-5100
Staff: Dr. Edward Dunbar, Chairman
Affiliation: Private, nonsectarian Christian university
Accreditation: State
Areas: App Mus; Th & An; Comp; Hist & Lit; Cond; Orch; Opera; Hist Musicol; Church Mus; Intro; Mus Ed (Elem & HS); Perf
Degrees: BA; BS, Mus Ed; MA; MFA

CENTRAL WESLEYAN COLLEGE[1]
Division of Humanities
Central, SC 29630
(803) 639-2453
Staff: Gloria Bell, Chairman
Affiliation: Church-related liberal arts college (Wesleyan Church)
Accreditation: SACS
Areas: App Mus; Hist & Lit; Th & An;

Cond; Orch; Church Mus; Mus Ed (Elem & HS)
Degrees: BA
Scholarships: National Merit Scholars and semifinalists may attend with full-tuition scholarship; members of the Wesleyan Church are given 10-percent reduction in tuition

CLAFLIN COLLEGE
Department of Music
Orangeburg, SC 29115
(803) 534-2710, x47
Staff: Fredricka R. Young, Chairman
Affiliation: Church-related college (United Methodist)
Accreditation: SACS
Areas: Th & An; Cond; Hist & Lit; Mus Ed (Elem & HS); App Mus; Comp; Orch
Degrees: BA; BA, Mus Ed
Scholarships: Music aid for choir and band; tuition awards based on audition and competition

CLEMSON UNIVERSITY
Department of Music
Strode Tower
Clemson, SC 29631
(803) 656-3043
Staff: Dr. John H. Butler, Head
Affiliation: State-supported university
Accreditation: SACS
Areas: App Mus; Hist & Lit; Th & An; Orch; Mus Ed (Elem); Perf; American Mus

COKER COLLEGE
Department of Music
Hartsville, SC 29550
(803) 332-1381, x438
Staff: Kenneth L. Wilmot, Director
Affiliation: Privately endowed liberal arts college
Accreditation: NASM; SACS
Areas: App Mus; Mus Ed (Elem & HS); Intro; Hist & Lit; Th & An; Cond
Degrees: BA

COLUMBIA COLLEGE[1]
Department of Music
Columbia, SC 29203
(803) 786-3761
Staff: James L. Caldwell, Chairman
Affiliation: Private, independent, church-related liberal arts college for women
Accreditation: NASM; SACS
Areas: App Mus; Church Mus; Mus Ed; Piano Ped
Degrees: BA; BM

CONVERSE COLLEGE
School of Music
E. Main St.
Spartanburg, SC 29301
(803) 585-6421
Staff: Henry Janiec, Dean
Affiliation: Private liberal arts college
Accreditation: NASM; SACS
Areas: App Mus; Hist & Lit; Th & An; Comp; Cond; Orch; Opera; Hist Musicol; Mus Ed (Elem & HS); Piano Ped
Degrees: BA; BM; MM
Scholarships: Partial scholarships awarded by audition; full range of academic scholarships awarded on the basis of need

ERSKINE COLLEGE
Music Department
Due West, SC 29639
(803) 379-8829
Staff: Miss Shirley Lampson, Chairman
Affiliation: Church related, liberal-arts college (A.R. Presbyterian)
Accreditation: SACS
Areas: App Mus; Hist & Lit; Th & An; Cond; Church Mus; Mus Ed (Elem & HS); Piano Ped
Degrees: BA; BS
Scholarships: Harriette E. Spivey Scholarship of $1,000; W. A. Anthony Scholarship of $500; plus other scholarships up to $2,000 per year awarded for exceptional musical ability; auditions required for all

FURMAN UNIVERSITY
Music Department
Poinsett Hwy.
Greenville, SC 29613
(803) 294-2086
Staff: Dr. Frank Little, Chairman
Affiliation: Church-related liberal-arts college (Southern Baptist)
Accreditation: NASM; SACS
Areas: App Mus; Hist & Lit; Th & An; Cond; Orch; Opera; Church Mus; Intro; Mus Ed (Elem & HS); Perf
Degrees: BA; BM
Scholarships: $200 to $1,000 per year awarded on the basis of competitive auditions held in January

LANDER COLLEGE
Music Department
Greenwood, SC 29646
(803) 229-8323
Staff: Dr. Anthony Lenti, Chairman
Affiliation: State-supported college
Accreditation: SACS
Areas: App Mus; Hist & Lit; Th & An; Cond; Orch; Intro; Mus Ed (Elem & HS)
Degrees: BME
Scholarship: Scholarships available through entrance tests and audition

LIMESTONE COLLEGE
Division of Fine Arts
Gaffney, SC 29340
(803) 489-7151
Staff: Robert B. Welch, Chairman
Affiliation: Privately-endowed college
Accreditation: NASM; SACS
Areas: App Mus; Hist & Lit; Th & An; Comp; Cond; Orch; Hist Musicol; Mus Ed (Elem & HS); Piano Tech; Accomp; Mus Appr
Degrees: BA
Scholarships: Performance scholarships available

NEWBERRY COLLEGE
Music Department
2100 College St.
Newberry, SC 29108
(803) 276-5010
Staff: Dr. George Sistrunk, Chairman
Affiliation: Private church-related liberal arts college (Lutheran Church in America)
Accreditation: NASM; SACS
Areas: Th & An; Perf; Church Mus; Arts Mgmt; Comp; Cond; Orch; Hist Musicol; Mus Ed (Elem & HS); Piano Class; Band; Choir; String Class; Experiential Learning; Mus Mgmt Internship; Piano Ped; Counterpt; Ind Study; Analytical Listening; Church Mus
Degrees: BA; BM; BME
Scholarships: Small to full scholarships awarded on the basis of talent by audition

PRESBYTERIAN.COLLEGE
Department of Fine Arts
Clinton, SC 29325
(803) 833-2820
Staff: Dr. Charles T. Gaines, Chairman
Affiliation: Church-related liberal arts college (Presbyterian)
Accreditation: SACS
Areas: App Mus; Hist & Lit; Th & An; Church Mus; Mus Ed (Elem & HS)
Degrees: BA (Fine Arts or Mus)
Scholarships: Five renewable music scholarships of from $1,000 to $1,500 awarded on the basis of audition; other scholarships also available

SOUTH CAROLINA STATE COLLEGE
Music Department
Orangeburg, SC 29117
(803) 536-7101
Staff: Dr. Arthur L. Evans, Chairman
Affiliation: State-supported liberal arts and teachers college
Accreditation: SACS; NCATE
Areas: App Mus; Hist & Lit; Th & An; Cond; Orch; Mus Ed (Elem & HS)
Degrees: BS, Mus Ed

UNIVERSITY OF SOUTH CAROLINA[1]
Department of Music
Columbia, SC 29208
(803) 777-4280
Staff: Dr. William J. Moody, Chairman
Affiliation: State-supported university
Accreditation: SACS; NASM
Areas: App Mus; Hist & Lit; Comp; Th & An; Cond; Opera; Intro; Mus Ed (Elem & HS); Electr Mus; Perf
Degrees: BA; BM; BME; MM; MME
Scholarships: Awarded to music majors; apply to Department of Music

UNIVERSITY OF SOUTH CAROLINA, AT COASTAL CAROLINA
Music Department
P.O. Box 1954
Conway, SC 29526
(803) 347-3161

Staff: Carolyn G. Cox, Chairman
Affiliation: Credit branch of the University of South Carolina, four year program
Accreditation: SACS
Areas: App Mus; Mus Hist; Th & An; Cond; Mus Ed (Elem & HS)
Degrees: BA (Mus Ed); BA (Mus; Interdisciplinary Studies)
Scholarships: Audition for applied music scholarships

WINTHROP COLLEGE
School of Music
Rock Hill, SC 29733
(803) 323-2255
Staff: Dr. Jess T. Casey, Dean
Affiliation: State-supported college
Accreditation: NASM; SACS
Areas: App Mus; Hist & Lit; Th & An; Cond; Opera; Church Mus; Intro; Mus Ed (Elem & HS); Piano Ped; Perf
Degrees: BM; BME; MM; MME
Scholarships: 4-year scholarships of varying amounts awarded through competition

SOUTH DAKOTA

AUGUSTANA COLLEGE
Department of Music
Sioux Falls, SD 57197
(605) 336-5451
Staff: Dr. Walter B. May, Chairman
Affiliation: Church-related liberal arts college (American Lutheran)
Accreditation: NASM; NCATE; NCA
Areas: App Mus; Hist & Lit; Th & An; Comp; Cond; Orch (instr arrang); Opera; Mus Ed (Elem & HS)
Degrees: BA
Scholarships: Scholarships of $600 to $6,000 (4 years) available to candidates who pass a performance audition and interview; maintenance of scholarship depends on progress in music study and performance as well as acceptable academic progress

BLACK HILLS STATE COLLEGE
Division of Fine Arts
Spearfish, SD 57783
(605) 642-6626
Staff: Dr. Victor Weidensee, Chairman
Affiliation: State-supported liberal arts and teacher education college
Accreditation: NCA; NCATE; NASM
Areas: App Mus; Hist & Lit; Th & An; Cond; Orch; Opera; Mus Ed (Elem & HS)
Degrees: BA; BS, Mus Ed

DAKOTA STATE COLLEGE
Music Department, Division of Humanities
Madison, SD 57042
(605) 256-3551
Staff: Dr. Donald J. Larsen, Coordinator
Affiliation: State-supported; primarily a teachers college
Accreditation: NCA
Areas: App Mus; Hist & Lit; Th & An; Comp; Cond; Orch; Mus Ed (Elem & HS); Perf
Degrees: BS, Mus Ed; BS, Mus
Scholarships: Performance scholarships available

MOUNT MARTY COLLEGE[1]
Music Department
Yankton, SD 57078
(605) 668-1011
Staff: John A. Lyons, Chairman
Affiliation: Church-related liberal arts college (Roman Catholic)
Accreditation: NCA; NCATE
Areas: App Mus; Hist & Lit; Th & An; Comp; Cond; Church Mus; Mus Ed (Elem & HS)
Degrees: BA
Scholarships: Awarded through audition

NORTHERN STATE COLLEGE
Music and Drama Department, Division of Arts and Sciences
Aberdeen, SD 57401
(605) 622-2497
Staff: Lonn M. Sweet, Chairman
Affiliation: State-supported college
Accreditation: NASM; NCA
Areas: App Mus; Hist & Lit; Th & An; Comp; Cond; Intro; Mus Ed (Elem & HS); Perf
Degrees: BA; BME; BS
Scholarships: Awards based on scholarship and performance

SIOUX FALLS COLLEGE
Department of Fine Arts
Sioux Falls, SD 57101
(605) 331-6628
Staff: Kerchal Armstrong, Chairman
Affiliation: Church-related liberal arts college (American Baptist)
Accreditation: NCA; NCATE
Areas: App Mus; Hist & Lit; Th & An; Comp; Cond; Hist Musicol; Mus Ed (Elem & HS)
Degrees: BA
Scholarships: Awarded by audition

SOUTH DAKOTA STATE UNIVERSITY
Music Department
Brookings, SD 57007
(605) 688-5187
Staff: Dr. Warren G. Hatfield, Head
Affiliation: State-supported university
Accreditation: NASM; NCATE; NCA
Areas: App Mus; Hist & Lit; Th & An; Comp; Cond; Orch; Opera; Mus Ed (Elem & HS); Jazz; Intro; Theater Mus; Instr Rep; Electr Mus; Perf
Degrees: BA; BME
Scholarships: Performance scholarships awarded by audition

UNIVERSITY OF SOUTH DAKOTA[1]
Department of Music
Vermillion, SD 57069
(605) 677-5274
Staff: Dennis Ondrozeck, Chairman
Affiliation: State-supported university
Accreditation: NASM; NCA
Areas: App Mus; Hist & Lit; Th & An; Comp; Cond; Orch; Opera; Hist Musicol; Intro; Mus Ed (Elem & HS); Perf
Degrees: BFA; MM
Scholarships: Wide range of scholarships available, from $100 to $600 per academic year

YANKTON COLLEGE
Conservatory of Music
12th and Douglas
Yankton, SD 57078
(605) 665-3661
Staff: J. Laiten Weed, Director
Affiliation: Church-related liberal arts college (United Church of Christ-Congregational)
Accreditation: NASM; NCA
Areas: App Mus; Hist & Lit; Th & An; Comp; Cond; Orch; Intro; Mus Ed (Elem & HS); Theater Mus; Perf; Mus Bus; Mus Mgmt
Degrees: BA; BM
Scholarships: Some full tuition scholarships, Presidential Scholarships, Dean's Music Schoalrships, talent scholarships; based on auditions, admittance to college, financial need; talent, grade point average

TENNESSEE

AUSTIN PEAY STATE UNIVERSITY
Music Department
Clarksville, TN 37040
(615) 648-7818
Staff: Dr. Solie Fott, Chairman
Affiliation: State-supported university
Accreditation: NASM; NCATE; SACS
Areas: App Mus; Hist & Lit; Th & An; Comp; Cond; Orch; Opera; Intro; Mus Ed (Elem & HS); Perf
Degrees: BA; BS, Mus Ed; MME
Scholarships: Performance-work scholarships awarded by audition

BELMONT COLLEGE
Music Department
Belmont Blvd.
Nashville, TN 37203
(615) 383-7001
Staff: Dr. Jerry L. Warren, Chairman
Affiliation: Church-related liberal arts college (Southern Baptist)
Accreditation: NASM; SACS
Areas: App Mus; Hist & Lit; Th & An; Comp; Cond; Church Mus; Intro; Mus Ed (Elem & HS); Theater Mus; Perf; Orch; Opera; Electr Mus; Commer Mus; Piano Ped
Degrees: BA; BM; BME; BM, Church Mus; BM, Piano Ped; BM, Commer Mus; BM, The & Comp
Scholarships: Awarded on the basis of performance ability and high academic achievements

BRYAN COLLEGE[1]
Division of Fine Arts
Bryan Hill
Dayton, TN 37321
(615) 775-2041, x288
Staff: David Friberg, Chairman
Affiliation: Private liberal arts college (Interdenominational)
Accreditation: SACS
Areas: App Mus; Hist & Lit; Th & An; Comp; Cond; Orch; Opera; Church Mus; Mus Ed (Elem)
Degrees: BA; BS, Mus Ed

CARSON-NEWMAN COLLEGE
Music Department
Jefferson City, TN 37760
(615) 475-9061
Staff: Dr. Louis O. Ball, Jr., Chairman
Affiliation: Church-related liberal arts college (Tennessee Baptists)
Accreditation: NASM; NCATE; SACS
Areas: App Mus; Comp; Church Mus; Mus Ed (Elem & HS); Theater Mus; Piano Ped
Degrees: BA; BM
Scholarships: Scholarships of $300 to $800 awarded on the basis of talent and need; audition required

COVENANT COLLEGE
Music Department
Lookout Mountain, TN 37350
(404) 820-1560
Staff: Craig A. Parker, Chairman
Affiliation: Church-related liberal arts college (Presbyterian Church in America)
Accreditation: SACS
Areas: App Mus; Hist & Lit; Th & An; Comp; Cond; Orch; Opera; Hist Musicol; Church Mus; Mus Ed (Elem & HS); Instr Rep (Strings)
Degrees: BA; BM; BME
Scholarships: Awarded on the basis of performance proficiency and need

DAVID LIPSCOMB COLLEGE
Department of Music
Nashville, TN 37203
(615) 385-3855
Staff: James Jackson, Chairman, Department of Music
Affiliation: Church-related college (Church of Christ)
Accreditation: SACS
Areas: App Mus; Th & An; Orch; Cond; Intro; Hist & Lit; Mus Ed (Elem & HS)
Degrees: BA; BS, Mus Ed

EAST TENNESSEE STATE UNIVERSITY
Department of Music
Johnson City, TN 37614
(615) 929-4270
Staff: Dr. Richard Compton, Chairman
Affiliation: State-supported university
Accreditation: NASM; SACS
Areas: App Mus; Hist & Lit; Th & An; Comp; Cond; Orch; Opera Workshop; Hist Musicol; Church Mus; Intro; Mus Ed (Elem & HS); Perf
Degrees: BA; BME; BS, Mus Ed
Scholarships: Work-study program (Tennessee residents); college work-study program; regular student work program; performance scholarships awarded through the Friends of Music, ETSU Foundation

FISK UNIVERSITY
Department of Music
17th Ave. N.
Nashville, TN 37203
(615) 329-8528
Staff: Valija Bumbulis, Acting Chairman
Affiliation: Private liberal arts college
Accreditation: NASM; SACS
Areas: App Mus; Hist & Lit; Cond; Orch; Hist Musicol; Ethnomusicol; Intro; Mus Ed (Elem & HS); Perf; Opera
Degrees: BA; BM; BS, Mus Ed
Scholarships: Very limited scholarships available; awards based on financial need, aptitude and promise, GPA, and performance in music courses

FREED-HARDEMAN COLLEGE[1]
Department of Music
158 E. Main St.
Henderson, TN 38340
(901) 989-5269
Staff: Arthur L. Shearin, Chairman
Affiliation: Private church-related liberal arts college (Church of Christ)
Accreditation: SACS
Areas: App Mus; Hist & Lit; Th & An; Cond; Orch; Opera; Church Mus; Mus Ed (Elem & HS); Theater Mus; Mus Apprec
Degrees: BA
Scholarships: Scholarships of up to $500 awarded for special ability

JOHNSON BIBLE COLLEGE[1]
Church Music Department
Kimberlin Heights Station
Knoxville, TN 37920
(615) 573-4517
Staff: Michael J. Dunn, Chairman
Affiliation: Church-related college (Christian)
Accreditation: SACS; AABC
Areas: App Mus; Hist & Lit; Theory; Cond; Church Mus; Mus Ed (Elem)
Degrees: BA, Church Mus

KNOXVILLE COLLEGE[1]
Music Department
901 College St.
Knoxville, TN 37921
(615) 524-6500
Staff: Dr. Walter Harris, Chairman
Affiliation: Church-related liberal arts college (Presbyterian)
Accreditation: SACS
Areas: App Mus; Hist & Lit; Th & An; Cond; Orch; Ethnomusicol; Church Mus; Intro; Mus Ed (Elem & HS)
Degrees: BA; BS, Mus Ed

LAMBUTH COLLEGE
Department of Music
Lambuth Blvd.
Jackson, TN 38301
(901) 427-6743
Staff: Don L. Huneycatt, Chairman
Affiliation: Church-related college (United Methodist)
Accreditation: SACS
Areas: Th & An; Cond; Intro; Hist & Lit; Mus Ed (Elem & HS); Church Mus
Degrees: BA; BA, Mus Ed; BS; BS, Mus Ed; BM, Church Mus; BM, Mus Ed

LANE COLLEGE[1]
Division of Humanities
Lane Ave.
Jackson, TN 38301
(901) 424-4600
Staff: Kenneth C. Sampson, Chairman
Affiliation: Private church-related liberal arts college (CME) **Accreditation:** SACS
Areas: App Mus; Hist & Lit; Th & An; Comp; Cond; Orch; Mus Ed (Elem & HS); Piano Tech
Degrees: BA

LEE COLLEGE
Department of Music and Fine Arts
Cleveland, TN 37311
(615) 472-2111
Staff: Dr. Jimmy W. Burns, Chairman
Affiliation: Church-sponsored college (Church of God)
Accreditation: SACS
Areas: App Mus; Hist & Lit; Th & An; Comp; Cond; Orch; Church Mus; Mus Ed (Elem & HS); Theater Mus
Degrees: BA; BME
Scholarships: Performing scholarships and academic scholarships awarded by audition

LINCOLN MEMORIAL UNIVERSITY[1]
Music Department, Fine Arts Division
Harrogate, TN 37752
(615) 869-3611
Staff: Dr. Robert L. Brown, Head, Fine Arts Division
Affiliation: Independent college of arts and sciences
Accreditation: SACS
Areas: App Mus; Hist & Lit; Th & An; Cond; Intro; Mus Ed (Elem & HS); Electr Mus
Degrees: BA

MARYVILLE COLLEGE
Department of Fine Arts
Maryville, TN 37801
(615) 982-6412
Staff: Dr. James A. Bloy, Chairman
Affiliation: Church-related liberal arts college (Presbyterian)
Accreditation: NASM; SACS
Areas: App Mus; Hist & Lit; Th & An; Comp; Cond; Orch; Church Mus; Mus Ed (Elem & HS)
Degrees: BA; BM; BM, Mus Ed

MEMPHIS STATE UNIVERSITY
Music Department

Memphis, TN 38111
(901) 454-2541
Staff: David Russell Williams, Chairman
Affiliation: State-supported university
Accreditation: NASM; NCATE; SACS
Areas: App Mus; Hist & Lit; Th & An; Comp; Cond; Orch; Opera; Hist Musicol; Ethnomusicol; Church Mus; Intro; Mus Ed (Elem & HS); Electr Mus; Perf; Commer Mus
Degrees: BM; BME; BS, Mus Ed; BFA; MA; MM; DMA; MEd, Mus Ed; PhD
Scholarships: Many types of scholarships available

MIDDLE TENNESSEE STATE UNIVERSITY
Music Department
Murfreesboro, TN 37130
(615) 898-2469
Staff: Tom L. Naylor, Chairman
Affiliation: State-supported liberal arts and teacher education institution
Accreditation: NASM; SACS
Areas: App Mus; Hist & Lit; Th & An; Comp; Cond; Orch; Opera; Intro; Mus Ed (Elem & HS); Electr Mus; Perf
Degrees: BM; MA; MAT
Scholarships: Work-study programs

SOUTHERN COLLEGE
Division of Music
Collegedale, TN 37315
(615) 396-2111
Staff: Dr. Marvin L. Robertson, Chairman
Affiliation: Church-related, liberal-arts college (Seventh-day Adventist)
Accreditation: NASM; SACS; NCATE
Areas: App Mus; Hist & Lit; Th & An; Cond; Orch; Church Mus; Mus Ed (Elem & HS)
Degrees: BA; BME
Scholarships: Music Education Scholarship, Theodore Presser Foundation; Performance Scholarships, awarded on the basis of level of performance, academics, and need

SOUTHWESTERN AT MEMPHIS
Department of Music
Memphis, TN 38112
(901) 278-2030
Staff: Prof. Robert C. Eckert, Chairman
Affiliation: Church-related college of liberal arts and sciences (Presbyterian, U.S.)
Accreditation: NASM; SACS
Areas: App Mus; Hist & Lit; Th & An; Cond; Church Mus; Mus Ed (Elem & HS); Intro; Perf
Degrees: BA, BM
Scholarships: Special achievement awards granted on the basis of academics and musical potential

TENNESSEE STATE UNIVERSITY[1]
Department of Music
3500 Centennial Blvd.
Nashville, TN 37203
(615) 320-3544
Staff: Ralph R. Simpson, Head
Affiliation: State-supported university
Accreditation: NASM; SACS
Areas: App Mus; Hist & Lit; Th & An; Comp; Cond; Orch; Opera; Hist Musicol; Mus Ed (Elem & HS)
Degrees: BA; BS, Mus Ed; MA; MS

TENNESSEE TECHNOLOGICAL UNIVERSITY[1]
Department of Music
Cookeville, TN 38501
(615) 528-3161
Staff: Marvin L. Lamb, Chairman
Affiliation: State-supported university
Accreditation: NASM; SACS
Areas: App Mus; Hist & Lit; Th & An; Comp; Cond; Orch; Opera; Mus Ed (Elem & HS)
Degrees: BS, Mus Ed, Mus Therapy

TENNESSEE TEMPLE UNIVERSITY
Music Department
1815 Union Ave.
Chattanooga, TN 37404
(615) 698-6021
Staff: Donella C. Brown, Chairman
Affiliation: Church-related liberal arts college (Baptist)
Accreditation: Candidate AABC
Areas: App Mus; Hist & Lit; Th; Cond; Orch; Church Mus; Mus Ed (Elem & HS); Perf
Degrees: BA; BS, Mus Ed; BSM
Scholarships: Awarded to student who assists choir director of Highland Park Baptist Church; awards to applied music students for vocal and instrumental private lessons

TENNESSEE WESLEYAN COLLEGE
Music Department
PO Box 40
Athens, TN 37303
(615) 745-9269
Staff: Dr. Janice L. Ryberg, Chairman
Affiliation: Church-related liberal arts college (United Methodist)
Accreditation: SACS
Areas: App Mus; Hist & Lit; Th & An; Cond; Church Mus; Intro; Mus Ed (Elem & HS); Perf
Degrees: BME; BA
Scholarships: General scholarships available through the college; performance scholarships available through the music department

TREVECCA NAZARENE COLLEGE[1]
Department of Music
333 Murfreesboro Rd.
Nashville, TN 37210
(615) 248-1200, x1288
Staff: Frederick Allen Mund, Chairman
Affiliation: Church-related liberal arts college (Nazarene)
Accreditation: NASM; SACS
Areas: App Mus; Hist & Lit; Th & An; Cond; Orch; Church Mus; Mus Ed (Elem & HS); Intro
Degrees: BS, Mus Ed; BS, Church Mus; BS, Mus
Scholarships: Partial scholarships of $300 a year available to students who apply during the preceding year

TUSCULUM COLLEGE
Music Department in Creative Arts-Humanities Div.
Greeneville, TN 37743
(615) 639-2861
Staff: Ruth C. Thomas, Chairman
Affiliation: Church-related liberal arts college (Presbyterian)
Accreditation: SACS
Areas: Hist & Lit; Th & An; Mus Ed (Elem & HS); App Mus; Cond; Intro; Perf
Degrees: BA; BS, Mus Ed

UNION UNIVERSITY
Music Department
Jackson, TN 38301
(901) 668-1818
Staff: Dr. Kenneth R. Hartley, Chairman
Affiliation: Church-related liberal arts university (Southern Baptist)
Accreditation: NASM; SACS
Areas: App Mus; Hist & Lit; Th & An; Comp; Cond; Orch; Opera; Church Mus; Intro; Mus Ed (Elem & HS); Perf
Degrees: BA; BM
Scholarships: Applied scholarships awarded by audition

UNIVERSITY OF TENNESSEE AT CHATTANOOGA
Music Department
Fine Arts Complex
Chattanooga, TN 37402
(615) 755-4601
Staff: Dr. Peter E. Gerschefski, Head
Affiliation: State-supported university
Accreditation: NASM; SACS
Areas: App Mus; Hist & Lit; Th & An; Comp; Cond; Orch; Opera; Hist Musicol; Church Mus; Mus Ed (Elem & HS)
Degrees: BA; BM; BS, Mus Ed; B Sacr Mus; MM
Scholarships: Performance grants awarded to students who perform in various ensembles

UNIVERSITY OF TENNESSEE AT KNOXVILLE
Music Department
Music Building, 1741 Volunteer Blvd.
Knoxville, TN 37996-2600
(615) 974-3241
Staff: John Meacham, Head
Affiliation: State-supported university; college of liberal arts
Accreditation: NASM; SACS
Areas: Orch; Cond; Intro; Hist & Lit; Opera; Th & An; Mus Ed (Elem & HS); Perf; App Mus; Intro; Suzuk; Ped; Church Mus; Electr Mus; Studio Mus; Jazz
Degrees: BA; BS, Mus Ed; BM; MA; MM; MS, Mus Ed

UNIVERSITY OF TENNESSEE AT MARTIN
Department of Fine and Performing Arts
Martin, TN 38238
(901) 587-7400
Staff: Dr. Earl Norwood, Chairman
Affiliation: State-supported university
Accreditation: NASM; NCATE; SACS
Areas: App Mus; Hist & Lit; Th & An; Comp; Cond; Orch; Opera; Intro; Mus Ed (Elem & HS); Theater Mus; Piano Tech; Instr Rep; Electr Mus; Perf
Degrees: BA; BM; BS
Scholarships: Performance and general music aptitude awards available

UNIVERSITY OF THE SOUTH
Music Department
Sewanee, TN 37375
(615) 598-5931
Staff: Steven W. Shrader, Chairman
Affiliation: Church-related liberal arts college (Episcopal)
Accreditation: SACS
Areas: App Mus; Hist & Lit; Th & An; Cond; Opera; Hist Musicol; Church Mus
Degrees: BA
Scholarships: General scholarships only

TEXAS

ABILENE CHRISTIAN UNIVERSITY[1]
Department of Music
ACU Station, Box 8274
Abilene, TX 79699
(915) 677-1911, x2302
Staff: Dr. Sarah Johnston Reid, Chairman
Affiliation: Church-related liberal arts university (Church of Christ)
Accreditation: NASM; SACS
Areas: App Mus; Hist & Lit; Th & An; Comp; Cond; Orch; Opera; Church Mus; Intro; Mus Ed (Elem & HS); Theater Mus; Electr Mus; Perf
Degrees: BA; BME
Scholarships: Scholarships for music majors and organization participants awarded by auditions in April for following school year

ANGELO STATE UNIVERSITY
Department of Art and Music
2601 W. Ave. N.
San Angelo, TX 76909
(915) 942-2085
Staff: Dr. Charles Robison, Head
Affiliation: State-supported university
Accreditation: NASM; SACS
Areas: App Mus; Hist & Lit; Th & An; Comp; Cond; Orch; Opera; Intro; Mus Ed (Elem & HS); Perf
Degrees: BA; BME; MME
Scholarships: Choir, band, and applied music scholarships awarded by audition

ARLINGTON BAPTIST COLLEGE[1]
Music Department
3001 W. Division
Arlington, TX 76012
(817) 461-8741
Staff: Betty R. Riffee, Chairman
Affiliation: Church-related college (Baptist)
Accreditation: AABC
Areas: App Mus; Th & An; Comp; Hist & Lit
Degrees: BA; BS

AUSTIN COLLEGE
Music Department
Sherman, TX 75090
(214) 892-9101
Staff: Bruce G. Lunkley, Chairman
Affiliation: Church-related liberal arts college (Presbyterian, U.S.)
Accreditation: SACS
Areas: App Mus; Hist & Lit; Th & An; Cond; Opera; Church Mus
Degrees: BA
Scholarships: Renewable scholarships of $500 a year in applied music awarded on the basis of taped or in-person audition

BAYLOR UNIVERSITY
School of Music
Waco, TX 76798
(817) 755-1161
Staff: Elwyn A. Wlenandt, Acting Dean
Affiliation: Church-supported university (Baptist General Convention of Texas)
Accreditation: NASM; NCATE; SACS
Areas: App Mus; Hist & Lit; Th & An; Comp; Cond; Orch; Opera; Hist Musicol; Church Mus; Intro; Mus Ed (Elem & HS); Electr Mus; Perf
Degrees: BM; BME; MM
Scholarships: Undergraduate scholarships, need or ability; graduate scholarships, need and ability; graduate assistantships, outstanding ability

BISHOP COLLEGE[1]
Division of Fine Arts, Music Unit
3837 Simpson-Stuart Rd.
Dallas, TX 75241
(214) 372-8086
Staff: J. Van Bolden, Coordinator
Affiliation: Church-related liberal arts college (Baptist)
Accreditation: SACS
Areas: App Mus; Hist & Lit; Th & An; Comp; Cond; Orch; Opera; Mus Ed (Elem & HS); Piano Tech
Degrees: BS, Mus Ed
Scholarships: Merit scholarships available to members of choir and band

CORPUS CHRISTI STATE UNIVERSITY
Music Department
6300 Ocean Dr.
Corpus Christi, TX 78412
(512) 991-6810
Staff: Dr. Miriam Wagenscheim, Dean
Affiliation: State-supported liberal arts university
Accreditation: NASM; SACS
Areas: Keybd Ped; Mus Ed (Elem & HS); Perf
Degrees: BM
Scholarships: Scholarships of $100 to full tuition and fees awarded on the basis of musical ability and financial need

DALLAS BAPTIST COLLEGE
Music Discipline
7777 W. Kiest Blvd.
Dallas, TX 75211
(214) 331-8311
Affiliation: Church-related liberal arts college (Southern Baptist)
Accreditation: SACS
Areas: App Mus; Church Mus; Mus Ed (Elem & HS)
Degrees: BA; BM; BS, Mus Ed
Scholarships: Vocal, keyboard, and instrumental scholarships awarded through audition

EAST TEXAS BAPTIST COLLEGE
Department of Music
1209 N. Grove St.
Marshall, TX 75670
(214) 935-7963, x288
Staff: Robert L. Spencer, Chairman
Affiliation: Church-related liberal arts college (Southern Baptist)
Accreditation: NASM; SACS
Areas: App Mus; Hist & Lit; Th & An; Comp; Cond; Opera; Church Mus; Intro; Mus Ed (Elem & HS); Electr Mus; Perf
Degrees: BM
Scholarships: Applied music, band, and choral scholarships available

EAST TEXAS STATE UNIVERSITY
Music Department
Commerce, TX 75428
(214) 886-5303
Staff: Dr. Robert House, Head
Affiliation: State-supported university
Accreditation: NASM; SACS
Areas: App Mus; Hist & Lit; Th & An; Comp; Cond; Orch; Opera; Hist Musicol; Mus Ed (Elem & HS); Instr Rep
Degrees: BA; BM; BME; BS, Mus Ed; MA; MM; MS; EdD; PhD
Scholarships: Scholarships for vocal, keyboard, and instrumental performance awarded by audition

GULF-COAST BIBLE COLLEGE
Music Department, Division of General Studies
PO Box 7889
Houston, TX 77270
(713) 862-3800
Staff: Robert A. Adams, Chairman, Music Department
Affiliation: Church-related college (Church of God, Anderson, IN)
Accreditation: SACS; AABC
Areas: App Mus; Hist & Lit; Th & An; Cond; Church Mus; Comp
Degrees: BA; BSM; BS, Church Mus

HARDIN-SIMMONS UNIVERSITY
School of Music
Abilene, TX 79698
(915) 677-7281
Staff: Wesley S. Coffman, Dean
Affiliation: Church-related university (Southern Baptist)
Accreditation: NASM; NCATE; SACS
Areas: App Mus; Hist & Lit; Th & An; Comp; Cond; Orch; Opera; Hist Musicol; Church Mus; Intro; Mus Ed (Elem & HS); Electr Mus; Perf
Degrees: BA; BM; MM
Scholarships: Awards based on ability in performance and/or composition plus financial need

HOUSTON BAPTIST UNIVERSITY
School of Music, College of Fine Arts
7502 Fondren Rd.
Houston, TX 77074
(713) 774-7661
Staff: Robert Linder, Dean
Affiliation: Church-related liberal-arts university (Southern Baptist)
Accreditation: SACS
Areas: App Mus; Hist & Lit; Th & An; Comp; Cond; Orch; Opera; Church Mus; Mus Ed (Elem & HS); Perf
Degrees: BA; BM; BME
Scholarships: Performance scholarships awarded on the basis of potential ability and usefulness in ensembles

HUSTON-TILLOTSON COLLEGE[1]
Department of Music
1820 E. 8th St.
Austin, TX 78702
(512) 476-7421
Staff: Beulah A. Curry-Jones, Head
Affiliation: Church-related liberal arts college (United Methodist)
Accreditation: SACS
Areas: App Mus; Hist & Lit; Th & An; Cond; Orch; Mus Ed (Elem & HS); Choral and Instr Perf Groups
Degrees: BA; BS, Mus Ed
Scholarships: Music Grants awarded for demonstration of outstanding talent or potential, reliability, initiative, cooperation, character, ambition, diligence, inspiration to others

INCARNATE WORD COLLEGE[1]
Music Department
4301 Broadway
San Antonio, TX 78209
(512) 828-1261
Staff: Sr. Maria Goretti Zehr, Coordinator
Affiliation: Church-related liberal arts college (Roman Catholic)
Accreditation: SACS
Areas: App Mus; Hist & Lit; Th & An; Comp; Cond; Orch; Church Mus; Mus Ed (Elem & HS); Perf
Degrees: BM; BME
Scholarships: Grants awarded on basis of audition and interview

LAMAR UNIVERSITY
Music Department
PO Box 10044
Beaumont, TX 77710
(713) 838-8144
Staff: Dr. George L. Parks, Head
Affiliation: State-supported university
Accreditation: NASM: SACS
Areas: App Mus; Hist & Lit; Th & An; Comp; Cond; Orch; Opera; Hist Musicol; Intro; Mus Ed (Elem & HS); Perf
Degrees: BM; BME; BS, Mus Ed; MM; MME
Scholarships: Awarded on the basis of performing ability

LUBBOCK CHRISTIAN COLLEGE[1]
Music Department
5601 W. 19th
Lubbock, TX 79407
(806) 792-3221
Staff: B. Wayne Hinds, Chairman
Affiliation: Church-related arts college (Church of Christ)
Accreditation: SACS
Areas: App Mus; Hist & Lit; Th & An; Cond; Orch; Hist Musicol; Church Mus; Mus Ed (Elem & HS)
Degrees: BA; BS, Mus Ed
Scholarships: Awarded to band and choir participants through audition by faculty

MCMURRY COLLEGE[1]
Department of Music
Abilene, TX 79697
(915) 692-4130, x295
Staff: John Gibson, Chairman
Affiliation: Church-related college (Methodist—UMC)
Accreditation: SACS
Areas: App Mus; Hist & Lit; Th & An; Comp; Cond; Orch; Opera; Hist Musicol; Church Mus; Mus Ed (Elem & HS); Electr Mus
Degrees: BA; BM; BME; BM, Church Mus
Scholarships: Awarded for performance in band and choir

MIDWESTERN STATE UNIVERSITY
Music Department
3400 Taft Blvd.
Wichita Falls, TX 76308
(817) 692-6611
Staff: Don Maxwell, Head
Affiliation: State-supported university
Accreditation: NASM; SACS
Areas: App Mus; Th & An; Comp; Intro; Mus Ed (Elem & HS); Theater Mus; Perf
Degrees: BM; BME; MM; Mus Ed
Scholarships: Awarded solely on the basis of audition

NORTH TEXAS STATE UNIVERSITY
School of Music
Denton, TX 76203
(817) 565-2791
Staff: Marceau C. Myers, Dean
Affiliation: State-supported university
Accreditation: NASM; SACS
Areas: App Mus; Hist & Lit; Th & An; Comp; Cond; Orch; Opera; Hist Musicol; Ethnomusicol; Mus Ed (Elem & HS); Instr Rep; Electr Mus; Perf; Intro
Degrees: BA; BM; BME; MA; MM; MME; DMA; EdD; PhD
Scholarships: Competitive Music Scholarships and Music Service Awards for in-state and out-of-state students in band, choir, composition, instrumental areas, keyboard, jazz lab band, orchestra, and voice; audition required

OUR LADY OF THE LAKE UNIVERSITY[1]
Department of Music
411 SW 24th St.
San Antonio, TX 78285
(512) 434-6711, x221
Staff: Sr. Emelene Matocha, Chairman
Affiliation: Church-related liberal arts college (Roman Catholic)
Accreditation: SACS
Areas: Hist & Lit; Th & An; Comp; Cond; Orch; Mus Ed (Elem & HS)
Degrees: BM; BME

PAN AMERICAN UNIVERSITY
Music Department
Edinburg, TX 78539
(512) 381-3471
Staff: Dr. Carl Seale, Head
Affiliation: State-supported university
Accreditation: SACS
Areas: App Mus; Hist & Lit; Th & An; Cond; Orch; Hist Musicol; Mus Ed (Elem & HS)
Degrees: BA
Scholarships: Academic scholarships, scholarships for music ensemble participation, and work-study scholarships available

PRAIRIE VIEW A & M UNIVERSITY
Department of Music & Drama
Prairie View, TX 77445
(713) 857-3919
Staff: Lucius R. Wyatt, PhD, Head
Affiliation: State-supported university
Accreditation: NCATE; SACS
Areas: App Mus; Mus Ed (Elem & HS)
Degrees: BA; BM; MA
Scholarships: Music Scholarships available in piano, voice and wind; percussion instruments by audition

RICE UNIVERSITY
Shepherd School of Music
Houston, TX 77251
(713) 527-4854
Staff: Larry Livingston, Dean
Affiliation: Privately endowed university
Accreditation: SACS
Areas: App Mus; Hist & Lit; Th & An; Comp; Cond; Intro; Electr Mus; Perf
Degrees: BA; BM; MM
Scholarships: Honor awards based on financial need and talent

ST. MARY'S UNIVERSITY[1]
Music Department

One Camino Santa Maria
San Antonio, TX 78284
(512) 436-3011
Staff: John P. Moore, Chairman
Affiliation: Church-related university (Catholic—Society of Mary)
Accreditation: SACS
Areas: App Mus; Hist & Lit; Th & An; Comp; Cond; Orch; Opera; Church Mus; Mus Ed (HS)
Degrees: BA
Scholarships: Tuition waivers for participants in ensembles awarded by audition; tuition waivers also available to music majors

SAM HOUSTON STATE UNIVERSITY[1]
Department of Music
Huntsville, TX 77341
(713) 294-1360
Staff: Dr. Fisher A. Tull, Chairman
Affiliation: State-supported university
Accreditation: NASM; NCATE; SACS
Areas: App Mus; Hist & Lit; Th & An; Comp; Cond; Orch; Opera; Hist Musicol; Mus Ed (Elem & HS)
Degrees: BM; BME; MA; MEd
Scholarships: $100 to $500 awarded each year; application and audition (live or tape) required

SOUTHERN METHODIST UNIVERSITY
Division of Music, Meadows School of the Arts
Owens Arts Center
Dallas, TX 75275
(214) 692-2587
Staff: Dr. William Hipp, Chairman
Affiliation: Private institution
Accreditation: NASM; SACS
Areas: App Mus; Hist & Lit; Th & An; Comp; Cond; Orch; Opera; Church Mus; Intro; Mus Ed (Elem & HS); Mus Therapy; Electr Mus; Perf
Degrees: BM; BME; MM; M Sacr Mus; B Mus Therapy; M Mus Therapy
Scholarships: Undergraduate and graduate scholarships available; audition and interview required

SOUTHWEST TEXAS STATE UNIVERSITY
Music Department
San Marcos, TX 78666
(512) 245-2651
Staff: Arlis Hiebert, Chairman
Affiliation: State-supported university
Accreditation: NASM; SACS
Areas: App Mus; Hist & Lit; Th & An; Comp; Cond; Orch; Opera; Mus Ed (Elem & HS); Instr Rep; Electr Mus; Perf
Degrees: BM; MM
Scholarships: Performance scholarships and teaching assistantships for graduate students

SOUTHWESTERN ADVENTIST COLLEGE
Fine Arts Department
Keene, TX 76059
(817) 645-3921, x217
Staff: Dr. William R. Bromme, Chairman
Affiliation: Church-related college (Seventh-day Adventist)
Accreditation: SACS
Areas: App Mus; Hist & Lit; Th & An; Comp; Cond; Church Mus; Mus Ed (HS); Intro; Piano Tech
Degrees: BA; BM
Scholarships: Awarded on the basis of need and talent

SOUTHWESTERN BAPTIST THEOLOGICAL SEMINARY
School of Church Music
Box 22000 4-D
Fort Worth, TX 76122
(817) 923-1921, x310
Staff: Dr. James C. McKinney, Dean
Affiliation: School of Church Music in a theological seminary supported by Southern Baptist convention
Accreditation: NASM; SACS; ATS
Areas: App Mus; Hist & Lit; Th & An; Comp; Cond; Hist Musicol; Church Mus; Orch
Degrees: MM; DMA

SOUTHWESTERN UNIVERSITY[1]
School of Fine Arts,
Department of Music
Georgetown, TX 78626
(512) 863-1380
Staff: Theodore D. Lucas, Dean, School of Fine Arts; George Nelson, Chairman, Department of Music
Affiliation: Church-related liberal arts college (Methodist)
Accreditation: NASM; SACS
Areas: App Mus; Hist & Lit; Th & An; Cond; Hist Musicol; Church Mus; Mus Ed (Elem & HS)
Degrees: BM

STEPHEN F. AUSTIN STATE UNIVERSITY
Music Department
Box 13043, SFA Station
Nacogdoches, TX 75961
(713) 569-0764
Staff: Dr. Robert L. Blocker, Chairman
Affiliation: State-supported university
Accreditation: NASM; NCATE; SACS
Areas: App Mus; Hist & Lit; Th & An; Comp; Cond; Orch; Opera; Church Mus; Mus Ed (Elem & HS); Hist Musicol; Intro; Electr Mus; Perf; Computer Mus
Degrees: BA; BFA; BM; MA; MFA
Scholarships: Applied music scholarships awarded by audition

SUL ROSS STATE UNIVERSITY
Department of Music in the Division of Fine Arts
Alpine , TX 79830
(915) 837-8211
Staff: Samuel E. Davis, Chairman
Affiliation: State-supported university
Accreditation: SACS
Areas: App Mus; Th & An; Mus Ed (Elem & HS)
Degrees: BA; BM; MEd
Scholarships: Academic and music participation scholarships available

TARLETON STATE UNIVERSITY
Department of Fine Arts and Speech
PO Box 39 T
Stephenville, TX 76402
(817) 968-9245
Staff: Dr. C. John Keith, Head
Affiliation: State-supported university
Accreditation: SACS
Areas: Mus Ed (Elem & HS); Perf
Degrees: BM
Scholarships: Scholarships awarded for performance in band or choir and to accompanists and/or piano performers

TEXAS A & I UNIVERSITY
Music Department
Kingsville, TX 78363
(512) 595-2804
Staff: Dr. Robert Scott, Chairman
Affiliation: State-supported university
Accreditation: NASM; NCATE; SACS
Areas: App Mus; Hist & Lit; Th & An; Cond; Orch; Intro; Mus Ed (Elem & HS); Perf
Degrees: BA; BM; MM; MS
Scholarships: Available to students who participate in large ensemble

TEXAS CHRISTIAN UNIVERSITY
Department of Music, School of Fine Arts
Fort Worth, TX 76129
(817) 921-7602
Staff: Emmet G. Smith, Chairman
Affiliation: Church-related nonsectarian university (Disciples of Christ)
Accreditation: NASM; SACS
Areas: App Mus; Hist & Lit; Th & An; Comp; Cond; Orch; Opera; Hist Musicol; Church Mus; Mus Ed (Elem & HS); Theater Mus
Degrees: BA; BM; BME; MA; MM; MME
Scholarships: Awards based on academic achievement and excellent performance; many scholarships available for various areas of interest (i.e. choir, opera, band, performance)

TEXAS COLLEGE[1]
Music Department
2404 N. Grand
Tyler, TX 75702
(214) 593-8311, x48
Staff: Sibyl Claybon, Chairman
Affiliation: Private college (Christian Methodist Episcopal)
Accreditation: SACS
Areas: Th & An; Orch; Cond; Comp; Intro; Hist & Lit; Mus Ed (Elem & HS)
Degrees: BA; BA, Mus Ed

TEXAS LUTHERAN COLLEGE
Music Department
Seguin, TX 78155
(512) 379-4161
Staff: Dr. Sigurd O. Christiansen, Chairman
Affiliation: Church-related liberal arts college (American Lutheran)
Accreditation: SACS
Areas: App Mus; Hist & Lit; Cond;

Church Mus; Mus Ed (Elem & HS)
Degrees: BA; BME
Scholarships: Awarded through audition

TEXAS SOUTHERN UNIVERSITY
Music Department
3201 Wheeler Ave.
Houston, TX 77004
(713) 527-7011
Staff: Jack C. Bradley, Chairman
Affiliation: State-supported university
Accreditation: SACS; NCATE
Areas: App Mus; Hist & Lit; Th & An; Mus Ed (Elem & HS); Orch; Cond; Comp; Intro; Perf
Degrees: BM; BME; MA; MME
Scholarships: Band scholarships; limited shcolarships for voice and piano

TEXAS TECH UNIVERSITY[1]
Department of Music
Lubbock, TX 79409
(806) 742-2270
Staff: Harold Luce, Chairman
Affiliation: State-supported university
Accreditation: NASM; SACS
Areas: App Mus; Hist & Lit; Th & An; Comp; Cond; Orch; Opera; Intro; Mus Ed (Elem & HS); Theater Mus; Electr Mus; Perf
Degrees: BM; BME; MM; MME; PhD, Fine Arts
Scholarships: Available to any student participating in the music program; audition before scholarship committee required

TEXAS WESLEYAN COLLEGE
Music Department, School of Fine Arts
Fort Worth, TX 76105
(817) 531-4443
Staff: Karen Johnson Waters, Dean, Fine Arts
Affiliation: Church-related liberal arts college (United Methodist)
Accreditation: NASM; SACS
Areas: App Mus; Hist & Lit; Th & An; Comp; Cond; Orch; Mus Ed (Elem & HS); Opera; Perf
Degrees: BME; BA, App Mus
Scholarships: Awarded on the basis of ability, and GPA, up to full tuition

TEXAS WOMAN'S UNIVERSITY
Department of Music and Drama
PO Box 23865, TWU Station
Denton, TX 76204
(817) 387-1412
Staff: Richard Rodean, Chairman
Affiliation: State-supported university
Accreditation: NASM; SACS
Areas: App Mus; Hist & Lit; Comp; Cond; Orch; Opera; Church Mus; Mus Ed (Elem & HS); Mus Therapy
Degrees: BA; BS, Mus Ed; BS; MA, Mus Ed
Scholarships: music major performance scholarships; performance scholarships for nonmajors

TRINITY UNIVERSITY[1]
Music Department
715 Stadium Dr.
San Antonio, TX 78284
(512) 736-8211
Staff: Dr. James Ode, Chairman
Affiliation: Church-related, independent university (Presbyterian)
Accreditation: SACS
Areas: App Mus; Hist & Lit; Th & An; Comp; Cond; Orch; Hist Musicol; Mus Ed (Elem & HS); Intro; Electr Mus; Perf
Degrees: BA; BM; MA
Scholarships: Scholarships available in all areas awarded on the basis of performance audition and musical aptitude tests

UNIVERSITY OF HOUSTON
School of Music
Houston, TX 77004
(713) 749-1116
Staff: Milton Katims, Artistic Director
Affiliation: State-supported university
Accreditation: NASM; SACS
Areas: App Mus; Hist & Lit; Th & An; Comp; Cond; Orch; Opera; Hist Musicol; Intro; Mus Ed (Elem & HS); Electr Mus; Perf
Degrees: BA; BM; MM
Scholarships: Music scholarships awarded on the basis of audition and maintained GPA; band scholarships awarded on the basis of audition and participation in marching band

UNIVERSITY OF MARY HARDIN-BAYLOR
School of Creative Arts
Division of Music, Fine Arts Department
Box 421
Belton, TX 76513
(817) 939-5811, x253
Staff: Dr. George W. Stansburg, Dean
Affiliation: Private church-related liberal arts university (Southern Baptist)
Accreditation: SACS
Areas: App Mus; Hist & Lit; Th & An; Cond; Orch; Opera; Church Mus; Intro; Mus Ed (Elem & HS); Perf
Degrees: BM
Scholarships: Departmental scholarships awarded by audition

UNIVERSITY OF ST. THOMAS
Music Department
3812 Montrose Blvd.
Houston, TX 77006
(713) 522-7911, x240
Staff: Thomas Borling, Chairman
Affiliation: Church-related liberal arts university (Roman Catholic)
Accreditation: SACS
Areas: App Mus; Hist & Lit; Th & An; Comp; Cond; Opera; Church Mus; Intro; Mus Ed (Elem & HS); Perf; Jazz
Degrees: BA; BM; BME
Scholarships: Full-tuition scholarships awarded on the basis of 3.0 GPA and audition

UNIVERSITY OF TEXAS AT ARLINGTON[1]
Department of Music
Box 19105, UTA Station
Arlington, TX 76019
(817) 273-3471
Staff: Linton Powell, Chairman
Affiliation: State-supported university
Accreditation: NASM; SACS
Areas: App Mus; Hist & Lit; Th & An; Comp; Cond; Orch; Opera; Mus Ed (Elem & HS)
Degrees: BM
Scholarships: Band, choir, orchestra, jazz band, and opera scholarships awarded by audition

UNIVERSITY OF TEXAS AT AUSTIN
Department of Music
Austin, TX 78712
(512) 471-7764
Staff: Dr. Gerard Behague, Chairman
Affiliation: State-supported university
Accreditation: NASM; SACS
Areas: App Mus; Hist & Lit; Th & An; Comp; Cond; Orch; Opera; Hist Musicol; Church Mus; Mus Ed (Elem & HS); Piano Tech
Degrees: BA; BM; MM; DMA; PhD

UNIVERSITY OF TEXAS AT EL PASO
Department of Music
El Paso, TX 79968
(915) 747-5606
Staff: Dr. Richard E. Henderson, Chairman
Affiliation: State-supported university
Accreditation: NASM; SACS
Areas: App Mus; Hist & Lit; Th & An; Comp; Cond; Orch; Opera; Mus Ed (Elem & HS); Piano Tech; Electr Mus; Perf
Degrees: BM; MM
Scholarships: Service awards and scholarships available

UNIVERSITY OF TEXAS OF THE PERMIAN BASIN[1]
Music Discipline, Division of Arts and Sciences
Odessa, TX 79762
(915) 367-2233
Staff: Dr. Craig Lister, Chairman
Affiliation: State-supported university offering upper-level and graduate classes only
Accreditation: SACS
Areas: App Mus; Hist & Lit; Th & An; Comp; Cond; Orch; Hist Musicol; Church Mus; Mus Ed (Elem & HS); Theater Mus; Instr Rep; Perf Prac; Choral Arrang
Degrees: BA; BS; Mus Ed; MA; Mus Ed
Scholarships: Scholarships available

UNIVERSITY OF TEXAS AT SAN ANTONIO
Division of Music
San Antonio, TX 78285
(512) 691-4357

Staff: Dr. Joe Stuessy, Director
Affiliation: State-supported university
Accreditation: SACS; NASM
Areas: App Mus; Hist & Lit; Th & An; Comp; Cond; Orch; Mus Ed (Elem & HS); Mus Merch; Opera; Intro; Electr Mus; Perf
Degrees: BM; BME; MM
Scholarships: Talent and scholarship awards based on audition

UNIVERSITY OF TEXAS AT TYLER
Department of Music
3900 University Blvd.
Tyler, TX 75701
(214) 566-1471, x289
Staff: Dr. Kenneth Muckelroy, Chairman
Affiliation: An upper division university of the University of Texas System
Accreditation: SACS
Areas: App Mus; Hist & Lit; Cond; Hist Musicol; Church Mus; Mus Ed (Elem & HS); Theater Mus; Perf
Degrees: BA; BFA; MA
Scholarships: Performance scholarships in all performance areas, awarded on the basis of need after an audition

WAYLAND BAPTIST UNIVERSITY
Music Department
Plainview, TX 79072
(806) 296-5521
Staff: W. Duane Harris, Chairman
Affiliation: Private church-related liberal arts college (Southern Baptist)
Accreditation: SACS
Areas: App Mus; Hist & Lit; Th & An; Comp; Cond; Orch; Opera; Hist Musicol; Church Mus; Mus Ed (Elem & HS); Intro
Degrees: BA; BM; BS, Mus Ed
Scholarships: Applied music, theory and composition, choral, instrumental, student teaching scholarships awarded on the basis of instructor's recommendation and audition

WEST TEXAS STATE UNIVERSITY
Music Department
Canyon, TX 79015
(806) 656-2016
Staff: Dr. Harry Haines, Chairman
Affiliation: State-supported university
Accreditation: NASM; SACS
Areas: App Mus; Hist & Lit; Th & An; Comp; Cond; Orch; Opera; Hist Musicol; Intro; Mus Ed (Elem & HS); Mus Therapy; Theater Mus; Electr Mus; Perf; Mus Bus
Degrees: BM; BME; MA; MM
Scholarships: Awarded by audition

UTAH

BRIGHAM YOUNG UNIVERSITY
Music Department
Provo, UT 84602
(801) 378-1211, x3082
Staff: K. Newell Dayley, Chairman
Affiliation: Church-related university (Church of Jesus Christ of Latter-day Saints-Mormons)
Accreditation: NASM; NCATE; NASC
Areas: App Mus; Hist & Lit; Th & An; Comp; Cond; Orch; Opera; Hist Musicol; Church Mus; Intro; Mus Ed (Elem & HS); Theater Mus; Piano Tech; Electr Mus
Scholarships: Performance scholarships available to students who devote minimum number of hours to ensemble and private instruction; audition required

SOUTHERN UTAH STATE COLLEGE[1]
Music Department
Cedar City, UT 84720
(801) 586-4411, x263
Staff: C. David Nyman, Chairman
Affiliation: State-supported college
Accreditation: NASC
Areas: App Mus; Hist & Lit; Th & An; Comp; Cond; Orch; Opera; Hist Musicol; Mus Ed (Elem & HS); Instr Rep
Degrees: BA; BS, Mus Ed
Scholarships: Fee waivers awarded on the basis of talent, scholarship, and need

UNIVERSITY OF UTAH
Music Department
Gardner Hall
Salt Lake City, UT 84112
(801) 581-6765
Staff: Dr. Edgar Thompson, Chairman
Affiliation: State-supported university
Accreditation: NASM; NASC
Areas: App Mus; Hist & Lit; Th & An; Comp; Cond; Orch; Opera; Hist Musicol; Intro; Mus Ed (HS); Theater Mus; Electr Mus; Perf
Degrees: BA; BM; MM; MA; PhD
Scholarships: Academic, honors, departmental, and solicited scholarships available

UTAH STATE UNIVERSITY
Music Department
UMC 50
Logan, UT 84322
(801) 750-3000
Staff: Warren L. Burton, Head
Affiliation: State-supported university
Accreditation: NASM; NASC
Areas: App Mus; Hist & Lit; Th & An; Comp; Cond; Orch; Opera; Hist Musicol; Church Mus; Intro; Mus Ed (Elem & HS); Mus Therapy; Electr Mus; Perf; Piano Ped; Jazz Ens; Guitar Ped
Degrees: BA
Scholarships: Performance scholarships awarded through audition

WEBER STATE COLLEGE
Music Department
Ogden, UT 84408
(801) 626-6436
Staff: Dr. K. Earl Ericksen, Chairman
Affiliation: State-supported college
Accreditation: NASM; NCATE; NASC
Areas: App Mus; Hist & Lit; Th & An; Comp; Cond; Orch; Hist Musicol; Mus Ed (Elem & HS); Instr Rep; Perf; Theater Mus
Degrees: BA; BS, Mus Ed
Scholarships: Tuition waivers from state and sponsor awarded on the basis of musical ability

WESTMINSTER COLLEGE[1]
Music Program
1840 S. Thirteenth E. St.
Salt Lake City, UT 84105
(801) 484-7651
Staff: Kenneth Kuchler, Director
Affiliation: Church-related liberal arts college (United Methodist, United Presbyterian, United Church of Christ Church)
Accreditation: NASC
Areas: App Mus; Hist & Lit; Th & An; Comp; Cond; Orch; Hist Musicol; Mus Ed (Elem & HS)
Degrees: BA; BS

VERMONT

BENNINGTON COLLEGE[1]
Music Division
Bennington, VT 05201
(802) 442-5401
Staff: Gunnar Schonbeck, Chairman
Affiliation: Private liberal arts college
Accreditation: NEA
Areas: App Mus; Th & An; Comp; Cond; Orch; Intro; Instr Rep; Electr Mus; Perf
Degrees: BA; MA; MFA
Scholarships: General college scholarships awarded on the basis of need; Presser Scholarship in music awarded on the basis of faculty selection

GODDARD COLLEGE
Music Department
Plainfield, VT 05667
(802) 454-8311
Staff: Lois Harris, Chairman
Affiliation: Private liberal arts college
Accreditation: NEA
Areas: Hist & Lit; Th & An; Ethnomusicol
Degrees: BA

JOHNSON STATE COLLEGE
Department of Fine Arts
Johnson, VT 05656
(802) 635-2356, x255
Staff: Albert A. Swinchoski, Chairman
Affiliation: State-supported liberal arts and teacher training college
Accreditation: NEA
Areas: App Mus; Hist & Lit; Th & An; Comp; Cond; Mus Ed (Elem & HS); Intro; Perf
Degrees: BA; BFA
Scholarships: Honors scholarships available to promising musicians; require successful performing experience and recommendation of secondary school music teachers

MIDDLEBURY COLLEGE[1]
Music Department
Middlebury, VT 05753
(802) 388-3711
Staff: George Todd, Chairman
Affiliation: Private liberal arts college
Accreditation: NEA
Areas: App Mus; Hist & Lit; Th & An; Comp; Hist Musicol; Orch; Opera
Degrees: BA

SAINT MICHAEL'S COLLEGE
Fine Arts Department
Winooski Park, VT 05404
(802) 655-2000, x2449
Staff: Don Rathgeb, Chairman
Affiliation: Church-related liberal arts college (Roman Catholic)
Accreditation: NEA
Areas: Hist & Lit; Th & An; Church Mus; Mus Ed (Elem & HS)
Degrees: BA

UNIVERSITY OF VERMONT
Department of Music
Redstone Campus
Burlington, VT 05405
(802) 656-3040
Staff: Dr. James G. Chapman, Chairman
Affiliation: State-supported university
Accreditation: NASM; NEA
Areas: App Mus; Hist & Lit; Th & An; Comp; Cond; Orch; Intro; Mus Ed (Elem & HS); Mus Therapy; Piano Tech; Instr Rep; Perf; Intro
Degrees: BA; BM; BS, Mus Ed

VIRGINIA

BLUEFIELD COLLEGE
Division of Fine Arts
Bluefield, VA 24605
(304) 327-7137
Staff: Dr. R. Paul Jones, Chairman
Affiliation: Church-related liberal arts college (Baptist)
Accreditation: SACS
Areas: App Mus; Hist & Lit; Th & An; Comp; Cond; Church Mus; Mus Ed (Elem & HS)
Degrees: BA; BFA; BS, Mus Ed; BSM
Scholarships: Tuition grants awarded on the basis of audition, interview, and demonstrated scholastic achievement; fine arts scholarships based on performance in area of specialization, academic work, and character

BRIDGEWATER COLLEGE[1]
Music Department
Bridgewater, VA 22812
(703) 828-2401
Staff: Dr. Tom R. Thornley, Chairman
Affiliation: Church-related liberal arts college (Church of the Brethren)
Accreditation: SACS
Areas: App Mus; Hist & Lit; Th & An; Comp; Cond; Orch; Church Mus; Intro; Mus Ed (Elem & HS); Perf
Degrees: BA
Scholarships: Applied music and music education scholarships awarded on the basis of financial need

CHRISTOPHER NEWPORT COLLEGE
Department of Fine and Performing Arts
50 Shoe Ln.
Newport News, VA 23606
(804) 599-7000; Music, 599-7074
Staff: James R. Hines, Director of Music; Rita C. Hubbard, Chairman, Department of Fine and Performing Arts
Affiliation: State-supported college
Accreditation: SACS
Areas: App Mus; Hist & Lit; Th & An; Comp; Cond; Opera; Hist Musicol
Degrees: BA; BM
Scholarships: Applied music and general education scholarships available; contact Director of Music for information

CLINCH VALLEY COLLEGE OF THE UNIVERSITY OF VIRGINIA[1]
Department of Performing Arts
Wise, VA 24293
(703) 328-2431
Staff: Dr. Michael Donathan, Chairman
Affiliation: University college of the University of Virginia
Accreditation: SACS
Areas: App Mus; Hist & Lit; Th & An; Cond; Mus Ed (Elem); Theater Mus
Degrees: BA, Perf Arts (concentration in mus)

COLLEGE OF WILLIAM AND MARY IN VIRGINIA
Department of Music
Williamsburg, VA 23185
(804) 229-4374
Staff: Margaret Freeman, Chairman
Affiliation: State-supported university
Accreditation: SACS
Areas: App Mus; Hist & Lit; Th & An; Comp; Cond; Opera; Intro; Mus Ed (Elem & HS); Orch
Degrees: BA

EASTERN MENNONITE COLLEGE
Music Department
Harrisonburg, VA 22801
(703) 433-2771
Staff: Kenneth Nafziger, Chairman
Affiliation: Church-related liberal arts college (Mennonite)
Accreditation: SACS
Areas: App Mus; Hist & Lit; Th & An; Cond; Opera; Church Mus; Mus Ed (Elem & HS)
Degrees: BA; BA, Mus Ed

EMORY AND HENRY COLLEGE
Music Department
Emory, VA 24327
(703) 944-3121
Staff: Prof. Joseph E. Williams, Chairman
Affiliation: Church-related liberal arts college (United Methodist)
Accreditation: SACS
Areas: App Mus; Hist & Lit; Th & An; Comp; Cond (Choral); Opera; Church Mus; Mus Ed (Elem & HS); Intro; Perf
Degrees: BA

GEORGE MASON UNIVERSITY
Music Division, Department of Performing Arts
4400 University Dr.
Fairfax, VA 22030
(703) 691-7950
Staff: Dr. Thomas Brawley, Coordinator, Music Division
Affiliation: State university of northern Virginia
Accreditation: SACS; NCATE
Areas: App Mus; Hist & Lit; Th & An; Comp; Cond; Orch; Opera; Hist Musicol; Ethnomusicol; Mus Ed (Elem & HS)
Degrees: BA; BM; MA
Scholarships: Limited scholarships available

HAMPTON INSTITUTE
Department of Music
Hampton, VA 23668
(804) 727-5402
Staff: Dr. Willia E. Daughtry, Chairman
Affiliation: Privately endowed liberal arts college
Accreditation: NASM; NCATE; SACS
Areas: App Mus; Hist & Lit; Th & An; Comp; Cond; Orch; Opera; Intro; Mus Ed (Elem & HS); Theater Mus; Hist Jazz; Perf
Degrees: BA; BS, Mus Ed; MA

HOLLINS COLLEGE
Music Department
Hollins College, VA 24020
(703) 362-6511
Staff: Dr. John Diercks, Chairman
Affiliation: Independent liberal arts college
Accreditation: NASM; SACS
Areas: App Mus; Hist & Lit; Th & An; Comp; Cond; Opera
Degrees: BA
Scholarships: Awarded on the basis of performance and academic standing (grades in the top 10 percent; scores of at least 1300)

JAMES MADISON UNIVERSITY
Music Department
Harrisonburg, VA 22801
(703) 433-6197
Staff: Dr. Joseph J. Estock, Chairman
Affiliation: State-supported liberal arts university
Accreditation: NASM; NCATE; SACS
Areas: App Mus; Th & An; Comp; Mus Ed (Elem & HS); Perf; Church Mus; Intro; Mus Mgmt
Degrees: BM; BME; MM

Scholarships: Scholarships of $400 to $1,500, annually renewable, awarded by audition during admissions process

LIBERTY BAPTIST COLLEGE
Department of Music and Art
Lynchburg, VA 24506
(804) 237-5961
Staff: David P. Randlett, Chairman
Affiliation: Private church-related liberal arts college (Baptist)
Accreditation: SACS
Areas: App Mus; Hist & Lit; Th & An; Comp; Cond; Orch; Hist Musicol; Church Mus; Mus Ed (Elem & HS)
Degrees: BA; BS, Mus Ed; BS, Perf; BS, Sacr Mus; MM
Scholarships: Up to full tuition for violin, viola, cello, bass, oboe, bassoon, based on auditions; partial tuition for other winds

LONGWOOD COLLEGE[1]
Department of Music
Farmville, VA 23901
(804) 392-9251
Staff: Louard F. Egbert, Chairman
Affiliation: State-supported college
Accreditation: SACS; NCATE
Areas: Th & An; Cond; Comp; Intro; Hist & Lit; Opera; Mus Ed (Elem & HS); Chamber Mus
Degrees: BA; BME

LYNCHBURG COLLEGE
Music Department
Lynchburg, VA 24501
(804) 522-8100
Staff: Dr. Robert Ellinwood, Chairman
Affiliation: Church-related liberal arts college (Disciples of Christ)
Accreditation: SACS
Areas: App Mus; Hist & Lit; Th & An; Opera; Church Mus; Mus Ed (Elem & HS)
Degrees: BA

MARY BALDWIN COLLEGE
Music Department
Staunton, VA 24401
(703) 885-0811
Staff: Robert Allen, Instructor
Affiliation: Private church-related liberal arts college (Presbyterian)
Accreditation: SACS
Areas: App Mus; Hist & Lit; Th & An; Mus Ed (Elem); Choir
Degrees: BA

MARY WASHINGTON COLLEGE
Department of Music
Fredericksburg, VA 22401
(703) 899-4356
Staff: James F. Baker, Chairman
Affiliation: State-supported liberal arts college
Accreditation: NASM; SACS
Areas: App Mus; Hist & Lit; Th & An; Comp; Cond; Orch; Intro; Mus Ed (Elem & HS); Electr Mus (part of Th); Perf; Hist Musicol
Degrees: BA
Scholarships: Performance scholarships awarded through audition

NORFOLK STATE UNIVERSITY
Music Department
2401 Corprew Ave.
Norfolk, VA 23504
(804) 623-8735
Staff: Dr. James M. Reeves, Chairman
Affiliation: State-supported university
Accreditation: NASM; NCATE; SACS
Areas: App Mus; Hist & Lit; Th & An; Cond; Opera; Mus Ed (Elem & HS)
Degrees: BS, Mus Ed; MM

OLD DOMINION UNIVERSITY
Music Department
Norfolk, VA 23508
(804) 440-4061
Staff: Harold Protsman, Chairman
Affiliation: State-supported urban university
Accreditation: NASM; SACS
Areas: App Mus; Hist & Lit; Th & An; Comp; Cond; Orch; Opera; Intro; Mus Ed (Elem & HS); Theater Mus; Electr Mus; Perf
Degrees: BA; BA, Mus Hist; BM, Comp; BM, Perf; BS, Mus Ed; BS, Mus Perf
Scholarships: Organizational and solo (voice and all instruments) scholarships offered; audition required; work-study for accompanists

PRESBYTERIAN SCHOOL OF CHRISTIAN EDUCATION
Music Department
1205 Palmyra Ave.
Richmond, VA 23227
(804) 359-5031
Staff: David W. McCormick, Coordinator of Dual Competency Program in Church Music and Christian Education
Affiliation: Church-related graduate school (Presbyterian, U.S.)
Accreditation: ATS; SACS
Areas: Church Mus
Degrees: MA
Scholarships: Scholarships available to all students, including music students; work scholarships awarded on the basis of need

RADFORD UNIVERSITY[1]
Department of Music
East Norwood St.
Radford, VA 24142
(703) 731-5177
Staff: Dr. Eugene C. Fellin, Chairman
Affiliation: Comprehensive state university
Accreditation: NASM; SACS
Areas: App Mus; Hist & Lit; Th & An; Comp; Cond; Orch; Opera; Hist Musicol; Church Mus; Mus Ed (Elem & HS); Mus Therapy
Degrees: BA; BM; BS, Mus Ed; BS, Mus Therapy; MA; MA, Mus Ed; MS, Mus Ed
Scholarships: Scholarships for performance ability awarded by audition

RANDOLPH-MACON WOMAN'S COLLEGE
Department of Music
Rivermont Ave.
Lynchburg, VA 24503
(703) 846-7392
Staff: Assoc. Prof. Daniel M. Raessler, Chairman
Affiliation: Church-related liberal arts college (United Methodist)
Accreditation: SACS
Areas: App Mus; Hist & Lit; Th & An; Comp; Cond; Opera; Hist Musicol; Intro; Mus Ed (Elem); Perf
Degrees: BA
Scholarships: Grisard Scholarship, given to an instrumentalist based on need and merit; Hsieh Scholarship, $1500, 3.92 GPA required, one given annually to student with highest GPA over 3.92

ROANOKE COLLEGE
Department of Fine Arts
Salem, VA 24153
(703) 389-2351
Staff: Karen C. Adams, Chairperson
Affiliation: Church-related liberal arts college (Lutheran Church in America)
Accreditation: SACS
Areas: App Mus; Hist & Lit; Th & An; Church Mus; Mus Ed (Elem & HS)
Degrees: BA
Scholarships: Marion Scholarships, 2 at $400 each, awarded by fall audition; 2 at $1000, awarded by Feb/Mar audition

SHENANDOAH COLLEGE AND CONSERVATORY OF MUSIC
Winchester, VA 22601
(703) 667-8714
Staff: Dr. Charlotte Collins, Conservatory Faculty Chairperson
Affiliation: Church-related liberal arts college and conservatory of music (United Methodist)
Accreditation: NASM; NAMT; SACS
Areas: App Mus; Hist & Lit; Th & An; Comp; Cond; Orch; Opera; Church Mus; Mus Ed (Elem & HS); Mus Therapy; Theater Mus; Piano Tech; Instr Rep; Electr Mus; Perf; Intro
Degrees: AA, Piano Tech; BM; BME; BSM; BMT; B, Jazz Studies; MA, Mus Ed
Scholarships: Talent scholarships awarded on the basis of evaluation by faculty after initial faculty recommendation

SWEET BRIAR COLLEGE
Music Department
Sweet Briar, VA 24595
(804) 381-5100
Staff: Allen Huszti, Chairman
Affiliation: Private college for women
Accreditation: SACS

Areas: App Mus; Th & An; Intro; Hist & Lit
Degrees: BA

UNIVERSITY OF RICHMOND
Music Department
University of Richmond, VA 23173
(703) 285-6334
Staff: Suzanne Bunting, Chairman
Affiliation: Church-related liberal arts college (Baptist)
Accreditation: NASM; SACS
Areas: App Mus; Hist & Lit; Th & An; Comp; Cond; Orch; Hist Musicol; Ethnomusicol; Church Mus; Intro; Mus Ed (Elem & HS); Electr Mus; Perf
Degrees: BA; BM
Scholarships: Awarded on the basis of exceptional ability in music and/or need

UNIVERSITY OF VIRGINIA
McIntire Department of Music
112 Old Cabell Hall
Charlottesville, VA 22903
(804) 924-3052
Staff: Donald G. Loach, Chairman
Affiliation: State-supported university
Accreditation: SACS
Areas: App Mus; Hist & Lit; Th & An; Comp; Cond; Orch; Hist Musicol; Ethnomusicol; Intro; Electr Mus; Perf
Degrees: BA; MA; MAT
Scholarships: Music lesson scholarships for music majors

VIRGINIA COMMONWEALTH UNIVERSITY
Music Department
922 Park Ave.
Richmond, VA 23284
(804) 257-1166
Staff: Dr. Richard Koehler, Chairman
Affiliation: State-supported university
Accreditation: NASM; NCATE; SACS
Areas: App Mus; Hist & Lit; Th & An; Comp; Cond; Opera; Hist Musicol; Church Mus; Intro; Mus Ed (Elem & HS); Mus Therapy; Electr Mus; Perf
Degrees: BM; BME; BS, Mus Ed; MM; MME
Scholarships: Awarded on the basis of need and merit

VIRGINIA INTERMONT COLLEGE[1]
Department of Performing Arts
Bristol, VA 24201
(703) 669-6101
Staff: Stephen Hamilton, Chairman
Affiliation: Church-related liberal arts college (Southern Baptist)
Accreditation: SACS
Areas: App Mus; Hist & Lit; Th & An; Comp; Church Mus; Intro; Mus Ed (Elem & HS); Perf
Degrees: BA
Scholarships: Scholarships available to incoming freshmen; awarded by audition, not by financial need

VIRGINIA POLYTECHNIC INSTITUTE AND STATE UNIVERSITY
Department of Music
Blacksburg, VA 24061
(703) 961-5685
Staff: Jon J. Polifrone, Head
Affiliation: State-supported land grant university
Accreditation: SACS
Areas: App Mus; Hist & Lit; Th & An; Comp; Intro; Mus Ed (Elem & HS); Perf
Degrees: BA; MA; EdD

VIRGINIA STATE UNIVERSITY[1]
Department of Music
Box 7, VSU
Petersburg, VA 23803
(804) 520-5311, 5312
Staff: Dr. Carl G. Harris, Jr., Chairman
Affiliation: State-supported liberal arts and teachers college
Accreditation: NASM; SACS
Areas: App Mus; Hist & Lit; Th & An; Comp; Mus Ed (Elem & HS); Perf
Degrees: BM; MS; MEd
Scholarships: J. Binford Walford–Laurelia B. Walford Scholarship awarded on the basis of B average and musical talent

VIRGINIA UNION UNIVERSITY
Music Department
1500 N. Lombardy St.
Richmond, VA 23220
(703) 359-9331
Staff: Dr. Odell Hobbs, Director of Music
Affiliation: Church-related university (Baptist)
Accreditation: SACS
Areas: App Mus; Mus Ed (Elem & HS)
Degrees: BA
Scholarships: Voice and instrumental scholarships available

WASHINGTON AND LEE UNIVERSITY
Department of Fine Arts, Music Division
Lexington, VA 24450
(703) 463-9111, x232
Staff: Robert Stewart, Head
Affiliation: Private liberal arts college
Accreditation: SACS
Areas: App Mus; Hist & Lit; Th & An; Comp
Degrees: Independent music major with emphasis in musicology or composition

WASHINGTON

CENTRAL WASHINGTON UNIVERSITY
Department of Music
Ellensburg, WA 98926
(509) 963-1216
Staff: Dr. Donald H. White, Chairman
Affiliation: State-supported university
Accreditation: NASM; NASC
Areas: App Mus; Hist & Lit; Th & An; Comp; Cond; Orch; Opera; Mus Ed (Elem & HS); Instr Rep; Intro; Electr Mus; Perf
Degrees: BM; BA; MM
Scholarships: Available for specific instruments

CORNISH INSTITUTE
Music Department
710 East Roy
Seattle, WA 98102
(206) 323-1400
Staff: Roger Nelson and Julian Priester, Administrators
Affiliation: Private fine arts college
Accreditation: NASC
Areas: App Mus; Hist & Lit; Th & An; Comp; Cond; Orch; Opera; Ethnomusicol; Jazz; Perf
Degrees: BFA
Scholarships: Scholarships of partial tuition awarded on the basis of audition, interview, demonstrated potential in and knowledge of chosen field, and financial need

EASTERN WASHINGTON UNIVERSITY
Department of Music
Cheney, WA 99004
(509) 235-6221
Staff: William Maxson, Chairman
Affiliation: State-supported college
Accreditation: NASM; NCATE; NASC
Areas: App Mus; Hist & Lit; Th & An; Comp; Cond; Orch; Opera; Hist Musicol; Mus Ed (Elem & HS); Theater Mus; Instr Rep; Perf
Degrees: BA; BA, Mus Ed; MA; MA, Mus Ed; MM; BM

THE EVERGREEN STATE COLLEGE[1]
Department of Music
Olympia, WA 98505
(206) 866-6100
Staff: Donald W. Chan, Professor
Affiliation: State-supported college
Accreditation: NASC
Areas: Th & An; Comp; Hist & Lit; Hist Musicol; Ethnomusicol
Degrees: BA

PACIFIC LUTHERAN UNIVERSITY
Department of Music
Tacoma, WA 98447
(206) 535-7601
Staff: David P. Robbins, Chairman
Affiliation: Church-related liberal arts college (American Lutheran)
Accreditation: NASM; NASC
Areas: App Mus; Comp; Cond; Orch; Church Mus; Intro; Mus Ed (Elem & HS); Electr Mus; Perf; Commer Mus
Degrees: BA; BAE; BM; MM; MME
Scholarships: Talent award based on financial need and talent

SEATTLE PACIFIC UNIVERSITY
School of Fine and Performing Arts
Seattle, WA 98119
(206) 281-2205
Staff: Carl H. Reed, Director
Affiliation: Church-related liberal arts

college (Free Methodist)
Accreditation: NASM; NCATE; NASC
Areas: App Mus; Hist & Lit; Th & An; Comp; Cond; Orch; Opera; Church Mus; Intro; Mus Ed (Elem & HS); Perf
Degrees: BA
Scholarships: Scholarships for freshmen and incoming students awarded on the basis of talent and need; audition required

SEATTLE UNIVERSITY
Fine Arts Department
Seattle, WA 98122
(206) 626-6336
Staff: J. Kevin Waters, Chairman
Affiliation: Private university sponsored and directed by the Jesuit order (Catholic)
Accreditation: NCATE; NASC
Areas: App Mus; Hist & Lit; Th & An; Comp; Cond; Orch; Mus Ed (Elem & HS); Hist Jazz; Interdisc arts courses (team-teaching symposia)
Degrees: BA

UNIVERSITY OF PUGET SOUND
School of Music
1500 N. Warner
Tacoma, WA 98416
(206) 756-3253
Staff: Dr. James Sorensen, Director
Affiliation: Privately endowed university
Accreditation: NASM; NCATE; NASC
Areas: App Mus; Hist & Lit; Th & An; Comp; Cond; Orch; Opera; Hist Musicol; Church Mus; Intro; Mus Ed (Elem & HS); Theater Mus; Perf
Degrees: BA; BM; MM
Scholarships: University grants and endowed scholarships

UNIVERSITY OF WASHINGTON
School of Music
Seattle, WA 98105
(206) 543-1200
Staff: Dr. Frederic Lieberman, Director
Affiliation: State-supported university
Accreditation: NASM; NASC
Areas: App Mus; Hist & Lit; Th & An; Comp; Cond; Orch; Opera; Hist Musicol; Ethnomusicol; Intro; Mus Ed (Elem & HS); Piano Tech; Electr Mus; Perf
Degrees: BA; BM; MA; MM; MAT; DMA; PhD
Scholarships: Scholarships for financial need awarded on the basis of audition, 3.0 GPA, and full-time status

WALLA WALLA COLLEGE
Music Department
College Place, WA 99324
(509) 527-2562
Staff: Dan M. Shultz, Chairman
Affiliation: Church-related liberal arts college (Seventh-day Adventist)
Accreditation: NASM; NASC
Areas: App Mus; Hist & Lit; Th & An; Comp; Cond; Orch; Church Mus; Mus Ed (Elem & HS)
Degrees: BA; BM
Scholarships: Free music lessons available to music majors

WASHINGTON STATE UNIVERSITY
Music Department
Pullman, WA 99164
(509) 335-8524
Staff: Prof. Robert L. Miller, Chairman
Affiliation: State-supported university
Accreditation: NASM; NASC
Areas: App Mus; Hist & Lit; Th & An; Comp; Cond; Orch; Opera; Intro; Mus Ed (Elem & HS); Perf
Degrees: BA; BM; MA
Scholarships: Various scholarships awarded on the basis of audition or tape submission; write the Music Department for information and application

WESTERN WASHINGTON UNIVERSITY
Department of Music
Bellingham, WA 98225
(206) 676-3130
Staff: Dr. Albert C. Shaw, Chairman
Affiliation: State-supported university
Accreditation: NASM; NCATE; NASC
Areas: App Mus; Hist & Lit; Th & An; Comp; Cond; Orch; Opera; Hist Musicol; Mus Ed (Elem & HS); Jazz; Electr Mus; Perf
Degrees: BM; MM
Scholarships: Awarded on the basis of applied music auditions

WHITMAN COLLEGE[1]
Department of Music
345 Boyer Ave.
Walla Walla, WA 99362
(509) 527-5232
Staff: Robert A. Kvam, Chairman
Affiliation: Privately-endowed college
Accreditation: NASM; NASC
Areas: Hist & Lit; Th & An; Comp; Cond; Orch; Hist Musicol; Mus Ed (Elem & HS)
Degrees: BA

WHITWORTH COLLEGE[1]
Department of Fine Arts
Spokane, WA 99251
(509) 466-1000, x584
Staff: Richard V. Evans, Chairman
Affiliation: Private liberal arts college related to the Presbyterian Church
Accreditation: NASM; NASC
Degrees: BA

WEST VIRGINIA

ALDERSON-BROADDUS COLLEGE
Department of Music and Music Education
Philippi, WV 26416
(304) 457-1700
Staff: Charles Ervin, Chairman
Affiliation: Church-related liberal arts college (Baptist)
Accreditation: NCA
Areas: Hist & Lit; Th & An; Cond; Orch; Mus Ed (Elem & HS)
Degrees: BA; BA, Mus Ed

BETHANY COLLEGE[1]
Music Department
Bethany, WV 26032
(304) 829-7331
Staff: Dr. William P. Crosbie, Head
Affiliation: Private liberal arts college
Accreditation: NCA
Areas: App Mus; Hist & Lit; Th & An; Comp; Cond; Orch; Opera; Hist Musicol; Mus Ed (Elem & HS); Theater Mus
Degrees: BA
Scholarships: Scholarships of half and full tuition awarded on the basis of need and talent (audition)

BLUEFIELD STATE COLLEGE[1]
Division of Fine Arts
Bluefield, WV 24701
(304) 325-7102, x217
Staff: William B. Caruth, Sr., Chairman
Affiliation: State-supported teachers college and liberal arts college, with a technological division
Accreditation: NCA
Areas: App Mus; Hist & Lit; Th & An; Cond; Orch; Mus Ed (Elem & HS)
Degrees: BS, Mus Ed

CONCORD COLLEGE[1]
Department of Music, Division of Fine Arts
Athens, WV 24712
(304) 384-3115
Staff: Dr. Dean W. Turner, Chairman
Affiliation: State-supported college
Accreditation: NCA; NCATE
Areas: App Mus; Hist & Lit; Th & An; Comp; Cond; Orch; Mus Ed (Elem & HS); Instr Rep
Degrees: BS, Mus Ed
Scholarships: Institutional and departmental scholarships awarded through recommendation of music faculty following audition

FAIRMONT STATE COLLEGE
Fine Arts Division, Music Department
Fairmont, WV 26554
(304) 363-4219
Staff: Dr. Leta Carson, Chairman
Affiliation: State-supported college
Accreditation: NCA
Areas: App Mus; Hist & Lit; Th & An; Comp; Cond; Orch; Intro; Mus Ed (Elem & HS); Mus Therapy; Instr Rep; Perf
Degrees: BA; BA, Mus Ed
Scholarships: MENC 4-year scholarships available to freshmen

GLENVILLE STATE COLLEGE
Department of Fine Arts
200 High St.
Glenville, WV 26351
(304) 462-7361, x185
Staff: Gary Gillespie, Chairman
Affiliation: State-supported college
Accreditation: NCA; NCATE

Areas: App Mus; Th & An; Intro; Hist & Lit; Mus Ed (Elem & HS)
Degrees: BA; BA, Mus Ed; BA, Interdisciplinary
Scholarships: Shaw Scholarship and tuition waivers require audition

MARSHALL UNIVERSITY[1]
Department of Music
Fourth Ave. and Hal Greer Blvd.
Huntington, WV 25701
(304) 696-3117
Staff: Paul A. Balshaw, Chairman
Affiliation: State-supported university
Accreditation: NASM; NCA
Areas: App Mus; Hist & Lit; Th & An; Comp; Cond; Orch; Opera; Hist Musicol; Church Mus; Mus Ed (Elem & HS); Fine Arts Intro
Degrees: BA; BFA; MA
Scholarships: Graduate assistantships; undergraduate tuition waivers in strings, winds, brass, percussion; cash awards in keyboard and voice; all awarded on the basis of performance ability; apply by May 1

SHEPHERD COLLEGE
Division of Creative Arts
Shepherdstown, WV 25443
(304) 876-2511
Staff: Dr. Guy Frank, Chairman
Affiliation: State-supported liberal arts and teacher training college
Accreditation: NCATE; NCA
Areas: App Mus; Hist & Lit; Th & An; Comp; Cond; Mus Ed (Elem & HS); Instr Rep; Perf; Jazz; Orch; Intro; Electr Mus
Degrees: BA
Scholarships: Tuition waivers and private scholarships awarded through audition

WEST LIBERTY STATE COLLEGE[1]
Department of Music
Hall of Fine Arts
West Liberty, WV 26074
(304) 336-8006
Staff: Charles D. Boggess, Chairman
Affiliation: State-supported college
Accreditation: NASM; NCA
Areas: Mus Ed (Elem & HS)
Degrees: BA, Mus Ed
Scholarships: Tuition scholarships awarded by audition

WEST VIRGINIA INSTITUTE OF TECHNOLOGY
Department of Music
Montgomery, WV 25136
(304) 442-3192
Staff: Charles F. Martyn, Chairman
Affiliation: State-supported college
Accreditation: NCA
Areas: App Mus; Hist & Lit; Th & An; Cond; Orch; Intro; Mus Ed (Elem & HS)
Degrees: BA; BS, Mus Ed; BS, Mus Bus
Scholarships: Tuition scholarships awarded through audition in all performances

WEST VIRGINIA STATE COLLEGE[1]
Department of Music
Institute, WV 25112
(304) 766-3000
Staff: W. Kent Hall, Chairman
Affiliation: State-supported college
Accreditation: NCA; NCATE
Areas: Th & An; Orch; Cond; Hist & Lit; Mus Ed (Elem & HS); Church Mus
Degrees: BS, Mus Ed

WEST VIRGINIA UNIVERSITY
College of Creative Arts, Division of Music
Morgantown, WV 26506
(304) 293-4091
Staff: Dr. C. B. Wilson, Chairman
Affiliation: State-supported university
Accreditation: NASM; NCA
Areas: App Mus; Hist & Lit; Th & An; Comp; Hist Musicol; Mus Ed (Elem & HS); Piano Ped
Degrees: BM; MM; DMA; EdD; PhD
Scholarships: Performance grants awarded through audition

WEST VIRGINIA WESLEYAN COLLEGE
Music Department
Buckhannon, WV 26201
(304) 473-8051
Staff: Dr. Bobby H. Loftis, Chairman
Affiliation: Church-related liberal arts college (Methodist)
Accreditation: NASM; NCA
Areas: App Mus; Hist & Lit; Th & An; Comp; Cond; Orch; Mus Ed (Elem & HS)
Degrees: BA; BME
Scholarships: Merit awards of up to $1,000 based on performance

WISCONSIN

ALVERNO COLLEGE
Music Department
3401 S. 39th St.
Milwaukee, WI 53215
(414) 647-3908
Staff: Sr. Mary Hueller, Coordinator
Affiliation: Church-related liberal arts college (Catholic)
Accreditation: NASM; NCATE; NCA
Areas: App Mus; Church Mus; Mus Ed (Elem & HS); Mus Therapy
Degrees: BA; BM
Scholarships: Scholarship for music major awarded on the basis of musical ability demonstrated through audition and music theory test

BELOIT COLLEGE
Music Department
Beloit, WI 53511
(608) 365-3391
Staff: Crawford Gates, Chairman
Affiliation: Private liberal arts college
Accreditation: NCA
Areas: App Mus; Hist & Lit; Th & An; Comp; Cond; Orch; Opera; Mus Ed (Elem & HS); Theater Mus
Degrees: BA
Scholarships: Financial aid and merit awards available

CARDINAL STRITCH COLLEGE
Music Department
6801 N. Yates Rd.
Milwaukee, WI 53217
(414) 352-5400
Staff: Sr. Annice Diderrich, Chairman
Affiliation: Private church-related liberal arts college (Roman Catholic)
Accreditation: NCA; NCATE
Areas: App Mus; Hist & Lit; Th & An; Intro; Perf
Degrees: BA
Scholarships: Applied music scholarships awarded on the basis of audition and academic record

CARROLL COLLEGE
Music Department
100 N. East Ave.
Waukesha, WI 53186
(414) 547-1211
Staff: Harold S. Kacanek, Chairman
Affiliation: Church-related liberal arts college (Presbyterian)
Accreditation: NCA
Areas: App Mus; Hist & Lit; Th & An; Comp; Cond; Orch; Opera; Church Mus; Mus Ed (Elem & HS); Mus Bus
Degrees: BA
Scholarships: Scholarships available

CARTHAGE COLLEGE[1]
Department of Music
2001 Alford Dr.
Kenosha, WI 53141
(414) 551-8500, x448
Staff: Richard Dale Sjoerdsma, Chairman
Affiliation: Church-related liberal arts college (Lutheran—LCA and in cooperation with ALC)
Accreditation: NASM; NCA
Areas: App Mus; Hist & Lit; Th & An; Comp; Cond; Orch; Opera; Church Mus; Mus Ed (Elem & HS); Piano Tech; Instr Rep; Mus Merch
Degrees: BA; MEd (creative arts major)
Scholarships: Approximately 10 scholarships awarded to incoming freshmen by audition

LAWRENCE UNIVERSITY[1]
Conservatory of Music
Music-Drama Center
115 N. Park Ave.
Appleton, WI 54911
(414) 735-6611
Staff: Colin Murdoch, Dean
Affiliation: Private liberal arts college
Accreditation: NASM; NCA
Areas: App Mus; Hist & Lit; Th & An; Comp; Cond; Orch; Intro; Mus Ed (Elem & HS); Perf
Degrees: BA; BM
Scholarships: Scholarships available

MILTON COLLEGE[1]
Music Department
Milton, WI 53563

(608) 868-2912
Staff: Robert Bond, Chairman
Affiliation: Private liberal arts college
Accreditation: NCA
Areas: App Mus; Hist & Lit; Th & An; Comp; Cond; Orch; Intro; Mus Ed (Elem & HS); Theater Mus; Perf
Degrees: BA; BS, Mus Ed
Scholarships: Awarded by audition

MOUNT MARY COLLEGE
Music Department
2900 N. Menomonee River Pkwy.
Milwaukee, WI 53222
(414) 258-4810
Staff: Sr. Marcia Zofkie, Chairman
Affiliation: Private liberal arts college
Accreditation: NCATE; NCA
Areas: App Mus; Hist & Lit; Th & An; Cond; Ethnomusicol; Church Mus; Intro; Mus Ed (Elem & HS)
Degrees: BA
Scholarships: 1 endowed scholarship for needy music student (memorial); 4 endowed Madrigal Dinner scholarships for music majors

MOUNT SENARIO COLLEGE
Music Department, Division of Fine Arts
College Avenue West
Ladysmith, WI 54848
(715) 532-5511
Staff: Alan Arnold, Chairman
Affiliation: Private liberal arts college
Accreditation: NCA
Areas: App Mus; Mus Mgmt/Bus
Degrees: BA; BS, Mus Ed
Scholarships: Generous scholarships for woodwind, brass, string, vocal and keyboard majors and minors

NORTHLAND COLLEGE[1]
Music Department
Ashland, WI 54806
(715) 682-4531
Staff: Joel Glickman, Chairman
Affiliation: Church-related liberal arts college (United Church of Christ)
Accreditation: NCA
Areas: App Mus; Hist & Lit; Th & An; Comp; Cond; Orch; Opera; Mus Ed (Elem & HS); Intro; Perf
Degrees: BA
Scholarships: Awarded to members of choir or wind ensemble

RIPON COLLEGE
Music Department
300 Seward St., Box 248
Ripon, WI 54971
(414) 748-8120
Staff: Dr. Donald Spies, Chairman
Affiliation: Private liberal arts college
Accreditation: NCA
Areas: App Mus; Hist & Lit; Th & An; Cond; Orch; Intro; Mus Ed (Elem & HS); Perf
Degrees: BA
Scholarships: Music cash awards

ST. NORBERT COLLEGE
Humanities Division
De Pere, WI 54115
(414) 337-3181
Staff: Robert Vanden Burgt, Chairman
Affiliation: Church-related liberal arts college (Roman Catholic)
Accreditation: NCA; NCATE
Areas: App Mus; Hist & Lit; Th & An; Comp; Cond; Orch; Opera; Hist Musicol; Mus Ed (Elem & HS); Theater Mus
Degrees: BA; BM

SILVER LAKE COLLEGE
Music Department, Division of Fine Arts
2406 S. Alverno Rd.
Manitowoc, WI 54220
(414) 684-6691
Staff: Sr. Lorna Zemke, Head, Music Department, and Chairperson, Division of Fine Arts
Affiliation: Private church-related liberal arts college (Roman Catholic)
Accreditation: NASM (pending); NCATE; NCA
Areas: App Mus; Hist & Lit; Th & An; Comp; Cond; Orch; Opera; Hist Musicol; Ethnomusicol; Church Mus; Mus Ed (Elem & HS); Theater Mus; Instr Rep; Jazz; Electr Mus; Synth; Computer
Degrees: BM
Scholarships: Erno Daniel Music Scholarship; Phyllis Sayeski Mu Scholarship; Delta Mu Theta Music Scholarship; all awards based on audition, academic record, and references

UNIVERSITY OF WISCONSIN EAU CLAIRE
Department of Music
Fine Arts 156
Eau Claire, WI 54701
(715) 836-4954
Staff: Dr. M. M. Schimke, Chairman
Affiliation: State-supported university
Accreditation: NASM; NCA
Areas: App Mus; Hist & Lit; Th & An; Comp; Cond; Orch; Opera; Hist Musicol; Intro; Mus Ed (Elem & HS); Mus Therapy; Theater Mus; Electr Mus; Perf
Degrees: BA; BM; BME; MAT; MST
Scholarships: Cash awards based on audition

UNIVERSITY OF WISCONSIN GREEN BAY
Music Department, Performing Arts Division
Green Bay, WI 54302
(414) 465-2348
Staff: Wayne L. Jaeckel, Chairman
Affiliation: State-supported liberal arts university
Accreditation: NASM; NCA
Areas: App Mus; Hist & Lit; Th & An; Comp; Cond; Orch; Opera; Hist Musicol; Ethnomusicol; Mus Ed (Elem & HS); Theater Mus
Degrees: BA; BS
Scholarships: Awards based on ability by audition

UNIVERSITY OF WISCONSIN LA CROSSE
Music Department
La Crosse, WI 54601
(608) 785-8409
Staff: Dr. William V. Estes, Chairman
Affiliation: State-supported university
Accreditation: NCATE; NCA
Areas: App Mus; Hist & Lit; Th & An; Comp; Cond; Orch; Opera; Hist Musicol; Mus Ed (Elem & HS); Electr Mus; Rec Tech
Degrees: BA; BS, Mus Ed
Scholarships: Performance scholarships awarded by competition through taped auditions

UNIVERSITY OF WISCONSIN MADISON
School of Music
455 N. Park St.
Madison, WI 53706
(608) 263-1900
Staff: Dr. Eunice Meske, Director
Affiliation: State-supported university
Accreditation: NASM; NCA
Areas: App Mus; Hist & Lit; Th & An; Comp; Cond; Orch; Opera; Hist Musicol; Ethnomusicol; Intro; Mus Ed (Elem & HS); Piano Tech; Electr Mus; Perf
Degrees: BA; BM; BME; MA; MM; DMA; PhD
Scholarships: Various scholarships available; contact School of Music for information

UNIVERSITY OF WISCONSIN MILWAUKEE
Music Department, School of Fine Arts
3223 N. Downer Ave.
Milwaukee, WI 53201
(414) 963-4393, 6063
Staff: Dr. Gerard McKenna, Chairman
Affiliation: State-supported university
Accreditation: NASM; NCA
Areas: App Mus; Hist & Lit; Th & An; Comp; Cond; Orch; Opera; Hist Musicol; Mus Ed (Elem & HS); Mus Therapy; Perf; Jazz
Degrees: BFA; MM; MFA
Scholarships: Scholarships of approximately $500 to $2000 awarded per semester to music students; judged and awarded on the basis of need and musical ability and promise

UNIVERSITY OF WISCONSIN-OSHKOSH
Department of Music
800 Algoma Blvd.
Oshkosh, WI 54901
(414) 424-4224
Staff: Dr. Alvin J. Curtis, Chairman
Affiliation: State-supported university
Accreditation: NASM; NAMT; NCA

Areas: App Mus; Hist & Lit; Th & An; Comp; Cond; Orch; Opera; Mus Ed (Elem & HS); Mus Therapy; Piano Tech; Instr Rep; Electr Mus; Perf; Recording Tech
Degrees: BA; BM; BME; BS; MA
Scholarships: Awarded on the basis of scholarship and musical performance

UNIVERSITY OF WISCONSIN-PARKSIDE
Department of Music
Kenosha, WI 53141
(414) 553-2111
Staff: Dr. Frank Mueller, Coordinator of Music
Affiliation: State-supported university
Accreditation: NCA
Areas: Th & An; Cond; Intro; Hist & Lit; Hist Musicol; Mus Ed (Elem & HS); App Mus; Comp
Degrees: BA

UNIVERSITY OF WISCONSIN-PLATTEVILLE
Music Department
Platteville, WI 53818
(608) 342-1143
Staff: Dr. R. E. Anfinson, Chairman
Affiliation: State-supported university
Accreditation: NCATE; NCA
Areas: App Mus; Hist & Lit; Th & An; Comp; Cond; Orch; Opera; Mus Ed (Elem & HS); Electr Mus; Perf
Degrees: BA; BS, Mus Ed
Scholarships: Awarded by audition

UNIVERSITY OF WISCONSIN-RIVER FALLS
Music Department
River Falls, WI 54022
(715) 425-3183
Staff: Donald A. Nitz, Chairman
Affiliation: State-supported university
Accreditation: NCA; NCATE
Areas: App Mus; Hist & Lit; Th & An; Comp; Cond; Orch; Intro; Mus Ed (Elem & HS); Piano Tech; Electr Mus; Perf
Degrees: BA; BME; BS, Mus Ed
Scholarships: Various scholarships available

UNIVERSITY OF WISCONSIN-STEVENS POINT
Music Department
Stevens Point, WI 54481
(715) 346-3107
Staff: Charles Reichl, Chairman
Affiliation: State-supported university
Accreditation: NASM; NCA
Areas: App Mus; Hist & Lit; Th & An; Comp; Cond; Orch; Opera; Mus Ed (Elem & HS); App Ped; Instr Rep; Piano Tech
Degrees: BA; BM; BME; MME
Scholarships: Scholarships available for all music areas; audition and entrance exam required

UNIVERSITY OF WISCONSIN STOUT
Music Department
Menomonie, WI 54751
(715) 232-1335
Staff: Lynn Pritchard, Chairman
Affiliation: State-supported university
Accreditation: NCA
Areas: App Mus; Hist & Lit; Mus Ed (Elem); Perf; Mus Appreciation; App Voice, Guitar, Piano

UNIVERSITY OF WISCONSIN-SUPERIOR
Music Department
Superior, WI 54880
(715) 394-8115
Staff: Dr. T. A. Bumgardner, Chairman
Affiliation: State-supported university
Accreditation: NCA; NCATE
Areas: App Mus; Hist & Lit; Th & An; Comp; Cond; Orch; Opera; Ethnomusicol; Intro; Mus Ed (Elem & HS); Theater Mus; Perf
Degrees: BA; BM; BME; BS, Mus Ed; MEPD
Scholarships: Foundation scholarships granted on the basis of audition and academic achievement

UNIVERSITY OF WISCONSIN-WHITEWATER
Music Department
Whitewater, WI 53190
(414) 472-1310
Staff: Dr. Howard G. Inglefield, Chairman
Affiliation: State university
Accreditation: NASM; NCA; NCATE
Areas: App Mus; Hist & Lit; Th & An; Mus Ed (Elem & HS); Perf; Intro
Degrees: BM; MST
Scholarships: Scholarships for music majors and participants of band and choir awarded by audition

VITERBO COLLEGE
Department of Music
815 South 9th Street
LaCrosse, WI 54601
(608) 784-0040
Staff: S. Marlene Weisenbeck, Chairperson
Affiliation: Private liberal arts college
Accreditation: NASM; NCATE; NCA
Areas: App Mus; Hist & Lit; Th & An; Comp; Cond; Orch; Opera; Church Mus; Intro; Mus Ed (Elem & HS); Perf; Theater Mus
Degrees: BA; BM; BME
Scholarships: Kress Scholarship, junior or senior, based on need and merit, $500 per year, 3.0 in music required; departmental scholarships, college funds based on merit available to freshmen and transfer students, renewable for four years by maintaining a 2.75 grade point average

WISCONSIN CONSERVATORY OF MUSIC
1584 N. Prospect Ave.
Milwaukee, WI 53202
(414) 276-4350
Staff: Dr. Patricia Jones, Dean
Affiliation: Private college-conservatory
Accreditation: NASM; Candidate NCA
Areas: App Mus; Hist & Lit; Th & An; Comp; Cond; Orch; Opera; Electr Mus; Jazz; Theater Mus; Piano Tech; Perf
Degrees: BM; MM
Scholarships: Merit scholarships, financial need scholarships, internships, graduate assistantships, based on varying requirements

WYOMING

UNIVERSITY OF WYOMING
Department of Music
Laramie, WY 82070
(307) 766-5242
Staff: Dr. David Tomatz, Chairman, Department of Music
Affiliation: State-supported university
Accreditation: NASM; NCA
Areas: App Mus; Hist & Lit; Th & An; Comp; Cond; Orch; Opera; Intro; Mus Ed (Elem & HS); Perf
Degrees: BA; BM; MA; MM
Scholarships: Tuition waivers available for talented students in music

PUERTO RICO

CONSERVATORY OF MUSIC OF PUERTO RICO
PO Box 41227, Minillas Station
Santurce, PR 00940
(809) 751-0160
Staff: Mr. David Bourns, Dean of Studies
Accreditation: MSA
Areas: App Mus; Hist & Lit; Th & An; Comp; Cond; Orch; Opera; Music Ed (Elem & HS); Perf
Degrees: BA
Scholarships: Federal and institutional scholarships available; student must be enrolled in 12 credit hours per week, must maintain a general average of 2.0 (C), and meet economic elibigiblity required by the Federal Government

INTER-AMERICAN UNIVERSITY OF PUERTO RICO
Department of Music
San German, PR 00753
(809) 892-1095, x279/892-4700
Staff: Salvador Rivera, Chairman
Affiliation: Private liberal arts university
Accreditation: MSA
Areas: App Mus; Hist & Lit; Th & An; Cond; Intro; Mus Ed (Elem & HS); Perf
Degrees: BA

UNIVERSITY OF PUERTO RICO
Music Department
Rio Piedras, PR 00931
(809) 764-0000, x2293
Staff: Donald Thompson, Chairman
Affiliation: State-supported university

Accreditation: MSA
Areas: App Mus; Hist & Lit; Th & An; Comp; Cond; Orch; Opera; Ethnomusicol; Mus Ed (Elem & HS); Electr Mus; Puerto Rican Mus; Mus in the Americas
Degrees: BA; BA, Mus Ed
Scholarships: Tuition waiver for participation in principal performance ensembles, by audition

CANADA

ALBERTA

PRAIRIE BIBLE INSTITUTE
Music Department
Three Hills, AB T0M 2A0
(403) 443-5511, x72
Staff: Raymond C. Olson, Chairman
Affiliation: Private school, trans-denominational
Accreditation: Province of Alberta
Areas: App Mus; Hist & Lit; Th & An; Cond; Church Mus; Perf
Degrees: BRE (Bachelor of Religious Education), music minor

UNIVERSITY OF ALBERTA
Music Department
Edmonton, AB T6G 2C9
(403) 432-3263
Staff: Dr. R. A. Stangeland, Chairman
Affiliation: Provincial institution
Accreditation: CUMS
Areas: App Mus; Hist & Lit; Th & An; Comp; Opera; Hist Musicol; Church Mus; Intro; Mus Ed (Elem & HS); Perf; Electr Mus
Degrees: BA; BM; MM; DMA
Scholarships: Scholarships available

UNIVERSITY OF CALGARY
Department of Music
Calgary, AB T2N 1N4
(403) 284-5376
Staff: Dr. C.K. Mather, Head
Affiliation: Public university
Accreditation: CUMS
Areas: App Mus; Hist & Lit; Th & An; Comp; Cond; Orch; Mus Ed (Elem & HS); Electr Mus
Degrees: BM; MM; MA

THE UNIVERSITY OF LETHBRIDGE[1]
Music Department
4401 University Dr.
Lethbridge, AB T1K 3M4
(403) 329-2111
Staff: Dr. John Jackson, Chairman
Affiliation: Undergraduate liberal arts university
Accreditation: CUMS
Areas: App Mus; Hist & Lit; Th & An; Comp; Cond; Orch; Intro; Mus Ed (Elem & HS); Perf
Degrees: BA; BFA; BM

BRITISH COLUMBIA

CAPILANO COLLEGE
Music Department
2055 Purcell Way
North Vancouver, BC V7J 3H5
(604) 986-1911
Staff: Karl Kobylansky, Coordinator
Affiliation: Provincially supported college
Areas: App Mus; Hist & Lit; Th & An; Comp; Orch; Mus Therapy; Intro; Orch; Arrang; Hist Jazz
Degrees: BM; Arts & Science Diploma
Scholarships: Available to college students in general

UNIVERSITY OF BRITISH COLUMBIA
Department of Music
6361 Memorial Road
Vancouver, BC V6T 1W5
(604) 228-3113
Staff: Dr. Wallace Berry, Head
Affiliation: Public university
Accreditation: CUMS
Areas: Hist & Lit; Th & An; Comp; Cond; Orch; Opera; Hist Musicol; Ethnomusicol; Intro; Mus Ed (HS); Electr Mus; Perf
Degrees: BA; BM; MA; MM; DMA; PhD
Scholarships: Scholarships available

UNIVERSITY OF VICTORIA
School of Music
P.O. Box 1700
Victoria, BC V8W 2Y2
(604) 721-7902
Staff: Paul Kling, Director
Affiliation: Provincial university
Accreditation: CUMS
Areas: App Mus; Th & An; Cond; Comp; Intro; Hist & Lit; Hist Musicol; Mus Ed (Elem & HS); Opera; Electr Mus; Perf; Orch
Degrees: BM; BME; MA; MM; PhD
Scholarships: Limited scholarships and bursaries available for academic/performance excellence; some awards require demonstration of financial need

MANITOBA

BRANDON UNIVERSITY
School of Music
Brandon, MB R7A 6A9
(204) 728-7388
Staff: Prof. Gordon Macpherson, Director
Accreditation: NASM; CUMS
Areas: App Mus; Hist & Lit; Th & An; Comp; Cond; Orch; Intro; Mus Ed (Elem & HS); Electr Mus; Perf
Degrees: BA; MM
Scholarships: R.D. Bell String Scholarships; Sanders Scholarships in Music; Board of Governors Entrance Scholarship; graduate assistantships up to $4,500; many others in all applied areas

MENNONITE BRETHREN BIBLE COLLEGE AND COLLEGE OF ARTS
Music Department
77 Henderson Hwy.
Winnipeg, MB R2L 1L1
(204) 667-9560
Staff: Dr. William Baerg, Chairman
Affiliation: Music teaching center for University of Winnipeg
Areas: App Mus; Hist & Lit; Th & An; Comp; Cond; Church Mus; Perf
Degrees: BA; BRS (Bachelor of Religious Studies, music major)
Scholarships: Scholarships based on academic and musical ability

UNIVERSITY OF MANITOBA
School of Music
65 Dafoe Rd.
Winnipeg, MB R3T 2N2
(204) 474-9465
Staff: Paul W. Paterson, Director
Affiliation: Provincially supported university
Accreditation: CUMS
Areas: App Mus; Hist & Lit; Th & An; Comp; Cond; Opera; Hist Musicol; Ethnomusicol; Church Mus; Intro; Mus Ed (Elem & HS); Perf
Degrees: BM
Scholarships: Most awarded for academic standing or performance level

WINNIPEG BIBLE COLLEGE
Department of Church Music
Otterburne, MB R0A 1G0
(204) 284-2923
Staff: Don Thiessen, Chairman
Affiliation: Interdenominational Bible college
Accreditation: AABC
Areas: App Mus; Hist & Lit; Th & An; Comp; Cond; Church Mus
Degrees: BA, (Mus/Christian Ed major); BA (Mus/Gen. St. major); BA (Mus/Bible major)

NEW BRUNSWICK

MOUNT ALLISON UNIVERSITY
Music Department
Sackville, NB E0A 3C0
(506) 536-2040, local 250
Staff: Brian Ellard, Head
Affiliation: Private university
Accreditation: CUMS
Areas: App Mus; Hist & Lit; Th & An; Comp; Cond; Orch; Church Mus; Intro; Mus Ed (Elem & HS); Perf
Degrees: BA; BM
Scholarships: Awarded on the basis of scholarship and performance ability

UNIVERSITE DE MONCTON
Music Department
Moncton, NB E1A 3E9
(506) 858-4041
Staff: Martin Waltz, Head
Affiliation: Government-supported university

Accreditation: CUMS
Areas: App Mus; Hist & Lit; Th & An; Comp; Cond; Orch; Hist; Musicol; Mus Ed (Elem & HS); Electr Mus; Perf
Degrees: BM (with 4 concentrations: General, Music Education, History and Theory, Performance)

NEWFOUNDLAND

MEMORIAL UNIVERSITY OF NEWFOUNDLAND
Music Department
Elizabeth Ave.
St. John's, NF A1C 5S7
(709) 737-7486
Staff: Assoc. Prof. Donald F. Cook, Head
Affiliation: Provincially supported university
Accreditation: CUMS
Areas: App Mus; Hist & Lit; Th & An; Comp
Degrees: BM; BME
Scholarships: Scholarships available

NOVA SCOTIA

ACADIA UNIVERSITY
School of Music
Wolfville, NS B0P 1X0
(902) 542-2201
Staff: Owen Stephens, Dean
Accreditation: CUMS
Areas: App Mus; Hist & Lit; Th & An; Comp; Cond; Orch; Opera; Intro; Mus Ed (Elem & HS); Electr Mus; Perf
Degrees: BA; BM; BME
Scholarships: General university scholarships based on academic achievement; specific music awards controlled by music faculty

DALHOUSIE UNIVERSITY[1]
Department of Music
Coburg Rd.
Halifax, NS B3H 4H6
(902) 424-2418
Staff: R.D. Byham, Chairman
Affiliation: Privately-endowed university
Accreditation: CUMS
Areas: Th & An; Orch; Comp; Intro; Hist & Lit; Mus Ed (Elem & HS); Opera
Degrees: BA; BME

ST. FRANCIS XAVIER UNIVERSITY
Department of Music
Box 108
Antigonish, NS B2G 1C0
(902) 867-2106
Staff: John C. O'Donnell, Chairman
Affiliation: Province-supported university
Areas: App Mus; Hist & Lit; Th & An; Comp; Cond; Ethnomusicol; Church Mus, Mus Ed (Elem & HS); Perf
Degrees: BA; Diploma in Church Mus; Diploma in Jazz Studies
Scholarships: Admission scholarships for ability and scholarship

ONTARIO

BROCK UNIVERSITY
Music Division, Department of Fine Arts
St. Catharines, ON L2S 3A1
(416) 688-5550, x214
Staff: Dr. Ronald Tremain, Coordinator
Affiliation: Provincially supported university
Accreditation: CUMS
Areas: Hist & Lit; Th & An; Comp; Orch; Intro; Electr Mus; Perf
Degrees: BA
Scholarships: 2 scholarships awarded to students with highest standing entering second year; 1 scholarship awarded to student with highest standing entering third year; 1 scholarship for student showing all-around excellence in both theoretical and practical music

CARLETON UNIVERSITY
Music Department
Colonel By Dr.
Ottawa, ON K1S 5B6
(613) 231-3633
Staff: David Piper, Chairman
Affiliation: Provincially supported university
Accreditation: CUMS
Areas: Hist & Lit; Th & An; Comp; Orch; Hist Musicol; Ethnomusicol; Intro; Electr Mus
Degrees: BA; BM
Scholarships: Available to continuing students only

CONRAD GREBEL COLLEGE/UNIVERSITY OF WATERLOO
Music Department
Waterloo, ON N2L 3G6
(519) 886-4955
Staff: Leonard Enns, Chairman
Affiliation: Church-related liberal arts college affiliated with the University of Waterloo (Mennonite)
Areas: App Mus; Hist & Lit; Th & An; Cond; Church Mus; Intro; Electr Mus; Perf; Ens; Comp; Computer Mus
Degrees: BA
Scholarships: Awarded on the basis of academic achievement and performance

EMMANUEL BIBLE COLLEGE
Department of Music
100 Fergus Ave.
Kitchener, ON N2A 2H2
(519) 742-3572
Staff: Elizabeth Esau, Chairman
Affiliation: Bible college sponsored by the Missionary Church
Accreditation: AABC
Areas: App Mus; Hist & Lit; Th & An; Cond; Church Mus
Degrees: BRE

HUNTINGTON UNIVERSITY
Department of Music
Ramsey Lake Rd.
Sudbury, ON P3E 2C6
(705) 675-1151
Staff: Douglas J. Webb, Chairman
Affiliation: Liberal arts college federated with Laurentian University
Accreditation: AUCC
Areas: App Mus; Hist & Lit; Th & An; Cond; Mus Ed (Elem)
Degrees: BA
Scholarships: Tuition awards and scholarships awarded on the basis of academic excellence

LAKEHEAD UNIVERSITY
Oliver Rd.
Thunder Bay, ON P7B 5E1
(807) 345-2121, x607
Staff: Igor Markstein, Director of Music
Affiliation: State-supported university
Areas: App Mus; Hist & Lit; Th & An; Comp; Cond; Chamber Mus
Degrees: HBA

McMASTER UNIVERSITY
Music Department
1280 Main St., W.
Hamilton, ON L8S 4M2
(416) 525-9140, x4445
Staff: F. A. Hall, Chairman
Affiliation: Public university
Areas: App Mus; Th & An; Orch; Comp; Cond; Opera; Perf; Intro; Hist & Lit; Hist Musicol; Mus Ed (Elem & HS)
Degrees: BA; BM; BME; MA
Scholarships: University and department scholarships available for students with honors standing, by audition

ONTARIO BIBLE COLLEGE
Department of Sacred Music
25 Ballyconnor Ct.
Willowdale, ON M2M 4B3
(416) 226-6380
Staff: Bert F. Polman, Chairman
Affiliation: Private interdenominational Bible college
Accreditation: AABC
Areas: App Mus; Hist & Lit; Th & An; Comp; Cond; Orch; Church Mus; Intro; Mus Ed (Elem); Perf
Degrees: B Sacr Mus
Scholarships: 1 scholarship for pianists and 1 general music scholarship awarded by music faculty on the basis of musicianship; graduation music award based on overall musicianship and leadership/academic achievement

QUEEN'S UNIVERSITY
Music Department
Kingston, ON K7L 3N6
(613) 547-5783
Staff: Dr. F.R.C. Clarke, Head
Affiliation: Regular nonaffiliated university
Accreditation: CUMS
Areas: App Mus; Hist & Lit; Th & An; Comp; Cond; Orch; Hist Musicol; Ethnomusicol; Intro; Mus Ed (Elem & HS); Electr Mus; Perf; Mus Therapy

Degrees: BA; BM
Scholarships: Various scholarships available; contact Music Department for information

ROYAL CONSERVATORY OF MUSIC
273 Bloor St., W.
Toronto, ON M5S 1W2
(416) 978-3797
Staff: Ezra Schabas, Principal
Affiliation: University of Toronto
Accreditation: CUMS
Areas: App Mus; Hist & Lit; Th & An; Comp; Cond; Intro; Mus Ed (Elem); Electr Mus; Perf
Degrees: ARCT

UNIVERSITY OF GUELPH
College of Arts
Guelph, ON N1G 2W1
(519) 824-4120, x3127
Staff: Stanley Saunders, Director of Music; Sylvia Hunter, Arts Administrator; Patricia Law, Administrative Secretary; Dudley Gibbs, Concert Coordinator
Affiliation: Provincially supported university
Accreditation: CUMS
Areas: App Mus; Hist & Lit; Th & An; Comp; Cond; Orch; Opera; Hist Musicol; Ethnomusicol; Collegium Musicum
Degrees: BA; BS; BASc; BComm
Scholarships: Limited funds available to students majoring in music

UNIVERSITY OF TORONTO
Faculty of Music
Edward Johnson Building
Toronto, ON M5S 1A1
Staff: Gustav Ciamaga, Dean
Accreditation: CUMS
Areas: App Mus; Hist & Lit; Th & An; Comp; Cond; Orch; Opera; Hist Musicol; Church Mus; Ethnomusicol; Intro; Mus Ed (Elem & HS); Electr Mus; Perf
Degrees: Mus Bac; MA (musicol); MusM; MusDoc; PhD (musicol); Diploma in Operatic Perf
Scholarships: Entrance, in-course, and graduation scholarships available

UNIVERSITY OF WESTERN ONTARIO
London, ON N6A 3K7
(519) 679-2481
Staff: Jack Behrens, Dean
Accreditation: CUMS
Areas: Th & An; Comp; Hist Musicol; Mus Ed (Elem & HS); Hist & Lit; Orch; Cond; App Mus; Electr Mus; Church Mus; Intro; Perf
Degrees: BA; BM; BMA; MM; MA
Scholarships: 5 continuing scholarships ($1500 per year); 5 first year scholarships ($1100); instrumental and vocal scholarships; graduate teaching assistantships

UNIVERSITY OF WINDSOR
School of Music
Windsor, ON N9B 3P4
(519) 253-4232, x132
Staff: Richard Householder, Director
Affiliation: Provincial university
Accreditation: CUMS
Areas: App Mus; Hist & Lit; Th & An; Comp; Mus Ed (Elem & HS); Theater Mus; Church Mus; Intro
Degrees: BA; BFA; BMA; BM
Scholarships: Tamburini-Ursu (brass), Les Kersey Memorial (piano), Windsor Symphony (string) available through audition; various others available through academic standing

WILFRID LAURIER UNIVERSITY
Faculty of Music
Waterloo, ON N2L 3C5
(519) 884-1970
Staff: Dr. Gordon K. Greene, Dean
Affiliation: Public university
Accreditation: CUMS
Areas: App Mus; Hist & Lit; Th & An; Comp; Cond; Orch; Opera; Church Mus; Intro; Mus Ed (Elem & HS); Electr Mus; Perf
Degrees: BA; BM
Scholarships: Entrance scholarships available; undergraduate scholarships awarded for high achievement

YORK UNIVERSITY
Music Department
4700 Keele Street
Downsview, ON M3J 1P3
(416) 667-3246
Staff: Prof. James R. McKay, Chairman
Affiliation: Government-funded university
Accreditation: CUMS
Areas: App Mus; Hist & Lit; Th & An; Comp; Orch; Hist Musicol; Ethnomusicol; Intro; Electr Mus
Degrees: BA; BFA; MFA
Scholarships: Available primarily to students entering the graduate program; undergraduate entrance and continuing scholarships and bursaries available on a limited basis

PRINCE EDWARD ISLAND

UNIVERSITY OF PRINCE EDWARD ISLAND
Music Department
Charlottetown, PE C1A 4P3
(902) 892-4121
Staff: Hubert Tersteeg, Chairman
Affiliation: State-supported university
Accreditation: CUMS
Areas: App Mus; Hist & Lit; Th & An; Comp; Cond; Orch; Mus Ed (Elem & HS)
Degrees: BA; BM: BME
Scholarships: String scholarships; general entrance scholarships; R & B buraries for out-of-province students

QUEBEC

BISHOP'S UNIVERSITY
Music Department
Lennoxville, PQ J1M 1Z7
(819) 569-9551
Staff: Howard F. Brown, Chairman
Affiliation: Nondenominational university offering education in arts, sciences, and business administration
Areas: App Mus; Hist & Lit; Th & An; Opera
Degrees: BA
Scholarships: Awarded on the basis of general academic standing

COLLEGE D'ENSEIGNEMENT GENERAL ET PROFESSIONNEL DE TROIS-RIVIERES[1]
Department de Musique
3500 rue de Courval
Trois-Rivieres, PQ G9A 5E6
(819) 378-9171
Staff: Claude Parenteau, Directeur
Affiliation: State-supported college
Accreditation: Ministere de L'Education, Province de Quebec
Areas: App Mus; Hist & Lit; Th & An
Degrees: DEC-Arts; Diploma of Collegial Studies in Fine Arts (Music)
Scholarships: Scholarships available from "Service des Prets et Bourses," Ministere de l'Education, Province de Quebec

CONCORDIA UNIVERSITY[1]
Department of Music
1455 de Maisonnueve Blvd. W.
Montreal, PQ H3G 1M8
(514) 879-4233
Staff: A. Crossman, Director
Affiliation: Provincially supported university
Accreditation: CUMS
Areas: App Mus; Hist & Lit; Th & An; Comp; Orch; Hist Musicol; Ethnomusicol; Mus Ed (Elem & HS); Mus Therapy; Piano Tech; Jazz; Hist Jazz; Early Mus Perf
Degrees: BFA; Diploma, Adv Mus Perf

CONSERVATOIRE DE MUSIQUE DE MONTREAL
School of Music
100 est Notre-Dame
Montreal, PQ H2Y 1C1
(514) 873-4031
Staff: Albert Grenier, Director
Areas: Hist & Lit; Th & An; Comp; Cond; Orch; Opera; Hist Musicol; Electr Mus; Perf
Degrees: BA; MA
Scholarships: Tuition is free; candidates must be Canadian citizens or received immigrants

McGILL UNIVERSITY
555 Sherbrooke St., W.
Montreal, PQ H3A 1E3
(514) 392-4533
Staff: Paul Pedersen, Dean
Affiliation: Provincially supported private university
Areas: App Mus; Hist & Lit; Th & An;

Comp; Cond; Orch; Opera; Hist Musicol; Church Mus; Intro; Mus Ed (Elem & HS); Electr Mus; Perf
Degrees: BM; MA; MM; D Mus
Scholarships: Scholarships and assistantships in all fields

UNIVERSITE DE MONTREAL[1]
Faculte de Musique
Case Postale 6128, Succursale "A"
Montreal, PQ H3C 3J7
(514) 343-6427
Staff: Henri Favre, Dean
Affiliation: Private university
Accreditation: CUMS
Areas: App Mus; Th & An; Comp; Hist & Lit; Hist Musicol; Ethnomusicol; Church Mus; Intro; Theater Mus; Electr Mus; Perf
Degrees: BM; MA; MM; PhD; D Mus

UNIVERSITE LAVAL[1]
Ecole de Musique
Cite universitaire
Quebec, PQ G1K 7P4
(418) 656-5742
Staff: Pierre Thibault, Directeur
Accreditation: CUMS
Areas: Hist & Lit; Th & An; Comp; Orch; Hist Musicol; Church Mus; Intro; Mus Ed (Elem & HS); Instr Rep; Electr Mus; Perf
Degrees: BM; BS, Mus Ed; MA; MA, Mus Ed; PhD

SASKATCHEWAN

BRIERCREST BIBLE COLLEGE
Music Department
Caronport, SK S0H 0S0
(306) 756-2321
Staff: Wilfred Gaertner, Chairman
Affiliation: Interdenominational Bible college
Accreditation: AABC
Areas: App Mus; Hist & Lit; Th & An; Cond; Church Mus; Intro; Perf
Degrees: B Sacr Mus; BRE (music major)
Scholarships: 2 Sperling Memorial Music Scholarships; 20 other bursaries and scholarships available based on academic and personal standing and financial need

CANADIAN BIBLE COLLEGE AND CANADIAN THEOLOGICAL SEMINARY
Division of Sacred Music
4400 Fourth Ave.
Regina, Saskatchewan S4T 0H8
(306) 545-1515, x57
Staff: Duane D. Emch, Chairman
Affiliation: The official colleges of the Christian Alliance and Missionary Alliance Church (in Canada)
Accreditation: AABC
Areas: App Mus; Hist & Lit; Th & An; Comp; Cond; Church Mus; Intro
Degrees: BSM
Scholarships: Scholarships for music majors and applied music scholarships for nonmusic majors awarded on the basis of ability; some grants based on need

UNIVERSITY OF REGINA[1]
Music Department
Regina, SK S4S 0A2
(306) 584-4111
Staff: Prof. J. Richard Raum, Chairman
Accreditation: CUMS
Areas: App Mus; Hist & Lit; Th & An; Comp; Cond; Orch; Opera; Church Mus; Intro; Mus Ed (HS); Theater Mus; Electr Mus; Perf
Degrees: BA; BM; BME; MM
Scholarships: Entrance and various other scholarships available; 3.25 GPA and audition required

Colleges and Conservatories Index

A

B

C

D

E

F

G

H

I

J

K

L

M

N

O

P

Q

R

S

T

U

V

W

X

Y

Community Colleges

U.S. and Canadian community colleges that offer at least a two-year course of study leading to an Associate degree in Music are listed alphabetically by state or province; non-degree granting institutions are not included. The name of the head of the music department, institution's affiliation, accrediting agency, areas of study, degrees offered, and scholarships available are given for most schools. The number 1 following the name of the institution indicates that they did not respond to our questionnaire. An alphabetical cross-index appears at the end of this section.

The following abbreviations have been used for accrediting agencies:

ACCM - Association of Colleges and Conservatories of Music
CUMS - Canadian University Music Society
MSA - Middle States Association of Colleges and Schools
NASC - Northwest Association of Schools and Colleges
NASM - National Associaton of Schools of Music
NCA - North Central Association of Colleges and Schools
NEA - New England Association of Schools and Colleges
SACS - Southern Association of Colleges and Schools
WASC - Western Association of Schools and Colleges

The following abbreviations have been used for degrees offered:

AA - Associate in Arts
AAS - Associate in Applied Science
AFA - Associate in Fine Arts
ALA - Associate in Liberal Arts
AM - Associate in Music
AS - Associate in Science

The following abbreviations have been used for areas of study:

App Mus - Applied Music
Mus Hist - Music History
Mus Lit - Music Literature
Th & An - Theory & Analysis
Comp - Composition
Cond - Conducting
Orch - Orchestration
Church Mus - Church Music
Mus Ed (Elem) - Music Education (Elementary)
Mus Ed (HS) - Music Education (High School)
Mus Therapy - Music Therapy
Theater Mus - Theater Music
Piano Tech - Piano Technology (Tuning)
Inst Rep - Instrument Repair
Mus Appr - Music Appreciation
Perf - Performance
Intro - Introductory

ALABAMA

GEORGE C. WALLACE STATE COMMUNITY COLLEGE[1]
Division of Fine Arts
Dothan, AL 36301
(205) 983-3521
Staff: Ralph E. Purvis, Chairman
Affiliation: State community college
Accreditation: SACS
Areas: App Mus; Mus Lit; Cond; Opera; Theater Mus
Degrees: AM
Scholarships: In performance and accompanying

JOHN C. CALHOUN STATE COLLEGE
Department of Fine Arts, Music Programs
PO Box 2216
Decatur, AL 35602
(205) 353-3102
Staff: Dr. Art Bond, Chairperson, Fine Arts Department
Affiliation: State supported junior college
Accreditation: SACS
Areas: App Mus; Mus Hist; Th & An; Comp; Cond; Mus Ed (Elem & HS)
Degrees: AS
Scholarships: Performing arts; performing abilities in voice, piano, or instrumental

NORTHEAST ALABAMA STATE JUNIOR COLLEGE
Division of Fine Arts and Humanities
PO Box 159
Rainsville, AL 35986
(205) 228-6001
Staff: Charlene Larson, Instructor of Music/Speech; Daniel Knox, Instructor of Music
Affiliation: State-supported junior college
Accreditation: SACS
Areas: App Mus; Class Piano; Class Voice; Chorus; Ensemble; Hist & Apprec of Mus; Class Guitar; Class woodwinds; Class percussion; Band; Th & An
Degrees: AA; Transfer credit
Scholarships: For accompanying musical groups; performance arts scholarships in voice, piano, instruments

NORTHWEST ALABAMA STATE JUNIOR COLLEGE[1]
Arts & Skills division
Phil Campbell, AL 35581
(205) 993-5331
Staff: Jimmie Lee Sparks, Chairperson
Affiliation: State-supported junior college
Accreditation: SACS
Areas: App Mus; Mus Hist; Mus Lit; Th & An; Comp; Mus Ed (Elem & HS); Piano Tech
Degrees: AA; AAS
Scholarships: Yes, band

PATRICK HENRY STATE JUNIOR COLLEGE[1]
Language & Fine Arts Division
PO Box 646
Monroeville, AL 36460
(205) 575-3156
Staff: Dr. Margaret H. Murphy, Chairman
Affiliation: State
Accreditation: SACS
Areas: Intro courses
Degrees: AA
Scholarships: For 2.0 GPA and participation in campus presentations

SNEAD STATE JUNIOR COLLEGE
Music Department
Drawer D
Boaz, AL 35957
(215) 593-5261
Staff: Glenn L. Maze, Chairman
Affiliation: State-supported junior college
Accreditation: SACS
Areas: App Mus; Th & An; Church Mus; Mus Ed (Elem); Hist & Lit
Degrees: AA; AAS
Scholarships: Performing Arts; Grant-in-Aid Scholarships (full tuition)

ALASKA

SHELDON JACKSON COLLEGE
Music Department
Box 479
Sitka, AK 99835
(907) 747-5236
Staff: Patricia Oetken, Director of Music
Affiliation: Church-related two-year college (Presbyterian)
Accreditation: NASC
Areas: App Mus; Intro courses; Fundamentals of Mus; Intro; Mus Ed (Elem)
Degrees: AA; AS; BA (Elem Ed)
Scholarships: For degree programs

ARIZONA

EASTERN ARIZONA COLLEGE[1]
Division of Fine Arts
616 Church St.
Thatcher, AZ 85552
(602) 428-3281
Staff: J. Ronald Keith, Fine Arts Division Chairman and Music Department Chairman
Affiliation: State-supported junior college

Accreditation: NCA
Areas: App Mus; Mus Hist; Mus Lit; Th & An; Cond
Degrees: AA
Scholarships: Performance scholarships. Letter of recommendation from high school director is required. Tapes are required under certain circumstances. Applicants should contact the school for more information.

GLENDALE COMMUNITY COLLEGE
Music Department
6000 W. Olive Ave.
Glendale, AZ 85301
(602) 934-2211, x231
Staff: Dr. Lee Baxter, Chairman
Affiliation: Community college
Accreditation: NCA
Areas: Hist & Lit; Th & An; Opera; Intro; App Mus; Cond; Mus Ed (Elem & HS); Theater Mus; Chamber Singing; Band; Choir
Degrees: AA
Scholarships: Fees for vocal and instrumental

CALIFORNIA

ALLAN HANCOCK COLLEGE
Music Department
800 S. College Dr.
Santa Maria, CA 93454
(805) 922-6966
Staff: Prof. Glenn A. Montague, Chairman
Affiliation: State-supported community college
Accreditation: WASC
Areas: App Mus; Mus Hist; Th & An; Orch; Mus Ed (Elem); Theater Mus
Degrees: AA; Transfer credit

AMERICAN RIVER COLLEGE
Music Department
4700 College Oak Dr.
Sacramento, CA 95841
(916) 484-8433
Staff: Larry Anderson, Chairman
Affiliation: Community college division of fine and applied arts
Accreditation: WASC
Areas: App Mus; Hist & Lit; Th & An; Intro; Perf
Degrees: AA

BAKERSFIELD COLLEGE
Music Department
1801 Panorama Dr.
Bakersfield, CA 93305
(805) 395-4547
Staff: Robert Oliveira, Chairman
Affiliation: State and community supported community college
Accreditation: NASM; WASC
Areas: App Mus; Hist & Lit; Th & An; Intro
Degrees: AA; AS; Transfer credit
Scholarships: Private and general scholarships—by recommendation of instructors

CABRILLO COLLEGE
Music/Drama, Division of Performing Arts
6500 Soquel Dr.
Aptos, CA 95076
(408) 426-6288
Staff: Lile O. Cruse, Chairman, Division of Performing Arts
Affiliation: Community college
Accreditation: WASC
Areas: App Mus; Hist & Lit; Th & An; Comp; Cond; Orch; Theater Mus; Piano Tech; Jazz; Commer Mus
Degrees: AA

CHABOT COLLEGE[1]
Division of Humanities
25555 Hesperian Blvd.
Hayward, CA 94545
(415) 786-6828
Staff: Otto E. Mielenz, Music Coordinator
Affiliation: Community college
Accreditation: WASC
Areas: App Mus; Mus Hist; Mus Lit; Th & An; Mus Ed (Elem)
Degrees: AA; Transfer credit

CHAFFEY COMMUNITY COLLEGE
Music Department, Creative Arts Division
5885 Haven Ave.
Alta Loma, CA91701
(714) 987-1731
Staff: C.A. Sheppard, Chairman, Division
Affiliation: Community college
Accreditation: WASC
Areas: App Mus; Mus Hist; Th & An; Mus Lit; Commer Mus
Degrees: AA; Transfer credit
Scholarships: Vocal—audition; Winifred Bailey Scholarship for a transferring graduating sophomore, selected by music faculty based on outstanding music performance; instrumental scholarships in jazz to qualified performers based on need

CITRUS COLLEGE[1]
Department of Music
18824 E. Foothill Blvd.
Azusa, CA 91702
(213) 335-0521
Staff: Frank Magliocco, Chairman
Affiliation: Community college
Accreditation: WASC
Areas: App Mus; Mus Hist; Mus Lit; Th & An; Comp; Cond; Orch; Opera; Theater Mus; Instrument Repair
Degrees: AA
Scholarships: A number of \$100-\$150 scholarships to help students buy books

COLLEGE OF ALAMEDA[1]
Fine, Applied, and Language Arts Division
555 Atlantic Ave.
Alameda, CA 94501
(415) 522-7221, x236, 246
Staff: Dr. Barbara E. M. Cannon, Assistant Dean
Affiliation: Community college
Accreditation: WASC
Areas: App Mus; Hist & Lit; Th & An; Comp; Jazz Improv; Choir; Perc
Degrees: AA

COLLEGE OF SAN MATEO[1]
Fine & Performing Arts Division
1700 W. Hillsdale Blvd.
San Mateo, CA 94402
(415) 574-6288
Staff: Wilson G. Pinney, Division Director
Affiliation: State-supported community college
Accreditation: WASC
Areas: App Mus; Mus Hist; Mus Lit; Th & An; Comp
Degrees: AA

COLLEGE OF THE DESERT
Music Department
43-500 Monterey Ave.
Palm Desert, CA 92260
(714) 346-8041
Staff: Dr. John L. Norman, Chairman
Affiliation: State-supported junior college
Accreditation: WASC
Areas: App Mus; Mus Hist; Th & An; Opera; Church Mus
Degrees: AA; Transfer credit

COLLEGE OF THE REDWOODS[1]
Music Department
Eureka, CA 95501
(707) 443-8411
Staff: Dean Boyd, Chairman
Affiliation: State-supported junior college
Accreditation: WASC
Areas: App Mus; Mus Lit; Th & An; Cond
Degrees: AA; Transfer credit

COLLEGE OF THE SISKIYOUS
Music Department
800 College Ave.
Weed, CA 96094
(916) 938-4462
Affiliation: State-supported community college
Accreditation: NASM; WASC
Areas: App Mus; Th & An; Hist & Lit
Degrees: AA
Scholarships: \$150 annually-enrollment in 2 choral groups; \$200 annually—enrollment in 3 performance groups; \$100 annually—enrollment in 2 performance groups

CUESTA COLLEGE[1]
Fine Arts Division
PO Box J
San Luis Obispo, CA 93406
(805) 544-2943
Staff: Barry Frantz, Chairman
Affiliation: Community college
Accreditation: WASC
Areas: App Mus; Mus Hist; Th & An; Opera; Theater Mus; Stage Band;

Chorus
Degrees: AA; Transfer credit
Scholarships: For full time students only, $50 applicable for private lessons

CYPRESS COMMUNITY COLLEGE
Music Department
9200 Valley View St.
Cypress, CA 90630
(714) 826-2220, x139
Staff: Jack Leyda, Chairman
Affiliation: Community college
Accreditation: NASM; WASC
Areas: App Mus; Hist & Lit; Th & An; Comp; Cond; Opera; Mus Ed (Elem & HS); Mus Therapy; Theater Mus; Piano Tech; Intro; App Voice; Guitar; Piano; Brass; Woodwinds; Strings
Degrees: AA; AFA; Transfer credit
Scholarships: Piano, Vocal, Instrumental, Guitar

DE ANZA COLLEGE[1]
Fine Arts Division
21250 Stevens Creek Blvd.
Cupertino, CA 95014
(408) 996-4671
Staff: Dr. Here Patnoe, Chairman, Music Department
Affiliation: Public community college
Accreditation: WASC
Areas: App Mus; Mus Hist; Th & An; Comp; Cond; Counterpoint; Jazz Arranging; & Improv; Nursery School Mus; Perf; Voice; Choral; Band; Jazz Ensemble; Jazz Hist
Degrees: AA

EL CAMINO COLLEGE
Division of Fine Arts
Via Torrance, CA 90506
(213) 532-3670
Staff: Dr. Lewis E. Hiigel, Dean
Affiliation: Community (district) college
Accreditation: WASC
Areas: App Mus; Mus Hist; Th & An; Comp; Cond; Orch; Mus Ed (Elem); Voice; Piano
Degrees: AA; Tranfer credit
Scholarships: $150 per semester, renewable for three additional semesters, audition only

FOOTHILL COMMUNITY COLLEGE
Department of Fine Arts
12345 El Monte Rd.
Los Altos Hills, CA 94022
(415) 948-8590
Staff: John L. Mortarotti, Chairman of Fine Arts
Affiliation: State and locally supported college
Accreditation: WASC
Areas: App Mus; Cond; Comp; Mus Appr; Mus Hist & Lit
Degrees: AA

FRESNO CITY COLLEGE
Music Department
1101 E. University Ave.
Fresno, CA 93741
(209) 442-4600, x8463
Staff: W. Vincent Moats, Chairman
Affiliation: Public community college
Accreditation: WASC
Areas: App Mus; Hist & Lit; Th & An; Comp; Cond; Opera; Theater Mus; Commer Mus
Degrees: AA; Transfer credit
Scholarships: Several community-sponsored scholarships, based on ability and need

FULLERTON COLLEGE[1]
Division of Fine Arts
321 E. Chapman Ave.
Fullerton, CA 92634
(714) 871-8000, x88
Staff: Terry J. Blackley, Chairman
Affiliation: Two-year community college
Accreditation: WASC
Areas: App Mus; Mus Hist; Th & An; Comp; Orch; Mus Ed (Elem & HS); Theater Mus; Commercial Mus
Degrees: AA
Scholarships: Yes

GAVILAN COLLEGE
Humanities—Music Department
5055 Santa Teresa Blvd.
Gilroy, CA 95020
(408) 847-1400
Staff: Arthur Juncker, Chairman, Music Department
Affiliation: Community college
Accreditation: WASC
Areas: App Mus; Mus Hist; Mus Lit; Th & An; Comp; Commer Mus
Degrees: AA; AS; Transfer credit
Scholarships: Yes

GOLDEN WEST COLLEGE[1]
Institute of Arts, Humanities, and Social Sciences
15744 Golden West St.
Huntington Beach, CA 92647
(714) 842-5327
Staff: Mary Wise, Instructional Coordinator
Affiliation: Community college
Accreditation: WASC
Areas: App Mus; Th & An; Comp; Church Mus; Rec Arts; Commer Perf; Copyist-Comp-Arrang; Songwriting; Piano Teaching; Retail Mus
Degrees: AA, Commer Mus & Rec Arts

GROSSMONT COLLEGE
Music Department
8800 Grossmont College Dr.
El Cajon, CA 92020
(619) 465-1700, x235
Staff: Dr. Ronald J. Sherrod, Chairman
Affiliation: Community college
Accreditation: WASC
Areas: App Mus; Th & An; Mus Appr; Hist & Lit
Degrees: AA
Scholarships: Scholarships for private lessons, based on college level proficiency

HARTNELL COLLEGE
Fine Arts and Social Sciences
156 Homestead Ave.
Salinas, CA 93901
(408) 758-8211
Staff: Dr. Manuel G. Rivera, Dean
Affiliation: State-supported junior college
Accreditation: WASC
Areas: App Mus; Hist & Lit; Th & An; Comp; Theater Mus
Degrees: AA
Scholarships: Boronda Scholarship in the Fine Arts

IMPERIAL VALLEY COLLEGE
Music Department, Humanities Division
PO Box 158
Imperial, CA 92251
(714) 352-8320
Staff: Jack B. Fuesler, Chairperson
Affiliation: Public two-year community college
Accreditation: WASC
Accreditation: App Mus; Mus Hist; Mus Lit; Th & An; Mus Ed (Elem)
Degrees: AA; Transfer credit

LANEY COMMUNITY COLLEGE
Music Department
10th & Fallon Sts.
Oakland, CA 94606
(415) 834-5740
Staff: Elvo D'Amante, Chairman
Affiliation: Community college (urban) campus of Peralta Community College District in Alameda County
Accreditation: WASC
Areas: Mus Hist; Th & An; Comp; Orch; Church Mus; Jazz Hist; Jazz Workshop; Band; Ear-training; Chinese Orchestra
Degrees: AA; Transfer credit

LONG BEACH CITY COLLEGE
Music Department
4901 E. Carson St.
Long Beach, CA 90808
(213) 420-4309
Staff: Priscilla Remeta, Chairman
Affiliation: Community (city) college
Accreditation: WASC
Areas: App Mus; Mus Hist; Th & An; Comp; Cond; Orch; Mus Ed (Elem); Theater Mus
Degrees: AA, Commer Mus; Cert, Commer Mus

LOS ANGELES CITY COLLEGE
Music Department
855 N. Vermont Ave.
Los Angeles, CA 90029
(213) 669-4377
Staff: Dominick A. DiSarro, Chairman
Affiliation: Community (city) college
Accreditation: WASC
Areas: App Mus; Mus Hist; Mus Lit; Th & An; Comp; Orch;
Degrees: AA; Transfer credit
Scholarships: For academic excellence and performance proficiency $100 (per semester) Clausen; $100 (per semester) Altheuser, primarily for choral/vocal students; $1,000 (awarded annually) Alpert, for an incoming student

LOS ANGELES HARBOR COLLEGE[1]
Humanities & Fine Arts Division, Music Department
1111 Figueroa Pl.
Wilmington, CA 90744
(213) 518-1000
Staff: Robert H. Billings, Chairman, Humanities & Fine Arts Division
Affiliation: Part of Los Angeles Community College District
Accreditation: WASC
Areas: App Mus; Th & An; Orch; Electronic Mus; recording Arts; Jazz Apprec & Hist
Degrees: AA

LOS ANGELES VALLEY COLLEGE
Music Department
5800 Fulton Ave.
Van Nuys, CA 91401
(213) 781-1200
Staff: Richard D. Carlson, Chairman
Affiliation: Community (city) college
Accreditation: WASC
Areas: Th & An; Cond; Orch; Opera Workshop; Hist & Lit; Comp; Theater Mus
Degrees: AA; Transfer credit

MENLO COLLEGE
Music Department
Menlo Park, CA 94025
(415) 323-6141
Staff: Janis Wilcox, Professor
Affiliation: Private liberal arts junior college
Accreditation: NASM; WASC
Areas: Hist & Lit; Theater Mus; Intro courses
Degrees: AA; Transfer credit

MERCED COLLEGE[1]
Music Department
3600 M. St.
Merced, CA 95340
(209) 723-4321
Staff: Ronnie Williams, Dean of Arts and Science
Affiliation: State and locally supported junior college
Accreditation: WASC
Areas: App Mus; Th & An; Mus Appr; Ethnomusicol; Opera
Degrees: AA

MIRACOSTA COLLEGE
Music Department
One Barnard Dr.
Oceanside, CA 92054
(619) 757-2121
Staff: Jeffrey Sell, Chairperson, Music Department; Dr. Keith Broman, Vice-President, Instruction
Affiliation: State-supported community college
Accreditation: WASC
Areas: App Mus; Hist & Lit; Th & An; Mus Ed (Elem & HS); Piano Tech; Jazz; Theater Mus
Degrees: AA; AM; Transfer credit
Scholarships: Scholarships available; lesson fees for vocal

MODESTO JUNIOR COLLEGE[1]
Music Department
College Ave.
Modesto, CA 95350
(209) 526-2000
Staff: Robert W. Larson, Chairman
Affiliation: State and locally supported community college
Accreditation: WASC
Areas: App Mus; Mus Hist & Lit; Th & An; Cond; Opera; Mus Ed (Elem); Theater Mus
Degrees: AA

MOORPARK COLLEGE[1]
Performing Arts Department
7075 Campus Rd.
Moorpark, CA 93021
(805) 529-2321
Staff: Alan Hyams, Chairman
Affiliation: State and community supported college
Accreditation: WASC
Areas: App Mus; Th & An; Orch; Cond; Mus Appr; Mus Hist & Lit; Opera
Degrees: AA

MT. SAN ANTONIO COMMUNITY COLLEGE
Music Department
1100 N. Grand Ave.
Walnut, CA 91789
(714) 594-5611
Staff: Gary Toops, Chairperson
Affiliation: Community college
Accreditation: WASC
Areas: App Mus; Mus Hist; Mus Lit; Th & An; Theater Mus
Degrees: AA; Transfer credit

NAPA VALLEY COLLEGE
Music Department, Fine and Performing Arts Division
2277 Napa-Vallejo Hwy.
Napa, CA 94558
(707) 255-2100, x274
Staff: Michael R. Tausig, Chairman, Performing Arts Division
Affiliation: Community college for Napa County
Accreditation: WASC
Areas: App Mus; Hist & Lit; Th & An; Comp; Cond; Orch; Mus Therapy; Theater Mus; Piano Tech; Mus in Early Childhood Ed
Degrees: AA; Certificate in piano tuner/techncian/repair

ORANGE COAST COLLEGE
Fine Arts Division
2701 Fairview Rd.
Costa Mesa, CA 92626
(714) 556-5523
Staff: Edward R. Baker, Chairman
Affiliation: Community college
Accreditation: WASC
Areas: App Mus; Mus Hist; Th & An; Comp; Cond; Orch; Opera; Church Mus; Mus Ed (Elem); Mus Therapy; Theater Mus; Piano Tech; Instrument Repair
Degrees: AA; Transfer credit

PALOMAR COLLEGE
Music Department
1140 W. Mission
San Marcos, CA 92069
(619) 744-1150
Staff: Carol Dougan, Chairman
Affiliation: Community college
Accreditation: WASC
Areas: App Mus; Mus Hist; Mus Lit; Th & An; Mus Ed (Elem)
Degrees: AA
Scholarships: Hidden Valley Concert Prewers $300, audition in applied field; Ivie Wickam Scholarship, to a female student in arts for advanced study, amount determined by need and committee action, up to $10,000 or amount of trust

PALO VERDE COLLEGE
Music Department
811 W. Chancelor Way
Blythe, CA 92225
(714) 922-6168
Staff: Merrill L. Tew, Chairman
Affiliation: State-supported community college
Accreditation: WASC
Areas: Intro
Degrees: AA

PASADENA CITY COLLEGE
After School Music Conservatory
1570 E. Colorado Blvd.
Pasadena, CA 91106
(213) 578-7102
Staff: Michael Wilson, Chairman, Music Department
Affiliation: Community-suported junior college
Accreditation: WASC
Areas: App Mus; Hist & Lit; Th & An; Mus Appr; Ethnomusicol; Opera; Theater Mus
Degrees: AA

RIO HONDO COLLEGE
Fine Arts Department
3600 Workman Mill Rd.
Whittier, CA 90608
(213) 692-0921
Staff: Prof John R. Jacobs, Chairman
Affiliation: State-supported community college
Accreditation: WASC
Areas: App Mus; Hist & Lit; Th & An; Cond; Theater Mus; Commercial Mus
Degrees: AA

RIVERSIDE CITY COLLEGE[1]
Department of Performing Arts
4800 Magnolia Ave.
Riverside, CA 92506
(714) 684-3240
Staff: Darrell A. Sausser, Chairman
Affiliation: Tax-supported community college
Accreditation: WASC
Areas: App Mus; Hist & Lit; Th & An; Cond; Mus Ed (Elem); Hist Jazz; Jazz Ens; Class Piano; Class Guitar
Degrees: AA

SACRAMENTO CITY COLLEGE[1]
Music Department
3835 Freeport Blvd.
Sacramento, CA 95822
(916) 449-7531
Staff: Jane Milley, Assistant Dean
Affiliation: State and locally supported community college
Accreditation: WASC
Areas: App Mus; Th & An; Comp; Mus Appr; Mus Hist & Lit
Degrees: AA

SAN BERNARDINO VALLEY COLLEGE[1]
Music Department
701 S. Mt. Vernon Ave.
San Bernardino, CA 92410
(714) 888-6511, x510
Staff: C. Paul Oxley, Head
Affiliation: State supported junior college
Accreditation: WASC
Areas: App Mus; Mus Hist; Mus Lit; Th & An; Comp; Cond; Orch; Theater Mus; Piano Tech; Intro Courses; Electronic Mus; Jazz Improv & Th
Degrees: AA
Scholarships: Band and choir—five general scholarships for grade point, musicianship and performance

SAN DIEGO MESA COLLEGE[1]
Music Department
7250 Mesa College Dr.
San Diego, CA 92111
(714) 230-6700
Staff: Elogene Hughes, Chairman
Affiliation: State and locally supported college
Accreditation: WASC
Areas: Th & An; Cond; Comp; Mus Appr; Mus Hist & Lit; Mus Ed (Elem & HS)
Degrees: AA

SAN JOSE CITY COLLEGE[1]
Music Department
2100 Moorpark Ave.
San Jose, CA 95128
(408) 298-2181, x215
Staff: Darrell L. Johnston, Chairman
Affiliation: Community college
Accreditation: WASC
Areas: App Mus; Mus Hist & Lit; Th & An; Mus Ed (Elem)
Degrees: AA

SANTA ANA COMMUNITY COLLEGE
Music Department
1530 W. 17th St.
Santa Ana, CA 92706
(714) 667-3000
Staff: Marie Pooler, Chairman
Affiliation: Community college
Accreditation: WASC
Areas: App Mus (private & class lessons); Mus Hist; Th & An; Mus Ed (Elem); Jazz in America; Mus of Mexico; Choral & Instr Ensembles; Mus Copying
Degrees: AA; Transfer credit

SANTA BARBARA CITY COLLEGE
Music Department
721 Cliff Dr.
Santa Barbara, CA 93109-9990
(805) 865-0581, x230, 232, 234
Staff: Robert L. Davis, Chairman
Affiliation: State-supported community college
Accreditation: WASC
Areas: App Mus; Hist & Lit; Mus Lit; Th & An; Jazz Arrang; Improv; Electr Mus; Computer Mus; Perf Band; Orch; Choir; Musicianship; Piano
Degrees: AA; Transfer credit
Scholarships: College work study programs and tutoring only

SANTA MONICA COLLEGE
Music Department
1900 Pico Blvd.
Santa Monica, CA 90405
(213) 450-5150, x240, 241
Staff: Joan G. Mills, Chairman
Affiliation: Community college
Accreditation: WASC
Areas: App Mus; Mus Hist; Th & An; Comp; Cond; Orch; Theater Mus
Degrees: AA; Transfer credit
Scholarships: $300 scholarships for music majors

SANTA ROSA JUNIOR COLLEGE
Music Department
1501 Mendocino Ave.
Santa Rosa, CA 95401
(707) 527-4249
Staff: Dan Goulart, Chairman
Affiliation: District junior college
Accreditation: WASC
Areas: App Mus; Mus Hist; Th & An; Comp
Degrees: AA
Scholarships: Voice—auditions in May on campus

SHASTA COLLEGE
Music Department
PO Box 6006
Redding, CA 96099
(916) 241-3523, x361
Staff: Leighton Edelman, Division Director
Affiliation: Community college
Accreditation: WASC
Areas: App Mus; Mus Hist; Mus Appr; Th & An; Opera; Musicals; Theater Mus
Degrees: AA; Transfer credit; Certificate
Scholarships: Shasta Chorale (Vocal & Piano); Shasta Symphony (Instrumental); Most Outstanding Student (Department)

SKYLINE COLLEGE
Performing Arts Division
3300 College Dr.
San Bruno, CA 94066
(415) 355-7000
Staff: M. Judith Watkins, Division Director
Affiliation: State-supported community college
Accreditation: WASC
Areas: App Mus; Mus Lit; Th & An; Comp; Opera; Theater Mus
Degrees: AA
Scholarships: Small local stipends

SOLANO COMMUNITY COLLEGE
Music Department
Box 246
Suisun City, CA 94585
(707) 422-4750
Staff: Carol Bishop, Chairman, Fine and Applied Arts
Affiliation: Community college
Accreditation: WASC
Areas: App Mus; Mus Hist; Th & An; Comp; Cond
Degrees: AA; Transfer credit

VENTURA COLLEGE[1]
Performing Arts Department
4667 Telegraph Rd.
Ventura, CA 93003
(805) 642-3211, x349
Staff: Margaret Edwards, Chairman
Affiliation: Community college
Accreditation: WASC
Areas: App Mus; Mus Hist & Lit; Th & An; Intro
Degrees: AA

VICTOR VALLEY COMMUNITY COLLEGE
Music Department
PO Drawer 00
Victorville, CA 93292
(714) 245-4271, x236, 265
Staff: Thomas E. Miller, Chairman
Affiliation: Public two-year community college
Accreditation: WASC
Areas: App Mus; Hist & Lit; Th & An; Theater Mus; Perf Ensembles
Degrees: AA

WEST HILLS COLLEGE
Fine Arts Division
300 Cherry Ln.
Coalinga, CA 93210
(209) 935-0801
Staff: Gordon Smith, Chairman
Affiliation: State-supported junior college
Accreditation: WASC
Areas: App Mus; Hist & Lit; Th & An; Opera; Theater Mus; Intro
Degrees: AA
Scholarships: One private scholarship in voice by application and audition

WEST VALLEY COLLEGE
Music Department
14000 Fruitvale Ave.
Saratoga, CA 95070
(408) 867-2200, x320
Staff: Kenneth Jewell, Chairman
Affiliation: State-supported community college
Accreditation: WASC
Areas: App Mus; Hist & Lit; Th & An; Orch
Degrees: AA

COLORADO

ARAPAHOE COMMUNITY COLLEGE
Music Department
5900 S. Santa Fe. Dr.
Littleton, CO 80120
(303) 794-1550
Staff: Kevin Kennedy, Chairman
Affiliation: Community college
Accreditation: NCA
Areas: App Mus; Mus Hist; Mus Lit; Th & An; Mus Ed (Early Childhood)
Degrees: AA
Scholarships: Full tuition available, based on audition and 3.0 GPA

NORTHEASTERN JUNIOR COLLEGE[1]
Music Department
100 College Dr.
Sterling, CO 80751
(303) 522-6600
Staff: Dorothy Corsberg, Chairman, Humanities Department
Affiliation: County-supported junior college
Accreditation: NCA
Areas: App Mus; Th & An; Mus Ed (Elem)
Degrees: AA
Scholarships: Memorial scholarships for demonstrated desire and musical aptitude. Applied scholarships also available.

TRINIDAD STATE JUNIOR COLLEGE
Music Department
600 Prospect
Trinidad, CO 80182
(303) 846-5653
Staff: Charlotte Kilpatrick, Co-ordinator of Musical Activities
Affiliation: State-supported junior college
Accreditation: NCA
Areas: App Mus; Mus Hist; Th & An; Mus Ed (Elem); Theater Mus; Instr Rep
Degrees: AA; AAS
Scholarships: Audition for tuition scholarship

DELAWARE

WESLEY COLLEGE
Department of Music
Dover, DE 19901
(302) 736-2300
Staff: Robert W. Bailey, Chairman
Affiliation: Church-related junior college (United Methodist)
Accreditation: MSA
Areas: App Mus; Mus Hist; Th & An; Mus Ed (Elem & HS); Mus Therapy
Degrees: AA
Scholarships: Unlimited number of $1,000 scholarships for ability and training; not need

FLORIDA

BREVARD COMMUNITY COLLEGE[1]
Divison of Liberal Arts
1519 Clearlake Rd.
Cocoa, FL 32922
(305) 632-1111
Staff: Dr. Robert A. Aitken, Chairman
Affiliation: Community college
Accreditation: SACS
Areas: App Mus; Mus. Hist; Th & An; Mus Ed (Elem & HS)
Degrees: AA

BROWARD COMMUNITY COLLEGE
Music Department
3501 S.W. Davie Rd.
Fort Lauderdale, FL 33314
(305) 475-6726-27
Staff: Jimmy Woodle, Head
Affiliation: State-supported community college
Accreditation: SACS
Areas: App Mus; Hist & Lit; Th & An; Opera; Various Ensembles; Instl Techniques
Degrees: AA
Scholarships: Tuition waivers

CENTRAL FLORIDA COMMUNITY COLLEGE
Department of Music
PO Box 1388
Ocala, FL 32678
(904) 237-2111
Staff: Gene A. Lawton, Chairman
Affiliation: State-supported junior college
Accreditation: SACS
Areas: App Mus; Mus Hist; Th & An; Church Mus; Mus Ed (Elem & HS); Theater Mus
Degrees: AA; AS
Scholarships: Tuition waiver for performance in organizations

CHIPOLA JUNIOR COLLEGE[1]
Division of Fine Arts and Humanities
College St.
Marianna, FL 32446
(904) 526-2761
Staff: Lawrence R. Nelson, Chairman
Affiliation: State-supported junior college
Accreditation: SACS
Areas: App Mus; Mus Hist; Th & An
Degrees: AA
Scholarships: Tuition, fees, semi-private dormitory room

GULF COAST COMMUNITY COLLEGE
Division of Fine Arts
Highway 98
Panama City, Fl 32401
(904) 769-1551
Staff: Norman J. Hair, Chairman, Fine Arts
Affiliation: State-supported college
Accreditation: SACS
Areas: App Mus; Mus Lit; Th & An
Degrees: AA

HILLSBOROUGH COMMUNITY COLLEGE[1]
Music Department
PO Box 22127
Tampa, FL 33622
(813) 879-7222
Staff: C. Richard Rhoades, Chairman
Affiliation: State-supported community college
Accreditation: SACS
Areas: App Mus; Mus Hist; Mus Lit; Th & An; Class Piano; Fund of Mus
Degrees: AA
Scholarships: Full tuition by audition based on talent

INDIAN RIVER COMMUNITY COLLEGE[1]
Music Department
3209 Virginia Ave.
Fort Pierce, FL 33450
(305) 464-2000
Staff: Anthony Allo, Chairman, Fine Arts
Affiliation: State-supported community college
Accreditation: SACS
Areas: App Mus; Mus Hist; Th & An; Cond; Theater Mus
Degrees: AA
Scholarships: Performance through audition, tuition

LAKE-SUMTER COMMUNITY COLLEGE
Humanities Division
U.S. Highway 441, South
Leesburg, FL 32748
(904) 787-3747
Staff: Dr. Lavera Yarish, Chairman
Affiliation: State-supported community college
Accreditation: SACS
Areas: App Mus; Hist & Lit; Th & An; Theater Mus; Perf; Band; Chorus; Jazz-lab; Community Chorus
Degrees: AA
Scholarships: Tuition wavers - audition, perform in organizations, serve as student assistant. Applied music grants - audition, show promise as performer, financial need.

MANATEE JUNIOR COLLEGE[1]
Department of Fine Arts, Division of Music
5840 26th St. W.
Bradenton, FL 33506
(813) 755-1511
Staff: Cortez Francis, Chairman, Department of Fine Arts
Affiliation: State-supported junior college
Accreditation: SACS
Areas: App Mus; Mus Hist; Mus Lit; Th & An; Opera; Mus Ed (Elem); Piano Tech
Degrees: AA
Scholarships: Full and half tuition waivers; scholarships from local clubs; must audition, have need and average or above average grades

MIAMI-DADE COMMUNITY COLLEGE
Music Department
11011 S.W. 104th St.
Miami, FL 33176
(305) 596-1282
Staff: Jane Pyle, Chairman
Affiliation: State-supported junior college

Accreditation: SACS
Areas: App Mus; Th & An; Mus Ed (Elem & HS)
Degrees: AA; Transfer credit
Scholarships: Service grants-performance in ensemble proficiency

NORTH FLORIDA JUNIOR COLLEGE[1]
Division of Communications & Fine Arts
1000 Turner Davis Dr.
Madison, FL 32340
(904) 973-2288
Staff: Dr. Edith Day, Chairman
Affiliation: State-supported junior college
Accreditation: SACS
Areas: App Mus; Mus Hist; Th & An
Degrees: AA
Scholarships: Based on audition

PALM BEACH JUNIOR COLLEGE[1]
Deaprtment of Music
4200 S. Congress Ave.
Lake Worth, FL 33461
(305) 439-8144
Staff: Letha Madge Royce, Chairman
Affiliation: State-supported public junior college
Accreditation: SACS
Areas: App Mus; Mus Hist; Th & An; Jazz Orientation; Arranging; Improvisation; Perf
Degrees: AA; AS
Scholarships: By audition

PENSACOLA JUNIOR COLLEGE
Department of Music and Drama
1000 College Blvd.
Pensacola, FL 32504
(904) 476-5410, x1800
Staff: Sidney Kennedy, Head
Affiliation: State-supported junior college
Accreditation: SACS
Areas: App Mus; Hist & Lit; Th & An; Cond; Opera; Theater Mus
Degrees: AA
Scholarships: Based on auditions and grades

POLK COMMUNITY COLLEGE[1]
Department of Music & Art
999 Avenue H, N.E.
Winter Haven, FL 33880
(813) 294-7771
Staff: Dr. Bertram D. Gable, Head
Affiliation: State-supported junior college
Accreditation: SACS
Areas: App Mus; Mus Lit; Th & An; Mus Ed (Elem)
Degrees: AA; Transfer credit

ST. PETERSBURG JUNIOR COLLEGE[1]
Department of Humanities
PO Box 13489
St. Petersburg, FL 33733
(813) 546-0021
Staff: Joseph F. Madden, Chairman
Affiliation: State-supported junior college
Accreditation: SACS
Areas: Mus Hist & Lit; Th & An; Opera; Mus Appr
Degrees: AA

SEMINOLE COMMUNITY COLLEGE[1]
Humanities Division
Sanford, FL 32771
(305) 323-1450
Staff: Dr. Robert Leving, Chairman
Affiliation: State-supported community college
Accreditation: SACS
Areas: App Mus; Mus Hist; Th & An; Intro courses
Degrees: AA
Scholarships: Eight full or 16 half, by audition

SOUTH FLORIDA JUNIOR COLLEGE
Music Department
600 College Dr.
Avon Park, FL 33825
(813) 453-6661
Staff: Douglas M. Andrews, Academic Dean
Affiliation: State-supported junior college
Accreditation: NASM; SACS
Areas: App Mus; Mus Hist; TH & An
Degrees: AA
Scholarships: Heart of Highlands Chapter of Sweet Adelines, for women, based on need and talent; Wednesday Musicale, based on demonstrated talent

VALENCIA COMMUNITY COLLEGE
Music Department
PO Box 3028
Orlando, FL 32802
(305) 299-5000
Staff: Qurentia Throm, Chairman, Fine Arts and Social Sciences
Affiliation: State-supported community college
Accreditation: SACS
Areas: App Mus; Hist & Lit; Th & An; Mus Ed (Elem & HS)
Degrees: AA
Scholarships: Scholarships for music majors and non-majors, depending on needs of department, especially in ensembles

GEORGIA

ALBANY JUNIOR COLLEGE
Division of Humanities
2400 Gillionville Rd.
Albany, GA 31707
(912) 439-4203
Staff: Dr. James R. Saville, Acting Chairman
Affiliation: State-supported junior college
Accreditation: SACS
Areas: App Mus; Hist & Lit; Th & An
Degrees: AA
Scholarships: Albany Junior College Foundation Scholarship—high academic average; Fine Arts Scholarships—contributions to fine arts program

BREWTON-PARKER COLLEGE
Music Department
Mt. Vernon, GA 30445
(912) 583-2241
Staff: Hildegard Jo Stanley, Music Coordinator
Affiliation: Private (Baptist) junior college
Accreditation: SACS
Areas: App Mus; Hist & Lit; Th & An
Degrees: AA
Scholarships: In vocal, keyboard, instrumental, guitar and handbells, by audition

BRUNSWICK JUNIOR COLLEGE
Humanities Division
Altama at Fourth
Brunswick, GA 31520
(912) 264-7226
Staff: Donna Certain Nilsson, Instructor of Music
Affiliation: State-supported junior college; unit of the University of Georgia
Accreditation: SACS
Areas: App Mus; Hist & Lit; Th & An; Ensemble
Degrees: AA
Scholarships: Yes

CLAYTON JUNIOR COLLEGE[1]
PO Box 285
Morrow, GA 30260
(404) 961-3400
Staff: Larry Crose, Associate Professor
Affiliation: State-supported junior college
Accreditation: SACS
Areas: Th & An; Mus Appr
Degrees: AA

DEKALB COMMUNITY COLLEGE
Department of Music
555 N. Indian Creek Dr.
Clarkston, GA 30021
(404) 299-4136
Staff: Dr. Thomas J. Anderson, Chairman
Affiliation: Public community college
Accreditation: SACS
Areas: App Mus; Hist & Lit; Th & An; Comp; Opera
Degrees: AA
Scholarships: Yes

GORDON JUNIOR COLLEGE
Music Department, Humanities Division
Barnesville, GA 30204
(404) 358-1700
Staff: Dr. Mary Jean Simmons, Chairman, Music Department
Affiliation: State-supported liberal arts junior college
Accreditation: SACS
Areas: App Mus; Th & An; Cond; Church Mus; Theater Mus; Piano Ped
Degrees: AA

Scholarships: By audition for voice, piano

MIDDLE GEORGIA COLLEGE[1]
Music Department
South Second St.
Cochran, GA 31014
(912) 934-6621
Staff: Nat E. Frazer, Head
Affiliation: State university system—junior college
Accreditation: SACS
Areas: App Mus; Th & An; Cond; Church Mus; Intro to Mus for non-majors
Degrees: AA
Scholarships: Three student assistantships at $300/per quarter for accompanying or secretarial service

SOUTH GEORGIA COLLEGE
Fine Arts Department
Douglas, GA 31533
(912) 384-1100
Staff: Lee G. Barrow, Chairman, Music Department
Affiliation: State-supported junior college; Unit of U. of Georgia system
Accreditation: SACS
Areas: App Mus; Hist & Lit; Th & An; Theater Mus
Degrees: AA
Scholarships: Full tuition scholarships by audition

TRUETT MCCONNELL COLLEGE
Department of Music
Cleveland, GA 30528
(404) 865-5688
Staff: David N. George, Chairman, Division of Fine Arts
Affiliation: Private liberal arts, church-related junior college (Baptist)
Accreditation: NASM; SACS
Areas: App Mus; Mus Hist; Th & An
Degrees: AM
Scholarships: Based on talent and need

YOUNG HARRIS COLLEGE
Music Department, Division of Fine Arts
Young Harris, GA 30582
(404) 379-3746
Staff: William H. Fox, Chairman, Fine Arts Division
Affiliation: Private liberal arts, United Methodist affiliated junior college
Accreditation: SACS
Areas: App Mus; Mus Hist; Th & An; Opera Workshop; Choral Perf
Degrees: AFA; Transfer credit
Scholarships: For music majors only in piano, voice, organ, awarded on audition fulfillment

IDAHO

RICKS COLLEGE
Music Department
Rexburg, ID 83440
(208) 365-2275
Staff: Dr. M. David Chugg, Coordinator
Affiliation: Church-related junior college (Church of Jesus Christ of Latter-Day Saints)
Accreditation: NASM; NASC
NASM; NASC
Areas: App Mus; Th & An; Cond; Opera; Music Ed (Elem & HS)
Degrees: AA; AS; Transfer credit
Scholarships: By audition, make application, meet college entrance requirements

ILLINOIS

BLACK HAWK COLLEGE
Music Department
6600 34th Ave.
Moline, IL 61265
(309) 796-1311
Staff: Roger A. Perley, Chairman
Affiliation: Public area junior college
Accreditation: NCA
Areas: App Mus; Th & An; Opera; Church Mus; Mus Ed (Elem & HS); Mus Therapy
Degrees: AA
Scholarships: Yes, upon request

COLLEGE OF DUPAGE
Department of Performing Arts
Glen Ellyn, IL 60137
(312) 858-2800
Staff: Dr. Harold Bauer, Director of Orchestra and Opera; Lee R. Kesselman, Director of Choral Activities; Robert L. Marshall, Director of Bands
Affiliation: State-supported community college
Accreditation: NCA
Areas: App Mus; Th & An; Opera; Intro courses
Degrees: AA

THE COLLEGE OF LAKE COUNTY
Division of Communication Arts, Humanities and Fine Arts
19351 W. Washington St.
Grayslake, IL 60030
(312) 223-6601
Staff: Russell Hamm, Chairperson
Affiliation: State-supported community college
Accreditation: NCA
Areas: App Mus; Mus & Lit; Th & An; Mus Ed (Elem); Jazz Ensemble; Wind Ensemble; Vocal Groups
Degrees: AA

ELGIN COMMUNITY COLLEGE[1]
Division of Communications & Fine Arts
1700 Spartan Dr.
Elgin, IL 60120
(312) 697-1000
Staff: Dr. Gail Shadwell, Instructional Dean
Affiliation: State-supported community college
Accreditation: NCA
Areas: App Mus; Mus & Lit; Hist & Lit; Th & An; Comp; Cond; Mus Ed (Elem); Mus Apprec
Degrees: AA; AS

ILLINOIS CENTRAL COLLEGE[1]
Music Department, Division of Fine Arts
East Peoria, IL 61635
(309) 694-5113
Staff: Donald Lewellen, Coordinator, Music Department
Affiliation: Illinois community college
Accreditation: NASM; NCA
Areas: App Mus; Hist & Lit; Th & An; Comp; Orch; Mus Ed (Elem); Piano Tech
Degrees: AA; AS; Transfer credit
Scholarships: Tuition grants awarded to in-district high school graduates who audition successfully; talent grants

JOLIET JUNIOR COLLEGE
Fine Arts Department
1216 Houbolt Ave.
Joliet, IL 60436
(815) 729-4232
Staff: Jerry E. Lewis, Chairman
Affiliation: State-supported junior college
Accreditation: NCA
Areas: App Mus; Hist & Lit; Th & An; Cond; Concert Band & Choir; Jazz Band; Swing Choir; Community Band; Chamber Ensembles; Class Piano
Degrees: AA; AS
Scholarships: Services and performance—information available through fine arts department

KASKASKIA COLLEGE
Music Department
Shattuc Rd.
Centralia, IL 62801
(618) 532-1981
Staff: William Camphouse, Chairman
Affiliation: State-supported junior college
Accreditation: NCA
Areas: App Mus; Hist & Lit; Th & An; Mus Ed (Elem)
Degrees: AA; Transfer credit
Scholarships: Tuition waiver, apply by August 1

LEWIS AND CLARK COMMUNITY COLLEGE
Division of Fine & Performing Arts
Godfrey, IL 62035
(618) 466-3411
Staff: Harlan Hock, Music Coordinator
Affiliation: State-supported junior college
Accreditation: NCA
Areas: App Mus; Th & An
Degrees: AA; AS
Scholarships: Alumni, Talent Award Foundation (LCCC & Webb)

LINCOLN COLLEGE
Division of Fine Arts
300 Keokuk

Lincoln, IL 62656
(217) 732-3155
Staff: Concetta R. DiLillo, Director of Fine Arts
Affiliation: Private two-year liberal arts college
Accreditation: NCA
Areas: App Mus; Hist & Lit; Th & An; Theater Mus; Mus Apprec; Foundations of Mus
Degrees: AA
Scholarships: Vocal and instrumental scholarships of up to $2,000 awarded by audition

LINCOLN LAND COMMUNITY COLLEGE[1]
Division of Performing Arts & Languages
Shepherd Rd.
Springfield, IL 62708
(217) 786-2320
Staff: Howard Wooters, Chairman
Affiliation: Public community college
Accreditation: NCA
Areas: App Mus; Mus Hist; Mus Lit; Th & An; Mus Ed (Elem); Perf Ensembles (Band, Choir, Jazz Band, Orch)
Degrees: AA
Scholarships: Performance—by audition

OLIVE-HARVEY COLLEGE
Department of Humanities & Foreign Languages
10100 S. Woodlawn Ave.
Chicago, IL 60643
(312) 568-3700
Staff: Dr. Dieter Kober, Professor of Music; Ms. Jacqueline Anderson, Chairman, Department of Humanities & Foreign Languages
Affiliation: City Colleges of Chicago
Accreditation: NCA
Areas: App Mus; Mus Hist; Intro courses
Degrees: AA

PARKLAND COLLEGE[1]
Music Department
2400 W. Bradley Ave.
Champaign, IL 61820
(217) 351-2200
Staff: Prof. Muriel Lyke, Coordinator
Affiliation: State supported (plus district funds) two-year community college
Accreditation: NCA
Areas: App Mus; Mus Lit; Piano Tech (Tuning)
Degrees: AA; Transfer credit
Scholarships: Not presently

PRAIRIE STATE COLLEGE
Music Department
197th & Halsted St.
Chicago Heights, IL 60411
(312) 756-3110
Staff: John Paris, Chairman
Affiliation: State-supported junior college
Accreditation: NCA
Areas: App Mus; Th & An; Mus Ed (Elem & HS)
Degrees: AA; Transfer credit
Scholarships: Tuition audition; Lynn Rudy Memorial Performing Arts Scholarship for currently enrolled students, based on audition

REND LAKE COLLEGE[1]
Music Department
Rural Route 1
Ina, IL 62846
(618) 437-5321
Staff: Larry D. Phifer, Director, Music Program
Affiliation: State-supported junior college
Accreditation: NCA
Areas: App Mus; Th & An; Mus Ed (Elem & HS); Perf Groups (Collegiate Choir Community Chorus, Concert Band, Jazz Band, Orchestra)
Degrees: AA
Scholarships: Not specifically in music

SOUTHEASTERN ILLINOIS COLLEGE[1]
Humanities Division
Route 4 College Rd.
Harrisburg, IL 62946
(618) 252-4411
Staff: Bruce Boone, Music Instructor
Affiliation: State-supported junior college
Accreditation: NCA
Areas: App Mus; Th & An; Mus Ed (Elem)
Degrees: AA

SPRINGFIELD COLLEGE IN ILLINOIS
Music Department
Springfield, IL 62702
(217) 525-1420, x50
Staff: Fred Greenwald, Chairman
Affiliation: Fine arts division of a church-related, two-year college (Roman Catholic)
Accreditation: NASM; NCA
Areas: App Mus; Hist & Lit; Th & An
Degrees: AA
Scholarships: Honor scholarships available for high grades and good performance; work scholarships available for need and talent, accompanying, library work, etc.

THORNTON COMMUNITY COLLEGE[1]
Music Department
15800 S. State St.
South Holland, IL 60473
(312) 596-2000, x297
Staff: Fred Hanzelin, Director
Affiliation: State and locally supported community college
Accreditation: NCA; NASM
Areas: App Mus; Th & An; Comp; Mus Appr; Opera
Degrees: AA

WILBUR WRIGHT COLLEGE
Music Department
3400 N. Austin Ave.
Chicago, IL 60634
(312) 777-7900, x48
Staff: Prof. Michael Holian, Chairman
Affiliation: State-supported junior college
Accreditation: NASM; NCA
Areas: Mus Hist; Th & An; Cond; Orch; Mus Ed (Elem)
Degrees: AA; Transfer credit
Scholarships: Beginning 1981-82; cash award by audition to incoming freshman based on musicianship and academic ability. One annually between $200-$500. Renewable for second year, primarily for Chicago-area students.

WILLIAM RAINEY HARPER COLLEGE
Music Department
Palatine, IL 60067
(312) 397-3000
Staff: Dr. Robert Tillotson, Chairman
Affiliation: State and local-supported community college
Accreditation: NASM; NCA
Areas: App Mus; Mus Lit; Th & An
Degrees: AA
Scholarships: Trustees' scholarship offered to graduating seniors in local district.

INDIANA

INDIANA UNIVERSITY SOUTHEAST
Humanities Division
New Albany, IN 47150
(812) 945-2731
Staff: James H. Bowden, Chairman
Affiliation: State-supported university
Accreditation: NCA
Areas: App Mus; MusED (Elem); Theater Mus; Intro
Degrees: BA, Mus, under consideration for 1983
Scholarships: Awarded for participation in chamber orchestra.

IOWA

ELLSWORTH COMMUNITY COLLEGE[1]
Department of Music
1100 College Ave.
Iowa Falls, IA 50126
(515) 648-4611
Staff: Gary DeClue, Instructor of Music
Affiliation: Affiliated with the Iowa Valley Community College District
Accreditation: NCA
Areas: App Mus; Th & An; Mus Ed (HS); Mus Apprec
Degrees: AA
Scholarships: Yes

GRAND VIEW COLLEGE
Music Department
1200 Grandview
Des Moines, IA 50316
(515) 263-2891
Staff: Marian Y. Luke, Chairman
Affiliation: Church-related junior college (Lutheran L.C.A.)
Accreditation: NCA
Areas: App Mus; Th & An; Mus Ed (Elem)

Degrees: AA; ALA; Diploma (Junior college)
Scholarships: $500 maximum—available to both music and non-music majors. Participation in musical activity of school either as major or participant in Grand View Choir

INDIAN HILLS COMMUNITY COLLEGE[1]
Music Department
Ninth & College
Ottumwa, IA 52501
(515) 683-5111
Staff: Sister St. John Ven Horst, Music Department
Affiliation: State-supported community college
Accreditation: NCA
Areas: App Mus; Mus Th & Ear Training
Degrees: AA

IOWA LAKES COMMUNITY COLLEGE
Department of Fine Arts
300 S. 18th St.
Estherville, IA 51334
(712) 362-2604
Staff: Dallas Freeman, Department Head
Affiliation: State-supported community college
Accreditation: NCA
Areas: App Mus; Mus Lit; Th & An; Comp; Cond; Orch; Mus Ed (Elem & HS); Jazz Hist; Arranging; Improv
Degrees: AA; AS; Transfer credit
Scholarships: For music activity—2.5 GPA must be maintained to receive scholarship and performance in two ensembles, subject to quarterly review

SOUTHEASTERN COMMUNITY COLLEGE, SOUTH CAMPUS
Music Department
285 Messenger Rd.
Keokuk, IA 52632
(319) 524-3221
Staff: Raymond E. Goeke, Music Director
Affiliation: State-supported community college
Accreditation: NCA
Areas: App Mus; Hist & Lit; Th & An
Degrees: AA; AS; Transfer credit
Scholarships: For music major or minor

SOUTHWESTERN COMMUNITY COLLEGE
Townline Rd.
Creston, IA 50801
(515) 782-7081
Staff: Dick Bauman, Director of Instrumental Music
Accreditation: NCA
Areas: App Mus; Th & An; Perf
Degrees: AA
Scholarships: Audition for scholarships; also depends on need and ability of student.

WALDORF COLLEGE
Music Department
Forest City, IA 50436
(515) 582-4145
Staff: Michael Van Auken, Chairman
Affiliation: Church-related junior college (Lutheran)
Accreditation: NCA
Areas: Hist & Lit; Th & An; Comp; Piano Tech
Degrees: AA
Scholarships: Scholarships available

KANSAS

CENTRAL COLLEGE
Department of Music
1200 S. Main
McPherson, KS 67460
(316) 241-0723
Staff: Daniel L. Hibbett, Chairman
Affiliation: Church-related liberal arts junior college with career programs (Free Methodist)
Accreditation: NCA
Areas: App Mus; Hist & Lit; Th & An; Cond; Church Mus; Mus Ed (Elem); Intro and technique courses
Degrees: AA
Scholarships: For students with demonstrated outstanding musical talent and promise. Awarded on basis of audition—amount depends on GPA

CLOUD COUNTY COMMUNITY COLLEGE
Music Department
2221 Campus Dr.
Concordia, KS 66901
(913) 243-1435
Staff: Dr. Everett Miller, Chairman
Affiliation: County/state-supported junior college
Accreditation: NCA
Areas: App Mus; Hist & Lit; Th & An
Degrees: AA
Scholarships: Tuition (full and partial), books, BEOG, work-study grants

COFFEYVILLE COMMUNITY COLLEGE[1]
Music Department
11th and Willow
Coffeyville, KS 67337
(316) 251-7700
Staff: James R. Criswell, Chairman
Affiliation: State-community supported
Accreditation: NCA
Areas: App Mus; Mus Hist; Mus Lit; Th & An; Cond; Piano Tech; Intro Courses
Degrees: AA; AS; Transfer credit
Scholarships: Music major scholarships for performance (instrumental and vocal)

COLBY COMMUNITY COLLEGE
Music Department
1255 S. Range
Colby, KS 67701
(913) 462-3984
Staff: Vaughn Lippoldt
Affiliation: Community college (16 northwest counties)
Accreditation: NCA
Areas: App Mus; Comp; Mus Ed (Elem & HS); Hist & Lit; Th & An
Degrees: AA
Scholarships: Up to $500/student, based on talent

COWLEY COUNTY COMMUNITY COLLEGE[1]
Humanities Department
125 S. Second St.
Arkansas City, KS 67005
(316) 442-0430
Staff: Kerry Hart, Instructor
Affiliation: County community college-public
Accreditation: NCA
Areas: App Mus; Th & An; Piano Tech
Degrees: AA
Scholarships: Full tuition, book grant; students must participate in two ensembles

DODGE CITY COMMUNITY COLLEGE
Music Department
North 14th Ave.
Dodge City, KS 67801
(316) 225-1321
Staff: Prof. Vernon R. Zollars, Chairman
Affiliation: County and state-supported junior college
Accreditation: NCA
Areas: App Mus; Comp; Cond; Church Mus; Mus Ed (Elem); Hist & Lit; Th & An; Perf
Degrees: AA
Scholarships: Academic and performing scholarships; some cover full tuition and books and applied music, others cover books only and applied music fees

LABETTE COMMUNITY COLLEGE[1]
Music Department
200 S. 14th St.
Parsons, KS 67357
(316) 421-6700
Staff: Dana Jane Saliba, Director
Affiliation: State-supported liberal arts junior college
Accreditation: NCA
Areas: App Mus; Mus Hist; Th & An; Mus Ed (Elem); Piano Tech; Mus Apprec; Piano Class; Voice Class; Choir; Orchestra; Jazz Workshop; Guitar Class
Degrees: AA
Scholarships: Departmental tuition scholarships and memorial endowment scholarships.

NEOSHO COUNTY COMMUNITY COLLEGE[1]
Music Department
1000 S. Allen
Chanute, KS 66720
(316) 431-2820
Staff: David R. Ludwick, Chairman; Leon Hazen, Division Coordinator of Fine Arts
Affiliation: State and locally supported junior college
Accreditation: NCA
Areas: Mus Appr; Band Instr; Voice Instr
Degrees: AA

ST. JOHN'S COLLEGE
Music Department
Winfield, KS 67156
(316) 221-4000
Staff: Lee Stocker, Assoc. Prof of Music
Affiliation: Church-related college (Lutheran)
Accreditation: NCA
Areas: App Mus; Mus Lit; Th & An; Cond; Church Mus; Mus Ed (Elem)
Degrees: AA; BA; BS
Scholarships: For choral, keyboard and instrumental by tape or personal audition; ensemble participation or lessons required

KENTUCKY

ALICE LLOYD COLLEGE
Music Department
Pippa Passes, KY 41844
(606) 368-2101
Staff: Richard Kennedy, Assistant Professor
Affiliation: Private senior college
Accreditation: SACS
Areas: App Mus; Mus Appr; Mus Fundamentals; Mus Ed (Elem); Band; Chorus
Degrees: AA; BA; BS

HOPKINSVILLE COMMUNITY COLLEGE[1]
Humanities Division
Hopkinsville, KY 42240
(502) 886-3921
Staff: JoAnne Gabbard, Chairman
Affiliation: State-supported community college
Accreditation: SACS
Areas: Mus Ed (Elem); Intro courses
Degrees: AA

LEES JUNIOR COLLEGE[1]
Music Department
601 Jefferson Ave.
Jackson, KY 41339
(606) 666-7521
Staff: Louard F. Egbert, Chairman
Affiliation: Church-related junior college (Presbyterian)
Accreditation: SACS
Areas: App Mus; Mus Appr; Piano
Degrees: AA

PADUCAH COMMUNITY COLLEGE
Division of Humanities and Related Technologies
Box 1380
Paducah, KY 42001
(502) 442-6131
Staff: Donald R. Maley, Chairman
Affiliation: Member, Community College System of the University of Kentucky
Accreditation: SACS
Areas: App Mus; Mus Lit; Th & An; Mus Ed (Elem)
Degrees: AA; AS
Scholarships: Freshmen are eligible for scholarships sponsored by local music clubs, based on high school academic standing and demonstrated performance capabilities; sophomores are eligible for divisional scholarships decided by faculty vote

SUE BENNETT COLLEGE
Music Department
London, KY 40741
(606) 864-2238
Staff: Jeanne Wintringham, Instructor, Department of Music
Affiliation: Church-related junior college (United Methodist)
Accreditation: SACS
Areas: App Mus; Mus Ed (Elem); Th & An; Intro courses (apprec)
Degrees: AA
Scholarships: Personal gift scholarships for those who plan to major in music and show promise; music scholarships of various amounts available, based on need, ability, and choir performance

LOUISIANA

SOUTHERN UNIVERSITY—SHREVEPORT-BOSSIER CITY CAMPUS
Division of Humanities (Music Department)
3050 Cooper Rd.
Shreveport, LA 71107
(318) 424-6552
Staff: Bobby Wiggins, Assistant Prof., Chairman (Coordinator)
Affiliation: Fully accredited part of Southern University System
Accreditation: SACS
Areas: App Mus; Hist & Lit; Th & An; Intro Courses; Mus Apprec
Degrees: AA
Scholarships: Merit scholarships

MAINE

UNIVERSITY OF MAINE AT AUGUSTA[1]
Division of Arts and Humanities
Augusta, ME 04330
(207) 622-7131
Staff: Charles D. Danforth, Chairman
Affiliation: Community college
Accreditation: NEA
Areas: App Mus; Mus Hist; Mus Lit; Th & An; Comp; Jazz; American Popular Mus
Degrees: Transfer credit; AS (American Popular Mus)

MARYLAND

ALLEGANY COMMUNITY COLLEGE
Division of Performing Arts, Department of Music
Willowbrook Rd.
Cumberland, MD 21502
(301) 724-7700
Staff: Ellynne Brice Yeager, Instructor, Music Department
Affiliation: Community (county) college-state & county-supported
Accreditation: MSA
Areas: Mus Ed (Elem); Intro; Choir
Degrees: AA
Scholarships: No, except through college workstudy

ESSEX COMMUNITY COLLEGE
Music Department, Division of Humanities & Arts
Baltimore County, MD 21237
(301) 682-6000, x1626, 1421
Staff: Carol Kingsmore, Head, Music Department
Affiliation: Community (county) college, state- and county-supported
Accreditation: NASM; MSA
Areas: App Mus; Hist & Lit; Th & An; Cond; Mus Ed (Elem & HS); Mus Therapy; Theater Mus
Degrees: AA; Transfer credit
Scholarships: Awarded on the basis of need and performance ability

MONTGOMERY COLLEGE
Music Department
51 Mannakee St.
Rockville, MD 20850
(301) 279-5209
Staff: Ervin O. Klinkon, Chairman
Affiliation: State supported community college
Accreditation: NASM; MSA
Areas: App Mus; Hist & Lit; Th & An; Comp; Cond; Orch; Opera Mus Ed (Elem & HS); Theater Mus; Piano Tech; Electronic Mus; Arranging; Class Piano; Class Guitar; Class Voice; Class Percussion; Ensembles
Degrees: AA
Scholarships: Available through Student Financial Aids Office

MONTGOMERY COLLEGE—TAKOMA PARK CAMPUS[1]
Institute for Humanities
Takoma & New York Ave.
Tacoma Park, MD 20912
(301) 587-4090
Staff: Gloria Monteiro, Dean
Affiliation: Public-supported community college
Accreditation: MSA
Areas: App Mus; Mus Hist; Th & An; Mus Ed (Elem)
Degrees: AA; Transfer credit

PRINCE GEORGE'S COMMUNITY COLLEGE
Humanities/Music Department
301 Largo Rd.
Largo, MD 20772
(301) 322-0955
Staff: Marcia Ward, Chairman, Music Department
Affiliation: Public state-supported community college
Accreditation: MSA
Areas: App Mus; Hist & Lit; Th & An; Cond; Choir; Band; Guitar/Bass Ensemble; Jazz Ensemble; Class Piano; Class Voice
Degrees: AA

Scholarships: Peter B. Miraglia Memorial Scholarship; Society of the Colonial Dames of America Scholarship

MASSACHUSETTS

BAY PATH JUNIOR COLLEGE
Music Department
588 Longmeadow St.
Longmeadow, MA 01106
(413) 567-0621
Staff: Charles E. Page, Chairman
Affiliation: Private liberal arts junior college for women
Accreditation: NEA
Areas: App Mus; Hist & Lit; Th & An; Intro
Degrees: AA

DEAN JUNIOR COLLEGE[1]
Visual and Performing Arts Department
99 Main St.
Franklin, MA 02038
(617) 528-9100
Staff: Lawry N. Reid, Chairman
Affiliation: Private liberal arts junior college
Accreditation: NEA
Areas: App Mus; Mus Lit; Th & An; Mus Therapy
Degrees: AA

HOLYOKE COMMUNITY COLLEGE
Music Department
303 Homestead Ave.
Holyoke, MA 01040
(413) 538-7000
Staff: Daniel Oberholtzer, Chairman
Affiliation: State of MA, two-year community college
Accreditation: NEA
Areas: App Mus; Hist & Lit; Th & An; Class Instruments (Percussion, Brass, Strings, Winds); Class Voice; Mus-Business; Class Piano; Orch; Small Ensembles; Theater Mus; Solfege; Mus Bus; Instr Ensembles; Early Mus
Degrees: AA
Scholarships: State and federal grants; work study

LASELL JUNIOR COLLEGE[1]
Department of Art & Music
Auburndale, MA 02166
(617) 243-2000
Staff: Leonie Bennett, Chairman
Affiliation: Private junior college for women
Accreditation: NEA
Areas: App Mus; Mus Hist; Th & An; Mus Ed (Elem); Intro courses
Degrees: AA
Scholarships: Dunham organ scholarship; audition

NORTHERN ESSEX COMMUNITY COLLEGE[1]
Division of Creative Arts
110 N. Elliott St.
Haverhill, MA 01830
(617) 374-0721
Staff: Michael G. Finegold, Coordinator of Music
Affiliation: State-supported community college
Accreditation: NEA
Areas: Mus Hist; Th & An; Intro courses
Degrees: AA

MICHIGAN

C.S. MOTT COMMUNITY COLLEGE
Music Area
1401 E. Court St.
Flint, MI 48503
(313) 762-0459
Staff: Samuel E. Morello, Chairman, Fine Arts Division
Affiliation: Public community college
Accreditation: NCA
Areas: App Mus; Mus Hist; Th & An; Cond; Mus Ed (Elem); Piano Tech
Degrees: AA
Scholarships: Various

GRAND RAPIDS JUNIOR COLLEGE[1]
Division of Fine Arts
143 Bostwick Ave., N.E.
Grand Rapids, MI 49503
(616) 456-4219
Staff: Lynn Asper, Chairperson
Affiliation: State-supported junior college; part of K-12 system city support also
Accreditation: NASM; NCA
Areas: App Mus; Mus Hist; Mus Lit; Th & An; Cond; Mus Ed (Elem & HS); Mus Therapy; Piano Tech; Guitar Technique (Class); Vocal & Instrumental Pop Classes
Degrees: AM
Scholarships: Vocal, instrumental & piano—based on audition proficiencies

JACKSON COMMUNITY COLLEGE[1]
Michigan School of the Arts
2111 Emmons Rd.
Jackson, MI 49201
(517) 787-0800, x274
Staff: Keith Drayton, Chairman
Affiliation: Locally-supported community college
Accreditation: NCA
Areas: Th & An; Mus Appr; Mus Hist & Lit; Mus Ed (Elem & HS)
Degrees: AA

SCHOOLCRAFT COLLEGE[1]
Fine Arts & Sciences
1860 Haggerty Rd.
Livonia, MI 48152
(313) 591-6400
Staff: Dr. Richard Saunders, Assistant Dean
Affiliation: Public community college
Accreditation: NCA
Areas: App Mus; Mus Hist; Mus Lit; Th & An; Comp; Cond; Mus Ed (Elem)
Degrees: AA
Scholarships: Full tuition; renewable upon the recommendation of the Music Faculty; based upon an audition and previous record of musical accomplishment

SUOMI COLLEGE[1]
Fine Arts Department
Hancock, MI 49930
(906) 482-5300
Staff: Jon Brookhouse, Head
Affiliation: Church-related liberal arts junior college (LCA)
Areas: App Mus; Mus Hist; Th & An; Comp; Intro Courses
Degrees: AA

MINNESOTA

ARROWHEAD COMMUNITY COLLEGE, HIBBING CAMPUS
Department of Music
Hibbing, MN 55746
(218) 262-3877
Staff: Thomas F. Palmersheim, Chairman
Affiliation: State junior college
Accreditation: NCA
Areas: App Mus; Th & An; Mus Ed (Elem)
Degrees: AA
Scholarships: Performance in vocal and instrumental

ARROWHEAD COMMUNITY COLLEGE, MESABI CAMPUS
Music Department
Virginia, MN 55792
(218) 741-9200
Staff: Jay H. Carlgaard, Head
Affiliation: State supported community college
Accreditation: NCA
Areas: App Mus; Th & An; Mus Ed (Elem)
Degrees: AA
Scholarships: Available for 2nd year students with high academic standing; scholarships are also available to cover cost of private instruction

NORTHLAND COMMUNITY COLLEGE
Music Department
Thief River Falls, MN 57601
(218) 681-2181
Staff: Les Torgerson, Chairman
Affiliation: State-supported junior college
Accreditation: NCA
Areas: App Mus; Hist & Lit; Th & An; Cond; Mus Ed (Elem & HS); Theater Mus; Intro courses
Degrees: AA
Scholarships: By audition for proficiency and need

ROCHESTER COMMUNITY COLLEGE
Music Department
East Highway No. 14
Rochester, MN 55901
(507) 288-6160
Staff: Willard C. Johnston, Music Chairman
Affiliation: State college
Accreditation: NCA
Areas: App Mus; Hist & Lit; Th & An
Degrees: AA
Scholarships: By audition, vocal and performance

WORTHINGTON COMMUNITY COLLEGE
Music Department
1450 Collegeway
Worthington, MN 56187
(507) 372-2107
Staff: Galen L. Benton, Chairman
Affiliation: State-supported junior college
Accreditation: NCA
Areas: App Mus; Th & An; Mus Appr; Piano, Voice Instr; Instrumental
Degrees: AA

MISSISSIPPI

EAST CENTRAL JUNIOR COLLEGE
Department of Music
Decatur, MS 39327
(601) 635-3246
Staff: Marion Thornton, Chairman; Robert Heritage, Director of Choral Activities
Affiliation: State-supported junior college
Accreditation: SACS
Areas: App Mus; Hist & Lit; Th & An; Mus Ed (Elem)
Degrees: AA
Scholarships: Tuition for band participation

EAST MISSISSIPPI JUNIOR COLLEGE[1]
Music Department
Scooba, MS 39358
(601) 476-2631
Staff: Glenda R. Malone, Chairman
Affiliation: State-supported junior college
Accreditation: SACS
Areas: App Mus; Mus Hist; Th & An; Mus Ed
Degrees: AA; Transfer credit
Scholarships: By audition, vocal and keyboard; band and stage band

HINDS JUNIOR COLLEGE[1]
Music Department
Raymond, MS 39154
(601) 857-5261, x42 or 43
Staff: James Leslie Reeves, Chairman
Affiliation: County-supported, state-supported, two-year college
Accreditation: SACS
Areas: App Mus; Mus Hist; Mus Lit; Theory
Degrees: AA

HOLMES JUNIOR COLLEGE
Division of Fine Arts
Goodman, MS 39079
(601) 472-2312
Staff: Ann Parker, Chairman
Affiliation: State-supported junior college
Accreditation: SACS
Areas: App Mus; Mus Lit
Degrees: AA; Transfer credit
Scholarships: Available in keyboard, voice and band instruments—based on ability and participation

NORTHEAST MISSISSIPPI JUNIOR COLLEGE
Music Department
Cunningham Blvd.
Booneville, MS 38829
(601) 728-6201
Staff: William T. Rutledge, Chairman
Affiliation: State-supported junior college
Accreditation: SACS
Areas: App Mus; Th & An; Theater Mus
Degrees: AA; Transfer credit
Scholarships: Performance

NORTHWEST MISSISSIPPI JUNIOR COLLEGE
Division of Fine Arts
Senatobia, MS 38668
(601) 562-5262
Staff: Glenn Triplett, Director of Fine Arts
Affiliation: State-supported junior college
Accreditation: SACS
Areas: App Mus; Mus Hist; Th & An; Mus Ed (Elem & HS)
Degrees: AA
Scholarships: Scholarships available for piano, voice, organ & band (must audition)

MISSOURI

COTTEY COLLEGE
Music Department
Nevada, MO 64772
(417) 667-8181
Staff: Michael Ashmore, Chairman
Affiliation: Liberal arts junior college for women supported by the PEO Sisterhood
Accreditation: NCA; NASM
Areas: App Mus; Mus Lit; Th & An
Degrees: AA

JEFFERSON COLLEGE
Music Department
Hillsboro, MO 63050
(314) 789-3951
Staff: Richard L. Bell, Chairman
Affiliation: Public junior college; local and state-supported
Accreditation: NCA
Areas: App Mus; Th & An; Mus Appr; Fundamentals of Mus; Perf
Degrees: AA

ST. LOUIS COMMUNITY COLLEGE AT FLORISSANT VALLEY
Music Department
3400 Pershall Rd.
St. Louis, MO 63115
(314) 595-4366
Staff: Dr. Henry Orland, Chairperson
Affiliation: State-supported junior college
Accreditation: NCA
Areas: App Mus; Hist & Lit; Th & An; Mus Ed (HS); Mus Therapy; Cond; Opera; Intro
Degrees: AA
Scholarships: For new students only—applicants must rank in upper 60% of high school class

ST. LOUIS COMMUNITY COLLEGE AT FOREST PARK
Music Department
5600 Oakland Ave.
St. Louis, MO 63110
(314) 644-9383
Staff: Stephen M. Curtis, Chairman
Affiliation: One of three campuses of St. Louis Community College
Accreditation: NASM; NCA
Areas: App Mus; Th & An; Class Piano; Voice; Basic Mus; Band; Chorus; Jazz; Guitar and Piano Tech; Hist & Lit
Degrees: AA
Scholarships: Activity and academic

ST. LOUIS COMMUNITY COLLEGE AT MERAMEC
Music Department
11333 Big Bend Blvd.
Kirkwood, MO 63122
(314) 966-7639
Staff: Dr. Richard Kalfus, Head, Humanities Department
Affiliation: Locally-supported junior college
Accreditation: NCA
Areas: Th & An; Mus Appr; Hist & Lit; Piano; Voice Instr; Jazz; Mus Therapy
Degrees: AA
Scholarships: Half tuition remission for performance in symphonic band, jazz lab band, orchestra, choir based on audition; jazz scholarship for one student annually, selected by audition and departmental recommendation

NEW JERSEY

BURLINGTON COUNTY COLLEGE[1]
Music Department
Pemberton-Browns Mills Rd.
Pemberton, NJ 08068
(609) 894-9311
Staff: Dr. William R. Rudolph, Associate Prof.
Affiliation: State-supported junior community college
Accreditation: MSA
Areas: App Mus; Mus Hist; Mus Lit; Th & An; Comp; Mus Ed (Elem & HS); Piano Tech; Diatonic Harmony, Chromatic Harmony; Piano Pedagogy
Degrees: AA; AS; Transfer credit
Scholarships: Excellence Award for performance of outstanding high school musicians

COUNTY COLLEGE OF MORRIS
Music Department
Route 10 and Center Grove Rd.
Randolph, NH 07869
(201) 361-5000, x419
Staff: Dr. John A. Gorman, Associate Professor of Music
Affiliation: County-supported community college
Accreditation: MSA
Areas: App Mus; Hist & Lit; Th & An;

Fund of Mus; 20th Cent Mus (Lit); Amer Mus (Lit); Musical Styles (Lit)
Degrees: AA
Scholarships: Small awards of about $100 available

NEW MEXICO

NEW MEXICO JUNIOR COLLEGE
Music Department
Lovington Highway
Hobbs, NM 88240
(505) 392-4510, x252
Staff: Prof. Lynn C. Dean, Chairman
Affiliation: State-supported junior college
Accreditation: NCA
Areas: App Mus; Th & An; Comp
Degrees: AA
Scholarships: Tuition scholarships based on audition and/or reference from high school choral or band director

NEW MEXICO STATE UNIVERSITY AT CARLSBAD
Music Department
1500 University Dr.
Carlsbad, NM 88220
(505) 885-8831
Staff: Barbara Carey, Chairman
Affiliation: Two-year branch of New Mexico State University
Accreditation: NCA
Areas: App Mus; Intro
Degrees: Transfer credit

NEW YORK

BOROUGH OF MANHATTAN COMMUNITY COLLEGE[1]
Department of Music and Art
199 Chambers St.
New York, NY 10007
(212) 262-5447
Staff: Professor Laurence Wilson, Chairman
Affiliation: Two-year college, unit of the City University of New York
Accreditation: MSA
Areas: App Mus; Th & An; Orch; Mus Lit
Degrees: AA

BRONX COMMUNITY COLLEGE[1]
Department of Music and Art
Bronx, NY 10453
(212) 220-6270
Staff: John C. Hamell, Chairman
Affiliation: A community college of the City University of New York
Accreditation: MSA
Areas: App Mus; Mus Lit; Th & An
Degrees: AAS

CAZENOVIA COLLEGE[1]
Music Department
Cazenovia, NY 13035
(315) 655-3466
Staff: Robert Capen, Lecturer
Affiliation: Private college for women
Accreditation: MSA
Areas: Mus Appr; Piano; Voice Instr
Degrees: AA

COMMUNITY COLLEGE OF THE FINGER LAKES
Visual/Performing Arts
100 Lincoln Hill Rd.
Canandaigua, NY 14424
(716) 394-3500, x243, 244
Staff: Dr. A. John Walker, Chairman
Affiliation: Community college—part of State University of New York/system
Accreditation: MSA
Areas: App Mus; Hist & Lit; Th & An; Comp; Orch; Instr Rep; Sound Tech
Degrees: AA

ERIE COMMUNITY COLLEGE[1]
City Campus
Music Department
121 Ellicott St.
Buffalo, NY 14203
(716) 842-2770
Staff: Michael De Yarmin, Instructor
Affiliation: State and locally-supported junior college
Accreditation: MSA
Areas: App Mus; Orch; Dance; Jazz Hist
Degrees: AA

FIVE TOWNS COLLEGE
Departments of Contemporary Music-Jazz, Music Business, and Music Instrument Technology
2165 Seaford Ave.
Seaford, NY 11783
(516) 783-8800
Staff: George Berordenelli, Chuck Mymit, and Martin Crafton, Coordinators
Affiliation: Private, independent, two-year co-educational college
Accreditation: MSA
Areas: App Mus; Th & An; Comp; Orch; Instr Rep; Intro; Mus Bus; Audio Recording Tech
Degrees: AAS
Scholarships: Scholarships awarded to advanced artistry students with proficiency of major instrument and admission to stage band at college

LAGUARDIA COMMUNITY COLLEGE
Music and Dance, Department of Humanities
31-10 Thomson Ave.
Long Island City, NY 11101
(212) 626-5089, 5572
Staff: Dr. Nick Rossi, Coordinator of Music
Affiliation: Two-year community college; branch of The City University of New York
Accreditation: MSA
Areas: App Mus; Hist & Lit; Th & An; Hist Musicol; Ethnomusicol; Theater Mus; Mus Bus; Mus Industry
Degrees: AA; AAS; AS; AS, Mus Bus; Transfer credit

MONROE COMMUNITY COLLEGE[1]
Music Department
1000 E. Henrietta Rd.
Rochester, NY 14623
(716) 424-5200
Staff: O. Whitney, Chairman
Affiliation: Community college of the State University of New York
Accreditation: MSA
Areas: App Mus; Mus Hist; Th & An; Comp; Theater Mus; Intro courses for non-mus majors; Piano; Voice; Guitar
Degrees: AS
Scholarships: Limited, half tuition

NASSAU COMMUNITY COLLEGE
Department of Music
Garden City, NY 11530
(516) 222-7447
Staff: Dr. Donald Gephardt, Chairman
Affiliation: Public (county) community college; part of SUNY
Accreditation: NASM; MSA
Areas: App Mus; Hist & Lit; Th & An
Degrees: AA; AAS

NEW YORK CITY TECHNICAL COLLEGE
Department of Humanities, Division of Liberal Arts
300 Jay St.
Brooklyn, NY 11201
(212) 643-8482
Staff: Dr. Eugene Armour, Associate Professor, Humanities and Performing Arts
Affiliation: Two-year community college of City University of New York
Accreditation: NASM; MSA
Areas: App Mus; Hist & Lit; Th & An; Intro courses
Degrees: AA; AS; Transfer credit

NIAGARA COUNTY COMMUNITY COLLEGE[1]
Music Department, Fine Arts Division
3111 Saunders Settlement Rd.
Sanborn, NY 14132
(716) 731-4101
Staff: Paul Ferington, Assistant Professor of Music
Affiliation: State supported community college, within State Univ. of New York system
Accreditation: MSA
Areas: App Mus; Mus Hist; Th & An; Comp; Cond; Mus Therapy; Piano Tech; American Popular Mus; Survey of Jazz & Rock Mus
Degrees: AS; Transfer credit
Scholarships: Full and partial awards for tuition and supplies—audition performance required

NORTH COUNTRY COMMUNITY COLLEGE
Music Department
20 Winona Ave.
Saranac Lake, NY 12983
(518) 891-2915
Staff: Prof. George F. Reynolds, Director of Music

Affiliation: Two-year community college, division of the State University of New York
Accreditation: MSA
Areas: App Mus; Piano Tech (every few years); Mus Apprec; 20th Century Mus; Concert Band; Chorale; Mus Th & Keyboard; Electr Mus; Computer Mus
Degrees: AA

ONONDAGA COMMUNITY COLLEGE
Music Department
Syracuse, NY 13215
(315) 469-7741, x5256-5257
Staff: Dr. Donald B. Miller, Chairman
Affiliation: State-supported community college—two-year transfer or professional program
Accreditation: MSA
Areas: App Mus; Mus Hist; Th & An; Orch; Opera; Church Mus; Theater Mus; Jazz Studies
Degrees: AAS
Scholarships: Barbara A. Micale Memorial Scholarship—open to any major—1st award in piano, subsequent awards in any applied area, yearly auditions, mid-year; Sweet Adeline Vocal Scholarship

QUEENSBOROUGH COMMUNITY COLLEGE
Music Department
56th Ave. & Springfield Blvd.
Bayside, NY 11364
(212) 428-0200, x410
Staff: Dr. Marvin Schwartz, Chairman
Affiliation: Community college of the City University of New York
Accreditation: MSA
Areas: App Mus; Hist & Lit; Th & An; Opera; Jazz Workshop; Piano Lab; Electr Mus Lab; Mus Therapy
Degrees: AA; AS; Transfer credit
Scholarships: Small scholarships available to students with a record of excellence in music; generally for private instruction in an instrument

ROCKLAND COMMUNITY COLLEGE[1]
Department of Performing Arts
145 College Rd.
Suffern, NY 10901
(914) 356-4650, x485
Staff: Isaiah Sheffer, Chairman
Affiliation: State-supported community college
Accreditation: MSA
Areas: Th & An; Cond; Orch; Violin
Degrees: AA

SCHENECTADY COUNTY COMMUNITY COLLEGE
Music Department
Washington Ave.
Schenectady, NY 12305
(518) 346-6211, x320
Staff: Dr. Gerald M. Hansen, Chairman
Affiliation: State-supported community colelge
Accreditation: NASM (cand.); MSA
Areas: App Mus; Hist & Lit; Mus & Lit; Th & An; Comp; Cond; Orch; Mus Ed (Elem & HS); Piano Tech
Areas: AS

SUFFOLK COUNTY COMMUNITY COLLEGE
Music Department
533 College Rd.
Selden, NY 11784
(516) 233-5254
Staff: Russell A. Stevenson, Department Head
Affiliation: SUNY; two-year college
Accreditation: MSA
Areas: App Mus; Mus Hist; Th; Mus in Recreation; Folk; Jazz; 20th Century; Sightsinging; Piano; Perf
Degrees: AS
Scholarships: For graduating students

ULSTER COUNTY COMMUNITY COLLEGE[1]
Music Department
Stone Ridge, NY 12484
(914) 687-7621
Staff: Prof. Richard Olsen, Coordinator of Music
Affiliation: State-supported community college
Accreditation: MSA
Areas: App Mus; Mus Hist; Mus Lit; Th & An
Degrees: AA; Transfer credit

VILLA MARIA COLLEGE OF BUFFALO
Music Department
240 Pine Ridge Rd.
Buffalo, NY 14225
(716) 896-0700
Staff: Andrew P. Ziemba, Chairperson
Affiliation: Private liberal arts junior college (administered by the Felician Sisters)
Accreditation: MSA
Areas: App Mus; Hist & Lit; Th & An
Degrees: AS
Scholarships: Two $500 scholarships, one to incoming freshman, and one to returning sophomore; based on audition, letter, interview and academic record

NORTH CAROLINA

BREVARD COLLEGE[1]
Division of Fine Arts
Brevard, NC 28712
(704) 883-8292, x211
Staff: Dr. John D. Upchurch, Chairman
Affiliation: Church-related liberal arts junior college (Methodist)
Accreditation: NASM; SACS
Areas: App Mus; Th & An; Comp
Degrees: AFA; JCD (junior college diploma)
Scholarships: Talent awards, performance awards, financial need

CHOWAN COLLEGE
Daniel School of Music
Murfreesboro, NC 27855
(919) 398-4101
Staff: Dr. James M. Chamblee, Chairman, Department of Fine Arts
Affiliation: Church-related liberal arts junior college (Baptist)
Accreditation: SACS
Areas: App Mus; Mus Lit; Th & An; Mus Ed (Elem & HS)
Degrees: AA; AS; AM
Scholarships: Three $1,000.00 departmental scholarships and two endowed scholarships (Barnes Scholarship - $1,200.00 and Futrell Scholarship - $400.00) awarded primarily on talent; campus visit and audition required

THE COLLEGE OF THE ALBEMARLE
Fine Arts Department
Elizabeth, NC 27909
(919) 335-0821
Staff: Dr. Leland, Chou, Chairman
Affiliation: State-supported community college
Accreditation: SACS
Areas: App Mus; Th & An; Mus Ed (Elem); Mus Fundamentals for Elem Classroom Teachers; Sightsinging & Dictation; Chorus; Hist & Lit
Degrees: AA
Scholarships: Anna and Clifford Bair Scholarships, tuition for piano, voice and organ; recipients of the scholarships must be a high school graduate, enroll at COA as a full-time student in the music curriculum, maintain a 3.0 or better GPA, participate in a performance competition with two compositions

DAVIDSON COUNTY COMMUNITY COLLEGE
Music Division, Department of Language & Fine Arts
P.O. Box 1287
Lexington, NC 27292
(704) 249-8186
Staff: Jo Ann D. Poston, Instructor
Affiliation: State-supported community college
Accreditation: SACS
Areas: Th & An; Cond; Choral Mus; Class Voice & Piano; Mus Apprec
Degrees: AA; AFA

LEES-MCRAE COLLEGE[1]
Music Department
Banner Elk, NC 28604
(704) 898-5241
Staff: Janet B. Carroll, Director
Affiliation: Privately-supported college
Accreditation: SACS
Areas: Mus Appr; Band; Piano
Degrees: AA

MITCHELL COMMUNITY COLLEGE[1]
Division of Fine Arts & Humanities
West Broad St.
Statesville, NC 28677
(704) 873-2201
Staff: Jane Heymann, Head
Affiliation: Community college
Accreditation: SACS
Areas: App Mus; Mus Hist; Mus Lit; Th & An
Degrees: AFA

Scholarships: Various—most based on financial need and scholarship

MONTREAT-ANDERSON COLLEGE[1]
Music Department
PO Box 1034
Montreat, NC 28757
(704) 669-8011
Staff: Lawrence Skinner, Chairman
Affiliation: Church-related college (U.S. Presbyterian)
Accreditation: SACS

MOUNT OLIVE COLLEGE
Music Department
PO Box 151
Mount Olive, NC 28365
(919) 658-2502
PO Box 151
Mount Olive, NC 28365
(919) 658-2502
Staff: Dr. Michael Pelt, Chairman
Affiliation: Church-related college (Free Will Baptist)
Accreditation: SACS
Areas: Th & An; Hist & Lit; Mus Ed (Elem & HS); Piano; Voice Instr; Organ; App Mus
Degrees: AA; AS

PEACE COLLEGE
Division of Fine Arts, Literature, and Languages—Music Area
15 E. Peace St.
Raleigh, NC 27604
(919) 832-2881
Staff: Virginia L. Vance, Music Area Coordinator
Affiliation: Private liberal arts college (Presbyterian)
Accreditation: SACS
Areas: App Mus; Hist & Lit; Th & An; Mus Lit
Degrees: AFAM (Associate of Fine Arts in Music)
Scholarships: Scholarship awards based on audition before music faculty

SOUTHEASTERN COMMUNITY COLLEGE
Department of Fine and Performing Arts
PO Box 151
Whiteville, NC 28472
(919) 642-7141, x221
Staff: Prof. Richard F. Burkhardt, Chairman
Affiliation: State-supported community college
Accreditation: SACS
Areas: App Mus; Mus Hist; Th & An; Cond; Opera; Church Mus; Music Ed (Elem & HS)
Degrees: AA; Transfer credit; AFA

NORTH DAKOTA

BISMARCK JUNIOR COLLEGE
Music Department
Schafer Heights
Bismarck, ND 58501
(701) 223-4500
Staff: Ervin Ely, Chairman
Affiliation: State-supported junior college
Accreditation: NASM; NCA
Areas: App Mus; Mus Hist; Cond; Mus Ed (Elem); Intro Courses
Degrees: AA
Scholarships: Full scholarships by audition

UNIVERSITY OF NORTH DAKOTA—WILLISTON CENTER
Humanities Division
Box 1326
Williston, ND 58801
(701) 572-6736
Staff: Davis J. Law, Chairman
Affiliation: State and locally supported junior college
Accreditation: NASM; NCA
Areas: App Mus; Mus Hist; Mus Ed (Elem); Intro
Degrees: AA
Scholarships: General college scholarships available

OHIO

CUYAHOGA COMMUNITY COLLEGE
Division of Humanities and Communications
11000 Pleasant Valley Rd.
Cleveland, OH 44130
(216) 845-4000
Staff: Toba Jeffery, Division Head
Affiliation: County & state-supported community colelge
Accreditation: NCA
Areas: App Mus; Hist & Lit; Mus Ed (Elem & HS); Jazz Apprec
Degrees: AA
Scholarships: Special talent awards: must be resident of Cuyahoga County, show special talent in music, maintain a 3.0 average

SHAWNEE STATE COMMUNITY COLLEGE
Division of Humanities
940 2nd St.
Portsmouth, OH 45662
(614) 354-3205
Staff: Shirley Evans Crothers, Associate Professor of Music
Affiliation: State-supported community college
Accreditation: NCA
Areas: App Mus; Hist & Lit; Mus Ed (Elem); Theater Mus; Intro; Comparative Arts
Degrees: AA; Arts Major

OKLAHOMA

BACONE COLLEGE[1]
Music Department
Division of Humanities
Muskogee, OK 74401
(918) 683-4581
Staff: Dr. George W. Stevenson, Chairman, Divison of Humanities
Affiliation: Church-related liberal arts junior college (American Baptist)
Accreditation: NCA
Areas: App Mus; Th & An; Cond
Degrees: AA
Scholarships: Choir—vocal and leadership ability; keyboard skills desired, although not required; ACT Financial Statement guidelines must be met

EASTERN OKLAHOMA STATE COLLEGE[1]
Music Department
Wilburton, OK 74578
(918) 465-2361
Staff: Bob G. Pratt, Chairman
Affiliation: State-supported college
Accreditation: NCA
Areas: Th & An; Intro; Mus Hist & Lit; Mus Ed (Elem & HS); Voice Instr; Theater Mus; Piano
Degrees: AA

OSCAR ROSE JUNIOR COLLEGE[1]
Music Department
6420 S.E. 15th St.
Midwest City, OK 73110
(405) 737-6611
Staff: Judith Torczynski, Instructor
Affiliation: State-supported junior college
Accreditation: NCA
Areas: Th & An; Mus Hist & Lit; Piano
Degrees: AA

WESTERN OKLAHOMA STATE COLLEGE[1]
Music Department
Altus, OK 73521
(405) 477-2000
Staff: Larry K. Duffy, Instructor
Affiliation: State-supported college
Accreditation: NCA
Areas: Th & An; Piano; Voice Instr
Degrees: AA

OREGON

BLUE MOUNTAIN COMMUNITY COLLEGE
Division of Fine Arts Department
2411 N.W. Carden (PO Box 100)
Pendleton, OR 97801
(503) 276-1260
Staff: John Weddle, Director of Music; William Hughes, Chairman, Fine Arts Department
Affiliation: Local and state-supported community college
Accreditation: NASC
Areas: App Mus; Th & An; Hist & Lit; Theater Mus
Degrees: AA
Scholarships: Tuition talent grant awards

CLACKAMAS COMMUNITY COLLEGE[1]
Music Department
19600 S. Molalla Ave.
Oregon City, OR 97045
(503) 656-2631, x293

Staff: LeRoy Anderson, Chairman
Affiliation: State and community supported community college
Accreditation: NASC
Areas: App Mus; Mus Lit; Th & An; Orch
Degrees: AA
Scholarships: Talent grants from one to six terms by audition

ROGUE COMMUNITY COLLEGE
Music Department
3345 Redwood Hwy.
Grants Pass, OR 97526
(503) 479-5541
Staff: JoAnn Pilcher, Music Coordinator
Affiliation: State-supported community college
Accreditation: NASC
Areas: App Mus; Hist & Lit; Comp; Th & An; Theater Mus
Degrees: AA; AS; Transfer credit
Scholarships: Performing arts scholarships to a full time student and members of RCC performing groups

TREASURE VALLEY COMMUNITY COLLEGE
Humanities Division
650 College Blvd.
Ontario, OR 97914
(503) 889-6493
Staff: Rodney N. Matson, Chairman, Music Department
Affiliation: Part of community college system of Oregon
Accreditation: NASC
Areas: App Mus; Mus Lit; Th & An
Degrees: AA; AS
Scholarships: Music talent grants available, based on performance proficiency and overall grade point average

PENNSYLVANIA

BUCKS COUNTY COMMUNITY COLLEGE
Media and Performing Arts Department
Swamp Rd.
Newtown, PA 18940
(215) 968-4261
Staff: William F. Brenner, Chairman
Affiliation: Public community college
Accreditation: MSA
Areas: App Mus; Mus Hist; Th & An; Comp; Cond; Mus Ed
Degrees: AA
Scholarships: Departmental scholarships to returning students, based on ability; partial tuition scholarships to new and returning students, based on ability

NORTHAMPTON COUNTY AREA COMMUNITY COLLEGE
Music Department
3835 Green Pond Rd.
Bethlehem, PA 18017
(215) 865-5351
Staff: Dr. Robert E. Schanck, Professor of Music
Affiliation: Community college
Accreditation: MSA
Areas: App Mus; Mus Hist; Th & An; Choral
Degrees: AA

SOUTH CAROLINA

ANDERSON COLLEGE
Fine Arts Division
316 Boulevard
Anderson, SC 29621
(803) 226-6181
Staff: Dr. Perry Carroll, Chairman, Fine Arts Division and Music Department
Affiliation: Church-related liberal arts college (Baptist)
Accreditation: SACS; NASM
Areas: App Mus; Hist & Lit; Th & An; Opera; Mus Apprec
Degrees: AA; AFA
Scholarships: By audition

NORTH GREENVILLE COLLEGE
Music Department
Tigerville, SC 29688
(803) 895-1410, x380
Staff: Jackie Griffin, Co-ordinator fo Fine Arts
Affiliation: Church-related college (Baptist)
Accreditation: SACS
Areas: Hist & Lit; Th & An; Cond; Piano; Voice Instr; App Mus
Degrees: AA; Mus; AM

TENNESSEE

CLEVELAND STATE COMMUNITY COLLEGE
Music Department
Cleveland, TN 37311
(615) 472-7141
Staff: Thomas R. Boles, Associate Prof. of Music
Affiliation: State-supported junior college
Accreditation: SACS
Areas: App Mus; Th & An; Cond; Choir; State Band; Mus Apprec
Degrees: AA
Scholarships: Applied music scholarships—audition

COLUMBIA STATE COMMUNITY COLLEGE[1]
Music Department
Hampshire Pike
Columbia, TN 38401
(615) 388-0120
Staff: Dr. Lee Roesti, Chairman
Affiliation: State-supported community college
Accreditation: SACS
Areas: App Mus; Mus Lit; Th & An; Mus Ed (Elem)
Degrees: AA
Scholarships: Available; must inquire for details

DYERSBURG STATE COMMUNITY COLLEGE
Division of Humanities
PO Box 648
Dyersburg, TN 38024
(901) 285-6910
Staff: Tom McCartney, Chairman, Division of Arts and Science
Affiliation: State-supported community college
Accreditation: SACS
Areas: App Mus; Mus Lit; Th & An; Mus Ed (Elem)
Degrees: AA
Scholarships: Scholarships awarded through auditions—must enroll in at least one music course per quarter

JACKSON STATE COMMUNITY COLLEGE
Music Department
North Parkway Dr.
Jackson, TN 38301
(901) 424-3520
Staff: Donnie Adams, Head
Affiliation: State-supported community college
Accreditation: SACS
Areas: App Mus; Hist & Lit; Th & An; Mus Ed (Elem)
Degrees: AA; AS
Scholarships: Scholarships for Tennessee residents (must audition)

MARTIN COLLEGE
Music Department
Pulaski, TN 38478
(615) 363-7456
Staff: Dr. Fred E. Ford, Chairman
Affiliation: Private, liberal arts two year college (Methodist)
Accreditation: SACS
Areas: App Mus; Mus Hist; Th & An; Mus Ed (Elem); Intro courses
Degrees: AA
Scholarships: By audition for vocal and instrumental performance

ROANE STATE COMMUNITY COLLEGE
Music Department
Harriman, TN 37748
(615) 354-3000, x298
Staff: Anna Miller, Music Coordinator
Affiliation: State-supported community college
Accreditation: SACS
Areas: App Mus; Th & An; Intro; Piano; Voice Instr; Hist & Lit
Degrees: AA
Scholarships: Available for accompanying and voice; one full scholarship for outstanding freshman music major

SHELBY STATE COMMUNITY COLLEGE
Music Department
PO Box 40568
Memphis, TN 38104
(901) 528-6841
Staff: Dr. Russ A. Schultz, Head
Affiliation: State-supported community college

Accreditation: SACS; NASM
Areas: App Mus; Mus Lit; Th & An; Orch; Arranging; Improv; Ensembles
Degrees: AA; AS

VOLUNTEER STATE COMMUNITY COLLEGE
Division of Humanities
Nashville Pike
Gallatin, TN 37066
(615) 452-8600
Staff: Dr. Donald R. Goss, Chairman, Division of Humanities; Dr. Bruce R. Smedley, Coordinator of Art & Music
Affiliation: State-supported; one of ten Tennessee community colleges
Accreditation: SACS
Areas: App Mus; Mus Lit; Th & An; Comp; Mus Ed (Elem); Mus Apprec (non-majors); Choral Groups; Chamber Mus; Ensemble (brass)
Degrees: AA; AS; Transfer credit

TEXAS

AMARILLO COLLEGE[1]
Music Department
2201 S. Washington St.
PO Box 447
Amarillo, TX 79178
(806) 376-5111
Staff: Robert E. Hoffman, Chairman
Affiliation: State-supported community college
Accreditation: NASM; SACS
Areas: App Mus; Mus Hist & Lit; Th & An; Mus Ed (elem & HS); Instr; Vocal Ensembles
Degrees: AA; AS

BEE COUNTY COLLEGE
Music Department, Division of Fine Arts
Foute 1, 3800 Charco Rd.
Beeville, TX 78102
(512) 358-7031
Staff: Dr. Jerry R. Hill, Chairman, Division of Fine Arts
Affiliation: State-supported junior college
Accreditation: SACS
Areas: App Mus; Th & An; Mus Ed (Elem & HS); Hist & Lit; Cond
Degrees: AA; AS; Transfer credit
Scholarships: Divisional, academic performance and private

BLINN COLLEGE
Division of Fine Arts
Brenham, TX 77833
(713) 836-9311
Staff: Bob Ham, Chairman
Affiliation: County-owned junior college
Accreditation: SACS
Areas: App Mus; Hist & Lit; Th & An; Mus Ed (Elem)
Degrees: AA
Scholarships: Band

BRAZOSPORT COLLEGE[1]
Music Department
500 College Dr.
Lake Jackson, TX 77566
(713) 265-6131
Staff: James A. Cargill, Chairman
Affiliation: State and locally-supported college
Accreditation: SACS
Areas: Th & An; Mus Hist & Lit; Voice Instr; Mus Ed (Elem); Piano
Degrees: AA

CISCO JUNIOR COLLEGE
Fine Arts Department
Cisco, TX 76437
(817) 442-2567
Staff: Wyley M. Peebles, Chairperson
Affiliation: State-supported, locally controlled public liberal arts junior college
Accreditation: SACS
Areas: App Mus; Mus Lit; Th & An
Degrees: AA
Scholarships: Cash awards in varying amounts for up to one-half total expenses, except lab fees

DEL MAR COLLEGE
Fine Arts Department
Corpus Christi, TX 78404
(512) 881-6211
Staff: Dr. Merton B. Johnson, Dean of Fine Arts
Affiliation: Community college
Accreditation: NASM; SACS
Areas: App Mus; Hist & Lit; Th & An; Comp; Mus Ed (Elem & HS)
Degrees: AA
Scholarships: All scholarships are by audition, based on talent and need, up to full tuition: Carl Duckwall Memorial Award, voice, entering freshmen; Blaise Montandon Memorial Piano Scholarship; entering freshmen; John R. Mertzen Scholarship for Brass, sophomore; Rabbi Sidney Wolf Orchestral Scholarship, entering freshmen

EL CENTRO COLLEGE[1]
Music Department
Main and Lamar Sts.
Dallas, TX 75202
(214) 746-2353
Staff: John Gunter, Chairman, Division of Humanities
Affiliation: Community college
Accreditation: SACS
Areas: App Mus; Mus Lit; Th & An; Mus Appr; Mus Fundamentals; Vocal Ensembles; Voice; Piano
Degrees: AA

HENDERSON COUNTY JUNIOR COLLEGE
Division of Fine Arts
Athens, TX 75751
(214) 675-6242
Staff: Dr. J.W. Smith, Chairman, Division of Fine Arts & Communications
Affiliation: State-supported junior college
Accreditation: SACS
Areas: App Mus; Th & An; Mus Ed (Elem)
Degrees: AA
Scholarships: Performance scholarships available in voice and instrumental music

HILL JUNIOR COLLEGE
Music Department
PO Box 619
Hillsboro, TX 76645
(817) 582-2555
Staff: Leland Lundgren, Chairman of Music and Fine Arts Department
Affiliation: State-supported junior college
Accreditation: NASM; SACS
Areas: App Mus; Mus Lit; Th & An; Cond; Mus Ed (Elem); Band; Stage Band; Choir; Ensemble; Brass Methods
Degrees: AA; Transfer credit; Diploma (Certificate of Completion)
Scholarships: Band or choir for performance

HOWARD COLLEGE AT BIG SPRING[1]
Music Department
Birdwell Ln. at Eleventh Pl.
Big Spring, TX 79720
(915) 267-6311, x44
Staff: Kenneth Sprinkle, Head
Affiliation: State and locally-supported junior college
Accreditation: SACS
Areas: App Mus; Th & An; Mus Ed (Elem); Opera; Mus Hist & Lit
Degrees: AA

KILGORE COLLEGE
Division of Fine Arts
1100 Broadway
Kilgore, TX 75662
(214) 984-8531
Staff: Jeanne Johnson, Chairman
Affiliation: State-supported community college
Accreditation: SACS
Areas: App Mus; Mus Lit; Th & An; Comp; Church Mus; Mus Ed (Elem)
Degrees: AA; AAS; AFA; AS
Scholarships: Available in varying amounts for participation in ensembles

LEE COLLEGE
Division of Fine Arts, Music Department
Box 818
Baytown, TX 77520
(713) 427-5611
Staff: Charles A. Stephenson, Chairperson, Fine Arts
Affiliation: Public-supported two-year community college
Accreditation: SACS
Areas: App Mus; Mus Lit; Th & An; Mus Ed (Elem); Ensembles
Degrees: AA; AS; Transfer credit
Scholarships: Organizational, foundation, departmental; requirements vary; scholarships available for private study

LON MORRIS JUNIOR COLLEGE
Music Department

Lon Morris Station
Jacksonville, TX 75766
(214) 214-2471
Staff: Robert Fordyce
Affiliation: Church-related liberal arts college (Methodist)
Accreditation: SACS
Areas: App Mus; Th & An; Choral; Band
Degrees: AA
Scholarships: For choir and band, by audition

MCLENNAN COMMUNITY COLLEGE[1]
Division of Fine Arts
1400 College Dr.
Waco, TX 76708
(817) 756-6551
Staff: Dr. William R. Haskett, Chairman
Affiliation: State-supported two year college
Accreditation: SACS
Areas: App Mus; Mus Hist; Mus Lit; Mus Ed (Elem)
Degrees: AA
Scholarships: 30 for half tuition; 30 for full tuition; 8 for full tuition and fees

NAVARRO COLLEGE
Music Department
PO Box 1170
Corsicana, TX 75110
(214) 874-6501
Staff: Edmond B. Hickman, Chairman, Band Division
Affiliation: State-supported college (community)
Accreditation: SACS
Areas: App Mus; Hist & Lit; Th & An; Orch; Mus Ed (Elem & HS) Band; Choir
Degrees: AA
Scholarships: Band

ODESSA COLLEGE
Music Department
201 W. University Blvd.
Odessa, TX 79762
(915) 335-6626
Staff: Dr. Jack W. Hendrix, Chairman
Affiliation: State-supported junior college
Accreditation: NASM; SACS
Areas: App Mus; Th & An; comp; Opera; Accoustics of Mus; Hist & Lit
Degrees: AA
Scholarships: Audition

PARIS JUNIOR COLLEGE[1]
Division of Fine Arts—Music
2400 Clarksville St.
Paris, TX 75460
(214) 785-7661
Staff: Dr. David Herfort, Coordinator
Affiliation: Local & state-supported community college
Accreditation: SACS
Areas: App Mus; Mus Lit; Th & An; Mus Ed (Elem); Theater Mus
Degrees: AA; AS
Scholarships: Tuition and work in instrumental, keyboard and vocal by audition and/or recommendation of previous instructor

SOUTH PLAINS COLLEGE
Creative Arts Department
Levelland, TX 79336
(806) 894-9611
Staff: Don Stroud, Professor of Fine Arts
Affiliation: Locally-supported community college
Accreditation: SACS
Areas: Th & An; Comp; Hist & Lit; Mus Ed (Elem & HS); Country & Bluegrass Mus
Degrees: AA
Scholarships: Competitive scholarship available to full time music student

SOUTHWESTERN ASSEMBLIES OF GOD COLLEGE[1]
Music Department
1200 Sycamore St.
Waxahachie, TX 75165
(214) 937-4010
Staff: William A. Bruton, Chairman
Affiliation: Church-related junior cole and Bible college
Accreditation: SACS
Areas: App Mus; Mus Hist; Th & An; Comp; Orch; Church Mus
Degrees: AA; Transfer credit; Diploma (Junior college)
Scholarships: Awarded to teen talent winners on district, regional and national levels

TEXARKANA COMMUNITY COLLEGE[1]
Music Department
2500 N. Robison Rd.
Texarkana, TX 75501
(214) 838-4541
Staff: Murray L. Alewine, Chairman
Affiliation: State and locally-supported community college
Accreditation: SACS; NASM
Areas: Th & An; Intro; Mus Hist & Lit; Mus Ed (Elem & HS); Opera; Voice Instr; Piano
Degrees: AA

TEXAS SOUTHMOST COLLEGE[1]
Music Department
83 Ft. Brown
Brownsville, TX 78520
(512) 546-7121
Staff: Lura Davidson, Chairperson
Affiliation: State-supported junior colge
Accreditation: SACS
Areas: App Mus; Mus Lit; Th & An; Comp; Mus Ed (Elem)
Degrees: AA
Scholarships: For stated music majors, not eligible for other types of grants

TYLER JUNIOR COLLEGE[1]
Music Department
PO Box 9020
Tyler, TX 75701
(214) 597-4351
Staff: J.W. Johnson, Chairman
Affiliation: District junior college
Accreditation: SACS
Areas: App Mus; Mus Lit; Th & An; Mus Ed (Elem); Perf Choral Groups; Instrl Perf Groups
Degrees: AA
Scholarships: Tuition and fees based on membership in performing groups and economic need

VICTORIA COLLEGE[1]
Music Department
2200 E. Red River
Victoria, TX 77901
(512) 573-3295
Staff: Wilbur L. Collins, Director of Bands
Affiliation: Public community college (state & county)
Accreditation: SACS
Areas: App Mus; Mus Lit; Th & An; Mus Ed (Elem & HS); Mus Therapy
Degrees: AA; Certificate of completion
Scholarships: By application and audition for applied music, band, jazz ensemble, choral and Madrigal singing

WEATHERFORD COLLEGE
Music Department
308 East Park
Weatherford, TX 76066
(817) 594-5471
Staff: Myrna Fields, Music Department
Affiliation: State-supported junior college
Accreditation: SACS
Areas: App Mus; Hist & Lit; Th & An; Mus Ed (Elem); Intro
Degrees: AA; ALA
Scholarships: Performance

WESTERN TEXAS COLLEGE
Music Department
Snyder, TX 79459
(915) 573-8511
Staff: Guy Gamble, Instructor; Jane Womack, Instructor
Affiliation: State and locally-supported college
Accreditation: SACS
Areas: Th & An; Comp; Voice Instr; Piano
Degrees: AA

UTAH

COLLEGE OF EASTERN UTAH[1]
Music Department, Humanities Division
451 E. 4th North
Price, UT 84501
(801) 637-2120
Staff: Prof. Derral L. Siggard, Music Department Head
Affiliation: State-supported two-year community college
Accreditation: NASC
Areas: App Mus; Mus Lit; Th & An; Cond; Mus Ed (Elem)
Degrees: AA; AAS
Scholarships: Instrumental and vocal music

VIRGINIA

FERRUM COLLEGE[1]
Division of Fine Arts
Ferrum, VA 24088
(703) 365-2121, x104
Staff: James E. McConnell, Chairman
Affiliation: Church-related college (Methodist)
Accreditation: SACS
Areas: Th & An; Cond; Comp; INtro; Mus Hist & Lit; Voice Instr; Piano
Degrees: AFA

NEW RIVER COMMUNITY COLLEGE[1]
Music Department
PO Drawer 1127
Dublin, VA 24084
(703) 674-4121, x300
Staff: Dr. Larry W. Long, Assistant Division Chairman, Humanities & Social Sciences
Affiliation: State-supported junior college
Accreditation: SACS
Areas: App Mus; Th & An; Cond; Church Mus; Mus Ed (Elem)
Degrees: AA

SOUTHERN SEMINARY JUNIOR COLLEGE
Music Department, Arts & Humanities Division
Buena Vista, VA 24416
(703) 261-6181, x249
Staff: Lowell D. Cooper, Chairman, Music Department
Affiliation: Private liberal arts junior college for young women
Accreditation: SACS
Areas: Mus Hist; Th & An; Mus Ed (Pre-school)
Degrees: AA

TIDEWATER COMMUNITY COLLEGE[1]
Frederick Campus
Music Department
Portsmouth, VA 23703
(804) 484-2121
Staff: Donald Smith, Associate Professor
Affiliation: State-supported community college
Accreditation: SACS
Areas: Cond; Intro; Mus Ed (Elem & HS); Voice Instr; Piano
Degrees: BA; BS, Mus Ed

WASHINGTON

COLUMBIA BASIN COLLEGE
Performing Arts Division
2600 N. 20th St.
Pasco, WA 99301
(509) 547-0511
Staff: Ted Neth, Chairman
Affiliation: Junior college affiliated with Washington State system of Junior colleges
Accreditation: NASM; NASC
Areas: App Mus; Th & An
Degrees: AA
Scholarships: Grants for tuition determined by performance ability

EVERETT COMMUNITY COLLEGE[1]
Music Department (Arts Division)
801 Wetmore Ave.
Everett, WA 98201
(206) 259-7151
Staff: John D. Shawger, Music Administrator
Affiliation: State-supported junior college
Accreditation: NASC
Areas: App Mus; Mus Hist; Th & An; Cond
Degrees: AA

GREEN RIVER COMMUNITY COLLEGE
Music Department
12401 S.E. 320th
Auburn, WA 98002
(206) TE 3-9111
Staff: Ronald W. Smith, Music Chairman
Affiliation: State-supported community college
Accreditation: NASC
Areas: App Mus; Th & An; Theater Mus
Degrees: AA

OLYMPIC COLLEGE[1]
Music Department, Humanities Division
Bremerton, WA 98310
(206) 478-4537
Staff: Polly Zanetta, Division Chairman
Affiliation: Washington State community college
Accreditation: NASC
Areas: App Mus; Mus Hist; Mus Lit; Th & An; Orch; Jazz Workshop; Jazz Arranging
Degrees: AA
Scholarships: For second year continuing students

PENINSULA COLLEGE
Division of Social Sciences and Humanities
Boulevard & Ennis Sts.
Port Angeles, WA 98362
(206) 452-9277
Staff: Dr. J. Marvin Pollard, Director
Affiliation: State-supported junior college
Accreditation: NASC
Areas: App Mus; Mus Lit; Th & An; Theater Mus; Perf; Choir; Chamber Mus
Degrees: AA
Scholarships: Yes

SPOKANE FALLS COMMUNITY COLLEGE
Creative & Performing Arts Division—Music Department
3410 Fort George Wright Dr.
Spokane, WA 99204
(509) 456-3906
Staff: Donald Nepean, Division Supervisor; Charles Zimmerman, Department Chairman
Affiliation: State-supported community college; two-year liberal arts and vocational arts programs
Accreditation: NASC
Areas: App Mus; Mus Hist; Th & An; Piano Tech; Instr Rep; Hist & Lit; Comp; Intro
Degrees: AA
Scholarships: Financial aid and work study only

WENATCHEE VALLEY COLLEGE[1]
Performing Arts Division
1300 Fifth St.
Wenatchee, WA 98801
(509) 662-1651
Staff: Richard Lapo, Chairman
Affiliation: State-supported junior college
Accreditation: NASC
Areas: App Mus; Mus Hist; Th & An; Comp; Cond; Orch; Church Mus; Mus Ed (Elem & HS)
Degrees: AA
Scholarships: Performance abilities in chorus, orchestra and band

YAKIMA VALLEY COLLEGE[1]
Creative Arts Division
PO Box 1647
Yakima, WA 98907
Staff: Scott Peterson, Chairman
Affiliation: Community college
Accreditation: NASC
Areas: App Mus; Th & An; Comp; Intro; Mus Hist & Lit; Voice Instr; Piano
Degrees: AA

WEST VIRGINIA

PARKERSBURG COMMUNITY COLLEGE
Music Department, Humanities Division
Route 5, Box 167-A
Parkersburg, WV 26101
(304) 424-8000, x248
Staff: H.G. Young, III, Associate Professor and Coordinator of Music
Affiliation: Two-year state-supported non-residential community college
Accreditation: NCA
Areas: App Mus; Mus Lit; Th & An; Cond; Church Mus; Theater Mus; Intro; Mus Ed (Elem)
Degrees: AA; Transfer credit
Scholarships: Academic ability (3.0 GPA and 17 ACT) and/or financial need

POTOMAC STATE COLLEGE OF WEST VIRGINIA UNIVERSITY
Division of Arts and Humanities, Music Unit
Keyser, WV 26726
(304) 788-3011
Staff: Richard A. Davis, Coordinator, Music Unit
Affiliation: Junior college branch of West Virginia Univ; transfer and two-year programs with emphasis on transfer programs
Accreditation: NCA
Areas: App Mus; Hist & Lit; Th & An; Cond; Mus Apprec; Performing Groups
Degrees: AA
Scholarships: West Virginia Board of Regents

WISCONSIN

UNIVERSITY OF WISCONSIN CENTER—BARRON COUNTY[1]
1800 College Dr.
Rice Lake, WI 54868
(715) 234-8176
Staff: Dennis Harms, Coordinator
Affiliation: Two-year liberal arts college
Accreditation: NCA
Areas: App Mus; Mus Hist; Mus Lit; Th & An; Theater Mus; Intro courses
Degrees: AA
Scholarships: Foundation scholarships based on need of student

UNIVERSITY OF WISCONSIN CENTER—MANITOWOC[1]
Music Department
705 Viebahn St.
Manitowoc, WI 54220
(414) 683-4700
Staff: Michael J. Arendt, Chairman
Affiliation: State-suported two-year (freshman and sophomores) transfer institution
Accreditation: NCA
Areas: App Mus; Hist & Lit; Th & An; Cond; Opera; Mus Ed (Elem & HS)
Degrees: AA

UNIVERSITY OF WISCONSIN CENTER—MARATHON COUNTY
Music Department
518 S. 7th Ave.
Wausau, WI 54401
(715) 845-9802
Staff: John A. Fitzgerald, Chairman
Affiliation: One of 14 campuses called the University of Wisconsin Center System (Freshman-sophomore)
Accreditation: NCA
Areas: App Mus; Hist & Lit; Th & An; Mus Ed (Elem)
Degrees: AA

UNIVERSITY OF WISCONSIN CENTER—MARSHFIELD
Music Department
2000 W. Fifth St., Box 150
Marshfield, WI 54449
(715) 387-1147
Staff: Robert Biederwolf, Associate Professor of Music
Affiliation: Two-year branch of the University of Wisconsin
Accreditation: NCA
Areas: App Mus; Hist & Lit; Mus Lit; Th & An; Orch; Choral; Instrumental Performing Organizations
Degrees: AFA
Scholarships: Scholarships available

UNIVERSITY OF WISCONSIN CENTER—RICHLAND
Music Department
Richland Center, WI 53581
(608) 647-6186
Staff: James K. Aagaard, Director of Music
Affiliation: Two-year campus of the U.W. Center System
Accreditation: NCA
Areas: App Mus; Th & An; Mus Ed (Elem & HS); Mus Lit & Fundamentals; Band; Choir; Ensembles
Degrees: AA; Transfer credit
Scholarships: Several scholarships ranging from $100 to $800 available to students in various musical specialties

UNIVERSITY OF WISCONSIN CENTER—SHEBOYGAN[1]
Music Department
One University Dr.
Sheyboygan, WI 53081
(414) 459-3708
Staff: Professor William E. Hughes, Professor of Music
Affiliation: Two year university level—Center System
Accreditation: NCA
Areas: App Mus; Mus Hist; Mus Lit; Th & An; Comp
Degrees: AA; AS

WYOMING

CASPER COLLEGE
Music Department
125 College Dr.
Casper, WY 82601
(307) 268-2606
Staff: Dr. Thomas Kinser, Chairman, Fine Arts Division
Affiliation: State-supported junior college
Accreditation: NCA
Areas: App Mus; Hist & Lit; Th & An; Mus Ed (Elem & HS); Theater Mus
Degrees: AA
Scholarships: Fine Arts Division: based on past GPA; Music Activity: participation in four performance groups for full tuition waiver; two groups for half tuition waiver

EASTERN WYOMING COLLEGE
Music Department
3200 West C
Torrington, WY 82240
(307) 532-7111
Staff: Jeanne Huntington Hamer, Chairperson
Affiliation: Community college, University of Wyoming
Accreditation: NCA
Areas: App Mus; Mus Hist; Th & An; Mus Ed (Elem & HS); Mus Therapy
Degrees: AA
Scholarships: Activity grant; tuition waivers

SHERIDAN COLLEGE[1]
Music Department
Sheridan, WY 82801
(307) 674-6446, x138
Staff: Kit Johnson, Chairman
Affiliation: Locally-supported college
Accreditation: NCA
Areas: Choral Groups; Piano; Jazz Ensemble; Jazz
Degrees: AA

CANADA

ALBERTA

GRANDE PRAIRIE REGIONAL COLLEGE[1]
Department of Fine Arts
Grande Prairie, AB T8V 4C4
(403) 539-2911
Staff: Sukumar Nayar, Chairman
Affiliation: Community college
Accreditation: ACCM
Areas: App Mus; Mus Hist; Mus Lit; Th & An; comp; cond; Orch; Opera; Mus Ed (Elem)
Degrees: Diploma in Visual & Performing Arts
Scholarships: Yes

MOUNT ROYAL COLLEGE
Conservatory of Music and Speech Arts
4825 Richard Rd., S.W.
Calgary, AB T3E 6K6
(403) 240-6821
Staff: Dr. Norman Burgess, Director
Affiliation: Publicly supported community college
Accreditation: ACCM (Association of colleges and Conservatories of Music); CMS (College Music Society)
Areas: App Mus; Hist & Lit; Mus Lit; Th & An; Studio Music; Orchestral Instruments
Degrees: Transfer credit; Diploma Music Performance (2 years)
Scholarships: Through the conservatory's own accredited examination system (all grades and instruments); in addition to exam-based scholarships, there are special scholarships awarded on the basis of merit/need

ONTARIO

FANSHAWE COLLEGE
Music Industry Arts, Communications Arts Division
PO Box 4005
London, ON N5W 5H1
(519) 452-4470
Staff: Terry McManus, Coordinator
Affiliation: Community college of applied arts & technology
Accreditation: Ontario Ministry of Education
Areas: Recorded Mus Production; Recording Engin; Th & An
Degrees: Diploma Course

QUEBEC

VANIER COLLEGE
Music Department
821 Ste. Croix Blvd.
St. Laurent, PQ H4L 3X9
(514) 333-3897
Staff: Raymond Laliberte, Coordinator
Affiliation: Government-sponsored junior college
Areas: App Mus; Hist & Lit; Th & An
Degrees: Diploma of Collegial Studies
Scholarships: Performance awards only

Community Colleges Index

A

B

C

D

E

F

G

H

I

J

K

L

M

N

O

P

Q

R

S

T

U

V

W

Y

Music Schools

U.S. and Canadian schools and conservatories of music that do not offer degrees are listed alphabetically by state or province. The name of the school's administrator, affiliation, level of instruction, specialty areas, private instruction offered, and scholarships available are given for most schools. Summer sessions, where available, are also noted. The number 1 following the name of the school indicates that they did not respond to our questionnaire. An alphabetical cross-index appears at the end of this section.

The following abbreviations have been used for accrediting agencies and affiliation:

NASM - National Association of Schools of Music
NATTS - National Association of Trade and Technical Schools
NGCSA - National Guild of Community Schools of the Arts

CALIFORNIA

CLAREMONT COMMUNITY SCHOOL OF MUSIC

PO Box 53
Claremont, CA 91711
(714) 624-3012
Staff: Debora L. Huffman, Executive Director
Affiliation: Community school, nonprofit; member, NGCSA
Level: Preschool through adult
Specialties: All instruments and voice, Suzuki instruction, music for young children, student recitals, faculty concerts. Summer sessions offered.
Private Instruction: Piano, violin, viola, cello, voice, flute, clarinet, saxophone, guitar, trumpet, trombone, French horn, harp, bassoon, oboe, and recorder
Scholarships: Scholarships available based on need.

COLLEGE FOR RECORDING ARTS

665 Harrison St.
San Francisco,CA 94107
(415) 781-6306
Staff: Robert G. Berlin, Operations Director
Affiliation: Private technical school, accredited by NATTS and approved by the California Department of Post-Secondary Education
Level: Post-secondary
Specialties: Recording engineering, music production, studio electronics and maintenance, music law (basic), music business and finance. Summer term offered.

COMMUNITY MUSIC CENTER

544 Capp St.
San Francisco, CA 94110
(415) 647-6015
Staff: Stephen R. Shapiro, Director
Affiliation: Private, non-boarding community school
Specialties: Group classes in theory and eurhythmics are offered, as well as a community chorus and a children's chorus.
Private Instruction: Strings, woodwinds, brass, percussion, voice, guitar, recorder, mandolin, banjo
Scholarships: All fees on a sliding scale. Limited scholarships available on faculty recommendation.

COMMUNITY SCHOOL OF MUSIC AND ARTS

405 Ortega Ave.
Mountain View, CA 94040
(415) 961-0342
Staff: Nancy Lawrence Glaze, Executive Director
Affiliation: Community school; member, NGCSA
Level: All levels
Specialties: Art classes; artists in the schools programs; all orchestral instruments, voice; specialize in jazz, Brazilian and Latino percussion. Summer sessions offered.
Private Instruction: Piano, flute, violin, viola, voice, oboe, recorder, vibraphone, string bass, electric bass, clarinet, saxophone, trumpet, trombone, marimba, guitar, percussion
Scholarships: Tuition aid available based on financial need and desire to learn.

THE COMMUNITY SCHOOL OF PERFORMING ARTS

3131 S. Figueroa St.
Los Angeles, CA 90007
(213) 743-6919
Staff: Toby E. Mayman, Executive Director
Affiliation: Private, nonprofit school; member, NGCSA, NASM, Federation of the Arts, and Los Angeles Area Dance Alliance
Level: Preschool through adult
Specialties: Classes in piano, cello, violin, orchestral instruments, guitar, voice, theory, chamber music, music appreciation. Concerts, recitals, workshops and special performances. A full course of dance study includes tap, ballet, and modern dance with support classes in creative dance, jazz, dance notation, history of dance, music for dancers, stage make-up. Professional training program is available. Summer sessions offered.
Private Instruction: Piano, cello, violin, orchestral instruments, guitar, voice
Scholarships: Scholarships available based on talent, motivation and progress.

EUBANKS CONSERVATORY OF MUSIC AND ARTS

4928 Crenshaw Blvd.
Los Angeles, CA 90043
(213) 291-7821
Staff: Dr. Rachel Eubanks, President
Affiliation: Private conservatory
Level: Preparatory and collegiate
Specialties: Instruction areas include performance (instruments, voice, accompanying), workshops, concerts, theory, composition, and church music. Summer sessions available. The complete curriculum, ranging from music history to orchestration, may be obtained by writing for the catalog.
Private Instruction: Any course listed with the conservatory may be taken privately.
Scholarships: Scholarships available. Requirements vary according to age and level of applicant.

MUSIC ACADEMY OF THE WEST SUMMER FESTIVAL[1]
1070 Fairway Rd.
PO Box 5737
Santa Barbara, CA 93108
(805) 969-4726
Staff: Susanne L. Byars, Executive Director
Affiliation: Summer boarding conservatory
Specialties: Vocal (opera, song and lieder), instrumental (symphony, chamber music), piano instruction during eight-week summer session only.

PALOS VERDES ACADEMY OF ARTS
727 Silver Spur Rd.
Rolling Hills Estates, CA 90274
(213) 377-4583
Staff: Alice Leggett LaMar, Owner
Affiliation: Dance community school
Level: Primary through adult
Specialties: Classical ballet, pointe, jazz dancing lessons. Home of the Peninsula Civic Ballet. Summer sessions offered.
Private Instruction: Ballet, pointe
Scholarships: Scholarships available based on ability and need.

SOUND MASTER RECORDING ENGINEER SCHOOLS
10747 Magnolia Blvd.
North Hollywood, CA 91601
(213) 650-8000
Staff: Barbara Ingoldsby, Dean of Administration
Affiliation: Private trade school, approved by the California State Department of Education; also approved by the Federal Immigration Department for foreign students
Level: Postsecondary
Specialties: Comprehensive training in multi-track recording, live concert sound, disc mastering, repair of studio equipment, and complete video production training from camera to computer editing. Summer sessions offered.
Scholarships: Available through state agencies.

COLORADO

COLORADO AUDIO INSTITUTE
680 Indiana St.
Golden, CO 80401
(303) 278-2551
Staff: Dennis Kitchens, Director of Admissions
Affiliation: Avocational school.
Level: Secondary through adult
Specialties: Comprehensive in-depth training in subjects relating to professional sound. Beginning and advanced courses in recording studio engineering, live sound engineering, music production, music business, concert lighting. Emphasis on hands-on experience. Summer sessions offered.

CONNECTICUT

ALBANO BALLET AND PERFORMING ARTS ACADEMY
15 Girard Ave
Hartford, CT 06105
(203) 232-8898
Staff: Joseph Albano, Director
Affiliation: Private music conservatory, boarding academy
Level: Children through adult
Specialties: Instruction in all instruments. Voice-classical and popular-also offered. Summer sessions offered.
Private Instruction: All instruments, voice and musical coaching

HARTFORD CONSERVATORY
834 Asylum Ave.
Hartford, CT 06103
(203) 246-2588
Staff: Donald J. Minutillo, Dean
Affiliation: Two-year diploma program in music and dance as private general enrollment community school. Member, NGCSA
Level: High school
Specialties: Modern dance, ballet, jazz dance, dance pedagogy, general music, jazz studies, record production. Summer sessions offered.
Private Instruction: All fields
Scholarships: Scholarships available.

NEIGHBORHOOD MUSIC SCHOOL[1]
100 Audubon St.
New Haven, CT 06511
(203) 624-5189
Staff: Peter Mansfield, Executive Director
Affiliation: Non-boarding community school; member, NGCSA and NASM
Specialties: Classes in theory, musicianship, rhythmic movement, Introduction to Music (Kodaly/Orff-based program for young children), opera workshop, piano literature, Suzuki piano and strings, chorus, madrigals, small and large ensembles, youth orchestras and early music consorts. Summer sessions offered.
Private Instruction: Piano, strings, voice, woodwinds, brass, percussion, guitar, recorder

DELAWARE

WILMINGTON MUSIC SCHOOL
4101 Washington St.
Wilmington, DE 19802
(302) 762-1132
Staff: Stephen Gunzenhauser, Artistic Director; Martha Collins, Administrative Director
Affiliation: Community school; member, NGCSA
Level: Preschool through adult
Specialties: Ensembles, jazz, theory classes, Suzuki classes, master classes, workshops, orchestra and string classes. Summer session workshops offered.
Private Instruction: Piano, voice, instruments, classical and folk guitar, jazz
Scholarships: Scholarships available based on ability and need.

DISTRICT OF COLUMBIA

LEVINE SCHOOL OF MUSIC
1655 Foxhall Rd., NW
Washington, DC 20007
(202) 965-6622
Staff: Joanne Hoover, Director
Affiliation: Private nonprofit preparatory school of music; member, NGCSA
Level: Preschool through adulty
Specialties: Classical music instruction in all instruments and voice; theory and musicianship; eurhythmics and Suzuki violin for younger children. Classes in early music, including harpsichord, viol and recorder; extensive chamber music program. Summer sessions offered.
Private Instruction: All areas
Scholarships: Scholarships, based on need plus merit, available in all areas; auditions held in spring for the next academic year.

GEORGIA

THE MUSIC BUSINESS INSTITUTE
2970 Peachtree Rd., NW, Ste. 400
Atlanta, GA 30305
(404) 231-3303
Staff: Vicki Tunstall, Admissions Coordinator
Affiliation: Proprietary vocational school
Level: Post secondary and college
Specialties: Instruction offered for post-high school and college levels. Artist representation; record promotion, marketing, and airplay; concert production and promotion; video production; copyright law/music legalities; recording and studio production; songwriting and music publishing; and music business (wholesaling, distribution, retailing, merchandising recorded music). Summer sessions offered.
Scholarships: Georgia Private School Association Scholarships; financial aid available (Pell Grant, GSL, NDSL, College Work-Study).

ILLINOIS

THE DR. JULIUS D'ALBERT ACADEMY AND INSTITUTE
2540 N. Spaulding Ave.
Chicago, IL 60647
(312) 342-0074
Staff: Dr. Francois D'Albert, President-Dean
Affiliation: Private conservatory
Level: All levels
Specialties: Strings, piano, voice; workshops; concerts. Summer sessions offered.
Private Instruction: Individual instruction in all applied music

IVS SCHOOL OF MUSIC
720 Lake St.
Oak Park, IL 60301
(312) 848-3008
Staff: William G. Messner, Executive Director
Affiliation: Private conservatory; member, NGCSA
Level: Preschool through adult
Specialties: Voice, piano, organ, musicianship (Kodaly) and voice therapy. Summer sessions offered.
Private Instruction: Voice, piano, organ
Scholarships: Scholarships available.

JACK BENNY CENTER FOR THE ARTS
Waukegan Park District
2000 Belvidere
Waukegan, IL 60085
(312) 244-1660
Staff: Lynn Schornick, Supervisor of Cultural Arts
Affiliation: Waukegan Park District community fine arts school
Level: Preschool through adult
Specialties: All band and orchestra instruments, voice, piano, guitar. Classes in dramatics, art and dance are also offered. Summer sessions offered.
Private Instruction: All band and orchestra instruments, voice, piano, guitar
Scholarships: Partial scholarships available based on desire and potential.

MU PHI EPSILON SCHOOL OF MUSIC
Gads Hill Center
1919 W. Cullerton Ave.
Chicago, IL 60608
(312) 743-7234
Staff: Mira Levi, Director
Affiliation: Part of an international music fraternity in the professional field, nationally funded by women musicians
Level: All ages
Specialties: Quality, professional instruction to minorities and low-income families. The school presents its students in concerts and performances both in the city and nationally.
Private Instruction: Piano, flute, clarinet, theory, voice, opera and musical comedy studies, movement for stage, and acting techniques
Scholarships: Adjusted fees available based on demonstrated need.

MUSIC CENTER OF THE NORTH SHORE[1]
300 Green Bay Rd.
Winnetka, IL 60093
(312) 446-3822
Staff: Kalman Novak, Director
Affiliation: Nonprofit, private corporation; member, NGCSA and NASM
Level: Piano, voice, all strings and winds. Summer sessions offered.
Private Instruction: Piano, voice, guitar, recorder, all orchestral instruments

MUSIC INSTITUTE OF THE LAKE FOREST SYMPHONY ASSOCIATION
PO Box 748
Lake Forest, IL 60045
(312) 295-2135
Staff: Mrs. Ellen Eastman, Chairman; Marc Levy, Registrar
Affiliation: Community school, emphasis on private instruction and preschool; member, NGCSA
Level: Preschool through adult
Specialties: Instrumental, voice, Orff and Suzuki lessons; in coordination with Lake Forest Symphony Concerts and concerts for young people. Summer sessions offered.
Private Instruction: Instrumental, voice
Scholarships: Scholarships available based on need.

THE PEOPLE'S MUSIC SCHOOL
4417 N. Sheridan Rd.
Chicago, IL 60640
(312) 784-7032
Staff: Rita Simo, Director
Affiliation: Community music school
Level: Preschool through adult
Specialties: Every student receives a one hour theory class each week and a one-half hour private lesson. Summer sessions offered.
Private Instruction: Piano, violin, flute, voice, woodwind, percussion
Scholarships: All lessons are free.

IOWA

PREUCIL SCHOOL OF MUSIC
524 N. Johnson St.
Iowa City, IA 52240
(319) 337-4156
Staff: Doris B. Preucil, Director
Affiliation: Community school; member, NGCSA
Level: Preschool through adult
Specialties: Pedagogy organization using the Suzuki method of instruction in violin, viola, cello, piano, and flute; fine arts preschool and Orff classes offered to ages 3-5. Orchestra, string quartet, violin, viola, cello, piano and flute classes offered. Summer sessions offered.
Private Instruction: Available
Scholarships: Scholarships available to those who require financial assistance and have been with the school for one year; scholarship applied to a percentage of the tuition.

MARYLAND

OMEGA STUDIOS' SCHOOL OF APPLIED RECORDING ARTS AND SCIENCES
10518 Connecticut Ave.
Kensington, MD 20895
(301) 946-4686
Staff: W. Robert Yesbek, Owner/Chief Engineer
Affiliation: Private vocational school, accredited by Maryland State Board for Higher Education; boarding during summers
Level: Post secondary and adult
Specialties: Professional practical recording engineering including theory, demonstration/workshop and hands-on experience in a modern Washington control room. Summer seminary (intensive ten-day program) includes lectures and workshops by experts in the field.

MASSACHUSETTS

ALL NEWTON MUSIC SCHOOL[1]
321 Chestnut St.
West Newton, MA 02165
(615) 527-4553
Staff: Andrew Wolf, Director
Affiliation: Community school; member, NGCSA
Specialties: Voice classes, individual instruction for all instruments, dance, ballet, opera, exercises, concerts, lectures. Summer session offered.
Private Instruction: All instruments, voice

BELMONT MUSIC SCHOOL
582 A Pleasant St.
Belmont, MA 02170
(617) 484-4696
Staff: Ellen Powers, Director
Affiliation: Community school
Specialties: All major orchestral instruments, plus theory, ensemble, eurhythmics, folk guitar and recorder.
Private Instruction: Baroque flute, banjo, bassoon, cello, clarinet, classical guitar, dulcimer, double bass, flute, folk guitar, French horn, harpsichord, oboe, organ, percussion, piano, recorder, saxophone, Suzuki cello, Suzuki violin, trombone, trumpet, viol, viola, violin, voice

BERKSHIRE MUSIC CENTER
(Winter)
Symphony Hall
Boston, MA 02115
(Summer)
Tanglewood
Lenox, MA 01240
(617) 266-5241
(413) 637-1600 (summer)
Staff: Daniel R. Gustin, Administrator
Affiliation: Boston Symphony Orchestra's private, boarding academy
Level: An academy for advanced training in music, operated at the summer home of the Boston Symphony Orchestra. For those 18 or more years of age, the fellowship program offers intensive coaching leading to public performance in instrumental music, vocal music, composition, and conducting. Other programs include seminars (no performance) for singers and conductors and various programs for high-school musicians. Summer sessions only.
Private Instruction: All instrumental disciplines

CAPE COD CONSERVATORY OF MUSIC & ARTS[1]
Route 132
West Barnstable, MA 02668
(617) 362-2772
Staff: Richard Casper, Director
Affiliation: Community school; member, NGCSA
Specialties: Offers instruction in musical instruments and voice, as well as dance classes in ballet, modern, jazz; art classes in all media, music theory and musical theater. Summer sessions offered.
Private Instruction: All musical instruments and voice

THE MUSIC SCHOOL AT RIVERS
337 Winter St.
Weston, MA 02193
(617) 235-6840
Staff: Richard S. Robbins, Director
Affiliation: Community music school on the campus of the Rivers School (a private day school for boys); member, NGCSA
Level: Preschool through adult
Private Instruction: Piano, voice, all orchestral instruments
Scholarships: Scholarships available according to need and merit.

THE MUSIC SCHOOL OF NORTH SHORE COMMUNITY COLLEGE
Box 276
South Hamilton, MA 01982
(617) 468-1201
Staff: Ernest M. Clark, Director
Affiliation: Part of North Shore Community Colleges Division of Continuing Education with three divisions: preparatory (5-18), Collegiate (NSCC), and Extension (Adult); member, NGCSA
Level: Preschool through adult
Specialties: Suzuki violin, cello, recorder; most orchestral instruments, workshops, recitals, ensembles, voice. Eight-week summer session offered.
Private Instruction: Theory, arrangement, composition, jazz improvisation
Scholarships: Scholarships available based on audition and need.

NEW ENGLAND CONSERVATORY EXTENSION DIVISION
290 Huntington Ave.
Boston, MA 02115
(617) 262-1133
Staff: Mark Churchill, Director, Extension Division
Affiliation: Noncredit extension of the New England Conservatory, with prep school and adult education department; member, NGCSA
Level: Preschool through adult
Specialties: All instruments, voice, classical and jazz styles; music theory, chamber music programs for prep and adult levels, three prep level orchestras and two wind ensembles for adults; opera workshop; master classes; recitals by students and faculty. Summer sessions offered.
Private Instruction: All instruments, voice (Alexander Technique) in jazz and classical styles
Scholarships: Limited assistance for prep level students only, based on demonstrated musical ability and financial need.

PITTSFIELD COMMUNITY MUSIC SCHOOL[1]
30 Wendell Ave.
Pittsfield, MA 01201
(413) 442-1411
Staff: Marion Maby Wells, Director
Affiliation: Private community school; member, NGCSA
Level: Keyboard, all orchestral instruments, voice, folk and classical guitar.
Private Instruction: See above

THE SOUTH SHORE CONSERVATORY OF MUSIC[1]
Cedar Hill, off Fort Hill St.
Hingham, MA 02043
(617) 749-7565
Staff: James C. Simpson, Jr., Director
Affiliation: Non-boarding, community school and conservatory; member, NGCSA
Level: Preschool through adult; senior citizens receive a private lesson discount. Summer sessions offered.
Private Instruction: Voice, most musical instruments, including guitar, piano, organ, flute, oboe, clarinet, French horn, trumpet, trombone, tuba, violin, cello, bassoon, recorder, etc.

WALNUT HILL SCHOOL OF PERFORMING ARTS
121 Highland St.
Natick, MA 01760
(617) 653-4312
Staff: H. Beresford Menagh, President
Affiliation: Private boarding school with emphasis on chamber music through Greater Boston Youth Symphony, N.E. Conservatory Youth Chamber Orchestra, Massachusetts Wind Ensemble, Brandeis or Young Artist Program
Specialties: Ballet, modern dance, voice, strings, woodwinds, keyboard, harp, theater, visual arts. Summer session offered.
Private Instruction: Voice, strings, with Boston Symphony Orchestra personnel; woodwinds and keyboard with Walnut Hill faculty or from Boston University, N.E. Conservatory or Brandeis

MICHIGAN

BAY VIEW MUSIC FESTIVAL AND CONSERVATORY OF MUSIC
Box 1596
Bay View, MI 49770 (May 15 to Oct. 14)
Box 322
Alma, MI 48801 (Oct. 15 to May 14)
(616) 347-4210 (Bay View)
(517) 463-1517 (Alma)
Staff: Dr. Ernest G. Sullivan, Director of Music
Affiliation: Eight-week, artists-in-residence program, sponsored by the Bay View Association of the United Methodist Church.
Level: Secondary through adult
Specialties: Voice, piano, organ, harp, violin, viola, violoncello, double bass, flute, oboe, clarinet, bassoon, saxophone, trumpet, French horn, trombone, vocal coaching, accompanying, music theory classes, performances practices for singers, conducting and score reading, opera workshop, piano master class, organ master class, theatre techniques, movement for the singer; concerts, student/faculty chamber orchestra, handbell workshop, and 80 to 90 voice choir. Summer session only.
Private Instruction: All areas
Scholarships: Scholarships available based on talent, demonstrated proficiency and financial need.

COMMUNITY SCHOOL OF THE ARTS, INC.
292 Bellview
Benton Harbor, MI 49022
(616) 925-7746
Staff: Merry Stover, Executive Director
Affiliation: Community school; member, NGCSA
Level: Preschool through adult
Specialties: All instruments, voice, organ, piano, percussion, musicianship, kinder piano, creative dramatics,

Nightingale's Chorus (children ages 7-11). Summer sessions offered.
Private Instruction: Strings, woodwinds, percussion, keyboard
Scholarships: Scholarships available based on need.

DETROIT COMMUNITY MUSIC SCHOOL[1]
200 E. Kirby St.
Detroit, MI 48202
(313) 831-2870
Staff: John A. Smith, Director
Affiliation: Private, non-boarding community school; member, NGCSA and NASM
Specialties: Nonprofit insitution offers group classes for children and adults. Children's classes include Orff-Schulwerk, Contemporary Group Piano, and Suzuki Violin. Dance division offers modern dance and ballet for children and adults. Also has jazz studies, music therapy division, ensembles and string orchestra, certificate program, children's choir, Creative Drama workshop for ages 7-19 and opera workshop. Has summer session.
Private Instruction: Most orchestral instruments, piano, voice, harp, organ

FLINT INSTITUTE OF MUSIC COMMUNITY MUSIC SCHOOL
1025 E. Kearsley
Flint, MI 48503
(313) 238-9651
Staff: Thomas Gerdom, Executive Director; Paul Torre, Director of Education
Affiliation: Community music school
Level: Preschool through adult
Specialties: Voice, woodwind, brass, percussion, strings; chamber music groups, bands and orchestras. Two summer camps offered.
Private Instruction: All instruments
Scholarships: Scholarships based on merit and need.

INTERLOCHEN ARTS ACADEMY
Division Interlochen Center for the Arts
Interlochen, MI 49643
(616) 276-9221
Staff: Bruce W. Galbraith, Director
Affiliation: Private, boarding college prep school.
Level: Grades 9 through 12 offering all academic subjects.
Specialties: Preprofessional training in music, dance, theater arts, visual arts, creative writing, and design/production. Students can concentrate on a specific instrument or area, learn how to play additional instruments, explore their potential as composers, gain a broad background in music literature and theory, and expand their appreciation of music and other arts. Academy has various large and small ensembles, chamber music groups, solo recitals, and on and off-campus recitals. Guest conductors and other artists may present concerts and workshops.
Private Instruction: Piano, organ, voice, violin, viola, cello, double bass, harp, horn, trumpet, trombone, euphonium, tuba, percussion, flute, oboe, saxophone, bassoon

NATIONAL MUSIC CAMP
Division Interlochen Center for the Arts
Interlochen, MI 49643
(616) 276-9221
Staff: Edward J. Downing, Director
Affiliation: Private, eight-week summer fine arts camp, affiliated with the University of Michigan and the Interlochen Arts Academy
Level: Preschool through college
Specialties: Intensive training in music, dance, drama, and the visual arts, under the direction of some 190 artist-teachers. Several performance events occur daily. The camp's eight orchestras, seven bands, four jazz bands, and the departments of dance, drama and visual arts present between 350 and 375 programs each summer. Numerous guest conductors and other artists are also engaged to present concerts and workshops.
Private Instruction: Piano, organ, voice, violin, viola, cello, double bass, harp, horn, trumpet, trombone, euphonium, tuba, percussion, flute, oboe, clarinet, saxophone, bassoon
Scholarships: Numerous scholarships available.

MINNESOTA

MACPHAIL CENTER FOR THE ARTS
1128 LaSalle Ave.
Minneapolis, MN 55403
(612) 373-1925
Staff: Joanna Cortright, Acting Director
Affiliation: Community school of the arts, affiliated with Continuing Education and Extension, University of Minnesota; member, NGCSA
Level: Preschool through adult
Specialties: Keyboard, other instrumental, voice, guitar, dance, speech, photography, early childhood arts exploration, theory, pedagogy, ensembles, workshops, conducting, performance, jazz/folk/pop. Summer sessions offered.
Private Instruction: All instruments, voice, speech
Scholarships: Scholarship program in developmental stages.

MISSOURI

SAINT LOUIS CONSERVATORY AND SCHOOLS FOR THE ARTS
560 Trinity Ave.
St. Louis, MO 63130
(314) 863-3033
Staff: Shirley Bartzen, Dean
Affiliation: Community school associated with private independent conservatory; members, NGCSA and NASM
Level: All ages
Specialties: All instruments, voice. Summer sessions offered.
Private Instruction: All instruments, voice
Scholarships: Scholarships available based on need.

NEW HAMPSHIRE

APPLE HILL CENTER FOR CHAMBER MUSIC
East Sullivan, NH 03445
(603) 847-3371
Affiliation: Private boarding summer camp
Level: All ages
Specialties: Summer music camp specializes in chamber music. Three ten-day sessions are offered, as well as one five-week session for more advanced musicians between 13 and 35 years old.
Private Instruction: String instruments, piano, woodwinds, horn
Scholarships: Information available on request.

NEW JERSEY

MONTCLAIR STATE COLLEGE MUSIC PREPARATORY DIVISION
Montclair State College
Upper Montclair, NJ 07043
(201) 893-4443
Staff: Sheila E. McKenna, Director
Affiliation: A division of the Department of Music of the School of Fine and Performing Arts of MSC; member, NGCSA
Level: Preschool through secondary
Specialties: Suzuki violin, Dalcroze eurythmics, kinder keyboard, theory, string ensembles, percussion ensembles, prep youth chorus, orchestral instruments, electronic music, musical theatre styles, sight singing, composition, guitar, The Robert Pace Piano Program. Summer sessions offered.
Private Instruction: All instruments, voice, theory, composition and other areas
Scholarships: Scholarships available based on financial need, demonstrated talent in instrument or voice.

NEIGHBORHOOD HOUSE MUSIC SCHOOL
12 Flagler St.
Morristown, NJ 07960
(201) 538-1229
Staff: Madelyn H. Aubin, Director
Affiliation: Community school
Level: Children and adults

Specialties: Piano, voice, guitar, plus classes in musicianship and music appreciation, employing the Orff philosophy to teach very young children.
Private Instruction: Guitar, piano, voice, violin

NEWARK COMMUNITY SCHOOL OF THE ARTS
89 Lincoln Park
Newark, NJ 07102
(201) 642-0133
Staff: Stephen L. Shiman, Executive Director
Affiliation: Community arts school; member, NGCSA
Level: Preschool through adult
Specialties: All musical instruments, voice, six forms of dance, music theory, drama, visual arts, 75 concerts a year, intensive gifted student program, training for handicapped. Summer sessions offered.
Private Instruction: All instruments, voice
Scholarships: Scholarships based on need using New Jersey guidelines for income; based on merit for Gifted Student Program.

NEW SCHOOL FOR MUSIC STUDY
Box 407
Princeton, NJ 08540
(609) 921-2900
Staff: Louise L. Goss, Executive Vice President
Affiliation: Center for piano pedagogy and music research, affiliated with Westminster Choir College
Level: Graduate music students; a preparatory department for children for private and group piano study
Specialties: Piano and piano pedagogy, program leading to a certificate of professional achievement or a Master's Degree in Piano Pedagogy and performance. Summer seminars offered.
Private Instruction: Piano
Scholarships: Interships available to qualified candidates with undergraduate degrees.

VILLAGE SCHOOL OF PERFORMING ARTS
1130 Mountain Ave.
PO Box 4214
Berkeley Heights, NJ 07922
(201) 647-6685
Staff: Sharon L. Vasile, Artistic Director
Affiliation: Community performing arts school
Level: Preschool through adult
Specialties: Class instruction provided in voice, piano, guitar, banjo, cello, violin, Suzuki violin, dramatics, flute and recorder. Performance and theory classes also held. Summer sessions offered.
Private Instruction: Instruments, voice

WATERLOO MUSIC SCHOOL
Waterloo Village
Stanhope, NJ 07874
(201) 347-0900
Staff: Mrs. Shirley Greitzer, Music School Director
Affiliation: Run by the Waterloo Foundation for the Arts, a public nonprofit foundation
Level: Advanced and post-college
Specialties: Instrument and concert performance. Summer sesions only.
Private Instruction: Yes
Scholarships: All students accepted are given full fellowships.

NEW MEXICO

TAOS SCHOOL OF MUSIC
PO Box 1879
Taos, NM 87571
(505) 776-2388
Staff: Chilton Anderson, Director
Affiliation: Private, boarding school devoted solely to the study and performance of chamber music
Specialties: Chamber music study and performance for eight weeks, eight student concerts. Also sponsor the Toas School of Music Chamber Music Festival series. Summer sessions only.
Private Instruction: Offered as part of coaching
Fees: $300 all-inclusive.

NEW YORK

ASPEN MUSIC SCHOOL
1860 Broadway, Ste. 401
New York, NY 10023
(212) 581-2196
Staff: Gordon Hardy, President and Dean
Affiliation: Private, boarding conservatory
Specialties: All orchestral instruments are taught, plus voice, piano. Opera Theatre, Choral Institute, Audio Recording Institute, Center for Advanced Quartet Studies, Conference on Contemporary Music.
Specialties: All strings, winds, voice, piano, choral, quartet
Scholarships: Available by audition and upon faculty recommendation.

BRONX HOUSE MUSIC SCHOOL
990 Pelham Parkway South
Bronx, NY 10461
(212) 792-9720
Staff: Amory Williams, Director
Affiliation: Community music school, division of Bronx House, Inc., a social services agency; member, NGCSA
Level: Preschool through adult
Specialties: Music classes for preschool children. Suzuki piano, violin, and cello. Classical ballet classes. Concerts by faculty, students, and guest artists. Summer sessions offered; lessons on an informal basis.
Private Instruction: Most instruments, voice
Scholarships: Scholarships limited to proven financial need.

BROOKLYN CONSERVATORY OF MUSIC
(In Brooklyn)
58 Seventh Ave.
Brooklyn, NY 11217
(212) 622-3300
(In Queens)
140-26 Franklin Ave.
Flushing, NY 11355
(212) 461-8910
Staff: Jess Smith, President-Director
Affiliation: Private, nonboarding conservatories
Specialties: All instruments, voice, composition, theory classes.
Private Instruction: All instruments, voice

THE BROOKLYN MUSIC SCHOOL AND PLAYHOUSE
126 St. Felix St.
Brooklyn, NY 11217
(212) 638-5660
Staff: Donna R. Merris, Executive Director
Affiliation: Community music school serving all five boroughs in New York City; member, NGCSA
Level: Preschool through adult
Specialties: All orchestral and band instruments, voice, classes in music theory and composition, introduction to music, classical ballet, modern dance, and drama. Professional chamber music concert series.
Private Instruction: Piano, stringed instruments, guitar, wind instruments, voice
Scholarships: Competitive scholarships available, criteria includes potential for professional performance.

CENTER MUSIC SCHOOL OF YONKERS
122 South Broadway
Yonkers, NY 10701
(914) 963-8457
Staff: Mrs. Aviva Domb, Director
Affiliation: Community school
Level: High school through adult
Specialties: Instruments and voice
Private Instruction: Instruments, voice

CHAUTAUQUA INSTITUTION SUMMER SCHOOL OF MUSIC
Box 1098
Chautauqua, NY 14722
(716) 357-4411
Staff: Dr. Nathan Gottschalk, Director
Affiliation: Nonprofit summer center for arts, education, religion, and recreation
Level: Secondary through adult
Specialties: Chautauqua Festival Orchestra (college age students);

Chautauqua Youth Orchestra (high school age); voice, piano, and organ, master and interpretation classes, chamber music workshops, opera musical theatre, English handbell directors' workshop, Vivaldi Chamber Orchestra, Suzuki piano pedagogy. Summer sessions only.
Private Instruction: Instrumental instruction in both orchestras, voice, piano, organ
Scholarships: Orchestral, piano, voice, and organ awards based on proficiency during national auditions; financial need considered.

COMMUNITY MUSIC SCHOOL OF SPRING VALLEY
185 N. Main St.
Spring Valley, NY 10977
(914) 356-1522 or 354-1593
Staff: Janet Simons, Program Director
Affiliation: Community school; member, NGCSA; also affiliated with Rockland County Music Teachers Arts Council
Level: Preschool through adult
Specialties: All orchestral instruments, voice, piano, guitar, recorder, theory, music and movement ensemble, chamber music, and early music ensemble.
Private Instruction: All orchestral instruments, piano, recorder, guitar, voice
Scholarships: Scholarships available based on interest, need and merit.

DALCROZE SCHOOL OF MUSIC
161 East 73rd St.
New York, NY 10021
(212) 879-0316
Staff: Hilda M. Schuster, Director
Affiliation: Private nonboarding school and conservatory
Level: Preschool to 16 in preparatory department; 18 to 60+ in teachers training department and extension divison.
Specialties: Eurhythmics, Solfege and Improvisation, and Methods for music and dance specialists, teachers, conductors, composers, and performers. Classes are offered in ear-training, sight-singing, piano improvisation, body technique, rhythmic movement, harmony, counterpoint, composition, orchestration, history of music, choral and instrumental conducting, strings, woodwinds, French horn, piano and choral ensemble, singing principles and musicianship. Summer sessions offered.
Private Instruction: Piano, voice, woodwinds, strings, French horn, harmony counterpoint, composition, orchestration, musicianship
Scholarships: A limited number of scholarships for class instruction and private lessons, based on talent and need, are available.

DAVID HOCHSTEIN MEMORIAL MUSIC SCHOOL
50 N. Plymouth Ave.
Rochester, NY 14614
(716) 454-4596
Staff: Helen Jackson, Executive Director
Affiliation: Community school of music and dance; member, NGCSA and NASM
Level: Preschool through adult
Specialties: All orchestral instruments, piano, guitar, voice, jazz workshop, Orff schulwerk, woodwind ensembles, theory, certificate program, music therapy, ballet, jazz dance, choirs (children). Summer sessions offered.
Private Instruction: Orchestral instruments, electric guitar, acoustic guitar, piano, voice
Scholarships: Scholarships available for tuition and partial tuition based on merit or need.

GREENWICH HOUSE MUSIC SCHOOL
46 Barrow St.
New York, NY 10014
(212) 242-4770
Staff: Edward Houser, Director
Affiliation: Community school; member, NGCSA
Level: Preschool through adult
Specialties: All instruments and voice; child and adult classes in theory; ear-training, and harmony, master classes; Greenwich House Opera Project; piano competition. Summer sessions offered.
Private Instruction: Lessons in all instruments and voice for children and adults, beginners and advanced
Scholarships: Scholarships available through application and interview.

HARLEM SCHOOL OF THE ARTS
645 Saint Nicholas Ave.
New York, NY 10030
(212) 926-4100
Staff: Betty Allen, Executive Director
Affiliation: Private community school of the arts; member, NGCSA
Level: Preschool through adult; special classes for senior citizens
Specialties: Instruction in art, dance (ballet, creative, modern, ethnic, and tap), chamber music, chorus, drama, ensembles (guitar, percussion, strings, Suzuki violin and woodwinds), eurythmics, master voice, piano class, piano master class, theory and composition. Summer session offered.
Private Instruction: Brass (trombone and trumpet), percussion instruments, piano, strings (cello, guitar, viola and violin), vocal repertoire, voice, woodwinds (clarinet, flute, oboe and saxophone)
Scholarships: Scholarships based on economic need are available

MID-WESTCHESTER YM-YWHA MUSIC SCHOOL
999 Wilmont Rd.
Scarsdale, NY 10583
(914) 472-3300
Staff: Mrs. Aviva Domb, Director
Affiliation: Community school; member, NGCSA
Level: Grade school through adult
Specialties: Piano ensembles, recorder ensembles, string and wind ensembles, "Y" String Ensemble, jazz workshop, preinstrument workshop, theory.
Private Instruction: Piano, violin, viola, cello, double bass, flute, recorder, clarinet, oboe, saxophone, trumpet, trombone, French horn, percussion, guitar, voice

MUSIC INSTITUTE OF THE JEWISH COMMUNITY CENTER
485 Victory Blvd.
Staten Island, NY 10301
(212) 981-1500
Staff: Saul J. Rosenfeld, Director of Music
Affiliation: Private, nonprofit music school affiliated with the Jewish Community Center; member, NGCSA
Level: Preschool through adult
Specialties: All instruments, voice, Suzuki violin, theory, improvisation; wind, flute, and string ensembles for elementary and advanced, concerts (faculty and children). Summer sessions offered.
Private Instruction: All instruments, voice
Scholarships: Scholarships available primarily for strings, woodwinds and brass; voice and piano scholarships are sometimes available based on need and talent.

RIVERDALE SCHOOL OF MUSIC[1]
253rd St. and Post Rd.
Bronx, NY 10471
(212) 549-8034
Staff: Robert Rudie, Director
Affiliation: Private conservatory
Level: Adults and children
Specialties: All instruments, voice, theory, chamber music, and classes for little children. Summer sessions offered.
Private Instruction: All instruments, voice

THE ROOSA SCHOOL OF MUSIC
26 Willow Pl.
Brooklyn, NY 11201
(212) 875-7371
Staff: Jeanne Lowe, Executive Director
Affiliation: Community school; member, NGCSA
Level: Preschool through adult
Specialties: All orchestral instruments, guitar, recorder, piano, harpsichord, voice; chamber ensembles; theory and musicianship classes; music therapy; workshops, recitals, faculty concerts. Six-week on site summer program.

Community programs at various sites throughout Brooklyn.
Private Instruction: All orchestral instruments, piano, harpsichord, recorder, guitar, voice, strings, woodwinds, brass, percussion
Scholarships: Partial only, based primarily on financial need; minority scholarships; some special memorials for specified instruments, backgrounds.

SONGWRITER SEMINARS AND WORKSHOPS
928 Broadway, Ste. 614
New York, NY 10010
(212) 505-7332
Staff: Libby Bush, Co-Director; Ted Lehrman, Co-Director
Affiliation: Consultant organization servicing songwriters
Specialties: Popular songwriting, lyrics, music, and business aspects fo the pop-music industry. Group workshops and private consultations. At-Home-Workshop program available to songwriters outside the New York metropolitan area. Summer sessions offered.

THE STECHER AND HOROWITZ SCHOOL OF THE ARTS, INC.
74 Maple Ave.
Cedarhurst, NY 11516
(516) 569-2313
Staff: Melvin Stecher, Co-Director; Norman Horowitz, Co-Director
Affiliation: Community school
Level: Preschool through adult
Specialties: Offers instruction in piano, strings, woodwinds, brass, voice, guitar. 70-piece Youth Orchestra; chamber, vocal and guitar ensembles; concert series. Summer sessions offered.
Private Instruction: Piano, strings, woodwinds, brass, voice, guitar
Scholarships: Scholarships available based on talent and need.

THIRD STREET MUSIC SCHOOL SETTLEMENT
235 E. 11th St.
New York, NY 10003
(212) 777-3240
Staff: MaryLou Francis, Associate Director
Affiliation: Community school; member, NGCSA
Level: Preschool through adult
Specialties: All orchestral instruments, piano, voice, guitar, dance, art and musical theatre; preschool arts nursery, Suzuki piano and violin. Professional concert series. Summer sessions offered.
Private Instruction: All orchestral instruments, piano (traditional, popular, and Suzuki), voice (traditional and popular), guitar (classical, folk, Latin, jazz, electric), recorder, theory, composition
Scholarships: By audition.

WESTCHESTER CONSERVATORY OF MUSIC
20 Soundview Ave.
White Plains, NY 10606
(914) 761-3715
Staff: Michael Pollon, Executive Director
Affiliation: Nonboarding, private community school and conservatory; member, NGCSA and NASM
Level: Preschool through adult
Specialties: A nonprofit education institution offering instruction on all instruments, voice, theory, compostiion; classical and jazz programs offered, along with ensembles, opera workshops and orchestra. Summer sessions offered.
Private Instruction: Voice, all instruments, theory
Scholarships: Scholarships available based on talent and need.

"Y" SCHOOL OF MUSIC
92nd St., YM-YWHA
1395 Lexington Ave.
New York, NY 10028
(212) 427-6000, x129
Staff: Mrs. Hadassah B. Markson, Director
Affiliation: Music Department of the Jewish Community Center; member, NGCSA
Level: Preschool through adult
Specialties: The school offers a spectrum of private and class lessons, lectures on musicology, workshops in musical theater, opera singers' master class, language and diction for singers, Dalcroze method taught for children and adults, jazz improvisation and workshops. For adults, Y Chorale and Y Symphonic Workshop; for boys, Y Boys Chorus.
Private Instruction: All instruments except the accordion
Scholarships: Scholarships awarded for individual instruction, classes and workshops; available for all ages based on need and talent.

NORTH CAROLINA

COMMUNITY SCHOOL OF THE ARTS
200 West Trade St.
Charlotte, NC 28202
(704) 377-4187
Staff: Dr. Ann Britt, Executive Director
Affiliation: Community school; member, NGCSA and The Arts and Science Council of Charlotte/Mecklenburg, Inc.
Level: Preschool through adult
Specialties: Arts instruction in the visual arts, all band and orchestra instruments, recorder, guitar, voice, music and arts appreciation. Summer sessions offered at community-wide sites (no individual lessons).
Private Instruction: All band and orchestral instruments, recorder, guitar, voice
Scholarships: Student tuition is based on a sliding fee scale, dependent solely upon family income and number of household members in the family.

OHIO

CLEVELAND MUSIC SCHOOL SETTLEMENT
11125 Magnolia Dr.
Cleveland, OH 44106
(216) 421-5806
Staff: Howard Whittaker, Executive Director
Affiliation: Private, non-boarding community school
Level: Preschool through adult
Specialties: Music lessons in all orchestral insturments, jazz studies, recorder, organ, theory, composition, music appreciation, theory, Dalcroze, Orff, kinderdance, modern dance, ballet, voice, vocal theory, guitar and group keyboard. Group also has music therapy department, arts-oriented preschool. Lessons are offered at two branches and two affiliates and in some 30 neighborhood agencies under auspices of the extension department.
Private Instruction: Theory, composition, percussion, piano, jazz instruments, woodwinds, brass, string instruments, organ, recorder, voice, guitar

THE EARLY MUSIC CENTER
242 Northwood Dr.
Yellow Springs, OH 45387
(513) 767-8181
Staff: Patricia Olds, Dirctor
Affiliation: Nonprofit, tax-exempt center
Level: All ages; primarily adult
Specialties: Study and performance of Medieval, Renaissance, and Baroque music. Staff at Center performs as the Early Music Group. Ensemble training and ensemble classes; basic ear training and vocal ensemble. Frequent workshops. Summer sessions offered.
Private Instruction: Recorder, viola da gamba, harpsichord
Scholarships: Full and half tuition scholarships available.

THE SCHOOL OF FINE ARTS
38660 Mentor Ave.
Willoughby, OH 44094
(216) 951-7500
Staff: James J. Savage, Executive Director
Affiliation: Operated by The Fine Arts Association as a cultural center to encourage and educate for all the arts
Specialties: Applied music, art, dance, and drama, offering instruction and performance in all arts. Summer session offered.
Private Instruction: All musical instruments and art forms

OREGON

PORTLAND COMMUNITY MUSIC CENTER
3350 S.E. Francis St.
Portland, OR 97202
(503) 231-5697
Staff: Charles Farmer, Director
Affiliation: Community school for City of Portland Bureau of Parks and Recreation
Level: Preschool through adult
Specialties: Programs and classes in musicianship, harmony and music analysis. Group piano for all ages. For adults and teens: chorus, recorder and guitar classes, music appreciation, jazz history, world music, folk singing and music theory. For children: Suzuki violin classes and string ensembles.
Private Instruction: Violin, viola, cello, bass

PENNSYLVANIA

ACADEMY OF VOCAL ARTS[1]
1920 Spruce St.
Philadelphia, PA 19103
(215) 735-1685
Staff: Dino Yannopoulos, Director
Affiliation: Private conservatory, nonprofit, for training exceptionally talented singers for the professional opera stage
Specialties: Instruction is given in voice, operatic staging, theater history, stage make-up, repertoire, solfege, piano, languages and related subjects. Admission for a limited number of students is full-scholarship. Competitive auditions are held annually for entrance.

ANNA L. PERLOW MUSIC SCHOOL OF THE JEWISH COMMUNITY CENTER
5738 Forbes Ave.
Pittsburgh, PA 15217
(412) 521-8010
Staff: Allen Sher, Director
Affiliation: Community school; member, NGCSA
Level: Preschool through adult
Specialties: All instruments and voice. Suzuki program in violin and piano. Monthly student recitals. Summer sessions offered.
Private Instruction: All instruments, voice
Scholarships: Scholarships available based on need.

JENKINTOWN MUSIC SCHOOL[1]
515 Meetinhouse Rd.
Jenkintown, PA 19046
(215) 885-6166
Staff: Monroe Levin, Co-Director; Cameron McGraw, Co-Director
Affiliation: Non-boarding community school; member, NGCSA
Specialties: All instrumens, dance, ensemble; adult classes offered.
Private Instruction: All instruments except harp

JON MILLER SCHOOL FOR RECORDING ARTS AND SCIENCES
7249 Airport Rd.
Bath, PA 18014
(215) 837-7550
Staff: Jon K. Miller, Director
Affiliation: Private trade school
Level: Adult
Specialties: Audio engineering; operation of reel to reel tape machines, consoles, microphones; video engineering: operation of videotape machines, cameras, and editing equipment; sound reinforcement: set up and operation of sound systems. Summer sessions offered.

NEUPAUER CONSERVATORY OF MUSIC
105 S. 18th St.
Philadelphia, PA 19103
(215) 567-6720
Staff: William Schimmel, Dean
Affiliation: Private Conservatory
Level: College level with high school preparatory program
Specialties: Program specializes in preparing students for the music industry by way of related courses, e.g., commercial musicology. Summer sessions offered.
Private Instruction: All instruments, voice, composition, arranging, ballet, modern dance
Scholarships: Semester scholarships available based on outstanding achievement.

SETTLEMENT MUSIC SCHOOL
PO Box 25120
Philadelphia, PA 19147
(215) 336-0400
Staff: Robert Capanna, Executive Director
Affiliation: Community school; member, NGCSA
Level: Preschool through adult
Specialties: Instruments, voice, workshops, concerts, recitals; specialized instruction for the handicapped. Summer sessions offered.
Private Instruction: All orchestral, keyboard and fingerboard instruments, voice
Scholarships: Financial assistance available based on need; scholarships available based on need and ability.

SUBURBAN MUSIC SCHOOL
The Media Elementary School
Media, PA 19063
(215) 566-4215 or 874-4895
Staff: Beatrice Wernick, Director
Affiliation: Nonprofit community music school; member, NGCSA
Level: Preschool through adult
Specialties: All orchestral instruments, voice, guitar; classes in recorder, Kodaly concepts, choral ensemble. Periodic concerts are given by students and faculty.
Private Instruction: All orchestral instruments, piano, voice, guitar, recorder

TENNESSEE

CADEK CONSERVATORY OF MUSIC[1]
615 McCallie Ave.
Chattanooga, TN 37402
(615) 755-4624
Staff: Marc Peretz, Director
Affiliation: Conservatory of music in the University of Tennessee at Chattanooga; member, NASM
Specialties: Pre-college instruction in applied music.
Private Instruction: Piano, guitar, flute, clarinet, percussion, trombone, trumpet, violin, viola, voice, French horn, string bass, banjo, oboe, harp, cello, bassoon, organ

TEXAS

AMERICAN INSTITUTE OF MUSICAL STUDIES
2701 Fondren Dr.
Dallas, TX 75206
(214) 691-6451
Staff: Nora S. Owens, President
Affiliation: Summer Vocal Institute
Level: Professional adult
Specialties: Two-month summer program in voice, piano, opera and lieder coaching, diction, German language program for musicians, full symphony orchestra. The Institute is held in Graz, Austria.
Private Instruction: Voice, opera coaching, lieder coaching, diction, dramatic aria preparation, audition training
Scholarships: Limited number of work grants available

VERMONT

BRATTLEBORO MUSIC SCHOOL
15 Walnut St.
Brattleboro, VT 05301
(802) 257-4523
Staff: Catherine Stockman, Administrative Director
Affiliation: Community school, part of Brattleboro Music Center; member, NGCSA
Level: Preschool through adult
Specialties: Preschool Suzuki and Dalcroze; instrumental and voice instruction, with emphasis on classical music; Bach performance workshop; faculty and student concerts; orchestra and chorus. Summer day-camps for children, Bach workshop for adults.

Private Instruction: All instruments, voice
Scholarships: Scholarships available based on need.

VERMONT CONSERVATORY OF THE ARTS
24 Elm St.
Montpelier, VT 05602
(802) 229-0769
Staff: Philip L. Stimmel, Executive Director
Affiliation: Community school of the arts; member, NGCSA
Level: All ages
Specialties: All instruments, voice, theory; modern dance, ballet. Summer sessions offered.
Private Instruction: All instruments, voice
Scholarships: Scholarships available based on need.

WISCONSIN

SYMPHONY SCHOOL OF AMERICA
PO Box 2554
LaCrosse, WI 54601
(608) 785-1555
Staff: Barbara Laga, Executive Secretary
Affiliation: Summer music camp
Level: Secondary through young adult
Specialties: Apprenticeship training with professionals; repertoire/ear training/rhythm classes; forums and master classes; conducting apprenticeship, ensemble, solo and ensemble recitals, concerts. Five-week summer camp.
Private Instruction: Weekly private lessons, all instruments
Scholarships: Full and partial scholarships available.

VIRGIN ISLANDS

TONESKOLEN SCHOOL OF MUSIC
PO Box 908
St. Thomas, USVI 00801
(809) 774-6153
Staff: Agatha Canfield, Director
Affiliation: Nonprofit cultural organization; member, NGCSA
Level: Preschool through adult
Specialties: Piano, guitar, woodwinds, brasses, percussion handbells, voice, jazz, organ; sight reading/ear training, dictation, theory, keyboard harmony; music history; appreciation; ensembles in instrumental, piano, handbells, and jazz. Programs include the Miniskole (ages 4-7); Preparatory (junior, intermediate, and high school); Music major (high school and adult). Summer session offered.

CANADA

ALBERTA

THE BANFF CENTRE, SCHOOL OF FINE ARTS
Box 1020
Banff, AB T0L 0C0
Staff: Jorie Adams, Manager, Music Programs; Thomas Rolston, Artistic Director of Music
Affiliation: Independent, nondegree granting music center
Level: Collegiate through adult
Specialties: Offers short, intensive master classes and training programs May to August and a post-university, pre-professional winter program September to April, including orchestral and academic sabbatical. Instruction areas for brass, woodwinds, piano, orchestral, chamber music, guitar, jazz, strings, piano. Concert opportunities, master classes, coaching sessions, extensive rehearsal and performance facilities. Professional development resources available. Summer sessions offered.
Private Instruction: In conjunction with both summer and winter programs. Lessons include technique, musicianship, concert preparation.
Scholarships: Limited scholarships available.

BRITISH COLUMBIA

ADVANCED TRAINING OPERA CENTRE
3737 Oak St.
Vancouver, BC V6H 2M4
(604) 736-1916
Staff: Mr. Leopold Simoneau, Director; Madame Pierrette Alarie, Artistic Director
Affiliation: Opera program affiliated with Canada Opera Piccola.
Level: Limited to 12 preadjudicated profession singers, between ages 22 and 34, who have completed formal studies with some initial experience.
Specialties: A three-month program of intensive studies involving all facets of opera. The voice program concentrates on the study of operatic repertoire, master classes in voice, practice with a coach supplied, study in acting, movement, fencing and make-up; participation in actual operatic production presented in public. Summer sessions offered. No fee requested. Reserved primarily for Canadian citizens or landed immigrants.
Private Instruction: As part of master classes
Scholarships: No fee; students will receive $200 per week.

JOHANNESEN INTERNATIONAL SCHOOL OF THE ARTS
3737 Oak St.
Vancouver, BC V6H 2M4
(604) 736-1611
Staff: J.J. Johannesen, Founder/Director
Affiliation: Summer program in close cooperation with the University of Victoria.
Level: Secondary through adult
Specialties: Stringed instruments excluding guitar, flute, oboe, clarinet, bassoon and piano; daily master classes, chamber music sessions; free admission to 26 concerts featuring teacher soloists and symphony orchestra. Six-week summer program only.
Private Instruction: Limited private instruction as can be arranged with teachers. No additional fee required.
Scholarships: Limited scholarships available based on merit and need.

VICTORIA CONSERVATORY OF MUSIC
839 Academy Close
Victoria, BC V8V 2X8
(604) 383-5311
Staff: Martin James, Director of Studies
Affiliation: Conservatory of Music
Level: Preschool through adult
Specialties: Offers comprehensive music training to the professional level and fits graduates for careers in music as performers and teachers. Instruction for preschoolers to adult in piano, strings, voice, opera, theory, ballet, wind, and brass. Summer sessions offered.
Private Instruction: Piano, strings, voice, opera, theory, ballet, wind, brass
Scholarships: Scholarships available by assessment or examination and recommendation of the teacher and department head.

NOVA SCOTIA

MARITIME CONSERVATORY OF MUSIC
5920 Gorsebrook Ave.
Halifax, NS B3H 192
(902) 423-6995
Staff: Klaro M. Mizerit, Director
Affiliation: Private conservatory, nonprofit organization
Level: All levels
Specialties: All instruments, voice, theory, ballet, social dance. No summer sessions offered.
Private Instruction: All areas
Scholarships: Scholarships available; a year's tuition, competitive awards, prizes, and bursaries.

ONTARIO

MUSIC SCHOOL OF THE ST. CHRISTOPHER HOUSE
84 Augusta Ave.
Toronto, ON M5T 2L1
(416) 364-8456
Staff: Mary Paton Leggatt, Music School Director
Affiliation: Department of the St. Christopher House, a neighborhood centre (settlement); member, NGCSA
Level: Preschool through adults; beginners through A.R.C.T. level
Specialties: Piano, violin, viola, cello, singing, guitar, accordion, and related theories. Summer sessions for individual lessons only.
Private Instruction: Piano, singing, violin, viola, cello, guitar, accordion

NATIONAL YOUTH ORCHESTRA ASSOCIATION
76 Charles St., W
Toronto, ON M5S 1K6
(416) 922-5031
Staff: Mr. John Pellerin, Executive Director
Affiliation: Summer musical training program
Level: All ages 14 to 26
Specialties: All students are under the direction of a professional international faculty during the training session (July-August).
Private Instruction: Individual faculty members instruct individual students in private and group sessions.
Scholarships: Any student accepted into the orchestra after successfully completing an audition is subsidized. A fee of $50 is required.

NEPEAN SCHOOL OF MUSIC
25 Esquimault Ave.
Nepean, ON K2H 6Z5
(613) 820-7482
Staff: Peter Morris, Program Director
Affiliation: Community school; member, NGCSA
Level: Preschool through adult
Specialties: Orchestral instruments, piano, recorder, guitar, theory. Summer sessions offered.
Private Instruction: All instruments

TREBAS INSTITUTE OF RECORDING ARTS
225 Mutual St.
Toronto, ON M5B 2B4
(416) 977-9797

290 Nepean St.
Ottawa, ON K1R 5G3
(613) 232-7104

1435 Bleury, Ste. 301
Montreal, PQ H3A 2H7
(514) 845-4141
Staff: David P. Leonard, Executive Director
Affiliation: Private independent nonprofit institution
Level: College through adult
Specialties: Two-year full-time professional training program in the recording arts and sciences offering eighty courses. Three programs of study: record producing, sound engineering, management for the music business. Facilities include 24-track professional recording studio, electronics lab, electronic music lab. Summer sessions offered.
Scholarships: Two scholarships available, plus awards of merit. Contact Scholarship Office for details.

UNIVERSITY SETTLEMENT MUSIC SCHOOL
23 Grange Rd.
Toronto, ON M5T 1C3
(416) 598-3444
Staff: George W. White, Director
Affiliation: Community school; member, NGCSA
Level: Preschool through adult
Specialties: Piano, violin, viola, cello, guitar, recorder, voice, theory, preinstrumental music, ear training, orchestra, flute, music therapy; monthly student recitals and faculty recital series. Summer sessions offered.
Private Instruction: Private lessons available
Scholarships: Scholarships available based on need.

QUEBEC

ECOLE VINCENT-D'INDY
628, chemin de la Cote Ste-Catherine
Outrement, PQ H2V 2C5
(514) 735-5261
Staff: Madeleine Tanguay, Directress of Musical Studies
Affiliation: Private school; member of ACQ (Association du Colleges du Quebec)
Level: Primary through college
Specialties: All instruments, music theory, classical music only. At college level: academic subjects, such as French, humanities, psychology, religious studies, and musical literature. Contests and concerts.
Private Instruction: Voice and all instruments; pedagogical individual aid if needed, individual contracts

TREBAS INSTITUTE OF RECORDING ARTS
(*See* listing under Ontario)

Music Schools Index

M

N

O

P

R

S

T

U

V

W

Y

Careers in Music

This information was originally published by the Music Educators National Conference, the Music Teachers National Association, Inc., and the National Association of Schools of Music. These three associations represent approximately 80,000 teachers and prospective teachers of music and 520 accredited collegiate schools of music. Careers in music education and performance are treated briefly on this page, with therapy, library, and industrial music careers summarized on page 272. A chart of ten career areas and over fifty specialties, containing salary information, personal qualifications, and education requirements, begins on the next page.

Studio Teaching

Individual instruction is the chief means through which a person becomes accomplished in the art of music-making. Private teachers, instructing one student at a time, comprise the largest group of music teachers in America. They sometimes teach small groups, particularly in piano.

The studio of a private teacher may be located in a home, school, office building, or music store. Those who teach in the home are self-employed, whereas others have a business relationship with the school or store. Many self-employed music teachers teach only part-time due to other responsibilities.

Individual instruction is most often given in piano or guitar. Teachers of voice and other instruments are in demand in varying degrees. Satisfactory teaching arrangements sometimes can be made with the various types of schools that are in need of individual music instructors.

Music Teaching in Elementary and Secondary Schools

Clearly, the largest number of full-time music teaching positions exist in public and private schools. In nursery, kindergarten, and elementary schools, the music teacher provides guidance for activities such as singing, listening, playing instruments, moving and dancing, composing, and experimenting with music patterns.

Teachers, supervisors, or directors of music in middle, junior high, and senior high schools provide direction for choral and instrumental organizations, small ensembles, and music theater productions. Music instruction in the secondary school also includes courses in general music, theory, music history, literature, and the related arts.

Music educators in the public schools may find opportunities for extra remuneration for service as conductors of church choirs, community music organizations, or recreational programs. In many communities, the music department of the public schools is the focal point of the musical life of the community.

Music Teaching in Colleges and Other Schools

Music teachers in institutions of higher education usually are expected to specialize in one or two areas such as music theory, music history and literature, music education, musicology, performance, electronic music, instrument repair, composition, conducting, or music therapy. The salaries for college or university music teaching vary considerably with the type of institution and its location.

In many cases, college faculties are recruited from people who have had successful professional careers as performers or success as teachers of music. However, a college music educator usually must have earned at least a master's degree in music. The music programs in institutions of higher education constitute one of the main sources of music standards and performances.

Performance

To many young people music performance as a career means giving concerts. The glamour of becoming a concert artist attracts many people, but it should be realized from the outset that opportunities for a career in music performance are very limited and that great perseverance and stamina are required for success. The vast majority of performers combine their activities with other careers in music. Concert performers pay their own travel and promotional expenses and management fees.

Composer and Conductor

Very few composers make a living from composing, but the nonmonetary rewards for writing classical or popular music are great. Some composers earn a living arranging music for school performance groups or writing music for radio or television advertising. Conductors, like composers, usually rely on supplemental income from teaching or guest appearances.

Careers in Music	Opportunity for Employment	Approximate Earnings
Teacher/Supervisor	1. Public school 2. Parochial school 3. College, university, conservatory 4. Private school, studio 5. Supervisor, consultant 6. Administrator, university	1. $8,250-$24,000 2. $8,000-$20,500 3. $10,000-$36,000 4. $5-$60 per lesson 5. $12,500-$36,000 6. $20,000-$48,000 *Some positions are less than 12 months.
Music Therapist	1. Hospitals: civilian, veteran 2. Clinics for handicapped children 3. Corrective institutions 4. Special education facilities 5. Nursing homes 6. Private practice	$14,000-$30,000
Instrumentalist	1. Armed forces: bands, orchestras 2. Symphony orchestra 3. Concert band (very limited) 4. Dance band, nightclub 5. Radio (very limited) 6. National TV (very limited) 7. Small ensemble 8. Concert soloist (very limited) 9. Rock or jazz group 10. Clinician	1. Base pay 2. $200-$650 per week (22-52 weeks) 3. $400-$500 per week 4. $250-$450 per week 5. $280+ per week 6. $1,000-$1,500 per week 7. $20-$750 per concert 8. $500-open per concert 9. Great variance in income 10. $0-$600 per day
Vocalist	1. Church choir soloist 2. Community choral group 3. Radio, TV shows 4. Dance band, nightclub 5. Concert choral group 6. Opera chorus (professional) 7. Opera soloist (very limited) 8. Concert soloist (very limited)	1. $30-$500 per performance 2. $100-$1,500 yearly 3. Local: $50 and up per show Network: $85 and up per show 4. $165 and up per week 5. $45 and up per performance 6. $220-$420 per week 7. $220-$4,800 per performance 8. $220-open
Religious Musician	1. Religious choir soloist 2. Minister of music 3. Choir director	$2,500-$22,500 part-time (less than 35 hours per week) $12,000-$35,000 full-time
Composer **Arranger** **Orchestrator** **Copyist**	1. Educational music, art music 2. Commercial: popular, films, TV	Commissions vary. Performance rights fees—10% composer, 5% arranger. Royalties: 2¢ per sale on music recordings.
Conductor	1. Choir 2. Dance bands 3. Concert band (very limited) 4. Symphony (very limited) 5. Opera (very limited) 6. Choral group (very limited)	1. See: Religious Musician (above) 2. $220-$900 per week 3. $500-$780 per week 4. $1,750-open* 5. $6,500-open* 6. $6,500-open* *Depends on amount of work.
Related Careers		
Tuner/Technician **Instrument Repair**	1. Private business 2. Dealer 3. Factory 4. Contract with college, university, conservatory	1. $10,000-$26,500 (pays own expenses) 2. $10,000-$26,500 3. $8,000-$20,000 4. $8,000-$24,000
Music Industry	1. Publisher or editor: music, books, periodicals 2. Manufacturer: instruments, recordings 3. Manager, booking agent 4. Music theater 5. Music dealer 6. Salesperson 7. Newspaper critic, reporter 8. Radio music producer	According to the wage and salary scale of each industry. Varies widely.
Music Librarian	1. College, university, conservatory 2. Public library 3. Orchestra, band, chorus (very limited) 4. Radio, TV station music coordinator	1. $10,000-$20,000 (may be augmented by teaching) 2. $9,000-$20,000 3. Up to $15,000 4. $9,500-$17,000

Personal Qualifications	Knowledge and Skills Required	Recommended Precollege Training	Minimum College Training Required
Musical talent Ability to work with people Ambition to continually study and improve Be inspiring, convincing, patient Enjoy people and desire to help them learn	Broad cultural background Extensive knowledge of music Performance skill on one instrument or voice Ability and skill in teaching people Administrative ability necessary for supervisor	Completion of high school Ability to read music Some performance skill on one instrument or voice Study of music in school and privately as much as possible Keyboard skill recommended	Public school: teaching certificate, bachelor's degree College, university: doctoral degree or equivalent training All others: degrees not always required but the equivalent training is necessary
Musical talent and skill Ability to work with handicapped people Human understanding Enjoy people and desire to help them attain physical and mental health	Competent and versatile musician Practical facility on piano, guitar, or other instruments Knowledge of instruments and voice, behavioral and physical sciences	Same as for teachers	Bachelor's degree in music therapy
Musical talent and skill Ability to work with people Ambition to continually study and improve	Specialized skill in one or more instruments Fluency in sight-reading, transposing, improvising Skill in ensemble playing Knowledge of instrumental literature	Completion of high school Ability to read music Some performance skill on one instrument Experience in high school orchestra, band, or small ensembles Solo experience	Degrees not always required but the equivalent training is usually necessary
Musical talent and skill Ability to work with people Ambition to continually study and improve Fine voice Showmanship	Specialized skill in singing and interpretation of songs Knowledge of choral music techniques Knowledge of foreign languages and vocal literature Skill in sightsinging and quick memorizing Practical facility at the piano	Completion of high school Ability to read music Background in piano Some performance skill in singing Experience in singing groups	Degrees not always required but the equivalent training is usually necessary
Musical talent Interest in religion and religious music Ability to work with people	Understanding of liturgy Conducting Voice instruction techniques Fluency in sight-reading, transposing, improvising on the organ	Completion of high school Ability to read music Keyboard skill	Degrees in organ or sacred music not always required but the equivalent training is necessary
Great musical talent Creativity Continual perseverance Confidence	Superior musicianship in theory, literature Understanding of qualities and limitations of instruments and voices Experience in playing, singing	Completion of high school Ability to read music Some performance skill on one or more instruments Experience in playing, singing	College degrees not always required but the equivalent training is necessary
Great musical talent Leadership Superior diplomacy Dynamic and unique stage personality	Superior musicianship Skill in group management Decisive and expressive baton technique Specialized skill on one instrument or voice	Completion of high school Ability to read music Some performance skill on piano and one instrument or voice Experience in vocal or instrumental groups	Graduate music degree not always required but the equivalent training is necessary
Mechanical talent Ability to work with people Interest in music and instruments	Specialized skill in tuning, rebuilding, or repairing instruments	Completion of high school Work experience in one or more areas of tuning, rebuilding, and repairing instruments	College degrees not usually required. At least 2-3 years training or apprenticeship is generally necessary.
Ability to work with people Interest in music and business	Specialized skill and knowledge in one or more of the music industries	Completion of high school Experience in one or more of the music industries	College degrees not always required but recommended
Ability to work with people Interest in music, books, recordings, professional problems, and research	Thorough knowledge of music and musicology Working knowledge of foreign languages (German and French) Library training or some knowledge of library and research techniques Some knowledge of copyright and performance rights	Completion of high school	Bachelor's degree with major in music history or theory (preferably plus at least one year graduate study in musicology) Graduate library degree

Music Industry

Many communities throughout the country use staffs experienced in performance management. The music industry absorbs people trained in music for designing, manufacturing, and selling music instruments, accessories, and music. In the field of general industry, there has been a demand for knowledgeable and experienced musicians to direct the many phases of music programs. Music tuners, technicians, repairpersons, and instrument restorers are in demand in most areas of the country. The broadcasting industry employs television and radio music directors, producers, recording engineers, and announcers.

Music Therapist

With increased awareness of the rights of handicapped children and adults, the importance of trained music therapists has increased. These highly skilled individuals combine music, teaching, and therapy to help persons with disabilities attain physical and mental health. Emotional stability and physical stamina are essential for competent therapists.

Music Librarian

Colleges and public libraries offer opportunities for trained music specialists with a knowledge of library and research techniques. Music librarians are involved in research and reference, indexing, cataloging, selecting materials for purchase, and community relations. Some opportunities for music librarians also exist in radio, television, and motion pictures.

Church/Synagogue Musician

A career as a church or synagogue music director or organist combines music performance and teaching. Most musicians for religious institutions are employed part-time, although large congregations may employ a full-time music director or minister of music. In addition to being competent performers, religious musicians must understand music composition, transposition, and arranging, and must be familiar with the theology and liturgy of worship.

In addition to the careers in music mentioned above, some opportunities exist for musicologists, music business attorneys, architectural acoustics consultants, and community arts program managers. In the publishing industry, most large newspapers and magazines, and many smaller periodicals, hire a music reporter or critic who combines knowledge and enjoyment of music with a writing or editing career. Other careers include music historian, biographer, and lyricist. Each of the various music careers reflects dignity and prestige, and serves to bring satisfaction and happiness to the lives of countless people. Thousands of persons in the United States find great pleasure through music as an avocation. A number of the occupational areas described in this brochure are carried out on a nonprofessional basis, particularly in small communities.

IV. RESOURCES

Music Libraries
Music Periodicals
Music Book Publishers

Music Libraries

U.S. and Canadian libraries are listed alphabetically by state or province. Phone number, name of the music librarian or person to contact, description of music holdings and special collections, and services and access information are given for most libraries. The number 1 following the library's name indicates that they did not respond to our questionnaire. An alphabetical cross-index appears at the end of this section.

ALABAMA

BIRMINGHAM AND JEFFERSON COUNTY FREE LIBRARY
Art and Music Department
2020 Park Pl.
Birmingham, AL 35203
(205) 254-2538
Contact: Jane Fackler Greene, Department Head
Music Collection/Holdings: 10,000 music books; 500 scores; 18,000 recordings.
Services/Access Information: Most materials circulate.

HUNTINGDON COLLEGE
Music Library
1500 E. Fairview Ave.
Montgomery, AL 36106
(205) 265-0511, x257
Contact: Kathryn Berry, Secretary-Librarian
Music Collection/Holdings: Records; scores; music-related books and references.
Services/Access Information: Card catalogues.

SAMFORD UNIVERSITY
Music Library
800 Lakeshore Dr.
Birmingham, AL 35229
(205) 870-2851
Contact: Eva White, Music Librarian
Music Collection/Holdings: 4,271 recordings, 1,875 scores; 1,292 audiocassettes; 11 reel-to-reel tapes; 330 videocasettes; 57 filmstrips; 81 slides; and 17 books of microfiche.
Services/Access Information: All materials are checked out for use in library's listening facilities only.

UNIVERSITY OF ALABAMA IN HUNTSVILLE
Library
Huntsville, AL 35899
(205) 895-6540/895-6529
Contact: Elizabeth B. Pollard, Acting Subject Specialist for Fine Arts
Music Collection/Holdings: 5,000 volumes, including critical and performing editions of scores and books on music history, theory, and education; 850 musical recordings; 30 current periodical subscriptions.
Services/Access Information: Open to students, faculty, and staff; limited access to affiliates of other area colleges through interlibrary loan; surrounding community may purchase user's card. Records do not circulate. Reference service by traditional methods and on-line through DIALOG. Listening facilities available; records and tapes may be checked out for classroom instruction use.

ARIZONA

ARIZONA STATE UNIVERSITY
Music Library
Tempe, AZ 85287
(602) 965-3513
Contact: Arlys L. McDonald, Music Librarian
Music Collection/Holdings: 35,000 books and scores; 1,500 microforms; 1,600 recordings; 150 journal and serial subscriptions. Special collections: International Percussion Reference Library of 3,500 titles; Wayne King Collection of 5,400 popular music titles with parts, and 150 television films and recordings; sheet music collection of 5,500 titles.
Services/Access Information: Interlibrary loan through main library (Hayden Library); open to public for reference use.

TUCSON PUBLIC LIBRARY
Main Library
200 S. 6th Ave.
Tucson, AZ 85701
(602) 791-4393
Music Collection/Holdings: General reference and circulating book collections, including *New Grove Dictionary of Music and Musicians* and other standard works; records and cassette tapes; periodicals; and limited number of vertical files and videocassettes.
Services/Access Information: Reference assistance; telephone reference. Circulating collection may be checked out to holders of the library card.

UNIVERSITY OF ARIZONA
Music Collection
115 Music Building
Tucson, AZ 85721
(602) 626-2140
Contact: Dorman H. Smith, Head, Music Collection
Music Collection/Holdings: 46,000 scores; 25,000 pieces of sheet music; 50,000 pieces of popular sheet music; 24,000 sound recordings; 35,000 volumes of books and periodicals housed in main library; special collections: National Flute Association Library; International Trombone Association Resource Library; also strong in guitar, harp, and chamber music.
Services/Access Information: Catalogs and references housed in main library; recordings, historical sets and pop music for local use only.

ARKANSAS

ARKANSAS ARTS CENTER[1]
Elizabeth Prewitt Taylor Memorial Library
Box 2137, MacArthur Park

Little Rock, AR 72203
(501) 372-4000
Contact: Mrs. Travis McCoy, Librarian

OUACHITA BAPTIST UNIVERSITY[1]
Riley Library
Arkadelphia, AR 71923
(501) 246-4531
Contact: Juanita Barnett, Music Librarian

SOUTHERN ARKANSAS UNIVERSITY
Fine Arts Record Library
Magnolia, AR 71753
Contact: Robert G. Campbell
Music Collection/Holdings: 7,000 recordings; tape recordings of Music Department programs; and disks for computer instruction.
Services/Access Information: Record players, tape recorders, and computer terminals for instructional use. Open 5 days a week.

SOUTHERN ARKANSAS UNIVERSITY
Magale Library
Magnolia, AR 71753
(501) 234-5120
Contact: Robert Reid, Head Librarian
Music Collection/Holdings: Large collection of music-related books, scores, and periodicals. Scores include many collected editions as well as complete works for 40 composers; 28 periodical subscriptions.
Services/Access Information: Access through Arkansas Union Catalogue; interlibrary loan; and OCL. Microform and microfiche readers/printers. Open daily.

UNIVERSITY OF ARKANSAS
Fine Arts Library
FA 104
Fayetteville, AR 72701
(501) 575-3498/575-4708
Contact: Joyce M. Clinkscales, Fine Arts Librarian
Music Collection/Holdings: 14,000 scores, books on music, and periodicals; strong in monumenta and collected editions; sound recordings and materials related to folk music housed in the David W. Mullins Library. Music-related archives housed in the Special Collections Department of Mullins Library: records pertaining to Arkansas musicians, composers, lyricists, and arrangers; the Arkansas Folklore Collection; gifts of Mary Dengler Hudgins and individual collections on Florence Beatrice Price, Laurence Powell, and William Grant Still.
Services/Access Information: Open to the public 79 hours a week during the academic year, 55 hours during the summer; closed the week after Christmas and other school vacations. Books and scores circulate on ALA or OCLC interlibrary loan; collected editions and journals do no circulate.

CALIFORNIA

AZUSA PACIFIC UNIVERSITY
Marshburn Memorial Library
Citrus and Alosta
Azusa, CA 91702
(213) 969-3434
Contact: Prof. Virginia King, Fine Arts/Music Librarian
Music Collection/Holdings: Average-size music collection includes books, scores, periodicals; recordings and tapes; and films. Media center houses the recordings, tapes and films.
Services/Access Information: Listening and viewing facilities; videotaping available; and OCLC.

BERKELEY PUBLIC LIBRARY[1]
Art and Music Division
2090 Kittredge St.
Berkeley, CA 94704
(415) 644-6785
Contact: Anne C. Nutting, Head Librarian

CALIFORNIA STATE UNIVERSITY, FRESNO
Music Department Library
Department of Music
Fresno, CA 93740
(209) 294-2821
Contact: Karl Rubrecht, Music Department Librarian
Music Collection/Holdings: Serves the music faculty. Mostly music for chorus, orchestra, band and jazz ensemble; small archive of departmental history.
Services/Access Information: Outside organizations may borrow materials; write or call for details.

CALIFORNIA STATE UNIVERSITY, FULLERTON
Donal Michalsky Memorial Faculty Library
Fullerton, CA 92634
(714) 773-2481
Contact: Kurt Lautenschlager, Music Librarian
Music Collection/Holdings: Recordings; scores; books and graduate theses; recital tapes; music for major performing groups and chamber ensembles on campus.
Services/Access Information: Resource for faculty; reference source; 24-station ear-training and listening laboratory.

CALIFORNIA STATE UNIVERSITY, HAYWARD
Music Library
25800 Carlos Bee Blvd.
Hayward, CA 94542
(415) 881-3778
Contact: Ray A. Reeder, Music Librarian
Music Collection/Holdings: Primarily an academic collection, but contains representative material from all periods, including popular music, jazz, and ethnomusicological recordings. Over 17,300 scores; 9,900 books; 15,500 recordings; and 125 periodical titles.
Services/Access Information: Books and scores circulate to members of campus community, also through interlibrary loan. All materials and facilities open to users; access through OCLC data base.

CALIFORNIA STATE UNIVERSITY, LONG BEACH
Library-Reference Center
1250 Bellflower Blvd.
Long Beach, CA 90840
(213) 498-4029
Contact: Marilyn Bergin, Senior Assistant Librarian
Music Collection/Holdings: Music references are integrated into central collection, 12,900 score titles, including collected works, monumenta, and performance parts; 12,700 books and bound journal titles; 79 current journal subscriptions and 200 active serials; 73 titles on microform; 9,100 recording titles, 1,300 cassettes. Additional music holdings on campus in the Music Resource Center.
Services/Access Information: Reference services Monday through Thursday; open daily.

CALIFORNIA STATE UNIVERSITY, LONG BEACH
Music Resource Center
Department of Music
1250 Bellflower Blvd.
Long Beach, CA 90840
(213) 498-4786
Contact: Valencia Williams, Coordinator
Music Collection/Holdings: 6,900 volumes of print material: bound scores; performance parts for choral, solo, instrumental, chamber, orchestra, and band music; and basic music references; 3,700 recordings, including an historical jazz collection of 78 and 33⅓ rpm records, and tapes. Sheet music collection of songs dating from 1880, music reference collection and scores housed in centralized Reference Center.
Services/Access Information: Open to faculty and students. Reference service for on-campus and outside inquiries; listening facilities. Open weekdays.

CHAFFEY COMMUNITY COLLEGE
Music Library
5885 Haven Ave.
Alta Loma, CA 91701
(714) 987-1737, x538
Contact: Gustavo Gil, Music Librarian
Music Collection/Holdings: 2,000 recordings, mainly of Western European music; small holdings of jazz, ethnic, musical theater, and American music; educational records; 700 scores and books, primarily vocal and symphonic scores and piano literature; some reference materials.

Services/Access Information: Primarily a listening library with facilities for records and tapes; records do not circulate, but students may check out scores.

COLLEGE OF NOTRE DAME
Music Library, Music Department
1500 Ralston Ave.
Belmont, CA 94002
(415) 593-1601, x427
Contact: Ruth Warren, Music Librarian
Music Collection/Holdings: Extensive score and record collection. Organ, piano, chamber and orchestral music, vocal solo and choral scores; 5,000 records, all classical. Books on music and musicians are held in the main library.
Services/Access Information: Reference assistance for this collection for students and faculty; performance scores loaned to faculty.

GLENDALE PUBLIC LIBRARY
Brand Library
1601 W. Mountain St.
Glendale, CA 91201
(213) 956-2051
Contact: Jane Hagan, Library Services Supervisor; Joseph Fuchs, Senior Librarian
Music Collection/Holdings: 25,000 records; 2,500 cassettes; 200 piano rolls; 15,000 books and musical scores; sheet music; and clipping files.
Services/Access Information: Open to anyone high-school-age and over.

LIBRARY ASSOCIATION OF LA JOLLA
Athenaeum Music and Arts Library
1008 Wall St.
La Jolla, CA 92037
(619) 454-5872
Contact: Carole R. Shipley, Music Librarian
Music Collection/Holdings: 700 music-related books; 3,000-item collection of sheet music and scores, including the Breitkopf & Hartel edition of the works of Bach in 47 volumes, edited by the Bach Gessellschaft; 3,800 stereo and monaural records, mostly classical, but also spoken-word, children's, musical theatre, folk and jazz; 2,000 cassettes circulate.
Services/Access Information: Members may check out any material for 4 weeks.

LOS ANGELES PUBLIC LIBRARY
Art, Music and Recreation Department
630 W. 5th St.
Los Angeles, CA 90071
(213) 626-7555, x258
Contact: Judy M. Horton, Department Manager
Music Collection/Holdings: 25,000 books; 45,000 scores; 350 periodicals; 2,000 orchestral scores and parts; and 75,000 pieces of sheet music.
Services/Access Information: Interlibrary loan; photocopying; song index.

MUSIC AND ARTS INSTITUTE OF SAN FRANCISCO
College Library
2622 Jackson St.
San Francisco, CA 94115
(415) 567-1445
Contact: R. McKee, Director
Music Collection/Holdings: Scores; recordings and tapes; musical textbooks and references; musical instruments and equipment collection; books generally relating to the arts and literature; and art work.
Services/Access Information: For use of the faculty and students.

OAKLAND PUBLIC LIBRARY
Art, Music & Recreation
125 14th St.
Oakland, CA 94612
(415) 273-3178
Contact: Richard Colvig, Senior Librarian
Music Collection/Holdings: Books and reference materials; large collection of performance scores; choral collection; popular sheet music; records and cassettes.

OCCIDENTAL COLLEGE
Music Library
1600 Campus Rd.
Los Angeles, CA 90041
(213) 259-2577
Contact: Deborah Smith, Music Librarian
Music Collection/Holdings: 3,700 scores and 3,500 records.
Services/Access Information: Listening facilities for students.

PACIFIC UNION COLLEGE
Angwin, CA 94508
(707) 965-6241
Contact: Taylor Ruhl, Music Librarian
Music Collection/Holdings: Broad collection of records and scores; monumenta; and books to support the undergraduate music program.

PALOS VERDES LIBRARY DISTRICT
Music Department
650 Deep Valley Dr.
Rolling Hill Estates, CA 90274
(213) 377-9584
Contact: Sylvia Norris, Librarian
Music Collection/Holdings: Record collection contains jazz; pop; classical; spoken-word; folk; opera; instructional; Audiocassettes of books and instructional materials; selected references; scores.
Services/Access Information: Separate audio catalog with reference-service access at all times; score collection indexed. Open 6 days a week.

PASADENA PUBLIC LIBRARY[1]
Alice Coleman Batchelder Music Library
285 E. Walnut St.
Pasadena, CA 91101
(213) 577-4049
Contact: Josephine M. Pletscher, Coordinator, Fine Arts Division

SAN DIEGO PUBLIC LIBRARY
Art, Music, and Recreation Section
820 E Street
San Diego, CA 92101
(619) 236-5810
Contact: Evelyn Kooperman, Music Librarian
Music Collection/Holdings: Scores; books about music; recordings; song index to anthologies in collection.

SAN FRANCISCO CONSERVATORY OF MUSIC
Bothine Library
1201 Ortega St.
San Francisco, CA 94122
(415) 564-8086
Contact: Lucretia Wolfe, Music Librarian

SAN FRANCISCO STATE UNIVERSITY
Frank V. de Bellis Collection of the California State University
1630 Holloway Ave.
San Francisco, CA 94132
(415) 469-1649
Contact: Serena de Bellis, Curator
Music Collection/Holdings: Part of a larger collection on the history and culture of Italy; music holdings include 25,000 recordings; 10,000 scores; 700 manuscripts; and 500 microfilms.
Services/Access Information: Research materials for in-house use only; microfilm and copying. Open weekdays.

SAN JOSE PUBLIC LIBRARY
180 W. San Carlos St.
San Jose, CA 95113
(408) 277-4815
Contact: Phyllis Terra, Librarian
Music Collection/Holdings: Strong collection of sheet music, mostly from the 19th century; a collection of stock music for small popular and jazz combos; a good selection of both reference and circulating music books including sheet music anthologies; large collection of recordings housed in the Media Center.
Services/Access Information: Interlibrary loan. Open 5 days a week; Media Center, 2 days a week.

SAN JOSE STATE UNIVERSITY
Clark Library
Reference Department
San Jose, CA 95114
(408) 277-3784
Contact: Barbara J. Jeskalian, Music Librarian
Music Collection/Holdings: Scores; books on music, including biographies, histories, and monographs; books on

music education and music theory; records house in the Media Division; reference materials. Rare and/or complete works kept in locked case.

SCRIPPS COLLEGE
Caster Music Room
Claremont, CA 91711
(714) 621-8000, x3266
Contact: Edris Boyll Brady, Music Section
Music Collection/Holdings: Records; scores; keyboard, vocal, and instrumental sheet music.
Services/Access Information: Open daily.

SOCIETY OF CALIFORNIA PIONEERS LIBRARY
456 McAllister St.
San Francisco, CA 94102
(415) 861-5278
Contact: Grace E. Baker, Librarian
Music Collection/Holdings: Sheet music of early California publishers, composers, and lyricists; playbills; theatre programs; biographies of California musicians and performing artists.
Services/Access Information: Open to the public. Sheet music cataloged by composer, lyricists, date of publication, publishers, subject, title, type of music, and so forth.

SONOMA STATE UNIVERSITY
Music Library
1801 E. Cotati Ave.
Rohnert Park, CA 94928
(707) 664-2460
Contact: Ruth Hafter, Director
Music Collection/Holdings: Supports general undergraduate curriculum. Monographs; scores; periodicals; and records.

STANFORD UNIVERSITY
Music Library
The Knoll
Stanford, CA 94305
(415) 497-2463
Contact: Jerry Persons, Music Librarian
Music Collection/Holdings: 56,000 books and scores; 14,000 sound recordings; 1,400 reels of microfilm and 1,000 other microforms; parts for solo and chamber music; journals.
Services/Access Information: Appropriate identification to borrow materials or to have access to closed stacks of sound recordings, microforms, and items kept in locked case. Listening facilities; microform readers; photocopier.

UNIVERSITY OF CALIFORNIA AT BERKELEY
Music Library
240 Morrison Hall
Berkeley, CA 94720
(415) 642-2623
Contact: Michael A. Keller, Head
Music Collection/Holdings: Collection for research in music, incorporating important holding in opera scores and libretti; early imprints; music manuscripts (10th through 20th centuries); archival materials; microfilm copies of manuscripts from other libraries; and references. 115,000 catalogued volumes; 1,200 current serial subscriptions; and 20,000 sound recordings.
Services/Access Information: Reference; interlibrary loan; microform readers; photocopying and microfilm.

UNIVERSITY OF CALIFORNIA AT DAVIS[1]
Music Library
Davis, CA 95616
(916) 752-2110
Contact: Jean Lokis, Music Librarian

UNIVERSITY OF CALIFORNIA, IRVINE
University Library
PO Box 19557
Irvine, CA 92713
(714) 883-7178
Contact: Don L. Hixon, Fine Arts Librarian
Music Collection/Holdings: 17,000 scores; 15,000 monograph titles; 165 serial titles; and 500 cassettes.
Services/Access Information: Open to public; borrowing by qualified card holders. All titles on interlibrary loan.

UNIVERSITY OF CALIFORNIA, LOS ANGELES
Music Library
1102 Schoenberg Hall
University of California
Los Angeles, CA 90024
(213) 825-4882
Contact: Stephen M. Fry, Head
Music Collection/Holdings: Central facility for music study and research at UCLA. 40,000 volumes of books; 50,000 scores; and 35,000 records and tape recordings. Special research materials: microforms of music manuscripts; early printed books and treatises; international dissertations; rare book collection of scores and books published before 1850, holograph manuscripts, and facsimiles of music manuscripts; notable are the Archive of Popular American Sheet Music; the Film and Television Music Archive; affiliated Ethnomusicology Archive devoted to non-Western music.
Services/Access Information: Open to all qualified patrons. Most books and scores circulate for 4 weeks to cardholders; recordings do not circulate and may be heard on the library's listening equipment. Reference staff most hours.

UNIVERSITY OF CALIFORNIA, RIVERSIDE
Music Library
PO Box 5900
Riverside, CA 92517
(714) 787-3137
Contact: John W. Tanno, Music Librarian
Music Collection/Holdings: 14,000 books about music housed in main library; 15,000 scores and 9,000 recordings housed in Music Library. Special collections: Harry and Grace James Recorded Sound Archive of 10,000-78rpm records; bells and carrillons; organology; Danish Music, including all editions of the music of Niels Wilhelm Gade; the Oswald Jonas Memorial Collection, incorporating the Heinrich Schenker Archive; 500 first and early editions of 18th and 19th century composers, e.g., Brahms, Shumann, Schubert, Chopin; 750 scores from the WPA Southern California Project and the Marcella Craft Collection.

UNIVERSITY OF CALIFORNIA AT SAN DIEGO
Music Collection
Central University Library
La Jolla, CA 92093
(619) 452-2759
Contact: Garrett H. Bowles, Music Librarian
Music Collection/Holdings: Strong general collection; specializes in new and computer music supporting a Ph.D. program in composition and contemporary music performance. Four special archives of manuscripts, correspondence, and recordings of Ernst Krenek, Peter Yates, Pauline Oliveros, Lawrence Morten; Center for Music Experiment Archive; Music Department Tape Archive.
Services/Access Information: Access to contemporary music collections through Music Librarian; open stacks for in-house use by the public, may be borrowed by faculty and students. Record collection in closed stacks, recordings do not circulate; 40 listening stations.

UNIVERSITY OF CALIFORNIA, SANTA BARBARA
Music Library
Santa Barbara, CA 93106
(805) 961-2641
Contact: Martin Silver, Music Librarian; Susan Sonnet, Assistant Music Librarian
Music Collection/Holdings: 55,000 volumes of books, scores, and periodicals supporting graduate programs in performance, composition, theory, and historical musicology. Includes a working record collection of 22,000 33⅓rpm records, and 20,000 historical 78rpms, mainly of vocal performances.
Services/Access Information: Open stack for circulating collection, except

for recordings and reference; interlibrary loan for circulating items. Limted access through a local computerized catalog in the Archive of Recorded Vocal Music, by appointment.

UNIVERSITY OF SOUTHERN CALIFORNIA
Doheney Library, Music Library
University Park
Los Angeles, CA 90089-0182
(213) 743-2525
Contact: Rodney D. Rolfs, Music Librarian
Music Collection/Holdings: 3,300 cassette recordings; 15,000 records; 33,000 scores; 165 periodical titles; most books housed in main library stacks.
Services/Access Information: Open to the faculty and students; interlibrary loan. Open daily.

COLORADO

COLORADO COLLEGE
Music Library
Packard Hall
Colorado Springs, CO 80903
(303) 473-2233, x560
Contact: Janine Seay, Music Librarian
Music Collection/Holdings: Over 10,000 music-related books and scores, supplemented by 5,000 books housed in main library (Tutt Library); Over 10,000 recordings on disc and tape. Strength in monumenta and reference materials.
Services/Access Information: Listening facilities; microfilm and microfiche readers.

COLORADO STATE UNIVERSITY
William E. Morgan Library
Fort Collins, CO 80523
(303) 491-5911
Contact: Ronald Burt DeWaal, Humanities Librarian
Music Collection/Holdings: Materials to support undergraduate and graduate music programs: music therapy and education; performance; conducting; music literature and theory; composition. Emphasis is European and American materials, and those in Western languages, primarily English; score collection represents Medieval, Renaissance, Baroque, Classical, Romantic and Modern (primarily post-World War I American) periods.
Services/Access Information: Open dialy during school session.

DENVER PUBLIC LIBRARY
Arts and Recreation Department
1357 Broadway
Denver, Co 80203
(303) 571-2070
Contact: Georgiana Tiff, Department Manager
Music Collection/Holdings: Books, scores and recordings; folk music collection.
Services/Access Information: Open to public; borrowing by valid cardholders.

UNIVERSITY OF COLORADO AT BOULDER
Music Library
N-290 Warner Imig Music Bldg.
PO Box 184
Boulder, CO 80309
(303) 492-8093
Contact: Karl Kroeger, Head
Music Collection/Holdings: 20,000 scores; 20,000 books; 15,000 records; 1,000 microfiche; 500 microfilms; and 150 periodical titles.
Services/Access Information: Borrowing by Colorado residents only; reference service for anyone; interlibrary loan.

UNIVERSITY OF COLORADO AT DENVER
Auraria Library
Lawrence at 11th St.
Denver, CO 80204
(303) 629-3451/629-2710
Contact: Robert L. Wick, Assistant Professor and Music Librarian
Music Collection/Holdings: 8,000 records; 20,000 monographs; 3,000 scores; 1,500 reference works; and 300 nonprint items.
Services/Access Information: Special service desk for collection in main library. Viewing and listening facilities include video distribution system to over 300 classrooms on campus. All materials for individual use, including the nonprint items; records must stay within the library, but circulate to faculty.

UNIVERSITY OF NORTHERN COLORADO
Music Library
Frasier 200
Greeley, CO 80639
(303) 351-2439
Contact: Norman Savig, Coordinator
Music Collection/Holdings: 22,000 volumes in music literature and theory and general music topics; 10,000 records; 193 periodical titles.
Services/Access Information: Serves university and surrounding community. Listening facilities; microfilm, microfiche, and microcard readers. Open daily.

CONNECTICUT

CONNECTICUT COLLEGE
Greer Music Library
Box 1534
New London, CT 06320
(203) 447-7535
Contact: Philip Youngholm, Music Librarian
Music Collection/Holdings: 5,000 volumes of books; 9,000 volumes of printed music; 750 volumes of bound periodicals; 30 microforms; sound recordings: 11,000 records and 300 tapes.
Services/Access Information: 10 listening booths, 4 listening rooms; photocopier. All materials available to public for in-library use.

HARTFORD PUBLIC LIBRARY
Art and Music Department
500 Main St.
Hartford, CT 06103
(203) 525-9121
Contact: Vernon Martin, Head, Art and Music Department
Music Collection/Holdings: Books, scores, orchestral sets, and musical recordings.
Services/Access Information: On-site listening; performing arts programs.

NEIGHBORHOOD MUSIC SCHOOL
Elizabeth Licht Library/Learning Center
100 Audubon St.
New Haven, CT 06511
(203) 624-5189
Contact: Jeanne B. D'Angelo, Librarian
Music Collection/Holdings: Extensive chamber music collection, including youth orchestra library; scores; books and periodicals; recordings library; instructional materials on individual instruments.
Services/Access Information: Research and reference services; listening facilities; and performance parts distribution. Currently open afternoons and Saturday morning only.

TRINITY COLLEGE
Watkinson Library
300 Summit St.
Hartford, CT 06100
(203) 527-3151, x307
Contact: Margaret Sax, Associate Curator
Music Collection/Holdings: Primary interest in 18th and 19th century American music: tunebooks; manuscript music. 40,000 pieces of sheet music; music ephemera; Abbe Niles Jazz Collection.
Services/Access Information: Open to public. Free guide to collection; no interlibrary loan, but will supply photocopies. Open weekdays.

UNIVERSITY OF CONNECTICUT
Music Library
U-Box 12
Storrs, CT 06268
(203) 486-2502
Contact: Dorothy Bognar, Music Librarian (Head)
Music Collection/Holdings: 35,000 volumes of books; wide variety of performance and scholarly scores; all types of sound recordings; journals; and microforms. Collection supports undergraduate and graduate programs.

Services/Access Information: Borrowing with a valid ID; class reserve; reference; and listening facilities. Interlibrary loans through department in main library; certain sound recordings and other material do not circulate. Open daily during school session.

UNIVERSITY OF HARTFORD, HARTT SCHOOL OF MUSIC
Mildred P. Allen Memorial Library
200 Bloomfield Ave.
West Hartford, CT 06117
(203) 243-4492
Contact: Ethel Bacon, Music Librarian
Music Collection/Holdings: 12,000 books; 26,000 scores; 17,000 records; 2,000 audio tapes of Hartt School opera productions, concerts, and recitals. Strengths and special collections: practical editions of vocal and instrumental music; The Kalmen Opperman Collection, 500 titles of clarinet music for solos and ensembles; The Robert E. Smith Collection of 34,000 sound recordings.
Services/Access Information: Open to members of other communities or universities for study and listening only. Free interlibrary loan; sound recordings do not circulate.

WESTERN CONNECTICUT STATE UNIVERSITY
Charles E. Ives Music Room
Ruth A. Haas Library
181 White St.
Danbury, CT 06810
(203) 797-4118
Contact: Edith Godel, Music Librarian
Music Collection/Holdings: Supports undergraduate program in performance, music education, and liberal arts with music concentration; and master's program in music education.
Services/Access Information: Open to public for study and listening.

THE YALE COLLECTION OF HISTORICAL SOUND RECORDINGS
Yale University Library
PO Box 1603A, Yale Station
New Haven, CT 06520
(203) 436-1822
Contact: Richard Warren, Jr., Curator
Music Collection/Holdings: Over 100,000 recordings (78rpm and 33⅓rpm records, tapes, cylinders, and wires) of Western classical music; American musical theater; and literature and history (spoken-word). Emphasis on historical documentation through collection of important performers' recordings: The Yale Collection of the Papers of the American Musical Theater includes original cast recordings, sheet music, and personal archives of Cole Porter and E.Y. Harburg.
Services/Access Information: Open to Yale students, faculty, and staff, and to outside scholars regardless of affiliation. Open weekdays. Archives do not circulate; listening on premises by appointment.

YALE UNIVERSITY
Yale Music Library
98 Wall St.
New Haven, CT 06520
(203) 436-8240
Contact: Prof. Harold E. Samuel, Music Librarian
Music Collection/Holdings: 100,000 circulating books and scores; 14,000 recordings. Special collections: 12,000 books and scores in Rare Book Collection; 100,000 recordings in Historical Sound Archive; 40 collections in the 20th-Century American Music Archive, including manuscripts and papers of Charles Ives, Carl Ruggles, Kurt Weill, and others; 600 miscellaneous manuscripts.
Services/Access Information: Open 78 hours a week.

YALE UNIVERSITY COLLECTION OF MUSICAL INSTRUMENTS
15 Hillhouse Ave.
PO Box 2117
New Haven, CT 06520
(203) 436-4935
Music Collection/Holdings: Over 800 musical instruments, the majority documenting the European art music tradition from the 16th century to 1900. 400-volume library of catalogues, books, brochures, treatises and facsimilies (catalogued in the Music Library of Yale University).
Services/Access Information: Limited admission days; closed August and holidays. Admission free; guided tours for fee by appointment.

DELAWARE

UNIVERSITY OF DELAWARE
Music Resource Center
Music Department
Newark, DE 19711
(302) 738-8130
Contact: J. Michael Foster, Music Resource Center Supervisor
Music Collection/Holdings: Materials supporting university music students and community: 4,500 scores; 3,000 records; 500 tape recordings; 1,200 books; and large collection of performing editions for large ensembles, band and chorus.
Services/Access Information: Books, scores, and performing editions circulate to the University and, with permission, to members of the community; recordings circulate to faculty only. Listening facility serves up to 60.

DISTRICT OF COLUMBIA

AMERICAN UNIVERSITY
Library-Record-Score Collection
Massachusetts and Nebraska Aves.
Washington, DC 20016
(202) 686-2165
Contact: James R. Heintze, Head
Music Collection/Holdings: 6,500 discs and 415 reel-to-reel tape recordings, representing all styles and periods of music, including classical, jazz, popular, and folk.
Services/Access Information: Access by card catalog; open daily.

DISTRICT OF COLUMBIA PUBLIC LIBRARY
Music and Recreation Division
Martin Luther King Memorial Library
901 G. St., N.W.
Washington, DC 20001
(202) 727-1285
Contact: Mary E. Elliott, Chief, Music and Recreation Division
Music Collection/Holdings: 24,494 scores; 6,229 pieces of sheet music; 16,604 records; 658 orchestral sets in Hans Kindler Collection; and 12,414 books

LIBRARY OF CONGRESS
Archive of Folk Culture
American Folklife Center
Washington, DC 20540
(202) 287-5510
Contact: Joseph C. Hickerson, Head, Archive of Folk Culture; or Gerald E. Parsons, Reference Librarian
Music Collection/Holdings: Over 35,000 field recordings of folksongs, folk music, folk tales, oral history and other types of folklore; 100,000 leaves of manuscript materials in folklore, folklife, and ethnomusicology with complete national and wide international representation; 3,500 selected books and periodicals; collection of magazines, newsletters, microforms, ephemera, and variety of unpublished theses and dissertations.
Services/Access Information: Public reading/listening room open weekdays, closed on national holidays; occasional listening by appointment; photocopying, phonocopying, reference, and referral services. 85 records available for public purchase; student intern program.

LIBRARY OF CONGRESS
Music Division
Washington, DC 20540
(202) 287-5503
Contact: Donald L. Leavitt, Chief
Music Collection/Holdings: More than 4 million scores; books about music and musicians, instruments, and so on.
Services/Access Information: Open to public. Interlibrary loan; photocopying; audio reproduction.

LIBRARY OF CONGRESS
National Library Service for the Blind and Physically Handicapped, Music Section
Washington, DC 20542
(202) 287-9257
Contact: Shirley P. Emanuel, Head, Music Section
Music Collection/Holdings: 30,000 titles containing braille scores and books about music; instructional recordings including self-instruction courses, lectures and master classes, on disc and cassette; and large print scores and books about music.
Services/Access Information: Library materials, reading equipment, and subscriptions available to individuals who cannot see or hold standard print publications. Free subscriptions available to: *High Fidelity/Musical America* (on 8rpm disc); *Music Article Guide* (in braille and on 15/16 ips cassette; and several specially produced and compiled music magazines. For further information about services and eligibility, use the toll-free number (800) 424-8567 to call the Music Section.

NATIONAL ENDOWMENT FOR THE ARTS[1]
Arts Library
2401 E St., N.W.
Room 1256
Washington, DC 20506
(202) 634-7640
Contact: Mary P. Morrison, Arts Librarian

SMITHSONIAN INSTITUTION
Division of Musical Instruments
Washington, DC 20560
(202) 357-1707
Music Collection/Holdings: Substantial collection of treatises concerning instrument manufacture and performance practices (no collection of music or records); trade catalog collection emphasizes the manufacture and use of instruments in the United States. Important collection of over 2,000 instruments from Western Europe and the United States.
Services/Access Information: Contact for information.

UNITED STATES MARINE CORPS[1]
Marine Band Library
Marine Barracks, Eighth and I Sts., S.E.
Washington, DC 20390
(202) 433-4298

FLORIDA

FLORIDA STATE UNIVERSITY
Warren D. Allen Music Library
Tallahassee, FL 32306
(904) 644-5028
Contact: Dale L. Hudson, Head
Music Collection/Holdings: Books and scores; recordings; journals supporting doctoral study in most areas of music.
Services/Access Information: Interlibrary loan. For more information contact the librarian.

MIAMI-DADE PUBLIC LIBRARY
Art and Music Department
One Biscayne Blvd.
Miami, FL 33132
(305) 579-5015
Contact: Kenneth R. Benoit, Librarian I
Music Collection/Holdings: 31,330 records; 1,512 scores; 8,252 pieces of sheet music; subscriptions to 27 music journals and other serials; 773 reference books; over 2,065 circulating books; 78 pieces of special collection materials.

SEMINOLE COMMUNITY COLLEGE
Fine Arts Library
Sanford, FL 32771-9990
(305) 323-1450
Contact: Patricia L. Meredith, Fine Arts Librarian
Music Collection/Holdings: Books, records, scores (orchestral and choral), scripts; music for wind and jazz ensembles and solos; piano, violin, vocal, march, studies.
Services/Access Information: Mainly a reference library; music is loaned to specific performing groups and classes.

STETSON UNIVERSITY[1]
Music Library
421 N. Woodland Blvd.
Deland, FL 32720
(904) 734-4121
Contact: Janice Jenkins, Music Librarian

UNIVERSITY OF FLORIDA[1]
Belknapp Collection for the Performing Arts
Gainesville, FL 32611
(904) 392-0322
Contact: Robena Eng, Music Librarian

UNIVERSITY OF MIAMI
Albert Pick Music Library
School of Music
PO Box 248165
Coral Gables, FL 33124
(305) 284-2429
Contact: Nancy Kobialka, Music Librarian
Music Collection/Holdings: 23,350 scores and 15,230 recordings; areas of specialization include: 1,000 jazz records; Latin-American scores and recordings; Yiddish folk-song collection.
Services/Access Information: Open to public for research only; borrowing by university faculty, students, and staff. Photocopier; no taping allowed in the library.

UNIVERSITY OF NORTH FLORIDA
Thomas G. Carpenter Library
PO Box 17605
St. Johns Bluff Rd., S.
Jacksonville, FL 32216
(904) 646-2553
Music Collection/Holdings: 4,000 scores, mostly of keyboard and chamber music; 6,000 music recordings; and 20,000 volumes of music literature.
Services/Access Information: General reference services. Open to adult public; borrowing by university community only; interlibrary loan; member, SOLINET/OCLC.

GEORGIA

DALTON JUNIOR COLLEGE
Music Library
Dalton, GA 30720
(404) 278-3113
Contact: Mary P. O'Neill, Assistant Librarian
Music Collection/Holdings: Core collection of notable music reference books; small circulating collection comprised of about 3,000 pieces of music-related material; 3,000 cassette recordings, classical to popular.

GEORGIA STATE UNIVERSITY
Department of Music Listening Library
200 Art and Music Bldg.
University Plaza
Atlanta, GA 30303
(404) 658-2349
Contact: James B. Kopp, Librarian
Music Collection/Holdings: 7,000 recordings of primarily classical music; 2,500 scores and music reference books; archives of departmental and guest recitals.
Services/Access Information: Strictly a reference and listening library. Main university library (Pullen Library) has larger collection of scores and books on music.

WEST GEORGIA COLLEGE[1]
Special Collections Department
Carrollton, GA 30117
(404) 834-1370
Contact: Susan Smith, Assistant Librarian

HAWAII

HAWAII STATE LIBRARY
Fine Arts-Audiovisual Section
478 South King St.
Honolulu, HI 96813
(808) 548-2340, x6283
Contact: Eloise S. Van Niel, Head
Music Collection/Holdings: 50,000 volumes, 10,000 of which are scores. Emphasis on song, with representative works for piano and chamber music; building collection strength in musical

theatre and opera. Song title index to sheet music file; Hawaiian music, primarily vocal, is included. Record collection of 11,000 titles (20,000 records).
Services/Access Information: For use by performers, auditioners, and by public for cultural purposes and enjoyment. Public reference desk, shared Social Science Section, open 54 hours a week.

UNIVERSITY OF HAWAII
Thomas Hale Hamilton Library
2550 The Mall
Honolulu, HI 96822
(808) 948-7205
Contact: Donald Matsumori
Music Collection/Holdings: 30,000 total pieces. Large Western art music collection housed in the Sinclair Library and selected Asian, Hawaiian, and Pacific titles, housed in the Hamilton Library. Holdings consist of music scores and printed music; books on music education, history, criticism, and analysis; monumenta, complete works of composers, and single works; reference collection of sources, bibliographies, thematic indexes, dictionaries, encyclopedias, and histories.
Services/Access Information: Open to faculty and students of the university and state residents, others selectively. The collection circulates except for the monumenta, the complete works of composers, and the references. Open daily.

IDAHO

RICKS COLLEGE
David O. McKay Learning Resources Center
College Ave.
Rexburg, ID 83440
(208) 356-2351
Contact: A. Graydon Burton, Circulation Supervisor
Music Collection/Holdings: 4,000 titles of choral music, primarily for the several college choirs; 1,000 volumes of scores and bound music books.
Services/Access Information: Materials are loaned to public and to the faculty, students, and staff for various lengths of time. Most sheet music circulates for 1 month; bound volumes and scores circulate for 2 weeks at at time.

ILLINOIS

AMERICAN CONSERVATORY OF MUSIC
Hattstaedt Memorial Library
116 S. Michigan Ave.
Chicago, IL 60603
(312) 263-4161
Contact: Lauren R. Denhardt, Music Librarian
Music Collection/Holdings: 8,000 volumes of books and scores; 2,000 sound recordings.
Services/Access Information: OCLC cataloging.

BRADLEY UNIVERSITY
Music Library
Peoria, IL 61625
(309) 676-7611, x583
Contact: Eleonore Hansen, Music Librarian
Music Collection/Holdings: 10,000 items of printed music; 6,000 records; 5,000 books about music; emphasis on classical music to support undergraduate programs.
Services/Access Information: OCLC, DIALOG, and BRS data bases; interlibrary loan.

CHICAGO MUSICAL COLLEGE OF ROOSEVELT UNIVERSITY
430 S. Michigan Ave.
Chicago, IL 60605
(312) 341-3651
Contact: Donald Draganski, Music Librarian
Music Collection/Holdings: 28,000 books and scores; 10,000 pieces of sheet music; 9,000 records; 80 periodical subscriptions. Strong in classical repertoire, with representative holdings in jazz and ethnomusicology; collected editions of all major composers and Denkmaler.
Services/Access Information: Open to public. Borrowing limited to faculty and students of the university and other schools in the CALC (Chicago Academic Library Council) Reciprocal Borrowing Program. Self-service audio equipment available on premises. Member OCLC and DIALOG data bases.

CHICAGO PUBLIC LIBRARY
Music Section, Fine Arts Divison
78 E. Washington
Chicago, IL 60602
(312) 269-2886
Contact: Ricahrd Schwegel, Head
Music Collection/Holdings: 8,000 titles emphasizing popular music, jazz, music business, discography, film music, and music therapy; over 320 current periodical subscriptions; 32,000 volumes of scores of all types and areas; 7,000 old popular songs in original covers; 52,000 recordings representing a wide range of performers and types of music; small, but growing Blues Archive collecting documentation, records, memorabilia, and video tapes.
Services/Access Information: Open 6 days a week; closed Sundays. Listening facilities: three practice rooms equipped with pianos and music stands.

CONCORDIA TEACHERS COLLEGE[1]
Klinck Memorial Library
7400 Augusta St.
River Forest, IL 60305
(312) 771-8300
Contact: Henry R. Latzke, Director of Library Services

DEPAUL UNIVERSITY
Lincoln Park Campus Library
2323 N. Seminary
Chicago, IL 60614
(312) 321-7939
Contact: Robert L. Acker, Music Librarian
Music Collection/Holdings: Core collection of scores, recordings, books, and periodicals; supports a School of Music curriculum emphasizing performance, composition, music education, and music therapy. Subject strengths: works of Alexander Tcherepnin and Leon Stein; music education; and music therapy.
Services/Access Information: Anyone may use materials within the library: reference service available to all patrons. Borrowing privileges restricted to the students, faculty, and staff, and to patrons of libraries in the LCS and CALC library networks.

ILLINOIS STATE UNIVERSITY
Milner Library Humanities-Fine Arts Division
Normal, IL 61761
(309) 438-7447
Contact: Mary Jo Brown, Music Librarian
Music Collection/Holdings: About 35,000 books and scores; 18,000 records; supports music curricula in performance; music history; theory; education; and therapy; 300 periodical titles.
Services/Access Information: Microfilm, microcard, and microfiche readers. Open daily except for major holidays.

ILLINOIS WESLEYAN UNIVERSITY[1]
Music Library
PO Box 2900
Bloomington, IL 61701
(309) 556-3003
Contact: Glenn Patton, Fine Arts Librarian

THE NEWBERRY LIBRARY
60 W. Walton St.
Chicago, IL 60610
(312) 943-9090
Music Collection/Holdings: One of the four major collections of its kind in the United States: 200,000 items, including 45,000 books about music; 55,000 scores and performance editions; 100,000 pieces of sheet music. Collection contains primary and secondary source materials for the study of Western European music from its beginnings into the early 20th century; and American music from its

beginnings into the early 20th century. Strengths are divided into 5 categories: medieval music; renaissance and baroque music; music of the 18th and 19th centuries; Americana; music periodicals (esp. 19th century) and music manuscripts.
Services/Access Information: Collections do not circulate; full complement of photocopying services upon request to the reference department. Open to readers 5 days a week; closed Sunday and Monday.

NORTHERN ILLINOIS UNIVERSITY
Music Library
175 Music Bldg.
DeKalb, IL 60115
(815) 753-1426
Contact: Gordon Rowley, Assistant Director for Research Services
Music Collection/Holdings: 21,000 scores; 9,100 books; 196 periodical titles; 22,000 disc and tape sound recordings; microforms.
Services/Access Information: Interlibrary loan; photocopying. Open to Illinois residents; open to others for room use only. Member OCLC and LCS network.

NORTHWESTERN UNIVERSITY
Music Library
1937 Sheridan Rd.
Evanston, IL 60201
(312) 492-3434
Contact: Don L. Roberts, Head Music Librarian
Music Collection/Holdings: 65,000 scores; 30,000 books and serial volumes; 360 current periodical subscriptions; 34,000 sound recordings; and 2,000 manuscripts. Specializes in 20th century music with a concentration on the post-1945 period. Special collections: John Cage Archives and NOTATIONS Collection; portion of Moldernhauer Archives: microfilm archives of music published by Summy-Birchard Co. (Chicago WPA Music Periodical Index), among other special collections.
Services/Access Information: Member of the Research Libraries Group. Open to public weekdays; limted access on evenings and weekends.

OLIVET NAZARENE COLLEGE
Benner Library
240 E. Marsile
Bourbonnais, IL 60914
(815) 939-5356
Contact: Wanda Kranich, Assistant Professor of Music
Music Collection/Holdings: 2,400 catalogued classical records of all types; choral music for the use of the college's 3 choirs and student class projects; band and orchestra music available; but not all catalogued.
Services/Access Information: Listening facilities; records usually may not be checked out by students. Open to students 6 days a week.

SHERWOOD MUSIC SCHOOL
1014 S. Michigan Ave.
Chicago, IL 60605
(312) 427-6267
Contact: Michael F. Burdick, Librarian
Music Collection/Holdings: 6,000 books dealing with music history, performance, theory, pedagogy, appreciation, church music, folk music, and music education; 1,500 recordings; 3,000 music scores.
Services/Access Information: Open to students and faculty only.

SOUTHERN ILLINOIS UNIVERSITY, CARBONDALE
Morris Library
Carbondale, IL 62901
(618) 536-3391
Contact: Theophil M. Otto, Music Librarian
Music Collection/Holdings: 40,000 scores and books; 15,000 sound recordings; 175 periodicals; 1,500 pieces of popular sheet music.
Services/Access Information: All materials circulate; listening facilities accomodate 50; member OCLC and LCS.

SOUTHERN ILLINOIS UNIVERSITY, EDWARDSVILLE
Lovejoy Library
Edwardsville, IL 62026
(618) 692-2670
Contact: Philip M. Calcagno, Fine Arts Librarian
Music Collection/Holdings: General collection supports music education and performance programs; Special collections: Jazz; and "Music of the American People."
Services/Access Information: Interlibrary loan; member OCLC and LCS.

UNIVERSITY OF CHICAGO
Joseph Regenstein Library, Music Collection
1100 E. 57th St.
Chicago, IL 60637
(312) 962-8445
Contact: Hans Lenneberg, Music Librarian
Music Collection/Holdings: 80,000 volumes; 8,000 reels of microfilm; 8,000 records. Primary strength in music history and theory.
Services/Access Information: Open to students and faculty of other institutions on limited basis; interlibrary loan. Microfilm, photocopier.

UNIVERSITY OF ILLINOIS AT URBANA-CHAMPAIGN
Music Library
2136 Music Bldg.
1114 W. Nevada
Urbana, IL 62801
(217) 333-1173
Contact: William M. McClellan, Director
Music Collection/Holdings: About 1 million items; 65,000 book titles and editions of music, including 626,000 volumes of uncatalogued music editions and scores; 35,000 records and audio tapes; 10,000 titles on microform; performance library in multiple copies or sets of parts for choral groups, orchestra, and wind ensembles.
Services/Access Information: Reference; verification of citations: vertical files; in-depth consultation; orientation tours, lectures to classes, handouts, guides, and exhibits; search services and assistance in use of audio and viewing equipment.

VANDERCOOK COLLEGE OF MUSIC
Harry Ruppel Memorial Library
3209 S. Michigan Ave.
Chicago, IL 60616
(312) 225-6288
Contact: Peter L. Eisenberg, Music Librarian
Music Collection/Holdings: Over 18,000 volumes of books on music education, wind and brass instruments, music theory, and so forth. 95 current periodicals titles with 77 in music; 1,600 records; 3,000 catalogued scores, and over 10,000 uncatalogued scores, mostly study scores of symphonic band and wind ensembles.
Services/Access Information: Open during school session; anyone may use materials within the library, but only students may check out material. Member of the Chicago Library System. Interlibrary loan; listening facilities.

WESTERN ILLINOIS UNIVERSITY
Music Library
203 Browne Hall
Macomb, IL 61455
(309) 298-1105
Contact: Allie Wise Goudy, Music Librarian
Music Collection/Holdings: 5,800 books; 4,200 scores; and 4,200 recordings; 128 periodical titles and 41 titles in back-issues.
Services/Access Information: Evening and weekend hours during school session; daily hours during breaks and summer. Listening facilities.

WHEATON COLLEGE
Buswell Memorial Library
Wheaton, IL 60187
(312) 260-5092
Contact: Virginia L. Powell, Librarian of Music and Education
Music Collection/Holdings: Approximately 6,000 records, 6,000 scores; 450 music reference books; 150 music tapes and other audiovisual materials; 175 music education series. Other music books and periodicals

housed with main library collection.
Services/Access Information: Records and tapes checked out to faculty and staff; students may check out records and tapes for 1 class period; scores circulate for 1 month; music education curriculum texts for 24 hours; and music reference materials, in-house use only.

INDIANA

BALL STATE UNIVERSITY
Music Library
2000 University Ave.
Muncie, IN 47306
(317) 285-7356
Contact: Dr. Nyal Williams, Professor of Library Services; Chairperson, Department of Library Service
Music Collection/Holdings: Approximately 40,000 items, including books, scores, and recordings; periodicals are part of main collection. Four archives; International Horn Society Archives; Cecil Leeson Archival Saxophone Collection; Tubist's Universal Brotherhood Association's Library of Tuba Music; and a small collection of early 20th century popular music.
Services/Access Information: Housed in the main library; open daily.

BUTLER UNIVERSITY
Fine Arts Library
4600 Sunset
Indianapolis, IN 46208
(317) 283-9243
Contact: Phyllis J. Schoonover, Fine Arts Librarian
Music Collection/Holdings: Books and periodicals covering art, dance, drama, all facets of music and radio/television; classical repertory scores; sheet music for solo voice, individual instruments and small ensembles; vocal scores of operas and Broadway shows; choral music; recordings of classical, jazz, show tunes, and plays, poetry, and other spoken material.
Services/Access Information: Open to public; check-out privileges limited to students and faculty; interlibrary loan.

GOSHEN COLLEGE
1700 S. Main St.
Goshen, IN 46526
(219) 533-3161
Contact: Linda S. Richer, Associate Librarian
Music Collection/Holdings: General music collection supporting undergraduate program; J.D. Hartzler Collection of early American music, including hymnals, singing school books, tunebooks (1700-1920).

INDIANAPOLIS-MARION COUNTY PUBLIC LIBRARY
Arts Division
40 E. St. Clair St.
Indianapolis, IN 46204
(317) 269-1700
Contact: Daniel Gann, Head

INDIANA UNIVERSITY
Music Library
Sycamore Hall
Bloomington, IN 47405
(812) 335-2970
Contact: David Fenske, Head Music Librarian
Music Collection/Holdings: 46,000 books and bound periodicals; 65,000 scores; 12,000 microforms; 195,000 orchestral and choral performance parts; 35,000 records; and 38,000 reels of tape. Special collections: Willi Apel Collection of early keyboard music in photoreproduction; The Jussi Bjoerling Memorial Archive of sound recordings; and Robert Orchard Collection of opera recordings.
Services/Access Information: Circulation to students and faculty, state residents, and other qualified users. Open daily during the school term; closed school and major national holidays. Reference; interlibrary loan; and photocopying.

INDIANA UNIVERSITY AT SOUTH BEND
Library
1700 Mishawaka Ave.
PO Box 7111
South Bend, IN 46634
(219) 237-4440
Contact: James L. Mullins, Director of Library Services
Music Collection/Holdings: Basic collection supporting undergraduate program.

MUNCIE PUBLIC LIBRARY
Audio-Visual Center
200 E. Main St.
Muncie, IN 47305
(317) 288-1411
Contact: Patricia Schaefer, Assistant Library Director and Audio-Visual Librarian
Music Collection/Holdings: Reference collection; 1,500 scores; over 10,000 records; 600 audiocassettes; and sheet music.
Services/Access Information: Except for reference materials, all materials are loaned to patrons; interlibrary loan.

SAINT MARY'S COLLEGE[1]
Music Seminar Room
Notre Dame, IN 46556
(219) 284-4186
Contact: Sr. Rita Claire Lyons, Music Librarian

TAYLOR UNIVERSITY
Music Library
Upland, IN 46989
(317) 998-2751
Contact: Yetive Williams
Music Collection/Holdings: Approximately 2,185 recordings and 100 cassette tape recordings; over 1,000 scores in the Music Library and a large collection of scores in the Ayers Taylor University Library
Services/Access Information: Listening facilities in the Music Building; open 6 days a week.

UNIVERSITY OF EVANSVILLE
Music Library
PO Box 329
Evansville, IN 47702
(812) 479-2888
Contact: Betsy Hine, Music Librarian
Music Collection/Holdings: Sound recordings—records, reel-to-reel, tapes, cassettes; and scores.
Services/Access Information: Sound recordings for class and faculty use; scores circulate to students and faculty. No interlibrary loan.

UNIVERSITY OF NOTRE DAME
Memorial Library
Notre Dame, IN 46556
(219) 239-6257
Contact: Joseph H. Huebner, Fine Arts Bibliographer
Music Collection/Holdings: Score collection; monographs and serials; sound recordings held in Audio Learning Center. Current music journals are kept in separate Periodical Center. In process of building a collection of music manuscripts on microfilm.

VALPARAISO UNIVERSITY
Moellering Library
Valparaiso, IN 46383
(219) 464-5364
Contact: William Beermann, Music Librarian
Music Collection/Holdings: Sound recordings: 4,000 discs, 450 tapes of campus performances by faculty and student ensembles, scores and books: 5,265 scores; 4,263 books.
Services/Access Information: Listening facilities; sound recordings circulate to students and faculty of university.

IOWA

COE COLLEGE
Fisher Music Library
1220 1st Ave., N.E.
Cedar Rapids, IA 52402
(319) 399-8651
Contact: Richard C. Adkins, Fisher Music Library Supervisor
Music Collection/Holdings: 2,500 scores; over 4,000-33rpm records, periodicals; R.L. Moehlmann rental library (band transcriptions); George Rider collection of 78rpm records;

memorabilia of Frederick Schauwecker.
Services/Access Information: OCLC access. Records do not circulate; listening facilities. Address Moehlmann rental library requests to Music Librarian.

PUBLIC LIBRARY OF DES MOINES
Fine Arts Department
100 Locust St.
Des Moines, IA 50309
(515) 283-4267
Contact: Stephen R. Brogden, Head; Martha Gersten Berger, Music Librarian
Music Collection/Holdings: 14,000 recordings; 25,000 pieces of sheet music; and 6,200 scores.
Services/Access Information: Piano available for public use; listening facilities.

UNIVERSITY OF IOWA
Rita Benton Music Library
2000 MB
Iowa City, IA 52242
(319) 353-3797
Contact: Kathleen A. Haefliger, Acting Head
Music Collection/Holdings: Research and performance collection of 60,000 bound volumes; 2,300 reels of microfilm; over 12,500 recordings on disc or tapes; microfiche and microcards. Bound volumes include scores; books on musical subjects; periodicals; dissertations; chamber music parts; and monographic and serial publications including most major research journals and current music magazine titles; large reference collection. Rare Books Room contains 18th and 19th century treatises and chamber music.
Services/Access Information: Reference services on request; listening facilities; microfiche and microfilm readers. Accessed by a dictionary catalog of over 350 drawers.

KANSAS

BETHEL COLLEGE
Gustav Dunkelberger Memorial Music Library
Fine Arts Center
North Newton, KS 67117
(316) 283-2500, x281
Contact: Professor Shirley King
Music Collection/Holdings: Major holdings, especially piano scores, miniature study scores, and 78rpm records, donated by the estate of Gustave Dunkelberger. Extensive piano scores; approximately 1,500-33⅓ rpm and 1,000-78rpm records.
Services/Access Information: Main function is research; collection does not circulate. Piano, organ, and vocal scores may be checked out for 2 weeks; records, reference materials, and hard-bound score collections for use within the music library only.

EMPORIA STATE UNIVERSITY
William Allen White Library
1200 Commercial
Emporia, KS 66801
(316) 343-1200, x205
Contact: Barbara Robins, Head, Reference Department
Music Collection/Holdings: Published monumenta and collected works; single performing pieces for solo instruments; musical show and popular song anthologies.

KANSAS STATE UNIVERSITY
Farrell Library
Manhattan, KS 66506
(913) 532-6516
Contact: Paula Elliot, Reference Librarian/Performing Arts Specialist
Music Collection/Holdings: General collection includes: 5,000 scores; 6,500 books on history and criticism and 2,275 on music education; several Denkmaler editions, and numerous sets of complete works. Special collections houses about 300 scores and 755 additional volumes on music history and instruction, 19th and early 20th century imprints, notably early American hymnals. Audiovisual department holds 7,883 records and has special collections of 1,682-78rpm records, 4,602 scores, and 421 reel-to-reel tapes.
Services/Access Information: Borrowing by faculty, staff, students, and other cardholders (non-University card available on request); special collection does not circulate. Audiovisual department houses extensive listening facilities; reproduces recordings for educational use; and maintains a reserve collection for course-related listening.

UNIVERSITY OF KANSAS
Thomas Gorton Music Library
Lawrence, KS 66045
(913) 864-3496
Contact: Earl Gates, Music Librarian
Music Collection/Holdings: Over 34,000 books and scores; over 270 microfilms, 4,260 microcards, 340 microfiches; 46,000 records; 800 phonotapes; 425 cylinders. Sound recordings include three major archival collections: James E. Seaver Opera Collection; Robert L. Platzman Opera Collection; and Dick Wright Jazz Collection.
Services/Access Information: Catalog access to books, scores, and sound recordings; computerized serial holdings on microfiche; photocopy service. Open daily.

WICHITA PUBLIC LIBRARY
Art and Music Division
223 S. Main St.
Wichita, KS 67202
(316) 262-0611
Contact: Leonard Messineo, Division Head; Darlene E. Fawver, Music Librarian
Music Collection/Holdings: 25,000 books; 18,000 sound recordings; 1,000 scores; 100 audiocassettes; 1,300 framed prints and art objects. Also contains Joan O'Bryant Folklore Collection; Mr. & Mrs. Samuel H. Marcus Performing Arts Handbill Collection; and Alice Bauman American Dance Symposia Collection.
Services/Access Information: Utilized DataPhase's Automated Library Information System (ALIS). Division sponsors ongoing concert series. Open daily.

WICHITA STATE UNIVERSITY
Lieurance Music Library
1845 Fairmont St.
Wichita, KS 67208
(316) 689-3029
Contact: David Austin, Music Librarian
Music Collection/Holdings: 10,000 scores, parts, performance editions, research editions; 12,000 sound recordings. Specialized reference collection; Thurlow Lieurance archives.
Services/Access Information: Open to public. Material loaned to qualified borrowers; interlibrary loan. Open weekdays.

KENTUCKY

CUMBERLAND COLLEGE
Hagan Memorial Library
821 Walnut St.
Williamsburg, KY 40769
(606) 549-2200, x324
Contact: Robert Williams, Head Librarian; Ann Brigham, Music Specialist
Music Collection/Holdings: 10,050 volumes of scores, books, and reference materials; 55 boxes of loose sheet music; 77 periodical titles; 2,500 records; 1,000 microfiche. Main library houses 25,000 music-related books and 200 music-related periodicals.
Services/Access Information: Lockheed and DIALOG data bases; Southeastern Library Network; 11 microcomputers with music capability for student/faculty use.

EASTERN KENTUCKY UNIVERSITY
Foster Music Building
Richmond, KY 40475
(606) 622-4944
Contact: Elizabeth K. Baker, Music Librarian
Music Collection/Holdings: 14,000 books and scores; 6,900 recordings; 65 music periodical subscriptions, 500 bound volumes; 500 reels of microfilm, mostly periodicals. Large collection of jazz recordings and books.
Services/Access Information: Reference services; listening facilities for non-

circulating records and tapes; recordings loaned to faculty and graduate students only. Photocopying; interlibrary loan.

LOUISVILLE ACADEMY OF MUSIC[1]
Music Library
2740 Frankfort Ave.
Louisville, KY 40206
(502) 893-7885
Contact: Robert French, President

SOUTHERN BAPTIST THEOLOGICAL SEMINARY
Music Library
James P. Boyce Centennial Library
2825 Lexington Rd.
Louisville, KY 40280
(502) 897-4713, x556
Contact: Martha C. Powell, Music Librarian and Adjunct Professor of Music
Music Collection/Holdings: 15,000 volumes of books; 34,000 volumes of scores and sheet music; 3,500 titles of anthems in multiple copies and 15,000 single copies of anthems; 11,000 phonodiscs and tapes. Strong holdings in church music: hymnals; cantatas; and oratorios.
Services/Access Information: Open 6 days a week.

UNIVERSITY OF KENTUCKY
Music Library
116 Fine Arts Building
Lexington, KY 40506-0022
(606) 257-2800
Contact: Cathy S. Hunt, Music Librarian
Music Collection/Holdings: Over 40,000 books and scores; 5,600 microforms; and 10,400 records and tapes; current periodical subscriptions of over 217 titles. Emphasis on the history, literature, theory, and performance of Western art music; holds strong collection of historical sets, collected editions and monumenta. Special collections: Alfred Cortot collection of early music treatises; collection of recordings and books about Appalachian music housed in M.I. King Library.
Services/Access Information: Individual tours and instruction upon request; taping service for School of Music faculty; acquisitions lists updated biweekly; photocopier. On-line search of RILM Abstracts; other databases available in King library reference department.

UNIVERSITY OF LOUISVILLE
Dwight Anderson Memorial Music Library
School of Music
2301 S. Third St.
Louisville, KY 40292
(502) 588-5659
Contact: Marion Korda, Professor of Bibliography and Librarian, School of Music
Music Collection/Holdings: 50,000 titles and 20,000 uncatalogued items; definitive editions of major composers, historical sets, and microtext materials; expanded audio facilities house combined sound-recording collection of 13,000 items. Performance collections, important reference materials, and automated serials data support research and study programs. A special collection documents music in Kentucky, Kentucky composers, and Louisville imprints as represented in early American sheet music.

LOUISIANA

CENTENARY COLLEGE OF LOUISIANA
Hurley School of Music
Music Library
Shreveport, LA 71134-0188
(318) 869-5235
Contact: Carolyn Garison, Music LIbrarian
Music Collection/Holdings: Approximately 3,000 scores and 4,000 discs supporting academic programs. Books and periodicals housed in the main library (Magale Library).
Services/Access Information: Scores may be checked out by students and faculty; recordings by faculty only; reference services.

DILLARD UNIVERSITY
Will W. Alexander Library
2601 Gentilly Blvd.
New Orleans, LA 70122
(504) 283-8822, x300
Music Collection/Holdings: 1,500 records; 2,100 volumes.
Services/Access Information: Open daily.

LOUISIANA STATE UNIVERSITY
Listening Rooms, Troy H. Middleton Library
Baton Rouge, LA 70803-3321
(504) 388-2900
Contact: Glenn Walden, Listening Rooms Library Assistant
Music Collection/Holdings: Approximately 10,000 items primarily related to classical music; also historical popular music, soundtracks, native Louisiana music (cajun, jazz, spiritual), and spoken-word recordings.
Services/Access Information: Collection does not circulate.

LOYOLA UNIVERSITY, NEW ORLEANS
Music Library
6363 St. Charles Ave.
New Orleans, LA 70118
(504) 865-2774
Contact: Laura Dankner, Assistant Professor/Music Librarian
Music Collection/Holdings: Scores; sound recordings; books on music; periodicals; microfilm and microfiche.
Services/Access Information: Serves University community, particularly, students and faculty of School of Music, but New Orleans residents welcome. Bibliographic instruction; on-line data base searches; listening facilities.

NEW ORLEANS BAPTIST THEOLOGICAL SEMINARY
Martin Music Library
4110 Seminary Pl.
New Orleans, LA 70126
(504) 282-4455, x289
Contact: Douglas G. Broome, Music Librarian
Music Collection/Holdings: 16,000 volumes, concentrating on liturgical and hymnological works; 3,000-volume hymnal collection, nearly 600 rare; oldest holdings from 17th century. Also included are current or popular church music publications. Listening library holds 3,400 sound recordings.
Services/Access Information: Media center includes an operating radio station; audiovisual, video recording and broadcasting equipment. Microfilm access to many primary source documents; listening facilities; member OCLC network.

NEW ORLEANS PUBLIC LIBRARY
Art, Music and Recreation Division
219 Loyola Ave.
New Orleans, LA 70140
(504) 586-7382, x40
Contact: Marilyn Wilkins, Head
Music Collection/Holdings: Over 20,000 records; music-related books; sheet music, single sheets, bound scores, miniature scores, and a historical early New Orleans collection; Fischer Collection of early acoustical records.
Services/Access Information: Audiovisual services include cassettes, 8mm films, extensive picture file, 100 videocassettes of feature films; 500 framed art prints. All materials circulate. Open 5 days a week; closed Sunday and Monday.

SOCIETY FOR COMMISSIONING NEW MUSIC[1]
Music Library
Box 19390-A, University Station
Baton Rouge, LA 70893
Contact: William Blackwell, Music Librarian

SOUTHEASTERN LOUISIANA UNIVERSITY[1]
Music Department Library
Hammond, LA 70402
(504) 549-2234
Contact: F. Landon Greaves, Jr., Head Librarian

TULANE UNIVERSITY
Maxwell Music Library
New Orleans, LA 70118
(504) 865-5642
Contact: Liselotte Andersson, Music Librarian
Music Collection/Holdings: Books and periodical literature on music; historical and national monumenta of music; music scores; dissertations and master theses in music; discs and tapes.
Services/Access Information: Generally open stacks for book materials; reference section; reference and assistance desk; listening facilities.

TULANE UNIVERSITY OF LOUISIANA[1]
Hogan Jazz Archive
Howard-Tilton Memorial Library
New Orleans, LA 70118
(504) 865-6634
Contact: Richard B. Allen, Curator

UNIVERSITY OF NEW ORLEANS
The Listening Room
Earl K. Long Library
New Orleans, LA 70148
(504) 286-6544
Contact: Charles A. Gholz, Head, The Listening Room
Music Collection/Holdings: 20,000 records; 100 reel-to-reel tapes; a small number of cassettes.
Services/Access Information: Collection does not circulate; for use in the Listening Room only.

MAINE

UNIVERSITY OF MAINE AT ORONO
Raymond H. Fogler Library
Orono, ME 04469
(207) 581-1661
Music Collection/Holdings: Primarily classical collection emphasizes music history, performance, and music education; a record and tape collection; performance editions for various instrumental combinations and solo instruments.
Services/Access Information: Open daily. Books circulate on interlibrary loan 4 weeks; records do not circulate; performance editions circulated to campus community only.

MARYLAND

CLARINETWORK INTERNATIONAL PERFORMANCE LIBRARY
13316 Bayberry Dr.
Germantown, MD 20767
(301) 972-4180
Contact: Dr. Cecil Gold, Director
Music Collection/Holdings: Solo works for clarinet. In process of gathering research materials concerning clarinet performance.
Services/Access Information: For further information, contact the Director at the above address.

ENOCH PRATT FREE LIBRARY
Fine Arts and Recreation Department
400 Cathedral St.
Baltimore, MD 21201
(301) 396-5490
Contact: Joan Stahl, Head
Music Collection/Holdings: Large collection of books, scores, recordings representing all musical periods. Collection more popular than academic. Special files and collections. Large collection of popular sheet music; song index to songbook collections.
Services/Access Information: Books, scores, recordings circulate.

MARYLAND HISTORICAL SOCIETY
201 W. Monument St.
Baltimore, MD 21201
(301) 685-3750
Music Collection/Holdings: Books, magazines, clippings; manuscript materials; sheet music; photographs relevant to the history of music and music performance in Maryland, especially in the City of Baltimore.
Services/Access Information: Open Tuesday through Saturday; daily admission fee, reader's ticket.

MONTGOMERY COUNTY DEPARTMENT OF PUBLIC LIBRARIES
18330 Montgomery Village Ave.
Gaithersburg, MD 20879
(301) 840-2515
Contact: Luvia Morin Zusi
Music Collection/Holdings: Specializing in the fine and performing arts, music holdings consist of circulating books and non-circulating references; records; libretti, scores, and sheet music; and 1,000 classical compositions on microfiche Musicache.

PEABODY INSTITUTE OF THE JOHNS HOPKINS UNIVERSITY
Peabody Conservatory Library
21 E. Mt. Vernon Pl.
Baltimore, MD 21202
(301) 659-8154
Contact: Edwin A. Quist, Librarian
Music Collection/Holdings: Approximately 75,000 books, scores and sound recordings; strong in performing editions of classical and romantic music and general music literature. Special collections include manuscripts of Peabody and Baltimore composers; a rare book collection strong in 19th century operas and chamber music; and the Barringer Collection of 78rpm jazz recordings.
Services/Access Information: Open daily during academic year. Study facilities open to the public; interlibrary loan available through the Maryland Interlibrary Loan Organization and the Research Libraries Group.

UNIVERSITY OF MARYLAND AT COLLEGE PARK (IPAM)
International Piano Archives at Marland Music Library/Hornbake Library
College Park, MD 20742
(301) 454-6479
Contact: Neil Ratliff, Fine Arts Librarian and Head of the Music Library
Music Collection/Holdings: The Piano Archives contain a unique collection of materials relating to keyboard performance and literature: 7,650-78rpm and 6,200-33⅓rpm records; 2,300 reproducing piano rolls; 4,000 scores; 1,100 tapes; and assorted files of musical iconography, manuscripts, and clippings relating to pianists. Archives are housed in the Music Library.
Services/Access Information: Open to qualified scholars by appointment.

UNIVERSITY OF MARYLAND AT COLLEGE PARK[1]
Music Room
College Park, MD 20742
(301) 454-3036
Contact: Frederic A. Heutte, Fine Arts Librarian

MASSACHUSETTS

AMERICAN ANTIQUARIAN SOCIETY
185 Salisbury St.
Worcester, MA 01609
(617) 755-5221
Contact: Georgia Brady Bumgardner, Curator of Graphic Arts
Music Collection/Holdings: Sheet music printed in America before 1880; collections of songsters, hymnals, tunebooks, ballads, and sound recordings of 18th and 19th century American music.
Services/Access Information: Open weekdays to adults working on research projects; graduate students should write in advance.

AMERICAN JEWISH HISTORICAL SOCIETY
2 Thornton Rd.
Waltham, MA 02154
(617) 891-8110
Contact: Nathan M. Kaganoff, Librarian
Music Collection/Holdings: Large collection of published works on Jews and Jewish music in America includes the papers of Abraham Ellstein, Walter Hart Blumenthal, and Molly Picon, each having extensive collections of music. Several thousand items of published American Yiddish sheet music, much of it from the American Yiddish theater.
Services/Access Information: Open weekdays to serious researchers; photocopying.

AMHERST COLLEGE
Vincent Morgan Library
Amherst, MA 01002
(413) 542-2387

Contact: Sally Evans, Music Librarian
Music Collection/Holdings: Books, scores, and sound recordings supporting undergraduate liberal arts program

BERKLEE COLLEGE OF MUSIC
Library
1140 Boylston St.
Boston, MA 02215
(617) 266-1400, x258
Contact: John Voigt, Librarian
Music Collection/Holdings: Core collection of 14,000 scores and 6,000 recordings; extensive jazz and popular music, including jazz and popular music texts and jazz recordings; 16,000 books in music and the humanities.
Services/Access Information: Limited access to those outside the Berklee community; contact for more information.

BERKSHIRE ATHENAEUM
Music and Arts Department
1 Wendell Ave.
Pittsfield, MA 01201
(414) 442-1559
Contact: Mary Ann Knight, Department Head
Music Collection/Holdings: 14,000 recordings; 3,000 scores; 8,000 books; 1,000 tapes; and 2,000 mounted art prints.
Services/Access Information: Monthly year-round exhibits; free music programs. Listening facilities; reference services.

THE BOSTON CONSERVATORY
Albert Alphin Music Library
8 The Fenway
Boston, MA 02215
(617) 536-6340, x291
Contact: Cathy Balshone Becze, Head Librarian
Music Collection/Holdings: 30,000 volumes of books and scores with parts; 7,000 records, audiotapes, videotapes, and filmstrips; 76 periodical titles. Subject areas: music performance, music education, opera, musical theatre, music history, music as related to dance and theatre, performing arts collection.

BOSTON PUBLIC LIBRARY
Music Department
Copley Square
Boston, MA 02117
(617) 536-5400, x285
Contact: Mrs. Ruth M. Bleecker, Curator of Music
Music Collection/Holdings: More than 100,000 volumes representing every facet of music study; includes collected editions, many first editions and rare items; reference collection; thousands of scores, librettos, and sets of chamber music parts; more than 400 current periodicals; seven special collections. A retrospective collection of 200,000 recordings is presently being developed.
Services/Access Information: Open 6 days a week. Special collections are restricted to scholars; letters outlining specific needs are appreciated. Books and recordings circulate; expanded listening facilities under construction.

BOSTON UNIVERSITY
Music Library (Mugar Memorial Library)
771 Commonwealth Ave.
Boston, MA 02215
(617) 353-3705
Contact: Frank Gramenz, Head, Music Library
Music Collection/Holdings: Particularly strong in materials relating to the history of music theory. The Byzantine research materials of Egon Wellesz have been incorporated into the library's general collection. The Music Library serves as the Archive for the performance tapes of the Boston Symphony Orchestra; includes the Arthur Fiedler Reading Room, which houses Fiedler's books, scores, and his collection of recordings.
Services/Access Information: Open to members of the Greater Boston Library Consortium and the Boston Area Music Libraries (BAML). Letters of introduction are requested for others who need to consult materials.

BRANDEIS UNIVERSITY
Farber Library, Creative Arts Department
Waltham, MA 02254
(617) 647-2524
Contact: Robert L. Evensen, Creative Arts Librarian
Music Collection/Holdings: Approximately 15,000 books; 13,500 scores; 15,000 sound recordings; extensive, 4,200 piece microform collection. Subject strengths: Medieval and Renaissance music; H. Schutz; Wagner; and history of opera.
Services/Access Information: Most material available on interlibrary loan or for use within the library; microforms and sound recordings do not circulate.

FITCHBURG PUBLIC LIBRARY
Wallace Library
610 Main St.
Fitchburg, MA 01420
(617) 343-3096
Contact: Suzanne L. Moulton, Music Librarian/Performing Arts Coordinator
Music Collection/Holdings: 1,600 circulating monographs; 171 non-circulating reference items; 1,200 scores; 5,500 records; and 250 audiocassette tapes. A number of scores remain from the recently dismantled Francis H. Jenks Collection of 19th century musical scores; other scores include vocal, opera, and piano music with emphasis on European music; Handel Collected Works (Chrysander).
Services/Access Information: All items circulate except references; photocopying. Open 6 days a week.

FORBES LIBRARY
Art and Music Department
20 West St.
Northampton, MA 01060
(413) 586-0489
Contact: Angela M. Sciotti, Art and Music Librarian
Music Collection/Holdings: 5,000 music books; 25,000 scores and sheet music; 6,000 records and cassette tapes; strong in 19th century American hymn books and singing schools.
Services/Access Information: Open 6 days a week. All material circulates except reference books and pre-1920 imprints; interlibrary loan.

HARVARD MUSICAL ASSOCIATION
Library
57 E. Chestnut St.
Boston, MA 02108
(617) 523-2897
Contact: Barbara Winchester, Music Librarian

HARVARD UNIVERSITY
Eda Kuhn Loeb Music Library
Music Building
Cambridge, MA 02138
(617) 495-2794
Contact: Michael Ochs, Librarian
Music Collection/Holdings: Over 94,000 scores and books on music and musicology; 29,000 recordings; 14,000 microfilms; and 625 subscriptions to journals and other serials. Special collections include the Isham Memorial Library of rare materials and microfilms of early music prints and manuscripts.
Services/Access Information: Library use requires a letter of introduction; fee for extended use. Interlibrary loan

HARVARD UNIVERSITY
Hilles Library (Morse Music Collection)
59 Shepard St.
Cambridge, MA 02138
(617) 495-8730
Contact: Stephan B. Fuller, Music Librarian
Music Collection/Holdings: Undergraduate music collection of books, scores, and sound recordings.
Services/Access Information: Open to students and faculty only.

LONGY SCHOOL OF MUSIC
Longy School of Music Library
1 Follen St.
Cambridge, MA 02138
(617) 876-0956
Contact: Gail Hennig, Librarian
Music Collection/Holdings: Supports the curriculum of small, private music

school emphasizing performance. Includes books, scores, and recordings; principal strengths are performing scores of vocal, instrumental, and chamber music. Archival collections on Georges Longy; Nadia Boulanger; and the early history of the school.
Services/Access Information: Visitors with identification and references approved by the library may use the collection on a restricted basis.

MASSACHUSETTS INSTITUTE OF TECHNOLOGY
Music Library
14E-109
Cambridge, MA 02139
(607) 253-5689
Contact: Linda I. Solow, Music Librarian
Music Collection/Holdings: 10,000 books and periodicals; 20,000 scores and parts; 14,000 recordings. Circulating collection: books and periodicals on music history and theory; opera librettos; printed music through the 20th century. Non-circulating: collected editions and monumenta; sound recordings, except a small number of cassettes. Special collections: facsimilies of composers' manuscripts; MIT composers' scores and recordings; also jazz and ethnic folk recordings, Broadway show scores and recordings.
Services/Access Information: Borrowing of circulating collection limited to MIT community; limited room access to outsiders; member of Boston Library Consortium and Boston Area Music Libraries. Reference service weekdays. Listening facilities: records, reel-to-reel tapes, cassette; no audio copying.

NEW ENGLAND CONSERVATORY OF MUSIC[1]
Firestone Audio Library
290 Huntington Ave.
Boston, MA 02115
(617) 262-1120
Contact: Geraldine Ostrove, Music Librarian

NORTHEASTERN UNIVERSITY
Dodge Library
360 Huntington Ave.
Boston, MA 02115
(617) 437-2458
Contact: Vivian A. Rosenberg, Music Librarian
Music Collection/Holdings: Extensive collection of reference and circulating books includes scholarly encyclopedias and popular songbooks; scores; and music periodicals.
Services/Access Information: Reference service provided for students; card catalog lists recordings, books, and scores.

RELIGIOUS ARTS GUILD
Affiliate of the Unitarian Universalist Association
Loan Library of Anthems
25 Beacon St.
Boston, MA 02108
(617) 742-2100
Contact: Barbara M. Hutchins, Executive Secretary
Music Collection/Holdings: Over 300 anthems, 15 copies of each.
Services/Access Information: Loan catalog.

ROBBINS LIBRARY (PUBLIC)
Art & Music Department
700 Massachusetts Ave.
Arlington, MA 02174
(617) 643-0026
Contact: Larry Domingues, Art & Music Librarian
Music Collection/Holdings: References and circulating books; over 6,000 records, classical, jazz, popular, folk, and spoken-word; over 300 cassette tapes; 200 music scores; and over 100 libretti; song index of popular songs on record.
Services/Access Information: Materials circulate to all state residents. Information and reference services; sponsors local concerts.

SMITH COLLEGE[1]
Werner Josten Library
Northampton, MA 01063
(413) 584-2700
Contact: Mary Ankudowich, Music Librarian

SPRINGFIELD CITY LIBRARY
Art & Music Department
220 State St.
Springfield, MA 01103
(413) 739-3871
Contact: Sylvia A. St. Amand, Music Librarian
Music Collection/Holdings: 4,500 books; 10,000 scores; 15,000 records; 1,000 spoken-word recordings on cassette; 70 microfilms; 2,000-piece popular sheet music collection.
Services/Access Information: Open to cardholders from other communities and universities for study, listening, and loan purposes.

TUFTS UNIVERSITY
Music Laboratory and Wessell Library
Medford, MA 02155
(617) 381-3594
Contact: Brenda Chasen Goldman, Associate Librarian, Music
Music Collection/Holdings: Strengths in theory and composition; history and literature of western music; ethnomusicology; performance; and for general music needs of the Tufts community. Special collections: Ritter Collection of approximately 2,000 books and scores of the 16th through 19th centuries; including music dictionaries, histories, theoretical treatises, hymnals, operas. Asa Alford Tufts Collection of songbooks and sheet music, primarily Boston imprints of the 19th century.
Services/Access Information: Open to adults and students of any university for reference, study, and listening purposes, except during examination periods. Borrowing by cardholding members of Greater Boston Consortium of Academic and Research Libraries only; interlibrary loan. Rare books and reference books do not circulate.

UNIVERSITY OF LOWELL, SOUTH CAMPUS[1]
Daniel H. O'Leary Library
Wilder St.
Lowell, MA 01854
(617) 452-5000
Contact: Charles R. Meehan, Director

UNIVERSITY OF MASSACHUSETTS/AMHERST
Music Library
Fine Arts Center 149
Amherst, MA 01003
(413) 545-2879
Contact: Pamela Juengling, Music Librarian
Music Collection/Holdings: Books, scores, journals, sound recordings. Special collections: Howard Lebow; Philip Bezanson; Alma Werfel Mahler.
Services/Access Information: Open to state residents for listening and study; valid ID/library card required for borrowing; interlibrary loan; reference assistance; photocopier, listening facilities. Open daily.

WCRB LIBRARY
Charles River Broadcasting, Inc.
750 South St.
Waltham, MA 02154
(617) 893-7080
Contact: George C. Brown, Music Director; Louise Boyce, Record Librarian
Music Collection/Holdings: Over 35,000 classical music discs; tapes of live concerts, including new digital tapes and CD-4 Compact Discs (digital discs).
Services/Access Information: Not a lending library; otherwise open to public during regular business hours.

WELLESLEY COLLEGE
Music Library
Wellesley, MA 02181
(617) 235-0320, x2075
Contact: Mary Wallace Davidson, Music Librarian
Music Collection/Holdings: Academic collection of 18,000 volumes and 11,000 sound recordings, based primarily on Western art music curriculum.
Services/Access Information: Open to members of the college community; to

members of Boston Area Music Libraries and Boston Library Consortium, upon presentation of a letter from another (public or academic) librarian; to others by prior arrangement. Interlibrary loan. Open daily during school session.

WHEATON COLLEGE
Music Library
Norton, MA 02766
(617) 285-7722, x436, 529
Contact: Kersti Tannberg, Fine Arts Librarian
Music Collection/Holdings: 4,004 volumes, including periodicals; 4,786 scores; and 6,957 sound recordings, including 2,775-78rpm records.
Services/Access Information: Open to public for study and listening. Interlibrary loan. Periodicals, references, multivolume sets, and fragile items do not circulate; recordings circulate to college community only. Open daily; closed January and summer.

WORCESTER PUBLIC LIBRARY
Salem Square
Worcester, MA 01608
(617) 799-1655
Contact: Alan M. Catalano
Music Collection/Holdings: Books and scores; chamber music parts; song folios; sheet music; records and cassettes.
Services/Access Information: Telephone reference service; interlibrary loan.

MICHIGAN

ANDREWS UNIVERSITY
Music Materials Center
Music Department
University Station
Berrien Springs, MI 49104
(616) 471-3114
Contact: Mrs. Elaine L. Waller, Music Materials Librarian
Music Collection/Holdings: Supports graduate and undergraduate program emphasizing Wester European music. Adjunct to the collection of historical, critical, and biographical books in the main library (James White Library). Contains numerous composers' complete works; several monumenta, the old and *New Grove;* reference books; scores; and sound recordings.
Services/Access Information: Loaning limited to on-campus and room use. Exceptions are referred to the librarian.

DETROIT PUBLIC LIBRARY
Music & Performing Arts Department
5201 Woodward Ave.
Detroit, MI 48202
(313) 833-1460
Contact: Agatha Pfeiffer Kalkanis, Chief of Department
Music Collection/Holdings: 20,000 book titles; 77,000 scores; 17,000 popular sheet music titles; 25,000 recordings; and 250 periodicals; files documenting local musical and theatrical events. Special collections: E. Azalia Hackley Collection of materials relating to Blacks in the perfomring arts; and the Michigan Collection of books, musical scores, and recordings by members of Michigan associations in the performing arts.
Services/Access Information: Interlibrary loan. Open daily.

DETROIT SYMPHONY ORCHESTRA[1]
Music Library
Ford Auditorium
20 Auditorium Dr.
Detroit, MI 48226
(313) 961-0700
Contact: Albert P. Steger, Music Librarian

EASTERN MICHIGAN UNIVERSITY
University Libary
Ypsilanti, MI 48197
(313) 487-2288
Contact: Professor Fred Blum, Reference Librarian
Music Collection/Holdings: Approximately 10,000 scores and 9,600 books about music housed in main library building; 130 music periodicals. Audio and video materials located in the Instructional Support Center in the same building.
Services/Access Information: Interlibrary loan and other standard services.

FLINT PUBLIC LIBRARY
Art, Music & Drama Department
1026 E. Kearsley St.
Flint, MI 48506
(313) 232-7111, x213
Contact: James Kangas, Head
Music Collection/Holdings: 41,000 volume general collection, 22% of which are music books and scores; 12,000 sound recordings; 2,400 pieces of sheet music; 410 anthem titles, periodicals, librettos, and so forth.
Services/Access Information: Reference service; listening facilities. Music Index.

THE GUILD OF CARILLONNEURS IN NORTH AMERICA
Archives
900 Burton Tower
University of Michigan
Ann Arbor, MI 48109
(313) 764-2539
Contact: William De Turk, Archivist
Music Collection/Holdings: Carillon music: manuscripts; published music; books; tapes and records; journals; and artifacts.

HOPE COLLEGE
Music Library
Holland, MI 49423
(616) 392-5111
Contact: Diane E. Murray, Technical Services Librarian & Music Library; Dorothy Pearson, Music Library Clerk
Music Collection/Holdings: Scores; books; and recordings supporting undergraduate program; small reference collection; approximately 30 periodical titles with backfiles.
Services/Access Information: Recordings circulate to faculty only; books and scores circulate to faculty, students, and registered guests.

INTERLOCHEN CENTER FOR THE ARTS
Music Library
Interlochen, MI 49643
(616) 276-9221, x257
Contact: E. Delmer Weliver, Director
Music Collection/Holdings: Houses the performance materials used by the National Music Camp and the Interlochen Arts Academy; includes works for orchestra, band, choir, chamber and solo performance of all levels of difficulty.

MICHIGAN STATE UNIVERSITY[1]
G. Robert Vincent Voice Library
Main Library Building, W433-W437
East Lansing, MI 48824
(517) 335-5122
Contact: Roseann Hammill, Music Librarian

OAKLAND UNIVERSITY
Performing Arts Library
Instructional Technology Center
Rochester, MI 48063
(313) 377-3020
Contact: Robert Burns, Manager
Music Collection/Holdings: Library holdings related to dance, theater, film and music consist of 8,500 scores; 7,500 books; 7,000 records; and 4,000 reel-to-reel and cassette tapes.
Services/Access Information: Serves faculty, staff, and students. Access through the OCLC system; Interlibrary loan requests should be addressed to Kresge Library, same address as above.

THE UNIVERSITY OF MICHIGAN
Music Library
3239 Moore Bldg.
Ann Arbor, MI 48109
(313) 764-2512
Contact: Peggy E. Daub, Head
Music Collection/Holdings: Approximately 70,000 volumes of books and scores; 16,000 recordings; 2,000 microfilms/microfiche.
Services/Access Information: Open year-round; reference, reproduction services.

WESTERN MICHIGAN UNIVERSITY
Harper C. Maybee Music & Dance Library

3008 Dorothy U. Dalton Center
Kalamazoo, MI 49008
(616) 383-1817
Contact: Gregory Fitzgerald, Music Librarian
Music Collection/Holdings: 11,000 books and periodicals; 12,000 scores; 10,000 recordings, classical and jazz.
Services/Access Information: Interlibrary loan.

MINNESOTA

COLLEGE OF SAINT BENEDICT
Music Library
Benedicta Arts Center
ST. Joseph, MN 56374
(612) 363-5684
Contact: Theresa Kasling, Music Librarian
Music Collection/Holdings: Sound recordings; scores; select reference collection; limited number of general music literature and theory books.
Services/Access Information: Individual and group listening facilities.

MANKATO STATE UNIVERSITY
Music Library
Performing Arts Center
Mankato, MN 56001
(507) 389-1325
Contact: Kiyo Suyematsu, Music Librarian
Music Collection/Holdings: 4,500 volumes of books on music; 9,000 scores; 7,000 records; 550 recital tapes; 200 bound master's theses; 250 reels of microfilm, 300 microfiche cards; 1,000-piece Musicache microfiche library of complete scores of standard literature; 100 periodical titles; school song series books; and other curricular materials.
Services/Access Information: Access through main library computer catalog. Services include music reference; maintenance of reserve books/records and tapes; taping of student and faculty recitals; maintenance of tape file of concerts and recitals; provisions of listening facilities for students and faculty; interlibrary loan and MINITEX through the main library.

MINNEAPOLIS PUBLIC LIBRARY
Art, Music and Films Department
300 Nicollet Mall
Minneapolis, MN 55401
(612) 372-6520
Contact: Marlea R. Warren, Department Head
Music Collection/Holdings: Extensive holdings of scores and books on all aspects of music.
Services/Access Information: Reference; circulation.

MINNESOTA ORCHESTRA
1111 Nicollet Mall
Minneapolis, MN 55403
(612) 371-5622
Contact: James N. Berdahl, Librarian
Music Collection/Holdings: Orchestral music and scores.
Services/Access Information: No public access or services.

ST. CATHERINE COLLEGE[1]
Performing Arts Library
2004 Randolph Ave.
St. Paul, MN 55105
(612) 690-6696
Contact: Donald Bemis Jones, Music Librarian

ST. OLAF COLLEGE
Halvorsen Music Library
Northfield, MN 55057
(507) 663-3209
Contact: Beth Christensen, Music and Reference Librarian
Music Collection/Holdings: Houses all music scores and sound recordings: 15,000 books and scores; 6,000 sound recordings. Choral music collection housed in Music Library is operated by the music department.
Services/Access Information: Bibliographic instruction; self-guided tours; information sheets available; card catalog access. Open daily.

ST. PAUL PUBLIC LIBRARY
Art and Music Department
90 W. Fourth St.
St. Paul, MN 55102
(612) 292-6186
Contact: Delores Sundbye, Supervisor
Music Collection/Holdings: 440 reference books; 1,800 books on music history and biography; 1,500 books of music instruction; 2,700 pieces of piano music and piano anthologies; 900 opera and music review scores and libretti; 750 miniature orchestral scores; 3,500 works of choral, solo, and instrumental music; 6,000 pieces of old-time popular sheet music; 7,000 records; 300 cassettes, popular and classical.
Services/Access Information: All anthologies are indexed; files for all uncatalogued music; easy song access. Photocopying service by mail with prepayment; interlibrary loan.

UNIVERSITY OF MINNESOTA LIBRARIES
Performing Arts Archives
826 Berry St.
St. Paul, MN 55114
(612) 376-7271
Music Collection/Holdings: Alan K. Lathrop, Curator
Music Collection/Holdings: Minnesota Orchestra scrapbooks, correspondence, minutes, photos, and publications from 1909; St. Paul Opera Association scrapbooks, minutes, photos, and publications from 1933-1975; St. Paul Philharmonic Society correspondence, contracts, minutes, and reports, publicity, financial information from 1960-1970.
Services/Access Information: Reference service by mail or phone; limited copying services. Contact curator for information about restrictions on use of these collections.

MISSISSIPPI

BLUE MOUNTAIN COLLEGE
Music Library
Blue Mountain, MS 38610
(601) 685-5711

UNIVERSITY OF MISSISSIPPI
Music Library
209 Meek Hall
University, MS 38677
(601) 232-5904
Contact: Beth Bartlett, Senior Library Assistant
Music Collection/Holdings: 6,000 bound volumes, including collected sets, scores, instructional and study materials; 4,500 records; minor collection of cassette and reel-to-reel tapes, sheet music, microfiche, and filmstrips.
Services/Access Information: Books, records, and cassettes circulate; listening and taping facilities; OCLC interlibrary loan.

MISSOURI

KANSAS CITY PUBLIC LIBRARY
Art & Music Department
311 E. 12th St.
Kansas City, MO 64106
(816) 221-2685
Contact: Carol Wallace, Music Subject Specialist
Music Collection/Holdings: Books on music literature, history, and historical and popular biography; study scores; performing scores for solo instruments, ensemble combinations, and full orchestras; collections of popular and folk songs; vocal music for soloists and choirs; complete works, historical sets, collected editions, and monumenta. Record collection: classical,folk, jazz, and some popular music.
Services/Access Information: Borrowing by library cardholders for 3 weeks; reference materials do not circulate.

ST. LOUIS CONSERVATORY & SCHOOLS FOR THE ARTS
Mae M. Whitaker Library
560 Trinity
St. Louis, MO 63130
(314) 863-3033
Contact: Marion Sherman, Librarian
Music Collection/Holdings: 8,879 volumes of books and music; 5,097 records and tapes; 106 volumes of bound periodicals; 13 sets of complete

works on microfiche. Special collections: Thomas B. Sherman Collection; Robert Orchard Opera Collection.
Services/Access Information: Interlibrary loan.

ST. LOUIS PUBLIC LIBRARY
Music Room
1301 Olive St.
St. Louis, MO 63103
(314) 241-2288
Contact: Mary Lou Allen, Librarian
Music Collection/Holdings: Music recordings of solo instruments, ensembles, chamber music, vocal, art songs, operas, musicals and popular songs; nonmusical recordings of documentaries, drama, literature, languages; children's records and cassettes; music scores, including complete works; 4,600 music-related books.
Services/Access Information: Indexes to music subjects; listening facilities. Noonday recorded stereo concerts in Lucas Park.

SOUTHWEST MISSOURI STATE UNIVERSITY
Music Materials Library, Music Department
Ellis Hall
901 S. National
Springfield, MO 65802
(417) 836-5434
Contact: Mary E. Coward, Music Materials Librarian
Music Collection/Holdings: Recordings; tapes; opera, study, piano and solo vocal scores; choral, orchestral, and band music.
Services/Access Information: Listening lab serves 66 students at a time.

UNIVERSITY CITY PUBLIC LIBRARY
6701 Delmar
University City, MO 63130
(314) 727-3150
Contact: Robert L. Miller, Librarian

UNIVERSITY OF MISSOURI-COLUMBIA
Music Library
4D32 Elmer Ellis Library
Columbia, MO 65201
(314) 882-7634
Contact: Marcia Reed, Art, Archaeology and Music Librarian
Music Collection/Holdings: Focuses on the needs of faculty and students in music history, education and performance; stresses historical sets, monumenta, collected editions, and study scores, rather than performing editions with parts. Music Library housed within the main library; Music Library contains the Recorded Sound Collection, whose holdings include materials on classical music, jazz, folk, and spoken-word, mostly on discs, and several hundred tapes.
Services/Access Information: Reference service and the Recorded Sound Collection open weekdays; books and microfilms available during all regular library hours.

UNIVERSITY OF MISSOURI-KANSAS CITY[1]
Conservatory of Music Library
4420 Warwick Blvd.
Kansas City, MO 64111
(816) 276-2745
Contact: Jack L. Ralston, Music Librarian

WASHINGTON UNIVERSITY
Gaylord Music Library
6500 Forsyth Blvd.
St. Louis, MO 63130
(314) 889-5560
Music Collection/Holdings: Basic and research collections of books on music history and theory, periodicals; complete editions of major composers' works, monumenta, study and playing scores, chamber music with instrumental parts, and octavo choral music; recordings, tapes, and microforms. Special collections: rare books and scores; the Ernst C. Krohn Musicological Library; extensive sheet music collection; other archival materials.
Services/Access Information: Materials are available to outside researchers for use within the library. Interlibrary loan; holdings from 1974 in the OCLC data base.

NEBRASKA

CONCORDIA COLLEGE
Link Library
800 N. Columbia
Seward, NE 68434
(402) 643-3651, x7255
Contact: Marjorie Meier, Associate Professor of Music
Music Collection/Holdings: 2,300 books; 3,000 scores; 4,400 records; and 70 tapes and filmstrips.
Services/Access Information: Music reference titles shelved in the reference section of main library. Students may check out any non-reserved material; individual and group listening facilities.

LINCOLN CITY LIBRARIES
Polley Music Library
14th and N Sts.
Lincoln, NE 68508
(402) 435-2146, x219
Contact: Carolyn Dow, Music Librarian
Music Collection/Holdings: Books; periodicals; scores; performing editions of solo instrumental and vocal music; sets of performance parts for chamber music; uncatalogued collections of sheet music for popular songs with emphasis on 1900-1930 and historical vocal music. 5,700 volumes in the catalogued collections; about 10,000 additional uncatalogued items.
Services/Access Information: All materials may be used in-house without charge. Residents of Lancaster County get free library card; nonresidents must pay $30 per year for a library card. Circulating items available through interlibrary loan at no charge; photocopying service for fee.

UNIVERSITY OF NEBRASKA-LINCOLN
Music Library
30 Westbrook Music Bldg.
Lincoln, NE 68588-0101
(402) 472-6300
Contact: Susan R. Messerli, Music Llbrarian
Music Collection/Holdings: Approximately 27,000 books, microforms, and scores; 8,000 sound recordings; 139 periodical subscription titles. Core collection consists of major bibliographic titles; collected editions and complete works; bound periodicals; and important biographical works and treatises.
Services/Access Information: Recordings do not circulate. Listening facilities; microfilm and microfiche readers; photocopier; reference and information assistance; interlibrary loan. Open daily.

NEW HAMPSHIRE

DARTMOUTH COLLEGE
Paddock Music Library
H.B. 6187
Hopkins Center
Hanover, NH 03755
(802) 646-3234
Contact: Particia Butler Fisken, Music Librarian
Music Collection/Holdings: 11,500 records; 500 cassette tapes; 9,000 scores; 2,000 monographs and bound journals. Main library (Baker Library) houses 6,000 scores and 18,000 music-related monographs and majority of bound periodicals. 20,000 pieces of sheet music in Special Collections.
Services/Access Information: Borrowing by students, faculty and staff; sound recordings do not circulate outside the library; references and current periodicals do not circulate. References and computer searches; interlibrary loan; photocopying; listening facilities and practice room.

MANCHESTER CITY LIBRARY
Carpenter Memorial Bldg.
405 Pine St.
Manchester, NH 03104
(603) 625-6485
Contact: Theresa Snow Toy, Art and Music Librarian
Music Collection/Holdings: Books; recordings; scores; sheet music;

libretti, popular and standard repertoire.
Services/Access Information: Books accessed through state library union catalog and on-site catalog; separate catalog for recordings.

PLYMOUTH STATE COLLEGE
Herbert H. Lamson Library
Plymouth, NH 03264
(603) 536-1550
Music Collection/Holdings: 5,000 books; 3,000 scores; 35 periodical titles and indexes; over 4,000 recordings; 275-volume reference collection; 50 audio tapes and 50 sound filmstrips. Includes children's literature and recordings.
Services/Access Information: All but reference books and recordings circulate; listening facilities. Open daily.

NEW JERSEY

FREE PUBLIC LIBRARY OF ELIZABETH
11 S. Broad St.
Elizabeth, NJ 07202
(201) 354-6060
Contact: Mrs. Doris Fichtelberg, Music Librarian
Music Collection/Holdings: Music score collection: 2,250 titles of art songs, folk songs, operettas, musical theatre, oratorios, hymns, and single instrument instruction books; 5,000 single sheet music; 300 titles in miniature score collection. Books on all aspects of music study; basic musical and spoken-word record collection.
Services/Access Information: Scores used primarily by music students, teachers, organizations, professional and semi-professional performers, and other music lovers. Patrons may borrow 4 records for 2 weeks; interlibrary loan.

GLASSBORO STATE COLLEGE
Music Branch Library 615
Wilson Bldg.
Glassboro, NJ 08028
(609) 445-7306
Contact: Marjorie Travaline, Librarian
Music Collection/Holdings: 11,000 scores; 5,500 records.
Services/Access Information: Collection supports undergraduate program concentrating in performance and music education.
Services/Access Information: Member OCLC network.

NEWARK PUBLIC LIBRARY
Music Division
5 Washington St.
Newark, NJ 07101
(201) 733-7761
Contact: William J. Dane, Supervisor, Art & Music Department
Music Collection/Holdings: Extensive collections covering all periods of music history. Scores; music literature; periodicals; vertical files. Special collections: John Tasker Howard manuscript material; Schaaf Music manuscripts; song sheets; and historic sheet music.
Services/Access Information: Photocopying and reference service; listening facilities.

PATERSON FREE PUBLIC LIBRARY
AV/Music Department
250 Broadway
Paterson, NJ 07501
(201) 881-7038
Contact: Helen A. Kupferle, Reference Librarian
Music Collection/Holdings: 8,585 records; 600 books; 200 scores; some cassettes and slides.
Services/Access Information: Listening facilities.

PRINCETON UNIVERSITY[1]
Music Collection
Firestone Library
Princeton, NJ 08540
(609) 452-3230
Contact: Paula Morgan, Music Librarian

PRINCETON UNIVERSITY[1]
Phonograph Record Library
Woolworth Center of Musical Studies
Princeton, NJ 08540
(609) 452-4251
Contact: Ida Rosen, Record Librarian

RUTGERS UNIVERSITY
Institute of Jazz Studies
135 Bradley Hall
Newark, NJ 07102
(201) 648-5595
Contact: Edward Berger, Curator
Music Collection/Holdings: 60,000 sound recordings; 3,000 books; and periodicals on jazz and related musics; sheet music; piano rolls; memorabilia; research files on musicians of all eras. Special projects: NEA-sponsored Jazz Oral Histories comprising over 100 interviews; NEH-sponsored computerized catalog of recordings. Publishes periodicals and monographs on jazz, record series.
Services/Access Information: Open to the public by appointment. Materials do not circulate; copying out-of-print materials permitted within copyright restrictions.

RUTGERS UNIVERSITY
Music Library
Mabel Smith Douglass Library
New Brunswick, NJ 08903
(201) 932-9783
Contact: Jan R. Cody, Music Librarian
Music Collection/Holdings: Emphasis on musicology and composition; includes 30,000 volumes of scores, monographs, and periodicals; 10,000 recordings; and microfilms.
Services/Access Information: Full dictionary catalog; photocopiers and microfilm readers; listening facilities. Open daily during school session.

TRENTON FREE PUBLIC LIBRARY
Art and Music Department
Box 2448
120 Academy St.
Trenton, NJ 08607
(609) 392-7188
Contact: Alice F. Fullam, Head
Music Collection/Holdings: 420 scores; 480 music reference books; 1,820 books; 36 music periodicals; 3,100 records; 500 orchestral parts and scores; 250 opera libretti; 5 file drawers of choral music; large music-related picture collection; music catalog and vertical files. Music collection includes dance materials. Arts Management Collections from New Jersey State Council on the Arts.
Services/Access Information: Orchestras may borrow scores; library members may also borrow scores, books, records, pictures, and pamphlets. Reference service; interlibrary loan.

WESTMINSTER CHOIR COLLEGE[1]
Talbott Music Library
Princeton, NJ 08540
(609) 921-3658
Contact: John Peck, Music Librarian

NEW MEXICO

UNIVERSITY OF NEW MEXICO
Fine Arts Library
Fine Arts Center
Albuquerque, NM 87131
(505) 277-2357
Contact: James B. Wright, Head
Music Collection/Holdings: Fine Arts collection contains over 90,000 items including books; periodicals; microforms; sound recordings; music scores; exhibition catalogs; and works on photography, art, and music. Extensive music collection features scores; 20,000 non-circulating records and tapes; scholarly editions and collections of music literature; monographs; and periodicals. Classical, jazz, and folk music are emphasized.

NEW YORK

AMERICAN ACADEMY AND INSTITUTE OF ARTS AND LETTERS LIBRARY[1]
633 W. 155th St.
New York, NY 10032
(212) 368-5900
Contact: Hortense Zera, Music Librarian

AMERICAN MUSIC CENTER[1]
Music Library
250 W. 57th St.
New York, NY 10019
(212) 265-8190
Contact: Karen M. Famera, Music Librarian

ANTIQUE PHONOGRAPH MONTHLY
APM Library of Recorded Sound
502 E. 17th St.
Brooklyn, NY 11226
(212) 941-6835
Contact: Robert Feinstein, Archivist; Allen Koenigsberg, Director
Music Collection/Holdings: Over 5,000 cylinder recordings, dating from 1892 to 1929; 75 antique phonographs to play these records; patent files on 2,000 inventions pertaining to the history of recorded sound; facsimile publications of original company and dealers' manuals, posters and catalogs. Current research projects include discographies of early singers, political figures, vaudeville artists, and others.
Services/Access Information: Publishes newsletter, *Antique Phonograph Monthly;* list of publications in monograph series available on request. Maintains own typesetting/interface service.

BARUCH COLLEGE
Music Library
17 Lexington Ave.
New York, NY 10010
(212) 725-3268
Contact: George R. Hill, Associate Professor of Music
Music Collection/Holdings: 6,000-item collection of scores and recordings to support undergraduate program. Books on music housed in the main library.
Services/Access Information: By previous arrangement.

BRONX COMMUNITY COLLEGE
Music Library
W. 181st & University Ave.
Bronx, NY 10453
(212) 220-6095
Contact: Estelle Kissel, Director
Music Collection/Holdings: Collection of classical, ethnic, popular, and jazz records; orchestral scores and parts; miniature scores; piano-vocal scores; libretti; piano collection; choral collection; ear training and sight singing instruction tapes; filmstrips.
Services/Access Information: Open weekdays. Services students with listening material and study aids.

BROOKLYN COLLEGE OF THE CITY UNIVERSITY OF NEW YORK
Music Library
417 Gershwin Hall
Brooklyn, NY 11210
(212) 780-5289
Contact: Diette Baily, Head
Music Collection/Holdings: Books, scores, recordings, periodicals, microfilm supporting the undergraduate and graduate programs of the Conservatory of Music; emphasis on American music; musicological festschrift; and unpublished musicological translations.
Services/Access Information: Call for further information.

BROOKLYN PUBLIC LIBRARY
Art/Music Division
Grand Army Plaza
Brooklyn, NY 11238
(212) 780-7784
Contact: Sue H. Sharma, Division Chief
Music Collection/Holdings: 20,000 books on all areas of music, reference and circulating; 50,000 scores, reference and circulating; 3,500-piece collection of popular songs, reference; 700 sets of scores and parts for full symphony orchestra. Phonograph records and tapes housed in separate Audio/Visual Division.
Services/Access Information: Open daily. Photocopier.

BUFFALO AND ERIE COUNTY PUBLIC LIBRARY
Music Department
Lafayette Square
Buffalo, NY 14203
(716) 856-7525
Contact: Norma Jean Lamb, Head
Music Collection/Holdings: Approximately 74,000 books and scores; 67,000 records and tapes; 160 periodical titles; and 2,400 orchestral sets; Strong in musical Americana, including 78,600 pieces of sheet music and 657 bound volumes of music dating from the 1790's; tunebooks, hymnals, songsters, and broadsides.
Services/Access Information: All circulating materials except sheet music are on open stacks. Listening facilities; photocopying; microform readers.

BUREAU OF JEWISH EDUCATION[1]
Community Library
2600 N. Forest Rd.
West Amherst, NY 14228
(716) 686-8844
Contact: Abraham F. Yanover, Executive Director

THE CITY COLLEGE OF CITY UNIVERSITY OF NEW YORK
Music Library
138th St. & Covent Ave.
New York, NY 10031
(212) 690-4174
Contact: Melva Peterson, Chief, Music Library
Music Collection/Holdings: Approximately 7,700 books; 13,450 scores; 10,770 records; 350 tapes; 600 microforms; 60 periodical subscriptions and 100 other serials.
Services/Access Information: Open to public; borrowing priviliges limited to students, faculty, and staff; books and scores, but not recordings, available thorugh interlibrary loan, with certain restrictions. Listening facilities; photocopying. Open weekdays.

COLGATE UNIVERSITY
Music Library
Dana Arts Center
Hamilton, NY 13346
(315) 824-1800
Contact: M. Cheng, Chair
Music Collection/Holdings: Basic collection of classical music from 15th through 20th centuries; large collection of recordings of organ music.

COLUMBIA UNIVERSITY
Music Library
701 Dodge
Broadway & 116th St.
New York, NY 10027
(212) 280-4711
Contact: Thomas T. Watkins, Librarian
Music Collection/Holdings: Music scores, literature and recordings supporting undergraduate programs; research materials for instruction and study in the field of historical musicology, ethnomusicology, theory, and composition.

COMPOSERS AND CHOREOGRAPHERS THEATRE, INC.[1]
Master Tape Library
25 W. 19th St.
New York, NY 10011
(212) 989-2230
Contact: John Watts, President

CORNELL UNIVERSITY
Music Library
225 Lincoln Hall
Ithaca, NY 14853
(607) 256-4011/7216
Contact: Lenore Coral, Music Librarian and Senior Lecturer
Music Collection/Holdings: Strong research collection, notable microfilm holdings of 16th through 18th century sources, including Baroque opera libretti; Vaughn Williams' manuscripts. Especially strong in opera and 20th century music.

DAEMEN COLLEGE
Marian Library
4380 Main St.
Amherst, NY 14226
(716) 839-3600, x243
Contact: Glenn V. Woike, Head Librarian
Music Collection/Holdings: Books and journals; scores; records.

EASTMAN SCHOOL OF MUSIC
Sibley Music Library

University of Rochester
Rochester, NY 14604
(716) 275-3046
Contact: Prof. Ruth Watanabe, Librarian
Music Collection/Holdings: Particularly rich in research materials pertaining to the theory and history of music form the Middle Ages to the present, including original editions of treatises, related books about music, and music scores. Also included as the library's specialties are: opera scores; chamber music scores and performing parts; scores, books, periodicals, and recordings on American music and music by American composers from the Colonial times to the present; complete runs of periodicals. Also maintains a collection of autographed manuscripts and letters.
Services/Access Information: Reference service by letter, telephone, or in person. Microprint service for library materials in the public domain; interlibrary loan; rare-book services to qualified research scholars.

FIVE TOWNS COLLEGE LIBRARY
21 Seaford Ave.
Seaford, NY 11783
(516) 783-8800
Contact: Mildred Gardner, Director
Music Collection/Holdings: Strong collection of books, periodicals, and audiovisual material pertaining to the history and theory of jazz, rock, and popular music.
Services/Access Information: Open to public for use within library. Member Long Island Library Resources Council.

GALAXY MUSIC CORPORATION
131 W. 86th St.
New York, NY 10024
(212) 874-2100
Contact: Sallie Burrow, Orchestral Librarian/Rental Librarian
Music Collection/Holdings: Orchestra scores and parts; some rental material such as piano/vocal scores.
Services/Access Information: By telephone or mail. Rental of full sets of performing material and borrowers privileges to qualified conductors and librarians for perusal.

GRADUATE SCHOOL OF THE CITY UNIVERSITY OF NEW YORK
Music Collection
33 W. 42nd St.
New York, NY 10036
(212) 790-4541/4338
Contact: Prof. William Shank, Music Librarian
Music Collection/Holdings: Specialize in reference works; bibliography; thematic catalogues; iconography; monumenta and standard collections. Large collection of musical manuscripts on microfilm, principally medieval.
Services/Access Information: Serves primarily doctoral students and faculty; access to all City University of New York students and faculty. Courtesy access to others requiring use of the collections.

HARTWICK COLLEGE
Listening Center
222 Anderson
Oneonta, NY 13820
(607) 432-4200, x567
Contact: Rayna Baker, Music Librarian
Music Collection/Holdings: 4,000 recordings, primarily classical and jazz; 825 scores; basic music reference books and periodicals.
Services/Access Information: Collection does not circulate; short-term borrowing with librarian's permission.

HERBERT H. LEHMAN COLLEGE
Music and Fine Arts Division
Bedford Park Blvd., W.
Bronx, NY 10468
(212) 960-8830
Contact: Harold J. Diamond, Music and Fine Arts Librarian
Music Collection/Holdings: 10,000 volumes of scores and books on music, art, and dance; records and tapes of classical music support undergraduate program.
Services/Access Information: Open to students, faculty, and community. Open daily.

HEWLETT-WOODMERE PUBLIC LIBRARY
1125 Broadway
Hewlett, NY 11557
(516) 374-1967
Contact: Mrs. Lakshmi Kapoor, Senior Reference Librarian/Music Specialist
Music Collection/Holdings: 5,000 scores, including orchestral parts, choral parts, vocal and instrumental scores of both popular and classical music. Sheet music collection with titles dating from the early 20th century; musical monographs; 10,000 sound recording; multi-media kits; and music periodicals in bound volumes and/or microfilm.
Services/Access Information: Serves as a subject center in art and music for the Nassau Library System. Interlibrary loan for Nassau County residents through Nassau Library System, for non-residents through Long Island Library Resources Council.

INSTITUTE OF THE AMERICAN MUSICAL, INC.[1]
Music Library
220 W. 93rd St.
New York, NY 10025
(212) 787-1997
Contact: Miles M. Kreuger, Curator

ITHACA COLLEGE
Ithaca College Library
Ithaca, NY 14850
(607) 274-3887
Contact: Betty Birdsey, Music/Audio Librarian
Music Collection/Holdings: Supports undergraduate and graduate programs with 15,000 titles in scores, music-related books, and sound recordings.
Services/Access Information: Materials circulate to college personnel and holders of I.C. privilege cards. Anyone may use materials within the library; photocopying; no microfilming. Open daily during school session.

THE JUILLIARD SCHOOL
Lila Acheson Wallace Library
Lincoln Center
New York, NY 10023
(212) 799-5000, x265
Contact: Brinton Jackson, Librarian
Music Collection/Holdings: Music, dance, and drama books; scores; and recordings. Special collections of opera scores; 19th century chamber music.

MANHATTAN SCHOOL OF MUSIC
Frances Hall Ballard Library
120 Claremont Ave.
New York, NY 10027
(212) 749-2802, x511
Contact: Nina Davis-Millis, Librarian
Music Collection/Holdings: Collection emphasizes performance materials and music education. Approximately 55,000 scores; 20,000 recordings; 8,000 books; and 70 periodical subscriptions.
Services/Access Information: By special arrangement; please contact librarian.

MANHATTANVILLE COLLEGE
Library
Purchase, NY 10577
(914) 694-2200
Contact: Donna L. Nickerson, Cataloger/Special Collections Librarian
Music Collection/Holdings: Approximately 7,000 titles; 4,000 scores; and 80 periodical subscriptions, including serials and newspapers. Circulating collection includes scores and books; rare books include 35 scores (12 pre-1800 imprint) and 14 books; special collections include liturgical music of the Catholic Church (Gregorian chant, hymnals, songbooks, etc.). Sound recordings and listening equipment are located in the Music Department. Separate Music Reading Room house collected works and historical monumenta (Denkmaeler, Bach Gesellschaft, etc) and standard reference works.
Services/Access Information: Available during regular library house; some material available thorugh interlibrary loan.

MANNES COLLEGE OF MUSIC
The Harry Scherman Library
157 E. 74th St.
New York, NY 10021
(212) 737-0700
Contact: Barbara Railo, Head Librarian
Music Collection/Holdings: Performance collection of scores; books on music; and recordings.
Services/Access Information: Library for student and faculty use only; outside reference use upon request for specific materials.

MUNSON-WILLIAMS-PROCTOR INSTITUTE
Art Reference and Music Libraries
310 Genesee St.
Utica, NY 13501
(315) 797-0000, x69
Contact: Kim R. Wheatley, Music Library Assistant
Music Collection/Holdings: 5,500 records; 400 scores; a small collection of reference books.
Services/Access Information: Records circulate to members of the Institute; listening facility open to the public.

THE MUSICAL MUSEUM
Deansboro, NY 13328
(315) 841-8774
Contact: Arthur H. Sanders, Curator
Music Collection/Holdings: Large collection of automatic musical instruments, such as music boxes and grind organs, on display; and hundreds of pages of original data, original sales literature, and pamplets and books related to these units on file. Exhibit of early musical instruments from accordions to zithers, and descriptive information.
Services/Access Information: No public access, but will photocopy materials on request, depending on availability of staff time.

NEW YORK JAZZ MUSEUM[1]
Archives
125 W. 55th St.
New York, NY 10019
Contact: Douglas F. Gibbons, Music Librarian

NEW YORK PUBLIC LIBRARY[1]
Donnell Library Center, Record Library
20 W. 53rd St.
New York, NY 10019
(212) 790-6402
Contact: Margaret Pyle Greenhall, Supervisory Librarian

THE NEW YORK PUBLIC LIBRARY
Music Division
111 Amsterdam Ave.
New York, NY 10023
(212) 870-1650
Contact: Frank C. Campbell, Chief
Music Collection/Holdings: 350,000 books; 2,000,000 clips; 700 periodical subscriptions; 375,000 scores; 900,000 pieces of sheet music; and 6,250 microforms. Subject interests in: American music; theory; Beethoven's operas (19th century); autographed manuscripts of Western composers; fine prints; and opera scene designs.
Services/Access Information: Free access to those 18 years of age and older; telephone and mail reference service; photocopying; publicaitons series; published catalogs; cataloging in RLIN data base since 1972.

NEW YORK UNIVERSITY LIBRARY
E.H. Bobst Library
Washington Square S.
New York, NY 10012
(212) 598-3607
Contact: Ruth Hilton, Music Librarian

NUBIAN CONSERVATORY OF MUSIC
233 Winthrop St.
Brooklyn, NY 11225
(212) 773-1652
Contact: Ms. Eleanor Williams, Librarian
Music Collection/Holdings: In the process of building a library. Have complete works of Handel, some rare works by Black composers. Striving for unique collection of Black history books and music, and extensive research resources on the lives and music of Black composers.
Services/Access Information: For further information contact the librarian or E. Harrision Gordon, President

ONONDAGA COUNTY PUBLIC LIBRARY
Art and Music Department
535 Montgomery St.
Syracuse, NY 13202
(315) 473-4492
Music Collection/Holdings: 12,000 recordings; 1,000 cassettes; 2,000 monographs; 3,500 scores; 200 titles in sacred choral music collection, 25 to 30 copies each.
Services/Access Information: Loan period for records and cassettes, 1 week; for instrucitonal recordings, 3 weeks; for books and scores, 3 weeks; for choral music collection, 8 weeks.

OXFORD UNIVERSITY PRESS, INC.
Oxford Music Library
200 Madison Ave.
New York, NY 10016
(212) 679-7300
Music Collection/Holdings: All in-print and out-of-print music, books, and recordings published by all branches of the Oxford University Press.
Services/Access Information: Open weekdays by prior notification.

POLISH SINGERS ALLIANCE OF AMERICA
180 Second Ave.
New York, NY 10003
(212) 254-6642/(201) 997-8832
Contact: Walter Witkowicki, Librarian
Music Collection/Holdings: Polish sheet music for male, female, mixed, and children's choruses; some English songs; Polish operas; and orchestrations. Over 300 songs numbered 50,000 sheet music.
Services/Access Information: Supply own choruses with songs and offer help to other choruses and organizations.

QUEENSBOROUGH COMMUNITY COLLEGE LIBRARY
Music and Art Division
Springfield Blvd. & 56th Ave.
Bayside, NY 11364
(212) 631-6241, x6454
Music Collection/Holdings: General collection supporting undergraduate program consists of some 8,000 books and scores; over 3,000 records and tapes; and a pamphlet file.
Services/Access Information: For use by students, faculty, and the community. Listening Room with 36 stations and 5 booths.

QUEENS COLLEGE OF THE CITY UNIVERSITY OF NEW YORK
Music Library
65-30 Kissena Blvd.
Flushing, NY 11367
(212) 520-7345
Contact: Dr. Joseph Ponte, Acting Head
Music Collection/Holdings: 22,000 books on music; 27,000 scores; 11,600 sound recordings; 65,000 choral folios and instrumental parts; 330 periodical subscriptions; 8,400 microforms; and Karol Rathaus Archives.
Services/Access Information: Separate department microfilm and microcard readers; photocopying; dictionary catalog.

RADIO CITY MUSIC HALL PRODUCTIONS
Radio City Music Hall Archives
55 W. 50th St.
New York, NY 10020
(212) 246-4600, x310
Contact: Jaime Ramos, Coordinator of Archives
Music Collection/Holdings: 420 file drawers of manuscript music from every Radio City production since 1932. Popular song and stage band collections; published operatic and symphonic scores; reference books.
Services/Access Information: Answers all public and Radio City reference requests for musical information or historical material.

ROCHESTER PUBLIC LIBRARY[1]
Art and Music Division
115 South Ave.

Rochester, NY 14604
(716) 428-7332
Contact: Mary Lee Miller, Head Librarian

SCHUMANN MEMORIAL FOUNDATION, INC.[1]
2904 E. Lake Rd.
Livonia, NY 14487
(716) 346-2745
Contact: June M. Dickinson, President

STATE UNIVERSITY COLLEGE AT BUFFALO
E.H. Butler Library
1300 Elmwood Ave.
Buffalo, NY 14222
(716) 878-6313
Contact: Marjorie Lord, Senior Assistant Reference Librarian
Music Collection/Holdings: Medium-sized undergraduate library with a basic but substantial music collection of scores, literature, and records supporting liberal arts and education degrees programs.

STATE UNIVERSITY COLLEGE AT FREDONIA
Reed Library Music Section
Fredonia, NY 14063
(716) 673-3183
Contact: Joseph Chouinard, Senior Assistant Librarian for Music Service
Music Collection/Holdings: 10,321 books; 28,914 scores; 12,634 records and tapes; and 114 serial subscriptions.
Services/Access Information: Full reference services, including computerized bibliographic data base searches and interlibrary loan.

STATE UNIVERSITY COLLEGE AT GENESEO
Milne Library
Geneseo, NY 14454
(716) 245-5591
Contact: Richard C. Quick, Director of Libraries
Music Collection/Holdings: 6,500 books and scores, including reference books on music, and instructional materials; 700 music recordings and 1,200 non-music recordings for general browsing. Departmental library housed in Brodie Fine Arts Building contains 2,400 scores and 6,000 recordings supporting undergraduate program.
Services/Access Information: Open to public; most materials circulate, except recordings from the Brodie Collection. Open daily during school session.

STATE UNIVERSITY COLLEGE AT POTSDAM
Crane Music Library
Potsdam, NY 13676
(315) 267-2451
Contact: Sally Skyrm, Music Librarian
Music Collection/Holdings: 11,000 books; 1,650 bound periodical volumes; 20,000 scores; 12,000 recordings; 130 journal and other serial subscriptions.
Services/Access Information: Interlibrary loan; photocopying. Open to public for reference.

STATE UNIVERSITY OF NEW YORK AT ALBANY
Music Department Library
1400 Washington Ave.
PAC 306
Albany, NY 12222
(518) 457-4788
Contact: Nancy J. Smith, Music Librarian
Music Collection/Holdings: Reference books, texts, scores, chamber music, recordings, and periodicals supplementing the curriculum and assisting campus performing organizations. Extensive collection of classical recordings for listening, plus a representation of jazz, sitar, African, and electronic music.
Services/Access Information: Primarily for use of faculty and students. The University community is extended listening privileges; reference assistance.

STATE UNIVERSITY OF NEW YORK AT BINGHAMTON[1]
William Mitchell Music Library
Fine Arts Library
Vestal Parkway E.
Binghamton, NY 13901
(607) 798-4927
Contact: Philip Conole, Music Librarian

STATE UNIVERSITY OF NEW YORK AT BUFFALO
Music Library
Baird Hall
Amherst, NY 14260
(716) 636-2923
Contact: James Coover, Director
Music Collection/Holdings: 30,000 books and journals; 45,000 scores and parts; 25,000 records; 7,000 microforms; and 2,000 slides. Strengths are new music; historical musicology; ethnomusicology; jazz; opera; bibliography; primary sources in the history of music librarianship; Archives of the Center of the Creative and Performing Arts and the Evenings for New Music; song literature; music iconography; posters.
Services/Access Information: Open 6 days a week; closed Saturday. Interlibrary loan through main University Libraries; member RLG; automated record catalogue, 1982-. Microcard reader; microfilm and microfiche readers/printers.

STATE UNIVERSITY OF NEW YORK AT STONY BROOK
Music Library
W-2510 Library
Stony Brook, NY 11794
(516) 246-5660
Contact: Judith Kaufman, Head, Music Library
Music Collection/Holdings: 42,000 books and scores; 16,000 sound recordings; 5,500 microforms; primarily Western classical, but some jazz and popular music.
Services/Access Information: Open daily. Audio Center has 85 listening carrels.

NORTH CAROLINA

APPALACHIAN STATE UNIVERSITY
Music Library
Boone, NC 28608
(704) 262-2186, x263
Contact: Joan O. Falconer, Associate Professor and Music Librarian
Music Collection/Holdings: 11,500 volumes of scores and parts; 6,600 discs and prerecorded cassettes; and 1,700 basic reference books and instrumental methods and studies; most music-related books housed in main library (Belk Library).
Services/Access Information: Recorded materials for library use only, but circulate to Music Department faculty for 1 week and to other faculty for 24 hours. Music and non-reference books from the Music Library may be checked out by university students and faculty, but normally not loaned to persons not connected with this institution. Music books housed in the main library may be checked out by local residents; persons from other state institutions; and through interlibrary loan.

BREVARD COLLEGE[1]
Music Library
Brevard, NC 28712
(704) 883-8292
Contact: Laura McDowell, Music Librarian

CHOWAN COLLEGE
Music Library, Daniel Fine Arts Building
Murfreesboro, NC 27855
(919) 398-4104, x236
Contact: Dr. James M. Chamblee, Chairman, Department of Fine Arts
Music Collection/Holdings: Over 2,000 sound recordings; 600 musical scores; 1,300 music-related books and periodicals housed in main library (Whitaker Library).
Services/Access Information: Recordings do not circulate; for use only in Music Library listening facilities or in class; scores and books may be checked out.

DUKE UNIVERSITY[1]
Music Library
6695 College Station
Durham, NC 27708
(919) 684-6449
Contact: Louis Auld, Music Librarian

EAST CAROLINA UNIVERSITY
Music Library
Greenville, NC 27834
(919) 757-6250
Contact: Geraldine Laudati, Music Librarian
Music Collection/Holdings: 30,000 books, scores, sound recordings, and journals devoted to music; concentrated holdings in music education, music therapy, and performance materials. Large collection of microforms; strong reference collection; and band music on disc. United States depository items pertaining to music include materials for blind and physically challenged.
Services/Access Information: Borrowning privileges granted by main library (J.Y. Joyner Library). Listening facilities; microform readers/printers; photocopying. Reference services include telephone referral; data base searches; interlibrary loan. Open daily.

GREENSBORO COLLEGE
James Addison Jones Library
815 W. Market St.
Greensboro, NC 27401-1875
(919) 272-7102
Music Collection/Holdings: Over 1,000 records and scores of classical recordings.
Services/Access Information: Open to students, faculty, and staff of the college and Friends of the Library. Listening facilities; videotape equipment.

MORAVIAN MUSIC FOUNDATION, INC.[1]
Music Library
20 Cascade Ave.
Winston-Salem, NC 27108
(919) 725-0651
Contact: Karl Kroeger, Director

NORTH CAROLINA CENTRAL UNIVERSITY
Fine Arts Library, Music Department
PO Box 19845
Durham, NC 27707
(919) 683-6220
Contact: Gene W. Leonardi, Fine Arts Librarian
Music Collection/Holdings: Small general collection serving music department of 60 majors, faculty, and the general college community: 3,000 books; 3,500 scores; and 4,500 records.
Services/Access Information: Open weekdays. Small listening facility; records do not circulate, except for classroom use. Interlibrary loan through main library.

NORTH CAROLINA WESLEYAN COLLEGE
Music Library, Department of Music
Room 189, Pearsall Classroom Bldg.
Rocky Mount, NC 27801
(919) 442-7121
Contact: William G. Sasser, Director
Music Collection/Holdings: 8,000 scores for piano, organ, winds, and strings, operatic, vocal, choral, chamber, and orchestral; 11,000 recordings, including a large number of rare 78rpm records; The Lawrence Wingate Brown Memorial Collection of 800 items, mostly recordings of vocal music.
Services/Access Information: Open 6 days a week; closed Saturdays.

ST. ANDREW'S PRESBYTERIAN COLLEGE[1]
Music Library
Laurinburg, NC 28352
(919) 276-3652
Contact: Helen Rogers, Music Librarian

UNIVERSITY OF NORTH CAROLINA AT CHAPEL HILL[1]
Music Library
Chapel Hill, NC 27514
(919) 933-1030
Contact: Margaret Lospiniuso, Music Librarian

UNIVERSITY OF NORTH CAROLINA AT GREENSBORO[1]
Jackson Library Special Collections
Luigi Silva Collection
Greensboro, NC 27412
(919) 379-5246
Contact: Jean Lyle, Music Librarian

WARREN WILSON COLLEGE
Music Library
Swannanoa, NC 28753
(704) 298-3325
Contact: Lora Scott, Instructor
Music Collection/Holdings: 2,500 records, mostly classical; 4,000 scores; 175 reference books and the public school music series books; music journals, in print and on microfiche; file of old popular music; choral music reference file; piano pedagogy file; and 8-track tapes.
Services/Access Information: Scores may be checked out by students, faculty, and persons in the community for 8 weeks; records generally do not circulate; some music education materials circulate for only 1 week; microfiche reader. Open 48-57 hours a week.

OHIO

ANTIOCH COLLEGE
Olive Kettering Library
Yellow Springs, OH 45387
(513) 767-7331, x418
Contact: Joseph J. Cali, Associate Librarian
Music Collection/Holdings: 2,500 books; 1,400 scores; and 3,500 records.

ARCHIVE OF THE GUITAR FOUNDATION OF AMERICA
Music Library, Sullivant Hall
The Ohio State University
Columbus, OH 43210
(614) 422-2310
Contact: Thomas F. Heck, Archivist
Music Collection/Holdings: Special colelction of guitar music; periodicals; references and scores; and sound recordings, principally donated by members. Much of the music dates from the 19th century; available for photocopying at the Milwaukee repository and mail-order center.
Services/Access Information: Computerized catalog containing rare, out-of-print guitar music available to members of the FGA for nominal photocopying cost from George Lindquist, Associate Archivist, Wisconsin Conservatory of Music Library, 1584 N. Prospect Ave., Milwaukee, WI 53202. Open to non-members by appointment.

BALDWIN-WALLACE COLLEGE[1]
Riemenschneider Bach Institute
Merner-Pfeiffer Hall
49 Seminary St.
Berea, OH 44107
(216) 826-2207
Contact: Dr. Elinore Barber, Director, Bach Institute

BOWLING GREEN STATE UNIVERISTY
Music Library
Bowling Green, OH 43403
(419) 372-2307
Contact: Linda M. Fidler, Head; William L. Schurk, Sound Recordings Archivist
Music Collection/Holdings: 200,000 sound recordings, principally of popular music; books concerning all phases of music; score and research materials supporting graduate programs in music and popular culture.
Services/Access Information: Sound recordings do not circulate. Interlibrary loan; reference services provided by phone and mail. Open daily during school session.

CLEVELAND HEIGHTS-UNIVERSITY HEIGHTS PUBLIC LIBRARY
2345 Lee Rd.
Cleveland Heights, OH 44118
(216) 932-3600
Contact: Mrs. Helene Stern, Adult Services Assistant Librarian
Music Collection/Holdings: 1,525 books; 150 reference books; 420 uncatalogued libretti; 10,662 classical, popular, ethnomusicologial, and spoken-word recordings. Dance music collection donated by Cleveland Modern Dance Association housed in Lois C. Kenny Memorial Library.
Services/Access Information: OCLC and Cleveland Public Library data bases.

THE CLEVELAND INSTITUTE OF MUSIC
Music Library
11021 E. Blvd.
Cleveland, OH 44106
(216) 791-5165, x214
Contact: Karen K. Griffith, Director of the Library
Music Collection/Holdings: Performing editions of solo and chamber works; collected editions of major composer's works; orchestral scores and books; and music-related periodicals.
Services/Access Information: Circulating materials available to students and faculty of the Cleveland Institute of Music, the Music Department of Case Western Reserve University, and to other institutions through interlibrary loan; reference must be used within the library. Listening Room open to Institute and CWRU Music Department faculty and students only.

CLEVELAND MUSIC SCHOOL SETTLEMENT[1]
Kulas Library
11125 Magnolia St.
Cleveland, OH 44106
(216) 421-5809
Contact: Mary Louise Emery, Music Librarian

CLEVELAND PUBLIC LIBRARY
Fine Arts and Special Collections
325 Superior Ave.
Cleveland, OH 44114-1271
(216) 623-2848/49
Contact: Alice N. Loranth, Head
Music Collection/Holdings: 21,340 volumes, including 2,093 volumes of bound periodicals; 45,000 scores; 20,000 pieces of sheet music; 11,000 sound recordings; 233 music journal titles. Reference and circulating collections include world-wide bibliographic resources. Emphasis on building strong collection of study and vocal scores by classical and contemporary composers; included are 3,000 orchestrations; chamber music sets; and critical editions of collected and complete works of 50 composers; manuscript archives.
Services/Access Information: Indexes to pre-1975 songs, hymns, instrumental and organ music; to vertical files; and to current and historial materials. OCLC, OHIONET, and Cleveland Area Metropolitan Library Systems (CAMLS); interlibrary loan, out-of-state fee. Paid research service, "Facts-for-a-Fee"; prepay photocopying.

CUYAHOGA COUNTY PUBLIC LIBRARY
Mayfield Regional Library
6080 Wilson Mills Rd.
Cleveland, OH 44143
(216) 473-0350
Contact: Dr. Eric van der Schalie, Regional Subject Specialist
Music Collection/Holdings: Serves the general public but can support undergraduate course work. Contains 400 reference volumes; 3,000 general introductions, histories, methods, and biographies; 1,500 songbooks; 1,100 miniature scores; 7,500 records; 1,000 cassette tapes; and 60 periodical titles.
Services/Access Information: Open to public without restriction. Interlibrary loan through OCLC; borrowing at the Librarian's discretion; audiovisual items do not circulate.

HEBREW UNION COLLEGE
Jewish Institute of Religion Library
3101 Clifton Ave.
Cincinnati, OH 45220
(513) 221-1875
Contact: David J. Gilner, Public Services Librarian
Music Collection/Holdings: One of the world's most extensive collections of Jewish music: 12,000 volumes of books, scores, manuscripts, and liturgical materials; 3,500 records and 1,100 cassettes of Jewish secular and liturgical music. The Edward Birnbaum Collection contains a comprehensive series of manuscripts of 18th century Jewish songs; 19th century cantorial and synagogue music; and a partial thematic catalogue of European synagogue music, 1700-1900.
Services/Access Information: Printed music housed with main library collection. Borrowing of manuscripts, recordings, and special collections by application to the Public Services Librarian.

HIRAM COLLEGE
Teachout-Price Library
Geidlinger Listening Center
Hiram, OH 44234
(216) 569-5359
Contact: Marjorie Adams, Music Librarian
Music Collection/Holdings: The Geidlinger Music Center contains about 5,000 records and 2,000 scores. Music texts and reference materials are located in other parts of the library.
Services/Access Information: Serves faculty, staff, and students. Listening facilities for records and tapes; borrowing of some records and scores.

KENT STATE UNIVERSITY
Music Library
Music and Speech Bldg.
Kent, OH 44242
(216) 672-2004
Contact: Judith B. McCarron, Music Library Coordinator
Music Collection/Holdings: 14,560 books and bound periodicals; 99 periodical subscriptions; 18,850 scores; 10,000 pieces of sheet music; 9,800 volumes of choral music; 490 reels of microfilm; and 21,350 sound recordings.
Services/Access Information: All materials circulate except sound recordings. OCLC provides access to all holding except sheet music, choral music, and 2,000 of the sound recordings; choral music accessible through Choralist computer index.

MALONE COLLEGE
Everett L. Cattell Library
515 25th St., N.W.
Canton, OH 44709
(216) 489-0800, x482
Contact: Stanford Terhune, Director of Library Services
Music Collection/Holdings: 1,906 volumes of scores; 2,941 records; 1,967 books; 454 open-reel tapes.
Services/Access Information: Interlibrary loan available for books; scores circulate at college's discretion. No interlibrary loan for records or tapes.

MIAMI UNIVERSITY
Amos Music Library
120 Center for the Performing Arts
Oxford, OH 45056
(513) 529-2017
Contact: Edith Miller, Music Librarian
Music Collection/Holdings: 11,500 volumes of music; 10,000 books; 76 current periodical subscriptions; 81 monumenta and complete works standing orders; 14,000 sound recordings, including 30-year-old collection of jazz, blues, and folk music recordings. Microforms and special collections housed in library.
Services/Access Information: Interlibrary loan.

MOUNT UNION COLLEGE
Sturgeon Music Library
Cope Music Hall
Alliance, OH 44601
(216) 823-3206
Contact: Becky C. Thomas, Music Librarian
Music Collection/Holdings: General collection of scores, including early American and European organ, piano, ensemble and orchestral music, sacred vocal music, and folksongs; recordings of American and orchestral music, art songs, and operas; music education texts; histories and monographs; and periodicals. Special collections: local hymnals; Collegium Musicum Collection; Recorded Art Songs with index; the New World Recorded Anthology of American Music.
Services/Access Information: Open to music faculty and students; limited access to rest of College and surrounding community. Music publisher's catalogs and information on ordering music available.

OHIO STATE UNIVERSITY
Music/Dance Library
186 Sullivant Hall
1813 N. High St.
Columbus, OH 43210
(614) 422-2310
Contact: Dr. Thomas F. Heck, Head, Music/Dance Library, and Associate Professor of Music
Music Collection/Holdings: 70,000 musical scores and books; 24,000 sound recordings; recent doctoral dissertations in music history, music education, and music theory; research collections of American sheet music and 78rpm records. Special collections include the most complete sequence of microfilm copies of source materials from the Deutsches Musikgeschichtliches Archiv in North America; dance videotapes.
Services/Access Information: Research and reference assistance weekdays. Sound recordings are not available on interlibrary loan, but most books and scores are.

OHIO UNIVERSITY
Music/Dance Library
530 Music Bldg.
Athens, OH 45701
(614) 594-5733
Contact: Dan O. Clark, Music Bibliographer
Music Collection/Holdings: 20,000 books and scores; 10,000 recordings.
Services/Access Information: OCLC interlibrary loan.

OHIO WESLEYAN UNIVERSITY
Sanborn Music Library
Sanborn Hall
Delaware, OH 43015
(614) 369-4431, x700
Contact: Trudy D. Muegel, Music Librarian
Music Collection/Holdings: Books on music; recordings; reference scores; orchestra, band, choral, ensemble, and solo music for performance.
Services/Access Information: Available for faculty, staff, and students; and through interlibrary loan.

PUBLIC LIBRARY OF CINCINNATI AND HAMILTON COUNTY
Art and Music Department
800 Vine St., Library Square
Cincinnati, OH 45202-2071
(513) 369-6954/5
Contact: R. Jayne Craven, Department Head
Music Collection/Holdings: Over 22,000 books; and 24,000 catalogued scores. Special materials include libretto files; popular sheet music reference collection dating from the late 1790's; circulating collection of over 10,500 pieces of sheet music; vertical files and programs dealing with all aspects of Cincinnati music; Cincinnati composers' manuscripts collection; early American hymnals. Classified collection contains a large holding of opera, operetta, and musical comedy scores; chamber music in score and with performing parts; over 1,630 volumes of historical sets and collected works of single composers.
Services/Access Information: Reference and circulating services. Open 6 days a week; closed Sundays.

PUBLIC LIBRARY OF CINCINNATI AND HAMILTON COUNTY
Films and Recordings Department
800 Vine St., Library Square
Cincinnati, OH 45202-2071
(513) 369-6924
Contact: Patrice Callaghan, Head
Music Collection/Holdings: Over 30,000 classical, jazz, and popular recordings, including 3,000 reference (non-circulating) recordings: Cincinnati Symphony Orchestra recordings and others; reel-to-reel tapes of modern composers from the Koussevitzky Foundation. Over 4,000 audiocassette recordings of classical and popular music.
Services/Access Information: Recordings circulate to library cardholders. Listening facilities planned.

PUBLIC LIBRARY OF COLUMBUS AND FRANKLIN COUNTY
Humanities, Fine Arts & Recreation Division
96 South Grant Ave.
Columbus, OH 43215
(614) 222-7189
Contact: Suzanne Fisher, Librarian, Division Head
Music Collection/Holdings: Over 17,000 music titles in many forms: piano-vocal scores; piano-vocal collections, pop and contemporary; miniature scores; piano solos and duets; organ music; cantatas; instruction for piano, guitar, and other instruments; solo vocal; libretti; solo instrumental (flute, clarinet, trumpet, violin, bagpipe, and so forth); trio, quartet, and ensemble parts. Reference collection of over 500 titles; popular record collection.
Services/Access Information: Phonolog; Folio-Dex; List-O-Tapes.

TOLEDO-LUCAS COUNTY PUBLIC LIBRARY
Fine Arts Department
325 Michigan St.
Toledo, OH 43624
(419) 255-7055, x226
Contact: Paula J. Baker, Department Head
Music Collection/Holdings: Records; tapes; orchestral, chamber, solo, voice, and musical scores; sheet music, mostly from 1920-1940; book collection, including reference/research materials.
Services/Access Information: Lockheed, BRS, and NY Times data bases; photocopying services.

UNIVERSITY OF AKRON
Music Department
Guzzetta Hall
Akron, OH 44325
(216) 375-6989
Contact: Jaclyn Facinelli, Assistant Professor of Music and Music Librarian
Music Collection/Holdings: 2,000 records; 3,000 books; journals; recital tapes form 1974 to the present; cassettes; vidoe tapes of performances; operas; 10,000 scores and parts for performance.
Services/Access Information: Librarian on duty daily; open 70 hours during the week and on weekends. Bibliography courses offered for undergraduate and graduate student levels.

UNIVERSITY OF CINCINNATI
College Conservatory of Music
Gorno Memorial Music Library
101 Emery Hall
Cincinnati, OH 45221
(513) 475-4471
Contact: Robert O. Johnson, Head
Music Collection/Holdings: 80,000 books, scores, records, bound periodicals, and microforms.
Services/Access Information: Reference service; photocopying; microform readers. Open daily during school session.

WRIGHT STATE UNIVERISTY
Music Library
Dayton, OH 45435
(513) 873-2165
Contact: Elizabeth Schumann, Music Library Supervisor
Music Collection/Holdings: Scores; records; references; selected books; music education textbooks.
Services/Access Information: Listening facilities.

OKLAHOMA

OKLAHOMA STATE UNIVERSITY[1]
Music Library
121 Seretean Center for the Performing Arts
Stillwater, OK 74078
(405) 624-6133
Contact: Dr. William McMurty, Music Librarian

UNIVERSITY OF OKLAHOMA[1]
Music Library
560 Parrington Oval
Norman, OK 73019
(405) 325-4243
Contact: Vynola Newkumet, Music Librarian

THE UNIVERSITY OF SCIENCE AND ARTS OF OKLAHOMA

Nash Library
Chickasha, OK 73018
(405) 224-3140, x260
Contact: William A. Martin, Jr., Director
Music Collection/Holdings: General undergraduate music library collection; records and cassette tapes. No special collection in music.
Services/Access Information: Anyone may use facility. Bibliographic resource for vicinity.

OREGON

LIBRARY ASSOCIATION OF PORTLAND
(Multnomah County Library)
Henry Failing Art and Music Department
801 S.W. 10th Ave.
Portland, OR 97205
(503) 223-7201
Contact: Barbara K. Padden, Department Head
Music Collection/Holdings: Books on music; scores; sheet music; records of classical and popular music.
Services/Access Information: Interlibrary loan; photocopying.

OREGON STATE UNIVERSITY MUSIC DEPARTMENT
Music Learning Center
Benton Hall
Corvallis, OR 97331
(503) 754-3634
Contact: Judith A. Fortmiller, Clerical Specialist
Music Collection/Holdings: Over 8,000 records and 4,000 scores. Electronic support includes several Video Brains; Tap Master units for rhythm training; and two Apple computers with a variety of programs.
Services/Access Information: Records reserved for in-house listening; scores circulate. Over 300 cassette tapes and a flexible desk reserve system for non-sound materials to support music class assignments; LC card catalog access to records and scores. Listening of 15 headsets and 8 private listening rooms. Provides assistance in developing program music for class presentations by faculty and students.

PACIFIC UNIVERSITY
Music Library, Music Department
Visual and Performing Arts Division
Knight Hall, College Way
Forest Grove, OR 97116
(503) 357-6151, x291
Contact: Norma M. Cooper, Head Music Librarian
Music Collection/Holdings: 4,000 scores and books; 4,500 band, choir, and orchestra arrangements; 4,000 records; 225 reel-to-reel tapes; and 150 cassettes.
Services/Access Information: Records do not circulate except by special request. Open to students, faculty, staff, and the surrounding community. Open 42 hours a week.

PENNSYLVANIA

BRYN MAWR COLLEGE
Canaday Library and Goodhart Hall
Bryn Mawr, PA 19010
(215) 645-6235
Contact: Isabelle Cazeaux, Chairman, Music Department; Janice Bryson, Record Librarian
Music Collection/Holdings: Books, scores, and periodicals housed in Canaday Library; records in Goodhart Hall. Collections include a number of monumenta and opera omnia; many standard periodicals; some rare books; the Billings collection of rare records; and numerous operatic tapes.
Services/Access Information: Open to public weekdays. Contact in advance for access to record collection.

BUCKNELL UNIVERSITY
Music Department Library of Scores and Records
Lewisburg, PA 17837
(717) 524-1216
Music Collection/Holdings: 8,356 records of Western art music, jazz-rock-popular, and non-Western music; 9,752 volumes of scores and performing editions. Scholarly editions housed elsewhere.
Services/Access Information: Open 6 days a week. Closed Saturday.

CARNEGIE LIBRARY OF PITTSBURGH
Music and Art Department
4400 Forbes Ave.
Pittsburgh, PA 15213
(412) 622-3105
Contact: Ida Reed, Head
Music Collection/Holdings: Over 100,000 scores; 30,000 recordings and books on music. Strengths include performing editions of solo and chamber music; 18th and 19th century German and American music periodicals.
Services/Access Information: Member OCLC; score/part holdings not listed. Telephone or mail reference questions; photocopying charge on request. Interlibrary loan; recordings not available through interlibrary loan.

CARNEGIE-MELLON UNIVERISTY
Hunt Library, Music Division
Schenley Park
Pittsburgh, PA 15213
(412) 578-2452
Contact: Myrtle H. Nim, Music Librarian
Music Collection/Holdings: Large collection of vocal music and vocal collections supports class work and performance of students, faculty, and campus organizations. 6,000-33rpm and 1,000-78rpm records; 600 reel-to-reel tapes; and 70 cassette recordings of primarily classical music. Archive of performance recordings of the Music Department. Fine Arts section houses periodicals, monographs, and monumenta.
Services/Access Information: Listening materials and facilities for Music, Drama, History, Musical Theatre, and English Departments.

THE CURTIS INSTITUTE OF MUSIC[1]
Music Library
1726 Locust St.
Philadelphia, PA 19103
(215) 893-5265
Contact: Elizabeth Walker, Music Librarian

DUQUESNE UNIVERSITY
Duquesne University Library
Pittsburgh, PA 15282
(412) 434-6130/6131
Contact: Dena F. Jacobson, Reference Library
Music Collection/Holdings: 12,755 books and scores; 3,800 records, musical and spoken-word.
Services/Access Information: Serves college faculty and students; outside inquiries welcomed anytime. Open daily during school session.

EDINBORO UNIVERSITY OF PENNSYLVANIA
Baron-Forness Library
Edinboro, PA 16444
(814) 732-2509
Contact: John Z. Fleming, Librarian
Music Collection/Holdings: About 4,000 music-related titles, including most standard English-language references; over 1,000 volumes of scores; 7,500 phonodiscs devoted to music with a strong representation of band music.
Services/Access Information: Standard services available, including on-line data bases; interlibrary loan for all materials except recordings. Computerized listing of Bob Hoc Collection of Band Music available for purchase.

FREE LIBRARY OF PHILADELPHIA
Drinker Library of Choral Music
Logan Square
Philadelphia, PA 19103
(215) 686-5364
Contact: Frederick James Kent, Head, Music Department; Robert C. Williams, Clerk-in-Charge.
Music Collection/Holdings: Choral music from the 16th through early 20th centuries, including the Bach cantatas in English translation by the donor, Henry S. Drinker.
Services/Access Information: Provides standard choral repertoire to churches, colleges, and schools in multiple copies for handling charge. Orchestral parts available for loan. Subscription fee. Catalog available.

FREE LIBRARY OF PHILADELPHIA
Edwin A. Fleisher Collection of Orchestral Music
Logan Square
Philadelphia, PA 19103
(215) 686-5313
Contact: Sam Dennison, Curator
Music Collection/Holdings: Conductors' scores and complete instrumental parts for over 13,000 orchestral works; 1,500 reference scores; reference files on over 1,400 composers; Archives of select American composers, including Louis Gruenberg, La Salle Spier, and Harl McDonald; repository for discs and cassettes of works from the collection; repository for tapes of American-International Music Fund's Recording Guarantee Project.
Services/Access Information: Does not lend directly to individuals. Organizations wishing to borrow scores must send a written request on official stationary over the signature of a responsible officer. Request should include: dates of concert and of first rehearsal; number of string parts required; shipping and billing addresses; phone numbers; and any necessary clearance for copyrighted music. Loan for 8 weeks, plus shipping time. Borrowing organization will be billed for shipping and handling (fee determined by size of orchestration).

FREE LIBRARY OF PHILADELPHIA
Music Department
Logan Square
Philadelphia, PA 19103
(215) 686-5316
Contact: Frederick James Kent, Head
Music Collection/Holdings: Approximately 100,000 volumes of books, scores, and bound periodicals for both the general reader and specialist. Reserved for room use only are records; multi-volume musical anthologies; references; bibliographies; complete works; facsimiles and manuscripts; pamphlets, periodicals; newspaper clippings; psaltes and songsters; and popular sheet music. Browsing collection of circulating records since 1976. Dance-related materials housed in the Music Department include scores, biographies, dictionaries, plot synopses.
Services/Access Information: Orders received by mail are subject to copyright restrictions and availability of staff. Microfilm housed in MAN Department with microreaders and copiers; listening facilities; interlibrary loan; photocopying.

INDIANA UNIVERSITY OF PENNSYLVANIA
Cogswell Music Library
Cogswell Hall
Indiana, PA 15705
(412) 357-2892
Contact: Calvin Elliker, Music Librarian
Music Collection/Holdings: Approximately 6,000 monographs; 20,000 scores; and 16,000 recordings.
Services/Access Information: Holdings accessible through OCLC; interlibrary loan through office in main library.

KEAN ARCHIVES[1]
1320 Locust St.
Philadelphia, PA 19107
(215) 735-1812
Contact: Manuel Kean, Owner

MANSFIELD STATE COLLEGE
Butler Center Library
Mansfield, PA 16933
(717) 662-4365
Contact: Holly Ann Gardinier, Music Librarian
Music Collection/Holdings: Approximately 6,700 books; 8,600 scores; 9,600 records; 400 tapes; 130 titles in microform; 200 kits; 50 periodical titles.
Services/Access Information: OCLC or request by mail; interlibrary loan.

NEW SCHOOL OF MUSIC
Alice Tully Library
301 S. 21st St.
Philadelphia, PA 19103
(215) 732-3966
Contact: Susan L. Koenig, Librarian
Music Collection/Holdings: About 6,000 scores and performing editions; 1,800 music-related books; 2,000 records and tapes.
Services/Access Information: Students, faculty, and alumni have borrowing privileges; others may use materials within the library.

THE PENNSYLVANIA STATE UNIVERSITY
Arts Library
E405 Pattee Library
University Park, PA 16802
(814) 865-6481
Contact: Jean Smith, Arts Librarian
Music Collection/Holdings: Music collection of the Arts Library contains 18,000 volumes (including 10,000 scores); 520 journals and other serial subscriptions. Listening collection contains over 6,000 records and cassette recordings.
Services/Access Information: Open daily; closed weekends, evenings and between school sessions.

PHILADELPHIA COLLEGE OF BIBLE
Scofield Memorial Library
Langhorne Manor
Langhorne, PA 19047
(215) 752-5800
Contact: Dorothy M. Black, Assistant to Director, Music Librarian
Music Collection/Holdings: Music collection housed in main library contains 3,500 books and hymnals; over 3,650 scores; (orchestral, octavo, miniature, manuscript, facsimile and microfiche editions of early reference works); 50 periodical titles; 3,000 recordings; films, filmstrips, cassettes, and microforms; collected works, sets and monumenta.
Services/Access Information: Open to public for use within the library.

PHILADELPHIA COLLEGE OF PERFORMING ARTS[1]
Music Library
250 S. Broad St.
Philadelphia, PA 19102
(215) 545-6200
Contact: Kent Christensen, Music Librarian

PHILADELPHIA ORCHESTRA ASSOCIATION
Philadelphia Orchestra Library
Academy of Music, Stage Door
Broad and Locust Sts.
Philadelphia, PA 19102
(215) 893-1921/1954/1960
Contact: Clinton Nieweg, Prinicpal Librarian; Robert Grossman, Assistant Librarian; Nancy Bradburd, Assistant Librarian
Music Collection/Holdings: Sheet music for orchestral works; 3,000 sets of scores and parts; extensive reference materials for to locating orchestral works.
Services/Access Information: Reference, by appointment only.

RESSLER PRIVATE MUSIC LIBRARY
RD 2, Box 173
Quarryville, PA 17566
(717) 529-2463
Contact: Martin E. Ressler, Owner
Music Collection/Holdings: More than 4,00 volumes, primarily religious; majority are hymnals from every religious denomination, including over 800 in German; 200 oblong tunebooks; books on hymnology, music instruction, and general music history. No periodicals.
Services/Access Information: Phone or write for appointment. No photocopying servies.

ST. VINCENT COLLEGE AND ARCHABBEY[1]
Music Library
Latrobe, PA 15650
(412) 539-9761
Contact: Joseph Bronder, Chairman

SETTLEMENT MUSIC SCHOOL
Blanche Wolf Kohn Library
416 Queen St.
Philadelphia, PA 19147
(215) 336-0400
Contact: Laurel Wyckoff, Head Librarian
Music Collection/Holdings: Sheet music, including chamber music for all

instruments, solo piano repertoire, various ensemble combinations. Special collections: William Kincaid Collection of flute music and Mischa Schneider Collection of chamber music. Books about music and musicians; recordings, scores, and piano vocal scores for operas and libretti.
Services/Access Information: Listening facilities; Kardon Northeast and Germantown branches of Settlement Music School have audiovisual equipment.

STEPHEN COLLINS FOSTER MEMORIAL
Foster Hall Collection
University of Pittsburgh
Pittsburgh, PA 15260
(412) 624-4100
Contact: Dr. Deane L. Root, Curator
Music Collection/Holdings: Reference and archival collection devoted to American composer Stephen Collins Foster, and reflecting the role of music in American life. First and early editions of Foster compositions; manuscripts, arrangements, books, photographs, and other artifacts of the composer; writings about Foster and recordings of his music.
Services/Access Information: Partial access through card catalog. Publications list available upon request; reference service, photographs, and reproductions for scholars and publishers. Non-circulating holdings, no interlibrary loan. Museum and display open to public.

SWARTHMORE COLLEGE
Daniel Underhill Music Library
Swarthmore, PA 19081
(215) 447-7232
Contact: George K. Huber, Music Librarian
Music Collection/Holdings: Books on music and dance; scores; recordings or classical music and jazz; and music-related microforms.
Services/Access Information: Open to public for reference only.

TEMPLE UNIVERSITY
Samuel Paley Library
Philadelphia, PA 19122
(215) 787-8213
Contact: Richard M. Duris, Reference Librarian/Music Bibliographer
Music Collection/Holdings: 15,000 books; 15,000 scores; 12,000 records; and 100 music-related periodicals.
Services/Access Information: On-line search services; interlibrary loan; photocopiers, microfilm readers/printers.

UNIVERSITY OF PENNSYLVANIA
Otto E. Albrecht Music Library
Van Pelt Library
Philadelphia, PA 19104
(215) 898-3450
Contact: John H. Roberts, Music Librarian
Music Collection/Holdings: Music library is a special collection within the main library. Contains 50,000 books and scores and over 26,000 recordings, with emphasis on research and western classical music; many 18th and 19th century editions. Rare Books Collection of main library contains papers of Marian Anderson and Alma Mahler-Werfel, and the music library of Francis Hopkinson.
Services/Access Information: Open daily; weekends by appointment only. Listening facilities; microform readers; photocopiers.

UNIVERSITY OF PITTSBURGH
Theodore M. Finney Music Library
4337 Fifth Ave.
Pittsburgh, PA 15260
(412) 624-4130
Contact: Norris L. Stephens, Music Librarian
Music Collection/Holdings: Serves undergraduate and graduate programs, and research needs of faculty and graduate students. 32,000 books (over 1,000 pre-1800 imprints); 5,000 music scores; 15,000 records and tapes, 2,000 microforms; 100 serial subscriptions. Specific subject strengths: ethnomusicology; jazz, electronic, renaissance, baroque, and 20th century music. Numerous special collections.
Services/Access Information: Photocopier; microfilm printer/reader; microcard and microfiche readers; record, cassette, and tape players. Open daily; closed major and university holidays.

WARREN LIBRARY ASSOCIATION[1]
Music Library
205 Market St.
Warren, PA 16365
(814) 723-4650
Contact: Deborah J. Mongeau, Reference Librarian

WEST CHESTER STATE COLLEGE
School of Music Library
Swope Hall, College Ave.
West Chester, PA 19380
(215) 436-2430
Contact: Ruth Irwin Weidner, Music Librarian and Associate Professor
Music Collection/Holdings: 22,000 musical scores, strong in collected works, Denkmaeler, opera, miniature scores, keyboard music, and American music; 19,000 records, concentrating in classical music, jazz, and ethnomusicology; 1,000 reference books in music and allied fields; particularly dictionaries and thematic catalogs.
Services/Access Information: All materials fully cataloged with some supplementary analytical cataloging. Listening facilities for 40 persons; photocopying; interlibrary loan through main library (Francis Harvey Green Library).

RHODE ISLAND

PROVIDENCE PUBLIC LIBRARY[1]
Art and Music Department
150 Empire St.
Providence, RI 02903
(401) 521-7722
Contact: Susan R. Waddington, Department Head

SOUTH CAROLINA

BOB JONES UNIVERSITY[1]
Music Library
Greenville, SC 29614
(803) 242-5100
Contact: Karen S. Wilson, Supervisor

CONVERSE COLLEGE
Music Library
East Main St.
Spartanburg, SC 29301
(803) 585-6421
Contact: Lenore Mack, Music Librarian
Music Collection/Holdings: 5,000 books; 9,300 scores; over 5,700 recordings; 94 music periodical and newsletter titles. Collection covers all periods and aspects of music.
Services/Access Information: Books and scores may be checked out for 3 weeks with one renewal; recordings circulate, to faculty and students only, for 2 weeks, no renewal. Listening facilities; reference service weekdays.

MORRIS COLLEGE
Richardson-Johnson Learning Resource Center
North Main St.
Sumter, SC 29150
(803) 755-9371, x246
Contact: Paula Walters, Reference Librarian
Music Collection/Holdings: 690 titles in general music; music literature; musical instruction.
Services/Access Information: General materials circulate for 2 weeks; reference materials may be checked out overnight by special request; audiovisual materials circulate for 1 to 2 days.

UNIVERSITY OF SOUTH CAROLINA-UNIVERSITY LIBRARIES
Music Library
McMaster College
Columbia, SC 29208
(803) 777-5139
Contact: Thomas M. Parkman, Music Librarian

Music Collection/Holdings: Collections of recordings (almost entirely art music); tapes; numerous collected works; periodicals; scores; and most of the University Libraries' collection of music-related books.
Services/Access Information: Circulation privileges to members of the University community only; others may use materials within the library or request through interlibrary loan.

SOUTH DAKOTA

UNIVERSITY OF SOUTH DAKOTA
Shrine to Music Museum and Center for Study of the History of Musical Instruments
USD Box 194
Vermillion, SD 57069
(605) 677-5306
Contact: Dr. Andre P. Larson, Director
Music Collection/Holdings: The Arne B. Larson Collection of Musical Instruments and Library, which forms the nucleus of The Shrine to Music Museum's holdings, consists of more than 3,500 musical instruments; an extensive supporting library of reference books; music; periodicals; 8,000 sound recordings; photographs; and musical memorabilia.
Services/Access Information: The Museum is operated by the Center for Study of the History of Musical Instruments at the University of South Dakota, which provides staff and facilities for teaching and research, and Shrine to Music Museum, Inc. a nonprofit foundation responsible for acquisitions and public exhibition. The Museum operates a modern laboratory for conservation and restoration of musical instruments. Open to public daily except national holidays. Write for futher information and access policies.

YANKTON COLLEGE
Yankton College Library
1016 Douglas St.
Yankton, SD 57078
(605) 665-4662
Music Collection/Holdings: 2,000 scores; 5,300 records (mostly classical, some jazz, popular, and folk music); and 5,000 books.
Services/Access Information: Open daily; reference librarian available weekdays.

TENNESSEE

BELMONT COLLEGE
Williams Library
Belmont Blvd.
Nashville, TN 37203
(615) 385-6782
Contact: Timothy J. Gmeiner, Music Librarian
Music Collection/Holdings: 300 circulating scores and 1,000 reference scores; 4,000 musical and 500 literary records and tapes; 2,700 music-related books housed in main library.
Services/Access Information: Recordings and scores in multi-volume anthologies or complete works sets do not circulate. Listening facilities.

COUNTRY MUSIC FOUNDATION, INC.
Country Music Foundation Library and Media Center
4 Music Square E.
Nashville, TN 37203
(615) 256-1639
Contact: Ronnie Pugh, Reference Librarian
Music Collection/Holdings: A multi-media collection representing all styles of country music, including western swing, gospel, old-time, bluegrass, cowboy, honky-tonk, rockabilly, blues, and Nashville sound. Collection consists of more than 100,000 recordings; 3,500 books; 13,000 photographs; 2,000 bound volumes of periodicals; 400 periodical titles; sheet music; pamphlets; vertical files; songbooks; videotapes; microfilms; films, and audiotapes.
Reference services; research and consultation; rental of country music-related objects (primarily composed of vintage and contemporary musical instruments); audio lab. Rates and available services vary; clients are urged to make an initial phone call or letter of inquiry outlining the nature and scope of their project.

MARYVILLE COLLEGE
Music Library
Maryville, TN 37801
(615) 982-6412, x301
Contact: Carol Roberts, AV and Music Librarian
Music Collection/Holdings: 11,000 records (classical, contemporary and popular music); music reference works; extensive music history holdings.
Services/Access Information: Listening facilities; all items except reference circulate. Open on limited schedule.

MEMPHIS STATE UNIVERSITY
Music Library
Memphis, TN 38152
(901) 454-2556
Contact: Ann Viles, Head
Music Collection/Holdings: 40,000 volumes, including 11,000 books; 17,000 scores and sets of performing parts; and 8,000 records; 61 periodical subscriptions. Strongest in areas of historical sets, collected editions and bibliographical tools.
Services/Access Information: Open daily. Visitors welcome.

TENNESSEE STATE LIBRARY
State Library and Archives
403 Seventh Ave. N.
Nashville, TN 37219
(615) 741-2764
Contact: Kendall J. Cram, Director, State Library
Music Collection/Holdings: 10,000 titles of instrumetnal and vocal popular sheet music.
Services/Access Information: Catalogued by composer, lyricist, and title; subject headings are topical only.

TENNESSEE TEMPLE UNIVERSITY
Music Library
1815 Union Ave.
Chattanooga, TN 37404
(615) 698-6021
Contact: Daniel B. Shorb, Music Library Supervisor
Music Collection/Holdings: 2,300 records of most basic repertoire works; approximately 350 scores representing the best-known composers.
Services/Access Information: Open only to the student community. Works closely with main library (Cierpke Memorial Library), which houses 100,000 volumes and has access to most basic services.

UNIVERSITY OF TENNESSEE AT KNOXVILLE
Music Library
301 Music Building
Knoxville, TN 37996-2600
(615) 974-3474
Contact: Pauline S. Bayne, Head
Music Collection/Holdings: Approximately 32,800 volumes: 10,000 books; 12,000 scores; 9,500 sound recordings; 1,300 reels of microfilm dissertations and journals; 250 music periodical titles and other serials. Strengths include opera and song literature, complete works and historical sets, music history and biography. The Galston-Busoni Archive and Gottfried Galston Music Collection housed in Hoskins Library. Collection includes manuscripts and memorabilia associated with the composers' careers, as well as a 1,500 score collection of piano music used by Galston.

VANDERBILT UNIVERSITY LIBRARY
Music Library
419 21st Ave. S.
Nashville, TN 37240
(615) 322-8222
Contact: Shirley Marie Watts, Music Librarian
Music Collection/Holdings: 11,000 books on music; 12,000 scores; 11,000 sound recordings; 95 current periodical titles; microforms. Strong in music education and collected editions. Special collections: 700 recordings from personal collection of Frances Robinson; George Peabody College dissertations and theses; tapes of Peabody Piano Seminars.
Services/Access Information: Open to

visitors for in-house use only; photocopying. Open 6 days a week.

TEXAS

BAYLOR UNIVERSITY
Crouch Music Library
Box 6307
Waco, TX 76706
(817) 755-1366
Contact: Dr. Avery T. Sharp, Music Librarian
Music Collection/Holdings: 50,000 scores; 20,000 sound recordings; 10,000 books on music, sheet music collections; hymnal collection; and 140 current periodical titles.
Services/Access Information: Borrowing by faculty and students; visitors welcome. Reference service; interlibrary loan. Audio center has 30 electronic channels and 146 listening stations.

CORPUS CHRISTI STATE UNIVERSITY
University Library
6300 Ocean Dr.
Corpus Christi, TX 78412
(512) 991-6810, x243
Contact: Richard L. O'Keefe, University Librarian
Music Collection/Holdings: Large collection of scores, books, periodicals, and reference materials supporting upper-division and graduate courses in music education, music history, and music theory.

DALLAS PUBLIC LIBRARY
Fine Arts Division
1515 Young St.
Dallas, TX 75201
(214) 749-4100/4236
Contact: Jane Holahan, Division Head; James H. Calhoun, Music Librarian; Donna Mendro, Recordings Librarian
Music Collection/Holdings: Core of collection is formed 6,000 music-related books, including biographies; 12,000 scores; 8,000 pieces of sheet music; and 30,000 recordings. Clip files with promotional material about classical and popular musicians; historical information, reviews, etc. of Dallas music organizations. Special collections: Lawrence V. Kelly Collection of costume and set designs from Dallas Opera; Marion Flagg Collection; John R. Rosefield Collection; American International Music Fund Recording Guarantee Project of approximately 300 tapes of contemporary works by leading American symphony orchestras; Texas Federation of Music Clubs, Music Manuscript Archives Committee; John Ardoin Collection; manuscripts of works commissioned by the Fine Arts Division, Dallas Public Library; Rual Askew Estate Recordings Collections; Zelman Brounoff Baton Collection.
Services/Access Information: Piano room; listening facilities; videocassette equipment. Telephone reference; interlibrary loan.

FORT WORTH PUBLIC LIBRARY
Arts Unit
300 Taylor St.
Fort Worth, TX 76102
(817) 870-7739
Contact: Heather Goebel, Unit Manager
Music Collection/Holdings: Numerous books on music history and theory; biographies; vocal, choral and instrumental techniques. Large number of piano-vocal scores of operas, operettas, and musical comedies; pocket scores of orchestral, choral and chamber music; collections of popular, folk, and sacred songs; lieder collection; and sheet music.
Services/Access Information: Song-dex and Tune-dex car cataloging. Most books circulate for 3 weeks; sheet music and references do not circulate.

HARDIN-SIMMONS UNIVERSITY
Smith Music Library
Abilene, TX 79698
(915) 677-7281, x433
Contact: Robin Henderson Leech, Music Librarian

HOUSTON PUBLIC LIBRARY
Fine Arts & Recreation Department
500 McKinney
Houston, TX 77002
(713) 224-5441
Contact: Marcia Schemper, Dick Sligar, Music Librarians
Music Collection/Holdings: Broad general collection, strong in music biography; reference. Sheet music collection of 10,000 items emphasizes current and retrospective popular song sheets, with a special collection of pre-1900 music. Well-rounded record collection; limited tape collection.
Services/Access Information: Books, records and tapes circulate; sheet music access controlled through departmental catalog. Open daily.

NORTH TEXAS STATE UNIVERSITY
Music Library
Denton, TX 76203
(817) 565-2860
Contact: Morris Martin, Music Librarian
Music Collection/Holdings: The Music Library, one of the largest in the United States, holds 79,000 items, including music books, periodicals, scores, parts, and microforms; standard works of vocal and instrumental music for solo and ensemble; band, orchestra, and stage band scores and parts; complete works of over 200 different composers, among them new editions of the works of Bach, Handel, Berlioz, Mozart, and Schoenberg, together with well over 100 historical collections. Special collections: manuscript collection of early letters and compositions of Arnold Schoenberg; the 10,000-volume Lloyd Hibberd Collection of French baroque first editions and manuscripts; over 1,000 Duke Ellington records, tapes and transcriptions from the 1920s through the 1960s; sets of Hofmeister's *Handbuch der Msikalishcen Literatur,* Pazdirek's *Universal-Handbuch der Muskliteratur,* and the *Dictionary Catalog* of the *New York Public Library Music Division;* archive of scores and recordings of works composed by distinguished North Texas alumnus Don Gillis. Adjacent Audio-Center, contains over 30,000 recordings.
Services/Access Information: Listening facilities for individuals and groups.

RICE UNIVERSITY
Music Library
Fondren Library
PO Box 1892
Houston, TX 77251-1892
(713) 527-8101, x2593
Contact: Ralph Holibaugh, Music Librarian
Music Collection/Holdings: General collection of western art music, consisting of scholarly editions, performing editions, and study scores (7,000 titles); historical, theoretical, and instructional books (8,5000 title); and sound recordings (8,000 titles).
Services/Access Information: Printed materials and recordings available for use in library; books and scores may be checked out by faculty, staff, students, and alumni, and others with outside borrower's card.

SAM HOUSTON STATE UNIVERSITY
Music Library
Huntsville, TX 77341
(713) 294-1622
Contact: Dr. Robert Curtis, Music Librarian
Music Collection/Holdings: 25,000 volumes of books and scores; 7,200 sound recordings; 100 periodical titles; microforms and uncatalogued materials.
Services/Access Information: Library open 90 hours per week. Listening facilities; reference; interlibrary loan; photocopier; Microform Center.

SOUTHERN METHODIST UNIVERSITY
Music Library
Owen Arts Center F203
Dallas, TX 75275
(214) 692-2894
Contact: Robert Skinner, Music and Fine Arts Librarian
Music Collection/Holdings: 40,000 catalogued books, scores, recordings, microforms, and bound periodicals; 108 current periodical subscriptions; several thousand additional uncatalogued but accessible books and scores. Special collections include the Paul and Viola Katwijk Music

Collection, the DeGoyler Music Collection, the Ferde Grofe Collection, and the John Rosenfield Record Collection, among others.
Services/Access Information: Open to public for reference use; checkout via interlibrary loan or purchase of visitor's card.

SOUTHWESTERN BAPTIST THEOLOGICAL SEMINARY
Music Library
PO Box 22, 000-D4
Fort Worth, TX 76122
(817) 923-1921. x321
Contact: Phillip W. Simms, Music Librarian and Associate Professor of Music Bibliography
Music Collection/Holdings: The library of a graduate school of music. The collection includes books, scores, recordings, periodicals, and hymnals. Serious music of all periods, genres, and media, with special strength in church music (no popular music). Includes an antiquarian collection.
Services/Access Information: Interlibrary loan. Visiting scholars and researchers welcome.

SYMPHONY SOCIETY OF SAN ANTONIO[1]
Symphony Library
109 Lexington Ave., Ste. 207
San Antonio, TX 78205
(512) 255-6161
Contact: James R. Dotson, Music Librarian

TEXAS CHRISTIAN UNIVERSITY[1]
Music Library
Fort Worth, TX 76129
(817) 921-7000
Contact: Ann H. Heyer, Consultant

TEXAS TECH UNIVERSITY
Music Department Listening Library
PO Box 4239
Lubbock, TX 79409
(806) 742-2275
Contact: Priscilla C. Stoune, Librarian
Music Collection/Holdings: Approximately 7,000 records; 4,500 study scores; 1,050 reel-to-reel tapes; and small reference collection.
Services/Access Information: All materials may be used within the library; materials do not circulate.

UNIVERSITY OF HOUSTON[1]
Music Library
106 Fine Arts
Houston, TX 77004
(713) 749-2534
Contact: Helen Garrett, Music Librarian

UNIVERSITY OF TEXAS AT AUSTIN
Fine Arts Library
Austin, TX 78712
(512) 471-4777
Contact: Olga Buth, Music Librarian
Music Collection/Holdings: Supports instruction and research in applied music, composition, ethnomusicology, music education and theory, and musicology. All periods represented; emphasis on Western tradition with increasing interest in ethnic music. Scores and sound recordings are collected comprehensively for all major composers. Archive of recital tapes; 559 serial titles; 75,000 volumes of books, scores, bound periodical volumes, microforms, theses and sound recordings.
Services/Access Information: Interlibrary loan through main library (Perry-Castaneda Library). Listening facilities; microform readers. OCLC terminal for use by patrons. Open daily.

WEST TEXAS STATE UNIVERSITY
Music Library, Department of Music
WT Box 879
Canyon, TX 79016
(806) 656-2951
Contact: Martha Morris, Director, Music Library
Music Collection/Holdings: 3,200 records; 3,600 scores; Houston Bright manuscripts; Ruth Crawford (Seeger) materials. Main library (Cornette Library) contains 5,600 books/collected works.
Services/Access Information: CLOIS (Cornette Library Online Information Service) provides access to DIALOG data base; or contact by phone.

UTAH

BRIGHAM YOUNG UNIVERSITY
Harold B. Lee Library
Provo, UT 84602
(801) 378-6119
Contact: Beth R. Webb, Music Librarian
Music Collection/Holdings: Approximately 36,000 books, scores, and bound periodicals covering all chronological and geographical areas, supporting both graduate and undergraduate levels. Special collections of sheet music, Mormon hymnals, manuscript music, organization papaers, and personal papers; record collection includes about 18,000 recordings.
Services/Access Information: Most of the collection circulates to faculty, students, and visiting scholars. Reference and photocopy services; interlibrary loan. The record collection does not circulate.

VERMONT

MIDDLEBURY COLLEGE
Music Library
Johnson Bldg.
Middlebury, VT 05753
(802) 388-3711, x2218
Contact: Jeffrey Rehbach, Music Librarian
Music Collection/Holdings: All areas of music: 8,000 records, 8,000 scores; 1,000-volume reference collection; 4,500 monographs housed in main library with the Flanders Ballad Collection (5,000 recordings and transcriptions of folksongs, ballads, fiddle tunes, and folktales collected in New England between 1930 and 1960; and a 2,500-volume supporting collection of journals, monographs and scores.

UNIVERSITY OF VERMONT
Bailey/Howe Library
Burlington, VT 05405-0036
(802) 656-2020, x35
Contact: Ken Maracek, Audio-Visual Librarian
Music Collection/Holdings: 5,000 books; 5,500 scores; over 4,000 records. Scores are integrated into the regular stacks of the library; sound recordings are kept in a separate AV area.
Services/Access Information: Open to anyone for study purposes. Only Chittenden County residents may borrow materials; sound recordings do not circulate. For interlibrary loan, contact Sandra Gavett.

VIRGINIA

AMERICAN SYMPHONY ORCHESTRA LEAGUE[1]
Music Library
Box 669
Vienna, VA 22180
(703) 281-1230
Contact: Ralph Black, Executive Director

FAIRFAX COUNTY PUBLIC LIBRARY
Music Department
3915 Chain Bridge Rd.
Fairfax, VA 22030
(703) 691-2006
Contact: Anita Lamkin, Music Librarian
Music Collection/Holdings: Sets of orchestral parts; sets of octavo and choral music; band parts; dance band sets; vocal and instrumental music; chamber music parts; scores of operas and musicals; miniature orchestral scores; popular song collection; music reference books and circulating books on music-related subjects.
Services/Access Information: Music reference service; Sunday afternoon recital series; Washington Amateur Chamber Music Director (free clearinghouse for players); and Music Teachers' Registry.

HOLLINS COLLEGE
Eric Rath Music Library and Listening Center
Hollins College, VA 24020
(703) 362-6516/6511
Contact: Charlotte B. Becker, Coordinator; Thelma C. Diercks, Advisor
Music Collection/Holdings: General

collection of books, scores, records; selected complete sets and reference works. The collected Stephen Foster edition in mint condition; about 4,000 33⅓rpm and 1,500 78rpm records, and 200 tapes/cassettes.
Services/Access Information: Non-circulating, open stack library and listening center for the college community and others by arrangement; listening facilities. Open 6 days a week; closed Saturday.

LIBERTY BAPTIST COLLEGE
Candlers Mountain Rd.
Box 20000
Lynchburg, VA 24506
(804) 237-5961
Music Collection/Holdings: 2,000 records, scores (complete works of Beethoven, Mozart, Bach, Brahms); 2,000 books; and 28 periodical titles.
Services/Access Information: Records, scores and cassettes housed in Audio-Visual Library, which contains cassettes for Music Theory Ear Training Lab.

OLD DOMINION UNIVERSITY
University Library, Music Collection
Norfolk, VA 23508
(804) 440-4173
Music Collection/Holdings: Recorded classical, jazz and popular music; recordings of plays, poetry, and speeches; tapes of faculty and student recitals and concerts; scores for vocal and instrumental music; collected editions of major composers; multi-media material on videocassettes, filmstrips, slides, and auidocassettes. The record collection includes George Gay's classical collection and Clarence Walton's jazz collection.
Services/Access Information: Records and reserve material must be used within the library; scores circulate according to the same policies as the general library book collection. Borrowing privileges require student ID. Open daily during school session.

RICHMOND PUBLIC LIBRARY
Art and Music Department
101 E. Franklin St.
Richmond, VA 23219
(804) 780-4740
Contact: Myra L. Kight, Head
Music Collection/Holdings: Books, recordings (records & cassettes), and sheet music.

ROANOKE COLLEGE
Olin Fine Arts Library
Salem, VA 24135
(703) 389-2351, x356
Music Collection/Holdings: Basic collection of instrumental, vocal and choral scores; 2,000 records.
Services/Access Information: Scores may be checked out by students, faculty, and staff. Records are reserved for faculty use only, but may be used by students within the library.

SHENANDOAH COLLEGE AND CONSERVATORY OF MUSIC[1]
Howe Library
Winchester, VA 22601
(703) 667-8714
Contact: Nancy H. Moore, Administrative Librarian

SWEET BRIAR COLLEGE
Junius P. Fishburn Music Library
Sweet Briar, VA 24595
(804) 381-5541
Contact: Kathleen A. Lance, Branch Librarian
Music Collection/Holdings: General collection serving undergraduates, with emphasis on music history and scores.

UNIVERSITY OF RICHMOND
Music Library
Modlin Fine Arts Center
Richmond, VA 23173
(804) 285-6398
Contact: Bonlyn Hall, Music Librarian
Music Collection/Holdings: General collection of records, scores, and reference books supporting undergraduate music program. Includes music manuscripts of Hilton Rufty and Jacob Reinhardt. General collection of books on music housed in the main library (Boatwright Memorial Library).
Services/Access Information: Open to public daily. Interlibrary loan provided to other academic libraries free of charge.

UNIVERSITY OF VIRGINIA
Music Library
113 Old Cabell Hall
Charlottesville, VA 22901
(804) 924-7041
Contact: Evan Bonds, Music Librarian
Music Collection/Holdings: 40,000 bound volumes; 10,000 recordings.

WASHINGTON

CENTRAL WASHINGTON UNIVERSITY
Music Library
Ellensburg, WA 98926
(509) 963-1841
Contact: Paul R. Emmons, Music Librarian
Music Collection/Holdings: 4,500 scores; 5,500 books; 4,200-78rpm and 5,000-33⅓rpm records; Special Collection: Paul Creston Collection.
Services/Access Information: Reference service and listening facilities available to public; borrowing by university community or others by special arrangement.

CORNISH INSTITUTE
Cornish Library
1501 10th Ave. E.
Seattle, WA 98102
(206) 323-1400, x302
Contact: Ronald G. McComb, Head Librarian
Music Collection/Holdings: 1,500 scores (classical); 2,000 records (classical, ethnic, and jazz)

UNIVERSITY OF WASHINGTON
Music Library
113 Music Bldg.
Seattle, WA 98195
(206) 543-1168
Contact: David A. Wood, Head
Music Collection/Holdings: General academic collection of 45,000 volumes and 28,000 sound recordings. Special collections include the Hazel G. Kinscella collection of early hymnals and tunebooks; a collection of early opera scores; the Eric Offenbacher Mozart Collection (early recordings); and the Melvin Harris collection of early woodwind performances on disc.

WASHINGTON STATE UNIVERSITY[1]
Music Library
Pullman, WA 99164
(509) 335-8524
Contact: Phyllis M. Nilson, Music Librarian

WESTERN WASHINGTON UNIVERSITY
Music Library
Performing Arts Center, 376
Bellingham, WA 98225
(206) 676-3716
Contact: Marian Ritter, Music Librarian
Music Collection/Holdings: 18,500 volumes; 175 current periodical titles; and 10,000 recordings. Included are collected editions and complete works, bound and unbound periodicals, important bibliographical references.
Services/Access Information: Listening facilities; microfilm readers.

WEST VIRGINIA

MARSHALL UNIVERSITY
Music Library
3rd Ave. & Hal Greer Blvd.
Huntington, WV 25701
(304) 696-6647
Contact: Kay Wildman, Music Librarian
Music Collection/Holdings: 14,000 items including recordings, tapes, and scores supporting an undergraduate music curriculum. Books on music-related subjects are housed in the main library (James E. Morrow Library).

WEST VIRGINIA UNIVERSITY
Music Library, Division of Music
Creative Arts Center
Morgantown, WV 26506
(304) 293-4505
Contact: Ruby M. Canning, Supervisor
Music Collection/Holdings: 12,150 scores; 10,800 books, bound

periodicals, and journals; 130 current periodical subscriptions; 800 reels of microfilm; 6,000 recordings. Also houses Fry Jazz Collection (1920-1970) consisting 3,500-78rmp and 33rpm records.
Services/Access Information: For students, faculty and staff; honors state library cards. Interlibrary loan.

WEST VIRGINIA WESLEYAN COLLEGE
Music Library, Loar Hall
Loar Fine Arts Bldg.
Buckhannon, WV 26201
(304) 473-8360
Music Collection/Holdings: Reference; current periodicals; orchestral, vocal, operatic, chamber and solo instrumental scores and study scores; complete works; music anthologies; specialized texts. Majority of books and periodicals housed in the main library (Annie Merner Pfeiffer Library).
Services/Access Information: Listening room; LC listing for scores and books. Open daily.

WISCONSIN

ALVERNO COLLEGE
3401 S. 39th St.
Milwaukee, WI 53215
(414) 647-3723
Contact: Lola Stuller, Fine Arts Librarian
Music Collection/Holdings: Sound recordings and study scores.
Services/Access Information: Collection does not circulate; in-house use by any patron. Reference service.

BEIHOFF MUSIC CORPORATION[1]
Sheet Music Department Library
5040 W. North Ave.
Milwaukee, WI 53208
(414) 442-3920
Contact: Robert F. Loomer, Manager

LAWRENCE UNIVERSITY CONSERVATORY OF MUSIC
Music Library
115 N. Park St.
Appleton, WI 54911
(414) 735-6618
Contact: Paul Hollinger, Music Librarian
Music Collection/Holdings: 10,000 records; 1,500 books; 5,000 sheets of music and scores; periodicals; tapes. Nearby University library contains an extensive collection of music-related books and additional sound recordings and listening equipment.
Services/Access Information: Listening facilities.

MADISON PUBLIC LIBRARY
Art and Music Division
201 W. Mifflin
Madison, WI 53705
(608) 266-6311
Contact: Beverly Brager, Supervisor
Music Collection/Holdings: 2,600 scores, including miniatures, songbooks, and collections for various instruments; 15,000 records, primarily classical; 8,000 books on music-related subjects.
Services/Access Information: Anyone may use materials within the library; material may be checked out by any resident of Dane, Sauk, Green, or Columbia counties.

MILWAUKEE PUBLIC LIBRARY
Art, Music and Recreation Section
814 W. Wisconsin Ave.
Milwaukee, WI 53233
(414) 278-3000
Contact: Mrs. June Edlhauser, Fine Arts Coordinator
Music Collection/Holdings: Extensive general music literature collection including classical, contemporary, jazz, and musical biographies, as well as the most significant reference works. Also includes 46,708 sound recordings; 73,150 historical recorded sound collection; 24,500 historic popular song collection; and W.P.A. copied music; collection of local music materials includes concert programs and newspaper clippings.
Services/Access Information: Circulating material and reference services available with a Milwaukee County Federated Library card or a fee card for non-resident. Telephone reference for City of Milwaukee residents only.

MILWAUKEE SYMPHONY ORCHESTRA
Music Library
929 N. Water St.
Milwaukee, WI 53202
(414) 273-7121
Contact: Paul B. Gunther, Librarian
Music Collection/Holdings: About 1,200 orchestral sets; 500 additional scores; 75 choral sets; miscellaneous reference books, including publishers' and orchestral music catalogs; sound and video recordings; files of composer biographical information.
Services/Access Information: Notebooks, cards, and computerized data banks listing performances by date, location, type; and compositions by composer, arranger, title, type, etc.; catalog of combined choral holdings of several dozen institutions available on interorganizational loan.

UNIVERSITY OF WISCONSIN-MADISON
Mills Music Library
728 State St.
Madison, WI 53717
(608) 263-1884
Contact: Arne Jon Arneson, Music Librarian
Music Collection/Holdings: 47,000 scores; 40,000 sound recordings; 33,000 monographs; 364 current journal subscriptions.

UNIVERSITY OF WISCONSIN-MILWAUKEE
Music Library
PO Box 604
Milwaukee, WI 53211
(414) 963-5529
Contact: Richard E. Jones, Music Librarian
Music Collection/Holdings: Academic, scholarly collection specializing in reference materials; scholarly editions; monographs on music; and performing editions of chamber music. About 27,000 volumes of books and music; 8,500 records; and 25,000 pamphlets, catalogs, and so forth. Special collections: Archives of the American Arriaga Society; the Slovenian Music Collection; European Music Bibliography and Catalog Reference Files.
Services/Access Information: Listening, reading, and photocopying facilities available without restriction during music-audio hours.

UNIVERSITY OF WISCONSIN-STEVENS POINT
Music Library
Stevens Point, WI 54481
(715) 346-2569
Contact: Steven Sundell, Music Librarian
Music Collection/Holdings: Study scores; chamber music; band, choral, and orchestral music; sound recordings. Special collection: Wisconsin Music Archive.

VITERBO COLLEGE[1]
Music Library
La Crosse, WI 54601
(608) 784-0040
Contact: Sr. Rosella Namer, Music Librarian

WISCONSIN CONSERVATORY OF MUSIC[1]
Music Library
1584 N. Prospect Ave.
Milwaukee, WI 53202
(414) 276-4350
Contact: Brian Gerl, Music Librarian

WISCONSIN STATE DIVISION FOR LIBRARY SERVICES[1]
Fulcher Collection of Sacred Choral and Organ Music
Reference and Loan Library
3030 Darbo Dr.
Madison, WI 53714
(608) 266-8671
Contact: Willeen Tretheway, Music Librarian

PUERTO RICO

CONSERVATORY OF MUSIC OF PUERTO RICO
Library
350 Rafael Lamar St.
San Juan, PR 00918-2199
(809) 751-0160, x222
Contact: Alberto H. Hernandez, Director
Music Collection/Holdings: 15,950 book titles; 48 periodical subscriptions; and 3,500 recordings.

UNIVERSITY OF PUERTO RICO[1]
Sala de Musica, General Library
Rio Piedras, PR 00931
(809) 764-0000
Contact: Annie F. Thompson, Music Librarian

CANADA

ALBERTA

THE BANFF CENTRE-SCHOOL OF FINE ARTS
Library
Box 1020
Banff, AB T0L 0C0
(403) 762-6265
Contact: Robert J. Rosen, Music Librarian
Music Collection/Holdings: Scores, recordings, and books focusing on performance practice; supports all divisions of School of Fine Arts, including music, visual arts, theatre arts, and literary arts.
Services/Access Information: Free use of material within library; borrowing privileges restricted to students and staff.

GRANT MACEWAN COMMUNITY COLLEGE
Learning Resource Center
Jasper Place Campus
10045-156th St.
Edmonton, AB T5P 2P7
(403) 483-4410
Contact: Pat Lloyd, Jasper Place Librarian
Music Collection/Holdings: 2,200 books; 1,100 scores; 60 audiovisual items (video and films); 2,200 records, and 20 periodical titles.
Services/Access Information: Reference service and circulation for students and staff; computerized index of scores by song title.

LETHBRIDGE COMMUNITY COLLEGE
Buchanan Resource Centre
2210-30th Ave. S.
Lethbridge, AB T1K 1L6
(403) 320-3352
Contact: Kathy Lea, Library Supervisor
Music Collection/Holdings: Historical materials; piano song books, audiovisual materials, instruments descriptions, reference books, books on music theory, instruction, and instrumental descriptions.
Services/Access Information: Reference service or by phone. Open weekdays.

MOUNT ROYAL COLLEGE
Conservatory of Music Library
4825 Richard Rd., S.W.
Calgary, AB T3E 6K6
(403) 240-6111
Contact: Sydney Goldstein, Resource Librarian
Music Collection/Holdings: Basic scores for performance and study; records.
Services/Access Information: Records primarily for the use of students.

RED DEER COLLEGE
Learning Resources Centre
PO Box 5005
Red Deer, AB T4N 5H5
(403) 342-3344
Music Collection/Holdings: 675 monographs and 1,650 records, primarily classical; no individual scores.
Services/Access Information: Records for use only within the library; records may be borrowed with special permission. Listening facilities.

UNIVERSITY OF ALBERTA
Music Resources Centre
3-82 Fine Arts Bldg.
Edmonton, AB T6G 2C9
(403) 432-5708
Contact: James Whittle, Librarian
Music Collection/Holdings: Books; periodicals; scores; sheet music; performance materials; sound recordings; vertical files; concert programs; and pamphlets (libretti, programs, lectures, and short monographs).
Services/Access Information: Open to public for use within Centre; special borrowing privileges to those with legitimate scholarly need. Open weekdays.

UNIVERSITY OF CALGARY
Library, Music Division
2500 University Dr., N.W.
Calgary, AB T2N 1N4
(403) 284-6162
Contact: Rita F. Vine, Music Librarian
Music Collection/Holdings: Approximately 25,000 books; 15,000 scores; 12,000 records. Special collections include Canadian composers' manuscripts and supporting published materials.
Services/Access Information: Recordings do not circulate; in-house listening facilities available.

UNIVERSITY OF LETHBRIDGE
Library
4401 University Dr.
Lethbridge, AB T1K 3M4
(403) 329-2265
Contact: M. Louise Needham, Department of Music Library Representative, Associate Professor
Music Collection/Holdings: Scores (including complete works of several composers); music history and theory-related books; reference books; serials; large number of recordings; and films.
Services/Access Information: Information available from main library staff and Media Centre.

BRITISH COLUMBIA

CANADIAN MUSIC CENTRE/CENTRE DE MUSIQUE CANADIENNE
British Columbia Regional Branch
No. 3-2007 W. 4th Ave.
Vancouver, BC V6J 1N3
(604) 734-4622
Contact: Colin Miles, Regional Director
Music Collection/Holdings: Regional branch of the national music centre. Holdings include some 7,000 published and unpublished scores by Canadian composers; Reference collection includes an archive of 2,000 records and cassettes; biographical files on Canadian composers and program notes on their works; books, periodicals, catalogues and information about Canadian music are on hand.
Services/Access Information: Scores are loaned free of charge. The National Centre produces digital recordings on the Centredisc label; these and other Canadian records are available for sale from each office of the Centre. The British Columbia Centre issues *Centregramme,* a bi-monthly newsletter.

DOUGLAS COLLEGE
Library
PO Box 2503
New Westminster, BC V3L 5B2
(604) 520-5400
Contact: V. Chisholm, Director
Music Collection/Holdings: 5,000 books and records, primarily classical, history and some instrumentation.
Services/Access Information: Serves students of the college.

NEW WESTMINSTER PUBLIC LIBRARY
716 Sixth Ave.
New Westminster, BC V3M 2B3
(604) 521-8874
Contact: Jane Kupfer, Librarian
Music Collection/Holdings: 8,000 records; 700 cassette tapes; and song books indexed by song title.
Services/Access Information: Member of the Greater Vancouver Library Federation; accepts cards from all member libraries. Holdings can be borrowed for 2 weeks. Listening facilities.

UNIVERSITY OF BRITISH COLUMBIA
Music Library
6361 Memorial Rd.
Vancouver, BC V6T 1W5
(604) 228-3589
Contact: Hans Burndorfer, Head
Music Collection/Holdings: Scores; books; recordings; microfilms; and journals.

UNIVERSITY OF BRITISH COLUMBIA
Wilson Recordings Collection
1958 Main Mall
Vancouver, BC V6T 1W5
(604) 228-2534
Contact: R.G. Kaye, Head
Music Collection/Holdings: 35,000 records of poetry, drama, and other spoken material and music, excluding pop and ephemera.
Services/Access Information: Borrowing privileges for annual fee. Listening facilities. Open daily during winter session.

VICTORIA CONSERVATORY OF MUSIC
839 Academy Pl.
Victoria, BC V8V 2X8
(604) 386-5311
Contact: Lawrence de la Haye, Librarian
Music Collection/Holdings: Small library devoted to written music, mostly piano music, and books; also collection of musical recordings.
Services/Access Information: A $10 refundable deposit for library card. Borrowing by faculty and students; others on deposit basis. Open six days a week.

MANITOBA

CANADIAN BROADCASTING CORPORATION
Music and Record Library
PO Box 160
Winnipeg, MB R3C 2H1
(204) 775-8351
Contact: Don R. McLaren, Senior Music and Record Librarian
Music Collection/Holdings: Concert music; vocal selections; some choral works; religious books (hymns); show music vocal scores; copies of sheet music, old standards and current popular songs. Record library consists of 23,000 classical, country, jazz, rock, ethnic and popular recordings.
Services/Access Information: Material available for internal use only. As a broadcast library, services provided for program use exclusively.

UKRAINIAN CULTURAL AND EDUCATIONAL CENTRE
184 Alexander Ave., East
Winnepeg, MB R3B 0L6
(204) 942-0218
Contact: Daria Bajus, Librarian; Zenon Hluszok, Archivist
Music Collection/Holdings: Manuscripts of music and other archival materials relating to various Ukrainian arrangers, composers, and conductors; sheet music mainly of Ukrainian and non-Ukrainian songbooks and other music books; books, monographs, and serials, chiefly in Ukrainian.
Services/Access Information: Most material uncatalogued. Published books, monographs, and serials available for use within the library; other materials available subject to the condition and nature of the documents and agreements with donors. Prior inquiry advised; selective photocopying depending on above restrictions and copyright regulations.

UNIVERSITY OF MANITOBA
Music Library
Winnipeg, MB R3T 2N2
(204) 474-9567
Contact: Vladimir Simosko, Librarian
Music Collection/Holdings: 8,000 volumes, 5,000 of which are music scores; 70 current periodicals; 20,000 performance music titles (17,000 items of choral music); 500 audio tapes; 7,000 records. Circulation of 18,000 items annually.
Services/Access Information: Serves students and faculty of the School of Music; Arts students with a minor in music; and various cultural groups of the Winnipeg Community.

WINNIPEG PUBLIC LIBRARY
251 Donald St.
Winnipeg, MB R3C 3P5
(204) 985-6460
Contact: Carol Burns, Head, Audio Visual Services
Music Collection/Holdings: 3,000 books; 40 periodical titles; 580 scores and 1,000 microfiche of miniature scores; 3,000 pieces of performance material, such as choral sets; 50,000 records; 1,500 cassettes; and 250 vertical files, concert programs, and pamphlets.
Services/Access Information: Records and cassettes may be rented for 10 cents per item per week (max. 1 month); books, circulating periodicals, scores and performance materials borrowed free of charge for 1 month; reference periodicals, vertical files, concert programs and pamphlets may be used within the library.

NEW BRUNSWICK

MOUNT ALLISON UNIVERSITY
Alfred Whitehead Memorial Music Library
Sackville, NB E0A 3C0
(506) 536-2040, x326
Contact: Gwen Creelman, Music Librarian
Music Collection/Holdings: 5,900 books; 840 bound periodicals; 9,500 scores; 5,000 recordings; and 110 journal and serial subscriptions. Subject strengths are music-theory, history, criticism, biography, musicology, music education. Special collection: 20th century Canadian music scores and recordings. Publishes *Canadian Music Scores & Recordings,* and a bibliography, *Sources in Canadian Music,* 2nd ed.
Services/Access Information: Borrowing by non-university patrons upon librarian's approval; resources open for in-house use.

MOUNT ALLISON UNIVERSITY
Mary Mellish Archibald Memorial Library
Sackville, NB E0A 3C0
(506) 536-0857
Contact: Margaret Fancy, Special Collections Librarian
Music Collection/Holdings: Over 2,000 titles concentrating on Anglo-American folk music and music for children.
Services/Access Information: Access through public catalogue of the main library (Ralph Pickard Bell Library).

SAINT JOHN REGIONAL LIBRARY
Audio-Visual Services
1 Market Square
Saint John, NB E2L 4Z6
(506) 693-1191
Contact: Barbara M. Cowan, Adult Services Librarian
Music Collection/Holdings: 7,344 recordings representing all musical interests, including instructional materials; 294 cassettes, primarily popular music; books on broad spectrum of musical knowledge; no libretti scores or sheet music; miscellaneous songbooks.
Services/Access Information: Recording and cassette collection available to local borrowers; book material available through interlibrary loan.

NEWFOUNDLAND

MEMORIAL UNIVERSITY OF NEWFOUNDLAND
Queen Elizabeth II Library
Library Audio Resource Centre (LARC)
St. John's, NF A1B 3Y1
(709) 737-7472
Contact: Music Cataloguer
Music Collection/Holdings: 5,000 volumes of general music literature; 2,000 recordings; 2,000 volumes of scores. Collection is integrated into the general collection.
Services/Access Information: Usual library service.

NOVA SCOTIA

CANADIAN BROADCASTING CORPORATION[1]
Music and Record Library
5600 Sackville St.
Box 3000
Halifax, NS B3J 3E9
(902) 422-8311
Contact: David S. Leadbeater, Senior Record Librarian

DALHOUSIE UNIVERSITY
Killam Memorial Library
Halifax, NS B3H 4H8
(902) 424-3611
Music Collection/Holdings: 65 music journal subscriptions; over 5,000 volumes (monographs and bound journals); and over 10,000 other items (recordings and scores).
Services/Access Information: Public card catalog for books and libretti; computer printout for journal access; music card catalog for recordings and scores; listening facilities; electric piano. Borrowing privileges, on request, to any adult in Halifax/Dartmouth Metropolitan area.

DARTMOUTH REGIONAL LIBRARY
Music Collection
100 Wyse Rd.
Dartmouth, NS B3A 1M1
(902) 421-2310
Music Collection/Holdings: Records in all musical categories, including classical, folk, jazz, male and female vocalists, musical reviews, rock, and western.

ONTARIO

CAMBRIAN COLLEGE OF APPLIED ARTS AND TECHNOLOGY
1400 Barrydowne Rd.
Sudbury, ON P3A 3V8
(705) 566-8101
Contact: Diane Henry, Head Librarian
Music Collection/Holdings: Over 1,500 recordings; 900 scores; 1,000 microfiche; 600 books; films and videotapes.
Services/Access Information: Record players and videotape recorders for in-house use.

CANADIAN BROADCASTING CORPORATION
Music Library
Box 500, Station A
Toronto, ON M5W 1E6
(416) 925-3311
Contact: John P. Lawrence, Coordinator
Music Collection/Holdings: 70,000 pieces of sheet music, scores and parts; 200,000 records; 2,000 books; 200 periodical subscriptions and vertical file material.
Services/Access Information: In-house radio and television production material research. Private research consultation by appointment only.

CARLETON UNIVERSITY
Library
Colonel By Drive
Ottawa, ON K1S 1S4
Contact: Alison Hall, Music Cataloguer
Music Collection/Holdings: Supports undergraduate and graduate programs with emphasis on Canadian music, especially scores. Monumenta; complete works; music history relating to all periods and genres; serials; scores for all types of music and parts for chamber music.
Services/Access Information: Reference services; interlibrary loan; orientation sessions and library guides; audiovisual room with listening facilities for music and spoken-word cassettes, videotape viewing. Open daily during school session; not open to public.

CONRAD GREBEL COLLEGE/ UNIVERSITY OF WATERLOO
Music Department
Waterloo, ON N2L 3G6
(519) 885-0220
Contact: Sam Steiner, Head Librarian
Music Collection/Holdings: 2,000 books; 2,600 recordings; 1,200 scores.
Services/Access Information: Collection is housed partially at Conrad Grebel College and partially at the Dana Porter Arts Library, University of Waterloo.

HALTON HILLS PUBLIC LIBRARIES
9 Church St.
Georgetown, ON L7G 2A3
(416) 877-2681
Music Collection/Holdings: About 1,200 sound recordings, briefly catalogued; small collection of books; no scores, libretti or sheet music.
Services/Access Information: Borrowing privileges restricted to residents of municipality.

KINGSTON PUBLIC LIBRARY
130 Johnson St.
Kingston, ON K7L 1X8
(613) 549-8888
Contact: Sten Ardal, Head of Audio
Music Collection/Holdings: 3,000 records, classical, popular, jazz, spoken-word, folk, language and so forth; some music tapes are in circulation; most tapes are spoken-word.
Services/Access Information: Records circulate for 1 week; listening facility. Borrowing privileges restricted to cardholders.

LONDON PUBLIC LIBRARY
West-One Reference Department
305 Queen's Ave.
London, ON N6B 3L7
(519) 432-7166
Contact: Ruth Adams, Music Librarian
Music Collection/Holdings: Scores; records and cassettes; periodicals; 16mm film; 700 books relating to art, music, film, and sports.
Services/Access Information: Reference service.

MCMASTER UNIVERSITY
Mills Memorial Library
1280 Main St., W.
Hamilton, ON L8S 4L6
(416) 525-9140, x2069
Contact: Dennis J. Driscoll, Head, Music Section
Music Collection/Holdings: 15,000 records; 600 cassettes; and 12,000 books and scores. Borrowing privileges restricted to University community.

METROPOLITAN TORONTO LIBRARY
Music Department
789 Yonge St.
Toronto, ON M4W 2G8
(416) 928-5224
Contact: Isabel Rose, Department Head
Music Collection/Holdings: 16,000 books; over 35,000 scores of orchestral, operatic, vocal, and choral music; over 15,000 classical recordings; over 200 periodical titles. Canadian collection: 19th and 20th century sheet music; Toronto concert programs; early Canadian educational texts; Canadian hymnals (including native Indian hymnals); trade catalogues; clipping files; and Canadian folksong collections.
Services/Access Information: Performance editions of printed music circulate; in-library use of all other materials. Photocopying; microform readers/printers; piano studio.

NIAGARA FALLS PUBLIC LIBRARY
4848 Victoria Ave.
Niagara Falls, ON L2E 4C5
(416) 356-8080
Contact: Coleen Lambert, Music Librarian
Music Collection/Holdings: 2400 items from all musical categories, including classical, popular, musicals, children's, international folk and ethnic music, plays and instructional materials.
Services/Access Information: Records are classified by The ANSCR Classification Scheme (the alpha-numeric system for classification of recordings); LC for subject headings. Music catalogue separate from the general catalogue. Interlibrary privileges throughout Niagara Regional Library System.

OSHAWA PUBLIC LIBRARY
Music Services
65 Bagot St.
Oshawa, ON L1H 1N2
(416) 579-6111, x18
Contact: Samuel Schulze, Head of Music Services
Music Collection/Holdings: 9,000 records; 2,000 cassettes; 100 reel-to-

reel tapes; and 1,000 pieces of sheet music.
Services/Access Information: Materials may be borrowed. Listening facilities; cassette players for rent.

OTTAWA PUBLIC LIBRARY[1]
Music Department
120 Metcalfe St.
Ottawa, ON K1P 5M2
(613) 236-0301
Contact: Genevieve Thomson, Coordinator, Adult Services

QUEEN'S UNIVERSITY AT KINGSTON
Music Library
Harrison-Le Caine Hall
Kingston, ON K7L 5C4
(613) 547-2873
Contact: E. Albrich, Music/Art Librarian
Music Collection/Holdings: Collection of books (8,000) and scores (10,500) supporting undergraduate program in music history, music education, ethnomusicology; 5,500 records; some microforms and tapes.
Services/Access Information: Limited interlibrary loan; limited public access.

RYERSON POLYTECHNICAL INSTITUTE
50 Gould St.
Toronto, ON M5B 1E8
(416) 595-5398
Contact: E. Bishop, Art and Literature Librarian
Music Collection/Holdings: Supports curriculum in theatre, radio and television, and film studies. Primarily music history and appreciation materials; material on musical production and its relationship with visual images and as a form of artistic expression. Contains 3,000 monographs; 300 cassette recordings; and 1,100 records.
Services/Access Information: Membership fee for borrowing privileges.

SUDBURY PUBLIC LIBRARY
Audio Visual Services
74 Mackenzie St.
Sudbury, ON P3C 4X8
(705) 673-1155
Contact: Helen Halverson, Audio Visual Coordinator
Music Collection/Holdings: 4,913 recordings (records and cassettes), adult and juvenile (French and English).
Services/Access Information: Charges for borrowing records and cassettes; special charge for operas or multi-volume sets. List of new recordings available monthly; card catalogue of Song Index to book and recordings collection. Listening facilities.

THUNDER BAY PUBLIC LIBRARY
Brodie Resource Library
216 S. Brodie St.
Thunder Bay, ON P7E 1C2
(807) 622-6446
Contact: Janice Bick, Adult Services Librarian
Music Collection/Holdings: Wide selection of records and tapes, including popular, jazz, classical, and folk; fairly large music book collection, including major reference works, such as Phonolog.
Services/Access Information: Books, records, and tapes circulate; 16mm film bookings; film and slide projector loans; reference service; record and tape reserve; programs available. Borrowing privileges for all valid cardholders.

UNIVERSITY OF OTTAWA
Music Library
1 Stewart St.
Ottawa, ON K1N 6H5
(613) 231-5717
Contact: Debra Ann Begg, Music Librarian
Music Collection/Holdings: 17,000 scores; 10,700 books; and 5,000 recordings.
Services/Access Information: No direct borrowing privileges for non-university users.

UNIVERSITY OF TORONTO
Edward Johnson Music Library
Faculty of Music
Toronto, ON M5S 1A1
(416) 978-3734
Contact: Kathleen McMorrow, Librarian
Music Collection/Holdings: Over 100,000 books, journals, scores, and microform holdings. Acquisitions policy emphasizes historical editions, collected works editions of individual composers; with reference works, chamber music parts; a comprehensive collection of contemporary music; biographical and historical monographs; manuscript of early music from European libraries on microform; archival collection documenting careers of a number of musicians. Rare Book Room houses first editions of Mozart, Haydn, Beethoven, and Gershwin; early Canadian tune books; 18th and 19th century opera scores.
Services/Access Information: Circulation is restricted to staff and students and registered extramural readers; open to the public for reference use. Listening facilities; microform readers.

UNIVERSITY OF WESTERN ONTARIO[1]
Music Library
London, ON N6A 3K7
(519) 679-2466
Contact: Merwin Lewis, Librarian-In-Charge

WINDSOR PUBLIC LIBRARY
Arts and Recreation Division
850 Ouellette Ave.
Windsor, ON N9A 4M9
(519) 255-6770
Music Collection/Holdings: Canadian emphasis in all materials; records and audio-cassettes; scores and sheet music; periodicals; books, including biographies, music history, 20th century music, music theory, instrumental methods, and studies.
Services/Access Information: Reference services.

WOODSTOCK PUBLIC LIBRARY AND ART GALLERY
Audio-Visual Department
445 Hunter St.
Woodstock, ON N4S 4G7
(519) 539-4801
Contact: Irene Pollock, Head
Music Collection/Holdings: 2,000 musical recordings; 58 references; 500 circulating music books; periodicals; and vertical pamphlet files.
Services/Access Information: Interlibrary loan; listening facilities; reference services. Identification card required for borrowing privileges.

YORK UNIVERSITY
Scott Library, Listening Room
4700 Keele St.
Downsview, ON M3J 2R2
(416) 667-3694
Contact: Mary Williamson, Fine Arts Bibliographer; Julie Stockton, Listening Room Head
Music Collection/Holdings: Recordings; scores; discographies; and a small number of music periodicals. Collection also includes clips, microfiche, and an archive of 78rpm records. The recordings collection consists of plays, poetry, public affairs, lectures, and a large selection of music (classical, jazz, folk, rock, electronic, and ethnic). Scores collection contains performance scores, sheet music, and miniature study scores. Music-related books housed in general stacks of main library.
Services/Access Information: Recordings do not circulate outside Listening Room; most scores can be borrowed for 1 week, except anthologies and collected works, which can be signed out for photocopying. Maintains a reserve collection of recordings and scores; reference assistance available; catalogues and indexes for locating recordings and special collections; turntables, reel-to-reel and cassette players for use.

QUEBEC

BIBLIOTHEQUE DE QUEBEC
La Phonotheque
350 St.-Joseph est
Quebec, PQ G1K 8A3
(418) 692-2135
Contact: Gilles Bergeron, Head, Audio-Visual Services
Music Collection/Holdings: 10,000

records, including children's music, jazz, classical, popular, western, soundtracks, and so forth.
Services/Access Information: Audition center; small musical library; references.

BIBLIOTHEQUE MUNICIPALE DE HULL
Maison du citoyen
25, rue Laurier
C.P. 1970, Succ. B
Hull, PQ J8X 3Y9
(819) 777-4341
Contact: Denis Boyer, Director
Music Collection/Holdings: 65,000 records; 2,000-78rpm; 38,000-45rpm; 25,000-33⅓ rpm.
Services/Access Information: Listening facilities.

CANADIAN AMATEUR MUSICIANS/MUSICIENS AMATEURS DU CANADA (CAMMAC)
Music Centre
PO Box 353
Westmount, PQ H3Z 2T5
(514) 932-8755
Contact: Diane Duguay, Librarian-In-Charge
Music Collection/Holdings: Performance material for recorder (duos, trios, ensembles); chamber music (duos, trios, quartets, quintets); choral works (masses, cantatas); and orchestral music (symphonies for small orchestras).
Services/Access Information: Borrowing privileges restricted to CAMMAC members; fees for membership vary.

CANADIAN BROADCASTING CORPORATION
Music Services-Library
PO Box 6000
1400 Dorchester Blvd. E.
Montreal, PQ H3C 3A8
(514) 285-3900
Contact: Claude Gagnon, Head of Music Services
Music Collection/Holdings: 2,000 books; 175,000 titles in sheet music; 60,000-78rpm and 320,000-33⅓ rpm records.
Services/Access Information: Not open to public.

CEGEP DE DRUMMONDVILLE
Option musique
960, rue St-Georges
Drummondville, PQ J2C 6A2
(819) 472-4671, x255
Music Collection/Holdings: Symphonic music for brass ensemble (wood and wind); stage band (combos of all kinds); and chorus (choral).

CONSERVATOIRE DE MUSIQUE DE MONTREAL
Centre de Documentation
100, rue Notre-Dame est
Montreal, PQ H2Y 1C1
(514) 873-4031
Contact: Nicole M.-Boisclair, Director
Music Collection/Holdings: 51,000 books and scores; 58 periodical subscriptions; 9,000 audiovisual documents; Reference collections. Special collections: Cooper, Arthur Garami, and Jean Deslauriers Collections; scores and manuscripts of 16th, 17th, and 18th centuries.
Services/Access Information: Interlibrary loan; reference services. consultation of materials on the premises; no borrowing privileges to outside users.

CONSERVATOIRE DE MUSIQUE DE TROIS-RIVIERES
Bibliotheque
587, rue Raddison
C.P. 1146
Trois-Rivieres, PQ G9A 5K8
(819) 375-7748
Contact: Guy Lefebvre, Librarian
Music Collection/Holdings: Music literature, instructional material; instrumental, vocal and orchestral scores and parts; scores sets; sound recordings.
Services/Access Information: Borrowing by students, faculty and staff; available to students of other conservatories in the network through interlibrary loan. Orchestral material may be borrowed by groups by special arrangement.

MCGILL UNIVERSITY
Marvin Duchow Music Library
555 Sherbrooke St., W.
Montreal, PQ H3A 1E3
(514) 392-4530/4281
Contact: Kathleen M. Toomey, Librarian-In-Charge
Music Collection/Holdings: 17,500 monographs and journals; 184 periodical titles; 17,000 scores, 13,000 records; 200 tapes and cassettes.
Services/Access Information: Reference; interlibrary loan; telex; and computer access UTLAS, 1973-present.

UNIVERSITY DE MONTREAL
Bibliotheque de Musique
C.P. 6128, Succursale A
Montreal, PQ H3C 3J7
(514) 343-6432
Contact: M. Claude Soulard, Librarian
Music Collection/Holdings: 8,000 monographs; 330 periodical titles; 6,000 microfilms/-fiches; 10,400 recordings; 11,100 scores; collection of 3,000 documents concerning Canadian music.
Services/Access Information: Interlibrary loan. Open to public for reference; borrowing restricted to students and faculty.

UNIVERSITE LAVAL
Bibliotheque de Musique
Pavillon Bonenfant
Cite Universitaire
Sainte-Foy, PQ G1K 7P4
(418) 656-7039
Contact: Claude Beaudry, Music Librarian
Music Collection/Holdings: 22,000 scores; 15,000 volumes; 500 periodical titles; and 15,000 recordings. Emphasis is on musicology, music education, 19th century French music, and contemporary music.
Services/Access Information: Open daily. Catalogs of holdings; photocopy services; listening facilities; interlibrary loan; and reference services.

WESTMOUNT PUBLIC LIBRARY
4574 Sherbrooke St. W.
Westmount, PQ H3Z 1G1
(514) 935-8531
Contact: R.E. Lydon, Chief Librarian
Music Collection/Holdings: 5 periodical subscriptions; 600 books concerning music and musicians; 700 books of musical scores; and 1,000 cassettes.
Services/Access Information: Loans to library members; interlibrary loan, except periodicals and new titles.

SASKATCHEWAN

ALDERSGATE COLLEGE
Wilson Memorial Library
Victoria Ave.
Moose Jaw, SK S6H 4P1
(306) 693-7773
Contact: Ruth Huston, Director
Music Collection/Holdings: Rare books: The Poetical Works of John and Charles Wesley. References; 500 books (songs, hymn stories, hymnbooks, history, sound, instruments, biography, music appreciation, music periodicals); 300 choral scores with parts for performance groups, with records or tapes of 100 of these.

FRANCES MORRISON LIBRARY
Fine and Performing Arts Department
311 23rd St. E.
Saskatoon, SK S7K 0J6
(306) 664-9579
Contact: Frances Daw Bergles, Head
Music Collection/Holdings: 25,000 total record holdings. Strengths: classical recordings; ethnic folk music; jazz; opera; Canadiana. Includes representative popular vocalists; dance music; and spoken-word recordings. Reference and circulating collection of 3,600 volumes of books; 48 periodical subscriptions.
Services/Access Information: Record and books circulate at no charge to library members. Listening center; reference service; and interlibrary loan within provincial library system.

UNIVERSITY OF REGINA LIBRARY
Fine Arts Branch Library
Regina, SK S4S 0A2
(306) 584-4826
Contact: Margaret A. Hammond, Director
Music Collection/Holdings: 8,000 books and bound serial volumes; 4,209 scores; 4,049 records; 50 current periodical subscriptions; vertical files.
Services/Access Information: Listening facilities; computer reference searching available at main library. Borrowing privileges for annual fee.

UNIVERSITY OF SASKATCHEWAN
Library
Saskatoon, SK S7K 5Z9
(306) 343-4216
Contact: Terence M. Horner, Music Cataloguer
Music Collection/Holdings: Approximately 5,000 scores and 8,000 books on music; 6,000 sound recordings. Scores and some music instruction and study materials housed in the education library; the remainder of music instruction and study materials housed in the main library with books on music.
Services/Access Information: Music reference provided in the main and education libraries. No direct borrowing privileges to non-university users.

Music Libraries Index

A

B

C

D

E

F

G

H

I

J

K

L

M

N

O

P

Q

R

S

T

U

V

W

Y

Music Periodicals

U.S., Canadian, and International periodicals are listed alphabetically within each country. Phone number, editor's name, frequency of publication, description of coverage/audience, and subscription rate are given for most publications, when supplied by the publisher.

A

ACADEMY OF COUNTRY MUSIC NEWSLETTER
Academy of Country Music
P.O. Box 508
Hollywood, CA 90028
(213) 843-5695
Editors: Fran Boyd, Jeanne Marchand
Frequency: Monthly
Coverage/Audience: Country music and country music artists.
Subscription: Free with membership

ACCORDION FEDERATION OF NORTH AMERICA NEWSLETTER
11438 Elmcrest St.
El Monte, CA 91732
(213) 686-1769
Frequency: Semimonthly
Subscription: Contact for rates

ACM NEWSLETTER
Academy of Country Music
P.O. Box 508
Hollywood, CA 90028
(213) 462-2351
Frequency: Monthly
Subscription: Free to members

ACUCAA BULLETIN
Association of College, University and Community Arts Administrators
6225 University Ave.
Madison, WI 53705-1099
(608) 233-7400
Editor: Gayle Crim Stamler
Frequency: 11/year
Coverage/Audience: News, trends and how-to articles for administrators of performing arts programs.
Subscription: Free with membership

AFTRA
American Federation of Television and Radio Artists
1350 Ave. of the Americas
New York, NY 10019
(212) 265-7700
Frequency: Quarterly
Subscription: Free

AGAC/THE SONGWRITERS GUILD NEWS
The American Guild of Authors and Composers
(AGAC)/The Songwriters Guild
40 W. 57th St., Ste. 410
New York, NY 10019
(212) 757-8833
Editor: Bob Leone
Frequency: 3-4/year
Coverage/Audience: Songwriters (lyricists and composers).
Subscription: Free with membership

AGAC NEWS/WEST COAST WIRE
American Guild of Authors and Composers/The Songwriters Guild
40 W. 57th St., Ste. 410
New York, NY 10016
(212) 757-8833
Editor: Bob Leone
Frequency: 3-4/year
Coverage/Audience: An organization run by songwriters with a national base and a membership of over 3,500. The AGAC News provides information of importance to songwriters. Guild activities and services, legislative issues, anything relevant to the education of and protection of songwriters.
Subscription: Free with membership; also available to nonmembers

AGMAZINE
American Guild of Musical Artists
1841 Broadway
New York, NY 10023
(212) 265-3687
Editor: Ms. Annalise Kamada
Frequency: 5/year
Coverage/Audience: Union publication for members and interested parties representing singers, dancers, choreographers, and stage personnel in opera, ballet, and concert.
Subscription: Free

AMATEUR CHAMBER MUSIC PLAYERS NEWSLETTER
Amateur Chamber Music Players, Inc.
633 E St., N.W.
Washington, DC, 20004
(202) 628-0099
Editor: Susan Lloyd
Frequency: 1-2/year
Subscription: Free with membership or suggested contribution of $10

AMERICAN ACCORDIONISTS' ASSOCIATION NEWSLETTER
580 Kearny Ave.
Kearny, NJ 07032
(201) 991-5010
Frequency: Quarterly
Subscription: Contact for rates

AMERICAN ARTS
American Council for the Arts
570 7th Ave.
New York, NY 10018-1763
(212) 354-6655
Editor: William Keens
Frequency: Bimonthly
Coverage/Audience: Arts and arts management professionals and the general public.
Subscription: $15/year

AMERICAN ENSEMBLE
Chamber Music America
215 Park Ave., S.
New York, NY 10003
(212) 460-9030
Editor: Barbara L. Sand
Frequency: Quarterly
Coverage/Audience: Covers all aspects of activity in the chamber music field, including news on performers, funding opportunities, how-to articles for both performers and concerts presenters,

feature stories about individual groups and news about parent organization. Geared toward professional, but of interest to laypersons.
Subscription: $35 voting members; $25 associate members

AMERICAN GUILD ASSOCIATE NEWS
American Guild of Music
P.O. Box 3
Downers Grove, IL 60515
(312) 968-0173
Frequency: Every 2-3 months
Subscription: Free with membership

AMERICAN HARP JOURNAL
American Harp Society, Inc.
1374 Academy Lane
Teaneck, NJ 07666
(201) 836-8909
Editor: Jane Weidensaul
Frequency: 2/year
Subscription: $15/year

AMERICAN MUSIC
University of Illinois
(cosponsored with the Sonneck Society)
54 E. Gregory, Room 100
Champaign, IL 61820
(217) 333-0950
Editor: Allen P. Britton
Frequency: Quarterly
Coverage/Audience: All aspects of American music and music in America for specialists and interested lay readers. All genres and forms, composers, performers, the media, political, and economic issues, education, criticism and aesthetics. Also contains book reviews and record reviews.
Subscription: $17.50/year individuals, $18.50 foreign; $22.50 institutions, $23.50 foreign

AMERICAN MUSICAL INSTRUMENT SOCIETY NEWSLETTER
American Musical Instrument Society
AMIS Membership Office
USD Box 194
Vermillion, SD 57069
(605) 677-5306
Editor: Andre P. Larson
Frequency: 3/year
Coverage/Audience: Promotes the study of the history, design, and use of musical instruments in all cultures and from all periods.
Subscription: $20/year (includes Newsletter and Journal)

AMERICAN MUSIC CENTER NEWSLETTER
250 W. 54th St., Rm. 300
New York, NY 10019
(212) 247-3121
Editor: Margaret Jory
Frequency: Quarterly
Coverage/Audience: For composers, performers and patrons of contemporary music—critics, libraries.
Subscription: Free with membership; $7.50/year nonmembers

THE AMERICAN MUSIC TEACHER
Music Teachers National Association, Inc.
2113 Carew Tower
Cincinnati, OH 45202
(513) 421-1420
Editor: Homer Ulrich
Frequency: 6/year
Coverage/Audience: The American Music Teacher is edited for the MTNA and its 7 divisional organizations as well as affiliated state associations. It is also for music teachers in colleges and universities.
Subscription: $7.50

THE AMERICAN ORGANIST
American Guild of Organists
815 Second Ave., Ste. 318
New York, NY 10017
(212) 687-9188
Editor: Anthony Baglivi
Frequency: Monthly
Coverage/Audience: 24,000 subscribers include all members of the American Guild of Organists, the Royal Canadian College of Organists. Writers are outstanding musicians who cover organ building; purchasing an organ; choir training; reviews of new organ, harpsichord and choral music; book recordings; interpretation of avant-garde music as well as current events.
Subscription: $20/year

THE AMERICAN RECORDER
The American Recorder Society, Inc.
48 W. 21st St.
New York, NY 10010
(212) 675-9042
Editor: Sigrid Nagle
Frequency: Quarterly
Coverage/Audience: Early music with an emphasis on the recorder. Articles range from translations of scholarly treatises to reports on activities of our 85 plus chapters. Book and record reviews. Written for the knowledgeable amateur and the professional.
Subscription: $15 individuals; $16 institutions

AMERICAN STRING TEACHER
American String Teachers Association
Box 688
University of Texas at Dallas
Richardson, TX 75080
(214) 690-2231
Editor: Dr. Nancy Cluck
Frequency: Quarterly
Coverage/Audience: Contains articles on string teaching and playing for violin, vila, cello, double bass, and guitar; string ensemble and orchestra; also specialized forums.
Subscription: Free with membership

AMERICAN SUZUKI JOURNAL
Suzuki Association of the Americas, Inc.
319 E. Second St., Ste. 302
Muscatine, IA 52761
(319) 263-3071
Editor: Robert K. Reinsager
Frequency: 6/year
Coverage/Audience: Presents a broad spectrum of articles related to talent education as well as announcements of events and reports on the activities of the Association.
Subscription: Free with membership; $16 nonmembers

AMERICA'S BOYCHOIR FEDERATION NEWSLETTER
Division of International Federation of Children's choirs
P.O. Box 677
125 S. 4th St.
Connellsville, PA 15425
(412) 696-3636
Editor: John B. Shallenberger
Frequency: Quarterly
Subscription: $8/year

THE ANCIENT TIMES
Company of Fifers & Drummers
c/o H.L. Carlson
16 Winter Ave.
Deep River, CT 06417
Editor: Ed Olsen
Frequency: Quarterly
Subscription: $4/year

AND ALL THAT JAZZ
Jazz Research
Box 462
Ingram, TX 78025
(512) 896-2285
Editor: Ted Tarr
Frequency: 1/year plus 3 or 4 addenda
Coverage/Audience: Primarily jazz record buyers.
Subscription: No charge. Send #10 SASE or 2 International Reply Coupons

ANNUAL REVIEW OF JAZZ STUDIES
Transaction Books
Rutgers University
New Brunswick, NJ 08903
(201) 932-2280
Editors: Dan Morgenstern, Charles Nanry, David A. Cayer
Frequency: Annual
Coverage/Audience: The only English-language publication specifically devoted to scholarly research on jazz and related musical forms. It embraces such disciplines as musicology,musical analysis, discography, social history, oral history, black studies, social science and archival practice.
Subscription: $15 volume (published annually as a serial)

ANTIQUE PHONOGRAPH MONTHLY
APM Press
502 E. 17th St.
Brooklyn, NY 11226
(212) 941-6835
Editor: Allen Koenigsberg
Frequency: 10/year
Coverage/Audience: Devoted to

preservation and restoration of antique phonographs and records (1877-1930). Articles include history, biography, popular music, opera, advertising, patent research, question and answer column, book and record reviews, advertisements, etc. Audience includes primarily private collectors, but also historical societies, libraries and museums.
Subscription: $10/year

ARSC BULLETIN
Association for Recorded Sound Collections
P.O. Box 1643
Manassas, VA 22110
(703) 361-3901
Frequency: Annually
Subscription: Free with membership

ARSC JOURNAL
Association for Recorded Sound Collections
P.O. Box 1643
Manassas, VA 22110
(703) 361-3901
Frequency: 3/year
Subscription: Free with membership

ARSC NEWSLETTER
Association for Recorded Sound Collections
P.O. Box 1643
Manassas, VA 22110
(703) 361-3901
Frequency: Quarterly
Subscription: Free with membership

ARTS MANAGEMENT
Radius Group, Inc.
408 W. 57th St.
New York, NY 10019
(212) 245-3850
Editor: Alvin H. Reiss
Frequency: 5/year
Coverage/Audience: News developments and trends in the arts, case histories of successful arts organization approaches to specific problems. Reports on arts funding, promotion and legislation, and books and articles of interest to arts fields. Audience is administrators of cultural institutions, board members, volunteers, and individual, corporate, foundation and government supporters.
Subscription: $10/year

ASSOCIATE NEWS
American Guild of Music
P.O. Box 3
Downers Grove, IL 60515
(312) 968-0173
Editor: Mike McWilliams
Frequency: 3-4/year
Coverage/Audience: Teachers and studio operators.
Subscription: Free to members

AUDIO MAGAZINE
CBS Publications
1515 Broadway
New York, NY 10036
(212) 719-6330
Editor: Eugene Pitts III
Frequency: Monthly
Coverage/Audience: Directed to the sophisticated hi-fi buff, providing many pages of equipment test reports.
Subscription: $15.94/year

B

BALLET NEWS
The Metropolitan Opera Guild, Inc.
1865 Broadway
New York, NY 10023
(212) 582-3285
Editor: Robert Jacobson
Frequency: Monthly
Coverage/Audience: Ballet and dance in words and pictures. Addressed particularly to the dance audience as opposed to the dance professional.
Subscription: $18/year

BAND FAN
Detroit Concert Band, Inc.
20962 Mack Ave.
Grosse Pointe Woods, MI 48236
(313) 886-0394
Editor: John Stafford
Frequency: 3-4/year
Coverage/Audience: Concert band fans.
Subscription: $10 to members

BANJO NEWSLETTER
P.O. Box 364
Greensboro, MD 21639
(301) 482-6278
Editor: Hub Nitchie
Frequency: Monthly
Coverage/Audience: Devoted to 5-string banjo. Much tablature in classical, bluegrass, old time and jazz, Scruggs or Reno styles. Articles, interviews, evaluations, opinions.
Subscription: $12/year

THE BATON OF PHI BETA FRATERNITY
622 E. Main
Mulvane, KS 67110
(316) 777-0714
Editor: Sue Henderson Wenger
Frequency: 3/year
Coverage/Audience: Articles, reports of interest to persons within the realm of the creative and performing arts (music, speech, drama, dance, and art—music therapy, speech therapy).
Subscription: $4.50/year

THE BLACK PERSPECTIVE IN MUSIC
Foundation for Research in the Afro-American Creative Arts, Inc.
P.O. Drawer 1
Cambria Heights, NY 11411
Frequency: Semiannual
Subscription: $7/year individuals; $8/year institutions; $10/year foreign

BLITZ MAGAZINE
P.O. Box 48124
Los Angeles, CA 90048-0124
(213) 432-6121
Editor: Mike McDowell
Frequency: 6/year
Coverage/Audience: Blitz is billed as the rock and roll magazine for thinking people. Emphasis is on underrated and/or obscure artists, with an academic slant and record collector's perspective. Format covers a wide range of artists.
Subscription: $8.50 U.S.; $9.50 Canada; $11.00 others

BLUEGRASS CLUB OF NEW YORK NEWSLETTER
Bluegrass Club of New York
380 Lexington Ave., Ste. 1119
New York, NY 10017
(212) 687-9000
Editor: Douglas Tuchman
Frequency: Monthly
Coverage/Audience: Covers the field of bluegrass and traditional country music.
Subscription: $5 individual; $7 family

BLUEGRASS UNLIMITED
Bluegrass Unlimited, Inc.
P.O. Box 111
Broad Run, VA 22014
(703) 361-8992
Editor: Peter V. Kuykendall
Frequency: Monthly
Coverage/Audience: All aspects of bluegrass, old-time country music. Record and book reviews, artists' appearances, complete festival list, feature artist profiles and letters.
Subscription: $12/year

BMI: THE MANY WORLDS OF MUSIC
Broadcast Music, Inc.
321 W. 57th St.
New York, NY 10019
(212) 586-2000
Editor: Howard Colson
Frequency: Quarterly
Coverage/Audience: Activities of BMI affiliates (awards, concerts, visits, festivals, books, etc.); profiles on prominent BMI music figures; BMI award presentations and yearly dinners. Readers include music trade press, colleges, universities, grammar and high schools, music organizations, and associations, libraries, record and publishing companies.
Subscription: Free

BOOMBAH HERALD
A Journal of Band History
15 Park Blvd.
Lancaster, NY 14086
(716) 681-9720
Editor: Loren D. Geiger
Frequency: Christmas and Easter
Coverage/Audience: Devoted to biographical sketches of composers of band music, features on military, circus and civilian bands, and reviews of records and books on band music.
Subscription: $6/year

BULLETIN OF THE GUILD OF CARILLONNEURS IN NORTH AMERICA
The Guild of Carillonneurs in North America
3718 Settle Rd.
Cincinnati, OH 45327
Editors: Gordon and Elsa Slater
Frequency: Occasionally (normally each January)
Coverage/Audience: Members and libraries interested in information about the Guild of Carillonneurs
Subscription: Contact for rate

BULLETIN OF THE INTERNATIONAL COUNCIL FOR TRADITIONAL MUSIC
International Council for Traditional Music
Department of Music
Columbia University
New York, NY 10027
(212) 678-0332
Editor: Dr. Dieter Christensen
Frequency: 2/year
Coverage/Audience: Traditional music worldwide, book and record reviews. Audience is comprised of musicians, scholars in fields of ethnomusicology and musicology.
Subscription: $20 U.S.; $22 institutions. Subscription includes the Yearbook for Traditional Music

BUSINESS BAROMETER
National Association of Music Merchants
500 N. Michigan Ave.
Chicago, IL 60611
(312) 527-3200
Editor: Dr. Ray Williams
Frequency: Twice monthly
Coverage/Audience: Economic news geared to music retailers; monthly sales trend graphs for music products industry.
Subscription: Membership only

C

CADENCE
The American Review of Jazz & Blues
Cadence Building
Redwood, NY 13679-9612
(315) 287-2852
Editor: Bob Rusch
Frequency: Monthly
Coverage/Audience: Reviews records and books on jazz and blues from around the world.
Subscription: $20/year; $30, first class; $40 airmail/Asia, Australia, Africa; $35 airmail/Europe, South America

THE CALENDAR FOR NEW MUSIC
Sound Art Foundation, Inc.
45 Greene St.
New York, NY 10013
(212) 226-6213
Editor: William Hauermann
Frequency: Monthly (Oct.-May)
Coverage/Audience: To audiences principally in the NY metropolitan area; all are persons who have asked to receive information on new music concerts.
Subscription: $7 regular; $3.50 students; $13/two years

CARILLON NEWS
The Guild of Carillonneurs in North America
3718 Settle Rd.
Cincinnati, OH 45227
(513) 271-8519
Frequency: 2/year
Subscription: Contact for rates

CATGUT ACOUSTICAL SOCIETY NEWSLETTER
112 Essex Ave.
Montclair, NJ 07042
Editor: Dr. Robert E. Fryxell
Frequency: Semiannual
Coverage/Audience: Acoustics of the violin family instruments. A membership of 850 in 29 countries; includes laymen and professionals, musicians, musicologists, instrument makers, composers, scientists, and engineers.
Subscription: $15 members only; $20 overseas

CBDNA JOURNAL
College Band Directors' National Association
Baylor University
School of Music
Waco, TX 76798
(817) 755-3571
Frequency: 3/year
Subscription: Free with membership

CBDNA NEWSLETTER
College Band Directors' National Association
Baylor University
School of Music
Waco, TX 76798
(817) 755-3571
Frequency: Quarterly
Subscription: Free with membership

CDSS NEWS
Country Dance and Song Society of America
505 8th Ave.
New York, NY 10018
(212) 594-8833
Frequency: Bimonthly
Subscription: Free with membership

CENTRAL OPERA SERVICE BULLETIN
Metropolitan Opera
Lincoln Center
New York, NY 10023
(212) 799-3467
Frequency: Quarterly
Subscription: Free to members; $15/year individuals; $30/year groups; $50/year institutions

CHINESE MUSIC
Chinese Music Society of North America
2329 Charmingfare
Woodridge, IL 60517
(312) 985-1606
Editor: Sinyan Shen, Ph.D.
Frequency: Quarterly
Coverage/Audience: All phases of research and performance activities in Chinese music. It also publishes papers of general interest to the music community and the public as well as book and record reviews. Some topics covered: analysis, acoustics, ballad singing, musical instruments, musicology, etc.
Subscription: $10 U.S., individual; $18 U.S. institution

THE CHOIR HERALD
The Lorenz Publishing Company
501 E. Third St.
P.O. Box 802
Dayton, OH 45401
(513) 228-6118
Editor: Robert J. Hughes
Frequency: Monthly
Coverage/Audience: SATB anthems, with solos and other interesting variations, closed score.
Subscription: $15.50 individual

THE CHOIR LEADER
The Lorenz Publishing Company
501 E. Third St.
P.O. Box 802
Dayton, OH 45401
(513) 228-6118
Editor: Eugene McCluskey
Frequency: Monthly
Coverage/Audience: For the choir that has grown beyond the basics. Many of the selections are moderately difficult, but some are easier, and will stretch your members' skills to their limits.
Subscription: $15.50 individual

THE CHORAL JOURNAL
American Choral Directors Association
P.O. Box 5310
Lawton, OK 73504
(405) 355-8161
Editor: James McCray
Frequency: 9/year
Coverage/Audience: Choral Directors, Church, educational and professional.
Subscription: $12 libraries only

CHORD AND DISCORD
Bruckner Society of America, Inc.
P.O. Box 2570
Iowa City, IA 52244
(319) 338-0313
Frequency: Irregular
Subscription: Contact for rates

THE CHORISTER
Associated Male Choruses of America, Inc.
106 Maplefield
Pleasant Ridge, MI 48069
(313) 544-1995
Frequency: 9/year
Subscription: $7.50/year associate members

CHORISTERS GUILD LETTERS
Choristers Guild
2834 Kingsley Rd.
Garland, TX 75041
(214) 271-1521
Editor: Donald F. Jensen
Frequency: Monthly (10/year, September - June)
Coverage/Audience: Addresses itself to the needs of people working with young people in music in the church, offering vocal techniques, repertory, programming ideas, workshops and festival information, activities, etc., for directors and young people.
Subscription: $20/year

THE CHURCH MUSICIAN
The Sunday School Board of the Southern Baptist Convention
127 Ninth Ave., N.
Nashville, TN 37234
(615) 251-2961
Editor: William M. Anderson, Jr.
Frequency: Monthly
Coverage/Audience: For music directors and volunteers, pastors, organists, pianists, choir coordinators, and members of the music council and/or other planning committees or groups. Contents include articles for spiritual growth and enrichment, testimonials, human interest stories, and other materials related to music programs in local churches.
Subscription: $8/year; $15.75/two years; $21.75/three years

CIRCUS MAGAZINE
419 Park Ave. S.
New York, NY 10016
(212) 685-5050
Editor: Gerald Rothberg
Frequency: Monthly
Coverage/Audience: Of interest to 15-26 year olds; music oriented reader. Profiles, record reviews, concert reviews, and listings. Articles of interest to rock and roll reader.
Subscription: $19/year

THE CLAPPER
North American Guild of Change Ringers
17 Farmcrest Ave.
Lexington, MA 02173
(617) 861-1604
Editor: Elizabeth F. Davies
Frequency: Quarterly
Coverage/Audience: Most readers are ringers. News of progress, articles about technical aspects of ringing; business news and historical articles.
Subscription: Free with membership; $8/year nonmembers

THE CLARINET
The International Clarinet Society
Box 8099
Idaho State University
Pocatello, ID 83209
(208) 236-3108
Editor: James Gillespie (School of Music, North Texas State University, Denton, TX 76203)
Frequency: Quarterly
Coverage/Audience: For clarinet teachers, professional players, students, etc. Covers clarinet history, literature, recordings, manufacturer's products, music/record/concert reviews, articles on all aspects of the clarinet.
Subscription: $15 U.S. & Canada; $25 foreign

CLAVIER
1418 Lake
Evanston, IL 60201
(312) 328-6000
Editors: Lee Prater Yost, Barbara Kreader
Frequency: 10/year
Coverage/Audience: An internationally known journal which is an indispensable musical resource for questions regarding keyboard performance, literature, and pedagogy. Read by keyboard teachers and performers. Contains reviews of recently released records, books, and music for piano, organ, and harpsichord. It includes in-depth interviews for prominent performers, monthly masterlessons, and the newest ideas in teaching techniques and materials.
Subscription: $12.50

THE CLEF
Mu Beta Psi National Honorary Musical Fraternity
3041 Hickory Crest Dr.
Marietta, GA 30064
(404) 428-1748
Frequency: Semiannual
Subscription: Contact for rates

CLEVELAND INSTITUTE OF MUSIC NEWSLETTER
The Cleveland Institute of Music
11021 E. Boulevard
Cleveland, OH 44106
(216) 791-5165
Editor: Jean Caldwell
Frequency: Monthly
Coverage/Audience: Musicians and music publications; clubs throughout the world; includes music education institutions, alumni, supporters, students.
Subscription: Free to libraries, resource centers, and educational institutions

CLOSE UP
Country Music Association
P.O. Box 22299
7 Music Circle N.
Nashville, TN 37202
(615) 244-2840
Editor: Cathleen Gurley
Frequency: Monthly
Coverage/Audience: On trends in the country music industry.
Subscription: Free with membership

CMA CLOSE-UP
Country Music Association, Inc.
P.O. Box 22299
Nashville, TN 37202
(615) 244-2840
Editor: Cathy Gurley
Frequency: Monthly
Coverage/Audience: For professionals in the country music industry.
Subscription: Free to members

COLLEGE MUSIC SYMPOSIUM
The College Music Society
Regent Box 44
University of Colorado
Boulder, CO 80309
(303) 492-5049
Editor: Dr. Theodore Albrecht
Frequency: 2/year
Coverage/Audience: Reviews, current music research.
Subscription: $25 with membership

THE COMMUNIQUE
The International Rock 'n' Roll Music Association, Inc.
P.O. Box 50111
Nashville, TN 37205
(615) 297-9072
Frequency: 2/year
Subscription: $9/year student; $10/year enthusiast; $25/year professional

COMPOSERS, AUTHORS, AND ARTISTS OF AMERICA (CAAA)
355 East 86th St.
New York, NY 10028
Editor: Dr. Michaelina Bumocore
Frequency: Quarterly (sometimes two issues combined)
Coverage/Audience: All contributions by member artists, composers, and authors only, but subject to review by editor. Represents the professional standards in the three arts of its membership. It reaches its members, libraries, colleges, universities, and interested individuals.
Subscription: $3 U.S. & Canada; $2 libraries

COMPOSER/USA
National Association of Composers/USA
P.O. Box 49652
Barrington Station
Los Angeles, CA 90049
(213) 541-8213
Frequency: Quarterly
Subscription: $8/year with membership

CONTEMPORARY CHRISTIAN MUSIC
P.O. Box 6300
Laguna Hills, CA 92653
(714) 951-9106
Editor: Frank Edmondson
Frequency: Monthly
Coverage/Audience: Designed for those involved or interested in the gospel music of today. Its readers include recording and performing artists, record company executives,

broadcasters, retailers, promoters and fans. Serves as a line of communication and a forum through which important issues relating to Christian music can be discussed. Personality profiles, album reviews, charts and various regular columns and departments are featured.
Subscription: $15/year; $28/two years

COUNCIL FOR RESEARCH IN MUSIC EDUCATION BULLETIN
School of Music
University of Illinois
1205 W. California
Urbana, IL 61801
(217) 333-1027
Editor: Richard Colwell
Frequency: Quarterly
Coverage/Audience: Music educators; international audience.
Subscription: $10 individual; $15 libraries

COUNTRY DANCE AND SONG
Country Dance and Song Society of America
505 8th Ave.
New York, NY 10018
(212) 594-8833
Frequency: Annually
Subscription: Free with membership

COUNTRY HERITAGE
RR 1, Box 320
Madill, OK 73446
Editor: Beverly King
Frequency: Monthly
Coverage/Audience: Covers traditional country music (including mountain folk music, bluegrass, old time country, early western). Also covers resophonic guitar (Dobro; acoustical steel guitar). Readers are musicians or people interested in old time country music.
Subscription: $6.25/year (bulk mail); $8/year (U.S. 1st class); $9.40 Canada

COUNTRY MUSIC FOUNDATION OF COLORADO NEWS RELEASE
P.O. Box 19435
Denver, CO 80219
(303) 936-7762
Frequency: 6/year
Subscription: Free with membership

CRESCENDO
Interlochen Center for the Arts
Interlochen Arts Academy/National Music Camp
Interlochen, MI 49643
(616) 276-9221
Editor: Betty Parsons
Frequency: 3/year
Coverage/Audience: Alumni of Interlochen Arts Academy and National Music Camp, parents, friends, and donors as well as libraries and other reference centers. Covers all aspects of Interlochen.
Subscription: Free

CUM NOTIS VARIORUM
Music Library
University of California
Berkeley, CA 94720
(415) 642-2623
Editor: Ann Basart
Frequency: 10/year
Coverage/Audience: Music and other librarians; music faculty and UCB and other academic institutions, the users of our library. Covers news of recent publications, events, meetings, interviews, book reviews (particularly reference books in music), and descriptions of our collection and lists of our new acquisitions.
Subscription: Free

CURRENT MUSICOLOGY
709 Dodge
Department of Music
Columbia University
New York, NY 10027
(212) 280-3826
Editor: Jeanne Ryder
Frequency: 2/year
Coverage/Audience: Covers recent work in musicology, particularly that of younger scholars. Features book reviews, dissertation reviews, bibliographica, list of recent publications in music.
Subscription: $10 individual; $12 institutions; $8 students

D

DANCE CHRONICLE: STUDIES IN DANCE AND THE RELATED ARTS
Marcel Dekker, Inc.
270 Madison Ave.
New York, NY 10016
(212) 696-9000
Editors: George Dorris and Jack Anderson
Frequency: Quarterly
Coverage/Audience: Publishes articles, reviews, and primary documents on all aspects of dance history up to the present. Its readers include serious dance—goers, scholars and critics interested in exploring the too-long neglected history of this art.
Subscription: $27.50 individual; $57.50 institutional

DANCE FILMS ASSOCIATION NEWSLETTER
241 E. 34th St., Rm. 301
New York, NY 10016
(212) 686-7019
Frequency: Monthly
Subscription: Free with membership

DANCE NEWS
Dance News, Inc.
119 W. 57th St.
New York, NY 10019
(212) 757-6761
Editors: Helen V. Atlas
Frequency: Monthly except July and August
Coverage/Audience: News coverage of the dance world both here and abroad, including features on ballet and modern dancers, composers, and designers; reviews of performances and books, obituaries, schools, calendar and letters to the editor.
Subscription: $13 U.S.; $16 foreign

DANCE NOTATION BUREAU NEWSLETTER
Dance Notation Bureau
505 8th Ave., Rm. 2301
New York, NY 10018
(212) 736-4350
Frequency: Quarterly
Coverage/Audience: Membership information, job positions, research information, profiles, library services, staff news, bookstore bargains, etc.
Subscription: $35 with membership; $15 nonmembers

DANCE NOTATION JOURNAL
Dance Notation Bureau
505 8th Ave., Rm. 2301
New York, NY 10018
(212) 736-4350
Editor: Jill Beck
Frequency: 2/year
Coverage/Audience: It is not about dance or dance personalities. It takes as its premise written notation systems for dance and movement; these serve as a medium for the focused presentation of theory and philosophy, style analysis, and research in dance history and education.
Subscription: $35 with membership; $15 nonmembers

DB-THE SOUND ENGINEERING MAGAZINE
Sagamore Publishing Co., Inc.
1120 Old Country Rd.
Plainview, NY 11803
(516) 433-6530
Editor: John Woram
Frequency: Monthly
Coverage/Audience: Directed to the engineers in the recording, broadcast and sound reinforcement fields. The articles are quite technical in nature.
Subscription: $15/year

THE DIAPASON
Scranton-Gillette Communications, Inc.
380 Northwest Highway
Des Plaines, IL 60016
(312) 298-6622
Editor: David M. McCain
Frequency: Monthly
Coverage/Audience: Devoted to the interests of the organ, the harpsichord, the carillon and all phases of church music. The official journal of the American Institute of Organbuilders.
Subscription: $10/year

THE DIRECTOR OF THE COMPOSERS' FORUM
Composers' Forum, Inc.

One Fifth Ave.
New York, NY 10003
(212) 673-8794
Editor: Joel Chadabe
Frequency: Annually
Coverage/Audience: Professional composers, new music, classical and jazz.
Subscription: Free to members; $3/year others

DISC COLLECTOR
P.O. Box 315
Cheswold, DE 19936
(302) 674-3149
Editor: Lou Deneumoustier
Frequency: 10 times per year
Coverage/Audience: Record reviews, discographies, aids to record collectors, old time country, bluegrass, folk, traditional country music.
Subscription: Free with purchase

DIVA
37A Bedford St. #63
New York, NY 10014
(212) 243-7177
Editor: Peter Dvarackas
Frequency: 10/year
Coverage/Audience: A vocal-scene newsletter targeted to opera lovers, and also a journal which comments on current American music life, events and personalities—with special emphasis on New York City.
Subscription: $17.50/year

THE DOUBLE REED/JOURNAL OF THE INTERNATIONAL DOUBLE REED SOCIETY
Department of Music
Michigan State University
East Lansing, MI 48824
(517) 355-7727
Editors: Daniel Stolper, Ron Klimko
Frequency: *The Double Reed* - 3/year; *Journal* - Annually
Coverage/Audience: For professional and student oboists and bassoonists.
Subscription: $20/year; $10/year students

DRUM CORPS WORLD
Box 8052
Madison, WI 53708
(608) 241-2292
Editor: Linda Hilton
Frequency: 20/year
Coverage/Audience: Provides its readers with the most complete coverage of the drum and bugle corps and color guard activity available. Readership includes directors, instructors, management personnel, members, boosters, and fans of drum and bugle corps and competitive color guards.
Subscription: $20

DRUM MAJOR MAGAZINE
National Baton Twirling Association
300 S. Wright Rd.
Janesville, WI 53545
(608) 754-2238
Editor: Don Sartell
Frequency: Monthly, except August
Coverage/Audience: The voice of baton twirling: news, photos, contest results and articles about baton twirlers and baton twirling. The official organ of the National Baton Twirling Association.
Subscription: $7.50/year

DULCIMER PLAYERS NEWS
P.O. Box 2164
Winchester, VA 22601
(703) 667-2017/668-6152
Editor: Madeline MacNeil
Frequency: Quarterly
Coverage/Audience: For players and builders of hammered and fretted (mountain) dulcimers. Features playing styles, tunes for beginning to advanced players, tips for beginners, book and record reviews, instrument care and repairs, interviews, and extensive dulcimer festivals and gatherings information.
Subscription: $8/year, $15/2 years, U.S.: $10 Canada & Mexico

E

EAR MAGAZINE EAST
New Wilderness Foundation, Inc.
325 Spring St., Rm. 208
New York, NY 10013
(212) 807-7944/45
Editor: Carol Tuynman
Frequency: 5/year
Coverage/Audience: A new music/literary journal; research and documentation of contemporary music featuring original scores, interviews, reviews, and articles.
Subscription: $12, individual (U.S.), $15, Canada & Mexico; $20 foreign

EASTMAN NOTES
Eastman School of Music
University of Rochester
26 Gibbs St.
Rochester, NY 14604
(716) 275-3031
Editor: Robert Kraus
Frequency: Quarterly
Coverage/Audience: Mailed to friends and alumni of the Eastman school. Contents deal with newsworthy events at the school, faculty, and alumni.
Subscription: Free

ELECTRONOTES
1 Pheasant Lane
Ithaca, NY 14850
(607) 273-8030
Editor: Bernie Hutchins
Frequency: Monthly
Coverage/Audience: Devoted to musical engineering, electronic music equipment theory and design, and application suggestions. Technical level is fairly high, but approach is informal. Includes introductory material and building instructions.
Subscription: $25/year

EMPLOYMENT OPPORTUNITITES
National Guild of Community Schools of the Arts, Inc.
P.O. Box 583
(201) 836-5594
Editor: Lolita Mayadas
Frequency: Monthly
Coverage/Audience: Job opportunities for faculty and administrators in the arts world.
Subscription: $25/year

ENTERTAINMENT EYES
Alsaman Records and Communications Group, Inc.
P.O. Box 8263
Heladon, NY 07508
(201) 942-6810
Editor: Sam Cummings
Frequency: Quarterly
Coverage/Audience: Music in general, i.e., disco, rock, reggae, calypso, etc.
Subscription: $25/year

EQUITY NEWS
Actors Equity Association
165 W. 46th St.
New York, NY 10036
(212) 719-9570
Editor: Dick Moore
Frequency: Monthly
Coverage/Audience: For AEA members.
Subscription: Free to members; $3/year nonmembers

ERNEST BLOCH SOCIETY BULLETIN
Ernest Bloch Society
Star Route 2
Gualala, CA 95445
(707) 884-3473
Editor: Lucienne Bloch Dimitroff
Frequency: Annual
Coverage/Audience: Sent out to members, universities in the U.S., Canada and UK, conductors of large symphony orchestras and musical associations and aficionados of Bloch's music.
Subscription: $3.50

ETHNOMUSICOLOGY
Society for Ethnomusicology
P.O. Box 2984
Ann Arbor, MI 48106
(313) 665-9400
Editor: Timothy Rice
Frequency: 3/year
Coverage/Audience: World-wide coverage and audience.
Subscription: $35

ETHNOMUSICOLOGY NEWSLETTER
Society for Ethnomusicology
P.O. Box 2984
Ann Arbor, MI 48106
(313) 665-9400
Editor: Barbara Hampton
Frequency: 3/year
Coverage/Audience: The advancement of research and study in the field of ethnomusicology. Ethnomusicology is a field closely allied with the social

sciences and humanities. Newsletter contains scholarly articles on music throughout the world, current bibliograph and discography, and book, record and film reviews.
Subscription: $35, members; $20, student members; $30, institutions

F

FANFARE
Fanfare, Inc.
273 Woodland St.
Tenafly, NJ 07670
(201) 567-3908
Editor: Joel Flegler
Frequency: Bimonthly
Coverage/Audience: Classical record reviews
Subscription: $18/year

FCM NEWSLETTER
Fellowship of Christian Musicians
P.O. Box 55151
Tulsa, OK 74155
(918) 252-3862
Frequency: 3/year
Coverage/Audience: Provides information regarding meetings, activities of student chapters, significant events of membership.
Subscription: Free

FILM MUSIC BUYER'S GUIDE
P.O. Box 10687
Costa Mesa, CA 92627
(714) 544-0740
Editor: I Nii
Frequency: Annually (March)
Coverage/Audience: An extensive reference work listing over 5,000 soundtrack titles in 1983, with record numbers and composers.
Subscription: $10 U.S.; $15 foreign

FINLANDIA FOUNDATION NEWSLETTER
1433 San Vincente Blvd.
Santa Monica, CA 90402
(213) 451-5147
Frequency: 1-2/year
Subscription: Free with membership

FIRST CHAIR OF AMERICA
First Chair of America, Inc.
P.O. Box 125
Greenwood, MS 38930
(601) 453-4098
Editor: Roy M. Martin
Frequency: Annually
Coverage/Audience: For school bands and directors.
Subscription: $10/year members; $25/year nonmembers

5-STRINGER
American Banjo Fraternity
202 Colsen Blvd.
Amherst, NY 14226
(716) 836-6432
Editors: Elias & Madeleine Kaufman
Frequency: Quarterly
Coverage/Audience: For anyone interested in the classic banjo.
Subscription: $5/year with membership

FOLK HARP JOURNAL
P.O. Box 161
Mount Laguna, CA 92048
(619) 473-8556
Editor: R.L. Robinson
Frequency: Quarterly
Coverage/Audience: Folk harp, its history and development, its music and techniques of playing, its construction, and current use throughout the world. For amateur and professional harpists, harp makers, harp teachers, libraries.
Subscription: $12 U.S.; $14 foreign

FONTES ARTIS MUSICAE
International Association of Music Libraries
IAML-US Branch
Northwestern University Music Library
Evanston, IL 60201
(312) 492-3434
Editor: Andre Jurres
Frequency: Quarterly
Coverage/Audience: Music librarians, music archivists, music libraries, musicologists.
Subscription: $21 individuals; $36 institutions

FOR THE RECORD
National Academy of Recording Arts and Sciences
4444 Riverside Dr.
Burbank, CA 91505
(213) 843-8233
Editor: George Simon
Frequency: 2/year
Coverage/Audience: News about Academy events.
Subscription: Free to Academy members

FRETS
GPI Publications
20605 Lazaneo
Cupertino, CA 95014
(408) 446-1105
Editor: Jim Hatlo
Frequency: Monthly
Coverage/Audience: The magazine of acoustic string instruments, all styles, all levels. Artist interviews, features about instruments and history, repair and craft techniques, how-to columns, equipment, books, and record reviews.
Subscription: $17.95/year

FRETTED INSTRUMENT GUILD OF AMERICA
2344 S. Oakley Ave.
Chicago, IL 60608
(312) 376-1143
Editor: Ann Pertoney
Frequency: Bimonthly
Coverage/Audience: Articles on banjo, mandolin, guitar and membership activities.
Subscription: $12.50/year

G

GOLDMINE
Arena Magazine Co., Inc.
30691 Utica Rd.
Roseville, MI 48066
(313) 776-0540
Editor: Jeff Tamarkin
Frequency: Monthly
Coverage/Audience: World's largest record collecting publication. Each issue features about 50,000 different records and related items listed for auction or set sale by dealers and collectors worldwide, plus in-depth interviews, discographies, reviews, and other musical features. Concentrates on rock, blues, country-western, little or no jazz or clasical coverage. Tabloid format, average of 200 pages per issue.
Subscription: $20 U.S.; $75 Europe; $100 Asia, Japan

GOOD NEWS
Gospel Music Association
P.O. Box 23201
Nashville, TN 37202
(615) 242-0303
Frequency: Monthly
Subscription: Free with membership

GOSPEL CHOIR
Baptist Sunday School Board
1279th Ave., N.
Nashville, TN 37234
(615) 251-2000
Editor: Mark Blankenship
Frequency: Quarterly
Coverage/Audience: A music magazine of 4 to 6 choral octavos per issue. The style is contemporary gospel/hymn anthems. For all evangelical church choirs.
Subscription: $4.50/year; $8.75/2 years; $12.25/3 years

GRAMMY AWARDS PROGRAM BOOK
National Academy of Recording Arts and Sciences
4444 Riverside Dr.
Burbank, CA 91505
(213) 843-8233
Editors: Christine Farnon, Joan Rodrigues, George Simon
Frequency: Annual
Coverage/Audience: Listings of nominations and past winners plus special feature articles about the Academy, its events, and other articles relating to recordings.
Subscription: Free to members and guests at Grammy Awards ceremonies

GTM NEWSLETTER
Guild of Temple Musicians
6636 N. Talman
Chicago, IL 60645
(312) 761-1382
Editor: Judith H. Karzen
Frequency: 2/year
Coverage/Audience: Publication keeps members abreast of latest developments and sources in Jewish

music.
Subscription: $30/year

GUILDLETTER
National Guild of Community Schools of the Arts, Inc.
P.O. Box 583
Teaneck, NJ 07666
(201) 836-5594
Editor: Lolita Mayadas
Frequency: Quarterly
Coverage/Audience: Feature articles, profiles of schools, interviews, current news of general interest to administrators, trustees, and faculty of community arts organizations.
Subscription: Free upon request

GUILDNOTES
National Guild of Community Schools of the Arts, Inc.
P.O. Box 583
Teaneck, NJ 07666
(201) 836-5594
Editor: Lolita Mayadas
Frequency: Monthly
Coverage/Audience: Detailed current news about developments in the community arts education field, legislation and funding news pertinent to community arts schools.
Subscription: $25/year

GUILD OF AMERICAN LUTHIERS QUARTERLY
Guild of American Luthiers
8222 S. Park
Tacoma, WA 98408
(206) 472-7853
Editor: Timothy L. Olsen
Frequency: Quarterly
Coverage/Audience: An information sharing system for makers and repairers of all types of stringed instruments.
Subscription: $25/year, including membership

GUILDPEOPLE
National Guild of Community Schools of the Arts
P.O. Box 583
Teaneck, NJ 07666
(201) 836-5594
Editor: Caryl Bixon
Frequency: Quarterly
Coverage/Audience: Events, photo features, news about students and faculty at member institutions.
Subscription: Available for institutional members only, for students, and faculty

GUITAR & MANDOLIN
15 Arnold Pl.
New Bedford, MA 02740
(617) 993-0156
Editor: Michael I. Holmes
Frequency: Bimonthly
Coverage/Audience: Articles about playing, collecting, repairing and building guitars and mandolins. Interviews with famous players, biographies about old makers and players, plus music and tablature for several tunes in each issue.
Subscription: $12/year

GUITAR PLAYER
GPI Publication
20605 Lazaneo
Cupertino, CA 95014
(408) 446-1105
Editor: Tom Wheeler
Frequency: Monthly
Coverage/Audience: For serious guitar players, all styles, all levels. Artist interviews, guitar features, how-to columns, plus equipment, books, and records reviews.
Subscription: $18.95/year

GUITARRA MAGAZINE
Antigua Casa Sherry-Brener Inc. of Madrid
3145 W. 63rd St.
Chicago, IL 60629
(312) 737-1711
Editor: James Sherry
Frequency: Bimonthly
Coverage/Audience: Up-to-date news, a calendar of events, where and when the arts are performing; in-depth interviews with peforming guitarists, new music, publication and record reviews. Dedicated to the enlightenment of classical guitar artists and composers.
Subscription: $15.50 U.S.; $21.50 foreign

H

THE HARMONIZER
Society for the Preservation and Encouragement of Barber Shop Quartet Singing in America, Inc.
6315 Third Ave.
Kenosha, WI 53141
(414) 654-9111
Editor: Leo W. Fobart
Frequency: Bimonthly
Coverage/Audience: Members of Barber Shop Harmony Society.
Subscription: $6/year

HARMONY TIMES
United in Group Harmony Association
P.O. Box 185
Clifton, NJ 07011
(201) 365-0049
Editors: Ronnie Italiano, Karen Constantine
Frequency: Quarterly
Subscription: $6/year

HARP REVIEW
Harp Renaissance Society
1036 Beechwood Blvd.
Pittsburgh, PA 15206
(412) 661-6161
Editor: Lucien Ramcos
Frequency: Annually
Coverage/Audience: The magazine provides world-wide information on solo harp concert activities, research in solo harp music and provides profiles of concert harpists. Also, reviews of recordings and important concerts. Awards "Golden Harp" awards for best harp recording once a year.
Subscription: Free with $15 membership

HIT PARADER
Charlton Publications
Charlton Bldg.
Derby, CT 06418
(203) 735-3381
Editor: John Shelton Ivany
Frequency: Monthly
Coverage/Audience: Popular music, rock fans from 8 to 80.
Subscription: $17/year

THE HORN CALL
Journal of the International Horn Society
International Horn Society
Department of Music
Southeastern Oklahoma State University
Durant, OK 74701
(405) 924-0121, x244
Editor: Dr. Paul Mansur
Frequency: Semiannual
Subscription: $15/year; $40/3 years

HOT LINE NEWS
Musicians National Hot Line Association
277 E. 6100 S.
Salt Lake City, UT 84107
(801) 268-2000
Frequency: Bimonthly
Coverage/Audience: For musicians and people in related occupations. Also for suppliers of music products and services.
Subscription: $20/year with membership

HUMANITIES JOURNAL
National Association for Humanities Education
School of Humanities and Sciences
University of South Carolina
Spartanburg, SC 29303
Frequency: Semiannually
Coverage/Audience: *Humanities Journal* deals with the philosophy, pedagogy, and curriculum in humanities education.
Subscription: $8/year

HURDY GURDY
Amateur Organist Association International
7720 Morgan Ave.
Minneapolis, MN 55435
(612) 866-3421
Editor: E.J. Sampson
Frequency: Bimonthly
Coverage/Audience: For amateur organists. Organ music, features, advertisements, events, and news.
Subscription: $16.50/year

THE HYMN
The Hymn Society of America
National Headquarters

Wittenburg University
Springfield, OH 45501
(513) 327-6308
Editor: Harry Eskew
Frequency: Quarterly
Coverage/Audience: Scholarly and practical information for clergy, church musicians, hymnologists, and institutional libraries.
Subscription: $18/year, including membership

I

I.F.
National Association of Broadcasters
1771 N St., NW
Washington, DC 20036
(202) 293-3516
Frequency: Quarterly
Subscription: Contact for rates

ILWC NEWSLETTER
Internaional League of Women Composers
P.O. Box 42
Three Mile Bay, NY 13693
(315) 649-5086
Editor: Hilary Tann Presslaff
Frequency: Quarterly
Coverage/Audience: News and opportunities of and about women composers, musicians, educators and researchers.
Subscription: $20 composers & affiliates; $10 special (senior citizens, students); $15 institutions

INDIANA MUSICATOR
Indiana Music Educators Association
School of Music
Ball State University
Muncie, IN 47306
(317) 285-1845/285-7089
Editor: Earl Dunn
Frequency: Quarterly
Coverage/Audience: For public schools and university level music instructors, the music industry and editors of similar publications.
Subscription: Free with membership or $3/year

INSTITUTE FOR STUDIES IN AMERICAN MUSIC NEWSLETTER
Institute for Studies in American Music
Brooklyn College
Brooklyn, NY 11210
(212) 780-5655
Editor: H. Wiley Hitchcock
Frequency: 2/year
Coverage/Audience: Includes feature essays, reviews of books, records, and journals; brief research reports and accounts of work-in-progress, all geared toward studies in American music.
Subscription: Free

INTERCOMPANY ANNOUNCEMENTS
Opera America, Inc.
1010 Vermont Ave., NW, #702
Washington, DC 20005
(202) 347-9262
Editor: Ellen Blassingham
Frequency: 10/year
Coverage/Audience: Managers and artistic directors of professional opera companies in the U.S. Canada; funding agencies; national press; other arts service organizations; advocacy groups; state arts councils and opera guilds.
Subscription: Free to members

INTERNATIONAL BANJO
International Banjo, Inc.
2039 Valencia Circle
P.O. Box 328
Kissimmee, FL 32741
(305) 846-4106
Editor: Pat Terry, Jr.
Frequency: Quarterly
Coverage/Audience: Magazine for banjo players and enthusiasts throughout the world. All types of banjo styles covered with top experts; news, history, music, tablature, interviews, book and record reviews, repair, restoration, and records inserted occasionally.
Subscription: $16/year

INTERNATIONAL ALBAN BERG SOCIETY NEWSLETTER
Ph.D. Program in Music
City University of New York
33 W. 42nd St.
New York, NY 10036
Editor: Joan Smith
Frequency: Annually
Coverage/Audience: Research and publication of the works of Alban Berg.
Subscription: $10/year individuals; $15/year institutions; $6/year students

INTERNATIONAL FAN CLUB ORGANIZATION
P.O. Box 177
Wild Horse, CO 80862
(303) 962-3543 or 962-3506
Frequency: 3/year
Subscription: $20/year with membership

INTERNATIONAL FEDERATION OF CHILDREN'S CHOIRS NEWSLETTER
P.O. Box 677
125 S. Fourth St.
Connellsville, PA 15425
(412) 628-3939
Editor: John B. Shallenberger
Frequency: Quarterly
Coverage/Audience: "How-To" Papers.
Subscription: $8/year

INTERNATIONAL MUSICIAN
American Federation of Musicians
1500 Broadway
New York, NY 10036
(212) 869-1330
Editor: J. Martin Emerson
Frequency: Monthly
Coverage/Audience: The official journal of the American Federation of Musician covers union matters, legislation affecting musicians, articles on professional musicians, and musical happenings.
Subscription: $.60 members; $15 nonmembers; $20 Canada; $25 foreign

IN THEORY ONLY: JOURNAL OF THE MICHIGAN MUSIC THEORY SOCIETY
Michigan Music Theory Society
School of Music
The University of Michigan
Ann Arbor, MI 48109
(313) 764-0583
Editor: David C. Carlson
Frequency: 8/year
Coverage/Audience: Theories and analyses of music from all periods, addressed principally to college teachers and students of music theory.
Subscription: $10 U.S.; $15 Canada & foreign

IPA NEWS
International Polka Association
864 N. Ashland Ave.
Chicago, IL
(312) 421-4372
Editor: Chet Schaefer
Frequency: Monthly
Subscription: Free with membership

ITG JOURNAL
International Trumpet Guild
Box 50183
Columbia, SC 29250
Editor: L. Anne Farr
Frequency: Quarterly
Coverage/Audience: Trumpet players.
Subscription: $20/year

J

JAZZ BUSINESS USA
Jazz World Society (Formerly International Jazz Federation, Inc.)
P.O. Box 777
Times Square Station
New York, NY 10108-0777
(201) 939-0836
Editor: Jan A. Byrczek
Frequency: Bimonthly
Coverage/Audience: Serves as a market place for the jazz scene and offers jazz people world-wide opportunities for communication and cooperation.
Subscription: Free with membership

JAZZ EDUCATORS JOURNAL
National Association of Jazz Educators
P.O. Box 724
Manhattan, KS 66502
(913) 776-8744
Editor: Dr. John Kuzmich, Jr.
Frequency: Quarterly
Coverage/Audience: Articles on how-to, jazz curriculums, band aids, choral aids, surveys of teaching materials, etc. For jazz educators, students, professionals—anyone interested in jazz.

Subscription: Free with membership; $12 libraries; $14 foreign

THE JAZZOLOGIST
New Orleans Jazz Club of California
P.O. Box 1225
Kerrville, TX 78028
(512) 896-2285
Editor: Mort Enob
Frequency: 5/year
Coverage/Audience: Jazz musicians, fans, writers, collectors; international scope
Subscription: $7.50/year

JAZZ WORLD INDEX
Jazz World Society (Formerly Internatinal Jazz Federation, Inc.)
P.O. Box 777
Times Square Station
New York, NY 10108-0777
(201) 939-0836
Editor: Jan A. Byrczek
Frequency: Bimonthly
Coverage/Audience: Serves as a market place for the jazz scene and offers jazz people world-wide opportunities for communication and cooperation.
Subscription: Free with membership

JEMF QUARTERLY
John Edwards Memorial Foundation
Folklore & Mythology Center
University of California
Los Angeles, CA 90024
(213) 825-3777
Editor: Linda L. Painter
Frequency: Quarterly
Coverage/Audience: The contents of the periodical are devoted to the field of commercially recorded American traditional music, including country, hillbilly, bluegrass, rhythm and blues, jazz, gospel, cajun, and ethnic-American.
Subscription: $12 individuals; $14 foreign; $14 libraries; $16 libraries, foreign

JERSEY JAZZ
The New Jersey Jazz Society
836 W. Inman Ave.
Rahway, NJ 07065
(201) 388-8905
Editor: Warren W. Vache, Sr.
Frequency: 11/year
Coverage/Audience: Jazz; also sent to jazz clubs around the world and other jazz publications.
Subscription: $15 (cost of family membership in NJJS)

JOURNAL FOR ETHNOMUSICOLOGY
Society for Ethnomusicology
P.O. Box 2984
Ann Arbor, MI 48106
(313) 665-9400
Editor: Timothy F. Rice
Frequency: 3/year
Coverage/Audience: Devoted to the advancement of research and study in the field of ethnomusicology (a field closely allied with the social sciences and humanities). Contains scholarly articles on music throughout the world, current bibliography and discography, as well as book, record and film reviews.
Subscription: $35 members; $20 student members; $30 institutions

JOURNAL OF AESTHETICS AND ART CRITICISM
The American Society for Aesthetics
Temple University
Philadelphia, PA 19122
(215) 787-8290
Editor: John Fisher
Frequency: Quarterly
Coverage/Audience: Articles relating to all aspects of the arts; visual art, music, dance, film, literature, architecture, etc. Read by academicians, performers, studio artists and critics.
Subscription: $20 U.S.; $22 foreign

JOURNAL OF BAND RESEARCH
American Bandmaster Association
Troy State University
Troy, AL 36082
(205) 566-3000, x259
Editor: Jon R. Piersol
Frequency: 2/year (Spring and Fall)
Coverage/Audience: Contains articles on subjects that encompass the whole spectrum of band/wind ensemble research, ranging from historical, analytical, and descriptive research to experimental studies with important implications for band and instrumental pedagogy.
Subscription: $5/year; $9.50/2 years; $14/three years

THE JOURNAL OF COUNTRY MUSIC
Country Music Foundation Press
4 Music Square East
Nashville, TN 37203
(615) 256-1639
Editor: Kyle Young
Frequency: 3/year
Coverage/Audience: Devoted to the publication of primary source material and interpretive articles treating subjects related to the country music tradition.
Subscription: $10/year

JOURNAL OF GUITAR ACOUSTICS
P.O. Box 128
11000 Seymour Rd.
Grass Lake, MI 49240
(313) 665-7808
Editor: Timothy White
Frequency: Quarterly
Coverage/Audience: Mixture of state-of-the-art research results, narrative inquiries into strict non-science, patent reviews (complete in sequence), lay access to the science of sound production and perception in stringed instrument music and nature at large. Readership includes major musical manufacturers, luthiers, academic researchers and science libraries around the world.
Subscription: $38/year in U.S. and Canada; $52/year foreign

JOURNAL OF MUSIC THERAPY
National Association for Music Therapy
1001 Connecticut Ave., N.W., Ste. 800
Washington, DC 20036
(202) 331-7792
Editor: Janet Gilbert
Frequency: Quarterly
Coverage/Audience: Contains authoritative articles on current research and theoretical work in music therapy.
Subscription: $12 U.S.; $14 foreign

JOURNAL OF RESEARCH IN MUSIC EDUCATION
Music Educators National Conference
1902 Association Dr.
Reston, VA 22091
(703) 860-4000
Editor: Jack Taylor
Frequency: Quarterly
Coverage/Audience: Provides reports of recent significant research related to music teaching. The publication is available only to active research members and non-profit institutions, such as schools and libraries.
Subscription: $8 members; $10 institutions; $12 Canada and Mexico; $13 foreign

JOURNAL OF SYNAGOGUE MUSIC
Cantors Assembly
150 Fifth Ave.
New York, NY 10011
Editor: Hazzan Abraham Lubin
Frequency: 2/year
Coverage/Audience: Articles, scholarly papers and reviews of new music by prominent composers, conductors, peformers and musicologists.
Subscription: $7.50/year members; $12.50/year nonmembers

JOURNAL OF THE AMERICAN LISZT SOCIETY
American Liszt Society
2825 Lexington Rd.
Louisville, KY 40280
(502) 897-4421
Editor: Dr. Maurice Hinson
Frequency: 2/year
Coverage/Audience: To promote scholarship and general understanding of the full creative and historial significance of Franz Liszt in the development of 19th and 20th century western culture. Annual festivals are held.
Subscription: Free to members; $12 libraries

JOURNAL OF THE AMERICAN MUSICAL INSTRUMENT SOCIETY
American Musical Instrument Society
AMIS Membership Office

USD Box 194
Vermillion, SD 57069
(605) 677-5306
Editor: William Hettrick
Frequency: Annual
Coverage/Audience: An International organizational magazine of the AMIS devoted to promoting study of history, design, and use of musical instruments from all cultures and all periods.
Subscription: $20

JOURNAL OF THE AMERICAN MUSICOLOGICAL SOCIETY
American Musicological Society, Inc.
201 S. 34th St.
Philadelphia, PA 19104
(215) 898-8698
Editor: Ellen Rosand
Frequency: 3/year
Coverage/Audience: Scholarly articles on topics of interest in the field of music.
Subscription: $25 per volume, i.e., year

JOURNAL OF THE ARNOLD SHOENBERG INSTITUTE
Arnold Shoenberg Institute
University of Southern California
Los Angeles, CA 90089-1101
(213) 743-5362
Editor: Leonard Stein
Frequency: Semiannually
Coverage/Audience: Scholarly journal on the writings and music of Arnold Schoenberg.
Subscription: $20 per volume

JOURNAL OF THE CONDUCTOR'S GUILD
The American Symphony Orchestra League
633 E. Street, N.W.
Washington, DC 20004
(202) 628-0099
Editor: Jacques Voois
Frequency: Quarterly
Coverage/Audience: For conductors worldwide.
Subscription: $20 with membership

JOURNAL OF THE VIOLA DA GAMBA SOCIETY OF AMERICA
1536 Third St., Apt. 6
Charleston, IL 61920
(217) 345-3995
Editor : Efrim Fruchtman
Frequency: Annual
Coverage/Audience: Scholarly articles pertaining to the viola da gamba and related instruments. The history of the instruments, its composers, and its music are primary concerns. Also contains reviews of books, music, and recordings, bibliographies and discographies, and translations of primary source material.
Subscription: $12.50

JOURNAL OF THE VIOLIN SOCIETY OF AMERICA
23 Culver Hill
Southampton, NY 11968
(516) 283-8573
Editor: Albert Mell
Frequency: Quarterly
Coverage/Audience: Articles on all aspects of stringed instrument making—restoration, history, performance. Proceedings of meetings and competitions.
Subscription: $35/year with membership; $50/year overseas; $25/year domestic student; $30/year overseas student

K

KANSAS MUSIC REVIEW
Kansas Music Educators
Wichita, KS 67208
(316) 689-3500
Editor: J. Hardy
Frequency: 5/year
Coverage/Audience: Music Education and music events in Kansas.
Subscription: $2 with membership

KEEPING UP WITH ORFF SCHULWERK
Keeping Up with Music Education
P.O. Box 2712
Muncie, IN 47302
(317) 286-0277
Editor: Arnold E. Burkart
Frequency: 4/year
Coverage/Audience: Music education background, sources, procedures for classroom music teachers.
Subscription: $12.50

KEYBOARD
GPI Publications
20605 Lazaneo
Cupertino, CA 95014
(408) 446-1105
Editor: Tom Darter
Frequency: Monthly
Coverage/Audience: For serious keyboard players, all styles and all levels. Artist interviews, keyboard features, how-to columns, plus equipment, books and record reviews.
Subscription: $17.95/year

KEYBOARD ARTS MAGAZINE
National Keyboard Arts Associates
783 Westholme Ave.
Los Angeles, CA 90024
(213) 785-2102
Editor: Thomas McBeth
Frequency: 3/year
Coverage/Audience: Keyboard arts.
Subscription: $6/year

THE KEY NOTE
Route 3
Plymouth, WI 53073
Editor: Charlotte Berndt
Frequency: Quarterly
Coverage/Audience: Women barbershop singers.
Subscription: $3 non-members

KODALY ENVOY
Organization of American Kodaly Educators
University of Wisconsin-Whitewater
Continuing Education
Whitewater, WI 53190
(414) 472-3165
Editor: Dr. Margaret Stone
Frequency: Quarterly
Coverage/Audience: For members committed to Kodaly.
Subscription: $20/year

L

LATIN AMERICAN MUSIC REVIEW
University of Texas Press, Journals Division
Box 7819
Austin, TX 78722
(512) 471-4531
Editor: Gerard H. Behague, Ph.D.
Frequency: Semiannual
Coverage/Audience: Concentrates on Latin America's varied oral and written musical traditions. Emphasizes a variety of theoretical and methodological approaches to the historical, folkloric, and musicological study of music as an expressive behavior.
Subscription: $15 individuals; $25 institutions

LE GRAND BATON
Journal of the Sir Thomas Beecham Society
P.O. Box 6361
Cleveland, OH 44101
Editor: Thomas E. Patronite
Frequency: Quarterly
Coverage/Audience: Record and sound recording collectors of classical music, both commercial recordings and off-the-air or live performances, with an emphasis on the musicians of by-gone years, such as Toscanini, Beecham, Mengelberg, Furtwaengler, etc.
Subscription: $10 with membership

LIEDER KRANZ NEWS
6 E. 87th St.
New York, NY 10028
(212) 534-0880
Frequency: Bimonthly
Subscription: Contact for rates

LITURGICAL GUIDEBOOK
National Forum for Greek Orthodox Church Musicians
68 W. Cooke Rd.
Columbus, OH
(812) 339-3142
Editor: Peter Vatsures
Frequency: Annually
Coverage/Audience: For choir directors, clergy and chanters.
Subscription: $7/year

LIVING BLUES
Living Blues Publications
2615 N. Wilton Ave.

Chicago, IL 60614
(312) 281-3385
Editors: Jim & Amy O'Neal
Frequency: Quarterly (newsletter, monthly)
Coverage/Audience: Journal of the Black American Blues Tradition: Interviews, articles, record reviews and news about blues musicians, media and business. Audience: Blues enthusiasts, musicians, and tradespeople.
Subscription: $15/year

THE LOCATION
Amusement and Music Operators Association
2000 Spring Rd., Ste. 220
Oak Brook, IL 60521
(312) 654-2662
Editor: J.D. Meacham
Frequency: Monthly
Coverage/Audience: For those interested in the coin-operated amusement device industry.
Subscription: Free to members only.

LYRIC OPERA NEWS
Lyric Opera of Chicago
20 N. Wacker Dr.
Chicago, IL 60606
(312) 332-2244
Editor: Alfred Glasser
Frequency: 2/year
Coverage/Audience: Sent out to all Lyric contributors.
Subscription: Free to Lyric Opera contributors of $25 or more

M

MASSACHUSETTS MUSIC NEWS
Massachusetts Music Educators Association, Inc.
P.O. Box 532
West Springfield, MA 01090-0532
(413) 739-9065
Editor: Mr. J. Anthony Di Giore
Frequency: Quarterly
Coverage/Audience: Publication documenting the progress of music education in Massachusetts.
Subscription: $6/year

THE MATTHAY NEWS
American Matthay Association
305 W. First St.
Springfield, OH 45504
(513) 390-3381
Editor: Stephen Siek
Frequency: 3/year
Coverage/Audience: Offers articles, news, and other materials pertaining to the teaching principles of Tobias Matthay, and the Matthay influence in the US and Europe.
Subscription: $9/year

MENGELBERG NEWSLETTER
Willem Mengelberg Society
P.O. Box 232
Greendale, WI 53129
Editor: Ronald Klett
Frequency: Quarterly
Coverage/Audience: Music lovers, phonograph record collectors, musicologists, and music libraries
Subscription: $4, U.S.; $5, foreign

MICHIGAN MUSIC EDUCATOR
Michigan Music Education Association
Department of Music
Eastern Michigan University
Ypsilanti, MI 48197
(313) 487-2255/665-3219
Editor: Mary D. Teal
Frequency: 3/year
Coverage/Audience: Articles, announcements, advertisements of interest to all music educators. Circulation goes to all organization members, advertisers, student chapter members, libraries, school administrators, editors of state music publications, national officers of Music Educators National Conference, and other music executives.
Subscription: $4.50/year for non-members

MIEA NOTES
Music Industry Educators Association
c/o Music Department
Elmhurst College
Elmhurst, IL 60126
(312) 279-4100, x357
Editor: Paul Kelly
Frequency: 3-4/year
Coverage/Audience: For leaders in the music industry, music trade associations, and music industry educators.
Subscription: $24/year

MIMA NEWSLETTER
Music Industries Marketing Association
600 S. Dearborn St.
Chicago, IL 60605
(312) 922-2433
Editor: Charles Suber
Frequency: Monthly
Subscription: Free with membership; $24/year U.S.; $35/year foreign

THE MISSISSIPPI RAG
The Mississippi Rag, Inc.
5644 Morgan Ave., S.
Minneapolis, MN 55419
(612) 920-0312
Editor: Leslie Johnson
Frequency: Monthly
Coverage/Audience: Features recent and historic photos; stories of past and present jazz and ragtime performers and bands, festival coverage; record and book reviews; listing of playdates. Tabloid format. Readers include top professional jazz and ragtime musicians; writers; record and festival producers; amateur musicians; jazz and ragtime fans (many of whom are active jazz club members); international readership and coverage.
Subscription: $11/year, U.S. & Canada; $12/year foreign

MODERN RECORDING & MUSIC
1120 Old Country Rd.
Plainview, NY 11803
(516) 433-6530
Editor: John Woram
Frequency: Monthly
Coverage/Audience: Published for the smaller recording studio operator and the recording-oriented musician. Among its regular features are test reports on professional audio equipment; articles on usage of professional audio gear both in the studio and on the musical stage; interviews with musicians, producers, and engineers explaining how recordings were made, and listings of new products and services for the engineer/musician.
Subscription: $15/year

MUGWUMPS
15 Arnold Pl.
New Bedford, MA 02740
(617) 993-0156
Editor: Michael I. Holmes
Frequency: Bimonthly
Coverage/Audience: Articles about musical instruments, histories of the companies that made them, building and repair articles, profiles of contemporary makers, substantial classified advertising section.
Subscription: $12

MUSICAL HERITAGE REVIEW
Orchestra, Inc.
P.O. Box 427
Neptune, NJ 07753
(201) 544-8446
Editor: Denise Wagner
Frequency: 18/year
Coverage/Audience: Classical music, articles, record advertising.
Subscription: $12

MUSICAL SIX-SIX NEWSLETTER
(in Esperanto, Muzika Ses-Ses Bulteno)
P.O. Box 241
Kirksville, MO 63501
(816) 665-8098
Editor: Thomas S. Reed
Frequency: Semiannually
Coverage/Audience: *Musical 6-6 Newsletter/Muzika 6-6-Bulteno* presents articles, letters to the editor, news items, and pictures about the 6-6 arrangement of the 12 tones, compared with the traditional 7-5 arrangement. Audience incudes students, teachers, amateurs, professionals.
Subscription: $6/year; $5/year, students, pensioners. Foreign and domestic rates are the same

MUSIC ARTICLE GUIDE
Information Services Incorporated
P.O. Box 12216
Philadelphia, PA 19144

(215) 848-3540
Editor: Morris Henken
Frequency: Quarterly
Coverage/Audience: The nation's only annotated guide to feature articles in American music periodicals; geared exclusively to the special needs of school and college music educators.
Subscription: $32/year

MUSIC BUSINESS CONTACTS
Music-by-Mail
P.O. Box 6101, Broadway
Long Island City, NY 11106
(212) 729-2972
Editor: Sydney Berman
Frequency: 6/year
Coverage/Audience: Newsletter for songwriters who want to keep in touch with music business activities and in contact with users and buyers of songs; feature articles, columns, six pages per issue.
Subscription: $6

MUSIC CLUBS MAGAZINES
National Federation of Music Clubs
1336 North Delaware St.
Indianapolis, IN 46202
(317) 638-4003
Frequency: Quarterly
Subscription: $5/year

MUSIC EDUCATORS JOURNAL
Music Educators National Conference
1902 Association Dr.
Reston, VA 22091
(703) 860-4000
Editor: Rebecca Grier Taylor
Frequency: 9/year
Coverage/Audience: Of interest to music educators and music students and is dedicated to the coverage of all aspects of music from early childhood to adult level.
Subscription: $4 with membership; $12 institutions; $18 foreign; $14, Canada

MUSIC FROM COLORADO
University of Colorado
College of Music
Campus Box 301
Boulder, CO 80309
(303) 492-6352
Editor: Mahala Kephart
Frequency: 3/year
Coverage/Audience: Colorado University music alumni and friends, and selected National Association of Schools of Music member institutions.
Subscription: Free

MUSICIAN
Billboard Publications, Inc.
Box 701
31 Commercial St.
Gloucester, MA 01930
(617) 281-3110
Editor: Sam Holdsworth
Frequency: Monthly
Coverage/Audience: Explores contemporary music from the artists' perspective. Audience is 18-34 years old, 60% college educated, 90% professional or amateur musicians as well as active music consumers and aficionados.
Subscription: $18/year

MUSIC IN HIGHER EDUCATION
National Association of Schools of Music
11250 Roger Bacon Dr., No. 5
Reston, VA 22090
Editor: Michael Yaffe
Frequency: Annually
Coverage/Audience: Statistical information on music in higher education.
Subscription: $6

MUSIC JOURNAL
60 E. 42nd St.
New York, NY 10017
(212) 682-7320
Editor: Bert Wechsler
Frequency: Bimonthly
Coverage/Audience: Full coverage of classical music and dance, reviews and feature stories.
Subscription: Contact for rates

MUSIC MAKERS
The Sunday School Board of the Southern Baptist Convention
127 Ninth Ave., N.
Nashville, TN 37234
(615) 251-2000
Editor: Jimmy R. Key
Frequency: Quarterly
Coverage/Audience: For children ages 6-11. Focus: Younger children's choir. This magazine is for younger children to use in their choir and at home. It also contains help for parents in relating musical experience in the home to the work of the Music Ministry.
Subscription: $.54/quarter; $3/year

MUSIC NOTES
Silver Lake College Music Department
2406 S. Alverno Rd.
Manitowoc, WI 54220
(414) 684-6691
Editors: Sr. Marella Wagner, Sr. Mary Carol Kopecky
Frequency: 3/year
Coverage/Audience: Covers department news, past and future, as well as some feature articles. Audience consists of music alumnae, students, and faculty of the college.
Subscription: Free

MUSIC NOW
Southeastern Composer's League
Appalachian State University
Music Department
Boone, NC 28608
(704) 262-3020
Editor: Scott R. Meister
Frequency: 3/year
Coverage/Audience: Composers in the southeastern U.S.
Subscription: $15 members; $10 associate members; $3 libraries

MUSIC RETAILER NEWS
National Association of Music Merchants
500 N. Michigan Ave
Chicago, IL 60611
(312) 527-3200
Editor: Elizabeth Scott
Frequency: 6/year
Coverage/Audience: All retailer and commercial members of NAMM (music products industry); emphasis on trade show news; also contains articles geared to problems and/or interests of music retailers; features legislative notes from Washington.
Subscription: Membership only

MUSIC TEMPO
4136 Peak St.
Toledo, OH 43612
(419) 476-5839
Editor: W. Walter Kosakowski
Frequency: Bimonthly
Coverage/Audience: Songs, music, music articles, editorials, artists, music business, publishers, records, and radio stations.
Subscription: $8.95/year; $4.50/6 months

MUSIC THERAPY
American Association for Music Therapy
211 E. 43, Ste. 1601
New York, NY 10017
(212) 867-4480
Frequency: Annual
Coverage/Audience: Coverage of clinical, research and educational issues for those interested in the enhancement of music therapy, practicing clinicians, music therapy educators, and professionals in the field.
Subscription: $12

THE MUSIC TRADES
P.O. Box 432
80 West St.
Englewood, NJ 07631
(201) 871-1965
Editor: Brian T . Majeski
Frequency: Monthly
Coverage/Audience: Music dealers, wholesalers, manufacturers, publishers, and tuners.
Subscription: $10/year

MUSIC/VIDEO RETAILER
Larkin-Pluznick-Larkin, Inc.
210 Boylston St.
Chestnut Hill, MA 02167
(617) 964-5100
Editor: Sidney L. Davis
Frequency: Monthly
Coverage/Audience: For record and tape dealers, wholesalers, and

manufacturers. Covers merchandising news and information.
Subscription: $20/year

N

NACWPI JOURNAL
National Association of College Wind & Percussion Instructors
201 E. Illinois
Kirksville, MO 63501
(816) 665-7251
Editor: Dr. Richard Weerts
Frequency: Quarterly
Coverage/Audience: College and university professors of the woodwind, brasswind, and percussion instruments.
Subscription: $15/year

NASM DIRECTORY
National Association of Schools of Music
11250 Roger Bacon Dr., #5
Reston, VA 22090
(703) 437-0700
Editor: Michael Yaffe
Frequency: Annually
Coverage/Audience: A listing of accredited institutions offering degree programs in music, includes address, accredited status, and programs offered.
Subscription: $6

NASM HANDBOOK
National Association of Schools of Music
11250 Roger Bacon Dr., #5
Reston, VA 22090
(703) 437-0700
Editor: Michael Yaffe
Frequency: Every other year
Coverage/Audience: Provides accreditation standards for educational programs in music.
Subscription: $6

NASM PROCEEDINGS OF THE ANNUAL MEETING
National Association of Schools of Music
11250 Roger Bacon Dr., #5
Reston, VA 22090
(703) 437-0700
Editor: Michael Yaffe
Frequency: Annually
Coverage/Audience: Speeches presented at the NASM meeting on subjects relating to music in higher education.
Subscription: $7

NATIONAL COUNCIL OF MUSIC IMPORTERS AND EXPORTERS NEWSLETTER
135 W. 29th St.
New York, NY 10001
(212) 564-0251
Frequency: 10/year
Subscription: Free with membership

NATIONAL SHEET MUSIC SOCIETY NEWSLETTER
National Sheet Music Society, Inc.
1597 Fair Park Ave.
Los Angeles, CA 90041
Editors: Dr. David Morton, Marilyn Brees
Frequency: 10/year
Coverage/Audience: Sheet music and composers
Subscription: $10/year

THE NATS BULLETIN
National Association of Teachers of Singing, Inc.
250 W. 57th St., Ste. 2129
New York, NY 10107
(212) 582-4043
Editor: Richard Miller
Frequency: 5/year
Coverage/Audience: Devoted completely to the art of singing and its teaching. Articles covering repetoire, pedagogy, history, and voice research providing the most current information available to students, teachers, and performers. Book reviews, recent song material, and recordings included. Also dialogues with outstanding people in the profession.
Subscription: $11/year, U.S.; $13/year Canada and Mexico.

NBA JOURNAL
National Band Association
P.O. Box 3228
Augusta, GA 30904
(404) 736-4798
Frequency: Quarterly
Subscription: Contact for rates

NCBA NEWSLETTER
National Catholic Bandmasters Association
P.O. Box 523
Notre Dame, IN 46556
(219) 239-7136
Editor: Rev. George Wiskirchen, C.S.C.
Frequency: Monthly (September to May)
Coverage/Audience: Members of NCBA (Band Directors in the Catholic school—elementary, secondary, college). News of the members activities, material reviews, clinical features, problem solutions, implementation of NCBA projects.
Subscription: Free to members

THE NCCBMI NEWSLETTER/ADCIS NEWSLETTER
National Consortium for Computer-Based Music Instruction
c/o Michael Arenson
School of Music
University of Delaware
Newark, DE 19711
(302) 738-2577
Editor: Michael Arenson
Frequency: Bimonthly
Coverage/Audience: For public school and college music teachers using computers. Content is information-based announcements and summaries of current projects.
Subscription: Free with membership; $5/year nonmembers

NEBRASKA MUSIC EDUCATOR
Nebraska Music Educator's Association
2620 S. 40
Lincoln, NE 68506
(402) 488-7792
Editor: H. Arthur Schrepel
Frequency: 4 times during each school year
Coverage/Audience: Nebraska music teachers, school administrators, college student teachers, and libraries.
Subscription: $5

NEW MEXICO MUSICIAN
New Mexico Music Educators Association
Music Department
University of New Mexico
Albuquerque, NM 87131
(505) 277-4705
Editor: Tom Dodson
Frequency: 3/year
Coverage/Audience: Music educators, public school administrators, students, State legislators and government personnel, libraries and state supervisors of music.

NEW MUSIC
Composers' Forum, Inc.
One Fifth Ave.
New York, NY 10003
(212) 673-8794
Editor: Terry Ross
Frequency: Quarterly
Coverage/Audience: Professional composers, new music, classical and jazz.
Subscription: Free to members; $8/year

NEW MUSIC DISTRIBUTION SERVICE CATALOG
Jazz Composers Orchestra Association
500 Broadway
New York, NY 10012
(212) 925-2121
Frequency: Annually
Subscription: Contact for rates

NEW ON THE CHARTS
Music Business Reference, Inc.
70 Laurel Pl.
New Rochelle, NY 10801
(212) 921-0165
Editor: Leonard Kalikow
Frequency: Monthly
Coverage/Audience: A cross-reference index of individuals and companies involved with current hit pop singers and albums complete with addresses and phone contacts—for professional use only.
Subscription: $99 U.S. & Canada

THE NEW RECORDS
H. Royer Smith Co.
2019 Walnut St.
Philadelphia, PA 19103
(215) 567-1676
Editor: E.J. Hamilton
Frequency: Monthly
Coverage/Audience: America's oldest record review; reviews classical records and other recordings of permanent interest (no rock, pop, folk, etc.)
Subscription: $10.50 U.S.; $12.50 foreign

THE NEWS BULLETIN OF THE LESCHETIZKY ASSOCIATION
105 W. 72nd St.
New York, NY 10023
(212) 362-3912
Editor: Claire Kire
Frequency: Annually
Coverage/Audience: News of interest to members of the asociation.
Subscription: Free with membership

NEWS FROM RIAA
888 Seventh Ave., 9th Flr.
New York, NY 10106
(212) 765-4330
Frequency: Periodic
Subscription: Free

NEWS FROM THEATRE ROYAL AND SCOTTISH OPERA
American Friends of Scottish Opera, Inc.
281 Park Ave. S.
New York, NY 10010
(212) 674-7491
Editor: Miss Duncan MacDonald
Frequency: Quarterly
Subscription: $15/year

NEWSLETTER OF THE AMERICAN VIOLA SOCIETY/YEARBOOK
American Viola Society/American Chapter of the International Viola Research Society
512 Roosevelt Blvd.
Ypsilanti, MI 48197
(313) 482-6288
Frequency: *Newsletter*-2/year; *Yearbook* -Annually
Subscription: Contact for rates

NEWSLETTER OF THE MUSIC CRITICS ASSOCIATION
6201 Tuckerman Lane
Rockville, MD 20852
(301) 530-9527
Frequency: 3/year
Subscription: Free with membership

NEWSLETTER OF THE NATIONAL FLUTE ASSOCIATION, INC.
805 Laguna Dr.
Denton, TX 76201
(817) 387-9472
Editor: Eleanor Lawrence
Frequency: Quarterly
Coverage/Audience: Sent to all members of the National Flute Association. Libraries and educational institutions may subscribe. Primarily of interest to flutists.
Subscription: $15/year

NEWSREAL MAGAZINE
350 E. Prince Rd.
Tucson, AZ 85705
(602) 887-3982/887-7200
Editor: Joan Rosen
Frequency: Monthly
Coverage/Audience: Covers jazz, rock, country, classical, new music—all kinds of music, local & national consisting of interviews and features.
Subscription: $7/year

NEW YORK PINEWOODS FOLK MUSIC CLUB NEWSLETTER
c/o Country Dance & Song Society
505 8th Ave., Rm. 2500
New York, NY 10018
(212) 594-8833
Editors: Hazel Pilcher, Marie Mularczyk
Frequency: 11/year
Coverage/Audience: News and events. Emphasis on traditional folk music.
Subscription: Free to members

NEW YORK STATE SCHOOL MUSIC NEWS
New York State School Music Association
108 Brandywine Ave.
Schenectady, NY 12307
(518) 372-8349
Editor: Dr. Robert Campbell
Frequency: Monthly
Coverage/Audience: Music educators, public and private schools and colleges.
Subscription: $7/year

NGCSA CONFERENCE REPORT
National Guild of Community Schools of the Arts, Inc.
P.O. Box 583
Teaneck, NJ 07666
(201) 836-5594
Frequency: Annual
Coverage/Audience: Report of proceedings of annual conference.
Subscription: $10 (nonmembers)

19th CENTURY MUSIC
University of California Press
2223 Fulton St.
Berkeley, CA 94720
(415) 642-7485
Editor: Joseph Kerman
Frequency: 3/year
Coverage/Audience: Devoted to musicology, analysis, and criticism as well as interdisciplinary studies of music in the nineteenth century. Regular departments include Performer, Instruments, Reviews (books, records, live performance), Rehearings, and Viewpoint.
Subscription: $20 individuals; $40 institutions

NMPA BULLETIN
National Music Publishers' Association, Inc.
110 E. 59th St.
New York, NY 10022
(212) 751-1930
Frequency: Quarterly
Coverage/Audience: News relating to music publishers and music associations.
Subscription: Free

NOA NEWSLETTER
National Opera Association, Inc.
Music Department
Old Dominion University
Norfolk, VA 23508
(804) 440-4069
Editor: Dr. Harold G. Hawn
Frequency: Quarterly
Coverage/Audience: Convention news, special reports on opera, business news, advertising, regional and national information on members, job placement information, minutes of meetings at conventions, contest and audition announcements.
Subscription: $15/year

NOTES
The Quarterly Journal of the Music Library Association
Music Library Association, Inc.
2017 Walnut St.
Philadelphia, PA 19103
(215) 569-3948
Editor: Susan T. Sommer
Frequency: Quarterly
Coverage/Audience: Publishes professional and scholarly articles in the areas of music bibliography, discography, music librarionship, music history, and the music trade. Also includes newly issue materials and recent developments and trends through reviews and lists (books, music, and periodicals), indexes to record reviews and music necrology, communications, notes and queries, news items, lists of music publishers' catalogues, and advertisements.
Subscription: $21 individuals; $31 institutions

NOTES A TEMPO
West Virginia Music Educators Association, Inc.
Hall of Fine Arts
West Liberty State College
West Liberty, WV 26074
(304) 336-8006
Editor: Edward C. Wolf
Frequency: 7/year
Coverage/Audience: All active and student members of the Music Educators National Conference in the state; all secondary school administrators in the state, and about 150 libraries and music educators throughout the US.
Subscription: $2

NSOA BULLETIN
National School Orchestra Association
330 Bellevue Dr.,
NSOA Service Center
Bowling Green, KY 42101
(502) 842-7121
Editor: Donn Mills
Frequency: Quarterly
Coverage/Audience: Pertinent articles of information and teaching techniques for orchestra directors, music reviews, programs given by various groups, etc. Audience directed to orchestra directors in public school and college libraries.
Subscription: Free to members; $8 college libraries

NTSU NOTES
North Texas State University
School of Music
P.O. Box 13887, NT Station
Denton, TX 76203-3887
(817) 565-2791
Editor: Frank Mainous
Frequency: 2-3/year
Coverage/Audience: News of the School of Music and alumni.
Subscription: Free

NU QUARTER NOTES
Northwestern University Music Library
1935 Sheridan Rd.
Evanston, IL 60201
(312) 492-3434
Editor: Karen N. Nagy
Frequency: Quarterly
Coverage/Audience: A communications medium for the faculty, students, and staff of the NU school of Music. Its purpose is to note newsworthy events connected with the Music Library, to explain library policies and services, to list newly acquired and processed materials, and to offer bibliographic reviews of new music materials.
Subscription: Free

O

OKLAHOMA BLUEGRASS GAZETTE
Oklahoma Bluegrass Club
1001 N. Pine
Oklahoma City, OK 73130
(405) 769-3172
Editor: Jerri Hill
Frequency: Monthly
Coverage/Audience: All Oklahoma bluegrass club members; includes calendar of bluegrass festivals and shows in several states, lists of bluegrass bands, news and notes about people in the bluegrass music as well as personal notes about members.
Subscription: $8/year with membership

ONE-SPOT WEEKLY NEW RELEASE REPORTER
One-Spot Publishing Division
Trade Service Publications, Inc.
1000 W. Central Rd.
Mt. Prospect, IL 60056
(312) 392-1720
Editor: Ola Corelli
Frequency: Weekly
Coverage/Audience: Covers the latest popular recordings, singles and albums. Each issue covers a span of 13 weeks of releases.
Subscription: $72/year

OPERA AMERICAN INTERCOMPANY ANNOUNCEMENTS
OPERA America
633 E St. NW
Washington, DC 20004
(202) 347-9262
Editor: Ellen Blassingham
Frequency: Monthly
Coverage/Audience: Audience is staff opera companies, national press, service organizations, and funding agencies. Reports on Congress, the National Endowment of the Arts and other affiliate organizations and agencies. Presents information on meetings, hearings, plans and priorities.
Subscription: Write for subscription information.

THE OPERA JOURNAL
The National Opera Association, Inc.
University of Mississippi
University, MS 38677
(601) 232-7474
Editor: Leland Fox
Frequency: Quarterly
Coverage/Audience: A literary publication about opera, including scholarly articles, critical and practical articles, and reviews of productions and current publications in the field.
Subscription: $15 associate members and libraries; $20 active members; $25 organizations

OPERA NEWS
The Metropolitan Opera Guild, Inc.
1865 Broadway
New York, NY 10023
(212) 582-7500
Editor: Robert Jacobson
Frequency: Monthly-biweekly during opera season
Subscription: $30/year U.S.; $37.50/year elsewhere

THE ORFF ECHO
American Orff-Schulwerk Association
Cleveland State University
Department of Music
Cleveland, OH 44115
(216) 543-5366
Editor: Isabel McNeil Carley
Frequency: Quarterly
Coverage/Audience: Articles of professional interest to music teachers, preschool and classroom teachers, administrators, libraries concerned with the techniques, implications, and relevance of the Orff approach to music education.
Subscription: $20 with membership

THE ORGANIST
Lorenz Publishing Company
P.O. Box 802
501 E. Third St.
Dayton, OH 45401
(513) 228-6118
Editor: James Mansfield
Frequency: Bimonthly
Coverage/Audience: Designed for the organist of modest ability, or the organist with limited practice time. Includes preludes, offertories, and postludes. All timed and registrated for Hammond, pipe, and electronic organs.
Subscription: $9.95

THE ORGAN PORTFOLIO
Lorenz Publishing Company
P.O. Box 802
501 E. Third St.
Dayton, OH 45401
(513) 228-6118
Editor: Dorothy Wells
Frequency: Bimonthly
Coverage/Audience: For the trained organist who seeks moderately difficult music. Classics, chorale preludes, hymn tunes, and original compositions. Registrated for pipe, Hammond and electronic organs.
Subscription: $9.95

THE ORGAN TEACHER-OFFICIAL JOURNAL
International Association of Organ Teachers
7938 Bertram Ave.
Hammond, IN 46324
(219) 844-3395
Frequency: Bimonthly
Coverage/Audience: Organ teachers, teacher training, colleges and universities, organ manufacturers and dealers.
Subscription: $20 membership for teachers, schools, libraries; variable for associate members

OVATION
320 W. 57th St.
New York, NY 10019
(212) 765-5110
Editor: Sam Chase
Frequency: Monthly
Coverage/Audience: Features and interviews with or about classical music artists and composers, plus reviews of music books, records, and home music equipment.
Subscription: $15

OVERTONES
The American Guild of English Handbell Ringers, Inc.
601 W. Riverview Ave.
Dayton, OH 45406
(513) 223-5065
Frequency: 6/year
Subscription: Free with membership

P

PAVASTUFF
Performing and Visual Arts Society

(PAVA)
P.O. Box 102
Kinnelon, NJ 07405
(201) 838-5360
Frequency: Annually
Subscription: Free

PEABODY NEWS
Peabody Conservatory of Music
Peabody Institute of the Johns Hopkins University
One East Mount Vernon Pl.
Baltimore, MD 21202
(301) 659-8163
Editor: Anne Garside
Frequency: Bimonthly
Coverage/Audience: Edited for Peabody/Hopkins students, faculty, alumni and friends; contains articles of interest to the musical community of Baltimore and Washington, D.C.
Subscription: Free

THE PEDAL STEEL NEWSLETTER
The Pedal Steel Guitar Association, Inc.
P.O. Box 248
Floral Park, NY 11001
Editors: Tom Higgins, Doug Mack
Frequency: 10/year
Coverage/Audience: To musicians worldwide who are interested in learning the pedal steel guitar. Subject matter includes biographical sketches of noted steel guitarists, reference articles on construction, modification and repair of steel guitars, amplifiers and accessories. Each issue contains one or more diagrammed arrangements for pedal steel guitar.
Subscription: $15 members; $11 associate members; $20 foreign

PERCUSSIVE NOTES/PERCUSSIVE NOTES RESEARCH EDITION
Percussive Arts Society, Inc.
214 W. Main St., Box 697
Urbana, IL 61801-0697
(217) 367-4098
Editor: Robert Schietroma
Frequency: Annually
Coverage/Audience: For professional percussionists, students, educators, libraries and trade members.
Subscription: $15/year

PERFORMING ARTS
3680 Fifth Ave.
San Diego, CA 92103
(714) 297-6430
Editor: Herbert Glass
Frequency: Varies, but at least monthly
Coverage/Audience: Covers three major cities in California: Los Angeles, San Francisco, and San Diego on each of their respective performing arts companies, e.g., the opera, orchestra, ballet, and symphony.
Subscription: No

PIANO GUILD NOTES
National Guild of Piano Teachers, American College of Musicians, and National Fraternity of Student Musicians
Box 1807
Austin, TX 78767
(512) 478-5775
Frequency: Bimonthly
Subscription: $10/year

THE PIANO QUARTERLY
Rader Rd.
Wilmington, VT 05363
(802) 464-5149
Editor: Robert Silverman
Frequency: Quarterly
Coverage/Audience: Directed toward all who have a serious interest in the piano. Contains interviews, reviews of new music, and feature articles. Includes a phonograph record highlighting new music.
Subscription: $13

THE PITCH PIPE
Sweet Adelines, Inc.
P.O. Box 45168
Tulsa, OK 74145
(918) 622-1444
Editor: Christy Medina
Frequency: Quarterly
Coverage/Audience: Mailed to members of Sweet Adelines, Inc., an organization promoting four-part harmony, barbershop style, for women.
Subscription: $4 includes joint subscription to *Rechorder,* another publication of Sweet Adelines, Inc.

PITTSBURGH SYMPHONY PROGRAM MAGAZINE
Pittsburgh Symphony Society
Heinz Hall for the Performing Arts
600 Penn Ave.
Pittsburgh, PA 15222
(412) 392-4878
Editor: Yvonne P. Steele
Frequency: Weekly
Coverage/Audience: Music audiences at Heinz Hall, includes program notes and pertinent information for performances. Also news of the Pittsburgh Symphony Society, musicians, programming, tours, etc.
Subscription: Rates available upon request

PMEA NEWS
Pennsylvania Music Educators Association
823 Old Westtown Rd.
West Chester, PA 19380
(215) 436-9281
Editor: Richard C. Merrell
Frequency: Quarterly
Coverage/Audience: Music teachers in Pennsylvania.
Subscription: $6

P.M.O. NOTES
Purdue Musical Organization
Edward C. Elliott Hall of Music
West Lafayette, IN 47907
(317) 494-3941
Editor: Jill A. Coyner
Frequency: Bimonthly
Coverage/Audience: Mainly for PMO alumni; provides current news plus items of interest to alumni.
Subscription: $5/year

THE PODIUM
Kappa Kappa Psi and Tau Beta Sigma
National Honorary Band Fraternities
122 Seretean Center
Oklahoma State University
Stillwater, OK 74078
(405) 372-2333
Editor: Thomas F. Sirridge
Frequency: 2/year
Coverage/Audience: Fraternal news covering chapter activities as well as national events. Professional articles concerning topics of interest to persons associated with bands.
Subscription: $5

POPULAR MUSIC AND SOCIETY
Bowling Green State University
Department of Sociology
Bowling Green, OH 43403
Editor: R. Serge Denisoff
Frequency: Quarterly
Coverage/Audience: Concerned with music in the broadest sense of the term; there are no limits on musical genres or approaches to their study.
Subscription: $15/year; $28/2 years

PRAIRIE SUN
Prairie Sun Communications, Inc.
P.O. Box 885
Peoria, IL 61652
(309) 673-6624
Editor: Bill Knight
Frequency: Weekly
Coverage/Audience: Covers music and current events, with emphasis on the Midwest. Audience is 15-40 years old.
Subscription: $12/year

PSYCHOMUSICOLOGY
A Journal of Music Cognition
Stephen F. Austin State University
P.O. Box 13022, SFA Station
Nacogdoches, TX 75962
(713) 569-2801
Editor: R.G. Sidnell
Frequency: 2/year
Coverage/Audience: Musical topics with conclusions oriented toward the human processes of creating music, performing music, and listening to music.
Subscription: $18 U.S.; $21 elsewhere

Q

THE QUARTERNOTE
Amusement and Music Operators Association
2000 Spring Rd., Ste. 220
Oak Brook, IL 60521
(312) 654-2662

Editor: J.D. Meacham
Frequency: Quarterly
Coverage/Audience: For those interested in the coin-operated amusement device industry.
Subscription: Free to members

QUODLIBET
Intercollegiate Musical Council, Inc.
c/o Stanley Malinowski
Wabash College
Crawfordsville, IN 47933
(317) 362-1400, x398, 290
Editor: Stanley Malinowski, Ph.D.
Frequency: 3/year
Coverage/Audience: Brief articles of interest to male choruses and directors.
Subscription: $30/year with associate membership

R

RADIOACTIVE
National Association of Broadcasters
1771 N St., NW
Washington, DC 20036
(202) 293-3516
Frequency: Monthly
Subscription: Contact for rates

RAG TIMES
The Maple Leaf Club
5560 W. 62nd St.
Los Angeles, CA 90056
Editor: Dick Zimmerman
Frequency: Bimonthly
Coverage/Audience: Articles about ragtime past and present, reviews of ragtime records and books and information about ragtime concerts and performers.
Subscription: $7 US & Canada; $9 foreign

RATE NEWS
Big Band Collectors' Club
P.O. Box 3171
Pismo Beach, CA 93449
(805) 543-2952
Editor: Bob Connolly
Frequency: Quarterly
Coverage/Audience: Articles on member activities, lists of phonograph records, tapes, other music-related items, record reviews.
Subscription: $5/year with membership

RECAP
Music Department
Southwest Missouri State University
904 S. National
Springfield, MO 65804
(417) 836-5648
Editor: Michael Madden
Frequency: Once per semester
Subscription: Free

RECHORDER
Sweet Adelines, Inc.
P.O. Box 45168
Tulsa, OK 74135
(918) 622-1444
Editor: Christy Medina
Frequency: Quarterly
Coverage/Audience: Promotes four-part harmony, barbershop style, for women.
Subscription: $4 includes joint subscription to *The Pitch Pipe* another publication of Sweet Adelines.

RECORD EXCHANGER
Vintage Records
Box 6144
Orange, CA 92667
(714) 639-3383
Editor: Art Turco
Frequency: Quarterly
Coverage/Audience: Devoted exclusively to the history of rock and roll. Each issue contains detailed research into the background of the performers and the records they made. In-depth information for those interested in the 50's and 60's era of music.
Subscription: $11.50/6 issues

RECORDING INDUSTRY ASSOCIATION OF AMERICA NEWSLETTER
888 Seventh Ave., 9th Flr.
New York, NY 10106
(212) 765-4330
Frequency: Quarterly
Subscription: Free

RECORD RESEARCH
65 Grand Ave.
Brooklyn, NY 11205
(212) 857-7003
Editors: Len Kunstadt, Bob Colton
Frequency: 6/year
Coverage/Audience: A discographical magazine encompassing all kinds of research: record statistics and information, jazz, folk, vaudeville, ethnic to classical recordings with emphasis on record labels and accompanying historical lore, Also includes a sales outlet for rare out of print collectors recordings in the form of a mail record auction.
Subscription: $5/10 issues (5 double issues)

RECORD REVIEW
Ashley Communications, Inc.
19431 Business Center Dr.
Northridge, CA 91324
(213) 885-6800
Editor: Brian J. Ashley
Frequency: Bimonthly
Coverage/Audience: Rock, jazz, and country. Features interviews and retrospectives. For music fans.
Subscription: $9/year

THE RELIGIOUS ART GUILD NEWSLETTER
25 Beacon St.
Boston, MA 02108
(617) 742-2100
Editor: Barbara M. Hutchins
Frequency: 3/year
Coverage/Audience: For all Unitarian Universalist churches as well as individual members.
Subscription: $10/year individual; $20/year church

RELIX
Leslie D. Kippel
P.O. Box 94
Brooklyn, NY 11230
(212) 645-0818
Editor: Toni A. Brown
Frequency: Bimonthly
Coverage/Audience: Current rock music, specializing on the Grateful Dead.
Subscription: $10/year

REPLAY MAGAZINE
Replay Publishing, Inc.
P.O. Box 2550
Woodland Hills, CA 91365
(213) 347-3820
Editors: Kay Bowline, Kathy Brainard
Frequency: Monthly
Coverage/Audience: A trade publication for the coin-operation amusement industry. This includes jukeboxes, video games, pinballs, coin-op pool tables, foosballs, kiddie rides, etc.
Subscription: $40/year ($55, includes a jukebox record report)

ROCK & SOUL
Charlton Publications
Charlton Bldg.
Derby, CT 06418
(203) 735-3381
Editor: John Shelton Ivany
Frequency: Every 6 weeks
Coverage/Audience: For music fans from all ages and backgrounds
Subscription: $10/12 issues

ROCKINGCHAIR
Voice of Youth Advocates
P.O. Box 6569
University, AL 35486
(205) 556-2104
Editor: John Politis
Frequency: Bimonthly
Coverage/Audience: Reviews of all types of recordings except classical for inclusion in library collections in schools, universities, institutions, and public libraries.
Subscription: $24.95

RTS ANNUAL
P.O. Box 10687
Costa Mesa, CA 92627
(714) 544-0740
Editor: I Nii
Frequency: Annually (December)
Coverage/Audience: Contains information about the highlights of film music in any given year including new releases, reissues, and other reference information unavailable anywhere else.
Subscription: $5.50 U.S.; $7 foreign

RTS MUSIC GAZETTE
P.O. Box 10687
Costa Mesa, CA 92627
(714) 544-0740
Editor: I. Nii
Frequency: Monthly
Coverage/Audience: A monthly film music newsletter that provides reference information about film composers and related areas. Not involved in technical music aspects.
Subscription: $25 U.S.; $50 foreign

S

THE SAB CHOIR
Lorenz Publishing Company
501 E. Third St.
P.O. Box 802
Dayton, OH 45401
(513) 228-6118
Editor: Clark Pearson
Frequency: 8/year
Coverage/Audience: Full sound for the tenorless choir. A year-round program of balanced, usable music for soprano, alto,and baritone. Selections are right for services in any season.
Subscription: $6.50/year; quantity subscriptions for choirs (10 or more copies monthly to one address), $5.30

SACRED MUSIC
Church Music Association of America
548 Lafond Ave.
St. Paul, MN 55103
(612) 293-1710
Editor: Richard J. Schuler
Frequency: Quarterly
Coverage/Audience: Intended chiefly for choirmasters, organists, and others interested in the liturgical music of the Roman Catholic Church.
Subscription: $10/year

THE SACRED ORGAN JOURNAL
Lorenz Publishing Company
501 E. Third St.
P.O. Box 802
Dayton, OH 45401
(513) 228-6118
Editor: Howard Wells
Frequency: Bimonthly
Coverage/Audience: Designed to supplement the well-trained organist's repertoire of good liturgical service music; music that is also suitable for teaching. Mostly traditional.
Subscription: $9.95

SANGER-HILSEN SINGERS' GREETINGS
The Norwegian Singers Association of America, Inc.
3316 Xenwood Ave., S.
Minneapolis, MN 55416
(612) 925-4658
Editor: Erling Stone
Frequency: Bimonthly
Coverage/Audience: Mailed to all members of the Norwegian Singers Association and also to associate members.
Subscription: $5

THE SCHOOL MUSICIAN DIRECTOR AND TEACHER
Ammark Publishing Co., Inc.
4049 W. Peterson Ave.
Chicago, IL 60646
(312) 463-7484
Editor: Dr. Edgar B. Gangware
Frequency: 10/year
Coverage/Audience: For the school music education program from elementary to junior high, through the university. It is helpful to both students and teachers as well. It covers all major areas of music education.
Subscription: $12/year

SCHOOL MUSICIAN MAGAZINE
The Women Band Directors National Association
3580 Rothschild Dr.
Pensacola, FL 32503
(904) 432-2887
Editor: Laurie Neeb, Barbara Lovett
Frequency: Monthly
Subscription: Contact for rates

SCVA NEWSLETTER
Southern California Vocal Association
P.O. Box 6048
El Monte, CA 91743-2048
(213) 445-0311
Editor: Christine VanderLeest, Lawrence Warden
Frequency: 5-6/year
Coverage/Audience: Choral directors throughout southern California in high schools, junior colleges and colleges.
Subscription: $20/year with membership; $10/year student/retired

THE SECOND LINE
New Orleans Jazz Club
1312 Royal St.
New Orleans, LA 70116
(504) 525-9910
Editor: Don Marquis
Frequency: Quarterly
Coverage/Audience: Feature articles about musicians, bands and events pertaining to traditional New Orleans. Little outside that scope. Strong emphasis on historical material.
Subscription: $15 with membership

THE SENSIBLE SOUND
403 Darwin Dr.
Snyder, NY 14226
Editor: John A. Horan
Frequency: Quarterly
Coverage/Audience: An audio equipment and recording review publication. Audience is composed of devoted audio hobbyists and record collectors.
Subscription: $18/year; $35/2 years

SHEET MUSIC MAGAZINE
Shacor, Inc.
223 Katonah Ave.
Katonah, NY 10536
(914) 232-8108
Editor: Joseph Knowlton
Frequency: 9/year
Coverage/Audience: Primarily for the amateur pianist, organist and/or guitarist. Each issue contains music for 10 songs, arranged in both easy and standard formats for piano or organ. Also contains articles of general interest for musicians, and workshops on technique and music theory.
Subscription: $13.97/year

SIGMA ALPHA IOTA QUARTERLY: PAN PIPES
Sigma Alpha Iota International Music Fraternity for Women
2820 Webber St.
Sarasota, FL 33579
(813) 365-4135
Editor: Margaret Maxwell
Frequency: Quarterly
Coverage/Audience: College chapter members are music majors and minors. Alumnae are mostly active professional musicians. Also sent to music school libraries, public libraries, music organizations and professional musicians outside the fraternity.
Subscription: $10/year

THE SINFONIAN NEWSLETTER
Phi Mu Alpha Sinfonia Fraternity
10600 Old State Rd.
Evansville, IN 47711
(812) 867-2433
Editor: Dr. Maurice I. Laney
Frequency: Quarterly
Coverage/Audience: Music educators, students, and people with a strong avocational interest in music.
Subscription: Contact for rates

SINGERS BULLETIN (PRZEGLAD SPIEWACZY)
Polish Singers Alliance of America
180 - 2nd Ave.
New York, NY 10003
(212) 254-6642, 748-3817
Editor: Walter Falencki
Frequency: Quarterly
Subscription: Free to members

SING OUT!
P.O. Box 1071
Easton, PA 18042
(215) 253-8105
Editor: Mark Moss
Frequency: Quarterly
Coverage/Audience: Covers folk and ethnic music - songs and articles.
Subscription: $11/year; $21/2 years; $30/3 years

THE SONGSMITH JOURNAL
The Songsmith Society
P.O. Box 622
Northbrook, IL 60062
(312) 274-0054
Editor: James Durst

Frequency: Quarterly
Coverage/Audience: Dedicated to the use of song as an instrument for personal and global transformation.
Subscription: $5/year; $6 Canada & foreign

SOUNDBOARD
Guitar Foundation of America
Box 5311
Garden Grove, CA 92645
Editor: Jim Forrest
Frequency: Quarterly
Coverage/Audience: For guitarists, teachers, composers, musicologists, and publishers who take the guitar seriously.
Subscription: $15/year

SOUNDING BOARD
National Association of Recording Merchandisers
1008-F Astoria Blvd.
Cherry Hill, NJ 08034
(609) 424-7404
Frequency: Monthly
Subscription: Free to members

THE SOUNDPOST
American Federation of Musicians, Local 325
1717 Morena Blvd.
San Diego, CA 92110
(714) 276-4324
Editor: C. Patric Oakley
Frequency: Monthly
Subscription: $12/year

SOUNDS
Georgia State University Department of Music
University Plaza
Atlanta, GA 30303
(404) 658-2349
Editor: Barbara Klingman
Frequency: 3/year
Coverage/Audience: Distributed to music educators, administrators, media personnel, alumni, students, and members of music organizations and other interested audiences in the state of Georgia. Keeps readers up to date on the musical and academic offerings of the department, its faculty and students' achievements; seeks to introduce Georgia State University to the potential student.
Subscription: Free

SOUTH DAKOTA MUSICIAN
South Dakota Music Education Association
Northern State College
Music Department
Aberdeen, SD 57401
(605) 622-2497
Editor: Mavis Hamre
Frequency: 3/year
Coverage/Audience: Mailed to music educators, music education students, and other music associations.
Subscription: $2/year

SOUTHERN APPALACHIAN DULCIMER ASSOCIATION NEWSLETTER
Rt. 1, Box 473
Helena, AL 35080
(205) 988-3350
Frequency: Quarterly
Subscription: $2/year with membership

SRS NEWSLETTER
Songwriters Resources and Services
6318 Hollywood Blvd.
Hollywood, CA 90028
(213) 463-7178 or 463-5691
Editor: Billy James
Frequency: 6/year
Coverage/Audience: SRS member activities, many special features on all topics of interest to the songwriting community. Announcements of SRS programs and events.
Subscription: Free with membership

THE STANZA
The Hymn Society of America
National Headquarters
Wittenburg University
Springfield, OH 45501
(513) 327-6308
Editor: W. Thomas Smith
Frequency: 2/year
Coverage/Audience: Scholarly and practical information for clergy, church musicians, hymnologists, and institutional libraries.
Subscription: $18/year with membership

STEEL GUITAR INTERNATIONAL NEWSLETTER
Steel Guitar International
P.O. Box 2413
St. Louis, MO 63114
(314) 427-7794
Editor: DeWitt Scott, Sr.
Frequency: Quarterly
Coverage/Audience: News, instruction, gossip about steel guitars and related products.
Subscription: $15/year

STEREOPHILE MAGAZINE
P.O. Box 1948
Santa Fe, NM 87501
(505) 982-2366
Editor: J. Gordon Holt
Frequency: 10/year
Coverage/Audience: Provides technical information, for audio perfectionists as well as record reviews, equipment reviews, philosophical commentary, classified ads, recommended components, audio equipment, some video.
Subscription: $20 3rd class; $24 1st class; $25 Canada; $35 foreign

STEREO REVIEW
Ziff-Davis Publishing Company
One Park Ave.
New York, NY 10016
(212) 725-3500
Editor: William Livingstone
Frequency: Monthly
Coverage/Audience: Special-interest publication for the hi-fi enthusiast; contains reviews and comment on equipment and recordings.
Subscription: $9.98/year

SYMPHONY MAGAZINE
American Symphony Orchestra League
633 E St., N.W.
Washington, DC 20004
(202) 628-0099
Editor: Ms. Robin L. Perry
Frequency: Bimonthly
Coverage/Audience: Articles and information on orchestral activities and musicians and topics of concern to orchestra managers, board members, volunteers, and musicians; readership includes orchestra board members, managers, and volunteer orchestra guilds as well as conductors, orchestral players, music publishers, and artist managers.
Subscription: Free with membership

T

TECHNI-COM
The National Association of Professional Band Instrument Repair Technicians
P.O. Box 51
Normal, IL 61761
(309) 452-4257
Editor: Tom Chekouras
Frequency: Bimonthly
Subscription: Membership only

TENNESSEE FOLKLORE SOCIETY BULLETIN
Middle Tennessee State University
Box 201
Murfreesboro, TN 37132
(615) 898-2576
Editor: Charles K. Wolfe
Frequency: Quarterly
Coverage/Audience: Seeks to document and promote traditional folk culture and music of the mid-south. Also sponsors television documentaries and other research projects; issues phonograph records. Aimed at both a general and academic audience.
Subscription: $5/year with membership

THE TENNESSEE MUSICIAN
Tennessee Music Educators Association
P.O. Box 17657
Tampa, FL 33682
(813) 961-0038
Editor: Lawrence P. Cooney
Frequency: Quarterly
Coverage/Audience: Exclusively designed for music educators in Tennessee.
Subscription: $4/year

THEATRE CRAFTS MAGAZINE
250 W. 57th St., Ste. 312

New York, NY 10107
(212) 582-4110
Editor: Patricia MacKay
Frequency: 9/year
Coverage/Audience: For professionals and serious amateurs in performing arts and video; stresses design, technical, and management aspects.
Subscription: $17.95/year

THEATRE COMMUNICATIONS
Theatre Communications Group, Inc.
355 Lexington Ave.
New York, NY 10017
(212) 697-5230
Editor: Jim O'Quinn
Frequency: Monthly
Coverage/Audience: An illustrated monthly for theatre professionals. Regular columns include: Production Schedules, Plays and Playwrights, Government, Funding, In Print, Management, Stages, People, TCG Focus, Trends and Callboard (classified ads). Features and opinion columns include articles by a wide range of theatre critics, artists and other professionals in American and international theatre.
Subscription: $18/year individuals; $24/year institutions

THEATRE ORGAN
American Theatre Organ Society, Inc.
P.O. Box 3487
Irving, TX 75061
(619) 421-9629
Editor: Robert M. Gilbert
Frequency: Bimonthly
Coverage/Audience: Articles and information about theatre pipe organs.
Subscription: $20 with membership

TICKET TALK
Bass Tickets
363 22nd St.
Oakland, CA 94612
(415) 835-4100
Editor: Beverly Lohwasser
Frequency: Monthly
Coverage/Audience: News about upcoming productions on the BASS system along with promoter profiles, etc.
Subscription: Free

THE TRACKER
The Organ Historical Society
P.O. Box 26811
Richmond, VA 23261
(804) 264-2126
(717) 872-5190
Editor: Susan Friesen
Frequency: Quarterly
Coverage/Audience: Organists, organ builders, aficionados, historians, students and musicologists.
Subscription: $22/year

THE TRIANGLE OF MU PHI EPSILON
Mu Phi Epsilon, International Professional Music Fraternity
National Executive Office
25824 Sugar Pine Dr.
Pioneer, CA 95666
(209) 295-4787
Editor: Jean Crites Compton
Frequency: Quarterly
Coverage/Audience: Members of the fraternity and its chapters; also college and university music departments and libraries.
Subscription: $2/year

TRI-SON NEWS
Tri-Son Promotions
P.O. Box 177
Wild Horse, CO 80862
(303) 962-3543
Editor: Loudilla Johnson
Frequency: Monthly
Coverage/Audience: Radio stations, booking agencies, talent buyers, fans worldwide.
Subscription: $8 U.S.; $15 foreign

U

UP WITH PEOPLE NEWS
3103 N. Campbell Ave.
Tucson, AZ 87519
(602) 327-7351
Editor: Dana A. Cooper
Frequency: Quarterly
Coverage/Audience: Directed to Up With People donors, sponsors, former cast members, host families. Covers the activities of the five casts of UWP, and their activities and performances around the world.
Subscription: Free

V

VERDI NEWSLETTER
American Institute for Verdi Studies
Department of Music
New York University
24 Waverly Pl., Rm. 268
New York, NY 10003
Editor: Andrew Porter
Frequency: Annually
Coverage/Audience: Contains information on important Verdi events: performances, recordings, publications, meetings, lectures. Material on Verdi's life and music.
Subscription: Free with membership; $7.50/year nonmembers

VERMONT MUSIC EDUCATORS NEWS
Vermont Music Educators Association
Johnson State College
Johnson, VT 05656
(802) 635-2356, x255
Editor: Albert A. Swinchoski
Frequency: Quarterly
Coverage/Audience: Contains current news and items of particular interest to the membership.
Subscription: Free with membership; $5 nonmembers

VIOLA D'AMORE SOCIETY OF AMERICA NEWSLETTER
Viola D'Amore Society of America
39-23 47th St.
Sunnyside, NY 11104
(212) 786-1467

10917 Pickford Way
Culver City, CA 90230
(213) 837-7596
Editors: Dr. Myron Rosenblum, Dr. Daniel Thomason
Frequency: 2/year
Subscription: $9/year with membership

VOICE
Association of Professional Vocal Ensembles
1830 Spruce St.
Philadelphia, PA 19103
(215) 545-4444
Editor: Janice F. Kestler
Frequency: Bimonthly
Coverage/Audience: Received by artistic, managerial, administrative and governing personnel of choral arts organizations across the US and Canada and includes matters of significance and assistance to such organizations. Also mailed to educational institutions and state, province, and federal arts agencies, free of charge.
Subscription: Varies with membership

THE VOLUNTEER CHOIR
The Lorenz Publishing Company
501 E. Third St.
P.O. Box 802
Dayton,OH 45401
(513) 228-6118
Editor: Lani Smith
Frequency: Monthly
Coverage/Audience: Easy music for the small or beginning adult choir. All selections are easy to learn and can be sung without tenor or bass in an emergency; easy-to-read closed score.
Subscription: $14.75/year; quantity (10 plus), $6.50

W

WASHINGTON INTERNATIONAL ARTS LETTER
325 Pennsylvania Ave., S.E.
Washington, DC 20003
(202) 488-0800
Editor: Daniel Millsaps
Frequency: 10/year
Coverage/Audience: Publishes financial information about grants and assistance to arts organizations and individual artists.
Subscription: $24.50 individuals; $48 institutions

WFLN PHILADELPHIA GUIDE TO EVENTS AND PLACES
Franklin Broadcasting Co.
8200 Ridge Ave.

Philadelphia, PA 19128
(215) 482-6000
Editor: Morris Henken
Frequency: Monthly
Coverage/Audience: Aimed at listeners to WFLN radio; each issue contains complete listings of classical music to be heard that month.
Subscription: $10/year

THE WHEEL OF DELTA OMICRON
Delta Omicron International Music Fraternity
1352 Redwood Ct.
Columbus, OH 43229
(614) 888-2640
Editor: Patricia Almon
Frequency: Quarterly
Coverage/Audience: Fraternity membership, educational materials, and fraternity news.
Subscription: $3/year

THE WOMEN BAND DIRECTORS NATIONAL ASSOCIATION NEWSLETTER
3580 Rothschild Dr.
Pensacola, FL 32503
(904) 432-2887
Editors: Laurie Neeb, Barbara Lovett
Frequency: Quarterly
Subscription: Contact for rates

WOODWINDS • BRASS • PERCUSSION
Association of Concert Bands
25 Court St.
Deposit, NY 13754
(607) 467-2191
Editor: Sarah Evans
Frequency: 8/year
Subscription: $5/year with membership; $9/year nonmembers

WORDS ABOUT MUSIC
National Academy of Popular Music
One Times Square, 8th Fl.
New York, NY 10036
(212) 221-1252
Editor: W. Randall Poe
Frequency: Quarterly
Coverage/Audience: News and information on songwriters, both past and present. Also gives highlights of N.A.P.M. Museum activity as well as information on Songwriters Hall of Fame Annual Awards Dinner.
Subscription: $25 with membership

WPAS MUSELETTER
Washington Performing Arts Society
425 13th St., N.W., Ste. 712
Washington, DC 20004
(202) 393-3600
Editor: Linda A. Coleman
Frequency: 6-8/year
Coverage/Audience: A publication for members of the Washington Performing Arts Society. It includes a calendar of upcoming performances, a priority mail-order form, articles of interest, special offers to members (record discounts, invitations to free concerts in the area, etc.)
Subscription: $25 with membership

Y

THE YALE REVIEW
Yale University Press
1902 A Yale Station
New Haven, CT 06520
(203) 436-8307
Editor: Kai Erikson
Frequency: Quarterly
Coverage/Audience: A journal of literature, culture, politics, and the arts for a general audience.
Subscription: $12 individuals; $18 institutions

YEARBOOK: ANNUAL PROCEEDINGS
American Academy and Institute of Arts and Letters
633 W. 155th St.
New York, NY 10032
(212) 368-5900
Frequency: Annually
Subscription: Contact for rates

YEARBOOK FOR TRADITIONAL MUSIC
International Council for Traditional Music
Department of Music
Columbia University
New York, NY 10027
(212) 678-0332
Editor: Dr. Dieter Christensen
Frequency: Annually
Coverage/Audience: Traditional music worldwide, book and record reviews. Audience is comprised of musicians, scholars in the field of ethnomusicology and musicology.
Subscription: $20 U.S.; $22 institutions. Subscription includes the *Bulletin of the International Council for Traditional Music,* which is published semiannually

YOUNG MUSICIANS
The Sunday School Board of the Southern Baptist Convention
127 Ninth Ave., N.
Nashville, TN 37234
(615) 251-2000
Editor: Jimmy R. Key
Frequency: Quarterly
Coverage/Audience: For children ages 6-11; to use in their choir or at home.
Subscription: $4/year

CANADA

A

A L'ECOUTE
Alliance des Chorales du Quebec
1415 Est Rue Jarry
Montreal, PQ H2E 2Z7
(514) 374-4700, x419-459
Frequency: Monthly
Coverage/Audience: News of the association.
Subscription: $7

THE AMATEUR MUSICIAN/ LE MUSICIEN AMATEUR
Canadian Amateur Musicians
P.O. Box 353
Westmount, PQ H3Z 2T5
(514) 932-8755
Editor: Claire Heistek
Frequency: 3-4/year
Subscriptions: $20/year with adult membership; $10 students, senior citizens

ARTS BULLETIN
Canadian Conference of the Arts
141 Laurier Ave., W., Ste. 707
Ottawa, ON K1P 5J3
(613) 238-3561
Editor: Brian Anthony
Frequency: Bimonthly
Coverage/Audience: Bilingual tumble format, contains news and views on development in the arts in Canada. Mailed to all members of the CCA, press, members of Parliament, and members of provincial legislatures, etc.
Subscription: Free to members; $15 libraries

B

THE BRITISH COLUMBIA MUSIC EDUCATOR
British Columbia Music Educators' Association
2235 Burrard St.
Vancouver, BC V6J 3H9
(604) 731-8121
Editor: Leonard J. Kay
Frequency: 4/year
Coverage/Audience: Music teachers and administrators (elementary through university), teacher education institutions, music and music education undergraduates, college and university libraries, and the music industry.
Subscription: $20 with membership

C

CAML NEWSLETTER
Canadian Association of Music Libraries
Music Library
University of Western Ontario
London, ON N6A 3K7
(613) 996-3377
Editor: Merwin Lewis
Frequency: 3/year
Coverage/Audience: Covers association activities, annual reports, news of the International Association of Music Libraries, of which CAML is a national branch, letters to the editor, book reviews, and papers presented at the annual meeting.
Subscription: $25 individual; $45 institutional; $7.50 student; $50 sustaining

CANADIAN COMPOSER
Composers, Authors and Publishers Association of Canada Limited

1240 Bay St., 9th Flr.
Toronto, ON M5R 2C2
Editor: Richard Flohil
Frequency: Monthly, except July and August
Subscription: $2/year

CANADIAN FEDERATION OF MUSIC TEACHERS' ASSOCIATIONS NEWSLETTER
5 Weldon St.
Sackville, NB E0A 3C0
(506) 536-0143
Frequency: Quarterly
Subscription: Free with membership

CANADIAN FOLK MUSIC BULLETIN
Bulletin de Musique Folklorique Canadienne
Canadian Folk Music Society
1314 Shelbourne St., S.W.
Calgary, AB T3C 2K8
(403) 244-2804
Editor: T.B. Rogers
Frequency: Quarterly
Coverage/Audience: Articles, columns, commentary related to Canadian Folk music.
Subscription: $10 individuals; $20 institutions

CANADIAN FOLK MUSIC JOURNAL
Canadian Folk Music Society
5 Notley Pl.
Toronto, ON M4B 2M7
(416) 257-3984
Editor: Edith Fowke
Frequency: Annually
Coverage/Audience: Features articles on various aspects of Canadian folk music on a scholarly level. Articles are printed in either English or French, with abstracts in the other language. It includes notes and/or reviews of important Canadian folk music publications and records.
Subscription: $10/year with membership

CANADIAN MUSIC EDUCATOR
Canadian Music Educators' Association
CMEA-National Resource Center
P.O. Box 1461
St. Catharines, ON L2R 7J8
(416) 684-4664
Frequency: 3/year
Subscription: $15/year members/libraries; $20/year corporations

CANADIAN MUSICIAN
Norris Publications
832 Mount Pleasant Rd.
Toronto, ON M4P 2L3
(416) 485-8284
Editor: Kathy Whitney
Frequency: Bimonthly
Coverage/Audience: Of interest primarily to professional and amateur musicians. Includes profiles on prominent Canadian performers, music equipment, technique, industry news, product news, the business of music, etc.
Subscription: $10 Canada; $13 outside Canada

CANADIAN MUSIC TRADE
Norris Publications
832 Mount Plesant Rd.
Toronto, ON M4P 2L3
(416) 485-8284
Editor: Kathy Whitney
Frequency: Bimonthly
Coverage/Audience: Aimed primarily at musical instrument retailers covering industry news, product news, articles on running a more effective retail business and profiles on retailers and suppliers of musical instruments and related products.
Subscription: $10 Canada; $13 outside Canada

CANADIAN UNIVERSITY MUSIC REVIEW/REVUE DE MUSIQUE DES UNIVERSITES CANADIENNES
Canadian University Music Society
Department of Music
University of Alberta
Edmonton, AB T6G 2F1
(403) 432-3263
Editor: Dr. Alan M. Gillmor (English), Dr. Jean-Jacques Nattiez (French)
Frequency: Annually
Subscription: $10/year

C.B.D.A. NEWSLETTER
The Canadian Band Directors Association
21 Tecumseh St.
Brantford, ON N3S 2B3
(519) 753-1858
Editor: F. McKinnon
Frequency: Bimonthly
Coverage/Audience: For members in the province of Ontario.
Subscription: Free with membership

CHOIRS ONTARIO
Ontario Choral Federation
208 Bloor St., W. Ste. 303
Toronto, ON M5S 1T8
(416) 925-5525
Editor: Norah Bolton
Frequency: 6/year
Coverage/Audience: Contains coming events, calendar, help wanted ads, and monthly highlights of the Federation. Mailed to choirs, individuals, corporations.
Subscription: Free with membership

CHORUS
Nova Scotia Choral Federation
5516 Spring Garden Rd., Ste. 305
Halifax, NS B3J 1G6
(902) 423-4688
Editors: Rachel DeWolf-Swetnam, Anne Munro
Frequency: Quarterly
Coverage/Audience: Sent to members of NSCF and some government agencies; gives member news, upcoming events, programs, and more.
Subscription: Free with membership

CIRPA NEWSLETTER
Canadian Independent Record Production Association
144 Front St., W., Ste. 330
Toronto, ON M5J 2L7
(416) 593-4545
Editor: Mary Quartarone
Frequency: 8/year
Coverage/Audience: Promotes members' business and publicizes organization views on government and industry matters affecting membership.
Subscription: Free to members; $50/year in Canada; $75/year elsewhere

CMEA NEWSLETTER
Canadian Music Educators' Association
CMEA-National Resource Center
P.O. Box 1461
St. Catharines, ON L2R 7J8
(416) 684-4664
Frequency: Quarterly
Subscription: Free with membership

CODA MAGAZINE
Box 87, Station J
Toronto, ON M4J 4X8
(416) 593-0269
Editors: Bill Smith and David Lee
Frequency: 6/year
Coverage/Audience: Jazz; contains interviews, photographs, reviews, and news coverage.
Subscription: $12/year

CONTINUO
An Early Music Magazine
6 Dartnell Ave.
Toronto, ON M5R 3A4
(416) 964-0819
Editor: Wendy de Jong
Frequency: 11/year
Coverage/Audience: An early music magazine which provides concise information on current events, new ideas in performance practice, instrument building, etc., as well as concert listings, records and book reviews, profiles and bimonthly special feature inserts. Audience includes builders, performers, amateurs, and listeners of early music.
Subscription: $12 Canada; $15 U.S. and overseas

COUNTRY MUSIC NEWS
The Academy of Country Music Entertainment
P.O. Box 574
Thornhill, ON L3T 4A2
(416) 883-9294
Editor: Gordon Burnett
Frequency: Quarterly
Subscription: Free

G

GUITAR TORONTO
Guitar Society of Toronto
19 Belmont St.
Toronto, ON M4N 1K6
(416) 922-8002
Editor: Dr. Mike Hogino
Frequency: Monthly, September to May
Coverage/Audience: For classical guitarists and guitar aficionados.
Subscription: Free with membership; $5/year nonmembers

I

INFORMATION DRUM CORPS
Ontario Drum Corps Association
466 Lake Dr. South
Keswick, ON L4P 1R1
(415) 476-5472
Editor: Allen J. Tierney
Frequency: Monthly
Coverage/Audience: Directed mainly to the management of the drum corps in Ontario.
Subscription: Free with membership

M

MIAC NEWSLETTER
Music Industries Association of Canada
130 Bloor St., W., Ste. 1101
Toronto, ON M5S 2X7
(416) 964-2875
Editor: Al Kowalenko
Frequency: Bimonthly
Coverage/Audience: For the Canadian music industry; MIAC members.
Subscription: Free to members

MUSICANADA
Canadian Music Council
36 Elgin St.
Ottawa, ON K1P 5K5
(613) 238-5893
Editor: Guy Huot
Frequency: Quarterly
Coverage/Audience: Musicians and music lovers.
Subscription: $6 Canada; $7 outside Canada

MUSIC DIRECTORY CANADA
CM Books
832 Mount Pleasant Rd.
Toronto, ON M4P 2L3
(416) 485-1049
Editor: Kathryn Mills
Frequency: Annually
Coverage/Audience: Listings of companies and organizations involved in music in Canada.
Subscription: $19.95 per copy, plus $1 postage and handling

MUSIC MAGAZINE
56 The Esplanade, Ste. 202
Toronto, ON M5E 1A7
(416) 364-5938
Editor: Ulla Colgrass
Frequency: 6/year
Coverage/Audience: Interviews and articles pertaining to classical music, book reviews, record reviews, stereo news, columns. The only classical music publication in Canada. Readers are the general public as well as professional musicians.
Subscription: $10 Canada; $12 outside Canada

THE MUSIC SCENE/LA SCENE MUSICALE
Performing Rights Organization of Canada, Ltd.
41 Valleybrook Dr.
Toronto, ON M3B 2S6
(416) 445-8700
Editor: Nancy Gyokeres
Frequency: 6/year
Coverage/Audience: Covers only activities of Canadian affiliated composers and music publishers.
Subscription: Free

MUSIC RESEARCH NEWS
Canadian Music Research Council
Faculty of Music
University of Western Ontario
London, ON N6A 3T4
(519) 679-6035
Editor: Dr. Harold Fiske
Frequency: 2/year
Coverage/Audience: Primarily Canadian music education, a few foreign subscriptions; primarily reports and reviews of Canadian music research.
Subscription: Free with membership

MUSICWORKS
The Music Gallery
30 St. Patrick St.
Toronto, ON M5T 1V1
(416) 593-0300
Editor: Tina Pearson
Frequency: Quarterly
Coverage/Audience: A sounding of the world from a Canadian perspective. It is created by musicians and artists to provide insight into significant innovative and alternative approaches to music-making. Contains articles, scores, photos, interviews, poems, and drawings.
Subscription: $10 individuals; $15 institutions

O

ONTARIO CHORAL FEDERATION NEWSLETTER
208 Bloor St., W., Ste. 308
Toronto, ON M5S 1T8
(416) 925-5525
Editor: Norah Bolton
Frequency: 6/year
Subscription: $20/year individuals; $30/year choir; $45/year corporations

OPERA CANADA
Foundation for Coast to Coast Opera Publication
366 Adelaide St., E., #433
Toronto, ON M5A 3X9
(416) 363-0395
Editor: Ruby Mercer
Frequency: Quarterly
Coverage/Audience: Canada's only national magazine on opera, highlights Canadians at home and abroad, with international reviews and events.
Subscription: $12 Canada; $15 elsewhere

ORCHESTRA CANADA/ORCHESTRES CANADA
Association of Canadian Orchestras and the Ontario Federation of Symphony Orchestras
56 The Esplanade, Ste. 311
Toronto, ON M5E 1A7
(416) 366-8834
Editor: Jack Edds
Frequency: 10/year
Coverage/Audience: All information pertinent to the Ontario Federation and Canadian Orchestras; timely information on government communications, news, people, musical chairs, fund-raising ideas, volunteer news, a new classified section, and other happenings.
Subscription: $5; $6 overseas

P

PERFORMING ARTS IN CANADA
Canadian Stage and Arts Publications
52 Avenue Rd., 2nd Fl.
Toronot, ON M5R 2G3
(416) 921-2601
Editor: Don Rooke
Frequency: Quarterly
Coverage/Audience: Up-to-date information on what is going on in theatre, dance, and music plus feature articles on issues and personalities that affect the performing arts in Canada.
Subscription: $5/year; $8/2 years

PROVINCIAL NEWSLETTER
British Columbia Registered Music Teachers' Association
10956 Swan Crescent
Surrey, BC V3R 5B6
(604) 581-3041
Frequency: Quarterly
Subscription: Contact for rates

R

REVUE DE MUSIQUE DES UNIVERSITES CANADIENNES/CANADIAN UNIVERSITY MUSIC REVIEW
Société de Musique des Universités Canadiennes
Université de Montréal
Faculté de Musique

C.P. 6128
Montreal, PQ H3C 3J7
Editor: J.J. Nattiez
Frequency: Annually
Subscription: $10/year

RPM WEEKLY
6 Brentcliffe Rd.
Toronto, ON M4G 3Y2
(416) 425-0257
Editor: Walter Grealis
Frequency: Weekly
Coverage/Audience: Top 50 singles and top 100 albums; also top 50 country singles; information on Canadian music industry, artists, and companies.
Subscription: $75/year (second class); $95/year (first class)

S

SASKATCHEWAN MUSIC FESTIVAL ASSOCIATION OFFICIAL SYLLABUS
Saskatchewan Music Festival Association
2205 Victoria Ave.
Regina, SK S4P 0S4
(306) 522-3651
Editor: Doris Covey Lazecki
Frequency: Annually
Coverage/Audience: Music teachers, students, music publishers, composers, and adjudicators.
Subscription: Contact for rates

U

UNDERGROUND
Old Time Music Club of Canada
1421 Gohier St.
St. Laurent, PQ H4L 3K2
(514) 748-7251
Frequency: 2-3/year
Subscription: Free to members; $.50 to nonmembers

V

VANCOUVER OPERA JOURNAL
Vancouver Opera Association
548 Cambie St.
Vancouver, BC V6N 2B7
(604) 682-2871
Editor: Staff
Frequency: Quarterly
Subscription: Contact for rates

ARGENTINA

FICTA-DIFUSORA DE MUSICA ANTIQUA
Centrode Musica Antiqua
Mexico 1208
1097 Buenos Aires, Argentina
Editor: Jorge V. Gonzalez
Frequency: Semiannually
Subscription: Contact for rates

AUSTRALIA

ACROSS COUNTRY
Box 177
Ferntree Gully
Victoria 3156, Australia
Editors: James J. Smith, Christine Whyte
Frequency: Monthly
Subscription: Contact for rates

AUSTRALIAN COUNTRY MUSIC NEWSLETTER
Box 186
Murwillumbah, N.S.W., 2484, Australia
Editors: Don and Noela Gresham
Frequency: 3/year
Subscription: Contact for rates

AUSTRALIAN JOURNAL OF MUSIC EDUCATION
Australian Society for Music Education
c/o Prof. Sir Frank Callaway
Department of Music
University of Western Australia
Nedlands, W.A. 6009, Australia
Editor: Sir Frank Callaway
Frequency: Semiannually
Subscription: Contact for rates

AUSTRALIAN MUSICIAN
Overall Services
Box 124
Bondi Rd.,
Bondi, N.S.W. 2026, Australia
Editor: Michael Burgess
Frequency: Bimonthly
Subscription: Contact for rates

FLAUTIST
Victorian Flute Guild
c/o 26 Milton Parade
Malvern, Victoris 3144, Australia
Editor: S.G. Caple
Frequency: 5/year
Subscription: Contact for rates

JAMM/JOURNAL FOR AUSTRALIAN MUSIC AND MUSICIANS
J.A.M.M. Pty. Ltd.
35 Advantage Rd.
Highett, Victoria 3190, Australia
Editor: Doug Ennis
Frequency: 11/year
Subscription: Contact for rates

AUSTRIA

DER KOMPONIST
Oesterreichischer Komponistenbund
Baumannstrasse 8-10
A-1031, Vienna, Austria
Editor: Robert Schollum
Frequency: Bimonthly
Subscription: Contact for rates

DENMARK

ACTA CAMPANOLOGICA
Scriptor Publisher A-S
Gasvaerksvej 15, DK-1656
Copenhagen U, Denmark
Frequency: Semiannual
Subscription: Contact for rates

ENGLAND

BASCA NEWS
British Academy of Songwriters, Composers and Authors
148 Charing Cross Rd.
London WC2H, OLB, England
Frequency: Quarterly
Subscription: Contact for rates

BRITISH JOURNAL OF MUSIC THERAPY
British Society for Music Therapy
48, Lanchester Rd.
London N6 4TA, England
Editor: M. Campbell
Frequency: 3/year
Subscription: Contact for rates

BUCKETFULL OF BRAINS
c/o Nighel Cross
25b Ridge Rd.
London N.8, England
Frequency: 3/year
Subscription: Contact for rates

CLARINET AND SAXOPHONE
Clarinet and Saxophone Society of Great Britain
26 Monks Orchard
Wilmington, Kent, England
Frequency: Quarterly
Subscription: Contact for rates

THE CONSORT
Journal of the Dolmetsch Foundation
14 Chestnut Way
Home Farm Rd.
Godalming, Surrey GU7 2TS, England 7725
Editor: S.M. Godwin
Frequency: Annually
Subscription: Contact for rates

COUNTRY MUSIC PEOPLE
Country Music Press, Ltd.
128A Lowfield St.
Dartford, Kent DA1 1JB, England
Editor: T. Byworth
Frequency: Monthly
Subscription: Contact for rates

EARLY MUSIC
Oxford University Press
Walton St.
Oxford OX2 6DP, England
Editor: J. Thomson
Frequency: Quarterly
Subscription: Contact for rates

EARLY MUSIC NEWS
27 Lanhill Rd.
London W9 2BS, England
Frequency: Monthly
Subscription: Contact for rates

ELGAR SOCIETY JOURNAL
Elgar Society
80 Langley Way
Watford, Herts WD1 3FF, England
Editor: R. Taylor
Frequency: 3/year
Subscription: Contact for rates

EXTRO
Constellation Publications
127a Oxford Rd.
All Saints, Manchester, England
Frequency: 8/year
Subscription: Contact for rates

THE FACE
43-47 Broadwick St.
London W. 1, England
Editor: N. Logan
Frequency: Monthly
Subscription: Contact for rates

GUITAR
Musical New Services Ltd.
Guitar House, Bimport
Shaftesbury, Dorset, England
Editor: G. Clinton
Frequency: Monthly
Subscription: Contact for rates

HARPSICHORD MAGAZINE
Rose Cottage, Bois Lane
Chesham Bois, Bucks, England
Editor: Edgar Hunt
Frequency: Semiannually
Subscription: Contact for rates

JAZZ JOURNAL INTERNATIONAL
Pitman Periodicals Ltd.
128 Long Acre
London WC2E 9AN, England
Editor: E. Cook
Frequency: Monthly
Subscription: Contact for rates

JOURNAL OF MUSICOLOGICAL RESEARCH
42 William IV St.
London WC2N 4DE, England
Editor: F. Smith
Frequency: Quarterly
Subscription: Contact for rates

LISZT SAECULUM
International LIszt Centre for 19th Century Music
35 Stanhope Rd.
Deal, Kent CT14 6AD, England
Editor: L. Rabes
Frequency: Semiannually
Subscription: Contact for rates

METHODIST CHURCH MUSIC SOCIETY BULLETIN
17 First Avenue
St. Anne's Park
Bristol BS4 4DV, England
Editor: Rev. B.F. Spinney
Frequency: Semiannually
Subscription: Contact for rates

MUSICAL WORLD
Turret Press Ltd.
886 High Rd.
London N12 9SB, England
Editor: P. Pulham
Frequency: Monthly
Subscription: Contact for rates

MUSIC ANALYSIS
108 Cowley Rd.
Oxford, OX4 1JF, England
Editor: J. Dunsby
Frequency: 3/year
Subscription: Contact for rates

MUSIC AND LETTERS
Oxford University Press
Walton St.
Oxford, OX2 6DP, England
Editor: E. Olleson
Frequency: Quarterly
Subscription: Contact for rates

MUSIC AND VIDEO
Music and Video Review, Ltd.
11 St. Bride St.
London, EC4, England
Frequency: Monthly
Subscription: Contact for rates

MUSIC AND VIDEO WEEK
Consumer Press
40 Long Acre
London WC2 9JT, England
Editor: R. Burbeck
Frequency: Weekly
Subscription: Contact for rates

MUSIC BOX
Musical Box Society of Great Britain
31 Perry Hill
London SE6, 4LF, England
Editor: R. Clarson-Leach
Frequency: Quarterly
Subscription: Contact for rates

MUSIC TEACHER
Scholastic Publications Ltd.
141-143 Drury Lane
London, WC2B 5TG, England
Editor: Leonard Pearcey
Frequency: Monthly
Subscription: Contact for rates

MUSICIAN
Salvation Army
101 Queen Victoria St.
London EC4P 4EP, England
Editor: T. Howes
Frequency: Weekly
Subscription: Contact for rates

NEW CHRISTIAN MUSIC
259 Marvels Lane
Grove Park
London SE12 9PT, England
Editor: P. Davis
Frequency: Quarterly
Subscription: Contact for rates

NEW GANDY DANCER
7 Corsair
Fellside Park
Whickham, Newcastle on Tyne
NE16 5YA, England
Editor: D. Peckett
Frequency: Semiannually
Subscription: Contact for rates

FINLAND

MUSIIKKI
Suomen Musiikkitieteellinen Seura
Vironkatu 1C17
00170 Helsinki 17, Finland
Frequency: Quarterly
Subscription: Contact for rates

FRANCE

AMIS DE 'OEUVRE ET LA PENSEE DE GEORGES MIGOT
Institut de Musicologie
22, rue Descartes
67084 Strasbourg Cedex, France
Editor: Dr. M. Honegger
Frequency: Semiannually
Subscription: Contact for rates

AVANT-SCENE OPERA
Editions de l'Avant Scene
27 rue St. Andre des Arts
75006 Paris, France
Frequency: Semiannually
Subscription: Contact for rates

CONFEDERATION MUSICALE DE FRANCE
121 rue la Fayette
75010 Paris, France
Frequency: 10/year
Subscription: Contact for rates

D.I.S.C. INTERNATIONAL
Mediapresse
32 rue Jean Bleuzen
92170 Vanves, France
Editor: J. Jordy
Frequency: Monthly
Subscription: Contact for rates

GERMAN DEMOCRATIC REPUBLIC

MUSIK IN DER SCHULE
Verlag Volk und Wissen
Krausenstrasse 50
108 Berlin, GDR
Editor: Wolfgang Wunder
Frequency: Monthly
Subscription: Contact for rates

GERMAN FEDERAL REPUBLIC

EURO PIANO
Verlag das Musikinstrument
Kleuberstrasse 9
6000 Frankfurt 1, GFR
Editor: Winfried Baumbach

Frequency: Quarterly
Subscription: Contact for rates

FORUM MUSIKBIBLIOTHEK
Deutsches Bibliothesinstitut
Bundesallee 184/185
1000 Berlin 31, GFR
Frequency: Quarterly
Subscription: Contact for rates

HANS-PFITZNER-GESELLSCHAFT. MITTEILUNGEN
Mozartstrasse 6
8132 Tutzing, GFR
Editor: W.F. Kreim
Frequency: Semiannually
Subscription: Contact for rates

MUSICA SACRA
Allgemeiner Caecilien-Verdand
Koelnstrasse 415
5300 Bonn, GFR
Frequency: Bimonthly
Subscription: Contact for rates

MUSICAE SACRAE MINISTERIUM
Consociato Internationalis Musicae Sacrae
Koeln 1
Burgmauer 1, GFR
Editor: J. Overath
Frequency: Quarterly
Subscription: Contact for rates

MUSIK EXPRESS
Christian Krummer Verlag GmbH
Winterhuder Weg 29
2000 Hamburg 76, GFR
Frequency: Monthly
Subscription: Contact for rates

MUSIK INTERNATIONAL
Verlag Franz Schmitt
Kaiserstrasse 99
5200 Siegburg, GFR
Subscription: Contact for rates

NEUE MUSIKZEITUNG
Gustav Bosse Verlag
Von-der-Tann-Str. 38
Posttach 417
8400 Regensburg 1, GFR
Editor: B. Bosse
Frequency: Bimonthly
Subscription: Contact for rates

ITALY

ALMANACCO DELLA CANZONE E DEL CINEMA
Editrice VIP
Via del Babuino 181
00187 Rome, Italy
Editor: N. Lusso
Frequency: Monthly
Subscription: Contact for rates

ANNO DISCOGRAFICO
Gruppo Editoriale Suono
Via del Casaletto 380
00151 Rome, Italy
Frequency: Semiannually
Subscription: Contact for rates

DISCOTECA HI FI
Casa Editrice Discoteca
Via Martignoni 1
20144 Milan, Italy
Editor: O.Z. Mauri
Frequency: Monthly
Subscription: Contact for rates

FLAUTO DOLCE
Societa Italiana del Flauto Dolce
Viale Angelico 67
00195 Rome, Italy
Editor: Giancarlo Rostirollo
Frequency: Semiannually
Subscription: Contact for rates

HI-FI MUSICA
Via A. Caroncini 43
00197 Rome, Italy
Subscription: Contact for rates

LABORATORIO MUSICA
Cooperativa Nuova Comunicazione
Via F. Carrara 27
00196 Rome, Italy
Editor: L. Nono
Frequency: Monthly
Subscription: Contact for rates

MUSIC
Edizioni Leti S.R.I.
Via Boezio 2
00192 Rome, Italy
Frequency: Monthly
Subscription: Contact for rates

MUSICA E DISCHI
Via Giannone 2
20154 Milan, Italy
Editor: M. DeLuigi, Jr.
Frequency: Monthly
Subscription: Contact for rates

MUSICA/REALTA
Edizioni Dedalo
Casella Postale 362
70100 Bari, Italy
Editor: L. Pestalozza
Frequency: Monthly
Subscription: Contact for rates

MUSICA VIVA
New International Media S.p.A.
Via Revere 16
20123 Milan, Italy
Editor: N. Geron
Frequency: Monthly
Subscription: Contact for rates

JAPAN

CASSETTE LIFE
4200 Yen. Shinko Music Publishing Co., Ltd.
2-12 Ogawa-Machi, Kanda
Chiyoda-Ku, Tokyo, Japan
Editor: Hirokazu Yoshida
Frequency: Bimonthly
Subscription: Contact for rates

MUSICA IBEROAMERICANA/CHUNAMBEI ONGAKU
Musica Iberoamericana Co.
1-21-6 Ebisu
Shibuya-Ku, Tokyo, Japan
Editor: Yoshio Nakanishi
Frequency: Monthly
Subscription: Contact for rates

MUSICA NOVA
Ongaku No Tomo Sha Corp.
Kagurazak 6-30
Shinjuku-Ku, Tokyo, Japan
Frequency: Monthly
Subscription: Contact for rates

MUSIC TRADE IN JAPAN/GAKKI SHOHO
Gakki Shohosha
c/o Gakki-Kaikan Bldg.
2-18-21 Soto Kanda
Chiyoda-Ku, Tokyo 101, Japan
Editor: Yoshio Miyauchi
Frequency: Monthly
Subscription: Contact for rates

MEXICO

HETEROFONIA
Conservatorio Nacional de Musica
Department of Musicology
Masaryk 582
Mexico 5, D.F., Mexico
Editor: E. Pulido
Frequency: Quarterly
Subscription: Contact for rates

MUNDO MUSICAL
Industrias Nacionales de Sonido, S.A.
Baja California 196-103
Mexico 7, D.F., Mexico
Editor: Raul Romero
Frequency: Monthly
Subscription: Contact for rates

OAXACA CULTURAL: SU MUSICA
Ediciones Culturales
5 de Febrero No. 115
Oaxaca, Mexico
Frequency: Monthly
Subscription: Contact for rates

NETHERLANDS

ABBA MAGAZINE
AKTV B.V.
Postbus 174
1380 AD Weesp, Netherlands
Frequency: 8/year
Subscription: Contact for rates

BEATLES VISIE
Nederlandse Beatles Fanclub
Box 1464
1000 BL Amsterdam, Netherlands
Editor: H. van der Woude

Frequency: Quarterly
Subscription: Contact for rates

BLOCK
c/o M.A. Wisse
Box 244
7600 AE Almelo, Netherlands
Editor: R. Wisse
Frequency: Quarterly
Subscription: Contact for rates

BOUWBRIEF
Verenigin voor Huismuziek
Catharynesingel 85
Utrecht, Netherlands
Editor: D.J. Hamden
Frequency: Quarterly
Subscription: Contact for rates

BULLETIN AANGESLOTENEN
Postbus 90507
1006 BM Amsterdam, Netherlands
Subscription: Contact for rates

DYNAMITE/INTERNATIONAL
International Cliff Richard Movement
Box 4164
1009 AD Amsterdam, Netherlands
Editor: Anton Husmann Jr.
Frequency: Bimonthly
Subscription: Contact for rates

EX ORE INFANTIUM
Lennards - Instituut
Steegstraat 16
6041 EA Roermond, Netherlands
Editor: L.P.M. Lindeman
Frequency: Quarterly
Subscription: Contact for rates

INFORMATIEBLAD 2112
2112 Productions
Postbus 906
6800 AX Arnhem, Netherlands
Frequency: Quarterly
Subscription: Contact for rates

JAZZ NU
Stichting Jazzonderzoek
Postbus 16719
1001 RE Amsterdam, Netherlands
Editor: Frans van Leeuwen
Frequency: Monthly
Subscription: Contact for rates

KLOK EN KLEPEL
Nederlandse Klokkenspel - Vereniging
Helenahoeve 13
2804 HN Gouda, Netherlands
Subscription: Contact for rates

MENS EN MELODIE
Uitgeverij Frits Knuf
Box 720
4116 ZJ Buren, Netherlands
Editors: L. van Hasselt, E. Vermeulen, B. Willink
Frequency: Monthly
Subscription: Contact for rates

MUZIEK EXPRES
Oberon B.V.
Postbus 63
Haarlem, Netherlands
Editor: D.R.J. Kooiman
Frequency: Monthly
Subscription: Contact for rates

NEW ZEALAND

COUNTRY SIDE OF MUSIC
New Zealand Country Music Association
29 Mayflower Close
Mangere East, New Zealand
Editor: C. Brickland
Subscription: Contact for rates

SOUTH AFRICA

AFRICAN MUSIC
Journal of the African Music Society
International Library of African Music
Rhodes University
Grahamstown, 6140, South Africa
Editor: A. Tracey
Frequency: Annually
Subscription: Contact for rates

KONSERVATORIUM NUUS
Konservatorium - Vereniging
Konservatorium vir Musiek
Private Bag 315
Pretoria, South Africa
Frequency: Semiannually
Subscription: Free

MUSICUS
University of South Africa
Department of Music Examinations
Box 392
Pretoria 0001, South Africa
Editor: H. Joubert
Frequency: Semiannually
Subscription: Contact for rates

SPAIN

ASOCIACION DE COMPOSITORES SINFONICOS ESPANOLES BOLETIN
Francisco de Rojas 5
Madrid 10, Spain
Frequency: Semiannually
Subscription: Contact for rates

MONSALVAT
Ediciones de Nuevo Arte Thor
Plaza Gala Placidia 1
Barcelona 6, Spain
Frequency: Monthly
Subscription: Contact for rates

SWEDEN

JEFFERSON
Scandinavian Blues Association
Zetterlunds Vaag 90 B
18600 Vallentuna, Sweden
Editor: Tom Loefgren
Frequency: Quarterly
Subscription: Contact for rates

MUSIKERN
Svenska Musikerfoerbundet
Box 4
10120 Stockholm, Sweden
Editor: Yngve Aakerberg
Frequency: 11/year
Subscription: Contact for rates

SWITZERLAND

NUTIDA MUSIK/CONTEMPORARY MUSIC
Sveriges Riksradig
S-105 10 Stockholm, Sweden
Editor: C. Tobeck
Frequency: Quarterly
Subscription: Contact for rates

U.S.S.R.

MUZYKAL 'NAYA ZHIZN'
Izdatel 'stvo Sovetskii Kompozitor
14-12 Sadovaya-Triumfalnaya St.
103006, Moscow, U.S.S.R.
Subscription: Contact for rates

Music Book Publishers

U.S. and Canadian publishers of reference works, trade books, textbooks, and monographs in the field of music or the performing arts are listed alphabetically within each country.

A

ABILITY DEVELOPMENT ASSOC., INC.
PO Box 887
93 W. Union St.
Athens, OH 45701
(614) 594-3547
Reginald H. Fink, President

ACCURA MUSIC
PO Box 887
93 E. Union St.
Athens, OH 45701
(614) 594-3547
Reginald H. Fink, President

ADRIAN PRESS
157 W. 57th St.
New York, NY 10019
(212) 265-6637
Vera Miller, Director

ALFRED PUBLISHING CO., INC.
Box 5964
15335 Morrison St.
Sherman Oaks, CA 91403
(213) 995-8811
John O'Reilly, Music Editor-in-Chief

AMERICAN COUNCIL FOR THE ARTS
570 Seventh Ave.
New York, NY 10018
(212) 354-6655
W. Glant Brownrice, Director

AMERICAN MUSIC CONFERENCE
1000 Skokie Blvd.
Wilmette, IL 60091
(312) 251-1600
Gene C. Wenner, President

AMERICAN RECORD COLLECTORS' EXCHANGE
PO Box 1377
FDR Station
New York, NY 10150
(212) 688-8426
J.M. Moses, President

APM PRESS
650 Ocean Ave.
Brooklyn, NY 11226
(212) 941-6835
Allen S. Koenigsberg, Director

APPLAUSE PUBLICATIONS
2234 S. Shady Hills Dr.
Diamond Bar, CA 91765
(714) 595-9380
John D. Pearson, President

ARARAT PRESS
585 Saddle River Rd.
Saddle Brook, NJ 07662
(201) 797-7600
Edward Mardigian, President

B

BELL SPRINGS PUBLISHING CO.
PO Box 640
Laytonville, CA 95454
(707) 984-6746
Bernard Kamoroff, President

BERKLEE PRESS PUBLICATIONS
1140 Boylston St.
Boston, MA 02215
(617) 262-4133
Lawrence Berk, President

BIRCH TREE GROUP LTD.
Box 2072
180 Alexander St.
Princeton, NJ 08540
(609) 683-0090
David K. Sengstack, President

BLACK SWAN BOOKS LTD.
PO Box 327
Redding Ridge, CT 06876
(203) 938-9548
John J. Walsh, Publisher

THE BOLD STRUMMER LTD.
1 Webb Rd.
Westport, CT 06880
(203) 226-8230
Nicholas R. Clarke, President

BOOSEY AND HAWKES, INC.
PO Box 130
Oceanside, NY 11572
(516) 678-2500
W. Stuart Pope, President

THE BOSTON MUSIC COMPANY
116 Boylston St.
Boston, MA 02116
(617) 426-5100
Warren W. Morris, General Manager

BRAILLE, INC.
44 Scranton Ave.
Falmouth, MA 02540
(617) 540-0800
Joan B. Rose, Executive Director

BRANDEN PRESS, INC.
Box 843
21 Station St., Brookline Village
Boston, MA 02147
(617) 734-2045
Adolph Caso, President and Treasurer

THE BRASS PRESS
136 Eighth Ave. N.
Nashville, TN 37203
(615) 254-8969
Stephen Glover, Editor

BROAD RIVER PRESS, INC.
PO Box 50329
Columbia, SC 29250
G.B. Lane, President

BROOKLYN COLLEGE INSTITUTE FOR STUDIES IN AMERICAN MUSIC
Brooklyn, NY 11210
(212) 780-5655
Prof. H. Wiley Hitchcock, Director

C

IRVING CAESAR MUSIC CORP.
850 Seventh Ave.
New York, NY 10019
(212) 265-7868
Irving Caesar, President

CDE
PO Box 41551
Atlanta, GA 30331
Charles D. Edwards, President

CENTER FOR SOUTHERN FOLKLORE
1216 Peabody Ave.
PO Box 40105
Memphis, TN 38104
(901) 726-4205
Judy Peiser, Executive Director

CHANTEYMAN PRESS
42 Crocus St.
Woodbridge, NJ 07095
(201) 634-4123
Eric P. Russell, Owner

CHARTMASTERS
PO Box 1264
Covington, LA 70434
James D. Quirin, Executive Director

COLUMBIA PUBLISHING CO.
Frenchtown, NJ 08825
(201) 996-2141
Bernard Rabb, President

COMSTOCK EDITIONS, INC.
3030 Bridgeway
Sausalito, CA 94965
(415) 332-3216
Richard N. Gould, President & Publisher

CONCORDIA PUBLISHING HOUSE
3558 S. Jefferson Ave.
St. Louis, MO 63118
(314) 664-7000
Edward Klammer, Music Production Manager

CONVEX INDUSTRIES
4720 Cheyenne
Boulder, CO 80303
(303) 494-4176
Daniel J. Miles, Co-Owner

THE CORINTHIAN PRESS
3592 Lee Rd.
Shaker Heights, OH 44120
(216) 751-7300
Daniel F. Eiben, Editor-in-Chief

COUNTRY DANCE AND SONG SOCIETY OF AMERICA
505 Eighth Ave., Room 2500
New York, NY 10018
(212) 594-8833
Jeff Warner, President

COUNTRY MUSIC FOUNDATION PRESS
4 Music Square
Nashville, TN 37215
(615) 256-1639
Kyle D. Young, Head of Publications

CRITERION MUSIC CORPORATION
6124 Selma Ave.
Hollywood, CA 90028
(213) 469-2296
Michael H. Goldsen, President

CROSS HARP PRESS
1016 Flora
Coronado, CA 92118
(714) 437-1357
Jon Ginidick, President

D

DA CAPO PRESS, INC.
233 Spring St.
New York, NY 10013
(212) 620-8000
Martin E. Tash, President

VINCE DANCA
2418 Barrington Pl.
Rockford, IL 61107
(815) 398-3620

DELILAH COMMUNICATIONS LTD.
118 E. 25th St.
New York, NY 10010
(212) 477-2100
Stephanie Bennett, President

DONATO MUSIC PUBLISHING CO.
PO Box 415
New York, NY 10011
(212) 877-2741
Daniel A. Ricigliano, Owner

E

EPOCH UNIVERSAL PUBLICATIONS
10802 N. 23rd. Ave.
Phoenix, AZ 85029
(602) 943-7229
Ray Bruno, President

EUROPEAN AMERICAN MUSIC DISTRIBUTORS CORPORATION
195 Allwood Rd.
Clifton, NJ 07012
(201) 777-2680
Ronald Freed, President

EXPRESSALL
260 Dean Rd.
PO Box 427
Brookline, MA 02146
(617) 734-1297
Thelma Gruenbaum, Owner

E-Z LEARNING METHODS
PO Box 2582
Pomona, CA 91766
(714) 622-6835
Donna Shannon, Sales

F

FACTS ON FILE, INC.
460 Park Ave. S.
New York, NY 10016
(212) 683-2244
Howard M. Epstein, President

BRICE FARWELL
5 Deer Trail
Briarcliff Manor, NY 10510
(914) 941-5144
Brice Farwell, Publisher

F. FERGESON PRODUCTIONS
PO Box 433
Lake Bluff, IL 60044
(312) 864-7696
David Jeffrey Fletcher, M.D., Owner/Publisher

FESTIVAL PUBLICATIONS
Box 10180
Glendale, CA 91209
(213) 222-8626
Alan Gadney, President

H. T. FITZSIMONS COMPANY, INC.
357 W. Erie St.
Chicago, IL 60610
(312) 944-1841
R. E. Fitzsimons, President/Treasurer

FOLK-LEGACY RECORDS, INC.
Sharon Mountain Rd.
Sharon, CT 06069
(203) 364-5661
Lee B. Haggerty, President

MARK FOSTER MUSIC COMPANY
PO Box 4012
Champaign, IL 61820
(217) 367-9932
James McKelvy, Editor

FUNK & WAGNALLS, INC.
53 E. 77th St.
New York, NY 10021
(212) 570-4500
James L. Stoltzfus, President & Chief Exec. Officer

G

GALAXY MUSIC CORPORATION
2121 Broadway
New York, NY 10023

(212) 874-2100
John Kernochan, President

GAMUT MUSIC COMPANY
PO Box 74
Mattapan, MA 02126
(617) 244-3305
Sewall B. Potter, Proprietor

GLOUCHESTER PRESS
PO Box 1044
Fairmont, WV 26554
(304) 366-3758
William R. Tudor, Manager

HERBERT K. GOODKIND
25 Helena Ave.
Larchmont, NY 10538
(914) 834-1448
Herbert K. Goodkind, Owner and Author

GPI PUBLICATIONS
20605 Lazanco
Cupertino, CA 95014
(408) 446-1105
Jim Crockett, Executive Director

GREAT OCEAN PUBLISHERS
1823 N. Lincoln St.
Arlington, VA 22207
(703) 525-0909
Mark Esterman, President & Editor-in-Chief

GREGORIAN INSTITUTE OF AMERICA PUBLICATIONS, INC.
7404 S. Mason Ave.
Chicago, IL 60638
(312) 496-3800
Edward Harris, President

GROVE'S DICTIONARIES OF MUSIC, INC.
15 E. 26th St., Ste. 1503
New York, NY 10010
(212) 532-4811
Nicholas Byam Shaw, President

H

HEATHCOTE PUBLISHERS
PO Box 135
Monmouth Junction, NJ 08852
(201) 297-4891
William R. Palmer, Owner

HIPPOCRENE BOOKS, INC.
171 Madison Ave.
New York, NY 10016
(212) 685-4371
George Blagowidow, President

HOPE PUBLISHING CO.
Carol Stream, IL 60187
(312) 665-3200
George H. Shorney, President

HYPERION PRESS, INC.
45 Riverside Ave.
Westport, CT 06880
(203) 226-1091
Hal Dareff, President

I

INFORMATION COORDINATORS, INC.
1435-37 Randolph St.
Detroit, MI 48226
(313) 962-9720
Florence Kretzschmar, President & Editor-in-Chief

INSTITUTE OF MEDIEVAL MUSIC, LTD.
PO Box 295
Henryville, PA 18332
Luther A. Dittmer, President

INTERNATIONAL ASSOCIATION OF ORGAN TEACHERS USA
7938 Bertram Ave.
Hammond, IN 46324
(219) 844-3395
Dorothy S. Greig, President

J

JAZZ DISCOGRAPHIES UNLIMITED
337 Ellerton S.
Laurel, MD 20810
George I. Hall, Editor-in-Chief

K

KASTLEMUSICK, INC.
901 Washington St.
Wilmington, DE 19801
Robert A. Hill, Vice-President & Editor-in-Chief

KENYON PUBLICATIONS
170 N.E. 33rd St.
Fourt Lauderdale, FL 33334
(305) 563-1844
Albert De Vito, Owner

KIKIMORA PUBLISHING CO.
PO Box 1107
Los Altos, CA 94022
(415) 941-3120
David Peterson, President

L

AL LEICHTER
580 Hilltop Dr.
Staunton, VA 24401
(703) 885-6614

LERNER PUBLICATIONS CO.
241 First Ave. N.
Minneapolis, MN 55401
(612) 332-3345
Harry J. Lerner, President

LEYERLE PUBLICATIONS
PO Box 384
Geneseo, NY 14454
(716) 658-2193
William D. Leyerle, Publisher

ROBERT B. LUCE, INC.
540 Barnum Ave.
Bridgeport, CT 06608
(203) 366-1900
Martin B. Berke, President & Editor

M

SCOTTY MACGREGOR PUBLICATIONS
10 Pineacre Dr.
Smithtown, NY 11787
(516) 269-6532
I.T. MacGregor, Owner

MAGNAMUSIC DISTRIBUTORS, INC.
Sharon, CT 06069
(203) 364-5431
Alice S. Mix, President

REESE MARKEWICH
Bacon Hill Rd.
Pleasantville, NY 10570
(212) 674-2979
Reese Markewich, Publisher

MCFARLAND & CO., INC.
Box 611
Jefferson, NC 28640
(919) 246-4460
Robert Franklin, President & Editor-in-Chief

THE MELROSE PUBLISHING COMPANY
384 N. San Vicente Blvd.
Los Angeles, CA 90048
(213) 655-5177
Al Berkman, Owner

THE MERRIAM-EDDY COMPANY, INC.
Sweden Rd., PO Box 25
South Waterford, ME 04081
(207) 583-4645
Eleanor M. Edwards, Executive Vice-President

MIDWEST PUBLISHING COMPANY
PO Box 33
Ceresco, NE 68017
(402) 665-5351
Elinor L. Brown, Owner and Manager

M.I.H. PUBLICATIONS
1600 Billman Ln.
Silver Spring, MD 20902
(301) 946-2243
Michael I. Holmes, Publisher & Editor

MOCKINGBIRD PRESS
1407 N. 9th, PO Box 7
Alpine, TX 79830
(915) 837-7398
Jeremy H. M. Mock, Publisher

MUSICDATA, INC.
3 Maplewood Mall
Philadelphia, PA 19144
(215) 842-0555

Nancy K. Nardone and Walter A. Frankel, Editors

MUSIC EDUCATORS NATIONAL CONFERENCE
1902 Association Dr.
Reston, VA 22091
(703) 860-4000

Donald W. Dillon, Executive Director

MUSICPRINT CORPORATION
225 W. 57th St., 5th Flr.
New York, NY 10019
(212) 582-2642

Gene Frank

MUSIC SALES CORP.
799 Broadway
New York, NY 10003
(212) 254-2100

Eugene Weintraub, Editor-in-Chief & Executive Music Editor

MUSIC TREASURE PUBLICATIONS
620 Fort Washington Ave. (1-F)
New York, NY 10040

Donald Garvelmann, Manager and Director

N

NATIONAL OPERA ASSOCIATION
823 Hotel Wellington
7th Ave. at 55th St.
New York, NY 10019
(212) 247-3900

Natalie Limonick, President

NIGHTHAWK PRESS
PO Box 813
Forest Grove, OR 97116

Cliff Martin, Presdient

O

ORGAN LITERATURE FOUNDATION
45 Norfolk Rd.
Braintree, MA 02184
(617) 848-1388

Henry Karl Baker, President

O'SULLIVAN WOODSIDE & CO.
2218 E. Magnolia
Phoenix, AZ 85034
(602) 244-1000

Donald S. Woodside, President

P

PAGANINIANA PUBLICATIONS
211 W. Sylvania Ave.
Neptune, NJ 07753
(201) 988-8400

Herbert R. Axelrod, President

PANJANDRUM BOOKS
11321 Iowa Ave., Ste. 1
Los Angeles, CA 90025
(213) 477-8771

Dennis Koran, Editor & Publisher

PARAGON PRODUCTIONS
817 Pearl St.
Denver, CO 80203
(303) 321-8159

Hugh A. Grant, Owner

JOSEPH PATELSON MUSIC HOUSE LTD.
160 W. 56th St.
New York, NY 10019
(212) 757-5587

Joseph Patelson, Owner

PENDRAGON PRESS
162 W. 13th St.
New York, NY 10011
(212) 243-3494

Robert J. Kessler, President

PERCEPTION DEVELOPMENT TECHNIQUES
PO Box 1068
Cathedral Station
New York, NY 10025
(212) 663-5220

Burton Kaplan, President/Owner

PHOENIXONGS
PO Box 622
Northbrook, IL 60062
(312) 564-2484

PIANO UNIVERSITY
5090 Dobrot
Central Point, OR 97502
(503) 664-6037

Duane Shinn, Owner

PINK HOUSE PUBLISHING CO.
410 Magellan Ave.
Penthouse 1002
Honolulu, HI 96813
(808) 949-8051

Heinz-Guenther Pink, President

POLY TONE PRESS
16027 Sunburst St.
Sepulveda, CA 91343
(213) 892-0044

Larry Fotine, Owner

THE PRAESTANT PRESS
PO Box 43
Delaware, OH 43015
(614) 363-1458

Homer D. Blanchard, Publisher/Editor

PRINCETON BOOK COMPANY PUBLISHERS
Box 109
Princeton, NJ 08540
(201) 297-8370

Charles Woodford, President

PRINTED EDITIONS
Box 27, Station Hill Rd.
Barrytown, NY 12507
(914) 758-6488

Dick Higgins, President & Editor

THE PUTNAM PUBLISHING GROUP
200 Madison Ave.
New York, NY 10016
(212) 576-8900

Samuel A. Mitnick, Vice-President & Publisher

Q

QUEST PUBLISHING COMPANY
5023 Kentucky St.
South Carolina, WV 25309

Charles Bradley, Editor/Publisher

R

RECORD RESEARCH, INC.
PO Box 200
Menomonee Falls, WI 53051
(414) 251-5408

Joel Whitburn, President

RIVERRUN PRESS, INC.
175 Fifth Ave.
New York, NY 10010
(212) 228-0390

John Calder, President & Editor-in-Chief

ROSS BOOKS
Box 4340
Berkeley, CA 94704
(415) 841-2474

Franz Ross, President

S

ST. MAWR OF VERMONT
PO Box 356
Randolph Center, VT 05060

John H. Kennedy, Director

DUNCAN P. SCHIEDT
R.R. 1, Box 217-A
Pittsboro, IN 46167
(317) 852-8528

SCHIRMER BOOKS
866 Third Ave.
New York, NY 10022
(212) 935-5521

Charles E. Smith, Publisher

ANNEMARIE SCHNASE-REPRINT DEPARTMENT
120 Brown Rd.
PO Box 119
Scarsdale, NY 10583
(914) 725-1284

SCHRODER MUSIC CO.
2027 Parker St.
Berkeley, CA 94704
(415) 843-2365
Nancy Schimmel, Owner

SEVEN ARTS PRESS, INC.
6253 Hollywood Blvd.
No. 1100
Hollywood, CA 90028
(213) 469-1095
Walter E. Hurst, President

THE SHERWOOD COMPANY
PO Box 21645
Denver, CO 80221
(303) 423-6481
Conrad Kracht, Director of Marketing

DUANE SHINN PUBLICATIONS
5090 Dobrot
Central Point, OR 97502
(503) 664-6037
Duane Shinn, Owner and Author

SILVER BURDETT CO.
250 James St.
Morristown, NJ 07960
(201) 285-7700
Patrick Donaghy, President

SOLO MUSIC, INC.
4708 Van Noord Ave.
Sherman Oaks, CA 91423
(213) 762-2219
Paul Mills, President and General Manager

JACK SPRATT WOODWIND SHOP
199 Sound Beach
Old Greenwich, CT 06870
(203) 637-3812
Jack Spratt, Owner

STANDARD EDITIONS
PO Box 1297
Stuyvesant Sta.
New York, NY 10009
(212) 473-2807
Constance DeJong, Co-founder

STERLING PUBLISHING CO., INC.
2 Park Ave.
New York, NY 10016
(212) 532-7160
Burton Hobson, President & Editor

SUMA
RD 1, Box 26
Huntington, VT 05462
(802) 434-3330
Mary Marguerite Jaquier, Publisher

THE SUNBURY PRESS
PO Box 1778
Raleigh, NC 27602
(919) 832-6417
Richard Parsons

T

TAB BOOKS, INC.
Blue Ridge Summit, PA 17214
(717) 794-2191
Lawrence Jackel, President

THAMES AND HUDSON, INC.
500 Fifth Ave.
New York, NY 10110
(212) 354-3763
Peter Warner, President

THEATER COMMUNICATIONS GROUP
355 Lexington Ave.
New York, NY 10017
(212) 697-5230

THREE CONTINENTS PRESS
1346 Connecticut Ave., N.W.
Ste. 224
Washington, DC 20036
(202) 457-0288
Donald E. Herdeck, President and Editor

TREE BY THE RIVER PUBLISHING
Box 413
Riverside, CA 92502
(714) 682-8942
George Williams III

TWO-EIGHTEEN PRESS
PO Box 218
Village Station
New York, NY 10014
(212) 966-5877
Tom Johnson, Owner

U

UMI RESEARCH PRESS
300 N. Zeeb Rd.
Ann Arbor, MI 48106
(313) 761-4700
Joseph J. Fitzsimmons, President

UNITED SYNAGOGUE BOOK SERVICE
155 Fifth Ave.
New York, NY 10010
(212) 533-7800
Morton Siegel, Educational Director

UNIVERSE BOOKS
381 Park Ave. S
New York, NY 10016
(212) 685-7400
Gilman Park, President

UNIVERSITY OF ILLINOIS PRESS
Box 5081, Station A
54 E. Gregory Dr.
Champaign, IL 61820
(217) 333-0950
Richard L. Wentworth, Director

UNIVERSITY OF PENNSYLVANIA PRESS
3933 Walnut St.
Philadelphia, PA 19104
(215) 898-6261
Maurice English, Director

UNIVERSITY OF WASHINGTON ASIAN MUSIC PUBLICATIONS
School of Music
Seattle, WA 98195
(206) 543-0974
Fredric Lieberman, Editor

V

VESTAL PRESS LTD.
PO Box 97
320 N. Jensen Rd.
Vestal, NY 13850
(607) 797-4872
Harvey N. Roehl, Owner and President

VIRTUE NOTAGRAPH EDITIONS
4940 Beaumont Dr.
La Mesa, CA 92041
(714) 469-6634
Constance Virtue, Partner

VOLKWEIN BROS, INC.
117 Sandusky St.
Pittsburgh, PA 15212
(412) 322-5100
Walter E. Volkwein, Secretary and Trasurer

W

WOODS BOOKS
PO Box 29521
Los Angeles, CA 90029
(213) 247-4177
Sylvia Woods, President

THE WORLD OF PERIPOLE, INC.
Browns Mills, NJ 08015
(609) 893-9111
M. Perry, President

WRITER'S DIGEST BOOKS
9933 Alliance Rd.
Cincinnati, OH 45242
(513) 984-0717
Richard Rosenthal, President

WYETH PRESS
PO Box 550
Great Barrington, MA 01230
(413) 528-1300
John W.P. Mooney, General Manager

Z

ZALO PUBLICATIONS & SERVICES, INC.
PO Box 6858
Santa Barbara, CA 93111
(805) 964-7190
James Pellerite, President

DALE ZDENEK PUBLISHING
31352 Via Colinas
Westlake Village, CA 91362
(213) 991-4334

Dale Zdenek, President

CANADA

THE AVONDALE PRESS
PO Box 451
Willowdale, ON M2N 5T1

Ronald Napier, Owner

BLACK RAINBOW PUBLICATIONS
193 Lord Seaton Rd.
Willowdale, ON M2P 1L1
(416) 225-3197

John Tapscott, President

BOLD BRASS STUDIOS & PUBLICATIONS
PO Box 77101
Vancouver, VC V5R 5T4
(604) 438-1111

Alexander Albert Adam, Proprietor

ROBERT GARBUTT PRODUCTIONS
219 Ronan Ave.
Toronto, ON M4N 2Y7
(416) 489-9034

Robert B. Garbutt, Proprietor

LESLIE MUSIC SUPPLY
PO Box 471
Oakville, ON L6J 5A8
(416) 844-3109

Mrs. W. Leslie, Owner

MILLAR PUBLICATIONS
PO Box 69
Exshaw, AB T0L 2C0

G. W. Millar, Owner

ROCKOLA ENTERPRISES
178 Gillard Ave.
Toronto, ON M4J 4N8
(416) 463-9078

Sharon Ablett, Partner

SONANTE PUBLICATIONS
PO Box 74, Station F
Toronto, ON M4Y 2L4

J. Kent Mason, Proprietor

WATERLOO MUSIC COMPANY LTD.
3 Regina St., N.
Box 250
Waterloo, ON N2J 4A5
(519) 886-4990

Willikam Brubacher, Vice-President and Managing Director

V. PERFORMANCE

Symphony Orchestras
Opera Companies
Music Festivals

Symphony Orchestras

U.S. and Canadian symphony orchestras are listed alphabetically by state or province. Phone number and principal personnel are given for most orchestras. The letter in parentheses following the orchestra's name indicates classification, based on the rating system developed by the American Symphony Orchestra League (ASOL).

A* Major orchestra (annual budget more than $3.25 million)
A Regional orchestra (annual budget $900,000 - $3.25 million)
B Metropolitan orchestra (annual budget $250,000 - $900,000)
C Urban orchestra (annual budget $115,000 - $250,000)
D Community orchestra (annual budget less than $115,000)
E College orchestra
F Youth orchestra

An asterisk following an orchestra's name indicates membership in the ASOL. An alphabetical cross-index appears at the end of this section.

ALABAMA

ALABAMA SYMPHONY ORCHESTRA (A)*
P.O. Box 2125
Birmingham, AL 35201
(205) 326-0100
Staff: Carl Fasshauer, Executive Vice President and General Manager; Amerigo Marino, Musical Director and Conductor; Jo Campbell, Assistant Manager

ALABAMA YOUTH SYMPHONY (F)*
P.O. Box 2125
Birmingham, AL 35201
(205) 326-0100
Staff: Bonnie Lipscomb, Administrative Director

HUNTSVILLE SYMPHONY ORCHESTRA (C)*
P.O. Box 2340
Huntsville, AL 35804
(205) 539-4818
Staff: Ellen A. Harris, Executive Secretary; Dr. Marx Pales, Musical Director and Conductor

HUNTSVILLE YOUTH ORCHESTRA (F)*
7910-A. South Parkway
Huntsville, AL 35802
(205) 881-2949
Staff: Hugh McInnish, President; Gary S. Parks, Conductor

MONTGOMERY SYMPHONY (D)*
1010 Forest Ave.
Montgomery, AL 36106
(205) 265-8593
Staff: Joanna Bosko, Administrator; Max Kaplan, Musical Advisor

UNIVERSITY OF ALABAMA/ BIRMINGHAM ORCHESTRA (E)
Dept. of Music
Birmingham, AL 35294
(205) 934-7375
Staff: Thomas Hinds, Conductor

UNIVERSITY OF ALABAMA SYMPHONY ORCHESTRA (E)
P.O. Box 2876
University, AL 35486
(205) 348-7110
Staff: J. Terry Gates, Conductor

ALASKA

ANCHORAGE SYMPHONY ORCHESTRA (C)*
524 W. Fourth Ave.
Ste. 205
Anchorage, AK 99501
(907) 274-8668
Staff: Patricia M. Lombard, General Manager; Isaiah Jackson, Musical Director and Conductor

ANCHORAGE YOUTH SYMPHONY (F)*
3331 Lake Otis Pkwy.
Anchorage, AK 99502
(907) 279-6465
Staff: Dewey W. Ehling, Conductor; Bob Amos, Manager

FAIRBANKS SYMPHONY ORCHESTRA (C)*
P.O. Box 82104
Fairbanks, AK 99708
(907) 479-3407
Staff: Jane Aspnes, General Manager; Gordon B. Wright, Conductor and Musical Director

ARIZONA

ARIZONA STATE UNIVERSITY SYMPHONY ORCHESTRA (E)
School of Music
Tempe, AZ 85281
(602) 965-3430
Staff: Eugene P. Lombardi, Conductor

CIVIC ORCHESTRA OF TUCSON (D)*
3316 E. Navajo Pl.
Tucson, AZ 85716
(602) 326-7844
Staff: Frieda K. Schwartz, General Manager; Dr. Herschel Kreloff, Musical Director and Conductor

EASTERN ARIZONA SYMPHONY ORCHESTRA (E)
Eastern Arizona College
616 Church St.
Thatcher, AZ 85552
(602) 428-3281
Staff: J. Ronald Keith, Conductor

FLAGSTAFF FESTIVAL SYMPHONY AND CONCERT ORCHESTRAS (D)*
P.O. Box 1607
Flagstaff, AZ 86002
(602) 774-5055
Staff: Denis de Coteau, Conductor

FLAGSTAFF SYMPHONY ORCHESTRA (C)*
P.O. Box 122
Flagstaff, AZ 86002
(602) 774-4231
Staff: Harold L. Weller, Musical Director and Manager; Patricia Valdez, Executive Secretary

MESA SYMPHONY ORCHESTRA ASSOCIATION (D)*
55 E. Main St., Ste. 106
Mesa, AZ 85201
(602) 969-1226
Staff: Mary Ann Aufderheide, Business Manager; Maurice Dubonnet, Musical Director and Conductor

PHILHARMONIA ORCHESTRA OF TUCSON (F)*
2301 E. Drachman
Tucson, AZ 85719
(602) 323-6565
Staff: Mrs. Dorle Stavroudis, Manager; Laszlo Veres, Conductor and Musical Director

PHOENIX COLLEGE ORCHESTRA (E)*
1202 W. Thomas St.
Phoenix, AZ 85013
Staff: Dr. Carlo Veronda, Musical Advisor

PHOENIX SYMPHONY ORCHESTRA (A)*
6328 N. Seventh St.
Phoenix, AZ 85014
(602) 277-7291
Staff: Leslie Lerman. Executive Vice President and Managing Director: Theor Alcantara, Musical Director and Principal Conductor; Dennis Sage, Orchestral Manager

PHOENIX SYMPHONY YOUTH ORCHESTRA (F)*
444 W. Camelback Rd., #202
Phoenix, AZ 85013
(602) 277-7013
Staff: Mrs. Lattimer Ford, Director; Bruce Polay, Conductor

SCOTTSDALE SYMPHONY ORCHESTRA (D)*
P.O. Box 664
Scottsdale, AZ 85252
(602) 945-8071
Staff: K. Dona Roberson, Business Manager; Irving A. Fleming, Musical Director

SUN CITY SYMPHONY ORCHESTRA (D)*
P.O. Box 1417
Sun City, AZ 85372
(602) 972-4484
Staff: George M. Blaesi, President; Bernard Goodman, Musical Director and Conductor

TUCSON SYMPHONY ORCHESTRA (B)*
443 S. Stone Ave.
Tucson, AZ 85701
(602) 792-9155
Staff: Eric Meyer, General Manager; William McGlaughlin, Musical Director and Conductor; Steven J. Bronfenbrenner, Assistant Manager

UNIVERSITY OF ARIZONA SYMPHONY ORCHESTRA/CHAMBER ORCHESTRA (E)
School of Music
Tucson, AZ 85721
(602) 884-1655
Staff: Dr. Leonard Pearlman, Conductor

YUMA COMMUNITY ORCHESTRA(D)*
P.O. Box 5533
Yuma, AZ 85364
(602) 344-1022
Staff: Alice H. Francis, Orchestral Manager; Charles Smalley, Conductor

ARKANSAS

ARKANSAS SYMPHONY ORCHESTRA (B)*
P.O. Box 3295
Little Rock, AR 72203
(501) 375-8261
Staff: Dr. Frederick Schuyler Fox, Executive Director; Robert Henderson, Musical Director and Conductor

FORT SMITH SYMPHONY (D)*
P.O. Box 3151
Fort Smith, AR 72913
(501) 452-2833
Staff: Carol Sue Wooten, Administrative Director; Walter C. Minniear, Musical Director

HARDING UNIVERSITY CHAMBER STRING ENSEMBLE (E)
Music Dept.
Box 772
Searcy, AR 72143
(501) 268-6161, x 343
Staff: Travis A. Cox, Conductor

NORTH ARKANSAS SYMPHONY ORCHESTRA (C)*
221 N. College Ave.
Fayetteville, AR 72701
(501) 521-4166
Staff: David C. Sloan, Executive Director; Dr. Carlton R. Woods, Musical Director and Conductor

NORTHEAST ARKANSAS SYMPHONY (D)*
Jonesboro Fine Arts Council
P.O. Box 224
Jonesborao, AR 72401
(501) 935-7181
Staff: Dan Urton, Executive Director; Dr. Neale Bartee, Musical Director

SOUTH ARKANSAS SYMPHONY (C)*
110 E. Fifth St.
El Dorado, AR 71753
(501) 862-0521
Staff: Brenda Works, Executive Director; Dr. Richard A. Worthington, Musical Director

UNIVERSITY OF CENTRAL ARKANSAS LITTLE SYMPHONY (E)*
Dept. of Music
Conway, AR 72032
(501) 329-2931
Staff: Carl Forsberg, Conductor

CALIFORNIA

AMERICAN RIVER COLLEGE ORCHESTRA (E)
Music Dept.
4700 College Oak Dr.
Sacramento, CA 95841
(916) 484-8433
Staff: Walter Kerfoot, Conductor

AMERICAN YOUTH SYMPHONY (F)*
Ste. 800
10850 Wilshire Blvd.
Los Angeles, CA 90024
(213) 475-7633
Staff: Thomas Neenan, Executive Manager; Mehli Mehta, Musical Director and Conductor

BAKERSFIELD COLLEGE CHAMBER ORCHESTRA (E)
Music Dept.
1801 Panorama Dr.
Bakersfield, CA 93305
(805) 395-4547
Staff: James Mason, Conductor

BAKERSFIELD SYMPHONY ORCHESTRA (B)*
400 Truxton Ave., Ste. 201
Bakersfield, CA 93301
(805) 323-7928
Staff: John Farrer, Musical Director; Patricia Huey, Executive Secretary

BERKELEY YOUTH ORCHESTRA (F)*
620 Spokane Ave.
Albany, CA 94706
Staff: George Zender, Manager; J. Karla Lemon, Conductor

BRENTWOOD-WESTWOOD SYMPHONY ORCHESTRA (D)
2303 27th ST.
Santa Monica, CA 90405
(213) 450-3061
Staff: Alvin Mills, Conductor; Lillian Evans Heuring, Manager

BAY AREA WOMEN'S PHILHARMONIC (D)*
3543 Eighteenth St.
San Francisco, CA 94110
(415) 652-7157
Staff: Miriam Abrams, Managing Director; Elizabeth Min, Musical Director

BEACH CITIES SYMPHONY ORCHESTRA (D)*
P.O. Box 248
Redondo Beach, Ca 90277
(213) 379-7654
Staff: David D. Bradburn, Board Chairman; Herman Clebanoff, Musical Director

CABRILLO COLLEGE ORCHESTRA (E)
Division of Performing Arts
6500 Soquel Dr.
Aptos, CA 95076
(408) 426-6288
Staff: Vincent Gomez, Conductor

CABRILLO MUSIC FESTIVAL (B)*
6500 Soquel Dr.
Aptos, CA 95003
(408) 425-6339
Staff: Lauie MacDougall, Executive Director; Dennis Russel Davies, Musical Director

CALIFORNIA CHAMBER SYMPHONY (B)
2219 S. Bentley Ave., Ste. 202
Los Angeles, Ca 90064
(213) 478-0581
Staff: Karen Kimes, General Manager; Henri Temianka, Musical Director

CALIFORNIA STATE COLLEGE/ STANISLAUS-COMMUNITY ORCHESTRA (E)
800 Monte Vista Ave.
Turlock, CA 95380
(209) 667-3421
Staff: Michael McArtor, Conductor

CALIFORNIA STATE POLYTECHNIC UNIVERSITY CHAMBER ORCHESTRA (E)
Music Dept.
3801 W. Temple Ave.
Pomona, CA 91768
(714) 598-4587
Staff: Dr. Donald Ambroson, Conductor

CALIFORNIA STATE UNIVERSITY/ FULLERTON ORCHESTRA, PACIFIC SYMPHONY ORCHESTRA (E)
Dept. of Music
800 N. State College Blvd.
Fullerton, CA 92634
(714) 773-3511
Staff: Keith Clark, Conductor

CALIFORNIA STATE UNIVERSITY/ HAYWARD SYMPHONY ORCHESTRA (E)
Music Dept.
Hayward, CA 94542
(415) 881-3135
Staff: Denis de Coteau, Conductor

CALIFORNIA STATE UNIVERITY/ LONG BEACH SYMPHONY (E)
Dept. of Music
1250 Bellflower Blvd.
Long Beach, Ca 90840
(213) 498-4781
Staff: Ruben Gurevich, Conductor

CALIFORNIA STATE UNIVERSITY/ SACRAMENTO ORCHESTRA (E)
Music Dept.
6000 Jay St.
Sacramento, CA 95819
(916) 454-6514
Staff: Ward G. Fenley, Conductor

CALIFORNIA WOMEN'S SYMPHONY (D)
2723 Via Verbena
San Clemente, CA 92672
(714) 492-9421
Staff: Ruth Haroldson, Conductor

CALIFORNIA YOUTH SYMPHONY (F)*
P.O. Box 1441
Palo Alto, CA 94302
(415) 325-6666
Staff: James Hogan, Executive Director; Lauren Jakey, Conductor

CAMELLIA SYMPHONY ORCHESTRA (D)*
P.O. Box 160145
Sacramento, CA 95816
(916) 441-1184
Staff: Sherry Hatch, General Manager; Daniel Kingman, Musical Director and Conductor

CAMERATA ORCHESTRA AND CHORUS OF LOS ANGELES (C)
23203 Yvette Ln.
Valencia, CA 91355
(805) 255-9138
Staff: H. Vincent Mitzelfelt, Conductor and President; Karin M. MItzelfelt, Manager

CARSON/DOMINGUEZ HILLS SYMPHONY ORCHESTRA (E)
California State University, Dominguez Hills
Dept. of Music
Carson, CA 90747
(213) 516-3543
Staff: Dr. Frances Steiner, Musical Director and Conductor

CHAPMAN SYMPHONY ORCHESTRA (E)*
Chapman College
Orange, CA 92666
(714) 997-6774
Staff: John Koshak, Musical Director and Conductor; G.T. Smith, President

CHICO SYMPHONY ORCHESTRA (E)
Chico State College, Music Dept.
P.O. Box 1756
Chico, CA 95927
(916) 895-5500
Staff: Walter Dahlin, Conductor

CLAREMONT SYMPHONY ORCHESTRA (D)*
840 N. Indian Hill Blvd.
Claremont, CA 91711
(714) 621-5194
Staff: Sidney Orlov, Business Manager; James Fahringer, Musical Director and Conductor

CLC-CONEJO SYMPHONY ORCHESTRA (D)*
60 West Olsen Rd.
Thousand Oaks, CA 91360
(805) 492-2411
Staff: Mildred B. Rinaman, Secretary; Elmer H. Ramsey, Musical Director and Conductor

COLLEGE OF NOTRE DAME ORCHESTRA (E)
Music Dept.
Ralston Ave.
Belmont, CA 94002
(415) 593-1601, x425
Staff: Dr. Henry Rosack, Conductor

CONTRA COSTA CHAMBER ORCHESTRA (D)*
1728 Camino Verde
Walnut Creek, CA 94596
(415) 933-5948
Staff: H.T. Payne, Musical Director and Conductor; Robert Mathews, General Manager

COTERIE SYMPHONIQUE (E)
Long Beach City College
Music Dept.
4901 E. Carson St.
Long Beach, CA 90808
(213) 420-4309
Staff: Dr. Michael Pappone, Conductor

CSUN SYMPHONY ORCHESTRA (E)
California State University, Northridge
Dept. of Music
18111 Nordhoff St.
Northridge, CA 91330
(213) 885-3184
Staff: Larry Christianson, Conductor

CYPRESS COLLEGE STRING ORCHESTRA (E)
Music Dept.
9200 Valley View
Cypress, CA 90630
(714) 826-2220, x 139
Staff: Lila Parrish, Conductor

DE ANZA CHAMBER ORCHESTRA (E)*
De Anza College
Cupertino, CA 95014
(408) 996-4752
Staff: Nelson Tandoc, Conductor

DIABLO SYMPHONY ORCHESTRA (D)
1777 Danesta Dr.
Concord, CA 94519
(415) 685-1489
Staff: Joyce Johnson-Hamilton, Musical Director and Conductor

DIABLO VALLEY PHILHARMONIC (D)*
321 Golf Club Rd.
Pleasant Hill, CA 94523
(415) 865-1230
Staff: Frederic Johnson, Conductor; John Gibson, General Manager

DIABLO YOUTH ORCHESTRA (F)*
2846 Deerpark Dr.
Walnut Creek, CA 94598
(415) 933-3773
Staff: Joyce E. Anderson, Manager; Jonathan Khuner, Conductor

DOMINICAN COLLEGE ORCHESTRA (E)
Dominican College of San Rafael
Music Dept.
San Rafael, CA 94901
(415) 457-4440
Staff: Hugo Rinaldi, Conductor

DOWNEY SYMPHONIC SOCIETY (D)
P.O. Box 763
Downey, CA 90241
Staff: Alberto Bolet, Musical Director and Conductor

EL CAMINO COLLEGE/COMMUNITY ORCHESTRA (E)
Division of Fine Arts
Via Torrance, CA 90506
(213) 532-3670
Staff: James Mack, Conductor

EL CAMINO YOUTH SYMPHONY (F)*
886 Colorado Ave.
Palo Alto, CA 94303
(415) 856-9821
Staff: Stephanie Smith, Publicist; Dr. Arthur P. Barnes, Conductor

FRESNO CITY COLLEGE/ COMMUNITY SYMPHONY ORCHESTRA (E)
Music Dept.
1101 E. University Ave.
Fresno, CA 93741
(209) 442-4600, x 8463
Staff: Alex Molnar, Conductor

FRESNO JUNIOR PHILHARMONIC ORCHESTRA (F)*
1362 N. Fresno St.
Fresno, CA 93703
(209) 485-3020
Staff: Gary Deeter, Conductor; Celina Bowen, Committee Chairman

FRESNO-PHILHARMONIC ORCHESTRA (B)*
1362 N. Fresno St.
Fresno, CA 93703
(209) 485-3020
Staff: Stewart Comer, General Manager; Guy Taylor, Conductor

GLENDALE SYMPHONY ORCHESTRA (B)*
401 N. Brand Blvd., Ste. 712
Glendale, CA 91203
(213) 241-9413
Staff: Shirley Seely, Vice President of Administration; Carmen Dragon, Musical Director and Conductor

GROSSMONT SINFONIA (E)
Grossmont College
Music Dept.
8800 Grossmont College Dr.
El Cajon, CA 92020
(619) 465-1700, x235
Staff: Anthony Porto, Conductor

HEARTLAND YOUTH PHILHARMONIA (F)*
380 Minnesota Ave.
El Cajon, CA 92020
(714) 447-4813
Staff: Charles Macleod, Conductor

HIGH DESERT SYMPHONY (E)
Victor Valley Community College
Music Dept.
P.O. Drawer 00
Victorville, CA 92392
(714) 245-4271
Staff: Leo Cichocki, Conductor

HOLY NAMES SYMPHONY ORCHESTRA (E)
Holy Names College
Music Dept.
3500 Mountain Blvd.
Oakland, CA 94619
(415) 436-1052
Staff: Sr. Xavier Courvoisier, Conductor

HUMBOLDT SYMPHONY ORCHESTRA (E)*
Humboldt State University
Music Department
Arcata, CA 95521
(707) 826-3531
Staff: Dr. Madeline F. Schatz, Conductor

IMPERIAL VALLEY CHAMBER ORCHESTRA (D)*
P.O. Box 713
El Centro, CA 92243
Staff: Dr. Keith MacGaffey, Manager; Joel Jacklich, Conductor

INGLEWOOD PHILHARMONIC SYMPHONY ORCHESTRA (D)
P.O. Box 2055
Inglewood, CA 90305
(213) 778-7600
Staff: Leroy E. Hurte, Musical Director and Conductor

JEWISH COMMUNITY CENTER SYMPHONY* ORCHESTRA (D)
4079 54th St.
San Diego, CA 92105
(714) 583-3300
Staff: Ilene Hubbs, Manager; David Amos, Conductor

LA JOLLA CHAMBER ORCHESTRA (C)*
P.O. Box 2168
La Jolla, CA 92038
(714) 459-3724
Staff: Peter Eros, Conductor

LA JOLLA CIVIC/UNIVERSITY SYMPHONY (D)*
University of Claifornia, San Diego
Music Department, Q-038
La Jolla, CA 92093
(714) 452-4637
Staff: Morrey H. Feldman, Business Consultant; Thomas Nee, Musical Director

LIVERMORE-AMADOR SYMPHONY (D)*
P.O. Box 1049
Livermore, CA 94550
(415) 447-2530
Staff: Thomas Raison, President; Dr. Arthur Barnes, Conductor and Musical Director

LONG BEACH SYMPHONY ORCHESTRA (A)*
121 Linden Ave.
Long Beach, CA 90802
(213) 436-3203
Staff: Dan Pavillard, Executive Director; Murry Sidlin, Musical Director and Conductor; Jim Feichtmann, General Manager

LOS ANGELES CHAMBER ORCHESTRA (A)*
285 W. Green St.
Pasadena, CA 91105
(213) 796-2200
Staff: Herbert A. Rankin, General Manager; Gerard Schwarz, Musical Director

LOS ANGELES CITY COLLEGE COMMUNITY ORCHESTRA (E)
Music Dept.
855 N. Vermont Ave.
Los Angeles, CA 90029
(213) 669-4377
Staff; Dominick Di Sarro, Conductor

LOS ANGELES DOCTORS SYMPHONY (D)
521 N. Maple Dr.
Beverly Hills, CA 90210
(213) 550-0691
Staff: David Avshalomov, Conductor; Shirley Brody, Manager

LOS ANGELES MOZART ORCHESTRA (D)
444 S. Kingsley Dr., St. 355
Los Angeles, CA 90020
(213) 383-8589
Staff: David Keith, Conductor; Ginni Keith, Manager

LOS ANGELES PHILHARMONIC (A)*
135 N. Grand Ave.
Los Angeles, CA 90012
(213) 972-7300
Staff: Ernest Fleischmann, Executive Director; Carlo Maria Giulini, Musical Director; Robert Harth, General Manager

LOS ANGELES SOLO REPERTORY ORCHESTRA (D)*
6931 Van Nuys Blvd., No. 203
Van Nuys, CA 91405
(213) 988-2508
Staff: Jane Wright, Librarian; James A. Swift, Musical Director

LOS ANGELES VALLEY COLLEGE SYMPHONY ORCHESTRA (E)
Music Dept.
5800 Fulton Ave.
Van Nuys, CA 91401
(213) 781-1200
Staff: Theodore A. Lynn, Conductor

LOYOLA MARYMOUNT UNIVERSITY SYMPHONY ORCHESTRA (E)*
Music Dept.
7101 W. 80th St.
Los Angeles, CA 90045
Staff: Tom Donlon, Manager; Bogidar Avramov, Musical Director

MARIN SYMPHONY ORCHESTRA (B)*
4172 Redwood Highway
San Rafael, CA 94903
(415) 479-8100
Staff: Betty Mulryan, General Manager; Sandor Salgo, Conductor

MARIN SYMPHONY YOUTH ORCHESTRA (F)*
4172 Redwood Hwy.
San Rafael, CA 94903
(415) 479-8100
Staff: Primula Kennedy, Manager; Hugo Rinaldi, Conductor

MERCED SYMPHONY ORCHESTRA (D)*
P.O. Box 454
Merced, CA 95340
(209) 384-0676
Staff: Sonja Headings, Orchestral Manager; Llogy Elliott, Conductor and Musical Director

MIRACOSTA COLLEGE SYMPHONY ORCHESTRA (E)
Music Dept.
One Barnard Dr.
Oceanside, CA 92054
(619) 757-2121
Staff: Dan Swen, Conductor

MODESTO SYMPHONY ORCHESTRA (C)
P.O. Box 1361
Modesto, CA 95353
(209) 523-4156
Staff: Fay Gartin, General Manager; Sandor Salgo, Musical Director and Conductor

MONTEREY COUNTY SYMPHONY ORCHESTRA (B)*
P.O. Box 3965
Carmel, CA 93921
(408) 624-8511
Staff: Elizabeth Pasquinelli, General Manager; Haymo Taeuber, Musical Director and Conductor; Mausita Jennings, Assistant Manager

MUSIC ACADEMY OF THE WEST FESTIVAL ORCHESTRA (A)
P.O. Box 4726
Santa Barbara, CA 93108
(805) 969-4726
Staff: Theo Alcantara, Conductor

NAPA VALLEY COLLEGE/NORTH BAY PHILHARMONIC (E)
Music Dept.
2277 Napa Vallejo Hwy.
Napa, CA 94558
(707) 255-2100, x274

NAPA VALLEY SYMPHONY ASSOCIATION (D)*
P.O. Box 2434
Napa, CA 94558
(707) 226-6872
Staff: George A. Sinclair, General Manager; Joyce Johnson-Hamilton, Musical Director and Conductor

NORTHRIDGE YOUTH ORCHESTRA (F)*
14249 Sylvan St.
Van Nuys, CA 91401
(213) 785-2224
Staff: Thomas M. Osborn, Musical Director and Conductor; Darlene J. Hopkins, Secretary

NOVA VISTA SYMPHONY (D)*
P.O. Box 11294
Palo Alto, CA 94306
(415) 854-5531
Staff: Beatrice Fenn, President; Dr. Lauren Jakey, Conductor

OAKLAND SYMPHONY ORCHESTRA (A)*
The Paramount Theater
2025 Broadway
Oakland, CA 94612
(415) 444-3531
Staff: Arthur D. Jacobs, General Manager; Leonard Slatkin, Artistic Counselor

OAKLAND SYMPHONY YOUTH ORCHESTRA (F)*
2025 Broadway
Oakland, CA 94612
(415) 444-3531
Staff: Ethel London, Manager; Kent Nagano, Conductor

OCCIDENTAL/CAL TECH ORCHESTRA (E)
Occidental College
Dept. of Music
1600 Campus Rd.
Los Angeles, CA 90041
(213) 259-2785
Staff: Dr. Kim Kowalke, Conductor

ORANGE COUNTRY PACIFIC SYMPHONY (B)*
100 W. Valencia Mesa, Ste. 204
Fullerton, CA 92635
(714) 680-3444
Staff: Doris Dressler, Acting Manager; Keith Clark, Conductor

ORANGE COUNTY YOUTH SYMPHONY (F)*
Music Dept.
Chapman College
Orange, CA 92666
(714) 997-6774
Staff: John Koshak, Musical Director and Conductor; Irene Kroesen, Manager

PACIFIC UNION COLLEGE ORCHESTRA (E)
Dept. of Music
Angwin, CA 94508
(707) 965-6201
Staff: Dr. George Wargo, Conductor

PALISADES SYMPHONY ORCHESTRA (D)*
1081 Palisair Pl.
Pacific Palisades, CA 90272
(213) 454-1241
Staff: Eva Holberg, President and Manager; Joel B. Lish, Musical Director

PALOMAR COLLEGE COMMUNITY ORCHESTRA (E)
Music Dept.
1140 W. Mission
San Marcos, CA 92069
(619) 744-1150

PARADISE SYMPHONY ORCHESTRA (D)*
6626 Skyway
Paradise, CA 95969
(916) 877-6211
Staff: Thomas E. Wilson, Musical Director and Conductor; Dean Kruta, President

PASADENA CHAMBER ORCHESTRA (C)*
16 S. Oakland Ave., No. 204
Pasadena, CA 91105
(213) 578-1848
Staff: Robert Duerr, Musical Director

PASADENA SYMPHONY ORCHESTRA (B)
300 E. Green St.
Pasadena, CA 91101
(213) 793-7172
Staff: Katherine K. Adkinson, Executive Director; Daniel G. Lewis, Musical Director; David M. Berggren, Assistant Director

PASADENA YOUNG MUSICIANS ORCHESTRA (F)*
c/o Pasadena Symphony Association
300 E. Green St.
Pasadena, CA 91101
(213) 793-7112
Staff: Adrienne Morgan, Manager; Richard Rintoul, Musical Director

PASADENA YOUTH SYMPHONY ORCHESTRA (F)*
300 E. Green St.
Pasadena, CA 91101
(213) 793-7172
Staff: David M. Berggren, Manager, Donn Lawrence Mills, Conductor

PENINSULA SYMPHONY (D)*
P.O. Box 2602
Palos Verdes Peninsula, CA 90274
(213) 375-8801
Staff: Joseph A. Valenti, Musical Director and Conductor; Ruth Springer, Office Manager

PENINSULA SYMPHONY ORCHESTRA (C)*
494 W. Portola Ave.
Los Altos, CA 94022
(415) 941-2090
Staff: Dorothy V. Norman, Business Manager; Aaron Sten, Conductor and Musical Director

POINT LOMA COLLEGE/COMMUNITY ORCHESTRA (E)
Music Dept.
3900 Lomaland Dr.
San Diego, CA 92106
(714) 222-6474, x210
Staff: Charles Hansen, Conductor

POMONA COLLEGE SYMPHONY ORCHESTRA (E)*
Thatcher Music Building
Claremont, CA 91711
(714) 621-8155
Staff: Raphael Metzger, Conductor; Debbi Daniel, Manager

REDLANDS SYMPHONY ORCHESTRA (D)*
University of Redlands
Watchorn Hall
Redlands, Ca 92373
(714) 793-2121
Staff: Dr. James Keays, Manager; Dr. Jon Robertson, Conductor

REPERTOIRE CHAMBER ORCHESTRA (D)*
12655 Homewood Way
Los Angeles, CA 90049
Staff: Beth Jones, President; Robert Turner, Conductor

SACRAMENTO SYMPHONY ORCHESTRA (A)*
451 Parkfair Dr., Ste. 11
Sacramento, CA 95825
(916) 488-0800
Staff: David M. Wax, General Manager; Carter Nice, Musical Director and Conductor; Edward Doehne, Assistant Manager

SACRAMENTO YOUTH SYMPHONY (F)*
451 Parkfair Dr., Ste. 11
Sacramento, CA 95825
(916) 488-0800
Staff: Doreen Mauk, Manager; Michael Neumann, Conductor

SADDLEBACK SYMPHONY ORCHESTRA (E)
Saddleback College, Music Faculty
28000 Marguerite Pkwy.
Mission Viejo, CA 92692
(714) 831-4747
Staff: Kay Andreas, Musical Director

SAN BERNARDINO CHAMBER ORCHESTRA (E)*
5500 State College Pkwy.
San Bernardino, CA 92407
(714) 887-7454
Staff: Dr. Richard Saylor, Conductor

SAN BERNARDINO SYMPHONY ORCHESTRA (D)*
P.O. Box 2312, Uptown Station
San Bernardino, CA 92406
(714) 883-7920
Staff: Evelyn Krzuetz, President; Alberto Bolet, Director and Conductor

SAN DIEGO STATE UNIVERSITY PHILHARMONIA (E)
Music Dept.
San Diego, CA 92182
(714) 265-6031
Staff: Ronald Stoffel, Musical Director and Conductor

SAN DIEGO SYMPHONY ORCHESTRA (A)*
P.O. Box 3175
San Diego, CA 92103
(714) 239-9721
Staff: Robert G. Boyd, Jr., Managing Director; David Atherton, Musical Director

SAN DIEGO YOUTH SYMPHONY (F)*
San Diego City Park/Rec. Dept.
Casa Del Prado, Balboa park
San Diego, CA 92101
(714) 233-3232
Staff: Kenneth Hayward, Vice President; Louis J. Campiglia, Conductor and Musical Director

SAN FRANCISCO CHAMBER ORCHESTRA (B)
840 Battery St.
San Francisco, CA 94111
(415) 788-1240
Staff: Richard Schober, General Manager; Edgar J. Braun, Musical Director

SAN FRANCISCO CHAMBER PLAYERS (D)*
138 Belvedere
San Francisco, CA 94117
Staff: Dusan Bobb, Director and Conductor

SAN FRANCISCO CONCERT ORCHESTRA (C)
520-A Clement St.
San Francisco, CA 94118
(415) 751-3955
Staff: Robert Sayre, Musical Director and Conductor

SAN FRANCISCO CONSERVATORY OF MUSIC ORCHESTRA (E)*
1201 Ortega St.
San Francisco, CA 94122
(415) 564-8086
Staff: Laurie Steele, Manager; David Agler, Conductor

SAN FRANCISCO STATE UNIVERSITY SYMPHONY ORCHESTRA (E)*
Music Dept.
1600 Holloway Ave.
San Francisco, CA 94132
(415) 469-1431
Staff: Laszlo Varga, Conductor

SAN FRANCISCO SYMPHONY (A)*
Davies Symphony Hall
San Francisco, CA 94102
(415) 552-8000
Staff: Peter Pastreich, Executive Director; Edo de Waart, Musical Director and Conductor; John Gidwitz, Manager

SAN FRANCISCO SYMPHONY YOUTH ORCHESTRA (F)*
Davies Symphony Hall
San Francisco, CA 94102
(415) 552-8000
Staff: Elena Biles, Youth Orchestra Coordinator; Jahja Ling, Musical Director

SAN JOSE STATE UNIVERSITY ORCHESTRA (E)
Music Dept.
125 S. Seventh
San Jose, CA 95192
(408) 277-2905
Staff: Dr. Lauren Jakey, Conductor

SAN JOSE SYMPHONY ORCHESTRA (A)*
170 Park Center Plaza, Ste. 100
San Jose, CA 95113
(408) 287-7383
Staff: Richard H. Wright, General Manager; George Cleve, Musical Director and Conductor; Michael Eshoff, Orchestral Manager

SAN LUIS OBISPO COUNTY SYMPHONY ORCHESTRA (E)*
California Polytechnic State University
Music Dept.
San Luis Obispo, CA 93407
(805) 546-2406
Staff: Clifton Swanson, Conductor

SAN LUIS OBISPO COUNTY YOUTH SYMPHONY (F)*
P.O. Box 430
San Luis Obispo, CA 93406
(805) 595-2576
Staff: Walter Shwetz, President; Loal Davis, Conductor

SANTA BARBARA CITY COLLEGE ORCHESTRA (E)
Music Dept.
721 Cliff Dr.
Santa Barbara, Ca 93109
(805) 965-]581, x230
Staff: Dr. Jack Ullom, Conductor

SANTA BARBARA SYMPHONY ORCHESTRA (B)*
3 W. Carrillo, Ste. 9
Santa Barbara, CA 93101
(805) 965-6596
Staff: Genevieve S. Fisher, Managing Director; Frank Collura, Musical Director

SANTA CRUZ COUNTY SYMPHONY (C)*
6500 Soquel Dr.
Aptos, CA 95003
(408) 462-0553

Staff: Michael Stamp, General Manager; Kenneth Klein, Musical Director and Conductor

SANTA CRUZ COUNTY YOUTH SYMPHONY (F)*
P.O. Box 154
Soquel, CA 95073
(408) 722-8206
Staff: Ruth Fesmire, President; Vincent Gomez, Conductor and Director; Ann McSweaney, Executive Director

SANTA MARIA SYMPHONY ORCHESTRA (E)
Allan Hancock College
Music Dept.
800 S. College Dr.
Santa Maria, CA 93454
(805) 922-6966
Staff: Samuel Simca Gorbach, Conductor

SANTA ROSA SYMPHONY (B)*
P.O. Box 1081
Santa Rosa, CA 95402
(707) 546-8742
Staff: Pauline Fisher, Manager; Corrick L. Brown, Conductor and Musical Director

SHASTA SYMPHONY (D)*
1065 N. Old Oregon Trail Rd.
Redding, CA 96001
(916) 241-3523
Staff: Dr. Olando Tognozzi, Conductor; William Palin, General Manager

SIERRA MUSICAL ARTS ASSOCIATION (D)*
P.O. Box 1444
Nevada City, CA 95959
(916) 273-6875
Staff: Richard Anshutz, Musical Director

SONOMA COUNTY JUNIOR SYMPHONY (F)*
P.O. Box 9261
Santa Rosa, CA 95405
(707) 545-5516
Staff: Marjorie March, Manager; Eugene Shepherd, Conductor

SONOMA STATE UNIVERSITY CHAMBER ORCHESTRA (E)
Dept. of Music
1801 E. Cotati Ave.
Rohnert Park, CA 94928
(707) 664-2324
Staff: David Sloss, Conductor

SOUTHEAST YOUTH SYMPHONY ORCHESTRA (F)*
2610 Manly Ave.
Santa Ana, CA 92704
(714) 546-5288
Staff: John Larry Granger, Director

SOUTH VALLEY SYMPHONY (D)*
P.O. Box 598
Morgan Hill, CA 95037
(408) 779-3453
Staff: Nancy Marselis, President; Kathleen Ash Barraclough, Musical Director and Conductor

STANFORD SYMPHONY ORCHESTRA (E)
Stanford University
Dept. of Music
Stanford, CA 94305
(415) 497-3812
Staff: Andor Toth, Conductor; John Planting, Administrator

STOCKTON SYMPHONY (B)*
P.O. Box 4273
Stockton, CA 95204
(209) 462-1533
Staff: Peter J. Ottesen, Manager; Kyung-Soo Won, Musical Director and Conductor

SYMPHONY OF THE VERDUGOS (D)*
P.O. Box 2043
Glendale, CA 91209
(213) 661-8527
Staff: Lee Trippett, General Manager; Wesley Cease, Musical Director

SYMPHONY WEST (C)
1729 E. Palm Canyon Dr., Ste. 106
Palm Springs, CA 92262
(714) 320-2778
Staff: Gregory Millar, Conductor

UNIVERSITY OF CALIFORNIA/BERKELEY SYMPHONY (E)
Music Dept.
Berkeley, CA 94720
(415) 642-2678
Staff: Michael Senturia, Conductor

UNIVERSITY OF CALIFORNIA/DAVIS SYMPHONY (E)
Dept. of Music
Davis, CA 95616
(916) 752-0666
Staff: D. Kern Holoman, Conductor

UNIVERSITY OF CALIFORNIA/IRVINE SYMPHONY ORCHESTRA (E)
Music Dept.
Irvine, CA 92717
(714) 833-6615
Staff: Bernard Gilmore, Conductor

UNIVERSITY OF CALIFORNIA/LOS ANGELES SYMPHONY ORCHESTRA (E)
Dept. of Music
405 Hilgard Ave.
Los Angeles, CA 90024
(213) 825-4761
Staff: Samuel Krachmalnick, Conductor

UNIVERSITY OF CALIFORNIA/RIVERSIDE ORCHESTRA (E)
Dept. of Music
Riverside, Ca 92502
(714) 787-3138
Staff: Anthony F. Ginter, Conductor

UNIVERSITY OF CALIFORNIA/SANTA BARBARA SYMPHONY ORCHESTRA (E)
Dept. of Music
Santa Barbara, CA 93106
(805) 961-2066
Staff: Serge Zehnacker, Conductor

UNIVERSITY OF SAN DIEGO SYMPHONY ORCHESTRA (E)
San Diego, CA 92110
(714) 291-6480, x 4426
Staff: Dr. Henry Kolar, Conductor

UNIVERSITY OF SOUTHERN CALIFORNIA SYMPHONY (E)*
School of Music, MUS 312
University Park
Los Angeles, CA 90089
(213) 743-6580
Staff: Daniel G. Lewis, Conductor

UNIVERSITY OF THE PACIFIC SYMPHONY ORCHESTRA (E)
Conservatory of Music
3601 Pacific Ave.
Stockton, CA 95211
(209) 946-2415
Staff: Thomas Tatton, Conductor

VALLEY SYMPHONY (C)
P.O. Box 39
Van Nuys, CA 91408
(213) 508-0623
Staff: Larry Christianson, Conductor

VENTURA COUNTY SYMPHONY ORCHESTRA (C)*
P.O. Box 1085
Ventura, CA 93002
(805) 643-8646
Staff: Ila G. Winterbourne, Manager; Frank Salazar, Musical Director and Conductor

WEST HILLS LITTLE SYMPHONY (E)
West Hills College
Fine Arts Division
300 Cherry Ln.
Coalinga, CA 93210
(209) 935-0801
Staff: T. Dean Perry, Conductor

WESTSIDE SYMPHONY OF BEVERLY HILLS (D)
321 N. Rexford Dr.
Beverly Hills, CA 90210
(213) 342-1551
Staff: Bogidar Avramov, Conductor

WEST VALLEY COMMUNITY SYMPHONY (D)*
P.O. Box 2263
Saratoga, CA 95070
(408) 463-0642
Staff: Barbara Kuklewicz, President; G. Ross Bergantz, Conductor

YOUNG MUSICIANS FOUNDATION DEBUT ORCHESTRA (F)*
914 S. Robertson Blvd.
Los Angeles, Ca 90035
(213) 659-3766
Staff: Judy Dubin, Manager; Neal Stulberg, Conductor

YOUNG PEOPLE'S SYMPHONY ORCHESTRA (F)*
P.O. Box 1296
Berkeley, CA 94701
(415) 526-3890
Staff: Eric Hansen, Musical Director and Conductor; Si Gershenson, President

COLORADO

ASPEN CHAMBER SYMPHONY/ASPEN FESTIVAL ORCHESTRA (D)
P.O. Box AA
Aspen, CO 81612
Winter Address: 1860 Broadway, New York NY 10023
(212) 581-2196
Staff: Jorge Mester, Musical Director; Robert Biddlecome, Manager

BOULDER CHAMBER ORCHESTRA (D)*
P.O. Box 826
Boulder, CO 80306
(303) 449-1343
Staff: Joan McLean-Braun, Manager; Oswald Lehnert, Conductor and Musical Director

BOULDER PHILHARMONIC (C)*
P.O. Box 826
Boulder, CO 80306
(303) 449-1343
Staff: Gene A. Bircher, General Manager; Oswald Lehnert, Musical Director and Conductor; Joan Mclean-Braun, Assistant Manager

COLORADO MUSIC FESTIVAL (B)*
1245 Pearl, No. 210
Boulder, Co 80302
(303) 449-1397
Staff: Philip Haimm, General Manager; Giora Bernstein, Musical Director; Marcia Schirmer, Administrative Manager

COLORADO PHILHARMONIC (C)*
P.O. Box 975
Evergreen, CO 80439
(303) 674-5161
Staff: Richard Zellner, General Manager; Carl Topilow, Musical Director and Conductor; Margaret Jones, Operations Manager

COLORADO SPRINGS SYMPHONY ORCHESTRA (B)*
P.O. Box 1692
Colorado Springs, Co 80901
(303) 633-4611
Staff: Beatrice W. Vradenburg, General manager; Charles A. Ansbacher, Conductor and Musical Director

COLORADO STATE UNIVERSITY ORCHESTRA (E)
Music Dept.
Fort Collins, Co 80521
(303) 491-5528
Staff: Wilfred Schwartz, Conductor

COMMUNITY ARTS SYMPHONY (D)*
P.O. Box 1222
Engelwood, CO 80110
(303) 795-7670
Carol E. Hays, Business Manager; T. Gordon Parks, Musical Director

CRYSTAL RIVER COMMUNITY ORCHESTRA (D)*
P.O. Box 9290
Aspen, CO 81612
(303) 925-2267
Staff: Ray V. Adams, Musical Director; Laurie Loeb, Manager

DENVER CHAMBER ORCHESTRA (D)*
P.O. Box 6545
Denver, CO 80206
(303) 322-9359
Staff: Joan E. Cotton, Business Manager; James Setapen, Musical Advisor

DENVER SYMPHONY ORCHESTRA (A)*
1245 Champa St.
Denver, Co 80204
(303) 572-1151
Staff: Stephen Klein, Executive Director; Gaetano Delogu, Musical Director; Robert Stiles, General Manager

DURANGO CIVIC SYMPHONY (E)
Fort Lewis College
Music Dept.
Durango, CO 81301
(303) 247-7329
Staff: Richard Strawn, Conductor

FORT COLLINS SYMPHONY ORCHESTRA (D)*
P.O. Box 1963
Fort Collins, CO 80522
(303) 482-4823
Staff: Clare M. Wilber, Executive Director; Will Schwartz, Musical Director and Conductor

GOLDEN YOUTH SYMPHONY (F)*
6668 Vivian St.
Arvada, CO 80004
(303) 421-1452
Staff: Jane W. Diggs, Business Manager; Leonard L. Diggs, Musical Director and Conductor

GRAND JUNCTION SYMPHONY ORCHESTRA (D)*
P.O. Box 3039
Grand Junction, CO 81502
(303) 242-8822
Staff: Lucille J. Crumbaker, Manager; Alan Burdick, Musical Director and Conductor

GREELEY PHILHARMONIC ORCHESTRA (C)
P.O. Box 1535
Greeley, CO 80632
(303) 351-2612
Staff: Dr. Howard Skinner, Musical Director and Conductor; Shirley Howell, Business Manager

JEFFERSON SYMPHONY ORCHESTRA (D)
1938 Mt. Zion Dr.
Golden, CO 80401
(303) 279-3134
Staff: T. Gordon Parks, Conductor; Jack Galland, President

PUEBLO SYMPHONY ORCHESTRA (C)*
431 E. Pitkin
Pueblo, CO 81004
(303) 546-0333
Staff: Rita Horvat, Manager; Gerhard Track, Musical Director and Conductor

UNIVERSITY OF COLORADO SYMPHONY ORCHESTRA (E)
College of Music
Boulder, CO 80309
(303) 492-6532
Staff: Giora Bernstein, Musical Director and Conductor

UNIVERSITY OF NORTHERN COLORADO SYMPHONY ORCHESTRA (E)
School of Music
Greeley, CO 80639
(303) 351-2678
Staff: Howard Skinner, Conductor

VALLEY SYMPHONY ORCHESTRA (D)*
18 Columbia Way
Montrose, CO 81401
Staff: Norma Vold, Treasurer; Dr. Rodney Ash, Conductor

WESTERN STATE COLLEGE CHAMBER ORCHESTRA (E)
Western State College of Colorado
Division of Music and the Arts
Gunnison, CO 81230
(303) 943-3093
Staff: Michael Jacobson, Conductor

YOUNG ARTISTS ORCHESTRA OF DENVER (F)*
1415 Larimer St., #306
Denver, CO 80202
(303) 571-1935
Staff: Jhyree Burkepile, Administrative Assistant; Charles A. Ansbacher, Musical Director and Conductor; Suzanne Ryan, Managing Director

CONNECTICUT

CHAMBER ORCHESTRA OF NEW ENGLAND (E)*
254 College St., Ste. 305
New Haven, CT 06510
(203) 777-0790

Staff: Christopher Rude, General Manager; James B. Sinclair, Musical Director

CONNECTICUT CHAMBER ORCHESTRA (D)
50 Trumbull St.
New Haven, CT 06510
(203) 288-4633
Staff: Sayard Stone, Musical Director and Conductor

CONNECTICUT COLLEGE ORCHESTRA (E)
Dept. of Music
Mohegan Ave.
New London, CT 06320
(203) 447-1911
Staff: Peter J. Sacco, Conductor

CONNECTICUT PHILHARMONIC ORCHESTRA (D)*
283 Greenwich Ave.
Greenwich, CT 06830
(704) 258-0989
Staff: Alexander Kopple, Manager; Robert Hart Baker, Musical Director and Conductor

CONNECTICUT SYMPHONY ORCHESTRA (D)*
35 Golf Ln.
Ridgefield, CT 06877
(203) 438-2685
Staff: Audrey J. Marino, Administrator; Skitch Henderson, Musical Director and Conductor

EASTERN CONNECTICUT SYMPHONY (C)*
63 Huntington St.
New London, CT 06320
(203) 443-2876
Staff: David C. Snead, General Manager; George Baziotopoulos, Musical Director

GREATER BRIDGEPORT SYMPHONY ORCHESTRA (B)*
Bernhard Center
University of Bridgeport
Bridgeport, CT 06602
(203) 576-0263
Staff: Audrey Thomson, General Manager; Gustav Meier, Musical Director and Conductor

GREENWICH PHILHARMONIA ORCHESTRA (C)*
P.O. Box 35
Greenwich, CT 06836
(203) 869-2664
Staff: Mahlon F. Perkins, Jr., President; David Gilber, Conductor and Musical Director

HARTFORD CHAMBER ORCHESTRA (B)*
15 Lewis St., Rm. 405
Hartford, CT 06103
(203) 727-0066
Staff: George Osborne, General Manager; Daniel Parker, Musical Director; James H. Marton, Manager

HARTFORD SYMPHONY ORCHESTRA (A)*
609 Farminton Ave.
Hartford, CT 06105
(203) 236-6101
Staff: Don F. Roth, Managing Director; Arthur Winograd, Musical Director; Paul Reuter, Assistant Manager

HARTT SYMPHONY ORCHESTRA (E)*
University of Hartford
200 Bloomfield Ave.
West Hartford, CT 06117
(203) 243-4410
Staff: Diane Kern, Manager of Performing Organization; Charles Bruck, Conductor

MERIDEN SYMPHONY ORCHESTRA (D)*
P.O. Box 2144
Meriden, CT 06450
(203) 237-1239
Staff: Irma Zola, Manager; Bruin Lipman, Musical Director and Conductor

NEW BRITAIN SYMPHONY ORCHESTRA (D)*
P.O. Box 1253
New Britain, CT 06050
(203) 225-2291
Staff: Phyllis A. Jehrpe, President; Dr. Jerome Laszloffy, Conductor

NEW HAVEN SYMPHONY ORCHESTRA
33 Whitney Ave.
New Haven, CT 06511
(203) 865-0831
Staff: Catherine Lacny, General Manager; Murry Sidlin, Musical Director and Conductor

NORWALK SYMPHONY ORCHESTRA (D)*
P.O. Box 174, Belden Station
Norwalk, CT 06852
(203) 847-2986
Staff: Culver Griffin, General Manager; Jesse Levine, Musical Director

NORWALK YOUTH SYMPHONY (F)*
P.O. Box 73
Norwalk, CT 06856
(203) 227-1108
Staff: Carol Mikesell, President; John N. Huwiler, Conductor; Marilyn Fitch, Manager

PHILHARMONIA ORCHESTRA OF YALE (E)*
Yale University School of Music
P.O. Box 2140 A, Yale Station
New Haven, CT 06520
(203) 436-2080
Staff: Vincent P. Oneppo, General Manager; Otto-Werner Mueller, Musical Director

RIDGEFIELD ORCHESTRA (D)*
P.O. Box 613
Ridgefield, CT 06877
(203) 327-2484
Staff: Beatrice Brown, Conductor and Musical Director; Moses Katz, President

RIDGEFIELD YOUTH ORCHESTRA (F)*
Ridgefield High School
North Salem Rd.
Ridgefield, CT 06877
(203) 438-5412
Staff: Charles A. Spire, Musical Director and Conductor

STAMFORD SYMPHONY ORCHESTRA (C)*
P.O. Box 3263
Stamford, CT 06905
(203) 322-5623
Staff: Barbara J. Soroca, General Manager; Roger Nierenberg, Musical Director and Conductor

SYMPHONY ON THE SOUND (D)
RD 1, 18 Zygmont Ln.
Greenwich, CT 06830
(203) 661-7413
Staff: Joseph Leniado-Chira, Musical Director and Conductor; Charlotte Schneider, Manager

UNIVERSITY OF CONNECTICUT SYMPHONY ORCHESTRA (E)
Music Dept.
Storrs, CT 06268
(203) 486-3728
Staff: Jack Heller, Conductor; D.J. Patrylak, Head

WALLINGFORD SYMPHONY ORCHESTRA (D)*
Paul Mellon Arts Center
Christian St.
Wallingford, CT 06492
(203) 269-7722
Staff: Philip T. Ventre, Musical Director; Thomas Hintz, Manager

WATERBURY SYMPHONY ORCHESTRA (D)*
P.O. Box 1762
Waterbury, CT 06721
(203) 574-4283
Staff: Dante Galuppo, Manager; Frank Brieff, Musical Director

YALE SYMPHONY (E)
Yale University
Dept. of Music
143 Elm St.
New Haven, CT 06520
(203) 436-4933
Staff: Robert Kapilow, Conductor

YOUNG ARTISTS PHILHARMONIC (F)*
P.O. Box 3301
Ridgeway Station
Stamford, CT 06905
(203) 329-2231
Staff: Linda L. Nielsen, Vice President; Salvatore Princiotti, Musical Director/Conductor

DELAWARE

DELAWARE SYMPHONY (B)*
P.O. Box 1870
Wilmington, DE 19899
(302) 656-7374
Staff: Jeffrey M. Ruben, Manager; Stephen Gunzenhauser, Musical Director

DISTRICT OF COLUMBIA

THE AMERICAN UNIVERSITY ORCHESTRA (E)
Division of Music
Massachusetts and Nebraska Aves.
Washington, DC 20016
(202) 686-2162
Staff: Thomas Ludwig, Conductor

THE CATHOLIC UNIVERSITY OF AMERICA SYMPHONY ORCHESTRA (E)
School of Music
Washington, DC 20064
(202) 635-5414
Staff: Robert Ricks, Conductor

D.C. YOUTH ORCHESTRA (F)*
Coolidge High School
5th & Tuckerman Sts., NW
Washington, DC 20011
(202) 723-1612
Staff: Lyn McLain, Director and Conductor

GEORGETOWN SYMPHONY (D)*
Georgetown University
Box 984, Hoya Station
Washington, DC 20057
(202) 625-4279
Staff: Deborah Pflieger, Manager, John Welsh, Musical Director

GEORGE WASHINGTON UNIVERSITY ORCHESTRA (E)
Dept. of Music
Washington, DC 20052
(202) 676-6245
Staff: George Steiner, Conductor

NATIONAL GALLERY ORCHESTRA (D)
Sixth St. & Constituion Ave. NW
Washington, DC 20565
(202) 737-4215
Staff: Richard Bales, Conductor

NATIONAL SYMPHONY ORCHESTRA (A)*
John F. Kennedy Center for the Performing Arts
Washington, DC 20566
(202) 785-8100
Staff: Henry Fogel, Executive Director; Mstislav Rostropovich, Musical Director; Anne H. Parsons, Orchestral Manager

THEATER CHAMBER PLAYERS OF KENNEDY CENTER (D)
John F. Kennedy Center for the Performing Arts
Washington, DC 20566
(202) 265-3990
Staff: Leon Fleisher and Dina Koston, Musical Directors

FLORIDA

BREVARD SYMPHONY ORCHESTRA (C)*
P.O. Box 1174
Melbourne, FL 32901
(305) 259-1926
Staff: Cynthia A. Skyrm, Business Manager; Maria Tunicka, Conductor and Director

BROWARD COMMUNITY COLLEGE YOUTH SYMPHONY (F)*
c/o Florida Chamber Orchestra
120 E. Oakland Pk. Blvd., #202
Fort Lauderdale, FL 33334
(305) 563-9606
Staff: Charles W. Noble, Conductor; Paul David Seltzer, Manager

BROWARD SYMPHONY ORCHESTRA (D)*
Broward Community College
3501 Southwest Davie Rd.
Ft. Lauderdale, Fl 33314
(305) 475-6500
Staff: Jimmy O. Woodle, Musical Director

CENTRAL FLORIDA COMMUNITY COLLEGE AEOLIAN PLAYERS (E)
Music Department
P.O. Box 1388
Ocala, FL 32678
(904) 237-2111
Staff: Gene A. Lawton, Conductor

CHARLOTTE CHAMBER ORCHESTRA (D)*
4158 Tamiami Trail, Apt. F-3
Charlotte Harbor, Fl 33952
(813) 625-5384
Staff: Frank Streny, General Manager; Fred Blake, Musical Director

FLORIDA CHAMBER ORCHESTRA (B)*
120 East Oakland Pk. Blvd., No. 202
Fort Lauderdale, FL 33334
(305) 563-9606
Staff: Paul David Seltzer, Manager; Dr. James A. Brooks, Conductor

FLORIDA GULF COAST SYMPHONY ORCHESTRA (A)*
3430 West Kennedy Blvd.
Tampa, FL 33609
(813) 877-7380
Staff: Horace T. Maddux, Executive Director; Irwin Hoffman, Conductor

FLORIDA STATE UNIVERSITY SYMPHONY ORCHESTRA (E)
School of Music
Tallahassee, FL 32306
(904) 644-3424
Staff: Phillip Spurgeon, Conductor

FLORIDA SYMPHONY ORCHESTRA (A)*
P.O. Box 782
Orlando, FL 32802
(305) 629-4545
Staff: Robert S. Gross, Executive Vice President and General Manager; Sidney Rothstein, Musical Director

FLORIDA SYMPHONY YOUTH ORCHESTRA (F)*
P.O. Box 782
Orlando, Fl 32802
(305) 841-1280
Staff: Charles M. Gottschalk, Conductor/Musical Director; Alexander J. Friedman, President

FLORIDA WEST COAST SYMPHONY ORCHESTRA (B)*
709 N. Tamiami Trail
Sarasota, FL 33577
(813) 955-4562
Staff: Gretchen Serrie, General Manager; Paul C. Wolfe, Musical Director

FLORIDA WEST COAST YOUTH ORCHESTRA (F)*
709 N. Tamiami Trail
Sarasota, FL 33577
(813) 955-4562
Staff: Gretchen I. Serrie, General Manager; Paul C. Wolfe, Musical Director and Conductor

FORT LAUDERDALE SYMPHONY ORCHESTRA (B)*
1430 N. Federal Highway
Fort Lauderdale, FL 33304
(305) 561-2997
Staff: Herbert W. Bromberg, Executive Director, Emerson Buckley, Musical Director

GREATER MIAMI YOUTH SYMPHONY (F)*
P.O. Box 431125
Miami, Fl 33143
(305) 233-9615
Staff: David Becker, Conductor; Kenneth Woodside, President

GREATER PALM BEACH SYMPHONY (B)*
P.O. Box 2232
Palm Beach, Fl 33480
(305) 655-2657
Staff: Barbara Hughes, Secretary; John Iuele, Conductor

GREATER PENSACOLA SYMPHONY ORCHESTRA (C)*
P.O. Box 1705
Pensacola, Fl 32598
(904) 455-0609
Staff: Dr. Philip Payne, President; Grier Williams, Musical Director

GULF COAST COLLEGE/COMMUNITY ORCHESTRA (E)
Gulf Coast Community College
Division of Fine Arts

Highway 98
Panama City, FL 32401
(904) 769-1551
Staff: James W. Smith, Conductor

JACKSONVILLE SYMPHONY ORCHESTRA (A)*
580 W. Eighth St., Ste. 9009
Jacksonville, Fl 32209
(904) 354-5479
Staff: Susan M. Sager, General Manager; Willis Page, Conductor and Musical Director

JACKSONVILLE UNIVERSITY COMMUNITY ORCHESTRA (E)
Division of Music
Jacksonville, Fl 32211
(904) 744-3950
Staff: Willaim McNeiland, Conductor

LAKELAND SYMPHONY ORCHESTRA (D)*
P.O. Box 2623
Lakeland, FL 33806
(813) 688-3743
Staff: Keith Sheldon, President; Dr. Larry Culleson, Conductor and Musical Director

MIAMI BEACH SYMPHONY ORCHESTRA (B)*
420 Lincoln Rd.
Miami Beach, Fl 33139
(305) 532-4421
Staff: Barnett Breeskin, Conductor and Manager

MIAMI CHAMBER SYMPHONY (D)*
7820 Southwest 148th Ave.
Miami, Fl 33193
Staff: Burton Dines, Musical Director; Kay Schaffer, Scretary

MIAMI-DADE COMMUNITY ORCHESTRA (E)
Miami-Dade Community College
Music Dept.
11011 S.W. 104th St.
Miami, Fl 33176
(305) 596-1282
Staff: Robert Bobo, Conductor

OCALA FESTIVAL ORCHESTRA & AEOLIAN PLAYERS (E)*
Central Florida Community College
Dept. of Music
P.O. Box 1388
Ocala, FL 32678
(904) 237-2111
Staff: Gene A. Lawton, Conductor

PENSACOLA SYMPHONY ORCHESTRA (E)
University of West Florida
Dept. of Music/Theatre
Pensacola, FL 32504
(904) 476-9500, x317
Staff: Grier M. Williams, Conductor

PINELLAS YOUTH SYMPHONY (F)*
P.O. Box 40044
Saint Petersburg, FL 33743
Staff: Bruce LeBaron, Conductor and Musical Director; Mrs. William Justice, President

ROLLINS CHAMBER ORCHESTRA (D)*
Rollins College
Box 2731
Winter Park, Fl 32789
(305) 646-2233
Staff: Tiedtke, President; Dr. Ward Woodbury, Conductor

SAINT PETERSBURG COMMUNITY SYMPHONY (D)*
1728 Delaware Ave., NE.
Saint Petersburg, FL 33703
(813) 522-5100
Staff: Kathy Del Grande, Vice President and Executive Director; Michael Ficocelli, Musical Director and Conductor

SARASOTA COMMUNITY ORCHESTRA (D)*
P.O. Box 15485
Sarasota, FL 33579
(813) 366-7473
Staff: Arlene C. Stein, Musical Director and Conductor; Dorothen Smart, President

SOUTH FLORIDA YOUTH SYMPHONY (F)*
555 N.W. 152nd. St.
Miami, Fl 33169
(305) 672-3905
Staff: Al Babcock, President; Peter Fuchs and Marjorie Hahn, Co-Conductors

SOUTHWEST FLORIDA SYMPHONY ORCHESTRA (C)*
P.O. Box 1534
Fort Myers, FL 33902
(813) 334-3526
Staff: Timothy J. Tigges, General Manager, Dr. Arlo C.I. Deibler, Musical Director and Conductor

STETSON UNIVERSITY ORCHESTRA (E)
School of Music
DeLand, FL 32720
(904) 734-4121
Staff: Paul Phillips, Conductor

SUN COAST SYMPHONY OF VENICE (D)*
P.O. Box 1561
Venice, FL 33595
(813) 484-2387
Staff: Margaret Strong, President; Hartley Haines, Conductor

UNIVERSITY OF CENTRAL FLORIDA COMMUNITY SYMPHONY (E)*
Music Dept.
Orland, FL 32816
Staff: John C. Whitney, Conductor and Musical Director; Lillian Bagley, President

UNIVERSITY OF FLORIDA SYMPHONY ORCHESTRA (E)*
Music Dept.
Gainesville, Fl 32611
(904) 392-0223
Staff: Dr. Raymond Chobaz, Conductor

WINTER HAVEN YOUTH SYMPHONY (F)*
841 Oleander Dr., SE
Winter Haven, FL 33880
(813) 293-1647

GEORGIA

ALBANY SYMPHONY ORCHESTRA (D)*
P.O. Box 1222
Albany, GA 31702
(912) 439-4377
Staff: Anne V.Crain, General Manager; Charles DeLaney, Musical Director and Conductor

ATLANTA COMMUNITY ORCHESTRA (D)*
2531 Henderson Mill Rd., NE
Atlanta, GA 30345
(404) 938-0420
Staff: Irene M. Constantinides, Vice President; John N. Demos, Conductor and Director

ATLANTA-EMORY ORCHESTRA (E)*
Emory University
Department of Music
Atlanta, GA 30322
(404) 329-6445
Staff: Dr. Bruce Dinkins, Conductor; Carolyn Butcher, Manager

ATLANTA POPS ORCHESTRA (D)
P.O. Box 723172
Atlanta, GA 30339
(404) 435-1222
Staff: Albert Coleman, Conductor

ATLANTA SYMPHONY ORCHESTRA (A)*
1280 Peachtree St., NE
Atlanta, GA 30309
(404) 898-1182
Staff: J. Thomas Bacchetti, Executive Vice President and General Manager; Robert Shaw, Musical Director and Conductor; Pat Upshaw, Assistant Manager

ATLANTA SYMPHONY YOUTH ORCHESTRA (F)*
1280 Peachtree St.
Atlanta, GA 30309
(404) 898-1177
Staff: Pat Upshaw, Manager; Jere Flint, Conductor

AUGUSTA SYMPHONY ORCHESTRA (C)*
Box 3684 Hill Station
Augusta, GA 30904
(404) 733-9739
Staff: Tona R. Bays, Manager; Harry Jacobs, Musical Director

BRUNSWICK COMMUNITY ORCHESTRA (E)
Brunswick Junior College
Altama at Fourth
Brunswick, Ga 31520
(912) 264-7226
Staff: Michelle Clingman, Conductor

COLUMBUS SYMPHONY ORCHESTRA (C)*
P.O. Box 5361
Columbus, GA 31906
(404) 323-5059
Staff: Andy Anderson, Manager; Harry Kruger, Conductor

DEKALB SYMPHONY ORCHESTRA (D)*
555 North Indian Creek Dr.
Clarkston, GA 30021
(404) 299-4135
Staff: Dr. Thomas J. Anderson, Conductor

GEORGIA STATE UNIVERSITY ORCHESTRA (E)
Dept. of Music
University Plaza
Atlanta, GA 30303
(404) 658-2349
Staff: David MacKenzie, Conductor

MERCER-ATLANTA CHAMBER ORCHESTRA (E)
Mercer University, Atlanta
Music Dept.
3000 Flowers Rd., South
Atlanta, GA 30341
(404) 451-0331
Staff: Norman Bernal, Conductor

MIDDLE GEORGIA SYMPHONY ORCHESTRA (D)*
P.O. Box 5700
Macon, Ga 31208
(912) 474-5700
Staff: George L. Grace, Manager; Harry Kruger, Musical Director and Conductor

MILLEDGEVILLE CHAMBER ORCHESTRA (E)
Georgia College
Music Dept.
Milledgeville, GA 31061
(912) 453-4226
Staff: Conrad Douglas, Conductor

SAVANNAH SYMPHONY ORCHESTRA (B)
P.O. Box 9505
Savannah, GA 31412
(912) 236-9536
Staff: David T. Guernsey, Jr., General Manager; Christian Badea, Musical Director and Conductor

STATESBORO-GEORGIA SOUTHERN SYMPHONY ORCHESTRA (E)
Georgia Southern College
Music Dept.
Box 8052, Landrum Center
Statesboro, GA 30460
(912) 681-5396
Staff: Warren Fields, Conductor

TOCCOA/STEPHENS COUNTY ORCHESTRA (E)
Toccoa Falls College
School of Music
Toccoa Falls, GA 30598
(404) 886-6831
Staff: Archie Sharretts, Conductor

HAWAII

HAWAII CHAMBER ORCHESTRA (D)
838 S. Beretania St., No. 207
Honolulu, HI 96813
(808) 537-4079
Staff: Richard W. Cornwell, Manager

HONOLULU SYMPHONY ORCHESTRA (A)*
1000 Bishop St., Ste. 901
Honolulu, HI 96813
(808) 537-6171
Staff: Robert S. Sandla, Executive Director; Donal Johanos, Musical Director; Catharine L. Hite, Orchestral Manager

UNIVERSITY OF HAWAII/HILO-COMMUNITY CHAMBER ORCHESTRA (E)
Performing Arts Dept.
1400 Kapolani St.
Hilo, HI 96720
(808) 961-9352
Staff: Takeo Kudo, Conductor

UNIVERSITY OF HAWAII SYMPHONY ORCHESTRA (E)
Music Dept.
2411 Dole St.
Honolulu, HI 96822
(808) 948-8091
Staff: Henry Miyamura, Conductor

IDAHO

BOISE PHILHARMONIC (B)*
P.O. Box 2205
Boise, ID 83701
(208) 344-7849
Staff: Michael Winter, General Manager; Dr. Daniel Stern, Conductor and Musical Director

COLLEGE OF IDAHO-COMMUNITY ORCHESTRA (E)
Music Dept.
Cleveland Blvd.
Caldwell, ID 83605
(208) 459-5011
Staff: Walter Cerveny, Conductor

IDAHO FALLS SYMPHONY ORCHESTRA (D)*
P.O. Box 604
Idaho Falls, ID 83401
(208) 529-1080
Staff: Mary V. Arnold, Business Manager; Carl J. Eberl, Conductor and Musical Director

IDAHO STATE CIVIC SYMPHONY (D)*
P.O. Box 4852
Pocatello, ID 83201
Staff: Nancy Thomas, Secretary; Gregory Fried, Conductor

MAGIC VALLEY SYMPHONY ORCHESTRA (D)*
P.O. Box 1805
Twin Falls, ID 83301
(208) 734-8511
Staff: Patricia Hadley, Business Manager; Lawrence Curtis, Musical Director

TREASURE VALLEY YOUTH SYMPHONY (F)*
P.O. Box 2205
Boise, ID 83701
Staff: John E. Hamilton, Musical Director and Conductor

UNIVERSITY OF IDAHO SYMPHONY ORCHESTRA (E)
School of Music
Moscow, ID 83843
(208) 885-6111
Staff: Stephen Folks, Conductor

WASHINGTON-IDAHO SYMPHONY (D)*
P.O. Box 9185
Moscow, ID 83843
(208) 882-6555
Staff: Jean Bonifas, Manager; Dr. H. James Schoepflin, Musical Director and Conductor

ILLINOIS

ALTON CIVIC ORCHESTRA (D)
1623 Washington Ave.
Alton, IL 62002
(618) 465-3921
Staff: Clarence J. Crichta, conductor; Frank M. Boals, President

AUGUSTANA COLLEGE SYMPHONY ORCHESTRA (E)*
Office of Cultural Events
Rock Island, IL 61201
(309) 794-7307
Staff: Dennis Loftin, Manager; Daniel Culver, Conductor

BLOOMINGTON-NORMAL SYMPHONY (D)*
P.O. Box 375
Bloomington, IL 61701
(309) 829-0011
Staff: Carole Ringer, General Manager; Julian Dawson and Robert Luke, Co-Musical Directors

CHAMPAIGN COUNTY YOUTH SYMPHONY (F)*
402 S. Coler Ave.
Urbana, IL 61801
(217) 344-5561
Staff: Marilyn Rasmusen, Manager; Paul Vermel, Conductor

CHAMPAIGN-URBANA SYMPHONY ORCHESTRA (C)*
Box 2079, Station A
Champaign, IL 61820
(217) 356-6037
Staff: Jerry Tessin, Concert Manager; Paul Vermel, Conductor

CHICAGO ARTISTS ORCHESTRA (D)
505 N. Lake Shore Dr., Apt. 2218
Chicago, IL 60611
(312) 372-2213
Staff: James N. Dutton, Conductor and Manager

CHICAGO CHAMBER ORCHESTRA (C)*
410 S. Michigan Ave.
Chicago, IL 60605
(312) 922-5570
Staff: Randolph A. Alexander, General Manager; Dr. Dieter Kober, Musical Director

CHICAGO POPS ORCHESTRA (D)*
100 N. LaSalle St., Rm. 1215
Chicago, IL 60602
(312) 332-3888
Staff: Sandi Goodman and Linda Grade, Administrators

CHICAGO STRING ENSEMBLE (D)*
2944 N. Lincoln
Chicago, IL 60657
(312) 880-5255
Staff: Donna Hapac, General Manager; Alan Heatherington, Musical Director

CHICAGO SYMPHONIC WIND ENSEMBLE*
P.O. Box 25782
Chicago, IL 60625
(312) 631-5800
Staff: Lloyd Vincent Bycz, Executive Director and Musical Director

CHICAGO SYMPHONY ORCHESTRA (A)*
220 S. Michigan Ave.
Chicago, IL 60604
(312) 435-8122
Staff: John S. Edwards, Executive Vice President and General Manager; Sir George Solti, Musical Director; Paul Chummers, Manager

CIVIC ORCHESTRA OF CHICAGO (F)*
220 S. Michigan Ave.
Chicago, IL 60604
Staff: Gordon B. Peters, Conductor and Administrator; Lowell S. Davis, Administrative Assistant/Librarian

CLASSICAL YOUTH SYMPHONY (F)*
534 N. Gove Ave.
Oak Park, IL 60302
Staff: Joseph Glymph, Conductor; Daniel C. Kielson, Business Manager

CONCERTS SYMPHONIQUES (D)
1439 Brassie Ave.
Flossmoor, IL 60422
(312) 799-1926
Staff: Emmett Mitchele Steele, Conductor; Carl Burkle, Manager

DANVILLE SYMPHONY ORCHESTRA (D)*
205½ N. Walnut St.
Danville, IL 61832
(217) 443-5300
Staff: Saundra Wilson, Administrative Director; William B. Handley, Musical Director

DEPAUL UNIVERSITY SYMPHONY (E)*
School of Music
804 W. Belden Ave.
Chicago, IL 60614
(312) 321-7760
Staff: Meng-Kong Tham, Musical Director

EASTERN ILLINOIS UNIVERSITY SYMPHONY ORCHESTRA (E)
Music Dept.
Fine Arts Center
Charleston, IL 61920
(217) 581-2917
Staff: Dr. James Krehbiel, Conductor

ELGIN AREA YOUTH ORCHESTRAS (F)*
Elgin Community College
1700 Spartan Dr.
Elgin, IL 60120
(312) 697-1000
Staff: Sue Larson, Manager; Paul Patterson and Ann Rapp, Conductors

ELGIN SYMPHONY ORCHESTRA (C)*
Elgin Community College
1700 Spartan Dr.
Elgin, IL 60120
(312) 888-7389
Staff: Robert Hansen, Executive Director and Resident Conductor; Margaret Hillis, Musical Director

ELMHURST SYMPHONY ORCHESTRA (E)
Elmhurst College
Music Dept.
190 Prospect
Elmhurst, IL 60126
(312) 279-4100
Staff: Dale Clevenger, Conductor

EVANSTON SYMPHONY ORCHESTRA (D)*
P.O. Box 778
Evanston, IL 60204
(312) 675-0743
Staff: D.F. McCarthy, President; Frank Miller, Musical Director

FLUTE AND FIDDLE CLUB ORCHESTRA (D)*
1623 Sylvester Pl.
Highland Park, IL 60035
Staff: Everett L. Millard, Jr., Conductor

FOX RIVER VALLEY SYMPHONY ORCHESTRA (D)*
50 Le Grande Blvd.
Aurora, IL 60506
(312) 892-1427
Staff: Mardi Glenn, President; Frederick Ockwell, Conductor

GRANT PARK SYMPHONY ORCHESTRA (B)
425 East McFetridge Dr.
Chicago, IL 60605
(312) 294-2420

JACKSONVILLE SYMPHONY (D)
813 Freedman
Jacksonville, IL 62650
(217) 245-9415
Staff: Garrett Allman, Conductor

KANKAKEE SYMPHONY ORCHESTRA (D)
553 S. Nelson Ave.
Kankakee, IL 60901
(815) 939-5306
Staff: Ovid Young, Musical Director and Conductor

KNOX-GALESBURG SYMPHONY (D)*
Knox College
Box 31
Galesburg, IL 61401
(309) 343-0112
Staff: Mary Borden, Manager; Dr. Uri Barnea, Musical Director

LAKE FOREST SYMPHONY ASSOCIATION (C)*
P.O. Box 748
Lake Forest, IL 60045
(312) 295-2135
Staff: Thomas D. Wilson, General Manager; Victor Aitay, Musical Director

LEWIS UNIVERSITY COMMUNITY SYMPHONY ORCHESTRA (E)
Dept. of Music
Route 53
Lockport, IL 60441
(815) 838-0500, x415
Staff: Dr. Daniel A. Binder, Conductor

LINCOLN COMMUNITY SYMPHONY ORCHESTRA (E)
Lincoln College
300 Keokuk
Lincoln, IL 62656
(217) 732-3155
Staff: Alan Tidaback, Conductor

MCHENRY COUNTY YOUTH ORCHESTRA (F)*
46 S. Walkup Ave.
Crystal Lake, IL 60014
(815) 459-7664
Staff: Marie Ann Vos, Manager; Thomas D. Wilson, Conductor

MILLIKIN-DECATUR CIVIC SYMPHONY (D)*
Milliken University
School of Music
Decatur, IL 62522
(217) 423-6300
Staff: George Nagy, Personnel Manager; Dr. Ronald D. Gregory, Musical Director and Conductor

NEW PHILHARMONIC (D)*
College of DuPage
Glen Ellyn, IL 60137
(312) 858-2800
Staff: Harold Bauer, Musical Director

NORTHERN ILLINOIS UNIVERSITY PHILHARMONIC (E)
Dept. of Music
DeKalb, IL 60115
(815) 753-1551
Staff: Carl Roskott, Conductor

NORTH SHORE YOUTH ORCHESTRA (F)*
Music Center of the North Shore
300 Green Bay Rd.
Winnetka, IL 60093
(312) 446-3822
Staff: Kalman Novak and Carol A. Hall, Co-Conductors

NORTHWEST CHICAGO SYMPHONY ORCHESTRA (E)
Wilbur Wright College
Music Dept.
3400 N. Austin Ave.
Chicago, IL 60634
(312) 777-7900, x 48
Staff: Michael Holian, Conductor

ORCHESTRA OF ILLINOIS (B)*
6 West Randolph Dr.
Chicago, IL 60601
(312) 263-3786
Staff: William P. Prenevost, Executive Director; Guido Ajmone-Marsan, Musical Advisor; Kim Giddens, Business Manager

PEORIA SYMPHONY ORCHESTRA (B)*
714 Hamilton Blvd.
Peoria, IL 61602
(309) 673-4254
Staff: Cynthia A. Swinarski, Manager; William Wilsen, Conductor

PRINCIPIA COLLEGE ORCHESTRA (E)
Music Dept.
Elsah, IL 62028
(618) 374-2131
Staff: David Sussman, Conductor

QUINCY SYMPHONY ORCHESTRA (D)*
3207 Lindell
Quincy, IL 62301
(217) 222-1078
Staff: Dr. Thom Ritter George, Musical Director and Conductor; Nicholas N. Schildt, Manager

ROCKFORD AREA YOUTH SYMPHONY (F)*
Mezzanine Level
401 S. Main St.
Rockford, Il 61101
(815) 654-4365
Staff: Jack L. Simon, Conductor; Judith Pember, Manager

ROCKFORD SYMPHONY ORCHESTRA (B)*
401 S. Main St., Mezzanine Level
Rockford, IL 61101
(815) 965-0049
Staff: Richard K. Scharf, Exeuctive Director; Dr. Crawford Gates, Musical Director; Judity M. Pember, Orchestral Manager

ROOSEVELT UNIVERSITY SYMPHONY ORCHESTRA (E)
Chicago Musical College of Roosevelt University
430 S. Michigan Ave.
Chicago,IL 60605
(312) 341-3780
Staff: Dr. Donald Chen, Conductor

SHEFFIELD WINDS (D)*
410 S. Michigan Ave.
Chicago, IL 60605
(312) 337-7180
Staff: Robert G. Levine, President; Robert Morgan, Musical Coach

SHERWOOD SYMPHONY ORCHESTRA (E)
Sherwood Music School
1014 S. Michigan Ave.
Chicago, IL 60605
(312) 427-6267
Staff: Giulio Favario, Conductor

SKOKIE VALLEY SYMPHONY ORCHESTRA (D)*
P.O. Box 767
Skokie, IL 60077
(312) 675-3204
Staff: Leo Krakow, Musical Director and Conductor; Dr. Robert Komaiko, President and Executive Director

SOUTHERN ILLINOIS UNIVERSITY/ EDWARDSVILLE SYMPHONY ORCHESTRA (E)
Dept. of Music
Edwardsville, IL 62026
(618) 692-3900
Staff: Robert Schieber, Conductor

SOUTHWEST SYMPHONY ORCHESTRA (D)
9533 Minnick Ave.
Oak Lawn, IL 60453
(312) 422-3822
Staff: Alfred Aulwurm, Conductor; Martha M. Morris, Assistant

SPRINGFIELD SYMPHONY ORCHESTRA (C)*
1537 S. Douglas
Springfield, IL 62704
(217) 546-2880
Staff: Daniel R. Spreckelmeyer, Manager; Kenneth Kiesler, Conductor and Musical Director

TRINITY COLLEGE CHAMBER ORCHESTRA OF DEERFIELD (E)
Music Dept.
2045 Half Day Rd.
Deerfield, IL 60015
(312) 945-6700
Staff: Daniel Sommerville, Conductor

UNIVERSITY OF CHICAGO SYMPHONY ORCHESTRA (E)
Dept. of Music
5845 S. Ellis Ave.
Chicago, IL 60637
(312) 962-8484
Staff: Barbara Schubert, Conductor

WAUKEGAN SYMPHONY ORCHESTRA (D)*
326 E. Westminster Ave.
Lake Forest, IL 60045
(312) 948-4637
Staff: Henry M. Kusher, Correspondence Secretary; Lynn Schornick, Conductor

WESTERN ILLINOIS UNIVERSITY SYMPHONY ORCHESTRA (E)
Dept. of Music
128 Browne hall
Macomb, IL 61455
(309) 298-1245
Staff: Roland Vamos, Conductor

WEST SUBURBAN SYMPHONY ORCHESTRA (D)*
P.O. Box 63
Western Springs, IL 60558
(312) 579-5863
Staff: Jean Piper, President; Ralph Lane, Musical Director and Conductor

WHEATON COLLEGE SYMPHONY ORCHESTRA (E)
Conservatory of Music
Wheaton, IL 60187
(312) 260-5000
Staff: Howard Whitaker, Conductor; Harold M. Best, Manager

WHEATON SUMMER SYMPHONY (D)*
1600 E. Roosevelt Rd.
Wheaton, IL 60187
(312) 668-8585
Staff: Dr. Donald C. Mattison, General Manager; Ralph Lane, Conductor

YOUTH SYMPHONY ORCHESTRA OF GREATER CHICAGO (F)*
Fine Arts Building, Room 827
410 S. Michigan Ave.
Chicago, IL 60605
Staff: Grace L. Kemper, Business Manager and Treasurer; Orcenith Smith, Musical Director

ZION CHAMBER ORCHESTRA (D)*
Dowie Memorial Dr.
Zion, IL 60099
(312) 872-4803
Staff: Robert Oakes, Manager; Timothy Allen, Conductor

INDIANA

BALL STATE UNIVERSITY SYMPHONY ORCHESTRA (E)
School of Music
Muncie, IN 47306

(317) 285-4433
Staff: Leonard Atherton, Conductor

BLOOMINGTON SYMPHONY ORCHESTRA (D)*
P.O. Box 1823
Bloomington, IN 47402
(812) 336-1208
Staff: Joann Alexander, Manager; Carl Fuerstner, Musical Director

BUTLER UNIVERSITY SYMPHONY ORCHESTRA (E)*
Jordan College of Fine Arts
4600 Clarendon Rd.
Indianapolis, IN 46208
(317) 283-9231
Staff: Jackson Wiley, Conductor

CARMEL SYMPHONY ORCHESTRA (D)*
P.O. Box 761
Carmel, IN 46032
(317) 846-6779
Staff: Renee Rich, Manager; Benjamin G. Del Vecchio, Musical Director and Conductor

COLUMBUS SYMPHONY ORCHESTRA (D)*
302 Washington St.
Columbus, IN 47201
(812) 379-4192
Staff: Susan Anderson, President; Dale L. Spurlock, Musical Director

DEPAUW SYMPHONY ORCHESTRA (E)*
DePauw University
School of Music
Greencastle, IN 46135
(317) 658-4388
Staff: Orcenith Smith, Musical Director

ELKHART SYMPHONY ORCHESTRA (B)*
P.O. Box 144
Elkhart, IN 46514
(219) 293-1087
Staff: Robert J. Pickrell, General Manager; Dr. Michael J. Esselstrom, Musical Director and Conductor

EVANSVILLE PHILHARMONIC ORCHESTRA (B)*
P.O. Box 84
Evansville, IN 47701
(812) 425-8241
Staff: Emily H. Benham, General Manager; Stewart Kershaw, Musical Director

FORT WAYNE PHILHARMONIC (B)*
1107 S. Harrison
Fort Wayne, IN 46802
(219) 424-4134
Staff: Peter W. Smith, Managing Director; Ronal Ondrejka, Musical Director; Macy Glabreath, Operations Manager

INDIANAPOLIS SYMPHONY ORCHESTRA (A)*
P.O. Box 88207
Indianapolis, IN 46208
(317) 925-5853
Staff: Fred H. Kumb, Jr., General Manger; John Nelson, Musical Director; Sue K. Staton, Assistant General Manager

INDIANA UNIVERSITY ORCHESTRAS (E)*
School of Music
Bloomington, IN 47405
(812) 337-8357
Staff: George Calder, Manager

INDIANA UNIVERSITY SOUTHEAST CHAMBER ORCHESTRA (E)
New Albany, IN 47150
(812) 945-2731

KOKOMO SYMPHONY ORCHESTRA (D)*
P.O. Box 143
Kokomo, IN 46901
(317) 455-1659
Staff: Barbara M. Cassis, Manager; Dr. Michael J. Esselstrom, Musical Director and Conductor

LAFAYETTE SYMPHONY (D)*
P.O. Box 52
Lafayette, IN 47902
(317) 474-9507
Staff: Paul L. Van Cleef, Manager; Dr. Eduardo A. Ostergren, Conductor and Musical Director

MARION PHILHARMONIC ORCHESTRA (E)
Taylor University
Music Dept.
Upland, IN 46989
(317) 998-2751
Staff: Raymond Harvey, Conductor

MUNCIE SYMPHONY ORCHESTRA (C)*
203 N. College Ave.
Muncie, IN 47306
(317) 285-6969
Staff: Joan McKee, Business Manager; Leonard Atherton, Conductor and Musical Director

NORTH MANCHESTER CIVIC/ COLLEGE SYMPHONY*
Manchester College
Box 42
North Manchester, IN 46962
(219) 982-2141
Staff: Robert G. Jones, Conductor; Orrin Manifold, President

NORTHWEST INDIANA SYMPHONY (C)*
P.O. Box 2077
Gary, IN 46409
(219) 980-5840
Staff: Judith M. Levine, General Manager; Robet Vodnoy, Musical Director

NORTHWEST INDIANA YOUTH ORCHESTRA (F)*
P.O. Box 2077
Gary, IN 46409
(219) 980-5840
Staff: Mrs. Seymour Kaplan, President and Manager; Charles Mann, Conductor

PHILHARMONIC ORCHESTRA OF INDIANAPOLIS (D)
4925 Central Ave.
Indianapolis, IN 46205
(317) 283-5242
Staff: Benjamin Del Vecchio, Conductor; Carl Henn, Jr., Manager

PURDUE UNIVERSITY SYMPHONY ORCHESTRA (E)*
Hall of Music, Room 136
West Lafayette, IN 47907
(317) 494-3957
Staff: Frank L. Stubbs, Jr., Conductor

RICHMOND SYMPHONY ORCHESTRA (D)*
P.O. Box 982
Richmond, IN 47374
(317) 935-6434
Staff: Betty Becknell, Business Manager; Manfred Blum, Conductor

ST. MARY-OF-THE-WOODS COLLEGE/ COMMUNITY ORCHESTRA (E)
Music Dept.
St. Mary-of-the-Woods, IN 47876
(812) 535-4141
Staff: Sr. Carol Nolan, Conductor

SOUTH BEND SYMPHONY ORCHESTRA (B)*
215 W. North Shore Dr.
South Bend, IN 46617
(219) 232-6343
Staff: B.D. Cullity, Manager; Herbert Butler, Musical Director and Conductor

TERRE HAUTE SYMPHONY ORCHESTRA (C)*
P.O. Box 957
Terre Haute, IN 47808
(812) 232-6311
Staff: Susan E. Bruce, General Manager; Dr. Ramon E. Meyer, Musical Director and Conductor

UNIVERSITY OF EVANSVILLE SYMPHONY ORCHESTRA (E)
Dept. of Music
1800 Lincoln Ave., P.O. Box 329
Evansville, IN 47702
(812) 479-2742
Staff: David Littrell, Conductor

VALPARAISO UNIVERSITY SYMPHONY ORCHESTRA (E)
Music Dept.
University Place
Valparaiso, IN 46383
(219) 464-5454
Staff: James Klein, Conductor

IOWA

CEDAR RAPIDS SYMPHONY ORCHESTRA (B)*
201 Security Building
201 Second St., SE
Cedar Rapids, IA 52401
(319) 366-8203
Staff: Karla Mason, Manager; Dr. Christian Tiemeyer, Musical Director and Conductor

CEDAR RAPIDS YOUTH SYMPHONY (F)*
1220 First AVe., NE
Cedar Rapids, IA 52402
(319) 399-8560
Staff: Tim Topolewski, Conductor; Bob Horick, Business Manager

CENTRAL COLLEGE/COMMUNITY ORCHESTRA (E)
Music Dept.
Pella, IA 50219
(515) 628-4151
Staff: Raymond M. Martin, Conductor

CORNELL COLLEGE/COMMUNITY ORCHESTRA
Music Dept.
Mount Vernon, IA 52314
(319) 895-8911
Staff: John Klaus, Conductor

DES MOINES COMMUNITY ORCHESTRA (D)*
3444 Kinsey
Des Moines, IA 50317
(515) 266-7580
Staff: Janice Wade, Conductor; Ruth Kneile, Manager

DES MOINES SYMPHONY ORCHESTRA (B)*
411 Shops Building
Des Moines, IA 50309
(515) 244-0819
Staff: Roger A. Malfatti, Managing Director; Yuri Krasnapolsky, Musical Director

DORDT COLLEGE ORCHESTRA (E)
Music Dept.
Sioux Center, IA 51250
(712) 722-3771
Staff: Noel Magee, Conductor

DRAKE UNIVERSITY SYMPHONY ORCHESTRA (E)*
College of Fine Arts
Des Moines, IA 50311
(515) 271-3131
Staff: John Canarina, Conductor

DUBUQUE SYMPHONY ORCHESTRA (C)*
P.O. Box 881
Dubuque, IA 52001
(319) 557-1797
Staff: Dr. Parviz Mahmoud, Musical Director and Conductor; Ruth Mahmoud, Orchestral Manager

FORT DODGE SYMPHONY ORCHESTRA (D)*
P.O. Box 73
Eagle Grove, IA 50533
Staff: Peggy Nash, Business Manager; Ross A. Leeper, Conductor

GREATER DES MOINES YOUTH SYMPHONY (F)*
313 49th St.
Des Moines, IA 50312
Staff: Sandra Tatge, Director; Cindy Jensen, Assistant Administrator

GRINNELL ORCHESTRA (E)*
Grinnell College
Music Department
Grinnell, IA 50112
(515) 236-2911
Staff: Terry King, Musical Director and Conductor

IOWA STATE UNIVERSITY SYMPHONY (E)
Music Dept.
Ames, IA 50011
(515) 294-5364
Staff: N.L. Buarkhalter, Conductor

LUTHER COLLEGE SYMPHONY ORCHESTRA (E)*
Music Dept.
Decorah, IA 52101
(319) 387-1209
Staff: Jonathan Hallstrom, Conductor; Curtis Reiso, Manager

ST. AMBROSE CHAMBER ORCHESTRA (E)
St. Ambrose College
Music Dept.
518 W. Locust
Davenport, IA 52803
(319) 383-8800
Staff: Charles Abplanalp, Conductor

SIOUX CITY SYMPHONY ORCHESTRA (B)*
P.O. Box 754
Sioux City, IA 51102
(712) 277-2111
Staff: Dr. Sheffield Klein, General Manager; Thomas Lewis, Musical Director and Conductor

SIOUXLAND YOUTH SYMPHONY ORCHESTRA (F)*
264 Orpheum Electric Building
P.O. Box 754
Sioux City, IA 51101
(712) 277-2111
Staff: Mrs. James F. Boysen, Chairman; Jane Berger, Musical Director and Conductor

SOUTHEAST IOWA SYMPHONY ORCHESTRA (D)*
601 N. Main St.
Mount Pleasant, IA 52641
(319) 385-8021
Staff: Gay W. Stuntzner, Manager; Dr. Ruth Keraus, Conductor

TRI-CITY SYMPHONY ORCHESTRA (B)*
P.O. Box 67
Davenport, IA 52805
(319) 322-0931
Staff: Lance O. Willett, Manager; James Dixon, Musical Director and Conductor

TRI-CITY YOUTH SYMPHONY ORCHESTRA (F)*
P.O. Box 67
Davenport, IA 52805
(319) 322-0931
Staff: Eloise Smit, General Manager; James Dixon, Conductor

UNIVERSITY OF IOWA SYMPHONY (E)
School of Music
Iowa City, IA 52242
(319) 353-5424
Staff: James A. Dixon, Conductor; Chandler G. Schaffer, Manager

UNIVERSITY OF NORTHERN IOWA ORCHESTRA (E)
School of Music
Cedar Falls, IA 50613
(319) 273-2024
Staff: Jack Graham, Conductor

WARTBURG COMMUNITY SYMPHONY (E)
Wartburg College
Music Dept.
Waverly, IA 50677
(319) 352-1200
Staff: Franklin E. Williams, Conductor

WATERLOO-CEDAR FALLS SYMPHONY ORCHESTRA (C)*
P.O. Box 864
Waterloo, IA 50704
(319) 235-6331
Staff: Joseph Giunta, Musical Director and Conductor; Judy Pullin, Official Secretary

KANSAS

BENEDICTINE COLLEGE/ATCHISON SYMPHONY ORCHESTRA (E)
Music Dept.
South Campus
Atchison, KS 66002
(913) 367-6110
Staff: Russell T. Waite, Conductor

BETHANY COLLEGE COMMUNITY ORCHESTRA (E)
Music Dept.
Lindsborg, KS 67456
(913) 227-3311
Staff: David Higbee, Conductor

COLBY COMMUNITY COLLEGE ORCHESTRA (E)
Music Dept.
1255 S. Range
Colby, KS 67701
(913) 462-3984
Staff: Bill Beck, Conductor

DODGE CITY COMMUNITY ORCHESTRA (E)
St. Mary of the Plains College
Music Dept.
Dodge City, KS 67801
(316) 225-4171, x66

EMPORIA STATE UNIVERSITY/ EMPORIA SYMPHONY ORCHESTRA (E)
Dept. of Music
1200 Commercial St.
Emporia, KS 66801
(316) 343-1200, x431
Staff: Howard Halgedahl, Conductor

FRIENDS UNIVERSITY/COMMUNITY SYMPHONY (E)
Division of Fine Arts
2100 University
Wichita, KA 67213
(316) 261-5800, x734
Staff: William Wade Perry, Conductor; A.L. Perry, Manager

HAYS SYMPHONY (E)*
Fort Hays State University
Music Dept.
Hays, KS 67601
(913) 628-5353
Staff: Lyle Dilley, Conductor

HUTCHINSON SYMPHONY (D)*
P.O. Box 1241
Hutchinson, KS 67501
(316) 663-7121
Staff: William L. Hutchinson, Business Manager; Jeffrey Bell-Hanson, Conductor

LAWRENCE CHAMBER PLAYERS (D)*
803 Avalon Rd.
Lawrence, KS 66044
(913) 842-9312
Staff: Sue Himes, President; Leon Burke, III, Conductor

LAWRENCE SYMPHONY ORCHESTRA (E)
University of Kansas
School of Fine Arts
Lawrence, KS 66045
(913) 864-3421
Staff: Charles Hoag, Conductor

MCPHERSON SYMPHONY ORCHESTRA (D)*
614 E. Seitz
McPherson, KS 67460
(316) 241-0040
Staff: Eunice E. Tarum, Orchestral Manager; H. Jay Setter, Musical Director and Conductor; Lynnifa Harris, Assistant

NEWTON/MID-KANSAS SYMPHONY ORCHESTRA (E)
Bethel College
Music Dept.
North Newton, KS 67117
(316) 283-2500
Staff: Gerald Kiger, Conductor

SALINA SYMPHONY (D)*
P.O. Box 792
Salina, KS 67401
Staff: James T. Crawford, Administrative Manager; Eric Stein, Musical Director and Conductor

SOUTHEAST KANSAS SYMPHONY (E)
Pittsburg State University
Music Dept.
Pittsburg, KS 66762
(316) 231-7000, x273
Staff: Carolann Martin, Conductor

SOUTHWESTERN COLLEGE COMMUNITY ORCHESTRA (E)*
200 College St.
Winfield, KS 67156
(316) 221-4150
Staff: Larry R. Williams, Conductor

TOPEKA CIVIC SYMPHONY (E)
Washburn Universtiy of Topeka
Music Dept.
Topeka, KS 66621
(913) 295-6511
Staff: Jack Herriman, Conductor

WICHITA STATE UNIVERSITY SYMPHONY ORCHESTRA (E)*
Division of Music, Box 53
Wichita, KS 67208
(316) 689-3103
Staff: Dr. Jay Decker, Conductor

WICHITA SYMPHONY ORCHESTRA (A)*
Century II Concert Hall
225 W. Douglas, Ste. 207
Wichita, KS 67202
(316) 267-5259
Staff: Mitchell A. Berman, General Manager; Michael Palmer, Musical Director and Conductor; Glenn M. Lestz, Assistant Manager

WICHITA YOUTH ORCHESTRAS (F)*
Centry II Concert Hall
225 W. Douglas
Wichita, KS 67202
(316) 267-5259
Staff: Janice Hupp, Manager; Dr. Jay Decker, Musical Director and Conductor

YOUTH SYMPHONY OF KANSAS CITY (F)*
3514 W. 78th St.
Shawnee Mission, KS 66208
(913) 642-7141
Staff: Mrs. Michael Spielman, Business Manager; David E. Circle, Musical Director and Conductor

KENTUCKY

BEREA COLLEGE/COMMUNITY ORCHESTRA (E)
Music Dept.
CPO 2352
Beara, KY 40404
(606) 986-9341, x359
Staff: John Little, Conductor

BOWLING GREEN/WESTERN SYMPHONY (E)
Western Kentucky University
Dept. of Music
Bowling Green, KY 42101
(502) 745-3751
Staff: Gary Dilworth, Conductor

CENTRAL KENTUCKY YOUTH ORCHESTRA (F)*
P.O. Box 22013
Lexington, KY 40522
(606) 273-7328
Staff: Nick Michael Lacanski, Musical Director

CHAMBER ORCHESTRA OF THE CUMBERLANDS (E)
Cumberland College
Music Dept.
Williamsburg, KY 40769
(606) 549-2200, x332
Staff: W. Edwin Bingham, Conductor

EASTERN KENTUCKY UNIVERSITY SYMPHONY ORCHESTRA (E)
Dept. of Music
Richmond, KY 40475
(606) 622-3266
Staff: Dan Duncan, Conductor

LEXINGTON PHILHARMONIC ORCHESTRA (B)*
412 Rose St.
Lexington, KY 40508
(606) 233-4226
Staff: Linda G. Moore, General Manager; George Zack, Musical Director

LOUISVILLE/JEFFERSON COUNTY YOUTH ORCHESTRA (F)*
1517 S. Second St.
Louisville, KY 40208
(502) 426-4037
Staff: Nancy M. Vizer, General Manager; Daniel Spurlock, Musical Director

LOUISVILLE ORCHESTRA (A)*
609 W. Main St.
Louisville, KY 40202
(502) 587-8681
Staff: Karen R. Dobbs, General Manager; Akira Endo, Musical Director: Gregory Copenhefer, Assistant Manager

MOREHEAD STATE UNIVERSITY ORCHESTRA (E)
Dept. of Music
Morehead, KY 40351
(606) 783-2473
Staff: John Stetler, Conductor

MURRAY STATE UNIVERSITY SYMPHONY ORCHESTRA (E)
Dept. of Music
Box 2022, University Station
Murray, KY 42071
(502) 762-4288
Staff: C. Thompson, Conductor

OWENSBORO SYMPHONY ORCHESTRA (C)*
Symphony Center
122 E. 18th St.
Owensboro, KY 42301
(502) 684-0661
Staff: John E. Bauser, General Manager; Leon Gregorian, Musical Director and Conductor

PADUCAH SYMPHONY ORCHESTRA (D)*
P.O. Box 2242
Paducah, KY 42001
(502) 443-4516
Staff: Charles R. Manchester, General Manager; Robert K. Baar, Musical Director

UNIVERSITY OF KENTUCKY ORCHESTRA (E)
School of Music
Fine Arts Building
Lexington, KY 40506
(606) 258-4936
Staff: Phillip Miller, Conductor

LOUISIANA

BATON ROUGE SYMPHONY ORCHESTRA (B)*
P.O. Box 103
Baton Rouge, LA 70821
(504) 387-6166
Staff: Richard H. Mackie, Jr., General Manager; James Paul, Musical Director; Clara Leach, Operations Manager

LAKE CHARLES SYMPHONY ORCHESTRA (D)*
P.O. Box 3102
Lake Charles, LA 70602
Staff: C. King, General Manager; William Kushner, Conductor

L'ORCHESTRE (E)*
University of Southwestern Louisiana
School of Music
P.O. Drawer 41207
Lafayette, LA 70504
(318) 231-6016
Staff: Dr. Allan Dennis, Musical Director

LOUISIANA STATE UNIVERSITY/ BATON ROUGE SYMPHONY ORCHESTRA (E)
School of Music
Baton Rouge, LA 70803
(504) 388-3261
Staff: James Yestadt, Conductor

NATCHITOCHES/NORTHWESTERN SYMPHONY (E)
Northwestern State University of Louisiana
Music Dept.
Natchitoches, LA 71457
(318) 357-4436
Staff: J. Robert Smith, Conductor

NEW ORLEANS PHILHARMONIC-SYMPHONY ORCHESTRA (A)*
203 Carondelet St., Ste. 903
New Orleans, LA 70130
(504) 524-0404
Staff: James D. Hicks, Vice President and Executive Manager; Philippe Entremont, Musical Director and Conductor; Daniel Furnald, Assistant Manager

NEW ORLEANS SYMPHONY YOUTH ORCHESTRA (F)*
Loyola University
Music Dept.
6363 Saint Charles Ave.
New Orleans, LA 70118
Staff: Dean Angeles, Conductor; Allison Gruber, Manager

RAPIDES SYMPHONY ORCHESTRA (D)*
P.O. Box 4464
Alexandria, LA 71301
Staff: William A. Kushner, Musical Director

SHREVEPORT SYMPHONY ORCHESTRA (B)*
P.O. Box 4057
Shreveport, LA 71104
(318) 869-2559
Staff: Sandra V. Keiser, General Manager; Paul Strauss, Principal Guest Conductor

MAINE

BANGOR SYMPHONY ORCHESTRA (C)*
P.O. Box 1441
Bangor, ME 04401
(207) 945-6408
Staff: Kenneth J. Vaillancourt, Manager; Werner Torkanowsky, Musical Director and Conductor

BATES COLLEGE COMMUNITY ORCHESTRA (E)
Music Dept.
Lewiston, ME 04240
(207) 783-3323
Staff: William R. Matthews, Conductor

BOWDOIN COLLEGE ORCHESTRA (E)
Music Dept.
Brushwick, ME 04011
(207) 725-8731
Staff: Nalin T. Mukherjee, Conductor

COLBY COMMUNITY SYMPHONY ORCHESTRA (E)
Colby College
Music Dept.
Waterville, ME 04901
(207) 873-1131
Staff: Peter Re, Conductor

PORTLAND SYMPHONY ORCHESTRA (B)*
30 Myrtle St.
Portland, ME 04101
(207) 773-8191
Staff: Russell I. Burleigh, Manager; Bruce Hangen, Musical Director and Conductor; Linda S. Bliss, Assistant Manager

UNIVERSITY OF MAINE/ORONO ORCHESTRA (E)
Music Dept.
Orono, ME 04469
(207) 581-1240
Staff: Ludlow Hallman, Conductor

UNIVERSITY OF SOUTHERN MAINE CHAMBER ORCHESTRA (E)
Music Dept.
100 Corthell Hall, College Ave.
Gorham, ME 04038
(207) 780-5265
Staff: Jerry Bowder, Conductor

MARYLAND

ANNAPOLIS SYMPHONY ORCHESTRA (D)*
P.O. Box 761
Annapolis, MD 21404
(301) 263-6734
Staff: John P.C. McCarthy, Manager; Leon Fleisher, Musical Director

BALTIMORE SYMPHONY ORCHESTRA (A)*
1212 Cathedral St.
Baltimore, MD 21201
(301) 727-7300
Staff: Joseph Leavitt, Executive Director; Sergiou Comissiona, Musical Director

COLUMBIA CHAMBER ORCHESTRA OF HOWARD COUNTY (D)*
5226 Harpers Farm Rd.
Columbia, MD 21044
(301) 730-4304
Staff: Holly H. Thomas, President; Yong Ku Ahn, Musical Director

COLUMBIA COMMUNITY BAND (D)*
P.O. Box 181
Columbia, MD 21045
(301) 596-3186
Staff: Edward Kerman, Musical Director; Marilyn Kelsey, President

GETTYSBURG SYMPHONY ORCHESTRA (D)*
1800 Cromwell Bridge Rd.
Baltimore, MD 21234
(301) 823-4686
Staff: Dr. William Sebastian Hart, Musical Director

GREATER BALTIMORE YOUTH ORCHESTRA (F)*
Essex Community College
Baltimore, MD 21237
(301) 682-6000
Staff: Carol Kingsmore, Manager; Christopher Wolfe, Conductor

HANDEL FESTIVAL ORCHESTRA (C)
3 Orleans Terrace
Kensington, MD 20895
(301) 946-7988
Staff: Stephen A. Simon, Musical Director; Eugene Dreyer, Business Manager

HARFORD COMMUNITY ORCHESTRA (D)*
5 Linwood Ct.
Bel Air, MD 21014
(301) 879-8927
Staff: A. Brinton Cooper, Board Chairman; Sheldon E. Bair, Musical Director and Conductor

MARYLAND SYMPHONY ORCHESTRA (D)*
P.O. Box 2157
Hagerstown, MD 21740
(301) 797-4000
Staff: Stephen Moore, General Manager; Barry Tuckwell, Musical Director

MARYLAND YOUTH SYMPHONY ORCHESTRA (F)*
5161 Phantom Ct.
Columbia, MD 21044
Staff: Angelo Gatto, Conductor; Mrs. Marvin Ginsberg, President

MONTGOMERY COLLEGE/ROCKVILLE ORCHESTRA (E)
Music Dept.
51 Mannakee St.
Rockville, MD 20850
(301) 279-5209
Staff: Ervin O. Klinkon, Conductor

MONTGOMERY COUNTY YOUTH ORCHESTRAS (F)*
7441 Bee Bee Dr.
Rockville, MD 20855
(301) 869-1483
Staff: Shirley Mae Ross, Information Officer; Chester Petranek, Conductor

NEW HARBOR CHAMBER ORCHESTRA (D)*
16 E. Lombard St.
Baltimore, MD 21202
Staff: Armand Baklor, Manager; Donald Anderson, Conductor

PEABODY SYMPHONY ORCHESTRA (E)*
One East Mount Vernon Pl.
Baltimore, MD 21202
(301) 659-8142
Staff: Linda G. Goodwin, Manager; Peter Eros, Conductor

PRINCE GEORGE COUNTRY SENIOR YOUTH ORCHESTRA (F)*
Instructional Services Offices
PG County Public Schools
Upper Marlboro, MD 20870
(301) 952-4265
Staff: Donald K. Smith, Supervisor; Peter Bay, Conductor

PRINCE GEORGES PHILHARMONIC ORCHESTRA (D)*
P.O. Box 323
Lanham-Seabrook, MD 20706
(301) 699-2540
Staff: Mark Ohnmacht, General Manager; Ray Fowler, Musical Director

UNIVERSITY OF MARYLAND BALTIMORE COUNTY (UMBC) SYMPHONY (E)
Dept. of Music
5401 Wilkens Ave.
Baltimore, MD 21228
(301) 455-2942
Staff: Robert Gerle, Conductor; Paul Covey, Manager

UNIVERSITY OF MARYLAND SYMPHONY ORCHESTRA (E)
Dept. of Music
College Park, MD 20742
(301) 454-2501
Staff: William Hudson, Conductor

MASSACHUSETTS

BERKSHIRE SYMPHONY (E)*
Williams College
Bernhard Music Center
Williamstown, MA 02167
(413) 597-2127
Staff: Jean S. Donati, Manager; Julius Hegyi, Conductor

BOSTON CLASSICAL ORCHESTRA (D)
551 Tremont St.
Boston, MA 02116
(617) 426-2387
Staff: F. John Adams, Conductor; Robert Brink, Manager

BOSTON CONSERVATORY OF MUSIC ORCHESTRA (E)
8 The Fenway
Boston, MA 02215
(617) 536-6340
Staff: Max Hobart, Conductor

BOSTON SYMPHONY ORCHESTRA (A)*
301 Massachusetts Ave.
Boston, MA 02115
(617) 266-1492
Staff: Thomas W. Morris, General Manager; Seiji Ozawa, Musical Director; Edward R. Birdwell, Orchestral Manager

BOSTON UNIVERSITY SYMPHONY ORCHESTRA (E)
School of Music
855 Commonwealth Ave.
Boston, MA 02215
(617) 353-3341
Staff: Josephy Silverstein and Victor Yampolsky, Conductors

BOSTON UNIVERSITY/TANGLEWOOD YOUNG ARTISTS ORCHESTRA (F)*
Third Floor
1019 Commonwealth Ave.
Boston, MA 02215
(617) 353-3386
Staff: Scott Schillin, Executive Director; Victor Yampolsky, Conductor

BRANDEIS SYMPHONY ORCHESTRA (E)
Brandeis University
Dept. of Music
South St.
Waltham, MA 02254
(617) 647-2557
Staff: David Hoose, Conductor

BROCKTON SYMPHONY ORCHESTRA (D)
18 Perkins Ave.
Brockton, MA 02401
(617) 586-7949
Staff: Martin Fireman, Manager

BROOKLINE SYMPHONY ORCHESTRA (D)
52 Oak Cliff Rd.
Newtonville, MA 02160
(617) 332-8229
Staff: A. Fred Prager, Managing Director

CAPE ANN SYMPHONY ORCHESTRA (D)*
P.O. Box 1343
Gloucester, MA 01930
(617) 281-0543
Staff: David L. Benjamin, Manager

CAPE COD SYMPHONY ORCHESTRA (C)*
West Barnstable, MA 02668
(617) 362-3258
Staff: Wesley DeLacy, Executive Director; Royston Nash, Musical Director and Conductor

CHAMBER ORCHESTRA OF CAPE ANN (D)
P.O. Box 1244
Gloucester, MA 01930
(617) 283-5334
Staff: Davis B. Carter, Manager; David Morrow, Musical Director

CHAMBER ORCHESTRA OF THE COMMONWEALTH (D)*
140 Walden St.
Concord, MA 01742
(617) 536-5039
Staff: Roger Davidson, Musical Director

CONCORD ORCHESTRA (D)*
P.O. Box 381
Concord, MA 01742
Staff: Margaret Nichols, President; Richard Pittman, Conductor

FIVE-COLLEGE SYMPHONY ORCHESTRA (E)
University of Massachusetts
Dept. of Music and Dance
Amherst, MA 01003
(413) 545-0642
Staff: Wayne Abercrombie, Lewis Spratlan, and Donald Wheelock, Conductors

GORDON COLLEGE ORCHESTRA (E)
Music Dept.
255 Grapevine Rd.
Wenham, MA 01984
(617) 927-2300

GREATER BOSTON YOUTH SYMPHONY ORCHESTRAS (F)
855 Commonwealth Ave.
Boston, MA 02215
(617) 353-3348
Staff: Nancy Lee Patton, Manager; Eiji Oue, Musical Director

GREATER FALL RIVER SYMPHONY ORCHESTRA (D)*
P.O. Box 2101
Fall River, MA 02722
Staff: Faust D. Fiore, Musical Director; David M. Cucinotta, President

HANDEL AND HAYDN SOCIETY (B)*
158 Newbury St.
Boston, MA 02116
(617) 266-3605
Staff: Jeffrey K. Neilan, General Manager; Thomas Dunn, Artistic Director

HARVARD-RADCLIFFE ORCHESTRA (E)
Harvard University
Music Building
Cambridge, MA 02138
(617) 864-0500
Staff: Dr. James Yannatos, Conductor

HOLYOKE COLLEGE/CIVIC ORCHESTRA (D)*
Holyoke Community College
Homestead Ave.
Holyoke, MA 01040
(413) 538-7000
Staff: Elroy A. Barber, Manager; Neal Gittleman, Musical Director

LONGY CHAMBER ORCHESTRA (E)
Longy School of Music
1 Follen St.
Cambridge, MA 02128
(617) 876-0956
Staff: Endel Kalam, Conductor

MASSACHUSETTS INSTITUTE OF TECHNOLOGY SYMPHONY ORCHESTRA (E)
14N-430
77 Massachusetts Ave.
Cambridge, MA 02139
(617) 253-2826
Staff: Karen M. Sauer, Manager; David Epstein, Musical Director and Conductor

NEW BEDFORD SYMPHONY ORCHESTRA (E)
Southeastern Massachusetts University
Music Dept.
Old Westport Rd.
North Dartmouth, MA 02747
(617) 999-8568
Staff: Eigi Oue, Conductor

NEW ENGLAND CHAMBER ORCHESTRA (D)
24 Quincy Rd.
Chestnut Hill, MA 02167
(617) 965-9863
Staff: Endel Kalam, Musical Director

NEW ENGLAND CONSERVATORY SYMPHONY ORCHESTRA (E)
290 Huntington Ave.
Boston, MA 02115
(617) 262-1120
Staff: Laurence Lesser, Music Director

NEW ENGLAND CONSERVATORY YOUTH/CHAMBER ORCHESTRA (F)*
290 Huntington Ave.
Boston, MA 02115
(617) 262-1120
Staff: Paul Marotta, Orchestra Manager; Benjamin Zander, Musical Director

NEW ENGLAND SYMPHONY ORCHESTRA (D)*
37 Cleveland St.
Arlington, MA 02174
(616) 646-1304
Staff: James Forte, Director; Rouben Gregorian, Conductor

NEWTON SYMPHONY ORCHESTRA (D)*
P.O. Box 124
Waban, MA 02168
(617) 965-2555
Staff: Constance G. Kantar, President and General Manager; Ronald Knudsen, Musical Director and Conductor

NORTHEASTERN UNIVERSITY SYMPHONY (E)*
307 Ell Building
360 Huntington Ave.
Boston, MA 02115
(617) 437-4128
Staff: James Forte, Manager; Dr. David Sonneschein, Conductor

PLYMOUTH PHILHARMONIC ORCHESTRA (D)*
P.O. Box 174
Plymouth, MA 02360
(617) 746-8008
Staff: Roberta J. Otto, Manager; Rudolf Schlegel, Musical Director

SPRINGFIELD SYMPHONY ORCHESTRA (A)*
56 Dwight St.
Springfield, MA 01103
(413) 733-2291
Staff: Wayne S. Brown, Executive Director; Robert Gutter, Musical Director and Conductor; Jane Hunter, Orchestral Manager

THAYER CONSERVATORY ORCHESTRA (E)*
Atlantic Union College
Main St.
South Lancanster, MA 01561
(617) 368-0041
Staff: Willam A. Jacobson, M.D., President; Mark Churchill, Musical Director

TRI-TOWN SYMPHONY ORCHESTRA
12 Homestead Way
Topsfield, MA 01983
Staff: Alfred Paranay, President; John Finnegan, Conductor and Musical Director

TUFTS UNIVERSITY ORCHESTRA (E)
Music Dept.
Medford, MA 02155
(617) 628-5000
Staff: Daniel Abbott, Conductor

WESTERN MASSACHUSETTS YOUNG PEOPLE'S SYMPHONY (F)*
56 Dwight St.
Springfield, MA 01103
(413) 733-2291
Staff: Nancy H. Brose, Operations Manager; Robert Gutter and Michael Greenebaum, Conductors

WESTFIELD STATE COLLEGE COMMUNITY ORCHESTRA (E)
Dept. of Music
Western Ave.
Westfield, MA 01086
(413) 568-3311, x356
Staff: David Crowe, Conductor

WHEATON CHAMBER ORCHESTRA (E)
Wheaton College
Dept. of Music
Norton, MA 02766
(617) 285-7722
Staff: Sophia Vilker, Conductor

WORCESTER CONSORTIUM ORCHESTRA (D)
Anna Maria College
Music Dept.
Sunset Lane
Paxton, MA 01612
(617) 757-4586
Staff: Robert Manero, Conductor

WORCESTER ORCHESTRA (C)
Memorial Auditorium
Worcester, MA 01608
(617) 754-3231
Staff: Joseph Silverstein, Conductor; Stasia B. Hovenesian, Executive Director

MICHIGAN

ADRIAN SYMPHONY ORCHESTRA (D)*
Adrian College
Music Dept.
Adrian, MI 49221
(517) 265-5161
Staff: Kathy L. Metz, General Manager; Dr. Arthur E. Shaw, Musical Director and Conductor

ALBION COLLEGE CHAMBER ORCHESTRA (E)
Music Dept.
Albion, MI 49224
(517) 629-5511, x 251
Staff: Dr. Philip Mason, Conductor

ALLEN PARK SYMPHONY (D)*
P.O. Box 145
Allen Park, MI 48101
(313) 928-8777
Staff: Lyman C. Perry, Manager; Robert Sadin, Conductor

ALMA SYMPHONY ORCHESTRA (D)*
Alma College
Alma, MI 48801
(517) 463-7213
Staff: Mallory B. Thompson, Conductor and Musical Director; Elizabeth M. McLaughlin, Business Manager

ANDREWS UNIVERSITY SYMPHONY (E)
Dept. of Music
Berrien Springs, MI 49104
(616) 471-7771
Staff: Dr. Charles Davis, Conductor

ANN ARBOR CHAMBER ORCHESTRA (D)*
P.O. Box 7026
Ann Arbor, MI 48107
(313) 996-0066
Staff: Linda Y. Marder, Manager; F. Carl Daehler, Musical Director

ANN ARBOR SYMPHONY ORCHESTRA (D)*
P.O. Box 1412
Ann Arbor, MI 48106
(313) 994-4801
Staff: Dr. Edward Szabo, Musical Director and Conductor

ARS MUSICA-THE BAROQUE ORCHESTRA (B)
Box 7473
Ann ARbor,MI 48107
(313) 662-3976
Staff: Lyndon Lawless, Musical Director

BATTLE CREEK SYMPHONY ORCHESTRA (B)*
P.O. Box 1319
Battle Creek, MI 49106
(616) 962-2518
Staff: Judith M. Costello, General Manager; William Stein, Musical Director

BAY VIEW FESTIVAL CHAMBER ORCHESTRA (E)*
P.O. Box 322
Alma, MI 48801
Staff: Dr. Joseph Henry, Musical Director and Conductor

CADILLAC AREA SYMPHONY ORCHESTRA (D)*
P.O. Box 435
Cadillac, MI 49601
Staff: Kathleen B. Baleiko, President; William R. Hayes, Jrs., Musical Director and Conductor

CALVIN COLLEGE ORCHESTRA (E)
Fine Arts Center
1801 E. Belt Line Dr., SE
Grand Rapids, MI 49506
(616) 949-1294
Staff: Douglas Scripps, Conductor

CENTER SYMPHONY ORCHESTRA (D)
Jewish Community Center of Metropolitan Detroit
6600 W. Maple Rd.
West Bloomfield, MI 48033
(313) 661-1000
Staff: Julius Chajes, Musical Director and Conductor

CENTRAL MICHIGAN UNIVERSITY SYMPHONY (E)*
Music Dept.
Mount Pleasant, MI 48859
Staff: Douglas Scripps, Conductor

DEARBORN SYMPHONY ORCHESTRA (C)*
P.O. Box 2063
Dearborn, MI 48123
(313) 565-6744
Staff: Philip Dillingham, Manager; Nathan Gordon, Musical Director

DETROIT SYMPHONY ORCHESTRA (A)*
Ford Auditorium
Detroit, MI 48226
(313) 567-9000
Staff: Oleg Lobanov, Executive Vice President and Managing Director; Antal Dorati, Conductor Laureate; Michael A. Smith, General Manager

EASTERN MICHIGAN UNIVERSITY SYMPHONY ORCHESTRA (E)
Music Dept.
Ypsilanti, MI 48197
(313) 487-0244
Staff: Russell Reed, Conductor

FLINT SYMPHONY ORCHESTRA (A)*
1025 E. Kearlsey St.
Flint, MI 48503
(313) 238-9651
Staff: Thomas Gerdom, Executive Director; Isaiah Jackson, Musical Director

GERMANIA SYMPHONY ORCHESTRA (D)
2099 Wheeler St.
Saginaw, MI 48607
(517) 792-8004
Staff: Dr. Kurt Tintner, Musical Director and Conductor

GRAND RAPIDS SYMPHONY ORCHESTRA (A)*
Exhibitors Building, Ste. 802
Grand Rapids, MI 49503
(616) 454-9451
Staff: David L. Thompson, General Manager; Semyon Bychkov, Conductor

GRAND RAPIDS YOUTH SYMPHONY (F)*
Grand Rapids Symphony Society
5th Floor, Exhibitors Building
Grand Rapids, MI 49503
(616) 454-9451
Staff: David McCoy, Conductor; William Basham, General Manager

GROSSE POINTE SYMPHONY ORCHESTRA (D)
1 Stratford Pl.
Grosse Pointe, MI 48230
(313) 886-6234
Staff: Felix Resnick, Conductor

HOPE COLLEGE ORCHESTRA (E)*
Dept. of Music
Holland, MI 49423
Staff: R. Robert Ritsema, Conductor

INTERLOCHEN ARTS ACADEMY ORCHESTRA (F)*
Inerlochen Center for the Arts
Interlochen, MI 49643
(616) 276-9221
Staff: Byron Hanson, Resident Conductor' Robert Marcellus, Musical Director and Principal Conductor; Ann Louise Hanson, Orchestra Manager

JACKSON SYMPHONY ORCHESTRA (D)*
212 W. Michigan Ave.
Jackson, MI 49201
(517) 782-3221
Staff: Ty Cross, Board Chairman; Stephen Osmond, Musical Director

KALAMAZOO JUNIOR SYMPHONY (F)*
714 S. Westnedge Ave.
Kalamazoo, MI 49007
(616) 349-7557
Staff: Vera C. Molloy, Business Manager; Robert W. Ritsema, Musical Director

KALAMAZOO SYMPHONY ORCHESTRA (B)*
426 S. Park St.
Kalamazoo, MI 49007
(616) 349-7759
Staff: Paul Ferrone, General Manager' Yoshimi Takeda, Musical Director and Conductor; Jan Spierenburg, Assistant Manager

KENT PHILHARMONIC ORCHESTRA (D)
143 Bostwick, NE
Grand Rapids, MI 49503
(616) 456-4865
Staff: Lynn Asper, Conductor

KEWEENAW SYMPHONY ORCHESTRA (E)*
Michigan Tech University
Sherman Arts/Humanities Center
Houghton, MI 49931
(906) 487-2207
Staff: Dr. Milton L. Olsson, Musical Director

LANSING SYMPHONY ORCHESTRA (B)*
230 N. Washington Sq., Ste. F.
Lansing, MI 48933
(517) 487-5001
Staff: Sandra Sutton Gaffe, General Manager; Gustav Meier, Musical Director and Conductor

LIVONIA YOUTH SYMPHONY SOCIETY (F)*
P.O. Box 2191
Livonia, MI 48154
(313) 474-1952
Staff: Donald Lewsader, Musical Director; Joanne Bryngelson, President

METROPOLITAN YOUTH SYMPHONY (F)*
P.O. Box 842
Southfield, MI 48037
(313) 538-2950
Staff: Mrs. Avra Weiss, Corresponding Secretary; Leif Bjaland and Douglas Bianchi, Principal Conductors

MICHIGAN CHAMBER ORCHESTRA (D)
60 Farnsworth
Detroit, MI 48202
(313) 886-6242
Staff: Andrew Massey, Principal Conductor

MICHIGAN YOUTH ORCHESTRA (F)*
University of Michigan
School of Music
Ann Arbor, MI 48109
(313) 764-1405
Staff: Robert Culver, Conductor; David Aderente, Ensemble Manager

WEST SHORE YOUTH SYMPHONY ORCHESTRA (F)*
P.O. Box 714
Muskegon, MI 49443
(616) 726-3231
Staff: Susan M. Schwartz, General Manager; Bruce Harwood, Conductor

MIDLAND SYMPHONY ORCHESTRA (B)*
1801 W. St. Andrews
Midland, MI 48640
(517) 631-4160
Staff: Grover B. Proctor, Jr., General Manager, Adrian Gnam, Musical Director

NORTHWESTERN MICHIGAN SYMPHONY ORCHESTRA (D)*
P.O. Box 1247
Traverse City, MI 49684
(616) 947-7120
Staff: Patricia M. Anderson, Business Manager, Donald Lewsader, Musical Director and Conductor

NORTHWOOD SYMPHONETTE (C)*
Northwood Institute
Midland, MI 48640
(517) 631-1600
Staff: Judith O'Dell, Executive Director; Don Th. Jaeger, Musical Director and Conductor

OAKLAND YOUTH SYMPHONY (F)*
3034 Southwind Dr.
Walled Lake, MI 48088
(313) 624-1540
Staff: Rosemary Lewis, Executive Director; Ervin Monroe, Musical Director and Conductor

OAKWAY SYMPHONY ORCHESTRA (D)*
P.O. Box 171
Farmington, MI 48024
(313) 476-6544
Staff: Nelda Di Blasi, Executive Director; Francesco Di Blasi, Conductor and Musical Director

PLYMOUTH SYMPHONY ORCHESTRA (D)
P.O. Box 467
Plymouth, MI 48170
(313) 455-6420
Staff: Johan van der Merwe, Conductor

PONTIAC-OAKLAND SYMPHONY ORCHESTRA (D)*
35 East Huron
Pontiac, MI 48058
(313) 334-6024
Staff: Philip C. Fouts, Executive Director; Dr. David Daniels, Musical Director

SAGINAW SYMPHONY ORCHESTRA (B)*
P.O. Box 415
Saginaw, MI 48606
(517) 755-6471
Staff: Nancy S. Smith, Manager; Leo M. Najar, Musical Director and Conductor

SAGINAW SYMPHONY YOUTH ORCHESTRA (F)*
P.O. Box 415
Saginaw, MI 48606
(517) 755-6471
Staff: Nancy Smith, Manager; Roderick J. Bieber, Conductor

SAINT CLAIR SHORES SYMPHONY ORCHESTRA (D)*
P.O. Box 334
Saint Clair Shores, MI 48080
Staff: Michael Upton, Orchestra Manager; Michael Krajewski, Musical Director

TWIN CITIES SYMPHONY (C)*
615 Broad St.
Saint Joseph, MI 49085
(616) 983-4334
Staff: Patrick O'Neall, General Manager; Robert Vodnoy, Musical Director

UNIVERSITY OF MICHIGAN ORCHESTRA (E)*
School of Music
Ann Arbor, MI 48109
(313) 764-557
Staff: David Aderente, General Manager; Gustav Meier, Conductor

WARREN SYMPHONY ORCHESTRA (B)
4504 East Nine Mile Rd.
Warren, MI 48091
(313) 754-2950
Staff: Richard Palais Eisenstein, General Manager; David Daniels, Musical Director

WAYNE STATE UNIVERSITY SYMPHONY ORCHESTRA (E)
Music Dept.
Detroit, MI 48202
(313) 577-1795
Staff: Valter Poole, Conductor

WEST BLOOMFIELD SYMPHONY ORCHESTRA (C)*
5640 W. Maple Rd., Ste. 201
West bloomfield, MI 48033
(313) 626-1560
Staff: Harold M. Patrick, President; Felix Resnick, Conductor and Musical Director

WEST SHORE SYMPHONY ORCHESTRA (C)*
P.O. Box 714
Muskegon, MI 49443
(616) 726-3231
Staff: Susan M. Schwartz, General Manager; Murray Gross, Musical Director and Conductor

MINNESOTA

BEMIDJI SYMPHONY (E)
Bemidji State University
Dept. of Music
Bemidji, MN 56601
(218) 755-2915
Staff: Timothy Perry, Conductor

BETHEL COMMUNITY/COLLEGE ORCHESTRA (E)
Bethel College
Dept. of Music
3900 Bethell Dr.
St. Paul, MN 55112
(612) 638-6400
Staff: Charles Olson, Conductor

BLOOMINGTON SYMPHONY ORCHESTRA (D)*
Bloomington Park and Recreation Department
2215 W. Shakopee Rd.
Bloomington, MN 55431
(612) 887-9601
Staff: Ishaq Arazi, Managing Director; Raymond Cutting, Musical Director

CARLETON COLLEGE ORCHESTRA (E)
Dept. of Music
Northfield, MN 55057
(507) 663-4347
Staff: Leslie Dunner, Conductor

CIVIC ORCHESTRA OF MINNEAPOLIS (D)*
1803 Hubbard Ave.
St. Paul, MN 55104

(612) 929-8293
Staff: Jim Streich, Librarian; Robert Bobzin, Musical Director; Mary L. Weddle, Manager

COLLEGE OF ST. CATHERINE/ COLLEGE OF ST. THOMAS ORCHESTRA (E)
Music Dept.
2004 Randolph
St. Paul, MN 55105
(612) 690-6000
Staff: David Aks, Conductor

CONCORDIA COLLEGE STRING ORCHESTRA (E)
Music Dept.
Hamline and Marshall
St. Paul, MN 55104
(612) 641-8248
Staff: Friedrich E. Brauer, Conductor

DULUTH-SUPERIOR SYMPHONY ORCHESTRA (B)*
506 W. Michigan St.
Suluth, MN 55802
(218) 727-7429
Staff: Jeff Prauer, General Manager; Taavo Virkhaus, Musical Director

FARGO-MOORHEAD SYMPHONY (E)
Moorhead State University
Dept. of Music
Moorhead, MN 56560
(218) 236-2101
Staff: Dr. J. Robert Hanson, Conductor

GUSTAVUS ADOLPHUS COLLEGE ORCHESTRA (E)
Dept. of Music
Saint Peter, MN 56082
(507) 931-7364
Staff: Gerald Lewis, Conductor

HEARTLAND SYMPHONY ORCHESTRA (D)*
P.O. Box 368
Little Falls, MN 56345
(218) 829-7415
Staff: Jan Wilcox, Administrative Assistant; Felix Spooner, Musical Director

ITASCA SYMPHONY ORCHESTRA (D)*
729 Northeast Sixth Ave.
Grand Rapids, MN 55744
(218) 326-9163
Staff: James W. Clarke, President; Raymond Kuuti, Director

LAKEWOOD ORCHESTRA (E)*
Lakewood Community College
White Bear Lake, MN 55110
(612) 770-1331
Staff: Robert Bobzin, Musical Director

MANKATO STATE UNIVERSITY ORCHESTRA (E)
Music Dept.
Mankato, MN 56001
(507) 389-2119
Staff: Cary Franklin, Conductor

MANKATO SYMPHONY ORCHESTRA (D)*
520 W. 10th St.
Mankato, MN 56001
(507) 388-2068
Staff: Lucille A. Northenscold, Business Manager; Jere Lantz, Musical Advisor

MESABI COMMUNITY ORCHESTRA (E)
Arrowhead Community College
Music Dept.
Virginia, MN 55792
(218) 741-9200
Staff: Jeanne Santa Doty, Conductor

MINNESOTA ORCHESTRA (A)*
1111 Nicollet Mall
Minneapolis, MN 55403
(612) 371-5600
Staff: Richard M. Cisek, President; Nevile Marriner, Musical Director; Robert C. Jones, General Manager

MINNESOTA YOUTH SYMPHONY (F)*
6121 Ridgeway Rd.
Minneapolis, MN 55436
(612) 929-5959
Staff: Phyllis Patch, Manager; Dr. Clyn Dee Barrus, Musical Director

MINNETONKA SYMPHONY ORCHESTRA (D)*
1001 Highway 7
Hopkins, MN 55343
(612) 935-4615
Staff: Mary Beth Stull, Manager; Roger Satrang Hoel, Musical Director

NORTH CENTRAL BIBLE COLLEGE CHAMBER ORCHESTRA (E)
Music Dept.
910 Elliot Ave., S.
Minneapolis, MN 55404
(612) 332-3491, x232
Staff: Helen Sorbo, Conductor

NORTHWESTERN COLLEGE/ COMMUNITY ORCHESTRA (E)
Division of Music
3003 N. Snelling
Roseville, MN 55113
(612) 636-4840
Staff: Lynn Erickson, Conductor

ROCHESTER COMMUNITY COLLEGE ORCHESTRA (E)
Music Dept.
East Highway No. 14
Rochester, MN 55901
(507) 288-6160
Staff: Willard Johnson, Conductor

ROCHESTER SYMPHONY ORCHESTRA (C)*
City Hall, Room 109
Rochester, MN 55901
(507) 285-8076
Staff: Marianne Segura, General Manager; Jere Lantz, Musical Director

SAINT CLOUD CIVIC ORCHESTRA (D)*
P.O. Box 234
Saint Cloud, MN 56301
Staff: Lee Gutteter, President; Duilio Dobrin, Musical Director and Conductor

ST. OLAF COLLEGE ORCHESTRA (E)
Music Dept.
Northfield, MN 55057
(507) 663-3180
Staff: Steven Amundson, Conductor

SAINT PAUL CHAMBER ORCHESTRA (A)*
Landmark Center
75 W. Fifth St.
St. Paul, MN 55102
(612) 292-3248
Staff: Pinchas Zukerman, Musical Director, Salvatore Venittelli, Orchestral Manager

SOUTHWEST MINNESOTA ORCHESTRA (D)*
Southwest State University
Music Dept.
Marshall, MN 56258
(507) 537-6833
Staff: Dr. Donald Fouse, Musical Director

UNIVERSITY OF MINNESOTA SYMPHONY ORCHESTRA (E)
School of Music
104 Scott Hall
Minneapolis, MN 55455
(612) 373-3546
Staff: Richard Massmann, Conductor

WILLMAR COMMUNITY ORCHESTRA (D)*
Willmar Junior College
Music Dept.
Willmar, MN 56201
Staff: Dr. Chet Sommers, Conductor

MISSISSIPPI

GREENVILLE SYMPHONY ORCHESTRA (D)*
21 Carol St.
Greenville, MS 38701
(601) 335-6148
Staff: Dr. Alex Solomon, President

GULF COAST SYMPHONY ORCHESTRA (D)
P.O. Box 4303
Biloxi, MS 39531
Staff: James E. Shannon, Conductor

JACKSON STATE UNIVERSITY ORCHESTRA (E)*
Music Education Dept.
Jackson, MS 39217
Staff: Dr. John P. Jones, Manager; J.J. Sampson, Conductor

JACKSON SYMPHONY ORCHESTRA (B)*
P.O. Box 4584
Jackson, MS 39216
(601) 960-1565
Staff: Carolyn Newton McLendon, General Manager; Lewis D. Dalvit, Musical Director and Conductor

JACKSON SYMPHONY YOUTH ORCHESTRA (F)*
P.O. Box 4584
Jackson, MS 39216
(601) 960-1565
Staff: Carolyn S. McLendon, Manager; Kathleen S. Robinson and Claudette Hampton, Co-Conductors

MERIDIAN SYMPHONY ORCHESTRA (C)*
P.O. Box 3173
Meridian, MS 39301
Staff: Vernon Raines, Conductor; Ed Edwards, Business Manager

MISSISSIPPI UNIVERSITY FOR WOMEN/COLUMBUS SYMPHONY (E)
Music/Fine & Performing Arts Division
P.O. Box 250-MUW
Columbus, MS 39701
(601) 328-6202
Staff: William Graves, Conductor

STARKVILLE/MSU SYMPHONY (D)*
P.O. Box 1271
Starkville, MS 39759
Staff: Julia Vissotto Saunders, Manager; Dr. Guy A. Hargrove, Conductor

TUPELO SYMPHONY ORCHESTRA (C)*
P.O. Box 474
Tupelo, MS 38801
(601) 842-8433
Staff: Clifton R. Jones, General Manager; Robert C. Austin, Musical Advisor

UNIVERSITY OF SOUTHERN MISSISSIPPI SYMPHONY ORCHESTRA (E)
Music Dept.
Hattiesburg,MS 39406
(601) 266-5363
Staff: Ronald McCreery, Conductor

MISSOURI

AUDITORIUM SYMPHONY ORCHESTRA (D)*
Saints Auditorium
P.O. Box 1059
Independence, MO 64051
(816) 833-1000
Staff: Jack R. Ergo, Conductor

BRENTWOOD SYMPHONY ORCHESTRA (D)
7150 Wise Ave.
St. Louis, MO 63117
(314) 647-6284
Staff: Dr. Henry Orland, Conductor; Edith Hougland, Manager

CIVIC SYMPHONY OF WEBSTER GROVES (D)*
P.O. Box 23942
Webster Groves, MO 63119
(314) 968-7040
Staff: Janet Chamberlin, President; Dr. Allen C. Larson, Conductor

KANSAS CITY SYMPHONY ORCHESTRA (A)*
The Lyric Opera
1029 Central
Kansas City, MO 64105
(816) 471-4933
Staff: Nat Greenberg, General Manager; Russell Patterson, Artistic Manager

KIRKWOOD SYMPHONY ORCHESTRA (D)
P.O. Box 3795
Kirkwood, MO 63122
(314) 878-8050
Staff: James E. Richards, Conductor; Florence Frager, President

LIBERTY SYMPHONY (D)
William Jewell College
Dept. of Music
Liberty, MO 64068
(816) 781-3806
Staff: Dr. Phillip C. Posey, Conductor

MERAMEC ORCHESTRA (E)
St. Louis Community College, Meramec
Music Dept.
11333 Big Bend Blvd.
Kirkwood, MO 63122
(314) 966-7639
Staff: Robert Charles Howard, Conductor

MIDWEST CHAMBER ENSEMBLE (D)
21 Bon Price Terr.
St. Louis, MO 63132
(314) 991-2618
Staff: Henry Orland, Conductor

MISSOURI SOUTHERN STATE COLLEGE/JOPLIN AREA SYMPHONY ORCHESTRA (E)
Music Dept.
Newman and Duquesne Rds.
Joplin, MO 64801
(417) 624-8100
Staff: William Elliott, II, Conductor

MISSOURI SYMPHONY SOCIETY (D)*
811 Cherry
P.O. Box 1121
Columbia, MO 65205
(314) 442-6677
Staff: Hugo Vianello, General Director and Conductor; Lucy Marino, Associate Manager

NORTHEAST MISSOURI STATE UNIVERSITY SYMPHONY (E)*
100 East Normal St.
Kirksville, MO 63501
Staff: Dr. William E. Fitzsimmons, Conductor

NORTHLAND SYMPHONY ORCHESTRA (D)*
P.O. Box 12255
Kansas City, MO 64152
(816) 741-2000
Staff: Dr. Theordore Albrecht, Musical Director; James Hammond, Manager

ORCHESTRA & CHORUS OF ST. LOUIS (B)
6548 Clayton Rd., Ste. 204
St. Louis, MO 63117
(314) 644-4454
Staff: Joel Revzen, Musical Director

PHILHARMONIC SOCIETY OF ST. LOUIS (D)
P.O. Box 591
St. Louis, MO 63188
(314) 842-3784
Staff: Robert Hart Baker, Conductor; Ina McNary, President

ST. JOSEPH SYMPHONY ORCHESTRA (D)*
120 S. Eighth St.
St. Joseph, MO 64501
(816) 233-0231
Staff: Matt Gilmour, Executive Director; Semyon Vekshtein, Musical Director

ST. LOUIS COMMUNITY COLLEGE/ FLORISSANT VALLEY SYMPHONY ORCHESTRA (E)
Music Dept. 3400 Pershall Rd.
St. Louis, MO 63115
(314) 595-4366
Staff: Ivy Allen, Conductor

ST. LOUIS CONSERVATORY ORCHESTRA (E)
560 Trinity
St. Louis, MO 63130
(314) 863-3033
Staff: Richard Holmes, Conductor

ST. LOUIS STRING ENSEMBLE (D)
95-19 Crain Ct.
St. Louis, MO 63126
(314) 843-7036
Staff: Carmine Ficocelli, Conductor and Manager

ST. LOUIS SYMPHONY ORCHESTRA (A*)*
Powell Symphony Hall
718 N. Grand Blvd.
St. Louis, MO 63103
(314) 533-2500
Staff: David J. Hyslop, Executive Director; Leonard Slatkin, Musical

ST. LOUIS SYMPHONY YOUTH ORCHESTRA (F)*
Powell Symphony Hall
718 N. Grand Blvd.
St. Louis, MO 63103
(314) 644-1696
Staff: Edith Hougland, Manager; Catherine Comet, Conductor

Director and Conductor; Joan T. Briccetti, Manager

SOUTHEAST MISSOURI STATE UNIVERSITY SYMPHONY (E)
Music Dept.
Cape Girardeau, MO 63701
(314) 651-2141
Staff: Dr. Gary Miller, Conductor

SOUTHWEST MISSOURI STATE UNIVERSITY SYMPHONY (E)*
Music Dept.
Springfield, MO 65804
(417) 836-5648
Staff: Jordan Tang, Musical Director

SPRINGFIELD SYMPHONY ORCHESTRA (C)*
1675 E. Seminole, Ste. G-200
Springfield, MO 65804
(417) 881-1641
Staff: Doris Rikard, General Manager; Charles E. Bontrager, Musical Director and Conductor

UMSL SYMPHONY ORCHESTRA (E)
University of Missouri, St. Louis
Dept. of Music
8001 Natural Bridge Rd.
St. Louis, MO 63121
(314) 453-0111
Staff: James Richards, Conductor

UNIVERSITY OF MISSOURI/KANSAS CITY CONSERVATORY SYMPHONY ORCHESTRA (E)
4949 Cherry St.
Kansas City, MO 64111
(816) 363-4300
Staff: Glenn Block, Conductor

UNIVERSITY OF MISSOURI PHILHARMONIC (E)
Music Dept.
Columbia, MO 65201
(314) 882-2604
Staff: Dr. Harry Dunscombe, Conductor

WASHINGTON UNIVERSITY CHAMBER ORCHESTRA (E)
Music Dept.
St. Louis, MO 63130
(314) 863-0100
Staff: Catherine Comet, Conductor

MONTANA

BILLINGS SYMPHONY ORCHESTRA (C)*
P.O. Box 602
Billings, MT 59103
Staff: Nancy S. Simmons, Manager; George Perkins, Conductor

BOZEMAN SYMPHONY ORCHESTRA (D)
P.O. Box 1174
Bozeman, MT 59715
(406) 587-8317
Staff: Creech Reynolds, Conductor

BUTTE SYMPHONY (D)*
1009 Placer St.
Butte, MT 59701
(406) 792-2546
Staff: Robert T. Taylor, Manager; Leopoldo Medina, Conductor

GLACIER ORCHESTRA AND CHORALE (D)*
P.O. Box 184
Whitefish, MT 59937

GREAT FALLS SYMPHONY ORCHESTRA (C)*
P.O. Box 1090
Great Falls, MT 59403
(406) 453-4102
Staff: Ricky Weatherspoon, Manager; Gordon J. Johnson, Musical Director and Conductor

HELENA SYMPHONY SOCIETY (D)*
P.O. Box 1073
Helena, MT 59601
(406) 422-1860
Staff: Bruce R. Thomas, Business Manager; John Lo Piccolo, Musical Director and Conductor

MISSOULA SYMPHONY ORCHESTRA (D)*
1001-B S. Higgins Ave.
Missoula, MT 59801
(406) 721-3194
Staff: Barrying H. Morrison, Executive Director: Thomas Elefant, Musical Director and Conductor

NEBRASKA

HASTINGS CIVIC SYMPHONY (D)*
Fuhr Hall
Ninth and Ash Sts.
Hastings, NE 68901
(402) 463-2402
Staff: Mel Cooksey, President; Dr. James Johnson, Conductor and Musical Director

LINCOLN CIVIC ORCHESTRA (D)*
Engel Hall
3800 S. 48th
Lincoln, NE 68506
(402) 488-2331
Staff: Dr. Robert Walters, Musical Director and Conductor; Doug Higgins, President

LINCOLN SYMPHONY ORCHESTRA (B)*
206 South 13th, Ste. 1315
Lincoln, NE 68508
(402) 474-5610
Staff: Patricia J. Steinke, Manager; Robert Emile, Musical Director and Conductor

LINCOLN YOUTH SYMPHONY ORCHESTRA (F)*
Public School Administration Building
P.O. Box 82889
Lincoln, NE 68501
Staff: June Moore, Conductor; Joseph L. Neal, Business Manager

NEBRASKA CHAMBER ORCHESTRA (D)*
3800 S. 48th, Room 208-A
Lincoln, NE 68506
(402) 483-7373
Staff: Jere Torkelsen, Office Manager; Bruce Ferden, Musical Director and Principal Guest Conductor

NORTHEAST NEBRASKA SINFONIA (D)
Wayne State College
Music Dept.
Wyane, NE 68787
(402) 375-2200, x 359
Staff: Christopher Bonds, Conductor

OMAHA AREA YOUTH ORCHESTRAS (F)*
325 Aquila Ct.
Omaha, NE 68102
(402) 342-3560
Staff: Lawrence David Eckerling, Musical Director/Manager; Margarette Smith, President

OMAHA SYMPHONY ORCHESTRA (A)*
310 Aquila Court Building
1615 Howard St.
Omaha, NE 68102
(402) 342-3560
Staff: William F. Kessler, General Manager; Thomas Briccetti, Musical Director; Mary K. Rauscher, Concert and Touring Manager

UNIVERSITY OF NEBRASKA/ LINCOLN SYMPHONY (E)
School of Music
Lincoln, NE 68588
(402) 472-2503
Staff: Dr. Robert Emile, Conductor

NEVADA

LAS VEGAS CIVIC SYMPHONY (D)*
Reed Whipple Center
821 Las Vegas Blvd. North
Las Vegas, NV 89101
(702) 386-6383
Staff: Iris Newman, Center Supervisor; William Gromko, Conductor

NORTH TAHOE SYMPHONY ORCHESTRA (D)
Sierra Nevada College
Music Dept.
800 Campbell Rd.
P.O. Box 4269
Incline Village, NV 89450
(702) 831-1314
Staff: Vahe Kochayan, Conductor

RENO CHAMBER ORCHESTRA (D)*
P.O. Box 547
Reno, NV 89504
(702) 786-1222
Staff: Gloria D. Thomas, General Manager; Vahe Khochayan, Musical Director and Principal Conductor

RENO PHILHARMONIC ASSOCIATION (C)*
P.O. Box 2391
Reno, NV 89505
(702) 329-1324
Staff: Edward S. Parsons, Jr., Managing Director; Ron Daniels, Conductor; Sharon L. Payne, Administrative Director

UNIVERSITY OF NEVADA/RENO SYMPHONY (E)
Music Dept.
Reno, NV 89557
(702) 784-6145
Staff: John Lenz, Conductor

NEW HAMPSHIRE

APPLE HILL CHAMBER PLAYERS (C)
Center for Chamber Music at Apple Hill
East Sullivan, NH 03445
(603) 847-3371
Staff: Tony Zito, Concert Manager

DARTMOUTH SYMPHONY ORCHESTRA (E)
Dept. of Music
Hopkins Center
Hanover, NH 03755
(603) 646-2520
Staff: Efrain Guigui, Conductor

KEENE STATE COLLEGE/COMMUNITY ORCHESTRA (E)
Dept. of Music
229 Main St.
Keene, NH 03431
(603) 352-1909
Staff: Eric Stumacher, Conductor

NASHUA SYMPHONY ORCHESTRA (D)*
P.O. Box 324
Nashua, NH 03061
(603) 880-7538
Staff: Janet Cochran, General Manager; Walter Eisenberg, Conductor

NEW HAMPSHIRE MUSIC FESTIVAL (C)*
P.O. Box 147
Center Harbor, NH 03226
(603) 253-4331
Staff: Philip L. Walz, Executive Director; Thomas Nee, Musical Director; Candace R. Ports, Assistant Director

NEW HAMPSHIRE SYMPHONY ORCHESTRA (C)*
P.O. Box 243
Manchester, NH 03105
(603) 669-3559
Staff: Lawrence J. Tamburri, General Manager; James Bolle, Musical Director and Conductor

NEW HAMPSHIRE YOUTH ORCHESTRA (F)*
Wheeler Professional Park
Box 648
Hanover, NH 93755
(603) 643-5085
Staff: Jeanne Sachs, Executive Director; John Kucer, Musical Director

UNIVERSITY OF NEW HAMPSHIRE SYMPHONY (E
Dept. of Music
Paul Creative Arts Center
Durham, NH 03824
(603) 862-1234
Staff: David Seiler and Ray Mann, Conductors

WHITE MOUNTAINS FESTIVAL ORCHESTRA (C)*
c/o Strout Realty
Box 216
Whitefield, NH 03598
(603) 444-2928
Staff: Gerard Schwarz, Conductor

NEW JERSEY

BERGEN PHILHARMONIC ORCHESTRA (D)*
P.O. Box 174
Teaneck, NJ 07666
(201) 843-0680
Staff: Bernice Sjogren, Librarian; Peter Leonard, Conductor and Musical Director

BERGEN YOUTH ORCHESTRA (F)*
41 Joyce Rd.
Tenafly, NJ 07670
(201) 569-1625
Staff: Lois Hargrave, Manager; Eugene Minor, Musical Director

CHAMBER SYMPHONY OF NEW JERSEY (D)
69 Prospect St.
Summit, NJ 07901
(201) 522-0937
Staff: Garyth Nair, Musical Director

COLONIAL SYMPHONY (D)*
36 Madison Ave.
Madison, NJ 07940
(201) 377-1310
Staff: Virginia K. Pierson, Executive Director; Paul Zukofsky, Musical Director and Conductor

COSMOPOLITAN CHAMBER ENSEMBLE OF NEW JERSEY (D)
P.O. Box 595
Elizabeth, NJ 07270
(201) 241-7097
Staff: Ira Kraemer, Musical Director

ELIZABETH CIVIC ORCHESTRA (D)
559 Winthrop Rd.
Union, NJ 07083
(201) 686-9626
Staff: Herman Toplansky, Musical Director and Conductor

GARDEN STATE CHAMBER ORCHESTRA (D)*
446 Grand Ave.
Leonia, NJ 07605
(201) 944-0893
Staff: Marjorie Harrison, General Manager; Frederick Storfer, Conductor and Musical Director

GARDEN STATE PHILHARMONIC SYMPHONY ORCHESTRA (D)*
230 Main St.
P.O. Box 269
Toms River, NJ 08753
(201) 349-6277
Staff: Morris Adler, Executive Vice President; Robert Hall, Musical Director and Conductor

GARDEN STATE PHILHARMONIC YOUTH ORCHESTRA (F)*
P.O. Box 269
Toms River, NJ 08753
(201) 349-6277
Staff: Thomas Hutchinson, Musical Director and Conductor; Peter Szap, Manager

GLASSBORO STATE COLLEGE/ COMMUNITY ORCHESTRA (E)
Dept. of Music
Glassboro, NJ 08028
(609) 445-6041
Staff: Dr. Robert Taylor, Conductor

GREATER TRENTON SYMPHONY ORCHESTRA (C)
28 W. State St., Room 705
Trenton, NJ 08680
(609) 394-1338
Staff: Evelyn B. Riegel, Administrative Assistant

HADDONFIELD SYMPHONY SOCIETY (D)*
P.O. Box 212
Haddonfield, NJ 08033
(609) 428-7540
Staff: Dorothy A. Clouser, Manager; Arthur Cohn, Musical Director

JERSEY CITY STATE COLLEGE/ COMMUNITY ORCHESTRA (E)
Music Dept.
Jersey City, NJ 07305
(201) 547-3151
Staff: David Dworkin, Conductor

LIVINGSTON COMMUNITY SYMPHONY (D)*
P.O. Box 253
Livingston, NJ 07039
(201) 992-1330
Staff: Nancy Berkley, President; Carolyn Hill, Conductor

MASTERWORK ORCHESTRA/ MASTERWORK CHAMBER ORCHESTRA (D)
Box 1037
Morristown, NJ 07960
(201) 538-1860
Staff: David Randolph, Conductor; Shirley S. May, Board President

MERCER COUNTY SYMPHONIC ORCHESTRA (F)*
The Lawrenceville School
Lawrenceville, NJ 08648
(609) 896-0400
Staff: Evelyn R. Krosnick, Manager; Dr. Matteo Giammario, Conductor

METROPOLITAN Y ORCHESTRA (D)*
YM-YWHA of Metropolitan New Jersey
760 Northfield Ave.
West Orange, NJ 07052
(201) 736-3200
Staff: Eleanor Kostant, General Manager; Brad Keimach, Musical Director

MONMOUTH SYMPHONY ORCHESTRA (D)*
480 Ocean Blvd.
Long Beach, NJ 07740
(201) 229-9347
Staff: Michael H. Goldwasser, President; John Carr, Musical Director

NEW JERSEY PHILHARMONIC (D)*
P.O. Box 834
Palisade Station
For Lee, NJ 07024
(201) 886-2800
Staff: Dr. Alvin L. Hoffman, President; Walter F. Engel, Conductor

NEW JERSY STATE ORCHESTRA (D)
P.O. Box 427
Neptune, NJ 07753
(201) 988-4747
Staff: Murray Glass, Conductor

NEW JERSEY SYMPHONY ORCHESTRA (A)
213 Washington St.
Newark, NY 07101
(201) 624-3713
Staff: John L. Hyer, Executive Director; Thomas Michalak, Musical Director and Conductor

NEW JERSEY YOUTH SYMPHONY (F)*
P.O. Box 477
Summit, NJ 07901
(201) 522-0365
Staff: Jane Donnelly, General Manager; George Marriner Maull, Musical Director

NEW PHILHARMONIC OF NORTHWEST NEW JERSEY (D)*
P.O. Box 286
Montclair, NJ 07042
(201) 746-5613
Staff: Karen Pinoci, General Manager; Leon Hyman, Musical Director

NUTLEY SYMPHONY ORCHESTRA (D)*
300 Franklin Ave.
Nutley, NJ 07110
(201) 751-3865
Staff: Edith Lodge, President; Dr. Ernest J. Ersfeld, Conductor and Musical Director

PARADISE CHAMBER ORCHESTRA (D)
P.O. Box 27
Neptune, NJ 07753
(201) 774-0028
Staff: Paul L. Paradise, Conductor and Manager

PHILHARMONIC ORCHESTRA OF NORTHERN NEW JERSEY (D)*
839 Frankling Lake Rd.
Franklin Lakes, NJ 07417
Staff: Walter W. Schoeder, Musical Director and Conductor

PLAINFIELD SYMPHONY ORCHESTRA (D)*
232 E. Front St.
Plainfield, NJ 07060
(201) 561-5140
Staff: John Graf, Jr., General Manager; George Marriner Maull, Conductor and Musical Director

RIDGEWOOD SYMPHONY ORCHESTRA (D)
59 Andover Ave.
Dumont, NJ 07628
(201) 385-0433
Staff: Walter F. Engel, Conductor; Robert V. Keihner, Jr., President

RUTGERS UNIVERSITY ORCHESTRA (E)
Music Dept.
73 Easton Ave.
New Brunswick, NJ 08903
(201) 932-7020
Staff: Jens Nygaard, Conductor

SOUTH ORANGE SYMPHONY ORCHESTRA (D)
70 N. Ridgewood
South Orange, NJ 07079
(201) 762-2058
Staff: Robert Helmacy, Conductor; Norman Cox, President

SUBURBAN SYMPHONY ORCHESTRA OF NEW JERSEY (D)*
P.O. Box 393
Cranford, NJ 07016
(201) 276-3589
Staff: E. Kassouf, President; Ira Kraemer, Musical Director

SUMMIT SYMPHONY ORCHESTRA (D)*
5 Myrtle Ave.
Summit, NJ 07901
(201) 322-4469
Staff: Catherine S. Carr, General Manger; Ira B. Kraemer, Musical Director

TRENTON STATE COLLEGE/ COMMUNITY ORCHESTRA (E)
Music Dept.
Hillwood Lakes, CN 550
Trenton, NJ 08625
(609) 771-2551
Staff: Dr. Martin LeBeau, Conductor

WESTFIELD SYMPHONY (D)*
6 Thomas Ct.
Westfield, NJ 07090
(201) 233- 6386
Staff: Margaret A. Glauch, Manager; Brad M. Keimach, Conductor

NEW MEXICO

ALBUQUERQUE YOUTH SYMPHONY (F)*
Albuquerque Public Schools
P.O. Box 25704
Albuquerque, NM 87125
(505) 842-3684
Staff: Dale E. Kempter, Musical Director and Conductor

CHAMBER ORCHESTRA OF ALBUQUERQUE (D)*
P.O. Box 4627
Albuquerque, NM 87196
(505) 247-0262
Staff: David Oberg, Musical Director and Conductor; Marion Dietrich, Administrative Coordinator

EASTERN NEW MEXICO UNIVERSITY ORCHESTRA (E)
School of Music
Portales, NM 88130
(505) 562-2376
Staff: Arthur M. Welker, Conductor

LAS CRUCES SYMPHONY (E)
New Mexico State University
Music Dept.
Box 3F, University Branch
Las Cruces, NM 88003
(505) 646-2421
Staff: Marianna Gabbi, Conductor

NEW MEXICO SYMPHONY ORCHESTRA (B)*
P.O. Box 769
Albuquerque, NM 87103
(505) 843-7657
Staff: William L. Weinrod, Exeuctive Administrator; Yoshimi Takeda, Musical Director

ORCHESTRA OF SANTA FE (C)*
P.O. Box 2091
Santa Fe, NM 87501
(505) 988-4640
Staff: Martha Hanson, Administrative Director; William Kirschke, Artistic Director and Conductor

ROSWELL SYMPHONY ORCHESTRA (C)*
P.O. Box 1321
Roswell, NM 88201
(505) 622-4700
Staff: Marjorie Wagner, Executive Secretary; John Farrer, Musical Director

WESTERN NEW MEXICO UNIVERSITY/ CIVIC SYMPHONY (E)
Dept. of Music
Silver City, NM 88061
(505) 538-6226
Staff: William Tietze, Conductor

NEW YORK

ALBANY SYMPHONY ORCHESTRA (B)*
19 Clinton Ave.
Albany, NY 12207
(518) 465-4755
Staff: Susan Bush, Manager; Julius Hegyi, Musical Director

ALFRED UNIVERSITY CHAMBER ORCHESTRA (E)
Division of Performing Arts
Alfred, NY 14802
(607) 871-2251
Staff: James W. Chapman, Conductor

AMERICAN COMPOSERS ORCHESTRA (C)*
170 West 74th St.
New York, NY 10023
(212) 362-8900
Staff: Lynda Dunn, Orchestral Manager; Dennis Russell Davies, Musical Advisor and Principal Conductor

AMERICAN SYMPHONY ORCHESTRA (A)*
161 W. 54th St., Ste. 1202
New York, NY 10019
(212) 581-1365
Staff: Benjamin S. Dunham, Executive Director; Moshe Atzmon and Giuseppe Patane, Principal Conductors

AMHERST SYMPHONY ORCHESTRA (D)*
325 Hopkins Rd.
Williamsville, NY 14221
(716) 836-3000
Staff: Arthur E. Pankow, General Manager; Dr. Joseph Wincenc, Musical Director

B.C. POPS ORCHESTRA (B)
233 Main St.
Vestal City, NY 13850
(607) 748-3384
Staff: David L. Agard, Artistic Director and Business Manager

BINGHAMTON SYMPHONY AND CHORAL SOCIETY (C)*
334-N Press Building
Binghamton, NY 13901
(607) 723-8242
Staff: Ernest S. Rose, Executive Director; John T. Covelli, Musical Director

BINGHAMTON YOUTH SYMPHONY (F)*
P.O. Box 1152
Binghamton, NY 13902
(607) 723-9531
Staff: Bernard J. Shifrin, Musical Director; Philip Grady, President

THE BOSTON GROUP (D)
25-44 91st St.
New York, NY 11369
(212) 672-1751
Staff: Louis Lopardi, Musical Director; Margaret Lundin, Business Manager

BRIGHTON SYMPHONY ORCHESTRA (C)*
Brighton Recreation Agency
2310 Elmwood Ave.
Rochester, NY 14618
(716) 442-2480
Staff: Carmen Clark, Executive Director; Dr. John Marcellus, Musical Director

BROCKPORT SYMPHONY ORCHESTRA (D)*
P.O. Box 344
Brockport, NY 14420
(716) 637-2115
Staff: Judity C. Tryka, Business Manager; James Walker, Musical Director

BRONX ARTS ENSEMBLE CHAMBER ORCHESTRA (C)
4450 Fieldston Rd.
Bronx, NY 10471
(212) 548-4445
Staff: William Schribner, Artistic Director

BRONX PHILHARMONIC (D)*
2235 Cruger Ave.
Bronx, NY 10467
(212) 881-6142
Staff: William Gunther, President and Musical Director

BRONX SYMPHONY ORCHESTRA (D)*
Herbert H. Lehman College
Music Dept.
Bedford Park Blvd., West
Bronx, NY 10468
(212) 960-8247
Staff: Joseph DelliCarri, Director

BROOKLYN PHILHARMONIC SYMPHONY ORCHESTRA (B)*
30 Lafayette Ave.
Brooklyn, NY 11217
(212) 636-4120
Staff: Maurice Edwards, Managing Director; Lukas Foss, Musical Director

BUFFALO PHILHARMONIC ORCHESTRA (A)*
26 Richmond Ave.
Buffalo, NY 14222
(716) 885-0331
Staff: Gary L. Good, Executive Director; Julius Rudel, Musical Director

CAECILIAN CHAMBER ENSEMBLE (D)
324 W. 101st St.
New York, NY 10025
(212) 865-8687
Staff: Gerardo Levy, Conductor; Stephen Baum, Manager

CATSKILL SYMPHONY ORCHESTRA (D)*
P.O. Box 14
Oneonta, NY 13820
(607) 432-6670
Staff: Charles W. England, General Manager; Charles Schneider, Musical Director

CHAPPAQUA ORCHESTRA (D)
6 Hayrake Ln.
Chappaqua, NY 10514
(914) 238-4534
Staff: Georges Petitpas, Chairman

CHAUTAUQUA SYMPHONY ORCHESTRA (B)*
Chautauqua Institute
Chautauqua, NY 14722
(716) 357-5635
Staff: Eugene Simonel, Business Manager; Varujan Kojian, Musical Director

CHEEKTOWAGA COMMUNITY SYMPHONY (D)*
140 Meadowlawn Rd.
Cheektowaga, NY 14225
Staff: Andrew A. Kulyk, General Manager; Marylouise Nanna, Conductor

THE CITY COLLEGE ORCHESTRA (E)
The City College of the City University of New York
Music Dept.
Convent Ave. and W. 139th St.
New York, NY 10031
(212) 690-5411, x5412
Staff: Fred Hauptman, Conductor

CLARENCE SUMMER ORCHESTRA (D)
8211 Lower East Hill Rd.
Colden, NY 14033
(716) 941-9312
Staff: Dr. Joseph Wincenc, Conductor; ARthur E. Pankow, Manager

CLARION MUSIC SOCIETY (B)
1860 Broadway, Room, 418
New York, NY 10023
(212) 765-8008
Staff: Louise H. Simon, Executive Director; Newell Jenkins, Musical Director

COLGATE CONCERT ORCHESTRA (D)*
Colgate University
Music Dept.
Hamilton, NY 13346
(315) 824-1000
Staff: Joyce Hawkins, Concert Manager; William Skelton, Conductor

COLLEGE OF ST. ROSE SINFONIA (E)
Music Division
432 Western Ave.
Albany, NY 12203
(518) 454-5178
Staff: J. Robert Sheehan, Conductor

COLUMBIA UNIVERSITY ORCHESTRA (E)*
Dept. of Music
703 Dodge Hall
New York, NY 10027
(212) 280-3825
Staff: Howard Shanet, Conductor

CONCERT ORCHESTRA OF ASIAN CONTEMPORARY MUSIC (D)
48-11 91st St.
Elmhurst, NY 11373

(212) 699-1406
Staff: Henry Shek, Musical Director and Conductor

COSMOPOLITAN SYMPHONY ORCHESTRA (D)
P.O. Box 1045, Ansonia Station
New York, NY 10023
(212) 873-7784
Staff: Simon Asen, Manager

COUNTY SYMPHONY OF WESTCHESTER (B)*
58 W. 58th St.
New York, NY 10019
(212) 753-0450
Staff: Robert M. Gewald, General Manager; Stephen Simon, Musical Director

CRANE SYMPHONY ORCHESTRA (E)
Crane School of Music
State University College of Arts and Science at Potsdam
Potsdam, NY 13676
(315) 267-2413
Staff: Richard Stephan, Conductor

DOCTORS' ORCHESTRAL SOCIETY OF NEW YORK (D)*
P.O. Box 138
New York, NY 10163
Staff: Dr. Harvey Salomon, Manager; Dr. David Fein, Conductor

DOWNEAST CHAMBER ORCHESTRA (F)*
248 E. 78th St.
New York, NY 10021
(212) 734-3904
Staff: Patricia A. Winter, Manager; Burton Kaplan, Musical Director

EASTMAN PHILHARMONIA (E)
Eastman School of Music
Univerity of Rochester
26 Gibbs St.
Rochester, NY 14606
(716) 275-3040
Staff: David Effron, Conductor

ELMIRA SYMPHONY & CHORAL SOCIETY (C)*
P.O. Box 22
Elmira, NY 14902
(607) 732-3011
Staff: Darrel L. Barnes, Musical Director and Conductor

EMPIRE STATE YOUTH ORCHESTRA (F)*
Empire State Plaza
P.O. Box 2111
Albany, NY 12220
Staff: Barry L. Richman, President; Burton Kaplan, Musical Director

FESTIVAL ORCHESTRA (E)
Concordia College
171 White Plains Rd.
Bronxville, NY 10708
(914) 337-9300
Staff: Ralph C. Schultz, Conductor

FINGER LAKES SYMPHONY ORCHESTRA (D)*
P.O. Box 305
Newark, NY 14513
(315) 986-3782
Staff: Nancy Magee, Manager; Robert R. Dwelley, Musical Director

GENESEE SYMPHONY ORCHESTRA (D)*
64 Walnut St.
Batavia, NY 14020
(716) 343-1123
Staff: George H. Smith, President; Karl Atkins, Conductor

GENESEO CHAMBER SYMPHONY (E)
State University of New York at Geneseo
Music Dept.
Geneseo, NY 14454
(716) 245-5824
Staff: James Walker, Conductor

GLENS FALLS SYMPHONY ORCHESTRA (D)*
Adirondack Community College
Music Dept.
Glen Falls, NY 12801
Staff: Michael John Stone, Musical Director; Dr. Vincent Koh, Manager

GREATER BUFFALO YOUTH ORCHESTRA (F)*
2468 Whitehaven Rd.
Grand Island, NY 14072
(716) 773-2913
Staff: Richard Myers, President

GREAT NECK SYMPHONY (D)*
P.O. Box 230
Great Neck, NY 11022
(516) 482-9210
Staff: Barbara L. Marcus, Exeucitve Director; Herbert Grossman, Musical Director

GREENWICH HOUSE ORCHESTRA (E)*
Greenwich House Music School
46 Barrow St.
New York, NY 10014
(212) 242-4770
Staff: Alice Jaffe, Intern Director; Edward Houser, Musical Director and Conductor

HAMILTON COLLEGE CHAMBER ORCHESTRA (E)
Music Dept.
Clinton, NY 13323
(315) 859-7331
Staff: Charles Schneider, Conductor

HOFSTRA UNIVERSITY SYMPHONY ORCHESTRA (E)
Music Dept.
1000 Fulton Ave.
Hempstead, NY 11550
(516) 560-5490
Staff: Seymour Benstock, Conductor

HORNELL SYMPHONY (D)*
P.O. Box 315
Hornell, NY 14843
(607) 324-2976
Staff: William Loree, President; Robert Dwelley, Conductor

HOUGHTON COLLEGE PHILHARMONIA (E)
School of Music
Houghton, NY 14744
(716) 567-2211
Staff: Herman Dilmore, Conductor

HUDSON VALLEY PHILHARMONIC ORCHESTRA (B)*
P.O. Box 191
Poughkeepsie, NY 12602
(914) 454-1222
Staff: Carla T. Smith, General Manager; Imre Pallo, Musical Director

HUNTER COLLEGE SYMPHONY (E)
Music Dept.
695 Park Ave.
New York, NY 10021
(212) 570-5736
Staff: Clayton Westermann, Conductor

INDEPENDENT SCHOOL ORCHESTRA (F)*
125 E. 87th St.
New York, NY 10028
Staff: Ann McKinney, Manager; Jonathan Strasser, Conductor

JUILLIARD ORCHESTRA/JUILLIARD SYMPHONY/JUILLIARD PHILHARMONIA (E)
The Juilliard School
Lincoln Center
New York, NY 10023
(212) 799-5000
Staff: Jorge Mester, Conductor

JUNIOR STRING CAMERATA (F)*
81-10 135th St., No. 714
Kew Gardens NY 11435
(212) 544-1277
Staff: Roberta Kaufman, Musical Director

JUPITER SYMPHONY ORCHESTRA (C)*
155 W. 68th St., No. 319
New York, NY 10023
Staff: Jens Nygaard, Conductor; Mary Alderice, Manager

LEVITE SYMPHONY ORCHESTRA (D)*
601 E. 18th St., No. 605
Brooklyn, NY 11226
(212) 859-7929
Staff: Armand Grunberg, General Manager; Myron Levite, Musical Director and Conductor

LITTLE ORCHESTRA SOCIETY (C)*
1860 Broadway, Ste. 1714
New York, NY 10023
(212) 757-5496
John Kordel, Managing Director; Dr. Dino Anagnost, Musical Director and Conductor

LONG ISLAND PHILHARMONIC (B)*
100 Baylis Rd.
Melville, NY 11747
(516) 293-2222
Staff: Howard Grant, Manager; Christopher Keene, Musical Director; Stuart Weiser, Operations Manager

MANHATTAN SYMPHONY/ MANHATTAN PHILHARMONIA (E)
Manhattan School of Music
120 Claremont Ave.
New York, NY 10027
(212) 749-2802

MANHATTANVILLE COLLEGE COMMUNITY ORCHESTRA (E)
Dept. of Music
Purchase, NY 10577
(914) 694-2200
Staff: Elliot Magaziner, Conductor

THE MANNES ORCHESTRA (E)
The Mannes College of Music
157 E. 74th St.
New York, NY 10021
(212) 737-0700
Staff: Sidney Harth, Conductor

MOZART FESTIVAL ORCHESTRA (D)
33 Greenwich Ave.
New York, NY 10014
(212) 675-9127
Staff: Baird Hastings, Conductor; Lily Hastings, Manager

NASSAU COLLEGE/COMMUNITY ORCHESTRA (E)
Nassau Community College
Dept. of Music
Garden City, NY 11530
(516 222-7447
Staff: Dr. Richard Brooks, Conductor

NATIONAL ORCHESTRA OF NEW YORK (E)*
National Orchestra Assocation
111 W. 57th St., No. 1400
New York, NY 10019
(212) 247-1228
Staff: Carol P. Madeira, Administrative Director; Alvaro Cassuto, Musical Director

NEW PALTZ COLLEGE COMMUNITY ORCHESTRA (E)
State University College at New Paltz
Music Dept.
New Paltz, NY 12561
(914) 257-2404
Staff: Lance Premezzi, Conductor

NEW REPERTORY ENSEMBLE (D)
61-25 171st St.
Fresh Meadows, NY 11365
(212) 359-4505
Staff: Dinu Ghezzo and Leo Kraft, Conductors

NEW YORK CHAMBER SYMPHONY (D)*
100 Riverside Dr., No. 15-A
New York, NY 10024
(212) 799-7633
Staff: Lois Heywood, Managing Director; Ronald Schweitzer, Musical Director

NEW YORK ORCHESTRAL SOCIETY (D)
40 W. 67th St.
New York, NY 10023
(212) 873-2872
Staff: Joseph Eger, Conductor; Eline McKnight, Manager

NEW YORK PHILHARMONIC (A)*
Avery Fisher Hall
132 W. 65th St.
New York, NY 10023
(212) 580-8700
Staff: Albert K. Webster, Executive Vice President and Managing Director; Zubin Mehta, Musical Director; Edward L. Alley, Orchestral Manager

NEW YORK PRO ARTE CHAMBER ORCHESTRA (C)
P.O. Box 652, Gracie Station
New York, NY 10028
(212) 876-1084
Staff: Raffael Adler, Artistic Director and Conductor

NEW YORK SINFONIA ORCHESTRA (D)
264 W. 91st St.
New York, NY 10024
(212) 874-2269
Staff: Dirk-Holger Bambeck, Musical Director and Conductor; Peggy L. Weiner, Manager

NEW YORK UNIVERSITY SYMPHONY ORCHESTRA (E)*
35 W. Fourth St., No. 777
New York, NY 10003
Staff: Dr. Dinu Ghezzo, Conductor

NYACK COLLEGE CHAMBER ORCHESTRA (E)
Division of Music
Nyack, NY 10960
(914) 358-1710
Staff: Dr. Glenn Koponen, Conductor

ONONDAGA CIVIC SYMPHONY ORCHESTRA (D)*
101 Horace Dr.
Syracuse, NY 13219
(315) 488-1902
Staff: Yvonne Barber, Chairman; William J. Mercer, Conductor

YOUTH SYMPHONY ORCHESTRA OF NEW YORK (F)*
Carnegie Hall 504
881 Seventh Ave.
New York, NY 10019
(212) 799-7633
Staff: Lois Heywood, Managing Director; Ronald Schweitzer, Musical Director

OPERA ORCHESTRA OF NEW YORK (B)
211 W. 56th St., Ste. 9-C
New York, NY 10019
(212) 246-7107
Staff: John D. Broome, Business Manager; Eve Queler, Musical Director

ORCHARD PARK SYMPHONY (D)*
33 Sherburn Dr.
Hamburg, NY 14075
(716) 649-6155
Staff: Jack F. Jaffe, Business Manager; Dr. Joseph Wincenc, Musical Director

ORCHESTRA DA CAMERA (B)*
129 East Dr.
North Massapequa, NY 11758
(516) 694-4195
Staff: Flori Lorr, Executive Director; Jesse Levine, Conductor

PHILHARMONIC SYMPHONY OF WESTCHESTER (D)*
9 W. Prospect Ave.
Mount Vernon, NY 10550
(914) 664-4353
Staff: Martin Rich, Conductor and Musical Director

PLATTSBURGH COLLEGE/ COMMUNITY ORCHESTRA (E)*
SUNY College of Arts and Sciences
Plattsburgh, NY 12901
Staff: William Phillips, Conductor

PURCHASE SYMPHONY ORCHESTRA (E)
State University of New York at Purchase
School of the Arts
Purchase, NY 10577
(914) 253-5000

QUEENSBOROUGH ORCHESTRA (E)
Queensborough Community College
Music Dept.
Bayside, NY 11364
(212) 428-0200, x410
Staff: Martin Canellakis, Conductor

QUEENS COLLEGE ORCHESTRAL SOCIETY (E)
Music Dept.
65-30 Kissena Blvd.
Flushing, NY 11367
(212) 520-7340
Staff: Martin Canellakis, Conductor

QUEENS FESTIVAL ORCHESTRA (D)*
18 Crest Road
Merrick, NY 11566
(516) 785-2532
Staff: Franklin Verbsky, Musical Director and Conductor; Alan Kuras, Business Manager

QUEENS SYMPHONY ORCHESTRA (B)*
99-11 Queens Blvd.
Rego Park, NY 11374
(212) 275-5000
Staff: Judith M. Linden, Executive Director; David Katz, Musical Director; Suzanne K. Ponsot, Associate Director

ROBERTS WESLEYAN COLLEGE/ COMMUNITY ORCHESTRA (E)
Music Dept.
2301 Buffalo Rd.
Rochester, NY 14624
(716) 549-9471
Staff: Dr. David Fray, Conductor

ROCHESTER CHAMBER ORCHESTRA (D)
950 East Ave.
Rochester, NY 14607
(716) 473-6711
Staff: David Fetler, Musical Director; Robert Eames, Manager

ROCHESTER PHILHARMONIC ORCHESTRA (A)*
108 East Ave.
Rochester, NY 14604
(716) 454-2620
Staff: Tony H. Dechario, General Manager; David Zinman, Musical Director

ROCHESTER PHILHARMONIC YOUTH ORCHESTRA (F)*
108 East Ave.
Rochester, NY 14604
(716) 454-2620
Staff: Mrs. Bernard Astill, Chairman; Howard Weiss, Musical Director

SCHNECTADY SYMPHONY ORCHESTRA (D)*
108 Union St.
Schenectady, NY 12305
(518) 399-0490
Staff: Dr. Charles D. Thompson, President

SINFONIA DA CAMERA OF NEW YORK (D)
48-11 91st St.
Elmhurst, NY 11373
(212) 699-1406
Staff: Henry Shek, Musical Director and Conductor

SKIDMORE COLLEGE CHAMBER ORCHESTRA (E)
Dept. of Music
Saratoga Springs, NY 12866
(518) 584-5000, x604
Staff: Dr. Anthony Holland, Conductor

STATEN ISLAND SYMPHONY (D)*
311 Howard Ave.
Staten Island, NY 10301
(212) 727-4161
Staff: C.A.P. van Stolk, Secretary; Robert Kogan, Conductor; Eugenia Bisignano, Manager

STATE UNIVERSITY OF NEW YORK AT CORTLAND ORCHESTRA (E)
Music Dept.
Cortland, NY 13045
(607) 753-2811
Staff: Lutz Mayer, Conductor

STATE UNIVERSITY OF NEW YORK AT FREDONIA ORCHESTRA (E)
Dept. of Music
Fredonia, NY 14063
(716) 673-3151
Staff: Harry John Brown, Conductor

STATE UNIVERSITY OF NEW YORK AT STONY BROOK CHAMBER SYMPHONY ORCHESTRA (E)
Music Dept.
Stony Brook, NY 11794
(516) 246-5672
Staff: David Lawton, Conductor and Musical Director

SYMPHONY FOR UNITED NATIONS (C)
40 W. 67th St.
New York, NY 10023
(212) 873-2872
Staff: Joseph Eger, Musical Director; Eline McKnight, Manger

SYRACUSE SYMPHONY ORCHESTRA (A)*
Civic Center, Ste.40
411 Montgomery St.
Syracuse, NY 13202
(315) 424-8222
Staff: Eleanor M. Shopiro, General Manager; Christopher Keene, Musical Director; Betsy Drew Robertson, Operations Manager

SYRACUSE SYMPHONY YOUTH ORCHESTRA (F)*
Civic Center, Ste. 40
411 Montgomery St.
Syracuse, NY 13202
(315) 424-8222
Staff: Elisabeth Rigsbee, Executive Manager; Ernest Muzquiz, Musical Director

UNIVERSITY OF ROCHESTER SYMPHONY (E)
Music Office
Rochester, NY 14627
(716) 275-2828
Staff: James Walker, Conductor; Roger Wilheim, Musical Director

UTICA SYMPHONY (C)*
212 Rutger St.
Utica, NY 13501
(315) 732-5146
Staff: TerryW. Ibbotson, Executive Director; Charles Schneider, Musical Director and Conductor

VASSAR COLLEGE ORCHESTRA (E)
Music Dept.
Poughkeepsie, NY 12601
(914) 452-7000
Staff: Jeremy Balmuth, Conductor

WASHINGTON SQUARE CHAMBER ORCHESTRA (D)
35 W. Fourth St.
New York, NY 10003
(212) 598-3491
Staff: Dinu Ghezzo, Conductor and Manager

WESTCHESTER CONSERVATORY SYMPHONY ORCHESTRA (F)*
20 Soundview Ave.
White Plains, NY 10606
(914) 761-3715
Staff: Elliot Magaziner, Musical Director and Conductor; Michael Candeloro, Orchestra Manager

WESTCHESTER SYMPHONY ORCHESTRA (D)
20 Overhill Rd.
Scarsdale, NY 10583
(914) 472-3595
Staff: Martin Canellakis, Conductor; Phyllis Ruttenberg, Manager

WEST END SYMPHONY (D)*
685 West End Ave.
New York, NY 10025
Staff: Eugene Gamiel, Musical Director; Roslyn Gamiel, Educational Director

WHITE PLAINS SYMPHONY ORCHESTRA (B)*
P.O. Box 35, Gedney Station
White Plains, NY 10605
(914) 725-1880
Staff: Leonard M. Moss, Chairman; Paul Dunkel, Musical Director

YORK/JAMAICA SYMPHONY ORCHESTRA (E)
York College
Music Dept.
150-14 Jamaica Ave.
Jamaica, NY 11451
(212) 969-4114
Staff: David Moore, Conductor

NORTH CAROLINA

ASHEVILLE SYMPHONY ORCHESTRA (C)*
P.O. Box 2852
Asheville, NC 28802
(704) 254-7046
Staff: Robert Hart Baker, Musical Director

BREVARD CHAMBER ORCHESTRA (D)*
P.O. Box 1547
Brevard, NC 28712
(704) 885-2896
Staff: Virginia Tillotson, Conductor; Jo Ane Anderson, President

BREVARD MUSIC CENTER (D)*
P.O. Box 592
Brevard, NC 28712
(704) 884-2011
Staff: Henry Janiec, Director; Robert M. Wood, President

CHARLOTTE POPS ORCHESTRA (C)*
110 E. Seventh St.
Charlotte, NC 28202
(704) 334-9887
Staff: Dr. Robert Maddox, Conductor and Manager

CHARLOTTE SYMPHONY ORCHESTRA (A)*
Spirit Sq.
110 E. Seventh St.
Charlotte, NC 28202
(704) 332-6136
Staff: Douglas A. Patti, General Manager; Leo B. Driehuys, Musical Director; Susan Magnuson, Assistant Manager

DUKE UNIVERSITY SYMPHONY ORCHESTRA (E)
Music Dept.
Box 6695, College Station
Durham, NC 27708
(919) 684-2534

DURHAM SYMPHONY ORCHESTRA (D)*
P.O. Box 1993
Durham, NC 27702
(919) 682-3836
Staff: Mitchell G. Simon, General Manger; Vincent Simonetti, Musical Director and Conductor

EAST CAROLINA UNIVERSITY SYMPHONY ORCHESTRA (E)
School of Music
Greenville, NC 27834
(919) 757-6851
Staff: Robert L. Hause, Conductor

EASTERN PHILHARMONIC ORCHESTRA (B)*
c/o Eastern Music Festival
200 N. Davie St.
Greensboro, NC 27401
(919) 373-4712
Staff: Joyce Beidler, Director of Financial Affairs; Sheldon Morgenstern, Conductor

ELON COLLEGE COMMUNITY ORCHESTRA (E)
Dept. of Fine Arts
Elon College, NC 27244
(919) 584-9711, x440
Staff: Malvin N. Artley, Conductor

FAYETTEVILLE SYMPHONY ORCHESTRA (D)*
302 Rush Rd.
Fayetteville, NC 28305
Staff: Linwood I. Sibley, Manager; Harlan F. Duenow, Musical Director

GREENSBORO CIVIC/CHAMBER ORCHESTRAS (D)*
200 N. Davie St.
Greensboro, NC 27401
(919) 373-2026
Staff: Barry Auman, Musical Director and Conductor; Lisa J. Burton, Business Manager

GREENSBORO SYMPHONY ORCHESTRA (B)*
200 N. Davie St.
Greensboro, NC 27401
(919) 373-4523
Staff: Margaret Faison, General Manager; Peter Paul Fuchs, Musical Director and Conductor

HENDERSONVILLE SYMPHONY ORCHESTRA (D)*
P.O. Box 1811
Hendersonville, NC 28739
(704) 693-6479
Staff: Peter Rickett, Conductor; Flora Larsen, President

NORTH CAROLINA SYMPHONY ORCHESTRA (A)*
P.O. Box 28026
Raleigh, NC 27611
(919) 733-2750
Staff: Dr. Thomas H. McGuire, Jr., Executive Director; Gerhardt Zimmerman, Artistic Director and Conductor; Hiram B. Black, General Manager

PIEDMONT CHAMBER ORCHESTRA (C)
200 Waughtown
Winston-Salem, NC 27107
(919) 784-7170
Staff: Dr. George Trautwein, Conductor; Roger R. Jones, Executive Director

RALEIGH CIVIC SYMPHONY (D)
North Carolina State University
Music Dept.
Box 5937, University Station
Raleigh, NC 27650
(919) 737-2981
Staff: Dr. Robert Petters, Conductor

ROCKY MOUNT/WESLEYAN COMMUNITY ORCHESTRA (E)
North Carolina Wesleyan College
Dept. of Music
Rocky Mount, NC 27801
(919) 442-7121
Staff: Stephen B. Wilson, Conductor

SALISBURY-ROWAN SYMPHONY ORCHESTRA (D)*
P.O. Box 4264
Salisbury, NC 38144
(704) 637-4482
Staff: Dr. Douglas Meyer, Conductor; Dr. Charles Turney, President

UNIVERSITY OF NORTH CAROLINA/ CHAPEL HILL SYMPHONY ORCHESTRA (E)
Dept. of Music
Chapel Hill, NC 27514
(919) 933-1039
Staff: David Serrins, Conductor

UNIVERSITY OF NORTH CAROLINA/ CHARLOTTE SYMPHONY (E)
Music Dept.
Charlotte, NC 28211
(704) 597-2474
Staff: Robert Glazer, Conductor

UNIVERSITY OF NORTH CAROLINA/ GREENSBORO SYMPHONY (E)
School of Music
Greensboro, NC 27412
(919) 379-5789
Staff: David H. Moskovitz, Conductor

UNIVERSITY OF NORTH CAROLINA/ WILMINGTON COMMUNITY ORCHESTRA (E)
Music Division
P.O. Box 3725
Wilmington, NC 28401
(919) 791-4330, x70
Staff: Dr. Joe Hickman, Conductor

WAKE FOREST UNIVERSITY ORCHESTRA (E)
Music Dept.
Winston-Salem, NC 27109
(919) 725-5000
Staff: Dr. David Levy, Conductor

WESTERN CAROLINA SYMPHONY ORCHESTRA (D)*
P.O. Box AG
Cullowhee, NC 28723
Staff: Lantford Cox, II, Conductor

WESTERN CAROLINA UNIVERSITY/ COMMUNITY ORCHESTRA (E)
Music Dept.
Cullowhee, NC 28723
(704) 227-7242
Staff: Dr. Thomas Tyra, Conductor

WESTERN PIEDMONT SYMPHONY (C)*
Old City Hall
30 Third St., NW
Hickory, NC 28601
(704) 324-8603
Staff: Marian C. Belk, Manager; Martin Bellar, Musical Director

WINSTON-SALEM SYMPHONY ORCHESTRA (B)*
610 Coliseum Dr.
Winston-Salem, NC 27106
(919) 725-1035
Staff: Alan Wynn Cooper, General Manager; Peter J. Perret, Musical Director and Conductor

YOUTH SYMPHONY OF THE CAROLINAS (F)*
110 E. Seventh St.
Charlotte, NC 28202
(704) 332-6136
Staff: Kirk D.N. Trevor, Conductor; Jonathan M. Kromer, Staff Coordinator

NORTH DAKOTA

BISMARCK-MANDAN SYMPHONY ORCHESTRA (C)*
P.O. Box 2031
Bismarck, ND 58502
(701) 258-8345
Staff: Nancy A. Swenson, Executive Director; Loran L. Eckroth, Conductor and Musical Director

FARGO-MOORHEAD SYMPHONY ORCHESTRA (C)*
P.O. Box 1753
Fargo, ND 58107

(218) 233-8397
Staff: Evelyn Nelson, Manager; J. Robert Hanson, Conductor

GREATER GRAND FORKS SYMPHONY (D)*
P.O. Box 97
Grand Forks, ND 58201
(701) 775-6195
Staff: Ben G. Gustafson, Treasurer and Executive Secretary; Jack L. Miller, Conductor

MINOT SYMPHONY ORCHESTRA (D)*
P.O. Box 461
Minot, ND 58701
(701) 839-8844
Staff: Mary L. Leiphon, Manager; Dr. Robert C. Quebbeman, Musical Director and Conductor

WILLISTON STRINGS (E)
University of North Dakota, Williston Center
Box 1326
Williston, ND 58801
(701) 572-6736
Staff: Roberta Domrese, Conductor

OHIO

AKRON SYMPHONY ORCHESTRA (B)*
Edward J. Thomas Peforming Arts Hall
Center and Hill Sts.
Akron, OH 44325
(216) 535-8131
Staff: Robert L. Henke, General Manager; Louis Lane, Conductor Emeritus and Artistic Advisor

AKRON YOUTH SYMPHONY (F)*
Edward J. Thomas Performing Arts Hall
Center and Hill Sts.
Akron, OH 44325
(216) 535-8131
Staff: Robert L. Henke, General Manager; Frank Diliberto, Conductor

ALLEGRO CHAMBER PLAYERS (F)*
400 W. Dorothy Ln.
Kettering, OH 45429
Staff: Kenneth R. Miller, Conductor and Manager

ASHLAND SYMPHONY ORCHESTRA (E)
Ashland College
Music Dept.
Ashland, OH 44805
(419 289-4085
Staff: Albert-George Schram, Conductor

BALDWIN-WALLACE COLLEGE SYMPHONY ORCHESTRA (E)
Conservatory of Music
Berea, OH 44017
(216) 826-2377
Staff: Dwight Oltman, Conductor and Manager

BOWLING GREEN PHILHARMONIA (E)*
Bowling Green State University
College of Musical Arts
Bowling Green, OH 43403
(419) 372-2181
Staff: Grzegorz Nowak, Musical Director; Ron Brooker, Manager

CANTON SYMPHONY ORCHESTRA (B)*
1001 Market Ave., No.
Canton, OH 44702
(216) 452-3434
Staff: Linda V. Moorhouse, General Manager; Gerhardt Zimmermann, Musical Director

CANTON YOUTH SYMPHONY (F)*
1001 Market Ave., No.
Canton, OH 44702
(216) 452-3434
Staff: Linda V. Moorhouse, Manager; Peter Wilson, Conductor

CENTRAL OHIO SYMPHONY ORCHESTRA (D)*
Ohio Wesleyan University
Delaware, OH 43015
(614) 369-4431
Staff: Dr. Glenn A. Muegel, Musical Director and Conductor; Charles R. Houser, President

CINCINNATI CHAMBER ORCHESTRA (D)
700 Walnut St., Ste. 412
Cincinnati, OH 45202
(513) 241-6405
Staff: Paul Nadler, Conductor

CINCINNATI SYMPHONY ORCHESTRA (A)*
1241 Elm St.
Cincinnati, OH 45210
(513) 621-1919
Staff: Steven I. Monder, General Manager; Michael Gielen, Musical Director; Judith Arron, Manager

CINCINNATI YOUTH SYMPHONY ORCHESTRA (F)*
1241 Elm St.
Cincinnati, OH 45210
(513) 621-1919
Staff: Carol Hubler, Production Manager; Teri Murai, Musical Director and Conductor

CLEVELAND INSTITUTE OF MUSIC YOUTH ORCHESTRA (F)*
11021 East Blvd.
Cleveland, OH 44106
(216) 791-5165
Staff: Eleanor Holt, Manager; Carl Topilow, Conductor

CLEVELAND ORCHESTRA (A)*
Severance Hall
11001 Euclid Ave.
Cleveland, OH 44106
(216) 231-7300
Staff: Kenneth Haas, General Manager; Christoph von Dohnanyi, Musical Director and Designer; J. Christopher Fahlman, Assistant General Manager

CLEVELAND STATE UNIVERSITY CHAMBER SYMPHONY (E)
Music Dept.
Cleveland, OH 44115
(216) 687-2000
Staff: Edwin London, Conductor

COLUMBUS SYMPHONY ORCHESTRA (A)*
101 East Town St.
Columbus, OH 43215
(614) 224-5281
Staff: Darrell Edwards, General Manager; Gary Sheldon, Interim Musical Director; Rebecca Bass, Assistant Manager

COLUMBUS SYMPHONY YOUTH ORCHESTRA (F)*
101 East Town St.
Columbus, OH 43215
(614) 224-5281
Staff: Albert-George Schram, Musical Director and Conductor; Linda Pearlstein, President

DANA SYMPHONY ORCHESTRA (E)*
Youngstown State University
410 Wick Ave.
Youngstown, OH 44555
(216) 742-3624
Staff: Michael D. Gelfand and John Wilcox, Co-Conductors

DAYTON PHILHARMONIC ORCHESTRA (B)*
Montgomery County's Memorial Hall
125 E. First St.
Dayton, OH 45402
(513) 224-3521
Staff: David L. Pierson, General Manager; Charles Wendelken-Wilson, Musical Director

DAYTON PHILHARMONIC YOUTH ORCHESTRA (F)*
Montgomery County's Memorial Hal
125 E. First St.
Dayton, OH 45402
(513) 224-3521
Staff: William J. Steinhort, Conductor

HAMILTON-FAIRFIELD SYMPHONY (D)*
319 N. Third St.
Hamilton, OH 45011
(513) 863-8873
Staff: David L. Dunevant, Manager; H. Teri Murai, Musical Director and Conductor

HEIDELBERG SYMPHONY ORCHESTRA (E)
Heidelberg College
Tiffin, OH 44883
(419) 447-7552
Staff: Paul Schmid, Musical Director and Conductor

KENT STATE UNIVERSITY SINFONIA (E)
School of Music
Kent, OH 44242
(216) 672-2172

KNOX COUNTY SYMPHONY (E)
Mount Vernon Nazarene College
Music Dept.
Martinsburg Rd.
Mount Vernon, OH 43050
(614) 397-1244
Staff: Albert-George Schram, Conductor

LAKELAND CIVIC ORCHESTRA (D)*
Lakeland Community College
Mentor, OH 44060
(216) 953-7135
Staff: Charles Frank, Manager; Peter Wilson, Director

LICKING COUNTY SYMPHONY ORCHESTRA (E)
Denison University
Dept. of Music
Granville, OH 43023
(614) 587-6220
Staff: Frank J. Bellino, Conductor

LIMA SYMPHONY ORCHESTRA (C)*
P.O. Box 1651
Lima, OH 45802
(419) 222-5701
Staff: Joseph Firszt, Musical Director and Conductor; Estelle Blattner, Business Manager

MANSFIELD SYMPHONY ORCHESTRA (C)*
354 Park Ave. West
Mansfield, OH 44906
(419) 524-5927
Staff: Janet E. Keeler, Orchestral Manager; Jeff Holland Cook, Conductor and Musical Director

MARIETTA COLLEGE-CIVIC SYMPHONETTE (D)*
Edward McTaggart Dept. of Music
Marietta, OH 45750
(614) 374-4687
Staff: Dr. Harold Mueller, Conductor

MIDDLETOWN SYMPHONY ORCHESTRA (D)*
130 N. Verity Parkway
Middletown, OH 45042
(513) 422-4519
Staff: Gerald R. O'Connor, President; Carmon DeLoene, Conductor

MOUNT UNION COLLEGE ORCHESTRA (E)
Dept. of Music
Alliance, OH 44601
(216) 823-3206
Staff: Peter Synnestvedt, Conductor

NORTHERN OHIO YOUTH ORCHESTRAS (F)*
P.O. Box 427
Oberlin, OH 44074
(216) 774-1576
Staff: Karan Cutler, General Manager; Priscilla Smith, Musical Director

OBERLIN COLLEGE SYMPHONY AND CHAMBER ORCHESTRA (E)*
Oberlin Conservatory of Music
Oberlin, OH 44074
(216) 775-8200
Staff: Robert Baustian, Conductor

OHIO CHAMBER ORCHESTRA (B)*
11125 Magnolia Dr.
Cleveland, OH 44106
(216) 229-4144
Staff: Randall Rosenbaum, General Manager; Dwight Oltman, Musical Director

OHIO NORTHERN UNIVERSITY CHAMBER ORCHESTRA (E)
Music Dept.
525 S. Main St.
Ada, OH 45810
(419) 772-2150
Staff: Herbert Murphy, Conductor

OHIO UNIVERSITY SYMPHONY ORCHESTRA (E)
School of Music
Athens, OH 45701
(614) 594-5587
Staff: Joseph Henry, Conductor

PRO MUSICA CHAMBER ORCHESTRA (D)
1870 Madison Rd.
Cincinnati, OH 45206
(513) 281-1270
Staff: Thomas J. Widlar, Musical Director

PRO MUSICA CHAMBER ORCHESTRA OF COLUMBUS (C)*
444 E. Broad St.
Columbus, OH 43215
(614) 464-0066
Staff: Richard Early, General Manager; Dr. Timothy Russell, Musical Director

SHAKER SYMPHONY ORCHESTRA (D)
2843 Edgehill Rd.
Cleveland, OH 44118
(216) 321-3704
Staff: Tiberius Sylvani, Conductor; Dr. H.M. Schackne, Manager

SOUTHEASTERN OHIO SYMPHONY ORCHESTRA (D)*
P.O. Box 42
New Concord, OH 43762
Staff: Karen R. Brown, Manager; Dr. Donald G. McGinnis, Musical Director

SPRINGFIELD SYMPHONY ORCHESTRA (B)*
P.O. Box 1374
Springfield, OH 45501
(513) 325-8100
Staff: Janet Beck, General Manager; John E. Ferritto, Musical Director

TOLEDO SYMPHONY ORCHESTRA (A)
One Stranahan Square
Toledo, OH 43604
(419) 241-1272
Staff: Gary W. Batts, Managing Director; Yuval Zaliouk, Musical Director and Conductor

TOLEDO YOUTH ORCHESTRA (F)*
3709 Willys Pkwy.
Toledo, OH 43612
(419) 478-6934
Staff: Michael A. Miller, Conductor; Jane Zbinden and Sue Lynn Sess, Co-Managers

TUSCARAWAS PHILHARMONIC (D)*
P.O. Box 406
New Philadelphia, OH 44663
(216) 343-8430
Staff: Patricia A. Fritz, Business Manager; Margery Henke, Conductor

UNIVERSITY OF CINCINNATI PHILHARMONIA AND CONCERT ORCHESTRAS (E)*
College-Conservatory of Music
Cincinnati, OH 45221
(513) 475-2696
Staff: Mack Richardson, Assistant Conductor; Gerhard Samuel, Musical Director and Conductor of Philharmonic Orchestra; Teri Murai, Conductor of Concert Orchestra

UNIVERSITY OF DAYTON STRINGS (E)
Music Division
Dayton, OH 45469
(513) 229-3936
Staff: Dr. Phillip Magnuson, Conductor

UNIVERSITY OF TOLEDO ORCHESTRA (E)
Music Dept.
2801 W. Bancroft St.
Toledo, OH 43606
(419) 537-2447
Staff: Bernard Sanchez, Conductor

WARREN CHAMBER ORCHESTRA (D)*
P.O. Box 48
Warren, OH 44482
(216) 856-4444
Staff: Dr. George Zack, Conductor and Musical Director; Robert Faulkner, Manager

WESTERVILLE CIVIC SYMPHONY AT OTTERBEIN COLLEGE (E)
Dept. of Music
Westerville, OH 43081
(614) 890-3000
Staff: Bruce Wood, Conductor

WOOSTER SYMPHONY ORCHESTRA (E)
College of Wooster
Music Dept.
Wooster, OH 44691
(216) 264-1234
Staff: Nancy B. Garlick, Conductor

WRIGHT STATE UNIVERSITY/ COMMUNITY ORCHESTRA (E)
Music Dept.
Dayton, OH 45435
(513) 873-2346
Staff: Dr. Robert Young, Conductor

YOUNGSTOWN SYMPHONY ORCHESTRA (B)*
260 Federal Plaza West
Youngstown, OH 44503
(216) 744-4269
Staff: Paul R. Bunker, General Manager; Peter Leonard, Musical Director

OKLAHOMA

BARTLESVILLE SYMPHONY ORCHESTRA (D)*
P.O. Box 263
Bartlesville, OK 74003
(918) 333-6925
Staff: Latrice Ringham, Corresponding Secretary; Lauren Green, Musical Director

CENTRAL STATE UNIVERSITY ORCHESTRA (E)
Music Dept.
Edmond, OK 73034
(405) 341-2980
Staff: Dr. Robert Strong, Conductor

CHAMBER ORCHESTRA OF OKLAHOMA CITY (D)*
P.O. Box 54956
Oklahoma City, OK 73154
(405) 525-3112
Staff: Helen Roberts, General Manager; William Jenks, Musical Director

ENID-PHILLIPS SYMPHONY (D)*
2013 W. Garriott Rd.
Enid, OK 73701
(405) 237-0134
Staff: Al Jensen, Business Manager; Dr. Max Tromblee, Conductor

LAWTON PHILHARMONIC ORCHESTRA (C)*
P.O. Box 1473
Lawton, OK 73502
(405) 248-2001
Staff: K.T. Wiggins, General Manager; Dr. Jack W. Bowman, Conductor and Musical Director

OKLAHOMA CITY JUNIOR SYMPHONY (F)*
P.O. Box 92
Oklahoma City, OK 73101
Staff: T. Burns Westman, Conductor; Robert C. Van Laanen, President

OKLAHOMA CITY UNIVERSITY/ METROPOLITAN SYMPHONY ORCHESTRA (E)
School of Music & Performing Arts
2501 N. Blackwelder
Oklahoma City, OK 73106
(405) 521-5315
Staff: Dr. Ray Luke, Conductor

OKLAHOMA SINFONIA AND CHORALE (C)*
P.O. Box 4633
Tulsa, OK 74104
(918) 744-5069
Staff: Karen Walker, Administrative Manager; Dr. G. Barry Epperley, Musical Director

OKLAHOMA STATE UNIVERSITY SYMPHONY ORCHESTRA (E)
Dept. of Music
121 Seretean Center for the Performing Arts
Stillwater, OK 74078
(405) 624-6133
Staff: Eric Fried, Conductor

OKLAHOMA SYMPHONY ORCHESTRA (A)*
512 Civic Center Music Hall
Oklahoma City, OK 73102
(405) 232-4292
Staff: Patrick B. Alexander, General Manger; Luis Herrera de la Fuente, Musical Director; Terri L. Ledford, Assistant Manager

OKLAHOMA YOUTH ORCHESTRA (F)*
Route 1, Box 149 JJ
Norman, OK 73069
(405) 364-8850
Staff: Legh W. Burns, Conductor; Doug Freebern, President

PONCA CITY CIVIC ORCHESTRA (D)*
2413 Canterbury
Ponca City, OK 74601
(405) 762-8539
Staff: Mary E. Martin, Acting Manager; Wayne E. Muller, Conductor

TULSA PHILHARMONIC ORCHESTRA (A)*
Harwelden
2210 S. Main
Tulsa, OK 74114
(918) 584-2533
Staff: Nancy Sies, Executive Director; Joel Lazar, Musical Director and Conductor; John Scott, Orchestral Manager

TULSA YOUTH SYMPHONY ORCHESTRA (F)*
2210 S. Main St.
Tulsa, OK 74114
(918) 584-2533
Staff: Ronald Wheeler, Conductor and Administrator; Roxanna Lorton, President

UNIVERSITY OF OKLAHOMA SYMPHONY ORCHESTRA (E)
School of Music
Norman, OK 73019
(405) 325-2081
Staff: L.W. Burns, Conductor

UNIVERSITY OF TULSA SYMPHONY ORCHESTRA (E)
School of Music
600 S. College
Tulsa, OK 74104
(918) 592-6000

OREGON

BLUE MOUNTAIN COMMUNITY COLLEGE ORCHESTRA (E)
2411 N.W. Carden
P.O. Box 100
Pendleton, OR 97801
(503) 276-1260
Staff: John Weddle, Conductor

CHAMBER MUSIC SOCIETY OF OREGON (D)*
1935 N.E. 59th Ave.
Portland, OR 97213
(503) 287-2175
Staff: W. DeLorenzo, Executive Director; Eugene Kaza, Musical Director

CHEHALEM SYMPHONY ORCHESTRA (E)
George Fox College
Newberg, OR 97132
(503) 538-8383
Staff: Dr. Dennis Hagen, Conductor

EDINBORO COLLEGE/COMMUNITY ORCHESTRA (E)
Edinboro State College
201 Heather Hall
Edinboro, PA 16444
(814) 732-2507
Staff: Dr. Paul A. Martin, Conductor

EUGENE SYMPHONY ORCHESTRA (B)*
1231 Olive St.
Eugene, OR 97401
(503) 687-9487
Staff: James W. Reeves, General Manager; William McGlaughlin, Musical Director and Conductor

EUGENE YOUTH SYMPHONY (F)*
3750 University St.
Eugene, OR 97405
(503) 345-0715
Staff: Richard M. Long, Conductor and Musical Director; Richard Vanberg, President

GRANDE RONDE SYMPHONY ORCHESTRA (D)*
P.O. Box 842
La Grande, OR 97850
(503) 963-2171
Staff: John L. Cobb, Musical Director; Eric DeLora, Manager

MARYLHURST SYMPHONY ORCHESTRA (E)
Marylhurst College
Music Division
Marylhurst, OR 97036
(503) 636-8141
Staff: Lajos Balogh, Conductor

OREGON SYMPHONY ORCHESTRA (A)*
813 S.W. Alder St.
Portland, OR 97205
(503) 228-4294
Staff: John E. Graham, General Manager; James DePreist, Musical Director; Ralph Nelson, Orchestral Manager

PACIFIC UNIVERSITY COMMUNITY ORCHESTRA (E)
Music Dept.
Forst Gove, OR 97116
(503) 357-6151, x251
Staff: Kenneth Combs, Conductor

PALATINE HILL SYMPHONY ORCHESTRA (E)
Lewis and Clark College
School of Music
Portland, OR 97219
(503) 244-6161
Staff: Jerry D. Luadders, Conductor

PETER BRITT GARDENS MUSIC AND ARTS FESTIVAL (C)*
P.O. Box 1124
Medfor, OR 97501
(503) 779-0847
Staff: David Shaw, Interim General Manager; John Trudeau, Musical Director and Conductor

PLUM RIDGE SYMPHONY (D)*
1233 Pacific Terrace
Klamath Falls, OR 97601
(503) 882-3146
Staff: Suzanne Tritch, President; Yair Strauss, Conductor

PORTLAND STATE UNIVERSITY ORCHESTRA (E)
Music Dept.
P.O. Box 751
Portland, OR 97207
(503) 229-3011
Staff: Gordon Solie, Conductor

PORTLAND YOUTH PHILHARMONIC (F)*
922 S.W. Main
Portland, OR 97205
(503) 223-5939
Staff: Kay W. Young, Executive Secretary and Manager; Jacob Avshalomov, Conductor and Musical Director

ROGUE VALLEY SYMPHONY ORCHESTRA (E)
Southern Oregon State College
Music Dept.
1250 Siskiyou Blvd.
Ashland, OR 97520
(503) 482-6101
Staff: Yair Strauss, Conductor

SALEM SYMPHONY ORCHESTRA (C)*
445 Ferry St., S.E.
Salem, OR 97301
(503)364-5763
Staff: Nadine Heald, Assistant Manager; John Trudeau, Conductor

UNIVERSITY OF OREGON SYMPHONY ORCHESTRA (E)
School of Music
Eugene, OR 97403
(503) 686-5661
Staff: Marsha Maybrey, Conductor

WESTERN OREGON STATE COLLEGE CHAMBER SYMPHONY (E)
Creative Arts Dept.
Monmouth, OR 97361
(503) 838-1220, x461
Staff: Eugene Kaza, Conductor

PENNSYLVANIA

ALLEGHENY CIVIC SYMPHONY (D)*
Allegheny College
Music Dept.
Meadville, PA 16335
(814) 724-3356
Staff: Robert Bond, Conductor

ALLENTOWN SYMPHONY (D)*
23 N. Sixth St.
Allentown, Pa 18101
(215) 432-7961
Staff: Virginia E. Wartman, Executive Director; Donald Voorhees, Musical Director

ALTOONA SYMPHONY ORCHESTRA (D)*
P.O. Box 483
Altoona, PA 16603
(814) 943-2500
Staff: Becky Lee Rice, General Manager; Frederick Morden, Musical Director

AMERICAN YOUTH SYMPHONY & CHORUS (F)*
3651 Ashland Dr.
Bethel Park, PA 15102
Staff: Dr. Donald E. McCathren, Musical Director and President

BLOOMSBURG COLLEGE-COMMUNITY ORCHESTRA (E)*
Bloomsburg State College
Dept. of Music
Bloomsburg, PA 17815
(717) 389-4284
Staff: Dr. John P. Master, Director

BUCKNELL UNIVERSITY SYMPHONY ORCHESTRA (E)*
Music Dept.
Lewisburg, PA 17837
(717) 524-3893
Staff: Christopher McGahan, Musical Director

CARNEGIE-MELLON PHILHARMONIC (E)
Music Dept.
Schenley Park
Pittsburgh, PA 15213
(412) 578-2372
Staff: Werner Torkanowsky, Conductor

CARNEGIE SYMPHONY ORCHESTRA (D)*
P.O. Box 344
Carnegie, PA 15106
Staff: Ian Gallacher, Musical Director; Arnold Lustig, President

CONCERTO SOLOISTS OF PHILADELPHIA (B)*
1732 Spruce St.
Philadelphia, PA 19103
(215) 735-0202
Staff: Katherine Sokoloff, General Manager; Marc Mostovoy, Musical Director

DICKINSON COLLEGE/COMMUNITY ORCHESTRA (E)
Music Dept.
Carlisle, PA 17013
(717) 245-1568
Staff: Frederick Petty, Conductor

DUQUESNE UNIVERSITY SYMPHONY (D)*
School of Music
Pittsburgh, PA 15282
(412) 434-6083
Staff: Alan Grishman, Musical Director; Suzanne Vertosick, Graduate Assistant

ELIZABETHTOWN COLLEGE/ COMMUNITY ORCHESTRA (E)
Music Dept.
Elizabethtown, PA 17022
(717) 367-1151
Staff: David Leithmann, Conductor

ERIE PHILHARMONIC ORCHESTRA (B)*
409 G. Daniel Baldwin Building
Erie, PA 16501
(814) 455-1375
Staff: Gloria Amidon, Acting General Manager; Walter Hendl, Orchestral Manager

GENEVA COLLEGE STRING ENSEMBLE (E)
Dept. of Music
Beaver Falls, PA 15010
(412) 846-5100, x247
Staff: George Churm, Conductor

GETTYSBURG COLLEGE/COMMUNITY ORCHESTRA (E)*
Music Dept.
Gettysburg, PA 17325
(717) 334-3131
Staff: Dr. Norman K. Nunamaker, Conductor

GREENVILLE SYMPHONY ORCHESTRA (D)
P.O. Box 364
Greenville, PA 16125
(412) 588-2851
Staff: Ivan Romanenko, Musical Director and Conductor

GROVE CITY COLLEGE SYMPHONY ORCHESTRA (E)
Dept. of Music and Fine Arts
Grove City, PA 16127
(412) 458-6600
Staff: Francis Pittock, Conductor

HARRISBURG SYMPHONY ORCHESTRA (B)*
Keystone Building, Ste. 403
22 S. Third St.
Harrisburg, PA 17101
(717) 232-8751
Staff: Samuel Kuba, III, General Manager; Larry Newland, Musical Director and Conductor

HARRISBURG YOUTH SYMPHONY ORCHESTRA (F)*
1337 Rousch Rd.
Hummelstown, PA 17036
(717) 566-3360
Staff: Ronald E. Schafer, Musical Director and Conductor; Estelle Hartranft, Coordinator

HAVERFORD-BRYN MAWR CHAMBER ORCHESTRA (E)
Haverford College
Music Dept.
Haverford, PA 19041
(215) 896-1008
Staff: Steven Lipsitt, Conductor

HARRISBURG YOUTH SYMPHONY ORCHESTRA (F)*
1337 Rousch Rd.
Hummelstown, PA 17036
(717) 566-3360
Staff: Ronald E. Schafer, Musical Director and Conductor; Estelle Hartranft, Coordinator

HAVERFORD-BRYN MAWR CHAMBER ORCHESTRA (E)
Haverford College
Music Dept.
Haverford, PA 19041
(215) 896-1008
Staff: Steven Lipsitt, Conductor

HERSHEY SYMPHONY ORCHESTRA (D)*
P.O. Box 93
Hershey, PA 17033
(717) 534-1446
Staff: Earl T. Caton, Jr., General Manager; Gerald S. Feintuch, Musical Director and Conductor

IMMACULATA COLLEGE COMMUNITY ORCHESTRA (E)
Music Dept.
Immaculata, PA 19345
(215) 647-4400
Staff: Dr. Constantine John, Conductor

INDIANA UNIVERSITY OF PENNSYLVANIA SYMPHONY (E)
Music Dept.
Indiana, PA 15701
(412) 357-2390
Staff: Dr. Hugh Johnson, Conductor

JOHNSTOWN SYMPHONY ORCHESTRA (B)*
230 Walnut St.
Johnstown, PA 15901
(814) 535-6738
Staff: Jacet C. Emery, General Manager; Donald P. Barra, Musical Director

JOHNSTOWN YOUTH SYMPHONY (F)*
809 Franco Ave.
Johnstown, PA 15905
(814) 255-2033
Staff: Rebecca Catelinet, Manager; Donald P. Barra, Musical Director

KENNETT SYMPHONY ORCHESTRA (D)*
P.O. Box 72
Kennett Square, PA 19348
(215) 347-2111
Staff: Dr. Carl Baccellieri, Business Manager; Terry E. Guidetti, Conductor

LAFAYETTE COLLEGE CHAMBER ORCHESTRA (E)
Dept. of Music
Williams Center for the Arts
Easton, PA 18042
(215) 250-5000
Staff: William E. Melin, Conductor

LANCASTER SYMPHONY ORCHESTRA (D)
44 W. Main St.
Leola, PA 17540
(717) 656-6114
Staff: Stephen Gunzenhauser, Conductor; Jack B. Stambaugh, Business Manager

LANSDOWNE SYMPHONY ORCHESTRA (D)*
Lansdowne Professional Building
85 N. Lansdowne Ave.
Lansdowne, PA 19050
(215) 461-5154
Staff: Edward Norton, Manager; Jacques C. Voois, Conductor

LEBANON VALLEY COLLEGE ORCHESTRA (E)
Music Dept.
Annville, PA 17003
(717) 867-4411
Staff: Dr. Klement Hambourg, Conductor

LEHIGH VALLEY CHAMBER ORCHESTRA (D)*
P.O. Box 2641
Lehigh Valley, PA 18001
(215) 437-5401
Staff: Llyena Boylan, General Manager; Donald E. Spieth, Musical Director and Principal Conductor

MAIN LINE SYMPHONY ORCHESTRA (D)*
945 Conestoga Rd.
Berwyn, PA 19312
(215) 644-5687
Staff: Folkert H. Kadyk, President; Henry Scott, Conductor

MANSFIELD COLLEGE/COMMUNITY ORCHESTRA (E)
Mansfield State College
Music Dept.
Mansfield, PA 16933
(717) 662-4080
Staff: Edwin Zdzimski, Conductor

MARYWOOD COLLEGE/COMMUNITY ORCHESTRA (E)
Music Dept.
2300 Adams Ave.
Scranton, PA 18509
(717) 348-6268
Staff: Robert D. Herrema, Conductor

MCKEESPORT SYMPHONY ORCHESTRA (D)*
P.O. Box 354
McKeesport, PA 15134
(412) 327-8363
Staff: John Scandrett, Orchestral Manager; James Meena, Musical Director

MESSIAH COLLEGE ORCHESTRA (E)
Music Dept.
Grantham, PA 17027
(717) 766-2511
Staff: Dr. Ronald Schafer, Conductor

MILLERSVILLE COLLEGE/COMMUNITY ORCHESTRA (E)
Millersville State College
Music Dept.
Millersville, PA 17551
(717) 872-3357
Staff: Peter Brye, Conductor

MORAVIAN COLLEGE/COMMUNITY ORCHESTRA (E)
Music Dept.
Bethlehem, PA 18018
(215) 861-1459
Staff: Donald Spieth, Conductor

NEW PITTSBURGH CHAMBER ORCHESTRA (D)*
P.O. Box 11458
Pittsburgh, PA 15238
(412) 963-8318
Staff: Nora Eninger, General Manager; Grover Wilkins, III, Musical Director

NEW SCHOOL OF MUSIC ORCHESTRA (E)*
301 S. 21st. St.
Philadelphia, PA 19103
(215) 723-3966
Staff: George F. Wisor, Vice President; Tamara Brooks, President and Conductor

NITTANY VALLEY SYMPHONY (D)*
721 Thomas St.
State College, PA 16801
(814) 237-1814
Staff: Ann Keller, President; Frederick Morden, Musical Director and Conductor

NORTHEASTERN PENNSYLVANIA PHILHARMONIC (B)*
P.O. Box 71
Avoca, PA 18641
(717) 342-0920
Staff: Salley E. Preate, General Manager; Hugh H. Wolff, Musical Director

NORTH PENN SYMPHONY ORCHESTRA (D)*
P.O. Box 694
Lansdale, PA 19446
(215) 449-6378
Staff: Leonard Murphy, Musical Director; William A. Eckert, Business Manager

ORCHESTRA SOCIETY OF PHILADELPHIA (D)
1310 Medary Ave.
Philadelphia, PA 19141
(215) 924-2196
Staff: Morris Goldman, President

PENN STATE SYMPHONY ORCHESTRA (E)
Pennsylvania State University
School of Music
232 Music Building
University Park, Pa 16802
(814) 865-0431
Staff: Smith Toulson, Director

PHILADELPHIA COLLEGE OF BIBLE CHRISTIAN SYMPHONY ORCHESTRA (E)
Music Dept.
Langhorne Manor
Langhorne, PA 19047
(215) 752-5800, x329
Staff: Dale Shepfer, Conductor

PHILADELPHIA DOCTORS' SYMPHONY (D)*
831 Amies Lane
Bryn Mawr, PA 19010
(215) 563-5343
Staff: James J. Ferguson, M.D., President; Jonathan Sternberg, Conductor and Musical Director

PHILADELPHIA ORCHESTRA (A)*
1420 Locust St.
Philadelphia, PA 19102
(215) 893-1900
Staff: Stephen Sell, Executive Director; Riccardo Muti, Musical Director; Joseph H. Santarlasci, Manager

PITTSBURGH SYMPHONY ORCHESTRA (A)*
Heinz Hall
600 Penn Ave.
Pittsburgh, PA 15222
(412) 392-4800
Staff: Marshall W. Turkin, Vice President and Managing Director; Andre Previn, Musical Director; Sid Kaplan, Manager and Director of Operations

PITTSBURGH YOUTH SYMPHONY ORCHESTRA (F)*
Heinz Hall
600 Penn Ave.
Pittsburgh, PA 15222
(412) 392-4872
Staff: Marie Maazel, Managing Director; Michael Lankester, Musical Director

POTTSTOWN SYMPHONY ORCHESTRA (D)*
P.O. Box 675
Pottstown, PA 19464
Staff: Herbert H. Houston, Business Manager; William F. Lamb, Musical Director

READING SYMPHONY ORCHESTRA (C)*
500 Museum Rd.
Reading, PA 19611
(215) 373-7557
Staff: Wes Fisher, Manager; Sidney Rothstein, Musical Director and Conductor

ROMANENKO CHAMBER PLAYERS (D)*
119 S. Pitt St.
Mercer, PA 16137
(412) 588-9505
Staff: David Miller, Administrator; Ivan S. Romanenko, Musical Director

SLIPPERY ROCK STATE COLLEGE/ COMMUNITY ORCHESTRA (E)
Music Dept.
Slippery Rock, PA 16057
(412) 794-7276
Staff: Sandra Dackow, Conductor

SWARTHMORE COLLEGE ORCHESTRA (E)
Music Dept.
Swarthmore, PA 19081
(215) 447-7233
Staff: James Freeman, Conductor

SUSQUEHANNA VALLEY SYMPHONY ORCHESTRA (D)*
P.O. Box 274
Williamsport, PA 17701
(717) 326-4206
Staff: Carol Sides, Manager; Dr. Donald W. Beckie, Conductor

TEMPLE UNIVERSITY SYMPHONY ORCHESTRA (E)*
College of Music
13th and Norris Sts.
Philadelphia, PA 19122
(215) 787-8307
Staff: Irene McKinney, Manager; Lawrence Wagner, Conductor

THREE RIVERS TRAINING ORCHESTRA (F)*
1027 Morewood Ave.
Pittsburgh, PA 15213
(412) 681-2764
Staff: Phyllis B. Susen, Managing Director; Bernard Z. Goldberg, Musical Director

UNIVERSITY OF PITTSBURGH ORCHESTRA (E)*
Music Dept.
Pittsburgh, PA 15260
(412) 624-4061
Staff: Grover Wilkins, III, Conductor

UPPER MORELAND SYMPHONY ORCHESTRA (F)*
2666 Moreland Rd.
Willow Grove, PA 19090
Staff: Stephen L. Woytowicz, Conductor

WARMINSTER SYMPHONY ORCHESTRA (D)*
550 West Street Rd.
Warminster, PA 18974
Staff: Anthony Guerrelli, Manager

WEST CHESTER STATE COLLEGE SYMPHONY (E)*
School of Music
West Chester, PA 19380
(215) 436-2628
Staff: Jacques C. Voois, Conductor; Henry Pearlberg, Manager

WESTMORELAND SYMPHONY ORCHESTRA (C)*
P.O. Box 1025
Greensburg, PA 15601
(412) 837-1850
Staff: Christel Horner, Manager; Kypros Markou, Musical Director

WILKES COLLEGE CHAMBER ORCHESTRA (E)
Dept. of Music
170 S. Franklin St.
Wilkes-Barre, P A 18703
(717) 824-4651
Staff: Dr. Herbert Garber, Conductor

WILKINSBURG CIVIC SYMPHONY (D)*
1007 Ross Ave.
Wilkinsburg, PA 15221
(412) 241-3606
Staff: Eugene Reichenfeld, Conductor

YORK JUNIOR SYMPHONY ORCHESTRA (F)*
2750 Durham Rd.
York, PA 17402
Staff: Darrell E. Pav, President; Priscilla M. Howard, Conductor

YORK SYMPHONY ASSOCIATION (C)*
13 E. Market St.
York, PA 17401
(717) 854-0906
Staff: James C. Pfohl, Musical Director and Conductor

YORK YOUTH SYMPHONY (F)*
1732 Crescent Rd.
York, PA 17403
Staff: Catherine Overhauser, Conductor; James L. Mohatt, Secretary

YOUTH ORCHESTRA OF GREATER PHILADELPHIA (F)*
2425 Fairmount Ave.

Philadelphia, PA 19130
(215) 765-7587
Staff: Ruth Stewart, President; Joseph Primavera, Conductor

RHODE ISLAND

BROWN UNIVERSITY ORCHESTRA (E)*
Music Dept., Box 1924
Providence, RI 02912
(401) 863-3234
Staff: Wolfgang Balzer, Conductor

RHODE ISLAND CIVIC CHORALE & ORCHESTRA (E)
334 Westminster Mall
Providence, RI 02093
(401) 521-5670
Staff: Robert T. Bass, Conductor; Nancy M. Yeaw, Manager

RHODE ISLAND COLLEGE SYMPHONY ORCHESTRA
Music Dept.
Providence, RI 02908
(401) 831-6600
Staff: Edward W. Markward, Conductor

RHODE ISLAND PHILHARMONIC ORCHESTRA (B)*
334 Westminster Mall
Providence, RI 02903
(401) 831-3123
Staff: Muriel Port Stevens, Manager; Alvaro Cassuto, Musical Director; Bruce Murray, Associate Manager

RHODE ISLAND PHILHARMONIC YOUTH ORCHESTRA (F)*
334 Westminster Mall
Providence, RI 02903
(401) 831-3123
Staff: Bruce Murray, Associate Manager; Nedo Pandolfi, Conductor

UNIVERSITY OF RHODE ISLAND ORCHESTRA (E)
Music Dept.
Kingston, RI 02882
(401) 792-1000
Staff: Dr. Joseph Ceo, Conductor

YOUNG PEOPLES SYMPHONY OF RHODE ISLAND (F)*
131 Washington St.
Providence, RI 02903
(401) 421-0460
Staff: Elvira D. Conte, Vice President; Joseph Conte, Musical Director

SOUTH CAROLINA

ANDERSON COLLEGE SYMPHONY ORCHESTRA (E)
Fine Arts Division
316 Boulevard
Anderson, SC 29621
(803) 226-6181
Staff: Dr. Perry Carroll, Conductor

CAROLINA YOUTH SYMPHONY (F)*
P.O. Box 6401
Greenville, SC 29606
(803) 232-3233
Staff: Dr. Robert Chesebro, Musical Director and Conductor; Mrs. David W. Hiott, President

CHARLESTON SYMPHONY ORCHESTRA (B)*
3 Chisolm St.
Charleston, SC 29401
(803) 723-7528
Staff: Mark Cedel, Acting Musical Director

COLUMBIA PHILHARMONIC ORCHESTRA (C)*
1527 Senate St.
Columbia, SC 29201
(803) 771-6303
Staff: John Whitehead, Managing Director; Gordon Goodwin, Musical Director

COLUMBIA YOUTH ORCHESTRA (F)*
1527 Senate St.
Columbia, SC 29201
(803) 771-6303
Staff: John Whitehead, Managing Director; Charles Gatch, Conductor

FURMAN UNIVERSITY ORCHESTRA (E)
Music Dept.
Poinsett Hwy.
Greenville, SC 29613
(803) 294-2086
Staff: Dr. Daniel Boda, Conductor

GREENVILLE SYMPHONY ORCHESTRA (C)*
P.O. Box 10002
Greenville, SC 29603
(803) 232-0344
Staff: Patricia G. Quarles, Office Manager; Peter Rickett, Conductor

PALMETTO STATE ORCHESTRA ASSOCIATION (D)*
P.O. Box 5703
Columbia, SC 29250
(803) 771-7937
Staff: James C. Celestino, Executive Director; Einar Anderson, Conductor and Musical Director

SPARTANBURG SYMPHONY ORCHESTRA (D)*
P.O. Box 1274
Spartanburg, SC 29304
Staff: Jean Blackford, Business Manager; Henry Janiec, Conductor

SOUTH DAKOTA

RAPID CITY SYMPHONY ORCHESTRA (D)*
506 Kansas City St.
Rapid City, SD 57701
(605) 343-9653
Staff: Lowell C. Holmgren, Business Manager; Jack Knowles, Conductor

SOUTH DAKOTA STATE UNIVERSITY/ CIVIC ORCHESTRA (E)
Music Dept.
Brookings, SD 57007
(605) 688-5187
Staff: John Colsom, Conductor

SOUTH DAKOTA SYMPHONY (B)*
707 E. 41st St.
Sioux Falls, SD 57105
(605) 335-7933
Staff: Mary W. Sommervold, Manager; Newton Wayland, Musical Advisor; Kathy Bagasser, Operations Manager

UNIVERSITY OF SOUTH DAKOTA ORCHESTRA (E)
Dept. of Music
Vermillion, SD 57069
(605) 677-5274
Staff: Kirk E. Gustafson, Conductor

YANKTON COLLEGE CONSERVATORY ORCHESTRA (E)
Conservatory of Music
12th and Douglas
Yankton, SD 57078
(605) 665-3661
Staff: Dr. J. Laiten Weed, Conductor and Manager

TENNESSEE

AUSTIN PEAY STATE UNIVERSITY ORCHESTRA (E)
Music Dept.
Clarksville, TN 37040
(615) 648-7818
Staff: Solie Fott, Conductor

CHATTANOOGA SYMPHONY ORCHESTRA (B)*
615 Lindsay St., Ste. 20
Chattanooga, TN 37402
(615) 267-8583
Staff: John G. Wendt, Manager; Dr. Richard Cormier, Musical Director

JACKSON SYMPHONY ORCHESTRA (C)*
P.O. Box 3098
Jackson, TN 38301
Staff: Ted Cunningham, Management Consultant; James Petty, Musical Director

JOHNSON CITY SYMPHONY (D)*
P.O. Box 533
Johnson City, TN 37601
(615) 928-7957
Staff: Guy R. Mauldin, Manager; Thomas Hinds, Conductor

KINGSPORT SYMPHONY ORCHESTRA (D)*
Fine Arts Center
Church Circle
Kingsport, TN 37660
(615) 246-9351
Staff: John Gordon Ross, Musical Director and Conductor; Dr. Jackson E. Hicks, President

KNOXVILLE SYMPHONY ORCHESTRA (B)*
618 Gay St.
Knoxville, TN 37902
(615) 523-1178
Staff: Constance Harrison, General Manager; Zoltan Rozsnyai, Musical Director

KNOXVILLE SYMPHONY YOUTH ORCHESTRA (F)*
1224 Huntingdon Dr.
Knoxville, TN 37919
(615) 691-0216
Staff: Nancy Doane, Manager; W. Sande MacMorran, Musical Director

MARYVILLE-ALCOA COLLEGE COMMUNITY ORCHESTRA (D)*
Maryville College
Maryville, TN 37801
(615) 982-6412
Staff: David Hoffecker, Director: Dr. James Emert, President

MEMPHIS STATE UNIVERSITY ORCHESTRA (E)
Music Dept.
Memphis, TN 38111
(901) 454-2541
Staff: Max Huls and James Richens, Co-Conductors

MEMPHIS SYMPHONY ORCHESTRA (A)*
3100 Walnut Grove Rd.
Memphis, TN 38111
(901) 324-3627
Staff: Florence Young, General Manager; Vincent de Frank, Musical Director and Conductor

MEMPHIS YOUTH SYMPHONY ORCHESTRA (F)*
Ste. 402
3100 Walnut Grove RdMemphis, TN 38111
(901) 324-3627
Staff: Fred Cook, President; David Goza, Musical Director and Conductor

NASHVILLE COMMUNITY ORCHESTRA (D)*
1704 Bonner Ave.
Nashville, TN 37215
(615) 383-5799
Staff: James Sherrill, Manager; Robert J. Weingart, Conductor

NASHVILLE SYMPHONY ORCHESTRA (A)*
1805 West End Ave.
Nasville, TN 37203
(615) 329-3033
Staff: George Carpenter, General Manager; Kenneth Schermerhorn, Musical Advisor; Sandy Wiscarson, Assisant Manager

NASHVILLE YOUTH SYMPHONY (F)*
Blair School of Music
2400 Blakemore Ave.
Nashville, TN 37212
Staff: David C. Cassel, Conductor

OAK RIDGE SYMPHONY ORCHESTRA (D)*
P.O. Box 271
Oak Ridge, TN 37830
(615) 482-5553
Staff: Charles S. Yust, President; Dr. H. Robert Lyall, Musical Director

SEWANEE SUMMER MUSIC CENTER ORCHESTRA (D)
Sewanee, TN 37375
(615) 598-5931
Staff: Martha McCrory, Director

SOUTHERN COLLEGE SYMPHONY ORCHESTRA (E)
Division of Music
Collegedale, TN 37315
(615) 396-2111
Staff: Orle Gilbert, Conductor

TECH COMMUNITY SYMPHONY ORCHESTRA (D)*
Tennessee Tech University
Music Dept.
Cookeville, TN 38501
Staff: Dr. James A. Wattenbarger, Conductor; Hill Carlen, President

TEXAS

ABILENE PHILHARMONIC (C)*
310 N. Willis, No. 126
Abilene, TX 79603
(915) 677-6710
Staff: Ed Allcorn, Manager and Librarian; George Yaeger, Musical Director and Conductor

AIMS ORCHESTRA (E)*
2710 Fondren Dr. Ste. 115
Dallas, TX 75206
(214) 691-6451
Staff: Robert Wagner, Manager; Cornelius Eberhardt, Conductor

AMARILLO SYMPHONY (B)*
P.O. Box 2552
Amarillo, TX 79105
(806) 376-8782
Staff: James M. Alfonte, Managing Director; Thomas Conlin, Conductor

AUSTIN SYMPHONY ORCHESTRA (B)*
1101 Red River
Austin, TX 78701
(512) 476-6064
Staff: Kenneth K. Caswell, General Manager; Sung Kwak, Musical Director

BAYLOR UNIVERSITY SYMPHONY ORCHESTRA (E)
School of Music
Waco, TX 76798
(817) 755-1161

BAYTOWN COMMUNITY ORCHESTRA (E)
Lee College
Music Dept.
Box 818
Baytown, TX 77520
(713) 427-5611
Staff: Dr. David L. Corder, Conductor

BEAUMONT SYMPHONY ORCHESTRA
1615 Howell St.
Beaumont, TX 77706
(713) 892-4421
Staff: Rose B. Carlucci, Executive Secretary and Business Manager; Dr. Joseph B. Carlucci, Conductor and Musical Director

BIG BEND CHAMBER ORCHESTRA (E)
Sul Ross State University
Dept. of Music
Alpine, TX 79830
(915) 837-8211
Staff: John Faraone, Conductor

BRAZOS VALLEY SYMPHONY ORCHESTRA (D)*
Bryan High School
3401 E. 29th St.
Bryan, TX 77801
(713) 775-3308
Staff: Harold Turbyfill, Artistic Director and Conductor; Charles Peterson, Business Manager

CLEAR LAKE SYMPHONY (D)*
2700 Bay Area Blvd.
Houston, TX 77058
(713) 488-9390
Staff: Dr. G. Warren Smith, President; Dr. Charles Johnson, Conductor

COMMUNITY ORCHESTRA OF GREATER HOUSTON (D)*
7110 Langdon Ln.
Houston, TX 77074
(713) 774-1156
Staff: William F. Wilson, Conductor Paul Thomas, Manager

CORPUS CHRISTI SYMPHONY ORCHESTRA (B)
P.O. Box 495
Corpus Christi, TX 78403
(512) 882-4091
Staff: Litta R. Kline, Executive Director and Manager; Cornelius Eberhardt, Conductor

DALLAS SYMPHONY ORCHESTRA (A)*
P.O. Box 26207
Dallas, TX 75226
(214) 565-9100
Staff: Leonard David Stone, Executive Director; Eduardo Mata, Musical Director; Fred W. Hoster, Administrative Director

DENTON UNIVERSITY/COMMUNITY ORCHESTRA (E)*
Texas Western University
Dept. of Music 0721
Box 23865, TWU Station
Denton, TX 76204

(214) 328-8297
Staff: Nan Hudson, Conductor

EAST TEXAS STATE UNIVERSITY ORCHESTRA (E)
Music Dept.
Commerce, TX 75428
(214) 886-5303
Staff: David Sogin, Conductor

EAST TEXAS SYMPHONY ORCHESTRA (C)*
P.O. Box 6323
Tyler, TX 75711
(214) 561-7282
Staff: Jane T. Benghauser, Manager; Daniel Hornstein, Conductor and Musical Director

EL PASO SYMPHONY ORCHESTRA (B)*
P.O. Box 180
El Paso, TX 79942
(915) 532-8707
Staff: John Emory Bush, Managing Director; Abraham Chavez, Jr., Musical Director and Conductor

EL PASO YOUTH SYMPHONY (F)*
P.O. Box 12155
El Paso, TX 79912
Staff: Mrs. Otis C. Coles, Secretary

FORT WORTH SYMPHONY ORCHESTRA (A)*
4401 Trail Lake Dr.
Fort Worth, TX 76109
(817) 921-2676
Staff: Ann Koonsman, Executive Director; John Giordano, Musical Director and Conductor; Dean Corey, Orchestra Manager

GREATER DALLAS YOUTH ORCHESTRA (F)*
7610 Meadow Oaks
Dallas, TX 75230
(214) 368-8500
Staff: Joann Mintz, Manager and Executive Secretary; Richard Giangiulio, Conductor

HOUSTON CIVIC SYMPHONY (D)
Houston Baptist University
School of Music
7502 Fondren Rd.
Houston, TX 77074
(713) 774-7661
Staff: Robert Linder, Conductor

HOUSTON POPS ORCHESTRA (B)*
3000 S. Post Oak Blvd., Ste. 140
Houston, TX 77056
(713) 871-8300
Staff: B. Calvin Jones, Managing Director; Ned Battista, Conductor

HOUSTON SYMPHONY ORCHESTRA (A)*
615 Louisiana St.
Houston, TX 77002
(713) 224-4240
Staff: Gideon Toeplitz, Executive Director; Sergiu Comissiona, Artistic Advisor; Russell Allen, Orchestral Manager

HOUSTON YOUTH SYMPHONY AND BALLET (F)*
P.O. Box 741829
Houston, TX 77274
(713) 528-4663
Staff: Linda Hirsh, Manager; Paul H. Kirby, Musical Director

IRVING SYMPHONY ORCHESTRA (D)*
P.O. Box 268
Irving, TX 75060
(214) 255-8766
Staff: Mike Itashiki, Manager; Yves L'Helgoual'ch, Musical Director and Conductor

LAREDO PHILHARMONIC ORCHESTRA (D)*
1401 San Bernardo
Laredo, TX 78040
(512) 727-8886
Staff: Jeffrey Alexander, General Manager; Terence Frazor, Musical Director and Conductor

LONGVIEW SYMPHONY ORCHESTRA (D)*
P.O. Box 1825
Longview, TX 75606
(214) 753-4207
Staff: Sally Bommarito, Business Manager; Dr. Frank Carroll, Musical Director and Conductor

LUBBOCK SYMPHONY ORCHESTRA (B)*
1721 Broadway
Lubbock, TX 79401
(806) 762-4707
Staff: Benjamin N. Smith, Manager; William A. Harrod, Musical Director

MARSHALL SYMPHONY ORCHESTRA (D)*
P.O. Box 421
Marshall, TX 75670
(214) 935-3525
Staff: Louis Kariel, Jr., President; Leonard Kacenjar, Conductor

MIDLAND-ODESSA SYMPHONY AND CHORALE (B)*
P.O. Box 6266
Midland, TX 79701
(915) 563-0921
Staff: George M. Esparza, General Manager; Dr. Thomas Hohstadt, Conductor and Musical Director

MID-TEXAS SYMPHONY ORCHESTRA (D)*
Texas Lutheran College
Box 3762
Seguin, TX 78155
(512) 379-1226
Staff: Anita Windecker, President; Terence Frazor, Musical Director; Gayle Smith, Manager

NORTH TEXAS STATE UNIVERSITY SYMPHONY ORCHESTRA (E)
School of Music
Denton, TX 76203
(817) 788-2791
Staff: Geoffrey Simon, Conductor

PAN AMERICAN UNIVERSITY-VALLEY SYMPHONY (D)*
c/o South Texas Symphony Association
P.O. Box 2832
McAllen, TX 78501
(512) 381-8682
Staff: Dr. Carl Seale, Conductor; Ruth Crews, STSA Executive Director

PLAINVIEW SYMPHONY ORCHESTRA (D)*
P.O. Box 1857
Plainview, TX 79072
(806) 293-3658
Staff: Dale R. Daniels, Conductor; Frank Gabriel, President

RICE UNIVERSITY SYMPHONY ORCHESTRA/CAMPANILE ORCHESTRA (E)
Shepherd School of Music
Houston, TX 77251
(713) 527-4854
Staff: Toshiyuki Shimada, Conductor

RICHARDSON SYMPHONY ORCHESTRA (C)*
P.O. Box 891
Richardson, TX 75080
(214) 234-4195
Staff: Chris P. Xeros, Conductor

SAM HOUSTON STATE SYMPHONY ORCHESTRA (E)*
Sam Houston State University
Music Dept.
Huntsville, TX 77341
(713) 294-1359
Staff: Carol Smith, Conductor

SAN ANGELO SYMPHONY ORCHESTRA (C)*
P.O. Box 5922
San Angelo, TX 76902
(915) 658-5877
Staff: Gene C. Smith, Conductor and Manager

SAN ANTONIO SYMPHONY ORCHESTRA (A)*
109 Lexington Ave., Ste. 207
San Antonio, TX 78205
(512) 225-6161
Staff: Carlos E. Wilson, Managing Director; Lawrence Leighton Smith, Musical Director; Benjamin Greene, Assistant Manager

SHERMAN SYMPHONY ORCHESTRA (E)
Austin College
Box 1592
Sherman, TX 75090
(214) 892-9101, x462
Staff: Cecil Isaac, Conductor and Manager

SOUTHERN METHODIST UNIVERSITY SYMPHONY ORCHESTRA (E)
Owens Art Center
Dallas, TX 75275
(214) 692-2587
Staff: Anshel Brusilow, Conductor

SOUTHWEST TEXAS STATE UNIVERSITY SYMPHONY ORCHESTRA (E)
Music Dept.
San Marcos, TX 78666
(512) 245-2651
Staff: John C. Stansberry, Conductor

STEPHEN F. AUSTIN STATE UNIVERSITY SYMPHONY (E)
Music Dept.
Box 13043, SFA Station
Nacogdoches, TX 75961
(713) 569-0764
Staff: Kurt Gilman, Conductor

SYMPHONY NORTH OF HOUSTON (D)*
1602 Castlerock Rd.
Houston, TX 77090
(713) 444-3830
Staff: Shirley Schulz, General Manager; Dr. Herman Barlow, Musical Director

TEXAS CHAMBER ORCHESTRA (C)*
721 Algregg
Houston, TX 77008
(713) 862-7287
Staff: Jerry McCathern, General Director; Ronald Braunstein, Principal Conductor; Marshall Maxwell, Operations Manager

TEXAS CHRISTIAN UNIVERSITY SYMPHONY ORCHESTRA (E)
Dept. of Music
P.O. Box 32887
Forth Worth, TX 76129
(817) 921-7602
Staff: George Del Gobbo, Conductor

TEXAS WESLEYAN COLLEGE ORCHESTRA (E)
Music Dept.
Fort Worth, TX 76105
(817) 531-4443
Staff: Robert McCashin, Conductor

TRINITY UNIVERSITY COMMUNITY ORCHESTRA (E)
Music Dept.
715 Stadium Dr.
San Antonio, TX 78284
(512) 736-8211
Staff: Domenick Saharelli, Conductor

TYLER YOUTH SYMPHONY ORCHESTRA (F)*
420 Sutherland
Tyler, TX 75703
(214) 581-1841
Staff: Robyn Files, Manager; Beverly Harrison, Conductor

UNIVERSITY OF TEXAS/ARLINGTON SYMPHONY (E)*
Music Dept.
Arlington, TX 76019
(817) 273-3471
Staff: Daniel Hornstein Musical Director; Randy Thompson, Manager

UNIVERSITY OF TEXAS/EL PASO SYMPHONY (E)*
Music Dept.
El Paso, TX 79968
(915) 747-5606
Staff: Laurence Gibson, Conductor

UNIVERSITY OF TEXAS/SAN ANTONIO ORCHESTRA (E)
Division of Music
San Antonio, TX 78285
(512) 691-4357
Staff: Dr. Janice K. Hodges, Conductor

VICTORIA SYMPHONY ORCHESTRA (D)
P.O. Box 4500
Victoria, TX 77903
(512) 576-4500
Staff: Robert Lyall, Conductor

WACO SYMPHONY ORCHESTRA (D)*
P.O. Box 7400
Waco, TX 76710
(817) 754-0851
Staff: Daniel Sternberg, Musical Director; Susan Taylor, Executive Secretary

WEST TEXAS STATE UNIVERSITY ORCHESTRA (E)
Music Dept.
Canyon, TX 79015
(806) 656-2016
Staff: Dr. Gary T. Garner, Conductor

WEST TEXAS YOUTH ORCHESTRA (F)*
1301 W. Florida
Midland, TX 79701
Staff: Charles Nail, Conductor; Susan Leshnower, President

WICHITA FALLS SYMPHONY ORCHESTRA (C)*
702 Hamilton Building
Wichita Falls, TX 76301
(817) 322-4393
Staff: Virginia Pierce, Manager; William H. Boyer, Conductor

YOUTH ORCHESTRA OF GREATER FORT WORTH (F)*
4401 Trail Lake Dr.
Fort Worth, TX 76109
(817) 923-3121
Staff: Susan Roth Thomas, Executive Director; George Del Gobbo, Conductor

YOUTH ORCHESTRAS OF SAN ANTONIO (F)*
P.O. Box 215
San Antonio, TX 78291
(512) 225-7474
Staff: Dr. Gene Carinci, Conductor; Evelyn Berg, President

UTAH

BRIGHAM YOUNG UNIVERSITY PHILHARMONIC ORCHESTRA (E)
E 464 Harris Fine Arts Center
Provo, UT 84602
(801) 378-3310
Staff: Ralph G. Laycock, Conductor and Manager

GOLDEN SPIKE YOUTH SYMPHONY ORCHESTRA (F)*
2444 Adams Ave.
Ogden, UT 84401
(801) 399-3456
Staff: Dr. James D. Thomson, Conductor and Manager

MORMON YOUTH SYMPHONY (F)
50 E. North Temple
Salt Lake City, UT 84150
(801) 531-2524
Staff: Robert C. Bowden, Conductor; Ray Furgeson, President

MURRAY SYMPHONY ORCHESTRA (D)*
4914 S. State St.
Murray, UT 84107
(801) 262-3630
Staff: Claudia Jesperson, Manager; Robert L. Lentz, Conductor

ROCKY MOUNTAIN SYMPHONY (D)*
Eccles Community Art Center
2580 Jefferson Ave.
Ogden, UT 84401
(801) 399-3456
Staff: James D. Thomson, Musical Director and Conductor; Greta Thomson, Manager

SOUTHERN UTAH STATE COLLEGE SYMPHONY (E)
Music Dept.
Cedar City, UT 84720
(801) 586-4411, x263
Staff: C. David Nyman, Conductor and Manager

UNIVERSITY OF UTAH SYMPHONY ORCHESTRA (E)
Music Dept.
Salt Lake City, UT 84112
(801) 581-6692
Staff: Jason Klein, Conductor

UTAH STATE UNIVERSITY SYMPHONY ORCHESTRA (E)
Music Dept.
Logan, UT 84322
(801) 753-1813
Staff: Mark A. Emile, Conductor

UTAH SYMPHONY ORCHESTRA (A)*
123 W. South Temple
Salt Lake City, UT 84101
(801) 533-5626
Staff: Stephen W. Swaner, Executive Vice President, Varujan Kojian, Musical Director and Conductor; Herold L. Gregory, Executive Director

UTAH VALLEY SYMPHONY (D)
461 E. 2875 North
Provo, UT 84604
(801) 377-6995
Staff: Ralph G. Laycock, Conductor; Mrs. Rex Dunford, Business Manager

UTAH VALLEY YOUTH SYMPHONY ORCHESTRA (F)*
P.O. Box 1235
Provo, UT 84601
(801) 373-8090
Staff; Brent E. Taylor, Manager; Terry S. Hill, Conductor

UTAH YOUTH SYMPHONY (F)*
61 S. Main, Ste. 401
Salt Lake City, UT 84111
(801) 521-9540
Staff: Joe H. Milner, President; Jason Klein, Musical Director

VERMONT

SAGE CITY SYMPHONY (D)*
P.O. Box 258
Shaftsbury, VT 05262
(802) 375-6766
Staff: Christine Graham, Manager; Louis Calabro, Musical Director

UNIVERSITY OF VERMONT ORCHESTRA (E)
Dept. of Music
Redston Campus
Burlington, VT 05405
(802) 656-3040
Staff: Peter Brown, Conductor

VERMONT SYMPHONY ORCHESTRA (B)*
77 College St.
Burlington, VT 05401
(802) 864-5741
Staff: Morris Block, Manager; Efrain Guigui, Musical Director; Kristin Kerr, Administrator

VERMONT YOUTH ORCHESTRA (F)*
Burlington Friends of Music
14 S. Williams St.
Burlington, VT 05401
(802) 862-6732
Staff: Carolyn E. Long, Manager; Raymond Anderson, Director and Conductor

VIRGINIA

ALEXANDRIA SYMPHONY ORCHESTRA (D)*
P.O. Box 1035
Alexandria, VA 22313
(703) 780-3303
Staff: F. Argyle Crump, President; Dr. George Steiner, Musical Director and Conductor

ARLINGTON SYMPHONY (D)*
706 N. Frederick St.
Arlington, VA 22203
(703) 243-5136
Staff: T.W. Taylor, President; Karl Rucht, Musical Director

CHARLOTTESVILLE UNIVERSITY/ COMMUNITY SYMPHONY (E)*
University of Virginia
112 Old Cabell Hall
Charlottesville, VA 22903
(804) 924-3052
Staff: Janet E. Doane, General Manager; Douglas Hargrave, Musical Director

COLLEGE OF WILLIAM AND MARY/ COMMUNITY ORCHESTRA (E)
Dept. of Music
Williamsburg, VA 23185
(804) 229-4374
Staff: Edgar Williams, Conductor

FAIRFAX SYMPHONY ORCHESTRA (C)*
P.O. Box 934
McLean, VA 22101
(703) 821-8118
Staff: Barbara B. Serage, Managing Director; William Hudson, Musical Director and Conductor; Grace Haines, Assistant Manager

HAMPTON INSTITUTE COMMUNITY ORCHESTRA (E)
Dept. of Music
Hampton, VA 23668
(804) 727-5402
Staff: James P. Herbison, Conductor

JAMES MADISON UNIVERSITY SYMPHONY (E)*
Music Dept.
Harrisburg, VA 22807
(703) 433-6654
Staff: Dr. Ben E. Wright, Musical Director; Bruno M. Nasta, Manager

LIBERTY SYMPHONY (E)
Liberty Baptist College
Lynchburg, VA 24506
(804) 237-5961
Staff: William Hayden, Conductor

MARY WASHINGTON COLLEGE/ COMMUNITY ORCHESTRA (E)*
Dept. of Music
Fredericksburg, VA 22401
(703) 899-4340
Staff: Dr. James E. Baker, Conductor; Susan Ford Johnson, President

MCLEAN CHAMBER ORCHESTRA (D)*
1902 Miracle Lane
Falls Church, VA 22043
(703) 827-0133
Staff: Patricia B. Brock, Manager; Dingwall Fleary, Musical Director

NEW RIVER VALLEY SYMPHONY (E)*
PAB, VPI and SU
Blacksburg, VA 24061
Staff: Richard C. Cole, Conductor

NORFOLK STATE UNIVERSITY COMMUNITY ORCHESTRA (E)
Music Dept.
2401 Corprew Ave.
Norfolk,VA 23504
(804) 623-8735
Staff: James M. Reeves, Conductor

NORTHERN VIRGINIA YOUTH SYMPHONY (F)*
P.O. Box 382
Annandale, VA 22003
(703) 256-3508
Staff: Pat Payne, Manager; Guido Mansuino, Conductor

OLD DOMINION UNIVERSITY SYMPHONY (E)*
Dept. of Music
Norfolk, VA 23508
(804) 440-4061
Staff: Dr. Gordon Baughman, Musical Director; Linda Dennis, Manager and Librarian

PENINSULA ORCHESTRAL SOCIETY (D)*
P.O. Box 6301
Newport News, VA 23606
(804) 877-5629
Staff: Carl M. Anderson, Orchestral Manager; Joel Eric Suben, Musical Director

PENINSULA YOUTH ORCHESTRA (F)*
WGH-FM
P.O. Box 9347
Hampton, VA 23670
Staff: Vianne B. Webb, President; Roland Carter, Conductor

PRINCE WILLIAM SYMPHONY ORCHESTRA (D)*
P.O. Box 1451
Woodbridge, VA 22193
(703) 590-1120
Staff: Doris Galvin, General Manager; John D. Welsh, Musical Director and Conductor

RICHMOND SYMPHONY ORCHESTRA (A)*
211 W. Franklin St., 2nd Flr.
Richmond, VA 23220
(804) 788-4717
Staff: Richard W. Thompson, General Manager; Jacques Houtmann, Musical Director; Cecil S. Cole, Assistant Manager of Personnel and Operations

RICHMOND SYMPHONY YOUTH ORCHESTRA (F)*
211 W. Franklin St., 2nd Flr.
Richmond, VA 23220
(804) 788-4717
Staff: Sue H. Schutt, Manager; Stephen Kapeller, Conductor

ROANOKE SYMPHONY ORCHESTRA (C)*
P.O. Box 2433
Roanoke, VA 24010
(703) 343-9127
Staff: John D. Martin, Secretary and Assistant Treasurer; Jack Moehlenkamp, Musical Director and Conductor

ROCKBRIDGE ORCHESTRA (D)
Washington and Lee University
Dept. of Fine Arts
Lexington, VA 24450
(703) 463-9111, x232
Staff: Dr. Gordon Spice, Conductor

UNIVERSITY OF RICHMOND ORCHESTRA (E)
Music Dept.
University of Richmond, VA 23173
(804) 285-6334
Staff: Steven Errante, Conductor

VIRGINIA COMMONWEALTH UNIVERSITY SYMPHONY (E)
Music Dept.
922 Park Ave.
Richmond, VA 23284
(804) 257-1166
Staff: Jack Jarrett, Conductor

VIRGINIA ORCHESTRA GROUP (A)*
P.O. Box 26
Norfolk, VA 23501
(804) 623-8590
Staff: Jerry T. Haynie, Executive Director; Richard D. Williams, Musical Director and Conductor; Harriet Ervin, Operations Manager

YOUTH ORCHESTRA OF CHARLOTTESVILLE-ALBERMARLE (F)
P.O. Box 3167
Charlottesville, VA 22903
(804) 973-5222
Staff: Elizabeth Gatewood, General Manager; Dan Lind, Conductor

WASHINGTON

BELLEVUE PHILHARMONIC ORCHESTRA (D)*
P.O. Box 1582
Bellevue, WA 98009
(206) 455-4171
Staff: Lucille H. Garrett, Business Manager; R. Joseph Scott, Conductor

BREMERTON SYMPHONY ORCHESTRA (D)*
1113 Sixth St.
Bremerton, WA 98310
(206) 377-3992
Staff: Al Dillan, President; Joseph Levine, Musical Director and Conductor

CASCADE SYMPHONY ORCHESTRA (D)*
18310 Sunset Way
Edmonds, WA 98020
(206) 778-4737
Staff: Robert B. Anderson, Musical Director and Conductor; Phillip Elvrum President

THE CENTRAL SYMPHONY (E)
Central Washington University
Dept. of Music
Ellensburg, WA 98926
(509) 963-1216
Staff: Eric Roth, Conductor

CORNISH CHAMBER ORCHESTRA (E)
Cornish Institute
Music Dept.
710 E. Roy
Seattle, WA 98102
(206) 323-1400
Staff: Melvin Strauss, Conductor

EASTERN WASHINGTON UNIVERSITY SYMPHONY ORCHESTRA (E)*
Dept. of Music
Cheney, WA 99004
(509) 235-6221
Staff: Dennis M. Layendecker, Conductor

EVERETT SYMPHONY ORCHESTRA (D)*
Woodinville, WA 98072
(206) 788-3404
Staff: Dr. Stafford Miller, Musical Director and Conductor; Robert Graef, President

MID-COLUMBIA SYMPHONY ORCHESTRA (C)*
P.O. Box 65
Richland, WA 99352
(509) 735-7356
Staff: Alan D. Valentine, Business Manager; Michel Singher, Musical Director

NORTHWEST CHAMBER ORCHESTRA (B)*
119 S. Main, 2nd Flr.
Seattle, WA 98104
(206) 343-0445
Staff: George C. Gelles, General Manager; Alun Francis, Musical Director and Conductor; Connie Cooper, Administrator

OKANOGAN SYMPHONY (D)*
P.O. Box 2058
Omak, WA 98841
(509) 826-4901
Staff: Karen Bogaardt, General Manager; Jim Riggs, Conductor

OLYMPIA SYMPHONY ORCHESTRA (D)*
1622 Woodland Creek Dr., NE
Olympia, WA 98506
(206) 491-3931
Staff: Ian Edlund, Musical Director and Conductor; Raymond L. Abbott, President

OLYMPIC YOUTH SYMPHONIES (F)*
17021 Eleventh Pl., SW
Seattle, WA 98166
Staff: Natalia Price, Chairman; Frances Walton, Musical Director

PACIFIC LUTHERAN UNIVERSITY SYMPHONY ORCHESTRA (E)
Dept. of Music
Tacoma, WA 98447
(206) 535-7601
Staff: Jerry Kracht, Conductor

PORT ANGELES SYMPHONY ORCHESTRA (D)*
P.O. Box 2148
Port Angeles, WA 98362
(206) 452-7300
Staff: Marcia Switzer, Business Manager; Dr. David E. Andre, Director

SEATTLE SYMPHONY ORCHESTRA (A)*
305 Harrison St.
Seattle, WA 98109
(206) 447-4700
Staff: Dr. Charles Odegaard, Acting General Manager; Rainer Miedel, Musical Director and Conductor

SEATTLE YOUTH SYMPHONY ORCHESTRA (F)*
400 Boren Ave., N
Seattle, WA 98109
(206) 623-2001
Staff: Shirley G. Schultz, General Manager; Vilem Sokol, Musical Director

SOUTHWEST WASHINGTON CIVIC SYMPHONY (D)*
1632 Kessler Blvd.
Longview, WA 98632
Staff: R.P. Wollenberg, Personnel Manager; George Simonsen, Jr., Conductor and Musical Director

SPOKANE FALLS COMMUNITY SYMPHONY (E)
Spokane Falls Community College
Music Dept.
3410 Fort George Wright Dr.
Spokane, WA 99204
(509) 456-3906
Staff: Wayne C. Smith, Conductor

SPOKANE SYMPHONY ORCHESTRA (A)*
The Flour Mill, Ste. 203
West 621 Mallon
Spokane, WA 99201
(509) 326-3136
Staff: Wesley O. Brustad, Executive Director; Donald Thulean, Musical Director and Conductor

TACOMA SYMPHONY ORCHESTRA (B)*
P.O. Box 19
Tacoma, WA 98401
(206) 952-5706
Staff: Rhoda Sherlock, Business Manager; Edward Seferian, Musical Director and Conductor

TACOMA YOUTH SYMPHONY (F)*
P.O. Box 660
Tacoma, WA 98401
(206) 845-4780
Staff: Shirley M. Getzin, Manager; Harry L. Davidson, Jr., Musical Director and Conductor

THALIA SYMPHONY AND CHAMBER SYMPHONY (D)*
Thalia Conservatory
2626 Eastlake Ave., E.
Seattle, WA 98102
(206) 322-0554
Staff: Frances Walton, Conductor and Musical Director; Richard Polf, Manager; Stanley Chapple, Conductor and Musical Director

UNIVERSITY OF WASHINGTON SYMPHONY ORCHESTRA (E)*
102 Music Building DN-10
Seattle, WA 98195
(206) 543-1200
Staff: Robert Feist, Conductor

WALLA WALLA SYMPHONY SOCIETY (D)*
P.O. Box 92
Walla Walla, WA 99362
(509) 529-8020
Staff: R. Lee Friese, Musical Director and Conductor; Lila Fleming, Manager

WESTERN SYMPHONY ORCHESTRA (E)
Western Washington University
Dept. of Music
Bellingham, WA 98225
(206) 676-3130
Staff: Dr. Wayne D. Gorder, Conductor

YAKIMA SYMPHONY ORCHESTRA (D)*
P.O. Box 307
Yakima, WA 98907
(509) 248-1414
Staff: Sarah S. Marley, Manager; Brooke Creswell, Musical Director

YAKIMA YOUTH ORCHESTRA (F)*
P.O. Box 307
Yakima, WA 98907
(509) 248-1414
Staff: Brooke Creswell, Musical Director; Sarah S. Marley, Manager

WEST VIRGINIA

CHARLESTON SYMPHONY ORCHESTRA (B)*
P.O. Box 2292
Charleston, WV 25328
(304) 342-0151
Staff: William D. McNeil, General Manager; Sidney Rothstein, Musical Director and Conductor

CHARLESTON SYMPHONY YOUTH ORCHESTRA (F)*
1210 Virginia St., E
Charleston, WV 25311
(304) 342-0151
Staff: Catherine B. Martin, President; James McWhorter, Conductor

FAIRMONT COLLEGE/COMMUNITY SYMPHONY ORCHESTRA (E)
Music Dept.
Fairmont, WV 26554
(304) 363-4219
Staff: John H. Ashton, Conductor

HUNTINGTON CHAMBER ORCHESTRA (D)*
Huntington Galleries
Park Hills
Huntington, WV 25701
(304) 529-4262
Staff: Judith Casto, President; Paul W. Whear

LILLIPUT ORCHESTRA (D)*
16 Terrace Rd.
Charleston, WV 25314
(304) 346-6095
Staff: Suzanne Riggio, General Manager; Donald J. Riggio, Musical Director

MARSHALL UNIVERSITY SYMPHONY (E)
Music Dept.
Huntington, WV 25705
(304) 696-3117
Staff: James McWhorter, Conductor

MILLBROOK CENTER CHAMBER ORCHESTRA (D)*
P.O. Box 718
Shepherdstown, WV 25443
(301) 876-2294
Staff: Dr. James E. Pantle, Associate Director; Dr. Gerald E. Zimmerman, Musical Director

WEST VIRGINIA UNIVERSITY/COMMUNITY SYMPHONY (E)
Creative Arts Center
Morgantown, WV 26506
(304) 293-2901
Staff: Donald C. Portnoy, Conductor

WHEELING SYMPHONY ORCHESTRA (B)*
Hawley Building, Ste. 307
Wheeling, WV 26003
(304) 232-6191
Staff: Susan Cox Nelson, General Manager; Jeff Holland Cook, Musical Director

WISCONSIN

ALVERNO COLLEGE/COMMUNITY ORCHESTRA (E)
Music Dept.
3401 S. 39th St.
Milwaukee, WI 53215
(414) 647-3908
Staff: Gregory Schaffer, Conductor

AMERICAN COMMUNITY SYMPHONY ORCHESTRA (D)
P.O. Box 101
Eau Claire, WI 54701
(715) 836-3633
Staff: Dr. L. Rhodes Lewis, Musical Director and Conductor; Wallace Johnson, Manager

BELOIT SYMPHONY ORCHESTRA (D)*
P.O. Box 185
Beloit, WI 53511
(608) 365-2719
Staff: Martha Gammons, General Manager; Dr. Crawford Gates, Musical Director

CARROLL COLLEGE COMMUNITY ORCHESTRA (E)
Music Dept.
100 N. East Ave.
Waukesha, WI 53186
(414) 547-1211
Staff: Harold S. Kacanek, Conductor

CENTRAL WISCONSIN SYMPHONY ORCHESTRA (D)*
P.O. Box 566
Stevens Point, WI 54481
(715) 344-4384
Staff: Patricia D. Rodgers, Manager; Jon Borowicz, Musical Director

CHIPPEWA VALLEY SYMPHONY (D)*
P.O. Box 161
Eau Claire, WI 54701
(715) 832-0386
Staff: Alfred J. Anderson, Acting Manager; Ivar Lunde, Jr., Musical Director

FOX VALLEY SYMPHONY (C)*
Goodwill Offices, Ste. S
1800 Appleton Rd.
Menasha, WI 54952
(414) 734-9930
Staff: Ruth Haviland, Executive Director; Kate Tamarkin, Musical Director

GREEN BAY SYMPHONY ORCHESTRA (C)*
P.O. Box 222
Green Bay, WI 54305
(414) 435-3465
Staff: Marilyn Stasiak, General Manager; Miroslav J. Pansky, Conductor and Musical Director

KENOSHA SYMPHONY (D)*
2717 67th St.
Kenosha, WI 53140
(414) 657-3185
Staff: James J. Trebbin, Orchestral Manager; David H. Schripsema, Conductor and Musical Director

LA CROSSE SYMPHONY ORCHESTRA (D)*
119 King St.
La Crosse, WI 54601
(608) 785-1434
Staff: Thomas J. Carroll, President; Hugo Jan Huss, Musical Director and Conductor

LA CROSSE YOUTH SYMPHONY (F)*
P.O. Box 2511
La Crosse, WI 54601
(608) 788-3796
Staff: Lenore Italiano, Manager; Frank Italiano, Musical Director

MADISON SYMPHONY ORCHESTRA (B)*
211 N. Carroll St.
Madison, WI 53703
(608) 257-3734
Staff: Robert R. Palmer, General Manager; Roland Johnson, Musical Director

MARSHFIELD-WOOD COUNTY SYMPHONY ORCHESTRA (D)*
510 S. Birch Ave.
Marshfield, WI 54449
(715) 387-1147
Staff: Robert I. Biederwolf, Conductor and Manager

MILWAUKEE CHAMBER ORCHESTRA (D)
P.O. Box 11524
Milwaukee, WI 53211
(414) 964-0199
Staff: Stephen Colburn, General Director and Conductor

MILWAUKEE SYMPHONY ORCHESTRA (A)*
929 N. Water St.
Milwaukee, WI 53202
(414) 273-7121
Staff: Robert L. Caulfield, Executive Director; Lukas Foss, Musical Director; Richard C. Thomas, General Manager

MOUNT SENARIO COLLEGE SYMPHONY/CHAMBER ORCHESTRA (E)
Music Dept.
College Ave., W
Ladysmith, WI 54848
(715) 532-5511
Staff: Lisa Arnold, Conductor

MUSIC FOR YOUTH (F)*
929 N. Water St.
Milwaukee, WI 53202
(414) 272-8540
Staff: Marian Hansen, Administrator; Manuel Prestamo, Musical Director

OSHKOSH SYMPHONY ORCHESTRA (D)*
P.O. Box 522
Oshkosh, WI 54902
(414) 233-7510
Staff: Carol Niendorf, Business Manager; Henri B. Pensis, Musical Director and Conductor

RACINE SYMPHONY ORCHESTRA (D)*
P.O. Box 1751
Racine, WI 53401
(414) 633-4292
Staff: Karol Rehm, Administrative Coordinator; Stephen Colburn, Musical Director and Conductor

RIPON COLLEGE ORCHESTRA (E)
Music Dept.
300 Seward St., Box 248
Ripon, WI 54971
(414) 748-8120
Staff: Dr. Raymond Stahura, Conductor

SYMPHONY OF THE HILLS/GREAT RIVER SYMPHONY (C)*
P.O. Box 2554
La Crosse, WI 54601
(608) 788-3796
Staff: Lenore Italiano, Administrator; Francesco Italiano, Musical Director

UNIVERSITY OF WISCONSIN/EAU CLAIRE SYMPHONY (E)*
Eau Claire, WI 54701
(715) 836-2181
Staff: Dr. Rupert Hohmann, Conductor; Ada Bors, Manager

UNIVERSITY OF WISCONSIN/LA CROSSE SYMPHONY (E)*
Fine Arts Building
La Crosse, WI 54601
(608) 785-8416
Staff: Dr. Joseph Cordeiro, Conductor; Sonja Lee Schmitt, Manager

UNIVERSITY OF WISCONSIN/MADISON SYMPHONY (E)*
School of Music
455 N. Park St.
Madison, WI 53706
(608) 263-1892
Staff: Alice M. Kopp, Manager; Gary Fagin, Conductor

UNIVERSITY OF WISCONSIN/ PLATTEVILLE COMMUNITY SYMPHONY ORCHESTRA (E)
Music Dept.
Platteville, WI 53818
(608) 342-1143
Staff: G. Daniel Fairchild, Conductor

UNIVERSITY OF WISCONSIN/STEVENS POINT SYMPHONY ORCHESTRA (E)
Music Dept.
Stevens Point, WI 54481
(715) 346-2808
Staff: Jon Borowicz, Musical Director

UNIVERSITY OF WISCONSIN/SUPERIOR CHAMBER ORCHESTRA (E)
Music Dept.
Superior, WI 54880
(715) 394-8115
Staff: Diane Balko, Conductor

WAUKESHA SYMPHONY ORCHESTRA (C)*
P.O. Box 531
Waukesha, WI 53187
(414) 547-1858
Staff: Elaine Oldberg, General Manager; Daniel Forlano, Musical Director

WAUSAU SYMPHONY (E)
University of Wisconsin
Marathon County Campus
Music Dept.
518 W. 7th Ave.
Wausau, WI 54401
(715) 845-9802
Staff: Thomas Wellin, Conductor

WISCONSIN CHAMBER ORCHESTRA (D)*
Madison Civic Center
211 State St.
Madison, WI 53703
(608) 257-0638
Staff: Kathy Silbiger, General Manager; David Crosby, Musical Director

WISCONSIN CONSERVATORY OF MUSIC CHAMBER ORCHESTRA (E)*
1584 N. Prospect Ave.
Milwaukee, WI 53202
(414) 276-4350
Staff: Daniel Forlano, Musical Director

WISCONSIN YOUTH SYMPHONY ORCHESTRAS (F)*
455 N. Park St.
Madison, WI 53706
(608) 263-3320
Staff: Bruce Matthews, General Manager; David J. Nelson, Musical Director

WYOMING

CASPER SYMPHONY ORCHESTRA (C)*
140 N. Center St.
Casper, WY 82601
(307) 266-1478
Staff: Kenneth D. Steiger, General Manager; Curtis Peacock, Musical Director

CHEYENNE SYMPHONY ORCHESTRA (D)*
P.O. Box 851
Cheyenne, WY 82003
(307) 778-8561
Staff: Edward L. Bartholic, General Manager; Robert Carter Austin, Musical Director and Conductor

UNIVERSITY OF WYOMING SYMPHONY ORCHESTRA (E)
Dept. of Music
Laramie, WY 82070
(307) 766-5242
Staff: David Tomatz, Conductor

PUERTO RICO

CONSERVATORY OF MUSIC OF PUERTO RICO ORCHESTRA (E)
P.O. Box 41227, Minillas Station
Santurce, PR 00940
(809) 751-0160
Staff: Roselin Pabon, Conductor

ORQUESTA SINFONICA JUVENIL DE SAN JUAN (F)*
Ave. Americo Miranda #1104
Repto. Metro.
Rio Piedras, PR 00921
Staff: Randolfo Juarbe

PUERTO RICO SYMPHONY ORCHESTRA (A)*
c/o AFAC
Box 41227, Minillas Station
Santurce, PR 00940
(809) 727-2186
Staff: Sylvia M. Lamoutte, Executive Director; John Barnett, Musical Director; Angel A. Heredia, Substituting Director

CANADA

ALBERTA

CALGARY PHILHARMONIC ORCHESTRA (A)*
No. 200-505 Fifth St., SW
Calgary, AB T2P 3J2
(403) 269-8201
Staff: John F. Shaw, General Manager; Mario Bernardi, Musical Director

CALGARY YOUTH ORCHESTRA (F)
Mount Royal College
Conservatory of Music and Speech Arts
4825 Richard Rd., SW
Calgary, AB T3E 6K6
(403) 240-6821
Staff: Frank Simpson, Conductor

EDMONTON SYMPHONY ORCHESTRA (A)*
11712 87th Ave.
Edmonton, AB T6G 0Y3
(403) 439-2091
Staff: Gordon R. Neufeld, General Manager; Uri Mayer, Musical Director and Principal Conductor; Marlin Wolfe, Director of Operations

MOUNT ROYAL COLLEGE JUNIOR ORCHESTRA (F)
Conservatory of Music and Sppech Arts
4825 Richard Rd., SW
Calgary, AB T3E 6K6
(403) 240-6821
Staff: Dr. Norman Burgess, Conductor

UNIVERSITY OF CALGARY SYMPHONY ORCHESTRA (E)
Dept. of Music
Calgary, AB T2N 1N4
(403) 284-5376
Staff: K. Nielsen, Conductor

BRITISH COLUMBIA

SYMPHONIE CANADIANA (A)
P.O. Box 91432
West Vancouver, BC V7V 3P1
(604) 922-8859
Staff: Yondani Butt, Conductor; Ian Wenham, Manager

UNIVERSITY OF BRITISH COLUMBIA SYMPHONY ORCHESTRA (E)
Dept. of Music
6361 Memorial Rd.
Vancouver, BC V6T 1W5
(604) 228-3113
Staff: Douglas E. Talney, Conductor

UNIVERSITY OF VICTORIA ORCHESTRA (E)
P.O. Box 1700
Victoria, BC V8W 2Y2
(604) 721-7902
Staff: George Corwin, Conductor

VANCOUVER SYMPHONY ORCHESTRA (A)*
400 E. Broadway
Vancouver, BC V5T 1X2
(604) 875-1661
Staff: Michael J. Allerton, Managing Director; Kazuyoshi Akiyama, Resident Conductor and Musical Director; Robert J. McGifford, Director of Finance and Administration

VICTORIA SYMPHONY ORCHESTRA (A)*
631 Superior St.
Victoria, BC V8V 1V1
(604) 385-9771
Staff: Dr. Paul Freeman, Musical Director

MANITOBA

WINNIPEG SYMPHONY ORCHESTRA (A)*
Centennial Concert Hall
117-555 Main St.
Winnipeg, MB R3B 1C3
(204) 942-4576
Staff: Jack Mills, Executive Director; John Barrett, Director of Operations

NEW BRUNSWICK

LA CHORALE SYMPHONIQUE DE L'UNIVERSITE DE MONCTON (E)
Music Dept.
Moncton, NB E1A 3E9
(506) 858-4041
Staff: Richard Boulanger, Director

NEW BRUNSWICK YOUTH ORCHESTRA (F)
Mount Allison University
Music Dept.
Sackville, NB E0A 3C0
(506) 536-2040, local 250
Staff: Rodney O. McLeod, Conductor

NOVA SCOTIA

ACADIA UNIVERSITY ORCHESTRA (E)
School of Music
Wolfville, NS B0P 1X0
(902) 542-2201
Staff: Robert Raines, Conductor

ATLANTIC SYMPHONY ORCHESTRA (A)
5639 Spring Garden Rd.
Halifax, NS B3J 1G9
(902) 423-9294
Staff: Victor Yampolsky, Conductor; Mark J. Warren, Executive Director

ONTARIO

CHAMBER PLAYERS OF TORONTO (D)
Box 5428, Station A
Toronto, ON M5W 1N6
(416) 598-2873
Staff: Winston Webber, Musical Director; Alan Toff, Manager

COMMUNITY CHAMBER ORCHESTRA OF YORK UNIVERSITY (E)
Music Dept.
4700 Keele St.
Downsview, ON M3J 1P3
(416) 667-3246
Staff: James R. McKay, Conductor

DEEP RIVER SYMPHONY ORCHESTRA (D)
Box 829
Deep River, ON K0J 1P0
(613) 584-2715
Staff: James Wegg, Conductor

HAMILTON PHILHARMONIC ORCHESTRA (A)*
P.O. Box 2080, Station A
Hamilton, ON L8N 3Y7
(416) 526-8800
Staff: Hamish Robertson, General Manager; Boris Brott, Musical Director and Conductor

HAMILTON PHILHARMONIC YOUTH ORCHESTRA (F)*
50 Main St., W
Hamilton, ON L8N 3Y7
(416) 526-8800

HURONIA SYMPHONY ORCHESTRA (D)
3 Clapperton St.
Barrie, ON L4M 3E4
(705) 728-0871
Staff: Arthur Burgin, Conductor; Noel G. Stephenson, Business Manager

KINGSTON SYMPHONY (B)
86 Lakeshore Blvd.
Kingston, ON K7L 5C8
(613) 389-0578
Staff: Lotte Bright, Manager; Brian Jackson, Conductor

KITCHENER-WATERLOO SYMPHONY ORCHESTRA (B)
101 Queen St. N.
Kitchener, ON N2H 6P7
(519) 745-4711
Staff: Caroline Oliver, General Manager; Raffi Armenia, Musical Director

LONDON YOUTH SYMPHONY ORCHESTRA (F)*
203 Baseline Rd., E
London, ON N6C 2N6
Staff: Jerome D. Summers, Musical Director; John Sterne, Manager

MCMASTER UNIVERSITY SYMPHONY ORCHESTRA (E)
Dept. of Music
Hamilton, ON L8S 4M2
(416) 525-9140
Staff: Lee Hepner, Conductor

MISSISSAUGA SYMPHONY ORCHESTRA (C)
Symphony Centre
161 Lakeshore Rd., W
Mississauga, ON L5H 1G3
(416) 274-1571
Staff: John Barnum, Conductor; Lynn Osmond, Executive Director

NATIONAL ARTS CENTRE ORCHESTRA (B)
Box 1534, Station "B"
Ottawa, ON K1P 5W1
(613) 996-5051
Staff: Joanne Morrow, Musical Administrator; Franco Mannino, Musical Advisor

NATIONAL YOUTH ORCHESTRA OF CANADA (F)*
76 Charles St., W
Toronto, ON M5S 1K8
(416) 922-5031
Staff: John Pellerin, General Director

NEPEAN SYMPHONY ORCHESTRA (C)
65 Bentley Ave.
Nepean, ON K2E 6T7
(613) 224-5523

NIAGARA SYMPHONY ORCHESTRA (B)
P.O. Box 401
Saint Catharines, ON L2R 6V9
(416) 685-7358
Staff: Ian Spraggon, General Manager; Uri Mayer, Guest Conductor

NIAGARA YOUTH ORCHESTRA (F)*
24 The Cedars
Saint Catharines, ON L2M 6M8
(416) 934-3314
Staff: Joseph Bandi, Manager; Tak Ng Lai, Conductor

NORTH YORK SYMPHONY (C)
P.O. Box 20
1210 Sheppard Ave., E, Ste. 109
Willowdale, ON M2K 1E3
(416) 499-2204
Staff: William McCauley, Conductor; W.E. Ward, General Manager

ORCHESTRA LONDON CANADA (B)
520 Wellington St.
London, ON N6A 3P9
(519) 679-8558
Staff: Paul B. Eck, General Manager; Alexis Hauser, Musical Director

ROYAL CONSERVATORY ORCHESTRA (E)*
273 Bloor St. W
Toronto, ON M5S 1W2
(416) 978-3797
Staff: Andrew R. Shaw, Director

THUNDER BAY SYMPHONY ORCHESTRA (B)
P.O. Box 2004
Thunder Bay, ON P7B 5E7
(807) 344-0631
Staff: Bruce Chown, General Manager; Dwight Bennett, Musical Director

TORONTO SYMPHONY ORCHESTRA (A)*
60 Simcoe St., Ste. C-116
Toronto, ON M5J 2H5
(416) 593-7769
Staff: Walter Homburger, Managing Director; Andrew Davis, Musical Director; J. Wray Armstrong, Assistant Manager and Musical Administrator

TORONTO SYMPHONY YOUTH ORCHESTRA (F)*
60 Simcoe St., Ste.C-116
Toronto, ON M5J 2H5
(416) 593-7769
Staff: Loie Fallis, Manager; David Zafer, Conductor

UNIVERSITY OF TORONTO SYMPHONY ORCHESTRA (E)
Faculty of Music
Edward Johnson Building
Toronto, ON M5S 1A1

WINDSOR SYMPHONY (B)
586 Ouellette Ave., No. 307
Windsor, ON N9A 1B7
(519) 254-4337
Staff: Margaret Krause, Manager; Laszlo Gati, Musical Director and Conductor

WOODSTOCK STRINGS (D)
419 Drew St.
Woodstock, ON N4S 4V3
(519) 537-3959
Staff: Patrick Burroughs, Conductor

QUEBEC

MCGILL CHAMBER ORCHESTRA (D)
5459 Earnscliffe Ave.
Montreal, PQ H3X 2P8
(514) 487-5190
Staff: Dr. Alexander Brott, Conductor

MCGILL SYMPHONY ORCHESTRA (E)
McGill University
Faculty of Music
555 Sherbooke St., W
Montreal, PQ H3A 1E3
(514) 392-4533
Staff: Richard Hoenich, Conductor

MONTREAL CIVIC YOUTH ORCHESTRA (F)*
Sun Life Building
1155 Metcalfe, Ste. 809
Montreal, PQ H3B 2V6
(514) 878-9680
Staff: Sandra Wilson, President; Jacques D. Clement, Musical Director

MONTREAL SYMPHONY ORCHESTRA (A)*
200 de Maisonneuve Blvd. W.
Montreal, PQ H2X 1Y9
(514) 842-3402
Staff: Zarin Mehta, Managing Director; Charles Dutoit, Musical Director; Madeleine Panaccio, Assistant Managing Director

QUEBEC SYMPHONY ORCHESTRA (A)
350 E. St.-Cyrille Blvd., No. 201
Quebec, PQ G1R, 2B4
(418) 692-3931
Staff: Francois Magnan, General Manager; James DePreist, Musical Director

SASKATCHEWAN

REGINA SYMPHONY ORCHESTRA (B)
200 Lakeshore Dr.
Regina, SK S4S 0B3
(306) 586-9555
Staff: Ann Hewat, General Manager; Simon Streatfeild, Musical Director

SASKATOON SYMPHONY ORCHESTRA (B)
P.O. Box 1361
Saskatoon, SK S7K 3N9
(306) 665-6414
Staff: John Holland, General Manager; David Gray, Musical Director

Symphony Orchestras Index

A

B

C

D

E

F

G

H

I

J

K

L

M

N

S

V

W

Y

Z

Opera Companies

U.S. and Canadian opera companies are listed alphabetically by state or province. Professional, semi-professional, community, and college opera companies, musical theatre companies, and workshops are included. Phone number and principal personnel are given for most companies. The letter in parentheses following the company's name indicates classification, based on the rating system developed by the Central Opera Service.

A* Major opera company (annual budget more than $1 million)
A Opera company (annual budget $500,000 - $1 million)
B Opera company (annual budget $100,000 - $500,000
C Opera company (annual budget less than $100,000)
S Sponsoring organization
T Theatre company
W Academic workshop

Where information wasn't available, no code follows the listing. An alphabetical cross-index appears at the end of this section.

ALABAMA

AUBURN UNIVERSITY (W)
Opera Workshop
Goodwin Music Building
Auburn, AL 36830
(205) 826-4165
Staff: Mary Joe Howard, Director

BIRMINGHAM CIVIC OPERA ASSOCIATION (B)
Box 76230
Birmingham, AL 35253
(205) 322-6737
Staff: Robert C. Austin, Musical Director

BIRMINGHAM SOUTHERN COLLEGE (W)
Opera Workshop
800 8th Ave. W.
Birmingham, AL 35254
(205) 328-5250
Staff: Thomas Gibbs, Artistic Director

HUNTINGDON COLLEGE (W)
Summer Repertory
1500 E. Fairview Ave.
Montgomery, AL 36106
(205) 265-0511
Staff: Jeanne E. Shaffer, Opera Director

HUNTSVILLE COMMUNITY COLLEGE (W)
Music Dept.
Huntsville, AL 35805

HUNTSVILLE OPERA WORKSHOP
8802 Willow Hills
Huntsville, AL 35802
Staff: Helen Bargetzi, Manager

MOBILE OPERA (B)
Box 8366
Mobile, AL 36608
(205) 342-7863
Staff: Katherine Wilson, General Manager

SAMFORD UNIVERSITY (W)
Opera Workshop
800 Lakeshore Dr.
Birmingham, AL 35229
(205) 870-2768
Staff: G. William Bugg, Director

SOUTHERN REGIONAL OPERA
Box 2151
Birmingham, AL 35201
(205) 251-1228
Staff: W. Cassell Stewart, President

TROY STATE UNIVERSITY (W)
Opera Workshop
Troy, AL 36082
(205) 566-3000
Staff: Philip Kelley, Director

UNIVERSITY OF ALABAMA (W)
Opera Theater
University, AL 35486
Staff: Darleen Feist, Director

UNIVERSITY OF MONTEVALLO (W)
Lyric Theater
Station 291
Montevallo, AL 35115
(205) 665-2521
Staff: Benjamin Middaugh, Director

ALASKA

ANCHORAGE CIVIC OPERA (A)
Box 3316
Anchorage, AK 99510
(907) 276-8688
Staff: Elvera Voth, Artistic Director

UNIVERSITY OF ALASKA (W)
Opera Workshop
Music Dept.
Fairbanks, AK 99701
(907) 474-7555
Staff: John Hopkins, Director

ARIZONA

ARIZONA OPERA COMPANY (A)
3501 N. Mountain Ave.
Tucson, AZ 85719
(602) 293-4336
Staff: Suzanne Clark, Business Manager

ARIZONA STATE UNIVERSITY (W)
Lyric Opera Theater
Dept. of Music
Tempe, AZ 85287
(602) 965-2856
Staff: Sylvia Debenport, Director

GLENDALE COMMUNITY COLLEGE (W)
Opera Workshop
Glendale, AZ 85306
(602) 934-2211
Staff: Mary Ann Dutton, Director

GRAND CANYON COLLEGE (W)
Opera Workshop
3300 W. Camelback
Phoenix, AZ 85061
(602) 249-3300
Staff: Mozelle C. Sherman, Director

MESA COMMUNITY COLLEGE (W)
Chamber Opera Theater
Mesa, AZ 85203

NORTHERN ARIZONA UNIVERSTIY (W)
Opera Theater
Box 6040
Flagstaff, AZ 86011
(602) 523-3731
Staff: Harry Pickup, Director

PHOENIX COLLEGE (W)
Opera Workshop
1202 West Thomas Rd.
Phoenix, AZ 85013
(602) 264-2492
Staff: Kay Poore, Director

PRESCOTT FINE ARTS
201 N. Marine
Prescott, AZ 86301
(602) 445-9853
Staff: Robert Gray, President

UNIVERSITY OF ARIZONA (W)
Opera Theater
School of Music
Tucson, AZ 85721
(602) 626-4820
Staff: Larry Day, Director

ARKANSAS

ARKANSAS OPERA THEATER (B)
908 Rock St.
Little Rock, AR 72202
(501) 372-7863
Staff: Ann Chotard, General Director

ARKANSAS REPERTORY THEATER (T)
712 East 11th St.
Little Rock, AR 72202
(501) 378-0405
Staff: Steven Caffery, General Manager

ARKANSAS STATE UNIVERSITY (W)
Opera Productions
Box 1047
State University, AR 72467
(501) 972-2094
Staff: David Niederbrach, Director

HARDING UNIVERSITY (W)
Music & Drama Department
Searcy, AR 72143
Staff: Vicki Dell, Director

HENDERSON STATE UNIVERSITY (W)
Music Department
Arkadelphia, AR 71923
(501) 246-5511

INSPIRATION POINT FINE ARTS COLONY (W)
Box 127
Eureka Springs, AR 72132
(405) 670-2204
Staff: Wenonah Williams, General Director

OUACHITA BAPTIST UNIVERSITY (W)
Opera Workshop
Box 693
Arkadelphia, AR 71923
(501) 246-4531
Staff: Harold Jones, Director

UNIVERSITY OF ARKANSAS (W)
Opera Theater
Fayetteville, AR 72701
(501) 575-4701
Staff: Richard Brothers, Director

UNIVERSITY OF ARKANSAS (W)
Opera Workshop
Box 3607
Monticello, AR 71655
(501) 367-6811
Staff: John W. Dougherty, Jr., Director

UNIVERSITY OF ARKANSAS (W)
Music Department
North Cedar
Pine Bluff, AR 71601

UNIVERSITY OF CENTRAL ARKANSAS (W)
Opera Workshop
Conway, AR 72032
Staff: Kay Kraeft, Director

CALIFORNIA

CALIFORNIA INSTITUTE OF THE ARTS (W)
Opera Workshop
24700 McBean Parkway
Valencia, CA 91355
Staff: Henrietta Pelta, Director

CALIFORNIA LYRIC GRAND OPERA
Box 3937
Los Angeles, CA 90039
Staff: Erica Hughes, Artistic Director

CALIFORNIA STATE COLLEGE/ STANISLAUS (W)
800 Monte Vista
Turlock, CA 95380
(209) 633-2421
Staff: Rosalie Jacobson, Chairman

CALIFORNIA STATE UNIVERSITY (W)
Opera Workshop
Chico, CA 95926

CALIFORNIA STATE/DOMINGUEZ HILLS (W)
Music Department
Carson, CA 90747
(213) 532-4300
Staff: Frances Steiner, Chairman

CALIFORNIA STATE UNIVERSITY (W)
Opera Theater
800 North State College Blvd.
Fullerton, CA 92634
(714) 773-3552
Staff: Michael Kurjian, Director

CALIFORNIA STATE UNIVERSITY (W)
Opera Theater
25800 Carlos Bee Blvd.
Hayward, CA 94542
(415) 881-3149
Staff: Thomas Accord, Director

CALIFORNIA STATE UNIVERSITY (W)
Music Theater
1250 Bellflower Blvd.
Long Beach, CA 90840
(213) 498-4781
Staff: Hans Lampl, Director

CALIFORNIA STATE UNIVERSITY (W)
Opera Theater
5151 University Dr.
Los Angeles, CA 90032
(213) 224-3448
Staff: Helen Blackenburg, Director

CALIFORNIA STATE UNIVERSITY (W)
Opera Theater
18111 Nordhoff St.
Northridge, CA 91336
(213) 363-5651
Staff: David W. Scott, Director

CALIFORNIA STATE UNIVERSITY (W)
Sonoma Opera Workshop
1801 East Cotati
Rohnert Park, CA 94928
(707) 664-2324
Staff: Peggy Donovan-Jeffrey, Director

CALIFORNIA STATE UNIVERSITY (W)
Opera Workshop
5500 State College Parkway
San Bernardino, CA 92407
(714) 886-4240
Staff: Richard Saylor, Director

CAL-POLY UNIVERSITY (W)
Opera Workshop
3801 West Temple
Pomona, CA 91768
(714) 598-4580
Staff: Susan Burns, Director

CASA ITALIANA OPERA THEATER (T)
5959 Franklin, No. 212
Los Angeles, CA 90028
Staff: Mario Leonetti, General Director

CINNABAR OPERA THEATER
3333 Petaluma Blvd. North
Petaluma, CA 94952
(707) 763-8920
Staff: Marvin Klebe, Artistic Director

CITY COLLEGE OF SAN FRANCISCO (W)
Music Department
50 Phelan
San Francisco, CA 94112

COLLEGE OF NOTRE DAME (W)
Opera Workshop
1500 Ralston Ave.
Belmont, CA 94002
(415) 593-1601
Staff: Onnie Taylor, Musical Director

COLLEGE OF SAN MATEO (W)
Opera Workshop
San Mateo, CA 94402
Staff: R. Galen Marshall, Director

CUESTA COLLEGE (W)
Music Dept.
San Luis Obispo, CA 93401

DESERT OPERA THEATER (C)
Box 999
Palmdale, CA 93550
(805) 268-1417

Staff: Barbara Bowe, Business Administrator

DOMINICAN COLLEGE (W)
Opera Workshop
Grand Avenue
San Rafael, CA 94901
(415) 457-4440
Staff: Martin Frick, Director

EL CAMINO COLLEGE (W)
Opera Workshop
16007 Crenshaw Blvd.
Torrance, CA 90506
(213) 532-3670
Staff: Burnet Ferguson, Director

EL CAMINO OPERA
Box 5081
San Jose, CA 95150

EUTERPE OPERA OF SOUTHERN CALIFORNIA (C)
5453 Valley Ridge Ave.
Los Angeles, CA 90043
(213) 291-4156
Staff: Ruth L. Hitt, President

FIVE PENNY OPERA (T)
2701 Fairview Rd.
Costa Mesa, CA 92626
(714) 556-5972
Staff: Carole Chardonnay, Artistic Director

FRESNO CITY COLLEGE (W)
Lyric Opera
1101 East University
Fresno, CA 93741
Staff: L. LeGrand Anderson, Director

FULLERTON CIVIC LIGHT OPERA (B)
218 W. Commonwealth
Fullerton, CA 92632
(714) 526-3832
Staff: Grif Duncan, General Manager

GLENDALE COLLEGE (W)
Music Theater
1500 North Verdugo
Glendale, CA 91208
Staff: M. Young, Director

HIDDEN VALLEY OPERA (A)
Box 116
Carmel Valley, CA 93924
(408) 659-3115
Staff: Peter Meckel, General Director

HOLLYWOOD BOWL ASSOCIATION (S)
135 N. Grand Ave.
Los Angeles, CA 90012

HOLLYWOOD OPERA ENSEMBLE
7017 Willoughby Ave.
Los Angeles, CA 90038
(213) 851-0271
Staff: Alde Monte, General Director

HUMBOLDT LIGHT OPERA
Box 3327
Eureka, CA 95501
(701) 445-1954
Staff: James Stanard, Director

HUMBOLDT STATE UNIVERSITY (W)
Opera Workshop
Arcata, CA 95521
(707) 445-1954
Staff: James Stanard, Director

LA MIRADA CIVIC LIGHT OPERA (T)
14900 La Mirada Blvd.
La Mirada, CA 90638

LAMPLIGHTERS/OPERA WEST (B)
361 Dolores
San Francisco, CA 94110
(415) 621-2112
Staff: Spencer S. Beman, Executive Vice President

LONG BEACH CIVIC LIGHT OPERA (T)
Box 20280
Long Beach, CA 90801
(213) 432-7926
Staff: Harvey Waggoner, Executive Director

LONG BEACH GRAND OPERA (B)
300 East Ocean
Long Beach, CA 90802
(213) 426-9611
Staff: M. Milenski, General Director

L'OPERA COMIQUE
1022 Myra
Los Angeles, CA 90029

LOS ANGELES MASTER CHORALE
135 North Grand
Los Angeles, CA 90012
(213) 972-7282
Staff: Roger Wagner, Musical Director

LOS ANGELES OPERA REPERTORY THEATER (B)
218 South Orange Dr.
Los Angeles, CA 90036
(213) 937-2491
Staff: Johanna Dordick, Artistic Director

LOS MEDANOS COLLEGE (W)
Music Department
Pittsburg, CA 94565

LYRIC OPERA OF ORANGE COUNTY
Box 514
Laguna Beach, CA 92653
Staff: Nunzio Crisci, Director

MARIN OPERA
25 Pepper Way
San Rafael, CA 94901
Staff: Ingrid Martinez, Artistic Director

MARQUIS PUBLIC THEATER
3717 India
San Diego, CA 92103
Staff: Scott Busrath, Manager

MEROLA OPERA PROGRAM (B)
War Memorial Opera House
San Francisco, CA 94102
(415) 861-4008
Staff: Alice Cunningham, Coordinator

MODESTO JUNIOR COLLEGE (W)
Opera Theater
435 College Ave.
Modesto, CA 95350
(209) 526-2000
Staff: Lewis Woodward, Director

MOUNT ST. MARY'S COLLEGE (W)
Music Department
Los Angeles, CA 90049
(213) 476-2237
Staff: Sr. T. Espinoza, Chairman

MOUNT SAN JACINTO COLLEGE (W)
Music Department
Gilman Hot Springs, CA 92383
(714) 658-1035
Staff: A. Ayers, Director

MUSIC ACADEMY OF THE WEST (W)
1070 Fairway Rd.
Santa Barbara, CA 93108
(805) 969-4726
Staff: Theo Alcantara, Artistic Director

MUSICAL MASQUERS
Box 1253
Claremont, CA 91711
Staff: Sara Drucker, Director

MUSIC AT THE VINEYARDS (S)
Box 97
Saratoga, CA 95070
Staff: Opal Armstrong, Coordinator

NOVATO LYRIC OPERA
5 Sunnyhill Dr.
Novato, CA 94947
Staff: Anna Secrist, Manager

OAKLAND OPERA THEATER (C)
2350 Park Blvd.
Oakland, CA 94606
(415) 832-0559
Staff: Alice Taylor, Artistic Director and General Manager

OCCIDENTAL COLLEGE (W)
Opera Workshop
1600 Campus Rd.
Los Angeles, CA 90041
Staff: Kim Kowalke, Director

ODYSSEY THEATER ENSEMBLE (T)
12111 Ohio Ave.
Los Angeles, CA 90025
(213) 879-5221
Staff: Ron Sossi, Artistic Director

OPERA A LA CARTE
Box 39606A
Los Angeles, CA 90039
Staff: Richard Sheldon, Director

OPERA COMPANY OF THE THEATER OF LIGHT (T)
6817 Franklin Ave.
Los Angeles, CA 90028
(213) 876-6702
Staff: Charles O'Connor, General Director

OPERA IN WORKSHOP
Box 544
Los Angeles, CA 90028
Staff: Rosemarie Lappano, General Director

ORANGE COUNTY OPERA
1617 West Fourth St.
Santa Ana, CA 92701
(714) 543-1404
Staff: Christopher Webb, Associate Director

PACIFIC LYRIC THEATER
Box 86288
San Diego, CA 92138
(714) 287-7260
Staff: Kellie Elaina Evans, General Manager

PACIFIC OPERA
2624 Pacific Ave.
Stockton, CA 95204
Staff: Richard Frazier, Manager

PEPPERDINE UNIVERSITY (W)
Opera Workshop
24255 Pacific Coast Highway
Malibu, CA 90265
(213) 456-4580
Staff: Violet McMahon, Director

PIERCE COLLEGE (W)
Opera Workshop
6201 Winnetka Ave.
Woodland Hills, CA 91371
Staff: Jim Warren, Director

PLACER CLASSIC THEATER (T)
275 Orange
Auburn, CA 95603
Staff: Ron Garrison, Executive Director

POCKET OPERA (B)
1370 Taylor, No. 10
San Francisco, CA 94108
(415) 474-3226
Staff: Mark Warwarick, General Manager

POINT LOMA COLLEGE (W)
Music Department
3900 Lomaland Dr.
San Diego, CA 92106

RIVERSIDE OPERA
Box 2353
Riverside, CA 92506
(714) 682-1960
Staff: Frances Calkins, General Manager

SACRAMENTO COMMUNITY OPERA THEATER
Box 13782
Sacramento, CA 95813

SACRAMENTO OPERA (B)
5380 Elvas
Sacramento, CA 95819
(916) 739-6924
Staff: Marianne Oaks, General Director

SAN CLEMENTE OPERA
Box 485
San Clemente, CA 92672
Staff: Dino Palazzi, Director

SAN DIEGO CIVIC LIGHT OPERA (T)
4408 Twain Avenue
San Diego, CA 92120
(714) 280-9111
Staff: J. Howard Stein, Executive Producer and Manager

SAN DIEGO OPERA (A*)
Box 988
San Diego, CA 92112
(714) 232-7636
Staff: Tito Capobianco, General Director

SAN DIEGO STATE UNIVERSITY (W)
Opera Center
217 College
San Diego, CA 92182
Staff: Tito Capobianco, Director

SAN FRANCISCO CHILDREN'S OPERA
245 Tenth Ave.
Box 18143
San Francisco, CA 94118
(415) 386-9622
Staff: Norbert Gingold, Director

SAN FRANCISCO CONSERVATORY OF MUSIC (W)
Opera Theater
1201 Ortega
San Francisco, CA 94122
(415) 564-8086
Staff: Susan Webb, Director

SAN FRANCISCO OPERA (A*)
War Memorial Opera House
San Francisco, CA 94102
(415) 861-4008
Staff: Terence McEwen, General Director

SAN FRANCISCO OPERA CENTER (B)
War Memorial Opera House
San Francisco, CA 94102
(415) 861-4008
Staff: Christine Bullin, Manager

SAN FRANCISCO STATE UNIVERSITY (W)
Opera Workshop
1600 Holloway
San Francisco, CA 94132
(415) 469-1432
Staff: Blanche Thebom, Director

SAN FRANCISCO TALENT BANK (C)
2100 Green St.
San Francisco, CA 94123
(415) 922-6072
Staff: Clara Dayton, Manager

SAN JOSE STATE UNIVERSITY (W)
Opera Theater
San Jose, CA 95192
(408) 277-2918
Staff: Irene Dalis, Production Director

SANTA MONICA CIVIC OPERA
1322 Tenth St.
Santa Monica, CA 90401
(213) 395-9703
Staff: Mario Lanza, Musical Director

SCHOLAR OPERA (B)
877 Moana Ct.
Palo Alto, CA 94306
(415) 858-2224
Staff: Donald Straka, General Director

SHASTA COLLEGE (W)
Fine Arts
Box 6006
Redding, CA 96099
(916) 214-3523
Staff: Cecil Johnson, Director

SIERRA CHAMBER OPERA
834 East Alamos
Fresno, CA 93704
(209) 227-4377
Staff: Alan Rea, Director

SKYLINE COLLEGE (W)
Opera Workshop
San Bruno, CA 94066
(415) 355-7000, ext. 121
Staff: Robert Conrad, Director

SONOMA OPERA WORKSHOP
(See California State University)

SOUTH COAST REPERTORY (W)
Box 2197
Costa Mesa, CA 92626
(714) 957-2602
Staff: David Emmes, Production Art Director

SOUTHERN CALIFORNIA CONSERVATORY (W)
Children's Opera Workshop
8711 Sunland Blvd.
Sun Valley, CA 91352
(213) 767-6554
Staff: Lurrine Burgess, Director

STANFORD SAVOYARDS
Stanford University
Tresidder Union
Stanford, CA 94305
(415) 497-2300, ext. 2411
Staff: Rita Taylor, Director

STANFORD UNIVERSITY (W)
Opera Theater
Music Department
Stanford, CA 94305
(415) 497-4304
Staff: Andor Toth, Director

STOCKTON OPERA (C)
Box 7883
Stockton, CA 95207
(209) 946-2415
Staff: Lucas Underwood, Artistic Director

UNIVERSITY OF CALIFORNIA (W)
Music Department
Irvine, CA 92664

(714) 833-6615
Staff: Peter Odegard, Chairman

UNIVERSITY OF CALIFORNIA (W)
Opera Theater
405 Hilgard Ave.
Los Angeles, CA 90024
(213) 825-4761
Staff: Samuel Krachmalnick, Musical Director

UNIVERSITY OF CALIFORNIA AT SAN DIEGO (W)
Opera Workshop
La Jolla, CA 92037
Staff: Thomas Nee, Director

UNIVERSITY OF CALIFORNIA (W)
Opera Theater
Santa Barbara, CA 93106
(805) 961-3484
Staff: Carl Zytowski, Director

UNIVERSITY OF THE PACIFIC (W)
Opera Theater
3601 Pacific Ave.
Stockton, CA 95211
(209) 946-2415
Staff: George Buckbee, Director

UNIVERSITY OF REDLANDS (W)
Music Theater
Redlands, CA 92373
(714) 793-2121
Staff: Jack Wilson, Director

UNIVERSITY OF SOUTHERN CALIFORNIA (W)
USC Opera
Ramo Hall
University Park
Los Angeles, CA 90007
(213) 743-7153
Staff: Natalie Limonick, General Director

VALLEY OPERA
Box 3292
Van Nuys, CA 91407
(213) 990-3761
Staff: Robert Chauls, Directors

VENTURA COLLEGE (W)
Music Department
Ventura, CA 93003

WEST BAY OPERA (C)
Box 231
Palo Alto, CA 94303
(415) 321-3471
Staff: Maria Holt, General Director

WEST COAST OPERA COMPANY (C)
776 King St.
San Gabriel, CA 91776
(213) 283-0079
Staff: Josephine Lombardo, General Director

WEST END OPERA
Box 172
Upland, CA 91786
(714) 981-3311
Staff: Frank Fetta, Musical Director

WEST HILLS COLLEGE(W)
Opera Workshop
300 Cherry Lane
Coalings, CA 93210
(209) 935-0801
Staff: Bernice Isham, Director

WESTERN OPERA THEATER (A)
War Memorial Opera House
San Francisco, CA 94102
(415) 861-4008
Staff: Terence McEwen, General Director

YOUTH IN ARTS (T)
74 Eliseo Dr.
Greenbrae, CA 94904
(415) 461-8155
Staff: Nyna Koppich, Executive Director

COLORADO

ADAMS STATE COLLEGE (W)
Music Theater Workshop
Alamosa, CO 81101
Staff: Randolph Jones, Director

CENTRAL CITY OPERA HOUSE ASSOCIATION (A)
1615 California St., No. 510
Denver, CO 80202
(303) 623-7167
Staff: John Moriarty, Artistic Director

COLORADO COLLEGE (W)
Music Dept.
Colorado Springs, CO 80903
(303) 473-2233
Staff: Albert Seay, Chairman

COLORADO STATE UNIVERSITY (W)
Opera Theater
Fort Collins, CO 80523
(303) 491-6780
Staff: John Lueck, Director

EVERGREEN CHORALE
c/o Weiker
6376 South Gray Ct.
Littleton, CO 80123
Staff: Marcia Phelps, Business Manager

OPERA COLORADO (A*)
121 Pearl
Denver, CO 80203
(303) 778-6464
Staff: Nathaniel Merrill, Artistic Director

ROCKMOUNT COLLEGE (W)
Music Dept.
Denver, CO 80226

SAN LUIS VALLEY OPERA THEATER
205 West Ave.
Alamosa, CO 81101
(303) 589-4541
Staff: Marilyn Wienand, Director

STEAMBOAT REPERTORY THEATER (T)
Box 771589
Steamboat Springs, CO 80477
(303) 879-6900
Staff: Andrew Eiseman, Managing Director

UNIVERSITY OF COLORADO (W)
Opera Theater
Boulder, CO 80309
(303) 492-6352
Staff: Dennis Jackson, Director

UNIVERSITY OF DENVER (W)
Lamont School of Music Opera Theater
Denver, CO 80208
(303) 753-2705
Staff: Ronald Worstell, Director

UNIVERSITY OF NORTHERN COLORADO (W)
Opera Theater
Greely, CO 80631
(303) 351-2248
Staff: Claude M. Schmitz, Producer

WESTERN STATE COLLEGE (W)
Opera Workshop
Gunnison, CO 81230
(303) 943-3093
Staff: Linda Marra, Director

CONNECTICUT

COMPOSER/LIBRETTIST CONFERENCE (C)
O'Neill Center
305 Great Neck Rd.
Waterford, CT 06385
(203) 443-5378
Staff: Marilyn Glassman, Administrator

CONNECTICUT GRAND OPERA (B)
576 Post Rd.
Darien, CT 06820
(203) 655-2332
Staff: John Hiddlestone, General Manager

CONNECTICUT OPERA (A)
15 Lewis St.
Hartford, CT 06103
(203) 527-0713
Staff: George Osborne, General Director

ELM CITY REPERTORY
Box 2021
New Haven, CT 06511

GOODSPEED OPERA HOUSE (T)
East Haddam, CT 06423
(203) 873-8664
Staff: Michael Price, Exeuctive Director

GREATER NEW BRITAIN OPERA
Box 664
New Britain, CT 06050

HARTMAN THEATER COMPANY (T)
Box 521
Stamford, CT 06904
(203) 324-6781
Staff: Harris Goldman, Exeuctive Director

HARTT COLLEGE OF MUSIC (W)
Opera Theater
200 Bloomfield Ave.
West Hartford, CT 06117
(203) 243-4469
Staff: Adelaide Bishop, Director

OPERA EXPRESS
15 Lewis St.
Hartford, CT 06103
(203) 527-0713
Staff: George Osborne, General Director

STAMFORD STATE OPERA (C)
1 Landmark Sq., 20th Flr.
Stamford, CT 06901
(203) 325-0686
Staff: Giovanni Corsiglio, Artistic Director

TROUPERS LIGHT OPERA
357 Highland
South Norwalk, CT 06854
(203) 853-4843
Staff: Diane Platenyk, President

WESTERN CONNECTICUT STATE COLLEGE (W)
Music Department
Danbury, CT 06810
(203) 747-4320

YALE UNIVERSITY (W)
School of Music
96 Wall St.
New Haven, CT 06520
(203) 436-8740
Staff: Phyllis Curtin, Opera Director

DELAWARE

MINIKIN OPERA COMPANY
4101 Washington St.
Wilmington, DE 19802
(302) 762-1132
Staff: June Cason, General Manager

OPERA DELAWARE (B)
Box 3553
Greenville, DE 19807
(302) 658-2507
Staff: Eric Kjellmark, President

UNIVERSITY OF DELAWARE (W)
Music Department
Newark,DE 19711
(302) 738-2577
Staff: Henry Cody, Chairman

WILMINGTON DRAMA LEAGUE
Box 504
Wilmington, DE 19899
Staff: Anne Grass, Managing Director

DISTRICT OF COLUMBIA

ARENA STAGE (T)
Sixth & Maine, SW
Washington, DC 20024
(202) 554-9066
Staff: Thomas Fichandler, Executive Director

CATHOLIC UNIVERSITY OF AMERICA (W)
Opera Workshop
Fourth and Michigan Ave., NE
Washington, DC 20064
(202) 635-5418
Staff: Michael Cordovana, Director

CHILDREN'S OPERA THEATER
1435 Fourth St., SW
Washington, DC 20024
Staff: Michael Kaye, Artistic Director

GEORGE WASHINGTON UNIVERSITY (W)
Music Dept.
2029 "G" St., NW
Washington, DC 20052
(202) 676-6245
Staff: George Steiner, Chairman

KENNEDY CENTER FOR THE PERFORMING ARTS (S)
Kennedy Center
Washington, DC 20566
Staff: Sir Roger L. Stevens, Chairman

NATIONAL LYRIC OPERA
5332 Sherrier Pl., NW
Washington, DC 20016
(703) 241-0008
Staff: Nikita Wells, General Manager

OPERA, SW
400 "T" St., SW
Washington, DC 20024
Staff: Susan Palmer, Producer

OPERA THEATER OF WASHINGTON
Box 40154
Washington, DC 20016
(301) 434-9082
Staff: Scott Mattingly, General Director

SOKOL OPERA
4529 Grant Rd., NW
Washington, DC 20016
(202) 363-8415
Staff: Lida Brodenova, Artistic Director

SUMMER OPERA THEATER COMPANY (C)
620 Michigan Ave., NE
Washington, DC 20064
(202) 526-1669
Staff: Elaine Walter, Executive Director

TRINITY COLLEGE (W)
Music Dept.
Washington, DC 20017
(202) 269-2270
Staff: Sharon Shafer, Chairman

WASHINGTON CIVIC OPERA (C)
3149 16th St., NW
Washington, DC 20010
(703) 527-0734
Staff: Richard Weilemann, Artistic Director

WASHINGTON OPERA (A*)
Kennedy Center
Washington, DC 20566
(202) 822-4700
Staff: Martin Feinstein, General Director

FLORIDA

ASOLO OPERA COMPANY (B)
61 North Pineapple
Sarasota, FL 33577
(813) 366-8450
Staff: Philip Hall, Executive Director

BROWARD COMMUNITY COLLEGE (W)
Opera Workshop
3501 Davie Rd.
Davie, FL 33324
(305) 475-6879
Staff: Richard Crawford, Director

FLORIDA ATLANTIC UNIVERSITY (W)
Opera Theater
Boca Raton, FL 33431
(305) 395-5100
Staff: Richard Wright, Director

FLORIDA LYRIC OPERA
1055 Stephen Foster Dr.
Largo, FL 33541
(813) 531-9116
Staff: Rosalia Maresca, Director

FLORIDA OPERA FOR YOUTH
3687 Southwest First St.
Fort Lauderdale, FL 33312
(305) 583-8799
Staff: G. Robert Smith, Director

FLORIDA OPERA REPERTORY
700 Santander Ave.
Coral Gables, FL 33134
(305) 443-7370
Staff: Bella Smith, Executive Director and President

FLORIDA OPERA WEST (B)
75 Pinellas Way North
St. Petersburg, FL 33710
(813) 381-2151
Staff: Thomas Palmer, General Manager

FLORIDA SOUTHERN COLLEGE (W)
Music Department
Lakeland, FL 33802

FLORIDA STATE UNIVERSITY (W)
Opera Department
Tallahassee, FL 32306
(904) 644-5248
Staff: F. Eugene Dybdahl, Director

GREATER MIAMI OPERA ASSOCIATION (A*)
1200 Coral Way
Miami, FL 33145
(305) 854-1643
Staff: Robert Herman, General Manager

JACKSONVILLE UNIVERSITY (W)
Opera Workshop
College of Fine Arts
Jacksonville, FL 32211
(904) 744-3950
Staff: William Vessel, Director

MANATEE JUNIOR COLLEGE (W)
Music Department
Bradenton, FL 33505

MIAMI-DADE COMMUNITY COLLEGE (W)
Music Department
Miami, FL 33176
(305) 596-1284
Staff: Jane Pyle, Chairman

NORTH MIAMI BEACH OPERA COMPANY
5225 La Gorce Dr.
North Miami Beach, FL 33140
(305) 864-7984
Staff: Laurence Siegel, Musical Director

OPERA JACKSONVILLE/OPERA A LA CARTE, INC.(C)
4227 Peachtree Circle East
Jacksonville, FL 32207
(904) 737-7858
Staff: Amelia Smith, General Manager

ORLANDO OPERA COMPANY (B)
801 N. Magnolia Ave., No. 212B
Orlando, FL 32803
(305) 423-9527
Staff: Dwight Bowes, General Manager

PALISADES THEATER (T)
Box 10717
St. Petersburg, FL 33733
(813) 823-1600
Staff: Barbara Siefer, Managing Director

PALM BEACH OPERA (B)
500 North Congress, No. 141
Palm Beach, FL 33401
(305) 689-7000
Staff: Jean St. John, Acting General Director

PENSACOLA JUNIOR COLLEGE (W)
Summer Opera
100 College Boulevard
Pensacola, FL 32504
(904) 476-5410
Staff: Sidney Kennedy, Director

SPANISH LITTLE THEATER
1704 Seventh
Tampa, FL 33605
Staff: R. Gonzalez Director

UNIVERSITY OF CENTRAL FLORIDA (W)
Opera Workshop
Music Dept.
Box 25000
Orlando, FL 32816
(305) 275-2867
Staff: Elizabeth Wrancher, Director

UNIVERSITY OF FLORIDA (W)
Music Department
Gainesville, FL 32601
(904) 392-6629
Staff: Elizabeth Graham, Chairman

UNIVERSITY OF MIAMI (W)
Opera Workshop
Box 248165
Coral Gables, FL 33124
(305) 284-2470
Staff: Franklin Summers, Director

UNIVERSITY OF SOUTH FLORIDA (W)
Opera Workshop
Fowler Ave.
Tampa, FL 33620
(813) 974-2311
Staff: Annamary Dickey, Director

GEORGIA

ALLIANCE THEATER COMPANY (T)
1280 Peachtree Northeast
Atlanta, GA 30309
(404) 892-7529
Staff: Fred Chappell, Artistic Director

ARMSTRONG STATE COLLEGE (W)
Opera Workshop
11935 Abercorn
Savannah, GA 31406
(912) 927-5325
Staff: Dan Radebaugh, Director

ATLANTA CIVIC OPERA (B)
1293 Peachtree, Northeast, No. 830
Atlanta, GA 30309
(404) 872-1706
Staff: Marti Hagan, General Manager

AUGUSTA COLLEGE (W)
Opera Workshop
Augusta, GA 30910
(404) 828-3211
Staff: James Russey, Director

AUGUSTA OPERA ASSOCIATION (B)
Box 3865 Hill Station
Augusta, GA 30904
(404) 738-0451
Staff: Edward Bradberry, Artistic Director

BRENAU COLLEGE (W)
Music Department
Gainesville, GA 30501

CLAYTON JUNIOR COLLEGE (W)
Opera Workshop
Box 285
Morrow, GA 30260
(404) 474-2700
Staff: Jack L. Hutcheson, Director

DEKALB COLLEGE (W)
Opera Theater
555 North Indian Creek
Clarkston, GA 30021
(404) 292-1520
Staff: Jim Bradford, Director

GEORGIA SOUTHERN COLLEGE (W)
Opera Workshop
Statesboro, GA 30460
(912) 681-5396
Staff: Joseph Robbins, Director

GEORGIA STATE UNIVERSITY (W)
Summer Opera Workshop
University Plaza
Atlanta, GA 30303
(404) 658-2349
Staff: Peter Harrower, Director

MACON JUNIOR COLLEGE (W)
Opera Workshop
Macon, GA 31206
(912) 474-2700
Staff: Jack L. Hutcheson, Director

NORTH GEORGIA COLLEGE (W)
Music Department
Dahlonga, GA 30533
(404) 864-3391
Staff: David Barnett, Chairman

OPERA, INC.
297 Gordon Ave. Northeast
Atlanta, GA 30307
(404) 373-8169
Staff: Alice Bliss, Director

PHOENIX OPERA (C)
Box 28003
Atlanta, GA 30328
(404) 255-1128
Staff: Olga Loveland, Managing Director

SHOESTRING OPERA
30 Montclair Dr.
Atlanta, GA 30309
Staff: Marilyn Dietrichs, Director

SHORTER COLLEGE (W)
Opera Workshop
Box 434
Rome, GA 30161
(404) 291-2121
Staff: John Ramsaur, Director

SOUTHEASTERN SAVOYARDS
2300 Henderson Mill Rd., No. 310
Atlanta, GA 30345
Staff: Tedi Langdon, Manager

UNIVERSITY OF GEORGIA (W)
Opera Workshop
Athens, GA 30601
(404) 542-5255
Staff: David Stoffel, Director

VALDOSTA STATE COLLEGE (W)
Opera Theater
Valdosta, GA 31601
(912) 244-4699
Staff: Carol Mikkelsen, Director

WEST GEORGIA COLLEGE (W)
Opera Workshop
Carrollton, GA 30017
Staff: Inge Manski-Lundeen, Director

YOUNG HARRIS COLLEGE (W)
Music Theater
Box 233
Young Harris, GA 30582
(404) 379-3746
Staff: William Fox, Director

HAWAII

HAWAII OPERA THEATER (B)
987 Waimanu
Honolulu, HI 96814
(808) 521-6537
Staff: Rosanne Cribley, Associate Manager

UNIVERSITY OF HAWAII (W)
Performing Arts Department
1400 Kapiolani
Hilo, HI 96720
(808) 961-9352
Staff: Jackie Johnson Debus, Director

UNIVERSITY OF HAWAII (W)
Opera Workshop
2411 Dole St.
Honolulu, HI 96844
(808) 948-6384
Staff: John Mount, Director

IDAHO

BOISE STATE UNIVERSITY (W)
Opera Theater
1907 University Dr.
Boise, ID 83725
(208) 385-1954
Staff: Victor Chacon, Director

IDAHO FALLS SYMPHONY OPERA THEATER
1090 Bannock
Idaho Falls, ID 83401
Staff: Alvin Nelson, Director

RICKS COLLEGE (W)
Opera Workshop
Snow Building
Rexburg, ID 83440
(208) 356-2604
Staff: Inga Johnson, Director

UNIVERSITY OF IDAHO (W)
Opera Workshop
Moscow, ID 83843
(208) 885-6231
Staff: Charles W. Walton, Director

ILLINOIS

AMERICAN CONSERVATORY OF MUSIC (W)
116 South Michigan
Chicago, IL 60603
(312) 263-4161

BRADLEY UNIVERSITY (W)
Opera Workshop
Peoria, IL 61606
Staff: JoAnn Lacquet, Director

CHAMBER OPERA THEATER
805 Belle Plaine Ave.
Chicago, IL 60613
(312) 975-6520
Staff: Edward C. Starkeson, General Manager

CHICAGO OPERA REPERTORY THEATER
Box 921
Chicago, IL 60690
Staff: Bruce Kamsler, Executive Director

CHICAGO OPERA THEATER
410 S. Michigan Ave., No. 540
Chicago, IL 60605
(312) 663-0555
Staff: Alan Stone, Artistic Director

COLLEGE OF DUPAGE (W)
Opera Workshop
Music Department
Glen Ellyn, IL 60137
(312) 858-2800
Staff: Harold Bauer, Director

DEPAUL UNIVERSITY
Chamber Opera
804 West Belden
Chicago, IL 60614
(312) 321-7776
Staff: Frank Little, Director

DUPAGE/MID AMERICAN OPERA
1300 North Dearborn
Chicago, IL 60610
(312) 944-6250
Staff: Karen Black, General Director

EASTERN ILLINOIS UNIVERSITY (W)
Music Theater Workshop
Charleston, IL 61920
(217) 581-3110
Staff: G. Sullivan, Director

HINSDALE OPERA THEATER (B)
Box 414
Hinsdale, IL 60521
(312) 323-8989
Staff: Nancy Hotvhkiss, General Manager

ILLINOIS WESLEYAN UNIVERSITY (W)
Opera Theater
Presser Hall
Bloomington, IL 61701
(309) 556-3122
Staff: Linda June Snyder, Director

LIGHT OPERA WORKS
927 Noyes
Evanston, IL 60201
(312) 869-6300
Staff: Bridget McDonald, Managing Director

LITHUANIAN OPERA COMPANY (B)
6905 South Artesian Ave.
Chicago, IL 60629
(312) 737-0235
Staff: Vytautas Radzius, General Manager

LYRIC OPERA CENTER FOR AMERICAN ARTISTS
20 N. Wacker Dr.
Chicago, IL 60606
(312) 346-6047
Staff: Carol Yamamoto, Manager

LYRIC OPERA OF CHICAGO (A*)
20 North Wacker Dr.
Chicago, IL 60606
(312) 346-6111
Staff: Ardis Krainik, General Manager

MIDLAND REPERTORY PLAYERS
930 Henry St.
Alton, IL 62002
(618) 462-3948
Staff: Kaye Shanahan, Artistic Director

MILLIKEN UNIVERSITY (W)
Opera Theater
1184 West Main St.
Decatur, IL 62522
(217 424-6328
Staff: Stephen Fiol, Director

MUSIC OF THE BAROQUE
343 S. Dearborn
Chicago, IL 60604
Staff: Earl Westfall, Director

NORTHERN ILLINOIS UNIVERSITY (W)
Opera Workshop
Chicago, IL 60115
(615) 753-1841
Staff: Elwood Smith, Director

NORTHWESTERN UNIVERSITY (W)
Opera Theater
School of Music
Evanston, IL 60201
(312) 492-5090
Staff: Robert Gay, Director

PEORIA CIVIC OPERA (B)
6016 North Knoxville Ave., No. 304A
Peoria, IL 61614
(309) 692-1569
Staff: Cybelle Abt, Director

PICCOLO PRODUCTIONS
Box 156
Chicago, IL 60690
Staff: Marijo Richter, Director

ROOSEVELT UNIVERSITY (W)
Opera Theater
430 S. Michigan Ave.

Chicago, IL 60605
(312) 341-3794
Staff: Clifford Reims, Director

ST. CECILIA OPERA REPERTORY (C)
Box 701
Westmont, IL 60559
(312) 985-8497
Staff: Marsha Lopez, Managing Director

SOUTHERN ILLINOIS UNIVERSITY (W)
Marjorie Lawrence Opera Theater
Carbondale, IL 62901
(618) 453-2792
Staff: Mike Blum, Director

SOUTHERN ILLINOIS UNIVERSITY (W)
Opera Workshop
Edwardsville, IL 62026
(612) 692-2489
Staff: Luther Stripling, Director

THORNTON COMMUNITY COLLEGE (W)
Opera Workshop
South Holland, IL 60473
(312) 596-2000
Staff: Dimpna Clarin, Director

UNIVERSITY OF CHICAGO (W)
Music Department
5845 Ellis
Chicago, IL 60637
(312) 753-2612
Staff: Phillip Gossett, Chairman

UNIVERSITY OF ILLINOIS (W)
Opera Theater
School of Music
Urbana, IL 61801
(217) 596-3254
Staff: David Lloyd, Artistic Director

WESTERN ILLINOIS UNIVERSITY (W)
Opera Workshop
Macomb, IL 61455
(309) 298-1544
Staff: Bruce Gardner, Director

WHEATON COLLEGE (W)
Opera Workshop
Wheaton, IL 60187
(312) 260-5100
Staff: Mary Hopper, Director

INDIANA

ANDERSON COLLEGE (W)
Music Department
Anderson, IN 46012
(317) 649-9071, ext. 2414
Staff: Greta Dominic, Artistic Director

BALL STATE UNIVERSITY (W)
Opera Workshop
Muncie, IN 47306
(317) 285-7334
Staff: Philip Ewart, Director

DEPAUW UNIVERSITY (W)
Opera/Musical Theater
134-E Performing Arts Center
Greencastle, IN 46135
(317) 658-4800
Staff: Thomas Fitzpatrick, Director

GOSHEN COLLEGE (W)
Opera Workshop
Goshen, IN 46526
(219) 533-3161
Staff: Doyle Preheim, Director

INDIANAPOLIS OPERA COMPANY (B)
708 E. Michigan
Indianapolis, IN 46202
(317) 638-4600
Staff: Vance du Rivage, Managing Director

INDIANA-PURDUE UNIVERSITY (W)
Opera Workshop
2101 Coliseum Blvd. East
Fort Wayne, IN 46805
(219) 482-5526
Staff: Joseph Meyers, Director

INDIANA STATE UNIVERSITY (W)
Opera Workshop
Terre Haute, IN 47809
(812) 232-6311, ext. 2123
Staff: Robert Hounchell, Director

INDIANA UNIVERSITY (W)
Opera Theater
School of Music
Bloomington, IN 47405
(812) 335-1582
Staff: Charles Webb, General Manager

INDIANA UNIVERSITY (W)
Opera Theater
1700 Mishawaka
South Bend, IN 46615
(219) 237-4100
Staff: Michael Esselstrom, Director

MICHIANA OPERA (C)
Box 1271
South Bend, IN 46624
(219) 233-2233
Staff: Robert DeMaree, Artistic Director

NORTHERN INDIANA OPERA ASSOCIATION
2303 College Ave.
Huntington, IN 46750
(219) 356-6000
Staff: Warren Jaworaski, Artistic Director

OPERA DE LAFAYETTE
Center for Performing Arts
Box 13
Lafayette, IN 47902
Staff: Ora McGuire, Manager

VALPARAISO UNIVERSITY (W)
Opera Workshop
Valparaiso, IN 46383
Staff: Joseph F. McCall, Director

WHITEWATER OPERA (B)
805 Promenade
Box 633
Richmond, IN 47374
(317) 962-7106
Staff: Charles Combopiano, General Manager and Artistic Director

IOWA

COE COLLEGE (W)
Opera Workshop
1220 First Ave., NE
Cedar Rapids, IA 52402
(319) 399-8521
Staff: Allan D. Kellar, Director

CORNELL COLLEGE (W)
Opera Workshop
Mount Vernon, IA 52314
(319) 895-8811
Staff: Marcella Lee, Director

DES MOINES METRO OPERA (B)
600 North Buxton
Indianola, IA 50125
(515) 961-6221
Staff: Douglas Duncan, Managing Director

DRAKE UNIVERSITY (W)
Opera Theater
Des Moines, IA 50311
(515) 271-3879
Staff: Marion Hall, Director

FAITH BAPTIST BIBLE COLLEGE (W)
Opera Workshop
1900 Northwest Fourth St.
Ankeny, IA 50021
(515) 964-0601
Staff: Michael Doonan, Director

IOWA STATE UNIVERSITY (W)
Opera Studio
Music Hall 104
Ames, IA 50010
(515) 294-2911
Staff: Donald Simonson, Director

LUTHER COLLEGE (W)
Opera Workshop
Decorah, IA 52101
(319) 387-1203
Staff: David F. Greedy, Director

ST. AMBROSE COLLEGE (W)
Opera Workshop
518 Locust St.
Davenport, IA 52803
(319) 383-8875
Staff: J.E. Greene, Director

SIMPSON COLLEGE (W)
Opera Workshop
Indianola, IA 50125
(515) 961-6251, est 637
Staff: Robert L. Larsen, Director

UNIVERSITY OF IOWA (W)
Opera Theater
Iowa City, IA 52242
Staff: James Dixon, Director

UNIVERSITY OF NORTHERN IOWA (W)
Lyric Theater
Cedar Falls, IA 50614
(319) 273-2353
Staff: John Pape, Director

KANSAS

BETHEL COLLEGE (W)
Opera Workshop
North Newton, KS 67117
(316) 283-2500
Staff: Walter Just, Director

EMPORIA STATE UNIVERSITY (W)
Opera Theater
1200 Commercial St.
Emporia, KS 66801
(316) 343-1200
Staff: H.J. Lennon, Director

FORT HAYS KANSAS STATE UNIVERSITY (W)
Opera Workshop
Malloy Hall
Hays, KS 67601
(913) 628-4258
Staff: Donald E. Stout, Director

KANSAS STATE UNIVERSITY (W)
Opera Theater
Manhattan, KS 66502
(913) 532-5740
Staff: Tomas Hernandez, Director

MUSIC THEATER OF WICHITA (B)
225 West Douglas, No. 201-L
Wichita, KS 67202
(316) 265-3253
Staff: John Holly, Production Director

PITTSBURG STATE UNIVERSITY (W)
Opera Workshop
Pittsburg, KS 66762
(316) 231-7000
Staff: Burton Parker, Director

ST. MARY'S COLLEGE (W)
Music Dept.
Levenworth, KS 66048
(913) 682-5151
Staff: William Krusemark, Director

TOPEKA CIVIC THEATER (T)
Box 893
Topeka, KS 66601
(913) 357-5213
Staff: Jim Robertson, Managing Director

UNIVERSITY OF KANSAS (W)
Opera Theater
Lawrence, KS 66045
(913) 864-3380
Staff: George Lawner, Director

WASHBURN UNIVERSITY (W)
Opera Theater
1700 College
Topeka, KS 66604
(913) 295-6511
Staff: Frederik Schuetze, Director

WICHITA STATE UNIVERSITY (W)
Opera Theater
1845 Fairmount
Wichita, KA 67208
(316) 689-3103
Staff: George H. Gibson, Director

KENTUCKY

BEREA COLLEGE (W)
Opera Workshop
Box 2352
Berea, KY 40404
(606) 986-9341
Staff: J. Ambroise-Chaumont, Director

CENTER CIVIC OPERA (C)
524 Madison
Covington, KY 41011
(606) 261-8617
Staff: Paul Zappa, Director

KENTUCKY OPERA ASSOCIATION (A)
631 South Fifth St.
Louisville, KY 40202
(502) 584-4500
Staff: Thomson Smillie, General Director

MURRAY STATE UNIVERSITY (W)
Opera Workshop
Murray, KY 42071
(502) 762-4288
Staff: Henry Bannon, Director

SOUTHERN BAPTIST THEOLOGICAL SEMINARY (W)
Opera Workshop
2825 Lexington Rd.
Louisville, KY 40280
(502) 897-4356
Staff: Carl Gerbrandt, Director

UNIVERSITY OF KENTUCKY (W)
Opera Workshop
Lexington, KY 40506
Staff: Phyllis Jenness, Director

UNIVERSITY OF LOUISVILLE (W)
Opera Theater
Belknap Campus
Louisville, KY 40292
(502) 588-5609
Staff: Allen Gross, Director

WESTERN KENTUCKY STATE UNIVERSITY (W)
Opera Theater
Bowling Green, KY 42101
(502) 745-3751
Staff: Virgil Hale, Director

LOUISIANA

BATON ROUGE OPERA
Box 2269
Baton Rouge, LA 70821
(504) 383-0554
Staff: Doores Ardoyno, General Manager

CENTENARY COLLEGE (W)
Opera Theater
Shreveport, LA 71104
(318) 869-0933
Staff: William Riley, Director

LOUISIANA OPERA THEATER (B)
Box 4057
2803 Woodlawn Ave.
Shreveport, LA 71104
(318) 869-2559

LOUISIANA STATE UNIVERSITY (W)
Opera Theater
Baton Rouge, LA 70803
(504) 389-6446
Staff: Richard Asianian, Director

LOUISIANA TECH UNIVERSITY (W)
Opera Workshop
Tech Station
Ruston, LA 71272
(318) 257-3536
Staff: Schuman Yang, Director

MCNEESE STATE UNIVERSITY (W)
Opera Workshop
Lake Charles, LA 70601
Staff: Michele Derrick-Gehrig, Director

NEW ORLEANS OPERA ASSOCIATION, INC. (A)
333 St. Charles Ave., No. 907
New Orleans, LA 70130
(504) 529-2278
Staff: Arthur Cosenza, General Director

NORTHEAST LOUISIANA UNIVERSITY (W)
Opera Workshop
Monroe, LA 71209
(318) 342-4118
Staff: Suzanne Hickman, Director

NORTHWESTERN STATE UNIVERSITY (W)
Opera Theater
Natchitoches, LA 71457
(318) 357-6444
Staff: John E. Taylor, Director

SHREVEPORT OPERA (B)
515 Spring St.
Shreveport, LA 71101
(318) 227-9503
Staff: Robert Murray, General Director

SOUTHEASTERN LOUISIANA UNIVERSITY (W)
Opera Workshop
Box 815
Hammond, LA 70402
Staff: Scharmal Schrock, Director

TULANE UNIVERSITY (W)
Opera Theater
Dixon Hall
New Orleans, LA 70118
(504) 865-5269
Staff: Francis Monachino, Director

UNIVERSITY OF NEW ORLEANS (W)
Opera Theater

Lakefront
New Orleans, LA 70148
(504) 286-6381
Staff: Raquel Cortina, Director

UNIVERSITY OF SOUTHWESTERN LOUISIANA (W)
Opera Guild
Box 41534
Lafayette, LA 70504
(318) 231-6016
Staff: G.S. Beman Griffin, Director

MAINE

MAINE OPERA ASSOCIATION (C)
Box 4404 Station A
Portland, ME 04101
(207) 799-7137
Staff: Andrew McMullan, General and Artistic Director

UNIVERSITY OF MAINE(W)
Opera Workshop
Pleasant St.
Fort Kent, ME 04743
(207) 834-3162
Staff: Charles Closser, Jr., Director

UNIVERSITY OF MAINE (W)
Opera Theater
209 Lord Hall
Orono, ME 04473
(207) 581-7656
Staff: Ludlow Hallman, Artistic Director

UNIVERSITY OF SOUTHERN MAINE (W)
Opera Workshop
Gorham, ME 04038
(207) 780-5272
Staff: Robert Russell, Director

MARYLAND

BALTIMORE CHAMBER OPERA (C)
Box 5654
Baltimore, MD 21210
(301) 752-1216
Staff: Matthew Sternberg, General Manager

BALTIMORE OPERA COMPANY (A*)
40 West Chase St.
Baltimore, MD 21201
(301) 727-0592
Staff: Jay Holbrook, General Manager

EASTERN OPERA THEATER
40 West Chase St.
Baltimore, MD 21201
(301) 727-0592
Staff: J.J. Lehmeyer, Producer

JOHNS HOPKINS UNIVERSITY
(See Peabody Conservatory)

MONTGOMERY COLLEGE (W)
Opera Theater
51 Mannakee St.
Rockville, MD 20850
Staff: Donald Miller, Director

OPERA PARADE
927 North Calvert
Baltimore, MD 21202
(301) 730-6488
Staff: Sally Stunkel, Artistic Director

PEABODY CONSERVATORY (W)
Opera Workshop
Johns Hopkins University
21 East Mount Vernon
Baltimore, MD 21202
(301) 235-1164
Staff: Roger Brunyate, Director

PRINCE GEORGE'S CIVIC OPERA (C)
Box 551
Riverdale, MD 20840
(301) 699-2459
Staff: Dorothy Biondi, General Manager

TOWSON STATE COLLEGE (W)
Opera Workshop
8000 York Rd.
Baltimore, MD 21204
(301) 321-2815
Staff: Phyllis Frankel, Director

UNIVERSITY OF MARYLAND (W)
Music Department
Catonsville, MD 21228

UNIVERSITY OF MARYLAND (W)
Opera Theater
College Park, MD 20742
(301) 454-2501
Staff: Martin Mangold, Director

WASHINGTON SAVOYARDS
Box 6422 Aspen Hill
Silver Spring, MD 20906

YOUNG VICTORIAN THEATER COMPANY (C)
5407 Roland Ave.
Baltimore, MD 21210
(301) 323-3800
Staff: Brian Goodman, General Manager

MASSACHUSETTS

AMERICAN REPERTORY THEATER (T)
64 Brattle
Cambridge, MA 02138
(617) 495-2668
Staff: Robert Brustein, Artistic Director

BOSTON CONCERT OPERA ORCHESTRA (B)
Box 459 Astor Station
Boston, MA 02123
(617) 542-3200
Staff: Michael Feibish, Manager

BOSTON CONSERVATORY (W)
Opera Theater
8 The Fenway
Boston, MA 02215
(617) 536-6340
Staff: John Moriarty, Chairman

BOSTON LYRIC OPERA (B)
102 The Fenway
Boston, MA 02115
(617) 267-1512
Staff: John Baine, General Director

BOSTON MUSICA VIVA
551 Tremont
Boston, MA 02116
(617) 451-1342
Staff: Richard Pittman, Musical Director

BOSTON UNIVERSITY (W)
Opera Department
855 Commonwealth
Boston, MA 02115
(617) 353-3396

CHAMBER CONCERTS OF NEWTON
85 Chestnut Hill Rd.
Chestnut Hill, MA 02167
Staff: Philip Morehead, Musical Director

CHAMINADE OPERA GROUP
77 Holden
Attleboro, MA 02703
Staff: Louise Pettitt, Director

COLLEGE LIGHT OPERA (B)
Drawer F
Falmouth, MA 02541
(617) 548-2211
Staff: Robert Hashun, General Manager and Producer

EMERSON COLLEGE (W)
Opera Workshop
100 Beacon
Boston, MA 02116
(617) 262-2010
Staff: Anthony Tommasini, Director

HANDEL AND HAYDN SOCIETY
158 Newbury
Boston, MA 02116
(617) 266-3605
Staff: Thomas Dunn, Musical Director

HARVARD UNIVERSITY
(See North House Music Society)

NEW ENGLAND CONSERVATORY (W)
Opera Theater
290 Huntington
Boston, MA 02115
Staff: David Bartholomew, Chairman

NORTH HOUSE MUSIC SOCIETY (W)
Harvard University
Cambridge, MA 02138
Staff: Nalin Mukherjee, Director

OPERA COMPANY OF BOSTON (A*)
539 Washington St.
Boston, MA 02111
(617) 426-5300
Staff: Robert Reilly, Associate Manager

OPERA NEW ENGLAND (B)
539 Washington St.
Boston, MA 02111
(617) 426-5300
Staff: Kenneth Porter, Manager

PRO ARTE CHAMBER ORCHESTRA OF BOSTON
104 Charles
Boston, MA 02114
Staff: Joyce Byrum, Manager

PROJECT OPERA (C)
160 Maine St.
Northampton, MA 01060
(413) 584-8811
Staff: Richard Rescia, Artistic Director

WILLIAMS COLLEGE (W)
Music Department
Williamstown, MA 01267

MICHIGAN

ATTIC THEATER (T)
525 Lafayette
Detroit, MI 48226
(313) 963-7750
Staff: Herbert Ferrer, Managing Director

CENTRAL MICHIGAN UNIVERSITY (W)
Opera Workshop
Mount Pleasant, MI 48858
(517) 774-3433
Staff: Mary Kiesgen, Director

EASTERN MICHIGAN UNIVERSITY (W)
Opera Workshop
Ypsilanti, MI 48197
(318) 487-0331
Staff: Glenda Kirkland, Director

HIGHLAND PARK COMMUNITY COLLEGE (W)
Opera Workshop
Glendale at Third
Highland Park, MI 48203
(313) 254-0475, Ext. 322

INTERLOCHEN OPERA THEATER (W)
National Music Camp
Interlochen, MI 49643
Staff: E. Downing, Director

LANSING COMMUNITY COLLEGE (W)
Opera Workshop
500 North Washington Sq.
Box 40010
Lansing, MI 48901
(517) 483-1496
Staff: John Dale Smith, Music Program Director

MICHIGAN OPERA THEATER (A*)
350 Madison Ave.
Detroit, MI 48226
(313) 963-3717
Staff: David DiChiera, General Director

MICHIGAN STATE UNIVERSITY (W)
Opera Workshop
East Lansing, MI 48823
(517) 353-5340
Staff: Jean Herzberg, Director

MIDLAND CENTER FOR THE ARTS MUSIC SOCIETY
1801 West. St. Andrews
Midland, MI 48640
(517) 631-1072
Staff: G. Richard Ryan, Musical Director

NORTHERN MICHIGAN UNIVERSITY (W)
Opera Theater
Marquette, MI 49855
(906) 227-3540
Staff: Peter Zellner, Director

OLIVET COLLEGE (W)
Opera Workshop
Olivet, MI 49076
(616) 749-7654
Staff: Ken Kleszynski, Director

OPERA COMPANY OF GREATER LANSING (C)
Box 903
East Lansing, MI 48823
(517) 353-6485
Staff: Dennis Burkh, General Manager

OPERA GRAND RAPIDS (B)
Waters Building, No. 203-D
Grand Rapids, MI 49503
(616) 451-2741
Staff: Robert Peterson, General Director

PICCOLO OPERA
18662 Fairfield Ave.
Detroit, MI 48221
(313) 861-6930
Staff: Marjorie Gordon, General Director

ST. BEDE PLAYERS
29239 Somerset
Southfield, MI 48076
Staff: J. Gamache, Manager

UNIVERSITY OF MICHIGAN (W)
Opera Theater
School of Music
Ann Arbor, MI 48109
(313) 763-5851
Staff: Gustav Meier, Musical Director

WESTERN MICHIGAN UNIVERSITY (W)
Opera Workshop
Main St.
Kalamazoo, MI 49007
(616) 383-0910
Staff: William Appel, Director

MINNESOTA

BEMIDJI STATE UNIVERSITY (W)
Opera Theater
Bemidji, MN 56601
(218) 755-3928
Staff: Thomas Swanson, Chairman

CARLETON COLLEGE (W)
Chamber Singers
Music Department
Northfield, MN 55057
(507) 663-4347
Staff: William Wells, Director

CHILDREN'S THEATER COMPANY (T)
2400 Third Ave. South
Minneapolis, MN 55404
(612) 874-0500
Staff: John Donahue, Artistic Director

COLLEGE OF ST. BENEDICT (W)
Opera Theater
St. Joseph, MN 56374
(612) 363-5888
Staff: Philip Welter, Director

COLLEGE OF ST. CATHERINE (W)
Opera Workshop
2004 Randolph St.
St. Paul, MN 55105
(612) 690-6691
Staff: Marguerite Hedges, Artistic Director

CRICKET THEATER (T)
528 Hennepin
Minneapolis, MN 55402
(612) 333-5241
Staff: Louis Salerni, Artistic Director

MACALASTER COLLEGE (W)
Opera Workshop
St. Paul, MN 55105
Staff: Edouard Forner, Director

MANKATO STATE UNIVERSITY (W)
Opera Workshop
Mankato, MN 56001
(507) 389-1030
Staff: James P. Dunn, Director

MIDWEST OPERA THEATER AND SCHOOL (C)
850 Grand Ave.
St. Paul, MN 55105
(612) 221-0122
Staff: H. Wesley Balk, Artistic Director

MINNESOTA OPERA (A*)
850 Grand Ave.
St. Paul, MN 55105
(612) 221-0122
Staff: Edward Corn, General Manager

MOORHEAD STATE UNIVERSITY (W)
Opera Workshop
Moorhead, MN 56560
Staff: William Wilson, Director

NORTHFIELD ARTS GUILD
Opera Workshop
Box 21
411 West Third St.
Northfield, MN 55057
(507) 645-8877
Staff: Sue Shepard, Administrator

OPERA ST. PAUL (C)
485 Portland
St. Paul, MN 55102

(612) 225-5541
Staff: Virginia Olson, Manager

ST. CLOUD STATE UNIVERSITY (W)
Opera Theater
St. Cloud, MN 56301
(612) 255-3291
Staff: Charles Peterson, Director

UNIVERSITY OF MINNESOTA (W)
Opera Workshop
Duluth, MN 55812
(218) 726-8215
Staff: Donna Pegors, Director

UNIVERSITY OF MINNESOTA (W)
Opera Workshop
204 Scott Hall
Minneapolis, MN 55455
(612) 373-3442
Staff: Vern Sutton, Director

WINONA STATE COLLEGE (W)
Music Department
Winona, MN 55987

MISSISSIPPI

JACKSON STATE UNIVERSITY
(See Opera/South)

MISSISSIPPI OPERA ASSOCIATION (B)
Box 1551
Jackson, MS 39206
(601) 960-1528
Staff: Franklin Choset, Artistic Director

OPERA/SOUTH (D)
Box 18016
Jackson State University
Jackson, MS 39217
(601) 968-2700
Staff: E. Naymond Thomas, General Director

UNIVERSITY OF MISSISSIPPI (W)
Opera Theater
University, MS 38677
(601) 232-7268
Staff: Leland Fox, Director

UNIVERSITY OF SOUTHERN MISSISSIPPI (W)
Opera Theater
Box 8224 Southern Station
Hattiesburg, MS 39401
Staff: Patricia Hays, Director

MISSOURI

CENTRAL MISSOURI STATE UNIVERSITY (W)
Opera Workshop
Warrensburg, MO 64093
Staff: Edwin Quistorff, Director

CULVER-STOCKTON COLLEGE (W)
Opera Workshop
Canton, MO 63435
(314) 288-5221
Staff: Carol F. Mathieson, Director

LYRIC OPERA OF KANSAS CITY (A)
1029 Central
Kansas City, MO 64105
(816) 471-4933
Staff: Russell Patterson, General and Artistic Director

NORTHEAST MISSOURI STATE UNIVERSITY (W)
Opera Workshop
Kirksville, MO 63501
(816) 785-4417
Staff: Dale Jorgenson, Chairman

OPERA THEATER OF ST. LOUIS (A*)
Box 13148
St. Louis, MO 63119
(314) 961-0171
Staff: Richard Gaddes, General Director

SCHOOL OF THE OZARKS (W)
Theater Department
Point Lookout, MO 65726
(417) 334-6411
Staff: James Meikle, Theatre Chairman

SOUTHEAST MISSOURI STATE COLLEGE (W)
Opera Workshop
Cape Giradeau, MO 63701
Staff: Mary Lou Henry, Director

SOUTHWEST BAPTIST UNIVERSITY (W)
Opera Workshop
Bolivar, MO 65613
(417) 326-6961
Staff: Lee Snook, Director

SOUTHWEST MISSOURI STATE UNIVERSITY (W)
Opera Theater
901 South National
Springfield, MO 65802
(417) 836-5435
Staff: Dawin Emanuel, Director

ST. LOUIS CONSERVATORY (W)
560 Trinity
St. Louis, MO 63130
(314) 863-3033
Staff: Edward Zambara, Opera Director

ST. LOUIS MUNICIPAL OPERA
Forest Park
St. Louis, MO 63112
(314) 361-1900
Staff: Edward Greenberg, Executive Producer

SPRINGFIELD REGIONAL OPERA
Box 3942
Springfield, MO 65804

UNIVERSITY OF MISSOURI (W)
Opera Workshop
140 Fine Arts Building
Columbia, MO 65211
(314) 882-2604
Staff: Harry Morrison, Jr., Director

UNIVERSITY OF MISSOURI (W)
Opera Workshop
4949 Cherry
Kansas City, MO 64110
(816) 363-4300, ext. 266
Staff: William Graham, Director

UNIVERSITY OF MISSOURI (W)
8001 Natural Bridge
St. Louis, MO 63130
(314) 553-5992
Staff: Jerel Becker, Director

WASHINGTON UNIVERSITY (W)
Opera Studio
St. Louis, MO 63130
Staff: John Perkins, Director

WILLIAM JEWELL COLLEGE (W)
Opera Workshop
Liberty, MO 64068
(816) 781-3806
Staff: David Robinson, Director

MONTANA

INTERMOUNTAIN OPERA ASSOCIATION (C)
Box 37
Bozeman, MT 59715
(406) 284-3335
Staff: Pablo Elvira, Artistic Director

UNIVERSITY OF MONTANA (W)
Opera Workshop
Missoula, MT 59801
(406) 243-6880
Staff: Esther England, Director

NEBRASKA

NEBRASKA STATE UNIVERSITY (W)
Music Dept.
Kearney, NE 68847
(308) 236-4446
Staff: G.F. Thomas, Chairman

NEBRASKA WESLEYAN UNIVERSITY (W)
Opera Theater
50th and St. Paul Ave.
Lincoln, NE 68504
(402) 466-2371
Staff: William Wyman, Director

OPERA/OMAHA (B)
Box 807 DTS
Omaha, NE 68101
(402) 346-4398
Staff: Mary Robert, General Director

UNIVERSITY OF NEBRASKA (W)
Opera Theater
School of Music
Lincoln, NE 68588
(402) 472-2993
Staff: Gregg Tallman, Director

UNIVERSITY OF NEBRASKA (W)
Opera/Music Theater
124 Performing Arts Center
Omaha, NE 68182
(402) 554-2251
Staff: Roger Foltz, Chairman

NEVADA

NEVADA OPERA COMPANY (B)
Box 3256
Reno, NV 89505
(702) 786-4046
Staff: Ted Puffer, Director

UNIVERSITY OF NEVADA (W)
Opera Theater
4505 Maryland Parkway
Las Vegas, NV 89154
(702) 739-3713
Staff: Carol Kimball, Director

NEW HAMPSHIRE

COLBY-SAWYER COLLEGE (W)
Music Department
New London, NH 03257
Staff: Nancy Draper, Chairman

DARMOUTH COLLEGE
(See Hopkins Center Opera Cooperative)

HANOVER OPERA WORKSHOP
2 Webster Terr.
Hanover, NH 03755
(603) 643-4427
Staff: Ruth Morton, Director

HOPKINS CENTER OPERA COOPERATIVE (W)
Dartmouth College
Hanover, NH 03755
Staff: Shelton G. Stanfill, Director

KEENE STATE COLLEGE (W)
Opera Workshop
Keene, NH 03431
(603) 352-1909, ext. 511
Staff: Carroll Lehman, Director

PLYMOUTH STATE COLLEGE (W)
Music Department
Plymouth, NH 03264
(603) 536-1550
Staff: Stephen Squires, Director

THEATER BY THE SEA (T)
125 Bow
Portsmouth, NH 02801
(603) 431-5846
Staff: John Kimball, Director

NEW JERSEY

CAMARATA OPERA THEATER
19 Kingshighway
Haddonfield, NJ 08033
(609) 428-7999
Staff: Rita Dreyfus, Director

FAMILY OPERA
Box 7234
North Bergen, NJ 07047
(201) 869-5534
Staff: Josephine Ruffino, President

FAIRLEIGH DICKINSON UNIVERSITY (W)
Music Department
Rutherford, NJ 07668

FOUR CORNERS OPERA ASSOCIATION (B)
Box 897
Farmington, NJ 87401
(505) 325-9681
Staff: Robert Gregori, General Director

GLASSBORO STATE COLLEGE (W)
Opera Company
Glassboro, NJ 08028
(609) 445-6041
Staff: Bonita Bachman-Granite, Director

JERSEY LYRIC OPERA (B)
Box 452
Westfield, NJ 07091
(201) 232-0814
Staff: Sonja Lewis, General Manager and Artistic Director

LUBO OPERA COMPANY (C)
116 71st St.
Guttenberg, NJ 07093
(201) 854-4524
Staff: Jody Lasky, General Manager

METRO LYRIC OPERA (C)
40 Ocean Ave.
Allenhurst, NJ 07711
(201) 531-2378
Staff: Era Tognoli, Executive and Artistic Director

MONMOUTH CONSERVATORY OPERA SOCIETY (W)
2 Cross St.
Little Silver, NJ 07739
(201) 747-9035
Staff: Evelyn Johnson, Director

MONTCLAIR STATE COLLEGE (W)
Opera Workshop
Upper Montclair, NJ 07043
(201) 893-5226
Staff: Jack Sacher, Director

NEW JERSEY STATE OPERA (A)
1020 Broad St.
Newark, NJ 07102
(201) 623-5757
Staff: Alfredo Silipigni, Artistic Director

OPERA CLASSICS (B)
Box 394
Paramus, NJ 07652
(201) 265-8494
Staff: George Ungaro, Artistic Director and General Manager

OPERA IN A SUITCASE
793 Fourteenth
Paterson, NJ 07504
Staff: Theresa Minnocci, Manager

OPERA THEATER OF NEW JERSEY
148 George
New Brunswick, NJ 08901
Staff: Janet Stewart, Manager

PRINCETON UNIVERSITY (W)
Opera Theater
Woolworth Center
Princeton, NJ 08540
(609) 452-4241
Staff: Peter Westergaard, Artistic Director

RED OAK MUSIC THEATER (T)
472 Somerset
Lakewood, NJ 08701
(201) 367-1515
Staff: Chester Gertner, Producer

RIDGEWOOD GILBERT AND SULLIVAN OPERA COMPANY
975 East Ridgewood Ave.
Ridgewood, NJ 07450
(201) 444-1378
Staff: Ruth Weber, Business Manager

RUTGERS UNIVERSITY/DOUGLASS COLLEGE (W)
Opera Workshop
New Brunswick, NJ 08903
(201) 932-9302
Staff: Valerie Goodall, Director

SUBURBAN OPERA
363 West South Orange
South Orange, NJ 07079
Staff: Deta Delman, Director

WASHINGTON CROSSING STATE PARK SUMMER THEATER (T)
R.D. 1
Box 337-A
Titusville, NJ 08560

WESTMINSTER CHOIR COLLEGE (W)
Hamilton Ave. at Walnut Ln.
Princeton, NJ 08540
(609) 921-8071
Staff: Glen Parker, Director

NEW MEXICO

ALBUQUERQUE OPERA THEATER (B)
515 15th St. NW
Albuquerque, NM 87104
(505) 243-8492
Staff: Justine Opal, Administrator

EASTERN NEW MEXICO UNIVERSITY (W)
Music Theater
Portales, NM 88130
(505) 562-2735
Staff: Janice Redding, Director

GALLUP LITTLE THEATER
Box 1926
Gallup, NM 87301
Staff: Mary Brooks, Manager

SANTA FE OPERA ASSOCIATION (A*)
Box 2408
Santa Fe, NM 87501
(505) 982-3851
Staff: John Crosby, General Director

UNIVERSITY OF NEW MEXICO (W)
Opera Studio
Fine Arts Center
Albuquerque, NM 87112
(505) 277-4612
Staff: Sean Daniel, Director

NEW YORK

AFTER DINNER OPERA (C)
23 Stuyvesant St.
New York, NY 10003
(212) 477-6212
Staff: Beth Flusser, Administrative Director

AMAS REPERTORY THEATER (B)
1 East 104 St., Third Flr.
New York, NY 10029
(212) 369-8000
Staff: Gary Halcott, Business Manager

AMATO OPERA THEATER (C)
319 The Bowery
New York, NY 10003
(212) 228-8200
Staff: Anthony Amato, President

AMERICAN OPERA REPERTORY COMPANY
2101 Broadway, No. 5-104
New York, NY 10023
(212) 595-4472
Staff: David Montefiore, Executive Director

APOLLO OPERA
2130 Broadway, No. 1211
New York, NY 10023
(212) 877-4904
Staff: Nicoclis Moraitis, President

ARTPARK/NATURAL HERITAGE TRUST (A)
Box 371
Lewston, NY 14092
(716) 745-3377
Staff: Joanne Allison, Exeuctive Director

BEL CANTO OPERA (C)
220 East 76th St.
New York, NY 10021
(212) 535-5231
Staff: Theodore Sieh, Artistic Director

BRIGHTON LIGHT OPERA
317 Main
East Rochester, NY 14445
Staff: Paul Roxin, Producer

BRONX OPERA COMPANY (C)
5 Minerva Pl.
Bronx, NY 10468
(212) 365-4209
Staff: Michael Spierman, Artistic Director

BROOKLYN COLLEGE (W)
Opera Theater
Brooklyn, NY 11210

BROOKLYN LYRIC OPERA (C)
62 Bay 8 St.
Brooklyn, NY 11228
(212) 837-1176
Staff: Norman Myrvick, Artistic Director

BROOKLYN OPERA SOCIETY (C)
826 Union
Brooklyn, NY 11215
(212) 643-7115
Staff: Rinaldo Tazzini, Managing Director

BROQUE OPERA (C)
216 East 82nd St., No. 19
New York, NY 10028
(212) 535-6069
Staff: Anastasia Nichole, Managing Director

BUFFALO ARTS AND MUSIC LTD.
Box 49 Central Park Station
Buffalo, NY 14215

CHAMBER OPERA THEATER OF NEW YORK (B)
109 West 85th St.
New York, NY 10024
(212) 496-0058
Staff: Thaddeus Motyka, General Director

CHAUTAUQUA OPERA COMPANY (B)
Chautauqua Institution
Chautauqua, NY 14722
(716) 357-3285
Staff: Cynthia Auerbach, Artistic Director

CHILDREN'S FREE OPERA OF NEW YORK (B)
11 Broadway
New York, NY 10004
(212) 943-0950
Staff: Michael Feldman, Director

CLARION MUSIC SOCIETY (C)
1860 Broadway
New York, NY 10023
(212) 765-8008
Staff: Newell Jenkins, Musical Director

COLGATE UNIVERSITY (W)
Theater Department
Hamilton, NY 13346
(315) 824-1000
Staff: Gerda M. Judd, Manager

CONCERT ROYAL
280 Riverside, No. 5H
New York, NY 10025
Staff: James Richman, Artistic Director

CORNELL SAVOYARDS
Cornell University
Willard Straight Hall
Ithaca, NY 14853
(607) 256-7263
Staff: Jim Mueller, President

C.W. POST COLLEGE (W)
Music Dept.
Long Island University
Greenvale, NY 11548

DELAWARE VALLEY ARTS ALLIANCE
Box 170 Main St.
Narrowsburg, NY 12764
(914) 252-7576
Staff: Elaine DeGaetani, President

EASTERN OPERA THEATER OF NEW YORK (B)
530 East 89th St.
New York, NY 10028
(212) 921-1728
Staff: Donald Westwood, Managing Director

EASTMAN SCHOOL OF MUSIC (W)
Opera Theater
26 Gibbs St.
Rochester, NY 14604
(716) 275-2146
Staff: Richard Pearlman, Director

ENCOMPASS MUSIC THEATER (B)
Box 229
New York, NY 10108
(212) 575-1558
Staff: Nancy Rhodes, Artistic Director

FIRST ALL CHILDREN'S THEATER (T)
37 West 65th St.
New York, NY 10023
(212) 873-6400
Staff: Meridee Stein, Artistic Director and Producer

FIRST STAGE FIRST
Box 229
New York, NY 10108
(212) 575-1557
Staff: Nancy Rhodes, Artistic Director

GLIMMERGLASS OPERA THEATER (B)
Box 191
Cooperstown, NY 13326
(607) 547-8971
Staff: Paul Kellogg, Exeuctive Manager

GOLDEN FLEECE INC.
204 West 20th St.
New York, NY 10011
(212) 691-6105
Staff: Lou Rodgers, Artistic Director

GOLDOVSKY OPERA INSTITUTE AND THEATER (B)
154 West 57th St.
New York, NY 10019
(212) 581-7122
Staff: Boris Goldovsky, Artistic Director

GREATER UTICA OPERA GUILD
Box 930
Utica, NY 13503
(315) 732-4933
Staff: Pat Way, Executive Director

HENRY STREET CHORALE AND OPERA WORKSHOP (W)
466 Grand
New York, NY 10002
Staff: S. Barker, Director

HUNTER COLLEGE (W)
Music Dept.
695 Park Ave.
New York, NY 10021
(212) 570-5736
Staff: Myron Fink, Director

IMPACT PRODUCTIONS
400 West 43rd St.
New York, NY 10036
Staff: Saundra McClain, Manager

INWOOD CHAMBER OPERA PLAYERS
35 Orange St.
Brooklyn, NY 11201
(212) 875-1887
Staff: Susanne Popper Edelman, Director

ITHACA OPERA ASSOCIATION (C)
518 Warren Rd.
Ithaca, NY 14850
(607) 257-1089
Staff: Barbara Troxell, Artistic Director

JUILLIARD AMERICAN OPERA CENTER (W)
Lincoln Center
New York, NY 10023
(212) 799-5000, ext. 261
Staff: Erica Gastelli, Administrator

JUILLIARD OPERA TRAINING CENTER (W)
Lincoln Center
New York, NY 10023
(212) 799-5000
Staff: Erica Gastelli, Administrator

LA GUARDIA COMMUNITY COLLEGE (W)
Opera Workshop
31-10 Thomson Ave.
Long Island City, NY 11101
(212) 626-5089
Staff: Nick Rossi, Director

L'ENSEMBLE (C)
Content Farm Rd.
Cambridge, NY 12816
(518) 677-5455
Staff: Cynthia Wands, Managing Director

LIEDERKRANZ OPERA SHOWCASE
6 East 87th St.
New York, NY 10028
Staff: Thomas Martin, Director

LIGHTHOUSE OPERA WORKSHOP (W)
111 East 59th St.
New York, NY 10022
Staff: Richard E. Krause, Director

LIGHT OPERA OF MANHATTAN (B)
334 East 74th St.
New York, NY 10021
(212) 861-2288
Staff: William Mount-Burke, Production Director

LONG ISLAND OPERA SOCIETY (C)
3022 Ann
Baldwin, NY 11510
(212) 525-5020
Staff: Gordon Davis, Artistic Director

LONG ISLAND UNIVERSITY
(See C.W. Post College)

MAGIC CIRCLE OPERA REPERTORY
235 West 102nd St., No. 71
New York, NY 10025
Staff: Ray Harrell, Producer

MANHATTAN OPERA THEATER
104 West 71st St., No. 4D
New York, NY 10023
Staff: Allan Charlet, Artistic Director

MANHATTAN SCHOOL OF MUSIC (W)
Opera Workshop
120 Claremont Ave.
New York, NY 10027
(212) 749-2802
Staff: Carolyn Lockwood, Studio Director

MANHATTAN SCHOOL PREP DIVISION (W)
120 Claremont Ave.
New York, NY 10027
(212) 749-2802
Staff: Cynthia Auerbach, Artistic Director

MANHATTANVILLE COLLEGE (W)
Opera Workshop
Purchase, NY 10577
(914) 478-2681
Staff: Sofia Steffan, Director

MANNES COLLEGE OF MUSIC (W)
Opera Workshop
157 East 47th St.
New York, NY 10021
(212) 737-1546
Staff: Paul Wolfe, Dean

MARYMOUNT MANHATTAN COLLEGE (W)
Music Dept.
221 East 71st St.
New York, NY 10021

METROPOLITAN OPERA ASSOCIATION (A*)
Lincoln Center
New York, NY 10023
(212) 799-3100
Staff: Anthony A. Bliss, General Manager

NASSAU LYRIC OPERA COMPANY (C)
855 Middleneck Rd.
Great Neck, NY 11024
(516) 482-1547
Staff: Robley Lawson, Artistic Director

NATIONAL OPERA TOURING COMPANY (A)
c/o New York City Opera
Lincoln Center
New York, NY 10023
(212) 870-5635
Staff: Nancy Kelly, Administrator

NEW FEDERAL THEATER (T)
466 Grand
New York, NY 10002
(212) 598-0400
Staff: Woodie King, Producer

NEW YORK CITY OPERA (A*)
State Theater
Lincoln Center
New York, NY 10023
(212) 870-5500
Staff: Beverly Sills, General Director

NEW YORK GILBERT AND SULLIVAN PLAYERS (B)
251 West 91st St.
New York, NY 10024
(212) 724-9159
Staff: Albert Bergeret, Artistic Director

NEW YORK GRAND OPERA (C)
154 West 57th St.
New York, NY 10019
(212) 245-8837
Staff: Vincent LaSelva, Director

NEW YORK LIGHT OPERA (C)
345 Riverside Dr., No. 6D
New York, NY 10025
(212) 663-3505
Staff: Judith Neale, General Manager

NEW YORK LYRIC OPERA (B)
124 West 72nd St.
New York, NY 10023
(212) 874-0351
Staff: John Haber, Manager

NEW YORK OPERA REPERTORY THEATER
670 West End Ave., No. 12E
New York, NY 10025
(212) 874-7177
Staff: Leigh G. Gore, Director

NEW YORK PRO MUSICA ANTIQUA
245 West 52nd St.
New York, NY 10019
Staff: George Houle, Musical Director

NEW YORK UNIVERSITY (W)
Opera Studio
35 West Fourth St.
New York, NY 10003
(212) 929-0232
Staff: Thomas Martin, Director

OPERA AT THE 92ND STREET "Y"
1395 Lexington
New York, NY 10028
Staff: K. Newbern, Musical Director

OPERA CAMERATA
55 West 88th St., No. 3
New York, NY 10024
(212) 799-7973
Staff: Jane Holcombe, Artistic Director

OPERA ENSEMBLE OF NEW YORK (B)
45 East 81st St.

New York, NY 10028
(212) 288-1485
Staff: Ruth Bierhoff, Musical Director

OPERA ON THE SOUND
Box 414
Commack, NY 11725
(516) 499-3572
Staff: Helen Chiet, General Manager

OPERA ORCHESTRA OF NEW YORK (B)
211 West 56th St.
New York, NY 10019
(212) 246-7107
Staff: John Broome, Business Manager

OPERA REDIVIVA
61 West 62nd St., No. 6F
New York, NY 10023
(212) 246-2809
Staff: Richard Kipp, Artistic Director

OPERA SACRA
692 Auburn Ave.
Buffalo, NY 14222
(716) 882-7457
Staff: Jacob Ledwon, Artistic Director

OPERA STAGE
62 Bay 8 St.
Brooklyn, NY 11228
(212) 837-1176
Staff: Norman Myrvick, Director

OPERA THEATER OF NEW YORK
344 West 89th St.
New York, NY 10024
(212) 877-7507
Staff: Richard Barri, Director

OPERA THEATER OF ROCHESTER (B)
530 Powers Building
Rochester, NY 14604
(716) 325-6290
Staff: Ruth Rosenberg, Artistic Director

OPERA THEATER OF SYRACUSE (A)
215 East Water St.
Syracuse, NY 13202
(315) 475-5915
Staff: Christine Day, Manager

OSWEGO OPERA THEATER
10 Draper St.
Oswego, NY 13126
(315) 343-8955
Staff: James Solui, General Director

QUEENS COLLEGE (W)
Opera Studio
65-30 Kissena Blvd.
Flushing, NY 11367
(212) 520-7344
Staff: Hugo Weisgall, Director

QUEENS OPERA ASSOCIATION (D)
313 Bay 14 St.
Brooklyn, NY 11214
(212) 256-6045
Staff: Joseph Messina, General Director

SANTA FE OPERA (A*)
48 East 63rd St.
New York, NY 10021
(212) 832-8757
Staff: John Crosby, General Director

SCOVASSO OPERA
2480 West Third St.
Brooklyn, NY 11223
(212) 336-7931
Staff: Stephen Scovasso, General Manager

SEAGLE COLONY
Opera Guild
Schroon Lake, NY 12870
Staff: John Seagle, Director

SINFONIA D'OPERA
66 West 82nd St.
New York, NY 10024
(212) 874-0158
Staff: Mitchell Krieger, Musical Director

SINGERS THEATER (C)
1261 Williams Dr.
Shrub Oak, NY 10588
(914) 528-5402
Staff: Dorothy Drazhal, Executive Director

STATE UNIVERSITY COLLEGE (W)
Music Theater Workshop
Geneseo, NY 14454
Staff: Jack Johnston, Director

STATE UNIVERSITY OF NEW YORK-BINGHAMTON (W)
Music Dept.
Binghamton, NY 13901
(607) 798-2582
Staff: John Hanson, Director

STATE UNIVERSITY OF NEW YORK-BUFFALO (W)
Opera Studio
110 Pritchard Hall
Buffalo, NY 14214

STATE UNIVERSITY OF NEW YORK-FREDONIA (W)
Lyric Theater
Fredonia, NY 14063
(716) 673-3151
Staff: John A. Wiles, Director

STATE UNIVERSITY OF NEW YORK-ONEONTA (W)
Opera Studio
Oneonta, NY 13820
(607) 431-3419
Staff: William Cole, Director

STATE UNIVERSITY OF NEW YORK-POTSDAM (W)
Crane Opera/Music Theater
Potsdam, NY 13676
(315) 265-4476
Staff: Thomas Holliday, Director

STATE UNIVERSITY OF NEW YORK-PURCHASE (W)
Opera Workshop
Purchase, NY 10577
(914) 253-5031
Staff: Barbara Owens, Director

STATE UNIVERSITY OF NEW YORK-STONY BROOK (W)
Opera Workshop
Department of Theatre Arts
Stony Brook, NY 11794
(516) 246-5670
Staff: Tom Neumiller, Director

STORY CONCERT PLAYERS
Gregory Lane
Millwood, NY 10546
(914) 941-6313
Staff: Michael Leavitt, Managing Director

SYRACUSE UNIVERSITY (W)
Opera Workshop
215 Crouse College
Syracuse, NY 13210
(315) 423-2191
Staff: Donald Miller, Chairman

THEATRE FOR THE NEW CITY (T)
162 Second Ave.
New York, NY 10003
(212) 254-1109
Staff: George Bartenieff, President

THEATER OPERA MUSIC INSTITUTE
23 West 73rd St.
New York, NY 10023
(212) 787-3980
Staff: Jonathon Silver, General Manager

THIRD STREET DOWNTOWN PLAYERS
235 East 11th St.
New York, NY 10003
(212) 777-3240
Staff: Mimi Stern-Wolfe, Artistic Director

THIRD STREET SETTLEMENT MUSIC THEATER (W)
235 East 11th St.
New York, NY 10003
(212) 777-3240
Staff: Beth Flusser, Director of Concerts

TOURING CONCERT OPERA
228 East 80th St.
New York, NY 10021
(212) 988-2524
Staff: Anne deFigols, Artistic Director

TRAVERSE OPERA LTD. (B)
Box 346
Palenville, NY 12463
Staff: Jay Pouhe, Artistic Director

TRI-CITIES OPERA (B)
315 Clinton St.
Binghamton, NY 13905
(607) 767-6344
Staff: Sara Granier, Administrative Director

VIENNESE OPERETTA COMPANY OF NEW YORK (C)
400 West 43rd St., No. 45D
New York, NY 10036
(212) 695-1454
Staff: Lois Albright, Executive Director

VILLAGE LIGHT OPERA GROUP (C)
Box 143 Village Station
New York, NY 10014
(212) 243-6281
Staff: Jack Behonek, Production Manager

WESTERN NEW YORK OPERA THEATER
193 Altair Dr.
Getzville, NY 14068
(716) 688-5463
Staff: Donna Mathewson, General Manager

NORTH CAROLINA

APPALACHIAN STATE UNIVERSITY (W)
Opera Workshop
Boone, NC 28608
(704) 262-3020
Staff: Frances Redding, Director

ATLANTIC CHRISTIAN COLLEGE (W)
Opera Theater
West Lee St.
Wilson, NC 27893
(919) 237-3161
Staff: J. Ross Albert, Chairman

BREVARD MUSIC CENTER (W)
Opera Workshop
Box 582
Brevard, NC 28712
(704) 884-2011
Staff: John McCrae, Production Director

CENTRAL PIEDMONT COMMUNITY COLLEGE (W)
Opera Workshop
Box 4009
Charlotte, NC 28204
(704) 373-6618
Staff: Joyce Marshall, Director

CHARLOTTE OPERA ASSOCIATION, INC. (A)
110 East Seventh St.
Charlotte, NC 28202
(704) 332-7177
Staff: Bruce Chalmers, General Director

DUKE UNIVERSITY (W)
Opera Workshop
6695 College Station
Durham, NC 27708
(919) 828-2511
Staff: John Hanks, Director

EAST CAROLINA UNIVERSITY (W)
Opera Theater
School of Music
Greenville, NC 27834
(919) 757-6331
Staff: Clyde Hiss, Director

ELON COLLEGE (W)
Opera Workshop
Box 2121
Elon College, NC 27244
(919) 584-2282
Staff: Terrell Cofield, Director

GARDNER-WEBB COLLEGE (W)
Opera Workshop
Boiling Spring, NC 28017
Staff: Patricia Harrellson, Director

GREENSBORO OPERA COMPANY (C)
Box 29031
Greensboro, NC 27408
(919) 273-9472
Staff: Peter Paul Feuhs, Artistic Director

LENOIR RHYNE COLLEGE (W)
Music Department
Hickory, NC 28601

MARS HILL COLLEGE (W)
Music Department
Mars Hill, NC 28754

NATIONAL OPERA COMPANY (B)
Box 12800
Raleigh, NC 27608
(919) 821-8782
Staff: David Witherspoon, General Manager

NORTH CAROLINA OPERA
110 East Seventh St.
Charlotte, NC 28202
(704) 332-7177
Staff: Robert Swedberg, Manager and Artistic Director

NORTH CAROLINA SCHOOL OF THE ARTS (W)
Opera Workshop
Box 12189
Winston-Salem, NC 27107
(919) 784-7170
Staff: Norman Johnson, Director

PIEDMONT OPERA THEATER (C)
Box 12189
Winston-Salem, NC 27107
(919) 725-2022
Staff: Norman Johnson, Artistic Director

SALEM COLLEGE (W)
Opera Workshop
Winston-Salem, NC 27108

UNIVERSITY OF NORTH CAROLINA (W)
Opera Theater
Music Department
Hill Hall 020A
Chapel Hill, NC 27514
(919) 962-1042
Staff: Marajean Marvin, Director

UNIVERSITY OF NORTH CAROLINA (W)
Opera Workshop
Charlotte, NC 28223
(704) 597-4468
Staff: Jane Dillard, Director

UNIVERSITY OF NORTH CAROLINA (W)
Opera Theater
100 Spring Garden
Greensboro, NC 27412
(919) 379-5493
Staff: Arvid Knutsen, Director

WESTERN CAROLINA UNIVERSITY (W)
Music Department
Cullowhee, NC 28723
(704) 227-7242
Staff: C. Temple Smith, Director

NORTH DAKOTA

DICKINSON STATE COLLEGE (W)
Opera Workshop
Dickinson, ND 58601
(701) 227-2308
Staff: Elwood Brown, Director

FARGO-MOORHEAD CIVIC OPERA (B)
4510 13th Ave., SW
Fargo, ND 58121
(701) 282-1394
Staff: Hale Laybourn, President

MINOT OPERA ASSOCIATION
Box 2012
Minot, ND 58701
(701) 857-3190
Staff: Wayne Nelson, Artistic Director

OHIO

BALDWIN-WALLACE COLLEGE CONSERVATORY (W)
96 Point St.
Berea, OH 44017
Staff: Sophie Ginn-Paster, Director

BLOSSOM FESTIVAL SCHOOL
Kent State University
Kent, OH 44242
Staff: Walter Watson, Director

BLUFFTON COLLEGE (W)
Opera Workshop
Bluffton, OH 45817
(419) 358-8015
Staff: Stephen Jacoby, Director

BOWLING GREEN STATE UNIVERSITY (W)
Opera Theater
Bowling Green, OH 43403
(419) 372-2181
Staff: William Taylor, Director

CAPITAL UNIVERSITY-CONSERVATORY (W)
2199 Main St.
Columbus, OH 43209

(614) 236-6411
Staff: Gene Allen, Director

CINCINNATI OPERA ASSOCIATION (A*)
1241 Elm St.
Cincinnati, OH 45210
(513) 621-1919
Staff: James deBlassis, General Director

CLEVELAND INSTITUTE OF MUSIC (W)
Opera Theater
11021 East Blvd.
Cleveland, OH 44106
(216) 791-5165
Staff: Andrew Foldi, Director

CLEVELAND OPERA COMPANY (A)
1438 Euclid Ave.
Cleveland, OH 44115
(216) 575-0903
Staff: David Bamberger, General Manager and Artistic Director

CLEVELAND OPERA THEATER
1300 West Hill Dr.
Gates Mills, OH 44040
(216) 566-8789

CLEVELAND PLAYHOUSE (T)
Box 1949
Cleveland, OH 44106
(216) 795-7000
Staff: Nelson Iskeit, Business Manager

COLLEGE OF WOOSTER
(See Ohio Light Opera Company)

DAYTON OPERA ASSOCIATION (B)
125 East First St.
Memorial Hall
Dayton, OH 45402
(513) 228-0662
Staff: Dennis Hanthorn, Business Manager

DENISON UNIVERSITY (W)
Opera Workshop
Granville, OH 43023
(614) 587-6365
Staff: Frederick Frey, Director

FINE ARTS ASSOCIATION (C)
38660 Mentor Ave.
Willoughby, OH 44094
(216) 951-7500
Staff: James Savage, Executive Director

HEIDELBERG COLLEGE (W)
Opera Theater
Tiffin, OH 44883
(419) 448-2505
Staff: Pamela and Norman Wurgler, Directors

KENT STATE UNIVERSTIY
(See also Blossom Festival School)

KENT STATE UNIVERSITY (W)
Opera Workshop
Kent, OH 44240
Staff: Rhonda Cundy, Director

MAD ANTHONY OPERA COMPANY
319 North Third St.
Hamilton, OH 45011
(513) 863-8873

MALONE COLLEGE (W)
Opera Workshop
515 25th St. Northwest
Canton, OH 44709
(216) 489-0800

MIAMI UNIVERSITY (W)
Opera Theater
Oxford, OH 45056
(513) 529-3014
Staff: David van Abbema, Director

MUSKINGHAM COLLEGE (W)
Music Department
New Concord, OH 43762

OBERLIN COLLEGE-CONSERVATORY (W)
Opera Theater
Oberlin, OH 44074
(216) 775-8206
Staff: Judity Layng, Director

OHIO LIGHT OPERA COMPANY (C)
College of Wooster
Wooster, OH 44691
(216) 264-1234
Staff: Frank Knorr, Producer

OHIO LYRIC THEATER
Box 432
Springfield, OH 45501
(513) 323-7755
Staff: Jeanne Carter, General Manager

OHIO STATE UNIVERSITY (W)
Opera/Music Theater
1866 College Rd.
Columbus, OH 43210
(614) 469-0939
Staff: Roger L. Stevens, Director

OHIO UNIVERSITY
Opera Theater
305 Kanter Hall
Athens, OH 45701
(614) 594-5235
Staff: T. Payne, Managing Director

OPERA AT PETERLOON
728 Carew Tower
Cincinnati, OH 45202

OPERA/COLUMBUS (B)
121 East State St.
Columbus, OH 43215
(614) 461-8101
Staff: Vivian Zoe, Exeuctive Manager

OPERA FUNATICS
858 Pool Ave.
Vandalia, OH 45377
Staff: Ed Sabrack, Director

OTTERBEIN COLLEGE (W)
Opera Theater
Music Department
Westerville, OH 43081
(614) 890-3000

TOLEDO OPERA ASSOCIATION (B)
3540 Secor Rd., No. 212
Toledo, OH 43606
(419) 531-5511
Staff: Lester Freedman, General Manager

UNIVERSITY OF AKRON (W)
Opera Department
Akron, OH 44325
(216) 375-6915
Staff: Kerry Woodward, Director

UNIVERSITY OF CINCINNATI (W)
Opera Department
College-Conservatory of Music
Cincinnati, OH 45221
Staff: Italo Tajo, Artistic Director

UNIVERSITY OF TOLEDO (W)
Opera Workshop
2801 Bancroft
Toledo, OH 43606
(418) 537-2966
Staff: Thomas East, Director

YOUNGSTOWN STATE UNIVERSITY (W)
Opera Theater
Dana School of Music
Youngstown, OH 44555
(216) 742-8646

OKLAHOMA

AMERICAN THEATER COMPANY (T)
Box 1265
Tulsa, OK 74101
(918) 582-5353
Staff: Kitty Roberts, Managing Director

CAMERON UNIVERSITY (W)
Opera Workshop
2800 Gore Blvd.
Lawton, OK 73505
(405) 248-2200

CIMMARON CIRCUIT OPERA COMPANY (C)
Box 1085
Norman, OK 73070
(405) 364-8962
Staff: Debra Moore, General Manager

LYRIC THEATER OF OKLAHOMA (T)
2501 North Blackwelder
Oklahoma City, OK 73106
(405) 528-3636

OKLAHOMA BAPTIST UNIVERSITY (W)
Musical Theater
Shawnee, OK 74801
(405) 275-2850

OKLAHOMA CHRISTIAN COLLEGE (W)
Opera Workshop
Route 1, Box 141
Oklahoma City, OK 73111
(405) 478-1661

OKLAHOMA CITY SYMPHONY/OPERA
512 Civic Center Music Hall
Oklahoma City, OK 73102

OKLAHOMA CITY UNIVERSITY (W)
Opera Workshop
2501 North Blackwelder
Oklahoma City, OK 73106
(405) 521-5169

OKLAHOMA STATE UNIVERSITY (W)
Opera Theater
112 Seretean Center
Stillwater, OK 74074

ORAL ROBERTS UNIVERSITY (W)
Opera Workshop
Tulsa, OK 74105

SOUTHWESTERN OKLAHOMA STATE UNIVERSITY (W)
Opera Workshop
Department of Music
Weatherford, OK 73069
(405) 772-5012
Staff: Charles Chapman, Director

TULSA OPERA INC. (A*)
1610 South Boulder Ave.
Tulsa, OK 74119
(918) 582-4035
Staff: Edward Purrington, General Director

UNIVERSITY OF OKLAHOMA (W)
Music Theater
School of Music
Norman, OK 73019
(405) 325-4077

UNIVERSITY OF SCIENCE AND ARTS OF OKLAHOMA (W)
Theater Department
Box 2878
Chickasha, OK 73018

UNIVERSITY OF TULSA (W)
Opera Theater
600 South College Ave.
Tulsa, OK 74114
(918) 592-6000
Staff: Judith Auer, Director

OREGON

CENTRAL OREGON COMMUNITY COLLEGE (W)
Opera Workshop
Bend, OR 97701
Staff: Charles Heiden, Director

EUGENE OPERA (B)
Box 11200
Eugene, OR 97440
(503) 485-3985
Staff: James Toland, General Manager

OPERA ENSEMBLE OF PORTLAND
6809 Northeast Broadway
Portland, OR 97213
Staff: Robert Sherwin, Director

OREGON COLLEGE OF EDUCATION (W)
Opera Workshop
Monmouth, OR 97361
(503) 838-1220
Staff: Ewan Mitton, Director

PACIFIC UNIVERSITY (W)
Opera Workshop
School of Music
Forest Grove, OR 97116
(503) 357-6151
Staff: Charles Tromblay, Director

PORTLAND OPERA ASSOCIATION (A*)
922 Southwest Main
Box 8598
Portland, OR 97207
(503) 248-4741
Staff: Robert Bailey, Executive Director

PORTLAND STATE UNIVERSITY (W)
Opera Workshop
Box 751
Portland, OR 97207
(503) 641-2076
Staff: Ruth Dobson, Director

ROGUE VALLEY OPERA ASSOCIATION
Box 322
Grants Pass, OR 97526
Staff: Yair Strauss, Musical Director

SOUTHERN OREGON STATE COLLEGE (W)
Opera Workshop
1250 Siskiyou Blvd.
Ashland, OR 97520
(503) 482-6101
Staff: John R. Tumbleson, Production Director

UNIVERSITY OF OREGON (W)
Opera Workshop
Eugene, OR 97403
(503) 686-3761

UNIVERSITY OF PORTLAND (W)
Opera Workshop
5000 North Williamette
Portland, OR 97203
(503) 283-7382
Staff: Roger Doyle, Director

VERY LITTLE THEATER, INC. (T)
2350 Hillyard
Eugene, OR 97405

WILLAMETTE UNIVERSITY (W)
Opera Theater
State and Winter Streets
Salem, OR 97301
(503) 370-6320
Staff: Julio Viamonte, Director

PENNSYLVANIA

ACADEMY OF VOCAL ARTS (W)
Opera Theater
1920 Spruce St.
Philadelphia, PA 19103
(215) 735-1685
Staff: Dino Yanopoulos, Director

ALLEGHENY COLLEGE (W)
Opera Workshop
Meadville, PA 16335
(814) 724-5368
Staff: Ward Johnson, Director

BERKS GRAND OPERA (C)
Box 162
Reading, PA 19603
(215) 373-5044
Staff: Barry Long, Director

BLOOMSBURG STATE COLLEGE (W)
Opera Workshop
Main and Penn Streets
Bloomsburg, PA 17815
(717) 389-3107
Staff: William Decker, Director

BUCKNELL UNIVERSITY (W)
Opera Workshop
Lewisburg, PA 17837
(717) 523-1216
Staff: Justin Kelly, Director

CARNEGIE MELLON UNIVERSITY (W)
Opera Workshop
Schenley Park
Pittsburgh, PA 15213
Staff: Robert Page, Director

CIVIC LIGHT OPERA (T)
600 Penn Ave.
Pittsburgh, PA 15222
(412) 281-3973
Staff: W.L Thunhurst, Managing Director

CURTIS INSTITUTE OF MUSIC (W)
Opera Department
1726 Locust St.
Philadelphia, PA 19103
(215) 893-5252
Staff: John DeLancie, Director

DICKINSON COLLEGE (W)
Opera Workshop
Carlisle, PA 17013
(717) 245-1568
Staff: Fred C. Petty, Director

DUQUESNE UNIVERSITY (W)
Opera Workshop
Pittsburgh, PA 15219
(412) 434-6080
Staff: Robert Croan, Director

EDINBORO STATE COLLEGE (W)
Opera Workshop
Edinboro, PA 16444
(814) 732-2518
Staff: G.J. Klausman, Director

INDIANA UNIVERSITY OF PENNSYLVANIA (W)
Music Theater
Indiana, PA 15705
(412) 357-4493
Staff: J.H. Wildeboor, Director

LANCASTER OPERA WORKSHOP (C)
Box 91
Lancaster, PA 17603
(717) 392-9455
Staff: Dorothy Rose Smith, Artistic Director

LEBANON VALLEY COLLEGE (W)
Summer Theater
Music Department
Annville, PA 17003

MUHLENBERG COLLEGE (W)
Opera Group
Allentown, PA 18104
(215) 433-3191
Staff: Jeremy A. Slavin, Director

OPERA COMPANY OF PHILADELPHIA (A*)
1518 Walnut St.
Philadelphia, PA 19102
(215) 732-5811
Staff: Margaret Anne Everitt, Manager

OPERA EBONY (B)
151 West Susquehanna
Philadelphia, PA 19122
(215) 426-7589
Staff: Malcolm Poindexter, Business Manager

OPERA WORKSHOP, INC. (C)
6 Wilkins Rd.
Pittsburgh, PA 15221
(412) 243-9897
Staff: James Meena, Executive and Musical Director

PENN STATE UNIVERSITY (W)
Opera Society
203 Arts Building
University Park, PA 16802
(814) 865-0431
Staff: Bruce Trinckley, Director

PENNSYLVANIA OPERA THEATER (B)
1218 Chestnut St., No. 808
Philadelphia, PA 19107
(215) 923-8768
Staff: Barbara Silverstein, Artistic Director

PENNSYLVANIA STAGE COMPANY (T)
837 Linden
Allentown, PA 18101
(215) 434-6110
Staff: Linda Goldstein, Business Manager

PHILADELPHIA COLLEGE OF PERFORMING ARTS (W)
Opera Program
250 South Broad St.
Philadelphia, PA 19102
(215) 875-2279
Staff: Kay Walker, Coordinator

PITTSBURGH CHAMBER OPERA THEATER (C)
Box 71067
Pittsburgh, PA 15213
(412) 683-0725
Staff: Mildred Miller-Posvar, Artistic Director

PITTSBURGH OPERA COMPANY (A*)
600 Penn Ave.
Pittsburgh, PA 15222
(412) 281-0912
Staff: Vincent Artz, General Manager

RITTENHOUSE OPERA SOCIETY
336 South 15th St.
Philadelphia, PA 19102
(215) 546-1474
Staff: Marco Farnese, Artistic Director

SAVOY COMPANY (C)
1009 Western Savings Fund Building
Philadelphia, PA 19107
Staff: Gerald Rorer, Producer

SUSQUEHANNA UNIVERSITY (W)
Opera Workshop
Selinsgrove, PA 17815
(717) 784-9266
Staff: Harriet Couch, Director

TEMPLE UNIVERSITY (W)
Opera Theater
13th and Norris Sts.
Philadelphia, PA 19122
Staff: George McKinley, Director

THEATRE EXPRESS (T)
4615 Baum
Pittsburgh, PA 15213
(412) 621-5477
Staff: Caren Harder, General Manager

UNIVERSITY OF PENNSYLVANIA (W)
Penn Singers
Philadelphia, PA 19104
(215) 243-7569
Staff: Bruce Montgomery, Director

UNIVERSITY OF PITTSBURGH (W)
Music Department
Pittsburgh, PA 15260

WEST CHESTER STATE COLLEGE (W)
Opera Theater
School or Music
West Chester, PA 19380
Staff: Larry Dorminy, Director

SOUTH CAROLINA

BOB JONES UNIVERSITY (W)
Opera Association
Greenville, SC 29614
(803) 242-5100
Staff: Dwight Gustafson, Musical Director

CHARLESTON OPERA COMPANY (C)
Box 33
Charleston, SC 29402
(803) 723-2844
Staff: Nancy LeBoeuf, Business Manager

COLUMBIA COLLEGE (W)
Music Theater
Columbia College Dr.
Columbia, SC 29203
(803) 787-2278
Staff: Sidney Palmer, Artistic Director

COLUMBIA LYRIC OPERA (C)
1527 Senate St.
Columbia, SC 29208
(803) 777-2984
Staff: Donald Gray, Artistic Director

CONVERSE COLLEGE (W)
Opera Workshop
Box 349
Spartanburg, SC 29301
(803) 585-6423
Staff: John R. McCrae, Director

FURMAN UNIVERSITY (W)
Opera Theater
Greenville, SC 29613
(803) 294-2023
Staff: Bruce Schoonmaker, Director

SOUTH DAKOTA

SOUTH DAKOTA STATE UNIVERSITY (W)
Opera Workshop
Lincoln Music Hall
Brookings, SD 57007
(605) 688-4614
Staff: Kristi Vensand, Director

UNIVERSITY OF SOUTH DAKOTA (W)
Opera Workshop
Fine Arts Center
Vermillion, SD 57069
(605) 677-5274
Staff: Madonna Byrkeland, Director

TENNESSEE

AUSTIN PEAY STATE UNIVERSITY (W)
Opera Theater
Clarksville, TN 37040
(615) 648-7818
Staff: Patrick Woliver, Director

BELMONT COLLEGE (W)
Music Department
Nashville, TN 37203
(615) 383-7001
Staff: Keith Moore, Director

CARSON-NEWMAN COLLEGE (W)
Lyric Theater
Box 2017
Jefferson City, TN 37760
(615) 475-9061
Staff: Thomas S. Teague, Director

CHATTANOOGA OPERA ASSOCIATION (B)
801 Oak St.
Chattanooga, TN 37402
(615) 266-0034
Staff: Robert C. Austin, Artistic Director

EAST TENNESSEE STATE UNIVERSITY (W)
Opera Theater
Box 24427 University Station
Johnson City, TN 37614
(615) 929-4419
Staff: Robert LaPella, Director

FISKE UNIVERSITY (W)
Opera Workshop
17th Ave. N
Nashville, TN 37203
Staff: Edward Payne, Director

KNOXVILLE CIVIC OPERA (C)
Box 1746
Knoxville, TN 37901
(615) 524-0795
Staff: Van Noy Daniels, Director

MARYVILLE COLLEGE (W)
Opera Theater
Maryville, TN 37801
(615) 977-1318
Staff: Kent Skinner, Director

MEMPHIS STATE UNIVERSITY
(See Opera Memphis)

OPERA MEMPHIS (A)
Memphis State University
Memphis, TN 38152
(901) 454-2706
Staff: Anne Atherton Randolph, Executive Director

PLAYHOUSE ON THE SQUARE (T)
2121 Madison
Memphis, TN 38104
(901) 725-0776
Staff: Eva Guggenheim, Administrator

SOUTHERN OPERA THEATER
Memphis State University
Memphis, TN 38152
(901) 454-2706
Staff: Anne Atherton Randolph, Director

UNION UNIVERSITY (W)
Music Department
Jackson, TN 38301
Staff: Kenneth Hartley, Chairman

UNIVERSITY OF TENNESSEE (W)
Opera Theater
Chattanooga, TN 37401
(615) 755-4616
Staff: David Pennebaker, Director

UNIVERSITY OF TENNESSEE (W)
Opera Theater
Knoxville, TN 37996
(615) 974-4398

UNIVERSITY OF TENNESSEE (W)
Music Department
Martin, TN 38237

TEXAS

AMARILLO COLLEGE (W)
Opera Workshop
2200 Washington
Amarillo, TX 79105
(806) 376-5111
Staff: Celia Rosenwald, Director

BEAUMONT CIVIC OPERA (C)
1030 Harriot St.
Beaumont, TX 77705
(713) 833-2120
Staff: Charlene Kiker, Business Manager

BAYLOR UNIVERSITY (W)
Opera Theater
School of Music
Waco, TX 76798
(817) 753-3661
Staff: Daniel Scott, Staging Director

CASA MANANA MUSICALS (T)
Box 9054
Fort Worth, TX 76109
(817) 332-9319
Staff: Bud Franks, General Manager

DALLAS OPERA (A*)
3000 Turtle Creek Plaza, No. 100
Dallas, TX 75206
(214) 528-9850
Staff: Plato Karayanis, General Director

DEL MAR COLLEGE (W)
Music Department
Corpus Christi, TX 78404

EAST TEXAS STATE UNIVERSITY (W)
Opera Ensemble
Commerce, TX 75428
(214) 886-5294
Staff: Carol Cannon, Director

FORT WORTH OPERA ASSOCIATION (A)
3505 West Lancaster
Fort Worth, TX 76107
(817) 731-0833
Staff: Rudolf Kruger, General Manager and Musical Director

GALVESTON COLLEGE (W)
Music Department
Galveston, TX 77550
(713) 774-6122
Staff: Maureen Patton, Director

HARDIN-SIMMONS UNIVERSITY (W)
Opera Workshop
Drawer J
Abilene, TX 79698
(915) 677-7281, ext. 424
Staff: Jayne Middleton, Director

HIGH NOON OPERA
3000 Turtle Creek Plaza, No. 100
Dallas, TX 75219
(214) 528-9850
Staff: Charlotte Schumacher, Production Coordinator

HOUSTON BAPTIST UNIVERSITY (W)
Opera Workshop
7502 Fondren
Houston, TX 77074
(713) 774-7661, ext 219
Staff: Richard Collins, Director

HOUSTON GRAND OPERA ASSOCIATION (A*)
615 Louisiana St.
Houston, TX 77002
(713) 227-0126
Staff: David Gockley, General Director

HOUSTON OPERA STUDIO
615 Louisiana St.
Houston, TX 77002
(713) 227-1287
Staff: David Gockley, General Director

HOWARD PAYNE UNIVERSITY (W)
Music Theater Workshop
Brownwood, TX 76801
Staff: Joseph McClain, Director

LAMAR UNIVERSITY (W)
Opera Theater
Box 10044, Lamar Station
Beaumont, TX 77710
(713) 838-8144
Staff: Joseph Truncale, Director

MIDLAND COLLEGE (W)
Opera Workshop
3600 North Garfield
Midland, TX 79701
(915) 684-7851
Staff: D. Stewart, Director

MIDWESTERN STATE UNIVERSITY (W)
Opera Workshop
3400 Taft
Wichita Falls, TX 76308
(817) 692-6611
Staff: Robert Hansen, Director

NORTH TEXAS STATE UNIVERSITY (W)
Opera Theater and Workshop
Denton, TX 76203
(817) 788-2791
Staff: Dennis Wakeling, Director

PAN AMERICAN UNIVERSITY (W)
Music Department
Edinburgh, TX 78539
(512) 381-3471
Staff: James Stower, Director

RED RIVER LYRIC THEATER (C)
Box 475
Wichita Falls, TX 76307
(817) 767-0315
Staff: Robert Hansen, General Director

SAM HOUSTON STATE UNIVERSITY (W)
Opera Workshop
Huntsville, TX 77340
Staff: Barbara Corbin, Director

SAN ANTONIO SYMPHONY/GRAND OPERA (B)
109 Lexington, No. 207
San Antonio, TX 78205
(512) 225-6161
Staff: Lawrence Smith, Musical Director

SOUTHERN METHODIST UNIVERSITY (W)
Music Theater Company
Dallas, TX 75275
(214) 692-2839
Staff: John Burrows, Director

SOUTHWESTERN BAPTIST THEOLOGICAL SEMINARY (W)
Opera Workshop
Box 220004D
Fort Worth, TX 76122
(817) 923-1921
Staff: Scotty Gray, Director

SOUTHWESTERN OPERA THEATER (C)
3505 West Lancaster
Fort Worth, TX 76107
(617) 731-0833
Staff: Rudolf Kruger, General Manager and Musical Director

SOUTHWEST TEXAS STATE UNIVERSITY (W)
Opera Ensemble
San Marcos, TX 78666
(512) 245-2651
Staff: J. Belisle, Director

STEPHEN F. AUSTIN STATE UNIVERSITY (W)
Opera Workshop
Box 3043 SFA Station
Nacdoches, TX 75961
(713) 569-4602
Staff: David Jones, Director

TARLETON STATE UNIVERSITY (W)
Opera Workshop
Box T-39 Tarleton Station
Stephensville, TX 76402
(817) 968-9243
Staff: Janette Kavanaugh, Director

TARRANT COUNTY JUNIOR COLLEGE (W)
Opera Workshop
828 Harwood
Hurst, TX 76053
(817) 281-7860
Staff: Marion Nesvadba, Director

TEXARKANA COMMUNITY COLLEGE (W)
Music Theater
1023 Tucker St.
Texarkana, TX 75501
Staff: Mrs. J.H. McCrosson, Musical Director

TEXAS A & I UNIVERSITY (W)
Music Dept.
Kingsville, TX 78363
(512) 595-2803
Staff: Robert C. Scott, Director

TEXAS CHRISTIAN UNIVERSITY (W)
Opera Theater
Box 32887
Fort Worth, TX 76129
(817) 921-7605
Staff: Arden Hopkin, Director

TEXAS OPERA THEATER (A*)
401 Louisiana St.
Houston, TX 77002
(713) 225-2190
Staff: M. Jane Weaver, Managing Director

TEXAS TECH UNIVERSITY (W)
Music Theater
Box 4239
Lubbock, TX 79409
(806) 742-2279
Staff: John Gillas, Director

THEATRE THREE (T)
2800 Routh St.
Dallas, TX 75201
(214) 748-5193
Staff: Joe Adler, Production Director

THEATER UNDER THE STARS (T)
4235 San Felipe
Houston, TX 77027
Staff: Ange Finn, General Manager

TRINITY UNIVERSITY (W)
Opera Workshop
715 Stadium Dr.
San Antonio, TX 78284
(512) 736-8211
Staff: Ben Jenkins, Director

UNIVERSITY OF HOUSTON (W)
Opera Theater
Houston, TX 77004
(713) 749-1116
Staff: Carlisle Floyd, Director

UNIVERSITY OF ST. THOMAS (W)
Music Department
3812 Montrose
Houston, TX 77006

UNIVERSITY OF TEXAS (W)
Music Department
Arlington, TX 76019
Staff: James Connor, Director

UNIVERSITY OF TEXAS (W)
Opera Theater
Austin, TX 78712
(512) 471-7764
Staff: Walter Ducloux, Director

UNIVERSITY OF TEXAS CIVIC OPERA (W)
Music Department
El Paso, TX 79968
(915) 747-5606
Staff: David Yoss, Director

VICTORIA COLLEGE (W)
Opera Workshop
2200 Red River
Victoria, TX 77901
(512) 573-3295
Staff: Ruth Williams, Director

WEST TEXAS STATE UNIVERSITY (W)
Music Theater
Box 879 WT Station
Canyon, TX 79016
(806) 656-2016
Staff: Burt Rosevear, Director

WEYLAND BAPTIST COLLEGE (W)
Music Department
Plainview, TX 79072

UTAH

BRIGHAM YOUNG UNIVERSITY (W)
Music Theater
A-253 HFAC
Provo, UT 84601
(801) 378-4719
Staff: Clayne Robison, Artistic Director

PIONEER MEMORIAL THEATER (A*)
University of Utah
Salt Lake City, UT 84112
(801) 581-6356
Staff: Keith Enger, Executive Director

SALT LAKE OPERA THEATER
940 Donner Way, No. 170
Salt Lake City, UT 84108
Staff: Bob Zabriskie, Manager

SOUTHERN UTAH STATE COLLEGE (W)
Music Dept.
Cedar City, UT 84720
Staff: Ellison Glattly, Director

UNIVERSITY OF UTAH
(See Pioneer Memorial Theater)

UNIVERSITY OF UTAH (W)
Opera Workshop
204 Music Hall
Salt Lake City, UT 84112
Staff: Lowell Farr, Director

UTAH OPERA COMPANY (A)
50 West 200 South
Salt Lake City, UT 84101
(801) 534-0842
Staff: Glade Peterson, General Director

WEBER STATE COLLEGE (W)
Lyric Theater
Ogden, UT 84403
Staff: Ronald Ladwig, Theater Director

VIRGINIA

BARTER THEATER (T)
Abingdon, VA 24210
(703) 628-2281
Staff: Rex Partington, Production Director

HOLLINS COLLEGE (W)
Opera Workshop
Hollins College, VA 24020
(703) 362-6513
Staff: Milton Granger, Director

JAMES MADISON UNIVERSITY (W)
Opera Workshop
Harrisonburg, VA 22807
(703) 433-6253
Staff: John Little, Director

OLD DOMINION UNIVERSITY (W)
Opera Workshop
Music Department
Norfolk, VA 23508
(804) 440-4061
Staff: Janis-Rozena Peri, Director

OPERA THEATER OF NORTHERN VIRGINIA (C)
300 North Park Dr.
Arlington, VA 22203
(703) 558-2161
Staff: John Edward Niles, Artistic Director

SHENANDOAH COLLEGE CONSERVATORY OF MUSIC (W)
Millwood Ave.
Winchester, VA 22601
(703) 667-0187
Staff: Jackson Sheats, Musical Director

SOUTHWEST VIRGINIA OPERA SOCIETY (C)
Drawer 4863
Roanoke, VA 24015
(703) 343-0179
Staff: Milton Granger, Artistic Director

VIENNA LIGHT OPERA COMPANY
9751 Firth Court
Vienna, VA 22180
(703) 281-2570
Staff: Dagmar White, Director

VIRGINIA COMMONWEALTH UNIVERSITY (W)
Opera Department
1015 Grove Ave.
Richmond, VA 23284
(804) 257-1525
Staff: L. Wayne Batty, Director

VIRGINIA OPERA ASSOCIATION (A*)
261 West Bute
Norfolk, VA 23510
(804) 627-9545
Staff: Peter Mark, General Director

VIRGINIA OPERA THEATER
261 West Bute
Norfolk, VA 23510
(804) 627-9545
Staff: Peter Mark, General Director

VIRGINIA POLYTECHNIC INSTITUTE (W)
Music Department
Blacksburg, VA 24061

WOLF TRAP COMPANY (B)
1624 Trap Road
Vienna, VA 22180
(703) 938-3810
Staff: Dina Smith, Administrator

WOLF TRAP FARM PARK FOR PERFORMING ARTS (S)
1624 Trap Rd.
Vienna, VA 22180
(703) 938-3810
Staff: Carol Harford, President

WASHINGTON

CIVIC LIGHT OPERA (T)
Box 472 Northgate Station
Seattle, WA 98125
(206) 363-2809
Staff: Ann-Denise Ford, Artistic Director

CORNISH INSTITUTE (W)
Opera Theater
710 East Roy
Seattle, WA 98102
(203) 323-1400
Staff: Roger Nelson, Director

EASTERN WASHINGTON UNIVERSITY (W)
Music Theater
Cheney, WA 99004
(509) 359-7074
Staff: John Duenow, Director

EVERETT COMMUNITY COLLEGE (W)
Music Theater Workshop
Everett, WA 98201
Staff: J. Shawger, Director

PACIFIC LUTHERAN UNIVERSITY (W)
Opera Workshop
Tacoma, WA 98447
Staff: W. Sare, Director

SEATTLE OPERA ASSOCIATION (A*)
Box 9248
Seattle, WA 98109
(206) 447-4700
Staff: Glynn Ross, General Director

SEATTLE PACIFIC UNIVERSITY (W)
Opera Workshop
Third Street West and North Nickerson
Seattle, WA 98119
(206) 282-8834
Staff: Wadad Saba, Director

UNIVERSITY OF PUGET SOUND (W)
Opera Workshop
Tacoma, WA 98416
Staff: Tommy Goleeke, Director

UNIVERSITY OF WASHINGTON (W)
Opera Theater
102 Music Building
Seattle, WA 98105
(206) 543-8259
Staff: Ralph Rosinbum, Director

WASHINGTON STATE UNIVERSITY (W)
Opera Theater
Pullman, WA 99164
(509) 335-3564
Staff: Gary Grice, Director

WESTERN WASHINGTON STATE UNIVERSITY (W)
Opera Workshop
Bellingham, WA 98225
Staff: C. Bruce Pullan, Director

WEST VIRGINIA

OGLEBAY INSTITUTE (W)
Opera Workshop
Oglebay Park
Wheeling, WV 26003
(304) 242-4200
Staff: Susan Greer, Administrative Director

WEST VIRGINIA OPERA THEATER (C)
11 Terrace Rd.
Charleston, WV 25314
(304) 346-6095
Staff: Donald Riggio, Artistic Director

WEST VIRGINIA UNIVERSITY (W)
Opera Theater
Creative Arts Center
Morgantown, WV 26506
(304) 293-5511
Staff: James Benner, Director

WISCONSIN

FLORENTINE OPERA OF MILWAUKEE (A)
750 N. Lincoln Memorial Dr.
Milwaukee, WI 53202
(414) 273-1474
Staff: John Gage, General Director

INTERNATIONAL OPERA
515 Shady Lane
Sheboygan, WI 53081
Staff: Carl Kielisch, Executive Producer

LAWRENCE UNIVERSITY (W)
Opera Theater
115 North Park Dr.
Appleton, WI 54911
(414) 735-6623
Staff: John Koopman, Director

MADISON CIVIC OPERA ASSOCIATION (B)
3823 Birch Ave.
Madison, WI 53711
(608) 233-4002
Staff: Arlene Johnson, Artistic Director

OPERA RACINE, LTD. (C)
Box 1791
Racine, WI 53401
(414) 639-1316
Staff: Ralph Lane, General and Artistic Director

SKYLIGHT COMIC OPERA (B)
813 North Jefferson
Milwaukee, WI 53202
(414) 271-8815
Staff: Colin Cabot, Managing Director

UNIVERSITY OF WISCONSIN (W)
Opera Workshop
Eau Claire, WI 54701
Staff: R. Johnson, Director

UNIVERSITY OF WISCONSIN (W)
Music Department
Green Bay, WI 54302

UNIVERSITY OF WISCONSIN (W)
Opera Workshop
3581 Humanities Building
Madison, WI 53713
(608) 262-3142
Staff: Karlos Moser, Director

UNIVERSITY OF WISCONSIN (W)
White Heron Opera Workshop
Menasha, WI 54911
(414) 733-3123
Staff: Lisa James, Director

UNIVERSITY OF WISCONSIN (W)
Opera Theater
Box 413
Milwaukee, WI 53201
(414) 963-4947
Staff: Corliss Phillabaum, Director

UNIVERSITY OF WISCONSIN (W)
Music Department
Oshkosh, WI 54901

UNIVERSITY OF WISCONSIN (W)
Opera Theater
Superior, WI 54880
(713) 394-8255
Staff: Art Bumgardner, Director

UNIVERSITY OF WISCONSIN (W)
Opera Theater
Whitewater, WI 53190
Staff: D. Wadsworth, Director

VITERBO COLLEGE (W)
Opera Workshop
815 South Ninth St.
La Crosse, WI 54601
(608) 784-0040, ext 495
Staff: Daniel Johnson-Wilmot, Director

WISCONSIN OPERA THEATER
750 North Lincoln Memorial Dr.
Milwaukee, WI 53202
(414) 273-1474
Staff: John Gage, General Manager

WYOMING

UNIVERSITY OF WYOMING (W)
Opera Theater
Box 3037
Laramie, WY 82071
(307) 766-1121
Staff: Frederick Gersten, Director

PUERTO RICO

OPERA DA CAMERA DE PUERTO RICO (C)
Apt. Postale 22542 UPR Station
Rio Pedras, PR 00931
(809) 755-6433
Staff: Luis Pereira, Director

CANADA

ALBERTA

BANFF CENTRE MUSIC THEATER STUDIO (W)
Box 1020
Banff, AB T0L 0C0
(403) 762-6100
Staff: Michael Bawtree, Artistic Director

BANFF CENTRE SCHOOL OF THE ARTS (W)
Box 1020
Banff, AB T0L 0C0
(403) 762-3391
Staff: George Ross and Neil Armstrong, Managers

EDMONTON OPERA ASSOCIATION (A*)
10102 101st St., No. 503
Edmonton, AB T5J 0S5
(403) 422-4919
Staff: Lorin J. Moore, Administrative Director

SOUTHERN ALBERTA OPERA ASSOCIATION (A)
No. 3 6025 Twelfth St. Southeast
Calgary, AB T2H 2K1
(403) 252-9905
Staff: Brian Hanson, General Manager

BRITISH COLUMBIA

CANADA OPERA PICCOLA (B)
3737 Oak St., No. 103
Vancouver, BC V6H 2M4
(604) 736-1916
Staff: J.J. Johannesen, General Manager

PACIFIC OPERA ASSOCIATION (B)
Box 386 Station E
Victoria, BC V8W 2N2
(604) 385-0222
Staff: Cameron More, General Manager

UNIVERSITY OF BRITISH COLUMBIA (W)
Opera Theater
6361 Memorial Rd.
Vancouver, BC V6T 1W5
(604) 228-6434
Staff: French Tickner, Director

UNIVERSITY OF VICTORIA (W)
Opera Theater
Box 1700
Victoria, BC V8W, 2Y2
(604) 477-6911
Staff: George Corwin, Director

VANCOUVER OPERA (A*)
111 Dunsmuir St.
Vancouver, BC V6B 1W8
(604) 682-2871
Staff: Hamilton McClymont, General Manager

MANITOBA

MANITOBA OPERA ASSOCIATION (A)
555 Main St., No.121
Winnipeg, MB R3B 1C3
(204) 942-7479
Staff: Irving Guttman, Artistic Director

NOVA SCOTIA

DALHOUSIE UNIVERSITY (W)
Opera Workshop
Music Department
Halifax, NS B3H 4H6
(902) 865-5320
Staff: Jeff Morris, Director

ONTARIO

CANADIAN BROADCASTING COMPANY (S)
TV Opera Department
354 Jarvis St.
Toronto, ON M4Y 2G6
Staff: J. Roberts, Director

CANADIAN CHILDREN'S CHORUS
c/o Opera Canada
366 Adelaide St. East, No. 433
Toronto, ON M5A 1N4
Staff: Ruby Mercer, Director

CANADIAN OPERA COMPANY (A*)
417 Queen's Quay West
Toronto, ON M5V 1A2
(416) 363-6671
Staff: Lotfi Mansouri, General Director

CANADIAN OPERA ENSEMBLE
417 Queen's Quay West
Toronto, ON M5V 1A2
(416) 363-6671
Staff: Lotfi Mansouri, General Director

COMUS MUSIC THEATER (B)
95 Trinity
Toronto, ON M5A 3C7
Staff: Claire Hopkinson, General Manager

CO-OPERA THEATER (C)
15 D'Arcy St.
Toronto, ON M5T 1J8
(416) 977-5271
Staff: Raymond Pannell, Artistic Director

COSMOPOLITAN OPERA ASSOCIATION (C)
739 Lawrence Ave. West., No. 3
Toronto, ON M6A 1B7
(416) 783-0477
Staff: Michele Strano, President

NATIONAL ARTS CENTRE (S)
Box 1534 Station B
Ottawa, ON K1P 5W1
(613) 996-5051
Staff: Donald MacSween, General Director

OPERA HAMILTON (B)
Hamilton Place
Hamilton, ON L8N 3Y7
(416) 527-7672
Staff: Steven Thomas, Artistic and General Manager

OPERA IN CONCERT SERIES (C)
538 Eglinton Ave. East
Toronto, ON M4P 1N9
(416) 921-7463
Staff: Stuart Hamilton, Producer

TORONTO LYRIC THEATER
1613 Bloor Street West
Toronto, ON M6P 1A6
(416) 533-8240
Staff: Victoria Masnyk, Managing Director

UNIVERSITY OF TORONTO (W)
Opera Division
Faculty of Music
80 Queen's Park Crescent
Toronot, ON M5S 1A1
Staff: Michael Albano, Coordinator

UNIVERSITY OF WINDSOR (W)
Opera Workshop
400 Sunset
Windsor, ON N9B 3P4
(519) 253-4232
Staff: Steven Henrickson, Director

WILFRED LAURIER UNIVERSITY (W)
Opera Workshop
Waterloo, ON N2L 3C5
Staff: Jacqueline Richards, Director

QUEBEC

CARNIVAL SOUVENIER DE CHICOUTINI
67 Ouest Jacques-Cartier
Chicoutini, PQ
Staff: Real Mimeault, Manager

MCGILL UNIVERSITY (W)
Opera Studio
Strathcona Music Building
555 Sherbrooke West
Montreal, PQ H3A 1E3
(514) 393-5864
Staff: Edith and Lucien Della Pergola, Directors

L'OPERA DE MONTREAL (A*)
1501 rue Jeanne-Mance
Montreal, PQ H2X 1Z9
(514) 285-4290
Staff: Jean-Paul Jeanotte, Artistic Director

SASKATCHEWAN

SASKATOON OPERA ASSOCIATION
421 Hilliard St. East
Saskatoon, SK S7J 0E7
(306) 653-2100
Staff: Dennis Jones, President

Opera Companies Index

A

B

C

D

E

F

G

H

I

J

K

L

M

N

O

P

Q

R

S

T

U

V

W

Y

Music Festivals

U.S., Canadian, and International festivals are listed alphabetically by state or province, and in each country. The festival's directors, types of music performed, approximate dates, and address and phone number of the person or organization to contact for further information are given for most events, when supplied by the director. An alphabetical cross-index appears at the end of this section.

ALABAMA

BIRMINGHAM FESTIVAL OF THE ARTS
Birmingham, AL
Type: Classical music, folk, light opera, ballet; art and craft exhibits, lectures, films; theater
When: Mid-April
Contact for Further Information: Birmingham Festival of the Arts Association, Commerce Center, Ste. 910, 2027 First Ave. N, Birmingham, AL 35203, (205) 323-5461

ALASKA

SITKA SUMMER MUSIC FESTIVAL
Sitka, AK
Staff: Paul Rosenthal, Music Director
Type: Chamber music
When: June
Contact for Further Information: Sitka Summer Music Festival, P.O. Box 907, Sitka, AK 99835, (907) 747-6774

ARIZONA

COUNTRY MUSIC FESTIVAL
Payson, AZ
Staff: Jack B. Sheahan, Managing Director; Ben Sandoval, Artistic Director
Type: Any and all types of country music
When: Two days in June
Contact for Further Information: Payson Chamber of Commerce, Drawer A, Payson, AZ 85541, (602) 474-4515

FLAGSTAFF FESTIVAL OF THE ARTS
Flagstaff, AZ
Staff: Mr. Pat B. Curry, Director
Type: Musical theatre, jazz, ballet performance with orchestra; 4 chamber music and 6 symphony orchestra concerts; 2 art exhibits; and 10 film classics
When: Last weekend in June to August 1
Contact for Further Information: Pat B. Curry, P.O. Box 1607, Flagstaff, AZ 86002, (602) 774-5055

OLD TIME STATE FIDDLERS' CONTEST
Payson, AZ
Staff: Jack B. Sheahan, Managing Director; Ben Sandoval, Artistic Director
Type: Old time music and instruments only; no modern amps/electronic equipment
When: Two days in late September
Contact for Further Information: Payson Chamber of Commerce, Drawer A, Payson, AZ 85541, (602) 474-4515

ARKANSAS

OZARK FOLK FESTIVAL
Eureka Springs, AR
Type: Traditional Ozarks music and songs that are at least 70 years old, played on nonelectrical instruments
When: First Wednesday-Saturday in November
Contact for Further Information: Eureka Springs Chamber of Commerce, P.O. Box 551, Eureka Springs, AR 72632, (501) 253-8737

CALIFORNIA

CABRILLO MUSIC FESTIVAL
Aptos, CA
Staff: Laurie MacDougall, Executive Director; Dennis Russell Davies, Artistic Director
Type: Approximately 12 different concerts each year during a two-week period, featuring the work of living composers, primarily Americans, in the context of less frequently heard classics
When: Last two weeks in August
Contact for Further Information: Laurie MacDougall, Cabrillo Music Festival, 6500 Soquel Dr., Aptos, CA 95003, (408) 476-9064

CARMEL BACH FESTIVAL
Carmel, CA
Staff: Janet Eswein, Festival Administrator; Sandor Salgo, Music Director and Conductor
Type: Classical music of the Baroque period; 21 concerts, 17 recitals, and 9 lectures and symposia
When: Last three weeks in July
Contact for Further Information: Janet Eswein, P.O. Box 575, Carmel, CA 93921, (408) 624-1521

HOLLYWOOD BOWL SUMMER FESTIVAL
Hollywood, CA
Staff: Ernest Fleischmann, Director
Type: At least 40 symphonic concerts with the Los Angeles Philharmonic, 5 jazz events, and 5 recitals or performances by visiting ensembles
When: July through mid-September
Contact for Further Information: Los Angeles Philharmonic, 135 N. Grand Ave., Los Angeles, CA 90012, (213) 972-7300

IDYLLWILD FESTIVAL CONCERT SERIES
Idyllwild, CA
Staff: Dwight Holmes, Director; Patricia Clark, Artistic Director
Type: Jazz, chamber music, choral, orchestral, solo, musicals, theatrical, and dance
When: July through early September
Contact for Further Information: Dwight Holmes, Idyllwild School of Music and the Arts, University of Southern California, P.O. Box 38, Idyllwild, CA 92349

THE LIVELY ARTS AT STANFORD
Stanford, CA
Staff: Vicky Holt, Director
Type: General performing arts series, including solo recital, dance, theater, chamber music, jazz and pops; approximiately 35 events per year
When: Academic year (October through May)
Contact for Further Information: Nan Bentley, Lively Arts at Stanford, Press Courtyard, Stanford, CA 94305, (415) 497-2551

LOS ANGELES BACH FESTIVAL
Los Angeles, CA
Staff: Thomas Somerville, Director
Type: Music of Johann Sebastian Bach and his contemporaries
When: Ten days in late April or May
Contact for Further Information: Gail P. Green, Music Coordinator, First Congregational Church of Los Angeles, 540 S. Commonwealth Ave., Los Angeles, CA 90020, (213) 385-1341

MONTALVO SUMMER MUSIC
Saratoga, CA
Staff: Gardiner R. McCauley, Executive Director; Margaret Slemmons, Chairperson, Music Committee
Type: Classical (solo recital, chamber orchestra, opera) and jazz (traditional)
When: June, July, August at three-week intervals
Contact for Further Information: Margaret Slemmons, Montalvo Center for the Arts, P.O. Box 158, Saratoga, CA 95071, (408) 867-3421

MONTEREY JAZZ FESTIVAL
Monterey, CA
Staff: Jimmy Lyons, Director; John Lewis, Artistic Director
Type: Jazz
When: Third weekend in September
Contact for Further Information: Paul Fingerote, Public Relations Director, 411 Alvarado St., Monterey, CA 93940, (408) 649-4499

MUSIC ACADEMY OF THE WEST SUMMER FESTIVAL
Santa Barbara, CA
Staff: Freda J. Campbell, Manager; Theo Alcantara, Artistic Director
Type: Chamber Ensembles (4), Festival Orchestra (5), Recitals (3), Opera (4), Master Classes (88)
When: Late June through August
Contact for Further Information: Music Academy of the West Summer Festival, P.O. Box 5737, Santa Barbara, CA 93108, (805) 969-4726

OJAI MUSIC FESTIVAL
Ojai, CA
Staff: Jeanette O'Connor, Production Manager; Lawrence Morton, Artistic Director
Type: Guest artists, featured along with ochestra and chamber ensembles in an outdoor setting, an emphasis on new and rarely heard older works of serious music; 5-concert series
When: Late May or early June
Contact for Further Information: Ojai Festivals, Ltd., Box 185, Ojai, CA 93023, (805) 646-2094

PAUL MASSON SUMMER SERIES
Saratoga, CA
Staff: Bruce Labadie, Program Coordinator; Sandor Salgo, Musical Advisor (classical series)
Type: Series composed of three parts: Music at the Vineyards—classical solo, symphonic and chamber music; Vintage Sounds—jazz, blues, and folk; and the Valley Shakespeare Festival—one month of performances and related activites; 30-35 musical performances in the season; 35 theatrical peformances
When: Summer weekends between June and September
Contact for Further Information: Bruce Labadie, Paul Masson Vineyards, P.O. Box 1852, Saratoga, CA 95070, (408) 257-7800

REDLANDS BOWL SUMMER MUSIC FESTIVAL
Redlands, CA
Staff: Conant K. Halsey, President; Florence H. Beeler, Program Director
Type: Ballet, opera, musicals, recitals, folk dancing, and symphonies
When: Tuesday and Friday evenings from July 4th though the end of August
Contact for Further Information: Conant K. Halsey, Redlands Community Music Association, Inc., P.O. Box 466, Redlands, CA 92373, (714) 793-7316

ROBERT MONDAVI SUMMER FESTIVAL
Oakville, CA
Staff: Margrit Biever, Special Events Director
Type: Outdoor jazz concerts, featuring famous jazz artists; picnics on the lawn are encouraged, with wine and cheese tasting during the intermission
When: Last Sunday in June to the first Sunday in August (six consecutive Sundays)
Contact for Further Information: Margrit Biever, Special Events Director, Robert Mondavi Winery, P.O. Box 106, Oakville, CA 94562, (707) 963-9611

SAN DIEGO FOLK FESTIVAL
San Diego, CA
Staff: Louis F. Curtiss, Director
Type: Old time and traditional performers, artists who recorded in the era of 78 rpm records (country, blues, jazz, cajun, calypso, vaudeville, etc.)
When: Five days over the last weekend in April
Contact for Further Information: Louis F. Curtiss, 3611 Adams Ave., San Diego, CA 92116, (619) 282-7833

SAN LUIS OBISPO MOZART FESTIVAL
San Luis Obispo, CA
Staff: Joanna Ronyecz, Director; Clifton Swanson, Artistic Director and Conductor
Type: Classical; focus is on Mozart, but programming extends from Baroque through contemporary compositions; 16 concerts, including 4 orchestra (2 of which are with chorus), 2 chamber orchestra, 9 ensembles, and 1 solo recital. Choral concerts performed in historic San Luis Obispo de Tolossa Mission; candlelight concert in Mission San Miguel
When: First week in August
Contact for Further Information: Joanna Ronyecz, P.O. Box 311, San Luis Obispo, CA 93406 (805) 543-4580

STERN GROVE MIDSUMMER MUSIC FESTIVAL
San Francisco, CA
Staff: James M. Friedman, Director; Albert White, Artistic Director
Type: Symphonic, opera, jazz, operetta, and ballet
When: Mid-June through mid-August (ten successive Sunday afternoons)
Contact for Further Information: James M. Friedman, Stern Grove Festival Association, P.O. Box 3250, San Francisco, CA 94119, (415) 398-6551

COLORADO

ASPEN MUSIC FESTIVAL
Aspen, CO
Staff: Gordon Hardy, President/Dean; Jorge Mester, Music Director
Type: Classical, choral, opera, and jazz; incudes the Conference on Contemporary Music, and offers a music school in conjunction with the festival season
When: Late June to late August, for nine weeks
Contact for Further Information: Aspen Music Festival, P.O. Box AA, Aspen, CO 81612, (303) 925-3254. Winter address: Aspen Music Festival, 1860 Broadway, New York, NY 10023, (212) 581-2196

CENTRAL CITY OPERA FESTIVAL
Central City, CO
Staff: J. Glen Arko, Director; John Moriarty, Artistic Director

Type: Opera (2 mainstage productions); recitals, scenes programs, concerts, cabaret operas
When: July-first two weeks in August
Contact for Further Information: Central City Opera House Association, 1615 California St., Denver, CO 80202, (303) 623-7167

COLORADO MUSIC FESTIVAL
Boulder, CO
Staff: Philip Haimm, Director; Giora Bernstein, Musical Director
Type: Classical: symphony orchestra, chamber orchestra, and chamber music; 35 concerts
When: Last two weeks in June through July
Contact for Further Information: Marcia Schirmer, Administrative Manager, Colorado Music Festival, 1245 Pearl, Ste. 210, Boulder, CO 80302, (303) 449-1397

COLORADO OPERA FESTIVAL
Colorado Springs, CO
Staff: Diane Benninghoff, Director; Donald P. Jenkins, Artistic Director
Type: Two to three full productions of Grand Opera per season, for a total of 6-9 performances yearly; outreach programs include Performing Arts for Youth Organization's "Opera in the Schools Program" and The Company Singer Program for young professional singers at the start of their careers
When: Last week in July or first week in August
Contact for Further Information: Jayme L. Kelly, Colorado Opera Festival, P.O. Box 1484, Colorado Springs, CO 80901, (303) 473-0073

TELLURIDE BLUEGRASS AND MUSIC FESTIVAL
Telluride, CO
Staff: Fred Shellman, Director
Type: Bluegrass and country music; also full acoustic instrumental and harmony vocal workshops, with approximately 20 nationally recognized bluegrass and country acts; food, musical, and craft concessions
When: Last weekend in June (annually)
Contact for Further Information: Jane Dunham, Telluride Festival Corporation, P.O. Box 908, Telluride, CO 81435, (303) 728-4448

TELLURIDE CHAMBER MUSIC FESTIVAL
Telluride, CO
Staff: Randy Brown, Chairman, Chamber Music Festival Committee; Roy Malan and Robin Sutherland, Artistic Directors
Type: Chamber music; 5 evening concerts in the Sheridan Opera House; informal dessert concert; other special events
When: First two weeks in August
Contact for Further Information: Randy Brown, Telluride Council for the Arts and Humanities, P.O. Box 1040, Telluride, CO 81435, (303) 728-3974

CONNECTICUT

INTERNATIONAL CONTEMPORARY MUSIC FESTIVAL
West Hartford, CT
Staff: John Holtz, Director
Type: Comprehensive week-long survey of contemporary keyboard music; lectures, discussions, workshops, masterclasses, seminars, and evening concerts
When: One week in June
Contact for Further Information: Donna R. Nestler, Hartt School of Music Summerterm Office, University of Hartford, West Hartford, CT 06117

MUSIC MOUNTAIN
Falls Village, CT
Staff: Nicholas Gordon, President, Board of Managers; Eric Lewis, Artistic Director
Type: Chamber music festival with continuous summer concert series since 1930; Manhattan String Quartet in residence, assisted at weekend concerts by distinguished guest artists and ensembles; about 20 concerts
When: Mid-June thorugh mid-September
Contact for Further Information: Donald G. Kobler, Music Mountain, Inc., P.O. Box 217, Lakeville, CT 06039, (203) 435-9447

YALE'S NORFOLK CHAMBER MUSIC FESTIVAL
Norfolk, CT
Staff: Joan Panetti, Director; Anne Clark, Festival Manager
Type: Chamber music; approximately 10 concerts
When: June and July
Contact for Further Information: Anne Clark, Yale Summer School of Music, Rte. 44, Norfolk, CT 06058, (203) 542-5537. Before June 5: Anne Clark, Yale School of Music, 96 Wall St., New Haven, CT 06520, (203) 436-8740

DISTRICT OF COLUMBIA

AMERICAN MUSIC FESTIVAL
Washington, DC
Staff: Richard Bales, Music Director
Type: Classical (no stage works)
When: Sunday evenings during April and May
Contact for Further Information: R. Bales, National Gallery of Art, 6th St. and Constitution Ave., NW, Washington, DC, 20565, (202) 842-6075

NATIONAL FOLK FESTIVAL
Washington, DC
Staff: Joseph Wilson, Director
Type: Old time country, bluegrass, jazz, ethnic music and dance; 3 days/3 stages
When: August or September
Contact for Further Information: National Council for the Traditional Arts, 1346 Connecticut Ave., NW #1118, Washington, DC 20036

FLORIDA

BACH FESTIVAL SOCIETY OF WINTER PARK
Winter Park, FL
Staff: Dr. Ward Woodbury, Artistic Director; Mr. John Tiedtke, President
Type: Classical works of J.S. Bach and other major oratorio composers
When: Last weekend in February
Contact for Further Information: Mrs. Jean Woodbury, Bach Festival Secretary, Box 2731, Rollins College, Winter Park, FL 32789, (305) 646-2233

FLORIDA FOLK FESTIVAL
White Springs, FL
Staff: Ormond H. Loomis, Director, Florida Folklife Program; Barbara Beauchamp, Festival Coordinator
Type: Traditional music, folk songs and contemporary folk songs, blues interpretation and blues by tradition bearers
When: Friday, Saturday, Sunday preceeding Memorial Day (in May)
Contact for Further Information: Ormond H. Loomis, Director, Florida Folklife Program, White Springs, FL 32096; or Barbara Beauchamp (same address)

NEW COLLEGE MUSIC FESTIVAL
Sarasota, FL
Staff: Millicent C. Fleming, Administrative Director; Paul C. Wolfe, Artistic Director
Staff: Chamber music festival featuring internationally known guest artists who perform in a series of 6 major concerts and teach masterclasses, seminars, etc.; they also coach students who are selected from the most promising and talented young musicians across the country
When: First three weeks in June
Contact for Further Information: Millicent C. Fleming, Administrative Director, New College Music Festival, Inc., 5700 N. Tamiami Trail, Sarasota, FL 33580, (813) 355-2116 or 351-1969

PALM BEACH FESTIVAL OF THE PERFORMING ARTS
West Palm Beach and Palm Beach, FL
Staff: Mr. Dale Heapps, Director
Type: Ballet, dance, chamber orchestra, acting company, lectures, early music, and many special events
When: Last two weeks of March through mid-April
Contact for Further Information: Diana Fortune, P.O. Box 3511, West Palm Beach, FL 33402, (305) 686-6800

SPIFFS INTERNATIONAL FOLK FAIR
St. Petersburg, FL
Staff: Anna Trakas, Executive Director
Type: A three-day Ethnic Fok Fair with continuous entertainment by over 40 ethnic and national performing groups; folk dancing, singing and instrumentalists, authentic songs and dances in native languages and dress
When: Last weekend in February
Contact for Further Information: Anna Trakas, Executive Director, St. Petersburg International Folk Fair Society, Inc. 2201 First Ave. No., St. Petersburg, FL 33713, (813) 327-7999 or 327-7998

HAWAII

INTERARTS HAWAII
Honolulu, HI
Staff: Marian J. Kerr, Director; Robert Hines, Chairman, Department of Music
Type: Classical, ethnic (Japanese, Korean, Chinese, Filipino, Indonesian, Vietnamese, Indian, Thai, and Hawaiian/South Pacific) music with dance; also jazz and theatre music; credit and noncredit courses related to the festival performances and exhibitions; approximately 10 performances
When: Late May through early August
Contact for Further Information: Marian J. Kerr, Porteus Hall 720, University of Hawaii, Honolulu, HI 96822, (808) 948-8259; or Donald Mair, Executive Director, University of Hawaii Foundation, Bachmann Hall 101, University of Hawaii, 2444 Dole St., Honolulu, HI 96822, (808) 948-8849

IDAHO

NATIONAL OLDTIME FIDDLERS' CONTEST
Weiser, ID
Staff: Bruce Campbell, Chairman
Type: Oldtime fiddling
When: Third full week in June
Contact for Further Information: Judee Parsons, Secretary, Weiser Chamber of Commerce, 8 E. Idaho St., Weiser, ID 83672, (208) 549-0452

NORTHERN ROCKIES FOLK FESTIVAL
Hailey, ID
Staff: E. Richard Hart, Director
Type: Folk music from the northwest
When: First week in August
Contact for Further Information: E. Richard Hart, Sun Valley Center for the Arts and Humanities, Box 656, Sun Valley, ID 83353, (208) 622-9371

ILLINOIS

CHICAGOFEST
Chicago, IL
Staff: Tom Drilias, Director; Joel Gast, Artistic Director
Type: Rock, jazz, blues, country, pop comedy
When: First two weeks in August
Contact for Further Information: Joel Gast, ChicagoFest, 600 E. Grand Ave., Navy Pier, Chicago, IL 60611, (312) 644-7430

FALL FESTIVAL OF THE ARTS
Peoria, IL
Staff: James Ludwig, Director
Type: All types of music
When: Third week in October
Contact for Further Information: James Ludwig, Director of the Division of Theatre, Bradley University, Peoria, IL 61652, (309) 676-7611, x512

GRANT PARK CONCERTS
Chicago, IL
Type: Symphonic, opera, choral, vocal, concerti, and pops; ballet, dance theatrical and musical stage performances; jazz at the end of the summer
When: Last two weeks in June through the end of August; jazz festival first weeks in September
Contact for Further Information: Merrilee Clark, Office of Public Information, Chicago Park District, 425 E. McFetridge Dr., Chicago, IL 60605

RAVINIA FESTIVAL
Highland Park, IL
Staff: James Levine, Music Director; Edward Gordon, Executive Director
Type: Concerts by the resident Chicago Symphony Orchestra and visiting orchestras, including symphonic pops concerts, recitals, chamber music, jazz/pop/folk attractions, dance and theatre performances
When: Last week in June through first week in September
Contact for Further Information: Ravinia Festival Association, Communications Department, 22 W. Monroe St., Chicago, IL 60603, (312) 782-9696

INDIANA

THE FESTIVAL MUSIC SOCIETY OF INDIANA, INC.
"Music for Midsummer Eves"
Indianapolis, IN
Staff: Frank Cooper, Musical Director and General Manager
Type: Early music on authentic instruments; 12 concerts
When: Sunday, Tuesday, Friday evenings in July
Contact for Further Information: Mary Ellen Roberts, Executive Secretary, 6471 Central Ave., Indianapolis, IN 46220, (317) 251-5190

ROMANTIC MUSIC FESTIVAL
Indianapolis, IN
Staff: Louis F. Chenette, Dean; Jackson Wiley, Artistic Director
Type: Classical music; ballet with full symphony orchestra; arts and crafts exhibits; ethnic dinners
When: Last weekend in April
Contact for Further Information: Jordan College of Fine Arts of Butler University, 4600 Sunset Ave., Indianapolis, IN 46208, (317) 283-9231

IOWA

AMES INTERNATIONAL ORCHESTRA FESTIVAL
Ames, IA
Staff: Dr. Richard D. Snyder, Director
Type: Performances by world class symphony orchestras
When: Scheduled according to availability of orchestras, generally September through May
Contact for Further Information: Dr. Richard D. Snyder, Iowa State Center, Iowa State University, Ames, IA 50011

DES MOINES METRO SUMMER FESTIVAL OF OPERA
Indianola, IA
Staff: Douglas J. Duncan, Director; Robert L. Larsen, Artistic Director
Type: Standard and contemporary opera repertory (16 performances); chamber orchestra recitals (3) and opera scene recitals (15)
When: Mid-June to mid-July
Contact for Further Information: Jerilee M. Mace, 600 N. Buxton, Indianola, IA 50125, (515) 961-6221

NATIONAL OLD-TIME COUNTRY MUSIC CONTEST AND PIONEER EXPOSITION
Avoca, IA
Staff: Bob Everhart, Director
Type: Five stages run simultaneously with 25 categories of competition in old-time traditional American country music, bluegrass music, folk music, blues, and typical traditional music in an acoustic medium
When: Labor Day weekend
Contact for Further Information: Bob Everhart, Director, National Traditional Country Music Association, Inc., 106 Navajo Drive, Council Bluffs, IA 51501, (712) 366-1136

KANSAS

MESSIAH FESTIVAL
Lindsborg, KS
Staff: Elmer Copley, Music Director
Type: Handel's *Messiah,* Bach's *Passion According to Saint Matthew,* other choral works, oratorios and solo recitals
When: Holy Week, late March or early April
Contact for Further Information: Messiah Festival Ticket Office, Bethany College, Lindsborg, KS 67456, (913) 227-3312

WICHITA RIVER FESTIVAL
Wichita, KS
Staff: Elma Broadfoot, Executive Director

Type: country/bluegrass concert and light classical music concert by the Wichita Symphony Orchestra; many other events, including an ice cream social with barbershop chorus and a banjo band, a jazz/dixieland concert, outdoor pageant, etc.
When: Ten days beginning the first weekend in May
Contact for Further Information: Elma Broadfoot, 519 S. Broadway, Wichita, KS 67202, (316) 267-2817

LOUISIANA

FINE ARTS FESTIVAL
Lafayette, LA
Staff: Michael P. Curry, Director
Type: Classical
When: September
Contact for Further Information: Michael P. Curry, The Fine Arts Foundation, P.O. Box 53320, Lafayette, LA 70505, (318) 233-2045

LOUISIANA STATE UNIVERSITY FESTIVAL OF CONTEMPORARY MUSIC
Baton Rouge, LA
Staff: Dinos Constantinides, Chairman
Type: Nine events of 20th century classical music, including dance, lectures, and workshops; music for orchestra, opera, choir, wind ensemble, solo and chamber music groups
When: February
Contact for Further Information: Dr. Dinos Constantinides, School of Music, Louisiana State University, Baton Rouge, LA 70803, (504) 766-3487/388-4010

MADEWOOD ARTS FESTIVAL
Napoleonville, LA
Staff: Keith C. Marshall, Director
Type: Opera, chamber, classical, and gospel; other art forms in the past have included theater, ballet, and exhibits and demonstrations of regional arts and crafts; approximately 10 or 11 musical programs annually
When: Mid-April
Contact for Further Information: Madewood Arts Foundation, 530 Chartes St., New Orleans, LA 70130, (504) 524-1988

NEW ORLEANS JAZZ & HERITAGE FESTIVAL
New Orleans, LA
Type: 3,000 musicians perform cajun, jazz, R&B, country, Latin, blues and all music typical of New Orleans and Louisiana; food concessions with local delicacies and contemporary and traditional crafts
When: Last weekend in April to first weekend in May
Contact for Further Information: New Orleans Jazz & Heritage Foundation, P.O. Box 2530, New Orleans, LA 70176, (504) 522-4786

MAINE

BAR HARBOR FESTIVAL
Bar Harbor, ME
Staff: Francis Fortier, Director
Type: Classical music: solo recitals, chamber music, choral groups, plus at least one "Pops" concert (Broadway shows to Viennese light opera); approximately 6-8 concerts each festival; occasional photography exhibits, poetry readings, and dance performances
When: Last two weeks in July through the first two weeks in August
Contact for Further Information: YWCA Building, 36 Mount Desert St., Bar Harbor, ME 04609, (207) 288-5744. Winter address: 510 Fifth Ave., 4th Floor, New York, NY 10036, (212) 222-1026

BOWDOIN SUMMER MUSIC FESTIVAL
Brunswick, ME
Staff: Robert K. Beckwith, Director; Lewis Kaplan, Artistic Director
Type: Six-week chamber music school for talented young musicians pursuing professional careers in music (2 recitals weekly on campus); six Thursday night concerts presented by the professional musicians affiliated with the school
When: Last week in June through first week in August
Contact for Further Information: Anne Underwood, Acting Director, Hawthorne-Longfellow Hall, Bowdoin College, Bruswick, ME 04011, (207) 725-8731, x706

KNEISEL HALL CHAMBER MUSIC SERIES
Blue Hill, ME
Staff: Mrs. Ruth B. Kneisel, Director; Mr. Leslie Parnas, Artistic Director
Type: Classical chamber music works; 12 concerts
When: July and first two weeks in August
Contact for Further Information: Mrs. Ruth B. Kneisel, Box 251, Court St., Castine, ME 04421, (207) 326-8294

THE PIERRE MONTEUX DOMAINE SCHOOL CONCERTS
Hancock, ME
Staff: Charles Bruck, Artistic Director
Type: Orchestra repertoire from classics to contemporary
When: July-August (Sundays)
Contact for Further Information: Pierre Monteaux Domaine School, Hancock, ME 04401, (207) 422-6251

SACO RIVER FESTIVAL
Kezar Falls, ME
Staff: Ruth G. Glazer, Director
Type: Orchestral, choral, and chamber music, jazz and folk concerts; arts and crafts exhibits
When: July and August
Contact for Further Information: Saco River Festival, RFD 1, Kezar Falls, ME 04047, (207) 625-4439

MASSACHUSETTS

ASTON MAGNA SUMMER FESTIVAL
Great Barrington, MA
Staff: Marianne Carroll, Executive Director; Albert Fuller, Artistic Director
Type: 17th and 18th century music on historical instruments; 6 weekend concerts
When: First three weekends in July
Contact for Further Information: Marianne Carroll, Aston Magna Foundation for Music, Inc., 2248 Broadway, Room 21, New York, NY 10024, (212) 595-1651

BERKSHIRE MUSIC FESTIVAL
Lenox, MA
Staff: Seiji Ozawa, Music Director
Type: The Boston Symphony Orchestra presents orchestral works with vocal and instrumental soloists, choral works, and opera in concert form
When: July and August
Contact for Further Information: Festival Ticket Office, Tanglewood, Lenox, MA 01240, (413) 637-1600. Winter address: Festival Ticket Office, Symphony Hall, 301 Massachusetts Ave., Boston, MA 02115, (617) 266-1492

CAPE & ISLANDS CHAMBER MUSIC FESTIVAL
Yarmouth Port, Wellfleet, Woods Hole, Nantucket, and Martha's Vineyard, MA
Staff: Evelyn Velleman, Administrative Director; Samuel Sanders, Artistic Director
Type: Classical music; 8 concerts; annual composer-in-residence
When: First three weeks in August
Contact for Further Information: Evelyn Velleman, Administrative Director, Cape & Islands Chamber Music Festival, P.O. Box 72, Yarmouth Port, MA 02675, (617) 362-3935. Winter address: One Christopher St., (2-G), New York, NY 10014, (212) 989-1446

CASTLE HILL FESTIVAL
Ipswich, MA
Staff: William J. Conner, Executive Director
Type: Historic entertainments featuring the music of the 14th through 20th centuries, with theatre, dance, dressage, and fireworks; chamber music and straight theatre; house tours, annual crafts festival, and annual Independence day celebration
When: July and August
Contact for Further Information: William J. Conner, Executive Director, Castle Hill Foundation, Box 283, Ipswich, MA 01938, (617) 356-4070

COMPOSERS CONFERENCE AND CHAMBER MUSIC CENTER
Wellesley, MA
Staff: Mario Davidovsky, Conference Director; Efrain Guigui, Music Director
Type: Classical and contemporary concert music, chamber music, orchestral music; informal concerts by amateurs, and 4 staff concerts; fellowships awarded to composers
When: First two weeks in August
Contact for Further Information: Amelia Rogers, Composers Conference and Chamber Music Center, P.O. Box 157, Wellesley College, Wellesley, MA 02181, (617) 235-0320 x2069 or 787-0762

HAMMOND CASTLE CONCERT SERIES
Gloucester, MA
Staff: R. David Porper, Concert Manager
Type: Organ, piano, chamber orchestras; mostly classical programs, occasional jazz or other popular forms
When: Most weekends in February through December
Contact for Further Information: Hammond Castle Museum, 80 Hesperus Ave., Gloucester, MA 01930, (617) 283-2080

THE SEVENARS MUSIC FESTIVAL
Worthington, MA
Staff: Rolande Young Schrade, Director; Robert Schrade, Artistic Director
Type: Classical music programs—solo recitals, chamber music ensembles, vocal; art exhibits on concert days; approximately 7-10 concerts
When: Mid-July to mid-August
Contact for Further Information: Roland Young Schrade, Sevenars Concerts, Inc., Worthington, MA 01098, (413) 238-5854. Winter address: Roland Young Schrade, Suite 3A, 30 East End Ave., New York, NY 10028, (212) 288-4261

SOUTH MOUNTAIN CONCERTS
Pittsfield, MA
Staff: Lou R. Steigler, Executive Director; Sally Willeke, Music Director
Type: Chamber music; 4-6 concerts concerts
When: End of July through second week in October
Contact for Further Information: Mr. Lou R. Steigler, South Mountain Concerts, Box 23, Pittsfield, MA 01202, (413) 442-2106

WORCESTER MUSIC FESTIVAL
Worcester, MA
Staff: Stasia B. Hovenesian, Executive Director
Type: Series of 5 or 6 classical music concerts, inclujding international symphony orchestras, instrumentalists, vocalists, ballet, and opera
When: October and November
Contact for Further Information: Stasia B. Hovenesian, Executive Director, Worcester County Music Association, Memorial Auditorium, Worcester, MA 01608, (617) 754-3231

MICHIGAN

ANN ARBOR MAY FESTIVAL
Ann Arbor, MI
Staff: Mr. Gail W. Rector, President, University Musical Society
Type: Classical music
When: Four days in late April or early May
Contact for Further Information: University Musical Society, Burton Tower, Ann Arbor, MI 48109, (313) 665-3717 or 764-2538

BAY VIEW MUSIC FESTIVAL AND SUMMER CONSERVATORY OF MUSIC
Bay View, MI
Staff: Dr. Ernest G. Sullivan, Director
Type: Classical music, theatre, and dance
When: Mid-June to mid-August
Contact for Further Information: Dr. Ernest G. Sullivan, P.O. Box 1596, Bay View, MI 49770, (616) 347-4210. Winter address: Dr. Ernest G. Sullivan, P.O. Box 322, Alma, MI 48801, (517) 463-1518

DETROIT CONCERT BAND SUMMER MUSIC FESTIVAL
Metropolitan Detroit, MI
Staff: Dr. Leonard B. Smith, Director
Type: Varied repertoire in the classical professional concert band tradition, including overtures, waltzes, excerpts from opera, symphonies and ballet, novelties and stirring marches
When: June through August
Contact for Further Information: Helen Rowe, Director of Public Relations, Detroit Concert Band, Inc., 20962 Mack Ave., Grosse Pointe Woods, MI 48236, (313) 886-0394

INTERLOCHEN ARTS FESTIVAL
Interlochen, MI
Staff: Edward J. Downing, Director
Type: Orchestra and band concerts, recitals, dance and theatre productions, and art exhibitions by students, faculty, and guests; classical, jazz, contemporary, folk
When: June to the end of August
Contact for Further Information: Concert Manager, Interlochen Center for the Arts, Interlochen, MI 49643

KALAMAZOO BACH FESTIVAL
Kalamazoo, MI
Staff: Dr. Russell A. Hammar, Director
Sponsor: Community and Kalamazoo College
Type: Vocal and instrumental Baroque music; 3 concerts
When: First week in March
Contact for Further Information: Bach Festival, Kalamazoo College, Kalamazoo, MI 49007, (616) 383-8458/8511

MATRIZ: MIDLAND CELEBRATION OF THE ARTS AND SCIENCES
Midland, MI
Staff: Marilyn T. Brown, Coordinator
Type: Four musical programs: classical, popular, opera; dance; theatre, literature, art and science lectures, art exhibits
When: First three weeks in June
Contact for Further Information: Marilyn T. Brown, MATRIX:MIDLAND, Midland Center for the Arts, 1801 W. St. Andrews Dr., Midland, MI 48640

MEADOW BROOK MUSIC FESTIVAL
Rochester, MI
Staff: Stuart C. Hyke, Managing Director; Neville Marriner, Artistic Director
Type: Classical, jazz, folk, and pop music, as well as children's concerts and ballet
When: Late June to late August
Contact for Further Information: Meadow Brook Music Festival, Oakland University, P.O. Box 705, Rochester, MI 48063, (313) 377-3100

MISSOURI

THE MUNICIPAL THEATRE ASSOCIATION OF ST. LOUIS (THE MUNY)
St. Louis, MO
Staff: Edwin R. Culver, III, Director; Edward M. Greenberg, Artistic Director
Type: Traditional musical revivals, Broadway shows, renowned dance companies, operettas, and popular name entertainers
When: Summer, 11 weeks from mid-June through late August; winter, a minimum of 12 weeks, September through May
Contact for Further Information: Barbara Mahon, Advertising and Publicity Director, The Muny, Forest Park, St. Louis, MO 63112, (314) 361-1900

OPERA THEATRE OF ST. LOUIS
St. Louis, MO
Staff: Richard Gaddes, General Director; Thomas J. Rother, Business Manager; Mark Tiarks, Artistic Administrator
Type: Opera/musical theater; average season includes 4 operas, sung in English, with approximately 25 total performances
When: Second or third week in June first three weeks in June
Contact for Further Information: Thomas J. Rother, Business Manager, Opera Theatre of St. Louis, P.O. Box 13148, #1 Kirthom Lane, St. Louis, MO 63119, (314) 961-0171

ST. LOUIS COUNTY POPS
Manchester, MO
Staff: Richard Hayman, McDonnell Douglas Principal Pops Conductor
Type: Pops; Dixieland, music of the

20's, big band night, some ragtime, etc.
When: Every Wednesday, Thursday, Friday, and Saturday, July through mid-August
Contact for Further Information: St. Louis Symphony Society, 718 N. Grand Blvd., St. Louis, MO 63103, (314) 533-2500 or 534-1700 (box office)

ST. LOUIS NATIONAL RAGTIME AND TRADITIONAL JAZZ FESTIVAL
St. Louis, MO
Staff: G. William Oakley, Director
Type: Authentic ragtime and traditional jazz
When: Second ro third week in June
Contact for Further Information: Goldenrod Showboat, 400 N. Wharf St., St. Louis, MO 63102, (314) 621-3311

MONTANA

CHAMBER MUSIC FESTIVAL
Bozeman, MT
Staff: Mary C. Sanks, Director
Type: Classical chamber music, baroque thorough contemporary, for strings, winds and keyboard; a participation festival for all ages; 1 concert and 2 lecture demonstrations by coaches; small group coaching
When: Last full week in June
Contact for Further Information: Music Department, Montana State University, Bozeman, MT 59717, (406) 944-3561

NEBRASKA

HERITAGE DAYS
McCook, NE
Staff: Lester Harsh, Director
Type: Folk-German, polka, Irish; generally two musical performances
When: First full weekend in May
Contact for Further Information: Greater McCook Area Chamber of Commerce, P.O. Box 337, McCook, NE 69001, (308) 345-3200

NEW HAMPSHIRE

NEW HAMPSHIRE MUSIC FESTIVAL
Plymouth and Gilford, NH
Staff: Philip L. Walz, Executive Director; Thomas Nee, Music Director
Type: Six classical orchestra concerts and 6 classical chamber music concerts, dance groups and ensembles
When: Mid-July through mid-August
Contact for Further Information: New Hampshire Music Festival, Box 147, Center Harbor, NH 03226, (603) 253-4331

STRAWBERY BANKE CHAMBER MUSIC FESTIVAL, INC.
Portsmouth, NH
Staff: Kay Shelton, Director
Type: Chamber music from very early to 20th century
When: Last Saturday in July through Labor Day weekend (6 consecutive Saturday evenings)
Contact for Further Information: Kay Shelton, 200 Newcastle Ave., Portsmouth, NH 03801, (603) 431-5111

NEW JERSEY

FAIR LAWN SUMMER FESTIVAL
Fair Lawn, NJ 07410, (201) 796-5280
Staff: Isadore Freeman, Director
Type: Classical—symphonic, opera, operetta, jazz, big bands, symphonic brass bands
When: Last Sunday in June through first Sunday in September
Contact for Further Information: Isadore Freeman, 13-08 Bellair Ave., Fair Lawn, NJ 07410 (201) 796-5280

WATERLOO FESTIVAL FOR THE ARTS
Stanhope, NJ
Staff: David O. Zonker, Jr., Executive Director; Gerard Schwarz, Artistic Director
Type: Classical, jazz, country & western, bluegrass, dance, crafts, antiques, and opera; approximately 57 events
When: May through October
Contact for Further Information: D. Alden Smith, Director of Operations, Waterloo Foundation for the Arts, Waterloo Village, Stanhope, NJ 07874

NEW MEXICO

SANTA FE CHAMBER MUSIC FESTIVAL
Santa Fe, NM
Staff: Sheldon Rich, Festival Director; Alicia Schachter, Artistic Director
Type: Chamber music
When: July and August
Contact for Further Information: Santa Fe Chamber Music Festival, P.O. Box 853, Santa Fe, NM 87501, (505) 983-2075

THE SANTA FE OPERA
Santa Fe, NM
Staff: John O. Crosby, Director
Type: Opera; 5 productions every summer
When: July and August
Contact for Further Information: Santa Fe Opera, P.O. Box 2408, Santa Fe, NM 87501, (505) 982-3851

TAOS SCHOOL OF MUSIC CHAMBER MUSIC FESTIVAL
Taos, NM
Staff: Mr. Chilton Anderson, Director
Type: Chamber music (classical)
When: Mid-June to early August
Contact for Further Information: Taos School of Music, Box 1879, Taos, NM 87571, (505) 776-2388

NEW YORK

ADIRONDACK FESTIVAL OF AMERICAN MUSIC
Saranac Lake and Lake Placid, NY
Staff: Michael Leavitt, Director; Gregg Smith, Artistic Director
Type: Chamber music series (2), orchestra series, choral series, and outdoor park concerts
When: July 4th through mid-August (4 programs per week)
Contact for Further Information: Michael Leavitt, 195 Steamboat Rd., Great Neck, NY 11024, (516) 487-3216

ARTPARK
Lewiston, NY
Staff: Joanne Allison, Executive Director
Type: Two musicals and 2 operas; 3-4 dance companies; 15-20 special concerts including jazz, country, folk, etc; sculptors, craftsmen, storytellers, children's theater, musicians, and actors throughout the park
When: Late June through late August
Contact for Further Information: Janette Hickin, Public Relations/Marketing Director, Artpark, Box 371, Lewiston, NY 14092

BERKSHIRE MOUNTAINS BLUEGRASS FESTIVAL
Hillsdale/Ancram, NY
Staff: Nancy Talbott, Director
Type: Traditional bluegrass music, continuous stage performances (Thursday through Sunday); bluegrass instruments and accessories, record booth, and other displays
When: Usually the last full weekend in July
Contact for Further Information: Nancy Talbott, HAZARD Productions, Inc., Box 127, No. Cambridge, MA 02140, (617) 492-0415

CARAMOOR FESTIVAL
Katonah, NY
Staff: Michael Sweeley, Executive Director; John Nelson, Musical Director
Type: Orchestral, chamber, recitals, opera
When: Late June through August
Contact for Further Information: Michael Sweeley, Caramoor Center for Music and the Arts, Inc., Box R, Katonah, NY 10536, (914) 232-4206

CELEBRATION OF NATIONS
Utica, NY
Staff: Anne Peno, Coordinator; Maria Wallace, Production Coordinator
Type: Ethnic dance and song
When: First weekend in May
Contact for Further Information: Anne Peno, Central New York Community Arts Council, 800 Park Ave., Utica, NY 13501, (315) 798-5039

CHAUTAUQUA INSTITUTION
Chautauqua, NY
Staff: Robert R. Hesse, President; Varujan Kojian, Music Director; Cynthia Auerbach, Artistic Director of Opera
Type: Twenty-one concerts by Chautauqua Symphony Orchestra; operas by Chautauqua Opera Company; drama by The Acting Company; Chautauqua Festival Orchestra, Chautauqua Youth Orchestra; jazz, country, lectures, guest artists
When: Nine weeks beginning at the end of June
Contact for Further Information: Darlene Benson, Program Coordinator, Chautauqua Institution, Chautauqua, NY 14722
(716) 357-5635

INTERNATIONAL HARP FESTIVAL
New York, NY
Staff: Dr. Artistid von Wurtzler, Director
Type: Classical and contemporary harp music; resident ensemble is the New York Harp Ensemble
When: June
Contact for Further Information: Dr. Aristid von Wurtzler, 140 West End Ave., New York, NY 10023, (212) 362-9018

KOOL JAZZ FESTIVAL-NEW YORK
New York City, NY
Staff: George Wein, Director
Type: Mainstream jazz featuring the biggest names in jazz; some avant garde jazz
When: Late June to the beginning of July
Contact for Further Information: Kool Jazz Festival-New York, P.O. Box 1169, Ansonia Station, New York, NY 10023 (212) 787-2020

MAVERICK SUNDAY CONCERTS
Woodstock, NY
Staff: Leo Bernache, Music Director
Type: Chamber music, traditional and contemporary
When: Sunday afternoons, July thorugh mid-September
Contact for Further Information: Maverick Concerts, Inc., P.O. Box 102, Woodstock, NY 12498, (914) 679-8746

SARATOGA PERFORMING ARTS CENTER
Saratoga Springs, NY
Staff: Herbert A. Chesbrough, Executive Director
Type: Symphonic music, ballet, popular music, theatre
When: Mid-June through August
Contact for Further Information: Saratoga Performing Arts Center, Saratoga Springs, NY 12866 (518) 584-9330 or 587-3330 (box office)

SPRING FESTIVAL OF THE ARTS
Potsdam, NY
Staff: Salvatore Cania, Director; N. Brock McEheran, Artistic Director
Type: Works for chorus and orchestra (2 concerts); theatre, dance, and art programs
When: Last two weeks in April
Contact for Further Information: Salvatore Cania, Technical Assistant to the Dean of Music, Crane School of Music, State University of New York, Potsdam, NY 13676

SUMMER OF MUSIC ON THE HUDSON FESTIVAL
Tarrytown, NY
Staff: Robert M. Gewald, Director; Stephen Simon, Artistic Director
Type: Symphony concerts, pops concerts, and special music events such as country music, bluegrass, and performances of Gilbert & Sullivan (six-week season)
When: July and first weeks of August
Contact for Further Information: Robert M. Gewald, Country Symphony Association of Westchester, Inc., 58 W. 58th St., New York, NY 10019, (212) 753-0450

NORTH CAROLINA

AMERICAN DANCE FESTIVAL
Durham, NC
Staff: Charles Reinhart, Director
Type: Modern dance; informal concerts—jazz and contemporary
When: Mid-June through end of July
Contact for Further Information: American Dance Festival, P.O. Box 6097, College Station, Durham, NC 27708 (919) 684-6402

BREVARD MUSIC FESTIVAL
Brevard, NC
Staff: Henry Janiec, Artistic Director
Type: Chamber, band, and youth orchestra concerts; Broadway shows, opera, symphony, guest artists, concertos; approximately 50 performances
When: Late June through mid-August
Contact for Further Information: Don Nickson, PR Director, Brevard Music Center, Box 592, Brevard, NC 29712, (704) 884-2011

EASTERN MUSIC FESTIVAL
Greensboro, NC
Staff: Sheldon Morgenstern, Music Director
Type: Orchestral and chamber music performed by three different orchestras, one composed of professional musicians, and two composed of students who are attending the summer institution of music which is part of this festival
When: Mid-June through early August
Contact for Further Information: Eastern Music Festival, 200 N. Davie St., Greensboro, NC 27401, (919) 373-4712

MOUNTAIN DANCE AND FOLK FESTIVAL
Asheville, NC
Staff: Mrs. Jackie Ward, Director
Type: Bluegrass and traditional Southern Applachian Mountain string music
When: First Thursday, Friday, Saturday in August
Contact for Further Information: Mrs. Jackie Ward, Asheville Area Chamber of Commerce, P.O. Box 1011, Asheville, NC 28802 (704) 258-5200 or 274-1360

SHINDIG-ON-THE-GREEN
Asheville, NC
Staff: Mrs. Jackie Ward, Director
Type: Bluegrass and traditional Southern Applachian string music; outdoor festival
When: Every Saturday night, July through August
Contact for Further Information: Mrs. Jackie Ward, Director, Shindig-on-the-Green, Asheville Area Chamber of Commerce, P.O. Box 1011, Asheville, NC 28802, (704) 258-5200 or 274-1360

OHIO

BALDWIN-WALLACE BACH FESTIVAL
Berea, OH
Staff: Dwight Oltman, Music Director
Type: Mostly Bach, including rarely heard works, and other composers of his era, such as Vivaldi
When: Third weekend in May
Contact for Further Information: Baldwin-Wallace College, Conservatory of Music, 96 Front St., Berea, OH 44017, (216) 826-2369

BLOSSOM MUSIC CENTER
Cuyahoga Falls, OH
Staff: J. Christopher Fahlman, Director
Type: Cleveland Orchestra concerts, jazz, rock, pop, country; over 70 concerts; dance events and art exhibits
When: First week in June to second week in September
Contact for Further Information: Jan C. Snow, Director of Communications and Press Relations, 11001 Euclid Ave., Cleveland, OH 44106, (216) 231-7300

CINCINNATI MAY FESTIVAL
Cincinnati, OH
Staff: James Conlon, Music Director
Type: Choral concerts and audience sing-alongs
When: Late May
Contact for Further Information: May Festival Tickets, Music Hall, 1241 Elm St., Cincinnati, OH 45210, (513) 621-1919

CINCINNATI OPERA SUMMER FESTIVAL
Cincinnati, OH
Staff: James de Blasis, Director
Type: At least 4 grand operas, 1 operetta, and 1 musical theater piece
When: June and July
Contact for Further Information: Stephen Brock, Administrative Manager, or Betty Schulte, Executive Assistant, Music Hall, 1241 Elm St., Cincinnati, OH 45210

LAKESIDE MUSIC FESTIVAL
Lakeside, OH
Staff: Tom Edwards, Director; Robert L. Cronquist, Artistic Director
Type: Festival symphony; 9 concerts
When: August
Contact for Further Information: R.L. Cronquist, 236 Walnut, Lakeside, OH 43440, (419) 798-4461. Winter address: 12931 Shaker Blvd., Cleveland, OH 44120

OREGON

CHAMBER MUSIC NORTHWEST
Portland, OR
Staff: Linda Magee, Executive Director; David Shifrin, Music Director
Type: Chamber music; 25-28 concerts each six-week season
When: Mid-June through late July
Contact for Further Information: Linda Magee, Executive Director, Chamber Music Northwest, P.O. Box 751, Portland, OR 97207, (503) 229-4079

OREGON BACH FESTIVAL
Eugene, OR
Staff: H. Royce Saltzman, Executive Director; Helmuth Rilling, Artistic Director and Conductor
Type: Choral and orchestra concerts, chamber music, recitals, lectures, and masterclasses; special attention to the work of Johann Sebastian Bach and his choral music; 8 cantatas, various instrumental works, and 1 or more major Bach choral works
When: Two full weeks starting the end of June
Contact for Further Information: Henriette Heiny, Assistant Director, Oregon Bach Festival, School of Music, University of Oregon, Eugene, OR 97403, (503) 686-5667

PETER BRITT GARDENS MUSIC & ART FESTIVAL ASSOCIATION
Jacksonville, OR
Staff: David Shaw, General Manger; John Trudeau, conductor and Music Director
Type: Classical, full orchestra and some recitals; bluegrass and country music; jazz
When: Late July and August
Contact for Further Information: Britt Festival, P.O. Box 1124, Medford, OR 97501, (503) 779-0847

PENNSYLVANIA

BETHLEHEM BACH FESTIVAL
Bethlehem, PA
Staff: William Reese, Director; Mrs. Joyce G. Lukehart, Executive Secretary
Type: Music of Johann Sebastian Bach
When: Second and third weekends in May **Contact for Further Information:** Bach Choir of Bethlehem, 423 Heckwelder Pl., Bethlehem, PA 18018

PHILADELPHIA FOLK FESTIVAL
Schwenksville, PA
Type: Folk music, folk dancing; crafts demonstrations, workshops, children's concerts
When: Last week in August
Contact for Further Information: Philadelphia Folk Festival, 7113 Emlen St., Philadelphia, PA 19119, (215) 247-1300 or 242-0150

ROBIN HOOD DELL SUMMER FESTIVAL
Philadelphia, PA
Staff: Helen Martin, Executive Director
Type: Classical music played by the Philadelphia Symphony Orchestra
When: Mid-June to early August
Contact for Further Information: Robin Hood Dell Concerts, Inc., 1617 John F. Kennedy Blvd., Philadelphia, PA 19103, (215) 567-0707

RHODE ISLAND

NEWPORT MUSIC FESTIVAL
Newport, RI
Staff: Mark P. Malkovich III, General Director
Type: Rare, often never-before-heard classical music
When: Second and third weeks in July
Contact for Further Information: Newport Music Festival, 50 Washington Sq., Newport, RI 02840, (401) 846-1133

SOUTH CAROLINA

SPOLETO FESTIVAL U.S.A.
Charleston, SC
Staff: James T. Kearney, Director; Gian Carlo Menotti, Artistic Director
Type: Comprehensive performing arts festival including opera, symphonic programs and dance (some with live orchestra); orchestra selected by audition in approximately 7 cities in U.S.
When: Last two weeks in May through first week in June
Contact for Further Information: Carmen Kovens, Company Manager, Spoleto Festival U.S.A., P.O. Box 157, Charleston, SC 29402, (803) 722-2764

TENNESSEE

SEWANEE SUMMER MUSIC CENTER
Sewanee, TN
Staff: Martha McCrory, Director
Type: Classical music training for instrumentalists, and Concert Series (26 programs)
When: End of June through July (five weeks)
Contact for Further Information: Miss Martha McCrory, Sewanee Summer Music Center, University of the South, Sewanee, TN 37375, (615) 598-5931 x225

TEXAS

FESTIVAL-INSTITUTE AT ROUND TOP
Round Top, TX
Staff: Richard R. Royall, Director; James Dick, Artistic Director
Type: Classical, solo, chamber, vocal and orchestral works; over 40 concerts throughout the year
When: June and early July (Summer Festival)
Contact for Further Information: Festival-Institute, P.O. Box 89, Round Top, TX 78954, (713) 249-3129

KERRVILLE BLUEGRASS FESTIVAL
Kerrville, TX
Staff: Rod Kennedy, Director
Type: Traditional and contemporary bluegrass music
When: Labor Day weekend
Contact for Further Information: Kerrville Festivals, Inc., P.O. Box 1466, Kerrville, TX 78028, (512) 896-3800

KERRVILLE FOLK FESTIVAL
Kerrville, TX
Staff: Rod Kennedy, Director
Type: Traditional and contemporary folk music; original songs, songwriters' events, blues, crafts
When: Memorial Day weekend through the first weekend in June
Contact for Further Information: Kerrville Festivals, Inc., P.O. Box 1466, Kerrville, TX 78028, (512) 896-3800

KERRVILLE GOODTIME MUSIC FESTIVAL
Kerrville, TX
Staff: Rod Kennedy, Director
Type: Acoustic music or based on old-time traditional music
When: Second weekend in October
Contact for Further Information: Kerrville Festivals, Inc., P.O. Box 1466, Kerrville, TX 78028, (512) 896-3800

KERRVILLE SUMMER MUSIC FESTIVAL
Kerrville, TX
Staff: Rod Kennedy, Director
Type: Classical music for solo voice, solo instruments; chamber, choral, and orchestral music
When: Third weekend in July
Contact for Further Information: Kerrville Music Foundation, Inc., P.O. Box 1466, Kerrville, TX 78028, (512) 896-3800

UTAH

UTAH ARTS FESTIVAL
Salt Lake City, UT
Staff: Olivette Trotter, Director
Type: Symphony, ballet, modern dance, jazz, chamber ensembles, bluegrass, punk, rock & roll; 80-90 groups; visual artists, demonstrating craftsmen, film events, a children's art yard, literary performances, food arts, etc.
When: Five days the last week in June
Contact for Further Information: Olivette Trotter, Director, 617 E. South Temple, Salt Lake City, UT 84102, (801) 533-5895

VERMONT

MARLBORO SCHOOL OF MUSIC, INC.
Marlboro, VT
Staff: Anthony P. Checchia and Frank Salomon, Administrators; Rudolph Serkin, Artistic Director
Type: Summer Program for the advanced study of classical chamber music; weekend Festival concerts by participants
When: Seven weeks each summer, late June to mid-Agust
Contact for Further Information: Marlboro Music, Marlboro, VT 05344, (802) 254-2394. Winter address: Marlboro Music, 135 S. 18th St., Philadelphia, PA 19103, (215) 569-4690

VERMONT MOZART FESTIVAL
Burlington, VT
Staff: Gretchen Amussen, Director; Melvin Kaplan, Artistic Director
Type: Classical music in a variety of outdoor and indoor sites
When: Last two weeks in July through the first week in August
Contact for Further Information: Gretchen Amussen, P.O. Box 512, Burlington, VT 05402, (802) 862-7352

YELLOW BARN MUSIC FESTIVAL
Putney, VT
Staff: Linda Rubinstein, Director; David and Janet Wells, Artistic Directors
Type: Chamber music; approximately 20 concerts per season
When: Five weeks beginning in early July
Contact for Further Information: Linda Rubinstein, RFD #2, Box 71, Putney, VT 05346, (802) 387-6637

VIRGINIA

THE BARNS OF WOLF TRAP FOUNDATION
Vienna, VA
Staff: Edward Mattos, Executive Director
Type: Film, classical music, folk, poetry readings, dance, and drama
When: Early October through early May
Contact for Further Information: Wolf Trap Foundation, 1624 Trap Rd., Vienna, VA 22180, (703) 938-8463

OLD FIDDLERS CONVENTION
Galax, VA
Type: Bluegrass and old-time music; folk songs, dancing, crafts, and different types of arts
When: Second weekend in August
Contact for Further Information: Oscar Hall, 328A Kenbrook Dr., Galax, VA 24333, (703) 236-6355; or Galax Moose Lodge #733, P.O. Box 755, Galax, VA 24333

WOLF TRAP FARM PARK FOR THE PERFORMING ARTS
Vienna, VA
Staff: Edward Mattos, Executive Director
Type: The full spectrum of the performing arts, including classical, jazz, popular, bluegrass, opera, dance, and film
When: Mid-June through the end of August
Contact for Further Information: Wolf Trap Foundation, 1624 Trap Rd., Vienna, VA 22180, (703) 938-3810

WASHINGTON

NORTHWEST REGIONAL FOLKLIFE FESTIVAL
Seattle, WA
Staff: Scott Nagel, Director
Type: Folk music of all kinds with limitations on the use of electric instruments—ethnic music, old time, gospel, folk, bluegrass, string bands, Irish, etc.
When: Memorial Day weekend
Contact for Further Information: Northwest Regional Folklife Festival, Seattle Center, 305 Harrison, Seattle, WA 98109, (206) 625-4410

PACIFIC NORTHWEST WAGNER FESTIVAL
Seattle, WA
Staff: Glynn Ross, Director; Lincoln Clark, Stage Manager; Henry Holt, conductor
Type: Opera by Ricahrd Wagner (specifically, the four opera cycle "The Ring of the Nibelung"
When: End of July through early August
Contact for Further Information: Seattle Opera Association, P.O. Box 9248, Seattle, WA 98109, (206) 447-4700

WISCONSIN

MUSIC UNDER THE STARS
Milwaukee, WI
Staff: John D. Anello, Jr., Director; John-David Anello, Artistic Director
Type: Pops concerts, musical production, classical, opera production, chamber; approximately 15 programs
When: July through first or second week in August
Contact for Further Information: Stars Productions, Inc., John D. Anello, Jr., General Manager, 4420 W. Vliet St., Milwaukee, WI 53208, (414) 278-4389

PENINSULA MUSIC FESTIVAL
Fish Creek, WI
Staff: Michael Charry, Conductor and Music Director
Type: Classical music played by professional musicians from the area
When: Middle to late August
Contact for Further Information: Peninsula Music Festival, Ephraim, WI 54211, (414) 854-4060

SUMMERFEST
Milwaukee, WI
Staff: Rod Lanser, President
Type: A wide variety of musical styles; one of the largest festivals in the nation
When: Late June through early July
Contact for Further Information: Summerfest, 200 N. Harbor Dr., Milwaukee, WI 53202, (414) 273-2680

CANADA

BRITISH COLUMBIA

VICTORIA INTERNATIONAL FESTIVAL
Vancouver, BC
Staff: J.J. Johannesen, Director
Type: Series of 26 concerts, including 9 recitals featuring soloists and chamber ensembles, 3 keyboard recitals, 4 chamber opera productions, 1 "pop-opera" extravaganza, and 6 "concerti extravaganza" concerts featuring the Victoria Symphony Orchestra
When: Mid-July through late August
Contact for Further Information: J.J. Johannesen, 3737 Oak St., Vancouver, BC V6H 2M4

NEW BRUNSWICK

MIRAMICHI FOLK SONG FESTIVAL
Newcastle, NB
Staff: Mrs. Maisy Mitchell, Director
Type: Folk songs sung without accompaniment
When: First week in July
Contact for Further Information: Mrs. Maisy Mitchell, 356 Water St., Newcastle, NB E1V 1X3, (506) 622-1292

ONTARIO

FESTIVAL OF THE SOUND
Parry Sound, ON
Staff: Anton Keurti, Artistic Director
Type: Chamber music—orchestra, recitals
When: Mid-July through mid-August
Contact for Further Information: Festival of the Sound, P.O. Box 750, Parry Sound, ON P2A 2Z1, (705) 746-2410

FESTIVAL OTTAWA
Ottawa, ON
Staff: Costa Pilavachi, Director of the Music Department, National Arts Centre
Type: Opera (5 performances each of up to 3 productions); chamber music

(15 concerts and recitals); and opera films and special exhibitions
When: July
Contact for Further Information: Gary Hanson, Music Publicity Department, P.O. Box 1534, Station "B", Ottawa, ON K1P 5W1, (613) 996-5051 x326

GUELPH SPRING FESTIVAL
Guelph, ON
Staff: Marilyn Crooks, Administrator; Nicholas Goldschmidt, Artistic Director
Type: Opera, jazz, soloists, classical; orchestra, piano, and chamber music; approximately 20 performances
When: Last week in April and first two weeks in May
Contact for Further Information: Edwina Carson, Director of Publicity, Guelph Spring Festival, P.O. Box 1718, Guelph, ON N1H 6S7, (519) 821-7570

THE SHAW FESTIVAL THEATRE FOUNDATION, CANADA
Niagara-on-the-Lake, ON
Staff: Paul Reynolds, Producer; Christopher Newton, Artistic Director
Type: Devoted to performing plays by George Bernard Shaw and his contemporaries; Monday music series offering classical and jazz music concerts throughout July
When: May to October
Staff: Department of Communications, P.O. Box 774, Niagara-on-the-Lake, ON L0S 1J0, (416) 468-2153

QUEBEC

ORFORD INTERNATIONAL MUSIC FESTIVAL
Magog, PQ
Staff: Maurice Collette, Director; Pierre Rolland, Artistic Director
Type: Classical music, jazz, opera, chamber music; crafts exhibits, conferences, workshops, and masterclasses; 60 events over an eight-week period
When: Mid-June through August
Contact for Further Information: C.P. 280, Magog, PQ J1X 3W8, (819) 843-3981. Winter phone: (514) 866-1518

FOREIGN

AUSTRIA

BREGENZ FESTIVAL
Kornmarkstrasse, Austria
Type: Opera, operetta, symphony and chamber concerts and recitals, as well as ballet and theater productions
When: Mid-July through mid-August annually
Contact for Further Information: Mrs. Rosemarie Fliegel, 545 Fifth Avenue, Suite 207, New York, NY 10017 (212) 697-0656 or Bregenzer Festspiele, Kornmarkstrasse 6, A 6901 Bregenz, Austria, (05574) 22-811

BURGENLANDISCHE FESTSPIELE
Morbisch am See, Austria
Type: Classical operettas and theater
When: May to August annually
Contact for Further Information: Professor Fred Liewehr, Director, Burgenlandische Festspiele, A-7072 Morbisch am See, Austria

CARINTHIAN SUMMER FESTIVAL
Ossiach and Villach, Austria
Type: Orchestra and chamber concerts, lieder and instrumental recitals, operas, masses, opera workshops, seminars, master classes and conducting courses
When: Late June to the end of August annually
Contact for Further Information: Mrs. Rosemarie Fliegel, 545 Fifth Avenue, Suite 207, New York, NY 10017, (212) 697-0656 or Carinthischer Summer, A 9570 Ossaich, Austria, (04243) 510

EASTER FESTIVAL
Salzburg, Austria
Type: Opera, large orchestral works and choral compositions
When: Palm Sunday to Easter Monday annually
Contact for Further Information: Osterfestspiele Salzburg, Festspielhaus, A 5010 Salzburg, Austria, (6222) 42-5-41

HOHENEMS SCHUBERT FESTIVAL
Hohenems, Austria
Type: Lieder recitals, choir concerts, piano recitals, chamber concerts and orchestral performances
When: Mid to late June annually
Contact for Further Information: Schubertiade Hohenems, Schlossplatz 8, P.O. Box 61, A-6845 Hohenems, Austria, (05576) 20-91

INTERNATIONAL BRUCKNER FESTIVAL
Linz, Austria
Type: Symphonies, masses, sacred choral and orchestral works, piano and organ compositions and choruses
When: Four weeks in September annually
Contact for Further Information: Internationales Brucknerfest Lina, Brucknerhaus, Untere Donaulande 7, A-4020 Linz, Austria, (0732) 75-2-25

MOZART WEEK
Salzburg, Austria
Type: Chamber music, opera in concert form, masses and symphonic concerts
When: Last week in January annually
Contact for Further Information: Internationale Stiftung Mozarteum, Postfach 34, A-5024 Salzburg, Austria, (6222) 73-1-54

OPERETTA WEEKS
Bad Ischl, Austria
Type: Operettas
When: Early July to the first week of September annually
Contact for Further Information: Operettengemeinde Bad Ischl, Herrengasse, 32, A-4820 Bad Ischl, Austria, (06132) 38-39

OSTERFESTSPIELE
(See Easter Festival)

SCHUBERTAIDE HOHENEMS
(See Hohenems Schubert Festival)

SALZBURG FESTIVAL
Salzburg, Austria
Type: Chamber and orchestral concerts, lieder and instrument recitals, opera and theater performances
When: Late July to late August annually
Contact for Further Information: Salzburger Festspiele, Kartenburo, Postfach 140, A-5010 Salzburg, Austria, (06222) 42-5-41

STYRIAN AUTUMN
Graz, Austria
Type: Contemporary compositions, world premieres and workshops and symposiums on 20th century music
When: September to November
Contact for Further Information: Steirischer Herbst, Zentralkartenburo, Herrengasse 7, A-8010 Graz, Austria, (0316) 80-2-55

VIENNA WEEKS FESTIVAL
Vienna, Austria
Type: Lieder and instrument recitals, opera, operetta, chamber and symphonic concerts, jazz and symposiums
When: Mid-May to mid-June annually
Contact for Further Information: Wiener Festwochen, Vogelweidplatz 14, A-1150 Wien, Austria (222) 92-66-01

BELGIUM

FLANDERS FESTIVAL
Antwerp, Brugge, Brussels, Ghent, Kortrijk, Leuven, Limburg and Mechelen, Belgium
Type: Many modes of music from all musical periods
When: April to October annually
Contact for Further Information: Festival van Vlaanderen, BRT Omroepcentrum, Reyerslaan 52, B1040 Brussels, Belgium, (02) 737-3856

FESTIVAL OF WALLONIA
Brussels, Chimay, Hainaut, Huy, Liege, Luxembourg, Mons, Namur, Stavelot, Saint-Hubert, Belgium
Type: Recitals and orchestral, vocal and choral concerts
When: June to September annually
Contact for Further Information: Festival de Wallonie, rue Joseph Saintraint 12, 5000 Namur, Belgium, (081) 712-2700

BRAZIL

FESTIVAL VILLA-LOBOS
Rio de Janeiro, Brazil
Type: Classical music concerts, recitals, lectures and international choral contest
When: November
Contact for Further Information: Museu Villa-Lobos, rua da Imprensa 16, Rio de Janeiro 20-030, Brazil

BULGARIA

INTERNATIONAL FESTIVAL OF CHAMBER MUSIC
Plovdiv, Bulgaria
Type: Chamber music
When: Early June for 10 days annually
Contact for Further Information: International Festival of Chamber Music, Boris Dischlier St., 4000 Plovdiv, Bulgaria

CZECHOSLOVAKIA

BRATISLAVA MUSIC FESTIVAL
Bratislava, Czechoslovakia
Type: Classical symphonies, chamber music, opera and ballet
When: October
Contact for Further Information: Slovkoncert, Czechoslovak Artistic Agency, Palackeho ul 4/11, 898 20 Bratislava, Czechoslovakia, 331-064, 337-252

BRNO MUSICAL FESTIVAL
Brno, Czechoslovakia
Type: Various types of music
When: Late September to early October annually
Contact for Further Information: Brno Musical Festival, Radnicka 10, 658 78 Brno, Czechoslovakia, 271-51, 259-08

PRAGUE SPRING FESTIVAL
Prague, Czechoslovakia
Type: Symphonic, chamber and choral concerts, recitals, operas and ballet
When: Mid-May to early June
Contact for Further Information: Festival Internationale de Musique, Prague Spring Festival, House of Artists, 11000 Prague 1, Czechoslovakia, 635-82, or CEDOK, Na Prikope 18, Prague 1, Czechoslovakia, 22-42-51

DENMARK

ARHUS FESTIVAL WEEK
Arhus, Denmark
Type: Symphonies, operas and recitals, as well as ballet
When: September annually
Contact for Further Information: Arhus Festival Week, Tourist Office, Town Hall, 8000 Arhus C, Denmark, (06) 13-200

COPENHAGEN SUMMER FESTIVAL
Copenhagen, Denmark
Type: Chamber music
When: July to mid-August
Contact for Further Information: Copenhagen Summer Festival, Vollerslev Praestegaard, 4100 Ringsted, Denmark, or Dansmarks Turistrad Banegardspladsen 2, DK 1570 Copenhagen V, Denmark, (01) 11-14-15

RONNE MUSIC FESTIVAL
Ronne, Bornholm, Denmark
Type: Organ concerts and chamber music
When: Wednesdays and Fridays in July and August
Contact for Further Information: Ronne Musikfestival, Kirkeplads, DK 3700, Ronne, Bornholm, Denmark, (03) 95-3695

TIVOLI CONCERTS
Copenhagen, Denmark
Type: Symphonic concerts, operettas, recitals, jazz and folk music and ballet
When: May 1 to mid-September
Contact for Further Information: Tivoli Concerts Box Office, Vesterbrogade 3, DK 1570 Copenhagen, Denmark, (01) 15-10-12

ENGLAND

ALDEBURGH FESTIVAL OF MUSIC AND THE ARTS
Aldeburgh, England
Type: Chamber and symphonic concerts, operas, recitals, lectures, art exhibitions and school for advanced musical studies
When: Early June for two weeks annually
Contact for Further Information: Aldeburgh Festival, 5 Dryden Street, London WC2E 9NW (01) 836-6914, 240-2430

BATH FESTIVAL
Bath, England
Type: Concerts, recitals and operas
When: Late May to early June annually
Contact for Further Information: Bath Festival Society, Ltd., Linley House, 1 Pierrepont Place, Bath, Avon BA1 1JY, England, (0225) 63362

BRIGHTON FESTIVAL
Brighton, England
Type: Symphonic and chamber concerts, recitals, opera, ballet, theater and dance
When: First week in May for two weeks annually
Contact for Further Information: Brighton Festival Society, Ltd., Marleborough House, Old Steine, Brighton, Sussex BN1 1EQ, England (0273) 29801

BRISTOL FESTIVAL
Bristol, England
Type: Folk and jazz concerts
When: June for three days annually
Contact for Further Information: Bristol Festival, The Chequers, Hanham Mills, Bristol, England

BUXTON FESTIVAL
Buxton, England
Type: Opera
When: Late July to early August
Contact for Further Information: Buxton Festival, 1 Crescent View, Hall Bank, Buxton, Derbyshire, England, (273) 29801

CAMDEN FESTIVAL
London, England
Type: Symphonic, choral and chamber concerts, recitals, jazz, dance and lectures
When: Mid-March for two weeks
Contact for Further Information: Libraries and Arts Department, St. Pancras Library, 100 Euston Rd., London NW1 2AJ, England, (01) 278-444, ext. 2482

CHELTENHAM INTERNATIONAL FESTIVAL OF MUSIC
Cheltenham, England
Type: Symphonic, chamber and choral concerts, opera, master classes and seminars
Contact for Further Information: Cheltenham Festival Office, Town Hall, Imperial Square, Cheltenham, Gloucestershire GL50 1QA, England, (0242) 21621

COVENT GARDEN PROMS
London, England
Type: Opera and ballet
When: April for six days annually
Contact for Further Information: Covent Garden Proms, Royal Opera House, Covent Garden, London, England, (01) 240-1066

ENGLISH BACH FESTIVAL
Oxford and London, England
Type: Classical music in several modes
When: May annually
Contact for Further Information: English Bach Festival Trust, 15 S. Eaton Place, London SW1W 9ER, England, (01) 730-5925

FAKENHAM FESTIVAL OF MUSIC AND THE ARTS
Fakenham, England
Type: Orchestral concerts, choral works, celebrity concerts, theater, ballet and exhibitions
When: May in odd-numbered years
Contact for Further Information: Fakenham Festival Office, Royal Oak House, Oak St., Fakenham, Norfolk, England

GLYNDEBOURNE FESTIVAL OPERA
Glyndebourne, England
Type: Opera
When: Late May to early August annually

Contact for Further Information: Glyndebourne Festival Opera Box Office, Lewis, East Sussex BN8 5UU, England, (0273) 812-411

HARROGATE INTERNATIONAL FESTIVAL
Harrogate, England
Type: Clasical music and jazz, dance, theater, films, literary performances and lectures
When: First two weeks in August
Contact for Further Information: Harrogate International Festival, Festival Office, Royal Baths, Harrogate, North Yorkshire HG1 2RR, England, (0423) 62303

LEEDS MUSIC FESTIVAL
Leeds, England
Type: Choral, orchestral and chamber music concerts
When: May for two weeks
Contact for Further Information: Leeds Musical Festival, 40 Park Lane, Leeds, Yorkshire LS1 1LN England, (0523) 452153

MALVERN FESTIVAL
Malvern, England
Type: Different modes of music and drama
When: Last two weeks in May
Contact for Further Information: Malvern Festival Theatre, Grange Rd., Malvern, Worcs. WR14 3HB, England, (06845) 3377

NORFOLK AND NORWICH TRIENNIAL FESTIVAL OF MUSIC AND THE ARTS
Norfolk and Norwich, England
Type: Classical, jazz and folk music performances and theater
When: Mid-October for two weeks
Contact for Further Information: Norfolk and Norwich Triennial Festival of Music and the Arts, The Grove, 61 Bracondale, Norwich, Norfolk NR 1 2AT, England

ROYAL OPERA HOUSE PROMS
(See Covent Garden Proms)

THREE CHOIRS FESTIVAL
Gloucester, Hereford and Worcester, England
Type: Choral works, recitals, chamber music, children's concerts and lectures
Type: Mid-August
Contact for Further Information: Gloucester Festival Office, Community House, College Green, Gloucester GL1 2LX, England, or Hereford Festival Office, 25 Castle St, Hereford HR1 2NE, England, or Worcester Festival Office, 5 Deansway, Worcester WR1 2JG, England

TILFORD BACH FESTIVAL
Surrey, England
Type: Choral, orchestral, ensemble and solo performance
When: Mid-May for four days
Contact for Further Information: Tilford Bach Society, Ling Lea, Frensham, Farnham, Surrey GU10 3AZ, England

WINDSOR FESTIVAL
Windsor, England
Type: Recitals and small chamber group performances, as well as orchestral and choral concerts
When: Mid-September for two weeks
Contact for Further Information: Windsor Festival Society, Dial House, Englefield Green, Surrey, England

FINLAND

HELSINKI FESTIVAL
Helsinki, Finland
Type: Opera, symphonic, jazz and chamber works
When: Mid-August to early September
Contact for Further Information: Helsinki Festival, Unioninkatu 28, SF 00100 Helsinki 10, Finland, (90) 659-688

JYVASKYLA ARTS FESTIVAL
Jyvaskyla, Finland
Type: Classical orchestral concerts
When: June to July
Contact for Further Information: Jyvaskyla Arts Festival, Kauppakatu 41 B 11, SF-40100, Jyvaskyla, Finland

KUHMO CHAMBER MUSIC FESTIVAL
Kuhmo, Finland
Type: Chamber music
When: August for ten days
Contact for Further Information: Kuhmo Chamber Music Festival, c/o Finland Festivals, Simonkatu 12 B 15, SF-00100 Helsinki 10, Finland, (90) 642-272

KUOPIO DANCE AND MUSIC FESTIVAL
Kuopio, Finland
Type: Brass band and organ concerts, as well as dance
When: Early June for one week
Contact for Further Information: Kuopio Dance and Music Festival, Kuntokuja 4H, SF-70200 Kuopio 20, Finland

LAHTI ORGAN FESTIVAL
Lahti, Finland
Type: Organ concerts, seminars, courses and exhibitions
When: August
Contact for Further Information: Lahti Organ Festival, Kirkkokatu 5, SF-151100 Lahti 11, Finland

PORI INTERNATIONAL JAZZ FESTIVAL
Pori, Finland
Type: Jazz concerts and jam sessions
When: Mid-July for four days
Contact for Further Information: Pori International Jazz Festival, Luvianpuistokatu 2 D, SF-28100 Pori 10, Finland

SAVONLINNA OPERA FESTIVAL
Savonlinna, Finland
Type: Opera
When: July
Contact for Further Information: Savonlinna Opera Festival, Olavinkatu 35, SF-57130 Savonlinna 13, Finland

TURKU MUSIC FESTIVAL
Turku, Finland
Type: Classical, rock, folk, jazz and opera performances
When: August for six days
Contact for Further Information: Turku Music Festival, Sibeliuksenkatu 2 B, SF-20110 Turku 11, Finland

FRANCE

AIX-EN-PROVENCE INTERNATIONAL FESTIVAL OF OPERA AND MUSIC
Aix-en-Provence, France
Type: Opera, chamber and symphonic performances, films, art exhibits and lectures
When: Mid-July to early August
Contact for Further Information: Aix-en-Provence International Festival, Palais de l'Ancien Archeveche, F-13100 Aix-en-Provence, France, (42) 23-11-20

AUTUMN FESTIVAL
Paris, France
Type: Contemporary music and art
When: Mid-September through December
Contact for Further Information: Festival d'Automne, 156 rue de Rivoli, F-75001 Paris, France, (01) 296-12-27

AVIGNON FESTIVAL
Avignon, France
Type: Musical theater, sacred music concerts and organ solos
When: Mid-July to early August
Contact for Further Information: Festival d'Avignon—Jean Vilar, Bureau du Festival, 21 bis Place du Palais, F-84000 Avignon, France (90) 82-67-08

BACH FESTIVAL OF MAZAMET
Mazamet, France
Type: Organ concerts, chamber music recitals and vocal solos
When: Early September for six days
Contact for Further Information: Festival J.S. Bach, c/o Maison du Tourisme, Square Gaston-Tournier, F-81200 Mazamet, France, (63) 61-27-07

HECTOR BERLIOZ INTERNATIONAL FESTIVAL
Lyon and La Cote-Saint-Andre, France
Type: Orchestral performances and opera
When: Mid-September for one week
Contact for Further Information: Festival Perlioz, Auditorium Maurice Ravel, 149 Rue Garibaldi, F-69003 Lyon, France, (78) 71-05-73

BESANCON INTERNATIONAL FESTIVAL
Besancon, France
Type: Symphonic concerts and recitals
When: September for two weeks
Contact for Further Information: Festival International de Besancon, 2 D. rue Isenbart, F-25000 Besancon, France (81) 80-73-26

CHOREGIES D'ORANGE
(See Orange Festival)

FESTIVAL D'AUTOMNE
(See Autumn Festival)

FESTIVAL ESTIVAL OF PARIS
Paris, France
Type: Orchestral and chamber music, workshops, public courses and exhibitions
When: Mid-July to late September
Contact for Further Information: Festival Estival de Paris, 5 Place des Ternes, F-75017 Paris, France

FESTIVAL D'AVIGNON
(See Avignon Festival)

FESTIVAL INTERNATIONAL D'ART LYRIQUE ET DE MUSIQUE
(See Aix-en-Provence International Festival of Opera and Music)

FESTIVAL INTERNATIONAL DE BESANCON
(See Besancon International Festival)

FESTIVAL INTERNATIONAL DE LYON
(See Lyon International Festival)

FESTIVAL INTERNATIONAL DE MUSIQUE DE MENTON
(See Menton Music Festival)

FESTIVAL INTERNATIONAL DE MUSIQUE DE STRASBOURG
(See Strasbourg International Music Festival)

FESTIVAL J.S. BACH DE MAZAMET
(See Bach Festival of Mazamet)

FETES MUSICALES EN TOURAINE
(See Touraine Festival)

GRAND PARADE OF JAZZ
Nice, France
Type: Jazz
When: Early June
Contact for Further Information: Grande Parade du Jazz, Hotel Mercure, 2 rue Helevy, F-06000 Nice, France (93) 85-09-35

INTERNATIONALES FESTIVAL HECTOR BERLIOZ
(See Hector Berlioz International Festival)

INTERNATIONAL MAY MUSICAL
Bordeaux, France
Type: Symphonic and chamber concerts, opera, ballet, theater, film and art exhibits
When: First week in May for two weeks
Contact for Further Information: Mai Musical International, 252 Faubourg St. Honore, F-75008 Paris, France, (01) 563-97-28

LYON INTERNATIONAL FESTIVAL
Lyon, France
Type: Symphonic, choral and chamber concerts, recitals, opera, international competitions for organ, jazz and piano
When: Mid-June to mid-July
Contact for Further Information: Festival de Lyon, Hotel de Ville, Place de la Comedie, F-69268 Lyon, France (78) 27-71-31

MAI MUSICAL INTERNATIONAL
(See International May Musical)

MENTON MUSIC FESTIVAL
Menton, France
Type: Chamber music and recitals
When: August
Contact for Further Information: Festival International de Musique de Menton, palais de l'Europe, Avenue Boyer, F-06500 Menton, France, (93) 35-82-22

METZ INTERNATIONAL CONTEMPORARY MUSIC FESTIVAL
Metz, France
Type: New works by young composers
When: Mid-November
Contact for Further Information: Center Europeen pour la Recherche Musicale, c/o Rencontres Internationales de Musique Contemporaine, Hotel de Ville, F-57038 Metz, France, (87) 75-14-88

ORANGE FESTIVAL
Orange, France
Type: Opera and choral works
When: Late July to early August
Contact for Further Information: Choregies d'Orange, c/o Maison du Theatre, Place des Freres Mounet, F-84100 Orange, France, (90) 34-15-52

RENCONTRES INTERNATIONALES DE MUSIQUE CONTEMPORAIRE
(See Metz International Contemporary Music Festival)

STRASBOURG INTERNATIONAL MUSIC FESTIVAL
Strasbourg, France
Type: Classical and contemporary music
When: June for two weeks
Contact for Further Information: Festival International de Musique de Strasbourg, 24 rue de la Mesange, F-67081 Strasbourg, France, (88) 32-43-10

TOURAINE FESTIVAL
Tours, France
Type: Symphonies, choral works and chamber music
When: Late June or early July
Contact for Further Information: Fetes Musicales en Touraine, Hotel de Ville, F-37032 Tours, France, (47) 61-81-24

GERMAN DEMOCRATIC REPUBLIC

ARBELTERFESTSPIELE
Berlin, German Democratic Republic
Type: Concerts and theater
When: June
Contact for Further Information: Arbelterfestspiele, Fritz Heckert Strasse 70, DDR-102 Berlin, German Democratic Republic

BERLINER FESSTAGE
Berlin, German Democratic Republic
Type: Classical concerts and opera, theater and ballet
When: October
Contact for Further Information: Berliner Fesstage, Behrenstrasses 42-45, DDR-102 Berlin, German Democratic Republic

HANDELFESTSPIELE HALLE
Halle, German Democratic Republic
Type: Concerts, theater and choral works
When: June
Contact for Further Information: Handelfestspiele Halle, Grosse Nikolaistrasse 6, DDR-402 Halle, German Democratic Republic

GERMAN FEDERAL REPUBLIC

BACH WEEK
Ansbach, German Federal Republic
Type: Bach's vocal compositions, motets, secular cantatas, chamber, organ and orchestral performances
When: Late July in odd-numbered years
Contact for Further Information: Bachwoche Ansbach, Postfach 41, D-8800 Ansbach, German Federal Republic

BAYREUTHER FESTSPIELE
(See Richard Wagner Festival)

BERLIN FESTIVAL
Berlin, German Federal Republic
Type: Symphonic, chamber and choral concerts, recitals, opera, ballet, theater, film and art exhibitions
When: September for four weeks
Contact for Further Information: Berliner Festspiele, Budapester Strasses 48/50, D-1000 Berlin 30, German Federal Republic, (030) 26-34-1

DONAUESCHINGEN FESTIVAL OF CONTEMPORARY MUSIC
Donaueschingen, German Federal Republic
Type: Contemporary music
When: Mid-October
Contact for Further Information:

Donaueschingen Festival of Contemporary Music, Stadtisches Kultur-und Verkehrsamt, D-7710 Donaueschingen, German Federal Republic

INTERNATIONAL MAY FESTIVAL
Wiesbaden, German Federal Republic
Type: Opera, symphonic concerts, ballet, dance, drama and experimental theater
When: Month of May
Contact for Further Information: Internationale Maifestspiele, c/o Hessisches Staatstheater, D-6200 Wiesbaden 1, German Federal Republic

INTERNATIONAL MUSIC FESTIVAL
Constance, German Federal Republic
Type: Orchestral and chamber music and recitals
When: Mid-June to mid-July
Contact for Further Information: International Music Festival, Stadtisches Verkehrsamt, Bahnhofsplatz 6, D-7750 Constance, German Federal Republic

INTERNATIONAL ORGAN WEEK
Nuremberg, German Federal Republic
Type: Organ music
When: Mid-June for two weeks
Contact for Further Information: International Organ Week, Stadtisches Verkehrsamt, D-8500 Nuremberg, German Federal Republic

MOZART FESTIVAL
Wurzburg, German Federal Republic
Type: Symphonies, concertos, sonatas, motets, sacred choral music and one opera
When: June for two weeks
Contact for Further Information: Mozartfest, Haus zum Falken, D-8700 Wurzburg, German Federal Republic

MUNICH OPERA FESTIVAL
Munich, German Federal Republic
Type: Opera
When: First week in July for four weeks
Contact for Further Information: Munich Opera Festival, Brieffach, D-8000 Munich 1, German Federal Republic

SCHWETZINGEN FESTIVAL
Schwetzingen, German Federal Republic
Type: Opera, oratorio, symphonic, chamber and solo performances
When: May
Contact for Further Information: Schetzingen Festspiele, Scholossplatz, D-6830 Schwetzingen, German Federal Republic

RICHARD WAGNER FESTIVAL
Bayreuth, German Federal Republic
Type: Opera
When: Late July into August for five weeks
Contact for Further Information: Bayreuther Festspiele, P.O. Box 2320, D-8580 Bayreuth 2, German Federal Republic

GREECE

ATHENS FESTIVAL
Athens, Greece
Type: Symphonic concerts, operas, recitals, drama and ballet
When: First week in July to last week in September
Contact for Further Information: Athens Festival, 1 Voukourestiou St., Athens, Greece

THESSALONIKI FESTIVAL
Athens, Greece
Type: Classical music, opera, dance and drama
When: October
Contact for Further Information: Thessaloniki Festival, c/o National Tourist Organization, 2 Amerikis St., Athens, Greece

HUNGARY

BUDAPEST FESTIVAL
Budapest, Hungary
Type: Symphonic, chamber and organ concerts and recitals
When: Mid-September to mid-October
Contact for Further Information: Budapest Festival, c/o Office of International Music Competitions and Festivals, P.O. Box 80, H-1366 Budapest 5, Hungary

ICELAND

REYKJAVIK ARTS FESTIVAL
Reykjavik, Iceland
Type: Different modes of music
When: June, biennially
Contact for Further Information: Reykjavik Arts Festival, P.O. Box 88, 101 Reykjavik, Iceland

IRELAND

DUBLIN FESTIVAL OF 20TH CENTURY MUSIC
Dublin, Ireland
Type: Solo, chamber and orchestral music
When: Early January for one week, biennially
Contact for Further Information: Music Association of Ireland, 11 Suffolk St., Dublin 2, Ireland, (01) 770976

WATERFORD INTERNATIONAL FESTIVAL OF LIGHT OPERA
Waterford, Ireland
Type: Light opera
When: Mid-September for two weeks
Contact for Further Information: International Festival of Light Opera, 7 Berker St., Waterford, Ireland, (051) 75437

WEXFORD FESTIVAL OPERA
Wexford, Ireland
Type: Opera
When: Late October for two weeks
Contact for Further Information: Wexford Festival Opera, Theatre Royal, High St., Wexford, Ireland, (053) 22240

ISRAEL

EIN-GEV MUSIC FESTIVAL
Kibbutz Ein-Gev, Israel
Type: Classical music, dance and opera
When: Passover
Contact for Further Information: Yaacov Steinberger, Administrative Director, Ein-Gev Music Festival, Kibbutz Ein-Gev, Israel, (067) 50166

ISRAEL FESTIVAL
Caesarea, Jerusalem and Tel Aviv, Israel
Type: Multiple modes of music
When: August and September
Contact for Further Information: Israel Festival, P.O. Box 29874, Shalom Tower, Tel Aviv, Israel (03) 58812

ZIMRYA INTERNATIONAL CHOIR FESTIVAL
Tel Aviv, Israel
Type: Choral music
When: July, biennially
Contact for Further Information: Zimrya International Choir Festival, P.O. Box 29334, 4 Aharonovitch St., Tel Aviv, Israel, (03) 280233

ITALY

ENTE AUTONOMO SPETTACOLL LIRICI ARENA DI VERONA
(See Verona Opera Festival)

ESTATE MACERATESE
Macerata, Italy
Type: Opera and dance
When: July
Contact for Further Information: Estate Maceratese, Arena Sferisterio, I-62100 Macerata, Italy

FESTIVAL OF TWO WORLDS
Spoleto, Italy
Type: Opera, ballet, symphonic, chamber and choral music, theater and art exhibitions
When: Late June to mid-July for three weeks
Contact for Further Information: Festival of Two Worlds, 119 West 57th St., New York, NY 10019, (212) 582-2746

FLORENCE MUSICAL MAY
Florence, Italy
Type: Symphonic and chamber music, opera, ballet and dance
When: May and June for eight weeks
Contact for Further Information: Maggio Musicale Florentino, Teatro Communale, Via Solferino 15, I-50123 Florence, Italy

MAGGIO MUSICAL FLORENTINO
(See Florence Musical May)

ROSSINI OPERA FESTIVAL
Pesaro, Italy
Type: Opera
When: August and September
Contact for Further Information:
Rossini Opera Festival, Via Rossini, I-61100 Pesaro, Italy

SAGRA MUSICAL UMBRIA
(See Umbria Sacred Music Festival)

SPOLETO FESTIVAL OF TWO WORLDS
(See Festival of Two Worlds)

STRESA MUSICAL WEEKS
Stresa, Italy
Type: Symphonic and chamber ensembles, choruses and instrumental and vocal soloists
When: Late August to late September for one month
Contact for Further Information:
Settiman Musicali de Stresa, Via R. Borghi 4, I-28049 Stresa, Italy

UMBRIA SACRED MUSIC FESTIVAL
Perugia, Italy
Type: Oratorios, cantatas, choral masses, psalms and opera
When: Mid-September for two weeks
Contact for Further Information:
Associazione Sagra Musicale Umbra, Piazza Italia 12, Perugia, Italy

VERONA OPERA FESTIVAL
Verona, Italy
Type: Opera
When: Second week in July to the first week in September
Contact for Further Information: Ente Autonomo Spettacoll Lirici Arena di Verona, Piazza Bra 28, I-37100 Verona, Italy

MEXICO

INTERNATIONAL MUSIC FESTIVAL
Cuautia, Morelos, Mexico
Type: Symphonic, band and choral music
When: Mid-April
Contact for Further Information:
International Music Festival, c/o Office de Turismo, Palacio Municipal, Cuautia, Morelos, Mexico

NETHERLANDS

HOLLAND FESTIVAL
Amsterdam, The Hague, Rotterdam and other cities, Netherlands
Type: Opera, symphonic, choral, chamber and solo concerts, ballet, dance, jazz and folk music, theater and visual arts
When: June for three weeks
Contact for Further Information:
Holland Festival, Willemsparkweg 52, 1071 HJ Amsterdam, Netherlands

INTERNATIONAL GAUDEAMUS MUSIC WEEK
Throughout the Netherlands
Type: Contemporary chamber, solo and orchestral performances
When: Early to mid-September
Contact for Further Information:
International Gaudeamus Music Week, P.O. Box 30, 3720 AA Bilthoven, Netherlands, (030) 787-033

NEW ZEALAND

AUKLAND FESTIVAL
Aukland, New Zealand
Type: Classical concerts
When: March in even-numbered years
Contact for Further Information:
Aukland Festival Society, Inc., P.O. Box 1411, Aukland, New Zealand

CHRISTCHURCH ARTS FESTIVAL
Christchurch, New Zealand
Type: Orchestral music, recitals, opera, ballet and modern dance, choral music and popular performance
When: March of even-numbered years
Contact for Further Information:
Christchurch Arts Festival, P.O. Box 13-203, Christchurch, New Zealand

NORWAY

BERGEN INTERNATIONAL FESTIVAL
Bergen, Norway
Type: Symphonic, chamber and choral concerts, recitals, jazz and folk music, dance, drama, art exhibitions and seminars
When: Last week in May for two-and-a-half weeks
Contact for Further Information:
Bergen International Festival, P.O. Box 183, Sverresgate 11, N-5001 Bergen, Norway

MOLDE INTERNATIONAL JAZZ FESTIVAL
Molde, Norway
Type: Jazz
When: Late July to early August for one week
Contact for Further Information: Molde International Jazz Festival, Parkveien 42, N-6400 Molde, Norway

POLAND

DAYS OF ORGAN MUSIC
Kracow, Poland
Type: Organ music, choirs, chamber ensembles and symphony orchestra concerts
When: Late January for one week
Contact for Further Information: Dni Muzyki Organowej, Philharmonia, Zwierzyniecka 1, 31-1-03 Krakow, Poland

GRAZYNA BACEWICZ
(See Polish Violin Festival)

INTERNATIONAL FESTIVAL OF CONTEMPORARY MUSIC
Warsaw, Poland
Type: Contemporary music
When: Mid-September for a week and a half
Contact for Further Information:
Warsawka Jesien, Rynek Starego Miasta 27, 00-272 Warsaw, Poland

INTERNATIONAL ORATORIO AND CANTATA FESTIVAL
Wroclaw, Poland
Type: Oratorios and cantatas
When: First week in September
Contact for Further Information:
Wratislavia Cantans, Panstwowa Filharmonia, ul. Swierczewskiego 19, 50-044 Wroclaw, Poland, (871) 44-24-59

POLISH VIOLIN FESTIVAL
Czestochowa, Poland
Type: Violin music
When: March
Contact for Further Information:
Grazyna Bacewicz, c/o State Philharmonic Orchestra, Kakielow 16, 42-200 Czestochowa, Poland

WARSAW AUTUMN FESTIVAL
(See International Festival of Contemporary Music)

WRATISLAVIA CANTANS
(See International Oratorio and Cantata Festival)

PORTUGAL

ALGARVE MUSIC FESTIVAL
Faro, Portugal
Type: Various modes of music
When: July, August and September
Contact for Further Information:
Algarve Music Festival, c/o Comissao Regional de Turismo, Rua da Misericordia 8, Faro, Portugal

SCOTLAND

EDINBURGH INTERNATIONAL FESTIVAL
Edinburgh, Scotland
Type: Chamber, symphonic and choral concerts, recitals, opera, ballet, dance, theater and other activities
When: Third week in August for three weeks
Contact for Further Information:
Edinburgh International Festival, 21 Market St., Edinburgh EH1 1BW Scotland

INTERNATIONAL FESTIVAL OF YOUTH ORCHESTRAS AND THE PERFORMING ARTS
Aberdeen, Scotland
Type: Youth orchestral, band and choral concerts, as well as dance
When: August for two weeks
Contact for Further Information:
International Festival of Youth

Orchestras and the Performing Arts, 24 Cadogan Square, London SW1X OJP, England

SPAIN

BARCELONA INTERNATIONAL FESTIVAL OF MUSIC
Barcelona, Spain
Type: Symphonic, chamber and choral concerts, solos, films, art exhibitions and lectures
When: Month of October
Contact for Further Information: International Festival of Music, c/o Antonio Sabat, Amadeu Vives 3, Barcelona 3, Spain

GRANADA INTERNATIONAL MUSIC AND DANCE FESTIVAL
Granada, Spain
Type: Symphonic and chamber concerts, songs, recitals, ballet and folk dance
When: Mid-June for three weeks
Contact for Further Information: Festival Internacional de Musica y Danza de Granada, c/o Comisaria del Festival, Carrera del Darro 29, Apdo. de Correos 417, Granada, Spain

SANTANDER INTERNATIONAL FESTIVAL OF MUSIC AND DANCE
Santander, Spain
Type: Symphonic, chamber and choral performances, recitals, dance and jazz
When: First week in August for three weeks
Contact for Further Information: Festival Internacional de Santander, Ayuntamiento de Santander, Santander, Spain

SWITZERLAND

FESTIVAL OF MUSIC YEHUDI MENUHIN
Gstaad, Switzerland
Type: Classical music
When: August
Contact for Further Information: Festival of Music Yehudi Menuhin, c/o Verkehrsverein Gstaad, CH-3780 Gstaad, Switzerland

INTERNATIONAL JAZZ FESTIVAL OF BERN
Bern, Switzerland
Type: Jazz
When: April and May
Contact for Further Information: International Jazz Festival of Bern, c/o Verkehrsverein der Stadt Bern, Postfach 3700, Ch-3001 Bern, Switzerland

INTERNATIONAL JUNE FESTIVAL
Zurich, Switzerland
Type: Classical concerts and opera
When: Last week in May to the end of June
Contact for Further Information: International June Festival, c/o Verkehrsverein Zurich, Postfach 8023, CH-8023 Zurich, Switzerland

LAUSANNE INTERNATIONAL FESTIVAL
Lausanne, Switzerland
Type: Chamber and symphonic concerts, ballet, opera and jazz
When: May and June
Contact for Further Information: Festival International de Lausanne, Theatre de Beaulieu, CH-1000 Lausanne, Switzerland

LUCERNE INTERNATIONAL FESTIVAL OF MUSIC
Lucerne, Switzerland
Type: Symphonic and chamber music, recitals, opera and master courses
When: Mid-August to mid-September
Contact for Further Information: International Festival of Music, Postfach 424, Ch-6002 Lucerne, Switzerland

MENUHIN FESTIVAL
(See Festival of Music Yehudi Menuhin)

MONTREUX INTERNATIONAL JAZZ FESTIVAL
Montreux, Switzerland
Type: Jazz
When: First week in July for two weeks
Contact for Further Information: Montreux International Jazz Festival, c/o Office du Tourisme, 42 Grand St., Ch-1820 Montreux, Switzerland

MONTREUX-VEVEY MUSIC FESTIVAL
Montreux and Vevey, Switzerland
Type: Symphonic and chamber concerts, vocal and instrumental recitals
When: Late August for six weeks
Contact for Further Information: Montreux-Vevey Music Festival, 27 bis Av. des Alpes, CH-1820 Montreux, Switzerland

YEHUDI MENUHIN
(See Festival of Music Yehudi Menuhin)

ZURICH INTERNATIONAL JUNE FESTIVAL
(See International June Festival)

TURKEY

ISTANBUL INTERNATIONAL FESTIVAL
Istanbul, Turkey
Type: Various modes of music
When: Mid-June to mid-July
Contact for Further Information: Istanbul International Festival, c/o Foundation for Culture and the Arts, Inonu Caddesi 92-94, Mithatpasa, Apt. D3, Taksim-Istanbul, Turkey

U.S.S.R.

MOSCOW INTERNATIONAL MUSIC FESTIVAL
Moscow, U.S.S.R.
Type: Modern symphony, chamber and choral performances
When: May, biennially
Contact for Further Information: Moscow International Music Festival, c/o Union of Composers of the U.S.S.R., ul. Nezhdanovoi 8, Moscow, U.S.S.R.

WALES

LLANGOLLEN INTERNATIONAL MUSICAL EISTEDDFOD
Llangollen, Wales
Type: Choral works
When: First week in July
Contact for Further Information: International Eisteddfod Office, Llangolle' . Clywd, LL20 8NG, Wales

ROYAL NATIONAL EISTEDDFOD OF WALES
Mid, North and South, Wales, alternating each year
Type: Choral performances
When: First week in August
Contact for Further Information: Royal National Eisteddfod of Wales, 10 Park Grove, Caerdydd, Cardiff CF1 3BN, Wales

YUGOSLAVIA

DUBROVNIK FESTIVAL
Dubrovnik, Yugoslavia
Type: Symphonic, chamber and choral concerts, recitals, opera, folk dancing and ballet, theater, art exhibits and symposiums
When: Mid-July through mid-August for seven weeks
Contact for Further Information: Dubrovacke Letnje Igre, Od Sigurate 1, 50000 Dubrovnik, Yugoslavia

FESTIVAL OF CROATIAN CHOIRS
Zadar, Yugoslavia
Type: Choral music
When: October
Contact for Further Information: Festival Pjevackih Zborova Hrvatske, Obdor za Muzicku Kulturu, Socijalisticke Revolucije 17, 41000 Zagreb, Yugoslavia

INTERNATIONAL SLOVENE SONG FESTIVAL
Ljubljana, Yugoslavia
Type: Popular music
When: Mid-October
Contact for Further Information: Slovenska Popevka, c/o Radio-television Ljubljana, Tavcarjeva 17, 61000 Ljubljana, Yugoslavia

LJUBLJANA INTERNATIONAL SUMMER FESTIVAL

Ljubljana, Yugoslavia

Type: Symphonic, chamber, solo and choral performances, ballet, film, theater, folk songs and dance
When: Mid-June to the end of August

Contact for Further Information: Festival Ljubljana, Trg Francoske Revolucije 1-2, 61000 Ljubljana, Yugoslavia

Music Festivals Index

A

B

C

D

E

VI. PROFESSION

Newspaper Music Editors and Critics
Volunteer Lawyers for the Arts
Booking Agents
Personal Managers

Newspaper Music Editors and Critics

U.S. and Canadian newspapers are listed alphabetically by state or province and city. If more than one newspaper is published by the same firm, the titles are included within the same listing. An alphabetical cross-index appears at the end of this section.

ALABAMA

BIRMINGHAM

BIRMINGHAM NEWS
2200 N. 4th Ave.
Birmingham, AL 35202
(205) 325-2222
Music Editor: Oliver Roosevelt

BIRMINGHAM POST-HERALD
2200 N. 4th Ave.
Birmingham, AL 35202
(205) 325-2222
Music Editor: Emmett Weaver

GADSDEN

GADSDEN TIMES
PO Box 188
401 Locust St.
Gadsden, AL 35999
(205) 547-7521
Music Editor: M.D. Gorman

HUNTSVILLE

THE HUNTSVILLE TIMES
2317 Memorial Parkway
Huntsville, AL 35807
(205) 532-4000
Entertainment Editor: Judi Moon

MOBILE

MOBILE PRESS-REGISTER
MOBILE PRESS
MOBILE REGISTER
PO Box 2488
304 Government St.
Mobile, AL 36630
(205) 433-1551
Music Editor and Critic: Gordon Tatum, Jr.

ALASKA

ANCHORAGE

ANCHORAGE TIMES
820 4th Ave.
Box 40
Anchorage, AK 99501
(907) 279-5622
Entertainment Editor: Shannon Lowry

ARIZONA

FLAGSTAFF

ARIZONA DAILY SUN
PO Box 1849
Flagstaff, AZ 86002
(602) 744-4545
Music Editor: Paul Sweitzer

MESA

MESA TRIBUNE
120 W. First Ave.
Mesa, AZ 85202
(602) 898-6500
Music Editor: Stu Hackel

PHOENIX

THE ARIZONA REPUBLIC
120 E. Van Buren St.
Phoenix, AZ 85004
(602) 271-8000
Music Editor: Thomas Goldthwaite

THE PHOENIX GAZETTE
120 E. Van Buren St.
Phoenix, AZ 85004
(602) 271-8000
Entertainment Editor: Kyle Lawson

SCOTTSDALE

SCOTTSDALE DAILY PROGRESS
7302 E. Earl Dr.
Scottsdale, AZ 85252
(602) 941-2300
Entertainment Editor: Deborah Adler

TEMPE

TEMPE DAILY NEWS
607 Mill Ave.
Box 27087
Tempe, AZ 85282
(602) 967-3321
Music Editor: Joan Rosley

TUCSON

ARIZONA DAILY STAR
PO Box 26807
Tucson, AZ 85726
(602) 294-4433
Arts Editor: Sam Hundley

TUCSON CITIZEN
Box 26767
Tucson, AZ 85726
(602) 294-4433
Music Editor: Charles D. Graham

YUMA

THE YUMA DAILY SUN
2055 Arizona Ave.
Yuma, AZ 85364
(602) 783-3333
Entertainment Editor: Pat McCune

ARKANSAS

BATESVILLE

BATESVILLE GUARD
PO Box 2036
115 N. 4th St.
Batesville, AR 72501
(501) 793-2383
Music Editor: Terry Losee

LITTLE ROCK

ARKANSAS DEMOCRAT

Capitol Ave. & Scott St.
Little Rock, AR 72203
(501) 378-3400
Entertainment Editor: Eric E. Harrison

ARKANSAS GAZETTE
112 W. Third Ave.
PO Box 1821
Little Rock, AR 72203
Music Editor: Paul Johnson

PINE BLUFF
PINE BLUFF COMMERCIAL
300 Beech St.
Pine Bluff, AR 71601
(501) 534-3400
Music Editor: Joe Farmer

CALIFORNIA

BAKERSFIELD
THE BAKERSFIELD CALIFORNIAN
PO Box 440
Bakersfield, CA 93301
(805) 395-7500
Music Critic: Mark Stetz
Entertainment Editor: Mark Grossi

BANNING
BANNING RECORD-GAZETTE
218 N. Murray St.
Banning, CA 92220
(714) 849-4586
Arts Editor: Neil Harrand

BEVERLY HILLS
BEVERLY HILLS INDEPENDENT
1920 Colorado Ave.
Santa Monica, CA 90404
(213) 829-6811
Entertainment Editor: Ann Herold

BRAWLEY
THE BRAWLEY NEWS
PO Box 251
205 N. 8th St.
El Centro, CA 92244
(714) 344-1220
Entertainment Editor: Don Quinn

BURBANK
BURBANK DAILY REVIEW
PO Box 991
111 N. Isabel St.
Glendale, CA 91209
(213) 843-8700
Music Editor: Ellen Reagan

CONCORD
CONCORD TRANSCRIPT
PO Box 308
Concord, CA 94522
(415) 682-6440
Arts Editor: Brooks Kuehl

COSTA MESA
ORANGE COAST DAILY PILOT
330 W. Bay St.
PO Box 1560
Costa Mesa, CA 92626
(714) 642-4321
Music Critic: J. Johnson

DAVIS
THE DAVIS ENTERPRISE
PO Box 1078
302 G St.
Davis, CA 96516
(916) 756-0800
Arts Editor: Del McColm

EL CENTRO
IMPERIAL VALLEY PRESS
205 N. 8th St.
PO Box 251
El Centro, CA 92244
(714) 352-2211
Entertainment Editor: Don Quinn

FAIRFIELD
FAIRFIELD DAILY REPUBLIC
PO Box 47
1250 Texas St.
Fairfield, CA 94533
(707) 425-4646
Entertainment Editor: Jerry Beaulieu

FRESNO
THE FRESNO BEE
1626 E St.
Fresno, CA 93786
(209) 441-6233
Music Editor: David Hale
Music Critic: Allen B. Skei

FULLERTON
FULLERTON DAILY NEWS TRIBUNE
655 W. Valencia Dr.
Fullerton, CA 92632
(714) 871-2345
Entertainment Editor: Moira Shepard

LIVERMORE
TRI-VALLEY HERALD
PO Box 3000
Livermore, CA 94550
(415) 447-2111
Arts Editor: Judy Java

LONG BEACH
LONG BEACH PRESS-TELEGRAM
604 Pine Ave.
Long Beach, CA 90740
(213) 435-1161
Entertainment Editor: Al Rudis

LOS ANGELES
DAILY NEWS OF LOS ANGELES
14539 Sylvan St.
Van Nuys, CA 91411
(213) 873-2051
Music Critic: Richard S. Ginell
Entertainment Editor: Morgan A. Gendel

LOS ANGELES HERALD EXAMINER
1111 S. Broadway
Box 2416
Los Angeles, CA 90051
(213) 744-8000
Music Editors: Ken Tucker, Donna Perlmutter

LOS ANGELES TIMES
Times Mirror Square
Los Angeles, CA 90053
(213) 972-5000
Music Editors: Martin Bernheimer, Robert Hilburn, Leonard Feather

MODESTO
THE MODESTO BEE
PO Box 3928
1325 H St.
Modesto, CA 95352
(209) 578-2000
Music Critic: Elizabeth Leedom

MONTEREY
THE PENINSULA HERALD
Pacific & Jefferson Sts.
PO Box 271
Monterey, CA 93940
(408) 372-3311
Music Editor: Charles Davis

OAKLAND
EASTBAY TODAY
OAKLAND TRIBUNE
409 13th St.
Oakland, CA 94612
(415) 645-2647
Music Critic: Charles Shere

PALM SPRINGS-PALM DESERT
THE DESERT SUN
611 S. Palm Canyon Dr.
PO Box 190
Palm Springs, CA 92263
(714) 325-8666
Entertainment Editor: Bruce Fessier

PALO ALTO
THE PENINSULA TIMES-TRIBUNE
245 Lytton Ave.
Palo Alto, CA 94302
(415) 326-1200
Music Critic: William Ratliff

PASADENA
STAR-NEWS
525 E. Colorado Blvd.
Pasadena, CA 91109
(213) 578-6300
Music Critic: Richard W. Stiles

POMONA
PROGRESS BULLETIN
300 S. Thomas St.
PO Box 2708
Pomona, CA 91766
(714) 622-1201
Music Editor: Joseph Firman

RIVERSIDE
RIVERSIDE PRESS-ENTERPRISE
3512 14th St.
Riverside, CA 92502
(714) 684-1200
Entertainment Editor: T. Foreman

ROSEVILLE
THE DAILY TRIBUNE
413 N. Lincoln St.
PO Box 940
Roseville, CA 95661

(916) 786-8742
Music Editor: K.C. Swan

SACRAMENTO
THE SACRAMENTO BEE
21st & Q Sts.
PO Box 15779
Sacramento, CA 95852
(916) 446-9211
Music Editor: W.C. Glackin

THE SACRAMENTO UNION
301 Capitol Mall
Sacramento, CA 95812
(916) 442-7811
Music Critic: Richard Simon

SAN BERNARDINO
SAN BERNARDINO SUN
399 D St.
San Bernardino, CA 92401
(714) 889-9666
Arts Editor: Ray Cooklis

SAN DIEGO
SAN DIEGO EVENING TRIBUNE
SAN DIEGO UNION
350 Camino de la Reina
San Diego, CA 92108
(714) 299-3131
Music Critics: Andrea Herman (Tribune), Donald Dierks (Union)

SAN FRANCISCO
SAN FRANCISCO CHRONICLE
902 Mission St.
San Francisco, CA 94119
(415) 421-1111
Music Critic: Robert Commanday

SAN FRANCISCO EXAMINER
110 Fifth St.
San Francisco, CA 94103
(415) 777-7937
Music Critic: Richard Pontzious

SAN JOSE
SAN JOSE MERCURY-NEWS
750 Ridder Park Dr.
San Jose, CA 95190
(408) 920-5000
Music Critic: Paul Hertelendy

SAN MATEO
TIMES AND NEWS LEADER
1080 S. Amphlett Blvd.
San Mateo, CA 94402
(415) 348-4321
Music Editor: Barbara Bladen

SAN RAFAEL
INDEPENDENT-JOURNAL
PO Box 330
San Rafael, CA 94915
(415) 883-8600
Music Editor: George Frazier

SANTA ANA
REGISTER
625 N. Grand Ave.
Santa Ana, CA 92711
(714) 835-1234
Music Editor: C.P. Smith

SANTA BARBARA
SANTA BARBARA NEWS-PRESS
Drawer NN
De La Guerra Plaza
Santa Barbara, CA 93102
(805) 966-3911
Music Editor: Joan Crowder

SANTA CRUZ
SANTA CRUZ SENTINEL
207 Church St.
PO Box 638
Santa Cruz, CA 95061
(408) 423-4242
Entertainment Editor: Mel Bowen

SANTA MONICA
EVENING OUTLOOK
1920 Colorado Ave.
Santa Monica, CA 90404
(213) 829-6811
Entertainment Editor: Ann Herold

SANTA ROSA
THE PRESS DEMOCRAT
427 Mendocino Ave.
Santa Rosa, CA 95402
(707) 546-2020
Music Editor: Dan Taylor

STOCKTON
STOCKTON RECORD
530 E. Market St.
Stockton, CA 95202
(209) 466-2652
Music Editor: Tony Sauro

TORRANCE
THE DAILY BREEZE
5215 Torrance Blvd.
Torrance, CA 90509
(213) 540-5511
Music Editor: Joe Bensoua

TURLOCK
TURLOCK DAILY JOURNAL
138 S. Center
Turlock, CA 95380
(209) 634-9141
Music Editor: Doris Connolly

VALLEJO
VALLEJO TIMES-HERALD
500 Maryland St.
Vallejo, CA 94590
(707) 644-4121
Entertainment Editor: Jimmie Jones

WALNUT CREEK
CONTRA COSTA TIMES
2640 Shaderlands Dr.
Walnut Creek, CA 94598
(415) 935-2525
Arts Editor: Margaret Crum

WEST COVINA
SAN GABRIEL VALLEY TRIBUNE
1210 N. Azusa Canyon Rd.
West Covina, CA 91790
(213) 962-8811
Entertainment Editor: Joe Smilor

WOODLAND
THE DAILY DEMOCRAT
702 Court St.
Woodland, CA 95695
(916) 662-5421
Music Editor: Lollie Hernandez

COLORADO

COLORADO SPRINGS
GAZETTE TELEGRAPH
PO Box 1779
30 S. Prospect St.
Colorado Springs, CO 80901
(303) 632-5511
Entertainment Editor: Elena Jarvis

DENVER
DENVER POST
650 15th St.
Denver, CO 80202
(303) 820-1624
Music Editor: Glenn Giffin

ROCKY MOUNTAIN NEWS
400 W. Colfax Ave.
Denver, CO 80204
(303) 892-5000
Music Editor: Keith Raether

FT. MORGAN
FT. MORGAN TIMES
329 Main St.
Ft. Morgan, CO 80701
(303) 867-5651
Music Editor: Fern Spencer

PUEBLO
PUEBLO CHIEFTAIN
PUEBLO STAR-JOURNAL
PO Box 36
Peublo, CO 81002
(303) 544-3520
Music Editor: Bob Thomas

CONNECTICUT

BRIDGEPORT
BRIDGEPORT POST
BRIDGEPORT TELEGRAM
338 Beechwood Ave.
Bridgeport, CT 06604
(203) 366-9444
Arts Critic: Richard W. Day

DANBURY
DANBURY NEWS-TIMES
333 Main St.
Danbury, CT 06810
(203) 744-5100
Music Editor: Jean Buoy

HARTFORD
HARTFORD COURANT
285 Broad St.
Hartford, CT 06115
(203) 241-3745
Features Editor: Henry Scott

MANCHESTER
MANCHESTER EVENING HERALD
Herald Square
Manchester, CT 06040
(203) 643-2711
Music Editor: Helen Jaskiewiez

NEW BRITAIN
NEW BRITAIN HERALD
One Herald Square
New Britain, CT 06050
(203) 225-4601
Music Critic: Eugene Gorlewski

NEW HAVEN
NEW HAVEN JOURNAL-COURIER
40 Sargent Dr.
New Haven, CT 06511
(203) 562-3131
Music Editor: Melinda Robins

NEW HAVEN REGISTER
40 Sargent Dr.
New Haven, CT 06511
(203) 562-1121
Music Critic: Gordon Emerson

WATERBURY
WATERBURY AMERICAN
WATERBURY REPUBLICAN
PO Box 2090
389 Meadow St.
Waterbury, CT 06720
(203) 574-3636
Music Editor: Teresa Rousseau

DELAWARE

WILMINGTON
WILMINGTON MORNING NEWS
WILMINGTON EVENING JOURNAL
831 Orange St.
Wilmington, DE 19899
(302) 573-2000
Music Critics: Otto Dekom (News), David B. Kozinski (Journal)

DISTRICT OF COLUMBIA

WASHINGTON, D.C.
WASHINGTON POST
1150 15th St., NW
Washington, DC 20071
(202) 334-7549
Music Critic: Joseph McLellan

WASHINGTON STAR
225 Virginia Ave., SE
Washington, DC 20061
(202) 484-5000
Music Editor: Theodore Libbey, Jr.

FLORIDA

BRADENTON
BRADENTON HERALD
401 13th St., W.
Bradenton, FL 33505
(813) 748-0411
Music Editor: Chris Kotchi

DAYTONA BEACH
DAYTONA BEACH NEWS-JOURNAL
901 6th St.
Daytona Beach, FL 32015
(904) 252-1511
Fine Arts Writer: Drew B. Murphy

FORT LAUDERDALE
FORT LAUDERDALE HI-RISER
FORT LAUDERDALE JEWISH JOURNAL
FORT LAUDERDALE TRIBUNE
4009 NE 5th Terrace
Fort Lauderdale, FL 33334
(305) 563-3311
Music Critic & Editor: Bob Freund

FORT LAUDERDALE NEWS
FORT LAUDERDALE SUN-SENTINEL
101 N. New River Dr., E.
Fort Lauderdale, FL 33302
(305) 761-4000
Music Editor: Tim Smith

JACKSONVILLE
JACKSONVILLE JOURNAL
JACKSONVILLE TIMES-UNION
PO Box 1949-F
Jacksonville, FL 32231
(904) 359-4101
Music Editors: Jaime Lucke (Journal), Claire Martin (Times-Union)

LAKELAND
LAKELAND LEDGER
PO Box 408
401 S. Missouri Ave.
Lakeland, FL 33802
(813) 687-7000
Music Editor: Steve Turner

MIAMI BEACH
MIAMI BEACH SUN REPORTER
CORAL GABLES SUN REPORTER
NORTH MIAMI BEACH SUN REPORTER
NORTH MIAMI SUN REPORTER
1771 West Ave.
Miami Beach, FL 33139
(305) 532-4531
Entertainment Editor & Critic: Linda R. Thornton

ORLANDO
ORLANDO SENTINEL STAR
633 N. Orange Ave.
Orlando, FL 32802
(305) 420-5503
Music Editor: Sumner G. Rand

PALM BEACH
PALM BEACH DAILY NEWS
PO Box 1176
Palm Beach, FL 33480
(305) 655-5755
Critic: Juliette de Marcellus

PENSACOLA
PENSACOLA NEWS-JOURNAL
PENSACOLA NEWS
PO Box 12710
Pensacola, FL 32501
(904) 433-0041
Music Editors: Ginny Graybiel (News-Journal), Larry Wheeler (News)

ST. PETERSBURG
ST. PETERSBURG EVENING INDEPENDENT
ST. PETERSBURG TIMES
PO Box 1121
St. Petersburg, FL 33731
(813) 893-8527
News Features Editors: Janet Woods (Independent), Paul Neely (Times)

TALLAHASSEE
TALLAHASSEE DEMOCRAT
PO Box 990
Tallahassee, FL 32302
(904) 599-2100
Critics: Chris Farrell, John Habich

WEST PALM BEACH
WEST PALM BEACH POST
WEST PALM BEACH EVENING TIMES
PO Drawer T
2751 S. Dixie Hwy.
West Palm Beach, FL 33405
(305) 833-7411
Music Critic: Thelma Newman

GEORGIA

ALBANY
ALBANY HERALD
138 Pine Ave.
Albany, GA 31701
(912) 888-9345
Music Editor: David B. Fuller

ATLANTA
ATLANTA CONSTITUTION
PO BOX 4689
Atlanta, GA 30302
(404) 526-5151
Music & Art Editor: Paula Crouch

ATLANTA JOURNAL
72 Marietta St., NW
Atlanta, GA 30303
(404) 526-5396
Music Editor: Diane Goldsmith

AUGUSTA
AUGUSTA CHRONICLE
AUGUSTA HERALD
PO Box 1928
Augusta, GA 30913
(404) 724-0851
Arts Editor: Louise K. Claussen

COLUMBUS
COLUMBUS LEDGER & ENQUIRER
17 W. 12th St.
Columbus, GA 31901
(404) 571-8580
Music Editor: Glen Thomason

LAWRENCEVILLE
GWINNET DAILY NEWS
PO Box 367
Lawrenceville, GA 30246
(404) 963-0311
Music Editor: Art Bowman

MACON
MACON NEWS
MACON TELEGRAPH
PO Box 4167
120 Broadway
Macon, GA 31213
(912) 744-4345
Music Columnists: Melodie Palmer (News), Edith McNeill (Telegraph)

WAYCROSS
WAYCROSS JOURNAL-HERALD
PO Box 219
402 Isabella St.
Waycross, GA 31501
(912) 283-2244
Music Editor: Dorothy Smith

HAWAII

HONOLULU
HONOLULU ADVERTISER
HONOLULU STAR-BULLETIN
SUNDAY STAR-BULLETIN & ADVERTISER
PO Box 3110
Honolulu, HI 96802
(808) 525-8000
Amusements Editor: Wayne Harada

IDAHO

BOISE
IDAHO STATESMAN
PO Box 40
1200 N. Curtis St.
Boise, ID 83707
(208) 377-6200
Music Editor: Julie Titone

LEWISTON
LEWISTON TRIBUNE
505 C Ct.
Lewiston, ID 83501
(208) 743-9411
Music Editor: Bruce Spotlegon

MOSCOW
IDAHONIAN
PO Box 8187
409 S. Jackson St.
Moscow, ID 83843
(208) 882-5561
Music Editor: Loris Jones

ILLINOIS

AURORA
AURORA BEACON-NEWS
101 S. River St.
Aurora, IL 60506
(312) 844-5902
Music Editor: John C. Shaffer

BENTON
BENTON EVENING NEWS
111 Church St.
Benton, IL 62812
(618) 438-5611
Music Editor: Edna Choisser

BLOOMINGTON
BLOOMINGTON-NORMAL DAILY PANTAGRAPH
301 W. Washington St.
Bloomington, IL 61701
(309) 829-9411
Music Editor: Louise Donahue

CHICAGO
CHICAGO SUN-TIMES
401 N. Wabash Ave.
Chicago, IL 60611
(312) 321-2147
Music Critic: Robert C. Marsh

CHICAGO TRIBUNE
435 N. Michigan Ave.
Chicago, IL 60611
(312) 222-3570
Music Critic: John Von Rhein

CRYSTAL LAKE
DAILY CRYSTAL LAKE HERALD
7803 Pyott Rd.
Crystal Lake, IL 60014
(815) 459-4040
Arts Editor: Anna Williams

DECATUR
DECATUR HERALD & REVIEW
601 E. William St.
Decature, IL 62523
(217) 429-5151
Associate Arts Editor: Theresa Churchill

MOLINE
MOLINE DAILY DISPATCH
1720 Fifth Ave.
Moline, IL 61265
(309) 764-4344
Music Editor: Bill McElwain

PEORIA
PEORIA JOURNAL-STAR
1 News Plaza
Peoria, IL 61601
(309) 686-3000
Music Critic & Editor: Jerry Klein

ROCK ISLAND
ROCK ISLAND ARGUS
1724 Fourth Ave.
Rock Island, IL 61201
(309) 786-6441
Music Editor: Charles H. Sanders

ROCKFORD
ROCKFORD REGISTER STAR
99 E. State St.
Rockford, IL 61105
(815) 987-1200
Music Critic: Craig Wyatt

SPRINGFIELD
SPRINGFIELD STATE JOURNAL-REGISTER
PO Box 219
313 S. Sixth St.
Springfield, IL 62705
(217) 788-8600
Music Critic: Bob Mahlburg

WAUKEGAN
WAUKEGAN NEWS-SUN
100 W. Madison St.
Waukegan, IL 60085
(312) 578-7210
Music Editor: Bea Armstrong

INDIANA

EVANSVILLE
EVANSVILLE COURIER
201 NW Second St.
Evansville, IN 47702
(812) 464-7459
Entertainment Editor: Patrice Smith

FORT WAYNE
FORT WAYNE JOURNAL-GAZETTE
FORT WAYNE NEWS-SENTINEL
600 Main St.
Fort Wayne, IN 46802
(219) 461-8207
Music Critics: Robert Hertzberg (Gazette), Connie Trexler (Sentinel)

GARY
GARY POST-TRIBUNE
1065 Broadway
Gary, IN 46402
(219) 886-5094
Music Critic: Jean M. Isaacs

INDIANAPOLIS
INDIANAPOLIS NEWS
INDIANAPOLIS STAR
307 N. Pennsylvania St.
Indianapolis, IN 46204
(317) 633-9226
Music Editor & Critic: Charles B. Staff, Jr.

KOKOMO
KOKOMO TRIBUNE
300 N. Union St.
Kokomo, IN 46901
(317) 459-3121
Arts Editor: Bruce Van Dusen

MICHIGAN CITY
MICHIGAN CITY NEWS-DISPATCH
121 W. Michigan Blvd.
Michigan City, IN 46360
(219) 874-7211
Music Editor: Joe Pixler

ROCHESTER
ROCHESTER SENTINEL
118 E. Eighth St.
Rochester, IN 46975
(219) 223-2111
Music Editor: Jack Overmyer

SOUTH BEND
SOUTH BEND TRIBUNE
225 W. Colfax Ave.
South Bend, IN 46626
(219) 233-6161
Entertainment Editor: John D. Miller

TERRE HAUTE
TERRE HAUTE STAR
721 Wabash Ave.
Terre Haute, IN 47807
(812) 232-0581
Music Editor: Frederick Black

WARSAW
WARSAW TIMES-UNION
Times Bldg.
Warsaw, IN 46580
(219) 267-3111
Music Editor: Marie Snyder

IOWA

BURLINGTON
BURLINGTON HAWK EYE
PO Box 10
800 S. Main St.
Burlington, IA 52601
(319) 754-8461
Music Editor: Lloyd Mafitt

CEDAR RAPIDS
CEDAR RAPIDS GAZETTE
500 Third Ave., SE
Cedar Rapids, IA 52401
(319) 398-8329
Music Critics: Les Zacheis, Dick Hogan

COUNCIL BLUFFS
COUNCIL BLUFFS NONPAREIL
117 Pearl St.
Council Bluffs, IA 51501
(712) 328-1811
Music Critic: Jim Williams

DAVENPORT
DAVENPORT QUAD-CITY TIMES
PO Box 3828
Davenport, IA 52722
(319) 383-2279
Entertainment Editor: Marilyn Lane

DELWEIN
DELWEIN REGISTER
16-20 E. Charles St.
Delwein, IA 50662
(319) 283-2144
Music Editor: Solveig Larson

DES MOINES
DES MOINES REGISTER
715 Locust St.
Des Moines, IA 50304
(515) 284-8000
Classical Music Critic: Nick Baldwin

DUBUQUE
DUBUQUE TELEGRAPH-HERALD
8th & Bluff Sts.
Dubuque, IA 52001
(319) 588-5671
Entertainment Editor: Ken Amundson

MARSHALLTOWN
MARSHALLTOWN TIMES-REPUBLICAN
135 W. Main St.
Marshalltown, IA 50158
(515) 753-6611
Music Editor: Dorris Ruopp

MUSCATINE
MUSCATINE JOURNAL
301 E. Third St.
Muscatine, IA 52761
(319) 263-2331
Music Editor: Nancy Bauer

SIOUX CITY
SIOUX CITY JOURNAL
6th & Pavonia Sts.
Sioux City, IA 51102
(712) 279-5075
Music Editor: Bruce Miller

WATERLOO
WATERLOO COURIER
PO Box 540
Waterloo, IA 50704
(319) 291-1462
Music Critic: Deb Lorenzen

KANSAS

COFFEYVILLE
COFFEYVILLE JOURNAL
Eighth & Elm Sts.
Coffeyville, KS 67337
(316) 251-3300
Entertainment Editor: Robert Leger

DODGE CITY
DODGE CITY DAILY GLOBE
705 Second St.
Dodge City, KS 67801
(316) 225-4151
Music Editor: Jim Moran

EMPORIA
EMPORIA GAZETTE
517 Merchant St.
Emporia, KS 66801
(316) 342-4800
Music Editor: R.C. Owen

INDEPENDENCE
INDEPENDENCE REPORTER
PO Box 869
320 N. Sixth St.
Independence, KS 67301
(316) 331-3550
Music Editor: Pat Greenhaw

KANSAS CITY
KANSAS CITY KANSAN
901 N. 8th St.
Kansas City, KS 66104
(913) 371-4300
Entertainment Editor: Andrea Stewart

MANHATTAN
MANHATTAN MERAIRY
Fifth & Osage Sts.
Manhattan, KS 66502
(913) 776-8805
Arts Editor: Kent Donovan

OTTAWA
OTTAWA HERALD
104 S. Cedar St.
Ottawa, KS 66067
(913) 132-4700
Music Editor: Carol Murphy

TOPEKA
TOPEKA CAPITAL-JOURNAL
Sixth & Jefferson Sts.
Topeka, KS 66607
(913) 295-1111
Music Editor: Connie Strand

WICHITA
WICHITA EAGLE-BEACON
825 E. Douglas Ave.
Wichita, KS 67201
(316) 268-6000
Music Writers: Nancy Pate, Diane Rush

KENTUCKY

LOUISVILLE
LOUISVILLE COURIER-JOURNAL
LOUISVILLE TIMES
525 W. Broadway
Louisville, KY 40202
(502) 582-4011
Music Editors: William Mootz (Journal), F.W. Woolsey (Times)

OWENSBORO
OWENSBORO MESSENGER-INQUIRER
PO Box 1480
1401 Frederica St.
Owensboro, KY 42301
(502) 925-0123
Music Editor: Ann W. Whittinghill

LOUISIANA

BATON ROUGE
BATON ROUGE MORNING ADVOCATE
BATON ROUGE STATE-TIMES
PO Box 588
Baton Rouge, LA 70821
(504) 383-1111
Music Critics: David Foil (Advocate), Eddy Allman (Times)

LAFAYETTE
LAFAYETTE DAILY ADVERTISER
PO Box 3268
Lafayette, LA 70502
(318) 235-8511
Music Critic: Lynn M. Mills

LAKE CHARLES
LAKE CHARLES AMERICAN PRESS
327 Broad St.
Lake Charles, LA 70601
(318) 439-2781
Music Editor: Jim Beam

MONROE
MONROE NEWS-STAR-WORLD
411 N. Fourth St.
Monroe, LA 71203
(318) 322-5161
Music Editor: Kathy Spurlock

NEW ORLEANS
NEW ORLEANS TIMES-PICAYUNE
NEW ORLEANS STATES-ITEM
3800 Howard Ave.
New Orleans, LA 70140
(504) 586-3687
Music Critic: Frank Gagnard
Music Editor: Bruce W. Eggler

OPBOUSAS
OPBOUSAS DAILY WORLD
PO Box 1179
Opbousas, LA 70570
(318) 942-4971
Music Editor: Eva Hall

SHREVEPORT
SHREVEPORT JOURNAL
PO Box 31110
222 Lake St.
Shreveport, LA 71130
(318) 424-0373
Entertainment Editor: David Connelly

SHREVEPORT TIMES
PO Box 222
222 Lake St.
Shreveport, LA 71130
(318) 424-0373
Music Critic: Lane Crockett

SLIDELL
SLIDELL DAILY TIMES
1441 Short Cut Rd.
Slidell, LA 70458
(504) 643-5224
Entertainment Editor: T. Perkins

MAINE

BANGOR
BANGOR DAILY NEWS
491 Main St.
Bangor, ME 04401
(207) 942-4881
Arts Editor & Critic: Robert H. Newall

PORTLAND
PORTLAND EVENING EXPRESS
PORTLAND PRESS HERALD
MAINE SUNDAY TELEGRAM
PO Box 1460
Portland, ME 04104
(207) 775-5811
Music Critic: Clark T. Irwin, Jr. (Express & Herald)
Entertainment Editor: Jon Halvorsen (Telegram)

MARYLAND

BALTIMORE
BALTIMORE NEWS-AMERICAN
301 E. Lombard St.
Baltimore, MD 21202
(301) 752-1212
Entertainment Editor: Carol Herwig

BALTIMORE SUN
Calvert & Centre Sts.
Baltimore, MD 21203
(301) 332-6176
Music Editor: Stephen Cera

COLUMBIA
COLUMBIA FLIER
HOWARD COUNTY TIMES
CATONSVILLE TIMES
LAUREL LEADER
ARBUTUS TIMES
BELAIR BOOSTER
PARKVILLE REPORTER
10750 Little Patuxent Pkwy.
Columbia, MD 21044
(301) 730-3620
Music Critics: Geoffrey Himes, Bill Graves

HAGERSTOWN
HAGERSTOWN HERALD
HAGERSTOWN DAILY MAIL
100 Summit Ave.
Hagerstown, MD 21740
(301) 733-5131
Music Editor: H.B. Warner, Jr.

MASSACHUSETTS

BOSTON
CHRISTIAN SCIENCE MONITOR
1 Norway St.
Boston, MA 02115
(617) 262-2300

Branch Office:
220 E. 42nd St., Ste. 3006
New York, NY 10017
(212) 599-1850
Music Critic: Thor Eckert, Jr.

BOSTON HERALD-AMERICAN
300 Harrison Ave.
Boston, MA 02106
(617) 426-3000
Music Critic: Ellen Pfeifer

BOSTON PHOENIX
100 Massachusetts Ave.
Boston, MA 02115
(617) 536-5390
Music Critic: Lloyd Schwartz

BROCKTON
BROCKTON ENTERPRISE
60 Main St.
Brockton, MA 02403
(617) 586-6200
Music Editor: Joseph Sherman

DORCHESTER
BOSTON GLOBE
135 W.T. Morrissey Blvd.
Dorchester, MA 02107
(617) 929-2000
Music Critic: Richard Dyer

FALL RIVER
FALL RIVER HERALD-NEWS
207 Pocasset St.
Fall River, MAS 02722
(617) 676-8211
Music Critic: Marion Flanigan

FRAMINGHAM
FRAMINGHAM MIDDLESEX NEWS
33 New York Ave.
Framingham, MA 01701
(617) 872-4321
Music Critic: Virginia Lucier

NEW BEDFORD
NEW BEDFORD STANDARD-TIMES
555 Pleasant St.
New Bedford, MA 02742
(617) 997-7411
Music Editor: Earl J. Dias

PITTSFIELD
PITTSFIELD BERKSHIRE EAGLE
33 Eagle St.
Pittsfield, MA 01201
(413) 447-7311
Music Critic: Andrew L. Pincus

QUINCY
QUINCY PATRIOT LEDGER
13-19 Temple St.
Quincy, MA 02169
(617) 786-7067
Music Critic: Peter Knapp

SPRINGFIELD
SPRINGFIELD DAILY NEWS
SPRINGFIELD UNION & REPUBLICAN
1860 Main St.
Springfield, MA 01101
(413) 787-2470
Music Critics: William Poleri (News), Richard Hammerich (Republican)

WORCESTER
WORCESTER EVENING GAZETTE
WORCESTER TELEGRAM
20 Franklin St.
Worcester, MA 01608
(617) 755-4321
Music Critic: Lily Owyang

MICHIGAN

BAY CITY
BAY CITY TIMES
311 Fifth Ave.
Bay City, MI 48706
(517) 895-8551
Music Critic: Lois Town

DETROIT
DETROIT FREE PRESS
321 W. Lafayette Blvd.
Detroit, MI 48231
(313) 222-6459
Music Critic: John Guinn

DETROIT NEWS
615 Lafayette Blvd.
Detroit, MI 48231
(313) 222-2283
Music Critic: Jay P. Carr

ESCANABA
ESCANABA DAILY PRESS
600-2 Ludington St.
Escanaba, MI 49829
(906) 786-2021
Music Editor: Peggy Bryson

FLINT
FLINT JOURNAL
200 E. First St.
Flint, MI 48502
(313) 767-0660
Music Critic: Susan Raccoli

GRAND RAPIDS
GRAND RAPIDS PRESS
Vandenberg Ctr.
Press Plaza
Grand Rapids, MI
(616) 459-1400
Music Editors: Jerry Elliot, Mark Newman, Richard DeVinney

KALAMAZOO
KALAMAZOO GAZETTE
401 S. Burdick
Kalamazoo, MI 49008
(616) 345-3511
Music Critic: Dean Knuth

LANSING
STATE JOURNAL
120 E. Lenawee St.
Lansing, MI 48919
(517) 487-4611
Arts Editor: Mike Hughes

LUDINGTON
LUDINGTON DAILY NEWS
202 N. Rath Ave.
Ludington, MI 49431
(616) 845-5181
Music Editor: Mary Rose Furstenau

MARQUETTE
MINING JOURNAL
249 Washington St.
Marquette, MI 49855
(906) 226-2554
Entertainment Editor: Jeffery Eaton

PONTIAC
PONTIAC OAKLAND PRESS
PO Box 9
48 W. Huron St.
Pontiac, MI 48056
(313) 332-8181
Entertainment Editor: Kenneth Jones

SAGINAW
SAGINAW NEWS
203 S. Washington Ave.
Saginaw, MI 48605
(517) 752-7171
Entertainment Editor: Janet I. Martineau

MINNESOTA

DULUTH
DULUTH HERALD
DULUTH NEWS-TRIBUNE
424 W. First St.
Duluth, MN 55801
(218) 723-5281
Music Critic: Bob Ashenmacher

MANKATO
MANKATO FREE PRESS
418 S. Second St.
Mankato, MN 56001
(507) 625-4451
Music Critic: Dianne Goldstaub

MINNEAPOLIS
MINNEAPOLIS STAR
MINNEAPOLIS TRIBUNE
425 Portland Ave.
Minneapolis, MN 55488
(612) 372-4141
Music Critic: Michael Anthony

RED WING
RED WING REPUBLICAN-EAGLE
433 Third St.
Red Wing, MN 55066
(612) 388-8235
Music Editor: Ruth Nerhaugen

ST. CLOUD
ST. CLOUD DAILY TIMES
3000 N. Seventh St.
St. Cloud, MN 56301
(612) 255-8743
Music Editor: Bill McAllister

ST. PAUL
ST. PAUL DISPATCH
ST. PAUL PIONEER PRESS
55 E. Fourth St.
St. Paul, MN 55101
(612) 222-5011
Music Critic: Roy M. Close

MISSISSIPPI

BILOXI
BILOXI-GULFPORT DAILY HERALD
PO Box 4567
Biloxi, MS 39531
(601) 896-2331
Music Critic: Jerry Kinser

JACKSON
JACKSON CLARION-LEDGER
JACKSON DAILY NEWS
311 E. Pearl St.
Jackson, MS 39205
(601) 956-8501
Music Critic: Mike Hall

LAUREL
LAUREL LEADER-CALL
130 Beacon St.
Laurel, MS 39440
(601) 428-0551
Music Editor: Louise Simpson

MERIDIAN
MERIDIAN STAR
810-12 22nd Ave.
Meridian, MS 39301
(601) 693-1551
Music Critic: Betty L. Coffey

MISSOURI

KANSAS CITY
KANSAS CITY STAR
KANSAS CITY TIMES
1729 Grand Ave.
Kansas City, MO 64108
(816) 234-4380
Music Editor: Harry Haskell

ST. JOSEPH
ST. JOSEPH NEWS-PRESS
Ninth & Edmond Sts.
St. Joseph, MO 64502
(816) 279-5671
Music Editor: Don E. Thornton

ST. LOUIS
ST. LOUIS GLOBE-DEMOCRAT
710 N. Tucker Blvd.
St. Louis, MO 63101
(314) 342-1354
Music Critic: James Wierzbicki

ST. LOUIS POST-DISPATCH
900 N. 12th St.
St. Louis, MO 63101
(314) 622-7079
Music Editor: Frank Peters

SPRINGFIELD
SPRINGFIELD LEADER & PRESS
SPRINGFIELD DAILY NEWS
SPRINGFIELD NEWS-LEADER
651 Boonville Rd.
Springfield, MO 65801
(417) 836-1100
Features Editor: Bill Tatum

MONTANA

BILLINGS
BILLINGS GAZETTE

PO Box 2507
401 N. Broadway
Billings, MT 59101
(406) 657-1200
Arts Critic: Christene Meyers

BUTTE
MONTANA STANDARD
25 W. Granite St.
Butte, MT 59701
(406) 782-8301
Music Editor: Bert Gaskill

MISSOULA
MISSOULIAN
502 N. Higgins Ave.
Missoula, MT 59801
(406) 721-5200
Music Editor: Brian Howell

NEBRASKA

OMAHA
OMAHA WORLD-HERALD
World-Herald Sq.
Omaha, NE 68102
(402) 444-1000
Music Critic: Warren Prince

NEVADA

LAS VEGAS
LAS VEGAS REVIEW-JOURNAL
PO Box 70
Las Vegas, NV 89125-0070
(702) 383-0270
Music Editor: A.D. Hopkins

RENO
RENO EVENING GAZETTE
NEVADA STATE JOURNAL
PO Box 22000
Reno, NV 89520-2000
(702) 788-6397
Arts Editor: Tonia Cunning

NEW HAMPSHIRE

LACONIA
LACONIA CITIZEN
171 Fair St.
Laconia, NH 03246
(603) 524-3800
Music Editor: Eileen Jacobs

MANCHESTER
MANCHESTER UNION LEADER
35 Amherst St.
Manchester, NH 03105
(603) 668-4321
Music Editor & Critic: Meg Geraghty

NEW JERSEY

ASBURY PARK
ASBURY PARK PRESS
Press Plaza
Asbury Park, NJ 07712
(201) 774-7000
Arts Editor: Gretchen C. Van Benthuysen

ATLANTIC CITY
ATLANTIC CITY PRESS & SUNDAY PRESS
303 N. Harrisburg Ave.
Atlantic City, NJ 08401
(609) 345-6837
Music Critic: William McMahon

BRIDGEWATER
BRIDGEWATER COURIER-NEWS
1201 Route 22
Bridgewater, NJ 08807
(201) 722-8800
Music Critic: Frank Edwards

CAMDEN
CAMDEN COURIER-POST
Cuthbert Blvd.
Camden, NJ 08101
(609) 663-6000
Music Critic: Robert Baxter

ELIZABETH
ELIZABETH DAILY JOURNAL
295 Broad St.
Elizabeth, NJ 07207
(201) 354-5000
Music Editor: Victor Zak

HACKENSACK
BERGEN COUNTY RECORD
150 River St.
Hackensack, NJ 07602
(201) 646-4000
Music Critics: David Spengler, Peter Wynne

JERSEY CITY
JERSEY JOURNAL
30 Journal Sq.
Jersey City, NJ 07306
(201) 653-1000
Critic: Byron Belt

MORRISTOWN
MORRISTOWN DAILY RECORD
55 Park Pl.
Morristown, NJ 07960
(201) 538-2000
Music Editor: Jim Bohen

NEW BRUNSWICK
NEW BRUNSWICK HOME NEWS
PO Box 551
New Brunswick, NJ 08901
(201) 246-5558
Music Critic: Rena Fruchter

NEWARK
NEWARK STAR-LEDGER
Star-Ledger Plaza
Newark, NJ 07101
(201) 877-4275
Music Editor: Michael Redmond

PATERSON
PATERSON NEWS
1 News Plaza
Paterson, NJ 07509
(201) 684-3000
Critic: Kevin Coughlin

TRENTON
TRENTON TIMES
500 Perry St.
Trenton, NJ 08605
(609) 396-3232
Music Critic: Donald Delany

TRENTORIAN
Southard & Perry Sts.
Trenton, NJ 08602
(609) 989-7800
Music Editor: Ron Williams

UNION CITY
UNION CITY DISPATCH
400 38th St.
Union City, NJ 07087
(201) 863-2000
Critic: Kevin Coughlin

WILLINGBORO
BURLINGTON COUNTY TIMES
Route 130
Willingboro, NJ 08046
(609) 871-8000
Music Editor: Lou Gaul

NEW MEXICO

ALBUQUERQUE
ALBUQUERQUE JOURNAL
ALBUQUERQUE TRIBUNE
717 Silver Ave., SW
Albuquerque, NM 87102
(505) 842-2227
Music Critics: Tom Jacobs (Journal), Ollie Reed, Jr. (Tribune)

NEW YORK

ALBANY
ALBANY KNICKERBOCKER NEWS
ALBANY TIMES-UNION
Box 15-627
Albany, NY 12212
(518) 454-5460
Music Editors: Mary Anne Leonard (News), Fred LeBrun (Union)

BINGHAMTON
BINGHAMTON EVENING PRESS
BINGHAMTON SUN-BULLETIN
Vestal Pkwy., E.
Binghamton, NY 13902
(607) 798-1234
Music Editor: Gene Grey

BUFFALO
BUFFALO EVENING NEWS
1 News Plaza
Buffalo, NY 14240

(716) 849-4506
Music Editor: John P. Dwyer

ELMIRA
ELMIRA STAR-GAZETTE
ELMIRA SUNDAY TELEGRAM
201 Baldwin St.
Elmira, NY 14902
(607) 734-5151
Music Editor: Diane Bacha

MELVILLE
GARDEN CITY NEWSDAY
LONG ISLAND NEWSDAY
235 Pinelawn Rd.
Melville, NY 11747
(516) 454-2020
Music Critic: Peter Goodman

NEW YORK
NEW YORK DAILY NEWS
220 E. 42nd St.
New York, NY 10017
(212) 949-3796
Music Critic: Bill Zakariasen

NEW YORK FRANCE-AMERIQUE
PO Box 415
New York, NY 10028
(212) 534-5455
Music Critic: Herve LeMansec

NEW YORK NEWS WORLD
401 Fifth Ave.
New York, NY 10016
(212) 532-8300
Features Editor: Tom Clifford

NEW YORK POST
210 South St.
New York, NY 10002
(212) 349-5000
Music Editor: Harriett Johnson

NEW YORK TIMES
229 W. 43rd St.
New York, NY 10036
(212) 556-1341
Music Critic: Donald Henahan

VILLAGE VOICE
842 Broadway
New York, NY 10003
(212) 475-3300
Music Critics: Leighton Kerner, Tom Johnson, Gregory Sandow

NIAGARA FALLS
NIAGARA GAZETTE
310 Niagara St.
Niagara Falls, NY 14303
(716) 282-2311
Music Critic: C. Wloszczyna

ROCHESTER
ROCHESTER DEMOCRAT & CHRONICLE
ROCHESTER TIMES-UNION
55 Exchange St.
Rochester, NY 14614
(716) 232-7100
Music Critics: Stephen Wigler (Chronicle), David Stearns (Union)

SCHENECTADY
SCHENECTADY GAZETTE
334 State St.
Schenectady, NY 12301
(518) 374-4141
Music Editor: M.C. Wright

STATEN ISLAND
STATEN ISLAND ADVANCE
950 Fingerboard Rd.
Staten Island, NY 10305
(212) 981-1234
Entertainment Editor: Louis Bergonzi

SYRACUSE
SYRACUSE HERALD-JOURNAL
SYRACUSE HERALD-AMERICAN
SYRACUSE POST-STANDARD
Clinton Square
Syracuse, NY 13202
(315) 470-2263
Music Critic: Dr. Earl George

TROY
TROY-TIMES-RECORD
Broadway & Fifth Ave.
Troy, NY 12181
(518) 272-2000
Arts Editor: Doug de Lisle

UTICA
UTICA DAILY PRESS
UTICA OBSERVER-DISPATCH
221 Oriskany Plaza
Utica, NY 13503
(315) 797-9150
Music Editor: David R. Price

WHITE PLAINS
WESTCHESTER-ROCKLAND NEWSPAPERS, INC.
1 Gannett Dr.
White Plains, NY 10602
(914) 694-9300
Entertainment Editor: Nick Paradise

NORTH CAROLINA

CHARLOTTE
CHARLOTTE OBSERVER
PO Box 32188
Charlotte, NC 28232
(704) 379-6412
Music Critic: LaFleur Paysour

DURHAM
DURHAM MORNING HERALD
DURHAM SUN
115-19 Market St.
Durham, NC 27702
(919) 682-8181
Music Editor: Susan Broili (Sun)

FAYETTEVILLE
FAYETTEVILLE OBSERVER
FAYETTEVILLE TIMES
458 Whitfield St.
Fayetteville, NC 28306
(919) 323-4848
Music Editor: Nancy Oliver (Observer)

GREENSBORO
GREENSBORO DAILY NEWS
GREENSBORO RECORD
PO Box 20848
200 E. Market St.
Greensboro, NC 27420
(919) 373-7090
Music Critic: Marnie Ross (News)

HIGH POINT
HIGH POINT ENTERPRISE
PO Box 1009
High Point, NC 27261
(919) 885-2161
Music Editor: Meg Gunkel

RALEIGH
RALEIGH NEWS & OBSERVER
215 S. McDowell St.
Raleigh, NC 27597
(919) 829-4574
Music Critic: Bill Morrison

THOMASVILLE
THOMASVILLE TIMES
PO Box 549
Thomasville, NC 27360
(919) 475-2151
Music Editor: Wint Capel

WINSTON-SALEM
WINSTON-SALEM JOURNAL
416-20 N. Marshall St.
Winston-Salem, NC 27102
(919) 727-7360
Music Editor: Jim Shertzer

NORTH DAKOTA

BISMARCK
BISMARK TRIBUNE
707 Front Ave.
Bismark, ND 58501
(701) 223-2500
Music Editor: Vicki Russell

FARGO
FORUM OF FARGO-MOREHEAD
Box 2020
Fargo, ND 58107
(701) 235-7311
Entertainment Editor: Janna Anderson

OHIO

AKRON
AKRON BEACON-JOURNAL
44 E. Exchange St.
Akron, OH 44328
(216) 375-8161
Music Critic: Donald Rosenberg

CANTON
CANTON REPOSITORY
500 Market Ave., S.
Canton, OH 44702
(216) 454-5611
Music Editor: Don Kane

CINCINNATI
CINCINNATI ENQUIRER
617 Vine St.
Cincinnati, OH 45201
(513) 369-1972
Music Critic: Nancy Malitz

CINCINNATI POST
800 Broadway
Cincinnati, OH 45202
(513) 352-2790
Music Critic: James Chute

CLEVELAND
CLEVELAND PLAIN DEALER
1801 Superior Ave.
Cleveland, OH 44114
(216) 344-4269
Music Critics: Robert Finn, Wilma Salisbury

COLUMBUS
COLUMBUS CITIZEN JOURNAL
COLUMBUS DISPATCH
34 S. Third St.
Columbus, OH 43216
(614) 461-5000
Music Critic: Nancy Gilson (Journal)
Entertainment Editor: Shirley McNeely (Dispatch)

DAYTON
DAYTON DAILY NEWS
DAYTON JOURNAL-HERALD
Fourth & Ludlow Sts.
Dayton, OH 45401
(513) 225-2211/2427
Music Editors: Betty Krebs, Hal Lipper (News); Richard Schwarze, Terre Lawson (Herald)

FINDLAY
FINDLAY COURIER
701 W. Sandusky St.
Findlay, OH 45840
(419) 422-5151
Entertainment Editor: Bob Sterner

HAMILTON
HAMILTON JOURNAL-NEWS
PO Box 298
Court & Journal Square
Hamilton, OH 45012
(513) 863-8200
Music Editor: Mike Jones

KENT
KENT-RAVENNA RECORD-COURIER
206 E. Erie St.
Kent, OH 44240
(216) 673-3491
Entertainment Editor: LuAnn Worley

LIMA
LIMA NEWS
121 E. High St.
Lima, OH 45802
(419) 223-1010
Entertainment Editor: Gerri Willis

LORAIN
LORAIN JOURNAL
1657 Broadway
Lorain, OH 44052
(216) 245-6901
Music Editor: Howard Gollop

MIDDLETOWN
MIDDLETOWN JOURNAL
First Ave. & Broad St.
Middletown, OH 45042
(513) 442-3611
Entertainment Editor: Phyllis Cox

NEWARK
NEWARK ADVOCATE
25 W. Main St.
Newark, OH 43055
(614) 345-4053
Music Editor: Lori Green

SPRINGFIELD
SPRINGFIELD DAILY NEWS
202 N. Limestone St.
Springfield, OH 45501
(513) 323-3731
Music Critic: Jim Hays

TOLEDO
TOLEDO BLADE
541 Superior St.
Toledo, OH 43660
(419) 245-6152
Arts Editor: Boris E. Nelson

WARREN
WARREN TRIBUNE-CHRONICLE
240 Franklin St., SE
Warren, OH 44482
(216) 841-1600
Entertainment Editor: Marty Douce

YOUNGSTOWN
YOUNGSTOWN VINDICATOR
Vindicator Square
Youngstown, OH 44501
(216) 747-1471
Music Editor: Adrian M. Slifka

OKLAHOMA

ARDMORE
DAILY ARDMOREITE
PO Box 1328
Ardmore, OK 73401
(405) 223-2200
Music Editor: Pam Martin

LAWTON
LAWTON CONSTITUTION
LAWTON MORNING PRESS
PO Box 2069
Lawton, OK 73502
(405) 353-0620
Arts Critic: O'Dette Havel

NORMAN
NORMAN TRANSCRIPT
215 E. Comanche St.
Norman, OK 73070
(405) 321-1800
Entertainment Editor: DeLaine Dannelley

OKLAHOMA CITY
OKLAHOMA CITY TIMES
DAILY & SUNDAY OKLAHOMAN
Box 25125
Oklahoma City, OK 73125
(405) 231-3311
Music Editor: Gene Triplett

PERRY
PERRY JOURNAL
714 Delaware St.
Perry, OK 73077
(405) 336-2222
Music Editor: Milo W. Watson

TULSA
TULSA DAILY WORLD
315 S. Boulder Ave.
Tulsa, OK 74102
(918) 583-2161
Music Editor: David Mackenzie

TULSA TRIBUNE
PO Box 1770
Tulsa, OK 74102
(918) 581-8400
Music Critic: John Tums
Entertainment Editor: Ellis Widner

OREGON

ALBANY
ALBANY DEMOCRAT-HERALD
138 W. Sixth Ave.
Albany, OR 97321
(503) 926-2211
Music Editor: Robert Caldwell

ASTORIA
DAILY ASTORIAN
949 Exchange St.
Astoria, OR 97103
(503) 325-3211
Music Editor: Todd Merriman

EUGENE
EUGENE REGISTER-GUARD
PO Box 10188
Eugene, OR 97401
(503) 485-1234
Music Critic: Fred Crafts

ONTARIO
DAILY ARGUS OBSERVER
1160 SW Fourth St.
Ontario, OR 97914
(503) 889-5387
Music Editor: Joyce McLean

PORTLAND
OREGON JOURNAL
1320 SW Broadway
Portland, OR 97201
(503) 221-8366
Music Critic: Martin Clark

OREGONIAN
1320 SW Broadway
Portland, OR 97201
(503) 221-8188

Classical Music Critic: Robert Lindstrom
Rock & Jazz Critic: John Wendeborn

SALEM
SALEM STATESMAN-JOURNAL
280 Church St., NE
Salem, OR 97301
(503) 399-6611
Music Editor: Ron Cowen

PENNSYLVANIA

ALTOONA
ALTOONA MIRROR
PO Box 2008
Altoona, PA 16603
(814) 946-7454
Music Critic: Steven C. Helsel

EASTON
EASTON EXPRESS
PO Box 391
Easton, PA 18042
(215) 258-7171
Music Editor: Nick Cristino

ERIE
ERIE DAILY TIMES
ERIE MORNING NEWS
205 W. 12th St.
Erie, PA 16534
Entertainment Editor: Kevin Cuneo

HARRISBURG
HARRISBURG EVENING NEWS
HARRISBURG PATRIOT
812 Market St.
Harrisburg, PA 17105
(717) 255-8251
Music Critic: Barker Howland

JOHNSTOWN
JOHNSTOWN TRIBUNE-DEMOCRAT
425 Locust St.
Johnstown, PA 15907
(814) 536-0711
Music Editor: Harold Barkhimer

LEVITTOWN
BUCKS COUNTY COURIER-TIMES
8400 Route 13
Levittown, PA 19058
(215) 752-6894
Music Critic: John Fisher

NORRISTOWN
NORRISTOWN TIMES-HERALD
PO Box 591
Norristown, PA 19404
(215) 272-2500
Music Editor: Bessie Wilson

PHILADELPHIA
PHILADELPHIA DAILY NEWS
400 N. Broad St.
Philadelphia, PA 19101
(215) 854-2648
Music Critic: Johnathon Takiff

PHILADELPHIA INQUIRER
Box 8263
Philadelphia, PA 19101
(215) 854-2948
Music Editor: Samuel L. Singer
Music Critic: Daniel Webster

PITTSBURGH
PITTSBURGH POST-GAZETTE
50 Blvd. of the Allies
Pittsburgh, PA 15222
(412) 263-1577
Music Critics: Robert Croan, Bill Stieg

PITTSBURGH PRESS
34 Blvd. of the Allies
Pittsburgh, PA 15230
(412) 263-1514
Music Editor: Carl Apone

READING
READING TIMES
345 Penn St.
Reading, PA 19603
(215) 373-4221
Music Critic: Gary Catt

SCRANTON
SCRANTON TRIBUNE
SCRANTONIAN
338 N. Washington Ave.
Scranton, PA 18505
(717) 344-7221
Music Editor: William E. McDonald

SCRANTON TIMES
Penn & Spruce Sts.
Scranton, PA 18503
(717) 348-9100
Music Critic: Jean Krupa

WILKES-BARRE
WILKES-BARRE TIMES-LEADER
15 N. Main St.
Wilkes-Barre, PA 18711
(717) 829-7100
Features Editor: Catherine McMahon

RHODE ISLAND

PAWTUCKET
PAWTUCKET EVENING TIMES
23 Exchange St.
Pawtucket, RI 02860
(401) 722-4000
Music Editor: William Oziemblewski

PROVIDENCE
PROVIDENCE EVENING BULLETIN
PROVIDENCE JOURNAL
75 Fountain St.
Providence, RI 02902
(401) 277-7275
Music Critic: Edwin Stafford

WESTERLY
WESTERLY SUN
56 Main St.
Westerly, RI 02891
(401) 596-7791
Music Editor: George H. Utter

SOUTH CAROLINA

ANDERSON
ANDERSON INDEPENDENT
ANDERSON MAIL
1000 Williamston Rd.
Anderson, SC 29622
(803) 224-4321
Entertainment Editor: Joanne Thrift

CHARLESTON
CHARLESTON EVENING POST
CHARLESTON NEWS & COURIER
134 Columbus St.
Charleston, SC 29402
(803) 577-7111
Music Critic: Claire McPhail

GREENVILLE
GREENVILLE NEWS
GREENVILLE PLEDMONT
PO Box 1688
Greenville, SC 29602
(803) 298-4457
Entertainment Editor: Diane Norman

GREENWOOD
GREENWOOD INDEX-JOURNAL
Phoenix & Fair Sts.
Greenwood, SC 29646
(803) 223-1411
Music Editor: Leslie Brooks

SOUTH DAKOTA

ABERDEEN
ABERDEEN AMERICAN NEWS
PO Box 4430
Aberdeen, SD 57401
(605) 225-4100
Music Editor: Mary Just Coomes

RAPID CITY
RAPID CITY JOURNAL
Box 450
Rapid City, SD 57709
(605) 342-0280
Music Critics: Ruth Brennan, Tim Gebhart

TENNESSEE

CHATTANOOGA
CHATTANOOGA NEWS-FREE PRESS
400 E. 11th St.
Chattanooga, TN 37401
(615) 756-6900
Entertainment Editor: June Hatcher

CHATTANOOGA TIMES
PO Box 951
Chattanooga, TN 37401
(615) 756-1234
Music Critic: Wesley M. Hasden

CLARKSVILLE
CLARKSVILLE LEAF CHRONICLE
PO Box 829
200 Commerce St.
Clarksville, TN 37040
(615) 552-1808
Music Editor: Max Moss

KNOXVILLE
KNOXVILLE JOURNAL
KNOXVILLE NEWS-SENTINEL
PO Box 911
Knoxville, TN 37901
(615) 522-4141
Entertainment Editor: Paul Carlton

MEMPHIS
MEMPHIS COMMERCIAL APPEAL
MEMPHIS PRESS-SCIMITAR
495 Union Ave.
Memphis, TN 38101
(901) 529-2798
Music Editors: Robert Jennings (Appeal); Jane Sanderson (Scimitar)

MURFREESBORO
MURFREESBORO DAILY NEWS-JOURNAL
224 N. Walnut St.
Murfreesboro, TN 37101
(615) 893-5860
Music Editor: Etta Worthington

NASHVILLE
NASHVILLE BANNER
1100 Broadway
Nashville, TN 37202
(615) 255-5401
Music Editor: Henry Arnold

TENNESSEAN
1100 Broadway
Nashville, TN 37202
(615) 255-1221
Music Editor: Walter Carter

OAK RIDGE
OAK RIDGER
101 W. Tyrone Rd.
Oak Ridge, TN 37830
(615) 482-1021
Entertainment Editor: Jonell Schmidt

TEXAS

ABILENE
ABILENE REPORTER-NEWS
PO Box 30
N. Second & Cypress Sts.
Abilene, TX 79603
(915) 673-4271
Entertainment Editor: William Whitaker

AMARILLO
AMARILLO DAILY NEWS
AMARILLO GLOBE-TIMES
900 Harrison St.
Amarillo, TX 79105
(806) 376-4488
Music Editor: Bette Thompson

AUSTIN
AUSTIN AMERICAN
AUSTIN STATESMAN
308 Guadalupe St.
Austin, TX 78767
(512) 397-1285
Music Critic: Patrick Taggart

BEAUMONT
BEAUMONT ENTERPRISE
BEAUMONT JOURNAL
PO Box 3071
380 Walnut St.
Beaumont, TX 77704
(713) 833-3311
Music Editor: Lela Davis

DALLAS
DALLAS MORNING NEWS
Communications Center
Dallas, TX 75202
(214) 745-8222
Music Editor: John Ardoin

DALLAS TIMES-HERALD
1101 Pacific Ave.
Dallas, TX 75202
(214) 744-6111
Music Editor: Olin Chism

EL PASO
EL PASO HERALD-POST
PO Box 20
El Paso, TX 79999
(915) 546-6349
Arts Editor: Betty Ligon

FORT WORTH
FORT WORTH STAR-TELEGRAM
400 W. 7th St.
Fort Worth, TX 76102
(817) 390-7684
Music Editor: Michael Fleming

HOUSTON
HOUSTON CHRONICLE
801 Texas St.
Houston, TX 77002
(713) 220-7171
Music Editor: Ann Holmes

LONGVIEW
LONGVIEW JOURNAL
LONGVIEW NEWS
PO Box 1792
Longview, TX 75601
(214) 757-3311
Music Editor: Delores Brown

LUBBOCK
LUBBOCK AVALANCHE-JOURNAL
PO Box 491
Lubbock, TX 79408
(806) 762-8844
Music Editor: Bill Kerns

ODESSA
ODESSA AMERICAN
Box 2952
Odessa, TX 79760
(915) 337-4661
Music Editor: Alice Bertheisen

PORT ARTHUR
PORT ARTHUR NEWS
COMMUNITY NEWS
PO Box 789
549 Fourth St.
Port Arthur, TX 77640
(713) 985-5541
Music Editor: Denny Angelle

SAN ANGELO
SAN ANGELO STANDARD-TIMES
34 W. Harris St.
San Angelo, TX 76902
(915) 653-1221
Music Editor: Kandis S. Gatewood

SAN ANTONIO
SAN ANTONIO EXPRESS
SAN ANTONIO EXPRESS-NEWS
PO Box 2171
San Antonio, TX 78297
(512) 225-7411
Music Critics: David Richelieu (Express); Mike Greenberg (News)

SAN ANTONIO LIGHT
420 Broadway
San Antonio, TX 78205
(512) 226-4271
Entertainment Editor: Elizabeth McIlhaney

TYLER
TYLER COURIER-TIMES
TYLER TELEGRAPH
PO Box 1020
Tyler, TX 75701
(214) 597-9811
Music Editor: Dot Adkins

WACO
WACO TRIBUNE-HERALD
900 Franklin Ave.
Waco, TX 76703
(817) 753-1511
Music Editor: Bob Darden

WICHITA FALLS
WICHITA FALLS RECORD-NEWS
WICHITA FALLS TIMES
1301 Lamar St.
Wichita Falls, TX 76307
(817) 767-8341
Music Critic: Martha B. Steimel

UTAH

OGDEN
OGDEN STANDARD-EXAMINER
Box 951
Ogden, UT 84401
(801) 394-7711
Music Editor: Don Rosebrock

PROVO
PROVO DAILY HERALD
1555 N. 200th W.
Provo, UT 84601
(801) 373-5050
Music Editor: Charlene Winters

SALT LAKE CITY
DESERT NEWS
30 E. First S.
Salt Lake City, UT 84111
(801) 237-2147
Music Critic: William S. Goodfellow

SALT LAKE TRIBUNE
PO Box 867
Salt Lake City, UT 84110
(801) 237-2078
Music Critic: Paul Wetzel

VERMONT

BENNINGTON
BENNINGTON BANNER
425 Main St.
Bennington, VT 05201
(802) 477-7567
Arts Editor: David Clayton

WHITE RIVER JUNCTION
VALLEY NEWS
PO Box 877
White River Junction, VT 05001
(603) 298-8711
Entertainment Editor: Terri Dudley

VIRGINIA

ALEXANDRIA
ALEXANDRIA GAZETTE
717 N. Asaph St.
Alexandria, VA 22314
(703) 549-0004
Music Editor: Cathy Perkins

LYNCHBURG
LYNCHBURG NEWS & DAILY ADVANCE
PO Box 10129
Lynchburg, VA 24506
(804) 237-2941
Entertainment Editor: Kathy Kirby

NEWPORT NEWS
NEWPORT NEWS-HAMPTON DAILY PRESS
NEWPORT NEWS-HAMPTON TIMES-HERALD
7505 Warwick Blvd.
Newport News, VA 23607
(804) 244-8421
Music Editors: Joan Johnston (Press); Joe West (Herald)

NORFOLK
NORFOLK LEDGER-STAR
150 W. Brambleton Ave.
Norfolk, VA 23501
(804) 446-2298
Music Editor: Lynn Feigenbaum

RICHMOND
RICHMOND NEWS-LEADER
RICHMOND TIMES-DISPATCH
PO Box C-32333
Richmond, VA 23293
(804) 649-6000
Music Critic: Francis Church (News Leader)
Music Editor: Clarke Bustardil (Dispatch)

ROANOKE
ROANOKE TIMES & WORLD NEWS
201-209 W. Campbell Ave.
Roanoke, VA 24010
(703) 981-3000
Feature Editor: Sandra Kelly

WASHINGTON

ABERDEEN
ABERDEEN DAILY WORLD
PO Box 269
315 S. Michigan Ave.
Aberdeen, WA 98520
(206) 532-4000
Music Editor: Betty Butler

EVERETT
EVERETT HERALD
EVERETT WESTERN SUN
PO Box 930
Everett, WA 98206
(206) 339-3000
Music Critic: Eugene Smith

SEATTLE
SEATTLE POST-INTELLIGENCER
521 Wall St.
Seattle, WA 98111
(206) 628-8396
Music Critic: R.M. Campbell

SEATTLE TIMES
PO Box 70
Fairview Ave. N. & John St.
Seattle, WA 98111
(206) 464-2321
Entertainment Editor: Judy Thorne

SPOKANE
SPOKANE CHRONICLE
926 W. Sprague St.
Spokane, WA 99204
(509) 455-7131
Music Critic: Jennifer Williamson

SPOKANE SPOKESMAN-REVIEW
927 W. Riverside Ave.
Spokane, WA 99210
(509) 455-6990
Music Critic: Travis Rivers

VANCOUVER
VANCOUVER COLUMBIAN
701 W. 8th St.
Vancouver, WA 98860
(206) 694-3391
Music Editor: David Jewett

WEST VIRGINIA

HUNTINGTON
HUNTINGTON HERALD-DISPATCH
PO Box 2017
Huntington, WV 25720
(304) 696-5784
Entertainment Editor: Jim Ware

PARKERSBURG
PARKERSBURG NEWS
PARKERSBURG SENTINEL
519 Juliana St.
Parkersburg, WV 26101
(304) 485-1891
Music Editor: Richard Suter

WISCONSIN

APPLETON
APPLETON POST-CRESCENT
306 W. Washington St.
Appleton, WI 54911
(414) 733-4411
Music Editor: John W. Miner

GREEN BAY
GREEN BAY PRESS-GAZETTE
435 E. Walnut St.
Green Bay, WI 54305
(414) 435-4411
Music Critic: Warren Gerds

KENOSHA
KENOSHA NEWS
715 58th St.
Kenosha, WI 53140
(414) 657-1000
Music Editor: Elaine Edwards

LA CROSSE
LA CROSSE TRIBUNE
401 N. Third St.
La Crosse, WI 54601
(608) 782-9710
Music Editor: Ken Brekke

MADISON
CAPITAL TIMES
PO Box 8060
Madison, WI 53708
(608) 252-6481
Music Critic: Walt Trott

WISCONSIN STATE JOURNAL
PO Box 8058
Madison, WI 53708
(608) 252-6182
Music Editor: Carmen Elsner

MILWAUKEE
MILWAUKEE JOURNAL
333 W. State St.
Milwaukee, WI 53201
(414) 224-2369
Music Critic: Roxanne Orgili

MILWAUKEE SENTINEL
918 N. Fourth St.
Milwaukee, WI 53201
(414) 224-2269
Music Critic: Lawrence B. Johnson

RACINE

RACINE JOURNAL-TIMES
212 Fourth St.
Racine, WI 53403
(414) 634-3322
Music Critic: Chris Boultinghouse

WAUSAU

WAUSAU-MERRILL DAILY HERALD
800 Scott St.
Wausau, WI 55401
(715) 842-2101
Music Editor: Jaime Orcutt

WYOMING

CASPER

CASPER STAR-TRIBUNE
170 Star Ln.
Casper, WY 82601
(307) 266-0587
Music Editor: Clayton S. Clark

CHEYENNE

WYOMING EAGLE
WYOMING STATE TRIBUNE
110 E. 17th St.
Casper, WY 82001
(307) 634-3361
Music Critic: Kerry Drake

WORLAND

NORTHERN WYOMING DAILY NEWS
723 Robertson Ave.
Worland, WY 82401
(307) 347-3241
Music Editor: Hugh K. Knoefel

CANADA

ALBERTA

CALGARY

CALGARY HERALD
215 16th St., SE
Calgary, AB T2P OW8
(403) 235-7589
Music Critic: Roman Cooney

CALGARY SUN
830 10th Ave., SW
Calgara, AB T2R 0B1
(403) 263-7730
Entertainment Editor: James Muretich

EDMONTON

EDMONTON JOURNAL
Box 2421
Edmonton, AB T5J 2S6
(403) 420-1919
Music Critics: Clayton Lee, Alan Kellogg

EDMONTON SUN
9405 50th St.
Edmonton, AB T6B 2T4
(403) 468-5111
Music Critic: John Charles

LETHBRIDGE

LETHBRIDGE HERALD
504 Seventh St., S.
Lethbridge, AB T1J 3Z7
(403) 328-4411
Entertainment Editor: Al Scarth

BRITISH COLUMBIA

NEW WESTMINSTER

THE COLUMBIAN
PO Box 730
New Westminster, BC V3L 4Z7
(604) 521-2622
Music Editor: N. Graham

VANCOUVER

VANCOUVER PROVINCE
VANCOUVER SUN
2250 Granville St.
Vancouver, BC V6H 3G2
(604) 732-2497/2410
Music Critics: Ray Chatelin (Province); Lloyd Dyck (Sun)

NEW BRUNSWICK

ST. JOHN

ST. JOHN TELEGRAPH-JOURNAL
ST. JOHN EVENING TIMES-GLOBE
Crown & Union Sts.
St. John, NB E2L 3V8
(506) 657-1230
Music Editor: Helmer Biermann

NEWFOUNDLAND

ST. JOHN'S

ST. JOHN'S EVENING TELEGRAM
PO Box 5970
St. John's, NF A1C 5X7
(709) 364-6300
Music Editor: Sean Finlay

ONTARIO

CHATHAM

CHATHAM DAILY NEWS
PO Box 2007
Chatham, ON N7M 5M6
(519) 354-2000
Music Editor: Wayne Smith

GUELPH

GUELPH DAILY MERCURY
8-14 Macdonnell St.
Guelph, ON N1H 6P7
(519) 822-4310
Music Editor: Gerald Manning

KITCHENER

KITCHENER-WATERLOO RECORD
225 Fairway Rd.
Kitchener, ON N2G 4E5
(519) 894-2231
Music Critics: Pauline Durichen, John Kiely

LONDON

LONDON FREE PRESS
369 York St.
London, ON N6A 4G1
(519) 679-0230
Entertainment Editor: M.F. Mulhern

OSHAWA

OSHAWA TIMES
44 Richmond St., W.
Oshawa, ON L1G 1C8
(416) 723-3474
Music Critic: George Kaufman

OTTAWA

OTTAWA CITIZEN
1101 Baxter Rd.
Ottawa, ON K2C 3M4
(613) 829-9100
Music Critic: Jacob Siskind

OTTAWA LE DROIT
375 Rue Rideau
Ottawa, ON K1N 5Y7
(613) 560-2711
Music Critic: Jean Jacques Van Vlasselaer

SARNIA

SARNIA OBSERVER
140 S. Front St.
Sarnia, ON N7T 7M8
(519) 344-3641
Music Editor: S. Little

ST. CATHARINES

ST. CATHARINES STANDARD
17 Queen St.
St. Catharines, ON L2R 5G5
(416) 684-7251
Entertainment Editor: Lorraine LePage

TORONTO

TORONTO GLOBE & MAIL
444 Front St., W.
Toronto, ON M5V 2S9
(416) 598-5000
Music Editors: John Kraglund, Paul McGrath

TORONTO STAR
1 Yonge St.
Toronto, ON M5E 1E6
(416) 367-2000
Music Critic: William Littler

TORONTO SUN
333 King St., E.
Toronto, ON M5A 3X5
(416) 868-2222
Music Editor: Wilder Penfield III

WINDSOR

WINDSOR STAR

167 Ferry St.
Windsor, ON N9A 4M5
(519) 256-5533
Music Critics: Harry van Vugt, John Laycock

QUEBEC

MONTREAL

MONTREAL LE DEVOIR
211 Rue du St. Sacrement
Montreal, PQ H2Y 1X1
(514) 844-3361
Music Critic: Gilles Potvin

MONTREAL DIMANCHE MONTREAL DERNIERE HEURE
5699 Rue du Christophe Colomb
Montreal, PQ H2S 2E8
(514) 273-8336
Music Editor: Jean Laurac

MONTREAL GAZETTE
250 St. Antoine St., SW
Montreal, PQ H2Y 3R7
(514) 282-2222
Music Critic: Eric McLean

LE JOURNAL DE MONTREAL
155 Port Royal W.
Montreal, PQ H3L 2B1
(514) 382-8800
Music Critic: Manon Guilbert

MONTREAL LA PRESSE
7 St. Jacques St.
Montreal, PQ H2Y 1K9
(514) 285-7272
Music Editor: Claude Gingras

QUEBEC CITY

QUEBEC CITY LE SOLEIL
390 Rue St. Vallier E.
Quebec, PQ G1K 7J6
(418) 647-3400
Music Editor: Marc Samson

SHERBROOKE

SHERBROOKE LA TRIBUNE
1950 Roy St.
Sherbrooke, PQ J1K 2X8
(819) 569-9201
Music Editor: Pierrette Roy

TROIS RIVIERES

TROIS RIVIERES LE NOUVEILLSTE
500 St. Georges St.
Trois Rivieres, PQ G9A 5J6
(819) 376-2501
Music Editor: Andre Gaudreault

SASKATCHEWAN

REGINA

REGINA LEADER-POST
1964 Park St.
Regina, SK
(306) 565-8211
Music Critic: Denise Ball

Newspaper Music Editors and Critics Index

A

B

C

Q

R

S

T

U

V

W

Y

Volunteer Lawyers for the Arts

Affiliated chapters of Volunteer Lawyers for the Arts (VLA) are listed alphabetically by state. VLA provides free legal services and counseling to artists and arts organizations meeting specific eligibility requirements. This list was compiled by freelance writer Jerome Richard, and is reprinted by permission.

ALASKA

ARTSLAW REFERRAL SERVICE
Anchorage Arts Council
402 W. 3rd Ave., #7 Sunshine Plaza
Anchorage, AK 99501
Contact: Jim Murphy

CALIFORNIA

SAN DIEGO LAWYERS FOR THE ARTS
7730 Herschel Ave., Ste. A
La Jolla, CA 92037
(714) 454-9696
Contact: Peter Karlen

LOS ANGELES LAWYERS FOR THE ARTS
617 S. Olive St.
Los Angeles, CA 90014
(213) 688-7404
Contact: Frank Cox

BAY AREA LAWYERS FOR THE ARTS
Fort Mason Center, Bldg. 310
San Francisco, CA 94123
(415) 775-7200
Contact: Alma Robinson

COLORADO

COLORADO LAWYERS FOR THE ARTS
770 Pennsylvania St.
Denver, CO 80203
(303) 866-2617
Contact: Ms. Raule Nemer

CONNECTICUT

CONNECTICUT COMMISSION ON THE ARTS
340 Capitol Ave.
Hartford, CT 06106
(203) 566-4770
Contact: T.J. Norris

DISTRICT OF COLUMBIA MARYLAND

LAWYERS COMMITTEE FOR THE ARTS
2700 Q St. NW, Ste. 204
Washington DC 20007
(202) 483-6777
Contact: Joshua Kaufman

FLORIDA

BROWARD ARTS COUNCIL
Cultural Arts Div.
236 SE 1st Ave.
Ft. Lauderdale, FL 33301
(305) 765-8443
Contact: Bobbie Kane/Robert Garrett

GAINESVILLE DIVISION OF CULTURAL AFFAIRS
Box 490, Drop 30
Gainesville, FL 32602
(904) 374-2250
Contact: Dr. Lemuel Moore, III

JEFFREY D. DUNN
940 Atlantic National Bank Bldg.
Jacksonville, FL 32202
(904) 353-6440

THOMAS R. POST
25 W. Flagler St.. #1011
Miami, FL 33130
(305) 379-7661

VOLUNTEER LAWYERS FOR THE ARTS
Council of Arts & Sciences
200 S. Miami Ave., Ste. 281
Miami, FL 33130
(305) 579-4634

ARTS COUNCIL OF TAMPA-HILLSBOROUGH
1420 N. Tampa St.
Tampa, FL 33602
(813) 229-6547
Contact: Earl Schreiber

GEORGIA

GEORGIA VOLUNTEER LAWYERS FOR THE ARTS
32 Peachtree St. NW
Atlanta, GA 30303
(404) 577-7378
Contact: John Eaton

ILLINOIS

LAWYERS FOR THE CREATIVE ARTS
220 S. State St.
Chicago, IL 60604
(312) 987-0198
Contact: Clarice Hearne

IOWA

BARRY LINDAHL
491 W. 4th St., Box 741
Dubuque, IA 52201
(319) 556-8552

KENTUCKY

LEXINGTON COUNCIL OF THE ARTS
161 N. Mill St.
Lexington, KY 40507
(606) 255-2951
Contact: Peter A. Reynolds

PROFESSIONAL SERVICES TO THE ARTS
444 S. 3rd. St.
Louisville, KY 40202
(502) 582-1821
Contact: Catherine Ashabraner

MASSACHUSETTS

LAWYERS FOR THE ARTS
Artists Foundation
110 Broad St.
Boston, MA 02110
(617) 482-8100
Contact: Michelle Schofield

MINNESOTA

FREDERICK T. ROSENBLATT
1200 National City Bank Bldg.
Minneapolis, MN 55402
(612) 339-1200

MISSOURI

ST. LOUIS VOLUNTEER LAWYERS FOR THE ARTS
St. Louis University School of Law
3700 Lindell
St. Louis MO 63108
(314) 658-2778

NEW YORK

ALBANY LEAGUE OF THE ARTS
19 Clinton St.
Albany, NY 12207
(518) 449-5380
Contact: Margaret Lanoue

ARTS DEVELOPMENT SERVICES
237 Main St.
Buffalo, NY 14203
(716) 856-7520
Contact: Paulette Counts/Gracia Ginther

HUNTINGTON AREA ARTS COUNCIL
12 New St.
Huntington, NY 11743
(516) 271-8423
Contact: Cindy Kiebitz

VOLUNTEER LAWYERS FOR THE ARTS
1560 Broadway, Ste. 711
New York, NY 10036
(212) 575-1150
Contact: Arlene Shuler

DUTCHESS COUNTY ARTS COUNCIL
24 Vassar St.
Poughkeepsie, NY 12601
(914) 454-3222
Contact: Diane Martuscello

ARTS FOR GREATER ROCHESTER
930 East Ave.
Rochester, NY 14607
(716) 442-0570
Contact: Sesta Peekstok

CIVIC CENTER
411 Montgomery St.
Syracuse, NY 13202
(315) 425-2155
Contact: Carol Jeschke

NORTH CAROLINA

NORTH CAROLINA ASSOCIATION FOR ART-LAW EDUCATION
Box 2851
Chapel Hill, NC 27514
(919) 967-8989
Contact: Susan Lewis

DOUGLAS A. JOHNSTON
State of N. Carolina
Dept. of Justice
Box 629
Raleigh, NC 27602
(919) 733-6026

OHIO

ARNOLD GOTTLIEB
421 N. Michigan St.
Toledo, OH 43624
(419) 243-3125

OREGON

LEWIS & CLARK COLLEGE
Northwestern School of Law
Portland, OR 97219
(503) 244-1181
Contact: Prof. Leonard Duboff/ Melissa Michelle

PENNSYLVANIA

PHILADELPHIA VOLUNTEER LAWYERS FOR THE ARTS
260 S. Broad St.
Broad & Spruce Sts.
Philadelphia, PA 19102
(215) 545-3385

RHODE ISLAND

LAWYERS REFERRAL SERVICE
Rhode Island Bar Assoc.
1804 Industrial Bank Bldg.
Providence, RI 02903
(401) 421-7799
Contact: Sharon Diangeles

SOUTH CAROLINA

SOUTH CAROLINA VOLUNTEER LAWYERS FOR THE ARTS
Box 10084
Greenville, SC 29603
(803) 242-6624
Contact: C. Diane Smock

TEXAS

JAY M. VOGELSON
2400 One Dallas Center
Dallas, TX 75201
(214) 651-1721

VOLUNTEER LAWYERS & ACCOUNTANTS FOR THE ARTS
1540 Sul Ross
Houston, TX 77006
(713) 526-4876
Contact: Karen Leback

UTAH

MELVIN G. LAREW, JR.
175 Southwest Temple, #500
Salt Lake City, UT 84101
(801) 943-6809

WASHINGTON

WASHINGTON VOLUNTEER LAWYERS FOR THE ARTS
University of Puget Sound Law School
950 Broadway
Tacoma, WA 98402
(206) 627-5580
Contact: Barbara Hoffman

Booking Agents

U.S. and Canadian booking agents and agencies are listed alphabetically by state or province and city. The symbols * and † following a firm's name indicate membership.

- * Member of International Theatrical Agencies Association (ITAA)
- † Licensed member of American Federation of Musicians (AFM)

An alphabetical cross-index appears at the end of this section.

ALABAMA

BIRMINGHAM

ACT I BOOKING AGENCY†
546 Bessemer Super Hwy.
Birmingham AL 35228
(205) 923-1444
Contact: Edmond Leon Bowers

ASCOT TALENT AGENCY†
2400 Savoy St.
Birmingham, AL 35226
(205) 823-2863
Contact: Ruth E. Huey, Jim Costello, C.E. Huey, Sr.

ARIZONA

MESA

AXTZ INTERNATIONAL*
P.O. Box 4603
Mesa, AZ 85201
(602) 968-6145
Contact: Mark Anderson

PHOENIX

BOBBY BALL AGENCY†
808 East Osborn
Phoenix, AZ 85014
(602) 264-5007
Contact: Roberta H. Ball, *aka* Bobby Ball, John F. Ball, Edna Scott, Nancy H. Thomas

CHUCK EDDY AND ASSOCIATES†
4326 E. Yawepe
Phoenix, AZ 85044
(602) 893-3093
Contact: Chuck Eddy, Julianne M. Eddy, Charles B. Eddy, Julianne A. Eddy, Michelene Eddy

BOB MCGREW ASSOCIATES†
4319 E. Buena Terra Way
Phoenix, AZ 85018
(602) 959-8111
Contact: Barrie H. McGrew

PANACEA PRODUCTIONS, INC.†
2344 West Weldon
Phoenix, AZ 85015
(602) 279-3460
Contact: Mary Bishop, Phil Paul

SOUTHWEST BOOKING AGENCY, INC.†
100 West Clarendon, Ste. 2224
Phoenix, AZ 85013
(602) 277-3368; (602) 263-8067
Contact: Tommy Reed, Mary Lou Reed, Ray Starling, Ross E. (Skip) LeCompte, Lou Garno

TOR/ANN TALENT AND BOOKING AGENCY†
6711 North 21st Way
Phoenix, AZ 85016
(605) 263-8708
Contact: Mrs. Toni Rami Anthony

PAT TRAPANI AND ASSOCIATES†
2601 East Turney
Phoenix, AZ 85016
(602) 956-2296
Contact: Patrick D. Trapani

SCOTTSDALE

BOROS BOOKING AGENCY†
7074 East Aster Drive
Scottsdale, AZ 85254
(602) 948-5307
Contact: Leslie A. Boros

JAY DAVID MUSIC BOOKING AGENCY†
6125 E. Delcoa Ave.
Scottsdale, AZ 85253
(602) 991-6716
Contact: Jay David, Anna D. David

J. MICHAEL DUNHAM & ASSOCIATES, LTD.*
6716 E. North Lane
Scottsdale, AZ 85252
(602) 948-9642
Contact: Michael Dunham

ENTERTAINERS UNLIMITED†
8743 East Arlington Rd.
Scottsdale, AZ 85253
(602) 945-9440
Contact: Raymond Michael Rice, David L. Harris

SELECT ARTISTS ASSOCIATES*†
7300 E. Camelback Rd.
Scottsdale, AZ 85251
(601) 994-0471
Contact: Charles Johnston, Don Pogrant, Mark Marini

YOUNGTOWN

WILLIS LARRY LEWIS†
11125 Oregon Ave.
Youngtown, AZ 85363
(602) 974-4907
Contact: Willis Larry Lewis

ARKANSAS

LITTLE ROCK

RICK CALHOUN & ASSOCIATES†
305 East 16th Street
Little Rock, AR 72202
(501) 374-2376
Contact: Julie Calhoun

KALEIDOSCOPE ARTIST MANAGEMENT & THEATRICAL AGENCY†
Town & Country Shopping Center
P.O. Box 9554
Little Rock, AR 72219
1-(501) 562-1641
Contact: William W. Ferguson, Jr., Loretta J. Ferguson, George Parchman, David A. Deaton

RUSSELLVILLE

J.W. UTLEY†
201 N. Cumberland Ave.
Russellville, AR 72801
(501) 968-1538

CALIFORNIA

ANAHEIM

BERNIE BERNARD†
1237 Crestbrook Place
Anaheim, CA 92805
(714) 535-5504
Contact: Jack Hampton

SYD LEWIS AGENCY†
P.O. Box 970
Anaheim, CA 92805
(714) 538-0606

ROCSHIRE PRODUCTION, INC.†
4091 E. La Palma #S
Anaheim, CA 92803
(714) 632-6660
Contact: Clyde L. Davis, Shirley J. Lindsey

APPLE VALLEY

CURLY WIGGINS TALENT AGENCY†
20212 Monte Vista Road
Apple Valley, CA 92307
(714) 247-6520
Contact: M.J. "Curly" Wiggins, Noel Laursen, Richard A. Gaione, Frank Monte, Nick Dewald

BAKERSFIELD

JIMMIE ADDINGTON ENTERPRISE†
3650 Rosedale Highway
Bakersfield, CA 93308
(805) 323-0541
Contact: Robert James Addington, Robert Gonzales

BEVERLY HILLS

ASSOCIATED BOOKING CORPORATION (NY)†
Branch Office:
292 S. LaCienega Blvd., Ste. 316
Beverly Hills, CA 90211
(213) 855-8051
Contact: Tony Papa, Billy McDonald, Tom Jones

DAVID BENDETT AGENCY, INC.†
2431 Briarcrest Road
Beverly Hills, CA 90210
(213) 278-5657

THE CAROL FAITH AGENCY†
280 S. Beverly Dr., Ste. 411
Beverly Hills, CA 90212
(213) 274-0776
Contact: Carol Faith

THE JACK HAMPTON AGENCY†
226 S. Beverly Dr.
Beverly Hills, CA 90212
(213) 274-6075
Contact: Jack Hampton, Vicki R. Johnson

THE ROBERT LIGHT AGENCY†
8920 Wilshire Boulevard, Ste. 438
Beverly Hills, CA 90211
(213) 659-3333
Contact: Robert W. Light, Sr.

WILLIAM MORRIS AGENCY, INC.(NY)†
Branch Office:
151 El Camino
Beverly Hills, CA 90212
(213) 274-7451
Contact: Rober Davis, Morris Stoller, Sam Weisbord, Walter Zifkin, Tony Frantozzi, Dick Alen, Larry Auerback, Marty Beck, Norman Brokaw, Ruth Englehardt, Stanley Kamen, Abe Lastfogel, Fred Moch, Joe Rivkin, Peter Sheils, Carol Sidlow, Tome Illius, Sol Leon, Mike Zimring, Ronald Russom, Hal Ray, Jay Jacobs, Robyn S. Goldman, Jeffrey P. Kuklin, Ronald A. Kaye, Gary Lucchesi

RAPER ENTERPRISES AGENCY†
9441 Wilshire Blvd.
Suite 620-D
Beverly Hills, CA 90212
(213) 273-7704
Contact: H. Leon Raper

BUENA PARK

HOUSE OF TALENT, TALENT AGENCY†
6305 Manchester Blvd.
Buena Park, CA 90621
(714) 739-0406
Contact: Carl B. Cotner

CALABASAS

GEORGE SOARES ASSOCIATES(NV)†
Branch Office:
26060 Adamor Rd.
Calabasas, CA 91302
(213) 880-5757
Contact: Roy Baumgart

CAMARILLO

VAMP TALENT AGENCY†
713 E. La Loma Ave., Office "I"
Camarillo, CA 93010
(805) 485-2001
Contact: Vivienne Principe, Antoinette McDevitt

CARLSBAD

JON D. MCGUFFIN TALENT AGENCY†
2541 State St.
Carlsbad, CA 92008
(714) 729-4078
Contact: Jon D. McGuffin

CARMEL

CALIFORNIA BOOKING AND MANAGEMENT†
P.O. Box 3801
Carmel, CA 93921
(408) 625-3801
Contact: Paul E. Lippman, James Jenkins, Mary Jenkins, Stephen Barkley, Michael Skopes, Larry Vargo

Branch Office:
8831 Sunset Blvd., Ste. 202
Hollywood, CA 90069
(213) 659-9674
Contact: Robert Brondell, Steve Johnson

MONTEREY PENINSULA ARTISTS†
P.O. Box 7308
Carmel, CA 93921
(408) 624-4889
Contact: Daniel Weiner, Fred Bohlander, Paul Goldman

CHATSWORTH

AZTEC PRODUCTIONS†
20531 Plummer Street
Chatsworth, CA 91311
(213) 998-0443
Contact: Archie E. Sullivan

CHULA VISTA

AILEEN'S TALENT & TRAVEL AGENCY†
210 Third Ave.
Chula Vista, CA 92010
(714) 425-1812
Contact: Aileen Hernandez Montelongo

CLOVIS

SAM ROBINSON ENTERTAINMENT†
7283 N. DeWolf
Clovis, CA 93612
(209) 298-7886
Contact: Sammy Tyner Robinson

COMPTON

JOHNNY POPE, JR.†
102 No. Poincettia Ave., Ste. 206
Compton, CA 90221
(213) 979-7424

COSTA MESA

STAR PRODUCTIONS TALENT AGENCY†
695 Town Center Drive, #800
Costa Mesa, CA 92626
(714) 549-7028
Contact: Bob Lemon, Dean Richards, Ted Dean Lee

CYPRESS

BREE TALENT AGENCY†
10292 Aurelia
Cypress, CA 90630
(714) 761-4750
Contact: Rose Marie L. Bree

GOOD COMPANY MUSIC PRODUCTIONS, ARTISTS' MGR.†
5400 Orange Ave., Ste. 126
Cypress, CA 90630
(714) 827-0889
Contact: Richard A. Corsino, Genevieve L. Corsino

ENCINO

AMERICAN MANAGEMENT†
17530 Ventura Blvd., Ste. 108
Encino, CA 91316
(213) 981-6500
Contact: Jim Wagner

GEORGE MICHAUD†
4950 Densmore, Ste. 1
Encino, CA 91436
(213) 981-6680
Contact: Lloyd Lindroth, Jean Padden, Frank W. Waldeck

FRESNO

M. HARRIS AGENCY†

611 E. Belmont
Fresno, CA 93701
(209) 486-0781
Contact: Marjorie A. Harris-Henry

HEATH & CUNNING ASSOCIATES, INC.†
1121 Chance Ave.
Fresno, CA 93702
(209) 251-1478
Contact: Dannion Cunning, Leslie Heath, Leslie Cunning, Rick Fatland

SUN WEST ENTERTAINMENT†
4921 E. Tulare St.
Fresno, CA 93727
(209) 252-9417
Contact: John Anthony Dutra, Janice L. Baleme, Randy Marks, Daren Baleme

WHITE TREE ARTIST MANAGEMENT†
827 East Fairmont
Fresno, CA 93704
(209) 229-9588
Contact: Dennis Ottenbacher

FULLERTON

MIKE MILLER AGENCY†
255 E. Chapman, Ste. 315
Fullerton, CA 92631
(714) 992-6860

HOLLYWOOD

BUDDY ALTONI ESQUIRE, INC.
(See Newport Beach listing)

ARTIST TALENT AGENCY OF HOLLYWOOD†
P.O. Box 418
Hollywood, CA 90028
(213) 462-4152
Contact: Mildred L. Banks, Buddy Banks

AVALON PRODUCTIONS†
1588 Crossroads of the World
Hollywood, CA 90028
(213) 463-3138
Contact: Rrichard A. Waterman, Jeffrey E. Hersh

CALIFORNIA BOOKING AND MANAGEMENT
(See Carmel listing)

LIL CUMBER ATTRACTIONS AGENCY†
6515 Sunset Blvd., Ste. 300A
Hollywood, CA 90028
(213) 469-1919
Contacts: Lillian Cumber, Wilton A. Clarke, Ellen Jones

THE DEVROE AGENCY†
2700 Cahuenga Blvd., E., Ste. 1102
Hollywood, CA 90068
(213) 666-2666
Contact: Billy Devroe

WILLIAM FELBER & ASSOCIATES†
2126 Cahuenga Blvd.
Hollywood, CA 90068
(213) 466-7627
Contact: William Felber, Frank Lind, Larry Fonseca

MARKS ARTIST MANAGEMENT & TALENT AGENCY†
7033 Sunset Blvd., Ste. 309
Hollywood, CA 90028
(213) 463-8191
Contact: Bob Marks, Tony Tamburri, E. Aubrey Smith

Branch Office:
1779 S. Main #E
Irvine, CA 95713
(714) 549-7544
Contact: Bob Marks, Carolyn Williams, Jorge Armenta, E. Aubrey Smith

MCCONKEY ARTISTS CORPORATION*†
1822 N. Wilcox Ave.
Hollywood, CA 90028
(213) 463-7141
Contact: Gail McConkey, Ronnie Summers, Mack K. McConkey

SONNY MILLER AGENCY†
6223 Selma, Ste. 101-106
Hollywood, CA 90028
(213) 465-5868
Contact: Allia T. (Sonny) Miller

REDLINE TALENT AND BOOKING†
1525 North Formosa Ave.
Hollywood, CA 90046
(213) 851-8110
Contact: Mark R. Spencer Levy, Debbie Meister

LEW SHERRELL AGENCY LTD.†
7060 Hollywood Blvd.
Hollywood, CA 90028
(213) 461-9955
Contact: Lew Sherrell

TAPESTRY ARTISTS TALENT AGENCY†
1680 Vine St. #315
Hollywood, CA 90028
(213) 464-1438
Contact: Timothy Joseph Heyne, Ryan Douglas, Toni Grifasi

LEO WALKER AGENCY†
1680 Vine St., Ste. 1206
Hollywood, CA 90028
(213) 466-1498
Contact: Inez M. Walker

IRVINE

MARKS ARTIST MANAGEMENT & TALENT AGENCY
(See Hollywood listing)

TRIVISON & TROUT TALENT AGENCY†
4 Whitney
Irvine, CA 92714
(714) 559-6570
Contact: Michael D. Trout, James D. Trivison

LAFAYETTE

BETTE KAYE PRODUCTIONS, INC.
(See Sacramento listing)

LODI

A O K TALENT AGENCY†
25 N. Sunset Drive
Lodi, CA 95240
(209) 369-4344
Contact: Otto Kundert, Joyce Kundert

LONG BEACH

GREAT AMERICAN TALENT, INC.†
110 W. Ocean Blvd., Ste. 17
Long Beach, CA 90802
(213) 435-7051
Contact: James Summers, Burk Dennis, Ray Stayer

NORFLEET ENTERPRISES†
P.O. Box 5028
Long Beach, CA 90805
(213) 423-4394
Contact: Melvin R. Norfleet, Prysler Norfleet, Charles C. Guidry, Michael Norfleet, John Norfleet, Sr., Shirley Hughes

LOS ANGELES

AGENCY FOR THE PERFORMING ARTS(NY)†
Branch Office:
9000 Sunset Blvd., Ste. 315
Los Angeles, CA 90069
(213) 273-0744
Contact: John C. Gaines, Marty Klein, Fred Lawrence, Burt Taylor, Dick Gilmore, Danny Robinson, Bob Zievers

IRVIN ARTHUR ASSOCIATES, LTD.†
9200 Sunset Blvd., Ste. 621
Los Angeles, CA 90069
(213) 278-5934
Contact: Irving Arthur, Sondra Arthur, Bob Phillips

DIRECTION, ARTIST MANAGERS†
9200 Sunset Blvd., Ste. 418
Los Angeles, CA 90069
P.O. Box 2189
Hollywood, CA 90028
(213) 276-2063
Contact: Thomas Atkinson, Walter De La Brosse, Nicholas Bell, James Byron

ARTISTS'/HELLER AGENCY†
6430 Sunset Blvd., Ste. 1516
Los Angeles, CA 90028
(213) 462-1100
Contact: Jerry Heller, Alan Feldstein, Ken Holden

BART-MILANDER ASSOCIATES, INC.†
6671 Sunset Blvd., Ste. 1574
Los Angeles, CA 90028
(213) 658-5454
Contact: Alvin N. Bart, Stan Milander, Alexis C. Joseph

JOHN S. BUCK TALENT AGENCY†
6223 Selma Ave
Los Angeles, CA 90028
(213) 529-1443

DAIMLER ARTIST AGENCY†
2007 Wilshire Blvd. #808
Los Angeles, CA 90057
(213) 483-9783
Contact: Francis O. Matthews

D.L. ENTERPRISES, LTD.
(See Oceanside listing)

HARMONY ARTISTS, INC.†
8831 Sunset Blvd., Ste. 200
Los Angeles, CA 90069
(213) 659-9644
Contact: Michael Dixon, Jerold Ross, Tamara L. Caldwell

JOY HEALEY PRODUCTIONS, INC.†
8350 Santa Monica Boulevard
Los Angeles, CA 90069
(213) 654-3901
Contact: Joy Healey, Irene Healey, Mary Howe, Sharon Johnson, Amanda Richey

GEORGE B. HUNT & ASSOCIATES†
8350 Santa Monica Boulevard
Los Angeles, CA 90069
(213) 654-6600
Contact: Earlene Smith, Frank Konyi, Arlene W. Hunt, Phil Levant, Particia M. Doty

Branch Office:
1255 Post Street, Ste. 609
San Francisco, CA 94109
(415) 775-3155
Contact: Elizabeth Phillips

INTERNATIONAL CREATIVE MANAGEMENT(NY)†
Branch Office:
8899 Beverly Blvd.
Los Angeles, CA 90048
(213) 550-4000
Contact: William H. Maher, Gerald Saltzmann, Ben Benjamin, Michael Black, Barry Freed, Lee Gabler, Bonnie Sugarman, Hal Lazareff, Michael North, Thomas E. Ross, Jim Wiatt, John Marx, David J. Hansen, Elliott Kozak, Rich Ohlson

HOWARD KING AGENCY, INC.†
9060 Santa Monica Blvd., Ste. 104
Los Angeles, CA 90069
(213) 858-8408
Contact: Carol Gwenn

THE LANTZ OFFICE INC.(NY)†
Branch Office:
9255 Sunset Blvd
Los Angeles, Ca 90069
(213) 858-1144
Contact: Marion Rosenberg

JOHNNY LLOYD'S MANAGEMENT FIRM†
6381 Hollywood Blvd., Ste. 317
Los Angeles, CA 90028
(213) 464-2738
Contact: Johnny Lloyd

GILBERT MILLER AGENCY†
9000 Sunset Blvd., Ste. 504
Los Angeles, CA 90069
(213) 858-7196
Contact: Jeffrey Miller

PREMIERE ARTISTS & PRODUCTIONS AGENCY†
6399 Wilshire Boulevard
Los Angeles, CA 90048
(213) 651-3545
Contact: Harold Jovien, Ann Hilliard

REGENCY ARTISTS, LTD.†
9200 Sunset Blvd. #823
Los Angeles, CA 90069
(213) 273-7103
Contact: Richard Rosenberg, Peter L. Grosslight, Norton Brown, Frank Rio, Don Fischel, Roger Adams, Ben Bernstein, Gene Shore, David Snyder, Marshall Reznick, Alphonso White

HOWARD ROSE AGENCY, LTD.†
2029 Century Park East, Ste. 450
Los Angeles, CA 90067
(213) 277-3630
Contact: Stephen Smith

WILLIE R. THOMPSON TALENT AGENCY†
3902 W. 6th St., Ste. 213
Los Angeles, Ca 90020
(213) 380-0676

VARIETY ARTISTS INTERNATIONAL, INC.(MN)/EXCELSIOR TALENT†
(A Div. of Variety Artists International, Inc.)
Branch Office:
9000 Sunset Blvd., Ste. 911
Los Angeles, CA 90069
(213) 858-7800
Contact: Bob Engel, Richard W. Halem

LOS ALTOS

MAD MUSIC WORKS & TRADING CO. TALENT AGENCY†
268 Alicia Way
Los Altos, CA 94022
(415) 941-3418
Contact: Wynn Davis

LOS GATOS

SCORE IV†
(Division of Jim Lewis & Associates)
15720 Winchester Blvd.
Los Gatos, CA 95030
(408) 395-0640
Contact: Westin E. Lewis, Jr., aka Jim Lewis, Sandra L. Hall.

MANTECA

OMAC ARTIST CORPORATION
237 West Yosemite Avenue
Manteca, CA 95336
(209) 239-3333
Contact: Joe McFadden, Jack McFadden, Frank Plume

NEWPORT BEACH

BUDDY ALTONI ESQUIRE INC. ARTISTS' MANAGER†
3901 MacArthur Boulevard, Ste. 211
Newport Beach, CA 92660
(714) 851-1711
Contact: Altoni Lee, Gregory Wallace

Branch Office:
1680 No. Vine St., Ste. 1208
Hollywood, CA 90028
(213) 467-4939
Contact: Jackie Lynne

NORTH HOLLYWOOD

CASTLE-HILL ENTERPRISES†
11526 Burbank Boulevard, Ste. 3
North Hollywood, CA 91601
(213) 653-3535
Contact: Leigh Castle aka Lita D. Schloss

CORALIE JR. AGENCY†
4798 Vineland Ave.
North Hollywood, CA 91602
(213) 766-9501
Contact: Coralie Fitzharris Bryan

ENTERTAINMENT ASSOCIATES†
12125 Riverside Dr., Ste. 202
North Hollywood, CA 91607
(213) 980-7800
Contact: Stephen Bloch, John Janis

LONDON STAR PROMOTIONS†
10928 Magnolia Blvd.
North Hollywood, CA 91601
(213) 763-8102
Contact: Audrey Lerner, Lore London

ART RUSH, INC.†
10221 Riverside Drive, Ste. 219
North Hollywood, CA 91602
(213) 985-3033
Contact: William A. Rush, Mary Jo Rush, Mary Cave

ANN WAUGH TALENT AGENCY†
4731 Laurel Canyon Blvd. #5
North Hollywood, CA 91607
(213) 980-0141
Contact: Ann Waugh, Beverly Derby, Ed Nelson

NORTHRIDGE

RUTH BUTLER TALENT AGENCY†
8622 Reseda Blvd., Ste. 211
Northridge, CA 91324
(213) 886-8440

OAKLAND

AMBASSADOR MUSIC AGENCY†
P.O. Box 13272
Oakland, CA 94661
(415) 653-7007
Contact: Rodney J. Reed

DOROTHEA GRAY AGENCY†
1922 Montana St.
Oakland, CA 94602
(415) 531-3270

HAL MORRIS THEATRICAL ENTERPRISES AGENCY†
1440 Broadway, Rm. 600
Oakland, CA 94612
(415) 444-7213

WALT SJOBERG ENTERPRISES AGENCY†
600 16th St.
Oakland, CA 94612
(415) 834-6312

OCEANSIDE

D.L. ENTERPRISES, LTD.†
913 S. Hill Street, Ste. F
Oceanside, CA 92054
(714) 722-1795
Contact: Dennis P. Levinson, Joel Ferraro

Branch Office:
8330 West Third St.
Los Angeles, CA 90048
(213) 655-1296

PALMER ENTERPRISES†
913 S. Hill St., Ste. E
Oceanside, CA 92054
(714) 722-8266
Contact: Don Palmer, Donna Anderson, Jose E. Colon

PALM DESERT

GLORIA BECKER MUSIC†
73051 Guadalupe Avenue
Palm Desert, CA 92260
(714) 346-1285
Contact: Gloria Becker Shaver, James D. Shaver, Virginia DaSilva

PALM SPRINGS

TEX KIDWELL TALENT AGENCY†
1490 N. Palm Canyon Dr.
Palm Springs, CA 92262
(714) 325-1403
Contact: Tex Kidwell

PASADENA

BLAZING STAR TALENT AGENCY†
1489 E. Colorado, #204
Pasadena, CA 91106
(213) 681-6743
Contact: Timothy J. Shumaker

WALTER TRASK THEATRICAL AGENCY†
750 East Greet St., Ste. 305
Pasadena, CA 91101
(213) 795-7651

RESEDA

TRENDA ARTISTS†
18747 Sherman Way
Reseda, CA 91335
(213) 343-1266
Contact: Charles Trenda, Tony Trenda, Agens Trenda

SACRAMENTO

BETTE KAYE PRODUCTIONS, INC.†
2701 Cottage Way, #21
Sacramento, CA 95825
(916) 487-1923
Contact: Bette Kaye, Michelle Hughes, Charles (Kaye) Kappmeyer, Dennis Sacco, Sara Lee Weiser, Mary J. McConnell, Mike Vax, Jackie O'Dell

Branch Office:
928 21st St.
Santa Monica, CA 90402
(213) 395-0747
Contact: Leonard Moss

Branch Office:
3467 Monroe St.
Lafayette, CA 94549
(415) 284-5246
Contact: Mrs. Phyllis Parson, Terry Parsons, Lynn Parsons

SAN DIEGO

ALLIED BOOKING COMPANY TALENT AGENCY†
2321 Morena Blvd., Ste. J
San Diego, CA 92110
(714) 275-5030
Contact: Russell L. Melcher, Dorothy Ruth Melcher, Gary R. Evans, James L. Deacy, Frank E. Dito, Bob Banks

CROWN BOOKING SERVICE OF CALIFORNIA†
3543 Fifth Ave., Ste. C
San Diego, CA 92103
(714) 297-4067
Contact: Dorothy Gill, Walter M. Carlson, Gene Nelson

ERINI PRODUCTIONS†
4178 Adams Ave.
San Diego, CA 92116
(714) 284-1128
Contact: Irene Cantos, Earl Cantos, Jr., Cliff Asay

BILL GREEN'S MUSIC & ENTERTAINMENT AGENCY†
6322 Mission Gorge Road
San Diego, CA 92120
(714) 283-5443
Contact: Bill Green, Stuart Cooper, Jim Donahue

STAN JACOBS STAR PRODUCTIONS AGENCY†
2560 First Ave., #110
San Diego, CA 92103
(714) 233-1992
Contact: Jim Spellman

JEANNE JENNAY TALENT & ASSOCIATES†
Security Pacific Bank Bldg.
591 Camino de La Reina, Ste. 408
San Diego, CA 92108
(714) 291-0333

SAN FRANCISCO

GEORGE B.HUNT & ASSOCIATES
(See Los Angeles listing)

ROSEBUD MUSIC AGENCY†
P.O. Box 1897
San Francisco, CA 94101
(415) 566-7009
Contact: Robert M. Kappus, aka Michael Kappus, Lary Gene Youngsteadt

LAVONNE VALENTINE TALENT & MODELING AGENCY†
2113 Van Ness Avenue
San Francisco, CA 94109
(415) 673-7965

SAN JOSE

THE ENTERTAINMENT CONNECTION†
915 Meridian Ave., Ste. 107
San Jose, CA 95126
(408) 275-6325
Contact: Donald E. Owens

SAN MATEO

CONCERTO MUSIC AGENCY†
P.O. Box 933
San Mateo, CA 94403
(415) 341-2954
Contact: Al King

VINATIERI & ASSOCIATES*
1730 S. Amphlett Blvd., #314
San Mateo, CA 94402
(415) 574-5414
Contact; John Vinatieri

SANTA BARBARA

GLENN HENRY ENTERTAINMENT AGENCY†
55 South La Cumbre, Ste. 9
Santa Barbara, CA 93105
(805) 687-1131
Contact: Jerry Brown

SANTA MONICA

BETTE KAYE PRODUCTIONS, INC.
(See Sacramento listing)

SHERMAN OAKS

DELIDO ARTISTS AGENCY†
3240 Longridge Ave.
Sherman Oaks, CA 91423
P.O. Box 270
Hollywood, CA 90028
(213) 462-3559
Contact: Cecilia Brown

THE MUSIC OF IVAN LANE, INC†
13455 Ventura Blvd., Ste. 223
Sherman Oaks, CA 91423
(213) 501-2668
Contact: Ivan Lane

STUDIO CITY

F.A.M.E.†
4223 Vantage Ave.
Studio City, CA 91604
(213) 877-6461
Contact: Albert Lerner

PENNY MAYO AGENCY†
3763 Laurel Canyon Blvd.
Studio City, CA 91604
(213) 769-1133
Contact: Penny Mayo

MUS-ART CORPORATION*
12435 Ventura Court
Studio City, CA 91604
(213) 980-5900
Contact: Bob Vincent

TARZANA

THE CARR COMPANY†
P.O. Box U
Tarzana, CA 91356
(213) 705-2717
Contact: Budd Carr, Nancy Jean Carr

AL SHERMAN CELEBRITIES INC., THEATRICAL AGENCY†
19562 Ventura Blvd., #240
Tarzana, CA 91356
(213) 708-2044
Contact: Al Sherman

VAN NUYS

AIMEE ENTERTAINMENT ASSOCIATION†
13749 Victory Blvd.
Van Nuys, CA 91401
(213) 994-9354
Contact: Joyce Aimee, Allen W. Gildard, Larry K. Smith, David R. Azure

MARIS MANAGEMENT†
17620 Sherman Way #8
Van Nuys, CA 91406
(213) 708-2493
Contact: Stephen G. Mariscal

WALDON WEBB AGENCY†
13735 Victory Blvd.
Van Nuys, CA 91401
(213) 988-4331

VISALIA

CHUCK FAIRMAN TALENT AGENCY†
107 S. Church St., Ste. A
Visalia, CA 93291
(209) 733-2222
Contact: Charles Elma Fairman III

WOODLAND HILLS

AMERICANA CORPORATION†
P.O. Box 47
22500 Berdon
Woodland Hills, CA 91365
(213) 347-2976
Contact: Steve Stebbins, Robert P. Stebbins, A.K. Mitchell, Suzanne Hait

COCHRAN AGENCY†
P.O. Box 515 (91365)
22028 Ventura Blvd., Ste. 201
Woodland Hills, CA 91364
(213) 883-6950
Contact: Nadyne F. Cochran, Gil E. Robinson

COLORADO

ARVADA

NERO ENTERPRISES†
7709 Ralston Road
Arvada, CO 80002
(303) 425-0303
Contact: Anthony C. Streno, Scotty Rogers, Dave Sullivan, Tom Olsen

JAC WINROTH ASSOCIATES†
9170 W. 64th Ave.
Arvada, CO 80004
(303) 424-1314
Contact: Jane Winroth, Les Yoder, Pat Blake, Kerwyn Overy, Gary Hooper

COLORADO SPRINGS

MATTAS THEATRICAL AGENCY†
4615 Northpark Dr., Ste. 203
Colorado Spring, CO 80907
(303) 599-3533
Contact: Lucy M. Mattas, Daniel C. Mattas

DENVER

A.G.C. PRODUCTIONS, LTD.†
1441 Welton Street, #220
Denver, CO 80202
(303) 623-3454
Contact: Gay J. Columbe, Ruth E. Columbe, Bernar Schilt, Tippi Kelley, DeAnna White

AMERICAN MUSIC ENTERPRISES, INC. (AME)†
1602 So. Parker Rd., Ste. 305
Denver, CO 80218
(303) 696-6626
Contact: Sammy R. Mai, Karen Diekman, Brad Miller, Kenny Turner, Tony Rae Klumb, Matthew R. Cassidy

JACK BLUE AGENCY†
1554 Fairfax
Denver, CO 80220
(303) 333-4991
Contact: Diana Rollins, Dale Rollins

J.F. IMAGES, INC., TALENT AGENCY†
Southeast State Building, Ste. 700
3600 South Yosemite
Denver, CO 80237
(303) 779-8888
Contact: Mary J. Farrell, Annie Maloney, Dick Abel, Dianne Means, Frank Thorwald

MARY MITCHELL PRESENTS ENTERTAINMENT†
Rm. 350 Office Bldg.
1515 Cleveland Place
Denver, CO 80202
(303) 825-2069

THE TRIPLE AGENCY†
811 Lincoln St., Ste. 600
Denver, CO 80203
(303) 831-6379
Contact: Ronald M. Battles, Candi Magner

REED WILLIAMS ENTERTAINMENT, INC.†
2219 W. 32nd Ave.
Denver, CO 80211
(303) 433-7231
Contact: Tom Schneider

WINTERSET, INC.†
P.O. Box 22198
5777 E. Evans #205
Denver, CO 80222
(303) 759-2152
Contact: Dorothy Winters

LAKEWOOD

MICHAEL ANTHONY AGENCY*†
6007 W. 16th Ave.
Lakewood, CO 80214
(303) 233-2163
Contact: Michael Tolerico, Russell W. Colletti

CONNECTICUT

BERLIN

JAY-BEE PRODUCTIONS†
32 Wethersfield Road
Berlin, CT 06037
(203) 828-6009
Contact: John J. Borcyczki

BLOOMFIELD

ARCHIE D'AMATO ASSOCIATES†
16 Guernsey Rd.
Bloomfield, CT 06002
(203) 242-4712

DANBURY

MARK ROTHBAUM & ASSOCIATES†
225 Main Street
Danbury, CT 06810
(203) 792-2400
Contact: Mark Rothbaum

EAST HARTFORD

LANDERMAN AGENCY†
65 Connecticut Blvd.
East Hartford, CT 06108
(203) 289-0221
Contact: Morris Landerman, Paul C. Landerman, Mrs. Eleanor Golec

EAST NORWALK

HALLMARK GALLERY OF ARTISTS†
Shorehaven Road
East Norwalk, CT 06855
(203) 853-2732
Contact: Norman Lorain Flewwellin

FAIRFIELD

LEE VINE PRODUCTIONS†
34 Woodridge Ave.
Fairfield, CT 06430
1 (203) 374-6030

HARTFORD

JARVIS MUSIC & ENTERTAINMENT AGENCY, INC.†
37 Huntington St.
Hartford, CT 06105
(203) 247-4496
Contact: Joseph M. Ronan, Jr., Sam Pasco, Jack Turner, Larry A. Slack, Walter L. Sycz

MARANDINO'S AGENCY†
31 Colonial St.
Hartford, CT 06106
(203) 278-7290
Contact: Anthony J. Marandino

MIDDLETOWN

JIM CORVO ENTERTAINMENT AGENCY†
170 E. Liberty St.
Middletown, CT 06457
(203) 346-7241
Contact: Vincent Jimmie Corvo

NEW LONDON

FLASH GROUPS TALENT AGENCY†
302 Captain's Walk, Ste. 502-503
New London, CT 06320
(203) 443-5371
Contact: Marc Gentilella

OLD GREENWICH

SANDRA KATHRYN BENDFELDT†
68 Binney Lane
Old Greenwich, CT 06870
(203) 637-8760

PUTNAM

MUSIC UNLIMITED†

375 School St.
Putnam, CT 06260
(203) 928-2988
Contact: Robert H. Lussier, Sr.

SHELTON
WILD OATES MUSIC†
676 Howe Avenue
Shelton, CT 06484
(203) 735-0392
Contact: Davie W. Chrzanowski

SOUTHBURY
C.J.T & SONS†
Main St., So.
Southbury, CT 06488
(203) 264-1100
Contact: Constantino J. Thomas, David J. Thomas

SOUTHINGTON
MAPLEWOOD TALENT AGENCY†
62 Maplewood Rd.
Southington, CT 06489
(203) 628-6433
Contact: Joseph A. Abate

STAMFORD
DON C. MARINO†
32 Francis Ave.
Stamford, CT 06905
(203) 327-9895

AYERS PRODUCTIONS*
70 Clay Hill Rd.
Stamford, CT 06905
(203) 329-7335
Contact: Bud Ayers

TORRINGTON
JERRY P. CARILLO†
47 Circle Dr.
Torrington, CT 06790
(203) 482-5328
Contact: Jerry P. Carillo

HARRIS C. DAIGLE†
299 East Main St.
Torrington, CT 06790
(203) 482-1253

WALLINGFORD
AL GENTILE ORCHESTRA†
105 So. Elm St.
Wallingford, CT 06492
(203) 265-5170
Contact: Al Gentiel, Stanley Hall, Shirley Fidler

DELAWARE

NEW CASTLE
A.J. ROCKY ROMANO ENTERTAINMENT BUREAU†
211 West Ave.
New Castle, DE 19720
(302) 658-3350
Contact: Angelo J. Romano

SMYRNA
PENINSULA ENTERTAINMENT, INC.†
R.D. #2, Box 412
Smyrna, DE 19977
(302) 653-4446
Contact: Charles A. Wall

WILMINGTON
DELAWARE ENTERTAINMENT AGENCY†
2702 Tonbridge Dr.
Wilmington, DE 19810
(302) 475-5050
Contact: Lee J. McFadden

DISTRICT OF COLUMBIA

AFFILIATED ENTERPRISES, INC.†
1012 14th St., N.W., Ste. 906
Washington, D.C. 20005
P.O. Box 13037
Washington, D.C. 20009
(301) 593-6588
Contact: Mrs. Arletta R. Wood, Larry K. Wood, Aerial R. Simmons, Charles E. Crusoe, Ricardo J. Carpenter, John Freeman, Leroy Hubbard, Gregory Wood, Samuel McCombs, Leander Williams

MORGAN BAER ORCHESTRAS OF D.C, INC.†
4201 Connecticut Ave., N.W., Ste. 210
Washington, D.C. 20008
(202) 667-6316
Contact: Eugene Donati, Irv Rubin, Tom Moropoulos, Frank Lanciano

QUINN REVUE THEATRICAL AGENCY†
1341 G Street, N.W., Ste. 518
Washington, D.C. 20005
(202) 347-1611
Contact: Ruth O'Grady Quinn, Fred A. Quinn, Jr., Jay G.H. Pooler, Jr.

FLORIDA

ALTAMONTE SPRINGS
CONTEMPORARY ARTISTS, INC.*
P.O. Box 220
Altamonte Springs, FL 32701
(305) 834-6677
Contact: Monte Taylor

HOEKSTRA AGENCY*
P.O. Box 1360
Altamonte Spring, FL 32701
(305) 321-1890
Contact: Bob Hoekstra

BROOKSVILLE
JEAN MARTIN AGENCY†
320 Lockhart Rd.
Brooksville, FL 33512
(813) 996-3745
Contact: Dan Bradford Martin

CLEARWATER
JIM SALEEM ASSOCIATES†
4153 Mallard Dr.
Clearwater, FL 33519
(813) 726-7642
Contact: James F. Saleem

CORAL GABLES
RALPH KIRSCH AGENCY†
1320 S. Dixie Highway, Ste. 250
Coral Gables, FL 33146
(305) 666-4689
Contact: Judith K. Sheffield

CORAL SPRINGS
FJM PRODUCTIONS*
8974 N.W. 25th Court
Coral Springs, FL 33065
(305) 753-8591
Contact: Fred Montilla

DAYTONA BEACH
SHELLY TAYLOR THEATRICAL AGENCY†
736 Fairmont Road
Daytona Beach, FL 32014
(904) 255-7401
Contact: Shelly Taylor

DELAND
WARREN BILLS AGENCY†
709 South Pearl
DeLand, FL 32720
(904) 736-1092
Contact: Warren Bills, Eddie E. Rusk

EAGLE LAKE
CHUCK BASS ENTERTAINMENT AGENCY†
P.O. Box 1036
Eagle Lake, FL 33839
(813) 293-5647
Contact: Charles Bass

FT. LAUDERDALE
FLORIDA ATTRACTIONS*†
P.O. Box 7036
Ft. Lauderdale, FL 33338
(305) 772-4543
Contact: Milo Stelt, Elsie K. Stelt

HEADLINE VARIETY ATTRACTIONS†
1775 North Andrews Ave.
Ft. Lauderdale, FL 33311
(305) 463-2238
Contact: William Gallus Jallos, Domenico Capaldi, Ronald W. Campbell

KING MUSIC ASSOCIATES†
3030 N.E. 47th Street
Ft. Lauderdale, FL 33308
(305) 491-3710
Contact: Walter B. Walters

JOHNNY LEIGHTON THEATRICAL AGENCY†
2741 West Collins Road
Ft. Lauderdale, FL 33312
(305) 584-8203

FT. MYERS
ARTIST' IMAGE*
9600 S. Tamiami Trail
Ste. 103
Ft. Myers, FL 33907
(813) 936-3343
Contact: Robin L. Alvey

CAL CLAUDE THEATRICAL AGENCY†
4402 Tuscaloosa St.
Ft. Myers, FL 33905
(813) 694-4966
Contact: Helen H. Ladner

TOMMY MASON ENTERTAINMENT AGENCY†
4113 Mandarin Ct.
Ft. Myers, FL 33905
(813) 694-1967
Contact: David P. Wilkinson, Thomas Mason Thawley

GAINESVILLE

BLADE AGENCY†
P.O. Box 12239
Gainesville, FL 32604
(904) 372-8158
Contact: Charles V. Steadham, Jr., Allen McCollum

HALLENDALE

MORISON AGENCY†
1102 NE 2nd Ct.
Hallendale, FL 33009
(305) 458-0916
Contact: Howard Wilde

HOLIDAY

BILLY SPATA ALL STAR ENTERTAINMENT AGENCY†
5605 Star Island Dr., N.
Holiday, FL 33590
(813) 937-6427
Contact: William Spata

HOLLYWOOD

JERRY GRANT PRODUCTIONS INC.†
2741 North 29th Ave.
Hollywood, FL 33021
(305) 925-5885
Contact: Jerry Grant

LESTER WAGMAN ASSOCIATES†
4624 Hollywood Blvd.
Hollywood, FL 33021
(305) 981-2345
Contact: Lester Wagman

JACKSONVILLE

VIRGINIA HARRITT PRODUCTIONS, INC.†
120 No. 5th St.
Jacksonville, FL 32250
(904) 241-2061
Contact: Virginia Harritt, Daniel J. Harritt, Thomas H. Harritt

ALLISON HERBERT PRODUCTIONS†
4131 University Blvd. So.
Jacksonville, FL 32216
(904) 733-8425
Contact: Allison Ingram Herbert

JOHN JELINEK THEATRICAL AGENCY†
Room 502 First Federal Savings Bldg.
Jacksonville, FL 32202
(904) 353-7044

WILLIAM T. PATTERSON, JR.†
P.O. Box 313
Jacksonville, FL 32201-0313
(904) 768-5102

KISSIMMEE

ZELL MUSIC†
1021 No. Brack
Kissimmee, FL 32741
(305) 847-0677
Contact: Edward Benjamin Haines

LONGWOOD

BRUCE WESTCOTT AGENCY†
214 Sweet Gum Way
Longwood, FL 32750
(305) 862-0348

MAITLAND

CAROLE S. DEPINTO†
1811 Gladiolas Dr.
Maitland, FL 32751
(305) 671-9701

MELBOURNE

BRITISH-AMERICAN MUSICAL PRODUCTIONS, INC.†
500 Harbor City Blvd., Ste. D
Melbourne, FL 32935
(305) 254-3583
Contact: Leonard Turner

MIAMI

JACK W. YOUNG THEATRICAL AGENCY†
5555 Biscayne Blvd.
Miami, FL 33137
(305) 757-2211
Contact: Jack W. Young, Rita Shore

MIAMI BEACH

HERBERT MARKS TALENT AGENCY†
600 Lincoln Rd.
Miami Beach, FL 33139
(305) 534-2119

MIAMI LAKES

MARGE JONES AGENCY†
13980 Lake George Ct.
Miami Lake, FL 33014
(305) 821-7033
Contact: Marjorie Jones

NAPLES

KLEINER ENTERTAINMENT SERVICE†
3701 25th Ave., S.W.
Naples, FL 33999
(813) 455-2693
Contact: Sid Kleiner, Trudy Kleiner

NORTH PALM BEACH

SPOTLIGHT ENTERPRISES, INC.†
44 Yacht Club Dr.
No. Palm Beach, FL 33408
(305) 626-7080
Contact: Johnny Brown, Grace Mitchell Brown

ORLANDO

DALE BURKE AGENCY†
8506 Tasmayne Pl.
Orlando, FL 32810
P.O. Box 17946
Orlando, FL 32860
(305) 869-1927
Contact: Dale O. Burke, James Miller, Alan Ries, Bill Love, Betty Smith

ENTERTAINMENT "PLUS"*
Box 951
Route 5
Orlando, FL 32812
(305) 273-4330
Contact: Dave Bellagamba

LOU FELDMAN AGENCY†
999 Woodcock Rd., Ste. 100
Orlando, FL 32803
(305) 896-7735

MARK WAYNE†
P.O. Box 9058
Orlando, FL 32807
(305) 275-1021

PALM SPRINGS

RON REILLY MUSIC†
384 Lake Arbor Dr.
Palm Springs, FL 33461
(305) 968-2801
Contact; Ronald S. Reilly

PANAMA CITY

B & H ASSOCIATES†
P.O. Box 1414
Panama City, FL 32401
(904) 769-2486
Contact: Leon D. Braddock, Jr.

PINELLAS PARK

GLENN E. ABRAHAM & ASSOCIATES, INC.†
6131 - 107th Avenue North
Pinellas Park, FL 33565
(813) 544-5356
Contact: Glenn E. Abraham

POLK CITY

MIDDLETON'S PUBLIC RELATIONS & MANAGEMENT†
322 Smith Rd.
Polk City, FL 33868
(813) 984-1286
Contact: Benjamin Middleton

POMPANO BEACH

VACCARO TALENT AGENCY†
1070 SE 9th Ave.
Pompano Beach, FL 33060
(305) 941-2733
Contact: Michael A. Vaccaro

SARASOTA

OLER ENTERTAINMENT PRODUCTIONS†
3400 Bayshore Rd.
P.O. Box 1418
Sarasota, FL 33578
(813) 355-4687
Contact: Wesley N. Oler, Micki Lydolph

ST. AUGUSTINE

SOUND PROMOTIONS†
Atlantic Bank Bldg., Rm. 203
P.O. Box 3207

St. Augustine, FL 32084
(904) 824-8102
Contact: Ronald F. Sanchez

ST. PETERSBURG

AL DOWNING MUSIC ENTERPRISES, INC.†
2121 25th St., So.
St. Petersburg, FL 33712
(813) 867-6436
Contact: Alvin J. Downing

RAY W. JOHNSON†
10622 Poplar Street, N.E.
St. Petersburg, FL 33702
(813) 577-1086

HARRY LAWRENCE & ASSOCIATES†
185-24th Ave., No.
St. Petersburg, FL 33704
(813) 896-3245
Contact: Harry William Lawrence

SUNSET ENTERTAINMENT*
P.O. Box 21232
St. Petersburg, FL 33742
(813) 225-1179
Contact: Joe Hood

ROY TAYLOR AGENCY†
777 30th Ave., No.
St. Petersburg, FL 33704
P.O. Box 7707
St. Petersburg, FL 33734
(813) 896-8811

TAMPA

JAY BROWN AGENCY*
Ste. B
221 West Waters Ave.
Tampa, FL 33604
(813) 933-2456
Contact: Jay Brown

WINTER HAVEN

MIKE ROBINSON PRODUCTIONS*
211 Lake Otis Rd.
Winter Haven, FL 33880
(813) 229-7510
Contact: Mike Robinson

WINTER PARK

DOMARI THEATRICAL AGENCY†
646 N. Semoran Blvd.
Winter Park, FL 32792
(305) 677-6727
Contact: Fred John Smalls

FRED WEISS MANAGEMENT*
2676 Barbados Dr.
Winter Park, FL 32792
(305) 677-5995
Contact: Fred Weiss

GEORGIA

ATLANTA

ARNOLD AGENCY, INC.*†
1252 W. Peachtree Rd.
Atlanta, GA 30367
(404) 873-2001
Contact: Frank W. Hanshaw, Sr., Frank W. Hanshaw, Jr., Mrs. Jayne Hanshaw, M.L. Kamin

ATLANTA TALENT CONSULTANTS†
P.O. Box 9747
3958 Peachtree Rd.
Atlanta, GA 30319
(404) 237-8485
Contact: Clyde Allan Diggs, John Pennington, Frank Shane

CAMERON PRODUCTIONS†
3026 Clairmont Rd., N.E.
Apt. E
Atlanta, GA 30329
(404) 329-0167
Contact: Peter John Cameron

ALBERT COLEMAN PRODUCTIONS, INC.†
P.O. Box 723172
Atlanta, GA 30339
(404) 435-1222
Contact: Albert Coleman, Barbara L. O'Neill

GREER AGENCY, INC.†
3190 Combellton Rd., S.W.
Atlanta, GA 30311
(404) 346-3020
Contact: Helen Roberta Greer

MORNING STAR*
P.O. Box 29785
Atlanta, GA 30359
Contact: Scott Donalds

JOHNNY O'LEARY AGENCY†
P.O. Box 82272
Atlanta, GA 30354
(404) 763-8042
Contact: John Leary, Elsie J. Leary

RISING STAR PRODUCTIONS, INC. (OF ATLANTA)†
Box 723034
Atlanta, GA 30339
(404) 429-0838
Contact: Paul Barlow, Verne D. Barlow, Jr., Eve Selman

RODGERS AGENCY, INC.†
P.O. Box 76640
Atlanta, GA 30358-1640
(404) 992-1050
Contact: Hugh James Rodgers, Jr.

WES-POL PRODUCTIONS†
7200 Peachtree Dunwoody Rd. NE
Atlanta, GA 30328
1(404) 394-0917
Contact: John A. Tailor

AUGUSTA

MANGELLY ENTERTAINMENT UNLIMITED†
2506 Peach Orchard Road
Augusta, GA 30906
(404) 798-1831
Contact: La Rue Mangelly, Thomas Mangelly

CONYERS

JIM BELT AND ASSOCIATES†
P.O. Box 627
Conyers, GA 30207
(404) 483-3423
Contact: James P. Belt, Della Mae Belt

DOUGLASVILLE

ATLANTA ENTERTAINMENT AGENCY†
9249 Highway 5
Douglasville, GA 30134
(404) 942-9840
Contact: Charles S. Lyda

MACON

ADVANTAGE†
561 Cotton Ave.
Macon, GA 31208
(912) 745-8511
Contact: William M. Hall

RODGERS REDDING & ASSOCIATES†
P.O. Box 4603
Macon, GA 31208
(912) 742-8931
Contact: Luther Rodgers Redding

SEASIDE PRODUCTIONS†
P.O. Box 7771
Macon, GA 31210
(912) 474-4600
Contact: J. Paul Pannell, Jr., J. Paul Pannell, Sr.

MARIETTA

EMPIRE AGENCY, INC.†
401 Atlanta St.
Marietta, GA 30060
(404) 427-1200
Contact: Alex Hodges, Mrs. Carole Kinzel, Rick Alter

NORCROSS

THE STARMOUNT AGENCY†
3962 Spalding Hollow
Norcross, GA 30092
(404) 448-8040
Contact: Ken Hewitt

ROSSVILLE

THEATRICAL ARTIST REPRESENTATIVES†
574 Millport Rd.
Rossville, GA 30741
(404) 866-6666
Contact: John P. Fava, Janet L. Fava

SCOTTDALE

COUNTRY MUSIC TALENT†
582 Woodland Ave.
Scottdale, GA 30079
(404) 296-5425
Contact: Essie B. Ferguson, William H. (Billy) Ferguson

HAWAII

HONOLULU

A.I.M. TALENT AGENCY†
666 Prospect St. #309
Honolulu, HI 96813
(808) 531-1890
Contact: Clarence Hideo Uesato, Allan Uyesalo

LEROY K. AKAMINE†
3469 Kakawalu Drive
Honolulu, HI 96817
(808) 595-4946

AMERICAN PACIFIC ENTERTAINMENT, INC.†
P.O. Box 29181
Honolulu, HI 96820
(808) 836-3600
Contact: Bob Mitchell

JOSEPHINE FLANDERS†
Wailana, #1010
1860 Ala Moana Blvd.
Honolulu, HI 96815
(808) 947-5467
Contact: William D. Flanders

INTERNATIONAL SHOW BIZ†
1050 So. King #15
Honolulu, HI 96814
(808) 537-9160
Contact: William T. Jacobs, Jr.

ISLAND TALENT†
1550 Rycroft St., Ste. 102
Honolulu, HI 96814
(808) 946-1606
Contact: Marjorie E. Spencer, Albert M. Waterson

J.J. PRODUCTIONS†
Ala Moana Bldg., Ste. 1117
1441 Kapiolani Bldg.
Honolulu, HI 96814
(808) 947-6871
Contact: James C. Arnold

JOHNNY JORDAN†
1556 Aulena Place
Honolulu, HI 96821
(808) 373-4553

GREGG KENDALL & ASSOCIATES, INC.†
2003 Kalia Rd., 9-J
Honolulu, HI 96815
(808) 946-9577
Contact: Charles Peck

MILESTONE PRODUCTIONS BOOKING AGENCY†
P.O. Box 25412
Honolulu, HI 96825
(808) 922-3520
Contact: Miles M. Jackson, Mrs. Regina Jackson

MARK Y. NISHIMOTO†
1750 Kalakaua Ave., Ste. 605
Honolulu, HI 96826
(808) 734-2025

TERII RUA'S TAHITI-NUI†
353 Awini-Way
Honolulu, HI 96821
(808) 396-0071
Contact: Terii Rua

JAMES M. SUGIYAMA, JR.†
1018 Poe Poe Place
Honolulu, HI 96819
(808) 847-0651

UNIVERSAL ARTISTS MANAGEMENT, INC.†
P.O. Box 8612
Honolulu, HI 96815
(808) 942-2444
Contact: Rod Anderson

DOLLY WON ENTERPRISES†
3052 Hibiscus Dr.
Honolulu, HI 96815
(808) 923-3909
Contact: Dolly Kang Won

KAAWA

MILTON T. COSME†
C.R. Box 484
Kaawa, HI 96730
(808) 237-8131

KAILUA

WILLIAM GONSALVES AGENCY†
1484 Keolu Dr.
Kailua, HI 96734
(808) 262-8480

KIHEI

MAJESTIC PRODUCTIONS†
P.O. Box 967
Kihei, HI 96753
(808) 879-7069
Contact: William Kahele Nahalea, Jr.

PEARL CITY

HAWAII BOOKING SERVICES†
1559 Hoolehua St.
Pearl City, HI 96782
(808) 455-3109
Contact: Howard S. Furukawa

IDAHO

BOISE

AURORA ENTERTAINMENT†
11336 Valley Heights Circle
Boise, ID 83709
(208) 362-6035
Contact: Paula Chafetz Smith, Michael I. Smith

IDAHO FALLS

LANCE AGENCY*
213 Shane Bldg.
Idaho Falls, ID 83401
(208) 522-3747
Contact: Kent Lance

PAUL

FELTON AGENCY†
Box 740
Paul, ID 83347
(208) 438-5439
Contact: Leonard C. Felton, Mari E. Felton

ILLINOIS

ADDISON

VALENTI & VALENTI*
528 North Lincoln
Addison, IL 60101
(312) 628-8456
Contact: Gail Valenti

BENSENVILLE

DM PRODUCTIONS*
1320 Medinah
Bensenville, IL 60106
(312) 595-9100
Contact: Dave Mills

BLOOMINGTON

CENTER STAGE ENTERTAINMENT†
506½ N. East
Bloomington, IL 61701
1 (309) 829-6304
Contact: Michael D. Mocilan, Lynn Hutchinson

CASEYVILLE

PENN'S COUNTRY ATTRACTIONS†
113 Brookhaven Rd.
Caseyville, IL 62232
(618) 345-9980
Contact: Margaret G. Penn, Leah Deem, Catherine Bartels

CHAMPAIGN

BLYTHAM LTD.†
207 W. Clark Street
P.O. Box 701
Champaign, IL 61820
(217) 356-1857
Contact: Robert Dean Nutt, Darryl Coburn, Chris Bradley, Douglas R. Bauer, Robin Brown, Bill Stein, John Hayes, Richard Kleinman

JEWEL PRODUCTIONS†
1502 Waverly Drive
Champaign, IL 61820
(217) 356-0660
Contact: Jewel M. Kurland

RUDY JAMES ORCHESTRA AGENCY†
1104 W. Healy St.
P.O. Box 71
Champaign, IL 61820
(217) 356-9358
Contact: Lois S. James

CHICAGO

WILLARD ALEXANDER INC.(NY)†
Branch Office:
333 North Michigan Avenue
Chicago, IL 60601
(312) 236-2460
Contact: Thomas J. Cassidy, Carl Schunk, Gregg McFall, Linda Garcher

ANTONIO ATTRACTIONS†
1476 West Belle Plaine
Chicago, IL 60613
(312) 929-2737
Contact: Tony Marconi

MAX BORDE AGENCY†
203 N. Wabash Ave.
Chicago, IL 60601
(312) 236-5284

CENTRAL BOOKING OFFICE†
203 North Wabash Avenue
Chicago, IL 60601
(312) 372-4406
Contact: Albert H. Borde, John King, Ron T. Kubelik

CONSOLIDATED RADIO ARTISTS*†
P.O. Box 30009
Chicago, IL 60630
(312) 685-3505
Contact: Jerry "K"

AL CURTIS ENTERTAINMENT, INC.†

P.O. Box 48833
Chicago, IL 60648
(312) 697-7379
Contact: Margaret Galica

THE DIAMOND AGENCY†
8560 So. Bennett Ave.
Chicago, IL 60617
(312) 734-1698
Contact: Harold R. Harris, Charles Hines, Leo Walker

MARVIN HIMMEL & ASSOCIATES, INC.†
333 North Michigan Ave., Ste. 1632
Chicago, IL 60601
(312) 236-6470
Contact: Elbe Johnson, Tom Ferris

FRANK J. HOGAN, INC.†
307 No. Michigan Ave.
Chicago, IL 60601
(312) 263-6910
Contact: Margaret M. Richards

DORIS HURTIG†
400 E. Randolph St.
Chicago, IL 60601
(312) 332-2503

JAYDE ENTERPRISES, INC.†
203 No. Wabash Ave., Ste. 706
Chicago, IL 60601
(312) 726-0771
Contact: Melba R. Caldwell, Alfred T. Williams

JOHNNY JONES ARTISTS' REPRESENTATIVE†
5630 North Sheridan Road, Apt. 914
Chicago, IL 60660
(312) 275-6675
Contact: John Strickler Jones, Sr.

MELTZ, ROMEO-PRODUCTIONS, MUSIC & ENTERTAINMENT†
6099 N. Sauganash Ave.
Chicago, IL 60646
(312) 685-5566

MUSIC BY PHIL VARCHETTA†
233 East Erie St.
Chicago, IL 60611
(312) 640-0266

PARAMOUNT PRODUCTIONS, INC.†
640 No. LaSalle St.
Chicago, IL 60611
(312) 944-2650
Contact: William E. Goldsmith, Betty Sampson, Jane R. Marks, Roy Davis, Don Alan aka Don McWethy, Marianne Braun aka Marianne Bowles, Paulette Wolf, Joyce Murphy, Guy Aylward, Randy Nolen, Robert Barranco

RHYTHM AND BLUES ATTRACTIONS†
8959 S. Oglesby Ave.
Chicago, IL 60617
(312) 375-4276
Contact: Armond G. Jackson, Celoa Baker Jackson

HOWARD W. SCHULTZ THEATRICAL AGENCY, INC.†
2525 West Peterson Ave.
Chicago, IL 60659
(312) 769-2244

SEYMOUR SHAPIRO AGENCY†
307 No. Michigan Ave., #914
Chicago, IL 60601
(312) 236-9596
Contact: Gertrude Shapiro

BENNY SHARP & ASSOCIATES†
520 N. Michigan Ave.
Chicago, IL 60611
(312) 644-0818
Contact: Rennie Collins

TAMAR PRODUCTIONS, INC.†
2130 N. Lincoln Park West
Chicago, IL 60614
(312) 477-8789
Contact: Vi Daley, Kristen M. Widhamn

Branch Office:
1325 Wilson Blvd., Ste. 305
Arlington, VA 22209
(703) 527-3079
Contact: Mary Ann Rose

UNITED ATTRACTIONS, INC.†
22 E. Huron St.
Chicago, IL 60611
(312) 664-0200
Contact: Phillip J. Consolo, Elayne Consolo

VARIETY ENTERPRISES†
1646 No. Natoma
Chicago, IL 60635
(312) 745-0988
Contact: Georgia C. Ullo, Philip P. Ullo

CHICAGO HEIGHTS

JACK RUSSELL & ASSOCIATES†
244 Constance Lane
Chicago Heights, IL 60411
(312) 756-7060

COLLINSVILLE

ARTCO ENTERPRISES OF ILLINOIS*†
1312 Vandalia
Collinsville, IL 62234
(618) 345-6702
Contact: Arthur F. Risavy, Katie Garde

HAISLAR PRODUCTIONS†
225 West Main
P.O. Box 69
Collinsville, IL 62234
(618) 344-7910
Contact: Dennis Paul Haislar, Ted Minkanic, Jon Ubben, Neal Butler, Joyce Gobin

DEERFIELD

LARRY BASTIAN AGENCY†
2580 Crestwood Lane
Deerfield, IL 60015
(312) 945-9283
Contact: Phil Ford

DES PLAINES

ASSOCIATED BOOKING CORPORATION(NY)†
Branch Office:
2700 North River Rd.
Des Plaines, IL 60018
(312) 296-0930
Contact: Hal Munro

ELMHURST

BEST ENTERTAINMENT SERVICES OF ILLINOIS†
OS 701 Old York Road
Elmhurst, IL 60126
(312) 832-7654
Contact: Edward W. Vodica

EVANSTON

DON Q. DAVIDSON AGENCY, INC.*†
1854 Sherman Ave.
Evanston, IL 60201
(312) 864-0061
Contact: Ralph C. Berger, Ronald K. Phelps, Corin Gold, Jay Bieiman

JOY PRODUCTIONS†
9236 N. Springfield
Evanston, IL 60203
(312) 677-2643
Contact: Joy Dickens, Bill Torres, Cyvea Newman

GLEN ELLYN

JERRY ROSS AGENCY†
207 Kenilworth
Glen Ellyn, IL 60137
(312) 858-5355
Contact: Shirley Ross

HERRIN

BEAVER TALENT AGENCY†
821 South 12th
Herrin, IL 62948
(618) 942-7262
Contact: Ralph C. Beaver

JACKSONVILLE

THE BAND ORGANIZATION†
601 West Morgan, Ste. 201
P.O. Box 1284
Jacksonville, IL 62651
(217) 243-7434
Contact: Howard A. Bowe, Douglas W. Parker

Branch Office:
2332 No. Cotner Blvd., Ste. D-2
Lincoln, NE 68507
(402) 467-5457
Contact: Kris Mortensen

JOLIET

BILL DISERA'S ENTERTAINMENT AGENCY†
555 Westminster
Joliet, IL 60435
(815) 725-8584

LAKE FOREST

WILLIAM A. RICHARD, LTD.†
222 Wisconsin Ave.
Lake Forest, IL 60045
(312) 295-7703
Contact: William A. Richard, Patricia Richard

LINCOLN
UPBEAT AGENCY†
P.O. Box 223
Lincoln, IL 62656
(217) 732-6483
Contact: Dana Sue Smith

LINCOLNWOOD
ARNE PRAGER & ASSOCIATES*
4433 W. Touhy
Lincolnwood, IL 60645
(312) 579-4700
Contact: Arne Prager

MOLINE
FIAGLE BOOKING AGENCY†
2409-46 Street
Moline, IL 61265
1 (309) 762-4992
Contact: Lawrence M. Fiagle

NORTHBROOK
LOU BROWNIE ATTRACTIONS, INC.†
660 Ballantree Rd.
Northbrook, IL 60062
(312) 480-0900
Contact: Lou Brownie

PAUL E. WITTENMYER & ASSOCIATES†
2175 Brentwood Road
Northbrook, IL 60062
(312) 564-4515
Contact: Virginia A. Wittenmyer

OTTAWA
SANTUCCI MUSICAL AGENCY†
102 West Main St.
Ottawa, IL 61350
(815) 434-0807
Contact: Shirley Santucci

PARK FOREST
PAUL CARROLL ATTRACTIONS†
P.O. Box 421
Park Forest, IL 60466
(312) 957-3178
Contact: Paul Carroll, William H. Lester

RIVERWOODS
MUSICAL ENTERPRISES*
1404 Blackheath
Riverwoods, IL 60015
(312) 948-9510
Contact: Ted Allan

SKOKIE
FABER ENTERTAINMENT, INC.*†
P.O. Box 282
5148 West Main Street
Skokie, IL 60076
(312) 677-5944
Contact: Donald C. Faber, John M. Hughes, Sheila M. Faber, Gwen I. Faber, Gregory Hayes, Leo Provost, Carol M. Lewandowski

SOUTH HOLLAND
KENNAWAY ENTERTAINMENT CORPORATION†
20909 S. Torrence Ave.
South Holland, IL 60411
(312) 758-0070
Contact: Ronald D. Michalak, Norman R. Michalak, Patricia L. Michalak, Robert W. Pursell

SPRINGFIELD
GEORGE HARNESS ASSOCIATES*
27 North Lake Rd.
Springfield, IL 62707
(217) 529-8550
Contact: George Harness

ST. CHARLES
PARADISE PRODUCTIONS†
3N778 Hawthorn Dr.
St. Charles, IL 60174
(312) 584-8024
Contact: Kathy A. Koran

WAUKEGAN
AL SCHULTZ AGENCY†
38328 N. Sheridan Road
Waukegan, IL 60087
(312) 244-1550
Contact: Alfred W. Shultz, Barry Ano, Robert Lee, Robert King, Mark Schultz, Woodrow Woodruff, John Hall, Bill Monnot

WESTMONT
TOP NOTCH TALENT*
335 South Cass Ave.
Westmont, IL 60559
(312) 964-5874
Contact: Dick Smith

INDIANA

ANDERSON
BILL ALBERT'S AGENCY*
408 E. 38th St.
Anderson, IN 46014
(317) 642-6306
Contact: Bill Albert

CEDAR LAKE
MUSICAL PRODUCTIONS†
8514 W. 146th Avenue
Cedar Lake, IN 46303
(219) 374-7730
Contact: Kenneth M. Tease

CROWN POINT
OPUSOUND†
9790 Grant Pl., Ste. 101 S.
Crown Point, IN 46307
(219) 663-8408
Contact: Robert C. Shriver, Robet C. Luptak

ELKHART
IMPRO INTERNATIONAL, INC.†
P.O. Box 1072
Elkhart, IN 46515
(219) 679-4061
Contact: Trudy Hernicz, Christopher L. Thornton, L. Thomas Wibbels

FT. WAYNE
C-BOLD PROMOTIONS†
2516 Beacon St.
Ft. Wayne, IN 46805
(219) 483-6107
Contact: Charles W. Seybold

DANNY EUTSLER AGENCY†
645 Riverside Avenue
Ft. Wayne, IN 46805
(219) 426-8368

MAKIN ENTERTAINMENT, LTD. DBA MEL AGENCY†
P.O. Box 11594
Ft. Wayne, IN 46859
(219) 456-5954
Contact: John R. Makin, Ryan R. Aldrich, Tana L. Makin, Suzanne C. Aldrich

GARY
SUN JAMM ENTERTAINMENT†
2137 W. 49th Pl.
Gary, IN 46408
(219) 980-2218
Contact: Roger B. Des Rosiers

QUEENDOM ENTERPRISES, INC.†
P.O. Box M521
Gary, IN 46401
(219) 885-0690
Contact: Faye Beverly, Ruby J. Richmond

GREENTOWN
LO REIGN AGENCY†
500 West Payton #25
Greentown, IN 46936
(317) 628-2284
Contact: Nora L. Nelson, Betty Burns

HAMLET
ORR PRODUCTIONS†
Route 1 Box 35
Hamlet, IN 46532
(219) 867-9255
Contact: Garry R. Orr

HIGHLAND
KARL F. LINDEN MUSIC CONSULTANT†
2540 Wicker Street
Highland, IN 46322
(219) 923-8280
Contact: Karl Frederick Linden, Florence Gindl

INDIANAPOLIS
ALBERTA'S ENTERTAINMENT SERVICE†
5942 W. Thompson Road
Indianapolis, IN 46241
(317) 856-8008
Contact: Alberta June Shaw

H.T. THEATRICAL AGENCY†
3556 Carrollton Ave.
Indianapolis, IN 46205
(317) 926-1092
Contact: Marvin R. McCurty, Thelma M. McCurty

JADE PRODUCTIONS†
2026 Overlook Court
Indianapolis, IN 46219
(317) 894-7208

Contact: Jane Allen, Dorothy Lee Schwab, Suzanne Bavender, Edward Schwab

THE MUSIC BOOK†
617 East 38th St.
Indianapolis, IN 46205
(317) 926-1244
Contact: C. Ray Chenowith, Margaret Ramspacher, Dennis Lee, William S. Lowry

TONY SHOUSE ENTERPRISES†
2726 Sheffield Dr.
Indianapolis, IN 46229
(317) 894-2431

TIMELY MUSIC ENTERPRISES†
4888 Kesslerview Dr.
Indianapolis, IN 46220
(317) 253-4794
Contact: Ray Churchman, Carolyn Churchman

JOSEPH A. TRIPODI
599 West Westfield Blvd.
Apt. 25
Indianapolis, IN 46208
(317) 255-1074

JASPER

PROFESSIONAL ARTISTS UNLIMITED, INC.†
Rustic Acres
Jasper, IN 47546
(812) 482-6823
Contact: Paul J. Vogler, Jerry J. Fuhs, Vicky L. Vogler

KOKOMO

DORTHA TARKINGTON ENTERTAINMENT SERVICE†
4215 West Sycamore Land
Kokomo, IN 46901
(317) 452-4452

LAFAYETTE

BILL ANDERSON AGENCY*†
635 South 24th Street
Lafayette, IN 47904
(317) 447-4073
Contact: William Curtis Anderson, A. Michael Tucciarelli, Ruby Tucciarelli

Branch Office:
c/o Holiday Inn North
5601 S.R. 43 No.
West Lafayette, IN 47906
(317) 567-2111-12

MERRILLVILLE

L.R. WRIGHT ENTERTAINMENT CONSULTANT†
130 E. 73rd Ave.
Merrillville, IN 46410
(219) 769-8014
Contact: Linda R. Wright

MICHIGAN CITY

SUPERSHOWS LTD.†
P.O. Box 2135
Michigan City, IN 46360
(219) 879-2971
Contact: Duane Francis Svetic

MISHAWAKA

HIT SHOWCASE AGENCY†
121 Lincolnway West
Mishawaka, IN 46544
(219) 255-6100
Contact: Maurice Fredrick Paulsen, Richard R. Johnson, Mike Dzierla

MUNSTER

CELESTIAL PRODUCTIONS†
8718 Greenwood
Munster, IN 46321
(219) 838-5231
Contact: Barbara Eileen Nava

NEW ALBANY

GUY RHODES AGENCY*
2306 E. Spring St.
New Albany, IN 47150
(812) 944-7993
Contact: Guy Rhodes

SOUTH BEND

TONY RULLI BOOKING AGENCY†
1523 Lincoln Way West
South Bend, IN 46628
(219) 233-4767

VALPARAISO

VIRGINIA V. ATKINSON†
23 So. 578W.
Valparaiso, IN 46383
(219) 464-8232

WEST LAFAYETTE

BILL ANDERSON AGENCY
(See Lafayette listing)

WORTHINGTON

PAM HALE PRODUCTIONS†
Route #1, Box 49
Worthington, IN 47471
(812) 875-3664
Contact: Rodger L. Hale

IOWA

CHARLES CITY

BIG JACK PRODUCTIONS†
103 Sprigg St.
Charles City, IA 50616
Contact: Kaye Rodamaker, Jack Rodamaker

DAVENPORT

GALA PRODUCTIONS†
P.O. Box 3583
Davenport, IA 52808
(319) 326-0057
Contact: Theodore R. Hester, Sylvester P. Mitchell

DES MOINES

BOBBY BAKER ENTERPRISES*†
P.O. Box 684
Des Moines, IA 50303
(515) 282-8421
Contact: Bobby Baker

DUBUQUE

KEITH MARUGG ENTERPRISES†
769 Fenelon Pl.
Dubuque, IA 52001
(319) 556-8185
Contact: Keith F. Marugg

IOWA CITY

TOP NOTCH TALENT AGENCY†
630 Beldon St.
Iowa City, IA 52240
P.O. Box 122
Iowa City, IA 52244
(319) 351-4101
Contact: Patti G. Murray, Jim Murray, Tom Suter

RUNNELLS

2 "M" ENTERPRISES†
RR #1
Runnells, IA 50237
(515) 966-2211
Contact: Maurice Tidball, Maryellen Tidball

WEST DESMOINES

T.T. CORP.†
1912 Locust
West Des Moines, IA 50265
(515) 225-6169
Contact: Douglas L. Taylor

KANSAS

CLAYCENTER

DIVERSIFIED TALENT ASSOCIATES†
Route 5
Claycenter, KS 67432
(913) 632-3151
Contact: G.L. Amyotte

FT. SCOTT

ROADSTARS ENTERTAINMENT AGENCY†
Box 1088, 101 State St.
Ft. Scott, KS 66701
(316) 223-0669
Contact: Donald Scott

HAYS

DANCELAND ENTERPRISES†
Box 124
Hays, KS 67601
(913) 625-6035
Contact: Eddie Basgall, Lillian Basgall

KANSAS CITY

ED COLEMAN ORCHESTRAS†
1847 Minnesota Ave.
Kansas City, KS 66102
(913) 342-4648
Contact: Edward L. Coleman

LAWRENCE

GREAT PLAINS ASSOCIATES, INC.†
107 E. 8th
P.O. Box 634
Lawrence, KS 66044
(913) 841-4444
Contact: Mark R. Swanson, Kathleen A. Swanson

LENEXA

DAN SMITH AGENCY†
11906 W. 77 Terrace 1-P
Lenexa, KS 66216
(913) 677-3736

MARQUETTE

LINDH'S BOOKING AGENCY†
RR #1
Marquette, KS 67464
(913) 546-2418
Contact: William Robert Lindh, Rosalynd La Ruth Lindh

NORTH NEWTON

AMERICAN CENTRAL ENTERTAINMENT†
9 Regal Crescent
Box 461
North Newton, KS 67117
(316) 283-8165
Contact: Keith W. Woolery, Dave Olson

OVERLAND PARK

GARRY MAC PRODUCTIONS†
#35 Corporate Woods
9101 W. 110th St.
Overland Pk., KS 66210
(913) 642-0400

STEVE MILLER AGENCY†
7429 Woodson
Overland Park, KS 66204
(913) 722-0887

PARSONS

NITESIDE ENTERTAINMENT†
238 Southern
Parsons, KS 67357
(316) 421-6659
Contact: David Thomas Cramer

SHAWNEE MISSION

JACKSON ARTISTS CORPORATION*
Suite 200
7251 Lowell Dr.
Shawnee Mission, KS 66204
(913) 384-6688
Contact: Dave Jackson

WITCHITA

DORIS BUSS AGENCY†
6518 Magill
Wichita, KS 67206
(316) 685-7267
Contact: Doris M. Buss

KENTUCKY

ASHLAND

"HAL" SCOTT ENTERPRISES†
422-55th St.
P.O. Box 488
Ashland, KY 41101
(606) 324-2881
Contact: Hal Scott

BEREA

MARY BETH TOP TEN TALENT AGENCY, INC.†
Mountain View Estates
Berea, KY 40403
(606) 986-9248
Contact: Mary Beth Lewis

BLUE EAGLE ENTERTAINERS, INC.†
Peachbloom Hill
Berea, KY 40403
(606) 986-8888
Contact: Janet Britton Skidmore

CATLETTSBURG

JAMES TAYLOR ENTERTAINMENT AGENCY†
Route 3 - Box 98
Catlettsburg, KY 41129
(606) 324-3901
Contact: James C. Taylor

JEFFERSONTOWN

THOMAS E. YENOWINE II†
3302 McAdams Court
Jeffersontown, KY 40299
(502) 499-9893
Contact: Tom E. Yenowine

LEXINGTON

R & R PROMOTIONS†
2852-A Snow Rd.
Lexington, KY 40502
(606) 266-8461
Contact: Robert Mc Nel Moser II

LOUISVILLE

DERBY CITY ATTRACTIONS†
2511 West Broadway
Louisville, KY 40211
(502) 778-1754
Contact: Billy Harold Rudolph

HAROLD MCDONALD ASSOCIATES TALENT & BOOKING AGENCY†
43 Meadowview Dr.
Louisville, KY 40220
(502) 456-6337
Contact: Harold Morgan McDonald

MCKINNEY ASSOCIATES, INC.†
P.O. Box 5162
Louisville, KY 40205
(502) 583-8222
Contact: Michael A. McKinney, Nancy Ammerman

SOUNDS OF LEGEND†
6402 Riverdale Rd.
Louisville, KY 40272
(502) 937-5996
Contact: Jack Willis McGill, Douglas Sego

TRIANGLE TALENT, INC.*†
9701 Taylorsville Road
Louisville, KY 40299
(502) 267-5466
Contact: David H. Snowden, Hardison G. Martin, Neil Long, Steve M. Woodring, Lynn R. Murrell, David Baldwin, Henry Krupinski, Sid Yates, Debbie Hoffman, Daniel H. Green, Al Gorrell, Kurt Wallen, Thomas Wanca, Phil Coultrip, Dan Ash

LOUISIANA

BATON ROUGE

DYNASTY ONE PROMOTIONS†
(DIV. OF DYNASTY ONE CORP.)
12121 S. Choctaw
Baton Rouge, LA 70815
(504) 273-0933
Contact: John R. Natchez

BOSSIER CITY

ACE WILLIAMSON PRODUCTIONS†
1627 Holiday Circle
Bossier City, LA 71112
(318) 746-5211
Contact: A.C. "Ace" Williamson

GRETNA

PENUNBRA PHOTOS, INC.†
733 Hickory
Gretna, LA 70053
(504) 392-9249
Contact: Armand Joseph Richardson

HOUMA

NASHVILLE SOUTH†
242 Leslie St.
Houma, LA 70360
(504) 876-3935
Contact: Catherine B. Blanchard

KENNER

DRAGON PRODUCTIONS†
P.O. Box 2155
Kenner, LA 70063
(504) 467-5928
Contact: Mrs. June Dragon Hoepffner

PREJEAN TALENT AGENCY†
3410 Florida Avenue
Kenner, LA 70062
(504) 468-1094
Contact: George J. Prejean

METAIRIE

THE PAT BARBEROT ORCHESTRA & PRODUCTIONS†
P.O. Box 8411
Metairie, LA 70011
(504) 837-3621
Contact: Bonnie N. Barberot

MICHAEL RAYMOND TALENT AGENCY†
2812 Metairie Court
Metairie, LA 70002
(504) 833-6145
Contact: Michael Raymond, Mary Raye

MINDEN

THE DREW AGENCY†
1002 Broadway
Minden, LA 71055
(318) 377-8098
Contact: Harmon Drew, Jr., Jean Drew

NEW ORLEANS

ARTS NEW ORLEANS, INC.†
527 Burgundy St., #1
New Orleans, LA 70112
(504) 522-0434
Contact: Barbara Nauer

DIANNA L. CHENEVERT†
1516 Shirley Dr.
New Orleans, LA 70114
(504) 366-2785

INTERNATIONAL PRODUCTIONS OF NEW ORLEANS†
126 S. Gayoso St.
New Orleans, LA 70119

(504) 821-3320
Contact: Leon Cornman

K C AGENCY, INC.†
928 Moss Street
New Orleans, LA 70119
(504) 488-1126
Contact: Kathryn K. Copponex

LOUISIANA ENTERTAINMENT PRODUCTIONS†
313 Royal St.
New Orleans, LA 70130
(504) 568-0141
Contact: John F. Young

MUSICAL CONTRACTING AGENCY†
1221 Maison Blanche Bldg.
New Orleans, LA 70112
(504) 524-8359
Contact: Melba Honey Wolfe

NEW ORLEANS TALENT SERVICES†
628 Dauphine St.
New Orleans, LA 70112
(504) 522-3346
Contact: Harry Mayronne, Sharon Hix

OGDEN'S ARTIST VAN BOOKING AGENCY†
2620 Milan St.
New Orleans, LA 70115
(504) 891-0988
Contact: Dave R. Ogden, Robert Ogden, William Ogden, Peter Ogden, Robert Gibson

KEN PRINDLE AGENCY†
823 Audubon Bldg.
New Orleans, LA 70112
(504) 523-7416

SHREVEPORT

BOB COXSEY PRODUCTIONS†
1111 W. 70th #50
Shreveport, LA 71106
(318) 868-5630
Contact: Robert Louis Coxsey

TILLMAN B. FRANKS†
324 Johnson Building
Shreveport, LA 71101
(318) 221-5886

SLIDEL

MAJOR ARTISTS†
260 Whisperwood
Slidel (New Orleans), LA 70458
(504) 649-4392
Contact: Phil Bernie, Virginia Till, Lucille Vennen, Barbara Sukman

MAINE

BANGOR

DICK RAYMOND ENTERPRISES, INC.†
(See Gorham listing)

FAIRFIELD

CLIFF DUPHINEY ENTERPRISES†
The Riverside Ranch
Main St.
Fairfield, ME 04937
(207) 453-7859
Contact: Cliff Duphiney

GORHAM

DICK RAYMOND ENTERPRISES, INC.†
Longmeadow Drive
Gorham, ME 04038
(207) 839-2207

Branch Office;
15 Hudson Street
Bangon, ME 04401
(207) 942-2419
Contact: Ron Bouchard

LEWISTON

GOOD SOUNDS TALENT AGENCY†
182 Webster St.
Lewiston, ME 04240
(207) 782-1697
Contact: Elaine Kesaris

PORTLAND

ADVANCE ENTERTAINMENT†
1150 Forest Ave.
Portland, ME 04103
(207) 797-9836
Contact: Jonas Smith

ALBERT REALI AGENCY†
2 Byfield Road
Portland, ME 04103
(207) 773-3626

MARYLAND

BALTIMORE

CES TALENT INC.†
2631 N. Charles St.
Baltimore, MD 21218
(301) 889-3900
Contact: Nicholas Litrenta, Dennis C. Bernstein, Jeffrey N. Setren, Thomas Apple, Bryan Hodegson, Franklin Serio

DICK GRAY ENTERTAINMENT AGENCY†
4 Dutlow Ct. #3-C
Baltimore, MD 21237
(301) 866-8440
Contact: Dick Gray, Daniel W. Grauer, David W. Holttle, John McFadden

STARLEIGH ENTERPRISES*
205 E. Joppa Rd., #106
Baltimore, MD 21204
(301) 828-9400
Contact: Marc Loundas

FREDERICK

D/B TALENT†
Dance Hall Rd.
P.O. Box 614
Frederick, MD 21701
(301) 898-9936
Contact: Donald Charles Barnes, Sr., Nola R. Barnes

GEORGE RICHARD DELAWRENCE†
705 Maxwell Ave.
Frederick, MD 21701
(301) 662-6196

GAITHERSBURG

BARRY RICK ASSOCIATES*
2 Professional Dr., #240
Gaithersburg, MD 20760
Contact: Barry Rick

ODENTON

C & J AFFILIATES, INC. ENTERTAINMENT AGENCY†
516 Patricia Court
Odenton, MD 21113
(301) 551-5025
Contact: James J. Temple, Sr., David J. Temple, Scarlet Harmon

SILVER SPRING

P.H.L. ASSOCIATES†
721 Ellsworth Drive
Silver Spring, MD 20910
(301) 565-3015
Contact: Peter H. Lambros

TIMONIUM

IRV KLEIN THEATRICAL AGENCY†
7C Aylesbury Road
Timonium, MD 21093
(301) 252-2832
Contact: Irv Klein

MASSACHUSETTS

BELMONT

JOHN PENNY ENTERPRISES INC.†
259-A Beech St.
Belmont, MA 02178
(617) 924-6722
Contact: John A. Piantedosi, Vera Piantedosi, Jerry Fox

BOSTON

JAZZ TREE†
59 Bay State Road
Boston, MA 02215
(617) 267-0100
Contact: Mary Ann Topper

TED KURLAND ASSOCIATES†
46 Ashford St.
Boston, MA 02134
(617) 254-0007
Contact: Kent Farquhar

LORDLY & DAME, INC.†
51 Church St.
Boston, MA 02116
(617) 482-3593
Contact: Samuel Dame, Martin A. Forrest, William G. Thompson, Eleanor Tuttle, Peter Rabbitt

CHELMSFORD

LITTLEFIELD ENTERTAINMENT AGENCY, INC.†
93 Chelmsford St.
Chelmsford, MA 08124
1 (617) 256-5895
Contact: Chet A. Littlefield, Jr., Wayne A. Littlefield, Ken Gervais, Joe Armstrong, Sarah Duffy

CHESTNUT HILL

RUBY NEWMAN ORCHESTRAS†
160 Boylston St. (Susse Chalet)
Chestnut Hill, MA 02167
(617) 527-3210
Contact: Ruby Newman, William Kroner, Ted Phillips

HARWICH

JACK BRADLEY†
24 Skipper's Dr.
Harwich, MA 02645
(617) 432-3416

LYNN

TOM CARUSO THEATRICAL AGENCY†
82 Linwood Street
Lynn, MA 01905
(617) 598-5006
Contact: Armand Caruso

NEEDHAM

WILLIAM H. CURTIS†
1001 Central Avenue
Needham, MA 02192
(617) 444-5235

NEWTONVILLE

JERRY BENARD†
82 Wyoming Rd.
Newtonville, MA 02160
(617) 244-4464
Contact: Jerry Benard, Sherman Marcus

NATIONAL BOOKING CONSULTANTS, INC.†
14 Beach St.
Newtonville, MA 02160
(617) 523-1515
Contact: Anthony R. Desimone, Michael Carlin

NORTH ADAMS

JIM DAMI AGENCY†
17 Frederick Street
North Adams, MA 02147
(413) 663-7064

PITTSFIELD

FRAN-MAN ENTERTAINMENT AGENCY†
138 Gamwell Avenue
Pittsfield, MA 01201
(413) 442-8733
Contact: Frank C. Mancivalano

SALEM

TED CHARLES AGENCY, INC.*†
167 Boston St.
P.O. Box 390
Salem, MA 01970
(617) 744-9310
Contact: Andrew S. Friedman, Carl Ellsworth, Bob Colia, Steven Bussiere

SPENCER

CAMPUS SERVICES, INC.†
172 Main St.
Spencer, MA 01562
(617) 753-1318

Contact: Patrick J. George, Lucy George, Domenic Santora, Joseph George

WALTHAM

COLLINS & BARRASSO TALENT COORDINATION†
30 Grant St.
Waltham, MA 02154
(617) 893-2776
Contact: Timothy J. Collins, Stephen G. Barrasso, Bruce Houghton

WOBURN

FRANK PAUL ENTERPRISES†
P.O. Box 113-6 Carter Place
Woburn, MA 01801
(617) 993-1474
Contact: Frank Paul Pappalardo

MICHIGAN

ANN ARBOR

A & A PRODUCTIONS†
206 South Main, #207
Ann Arbor, MI 48104
(313) 769-0800
Contact: Raymond L. Shelide, Roger Shelide, James R. Barry

ASHLEY STREET TALENT, INC.†
312 S. Ashley Street
Ann Arbor, MI 48104
(313) 769-5454
Contact: Susan I. Nalli, Jay Frey, Al Nalli, Robert Young

PRISM PRODUCTIONS, INC.†
P.O. Box 8125
Ann Arbor, MI 48107
(313) 665-4755
Contact: Thomas R. Stachler

BIRMINGHAM

DJERKISS BROTHERS & ASSOCIATES†
6405 Westmoor Road
Birmingham, MI 48010
1 (313) 626-5330
Contact: Donald T. Dierkes, Walter E. Dierkes

CANTON

MUZACAN ASSOCIATES, INC.†
44844 Michigan Ave.
Canton, MI 48188
(313) 397-3444
Contact: Bruce A. Young, Elsie Young, Gregory A. Gomez, Michael Apel, Kathy Sarcone, Stephen G. Broyles

DEARBORN

AGENT WILLIAM CHARLES†
13600 Ford Rd.
Box 4421
Dearborn, MI 48126
1 (313) 846-4299

SHOWCASE PRODUCTIONS, INC.†
1800 Grindley Park, Ste. 4
Dearborn, MI 48124
(313) 563-6730

Contact: Lawrence J. Marshall, Phillip Morey

STERLING DIVERSION, INC.†
1800 Grindley Park
Dearborn, MI 48124
(313) 561-4404
Contact: Ronal Baltrusz, Joseph P. Peraino II, Mike Murdza, Ralph Rivett, James McCallum, Candy Bashor

DEARBORN HEIGHTS

COUNTRY MUSIC PROMOTIONS†
2036 Kinmore St.
Dearborn Heights, MI 44127
(313) 562-1000
Contact: Paul Wade, Bill Clayton

DETROIT

FIVE POINT PRODUCTIONS†
60 West Canfield
Detroit, MI 48201
(313) 832-2622
Contact: Keith Heavenridge, Daniel O'Connell, Raymond Kaczor, Brian Munce

FRAN LEE AGENCY†
1432 Ferry Park
Detroit, MI 48208
(313) 873-0479
Contact: Francine E. Lee

M.R.S. TALENT AGENCY†
14049 Gratiot
Detroit, MI 48205
(313) 521-4192
Contact: Victor Pettenuzzi, Salvitore G. Moceri, Dan Pifer

LOUIS PARENTI†
1059 Seminole
Detroit, MI 48214
(313) 331-1673

JERRY PATLOW & ASSOCIATES†
17429 Indian Ave.
Detroit, MI 48240
(313) 531-9330

EAST LANSING

SIDARTHA ENTERPRISES, LTD.†
1504 East Grand River Ave.
East Lansing, MI 48823
(517) 351-6780
Contact: Thomas R. Brunner, Dan Callihan, Wilson Gravenor

FARMINGTON HILLS

DICK STEIN ENTERPRISES, INC.†
31455 Northwestern Hwy.
Farmington Hills, MI 48018
1 (313) 855-1400

HARTLAND

JOE BANKET ENTERTAINMENT AGENCY, INC.†
6360 Bullard Road
Fenton, MI 48430
Mailing Address:
P.O. Box 257
Hartland, MI 48029
(313) 478-4035
Contact: Joe Banket

FLINT

FRED BUCHANAN ENTERTAINMENT AGENCY†
G-4170 Miller Road
Flint, MI 48507
(313) 733-0320
Contact: Fred Buchanan, Mrs. Reta Fagan, Rosana Bissonette, Dennis Niec, Ronald A. Fadell, Barry Duke, Freddie Buchanan, Jr.

FRASER

STARHEART TALENT AND BOOKING LTD.†
34687 Groesbeck HIghway
Fraser, MI 48026
(313) 791-8070
Contact: Giovanni Chiaramonti, Steven E. Zmuda, Larry Clinkscales, Lisa McFarland, Ben Furlow

FREELAND

RUSCH PRODUCTIONS†
3588 N. Thomas Road
Freeland, MI 48623
(517) 781-1553
Contact: Dean A. Rusch

GARDEN CITY

AL'S VARIETY SHOWS, INC.†
30400 Rush
Garden City, MI 48135
(313) 261-2141
Contact: Alva D. Cole

GRAND RAPIDS

JERRY MAGNAN AGENCY†
202 Brown St., S.E.
Grand Rapids, MI 49507
(616) CH 1-1130
Contact: Bill Farrow, Gertrude Barnes, Antonia Kiekoda, Tiny Young

TREECE TRADEWINDS PRODUCTIONS†
1531 Coit N.E.
Grand Rapids, MI 49505
(616) 459-9493
Contact: James Lee Treece, Lawrence Jay Treece, Judy Barr, Janice Keck, Aura Ulm, Dorothy Kelting

Branch Office:
3011 No. Garfield, Lot 4
Traverse City, MI 49684
(616) 941-0655

KALAMAZOO

MAIDA BOOKING AGENCY†
2917 Duchess Drive
Kalamazoo, MI 49008
(616) 349-4250

DON NEAL PRODUCTIONS†
521 East Michigan Avenue
Kalamazoo, MI 49007
(616) 382-1174
Contact: Donald B. Neal, Shelley A. Brye

LANSING

NORRIS AGENCY†
3904 South Logan St.
Lansing, MI 48910
(517) 882-4647
Contact: Gary Lynn Norris, Carol Mary Norris

LIVONIA

GAIL & RICE, INC.†
11845 Mayfield
Livonia, MI 48150
(313) 427-9300
Contact: Clarence Al Rice, John Bonino, H.E. Faulkner, Michael Williams, Bob Gentry, Max Gail, Jr., Jack Qualey, Barry Martin, Johnny Johnson, Timothy Rice, John R. Trudell, Warney Ruhl, Chris Nordman

MADISON HEIGHTS

GRENIER & MOORE ASSOCIATES†
32500 Concord Drive
Madison Heights, MI 48071
(313) 585-2552
Contact: John Grenier, Stephen Smorol, Jr., James Nantais, Greg Romain

JSF PRODUCTIONS, INC.†
27301 Dequindre, Ste. 307
Madison Heights, MI 48071
(313) 548-1932
Contact: Albert I. Fill, Jeffrey S. Fill, Judity A. Schefke

OAK PARK

DAVID J. HULL MUSIC ENTERPRISES†
13540 Dartmouth
Oak Park, MI 48237
(313) 542-1195

OKEMOS

ROBERT BALDORI & ASSOCIATES†
2719 Mt. Hope Road
Okemos, MI 48864
(517) 351-6555
Contact: Robert Baldori, Marvin Rank, Jean Standress

PORT HURON

BOB HERBER BOOKING AGENCY†
1515 Stone St.
Port Huron, MI 48060
1 (313) 985-7637
Contact: Robert C. Herber, Raymond D. McDonald

REDFORD

EMPIRE MANAGEMENT AGENCY†
24755 Five Mile Road
Redford, MI 48239
(313) 533-3134
Contact: Angel Gregory Gomez

ROYAL OAK

LORIO-ROSS ENTERTAINMENT*
505 S. Lafayette
Royal Oak, MI 48084
(313) 588-0441
Contact: Jerry Ross

SOUTHFIELD

DIVERSIFIED MANAGEMENT AGENCY†
17650 W. 12 Mile Rd.
Southfield, MI 48076
(313) 559-2600
Contact: David A. Leone, Nick Caris, Roger Alan Gacon, Donald "Trip" Brown, Mark Hyman

INTERNATIONAL TALENT ARTISTS†
24548 Pierce
Southfield, MI 48075
(313) 559-7630
Contact: Bruce Lorfel, Tom Wells, Steve Pic, Pamela Bates, Mark Isabel

SEYMOUR SCHWARTZ AGENCY†
19111 West 10 Mile Road
Southfield, MI 48075
(313) 356-8525

STERLING HEIGHTS

DAVID A. KIMLER & ASSOCIATES†
36712 Park Place Dr., Ste. 100
Sterling Heights, MI 48077
(313) 268-7468

TAYLOR

ED NEAGLE PRODUCTIONS†
8856 Caroline
Taylor, MI 48180
(313) 292-5767
Contact: Edwin Thomas Neagle, Gerald T. Harris

TRAVERSE CITY

TREECE TRADEWINDS PRODUCTIONS‡
(See Grand Rapids listing)

TROY

LORIO-ROSS ENTERTAINMENT AGENCY†
799 Stephenson Highway
Troy, MI 48084
(313) 588-0441
Contact: Jerry Ross, Leola Taylor, Nancy Witt, John Chervak, David Blake, Anne M. McPhail, Julie Ross, Ricky Dee

WARREN

BANDS GALORE ENTERPRISES†
14402 Peck Drive
Warren, MI 48093
(313) 293-4503
Contact: Richard A. Paul, Frank T. Paul, Thomas F. Paul

WEST BLOOMFIELD

MEL BALL PRODUCTIONS, INC.†
P.O. Box 5086
West Bloomfield, MI 48033
(313) 851-1992

WYANDOTTE

AL SPARER THEATRICAL AGENCY†
1685 Fort Street
Wyandotte, MI 48192
(313) 285-2520
Contact: Alexander Sparer, Dino Valle, Michael Matthews, James Brown, Hershel Stroud, Alfonso G. Pugh

WYOMING

MUSICAL TALENT SERVICE†
3860 Collingwood, S.W.
Wyoming, MI 49509
(616) 538-3293
Contact: Virginia E. Sasso

MINNESOTA

ALBERT LEA

NORCO ENTERTAINMENT†
139 E. William-Lea Center Plaza
P.O. Box 983
Albert Lea, MN 56007
(507) 373-8111
Contact: Paul S. Nordby, Shirley Gunderson

AUSTIN

D.C. MUSIC INC.†
2108 5th Ave., N.E.
Austin, MN 55912
(507) 437-6968
Contact: Dennis Lawrence Charnecki, Connie J. Warner

GEORGE A. HILLBERG†
2009 1st Ave., S.E.
Austin, MN 55912
1 (507) 437-2881

BLOOMINGTON

C & L PRODUCTIONS†
6124 W. 104th St.
Bloomington, MN 55438
(612) 831-7977
Contact: Charles William Loufek

BROOKLYN PARK

T.M.S. PRODUCTION†
817 Pearson Parkway
Brooklyn Park, MN 55444
(612) 561-2459
Contact: Theresa M. Skon

BURNSVILLE

JAN SESSIONS: JAZZ PRODUCTIONS†
170 Birnamwood Dr.
Burnsville, MN 55337
(612) 890-1700
Contact: Janice H. Hartley

EDEN PRAIRIE

O'BRIEN ENTERTAINMENT*
9975 Valley View Rd.
Eden Prairie, MN 55344
(612) 944-9000
Contact: Jerry O'Brien

EXCELSIOR

GOOD MUSIC AGENCY*
P.O. Box O
Excelsior, MN 55331
(612) 474-2581
Contact: Doug Brown

KEITH JOHNSON ENTERPRISES*
10 Water St.
Excelsior, MN 55331
(612) 474-8837
Contact: Keith Johnson

HOPKINS

DON BATES PRODUCTIONS†
251-21st Ave., N.
Hopkins, MN 55343
(612) 938-5598
Contact: Don A. Bates

HARRY HABATA ENTERTAINMENT†
106 Van Buren Avenue South
Hopkins, MN 55343
(612) 935-2139
Contact: Dorothy Habata, Barbara Riker, John Harrington

GEORGE THOMPSON AGENCY†
19 Loring Road
Hopkins, MN 55343
(612) 933-6493
Contact: Ronald E. Thompson, George E. Thompson, Jr., Patricia Pavey, Mary Jane Thompson

LAKE ELMO

JOHNSON DIVERSIFIED ENTERPRISES (JDE)†
Box 158
Lake Elmo, MN 55042
(612) 436-7271
Contact: Paul M. Johnson

LAKEVILLE

FAY'S MUSICAL SERVICES†
10530 175th St., W.
Lakeville, MN 55044
(612) 435-7766
Contact: Richard Harold Fay

MINNEAPOLIS

BARKER-THOMPSON ENTERPRISES†
6945 Harriet Avenue South
Minneapolis, MN 55423
(612) 866-4683
Contact: Paul Thompson, Barbara Barker

BLONS PRODUCTIONS†
4216 Queen Ave., S. #2
Minneapolis, MN 55410
(612) 927-0893
Contact: Steven G. Blons

RAY BOILES TALENT AGENCY†
3205 E. 37th St., Ste. 307
Minneapolis, MN 55406
1 (612) 722-4428
Contact: Raymond Foy Boiles

BPA PRODUCTIONS†
P.O. Box 22567
Minneapolis, MN 55422
(612) 544-3444
Contact: Bernie Aydt, Robet Dale Engquist, Shirley Aydt, George "Gus" Cambanes, Daniel M. Blair, Joe Campbell, Marjorie Douville, Bob Kahle, Diane Englin, Denice R. Aydt, Jim Feeny, Tom Barbeau

COURTNEY LEE (CORKY) FENSKE†
2818 Sunset Boulevard
Minneapolis, MN 55416
(612) 920-3511

NED KANTAR PRODUCTIONS, INC.†
6000 Oliver Ave., S.
Minneapolis, MN 55419
(612) 861-1212

MIKE MACKEN MUSIC & ASSOCIATES†
5001 W. 80th St., Ste. 710
Minneapolis, MN 55437
(612) 831-0270
Contact: Michael R. Macken

PETEY'S ENTERTAINMENT ENTERPRISE†
118 Wesley Temple Bldg.
Minneapolis, MN 55403
(612) 870-4141
Contact: Earl C. Peterson

RIVERA AGENCY†
2800 Grand Ave., S.
Minneapolis, MN 55408
(612) 823-5425
Contact: David Rivera

SHEEHAN ENTERTAINMENT CORPORATION†
625 Second Avenue South
Minneapolis, MN 55402
(612) 333-6464
Contact: Fred W. Smith, Bette B. Smith, Morrie Wilf

SOUNDINGS†
1834 Fremont, S.
Minneapolis, MN 55403
(612) 377-8582
Contact: Joanne M. Cierniak

BOB TERRI†
2301 Garfield Street, N.E.
Minneapolis, MN 55418
(612) 781-1061

VARIETY ARTISTS INTERNATIONAL, INC./EXCELSIOR TALENT†
(DIV. OF VARIETY ARTISTS INTERNATIONAL, INC.)
4120 Excelsior Blvd.
Minneapolis, MN 55416
(612) 925-3440
Contact: Gordon Singer, Rodney A. Essig, Allan Neuman, Lloyd St. Martin, Arne Brogger, David Milberg

Branch Office:
9000 Sunset Blvd., Ste. 911
Los Angeles, CA 90069
(213) 858-7800
Contact: Bob Engel, Richard W. Halem

MINNETONKA

M.J. PRODUCTIONS INC.†
4537 Highland Road
Minetonka, MN 55343
(612) 938-5181
Contact: Mari Jane Engebrit

NEW BRIGHTON

NINA E. CAFARO†
1500 Piper Drive
New Brighton, MN 55112
(414) 432-8852

PINE ISLAND

SHARYL A. SANFORD†

RR #1 Box 421
Pine Island, MN 55963
(507) 356-8970

PLAINVIEW

PARRISH TALENT AGENCY†
Lot 94 Edgewood Acres
Plainview, MN 55964
(507) 534-3203
Contact: Edward Odell Parrish

PRINCETON

MID FLIGHT PRODUCTIONS†
P.O. Box 162
Princeton, MN 55371
(612) 389-4735
Contact: Mitchell Allen Heyn, Gary Whitcomb

RICHFIELD

T.S.J. PRODUCTIONS†
7408 18th Ave., S.
Richfield, MN 55423
(612) 869-1779
Contact: Katherine J. Lange, Thomas St. James

ST. PAUL

CARTER COUNTRY BOOKING AGENCY†
786 E. Hyacinth Ave.
St. Paul, MN 55106
1 (612) 774-5392
Contact: Robert L. Carter

LARRY CORTEZ ENTERTAINMENT†
109 East Annapolis Street
St. Paul, MN 55118
(612) 226-3045
Contact: Lorenzo Cortez, Jr., Joe Gaona

DEWY ENGEL PRODUCTIONS†
272 East Congress
St. Paul, MN 55107
(612) 221-0132
Contact: Dewy A. Engel, Kathleen McPhillips, Kari Anderson

OAK ROOM MUSIC ENTERPRISES, INC.†
1021 Arcade St. (Upper)
St. Paul, MN 55106
(612) 774-6924
Contact: Jerry Russell, Lance Terrell

REFLECTION PRODUCTIONS†
P.O. Box 3131
St. Paul, MN 55165
(612) 455-5200
Contact: Michael J. Fendt

RONALD HENRY ROTTER†
1765 Reaney Ave.
St. Paul, MN 55106
(612) 771-7850
Contact: Deborah Rotter

TOM WIGGINS MUSIC†
821 Watson
St. Paul, MN 55102
(612) 225-1163
Contact: Thomas C. Wiesner

WAYZATA

PLUS THREE†
815 E. Rice
Wayzata, MN 55391
(612) 475-1710
Contact: Roy Lester Geidel

MISSISSIPPI

CORINTH

C.P. RAMER, AGENT†
P.O. Box 304
Corinth, MS 38834
(601) 287-2311
Contact: Cecil Philip Ramer

JACKSON

DELTA ENTERTAINMENT AGENCY†
5310 Jamaica Drive
Jackson, MS 39211
(601) 956-5495, 956-5532
Contact: James W. Sacca, Jr., James W. Sacca III

RALPH GIBBS ENTERTAINMENT AGENCY*†
P.O. Box 9965
Jackson, MS 39206
(601) 362-8306
Contact: Ralph Gibbs, Linda Philley

MISSOURI

ARNOLD

DON SCHERER PRODUCTIONS†
1440 Jeffco Boulevard
Arnold, MO 63010
(314) 296-9330
Contact: Donald J. Scherer

BERKELEY

JEAN'S LITTLE EGYPT BOOKING AGENCY†
8466 Alder Ave.
Berkeley, MO 63134
(314) 524-7043
Contact: Geneva Jean Scotland

CAPE GIRARDEAU

FORD BOOKING AGENCY*
P.O. Box 674
Cape Girardeau, MO 63701
(314) 335-5851
Contact: Mike Ford

CHESTERFIELD

JUDY ATWELL AGENCY†
1755 Golden Lake Court
Chesterfield, MO 63017
(314) 532-4738
Contact: Judy A. Atwell

HAZELWOOD

CONCERT CONNECTIONS UNLIMITED†
7583-G Hazelcrest Dr.
Hazelwood, MO 63042
(314) 837-7107
Contact: Geral G. Rowland, Dawnbeth Rowland

INDEPENDENCE

BILIN AGENCY(TX)†
Branch Office:
4413 Lee's Summit Road
Independence, MO 64057
(816) 373-1639
Contact: Mrs. Jean Echols

JOPLIN

LE-MO PRODUCTION AND TALENT AGENCY†
1700 West 7th
Joplin, MO 64801
(417) 781-4500
Contact: Leon A. Moser

OZARK TALENT†
2423 Mina
Joplin, MO 64801
(417) 781-1568
Contact: Linda J. Scheurich

KANSAS CITY

TONY DIPARDO MUSIC & ENTERTAINMENT†
510 East 31st Street
Kansas City, MO 64108
(815) 756-1515
Contact: Tony DiPardo, Doddie DiPardo, Patricia A. DiPardo

GOLDMAN-DELL MUSIC PRODUCTIONS†
421 W. 87th St., Ste. 29
P.O. Box 8680
Kansas City, MO 64114
(816) 333-8701
Contact: Irving S. Goldman, Ethel G. Dell

BUDDY LEE ATTRACTIONS, INC.(TN)†
Branch Office:
3821 West Park Dr.
Kansas City, MO 69116
(816) 454-0839
Contact: Joan Saltel

MARHILL AGENCY†
811 E. Linwood Blvd.
Kansas City, MO 64109
1 (816) 931-4397
Contact: Jack L. Marvin, Eugene E. Hill

JERRY PLANTZ PRODUCTIONS†
1703 Wyandotte
Kansas City, MO 64108
(816) 471-1501
Contact: Jan Mahaffey, Norm Gresham, Fred Hendrix, Jim Weinrich, Rex Calhoun, Candace Calhoun

PLAYHOUSE PRODUCTIONS†
1301 Traders Bank
1125 Grand Avenue
Kansas City, MO 64106
(816) 842-9700
Contact: Gerlarmo P.L. Cammisano, John Benson Williams

SANDUSKY'S ENTERTAINMENT, LTD.†
7540 Grand
Kansas City, MO 64114
(816) 363-6426
Contact: John W. Sandusky, Martha M. Sandusky, William E. Tobin, Chuck Mardee, Wilfred O. "Wink" Wright, Carl Russell

DAN SMITH AGENCY(KS)†
Branch Office:
100 W. 99 Terrace, #102
Kansas City, MO 64114
(816) 942-5344

MANCHESTER

JAY MCINTYRE, LTD.†
1583 Woodside Village Lane
Manchester, MO 63011
(314) 225-7254
Contact: James Jay McIntyre

NORTH KANSAS CITY

AMERICA'S BEST ATTRACTIONS†
310 Armour Rd., Ste. 104
North Kansas City, MO 64116
(816) 421-1124
Contact: Allan H. Bell, Carroll Jenkins, Stewart Farbman, Lana Finks, Catherine Szulc

SPRINGFIELD

ACE-ASSOCIATES FOR COMMUNITY ENTERTAINMENT†
324 St. Louis
P.O. Box 1924
Springfield, MO 65805
(417) 884-6600
Contact: John M. Gott, C. Robert McCroskey

SOUTHWESTERN MISSOURI BOOKING AGENCY†
1629 E. Walnut Lawn
Springfield, MO 65807
(417) 883-2043
Contact: Herman A. Lemmon

TOP TALENT, INC.†
1121 S. Glenstone
Springfield, MO 65804
(417) 869-6379
Contact: Ralph Foster, E.E. Siman, Jr.

ST. LOUIS

DON C. BUTLER†
6121 Garesche
St. Louis, MO 63136
(314) 382-8391

CONTINENTAL ENTERTAINMENT ASSOCIATES†
680 Craig Road
St. Louis, MO 63141
(314) 567-9880
Contact: Steve Madison, Susan Panitz, Paul L. Tassler, Kevin Dochtermann, Joyce Williams

CRESCENDO TALENT†
8510 Page
St. Louis, MO 63114
(314) 423-6688
Contact: Olinn E. Erb

E-G PRODUCTIONS†
1139 Olive St.
P.O. Box 596
St. Louis, MO 63101
(314) 231-6042
Contact: Eddie Gromacki, Cathy-Lynne Ficken, Patricia Holt

DICK HALL PRODUCTIONS, INC.*
2816 Breckinridge Industrial Park
St. Louis, MO 63144
(314) 961-2193
Contact: Dick Hall

BOB KUBAN ENTERTAINMENT AGENCY†
5 Biritz Drive
St. Louis, MO 63137
(314) 869-6056

HOWARD E. MCNIER†
7 N. Seventh St., Ste. 623
St. Louis, MO 63101
(314) 421-0326

JOHNNY POLZIN ENTERPRISES, INC.†
416 Oakley Drive
St. Louis, MO 63105
(314) 862-1114
Contact: Carleen C. Polzin, Sharon A. Diffley

CHARLES V. WELLS BOOKING AGENCY†
6841 Bartmer Ave.
St. Louis, MO 63130
(314) 863-2268

WARRENSBURG

UNITED ENTERTAINMENT AGENCY*†
P.O. Box 83
Warrensburg, MO 64093
(816) 747-3476
Contact: David McQuitty

NEBRASKA

KEARNEY

EDDIE OSBORN ENTERPRISES†
102 E. 28th St.
Kearney, NE 68847
(308) 237-9321
Contact: Ron Barker

LEIGH

REININGER ENTERTAINMENT AGENCY†
RR #2
P.O. Box 266
Leigh, NE 68643
(402) 487-2213
Contact: Roger E. Reininger

LINCOLN

THE BAND ORGANIZATION(IL)†
Branch Office:
2332 N. Cotner Blvd., Ste. D-2
Lincoln, NE 68507
(402) 467-5457
Contact: Kris Mortensen

LUTZ AGENCY*†
5625 "O" Street Building, Ste. 7
Lincoln, NE 68510
(402) 483-2241
Contact: Richard Lutz, Craig Lutz, Cherie Hanfelt, Jim Lawson, Brian Lutz

NATIONAL ENTERTAINMENT NETWORK†
5609 S. 49th St.
Lincoln, NE 68516
(402) 423-3863
Contact: Ronald K. Jester, J. Sherman Bixby

RAN-VIL MUSIC†
140 S. 48th, Ste. 1
Lincoln, NE 68510
P.O. Box 6407
Lincoln, NE 68506
(402) 483-6658
Contact: Vil Rizijs, Randy Stone, Bobbie Jo Carter

OMAHA

SUBBY ANZALDO ENTERTAINMENT AGENCY†
330 Aquila Court Bldg.
1615 Howard St.
Omaha, NE 68102
(402) 346-0100

EDDY HADDAD ENTERPRISES†
2202 S. 88th St.
Omaha, NE 68124
(402) 391-3653

PANCO ENTERTAINMENT AGENCY*†
P.O. Box 4169
Omaha, NE 68104
(402) 571-5222
Contact: Joseph Francis Pane, Jr.

NEVADA

CARSON CITY

GARFIN PRODUCTIONS†
1642 Camille Dr.
Carson City, NV 89701
(702) 883-9727
Contact: Howard "Speedy" Garfin

JACKPOT

J.L. TALENT & BOOKING AGENCY†
P.O. Box 388
Jackpot, NV 89825
(702) 755-2394
Contact: Verlin J. Logan

LAS VEGAS

AMERICAN CREATIVE ENTERTAINMENT, LTD.†
536 East St. Louis Avenue
Las Vegas, NV 89104
(702) 731-2322
Contact: Frank Moore, Joel Klein

Branch Office:
1616 Pacific Ave., Ste. 817
Atlantic City, NJ 08401
(609) 348-1809
Contact: Danny Luciano

B & G THEATRICAL AGENCY†
616 E. Carson
Las Vegas, NV 89101
(702) 384-9448
Contact: William H. Bailey, Anna L. Bailey, Roslynn Guy

J. BASKOW TALENT AGENCY & ASSOCIATES†

2770 S. Maryland Pkwy., Ste. 212
Las Vegas, NV 89109
(702) 733-7818
Contact: Jaki Iris Baskow, Daniel DeSimone, Stuart Grant

FRANKIE CARR PRODUCTIONS†
2301 Karli Dr. #1
Las Vegas, NV 89102
(702) 878-8684
Contact: Frankie Carr

CREATIVE ENTERTAINMENT ASSOCIATES†
1629 East Sahara Ave.
Las Vegas, NV 89104
(702) 733-7575
Contact: Robert Morris, Mrs. Diane Robinson, Eleanor Roth-Grasso

ART ENGLER, INC.†
4055 S. Spencer
Las Vegas, NV 89109
(702) 369-7208
Contact: Art Engler, Shirley Engler

MERLE HOWARD†
416 McArthur Way
Las Vegas, NV 89107
(702) 878-5518

REDBEARD PRESENTS PRODUCTIONS, LTD.†
1061 E. Flamingo Rd., Ste.7
Las Vegas, NV 89109
P.O. Box 19114
Las Vegas, NV 89132
(702) 361-4875
Contact: Robert Leonard

GEORGE SOARES ASSOCIATES†
2685 So. Tenaya Way
Las Vegas, NV 89117
(702) 876-3843
Contact: Jay Finger

Branch Office:
26060 Adamor Rd.
Calabasas, CA 91302
(213) 880-5757
Contact: Roy Baumgart

HOLLY STORM LTD.†
421 E. Carson #305
Las Vegas, NV 89101
(702) 384-2389
Contact: Holly Storm

TAYLOR ARTISTS MANAGEMENT*†
2874 La Canada
Las Vegas, NV 89109
(702) 734-6278
Contact: Donna Taylor

VEGAS INTERNATIONAL PERSONALITIES†
Bldg. 28B, Ste. 202
953 E. Sahara
Las Vegas, NV 89104
(702) 737-5177
Contact: Chris Columbo, Toni Columbo, Robert Allen

RENO

GAYLORDS ENTERTAINMENT COMPANY†
17 S. Virginia
Reno, NV 89501
(702) 322-2442
Contact: Burt Bonaldi, Ronald Fredianelli, Donald G. Rea

BIG TINY LITTLE ENTERTAINMENT AGENCY†
100 W. Grove #155
Reno, NV 89509
P.O. Box 12010
Reno, NV 89510
(702) 322-0791
Contact: Dudley R. Little

JOE MARTINI PRODUCTIONS†
6555 Plumas St., Ste. 153
Reno, NV 89509
(702) 825-4181
Contact: Joe Martini

NEVADA TALENT & BOOKING†
550 E. Plumb Lane
Reno, NV 89502
(702) 827-3648
Contact: Ward P. Johns, Sabian Simpson, Dennis Alexander, Karen Pugh

SCOTT DEAN AGENCY†
428 Hill St.
Reno, NV 89501
(702) 322-9426
Contact: Steve Cox, Ted Files

AL SHAY ARTISTS AGENCY†
2930 Outlook Dr.
Reno, NV 89509
(702) 825-8034

SPARKS

JAYBIRD ENTERPRISES†
P.O. Box 1493
Sparks, NV 89431
(702) 329-8122
Contact: Joan Hartley

DICK LINK ENTERTAINMENT AGENCY†
1215 Sullivan Lane, Apt. 47B
Sparks, NV 89431
(702) 359-3236

ZEPHYR COVE

J. FLETCHER AGENCY†
57 Crescent Drive
P.O. Box 770
Zephyr Cove, NV 89448
(702) 588-3660
Contact: Kathryn E. Fletcher

LAKE TAHOE TALENT AGENCY†
P.O. Box 1729
Zephyr Cove, NV 89448
(702) 588-4666
Contact: John Gehring Foster

NEW HAMPSHIRE

CONCORD

MUSIC ENTERTAINMENT SERVICES†
79 Fisherville Road
Concord, NH 03301
(603) 224-2452
Contact: Donald C. Lassonde, Barbara M. Lassonde

MANCHESTER

TED HERBERT ORCHESTRAS†
155 Cypress St.
Manchester, NH 03103
(603) 627-2122

MELVIN R. SIBULKIN†
298 Manchester St.
Manchester, NH 03103
(603) 622-9513

NEW JERSEY

ABERDEEN

ADMIRAL TALENT ASSOCIATES(NY)†
Branch Office:
39 Deerfield Lane
P.O. Box 523
Aberdeen, NJ 07747
(201) 566-5490
Contact: Ted Purcell, Wayne R. King

ATLANTIC CITY

AMERICAN CREATIVE ENTERTAINMENT, LTD.(NV)†
Branch Office:
1616 Pacific Ave., Ste. 817
Atlantic City, NJ 08401
(609) 348-1809
Contact: Danny Luciano

BRICKTOWN

R.P.M. PRODUCTIONS†
744 Midstreams Rd.
Bricktown, NJ 08723
(201) 892-5430
Contact: Roy Phillip Metz

BRIGANTINE

CASINO CITY ATTRACTIONS†
11 Heald Circle
Brigantine, NJ 08203
(609) 266-3679
Contact: Frank Vito

CHERRY HILL

R.J.K PRODUCTIONS†
1101 Kings Highway North, Ste. 107
Cherry Hill, NJ 08034
(609) 667-7200
Contact: Ronald Kyle

DUMONT

D C PRODUCTIONS, INC.†
102 McKinley Ave.
Dumont, NJ 07628
(201) 385-5143
Contact: Joseph J. Carroll, Victor Danzi

EAST BRUNSWICK

THE REDFIELD AGENCY†
102 Ryders Lane
East Brunswick, NJ 08816
(201) 846-9393
Contact: Robert Redfield, Tess Redfield, Tony Lento, Ron Whitney

EDGEWATER
SUZANNE HILL†
Caribbean House
1375 River Road
Edgewater, NJ 07020
(201) 886-0657

EDISON
DONATELLI THEATRICAL & ENTERTAINMENT AGENCY†
3 Sleepy Hollow Rd.
Edison, NJ 08820
(201) 548-5169
Contact: Robert J. Donatelli, Alfred Q. Cappeci, Paul L. Rhine, Al DePalma, Marge Varley, Mike Rotollo

FORDS
BROTHERS MANAGEMENT ASSOCIATES†
141 Dunbar Avenue
Fords, NJ 08863
(201) 738-0880
Contact: Allen A. Faucera, Nick Grant

LITTLE FALLS
TONY SHELDON†
70 Houston Rd.
Little Falls, NJ 07424
(201) 785-3697

LONG VALLEY
RALPH ROOD ORCHESTRA & ENTERTAINMENT†
139 West Springtown Road
Long Valley, NJ 07853
Contact: Ralph H. Rood III

MANASQUAN
FRANKIE RENDELL ASSOCIATES†
26 Broad St.
P.O. Box N
Manasquan, NJ 08736
(201) 899-7969
Contact: Frank Rendell

MERCHANTVILLE
KAYDEN PRODUCTIONS†
13 W. Park Avenue
Merchantville, NJ 08109
(609) 858-1633
Contact: Peter N. Paull

NORTH WILDWOOD
EDDIE SUEZ CAPE MAY COUNTY AGENCY†
1711 Surf Ave. (Rear)
North Wildwood, NJ 08260
(609) 522-2347
Contact: Ernest R. Morano

ORTLEY BEACH
JIMMY LAMARE AGENCY†
120 Fielder Ave.
Ortley Beach, NJ 08751
(201) 793-2152

PALMYRA
SHELDON EHRINGER ORCHESTRAS†
335 Leconey Avenue
Palmyra, NJ 08065
(609) 829-2789

PENNSAUKEN
GEORGE NARDELLO ENTERTAINMENT ASSOCIATES, INC.†
Prodigy Bldg., 6027 Route 130
Pennsauken, NJ 08105
(609) 662-3444
Contact: George Nardello, Jr.

POINT PLEASANT
JOSEPH F. BRADY†
2403 River Rd.
Point Pleasant, NJ 08742
(201) 892-5067

ROCKAWAY
LESTER PRODUCTIONS†
13 Wall St.
Box 225
Rockaway, NJ 07866
(201) 627-0690
Contact: Edward H. Lester

ROSELLE PARK
ENTERTAINMENT SHOP†
212 W. Grant Ave.
Roselle Park, NJ 07204
(201) 241-2451
Contact: Joseph Signorella

THOROFARE
JANET LYNNE THEATRICAL AGENCY†
2695 Queen St.
Thorofare, NJ 08086
(609) 848-5049

TOTOWA
TITAN PRODUCTIONS CORPORATION†
#1-Route 46
Totowa, NJ 07512
(201) 785-1740
Contact: James C. Amico

TOTOWA BORO
TY ANN MUSIC AGENCY*
2 DeNora Dr.
Totowa Boro, NJ 07512
(201) 256-7257
Contact: Charles Penta

TRENTON
JEAN FRANCIS AGENCY, INC.†
314 Whitehead Road
Trenton, NJ 08619
(609) 890-8524
Contact: Jean Francis Markowitz, Andro Markowitz

WEST CALDWEL
ENTERTAINMENT EAST, INC.†
1129 Bloomfield Avenue
West Caldwel, NJ 07006
(201) 227-0545
Contact: Samuel Boyd, Tom Scorsone, Michael Combardo, Louis Dobrolsky

NEW MEXICO

ALAMOGORDO
SUGAMOSTO PRODUCTIONS†
1705 - 13th St.
P.O. Box 1904
Alamogordo, NM 88310
(505) 437-0903
Contact: Gary D. Sugamosto

ALBUQUERQUE
JOE BUFALINO & ASSOCIATES*
4518 Fourth St., NW
Albuquerque, NM 87107
(505) 883-1433
Contact: Joe Bufalino

NEW YORK

BRENTWOOD
HELEN OF TROY ENTERTAINMENT AGENCY†
410 Mayflower Ave.
Brentwood, NY 11717
(516) 581-7347
Contact: Helen R. Ettl

BROOKLYN
LINDA MARQUETTE†
GPO Box 142
Brooklyn, NY 11201
(212) UL 5-8788

BINGHAMTON
CMK TALENT AGENCY†
66 Front St.
P.O. Box 1554
Binghamton, NY 13902
(607) 772-6240
Contact: Charles M. Ketchuck

BUFFALO
GENERAL PRODUCTIONS†
(DIV. GENERAL PERSONNEL AGENCY)
523 Delaware Ave.
Buffalo, NY 14202
(716) 885-3535
Contact: Donald F. Ketteman, Abe McLarahmore

STARSTUCK PRODUCTIONS†
2650 Delaware Ave.
Buffalo, NY 14216
(716) 873-8911
Contact: Frederick Caserta

MARY STOCK†
8 Oregon Pl.
Buffalo, NY 14207
1 (716) 877-0441

EAST WILLISTON
BETTY V. KELAPIRE†
15 Meritoria Dr.
East Williston, NY 11596
(516) 742-1169

FLORIDA
UNITED POLKA ARTISTS INC.†
Box 1

Florida, NY 10921
(914) 651-4266
Contact: James W. Sturr, Jr., Edward Kosior

GREAT NECK

CARNEGIE TALENT AGENCY, INC.†
300 Northern Blvd.
Great Neck, NY 11021
(516) 487-2260
Contact: Arnold Klein, Selma Klein, Julian Kamen

ITHACA

VALEX AGENCY†
105 E. Clinton St.
P.O. Box 241
Ithaca, NY 14850
(607) 273-3931
Contact: John Perialas, Crit Harmon

JAMAICA

H & S PRODUCTIONS†
170-19 Douglas Ave.
Jamaica, NY 11433
(212) AX 1-8832
Contact: Hilliar Saunders

KENMORE

ANTHONY PICCOLO†
41 Kenview Ave.
Kenmore, NY 14217
(716) 836-0412

MT. VERNON

CHARLES T. FLOOD†
160 Foster Ave.
Mt. Vernon, NY 10552
(914) 664-1412

NEW ROCHELLE

TONY CABOT MUSIC†
40 Hanson Lane
New Rochelle, NY 10804
(914) 576-2397

CREATIVE TALENT ASSOCIATES, INC./MASTER TALENT†
27 White Oak St.
New Rochelle, NY 10801
(914) 576-1100
Contact: Kevin Brenner, Michael D. Roviello, Bill Orensteen, Al Caccamo, Scott Neglia, Glen Katz

ENCHANTED DOOR MANAGEMENT CO., INC.†
P.O. Box 1235
New Rochelle, NY 10802
(914) 576-1211
Contact: Joseph Messina, Laurie Saperstein

NEW YORK

ADMIRAL TALENT ASSOCIATES†
111 W. 57th St.
New York, NY 10019
(212) 581-0665
Contact: Ted Purcell, Ed Risman, Penny Purcell

Branch Office:
39 Deerfield Lane
P.O. Box 523
Aberdeen, NJ 07747
(201) 566-5490
Contact: Ted Purcell, Wayne R. King

AGENCY FOR THE PERFORMING ARTS, INC.†
888 Seventh Ave.
New York, NY 10106
(212) 582-1500
Contact: David C. Baumgarten, Harvey Litwin, Roger Vorce, D.J. McLachlan

Branch Office:
9000 Sunset Blvd., Ste. 315
Los Angeles, CA 90069
(213) 273-0744
Contact: John C. Gaines, Marty Klein, Fred Lawrence, Burt Taylor, Dick Gilmore, Danny Robinson, Bob Zievers

BOB ALEXANDER†
1410 York Ave.
New York, NY 10021
(212) RH 4-6478
Contact: Bob Alexander, Mart Pedell Alexander

WILLARD ALEXANDER INC.†
660 Madison Ave.
New York, NY 10021
(212) 751-7070
Contact: Willard Alexander, Bob Kasha, Jerry Campbell, Irv Dinkin, Richard Barz

Branch Office:
333 No. Michigan Ave.
Chicago, IL 60601
(312) 236-2460
Contact: Thomas J. Cassidy, Carl Schunk, Gregg McFall, Linda Garcher

AMERICAN TALENT INTERNATIONAL, LTD.†
888 Seventh Ave., 21st Flr.
New York, NY 10021
(212) 977-2300
Contact: Jeffrey A. Franklin, William Elson, Doug Thaler, Randy Garelick, Ann Peterson, Marilyn Ford, Andy Waters, Jeff Rowland, Marsha Vlasic, Michael Lourie, Ronald M. Cohan

ASSOCIATED BOOKING CORPORATION†
1995 Broadway
New York, NY 10023
(212) 874-2400
Contact: Oscar Cohen, Joe Sully, Jody Wenig, Phil Friedensohn, Richie Schechner, Larry Tersigni, Paul LaMonica

Branch Office:
2700 North River Rd.
Des Plaines, IL 60018
(312) 296-0930
Contact: Hal Munro

Branch Office:
292 LaCienega Blvd., Ste. 316
Beverly Hills, CA 90211
(213) 855-8051
Contact: Tony Papa, Billy McDonald, Tom Jones

Branch Office:
3511 Hall St.
Lee Park Bldg.
Dallas, TX 75219
(214) 528-8296
Contact: Tony Papa

SAM BERK AGENCY†
159 W. 53rd. St.
New York, NY 10019
(212) CO 5-1984

MEYER DAVIS MUSIC†
119 W. 57th St.
New York, NY 10019
(212) 247-6161
Contact: Emery Davis

D.M.I TALENT ASSOCIATES, LTD.†
250 West 57th Street
New York, NY 10019
(212) 246-4650
Contact: Dolores Sancetta, Diane Cummins

STEVE ELLIS AGENCY, LTD.†
250 W. 57th St., Ste. 330
New York, NY 10019
(212) 757-5800
Contact: Nanci Ellis, Mark Siegel

JAMES EVANS MANAGEMENT†
1650 Broadway
New York, NY 10019
(212) 265-3553
Contact: James Evans

FRONTIER BOOKING INTERNATIONAL, INC.†
250 W. 57th St., Ste. 603
New York, NY 10107
(212) 246-1505
Contact: Ian Copeland, John Huie

GENERAL LIAISON ARTIST MGT. OF N.Y.(GLAMONY)†
P.O. Box 351
New York, NY 10101
Contact: George G. Evans

ABBY HOFFER ENTERPRISES†
515 Madison Ave.
New York, NY 10022
(212) 935-6350

INN TALENT†
175 West 73rd Street
New York, NY 10023
(212) TR 3-7167
Contact: Marlene H. Meyers

INTERNATIONAL CREATIVE MANAGEMENT, INC.†
40 W. 57th St.
New York, NY 10019
(212) 556-5600
Contact: Marvin Josephson, Ralph S. Mann, Sam Cohn

Branch Office:
8899 Beverly Blvd.
Los Angeles, CA 90048
(213) 550-4000
Contact: William H. Maher

INTERNATIONAL TALENT AGENCY, INC.†
166 West 125th Street
New York, NY 10027

(212) 663-4626
Contact: Wanza L. King

INTERNATIONAL TALENT GROUP†
200 W. 57th St., #1404
New York, NY 10019
(21) 246-8118
Contact: Wayne Forte, Mike Farrell

VAN JOYCE AGENCY†
453 E. 79th St.
New York, NY 10021
(212) 988-3371
Contact: Diane Keating

KOLMAR-LUTH ENTERTAINMENT, INC.†
1776 Broadway
New York, NY 10019
(212) 581-5833
Contact: Klaus W. Kolmar, Murray Luth, John M. Quinn, Ralph Bridges

CARYLL KRAMER†
345 East 56th St.
New York, NY 10022
(212) 759-4893

EDDIE LANE'S MUSIC†
45 East 89th Street
New York, NY 10028
(212) 534-5759

THE LANTZ OFFICE INC.†
888 Seventh Ave.
New York, NY 10019
(212) 586-0200
Contact: Robert Lantz, Barry Lee Cohen

Branch Office:
9255 Sunset Blvd.
Los Angeles, Ca 90069
(213) 858-1144
Contact: Marion Rosenberg

BUDDY LEE ATTRACTIONS, INC.(TN)†
Branch Office:
100 W. 57th St., Ste. 9E
New York, NY 10019
(212) 247-5216
Contact: Jim Gosnell, Joe Higgins

MAGNA ARTISTS CORPORATION†
595 Madison Ave., Ste. 901
New York, NY 10022
(212) 752-0363
Contact: Edwin Rubin, Chuck Ramsey, William Hahn, Bruce S. Eisenberg, Lee Eisenberg

CLIFF MARTINEZ ENTERPRISES†
1576 Broadway
New York, NY 10036
(212) 974-9866

RALPH MERCADO MANAGEMENT†
1650 Broadway, Ste. 310
New York, NY 10019
(212) 541-7950

WILLIAM MORRIS AGENCY, INC.†
1350 Ave. of the Americas
New York, NY 10019
(212) 586-5100
Contact: Nat Lefkowtiz, Lee Stevens, Jerome Talberg

Branch Office:
2325 Crestmoor Rd.
Nashville, TN 37215
(615) 385-0310
Contact: Dave Douds, Sonny Neal, Paul G. Moore, Ted Simmons

Branch Office:
151 El Camino
Beverly Hills, CA 90212
(213) 274-7451
Contact: Roger Davis, Morris Stoller, Sam Weisbord, Walter Zifkin, Tony Fantozzi

DOROTHY PALMER TALENT AGENCY†
250 West 57th Street
New York, NY 10019
(212) 765-4280
Contact: Dorothy Palmer

CHARLES PETERSON THEATRICAL PRODUCTIONS, INC.*
34 Metropolitan Oval
New York, NY 10462
(212) 863-8997
Contact: Charles Peterson

PREMIER TALENT ASSOCIATES†
Three East 54th Street
New York, NY 10022
(212) 758-4900
Contact: Frank Barsalona, Barbara Skydell, Jane Geraghty, Artie Patisiner, Barry Bell, Quevedo Hijosa, Tim McGrath, Kenneth Kohberger

RENAISSANCE TALENTS, LTD.†
39 West 55th Street
New York, NY 10019
(212) 586-6246
Contact: Billy W. Bowen, Carl Hunter

SHIRLEY MARCH SELZER†
1 Lincoln Plaza
New York, NY 10023
(212) 873-3069

SUBRENA ARTISTS CORPORATION†
1650 Broadway, Ste. 410
New York, NY 10019
(212) 757-8354
Contact: Henry Nash, Henry G. Nash, Jr., Carole Eldridge, Ruth D. Hunt

SUTTON ARTISTS CORPORATION†
119 West 57th St.
New York, NY 10019
(212) 977-4870
Contact: Frank Modica, Jr.

THAMES TALENT LTD.†
1345 Avenue of the Americas
New York, NY 10105
(212) 541-6740
Contact: Bruce A. Payne, Bruce Palley, Mary Roach

TIN-BAR AMUSEMENT CORPORATION†
11 West 69th St.
New York, NY 10023
(212) 586-1015
Contact: Joseph A. Saitta

UNITED ENTERTAINMENT COMPLEX, LTD.†
527 Madison Ave., Ste. 710
New York, NY 10022
(212) 753-7000
Contact: Charles E. Graziano, Seth Ullman

UNIVERSAL ATTRACTIONS, INC.†
218 W. 57th St., Ste. A
New York, NY 10019
(212) 582-7575
Contact: Jack Bart, Dolores Rosaler, Larry Myers, Jimmy Thomas, James Crawford, Rick Feldman, Bobby Schiffman

NORBY WALTERS ASSOCIATES, INC.†
200 West 51st St.
New York, NY 10019
(212) 245-3939
Contact: Bob Reid, Chuck Anthony, James Pinten, Adam Yallegio, Sal Aversano, Jerry Ade, Tommy Stagg

CARL WARWICK†
P.O. Box 351 - Canal St.
New York, NY 10013
(212) 374-4440

PAUL WILLIAMS ENTERTAINMENT BUREAU†
601 West 156th Street, Ste. 15
New York, NY 10032
(212) 234-6431

JACK WITTEMORE†
80 Park Avenue
New York, NY 10016
(212) 986-6854

ROCHESTER

M & M TALENT AGENCY OF ROCHESTER, NY†
22 Debby Lane
Rochester, NY 14606
(716) 247-6670
Contact: Marvin J. Pizzo

ROBERT L. MAXWELL AGENCY†
1031 Sibley Tower Bldg.
Rochester, NY 14604
(716) 232-7659

THE KENNETH J. MCNEILL AGENCY
49 Wilton Terrace
Rochester, NY 14619
(212) 436-4170

PELICAN PRODUCTIONS†
3700 East Ave.
Rochester, NY 14618
(716) 381-5224
Contact: Peter Morticeli

ROCHESTER TALENT UNLIMITED INC.†
346 Ridge Road, East
Rochester, NY 14621
(716) 342-4650
Contact: Thomas DiPoala, David Termotto, Katie Leone, Flo Gapsky

SCARSDALE

ROBERT HOUGH AGENCY†

71 Chase Rd.
P.O. Box 1023
Scarsdale, NY 10583
(914) 723-8446
Contact: Mrs. Ann J. Hough, Thomas J. Hough

SCHENEDTADY

CEASAR'S AGENCY†
12 St. Thomas Lane
Schenectady, NY 12304
(518) 346-7009
Contact: Carl P. Di Cesare

FRED GRAY AGENCY†
2410 First Ave.
Schenectady, NY 12303
(518) 355-6514
Additional Office:
Ramada Inn, corner of Nott St. & Erie Blvd.
Schenectady, NY
(518) 370-7151

SEAFORD

SAMMY MASLIN STUDIOS†
3742 Clark St.
Seaford, NY 11783
(212) 895-2834

ST. ALBANS

MILTON J. HINTON†
173-05 113th Avenue
St. Albans, L.I., NY 11433
(212) OL 8-8975
Contact: Mona Hinton, Charlotte Hinton

STATEN ISLAND

BEN CATTANO AGENCY†
491 Vanderbilt Ave.
Staten Island, NY 10304
(212) 727-8435
Contact: Benjamin Nunzio Cattano, Sr.

SYRACUSE

DMR ENTERPRISES†
Ste. 316, Wilson Bldg.
Syracuse, NY 13202
(315) 471-0868
Contact: David M. Rezak, Daniel Christy, Bob Perry, Mark Alexander, Greg Belinski, Joe DeGennaro, Paul Farley

TRADEWINDS TALENT AGENCY†
431 N. Salina St.
Syracuse, NY 13203
(315) 422-2795
Contact: Samuel M. Tassone

TONAWANDA

JR PRODUCTIONS*
1620 Niagra Falls Blvd.
Tonawanda, NY 14150
(716) 838-6330
Contact: John Sansone

TROY

ORIGINAL SOUNDS†
162 Delaware Ave., Apt. B
Troy, NY 12180
(518) 274-2140
Contact: Thomas F. McGrath, Jr.

VIC SPECIALE ENTERPRISES AGENCY†
31 Madison Avenue
Troy, NY 12180
(518) 272-0734
Contact: Vic Speciale

TRUMANSBURG

MCTARA AGENCY†
16 East Main Street
P.O. Box 539
Trumansburg, NY 14886
(607) 387-5880
Contact: Ms. Arden A. McCracken, Martha M. Taraszkiewicz

UTICA

JOHN SPIRSI ENTERTAINMENT AGENCY†
250 Genesee St.
Utica, NY 13501
(315) 732-1500
Contact: John A. Spirsi

WARRENSBURG

FLASH ATTRACTIONS AGENCY†
38 Prospect Street
Warrensburg, NY 12885
1 (518) 623-9313
Contact: Walter O. Brunner, Wally Chester Brunner, Dawn Brunner

NORTH CAROLINA

CHARLOTTE

ENTERTAINMENT CONSULTANTS†
Ste. 210 Colwick Towers
P.O. Box 220219
Charlotte, NC 28222
(704) 372-3111
Contact: Patricia B. Moser, Mrs. Patricia M. Turner, Thomas E. Smart, Judy Pierce

FISHER & ASSOCIATES ENTERTAINMENT*
P.O. Box 240802
Charlotte, NC 28224
(704) 525-9220
Contact: Brent Fisher

HIT ATTRACTIONS, INC.†
P.O. Box 4585
Charlotte, NC 28204
(704) 372-3955
Contact: Ted Hall, Larry Farber, Steve Haley, Bill Kennedy

INSIGHT TALENT, INC.†
2300 East Independence Boulevard
Charlotte, NC 28205
(704) 372-1970
Contact: Michael S. Branch, Johnnie C. Bailey, J.O. Vickers, Mace Brown, Sam Buxton

KEMP ATTRACTIONS†
Cameron Brown Bldg.
P.O. Box 4374
Charlotte, NC 28204
(704) 333-6151
Contact: Thomas Dupre Kemp

PRATHER ARTIST MANAGEMENT†
1748 Sterling Rd.
Charlotte, NC 28209
(704) 375-2015
Contact: Hugh C. Prather, Jr., Hugh C. Prather, Sr.

STALLINGS ENTERTAINMENT*
Ste. 255
1373 E. Morehead St.
Charlotte, NC 28204
(704) 375-1260
Contact: Jack Stallings

GREENSBORO

COTILLION ORCHESTRA AGENCY†
P.O. Box 5102
Greensboro, NC 27403
(919) 855-3628
Contact: Burt Massengale

KINSTON

LEN TALENT PRODUCTIONS†
P.O. Box 509
Kinston, NC 28501
(919) 523-6974
Contact: Leonard Loftin, David V. Barnes

RALEIGH

SIMMONS AGENCY†
200 Six Forks Rd., E.
Raleigh, NC 27609
(919) 828-1931
Contact: Harry Q. Simmons, Jr., Peggy N. Simmons, A.T. Simmons

NORTH DAKOTA

BISMARCK

EDDY'S MUSIC CORPORATION†
516 18th St.
Bismarck, ND 58501
(701) 255-4555
Contact: Charles E. Connell, Anna Marie Connell, Jo Ann Cooper

WALLY KITTLER PRODUCTIONS†
P.O. Box 491
200 W. Main
Bismarck, ND 58501
(701) 223-9259
Contact: Walter E. Kittler

TELSTAR MUSICAL PRODUCTIONS†
2428 Stevens Street
Bismarck, ND 58501
(701) 258-3748
Contact: Charles J. Kocher

GRAND FORKS

D.J. TRI-STATE PRODUCTIONS†
P.O. Box 1622
Grand Forks, ND 58201
1 (218) 773-1981
Contact: Dan Gefroh

SHOWBOAT TALENT MANAGEMENT AND PROMOTIONS†
124 Conklin Ave.
Grand Forks, ND 58201
(701) 746-6293
Contact: Barry Kent Land

VALLEY PRODUCTIONS, INC.†
Box 5038
Grand Forks, ND 58201
(701) 746-0552
Contact: Jerry Souder, Richard McLaughlin, Myra McLaughlin

OHIO

AKRON

DL AGENCY†
25 Brighton Dr.
Akron, OH 44301
(216) 773-5065
Contact: D.L. Donnella

AURORA

JOSEPH P. GADD†
227 Chelmsford Dr.
P.O. Box 13
Aurora, OH 44202
(216) 562-8431
Contact: Hank LeVine, Betty Gadd, Mary Jo Tyler

BEACHWOOD

ENERGY TALENT AGENCY†
26949 Chagrin Blvd., Ste. 209
Beachwood, OH 44122
(216) 464-4150
Contact: John Valent Tevis, George Annesley, Jim Quinn, Lee D. Marshall, Larry A. Main, Ed Botnick, Mark Litten, Lola J. Davis

BEACH CITY

LSB PRODUCTIONS†
122 Second St.
Box 527
Beach City, OH 44608
(216) 756-2360
Contact: Donald J. Dogwiler, Sherry J. Dogwiler

BEDFORD HEIGHTS

BOB BERRY ORCHESTRAS†
5427 Campton Court
Bedford Heights, OH 44146
(216) 232-9230
Contact: Donald P. Moyer

BEVERLY

NINA RUTH MILLER†
113 Sixth St.
P.O. Box 516
Beverly, OH 45715
(614) 984-2258
Contact: Rodger D. Unger, Stephen F. Miller

BRECKSVILLE

BOB LORENCE AGENCY†
(DIV. OF NOBLE-BERGNER AGY.)
6614 Greenbrier Drive
Brecksville, OH 44141
(216) 526-2470
Contact: Lois Lorence

CANTON

AKRON-CANTON MUSIC EXCHANGE†
2854 Farmington Cir., S.W.
Canton, OH 44706
(216) 477-2058
Contact: Andrew H. Fraga

PHYLLIS J. DUNHAM†
Wynnbrook Rd., S.W.
Canton, OH 44706
(216) 477-6193

CINCINNATI

ACCENT MUSIC†
19 West Court St.
Cincinnati, OH 45202
(513) 241-0903
Contact: Ruth R. Rekers

AJAYE ENTERTAINMENT CORPORATION†
2181 Victory Parkway
P.O. Box 6568
Cincinnati, OH 45206
(513) 221-2626
Contact: Stanford H. Silverman, Stanley B. Hertzman, Robert L. Schwartz

M.J. BELL AND ASSOCIATES†
998 Hatch St.
Cincinnati, OH 45202
(513) 241-6679
Contact: Mary Jo Bell, Mary L. Morrow

D/S TALENT AGENCY, INC.†
4243 Hunt Rd.
Cincinnati, OH 45242
(513) 984-2572
Contact: Don Sheets

BARNEY RAPP AGENCY, INC.†
Carew Tower - Lower Arcade
Cincinnati, OH 45202
(513) 381-7277
Contact: Ruby Rapp, Nancy J. Rapp, Susan Reisenfeld, Patty Rapp Nulsen, Jimmy Morgan

CLEVELAND

ALL STAR THEATRICAL AGENCY†
Cleveland Plaza
E. 12th & Euclid Ave., Rm. 840
Cleveland, OH 44115
(216) 781-2215
Contact: Syd Friedman

ARTIST ENTERTAINMENT CORPORATION†
23200 Chagrin Blvd., Bldg. #3
Cleveland, OH 44122
(216) 831-0240
Contact: Marty Conn, Billy Lang, Buddy Russell, Ronnie A. Nardi, Alan Wishard

Associate Office:
MUSIC CORPORATION ASSOCIATION†
5415 B-6 Yorkshire Terrace
Columbus, OH 43227
(614) 866-3046
Contact: Marty Conn, Steve Schaffer, David Allen, Tom Rodoski, Judith Kloss, Sandra Gustavson

AUGUST 81, INC.†
260 The Leader Bldg.
Cleveland, OH 44114
(216) 589-9999
Contact: Rita Franklin, Sharlot Fingerhut

CYBORG†
2944 East 121st
Cleveland, OH 44120
(216) 752-4255
Contact: William A. Berry, Jr.

G.G. GREG†
1686 Catalpa Ave.
Cleveland, OH 44112
(216) 692-1193
Contact: Greg C. Giancola

M. & A. THEATRICAL PRODUCTIONS†
28829 Chagrin Blvd., Ste. 111
Cleveland, OH 44122
(216) 831-9546
Contact: Michael Anthony Fugo

SUPER DIAMOND MANAGEMENT†
10537 Elk Ave.
Cleveland, OH 44108
(216) 761-4777
Contact: Delia L. Mines, Charles F. Mines

THIRD STREET EXIT, INC.†
4159 West 59 St.
Cleveland, OH 44144
(216) 398-7445
Contact: Raymond T. Lamatrice

TOP SHELF ENTERTAINMENT†
1314 Huron Rd.
Cleveland, OH 44115
(216) 861-1324
Contact: Stephen J. Knill, James J. Girard, Richard J. Kabat

V.C. PRODUCTIONS & PROMOTION†
27869 Lincoln Rd.
Cleveland, OH 44140
(216) 835-2727
Contact: Tom Claire

VIRGIL T. VINCENT†
1357 East Blvd.
Cleveland, OH 44106
(216) 231-0932

COLUMBUS

AMERICAN MUSIC, INC.*
Ste. 202
2151 Dublin-Granville Rd.
Columbus, OH 43229
(614) 882-8090
Contact: Mike Kapson

COUNTRY CONCERT PRODUCTIONS†
108-C Old Village Rd.
P.O. Box 28477
Columbus, OH 43228
(614) 878-2307
Contact: Steven V. Rutherford, Nancy K. Smith

DIVERSIFIED TALENT COMPANY†
843 Westbury Lane
Columbus, OH 43228
(614) 878-2992
Contact: Louis S. Kerr

DENNIS R. HULSE†
1317 Barnett Rd.
Columbus, OH 43227
(614) 231-3216

INTERNATIONAL ENTERTAINMENT UNLIMITED†
153 Leland
Columbus, OH 43214
(614) 888-1925
Contact: Bruno D. Mollica

JEM ENTERTAINMENT†
4714 Knightsbridge Blvd.
Columbus, OH 43214
P.O. Box 15794
Columbus, OH 43215
(614) 882-9272
Contact: Joyce E. Martin

KEY SOUND BOOKING AGENCY†
1667 Shanley Dr. #2
Columbus, OH 43224
(614) 267-9777
Contact: George L. Davis, Asa T. Featherstone, Jr., Ernest C. Bradley, Melven Griffin, Andrew D. Sahli, David S. Chandler, Jr.

JOHN M. MOORE ENTERTAINMENT†
16 East Broad St.
Columbus, OH 43215
(614) 461-6600
Contact: John M. Moore, Andi Robbins, Billy Scott, Robert E. Husted

MUSIC CORPORATION ASSOCIATION†
(See Cleveland listing, Artist Entertainment Corporation†)

FLORENCE SCHULZ AGENCY†
3253 W. Broad St.
Columbus, OH 43204
(614) 274-2400
Contact: Florence Schulz

SPECTRUM ENTERTAINMENT AGENCY†
P.O. Box 24063
Columbus, OH 43224
(614) 268-4137
Contact: Terry E. Adams, Dalton E. Bosley

SUMMIT ENTERPRISES*†
1391 Oakland Park Ave.
Columbus, OH 43224
(614) 263-4344
Contact: Barrie D. Brandt, Lee Foster, Rick Stevens, David Hickey, Charlie Cesner, Jr., Bob Murphy, Robert Lamp, Teresa Carlisle, Fred Francis

TCA ENTERTAINMENT†
P.O. Box 24172
Columbus, OH 43224
(614) 261-1107
Contact: Timothy D. Coulter

CRESTLINE

ANTONIO GIAMPIETRO†
P.O. Box 66
Crestline, OH 44827
(419) 683-1767

CUYAHOGA FALLS

JOEL A. BROWN, & ASSOCIATES*†
2045 Seventh St.
Cuyahoga Falls, OH 44221
(216) 928-4568
Contact: Joel Brown

DAYTON

ADVERTISING & TALENT ASSOCIATES, INC.†
132 Marbrook Dr.
Dayton, OH 45429
(513) 849-6334
Contact: Virginia Bennett, James W. Bennett

MARION F. GANGE TALENT AGENCY†
106 Squirrel Road
Dayton, OH 45405
(513) 228-2371
Contact: Marion F. Gange

JAMES B. MAY MANAGEMENT†
60 Forrer Boulevard
Dayton, OH 45419
(513) 293-9914
Contact: James B. May, Sr., Helen V. May

JIMMY MAY ORCHESTRAS & ENTERTAINMENT AGENCY†
400 Carrlands Dr.
Dayton, OH 45429
(513) 294-4646
Contact: James Brunell May, Jr.

EASTLAKE

POT OF GOLD†
34296 Waldmer Dr.
Eastlake, OH 44094
(216) 942-1555
Contact: Bobbie Greenberg

ELYRIA

H. SCOT KRAUSE AND ASSOCIATES†
122 Potomac Dr.
Elyria, OH 44035
(216) 323-9091
Contact: Herbert S. Krause

EUCLID

AFTER MIDNIGHT PRODUCTIONS†
709 Walnut Dr.
Euclid, OH 44132
(216) 261-6098
Contact: David E. Moye

GAHANNA

RISING SON PRODUCTIONS†
578 Rocky Fork Blvd.
Gahanna, OH 43230
(614) 475-8335
Contact: James L. Bradshaw

GIRARD

JMS PRODUCTIONS†
1120 North Ward Avenue
Girard, OH 44420
(216) 545-6096
Contact: Joseph R. Costarella, Joseph R. Costarella, Jr.

GRANVILLE

ARTISTIC MOVEMENT†
P.O. Box 24
Granville, OH 43023
(614) 587-3020
Contact: Stosh Yankowski

HAMILTON

MICHAEL P. MEHAS†
5975 Fairham Rd.
Hamilton, OH 45011
(513) 863-8172

HIGHLAND HEIGHTS

SANDBROOK ENTERTAINMENT AGENCY†
880 Stanwell Drive
Highland Heights, OH 44143
(216) 442-0106
Contact: Joann Bongiorno, Jane Stamm, Mary Bongiorno

HILLIARD

NEW WORLD ENTERTAINMENT†
4030 Columbia St.
Hilliard, OH 43026
(614) 876-1794
Contact: Thomas A. Gallagher

LORAIN

NATIONWIDE THEATRICAL AGENCY†
1629 Broadway
Lorain, OH 44052
(216) 244-6498
Contact: Frank Gimello

MANSFIELD

JODY VARGA BOOKING AGENCY†
1680 West Cook Rd.
Mansfield, OH 44906
(419) 756-5387
Contact: Jody Mary Varga

MASURY

PIERSON & ASSOCIATES†
Cleveland-Pittsburgh Office
8223 Loraine St., S.E.
Masury, OH 44438
1 (216) 448-6413
Contact: Harry A. Pierson

MAUMEE

THE J.R. AGENCY†
2548 Parkway Plaza
Maumee, OH 43537
(419) 893-0209
Contact: Jack Runyan

MENTOR

BOB READY & ASSOCIATES†
7088 West Jefferson Dr.
Mentor, OH 44060
(216) 951-4493
Contact: Robert James Ready

MILFORD CENTER

CONTINENTAL PROMOTIONS†
22121 Buck Run Rd.

Milford Center, OH 43045
(513) 349-5675
Contact: Gene A. Hanselman

NANKIN

JAMES CASE AGENCY†
Box 145
Nankin, OH 44848
(419) 289-8468
Contact: James I. Case

NEW PHILADELPHIA

FRONTIER ATTRACTIONS†
422 West High Ave.
New Philadelphia, OH 44663
(216) 339-5818
Contact: Norman G. Senhauser, Charlotte A. White

NORTH CANTON

NORTH ATLANTIC PRODUCTIONS†
5600 Chandler, N.W.
North Canton, OH 44720
(216) 494-1000
Contact: John Lazar, George M. Milosan, Mircea Cristea

POWHATAN POINT

INTERSTATE UNLIMITED BOOKING AGENCY†
Rt. 1, Box 3-A
Powhatan Point, OH 43942
(614) 458-1015
Contact: Sandra S. Sisson, Sondra E. Harvey

SALEM

COUNTRY WESTERN PRODUCTIONS†
442 Aetna Street
Salem, OH 44460
(216) 332-0112
Contact: Frank G. Coy, Winifred Coy, Judy L. Kelm, R.N. McLaughlin, Martha McLaughlin, Robert C.V. Roberts

SHAKER HEIGHTS

MAD-CAP PRODUCTIONS†
20899 Farnsleigh
Shaker Heights, OH 44122
(216) 751-6768
Contact: Bruce C. Dangler

SIDNEY

NEVILLE ORCHESTRAS & ENTERTAINMENT†
614 North Main Ave.
Sidney, OH 45365
(513) 492-5880
Contact: Barbara Jean Neville

STOW

GARRY L. ELLIOT†
4110 Vira Rd.
Stow, OH 44224
(216) 688-9113

SYLVANIA

A COMPANY CALLED BRADY, INC.†
5800 Monroe St.
Sylvania, OH 43560
(419) 885-5511
Contact: Thomas J. Brady, Richard G. Morris, Carole Seibert

TOLEDO

C.P.W. SHOWTIME, INC.†
5150 Lewis Ave.
Toledo, OH 43615
(419) 478-2333
Contact: Charles Le Vally, Walter C. Patton

JOHNNY KNORR†
1751 Fallbrook Rd.
Toledo, OH 43614
1 (419) 385-4241

MICHAEL PRODUCTIONS†
P.O. Box 6802
Toledo, OH 43612
(419) 385-3306
Contact: Michael W. Nitschke

MUSIC CO.†
The Hillcrest Hotel, Ste. 239
Madison at 16th Caller 10003
Toledo, OH 43699
(419) 241-1207
Contact: Marek R. Moldawsky, Linda Clifton

FRED WOOD ORCHESTRAS AND ENTERTAINMENT AGENCY†
4162 Dorchester Drive
Toledo, OH 43607
(419) 536-6227
Contact: Fred Wood, Stephanie Barnum

TWINSBURG

CREATIVE CLUSTERS & ENTERTAINMENT†
9076 Church St.
Twinsburg, OH 44087
(216) 425-2101
Contact: Jeannine M. Gurnack

WARRENSVILLE HEIGHTS

ART-TONE†
23308 Emery Rd.
Warrensville Heights, OH 44128
(216) 831-0172
Contact: Arthur G. Sutton, Fred Jenkins

WORTHINGTON

PARDO ENTERPRISES†
1724 Hightower Dr.
Worthington, OH 43085
1 (614) 889-6946
Contact: Mary L. Pardo

PARTY BANDS, LTD.†
163 E. Wilson Bridge Rd.
Worthington, OH 43085
(614) 436-8218
Contact: Donald A. Smathers

YOUNGSTOWN

RICHARD M. HAHN†
5645 Baylor Dr.
Youngstown, OH 44515
(216) 793-7295

PAT PRODUCTIONS†
93 Spring Garden Ct.
Youngstown, OH 44512
(216) 758-9446
Contact: Pat Puhalla, James Puhalla, Roy Guerrieri

JOSEPH A. RANALLI†
120 W. Florida Ave.
Youngstown, OH 44507
(216) 788-1323
Contact: James Ament, Sandy Jackintell

OKLAHOMA

JENKS

SPOT PRODUCTIONS†
1011 W. 121st St., So.
Jenks, OK 74037
(918) 299-2424
Contact: Sammy Pagna

NORMAN

STAGE II ATTRACTIONS(TN)†
Branch Office:
3701 Bellwood Dr.
Norman, OK 73069
(405) 360-1414
Contact: Phyllis McCraw

OKLAHOMA CITY

EVENING SUN ENTERPRISES†
3313 N. Broadway
Oklahoma City, OK 73118
(405) 528-6118
Contact: David Wilderson, Larrie E. Wilkerson

AL GOOD ARTISTS BUREAU†
2500 N.W. 39th St.
Oklahoma City, OK 73112
1 (405) 947-1503
Contact: Alan R. Good

FLOYD G. RICE†
10852 Sunnymeade Place
Oklahoma City, OK 73120
(405) 751-6034
Contact: Floyd G. Rice

RUTH SALLEE'S ENTERTAINMENT BOOKING AGENCY†
1315 North Shartel
Oklahoma City, OK 73103
(415) 232-3614

PETE TYLER ARTIST MANAGEMENT†
2708 N. Coltrane Road
Oklahoma City, OK 73121
(405) 427-7266
Contact: Pete F. Tyler, Octavia M. Tyler

TULSA

EVERYBODY'S TALKIN PRODUCTIONS†
5658 S. Peoria #106 No.
Tulsa, OK 74105
(918) 749-9277
Contact: Tommie P. Keys

ERNIE FIELDS ARTISTS REPRESENTATIVE AGENCY†
1852 N. Peoria Ave.
Tulsa, OK 74106
(918) 587-0421
Contact: Jean Wright

JIM HALSEY AGENCY†
5800 E. Skelly Drive/Penthouse
Tulsa, OK 74135
(918) 663-3883

SKYLINE TALENT†
P.O. Box 45855
Tulsa, OK 74145
(918)299-5054
Contact: Edwin E. Conley

THE A.J. SOLOW COMPANY†
410 S. Detroit
Tulsa, OK 74120
(918) 582-2178
Contact: Anthony J. Solow

OREGON

ASHLAND

CAGEY GREEN PRODUCTIONS†
944 Oak Knoll Drive
Ashland, OR 97520
(503) 482-0890
Contact: Johnny Green, Marilyn Green

BEAVERTON

SHOWCASE OF ENTERTAINMENT, INC.†
Park Plaza West Executive Bldg., Ste. 555
10700 Beaverton Hwy.
Beaverton, OR 97005
(503) 644-8300
Contact: David Bowen, Alma Faye Clark, Delinda Jones, Brenda J. Clark, Lee Clark, Virginia Clark, Bruce Bowen

LAKE OSWEGO

LIVE-STAR MANAGEMENT†
P.O. Box 2034
Lake Oswego, OR 97043
(503) 227-3227
Contact: Michal Ceglie

PORTLAND

BAND BOX ENTERTAINMENT†
2425 S.W. 76 Ave.
Portland, OR 97225
(503) 297-4334
Contact: Jolly D. Dawson

CONSUELO'S THEATRICAL AGENCY†
2530 N.E. Brazee
Portland, OR 97212
(503) 284-2310
Contact: Consuelo Routtu

PHIL DOWNING ASSOCIATES*†
3038 E. Burnside St.
Portland, OR 97214
(503) 235-8981
Contact: Phil Downing, Beth Anderson

SYLVIA EPSTEIN AGENCY‡
3445 N.E. 21st Ave.
Portland, OR 97212
(503) 287-1925

THE FUTURE AGENCY†
712 S.W. Salmon
Portland, OR 97205
(503) 224-1515
Contact: Frank Otto Butler

BETTE GALL-VAUGHN AGENCY†
9435 N.E. Marine Dr., J-7
Portland, OR 97220
1 (503) 253-7053
Contact: Bette M. Gall-Vaughn

LANE ENTERTAINMENT AGENCY†
P.O. Box 02068
Portland, OR 97202
(503) 653-6967
Contact: Lucille Lane Selvig, Kurt H. Selvig, Patti James, Bobby James

PACIFIC TALENT†
516 S.E. Morrison, Ste. 420
Portland, OR 97214
(503) 231-1797
Contact: Andrew R. Gilbert, Kathy Wellington

PICTURE MUSIC COMPANY†
P.O. Box 10794
Portland, OR 97210
(503) 224-9273
Contact: Terry T. Layne, Tina Layne

SIRIUS PRODUCTIONS†
3107 SE Ankeny
Portland, OR 97214
(503) 236-7329
Contact: Robert H. Melvin

TOM STINETTE AGENCY*
4157 E. Brooklyn
Portland, OR 97202
(503) 235-5988
Contact: Tom Stinette

SUNTRACK PRODUCTIONS†
P.O. Box 230315
Portland, OR 97223
(503) 232-5180
Contact: Michael D. Le Clair, Steve Hoyt

SEASIDE

PAT MASON AGENCY†
P.O. Box 286
444 Second St.
Seaside, OR 97138
(503) 738-7512

SPRINGFIELD

SILVERWING PRODUCTIONS†
485 W. Centennial #8
Springfield, OR 97477
(503) 741-2867
Contact: John Franklin Lee, John Rannells

TIGARD

NORTHWEST TALENT & BOOKING†
13230 S.W. Howard Dr.
Tigard, OR 97223
(503) 639-6082
Contact: Mildred L. Hoyt

TROUTDALE

MICHAEL KAU AGENCY†
23300 W. Arata Rd. #150
Troutdale, OR 97060
(503) 667-2661
Contact: Michael M. Kau

PENNSYLVANIA

ALTOONA

SUNDANCE PRODUCTIONS†
210 Ridge Ave., Ste. 1
Altoona, PA 16602
(814) 944-0931
Contact: Gregory S. Morris

BERWYN

NAMAR PRODUCTIONS, INC.†
456 Winston Way
Berwyn, PA 19312
(215) 647-4950
Contact: Nathan Golin, Mary E. Golin

BLOOMSBURG

ALBERT WHITENIGHT SUPER TALENTS†
84 Perry Avenue
Bloomsburg, PA 17815
(717) 784-2138
Contact: Mathias Albert Whitenight

CHAMBERSBURG

JONATHAN COOPER PRODUCTIONS†
153 South Main Street
Chamberburg, PA 17201
(717) 264-3005

CLIFTON HEIGHTS

APOLLO ARTISTS ATTRACTIONS†
427 North Springfield Avenue
Clifton Heights, PA 19018
(215) 583-2106
Contact: Freddy Baker, Mike Vanella, Joe Costello

EASTON

SAM LOSAGIO ENTERTAINMENT AGENCY†
295 Spring Valley Road
Easton, PA 18042
(215) 253-1117
Contact: Samuel C. Losagio, Jr.

MEDIA 5 ENTERTAINMENT AGENCY†
Ste. 600 - First Natl. Bank Bldg.
Easton, PA 18042
(215) 258-2308
Contact: David A. Sestak, Dennis Jones, John DiFrancisco, Thomas Scott Curdt

ERIE

ARTIST ENTERTAINMENT CORPORATION(OH)†
Branch Office:
2314 Peach St., Ste. One
Erie, PA 16502
(814) 455-7729
Contact: Frank J. Sonzala, Leo D. Shields, Mark Summers,

PROGRESSIVE TALENT MANAGEMENT, INC.†
824 Hillborne Ave.

Erie, PA 16505
(814) 833-2263
Contact: Dennia Jay Cohen, Daniel F. Lewis

FT. WASHINGTON
NINO BARI AGENCY†
6030 Sheaff Lane
Ft. Washington, PA 19034
(215) 646-1810

GLEN ROCK
BORTNER THEATRICAL AGENCY†
RD #3, Box 248
Glen Rock, PA 17327
(717) 235-2007
Contact: Gerald A. Bortner

HANOVER
FORTE ENTERPRISES†
P.O. Box 75
Hanover, PA 17331
(717) 632-7247
Contact: Donald Orndorff

HARRISBURG
PENN-WORLD ATTRACTIONS†
1416 N. Second St.
Harrisburg, PA 17102
(717) 233-7972
Contact: Mrs. Dorothy McKissick

VAN HORN MUSIC & TALENT AGENCY†
545 Marlborough Ave.
Harrisburg, PA 17111
(717) 564-5342
Contact: Charles B. Van Horn, Mary Ann Van Horn

HAZLETON
MEIER TALENT AGENCY*
511 W. Third St.
Hazleton, PA 18201
(717) 454-8767
Contact: Harold Meier

P & S ENTERPRISES†
P.O. Box 596
Hazleton, PA 18201
(717) 788-3892
Contact: Samuel Schalleat, Steve Wallmark, Judy Montgomery

HUNTINGDON VALLEY
RAY ROYAL AGENCY†
One Fairway Plaza, Ste. 311
Huntingdon Valley, PA 19006
(215) 947-7743
Contact: Ray A. Royal

KULPMONT
C.M. PRODUCTIONS†
528 Pine Street
Kulpmont, PA 17834
(717) 373-3258
Contact: Chuck Cesari, Donna Kay Cesari, Carmen Michael Cesari

LANCASTER
OLEGNA ENTERPRISES†
419 East King St.
Lancaster, PA 17602
(717) 299-5568
Contact: Jamie F. Rowley, Tony Angelo

LATROBE
KENDRA ENTERPRISES†
1593 Woodlawn Dr.
P.O. Box 242
Latrobe, PA 15650
(412) 537-2217
Contact: William George Kendra

MOHNTON
CRAIG WES FISHER'S MUSIC†
RD 2, Box 80
Mohnton, PA 19540
(215) 777-2411
Contact: Craig Wes Fisher

MONROEVILLE
KEN HILL PRODUCTIONS*
4232 Northern Pike
Ste. 204
Monroeville, PA 15146
(412) 856-9100
Contact: Rich Kaminsky

NEW KENSINGTON
CRYSTAL PRODUCTIONS*
300 Tarentum Bridge Rd.
New Kensington, PA 15068
(412) 339-1800
Contact: Kathy Renda

PHILADELPHIA
BB PRODUCTIONS†
4270 Lawnside Rd.
Philadelphia, PA 19154
(215) 824-1662
Contact: Robert H. Beato, Paul Beato

JOSEPH BUTLER ASSOCIATES*
2718 East Luzerne St.
Bldg. 2
Philadelphia, PA 19137
(215) 289-6241
Contact: Joseph Butler

JOLLY JOYCE AGENCY†
2028 Chestnut St.
P.O. Box 2349
Philadelphia, PA 19103
(215) 564-0982
Contact: Norman Joyce

JOE MARTIN MUSIC†
1901 J.F.K. Blvd.
Philadelphia, PA 19103
(215) 568-1478
Contact: Joseph Martin

ART RAYE ENTERTAINMENT AGENCY†
7845 Brous Ave.
Philadelphia, PA 19152
(215) 624-0758

PITTSBURGH
AQUARIAN ASSOCIATES, INC.*†
Ste. 1719 The Bigelow
One Bigelow Square
Pittsburgh, PA 15219
(412) 391-9640
Contact: Gerald V. Pace, Parris L. Westbrook, Tom Ingegno, John Desmone, Sam Manfredi, Richard Kaminsky

WALTER BROWN ASSOCIATES†
1300 Clark Bldg.
Pittsburgh, PA 15222
(412) 391-8788

FISHER ASSOCIATES†
P.O. Box 862
Pittsburgh, PA 15230
(412) 261-3970
Contact: Joseph J. Fisher

JACK PURCELL ORCHESTRA†
1621 Brookline Blvd.
Pittsburgh, PA 15226
(412) 881-4885
Contact: John E. Purcell

ROSETO
SOUND APPROACH ENTERTAINMENT AGENCY†
411 Front Ave.
Roseto, PA 18013
(215) 588-4524
Contact: David Mollo, Mary Jo Martino

SCRANTON
ED CURRY AGENCY†
431 Cedar Ave.
Scranton, PA 18505
(717) 347-3501
Contact: Ed Curry

SINKING SPRING
WOLFF & ADAMS ENTERTAINMENT BUREAU†
361 Weidman Avenue
Sinking Spring, PA 19608
(215) 678-2331
Contact: Gerard C. Ream, Caroline E. Ream

STATE COLLEGE
BOB DOYLE AGENCY†
Box 1199
State College, PA 16801
(814) 238-5478

STROUDBURG
RHYTHM PRODUCTIONS ENTERTAINMENT AGENCY†
588 Main St.
P.O. Box 819
Stroudsburg, PA 18360
(717) 421-2828
Contact: Frank M. Febbo

WILKES-BARRE
LEN BRADER AGENCY†
1 Sturdevant St.
Wilkes-Barre, PA 18702
(717) 829-1100
Contact: Len Brader

WYNDMOOR
A.C.I. PRODUCTIONS†
618 E. Willograve Ave.
Wyndmoor, PA 19118
1 (215) 355-0536
Contact: Anthony C. Iaquinto

WYOMISSING
EXECUTIVE ENTERPRISES†
P.O. Box 6148
Wyomissing, PA 19610
(215) 374-0320
Contact: Randall W. Stump

YORK
BOB ENGLAR THEATRICAL AGENCY†
2466 Wildon Dr.
York, PA 17403
(717) 741-2844
Contact: William R. Englar

RHODE ISLAND

JAMESTOWN
MUSIC 2000†
13 Standish Rd.
Jamestown, RI 02835
(401) 423-2979
Contact: Arthur Motycka

PROVIDENCE
MODERN BOOKING AGENCY†
112 Union St.
Providence, RI 02903
1 (401) 421-5197
Contact: Arthur Cabral

RALPH STUART MUSIC, INC.†
60 Broadway
Providence, RI 02903
(401) 274-4420
Contact: Janet Stuart, Shirley Sisson

WARWICK
ARTIST ENTERTAINMENT AGENCY†
70 Moccasin Dr.
Warwick, RI 02886
(401) 737-4983
Contact: Robert A. Romano

SOUTH CAROLINA

CHARLESTON
ACRES OF TALENT†
262 B Fleming Rd.
Charleston, SC 29412
(803) 795-9362
Contact: Lillian M. Mills, Jack Mills

COLUMBIA
SCORPIO ENTERPRISES, LTD.†
2513 Flamingo Drive
Columbia, SC 29209
(803) 771-7819
Contact: Donald Jennings

Branch Office:
8714 Bridington Street
San Antonio, TX 78239
(512) 656-7527
Contact: Lucille White

SOUTH DAKOTA

RAPID CITY
STERLING ENTERTAINMENT AGENCY†
2726 Eden Lane
P.O. Box 1096
Rapid City, SD 57701
(605) 342-2697
Contact: Lowell Burdette Sterling

TENNESSEE

ANTIOCH
AR-LANS TALENT AGENCY†
334 Cane Ridge Rd., Apt 213
Antioch, TN 37013
(615) 833-6950
Contact: Lana Sue Kerce

BRENTWOOD
DON C. WARDEN†
Box 3065
Brentwood, TN 37027
(615) 791-0000

FRANKLIN
A R BOOKING†
410 Stable Dr.
Franklin, TN 37064
(615) 790-6559
Contact: Jeannetta Lunsford, Mike Murphy

TALENTMASTER†
Route 12, Temple Rd.
Franklin, TN 37064
(615) 646-3764
Contact: Stephen F. Bess

GOODLETTSVILLE
ATLAS ARTIST BUREAU†
217 E. Cedar St.
P.O. Box 50
Goodlettsville, TN 37072
(615) 859-1343
Contact: Haze B. Jones

ENTERTAINMENT CORPORATION OF AMERICA†
P.O. Box 464
Goodlettsville, TN 37072
(615) 859-1319
Contact: J. Hal Smith, Velma E. Smith, Becky Bellar

WALLY HARDISON AGENCY†
Rt. 5, Long Hollow Pike
Goodlettsville, TN 37072
(615) 824-0991
Contact: Wallace E. Hardison II

TRANS WORLD ARTIST, INC.†
121 Two Mile Pike
P.O. Box 208
Goodlettsville, TN 37072
(615) 859-3800
Contact: John D. Swanner, Rosa L. Swanner, Wayne Gray

SMILEY WILSON AGENCY, INC.†
847 Springfield Hwy.
P.O. Box 125
Goodlettsville, TN 37072
(615) 859-2820
Contact: Rita Faye Sinks, Mary K. Wilson

GREENBRIER
ALL STAR TALENT AGENCY†
P.O. Box 82
Greenbrier, TN 37073
(615) 244-3237
Contact: Joyce R. Brown

HEISKELL
BLUEGRASS MUSIC CITY PROMOTIONS†
P.O. Box 21
Heiskell, TN 37754
(615) 938-1185
Contact: H. Earl Marlar

HENDERSONVILLE
ALLIED ENTERTAINERS, INC.†
P.O. Box 647
Hendersonville, TN 37075
(615) 824-0142
Contact: Bobby Osborne, Sonny Osborne

THE JONES-HAWKINS AGENCY†
P.O. Box 90
Hendersonville, TN 37075
(615) 824-1484
Contact: Eloise J. Hawkins

LANCER AGENCY†
P.O. Box 160
Hendersonville, TN 37075
(615) 822-0222
Contact: Lance LeRoy, Lester R. Flatt

NASHVILLE LIVE†
P.O. Box 1106
Hendersonville, TN 37075
(615) 822-4204
Contact: Walker Marsh Hudson

NORTH AMERICAN TALENT AGENCY†
128-C Volunteer Dr.
Hendersonville, TN 37075
(615) 822-1888
Contact: G. Gerald Roy, Gail Spurlock, Cathi Kragen

BOBBY ROBERTS ENTERTAINMENT*
P.O. Box 1006
Hendersonville, TN 37075
(615) 824-2719
Contact: Bobby Roberts

SANBORN BOOKING AGENCY†
P.O. Box 1680
Hendersonville, TN 37075
(615) 824-8601
Contact: Wesley E. Sanborn, Julia A. Abrams

UNITED TALENT, INC.†
Twitty City
#1 Music Village Blvd.
Hendersonville, TN 37075
(615) 822-3210
Contact: Jimmy Jay, Conway Twitty, Loretta Lynn, O.V. (Monney) Lynn, Jr., Reggie Mac, Tom Dean, Dave Schuder

HERMITAGE
DARLIN' TALENT AGENCY†
556 Augusta Dr.
P.O. Box 90
Hermitage, TN 37076

(615) 883-3506
Contact: David Pierce Rogers

PAT TRENT PROMOTIONS AGENCY†
742B Linden Green Dr.
Hermitage, TN 37076
(615) 889-4734
Contact: Pat S. Trent

KNOXVILLE

CLUB SERVICE BOOKING AGENT†
1209 Dartmouth Rd.
Knoxville, TN 37914
(615) 523-9455
Contact: John L. Harper

MUSICIANS UNLIMITED BOOKING AGENCY†
2450 McCalla Ave.
Knoxville, TN 37917
(615) 588-3056
Contact: Charles Houston, James E. Houston

TAYLOR TALENT AGENCY†
2906 Brabson Dr.
Knoxville, TN 37918
(615) 688-9642
Contact: John W. Taylor

THE VACCARO AGENCY†
P.O. Box 10872
Knoxville, TN 37919
(615) 584-1010
Contact: Gene C. Vaccaro, Brent Dalton, Phil Barber

MADISON

FUSE BOOKING AGENCY†
323 Forrest Park Rd.
P.O. Box 4343
Madison, TN 37115
1 (615) 865-9015
Contact: Eugene M. McLeod

BILL GOODWIN AGENCY, INC.†
P.O. Box 144
Madison, TN 37115
(615) 868-5380
Contact: William T. Goodwin, Robert Michael Feurt

L/S TALENT†
120 Hickory St.
Madison, TN 37115
(615) 868-7172
Contact: Lee Stoller

TESSIER TALENT, INC.†
505 Canton Pass
Madison, Tn 37115
(615) 865-6602
Contact: Roy Tessier, Jim Whitaker, Debra McClure

MEMPHIS

CENTER STAGE ATTRACTIONS†
4992 Yale Rd. #2
Memphis, TN 38128
(901) 372-0436
Contact: Lydle Dwight McClain

DON DORTCH INTERNATIONAL, INC.†
2272 Deadrick
Memphis, TN 38114
(901) 324-1900
Contact: Donald E. Dortch, E.L. Hutton, Olin D. Sharpe

ODYSSEY ENTERTAINMENT CORPORATION†
2842 Semmes Rd.
Memphis, TN 38114
(901) 942-2358
Contact: Donald T.A. Mitchell, Jr.

BEN WAGES ADVERTISING AND MUSIC ENTERPRISES†
2794 Clark Rd. #2
Memphis, TN 38115
(901) 794-4332
Contact: Bennie Gerry Wages

NASHVILLE

ACE PRODUCTIONS†
3407 Green Ridge Dr.
Nashville, TN 37214
(615) 883-3888
Contact: Jim Case

ACUFF-ROSE ARTISTS CORPORATION†
2510 Franklin Road
Nashville, TN 37204
(615) 385-3031
Contact: Roy Acuff, John R. Brown, Mildred Acuff, Margaret Rose, Howard W. Forrester

ARTA PRODUCTIONS INTERNATIONAL(API)†
P.O. Box 40271
Nashville, TN 37204
(615) 385-0164
Contact: Don M. Keirns, W.C. Westenberger

BOB BEAN TALENT†
50 Music Sq., W., Ste. 309
Nashville, TN 37203
(615) 329-0222
Contact: Robert L. Bean

DICK BLAKE INTERNATIONAL, INC.†
P.O. Box 24727
Nashville, TN 37202
(615) 244-9550
Contact: Dave Barton, Lincoln Lakoff, Pat Blake, Scott Faragher

CAN-AM (CANADIAN-AMERICAN) TALENT†
P.O. Box 60346
Nashville, TN 37206
(615) 226-2787
Contact: James K. Green

CENTURY II TALENT AGENCY†
63 Music Sq. W.
P.O. Box 22707
Nashville, TN 37202
(615) 327-9222
Contact: Dr. Cecil E. Simmons, D. Terry Simmons

CIRCUIT RIDER TALENT AGENCY†
508 Whispering Hills Dr.
Nashville, TN 37211
(615) 833-3170
Contact: Sheb Wooley, Linda S. Dotson

CRESCENT MOON TALENT†
20 Music Sq. W.
Nashville, TN 37203
(615) 254-7553
Contact: Anthony Joseph Moon, John L. Maxcy, Mike Hooks

BILLY DEATON ENTERPRISES†
1300 Division St., Ste. 102
Nashville, TN 37203
(615) 244-4259
Contact: Billy J. Deaton

MARV DENNIS & ARTISTS, INC.(WI)†
Branch Office:
214 Old Hickory Blvd., Ste. 198
Nashville, TN 37221
(615) 352-0580
Contact: Marv Dennis, Sharon Hrncir, Gene White

DIAMOND TALENT†
P.O. Box 120662
Nashville, TN 37212
(615) 790-2446
Contact: Jay Diamond

AL EMBRY INTERNATIONAL†
1719 West End Ave., 11th Floor
Nashville, TN 37203
Mailing Address:
P.O. Box 23162
Nashville, TN 37202
(615) 327-4074
Contact: Alton Embry

EXECUTIVE ENTERTAINMENT COMPANY†
Grantland House
2214 Grantland Ave.
Nashvill, TN 37204
(615) 297-4962
Contact: "Mikk" Mastin, Jr.

FARRIS INTERNATIONAL TALENT, INC.†
821 19th Ave., S.
Nashville, TN 37203
(615) 329-9264
Contact: Jerry West, Allen Farris, Pat Brewer

THE FORD AGENCY†
P.O. Box 22635
Nashville, TN 37202
(615) 383-8318
Contact: John W. Cale, Jennifer Bryant

FRONT ROW NASHVILLE†
2120 Crestmore Road #186
Nashville, TN 37215
(615) 292-7667
Contact: Marycarol Stone, Dale Stone

FULL HOUSE ARTIST MANAGEMENT, INC.†
50 Music Square West, Ste. 800
Nashville, TN 37203
(615) 320-1441
Contact: Terry W. Vester, Steve Sandefur, Roger L. Rollins, Frank J. Deeter, Joy McKissick

SUSAN HACKNEY ASSOCIATES†
7 Music Circle N.
Nashville, TN 37203
(615) 244-7976
Contact: Margaret Susan Hackney

GRACE HALL TALENT AGENCY†
P.O. Box 110142
125 Rolynn Drive
Nashville, TN 37211
(615) 833-5157

ROY HALL ATTRACTIONS†
P.O. Box 90462
Nashville, TN 37209
(615) 292-0734
Contact: Roy Hall

INTERNATIONAL CELEBRITY SERVICES†
1808 West End Building, Ste. 102
Nashville, TN 37203
(615) 327-1880
Contact: Berdena (Dean) M. Ramer, Andrea Smith

INTERNATIONAL HOUSE OF TALENT, INC.†
816 19th Ave., S.
Nashville, TN 37203
(615) 327-1763
Contact: Billy Wayne Craddock, Nancy C. Josie, Tony Entsminger

JACK D. JOHNSON TALENT, INC.†
P.O. Box 40484
Nashville, TN 37204
(615) 383-6564
Contact: Jack D. Johnson, Ray Singer

KEY TALENT, INC.†
11 Music Circle, S.
Nashville, TN 37203
(615) 242-2461
Contact: E. Jimmy Key

KIT TALENT AGENCY†
800 18th Ave., S.
Nashville, TN 37203
(615) 244-5290
Contact: Edwin E. Rowell, Edwin P. Rowell, W. Timothy Rowell, Gloria K. Rowell, Patsy R. Looney, Kelly Noblett

SHORTY LAVENDER TALENT AGENCY†
1300 Division St., #200
Nashville, TN 37203
(615) 327-9595
Contact: Barbara Lavender, Dan Wojcik, Robert A. Lavender

BUDDY LEE ATTRACTIONS, INC.†
38 Music Square East, Ste. 300
Nashville, TN 37203
(615) 244-4336
Contact: Buddy Lee, Tony Conway, Jerry Rivers, Don Helms, Joseph E. Harris, Steve Buchanan, J.R. Shipp

Branch Office:
100 W. 57th St., Ste. 9E
New York, NY 10019
(212) 247-5216
Contact: Jim Gosnell, Joe Higgins

Branch Office:
3821 West Park Dr.
Kansas City, MO 69116
(816) 454-0839
Contact: Joan Saltel

LET US ENTERTAIN YOU, INC.†
50 Music Square West, Ste. 901
Nashville, TN 37203
(615) 327-3222
Contact: Robert Lee Smith

DON LIGHT TALENT, INC.†
1100 17th Ave., S.
Nashville, TN 37212
(615) 244-3900
Contact: Herman Harper, Bobby Cudd

LIMELITERS, INC.*†
Ste. 804
50 Music Square, W.
Nashville, TN 37203
(615) 329-2292
Contact: Miles Bell, Peggy O'Bitts, Brian D. Ashton

MIDDLE OF THE ROAD TALENT†
904 Shauna Dr.
Nashville, TN 37214
(615) 883-0086
Contact: Hugh X. Lewis

DALE MORRIS & ASSOCIATES, INC.†
812 19th Ave., S.
Nashville, TN 37203
(615) 327-3400
Contact: Dale Morris, Barbara Hardin, Sue Leonard, Sue Brady, Ray Burdett

WILLIAM MORRIS AGENCY, INC.(NY)†
Branch Office:
2325 Crestmoor Rd.
Nashville, TN 37215
(615) 385-0310
Contact: Dave Douds, Sonny Neal, Paul G. Moore, Ted Simmons

MUSIC ROW TALENT†
50 Music Square, W., Ste. 309
Nashville, TN 37203
(615) 244-6427
Contact: Jim Greene, Nat Stuckey, Debbie Turner, Ann Stuckey, Eddie R. Rhines

NASHVILLE ARTISTS MANAGEMENT BUREAU†
730 Currey Road
Nashville, TN 37217
(615) 361-0779
Contact: Xavier B. Cosse

THE NEAL AGENCY, LTD.†
42 Music Square, W.
Nashville, TN 37203
P.O. Box 121153
Nashville, TN 37212
(615) 242-1192
Contact: Bob Neal, Helen Neal, Kevin Neal

ONE-NITERS, INC.†
Box 40686
Nashville, TN 37204
(615) 383-8412
Contact: Billy Smith

PARKER ENTERTAINMENT†
3603 Caldwell Court
Nashville, TN 37204
(615) 297-0213
Contact: Jeffrey R. Parker

PRODIGY MUSICAL ENTERPRISES†
2131 Elm Hill Pike, Bldg. J-188
Nashville, TN 37210
(615) 883-7801
Contact: Thomas Patrick Briley

R & W TALENT†
146-B Cross Timbers Dr.
Nashville, TN 37221
(615) 646-3007
Contact: Roger G. West

ROCK-A-BILLY ARTISTS (50'S THRU 80'S) AGENCY†
P.O. Box 4740
Nashville, TN 37216
(615) 859-0355
Contact: Wade Theodore Curtiss, Susan D. Curtiss

ROGER TALENT ENTERPRISES†
P.O. Box 120306
Nashville, TN 37212
(615) 362-3896
Contact: Roger L. Jaudon

RUSTY SCOTT TALENT AGENCY†
P.O. Box 22952
Nashville, TN 37202
(615) 255-1054
Contact: Thomas J. Kist

DENNY SKI THEATRICAL AGENCY†
1300 Division, St., Ste. 103
Nashville, TN 37203
(615) 242-1373
Contact: Dennis Drazkowski, Max Blakeway

SRO TALENT†
903 18th Ave., S.
P.O. Box 120368
Nashville, TN 37212
(615) 329-2010
Contact: Dolores B. Smiley, Jim Hartley, Nina Swallows

STAGE RIGHT PRODUCTIONS†
2014 Sweetbriar Avenue
Nashville, TN 37212
(615) 385-3460
Contact: David Foster Cannon, Toby G. Cannon

STARGOLD PRODUCTIONS†
(A DIV. OF STARGOLD PUBLICATIONS, INC.)
211 Cumberland Circle
P.O. Box 140542
Nashville, TN 37214
(615) 889-2320
Contact: Roy G. Edwards, Jr., John L. Weaver III, Fay Benson, James D. Dodson

BISHOP M. SYKES, AND ASSOCIATES, INC.†
713 18th Ave., S.

Nashville, TN 37203
(615) 329-9556
Contact: Joe Saperstein, Louis H. Dunn

JOE TAYLOR ARTIST AGENCY†
2401 Granny White Place
Nashville, TN 37204
(615) 385-0035
Contact: Bill Bleckley, Bob Benn, Frank D. Stephens, Robert J. Vandygriff, Florence J. Tessier

LARRY TAYLOR†
P.O. Box 23233
Nashville, TN 37202
(615) 292-3272
Contact: Larry Taylor

TOP BILLING, INC.*†
P.O. Box 121089
4301 Hillsboro Road
Nashville, TN 37212
(615) 383-8883
Contact: Tandy C. Rice, Jr., Dolores B. Rice, Don Fowler, Jack Sublette, Ginger Hennessy, Fred Chip Peay, Allen Whitcomb, Dan Goodman

TOP NOTCH BOOKING AGENCY†
141 Neese Dr. J-50
Nashville, TN 37211
(615) 832-8027
Contact: Marie C. Koehn

TOTAL CONCEPTS REPRESENTATION, INC.†
38 Music Square, East, Ste. 111
Nashville, TN 37203
(615) 255-4181
Contact: Robert F. Nacarato, Earl E. Owens, Michael J. Nacarato, Frank Auman

U.S. TALENT AGENCY†
60 Music Square, West
Nashville, TN 37203
(615) 327-2255
Contact: Doyle Wilburn, Leslie Wilburn

BOB WITTE'S BLUE RIBBON TALENT†
38 Music Square, E., Ste. 214
Nashville, Tn 37203
(615) 242-2548
Contact: Bob J. White

FRED ZINN PRODUCTIONS OF WORLD WIDE COUNTRY†
14 Music Circle East
Nashville, TN 37203
(615) 255-2547
Contact: W. Frederick Zinn

NOLENSVILLE

STAGE II ATTRACTIONS†
Box 344
Nolensville, TN 37135
(615) 776-2600
Contact: Norm Forrest

Branch Office:
3701 Bellwood Dr.
Norman, OK 73069
(405) 360-1414
Contact: Phyllis McCraw

OLD HICKORY

AQUILA†
4520 Woodside Rd.
Old Hickory, TN 37138
(615) 847-8610
Contact: Walter F. Sill, Jr.

M & R TALENTS†
32 San Gabriel Court
Old Hickory, TN 37138
(615) 754-4884
Contact: Robert D. Salyer

TEXAS

AMARILLO

BOBBY BURNS AGENCY†
P.O. Box 7632
Amarillo, TX 79109
(806) 352-0971
Contact: Dorothy Dee Burns, Dick Morton, C.W. (Bill) McGill, Jr.

ARLINGTON

BAMBI PRODUCTIONS†
2208 President's Corner #302
Arlington, TX 76011
(817) (Metro) 261-3253
Contact: Kenneth R. Hicks

AUSTIN

AUSTIN TEJAS SOUNDS†
3300 Hollywood
Austin, TX 78722
(512) 476-8195
Contact: Carlyne Majer

CASE-MUNSON ENTERTAINMENT*†
8220 Research Blvd. #132D
Austin, TX 78758
(512) 454-0408
Contact: Dusty Case

CLASSICAL BOOKING AGENCY†
1007 E. Rundberg Land #232
Austin, TX 78753
(512) 835-5910
Contact: Tracy Collins

COUNTRY TALENT†
9027 Northgate Blvd., Ste. 100
Austin, TX 78758
(512) 837-4332
Contact: James D. Louis

DOUBLE D PRODUCTIONS†
1005 Rocky Spring Rd.
Austin, TX 78753
(512) 836-7876
Contact: Dotty Buchanan

JUNIPER COUNTRY TALENT & REFERRAL AGENCY†
805 W. 10th St., Apt. 101
Austin, TX 78701
(512) 477-7015
Contact: Orville Laird

MCVAY AGENCY†
1781 Spyglass #221
Austin, TX 78746
(512) 327-0433
Contact: Kitty McVay

JOE MONTGOMERY BOOKING AGENCY†
8914 Georgian Dr.
Austin, TX 78753
(512) 836-3201
Contact: Roy J. Montgomery

ROCK ARTS, LTD.†
3839 Bee Cave Rd., #101
Austin, TX 78746
(512) 327-5320
Contact: Tim Neece, Joe Priesnitz, Kathleen Vick, Ethridge Hill, Sherwin Roden, Al Bettis, Tom Ordon

TOUR BOOKING AGENCY†
10508A Little Pebbles Dr.
Austin, TX 78758
(512) 837-8647
Contact: Julian Johnson, Jr.

BEAUMONT

SIMMONS MUSICAL SERVICES†
4620 Elmherst
Beaumont, TX 77706
(713) 898-1273
Contact: Dr. James M. Simmons

BELLAIRE

JEROME B. BORSKI & ASSOCIATES†
4501 Palmetto
Bellaire, TX 77401
(713) 664-2460

CONROE

JAMES A. VAUGHN†
212 Wroxton Dr.
Conroe, TX 77304
(713) 756-1508

CORPUS CHRISTI

ALEXANDER ENTERPRISES*†
P.O. Box 6219
Corpus Christi, TX 78411
(512) 853-3321
Contact: M.T. Alexander

AQUARIUS PRODUCTIONS & ASSOCIATES, INC.†
6245 Hanley Drive
Corpus Christi, TX 78412
(512) 991-2986
Contact: Robert E. McAuliffe, Helen M. McAuliffe aka Ginny Lamare

DON BENNETT AGENCY*†
4630 Deepdale
Corpus Christi, TX 78413
(512) 854-4871
Contact: Don Bennett

DALLAS

ASSOCIATED BOOKING CORPORATION(NY)†
Branch Office:
3511 Hall St.
Lee Park Bldg.
Dallas, TX 75219
(214) 528-8296
Contact: Tony Papa

BIG JIM PRODUCTION†
1915 Hall St.
Dallas, TX 75204

(214) 824-7548
Contact: William E. Harris, Eloise Harris

CABARET ATTRACTIONS & TALENT†
P.O. Box 64888
Dallas, TX 75206
(214) 349-0610
Contact: James A. Caterine, Skip Fritz, Charles Wythe, Mrs. Jane E. Tilford, Bob Endreson, Lee Harris

CENTRAL CASTING†
2522 McKinney Ave., Ste. 101
Dallas, TX 75219
(214) 747-9933
Contact: Angus G. Wynne III

CHARDON, INC.†
3198 Royal Lane, Ste. 204
Dallas, TX 75229
(214) 350-4650
Contact: Randy Jackson, Hortense C. Jones, Jerry Lastelick, Rozene Pride, Jim Prater

J. JEAN DIXON AGENCY†
P.O. Box 140443
Dallas, TX 75214
(214) 327-5385
Contact: Johnnie Jean Dixon Finley

EAGLE ATTRACTION†
3204 Oakland Ave.
Dallas, TX 75215
(214) 421-5544
Contact: Boyd Meshack

ENTERTAINMENT PRODUCTIONS, INC.†
2646 Andjon
Dallas, TX 75220
(214) 350-4974
Contact: George Michael Sanders, Hubert Knight

KEN-RAN ENTERPRISES*
P.O. Box 25505
Dallas, TX 75225
(214) 349-3025
Contact: C.W. Kendall

MUSIC PROMOTIONS†
11145 Lake Highlands Circle, Ste. 240
Dallas, TX 75218
(214) 343-6494
Contact: Thomas Gary Davidson, Laura S. Davidson, Winston C. Flood, II

RAY PRICE ENTERPRISES†
P.O. Box 30384
Dallas, TX 75230
(214) 750-9993
Contact: Janie Price

CYNTHIA MARIE SCOTT†
7522 Holly Hill, #20
Dallas, TX 75231
(214) 692-6041

SHORT BIGGY PRODUCTIONS†
5103 Skillman #218
Dallas, TX 75206
(214) 368-7209
Contact: D.W. Homes, Cathleen Bernier

SILVER STAR ENTERTAINMENT†
3883 Turtle Creek Blvd.
Dallas, TX 75219
(214) 528-8050
Contact: Rudolph Wilson, Tom Workman, Frederick Brodsky, Deborah Stuer

SOUTHWEST ORCHESTRA & THEATRICAL AGENCY†
1938 Las Cruces Lane
Dallas, TX 75217
(214) 391-5013
Contact: Joe Garcia, Sherry Lynn, Leo Peeper

VICAM PRODUCTIONS†
6001 Skillman Ave., Apt 176
Dallas, TX 75231
(214) 363-4889
Contact: Robert (Kin) King Via, Pedro M. Campos

EL PASO

IMAGE INTERNATIONAL†
2500 Scenic Crest Circle #1
El Paso, TX 79930
(915) 565-1413
Contact: Don Cange

FT. WORTH

C C & CO. TALENT BOOKING AGENCY†
4500 Westlake Dr.
Ft. Worth, TX 76109
(817) 926-6456
Contact: Nancy J. Carpenter

HUBBARD ENTERTAINMENT†
3420 Alemeda, Rt. 5
Ft. Worth, TX 76116
(817) 244-8114
Contact: Ora Mae Hubbard

GAINESVILLE

JOKER ENTERTAINMENT†
103 South Morris Street
Gainesville, TX 76240
1 (817) 665-0122
Contact: Jody Joseph Shotwell

GARLAND

NATIONAL BOOKING AGENCY†
2605 Northridge Dr.
Garland, TX 75043
(214) 840-8222
Contact: Jo Dee Morgan

HOUSTON

AARON AND WILLIAMS ENTERTAINMENT AGENCY†
2630 Fountainview, Ste., 300
Houston, TX 77057
P.O. Box 56789
Houston, TX 77027
(713) 961-2263
Contact: Joel D. Williams

ADAMS & GREEN ENTERTAINMENT, INC.*†
5414 Antoine, Ste. C
Houston, TX 77091
1 (713) 681-5200
Contact: William C. Green, Jr., Cheryle Green, Bonnie Jean Miller, Arthur Allen Henson

B.A.S. ENTERPRISES†
5925 Kirby Drive, Ste. 226
Houston, TX 77005
(713) 522-2713
Contact: Shelton O. Bissell

BILIN AGENCY†
16528 Kentwood Dr.
Houston, TX 77058
(713) 488-8339
Contact: Mrs. Linda L. Johnston

Branch Office:
4413 Lee's Summit Rd.
Independence, MO 64057
(816) 373-1639
Contact: Mrs. Jean Echols

BROCK AGENCY†
Hyatt Regency Houston Hotel
1200 Louisiana
Houston, TX 77002
(713) 652-2111
Contact: Buddy Brock, Frances Wilbanks, Col. Jack McKenzie, Frances Lauer, Wayne Johnson, Judy Johnson, Mark W. Taylor

H. HAL BURMAN & ASSOCIATES, INC.†
7634 Clarewood
Houston, TX 77036
(713) 776-8183
Contact: Jay Mark Burman, Sylvia R. Burman

SHIRLEY ANN CAMPBELL†
10622 Castleton
Houston, TX 77016
(713) 633-5313

ENTERTAINMENT AGENCY UNLIMITED, INC.†
6363 Richmond, Ste. 214
P.O. Box 8305
Houston, TX 77004
(713) 784-4125
Contact: Sirron Kyles, Alvin Terry, Brenda Terry, Aubrey Dunham, Murray Harris, K.K. Kenneth Kyles, Gregg Kyles, Janet Schoppe, Debbie Rogstad, Gordon Irwin

GERLACH ENTERTAINMENT, INC.†
1011 Augusta, Ste. 102
Houston, TX 77057
(713) 977-5010
Contact: Ed Gerlach, Jack R. Creel, Doris Gerlach, David H. Vandiver

PHIL GRAY ORCHESTRAS†
25 Champions Colony West
Houston, TX 77069
(713) 444-6656
Contact: Phil Gray

HOUSTON ENTERTAINMENT AGENCY†
6302 Glencoe
Houston, TX 77087
(713) 643-0946

Contact: J.A. Rudy Garcia, Gloria Garcia

CAROLYN HUGHES AGENCY, INC.†
9720 Town Park Dr., Ste. 101
Houston, TX 77036
(713) 270-5602
Contact: Carolyn A. Hughes, Wanda Berg

JONES AND JONES AGENCY†
5310 Trail Lake Drive
Houston, TX 77045
(713) 433-7415
Contact: Carolyn Jones, Mildred E. Jones, Bill Kouski

MILTON LARKIN ORCHESTRA AGENCY†
5911 Beldart
Houston, TX 77033
(713) 738-6247
Contact: Milton Larkin

THE LATEST RAGE TALENT AGENCY†
3519 Tanglewilde
Houston, TX 77063
(713) 974-2502
Contact: Charles Robert Bellomy

AL MARKS ORCHESTRA & ENTERTAINMENT AGENCY†
6218 Cheena Dr.
Houston, TX 77096
(713) 785-5301

MUSICIANS MANAGEMENT HEADLINER ATTRACTIONS†
59 Casa Grande Dr.
Houston, TX 77060
(713) 820-4991
Contact: Dave J. Holl, Dian Schoppa, Larry Holcombe

OTT MUSIC AGENCY†
2411 Wheeler Ave.
Houston, TX 77004
(713) 529-9387
Contact: Mary Ann Ott

RICKY'S ENTERTAINMENT AGENCY†
9327 Rentur
Houston, TX 77031
(713) 771-8922
Contact: Ricky Diaz, John Burchell, Ricky Diaz, Jr.

SHOWAY TALENT AGENCY†
2726 Ladin Dr.
Houston, TX 77039
(713) 449-1221
Contact: Wayne P. Falbe, Dorothy C. Hess, Darwin Lavelle Collins

BOB SMITH ORCHESTRAS†
The Warwick
5701 Main
Houston, TX 77001
(713) 526-3475
Contact: Robert E. Smith

THE LEON SPENCER AGENCY†
4830 Ligonberry St.
Houston, TX 77033
(713) 738-7788
Contact: Leon R. Spencer, Jr.

WORLD STAGE LTD.†
3620 Washington Ave., Ste. 340
Houston, TX 77007
(713) 861-5428
Contact: Angela Carolyn, Stewart Moore

WORLD TALENT ASSOCIATES, INC.†
1423 Sherwood Forest
P.O. Box 19647
Houston, TX 77024
(713) 461-0530
Contact: Bill Hamm, Buddy C. Howell, Edward Z. Fair, Stephen F. Moore

"YELLOW ROSE OF TEXAS IN HOUSTON"†
2516 Sunset
Houston, TX 77005
(713) 529-0100
Contact: Patricia J. McIntire

HUMBLE

DONNA PRIOR WAUHOB AGENCY†
P.O. Box 596
Humble, TX 77338-0596
(713) 852-8354
Contact: Donna Lou Wauhob

IOWA PARK

PARTYTIME ENTERTAINMENT SERVICE†
503 W. Magnolia
Iowa Park, TX 76367
(817) 592 5961
Contact: Jerry L. Matthews

ORANGE

BLACKWATER COMPANY†
P.O. Box 1787
Orange, TX 77630
(713) 883-9097
Contact: Gerald Green, Doug Childress

SAN ANGELO

ADVANCE PRODUCTIONS, INC.†
635 Cactus Lane
San Angelo, TX 76903
(915) 653-0068
Contact: Jacque Dendy

SAN ANTONIO

BILL BAILEY PRESENTS†
#507 Casino Club Bldg.
Corner/Presa at Crockett
San Antonio, TX 78205
P.O. Box 822
San Antonio, TX 78293
(512) 223-6784
Contact: A.D. Bill Bailey

BLUE HORIZONS ENTERTAINMENT†
304 East Craig
P.O. Box 12401
San Antonio, TX 78212
(512) 735-6946
Contact: Tony Rozance

SCOTTY CLOUDT & ASSOCIATES†
310 First International Bank Bldg.
San Antonio, TX 78201
(512) 736-3113
Contact: Scotty Cloudt

ENCORE TALENT, INC.†
2137 Zercher
San Antonio, TX 78209
(512) 822-2655
Contact: R.A. Spillman, Ray Baker, Marion Bandy

S & V BOOKING AGENCY†
122 Forrest Valley
San Antonio, TX 78227
(512) 674-7229
Contact: Samuel J. Smith

SCORPIO ENTERPRISES, LTD.(SC)†
Branch Office:
8714 Bridington Street
San Antonio, TX 78239
(512) 656-7527
Contact: Lucille White

TEXAS GREATS PROMOTIONS†
4047 Naco Perrin, Ste., 110
San Antonio, TX 78217
(512) 654-8773
Contact: David William Green

SPRING

STAR ATTRACTIONS, INC.†
7406 Theisswood Rd.
Spring, TX 77379
(713) 683-7171
Contact: J.R. Reeder, Gary Gene Watson, Jane Reeder

TEXAS CITY

RICK DOSS AGENCY†
P.O. Box 2479
Texas City, TX 77590
(713) 948-0679
Contact: Rickey Neal Doss

TOMBALL

FLETCHER'S MUSIC & BAND PLACEMENT†
14714 Brown Rd.
Tomball, TX 77375
(713) 351-8449
Contact: Roy M. Fletcher

WACO

ERNIE FIELDS ARTISTS REPRESENTATIVE AGENCY(OK)†
Branch Office:
204 Fissler
Waco, TX 76704
Contact: Classie Ballou, Sr.

HEART OF TEXAS TALENT†
1310 Crestline Dr.
Waco, TX 76705
(817) 799-8727
Contact: Joseph E. Callahan, Marilyn A. Callahan, James Dunn

WICHITA FALLS

SAM GIBBS AGENCY†
4117 Jacksboro Highway
Wichita Falls, TX 76302
(817) 767-1456
Contact: Robert L. Bollinger, Steven S. Moore

VIRGINIA

ARLINGTON

TAMAR PRODUCTIONS, INC.(IL)†
Branch Office:
1325 Wilson Blvd., Ste. 305
Arlington, VA 22209
(703) 527-3079
Contact: Mary Ann Rose

BURKEVILLE

DOOLEY ENTERPRISES†
Rt. 1, Box 189
Burkeville, VA 23922
(804) 767-4150
Contact: James Warren, Dooley, Jr.

CHESAPEAKE

BENJAMIN ROSS PRODUCTIONS†
1318 Wingfield Avenue
Chesapeake, VA 23325
1 (804) 545-3420
Contact: Bennie Hudgins

NEWPORT NEWS

GALAXY PRODUCTIONS†
P.O. Box 473
Newport News, VA 23607
(804) 874-2802
Contact: Alphonso D. Edwards

PORTSMOUTH

NEW SOUND BOOKING AGENCY†
904 Ann Street
Portsmouth, VA 23704
(804) 399-8088
Contact: Noah Deal, Sr.

ROANOKE

KINCER TALENT AGENCY†
2745 Calloway St., N.W.
Roanoke, VA 24012
(703) 563-0563
Contact: Cecil O. Kincer, Dorothy H. Kincer

VIRGINIA BEACH

SOUTHERN ORCHESTRAS CORPORATION*†
Ste. 303 Executive Center
1604 Hilltop West
Virginia Beach, VA 23451
(804) 422-9780
Contact: Margaret L. Cunniff, Darius C. Auman, III, Nell Z. Auman, William R. Fellion, Robert W. Morris

SPOTLITE ENTERPRISES, LTD. OF VIRGINIA†
2224 Commerce Parkway
Virginia Beach, VA 23454
(804) 481-5500
Contact: Roberts S. Williams

WINCHESTER

CLAY ENTERPRISES†
P.O. Box 705
Winchester, VA 22601
(703) 667-6076
Contact: Clay Ervin Smith, Jr.

WASHINGTON

BELLEVUE

WILLIAM STEPHAN & ASSOCIATES, INC.*†
1-100th Avenue N.E.
Bellevue, WA 98004
(206) 455-2224
Contact: William Stephan, Don Consold, Mark Wilson

CHATTAROY

FREADE' SOUNDS†
Route 1 - Box 231
Chattaroy, WA 99003
(509) 292-2201
Contact: Jeannie Carter, Verna Leoth Krakenberg, Thomas Michael Lapansky

PAUL HANDLER & ASSOCIATES†
Rt. 2, Box 167
Chattaroy, WA 99003
(509) 292-2670
Contact: Paul Handler

EVERETT

CHAPARRAL INVESTMENT CORPORATION†
13000 17th Ave. W., #105
Everett, WA 98204
(206) 355-8552
Contact: Gerald G. Albin, Virginia L. Bath, Theodore Ginty

GREENACRES

GLENN SZABO AGENCY†
18909 Alki Avenue
Greenacres, WA 99016
(509) 924-3891
Contact: Glenn Szabo, Keith Terhune

LONGVIEW

MOTION MUSIC†
P.O. Box 1463
Longview, WA 98632
(206) 423-7722
Contact: Jeff W. Whitted

MARSHALL

FUTURE STAR PROMOTIONS†
P.O. Box 88
Marshall, WA 99020
(509) 625-5516
Contact: Frank P. Graham

MERCER

FRED RADKE ENTERTAINMENT†
P.O. Box 821
Mercer Island, WA 98040
(206) 232-3692
Contact: Fred Radke

MOUNTLAKE TERRACE

JACK BELMONT AGENCY*
21718 66th Ave., W.
Mountlake Terrace, WA 98043
(206) 771-3595
Contact: Jack Belmont

OLYMPIA

BOB WRIGHT MUSIC PRODUCTIONS†
5022 Racoon Valley Rd.
Olympia, WA 98503
(206) 459-1019
Contact: Robert Wright

Branch Office:
US Coast Guard Base
Westport, WA 98595
(206) 268-0586
Contact: Kristine Trapp

REDMOND

P.M. PROMOTIONS†
16636 N.E. 40th
Redmond, WA 98052
(206) 883-1654
Contact: Peggy McIntyre, Margot Miller

RENTON

TOM THRASHER AGENCY†
P.O. Box 74
Renton, WA 98057
(206) 271-4554
Contact: Thomas R. Thrasher, Doris J. Thrasher

SEATTLE

BRAVO ARTIST MANAGEMENT, INC.†
333 Taylor N., Ste. 202
Seattle, WA 98109
(206) 624-1492
Contact: Lauren E. Anderson, Alice B. Anderson, Teresa Tillson

GEORGE CARLSON & ASSOCIATES† WESTERN LECTURE/ ENTERTAINMENT BUREAU
113 Battery St.
Seattle, WA 98121
(206) 623-8045
Contact: George Carlson

FAR WEST ENTERTAINMENT*†
110 Baylston Ave., E.
Seattle, WA 98102
(206) 324-6750
Contact: John Nyberg, Paul Barbarus, Dennis P. Caldirola, Neil Rush, Douglas Boad

INDEPENDENT ENTERTAINERS†
2854 South 146th
Seattle, WA 98168
(206) 246-8740
Contact: William Robert Osborne

JERRY ROSS AGENCY†
Room 622 - Jones Bldg.
1331 Third Ave.
Seattle, WA 98101
(206) 624-3141
Contact: Jerry Ross, Lou Bianchi

SAVANT ENTERTAINMENT AGENCY*
Ste. 729
2200 6th Ave.
Seattle, WA 98121
(206) 622-6571
Contact: Bob Anderson

STINSON ENTERPRISES†
1224 S.W. 157th
Seattle, WA98166

(206) 244-4532
Contact: James Edward Stinson

P.A. TINSLEY & ASSOCIATES†
P.O. Box 12134
Seattle, WA 98112
(206) 632-2320
Contact: Preston A. Tinsley

WESTWIND ENTERTAINMENT†
6812 52nd N.E.
Seattle, WA 98115
(206) 522-2202
Contact: Gregory C. Erickson

SPOKANE

AUDIO PROMOTION†
P.O. Box 7141
Spokane, WA 99207
(509) 926-3132
Contact: Floyd Mark Ashley, David Brett Ashley, Stephen Duane La Londe

FROST & FROST ENTERTAINMENT†
W. 3985 Taft Drive
Spokane, WA 99208
(509) 325-1777
Contact: Dick Frost, Fay Ann Frost

ROBERT L. JASPER†
172 S. Madison
Spokane, WA 99204
(509) 624-5900

JOHN W. POWELL AND ASSOCIATES†
P.O. Box 8064, Manito Station
Spokane, WA 99203
(509) 838-3432
Contact: John W. Powell

DAVE SOBOL THEATRICAL AGENCY†
E. 8023 Sprague Ave.
Spokane, WA 99206
(509) 928-2132
Contact: Billy Tipton, Harley Reckord

TOPP NAME ENTERPRIZE†
S. 328 Pittsburg St.
Spokane, WA 99202
(509) 535-5881
Contact: Memphis Johnson, Jr.

DWIGHT S. VAN BRUNT†
Box 857
Spokane, WA 99210
(509) 235-5155

TACOMA

M.K. PRODUCTIONS*†
10602 Butte Dr., SW
Tacoma, WA 98498
(206) 582-4422
Contact: Mary Kaye Moisio

SHOOTING STARR PRODUCTIONS†
6610 S. Madison
Tacoma, WA 98409
(206) 472-3839
Contact: Jose Luis Garcia

VANCOUVER

B-LEE ENTERTAINMENT SERVICE†
6104 N.E. 74th Street
Vancouver, WA 98661
(206) 695-0268
Contact: Mickey Jean LeGerrette aka Micki Lee

JACK HART AGENCY†
102 E. 43rd St.
Vancouver, WAS 98663
(206) 694-5520
Contact: Jack A. Hart

HCC BOOKING AGENCY†
10013 NE 35th St.
Vancouver, WA 98662
(206) 254-8074
Contact: Higinio Camacho Cerdon

STAN KRAMIEN AND ASSOCIATES†
400 E. Evergreen, Ste. 9G (The Academy)
Vancouver, WA 98660
(206) 694-9444
Contact: Stanley R. Kramien, Stan Kramien, Jr., Carol D'Amico

WALLA WALLA

JUNO TALENT COORDINATION†
1319 Monroe
Walla Walla, WA 93362
(509) 529-2258
Contact: Orville Ott, June Ott, Wendell McKenzie

WESTPORT

BOB WRIGHT MUSIC PRODUCTION†
(See Olympia listing)

YAKIMA

MAE ALLEN ENTERTAINMENT PRODUCTIONS AGENCY†
7205 MacLaren St.
Yakima, WA 98908
(509) 965-1684
Contact: Florence M. Showman

WEST VIRGINIA

BELLE

A.B. PROMOTIONS†
3413 West 2nd Ave.
Belle, WV 25015
(304) 343-5142
Contact: Arthur I. Butler, Jr.

CHARLESTON

GREGORY & HILL ENTERPRISES†
24 Bradford St., No. 11
Charleston, WV 25301
(304) 343-7859
Contact: Mimi Methvin

SOUND SENSATIONS†
304 Antler Dr.
Charleston, WV 25314
(304) 744-6500
Contact: David V. Dodd, Dawn R. Young

FAYETTEVILLE

DONALD L. VEST BAND BOOKINGS†
P.O. Box 547
Fayetteville, WV 25840
(304) 469-6879
Contact: Donald L. Vest

HUNTINGTON

MEDIA PROMOTIONS ENTERPRISES*
2880 Third Ave.
Huntington, WV 25702
(304) 697-4222
Contact: Bell Heaberlin

MARTINSBURG

BIG "K" TALENT AGENCY†
Route 2 #92 J
Martinsburg, WV 25401
(304) 267-4469
Contact: James Grove Kretzer, J.R. Sanders

ST. ALBANS

CRIMCO AGENCY†
1291 Highland Drive
St. Albans, WV 25177
(304) 727-8222
Contact: Dewey M. Lester, Steve Morrison

PHIL RAMIREZ AGENCY†
P.O. Box 883
St. Albans, WV 25177
(304) 727-3253
Contact: Phil Ramirez

WEIRTON

RUTH BRODINE BOOKING AGENCY†
3840 Marlamont Way
Weirton, WV 26062
1 (304) 748-7689

WHEELING

WHEELING TALENT AGENCY†
P.O. Box 6687
Wheeling, WV 26003
(614) 758-5812
Contact: Robert H. Gallion, Sybil P. Tarpley

WHITE SULPHUR SPRINGS

BILL WALZ PRODUCTIONS†
107A Spring Street
White Sulphur Springs, WV 24986
(304) 563-1377
Contact: William F. Walz

WISCONSIN

APPLETON

RADTKE ENTERPRISES†
701 E. Pershing St.
Appleton, WI 54911
(414) 734-2551
Contact: Carl F. Radtke, Mary L. Radtke

BELOIT

SUNLIGHT PRODUCTIONS-MAGNET ATTRACTIONS†
731 Eighth Street
Beloit, WI 53511
(608) 362-4340
Contact: David C. Tasse

BENTON

BOB HARRIS ENTERTAINMENT*†
P.O. Box 366

Benton, WI 58303
(608) 759-2311
Contact: Bob Harris

BROOKFIELD

TALENT ASSOCIATES OF WISCONSIN, INC.†
P.O. Box 588
2840 N. Brookfield Rd.
Brookfield, WI 53005
(414) 786-8500
Contact: John A. Mangold, Jr., Lee G. Rinder

BUTLER

FOUR STAR PRODUCTIONS†
P.O. Box 176
Butler, WI 53007
(414) 438-0300
Contact: Jon Hall, Jeff Moylan, Mike L. Boelter

K.F. PRODUCTIONS, INC.†
P.O. Box 469
Butler, WI 53007
(414) 466-8055
Contact: Ken Felerski, Ann Marie Felerski

CLEAR LAKE

GRA-BON PRODUCTIONS†
P.O. Box 261
Clear Lake, WI 54005
(715) 263-2693
Contact: Graydon L. Jarvinen, Bonita M. Jarvinen, Bradley Blihovde

CUDAHY

BARRY'S SUNSHINE PRODUCTIONS†
3535 East Cudahy Ave.
Cudahy, WI 53110
(414) 481-3959
Contact: Paul Barry

DELAVAN

LES JAMES ENTERTAINMENT AGENCY†
Rt. 3, Box 345
Delavan, WI 53115
(414) 728-5693
Contact: Leslie J. Puttkammer

EAU CLAIRE

SHOW BIZ TALENT CORPORATION†
(See Marinette listing)

GREEN BAY

MRS. ELLEN M. PETERSON†
2248 University Ave.
Green Bay, WI 54302
(414) 468-8848

HALES CORNERS

THE EPICENTER ORGANIZATION†
P.O. Box 474
Hales Corners, WI 53130
Contact: John F. Ertl, Jr.

KENOSHA

LEE PRODUCTIONS†
6720 26th Ave.
Kenosha, WI 53140
(414) 657-4516
Contact: Fletcher Lee

FRANK MELLONE BOOKING AGENCY†
3109 24th Ave.
Kenosha, WI 53140
(414) 658-2259
Contact: Ronald Funk

ONE-WAY PRODUCTION LTD.†
5920 34th Ave.
Kenosha, WI 53142
(414) 652-3898
Contact: William J. Strupp, Jeffrey W. Stevens, Mitch W. Haberle

LACROSSE

MARV DENNIS & ARTISTS, INC.†
330 S. 6th St.
P.O. Box 1926
LaCrosse, WI 54601
(608) 782-0026
Contact: Marvin O. Blihovde aka Marv Dennis, Jerry Morrison, John McDonald, William E. Cree, Sharon Hrncir

Branch Office:
214 Old Hickory Blvd., Ste. 198
Nashville, TN 37221
(615) 352-0580
Contact: Marv Dennis, Sharon Hrncir, Gene White

INTENSE AGENCY†
411 S. 3rd.
LaCrosse, WI 54601
(608) 782-0120
Contact: Maurice O. Sherman

LIN-BECK ENTERPRISES†
804 S. 8th St.
LaCrosse, WI 54601
(608) 782-3743
Contact: Lindy Shannon

LITTLE CHUTE

GARY VAN ZEELAND TALENT, INC.*
1750 Freedom Road
Little Chute, WI 54140
(414) 788-5222
Contact: Gary Van Zeeland

MADISON

ACADEMY OF ARTIST PRODUCTIONS†
7105 Flower Lane #F
Madison, WI 53717
(608) 833-9262
Contact: Erin Smith, Louis Carlson

THE ACADEMY OF SWING†
3413 Dawes St.
Madison, WI 53714
(608) 244-6569
Contact: Steven J. Dahl, Michael Wilhelms, Dean Starkey

KEN ADAMANY ASSOCIATES†
315 W. Gorham St.
Madison, WI 53703
(608) 251-2644
Contact: Tom Hennick

BADGER ENTERTAINMENT†
3011 Todd Dr.
Madison, WI 53713
(608) 274-7330
Contact: Edward J. Weinberger, Dolores, Weinberger, Paul Thalmann

CLASS ACTS TALENT AGENCY†
7008 Tree Lane - Apt. F
Madison, WI 53717
P.O. Box 5636
Madison, WI 53705
(608) 833-5753
Contact: Lien T. Lemon

OPEN BOOKING AGENCY†
5601 Odana Road, Ste. 10
Madison, WI 53719
(608) 271-1190
Contact: Nels C. Christiansen, Sarah Peisch, Chad Dell

PARKEY AGENCY†
3134 Ashford Lane
Madison, WI 53713
(608) 271-6055
Contact: Parkis G. Waterbury

MARINETTE

SHOW BIZ TALENT CORPORATION†
1521 Oakes
Marinette, WI 54143
(715) 732-0659
Contact: Gene Michaels

Branch Office:
Rt. 6, Box 112
P.O. Box 1062
Eau Claire, WI 54701
(715) 832-9934

Branch Office:
747A S. 23 St.
Milwaukee, WI 53204
(414) 384-5799
Contact: Dan Bubnich

MILWAUKEE

ACA ENTERTAINMENT CONSULTANTS*
2421 North Mayfair Road
Milwaukee, WI 53226
(414) 778-0600
Contact: Bill Rothe

ARTISTS CORPORATION OF AMERICA*
Mayfair Plaza
2421 North Mayfair Road
Milwaukee, WI 53226
(414) 778-0600
Contact: William T. Rothe, Bernardine Rothe, Chuck Irvin, Bobbi Howe aka Roberta Howe, Mary Rothe, Louie Higgins, Pat McCants, Neil Hawes

CURT BERGER AGENCY†
1626-N. 57th St.
Milwaukee, WI 53208
(414) 476-3044

BURMEK THEATRICAL PRODUCTIONS†
101 East Wells Street
Milwaukee, WI 53202
(414) 276-8300
Contact: "C" Clifford Burmek

CLIMAX ENTERTAINMENT AGENCY†
P.O. Box 10128
Milwaukee, WI 53210
(414) 442-0272
Contact: Charles L. Offer, Vanett Swing

GREATER HEIGHTS IN ARTISTRY†
431 N. 31st. St.
Milwaukee, WI 53205
(414) 344-6663
Contact: Ralph M. Sanders, Harvey Godlstein, Jr., Doris Katz

THE HUNTER AGENCY†
2222 N. Farwell Ave.
Milwaukee, WI 53202
(414) 765-0307
Contact: Michael Hunter Short

JRL ENTERPRISES†
3005 W. Kilbourn
Milwaukee, WI 53208-3497
(414) 342-3436
Contact: John Langmesser

OVERLAND STAGE PRODUCTIONS†
P.O. Box 09479
Milwaukee, WI 53209
(414) 464-5568
Contact: Ricky H. Rumpel, Dale E. Ramthun

FRED J. PASCOE†
P.O. Box 19793
Milwaukee, WI 53219
(414) 355-5889

REYNOLDS MANAGEMENT†
P.O. Box 14636
Milwaukee, WI 53214
(414) 259-0154
Contact: Gary Michael Reynolds

RICHARD ROBBINS TALENT AGENT†
4224 N. 68th Street
Milwaukee, WI 53216
(414) 461-3421
Contact: Richard Robbins

SCARLET AGENCY†
2850 W. Highland #204
Milwaukee, WI 53208
(414) 933-2983
Contact: Deborah L. Williams, Hubbard Riley, Mary A. Button

SHOW BIZ TALENT CORPORATION†
(See Marinette listing)

NEENAH

ST. JOHN ARTISTS†
314 Cowling Bay Road, P.O. Box 619
Neenah, WI 54956
(414) 725-7949
Contact: Jon Bailey St. John

RACINE

PULICE BOOKING AGENCY†
2523 Green St.
Racine, WI 53402
(414) 639-5882
Contact: Joseph Pulice, Sr., Mrs. Helen M. Pulice

RIPON

ACOUSTIPHILE PRODUCTIONS†
107 Watson St.
Ripon, WI 54971
(414) 748-6195
Contact: John E. Stiernberg, Jeanne A. Stiernberg, Lori Schweder

SHEBOYGAN

MEL HUMMITZSCH THEATRICAL AGENCY, INC.†
2021 N. 19th St.
Sheboygan, WI 53081
(414) 458-3588

SILVER LAKE

RICHARD CARR ASSOCIATES†
Box 295
303 East Elm Street
Silver Lake, WI 53170
(414) 889-4123

STEVENS POINT

TRIANGLE TWO BOOKING†
2029 Portage Street
Stevens Point, WI 54481
(715) 341-4109
Contact: Peter J. Malischke

TWIN LAKES

BOB OBIE ENTERPRISES†
2001 East Lakeshore Dr.
Twin Lakes, WI 53181
(414) 877-3995
Contact: Robert H. Obermayer, Gini P. Obermayer

VERONA

ALPINE BRASS†
501 Edward St.
Verona, WI 53593
(608) 845-6820
Contact: Gertrude Trudy Inglin

WAUKESHA

DYNASTY PRODUCTIONS†
218 S. Washington Ave.
Waukesha, WI 53186
(414) 542-4668
Contact: Stephen Rohwer, Mark L. Rickards

WAUWATOSA

B.J. TALENT AGENCY†
2109 North 106th St.
P.O. Box 26396
Wauwatosa, WI 53226
(414) 257-3100
Contact: Robert J. Freund

WISCONSIN RAPIDS

D & R PRODUCTIONS†
P.O. Box 844
Wisconsin Rapids, WI 54494
(715) 421-0135
Contact: Donald Mikkelsen, Stewart Punsky

WYOMING

JACKSON

ART WHITING ATTRACTIONS*
P.O. Box 1185
Jackson, WY 83001
Contact: Edna Whiting

PUERTO RICO

RIO PIEDRAS

GOLDEN ARTISTS AGENCY†
Torrecillas St., #601 Summit Hills
Rio Piedras, PR 00920
(809) 792-1073
Contact: Aranias Gimenez Arias

SANTURCE

CA ADVERTISING PROMOTION†
1259 Ave. Ponce de Leon, Ste. 5-2
Santurce, PR 00907
(809) 723-8916
Contact: Jose Luis Quinones Concepcion

IDALI P. CAMACHO†
150 Diez De Andino
Santurce, PR 00911
(809) 722-3126 & 723-8908

EMPRESAS CAMACHO†
150 Diez De Andino
Santurce, PR 00911
(809) 722-3126
(809) 723-8908
Contact: Carlos Camacho

GUAM

TUMON

ROBERTO FRANCASSINI PRODUCTIONS†
Guam Reef Hotel, Rm. 1702
P.O. Box 8258
Tumon, Guam 96911
646-6881
Contact: Roberto N.A. Fracassini

VIRGIN ISLANDS

ST. CROIX

OZZIE JAMES BENNERSON†
39 Richmond-Christiansted
St. Croix, VI 00820
(809) 773-1718
Contact: Ozzie James Bennerson

CANADA

ALBERTA

EDMONTON

AUDIO ART PRODUCTIONS†
11333 - 101 St.
Edmonton, AB T5G 2AG
(403) 474-5983
Contact: J. Anna Kennedy

BANKS ASSOCIATED MUSIC LTD.†
305 - 10310 - 102 Ave.
Edmonton, AB T5J 2X6
(403) 424-0441
Contact: Ida E. Banks, Kathy Jowett, Jan Bell

CHORNOWOL MUSIC, LTD.†
9235 - 96th Street
Edmonton, AB T6C 3Y5
(403) 466-1958
Contact: Adrian Chornowol, Sheila Mayfield

DIMAS ENTERTAINMENT†
8028 -180th St.
Edmonton, AB T5T 0S8
(403) 487-0669
Contact: Luis Dimas Misle, Les Terrell

GUILDHALL PRODUCTIONS†
9912 - 109th St. #7
Edmonton, AB T5K 1H5
(403) 423-1231
Contact: Maureen Saumer

HERITAGE PRODUCTIONS†
1756 - 62nd St.
Edmonton, AB T6L 1M6
(403) 462-8070
Contact: Miguel Neri

J-S ENTERPRISES PRODUCTION, LTD.†
P.O. Box 11802, Main P.O.
Edmonton, AB T5J 3K4
(403) 433-8491
Contact: James Stewart

R & R MUSIC, LTD.†
12324 - 132 Ave.
Edmonton, AB T5L 3P7
(403) 454-7041
Contact: Raymond J. Dussome

ROYALTY SHOWS, LTD.†
9229 - 58 Ave.
Edmonton, AB T6E 0B7
(403) 436-0665
Contact: R. Harlan Smith, Danny Makarus, Brenda Rudiger

SEAHORSE SOUND PROMOTIONS†
10514 - 128 St.
Edmonton, AB T5N 1W4
(403) 454-6262
Contact: R. Christopher Lewis

SPANE INTERNATIONAL†
10534 - 109 St., Ste. 102
Edmonton, AB T5H 3B2
(403) 426-1362
Contact: Caryl L. Dakus

STUDIO CITY MUSICAL, LTD.*†
10528 - 108 St.
Edmonton, AB T5H 2Z9
(403) 425-0321
Contact: Donald H. McKenzie, Ross McKenzie, Dave Beck, Marg Zahn, Carol Duke, Rita Williamson

Branch Office:
1347 - 12th Ave., S.W.
Calgary, AB T3C 0P6
(403) 244-5572
Contact: Donald H. McKenzie, Greg Thomas, Al Gibson, Wayne Munson, Rick Nelson

20TH CENTURY MUSIC†
11528 - 96th St.
Edmonton, AB T5G 1T7
(403) 471-4196
Contact: Orville L. Williams

CALGARY

CALDWELL ENTERTAINMENT AGENCY*†
38-1011 Canterbury Dr., SW
Calgary, AB T2W 2S8
(403) 281-2040
Contact: Dick Caldwell, Dee Anna Caldwell, Audrey Huntley

CELEBRITY ENTERTAINMENT†
457-24 Avenue, N.W.
Calgary, AB T2M 1X3
(403) 276-4892
Contact: Dale A. Bohna

COMMODORE ENTERTAINMENT, LTD.†
7007 Silverview Rd., N.W.
Calgary, AB T3B 3L9
(403) 288-4752
Contact: Melvin R. McMurren, Pat McMurren Gail Stopyra, Van Louis aka Emile Van Sprang, Roy Beckman

KLAAS CRAATS PRODUCTIONS, LTD.†
808 Lake Lucerne Dr., S.E.
Calgary, AB T2J 3H3
(403) 278-1861
Contact: Klaas Craats

D & I ENTERTAINMENT AGENCIES†
630 - 8th Ave., S.W., Ste. 411
Calgary, AB T2P 1G6
(403) 242-3588
Contact: Mrs. Irene Marjoram, Derek Marjoram

DEW PRODUCTIONS, LTD.†
315 Deercliffe Rd., S.E.
Calgary, AB T2J 5K6
(403) 278-5330
Contact: MItzie M. Wasyliw

K.B.D. ENTERPRISES, LTD.†
#500 - 630 Eighth Ave. S.W.
Calgary, AB T2P 1G6
(403) 263-5480
Contact: Robert DiPaolo

JEFF PARRY & ASSOCIATES†
Box 1234, Stn. "M"
Calgary, AB T2P 2L7
(403) 230-5334
Contact: Jeff M. Parry

PERFORMING ARTISTS CONSULTANTS†
A16 - 6120 - 2nd St., S.E.
Calgary, AB T2H 2L8
(403) 253-0494
Contact: C. Dean Cross, Frank Scott, Eve Lee

ANN RANDALL PRODUCTIONS, LTD.†
Ste. 436, Palliser Hotel
133 - 9th Ave., S.W.
Calgary, AB T2P 1J1
(403) 266-7501
Contact: Ann Gray Randall, Donna M. Hopkins, Brenda S. Thomas, Terry Neubauer

SIENNA PROMOTION†
#405H-354-3 Ave., N.E.
Calgary, AB T2E 0H4
(403) 233-9406
Contact: Staccie N. Tayler, Laara Johns, Heater L. Sandvold

STUDIO CITY MUSICAL LTD.
(See Edmonton listing)

HIGH RIVER

HIGHWOOD PRODUCTIONS†
Box 44
High River, AB T0L 1B0
(403) 652-7784
Contact: Keith E. Hitchner

MEDICINE HAT

UNIVERSAL TALENT PRODUCTIONS†
437 - 1 Street N.W.
Medicine Hat, AB T1A 6H6
(403) 527-9639
Contact: Barry Wong

BRITISH COLUMBIA

BURNABY

KELLY LLOYD CROWE†
7079 Waverley Avenue
Burnaby, BC V5J 4A4
(6]4) 435-2649

NORTH VANCOUVER

KILLARNEY ENTERTAINMENT AGENCY, LTD.†
#101 - 310 E. 2nd St.
No. Vancouver, BC V7L 1C7
(604) 980-7192
Contact: Maria A. Lynch, Jane Cronin

PORT ALBERNI

DOUGIE DAY BOOKING AGENCY†
5251 Argyle St.
Port Alberni, BC V9Y 1V1
(604) 723-6276
Contact: Douglas Medina aka Doug Day, Barbara Medina aka Barbara Day

ROSSLAND

WINTERLAND ENTERTAINMENT, LTD.*†
Box 1007
Rossland, BC V0G 1Y0
(604) 362-7356
Contact: Thomas R. Jones, Irene Butler, Joseph A. Killough, R. Allen Cayen, Denis J.A. Gunn, Bruce Bromley

VANCOUVER

S.L. FELDMAN & ASSOCIATES†
#202 -1334 W. 6th Ave.
Vancouver, BC V6H 1A7
(604) 734-5945
Contact: Samuel L. Feldman, Brian Wadsworth, Rob Hoskin, Lach Buchanan, Elaine Chick, Len Godard, Michael B. Boyle

VALERIE A.H. KING†
2736 West 13th Avenue

Vancouver, BC V6K 2T4
(604) 738-7676

SHELBY TALENT AGENCY†
726 Richard St.
Vancouver, BC V6B 3L2
(615) JK 7-8270
Contact: MItzi Lee Knox

WHITEFOOT ENTERTAINMENTS, LTD.†
Box 35281, Post. Sta. E
Vancouver, BC V6M 2V7
(604) 266-7145
Contact: John W. Whitefoot, Shaw Saltzberg, Paul Bartram

VICTORIA

B.C. SOUND PRODUCTIONS, INTERNATIONAL†
P.O. Box 1384
Victoria, BC V8W 2W3
(604) 381-3003
Contact: David G. Ringland

GRACE GERMAIN PRODUCTIONS†
1934 Bee St., Apt. 204
Victoria, BC V8R 5E5
(604) 595-4821
Contact: Grace E. Germain

PRESTIGE ENTERTAINMENT AGENCIES, LTD.*†
4680 Elk Lake Drive, Ste. 304
Victoria, BC V8Z 5M1
(604) 658-5202
Contact: Paul Mascioli, Joan E. Mascioli, Marion Mitchell, Allen Cottell, Lawrie Hooper

SOUNDS GOOD ENTERTAINMENT SERVICES†
203, 620 View St.
Victoria, BC V8W 1J6
(604) 386-1695
Contact: Glenn A. Parfitt

WEST VANCOUVER

NOTE-ABLE ENTERTAINMENT†
4655 Rutland Road
West Vancouver, VC V7W 1G6
(604) 984-9674
Contact: Blaine O'Bray, Tommy Hiat, Jai Allan, Don Buchanan

MANITOBA

BRANDON

JASON DAVID BLAIR ENTERPRISES†
Box 1423
Brandon, MB R7A 6N2
(204) 727-4455 Ext. 5
Contact: Carol L. Bernier

WINNIPEG

ANDREE PRODUCTIONS, LTD.†
927 St. Mary's Rd.
Winnipeg, MB R2M 3R6
(204) 253-2658
Contact: Len E. Andree

HUNGRY I AGENCY*†
403-265 Portage Ave.
Winnipeg, MB R3C 0A2
(204) 947-0092
Contact: Frank Wiener

MORRIS THEATRICAL AGENCIES INC.†
#406 - 265 Portage Ave.
Winnipeg, MB R3B 2B2
(204) 943-7236
Contact: Terry Morris

MAURICE PROULX ENTERTAINMENT AGENCY†
51 St. Annes Rd.
Winnipeg, MB R2M 2Y4
(204) 237-4639
Contact: Maurice F. Proulx

SHOWCASE PRODUCTIONS, LTD.†
M-12, 2727 Portage Ave.
Winnipeg, MB R3J 0R2
(204) 889-5567
Contact: Douglas T. Mac Farlane, Terence O'Reilly, Barry Babiak

ZEE TALENT AGENCY, LTD.†
356 Royal Ave.
Winnipeg, MB R2V 1J2
(204) 338-7094
Contact: Linda S. Zagozewski

NEW BRUNSWICK

FREDERICTON

THE IDEA WORKS†
224 Argyle St.
Fredericton, NB E3B 1T7
(506) 454-6844
Contact: Ruth A. McAvity

MONCTON

ATLANTIC TALENT AGENCY†
1650 Main St.
Moncton, NB E1E 1G6
(506) 389-1718
Contact: George Manship, Douglas Taylor

CANADIAN ASSOCIATED TALENT†
681 Main Street, Ste. 21
Moncton, NB E1C 1E3
(506) 382-8673
Contact: Gregoire M. Cormier

Branch Office:
P.O. Box 257
Middletown, NS B0S 1P0
(902) 678-1898
Contact: John Eakin

SAINT JOHN

MUSICAL ENTERTAINMENT AGENCY LTD.†
P.O. Box 6025, Station A
Saint John, NB E2L 4R5
(506) 657-8005
Contact: Bill Wellington

NEWFOUNDLAND

WINDSOR

ARCTIC FOX PRODUCTIONS†
P.O. Box 9
Windsor, NF A0H 2H0
(709) 489-7726
Contact: Edward Casciato aka Jason Belmer, Donna Bursey

NOVA SCOTIA

ARMDALE

LONE WOLF MUSIC PRODUCTIONS†
Site 17, Box 37
R.R. #5
Armdale, NS B3L 4J5
(902) 477-0889
Contact: John W. Brennan, Patrick F. Brennan

DARTMOUTH

ARRANGE-A-PARTY†
139 Amaranth Cres.
Dartmouth, NS B2W 4C1
(902) 434-9794
Contact: Donald W. Estey, Michael F. Melvin

D.C. AGENCIES, LTD.†
18 Elmwood Ave.
Dartmouth, NS B3A 3E4
(902) 466-2411
Contact: Dwaine R. Coughlin, Blair Coughlin, Marcel Cloutier

HALIFAX

ABLE PRODUCTIONS†
c/o Robert Hope
R.R. #4, Lr. Sackville
Halifax, NS B4C 3B1
(902) 865-9516
Contact: Richard D. Bendokas, Robert A. Hope

JOHN J. ALPHONSE PRODUCTIONS, LTD.†
1649 Barrington St., Ste. 500
Halifax, NS B3J 1Z9
(902) 422-1451 (127)
Contact: John J. Alphonse

DEAN'S ENTERTAINMENT AGENCY†
41 Canary Cresc.
Halifax, NS B3M 1R2
(902) 443-0492
Contact: John J. Dean

ROBERT J. DOOLEY†
22 Mabou Avenue
Halifax, NS B3P 1V7
(902) 477-3130

IRIE PRODUCTIONS†
1146 Wellington St.
Halifax, NS B3H 2Z8
(902) 422-5407
Contact: Kevin J. Stephen, Michael Patriquen, Douglas Stephen

KIRBY-CHARLES ORGANIZATION†
P.O. Box 3606 South
Halifax, NS B3J 3K6
(902) 429-0174
Contact: Joan M. Kirby, C. Douglas Kirby

THE PEPPER AGENCY†
6336 London St.
Halifax, NS B3L 1X3
(902) 422-9663
Contact: Fiona M. Perina

REDLINE PRODUCTIONS†
c/o Vantage Ent., Ltd.

1855 Granville St.
Halifax, NS B3J 1Y1
(902) 422-6035
Contact: Eric P. Shields

SCORPIO TALENT†
1587 Dresden Row
Halifax, NS B3J 2K4
(902) 429-4781
Contact: Hazen L. Horseman, Michael Shepherd

JOSEPH SKOWRONSKI BOOKING AGENT†
19 Dipper Cres.
Halifax, NS B3M 1W5
(902) 443-0612
Contact: Joseph A. Skowronski

THREE FATHOM PRODUCTIONS†
P.O. Box 983, Armdale
Halifax, NS B3L 4K9
(902) 423-0786
Contact: Patrick Purcell, Sandy Greenberg

WIND RIDER PRODUCTIONS†
36 Hanover Court
Halifax, NS B3M 3K6
(902) 443-2280
Contact: R. Ian Fraser

LOWER SACKVILLE

HOUSE OF GOLD MANAGEMENT LTD.†
219 Danny Dr., Box 27
Lower Sackville, NS B4C 2S6
(902) 865-6425
Contact: John F. Gold aka Johnny Gold

SOUTH HALIFAX

BRUCE HUDSON PRODUCTIONS†
P.O. Box 3250
South Halifax, NS B3J 3H5
(902) 429-7007
Contact: G. Bruce Hudson, Ron B. Hudson

SYDNEY

THE MUSICAL CASTLE BOOKING AGENCY†
28 Castle Dr.
P.O. Box 584
Sydney, NS B1P 6H4
(902) 539-3452
Contact: Sylvia D. Milner, William D. Milner

ONTARIO

AGINCOURT

RON MARENGER PRODUCTIONS, INC.†
35 Brindley Dr.
Agincourt, ON M1V 1B1
(416) 293-3562
Contact: Ronald E. Marenger

STEVE THOMSON AGENCY†
62 Ardgowan Cresc.
Agincourt, ON M1V 1B3
(416) 291-4913
Contact: Stephen A. Thomson

AURORA

MARGARET J. GOOD†
R.R. #2
Aurora, ON L4G 3G8

ROGER A. POWELL†
39 Haida Dr.
Aurora, ON L4G 3C6
(416) 727-1635
Contact: Roger A. Powell

BELLEVILLE

SOUND WAVE'S MUSIC PRODUCTIONS†
375 Front St.
Bellevile, ON K8N 2Z9
(613) 962-7949
Contact: Mrs. Jodi Donovan, William Donovan

BRANTFORD

PAT ALONZO BOOKING AGENCY†
971 Colborne St.
Brantford, ON N3S 3T5
(519) 753-6804
Contact: Patrick W. Alonzo

MUSIC EXCHANGE TALENT AGENCY†
126 Charing Cross
Brantford, ON N3R 2J1
(519) 756-0192
Contact: Dale Page

Branch Office:
1342 King St., E.
Kitchener, ON N2G 2N7
(519) 578-7550
Contact: Dale Page

BRIDGENORTH

BLUE MOODS MUSIC, INC.†
Box 91
Bridgenorth, ON K0L 1H0
(705) 799-7160
Contact: Keith J. Burton, Mick McGrath, Steve Lynch

BROCKVILLE

GEORGE EARL ASSOCIATES†
234 Ormond St.
Brockville, ON K6V 2L5
(613) 342-0367
Contact: George Earl Elliott, Hazel E. Elliott, Ronald Schroeder, Art Mallet

BURLINGTON

VANDA KING ENTERTAINMENT, LTD.†
2256 Ireland Dr.
Burlington, ON L7P 3E9
(416) 335-5531

CALEDONIA

TOTEM AGENCY†
Box 1347
Caledonia, ON N0A 1A0
(519) 445-2701
Contact: MIchael G. Doxtater, Rick Hayes

CAMBRIDGE

ALGOWOOD AGENCY†
P.O. Box 3612
Cambridge, ON N3H 5C6
(519) 653-7474
Contact: James A. LeClair

CARLETON PLACE

FOXLAND ENTERPRISES†
Box 261
Carleton Place, ON K7C 3P4
(613) 257-3711
Contact: Ronald F. McMunn, Elizabeth Lang, Sheila Robillard

Branch Office:
227 Ayer Ave.
Moncton, NB E1C 8H1
Contact: Vernon Harrison

CORNWALL

THE CHARLES LANT AGENCY†
P.O. Box 1085
Cornwall, ON K6H 5V2
(613) 932-1532
Contact: Charles W.B. Lant

DON MILLS

CROSSROADS ENTERTAINMENT CONSULTANTS†
180 Duncan Mill Road, Ste. 400
Don Mills, ON M3B 1Z6
(416) 441-2144
Contact: S. Lawrence Cuthbertson

MUSIC AND ARTISTS PLACEMENT, LTD.†
65 Wynford Heights Cres. #909
Don Mills, ON M3C 1L6
(416) 445-4203
Contact: George B. Mitford, Maureen Enright

TAYLOR-FOTES ENTERTAINMENT AGENCY†
73 Railside Rd.
Don Mills, ON M3A 1B3
(416) 445-3660
Contact: Henry Taylor, Nick Fotes, Lucie Carr

CHICHO VALLE ORCHESTRAS & AGENCY, LTD.†
1100 Eglinton Ave. E., Ste. 223
Don Mills, ON M3C 1H8
(416) 445-6710
Contact: A. Chicho Valle, Luba Shemrey, Meron Kapuszczak, Valerie Ann Thompson, Rick Adamson

DOWNSVIEW

DAVE CAPLAN ENTERTAINMENT†
35 Canyon Avenue, Ste. 2009
Downsview, ON M3H 4Y2
(416) 630-1535

FLAMINGO TALENT SEARCH†
415 Oakdale Rd., Ste. 228
Downsview, ON M3N 1W7
(416) 749-3832
Contact: Glen G. Samuel

ELMIRA

MERCEY BROTHERS TALENT AGENCY†
38 Church St., W.
Elmira, ON N3B 1M5
(519) 669-5394

Contact: Lloyd J. Mercey, Larry Mercey, June Mercey, Connie Mercey

RAY MERCEY ENTERTAINMENT†
7 Victoria St.
Elmira, ON N3B 1R9
(519) 669-8840
Contact: Raymond G. Mercey

ETOBICOKE

CANADIAN ARTISTS REPRESENTATION SERVICES†
135 The West Mall
Unit 9
Etobicoke, ON M9C 1C2
(416) 626-1176
Contact: Salvatore S. Marchese

LYNN "NOVA" JOHNSTON'S ENTERTAINMENT†
476 Valermo Dr.
Etobicoke, ON M8W 2M7
(416) 252-3954
Contact: Lindo G. Payne

CHRIS O'TOOLE AGENCY†
3 Neilor Cres.
Etobicoke, ON M9C 1K3
(416) 626-3793
Contact: Christopher J. O'Toole

GRAND VALLEY

NORTH AMERICAN TALENT AGENCY†
84 Amaranth St., E.
Grand Valley, ON L0N 1G0
(519) 928-2833
Contact: Joe Firth

GUELPH

AUGUST MUSIC†
P.O. Box 1774
Guelph, ON N1E 6Z9
(519) 821-1023
Contact: Paul E. Embro, Randy Graham

OPEN DOOR TALENT AGENCY†
376 Woolwich St.
Guelph, ON N1H 3W7
(519) 836-9533
Contact: Larry G. Gregson

STEVENSON ENTERTAINMENT SERVICES†
165 London Rd. W
Guelph, ON N1H 2C4
(519) 824-8797
Contact: Marv. K. Stevenson

HAMILTON

BLUE OX TALENT AGENCY†
21 Woodside Dr.
Hamilton, ON L8T 1C4
(416) 385-5558
Contact: David S. Bach, Sylvia Messina

COUNTRY ARTISTS AGENCY, LTD.†
595 Upper Wellington St.
Hamilton, ON L9A 3P8
Box 6308, Station "F"
Hamilton, ON L9C 6L9
(416) 383-2111
Contact: Donald C. Gordon

DIAMOND MUSIC AGENCY†
37 Warren St.
Hamilton, ON L9A 3C7
(416) 385-8332
Contact: Stephan T. Sobolewski

D.R.A. AGENCY†
630½ Barton St. E.
Hamilton, ON L8L 3A1
(416) 549-5583
Contact: Douglas R. Ambrose

HAROLD KUDLETS AGENCY, LTD.†
4 Freeland Court
Hamilton ON L8S 3R5
(416) 522-0900

JASON MCKENZIE ENTERTAINMENT SPECIALISTS†
60 Arbour Rd.
P.O. Box 121
Hamilton, ON L0R 1P0
(416) 560-2602
Jason L.O. McKenzie

WILLIAM POWELL AGENCY†
21 Augusta St.
Hamilton, ON L8N 1P6
(416) 525-6644
Contact: William B. Powell, Tom Willey

SECRET AGENCY†
242 Emerald St., N.
Hamilton, ON L8L 5M8
(416) 523-7120
Contact: Randall D. Cousins

VEHICLE ENTERTAINMENT†
350 Quigley Rd., #513
Hamilton, ON L8K 5N2
(416) 560-9552
Contact: Carlo S.P. DiBattista

ISLINGTON

ROBERT TYRALA AGENCY (R.T.A.)†
11 Northhampton Dr.
Islington, ON M9B 4S5
(416) 622-4253
Contact: Robert J. Tyrala

KINGSTON

THE DOBBIN AGENCY†
477A Princess St.
Kingston, ON K7L 1C3
(613) 549-4401
Contact: Bernard F. Dobbin, Brian Hichey, David Butler

SOUND INVESTMENTS†
84 Brock St., Ste. 400
Kingston, ON K7L 1R9
(613) 549-6936
Contact: Frederick J. Pollitt

KITCHENER

D.A.R. BOOKING AGENCY†
1 Cedarwoods Cres., Apt. 811
Kitchener, ON N2C 2L8
(519) 576-9203
Contact: Dale A. Ruttkay

MR. OCTOBERFEST PRODUCTIONS, LTD.†
P.O. Box 94
Kitchener, ON N2G 3W9
(519) 743-7401
Contact: Gary Allan Dunn, Julius Rauchfuss, Ollie Lackenbauer

MUSIC EXCHANGE TALENT AGENCY
(See Brantford listing)

LONDON

ANDERSON ENTERTAINMENT AGENCY†
622 Wonderland Rd., S.
London, ON N6K 1L8
(519) 472-8918
Contact: John Anderson

ARJAY TALENT MARKETING†
197 Ridout St. South
London, ON N6C 3X8
(519) 679-1396 and (519) 434-2441
Contact: R. James Chapman

B.B.R AGENCY†
485 Queens Ave.
London, ON N6B 1Y3
(519) 679-8130
Contact: Brian E. Courtis, Ken Stewart

CANADIAN CREATIVE ENTERTAINMENT†
P.O. Box 2842
London, ON N6A 4H4
(519) 433-6995
Contact: Richard Lowry, Barbara Good, Gary Nichol

CHANTEL SHANE AGENCY†
31 - 825 Dundalk Drive
London, ON N6C 3V8
(519) 686-1368
Contact: Debra Marie Gilmore, Ben (Shane) Gilmore

VIC DENOMY ENTERTAINMENT AGENCY†
234 Holgate Rd.
London, ON N5V 1C2
(519) 452-1712
Contact: Victor P. Denomy

JOHNNY DOWNS ENTERTAINMENT†
132 Maple St., Apt. 4
London, ON N6A 1K6
(519) 433-1795
Contact: Johnny Downs

ROBERT GARDINER & ASSOCIATES, INC.†
529 Topping Lane
London, ON N6J 3M8
(519) 471-4331
Contact: Robert Gardiner

BILL GILROY ENTERTAINMENT AGENCY†
15 Villeneuve Cres.
London, ON N5V 1M7
(519) 455-0831
Contact: William Gilroy, William Genttner, Mike McCullough

J.G. HAM ENTERPRISES, LTD.†
714 Wonderland Rd.
London, ON N6K 1L8
(519) 472-8381
Contact: Joseph G. Ham

LUNASEE†
1802 Park Avenue
London, ON N5W 2J5
(519) 451-6530
Contact: Ron Schroeyens

M.C. TALENT AGENCY†
134 Odessa Ave.
London, ON N6J 2Z8
(519) 686-5400
Contact: Marilynne E. Caswell, Joseph Caswell, Merla Patterson

"RAM" ENTERTAINMENT AGENCY†
415 Merlin Street
London, ON N5W 5A9
(519) 453-0508
Contact: Bernard B. McKay

MISSISSAUGA

FESTIVAL PRODUCTIONS, LTD.†
1227 Mississauga Rd.
Mississauga, ON L5H 2J1
(416) 271-1680
Contact: Peter A. Groschel

DAMIAN KERR AGENCY†
2133 Royal Windsor Dr., Unit #3
Mississauga, ON L5J 1K5
(416) 823-7633
Contact: Damian McKerr, Robert Legault

LARK ENTERTAINMENT AND CONVENTION SERVICES†
1055 Bloor St., E., Ste. 212
Mississauga, ON L4Y 2N5
(416) 279-0930
Contact: S. Wray Featherston

KITTY MEREDITH, INC.†
1333 Bloor St. E., Ste. 2117
Mississauga, ON L4Y 3T6
(416) 625-4466
Contact: Rosann T. Meredity, George Wm. Mitchell

PEEVER TALENT & MANAGEMENT†
2464 Brasilia Circle
Mississauga, ON L5N 2G1
(416) 826-1701
Contact: David M. Peever

PERFORMANCE PRESENTS†
286 Willa Road
Mississauga, ON L5G 2G8
(41) 274-3055
Contact: Ann E. Footitt

PROGRESSIVE TALENT PRODUCTIONS, INC.*†
7270 Torbram Rd., Ste. 204
Mississauga, ON L4T 3Y2
(416) 678-1250
Contact: John Kondis, Dave Nicholls, Peter Dunn, Belinda Bebenek, Allan Nicholls

RICHARD RATIGAN AGENCY†
2133 Royal Windsor Dr., Unit 3
Mississauga, ON L5J 1K5
(416) 823-4781
Contact: Richard D. Ratigan

STARRIDER PRODUCTIONS*
16 Cayuga Ave.
Mississauga, ON L5G 3S7
(416) 274-8421
Contact: Wayne Baguley

TOWN & COUNTRY ENTERTAINMENT AGENCY†
1219 Ogden Ave.
Mississauga, ON L5E 2H2
(416) 274-2593
Contact: William J. Legere, Marie P. Legere

UNISTAR PRODUCTIONS†
3514 Credit Woodlands
Mississauga, ON L5C 2K6
(416) 275-5432
Contact: Ruth Anne Melito

BRUCE WEST AGENCY†
3580 Autumn Leaf Cr.
Mississauga, ON L5L 1K5
(416) 828-6758
Contact: Bruce G. West

NEPEAN

LAURIE-ANN ENTERTAINMENT AGENCY†
71 Birchview Rd.
Nepean, ON K2G 3G3
(613) 224-6530
Contact: Ronald P. Sparling, Laurie-Ann Sparling, Jo-Ann Adams

OSHAWA

MUSIC WORLD ATTRACTIONS†
410 Dean Avenue
Oshawa, ON L1H 3E2
(416) 576-5808
Contact: Steve H. Maley

OTTAWA

B & C PRODUCTIONS†
385 Winona Ave., Ste. 303
Ottawa, ON K1Z 5H8
(613) 728-1601
Contact: Rick Crepin, Bill Grella

BLUE SKY ENTERPRISES†
406 - 145 York St.
Ottawa, ON K1N 8Y3
(613) 235-6345
Contact: William J. Mackay

ROLLY HAMMOND PRODUCTIONS, INC.†
166 Elm St.
Ottawa, ON K1R 6N5
(613) 234-2886
Contact: L. Roland Hammond

HARMONY INTERNATIONAL†
150 Metcalfe St., Ste. 210
Ottawa, ON K2P 1P1
(613) 233-0106
Contact: Robert L. Fancy

NIGHT OWL BOOKING AGENCY†
376 Arlington Ave.
Ottawa, ON K1R 6Z5
(613) 234-4922
Contact: Bruce J. Declare

PHIL'S ENTERTAINMENT AGENCY†
899 Smyth Rd.
Ottawa, ON K1G 1P4
(613) 731-8983
Contact: Phyllis M. Woodstock

SCAM PROMOTIONS†
P.O. Box 4885
Station "E"
Ottawa, ON K1S 5J1
(613) 232-7446
Contact: Jamie M. Westell

Branch Office:
1378 - 1 Begbie St.
Victoria, BC
(604) 595-8386
Contact: Carrie Foster

PEMBROKE

THE ROCK SHOPPE†
P.O. Box 1329
Pembroke, ON K8A 6Y6
(613) 732-4985
Contact: Stuart J. Roberts

PETERBOROUGH

ADA LEE'S ENTERTAINMENT AGENCY†
813 Fairbairn St.
Peterborough, ON K9H 6B9
(705) 742-5250
Contact: Ada Lee Barker

ROCKLANDS TALENT & MANAGEMENT†
P.O. Box 1282
Peterborough, ON K9J 7H5
(705) 743-7354
Contact: Brian W. Edwards

PORT STANLEY

GARY BAILEY ENTERTAINMENT AGENCY†
207 Queen Street
Port Stanley, ON N0L 2A0
(519) 782-3570

T.N.T. ENTERTAINMENT AGENCY†
268 Frances St.
P.O. Box 337
Port Stanley, ON N0L 2A0
(519) 782-4378
Contact: S. Scott Hickson

REXDALE

HELEN CHILCOTT THEATRICAL AGENCY†
655 Dixon Road
Rexdale, ON M9W 1J4
(416) 244-6491
Contact: Roselle Stone, Evelyn Rosen

RUSSELL

C & S AGENCY†
P.O. Box 175
Russell, ON K0A 3B0
(613) 445-2996
Contact: Glenn D. Cochrane

SCARBOROUGH

RON ALBERT ENTERTAINMENT AGENCIES, LTD.†
55 Nugget Ave., Ste. 217
Scarborough, ON M1S 3L1
(416) 292-0433
Contact: Ronald D. Albert, Dave Blum

PETER APPLEYARD PRODUCTIONS†
25 Kingsbury Cres.
Scarborough, ON M1N 1E8
(416) 694-6717
Contact: Peter Appleyard

ENTERTAINMENT CENTRE†
2281 Kingston Rd.
Scarborough, ON M1N 1T8
(416) 266-4476
Contact: George H. Hood, Robby Tustin, Chris Bechard

KEY ARTISTS CORPORATION†
2061 McCowan Rd., Ste. 209
Scarborough, ON M1S 3Y6
(416) 298-8988
Contact: William C. McGrath, Michael Ryshouwer aka Michael Kuno, Richard Brown

MUSIC AND ENTERTAINMENT†
18 Fremont St.
Scarborough, ON M1N 2B9
(416) 691-4430
Contact: A. Zena Cheevers

ROSS BOOKING AGENCY†
273 Pharmacy Ave., Ste. 909
Scarborough, ON M1L 3E9
(416) 752-8317
Contact: Claudette Joan Ross-Johnson

DANTE YOUNG PRODUCTIONS†
78 Redheugh Cres.
Scarborough, ON M1W 3C3
(416) 596-0153
Contact: Dante A. Young

SIMCOE

BANDSTAND (INTERNATIONAL) ENTERTAINMENT AGENCY†
P.O. Box 844
Simcoe, ON N3Y 4T2
(519) 426-3799
Contact: C.G. Wayne Elliot, Sheila M. Elliot, Norbert Lava, Kirby Ellis, Mike Swainston

SMITH FALLS

K.B. PROMOTIONS†
P.O. Box 771
Smith Falls, ON K7A 4W6
(613) 283-2372
Contact: Elaine (Kitty) Bast, George Brothers

STEVENSVILLE

BRADY'S BOOKING AGENCY†
2991 Burger Road
Stevensville, ON L0S 1S0
(416) 382-2349
Contact: Desmond P. Brady

STONEY CREEK

CONCERTHOUSE ENTERTAINMENT†
P.O. Box 35
Stoney Creek, ON L8G 3X7
(416) 639-7578
Contact: Ross B. Tonkin, Rita Chirelli, Vicki Baker, Glen Montani

RAM-ON PRODUCTIONS†
500 Greens Rd., Unit 1012
Stoney Creek, ON L8E 3M6
(416) 662-3030
Contact: J. Richard McIsaac

ST. CATHARINES

HALLARY DWORET†
155 Riverview Blvd.
St. Catharines, ON L2T 3M6
(416) 685-7100
Contact: Hallary S. Dworet

MURRAY HUNT TALENT AGENCY†
P.O. Box 533
St. Catharines, ON L2R 6V9
(416) 685-7715
Contact: Murray J.T. Hunt, Gwen Hunt

ST. THOMAS

BUSKER ENTERTAINMENT AGENCY-B.E.A.†
R.R. #7
St. Thomas, ON N5P 3T2
(519) 633-6989
Contact: Randy C. Dawdy, John Dinsdale, Stephen McCann

PUPPET ENTERPRISES†
24 Fairview Ave., #4
St. Thomas, ON N5R 4X5
(519) 631-3214
Contact: Michelle A. Kerr

SUDBURY

THE TALENT SHOPPE†
P.O. Box 744
Sudbury, ON P3E 4R6
(705) 566-2550
Contact: Raymond F. Morel

THUNDER BAY

DEBBIE "K" DEBBIE ENTERTAINMENT BOOKING†
131 Rupert St.
Thunder Bay, ON P7B 3W8
(807) 345-1945
Contact: Deborah L. Vinneau

HORRICKS TALENT AGENCY†
324 N. Court S.
Thunder Bay, ON P7A 4W7
(807) 344-2675
Contact: Thomas M. Horricks

TORONTO

THE AGENCY†
376 George Street
Toronto, ON M5A 2N3
(416) 968-2222
Contact: David Bluestein, Andy McCreath, Steve Predergast, Robert Richards, Mike White, Ed Smeall, Wayne Dean, Lawrence Schuman, Gerry Blais, Cathie Faint

BAND AID ENTERTAINMENT†
270 Queensdale Ave.
Toronto, ON M4C 2B4
(416) 425-8433
Contact: Christopher Tassone

THE BATTEN GROUP†
11 Adelaide St. W., Ste. 803
Toronto, ON M5H 1L9
(416) 363-9453
Contact: Meline C. Batten

CARIBBEAN TALENT AGENCY†
688 St. Clair Ave., W.
Toronto, ON M6C 1B1
(416) 690-2567
Contact: Patrick E. McNeilly

CARLOMAR PRODUCTIONS, INC.†
404 Soudan Avenue
Toronto, ON M4S 1W9
(416) 484-0258
Contact: Marguerite K, Sakeris, Charles Rodrigues

CLASSIC ENTERPRISES†
P.O. Box 186, Postal Station B
Toronto, ON M5T 2W1
(416) 481-5327
Contact: John Monahan, Tom Williams

COPRA MANAGEMENT†
P.O. Box 666
Station F
Toronto, ON M4Y 2N6
(416) 922-5465
Contact: Kathryn P. Kates, Valerie Kates

COTTON/SMYTH, INC.†
42 Charles St., E., Ste. 510
Toronto, ON M4Y 1T4
(416) 921-2354
Contact: Catherine Smyth

CROWN COMMUNICATIONS†
P.O. Box 1070
Station "A"
Toronto, ON M5W 1G6
(416) 924-2638
Contact: John P. Pierre

GINO EMPRY PUBLIC RELATIONS, LTD.†
Ste. 104, The Maples
25 Wood St.
Toronto, ON M4Y 2P9
(416) 977-1153
Contact: Gino Empry

ENTERTAINMENT ASSOCIATES OF CANADA†
2828 Bathurst St., #601
Toronto, ON M6B 3A7
(416) 787-0277
Contact: Walter Pasko, Ron Cahute, Francesca Domingo

BUD MATTON ENTERPRISES, LTD.†
953 A Eglinton Ave., W.
Toronto, ON M6C 2C4
(416) 787-8881
Contact: Bud Matton, Brian Ayres, Dennis Matton

J.R. PRODUCTIONS†
22 College St.
Lower Concourse
Toronto, ON M5G 1K2
(416) 922-0448
Contact: Jules Rabkin

JONWITE PRODUCTIONS†
696 Yonge St., #601
Toronto, ON M4Y 2A7

(416) 968-0720
Contact: John W. White

KAYMAR ARTIST'S PRODUCTIONS†
2707 Yonge Street, Apt 2
Toronto, ON M4N 2H8
(416) 484-6939
Contact: Klaus Max J. Hartwig

GEORGE KING ENTERTAINMENT SERVICE†
404 Huron Street
Toronto, ON M5S 2G6
(416) 979-2121
Contact: Donald S. Cowan

JACK LANDER MUSIC†
30 Springhurst Ave., #1004
Toronto, ON M6K 1B3
(416) 533-1882

VITA LINDER AGENCY†
64 St. Clair Ave., W., Ste. 407
Toronto, ON M4V 1N1
(416) 921-9536

MONIKA LITTLE AGENCIES†
1013 Glengrove Ave., W.
Toronto,ON M6B 2J8
(416) 781-7132
Contact: Monika C. Little

MAR-LYN MUSIC†
251 Benson Ave.
Toronto, ON M6G 2J7
(416) 653-9419
Contact: Martin Warsh, Jacqueline Johnson

MARSON PRODUCTIONS, INC.†
2180 Yonge St., Ste. 1707
Box 18
Toronto, ON M4S 2B9
(416) 485-4653
Contact: David I. Matheson

NANCY MCCAIG ALL STAR PRODUCTIONS, LTD.†
19 Eastview Cres.
Toronto, ON M5M 2W4
(416) 486-0081
Contact: A. Nancy (McCaig) Higgins, Walter E. Higgins

MCCLUSKEY BOOKING AGENCY†
161 Bingham Ave.
Toronto, ON M4E 3R2
(416) 691-0829
Contact: Michael McCluskey

VIVIENNE MURPHY & ASSOCIATES†
81 Hiag Ave.
Toronto, ON M1N 2W2
(416) 694-2400
Contact: Vivienne H. Murphy

MUSIC ANYONE?, INC.†
121 Kennedy Ave.
Toronto, ON M6S 2X8
(416) 763-3888
Contact: Donald Facchini, Shirley Grenier

MUSIC COLLAGE, INC.†
524 Woburn Avenue
Toronto, ON M5M 1L9
(416) 789-4841
Contact: Peter C. Beecham

BILLY O'CONNOR ENTERPRISES, LTD.†
29 Grenville St.
Toronto, ON M4Y 1A1
(416) 924-1148
Contact: E. William O'Connor

PATRICIAN MANAGEMENT†
46 MacPherson Ave.
Toronto, ON M5R 1W8
(416) 964-7992
Contact: Patrician A. McKinnon

PIZAZZ PRODUCTIONS*†
35 Hambly Ave.
Toronto, ON M4E 2R5
(416) 699-3359
Contact: Craig Nicholson

PLATINUM ARTISTS, INC.†
20 Carlton St., Ste. 124
Toronto, ON M5B 1J2
(416) 596-1500
Contact: Ralph A. Jolivet, Mike Greggs, Vinny Cinquemani, Bruce Barrow, David Kirby, Mickey Quase

RENT AN EVENT, INC.†
P.O. Box 146, Station M
Toronto, ON M6S 4T2
(416) 624-9012
Contact: L. Anne Belvedere, Dale Biason

SHOE STRING BOOKING AGENCY†
935 The Queensway, Unit 340
Toronto, ON M8Z 5P7
(416) 259-4164
Contact: Armin O. Darmstadt

PAUL SIMMONS MANAGEMENT†
125 Dupont St.
Toronto, ON M5R 1V4
(416) 920-1500
Contact: Paul Simmons

JOANNE SMALE BOOKING AGENCY†
466 Spadina Ave. #2
Toronto, ON M5T 2G8
(416) 961-3424

SMOOTH SOUNDS†
145 Marlee Ave., #907
Toronto, ON M6B 3H3
(416) 741-4073
Contact: Francine Drubick

SPHERE†
49 Rainsford Rd.
Toronto, ON M4L 3N7
(416) 694-6900
Contact: Patricia S. Erlendson, Catherine Eckert, Paul Beedham

ULTIMATE SOUND, INC.†
400 Walmer Rd., #1428
Toronto, ON M5P 2X7
(416) 923-6464
Contact: Norman B. Bernard

VAN ENTERTAINMENT, LTD.†
11 Yorkville Ave., Ste. 501
Toronto, ON M4W 1L2
(416) 964-6462
Contact: Henk Vandenberg, Vera Milec, Sunday E. Hamilton, Carol Straight, Klaas Vangraft
Bob Erwig

THE WORLD OF MUSIC†
162 Silver Birch Ave.
Toronto, ON M4E 3L4
(416) 694-0723
Contact: Andre (Andy) S. Blumauer

VANIER

AXIOM AGENCY†
255 Rue Ste. Anne
Vanier, ON K1L 7C3
(613) 744-1040
Contact: Dayle R. Reynolds

CREATIVE ARTISTS OF CANADA†
25 Montreal Road
Vanier, ON K1L 6E8
(613) 745-0004
Contact: D. Ross McCallum, Richard Flanagan

MISSION AGENCY†
#5 - 389 MIller Ave.
Vanier, ON K1L 6V7
(613) 749-8606
Contact: Francois Y. Roberge

WATERLOO

OPUS WORLD OF MUSIC, INC.†
123 Columbia St. W.
Waterloo, ON N2L 3L1
(519) 885-0046
Contact: Mike Bergauer, Adie-Jane Bergauer, Robert McWade, Mark Kreller, Michelle Bergauer

WELLAND

FRED USKIN PRODUCTIONS†
306 Broadway Ave.
Welland, ON L3C 5L4
(416) 735-2943
Contact: Fred A. Uskin

WEST HILL

PAUL SUMMERVILLE†
62 Boydwood Lane
West Hill, ON M1B 1H2
(416) 284-5702
Contact: Paul W. Summerville

WESTON

ELTON ENTERTAINMENT AGENCY†
6 Manorhampton Dr.
Weston, ON M9P 1E2
(416) 244-1500
Contact: Evelyn Mishko

WILLOWDALE

BIG G ENTERPRISES†
5754 Yonge Street, #805
Willowdale, ON M2M 3T6
(416) 223-4771
Contact: Eardley A. Guthrie, Liz Litwiniok

JAN GOLDIN†
98 Burbank Dr.
Willowdale, ON M2K 1N4
(416) 223-3609
Contact: Jan Goldin

GROSNEY ENTERTAINMENT AGENCY†
412 Empress Ave.
Willowdale, ON M2N 3V8
(416) 225-7806
Contact: Paul Grosney

K-ALD PRODUCTIONS†
42 Lesgay Cres.
Willowdale, ON M2J 2H8
(416) 493-1964
Contact: F. Keith Alderson

PARTY PLANNERS†
4 Harrison Rd.
Willowdale, ON M2L 1V2
(416) 445-7953
Contact: (Kalef) Shirley Sobel

WINDSOR

FUNKENHAUSER PRODUCTIONS*†
P.O. Box 246
Windsor, ON N9A 6K7
(519) 258-3731
Contact: Barry Holden

QUEBEC

CHARLESBOURG

AGENCE MUSICALE ROLAND MARTEL, INC.†
6495 Place Monette
Charlesbourg, PQ G1H 6K1
(418) 626-0034
Contact: Roland J. Martel

CENTRE DES ORCHESTRES DU QUEBEC ALEX DROLET LTEE†
4765 - Lere Ave.
Charlesbourg, PQ G1H 2T3
(418) 628-9933
Contact: Alexandre Drolet

DANFORD LAKE

ZEB'S ENTERTAINMENT AGENCY†
Danford Lake, PQ J0X 1P0
(819) 467-2968
Contact: Jan McCambley

DUVERNAY-LAVAL

GEORGE ANGERS MUSICAL PRODUCTIONS†
1755 Concorde Blvd.
Duvernay-Laval, PQ H7G 2G1
(514) 668-4788
Contact: George J. Angers

GRANBY

PIERRE GRAVEL AGENCY†
89 Alexandra St.
Granby, PQ J2G 2P4
(514) 372-6725
Contact: Pierre Gravel, Lucie Trottier

KIRKLAND

MUSIC MARKET REG'D†
36 Daudelin
Kirkland, PQ H9J 1L8
(514) 694-3515
Contact: Lynda D. Moffet, Paul Church, Anne Field, Charlie Moore

LACHINE

LES PRODUCTIONS C.R. ENRG.†
1091 rue Notre Dame
Lachine, PQ H8S 2C3
(514) 637-4468
Contact: Raymond Lavoie, Ricky Edwards, Francine Hamel, Gilles Rouleau, Francine Hebert, Michel Laplante, Andre DiCesare

MONTREAL

AGENCE THEATRALE APOLLO LTEE†
1600 rue Berri, Ste. 3150
Montreal, PQ H2L 4E4
(514) 284-0808
Contact: Peter Belmont

BOB CARLISLE PRODUCTIONS ENRG.†
175 Sherbrooke St., W., Ste. 103
Montreal, PQ H2X 1X5
(514) 844-7075
Contact: R.L. Carlisle, Raymond Deguire, Jean-Louis Gladu, Raymond Sequin

DO-RE-MI AGENCY†
1055 Rochon St.
Ville St. Laurent
Montreal, PQ H4L 1V6
(514) 748-8270
Contact: Don Arres

A.P. GORDON PRODUCTIONS†
5380 Garland Place
Montreal, PQ H3X 1E4
(514) 739-3716
Contact: Anthony P. Gordon

MAY JOHNSON ASSOCIATES (CANADA), LTD.†
Sheraton Mount Royal Hotel
Peel St., Ste. M45
Montreal, PQ H3A 1T5
(514) 845-8265
Contact: James V. Nichols

BEN KAYE ASSOCIATES, INC.†
4824 cote Des Neiges, Ste. 38
Montreal, PQ H3V 1G4
(514) 739-4774
Contact: Ben Kaye

STEVE MICHAELS, INC.†
1 Redpath Row
Montreal, PQ H3G 1E4
(514) 931-5022
Contact: Saul Michael Shade

PARAMOUNT ENTERTAINMENT BUREAU, INC.†
1010 St. Catherine St. W., Ste. 904
Montreal, PQ H3B 3R7
(514) 878-1496
Contact: Roy Cooper

PIANO PLAYERS†
3420 Drummond St., Ste. 3
Montreal, PQ H3G 1Y1
(514) 849-9536
Contact: William B. Georgette

BRIAN POMBIERE PRODUCTIONS†
205 Ouest Mont-Royal, Ste. 4
Montreal, PQ H2T 2T2
(514) 849-5252
Contact: Brian Pombiere, David Byrne, Lyn Bartram

NAT RAIDER PRODUCTIONS, INC.†
5799 Eldridge Ave.
Montreal, PQ H4W 2E3
(514) 486-1676
Contact: Nat N. Raider, Buddy Hampton

Branch Office:
1248 The Queensway
Toronto, ON M8Z 1S2
(416) 869-0576
Contact: Nat N. Raider, Diane Karabinos, Cathy Ackerman

SILLERY

PETER NOVAK PRODUCTIONS†
2028 Masse
Sillery, PQ G1T 1S7
(418) 688-9349
Contact: Peter Novak

ST. LAURENT

PERRY CARMEN PRODUCTIONS†
2390 Frenette St.
St. Laurent, PQ H4R 1M4
(514) 331-7262
Contact: Perry Carmen

TEMISCAMING

CORY AGENCY†
960 Kipawa Rd.
Box 932
Temiscaming, PQ J0Z 3R0
(819) 627-9479
Contact: Simone E. Piquette

VALLEYFIELD

JEAN-MARIE PAYANT†
26 rue Lapointe
Valleyfield, PQ J6S 4R6
(514) 373-8854
Contact: Jean-Marie Payant, Nicole Payant

SASKATCHEWAN

REGINA

DRUMMOND MUSIC SERVICES, LTD.†
4332 Pasqua St.
Regina, SK S4S 6M5
(306) 584-8114
Contact: Doreen E. Brown

JK MUSICAL SERVICES, LTD.†
1127 Weaver St.
Regina, SK
(306) 949-6030
Contact: Kenneth G. Hartfield

MUSIC UNLIMITED 1979, LTD.†
2310 College Ave., 3rd Flr.
Regina, SK S4P 1C7
(306) 586-1333
Contact: Chris Siller

RAM TALENT AGENCY†
378 Rink Ave.
Regina, SK S4X 1K8
(306) 949-8911
Contact: Barry B. Karhut

VIKING PRODUCTIONS, LTD.†
144 Milne St., N.
Regina, SK S4R 5B7
(306) 949-0453
Contact: Dallas S. Gudmundson

SASKATOON

BOECHLER MUSIC WORLD†
514 Boychuk Drive
Saskatoon, SK S7H 4L5
(306) 343-1236
Contact: Guy J. Boechler, Wendy D. Boechler

CROSSTOWN BUS TALENT AGENCY†
1105 - 11th Street East
Saskatoon, SK S7H 0G1
(306) 343-8356
Contact: Bradley D. Welk, James Hodges

MUSIC CITY PROMOTIONS†
3410 Dieppe St.
Saskatoon, SK S7M 3S9
(306) 382-0330
Contact: David P. Calyniuk, Adeline Calyniuk

NORTHWIND TALENT AGENCY, LTD.†
Box 3065
Saskatoon, SK S7K 3S9
(306) 653-0901
Contact: Robert K. Hodgins, Michael C. Scott, Pat Cooney

D.V. OLSON PROMOTIONS†
1002 - 541- 5th Ave., N.
Saskatoon, SK S7K 2R1
(306) 664-2717
Contact: Dennis T. Olson, Lavina Olson

PRAIRIE PROMOTIONS, LTD.†
903 Coppermine Lane
Saskatoon, SK S7K 5H9
(306) 382-1944
Contact: William H. Kolter, Debra Chuka

Booking Agents Index

A

D

E

F

G

H

I

J

K

L

M

N

O

P

Q

R

S

T

U

V

W

Y

Z

Personal Managers

U.S. and Canadian personal managers and management firms are listed alphabetically by state or province. An alphabetical cross-index appears at the end of this section.

ALABAMA

LESUEUR MANAGEMENT
803 First Ave.
Athens, AL 35611
(205) 233-2462
Contact: Mike Lessor

JAMES R. SMITH-HANK WILLIAMS, JR.
P.O. Box 970
Cullman, AL 35055
(205) 734-8656
Contact: James R. Smith

SOUTHEASTERN ATTRACTIONS, INC.
120 Vulcan Rd.
Birmingham, AL 35202
(205) 942-6600

ARIZONA

JERRY HALE PRODUCTIONS
Box 5054, ELRB
Parker, AZ 85344
(602) 669-9274

MPL ASSOCIATES, LTD.
P.O. Box 2108
Phoenix, AZ 85001
Contact: Louis P. Goldstein

CALIFORNIA

AIMEE ENTERTAINMENT ASSOCIATION
13743 Victory Blvd.
Van Nuys, CA 91401
(213) 994-9709
Contact: Joyce Aimee

ALIVE ENTERPRISES
8600 Melrose Ave.
Los Angeles, CA 90069
(213) 659-7001
Contact: Bob Emmer

AMERICANA CORPORATION
P.O. Box. 47
Woodland Hills, CA 91365
(213) 347-2976
Contact: Steve Stebbins

AMUSEX CORPORATION
P.O. Box 902
Menlo Park, CA 94025
(415) 324-1444
Contact: David Elder

ANDERS ARTIST MANAGEMENT, INC.
535 El Camino del Mar
San Francisco, CA 94121
(415) 752-4404
Contact: Mariedi Anders

ANDERSON AGENCY, INC.
290 California Dr.
Burlingame, CA 94010
(415) 342-8500
Contact: Don Anderson

ANSON PRODUCTIONS
11350 Ventura Blvd., Ste. 206
Studio City, CA 91604
(213) 766-3896
Contact: Haskell Hal Heimlick

ARN-VACCHINA ASSOCIATES
Fontana West, Ste. 409
1050 North Point
San Francisco, CA 94109
(415) 776-7798
Contact: Irena Arn

ARTS UNLIMITED
515 John Muir Dr., Ste. 605
San Francisco, CA 94132
(415) 584-6333
Contact: Ruth McCreery

ASSOCIATED BOOKING CORPORATION
292 South La Cienega Blvd.
Beverly Hills, CA 90211
(213) 855-8051
Contact: Tony Papa

AZTEC PRODUCTIONS
20531 Plummer St.
Chatsworth, CA 91311
(213) 998-0443
Contact: A. Sullivan

RICK BERNSTEIN ENTERPRISES, INC.
9200 Sunset Blvd.
Los Angeles, CA 90069
(213) 275-6128
Contact: Rick Bernstein

SANDRA BLODGET
P.O. Box 6543
Carmel, CA 93921
(408) 624-7653

RICK BLOOM'S OFFICES
6338 Jackie Ave.
Woodland Hills, CA 91367
(213) 833-7160

BNB ASSOCIATES, LTD.
9454 Wilshire Blvd.
Beverly Hills, CA 90212
(213) 273-7020
Contact: Sherwin Bash

RAY BOWMAN
1903 Harriman Lane
Redondo Beach, CA 90278
(213) 379-2557

BUG MUSIC GROUP
6777 Hollywood Blvd.
Hollywood, CA 90028
(213) 466-4352
Contact: Fred Bourgoise

BOB BURTON MANAGEMENT
1248 Devon Ave.
Los Angeles, CA 90024
(213) 276-8684

CALIFORNIA ARTISTS MANAGEMENT
23 Liberty St., Ste. 4
San Francisco, CA 94110
(415) 824-8442
Contact: Susan Endrizzi

PAUL CANTOR ENTERPRISES, LTD.
144 South Beverly Dr.
Beverly Hills, CA 90212
(213) 274-9222

CARMAN PRODUCTIONS, INC.
15456 Cabrito Rd.
Van Nuys, CA 91406
(213) 787-6436
Contact: Tom Skeeter

CASA ITALIANA OPERA COMPANY
5959 Franklin Ave.
Hollywood, CA 90028
(213) 463-2996
Contact: Mario E. Leonetti

CLAYTON ENTERPRISES
8730 Sunset Blvd.
Los Angeles, CA 90069
(213) 659-5186
Contact: Dick Clayton

JOHN ALAN COHAN
2049 Century Park East, Ste. 1100
Los Angeles, CA 90067
(213) 557-9900

CREATIVE CORPS
6607 West Sunset Blvd., Ste. E
Hollywood, CA 90028
Contact: Kurt Hunter

CREATIVE MINDS, INC.
1560 North La Brea
Hollywood, CA 90028
Contact: Art Benson

DAWG MUSIC, INC.
P.O. Box 2999
San Rafael, CA 94912
(415) 457-5474
Contact: Craig or Isabel Miller

MARCIA LEE DAY
216 Chatsworth Dr.
San Fernando, CA 91340
(213) 365-9371
Contact: Sheila Moloney

ARLENE DAYTON PERSONAL MANAGEMENT
1490 Cardiff Ave.
Los Angeles, CA 90036
(213) 273-3161

DAVID DIAMOND MANAGEMENT
5446 Topeka Dr.
Tarzana, CA 91356
(213) 960-2395

DIAMONDACK MUSIC COMPANY
10 Waterville St.
San Francisco, CA 94124
Contact: Joseph Burchwald

BEA DONALDSON
P.O. Box 7088
Burbank, CA 91510
(213) 761-3796

GEORGE "BULLETS" DURGOM, INC.
9229 Sunset Blvd., Ste. 615
Los Angeles, CA 90069
(213) 278-8820
Contact: George "Bullets" Durgom

RICHARD LEE EMLER ENTERPRISES
8601 Wilshire Blvd., Ste. 1000
Los Angeles, CA 90211
(213) 659-3932

WILLIAM FELBER & ASSOCIATES
2126 Cahuenga Blvd.
Hollywood, CA 90068
(213) 466-7627
Contact: William Felber

ELIZABETH A. FERRELL ASSOCIATES
2451 Green Valley Rd.
Los Angeles, CA 90046
(213) 654-4175

FESTIVALS INTERNATIONAL
618 Emerald Hill Rd.
Redwood City, CA 94061
(415) 364-4769
Contact: Lynn Carpenter

THE FRANKLYN AGENCY
1010 Hammond St., Ste. 312
Los Angeles, CA 90069
(213) 272-6080
Contact: Audrey P. Franklyn

FREEMAN & DOFF, INC.
8732 Sunset Blvd.
Los Angeles, CA 90069
(213) 659-4700
Contact: Red Doff

ROBERT FRIEDMAN PRESENTS
530 Congo St.
San Francisco, CA 94131
(415) 469-7800

KEN FRITZ
444 South San Vincente
Los Angeles, CA 90048
(213) 651-5350
Contact: Dennis Turner

FRONT LINE MANAGEMENT
9044 Melrose Ave.
Los Angeles, CA 90069
(213) 859-1900
Contact: Irving Azoff

MICK GAMBILL ENTERPRISES, INC.
1617 North El Centro, Ste. 12
Hollywood, CA 90028
(213) 466-9777

LYNN GLASER & ASSOCIATES
3514 Dwight Way
Berkeley, CA 94704
(415) 849-1920

ZACH GLICKMAN
6430 Sunset Blvd.
Hollywood, CA 90028
(213) 461-2988

GLOTZER MANAGEMENT CORPORATION
7720 Sunset Blvd.
Los Angeles, CA 90046
(213) 851-9115
Contact: Bennett H. Glotzer

PETER GOLDEN & ASSOCIATES
1592 Crossroads of the World
Hollywood, CA 90028
(213) 462-6156
Contact: Bill Siddons

THE GOLDSTEIN COMPANY
10100 Santa Monica Blvd.
Los Angeles, CA 90067
(213) 557-2507
Contact: Jerry Goldstein

JOE GOTTFRIED MANAGEMENT
15456 Cabrito Rd.
Van Nuys, A 91406
(213) 873-7370

BILL GRAHAM MANAGEMENT
201 Eleventh St.
San Francisco, CA 94103
(415) 864-0815
Contact: Mick Bridgen

LEONARD J. GRANT
P.O. Box 69360
Los Angeles, CA 90069
(213) 274-9483

JOE GRAYDON & ASSOCIATES
P.O. Box 1
Toluca Lake, CA 91602
(213) 769-2424

GREAT PYRAMID MUSIC
P.O. Box 1340
Pacifica, CA 94044
Contact: Joseph Buchwald

FOREST HAMILTON PERSONAL MANAGEMENT
9022 Norma Pl.
Los Angeles, CA 90069
(213) 273-3710

THE JACK HAMPTON AGENCY
226 South Beverly Dr.
Beverly Hills, CA 90212
(213) 274-6075
Contact: Donovan Moore

GEOFFREY HANSEN ENTERPRISES, LTD.
P.O. Box 63
Orinda, CA 94563
(415) 937-6469
Contact: Marvin Farkelstein

HELLER, SEYMOUR & ASSOCIATES
7060 Hollywood Blvd., Ste. 1212
Los Angeles, CA 90028
(213) 462-7151

Contact: Seymour Heller, Bette Rosenthal, Raymond Harris

GORDON HERRITT
P.O. Box 194
Topanga, CA 90290
(213) 455-1973

GLENN HOLLAND MANAGEMENT
2368 Stanley Hills Dr.
Los Angeles, CA 90046
(213) 656-6834

GEORGE B. HUNT & ASSOCIATES
8350 Santa Monica Blvd.
Los Angeles, CA 90069
(213) 654-6600

ILRO PRODUCTIONS, LTD.
9056 Santa Monica Blvd.
Los Angeles, CA 90069
(213) 276-3532
Contact: Curtis Roberts

INDEPENDENT CONCERTS & ARTISTS INTERNATIONAL CONCERT EXCHANGE
1124 Summit Dr.
Beverly Hills, CA 90210
(213) 272-5539
Contact: Irwin Parnes

STAN IRWIN ENTERPRISES, INC.
8530 Wilshire Blvd., Ste. 500
Beverly Hills, CA 90211
(213) 659-5044

JAMES J. JAMES MANAGEMENT
2126 Cahuenga Blvd.
Hollywood, CA 90068
(213) 466-7626

KATZ-GALLIN ENTERPRISES, INC.
9255 Sunset Blvd., Ste. 1115
Los Angeles, CA 90069
(213) 273-4210
Contact: Raymond Katz, Sandy Gallin

JUNE KINGSLEY ARTISTS' MANAGEMENT
45 Raycliff Terrace
San Francisco, CA 94115
(415) 931-2574

KRAGEN & COMPANY
1112 North Sherbourne Dr.
Los Angeles, CA 90069
(213) 659-7914
Contact: Ken Kragen

RICHARD LAWRENCE ENTERPRISES, INC.
310 North San Vincente Blvd.
Los Angeles, CA 90048
(213) 659-3654

ED LEFFLER MANAGEMENT
9229 Sunset Blvd., Ste. 625
Los Angeles, CA 90069
(213) 550-8802

LEMOND-ZETTER, INC.
5160 Genesta Ave.
Encino, CA 91316
(213) 995-3403
Contact: Robert LeMond, Lois Zetter

JOHN LEVY ENTERPRISES, INC.
181 South Sycamore Ave., Ste. 101
Los Angeles, CA 90036
(213) 876-4071
Contact: Lew Linet

RICHARD O. LINKE & ASSOCIATES, INC.
4055 Kraft Ave.
Studio City, CA 91604
(213) 760-2500

SANDY LITTMAN
1707 Clearview Dr.
Beverly Hills, CA 90210
(213) 271-6239

SAM J. LUTZ ARTIST'S MANAGEMENT
1626 North Vine St.
Hollywood, CA 90028
(213) 469-1993

TAMI LYNN MANAGEMENT
20411 Chapter Dr.
Woodland Hills, CA 91364
(213) 881-1511

REUBEN MACK ASSOCIATES, INC.
5820 Wilshire Blvd., Ste. 300
Los Angeles, CA 90036
(213) 936-5123

LEE MAGID, INC.
P.O. Box 532
Malibu, CA 90265
(213) 858-7282

THE MANAGEMENT COMPANY
1438 North Gower St., Ste. 245
Hollywood, CA 90028
(213) 462-7421
Contact: Howard Hinderstein

THE MANAGEMENT TREE
1717 North Highland Ave.
Hollywood, CA 90028
(213) 466-6206
Contact: Ron Singer

MASTERSTAR MUSIC & MPM PRODUCTIONS
P.O. Box 727
Sunnymead, CA 92388
(714) 653-3328
Contact: Daniel Porter

MC QUEENY MANAGEMENT, INC.
146 North Almont Dr.
Los Angeles, CA 90048
(213) 273-1253
Contact: Pat Mc Queeny

LEE MCRAE, PERSONAL REPRESENTATIVE
2130 Carleton St.
Berkeley, CA 94704
(415) 848-5491

MERCANTILE PRODUCTIONS
P.O. Box 2271
Palm Springs, CA 92263
(714) 320-4848
Contact: Kent Fox

JON MERCEDES III
9110 Sunset Blvd., Ste. 120
Los Angeles, CA 90069
(213) 858-0277

ARNOLD MILLS & ASSOCIATES
8721 Sunset Blvd.
Los Angeles, CA 90069
(213) 657-2024

MONTCLAIR RECORDS
13755 Bayliss Rd.
Los Angeles, CA 90049
Contact: L.Z. Dough

RON MOSS MANAGEMENT
11257 Blix St.
North Hollywood, CA 91602
(213) 508-9865

MOUSEVILLE NOSTALGIA
5218 Almont St.
Los Angeles, CA 90032
(213) 223-2860
Contact: Mr. Perez

MR. I. MOUSE, LTD.
7876 Woodrow Wilson Dr.
Los Angeles, CA 90046
(213) 650-5930
Contact: Ira Bracker

NEW DIRECTIONS
9255 Sunset Blvd.
Los Angeles, CA 90069
(213) 550-7205
Contact: Kevin Hunter

PARC
2130 Carleton St.
Berkeley, CA 94704
(415) 848-5591
Contact: Lee McRae

TERESA PARKER ASSOCIATES
65 Cervantes Blvd., Ste. 10
San Francisco, CA 94123
(415) 567-3266

PATCO
10525 Strathmore Dr.
Los Angeles, CA 90024
(213) 472-7950
Contact: Pat Lynn

PATTACK PRODUCTIONS
314 Huntley Dr.
Los Angeles, CA 90048
(213) 652-2222
Contact: Jack Rael

PDQ DIRECTIONS, INC.
1474 North King's Rd.
Los Angeles, CA 90048
(213) 656-4870
Contact: Leo Leichter

PERFECTION LIGHT PRODUCTIONS
P.O. Box 690
San Francisco, CA 94101
(415) 626-0655
Contact: Gregory DiGiovine

PINECREST PRODUCTIONS, INC.
9229 Sunset Blvd., Ste. 613
Los Angeles, CA 90069
(213) 273-7070
Contact: Tom Sheils, Gloria Burke

PLAIN GREAT ENTERTAINMENT CORPORATION
6525 Sunset Blvd., Ste. 8
Hollywood, CA 90028
(213) 469-3936
Contact: Ron Henry

PROS FROM DOVER
P.O. Box 1211
Beverly Hills, CA 90213
Contact: Donovan Moore

ROBERT RAISON
9575 Lime Orchard Rd.
Beverly Hills, CA 90210
(213) 274-7217

JESS RAND, INC.
9460 Wilshire Blvd.
Beverly Hills, CA 90212
(213) 275-6000

ROBERT RAYMOND MANAGEMENT
15312 Longbow Dr.
Sherman Oaks, CA 91403
(213) 995-8999

RENAISSANCE MANAGEMENT
433 North Camden Dr.
Beverly Hills, CA 90210
(213) 273-4162
Contact: Elliott Abbott

RNJ PRODUCTIONS, INC.
11514 Calvert St.
North Hollywood, CA 91606
Contact: Rein Neggo, Jr., Roger Montesano

HERB ROBERS
621 North Beverly Dr.
Beverly Hills, CA 90210
(213) 273-1495

BUD ROBINSON PRODUCTIONS, INC.
1100 North Alta Loma Rd., Ste. 707
Los Angeles, CA 90069
(213) 652-3242

KAL ROSS MANAGEMENT, INC.
2029 Century Park East, Ste. 3585
Los Angeles, CA 90067
(213) 553-9757

SOUND III MANAGEMENT
9046 Sunset Blvd.
Los Angeles, CA 90069
(213) 271-7246
Contact: Bruce Berlow

MERVIN I. TARLOW
3812 Sepulveda Blvd., Ste. 400
Torrance, CA 90505
(213) 373-6821

PHYLLIS TEITLER
2411 Horseshoe Canyon Rd.
Los Angeles, CA 90046
(213) 650-7349

TELCO PRODUCTIONS, INC.
6525 Sunset Blvd.
Los Angeles, CA 90028
(213) 461-2888
Contact: Rudy Tellez

TODAY'S ARTISTS, INC.
P.O. Box 465
Berkeley, CA 94701
(415) 527-3622
Contact: Dr. W. Hazaiah Williams

TOWER ROAD PRODUCTIONS
9025 Wilshire Blvd.
Beverly Hills, CA 90212
(213) 271-5261
Contact: Peter Bayles

JIM WAGNER, INC.
17530 Ventura Blvd., Ste. 108
Encino, CA 91316
(213) 981-6500

WILLIAM F. WAGNER AGENCY
14343 Addison St., Ste. 218
Sherman Oaks, CA 91423
(213) 501-4161

ELLIOT WAX & ASSOCIATES, INC.
9255 Sunset Blvd.
Los Angeles, CA 90069
(213) 273-8217

MIMI WEBBER MANAGEMENT
9200 Sunset Blvd., Ste. 810
Los Angeles, CA 90069
(213) 278-8440

WEST COAST ARTISTS' MANAGEMENT
5820 Wilshire Blvd., Ste. 300
Los Angeles, CA 90036
(213) 938-5229
Contact: Dale Russell

WESTERLY ARTISTS' MANAGEMENT
P.O. Box 1325
Grass Valley, CA 95945
(916) 272-3068
Contact: Lauren Ernest West

SHANE WILDER MANAGEMENT
P.O. Box 3503
Hollywood, CA 90028

LOUISE WILLIAMS, PERSONAL MANAGEMENT
165 Northpoint St., Ste. 318
San Francisco, CA 94133
(415) 986-0519

HOWARD B. WOLF & ASSOCIATES
8601 Wilshire Blvd., Ste. 1000
Los Angeles, CA 90211
(213) 652-1983

WOODEN LADY PRODUCTIONS
1154 North Western Ave., Ste. 208
Los Angeles, CA 90029
(213) 463-7578
Contact: Albert Williams, Colleen Mickey

BONNIE YOUNG PERSONAL MANAGEMENT
8633 West Knoll Dr.
Los Angeles, CA 90069
(213) 657-7819

STANFORD ZUCKER & ASSOCIATES
9350 Wilshire Blvd.
Beverly Hills, CA 90212
(213) 274-6703
Contact: Stan Zucker

COLORADO

GIBSON GARDNER ASSOCIATES
P.O. Box 5362
Denver, CO 80217
(303) 399-2999

ROCK HARD, INC.
13010 West Thirtieth Dr.
Golden, CO 80401
(303) 278-8367
Contact: Barry Higgins, Mike Walsh

CONNECTICUT

ANTHONY ANGARANO
P.O. Box 136
New Hartford, CT 06057
(203) 379-1326

DOUGLASS ASSOCIATES
17 Haynes St.
Hartford, CT 06103
(203) 527-4980
Contact: Philip A. Douglass

EUROPEAN AMERICAN ARTISTS & AUTHORS AGENCY, INC.
27 Pine St.
New Canaan, CT 06804
(203) 966-4464
Contact: Henno Lohmeyer

DICK GRASS
585 Ellsworth Ave.
Bridgeport, CT 06601
(203) 334-9285

INTERMUSE PERFORMING ARTISTS BUREAU
P.O. Box 1163
New Haven, CT 06505
(203) 624-7485
Contact: Dr. Charles Borovsky

THE KOTULA COMPANY, INC.
37 Arch St.
Greenwich, CT 06830

(203) 661-6615
Contact: Stine Kotula

RICK MARTIN
125 Greld Point Rd.
Greenwich, CT 06830
(203) 661-1615

PHILLIP TRUCKENBROD CONCERT ARTISTS
P.O. Box 14600, Barry Square Station
Hartford, CT 06114
(203) 728-1096

DELAWARE

WHITE CLAY PRODUCTIONS, INC.
P.O. Box 324
Newark, DE 19711
(302) 368-1211
Contact: Nicholas C. Norris

DISTRICT OF COLUMBIA

DANIEL CAPLIN ARTISTS MANAGEMENT
1850 Mint Wood Pl., NW
Washington, D.C. 20009
(202) 332-8329

ELLIOT A. SIEGEL MUSIC MANAGEMENT, INC.
3003 Van Ness St. NW, Ste. W832
Washington, D.C. 20008
(202) 966-0003

FLORIDA

ARTISTS UNLIMITED, AGENTS
4117 Santa Maria
Coral Gables, FL 33146
(305) 661-7951
Contact: Arlene Huysman

BEACON INTERNATIONAL ARTISTS
P.O. Box 1746
Miami, FL 33176
(305) 255-4911
Contact: R.W. Augstroze

BLADE AGENCY
P.O. Box 12239
Gainesville, FL 32604
(904) 372-8158
Contact: Charles V. Steadham, Jr.

CFA
415 North Ridgewood Ave.
Edgewater, FL 32032
(904) 427-2480
Contact: Dick Conti

DOCTOR COOL PRODUCTIONS
P.O. Box 011321, Flagler Station
Miami, FL 33101
(305) 374-9717
Contact: Doctor Cool

DUO ASSOCIATES
2809 St. Leonard Dr.
Tallahassee, FL 32312
(904) 386-8730

FANTASMA PRODUCTIONS, INC.
1675 Palm Beach Lakes Building
Ste. 902
West Palm Beach, FL 33401
(305) 686-6397
Contact: Jon Stoll

LOCONTO PRODUCTIONS
7766 NW Forty-Fourth St.
Sunrise, FL 33321
(305) 741-7766
Contact: Frank X. Loconto

MANAGEMENT VII
1811 NE Fifty-Third St.
Fort Lauderdale, FL 33308
(305) 776-1004
Contact: Ramona Beri

NOVA ENTERTAINMENT, INC.
P.O. Box 521173
Miami, FL 33152
(305) 551-1866
Contact: Thomas Chelko

PRYOR-MENZ-LEE ATTRACTIONS, INC.
P.O. Box 9550
Panama City Beach, FL 32407
(904) 234-3326
Contact: David Lee

OTTO SCHMIDT
2116 Northeast Sixty-Second Ct.
Fort Lauderdale, FL 33308
(305) 771-4863

SCM INTERNATIONAL MANAGEMENT
P.O. Box 5208
Clearwater, FL 33518
(813) 446-2914

SOUTH WIND ENTERTAINMENT
2500 Forsyth Rd., Building 31
Orlando, FL 32807
(305) 677-5300
Contact: Michael Orlando

DON TAYLOR ARTIST MANAGEMENT
9400 South Dadeland Blvd., Ste. 220
Miami, FL 33156
(305) 665-2552

TDI DIRECTION & MANAGEMENT
4100 West Flagler St.
Miami, FL 33134
(305) 446-1900
Contact: Larry Brahms

GEORGIA

ALKAHEST AGENCY, INC.
P.O. Box 12403, Northside Station
Atlanta, GA 30355
(404) 237-1540
Contact: Ralph P. Bridges

THE MALCOLM GREENWOOD AGENCY
P.O. Box 72303
Atlanta, GA 30339
(404) 433-1979

THE GROUP, INC.
1957 Kilburn Dr.
Atlanta, GA 30324
(404) 872-6000
Contact: Hamilton Underwood

PRO TALENT CONSULTANTS
P.O. Box 29543
Atlanta, GA 30359
(404) 424-1684
Contact: John Eckert, Glenn Elliott

JULITA SHALLAL PERSONAL REPRESENTATIVE
312 Jackson Woods Boulevard
Savannah, GA 31405
(912) 352-9685

SOUTHERN TALENT INTERNATIONAL
2925 Fallowridge
Snellville, GA 30278
(404) 979-0847
Contact: John M. Titak

HAWAII

ASSOCIATED PACIFIC ARTISTS
838 South Beretania St., Ste. 207
Honolulu, HI 96813
(808) 537-4079
Contact: Richard W. Cornwell

BORISOFF-STARR ASSOCIATES
1860 Ala Moana Blvd., Ste. 1606
Honolulu, HI 96815
(808) 941-2443
Contact: Alexander Borisoff

MALAMA ARTS, INC.
P.O. Box 1761
Honolulu, HI 96806
(808) 988-7453
Contact: John P. Thomas

ILLINOIS

WILLARD ALEXANDER, INC. ARTISTS MANAGEMENT
333 North Michigan Ave.
Chicago, IL 60601
(312) 236-2460

ARMAGEDDON TALENT ASSOCIATES
1604 West Juneway Terrace
Chicago, IL 60626
(312) 465-3373
Contact: Gail Smith, Fred Tieken

ARTISTS MANAGEMENT OF AMERICA
800 Valley View Dr.
Downers Grove, IL 60516
(312) 968-0155
Contact: Robert Zechel

ASSOCIATED BOOKING CORPORATION
2700 River Rd.
Des Plaines, IL 60018
(312) 296-0930
Contact: Hak Munro

THE CAMERON ORGANIZATION, INC.
320 South Waiola Ave.
La Grange, IL 60525
(312) 352-2026
Contact: Scott A. Cameron

CORINNE CARPENTER COMMUNICATIONS
549 Roscoe St.
Chicago, IL 60657
(312) 248-1478

CLARK MUSICAL PRODUCTIONS
P.O. Box 299
Watseka, IL 60970
Contact: Paul E. Clark

CONTEMPORARY FORUM
2528 West Jerome St.
Chicago, IL 60645
(312) 764-4383
Contact: Beryl Zitch

DAWN TALENT
P.O. Box 48597
Niles, IL 60648
(312) 288-0969
Contact: Tiffany Dawn

DAVID GOLIATH AGENCY
1272 Lynn Terrace
Highland Park, IL 60035
(312) 266-0040
Contact: Cynthia Winston

GEORGE HARNESS ASSOCIATES
27 North Lake Rd.
Springfield, IL 62707
(217) 529-8550

SOUND RISING ARTISTIC MANAGEMENT
8941 North LaCrosse Ave.
Skokie, IL 60077
(312) 679-6512
Contact: Harmon Greenblatt

SOUTH PRODUCTIONS, LTD.
P.O. Box 227
Chicago Ridge, IL 60415
(312) 599-9178
Contact: Bud Monaco, Jerry Gamauf

STAR REPRESENTATION
4026 Bobby Lane
Schiller Park, IL 60176
(312) 678-2755
Contact: James Stella

RAY G. STEINER MANAGEMENT
1300 West Roscoe St.
Chicago, IL 60657
(312) 248-4849

TOPDRAW ARTIST MANAGEMENT
Box 2787, Station A
Champaign, IL 61820
(217) 398-1221
Contact: Jeff Ross

IOWA

ENTERTAINMENT SERVICES

CONCEPT
P.O. Box 2501
Des Moines, IA 50315
(515) 285-6564
Contact: Art Stenstrom

4-K PRODUCTIONS
P.O. Box 557
Knoxville, IA 50138
(515) 842-3723
Contact: Larry Heaberlin

JOHN HILL ASSOCIATES
Rural Route 2
Iowa City, IA 52240
(319) 353-3622

ONSTAGE MANAGEMENT, INC.
233 West Woodland Ave.
Ottumwa, IA 52501
(515) 682-8283
Contact: Nada C. Jones

KANSAS

INTERNATIONAL CELEBRITY REGISTER, INC.
First National Bank Towers, Box 4527
Topeka, KS 66604
(913) 233-9716
Contact: Kent Raine

JACKSON ARTISTS CORPORATION
7251 Lowell Dr., Ste. 200
Shawnee MIssion, KS 66204

MUTUAL MANAGEMENT ASSOCIATES
P.O. Box 3247
Shawnee, KS 66203
(913) 631-6060
Contact: Frank Fara

WINTERSWAN
P.O. Box 634
Lawrence, KS 66044
(913) 841-4444
Contact: Mark Swanson, Scott Winters

KENTUCKY

PREFERRED ARTIST MANAGEMENT, INC.
9701 Taylorsville Rd.
Louisville, KY 40299
(502) 267-5466
Contact: Dan Green

LOUISIANA

BOUQUET-ORCHID ENTERPRISES
P.O. Box 4220
Shreveport, LA 71104
(318) 686-7362
Contact: Bill Bohannon

RONALD L. EISENBERG
141 Tealwood St.
Shreveport, LA 71104
(318) 868-3266

RCS MANAGEMENT
5220 Essen Lane
Baton Rouge, LA 70898
(504) 766-3233
Contact: John Fred

MAINE

LINGERING MUSIC, INC.
2 Bay St.
Thomaston, ME 04861
(207) 354-8928
Contact: Chuck Kruger

MARYLAND

ARMSTRONG & DONALDSON MANAGEMENT, INC.
2 East Read St., Ste. 209
Baltimore, MD 21202
(301) 727-2220
Contact: Rod Armstrong

JACK BERRY & LAURA BECK
8715 First Ave.
Silver Springs, MD 20910
(301) 588-1890

CAPITOL ARTISTS MANAGEMENT
8717 Hidden Hill Lane
Potomac, MD 20854
(301) 299-8840
Contact: Inga Britta Elgcrona

CULTURAL ARTS MANAGEMENT
2819 St. Pauls St.
Baltimore, MD 21218
(301) 889-3712
Contact: Rosemary Fetter

INTERNATIONAL CONCERT ADMINISTRATION
2219 Eastridge Rd.
Timonium, MD 21093
(301) 252-1799
Contact: Harry de Freese

EMILY SATTELL ARTISTS' MANAGEMENT
3408 Tulsa Rd.
Baltimore, MD 21207
(301) 944-3978

TEILESCO ARTISTS
P.O. Box 2626
Baltimore, MD 21215
(301) 542-6666

R.J. THOMAS ASSOCIATES, INC.
1121 University Blvd. West, Ste. 1017
Silver Spring, MD 20902
(301) 649-5200
Contact: Ruth A. Patterson

MASSACHUSETTS

AMERICAN PROGRAM BUREAU, INC.
850 Boylston St.
Chestnut Hill, MA 02167
(617) 731-0500
Contact: June Karger

BAILEY ARTISTS INTERNATIONAL
171 Newbury Street
Boston, MA 02116
(617) 262-2530
Contact: Roberta Bailey

BOSTON CONCERT ARTISTS' MANAGEMENT
22 Seneca Rd.
Winchester, MA 01890
(617) 731-9786
Contact: John Parker Murdock

BUCHANAN ARTISTS, LTD.
Maple St.
Chester, MA 01011
(413) 354-7701
Contact: Lynn Edwards

CAMPUS SERVICES, INC.
172 Main St.
Spencer, MA 01562
(617) 753-1318
Contact: Patrick George

JOSEPH CASEY MANAGEMENT
739 Astor Station
Boston, MA 02123
(617) 545-6293

CLOCKWORK MANAGEMENT
P.O. Box 1600
Haverhill, MA 01830
(617) 374-4792
Contact: Bill Macek

JEAN DONATI
Care of Williams College Music Department
Williamstown, MA 01267
(413) 597-2127

FROTHINGHAM MANAGEMENT
384 Washington St.
Wellesley Hills, MA 02181
(617) 237-6141
Contact: Gelsey T. Frothingham

BETSY M. GREEN
36 Hampshire Rd.
Wayland, MA 01778
(617) 358-2939

HANDLEY MANAGEMENT
51 Church St.
Boston, MA 02116
(617) 542-2479
Contact: George Perry

ARNOLD G. HAYWOOD
11 Edmands Rd., #54
Framingham, MA 01201
(617) 877-2895

INNOVATIVE ARTISTS MANAGEMENT
172 Main St.
Spencer, MA 01562
(617) 885-6912
Contact: Patrick George

TED KURLAND ASSOCIATES, INC.
45 Ashford St.
Boston, MA 02134
(617) 254-0007

LORDLY & DAME, INC.
51 Church St.
Boston, MA 02116
(617) 482-3593
Contact: Samuel Dame

MANAGEMENT IN THE ARTS, INC.
551 Tremont St.
Boston, MA 02116
(617) 426-2387
Contact: Robert Brink

PERFORMING ARTIST ASSOCIATES OF NEW ENGLAND
161 Harvard Ave., Ste. 11
Allston, MA 02134
(617) 783-2060
Contact: Sandy Sheckman

MICHIGAN

BARBARA DILES MANAGEMENT COMPANY
4275 Compton Way
Bloomfield Hills, MI 48013
(313) 644-1095

GREAT LAKES PERFORMING ARTIST ASSOCIATES
310 East Washington St.
Ann Arbor, MI 48104
(313) 665-4029
Contact: Joan Lettvin

RICHARD HADDEN MANAGEMENT
Mackinac Island, MI 49757
(906) 847-3259

GARY LAZAR MANAGEMENT
3222 Belinda Dr.
Sterling Heights, MI 48077
(313) 977-0645
Contact: Robin Gaines

LEE JON ASSOCIATES
18662 Fairfield Ave.
Detroit, MI 48221
(313) 861-6930
Contact: Lee Merrill

LOUIS PARENTI ASSOCIATES
1059 Seminole St.
Detroit, MI 48214
(313) 331-1673

SAGITTARIAN ARTISTS INTERNATIONAL
970 Aztec Dr.
Muskegon, MI 49444
(616) 733-2329
Contact: G. Loren Ruhl

STAR ARTIST MANAGEMENT, INC.
P.O. Box 114
Fraser, MI 48026
(313) 979-5115
Contact: Ron Geddish

MINNESOTA

MARSH PRODUCTIONS, INC.
1704 West Lake St.
Minneapolis, MN 55408
(612) 827-6141
Contact: Marshall Edelstein

SRO PRODUCTIONS, INC.
Lumber Exchange Building
Minneapolis, MN 55401
(612) 341-4110
Contact: Larry Berle

MISSISSIPPI

LEGEND ENTERTAINMENT SERVICES
P.O. Box 1414
Vicksburg, MS 39180
(601) 638-5622
Contact: Robert Garner

MISSOURI

CONTINENTAL ENTERTAINMENT ASSOCIATES
680 Craig St., Ste. 4
St. Louis, MO 63141
(314) 567-9880
Contact: Stephanie Vermilyea

GOLDMAN-DELL MUSIC PRODUCTIONS
421 West Eighty-Seventh St.
Kansas City, MO 64114
(816) 333-8701
Contact: Irving Goldman

GOOD KARMA PRODUCTIONS, INC.
4218 Main St.
Kansas City, MO 64111
(816) 531-3857
Contact: Paul Peterson

JERRY PLANTZ PRODUCTIONS
1703 Wyandotte St.
Kansas City, MO 64108
(816) 471-1501

MONTANA

BOB HALE TALENT
423 Kuhlman Dr.
Billings, MT 59101
(406) 425-2174

MEADOWLARK VENTURES
P.O. Box 7218
Missoula, MT 59807
(406) 728-2180
Contact: Chris Roberts

NEBRASKA

RICHARD LUTZ ENTERTAINMENT AGENCY
5625 O Street
Lincoln, NE 68510
(402) 483-2241
Contact: Cherie Hanfelt

NEVADA

AMATO MANAGEMENT CORPORATION
1855 Sierra Sage Lane
Reno, NV 89509
(702) 826-5899
Contact: Tommy Amato

E. LEWIS ASSOCIATES
212 Colleen Dr.
Las Vegas, NV 89107
(702) 870-1358

REDBEARD PRESENTS PRODUCTIONS, LTD.
1061 East Flamingo Rd.
Las Vegas, NV 89119
(702) 739-6494
Contact: Robert Leonard

NEW JERSEY

AGENCY FOR OPERA, CONCERT & THEATRE AUTHORS, COMPOSERS & PERFORMERS
P.O. Box 131
Lake Hiawatha, NJ 07034
(201) 335-0111
Contact: Royall Rockefeller

AGENCY FOR STAGE & SCREEN PERFORMERS, AUTHORS & COMPOSERS
P.O. Box 131
Lake Hiawatha, NJ 07034
(201) 335-0111
Contact: Celia Goldstein

C & C MANAGEMENT
P.O. Box 109
Kingston, NJ 08528
(609) 924-0530
Contact: Louise Cheadle

COME ALIVE ARTIST MANAGEMENT
P.O. Box 86
Medford, NJ 08055
(609) 654-8440
Contact: Greg Menza

CONDUCTORS INTERNATIONAL MANAGEMENT
95 Cedar Road
Ringwood, NJ 07456
(201) 962-4504
Contact: Zola Shaulis

EAGLE PRODUCTIONS
P.O. Box 1274
Merchantville, NJ 08109
(609) 663-8910
Contact: Rob Russen, Jim Creech

EAT MUSIC
North Brewster Rd.
Newfield, NJ 08344
(609) 697-0850
Contact: Ernie Trionfo

WALT GOLLENDER ENTERPRISES
12 Marshall Street, Ste. 8Q
Irvington, NJ 07111
(201) 373-6050

HARRIET S. GREEN ARTISTS' REPRESENTATIVE
51 Hawthorne Ave.
Princeton, NJ 08540
(609) 924-2568

WILLIAM KNIGHT ARTISTS' REPRESENTATIVE
P.O. Box 345
Roosevelt, NJ 08555
(609) 448-4409

RON LUCIANO MUSIC COMPANY
P.O. Box 263
Hasbrouck Heights, NJ 07604
(201) 288-8935

SEYMOUR F. MALKIN
651 Colonial Blvd.
Westwood, NJ 07675
(201) 666-4400

ORPHEUS ENTERTAINMENT
P.O. Box 213
Vauxhall, NJ 07088
(201) 677-1090

RIDGEWOOD TALENT MANAGEMENT
1 Gilbert Rd.
Ho Ho Kus, NJ 07423
Contact: Michele Burk

PETE SALERNO ENTERPRISES
317 Temple Pl.
Westfield, NJ 07090
(201) 232-8766

FRANCES SCHRAM ARTISTS' MANAGEMENT
36 Park St.
Montclair, NJ 07042
(201) 744-7755

WHIMPIA MANAGEMENT, INC.
77 Milltown Rd.
East Brunswick, NJ 08816
(201) 254-3990
Contact: William Franzblau

PAUL WOLFE
Box 262, Abe Lincoln Station
Carteret, NJ 07008
(201) 541-9422

NEW YORK

BRET ADAMS, LTD.
36 East Sixty-First St.
New York, NY 10021
(212) 752-7864

CAROL ADLER ASSOCIATES, INC.
211 Central Park West
New York, NY 10024
(212) 595-5796

AFFILIATE ARTISTS, INC.
155 West Sixty-Eighth St.
New York, NY 10023
(212) 580-2000
Contact: Richard C. Clark

AKIVA ARTISTS
1755 Broadway
New York, NY 10019
(212) 246-9683
Contact: Akiva Kaminsky

WILLARD ALEXANDER, INC. ARTISTS MANAGEMENT
660 Madison Ave.
New York, NY 10021
(212) 751-7070

ALLIED ARTISTS BUREAU
195 Steamboat Road
Great Neck, NY 11024
(516) 487-3216
Contact: Michael Leavitt

RAMON ALSINA ARTIST REPRESENTATIVE
228 East Eightieth St.
New York, NY 10021
(212) 988-2542

AMERICAN ARTISTS MANAGEMENT, INC.
300 West End Ave., Ste. 13A
New York, NY 10023
(212) 362-7837
Contact: Sophie P.Q. Haynes

AMERICAN INTERNATIONAL ARTISTS
275 Madison Ave., Ste. 1618
New York, NY 10016
(212) 725-9812
Contact: Cynthia B. Herbst

AMERICAN THEATRE PRODUCTIONS, INC.
1500 Broadway, Ste. 1901
New York, NY 10036
(212) 391-8160
Contact: Thomas Mallow

ANDEL MANAGEMENT ASSOCIATES
1860 Broadway, Ste. 1714
New York, NY 10023
(212) 757-5496
Contact: John Kordel

ARS MUSICALI ARTISTS MANAGEMENT
276 Riverside Dr., Ste. 8F
New York, NY 10025
(212) 749-0458
Contact: Allen Robertson

ARTIST ASSOCIATES
265 Riverside Dr.
New York, NY 10025
(212) 662-8599

ARTISTS INTERNATIONAL PRESENTATIONS, INC.
663 Fifth Ave., Ste. 600
New York, NY 10022
(212) 757-6454
Contact: Leo B. Ruiz

ARTS ARCADIA ASSOCIATES, INC.
853 Broadway, Ste., 1208
New York, NY 10003
(212) 477-1850
Contact: Carolelinda Dickey

SIMON ASEN MANAGEMENT
110 West End Ave., Ste. 17H
New York, NY 10023
(212) 873-7784

WILLIAM ASHWOOD ORGANIZATION
230 Park Ave.
New York, NY 10169
(212) 682-5400
Contact: Artist Relations Department

ASIA SOCIETY, INC.
725 Park Ave.
New York, NY 10021
(212) 288-6400
Contact: Beate Gordon

ASSOCIATED BOOKING CORPORATION
1995 Broadway
New York, NY 10023
(212) 874-2400
Contact: David Gold

ASSOCIATED CONCERT ARTISTS
1 Sherman Square, Ste. 15C
201 West Seventieth St.
New York, NY 10023
(212) 362-5520
Contact: M. Irgen

AUGUST ARTISTS MANAGEMENT
584 Eighth Ave., Ste. 303
New York, NY 10018
(212) 869-3885
Contact: Camille Barbone

BANDANA ENTERTAINMENT, LTD.
595 Madison Ave.
New York, NY 10022
(212) 249-1250
Contact: Dee Anthony

BARRETT MANAGEMENT, INC.
1860 Broadway
New York, NY 10023
(212) 245-3530
Contact: Herbert Barrett

TINO BARZI
15 Central Park West
New York, NY 10023
(212) 586-1015

BAYVIEW MUSIC GROUP
51 Bayview Ave.
Great Neck, NY 11021
(516) 829-9841
Contact: Herbert B. Feldman

BEALI MANAGEMENT, INC.
119 West Fifty-Seventh St.
New York, NY 10019
(212) 586-8135
Contact: Harry Beali

HARVEY BELLOVIN
410 East Sixty-Fourth St.
New York, NY 10021
(212) 752-5181

GLORIA BERCHIELLI
67 Winfred Ave.
Yonkers, NY 10704
(914) 237-1308

BOBBY BERNARD
40 Central Park South
New York, NY 10019
(212) 753-9843

MARION BILLINGS
605 Park Ave.
New York, NY 10021
(212) 249-1368

BLYTH & HACKEL ARTS MANAGEMENT, LTD.
431 Hicks St.
Brooklyn, NY 11201
(212) 522-1284
Contact: Cheryl Weston

HERBERT H. BRESLIN, INC.
119 West Fifty-Seventh St., Ste. 1505
New York, NY 10019
(212) 246-5480
Contact: Herbert Breslin

JACKIE BRIGHT
850 Seventh Ave.
New York, NY 10019
(212) 247-2930

BROADWAY ARTISTS' MANAGEMENT CULTURAL TALENT EXCHANGE
99-46 Sixty-Fourth Ave.
New York, NY
(212) 897-6471
Contact: Dr. Sioma Glaser

AGNES BRUNEAU
711 West End Ave., Ste. 5GN
New York, NY 10025
(212) 222-7463

ESTHER BROWN
199 Park Ave., Ste. 1E
New York, NY 10028
(212) 289-4908

MELODY BUNTING
118 West Seventy-Second St., Ste. 1002
New York, NY 10023
(212) 799-4949

BYERS, SCHWALBE & ASSOCIATES, INC.
1 Fifth Ave.
New York, NY 10003
(212) 260-3320
Contact: Montgomery L. Byers

JAMES CALE
166-77 Twenty-Second Ave.
Flushing, NY 11357
(212) 352-5935

CAMEO PRODUCTIONS, LTD.
29 West Sixty-Fifth St.
New York, NY 10023
(212) 787-0244
Contact: Jacqueline Kroschell

CAPITOL STAR ARTIST ENTERPRISES, INC.
1159 Jay St.
Rochester, NY 14611
(716) 328-5565
Contact: Don Redanz

CARID: PERSONALIZED MANAGEMENT FOR THE ARTS
119 West Fifty-Seventh St., Ste. 1620
New York, NY 10019
(212) 586-2832
Contact: David R. Hatfield

CAVU MUSIC ASSOCIATES
15 West Seventy-Second St., Ste. 8D
New York, NY 10023
(212) 873-8110
Contact: Barberi Paull

CENTURY ARTISTS' BUREAU, INC.
866 Third Ave.
New York, NY 10022
(212) 752-3920
Contact: Walter Gould

CLABORNE & ASSOCIATES ARTISTS MANAGEMENT, INC.
166 Lexington Ave.
New York, NY 10016
(212) 288-9031
Contact: Conrad Claborne

GEORGE COCHRAN PRODUCTIONS
225 West Fifty-Seventh St., Ste. 802
New York, NY 10019
(212) 582-1222

COLBERT ARTISTS MANAGEMENT, INC.
111 West Fifty-Seventh St.
New York, NY 10019
(212) 757-0782
Contact: Ann Colbert

COLUMBIA ARTISTS MANAGEMENT, INC.
154 West Fifty-Seventh Street
New York, NY 10019
(212) 757-8344
Contact: Ronald A. Wilford

CONCERT ARTIST REPRESENTATIVE ASSOCIATES
160 East Sixty-Fifth St.
New York, NY 10021
(212) 472-3306
Contact: Natalie S. Lang

CONCERT ARTISTS GUILD, INC.
154 West Fifty-Seventh St.
New York, NY 10019
(212) 757-8344
Contact: Jerome Bunke

CONCERT IDEAS
P.O. Box 669
Woodstock, NY 12498
(914) 679-6069
Contact: Harris Goldberg

CONE ARTISTS REPRESENTATIVES, INC.
250 West Fifty-Seventh St.
New York, NY 10019
(212) 245-8451
Contact: Dorothy Cone

COOPER-GRANT, INC.
711 West End Ave., Ste. 4D North
New York, NY 10025
(212) 222-9539

CORSAIRE PRODUCTIONS
180 Thompson St.
New York, NY 10012
(212) 473-2310
Contact: Charles Marahrens

COUNTERPOINT CONCERTS, INC.
211 West Fifty-Sixth St.
New York, NY 10019
(212) 246-6400
Contact: Peter Mallon

COURTENAY ARTISTS, INC.
411 East Fifty-Third St., Ste. 6F
New York, NY 10022
(212) 832-7025
Contact: Elaine Courtenay

CRISGINA ENTERPRISES
900 Park Ave.
New York, NY 10021
(212) 249-0017

CRITICS CHOICE ARTISTS MANAGEMENT
2067 Broadway
New York, NY 10019
(212) 595-0351
Contact: Norman J. Seaman

WILLIAM DAILEY
226 Lafayette St.
New York, NY 10012
(212) 925-4550

DAIRYMPLE ASSOCIATES
150 West Fifty-Fifth St.
New York, NY 10011
(212) 246-7820
Contact: Jean Dairymple

FAYE DEAN
400 East Fifty-Second St., Ste. 9-F
New York, NY 10022
(212) 753-2492

JOE DEANGELIS MANAGEMENT
79 Kingsland Ave.
Brooklyn, NY 11211
(212) 389-2511

CONNIE DENAVE MANAGEMENT
300 East Seventy-Fourth St.
New York, NY 10021
(212) 737-4805

PETER S. DIGGINS ASSOCIATES
133 West Seventy-First St.
New York, NY 10023
(212) 874-4534

THEA DISPEKER
59 East Fifty-Fourth St.
New York, NY 10022
(212) 421-7676

KATHERINE DOWLING
149 Main St.
East Setauket, NY 11733
(212) 751-2442

BARRY DRAKE-JON IMS AGENCY
The Gables, Halcott Rd.
Fleischmanns, NY 12430
(914) 254-4565
Contact: Barry Drake, Patricia Padla

DREAMSPUN MANAGEMENT & PUBLICITY GROUP
11 Riverside Dr.
New York, NY 10023
(212) 581-1810
Contact: Nina Cranton, Lydia Lilli, Davina Wells

DUBE-ZAKIN MANAGEMENT, INC.
1841 Broadway
New York, NY 10023
(212) 582-0140
Contact: Alexander Dube

JUDITH FINELL MUSIC SERVICES, INC.
155 West Sixty-Eighth St.
New York, NY 10023
(212) 580-4500

DAVID FISHOF
1775 Broadway
New York, NY 10019
(212) 757-1605

JOE FONTANA ASSOCIATES
161 West Fifty-Fourth St.
New York, NY 10019
(212) 247-3043

FOR THE ARTS
33 East Sixtieth St.
New York, NY 10022
(212) 752-7812
Contact: Steven Keith

FRYCEK PRODUCTIONS COMPANY
P.O. Box 1492
Newburgh, NY 12550
(914) 561-6700
Contact: Patricia Smiley

RICHARD FULTON, INC.
101 West Fifty-Seventh St.
New York, NY 10019
(212) 582-4099

FUTERNICK ARTISTS MANAGEMENT, INC.
250 West Fifty-Seventh St.
New York, NY 10019
(212) 582-4222
Contact: Hadassah Futernick

ROBERT GARDINER
610 West End Ave., Ste. B
New York, NY 10024
(212) 873-5666

LYNN GARON MANAGEMENT
1199 Park Ave.
New York, NY 10028
(212) 876-1279

GERSHUNOFF ATTRACTIONS, INC.
502 Park Ave.
New York, NY 10022
(212) 752-5925
Contact: Maxim Gershunoff

CAROL GERSON
145 West Seventy-First St.
New York, NY 10023
(212) 362-4375

ROBERT M. GEWALD MANAGEMENT, INC.
58 West Fifty-Eighth St.
New York, NY 10019
(212) 753-0450

ERNEST GILBERT
61 West Sixty-Second St., Ste. 6F
New York, NY 10023
(212) 246-2809

DAVID GONYA
99 Sixth Ave.
Brooklyn, NY 11217
(212) 789-8528

CELIA B. GOODSTEIN ARTISTS' MANAGEMENT
Linden & Muttontown
East Norwich, NY 11732
(516) 922-0448

WALTER GOULD
866 Third Ave.
New York, NY 10022
(212) 752-3920

PETER GRAVINA
115 East Ninety-Second St.
New York, NY 10028
(212) 369-7086

LLOYD GREENFIELD
30 Rockefeller Plaza
New York, NY 10020
(212) 245-8130

GTN PRODUCTIONS
230 Park Ave., Ste. 460
New York, NY 10169
(212) 599-3032
Contact: George T. Nierenberg

REUBEN GUSS ENTERPRISES, INC.
215 West Ninety-Second St.
New York, NY 10025
(212) 580-7401

HAMLEN-LANDAU MANAGEMENT, INC.
125 West Eighty-Fifth St.
New York, NY 10024
(212) 877-8597
Contact: Charles Hamlen, Edna Landau

MARIKA HANDAKAS ARTISTS' REPRESENTATIVE
139 West Eighty-Second St., Ste. 6E
New York, NY 10024
(212) 787-1978

MICKEY HARMAN
215 Lexington Ave.
New York, NY 10016

TONY HARTMANN ASSOCIATES
250 West Fifty-Seventh St., Ste. 1120
New York, NY 10107
(212) 541-7592

KIM S. HARTSTEIN PERSONAL MANAGEMENT
145 West Fifty-Fifth St., Ste. 2B
New York, NY 10019
(212) 582-1992

DON HENRY
Care of Lyra House
133 West Sixty-Ninth St.
New York, NY 10023
(212) 874-3360

PAT HERMAN
300 Central Park West
New York, NY 10019
(212) 724-6476

KAZUKO HILLYER INTERNATIONAL, INC.
250 West Fifty-Seventh St.
New York, NY 10107
(212) 581-3644
Contact: Dennis Letzler

MARC HOFFMAN
113 Oxford St.
Brooklyn, NY 11235
(212) 889-7460

HOFFMANN MANAGEMENT ASSOCIATES
46 Broad St.
Staten Island, NY 10304
(212) 273-0929
Contact: Beverly Hoffmann

NORMA HURLBURT
2248 Broadway
New York, NY 10024
(212) 874-3710

ICM ARTISTS, LTD.
40 West Fifty-Seventh St.
New York, NY 10019
(212) 556-5600
Contact: Sheldon Gold

IF PRODUCTIONS, INC.
15 Glenby Lane
Brookville, NY 11545
(516) 626-9504

22240 Schoenborn St.
Canoga Park, CA 91304
(213) 883-4865

INTERNATIONAL ARTISTS' MANAGEMENT
111 West Fifty-Seventh St., Ste. 1115
New York, NY 10019
(212) 586-2127
Contact: Joseph A. Scuro

INTERNATIONAL BALLET & FESTIVAL CORPORATION
143 East Twenty-Seventh St.
New York, NY 10016
(212) 889-6000
Contact: Mel Howard

INTERNATIONAL CONCERTS MANAGEMENT
P.O. Box 748, Ansonia Station
New York, NY 10023
(212) 781-5663
Contact: Alexis Skidan

INTERNATIONAL CREATIVE MANAGEMENT
40 West Fifty-Seventh St.
New York, NY 10019
(212) 556-5600

8899 Beverly Blvd.
Los Angeles, CA 90048
(213) 550-4000

INVERSION MUSIC & ART COMPANY, INC.
421 West Fifty-Seventh St., Ste. 1D
New York, NY 10019
(212) 581-8562
Contact: Bozena Checinska

VAL IRVING
527 Madison Ave.
New York, NY 10021
(212) 755-8932

DAVID JONAS
101 West Fifty-Seventh St.
New York, NY 10019
(212) 247-5140

JOYCE AGENCY
435 East Seventy-Ninth St.
New York, NY 10021
(212) 988-3371
Contact: Van Joyce

MELVIN KAPLAN, INC.
1860 Broadway, Ste. 1010
New York, NY 10023
(212) 765-5901

115 College St.
Burlington, VT 05401
(802) 658-2592

H. KAPNER MANAGEMENT
67-24 One-Hundred-Sixty-First St.
Flushing, NY 11365
(212) 591-2773
Contact: Harriet Kapner

MARK KAPPEL
252 West Seventy-Sixth St., Ste. 6E
New York, NY 10023
(212) 724-3889

JERRY KATZ
340 East Sixty-Fourth St.
New York, NY 10021
(212) 421-1714

ALBERT KAY ASSOCIATES, INC. CONCERT ARTISTS' MANAGEMENT
58 West Fifty-Eighth St.
New York, NY 10019
(212) 759-7329

HELEN KEANE
49 East Ninety-Sixth St.
New York, NY 10028
(212) 722-2921

JOHANNA KELLER
54 West Eighty-Fifth St.
New York, NY 10024
(212) 873-2083

IRENE KESSLER, INC.
155 West Sixty-Eighth St.
New York, NY 10023
(212) 496-7292

ALAN KLAUM INTERNATIONAL
35 West Seventy-First St.
New York, NY 10023
(212) 724-0529

BOB KNIGHT AGENCY
185 Clinton Ave.
Staten Island, NY 10301
(212) 448-8420

KOLMAR-LUTH ENTERTAINMENT, INC.
1776 Broadway
New York, NY 10019
(212) 581-5833
Contact: Klaus W. Kolmar

KRAGEN & COMPANY
8 Cadman Plaza West
Brooklyn, NY 11201
(212) 858-2544
Contact: Lynn Volkman

JERRY KRAVAT ENTERTAINMENT SERVICES
205 Lexington Ave.
New York, NY 10016
(212) 758-3333

JUDITH KURZ ENTERPRISES
215 West Ninety-First St.
New York, NY 10024
(212) 873-5723, 737-1336

L&R PRODUCTIONS
16 East Broad St.

Mount Vernon, NY 10552
(914) 668-4488
Contact: Richard Rashbaum

LANDSLIDE MANAGEMENT
119 West Fifty-Seventh St.
New York, NY 10019
Contact: Ted Lehrman, Ruth Landers, Libby Bush

DODIE LEFEBRE ARTISTS' REPRESENTATIVE
498 West End Ave.
New York, NY 10024
(212) 724-8143

JACQUES LEISER ARTISTS' MANAGEMENT, INC.
155 West Sixty-Eighth St.
New York, NY 10023
(212) 595-6414

LEMOYNE MANAGEMENT
140-39 Thirty-Fourth Ave.
Flushing, NY 11354
(212) 539-3032
Contact: E. Schuman-LeMoyne

ADELINE LESLIE ARTISTS' REPRESENTATIVE
233 West Seventy-Seventh St.
New York, NY 10024
(212) 724-8565

HAROLD LEVENTHAL MANAGEMENT, INC.
250 West Fifty-Seventh St.
New York, NY 10107
(212) 586-6553

ROBERT LEVIN ASSOCIATES, INC.
250 West Fifty-Seventh St., Ste. 1332
New York, NY 10107
(212) 586-8906

LEW-BENSON ARTISTS' REPRESENTATIVES
204 West Tenth St.
New York, NY 10014
(212) 691-2571
Contact: Eddie Lew, Ken Benson

LIAISON CONCEPT, LTD.
39 East Seventy-Eighth St.
New York, NY 10021
(212) 988-8980
Contact: Lorraine J. Russo

IRA LIEBERMAN ARTIST REPRESENTATIVE, INC.
11 Riverside Dr.
New York, NY 10023
(212) 877-9859

LIEGNER MANAGEMENT
1860 Broadway
New York, NY 10023
(212) 582-5795
Contact: Judith Liegner

JOSEPH LODATO
111 West Fifty-Seventh St.
New York, NY 10019
(212) 957-9799

ROBERT LOMBARDO ASSOCIATES
61 West Sixty-Second St., Ste. 6F
New York, NY 10023
(212) 586-4453

LUDWIG LUSTIG ARTIST'S MANAGEMENT
225 West Fifty-Seventh St.
New York, NY 10019
(212) 265-1426

LYRA MANAGEMENT
210 Riverside Dr.
New York, NY 10025
(212) 663-4493
Contact: Robert W. Holton

MICHAEL MACE ASSOCIATES, LTD.
315 West Fifty-Seventh St.
New York, NY 10019
(212) 245-7760

ROBERT MARKS
850 Seventh Ave.
New York, NY 10019
(212) 664-1654

MARLOWE CONCERTS BUREAU
698 West End Ave., Ste. 5D
New York, NY 10025
(212) 864-5698
Contact: William E. Yacker

LLOYD MARX
364 West Eighteenth St.
New York, NY 10011
(212) 929-3184

MASADA MUSIC, INC.
888 Eighth Ave.
New York, NY 10019
(212) 757-1953
Contact: Gene Heimlich

MATTHEWS/NAPAL, LTD. ARTIST'S MANAGEMENT
270 West End Ave.
New York, NY 10023
(212) 873-2121
Contact: Ronald J.H. Napal, Thomas Matthews

MAUREL ENTERPRISES, INC.
225 West Thirty-Fourth St., Ste. 1012
New York, NY 10001
(212) 744-7380
Contact: Michael Maurel

MEMNON TALENT CORPORATION
P.O. Box 98
Forest Hills, NY 11375
Contact: Krzysztof Z. Purzycki

METROPOLITAN ARTIST'S MANAGEMENT
140 West End Ave., Ste. 3K
New York, NY 10023
(212) 362-9018
Contact: Ed Baron

RAE METZGER MANAGEMENT
110 West Ninety-Sixth St., Ste. 9D
New York, NY 10025
(212) 749-5464

BRUCE MICHAEL-NEIL FLECKMAN ASSOCIATES
327 Central Park West, Ste. 2-C
New York, NY 10025
(212) 662-5118

VERA MICHAELSON
70 East Tenth St.
New York, NY 10003
(212) 473-5203

GORDON MILLS
1 Rockefeller Plaza
New York, NY 10021
(212) 245-8130

WILLIAM MORRIS AGENCY, INC.
1350 Avenue of the Americas
New York, NY 10019
(212) 586-5100

151 El Camino Dr.
Beverly Hills, CA 90212
(213) 274-7451

2325 Crestmoor Rd.
Nashville, TN 37215
(615) 385-0310

JEFFREY MOSS
850 Seventh Ave.
New York, NY 10019
(212) 586-7344

MOVEMENT ARTS FOUNDATION, INC.
P.O. Box 182
Pomona, NY 10970
(914) 354-1110
Contact: Frances Cott

EDITH MUGDAN ARTISTS MANAGEMENT
84 Prospect Ave.
Douglaston, NY 11363
(212) 224-4415

MUNRO ARTISTS MANAGEMENT
344 West Seventy-Second St.
New York, NY 10023
(212) 877-0468
Contact: Martha Munro

MUSICAL ARTISTS, INC.
119 West Fifty-Seventh St.
New York, NY 10019
(212) 895-1872

120 Elder Rd.
Islip, Long Island, NY 11751
(516) 581-5204
Contact: Susan Pimsleur

MUSKRAT PRODUCTIONS, INC.
44 North Central Ave.
Elmsford, NY 10523
(914) 592-3144
Contact: Linda Simpson

NATIONAL ARTISTS MANAGEMENT COMPANY
165 West Forty-Sixth St., Ste. 1202
New York, NY 10036
(212) 575-1044
Contact: Barry Weissler

NEW YORK ARTISTS BUREAU, INC.
170 West End Ave., Ste. 3N
New York, NY 10023
(212) 799-4445
Contact: Clyde Keutzer

NEW YORK RECITAL ASSOCIATES, INC.
1776 Broadway
New York, NY 10019
(212) 581-1429
Contact: Anne J. O'Donnell

ORANGE BLOSSOM PRODUCTIONS
380 Lexington Ave., Ste. 1119
New York, NY 10017
(212) 687-9000
Contact: Douglas Tuchman

ORGANIC MANAGEMENT
745 Fifth Ave.
New York, NY 10022
(212) 751-3400

PARK RECORDING COMPANY, INC.
200 East Sixty-Sixth St.
New York, NY 10021
(212) 838-2090
Contact: Muriel Zuckerman

PELICAN PRODUCTIONS
3700 East Ave., Ste. 10
Rochester, NY 14618
Contact: Peter Morticelli

PENTACLE
104 Franklin St.
New York, NY 10013
(212) 226-2000
Contact: Ivan Sygoda, Mara Greenberg

PERFORMANCE MARKETING CONSULTANTS
1 Harkness Plaza, Ste. 20D
New York, NY 10023
(212) 581-2571
Contact: Richard Torrence

PERFORMING ARTSERVICES, INC.
325 Spring St.
New York, NY 10013
(212) 243-6153
Contact: Mimi Johnson, Jane Yockel

RENATE PERLS MANAGEMENT
7 West Ninety-Sixth St.
New York, NY 10025
(212) 648-0980

PERROTTA MANAGEMENT
211 West Fifty-Sixth St.
New York, NY 10019
(212) 247-2931

PERZANOWSKI MANAGEMENT
640 West End Ave., Ste. 1B
New York, NY 10024
(212) 787-0517
Contact: Judith Perzanowski

AMATO PETALE ASSOCIATES
415 West Twenty-Fourth St.
New York, NY 10011
(212) 807-8500
Contact: John Amato Petale

PMC INTERNATIONAL
1860 Broadway, Ste. 1201
New York, NY 10023
(212) 541-4620
Contact: Frances George

SUZANNE PRESTON, PERSONAL REPRESENTATIVE
15 West Seventy-Fifth St., Ste. 7D
New York, NY 10023
(212) 595-3734

ESTHER PRINCE MANAGEMENT
101 West Fifty-Seventh St.
New York, NY 10019
(212) 586-7137

PRO MUSICIS
140 West Seventy-Ninth St.
New York, NY 10024
(212) 787-0993
Contact: Jeanine Briefel

PRUITT ASSOCIATES, INC.
819 East 168th St.
Bronx, NY 10459
(212) 589-0400
Contact: Bessie J. Pruitt

GERALD PURCELL
133 Fifth Ave.
New York, NY 10003
(212) 475-7100

KRZYSTOF PURZYOKI
1619 Broadway
New York, NY 10019
(212) 245-8860

JOSEPH RAPP
1650 Broadway
New York, NY 10019
(212) 581-6162

GOMER REES PRODUCTIONS
325 Riverside Dr., Ste. 3
New York, NY 10025
(212) 865-7035

NAOMI RHODES ASSOCIATES, INC.
157 West Fifty-Seventh St.
New York, NY 10019
(212) 956-6544
Contact: Sanders D. Terkell

JOANNE RILE MANAGEMENT
485 Fifth Ave., Ste. 1042
New York, NY 10017
(212) 687-5047

P.O. Box 27539
Philadelphia, PA 19118
(215) 233-2333

RIVA MANAGEMENT
260 West End Ave., Ste. 7A
New York, NY 10023
(212) 874-4892
Contact: Bobbi Tillander

RIVERA MANAGEMENT
251 West Ninety-Eighth St.
New York, NY 10025
(212) 663-8616
Contact: Joseph Rivera, Richard Felton

JACK ROLLINS
130 West Fifty-Seventh St.
New York, NY 10019
(212) 582-1940

ROSATI ARTIST MANAGEMENT
210 East Sixty-Third St., Ste. 8D
New York, NY 10021
(212) 758-5189
Contact: Frank A. Rosati

DEL ROSENFIELD ASSOCIATES
714 Ladd Rd.
Bronx, NY 10471
(212) 549-5687
Contact: Del Rosenfield, Robert Rothschild

CHARLES R. ROTHSCHILD PRODUCTIONS, INC.
330 East Forty-Eighth St.
New York, NY 10017
(212) 752-8753
Contact: Charles R. Rothschild, Maxine Firestone

ROYCE CARLTON, INC.
866 United Nations Plaza
New York, NY 10017
(212) 355-3210
Contact: Carlton S. Sedgeley

HARRY RUBENSTEIN & ASSOCIATES
1 West Eighty-Fifth St.
New York, NY 10024
(212) 496-6958

DICK RUBIN, LTD.
60 West Fifty-Seventh St.
New York, NY 10019
(212) 541-6576

LINDA RUGOFF
135 East Fifty-Fourth St.
New York, NY 10022

RUNAWAY ENTERPRISES
225 Central Park West, Ste. 702A
New York, NY 10024
(212) 580-1747
Contact: Nina Marson

RUSTRON MUSIC PRODUCTIONS
200 Westmoreland Ave.
White Plains, NY 10606
(914) 946-1689
Contact: Rusty Gordon

SALMON & STOKES
380 Riverside Dr., Ste. 3B
New York, NY 10025
(212) 222-2862
Contact: Thomas Salmon, Ms. Sonny Stokes

FRANK SALOMON ASSOCIATES
201 West Fifty-Fourth St., Ste. 4C
New York, NY 10019
(212) 581-5197
Contact: Frank Salomon, Catherine Gevers

SARDOS ARTIST MANAGEMENT CORPORATION
180 West End Ave.
New York, NY 10023
(212) 874-2559
Contact: James Sardos

PHIL SCHAPIRO
1157 West Fifty-Seventh St.
New York, NY 10019
(212) 581-6830

DAVID SCHIFFMANN INTERNATIONAL ARTISTS' MANAGEMENT
58 West Seventy-Second St., Ste. 5A
New York, NY 10023
(212) 877-8111

EDIE F. SCHUR
176 East Seventy-First St.
New York, NY 10021
(212) 734-5100

GEORGE F. SCHUTZ PRESENTATIONS, INC.
320 West End Ave.
New York, NY 10023
(212) 580-7400
Contact: Valerie M. Velella

JIM SCOVOTTI MANAGEMENT
185 West End Ave.
New York, NY 10023
(212) 724-4509

NORMAN SEAMAN ASSOCIATES
2067 Broadway
New York, NY 10019
(212) 595-0351

JACK SEGAL
101 West Fifty-Seventh St.
New York, NY 10019
(212) 265-7489

ERIC SEMON ASSOCIATES, INC.
111 West Fifty-Seventh St., Ste. 1209
New York, NY 10019
(212) 765-1310
Contact: Marianne Semon

ARTHUR SHAFMAN INTERNATIONAL, LTD.
723 Seventh Ave.
New York, NY 10019
(212) 575-0488

BRAD SIMON ORGANIZATION
176 East Seventy-Seventh St.
New York, NY 10021
(212) 988-4962

LINWOOD N. SIMON
405 Park Ave.
New York, NY 10022
(212) 355-3270

JON SMALL MANAGEMENT
166 East Sixty-First St.
New York, NY 10021
(212) 888-0144

MARTHA MOORE SMITH ENTERPRISES
2109 Broadway, Ste. 13-102
New York, NY 10023
(212) 870-5251

E. SNAPP, INC.
87 Robinson Ave.
Glen Cove, NY 11542
(516) 671-9314
Contact: Bette Snapp

ELISE SOBOL MANAGEMENT, INC.
28 Marion Pl.
Huntington Station, NY 11746
(516) 427-5395

SHELDON SOFFER MANAGEMENT, INC.
130 West Fifty-Sixth St.
New York, NY 10019
(212) 757-8060

RUTH K. SOLOMON & ASSOCIATES
4544 Fieldston Rd.
Riverdale, NY 10471
(212) 548-9323

SONGSHOP RECORDING COMPANY
126 West Twenty-Second St.
New York, NY 10011
(212) 691-2707
Contact: Jean Petrucelli

SPECTRUM CONCERTBUREAU
205 East Sixty-Third St.
New York, NY 10021
(212) 753-9527

KUNO SPONHOLZ
350 West Fifty-Fifth St.
New York, NY 10019
(212) 265-3777

FONDA ST. PAUL
101 West Fifty-Seventh St.
New York, NY 10019
(212) 581-4164

STARSTRUCK PRODUCTIONS
701 Seneca St.
Buffalo, NY 14210
(716) 865-2984
Contact: Fred Caserta, Mike Faley

HARRY STEINMAN
15 Central Park West
New York, NY 10023
(212) 751-2156

STEORRA ENTERPRISES
243 West End Ave., Ste. 907
New York, NY 10023
(212) 799-5783
Contact: Lynda L. Ciolek

SULLIVAN & LINDSEY ASSOCIATES
133 West Eighty-Seventh St.
New York, NY 10024
(212) 799-8829

SUTTON ARTISTS' CORPORATION
119 West Fifty-Seventh St.
New York, NY 10019
(212) 977-4870
Contact: Frank Modica, Jr.

PAUL SZILARD PRODUCTIONS, INC.
161 West Seventy-Third St.
New York, NY 10023
(212) 799-4756

THEATOUR
Box 408, Ginger Rd.
High Falls, NY 12440
(914) 687-7522
Contact: Howard Crampton-Smith

TORNAY MANAGEMENT, INC.
127 West Seventy-Second St.
New York, NY 10023
(212) 580-8696
Contact: Sara Tornay

TRM MANAGEMENT, INC.
527 Madison Ave.
New York, NY 10022
(212) 838-3377
Contact: Tittica Roberts Mitchell

LARRY TUNNY
30 Lincoln Plaza
New York, NY 10023
(212) 582-2023

VALEX TALENT AGENCY
105 East Clinton St.
Ithica, NY 14850
(607) 273-3931
Contact: Tom Brennan

SHARON WAGNER ARTISTS' SERVICE
150 West End Ave.
New York, NY 10023
(212) 580-8828

NORBY WALTERS ASSOCIATES
1650 Broadway
New York, NY 10015
(212) 245-3939

WARDEN ASSOCIATES, LTD.
45 West Sixtieth St., Ste. 4K
New York, NY 10023
(212) 246-4994
Contact: William Warden

RAYMOND WEISS ARTIST MANAGEMENT, INC.
300 West Fifty-Fifth St.

New York, NY 10019
(212) 581-8478

JONATHAN WENTWORTH ASSOCIATES, LTD.
5 Lockwood Rd.
Scarsdale, NY 10583
(914) 472-4272
Contact: Kenneth Wentworth

WAYNE WILBUR MANAGEMENT
P.O. Box A-1378, Grand Central Station
New York, NY 10163
(212) 535-6024

WOEMER-BOBRICK ASSOCIATES
54 Greenwich Ave.
New York, NY 10011
(212) 242-3736
Contact: Danielle Woemer, Benson Bobrick

BEVERLY WRIGHT ARTISTS' REPRESENTATIVE
400 East Fifty-Second St.
New York, NY 10022
(212) 826-8806

YOUNG CONCERT ARTISTS, INC.
65 East Fifty-Fifth St.
New York, NY 10022
(212) 759-2541
Contact: Susan Wadsworth

ETHEL ZEVIN
134-45 166th Pl., Ste. 11G
Jamaica, NY 11434
(212) 525-2970

ARTHUR D. ZINBERG
11 East Forty-Fourth St.
New York, NY 10017
(212) 986-7077

MAX ZUBER MANAGEMENT
500 West End Ave.
New York, NY 10024
(212) 580-8241
Contact: Bob Combs

NORTH CAROLINA

ENTERTAINERS' MANAGEMENT & BOOKING AGENCY
P.O. Box 11306
Charlotte, NC 28220
(704) 364-1433
Contact: Bernard Bailey

LINDY S. MARTIN PERSONAL MANAGEMENT
Pinehurst, NC 28374
(919) 295-3303

MOVING MANAGEMENT, INC.
Charlotte, NC 28205
(704) 372-9563
Contact: Mike Wingate

NORTH-SOUTH ARTSCOPE
1914 White Plains Rd.
Chapel Hill, NC 27514
(919) 929-5508
Contact: Mary Nordstrom

SUREFIRE PRODUCTIONS
P.O. Box 1808
Asheville, NC 28802
Contact: Ron Weathers

NORTH DAKOTA

STARCREST PRODUCTIONS, INC.
2516 South Washington St.
Grand Forks, ND 58201
(701) 772-6831
Contact: George Hastings

OHIO

ARTIST PROMOTIONAL BUREAU
6072A Glenway
Brookpark, OH 44142
(216) 267-4537
Contact: Larry Rosen

THE BELKIN-MADURI ORGANIZATION
28001 Chagrin Blvd., Ste. 205
Cleveland, OH 44122
(216) 464-5990
Contact: Chris Maduri, Jim Fox

ELIZABETH BRETT MANAGEMENT
2654 Ruhl Ave.
Columbus, OH 43209
(614) 239-6901

ELWOOD EMERICK
596 Crystal Lake Rd.
Akron, OH 44313
(216) 666-2036

HITCH-A-RIDE MUSIC
P.O. Box 201
Cincinnati, OH 45201
Contact: J.H. Reno

INTERNATIONAL MANAGEMENT GROUP
Cuyahoga Savings Building, Ste. 1300
1 Erieview Plaza
Cleveland, OH 44114
(216) 522-1200
Contact: Arthur L. Lafave, Jr.

LAKEFRONT TALENT AGENCY
P.O. Box 2395
Sandusky, OH 44870
(419) 626-4987
Contact: Larry Myers

DANIEL MORGENSTERN ARTS CONSULTANT
8702 Bessemer Ave.
Cleveland, OH 44127
(216) 271-6247

MULTIPLE ARTS PERFORMANCES
302 South Ashburton, Ste. C100
Columbus, OH 43213
(614) 231-2004
Contact: James Westwater

NATIONAL SERVICES ARTISTS' BUREAU, INC.
2216 Bedford Terrace
Cincinnati, OH 45208
(513) 871-8330
Contact: Carl H.P. Dahlgren

SOLID SOUL PRODUCTIONS
3282 East 119th St.
Cleveland, OH 44120
(216) 231-0772
Contact: Anthony Luke

UMBRELLA ARTISTS MANAGEMENT, INC.
Box 6507, Victoria Parkway
Cincinnati, OH 45206
(513) 861-1500
Contact: Stan Hertzman

OKLAHOMA

ACTION TICKET AGENCY & PROMOTIONS
2609 NW Thirty-Sixth St.
Oklahoma City, OK 73112
(405) 942-0462
Contact: Bobby Boyd

JIM HALSEY COMPANY, INC.
5800 East Skelly St.
Tulsa, OK 74101
(918) 663-3883

OREGON

JEFFREY ROSS MUSIC
P.O. Box 5943
Portland, OR 97208
(503) 281-8322

TOM STINETTE ENTERTAINMENT AGENCY
P.O. Box 06404
Portland, OR 97206
(503) 235-5988

PENNSYLVANIA

CONCERT JAZZ, INC.
1635 Ritner St.
Philadelphia, PA 19145
(215) 755-8198
Contact: Edward Strauman

CULTURAL ENCOUNTERS, INC.
606 Ridge Ave.
Kennett Square, PA 19348
(215) 444-1157
Contact: Marc Pevar

EHRET MUSICAL MANAGEMENT
4622 Pine St.
Philadelphia, PA 19143
(609) 546-8170
Contact: Alexandra F. Ehret

GENERAL MANAGEMENT ASSOCIATES
4110 Monroeville Blvd.
Monroeville, PA 15146
(412) 373-3860
Contact: Richard Foreman

HARLEQUIN ENTERPRISES
604 North St. Clair St.
Pittsburgh, PA 15206
(412) 563-2070
Contact: John Watson

CHUCK KRONZEK MANAGEMENT
P.O. Box 8120
Pittsburgh, PA 15217
(412) 422-7052

STAN LAWRENCE PRODUCTIONS
191 Presidential Blvd.
Bala Cynwyd, PA 19004
(215) 664-4873

LOGSDON ASSOCIATES
P.O. Box 137
New Providence, PA 17560
(717) 284-2063
Contact: Paul K. Logsdon

MASCARA SNAKE PRODUCTIONS
1478 Crafton Blvd.
Pittsburgh, PA 15205
(412) 921-1319
Contact: Bob Bishop

JIM MCCLELLAND ASSOCIATES
2316 Lombard St.
Philadelphia, PA 19146
(215) 545-6856

MARA MEITIS
226 West Rittenhouse Sq., Ste. 2510
Philadelphia, PA 19103
(215) 546-3919

MOTOBOY MOTIONS
1145 East Hortter St.
Philadelphia, PA 19150
(215) 424-3394
Contact: Alan Moss

ALEXANDER MURPHY
Penn Square Building, Ste. 508
Filbert & Juniper Sts.
Philadelphia, PA 19107
(215) 567-2050

NIGHTSTREAM MUSIC
634 Washington Rd.
Pittsburgh, PA 15228
(412) 561-7111
Contact: Sam Balistreri

PROCESS TALENT MANAGEMENT
439 Wiley Ave.
Franklin, PA 16323
(814) 432-4633
Contact: Norman Kelly

F. RANDOLPH ASSOCIATES, INC.
P.O. Box 328
Philadelphia, PA 19105
(215) 567-6662
Contact: F. Randolph Swartz

RAY ROYAL AGENCY
1 Fairway Plaza, Ste. 311
Huntingdon Valley, PA 19006
(215) 947-7743

ALEXANDER J. SCHMERLING ARTISTS' MANAGEMENT
7901 Cobden Rd.
Laverock, PA 19118
(215) 836-7237

SHOWCASE ASSOCIATES, INC.
Benson East, Ste. A-200
Jenkintown, PA 19046
(215) 884-6205
Contact: Helen Adam

SOMMERS-ROSEN, INC.
1405 Locust St.
Philadelphia, PA 19102
(215) 735-8943

SOUTHERN MANAGEMENT BOOKINGS
Box 262, Route 2
Landenberg, PA 19350
Contact: Box Paisley

TENTH HOUR PRODUCTIONS
4470 Brownsville Rd.
Pittsburgh, PA 15236
(412) 621-4734
Contact: Carl M. Grefenstette

WETHERILL ARTIST MANAGEMENT
P.O. Box 45
821 King of Prussia Rd.
Radnor, PA 19087
(215) 688-3081
Contact: Jean Wetherill

ZANE MANAGEMENT, INC.
1529 Walnut St.
Philadelphia, PA 19119
(215) 568-0500
Contact: Lloyd Zane Remick

RHODE ISLAND

ANNE UTTER, PERSONAL REPRESENTATIVE
54 Elm St.
Westerly, RI 02819
(401) 596-2313

SOUTH CAROLINA

CAROLINA ATTRACTIONS, INC.
203 Culver Ave.
Charleston, SC 29407
(803) 766-2500
Contact: Harold Thomas

THE JOE PHILLIPS ORGANIZATION
P.O. Box 5981
Greenville, SC 29607
Contact: Joe Phillips

REED SOUND RECORDS, INC.
120 Mikel Dr.
Summerville, SC 29483
(803) 873-3324
Contact: Haden Reed

MIKE THOMAS MANAGEMENT
P.O. Box 70486
Charleston, SC 29405
(803) 554-6768

SOUTH DAKOTA

INTERMOUNTAIN CONCERTS
P.O. Box 942
Rapid City, SD 57709
(605) 342-7696
Contact: Ron Kohn

TENNESSEE

ALEXANDER TALENT AGENCY
190 Manchester Ave., Ste. B
Nashville, TN 37202
(615) 262-9031

AMERICAN MANAGEMENT
1300 Division St.
Nashville, TN 37202
(615) 256-6898

ATLAS ARTISTS BUREAU
217 East Cedar St.
Goodlettsville, TN 37072
(615) 859-1343

CLIFF AYERS PRODUCTIONS
62 Music Square West
Nashville, TN 37203
(615) 327-4538
Contact: Connie Wright

BOB BEAN TALENT
38 Music Square East
Nashville, TN 37202
(615) 244-9727

BEAVERWOOD TALENT AGENCY & RECORDING STUDIO
133 Walton Ferry Rd.
Hendersonville, TN 37075
(615) 824-2820
Contact: Clyde Beavers

CAJUN COUNTRY, INC.
200 Madison St.
Nashville, TN 37202
(615) 865-0783

X. COSSE MANAGEMENT
730 Curry Rd.
Nashville, TN 37217
(615) 361-0779

CRESCENT MOON TALENT
20 Music Square West
Nashville, TN 37202
(615) 254-7553

BILLY DEATON TALENT AGENCY
1300 Division St.
Nashville, TN 37202
(615) 244-4259

DE SANTO ENTERPRISES
P.O. Box 4796
Nashville, TN 37216
Contact: Duane De Santo

DHARMA ARTIST AGENCY
50 Music Square West

Nashville, TN 37202
(615) 329-0330

AL EMBRY INTERNATIONAL, INC.
1719 West End Ave.
Nashville, TN 37202
(615) 327-4074

THE EXCALIBUR GROUP
Route 3, Sweeney Hollow
Franklin, TN 37064
(615) 794-5712
Contact: Jeff Engle

FARRIS INTERNATIONAL TALENT, INC.
821 Nineteenth Ave., South
Nashville, TN 37202
(615) 329-9264

BILL GOODWIN TALENT AGENCY
1303 North Gallatin Rd.
Nashville, TN 37202
(615) 868-5380

SUSAN HACKNEY ASSOCIATES
7 Music Circle North
Nashville, TN 37202
(615) 244-7976

INTERNATIONAL TALENT MANAGEMENT
1300 Division St.
Nashville, TN 37202
(615) 256-7376

JACK D. JOHNSON
2803 Azalea Pl.
Nashville, TN 37202
(615) 383-6564

CRISTY LANE MUSIC
120 Hickory St.
Nashville, TN 37202
(615) 868-7171

BUDDY LEE ATTRACTIONS, INC.
38 Music Square East, Ste. 300
Nashville, TN 37203
(615) 244-4336
Contact: Tony Conway

DON LIGHT TALENT, INC.
1100 Seventeenth Ave. South
Nashville, TN 37202
(615) 244-3900

LIMELITERS, INC.
50 Music Square West
Nashville, TN 37203
(615) 329-2292

MAINSTREAM MUSIC GROUP
50 Music Square West
Nashville, TN 37203
(615) 320-0808

MANDRELL MANAGEMENT
38 Music Square East
Nashville, TN 37202
(615) 327-0298

MAXCY TALENT AGENCY
50 Music Square West, Ste. 102
Nashville, TN 37203
(615) 329-9671
Contact: Lee Maxcy

LINDA MILLER & ASSOCIATES
1009 Seventeenth Ave. South
Nashville, TN 37202
(615) 327-2026

MONROE'S BLUEGRASS TALENT AGENCY
3819 Dickerson Rd.
Nashville, TN 37202
(615) 868-3333

MUSIC PARK TALENT
50 Music Square West
Nashville, TN 37202
(615) 329-4111

MUSIC ROW TALENT
50 Music Square West, Ste. 501
Nashville, TN 37202
(615) 327-0222

NAPEG TALENT ASSOCIATES, INC.
50 Music Square West
Nashville, TN 37202
(615) 320-1177

CIT NEIFERT & ASSOCIATES
1555-C Lynnfield Rd., Ste. 159
Memphis, TN 38119
(901) 761-0573
Contact: Cit Neifert

NEW DIRECTION ARTIST GUILD
1816 Hayes St.
Nashville, TN 37202
(615) 327-2805

PATHFINDER MANAGEMENT, INC.
P.O. Box 30166
Memphis, TN 38130
(901) 324-5385
Contact: Naomi McGowan

PINNACLE PRODUCTIONS, INC.
P.O. Box 40662
Nashville, TN 37204
Contact: Tommy Overstreet

GEORGE RICHEY MANAGEMENT COMPANY
6 Music Circle North
Nashville, TN 37203
(615) 254-9605

SINGING HILLS TALENT
Ridgetop
Goodlettsville, TN 37072
(615) 859-9507

BOB SPARROW COMPANY
50 Music Square West
Nashville, TN 37202
(615) 327-0995

SRO TALENT
903 Eighteenth Ave. South
Nashville, TN 37202
(615) 329-2010

SSS MANAGEMENT, LTD.
3106 Belmont Blvd.
Nashville, TN 37202
(615) 385-1120

STAGE ONE DEVELOPMENT
2828 Dogwood Place
Nashville, TN 37202
(615) 383-6923

BISHOP SYKES & ASSOCIATES
713 Eighteenth Ave. South
Nashville, TN 37202
(615) 329-9556

TALENTHOUSE
1719 West End Ave., Ste. 1100
Nashville, TN 37202
(615) 320-1187
Contact: Robert Porter

JOE TAYLOR ARTIST AGENCY
2401 Twelfth Ave. South
Nashville, TN 37202
(615) 385-0035

TESSIER TALENT, INC.
505 Canton Pass
Nashville, TN 37202
(615) 865-6602

TOP BILLING, INC.
4301 Hillsboro Rd.
Nashville, TN 37202
(615) 383-8883

TRANS-WORLD ARTIST, INC.
121 Two Mile Pike
Goodlettsville, TN 37072
(615) 859-3800

VARNELL ENTERPRISES, INC.
311 Church St.
Nashville, TN 37202
(615) 259-3131

SMILEY WILSON
845 Springfield Highway
Goodlettsville, TN 37072
(615) 859-2820

LARRY WILT & ASSOCIATES
P.O. Box 22638
Nashville, TN 37202
(615) 859-4457

TEXAS

AMUSEMENT ENTERPRISES
610 White St.
Houston, TX 77007
(713) 864-6561
Contact: Bill Siros

COLONEL BUSTER DOSS PRESENTS
P.O. Box 927, Manchaca Station
Austin, TX 78652
Contact: Buster Doss

BILL FEGAN ATTRACTIONS
8945 Diplomacy Row
Dallas, TX 75247
(314) 725-5051
Contact: Bill Fegan

GDH ENTERPRISES
P.O. Box 634
Sugarland, TX 77478
(713) 980-1839
Contact: Michael K. Hollis

MAD MAN MANAGEMENT
P.O. Box 54
Man's Field, TX 76063
(817) 477-2897
Contact: James Michael Taylor

JANIE PRICE, PERSONAL MANAGER
Ray Price Enterprises
P.O. Box 30384
Dallas, TX 75230
(214) 750-9993

NINA UZICK
9611 Greenwillow Street
Houston, TX 77096
(713) 729-8833

UTAH

JOSEPH LAKE & ASSOCIATES
4105 Morning Star Dr.
Salt Lake City, UT 84117
(801) 278-3587

VERMONT

BRUCE JAMES COMPANY
P.O. Box 439
Lyndonville, VT 05851
(802) 626-3317

NORTHEAST PRODUCTIONS, LTD.
P.O. Box 555
Bristol, VT 05443
(802) 453-2411
Contact: Steven C. Wyer

VIRGINIA

CHECK PRODUCTIONS, INC.
936 Moyer Rd.
Newport News, VA 23602
(804) 877-0762
Contact: Wilson Harrell

EAST COAST ENTERTAINMENT
1901 North Hamilton St.
Richmond, VA 23230
(804) 355-2178
Contact: Dennis Huber

INTERNATIONAL ARTISTS ALLIANCE
P.O. Box 131
Springfield, VA 22150
(703) 451-1404

LEON I. SALOMON ARTISTS' MANAGEMENT
8301 Penobscot Rd.
Richmond, VA 23227
(804) 264-0123

SHORT PUMP ASSOCIATES
P.O. Box 11292
Richmond, VA 23230
(804) 355-4117
Contact: Ken Brown

STEVE THOMAS MANAGEMENT, INC.
P.O. Box 11283
Richmond, VA 23230
(804) 355-2178

WASHINGTON

ARTISTS' ALLIANCE
2235 Willida Lane
Sedro Wooley, WA 98284
(206) 856-4779
Contact: Carol Cunning

HELEN JENSEN ARTISTS' MANAGEMENT
716 Joseph Vance Building
Third & Union
Seattle, WA 98101
(206) 622-7896

WEST VIRGINIA

SHOWCASE ATTRACTIONS
P.O. Box 6687
Wheeling, WV 26003
(614) 758-5812
Contact: R.H. Gallion

WISCONSIN

ARTS SERVICES ASSOCIATES OF MILWAUKEE, INC.
P.O. Box 92222
Milwaukee, WI 53202
(414) 374-5599
Contact: Marc Haupert

SRO ARTISTS
P.O. Box 9532
Madison, WI 53715
(608) 256-9000
Contact: Jeffrey C. Laramie

SKYBLUE MANAGEMENT AGENCY
2323 East Newberry Blvd.
Milwaukee, WI 53211
(414) 963-9315
Contact: Marc M. Dulberger

CANADA

BRITISH COLUMBIA

ROBERT MEYER ARTIST MANAGEMENT
3871 Broadway
Richmond, BC V7E 2Y3
(604) 271-1081

THE MUSIC MANAGEMENT COMPANY
2729 Lake City Way
Burnaby, BC V5A 2Z6
(604) 420-3403
Contact: Donald W. Marsh

ONTARIO

BARR ARTISTS' MANAGEMENT
10 Kew Beach Ave.
Toronto, ON M4L 1B7
(416) 698-2249
Contact: Anne Barr

COLLEGIUM ARTISTS MANAGEMENT
427 Bloor St. West
Toronto, ON M5S 1X7
(416) 920-9797
Contact: Ottie Lockey

CREATIVE INTERNATIONAL, INC.
44 Charles St. West, Ste. 3703
Toronto, ON M4Y 1R8
(416) 967-0874
Contact: Robert J. Abraham

GENERAL ARTS MANAGEMENT, INC.
471 Queen St. East
Toronto, ON M5A 1T9
(416) 363-1468
Contact: Peter J. Sever

DAVID HABER ARTISTS' MANAGEMENT, INC.
553 Queen St. West, Ste. 400
Toronto, ON M5V 2B6
(416) 862-7267

HART-MURDOCK ARTISTS' MANAGEMENT
191 College St.
Toronto, ON M5T 1P9
(416) 595-1886
Contact: Joanne Hart, Anne Murdock

JOHN MEDLAND PRODUCTIONS
334 Dufferin St.
Toronto, ON
(416) 536-4882

PHOENIX ARTISTS' MANAGEMENT, LTD.
425½ Church St.
Toronto, ON M4Y 2C3
(416) 964-6464
Contact: Kathy Kernohan

PIZAZZ PRODUCTIONS
35 Hambly Ave.
Toronto, ON M4E 2R5
(416) 699-3359
Contact: Craig Nicholson

SRO PRODUCTIONS, INC.
Care of Oak Manor
12261 Yonge St.
Oak Ridges, ON L0G 1P0
(416) 881-3212

WILLIAM SEIP MANAGEMENT, INC.
P.O. Box 413
Waterloo, ON N2J 4A9
(519) 885-6570

STANLEY SOLOMON CONCERT ARTISTS' MANAGEMENT
290 Berkeley St.
Toronto, ON M5A 2X5
(416) 967-7755

Contact: Ray Danniels

ANN SUMMERS INTERNATIONAL
P.O. Box 188, Station A
Toronto, ON M5W 1B2
(416) 362-1422
Contact: Ann Summers Dossena

RICHARD VON HANDSCHUH
411 Duplex Ave. Ste. 2018
Toronto, ON M4R 1V2
(416) 489-2762

QUEBEC

ARS MUSICALI, INC.
231 Ouest Notre Dame
Montreal, PQ H2Y 1T4
(514) 849-6587
Contact: Marcel Bousquet

FRANCOISE CHARTRAND, INC.
129 Rue Prince Arthur, E
Montreal, PQ H2X 1B6
(514) 844-8694

PAUL EUGENE JOBIN
1036 Pere Marquette
Quebec, PQ G1S 2B2
(418) 688-1427

MICHAEL REGENSTREIF MANAGEMENT
200 Kensington Ave., Ste. 510
Westmount, PQ H3Z 2G7
(514) 935-5066

Personal Managers Index

A

B

C

D

E

F

G

H

I

J

K

L

M

N

O

P

R

S

T

VII. TRADE AND INDUSTRY

Record Companies
Independent Record Producers
Music Publishers

Record Companies

U.S. record companies are listed alphabetically. If a firm has more than one office, all addresses are included within the same listing.

A

A&M RECORDS
1416 North LaBrea
Los Angeles, CA 90028
(213) 469-2411

595 Madison Avenue
New York, NY 10022
(212) 826-0477

ATV MUSIC CORPORATION
6255 Sunset Boulevard
Hollywood, CA 90028
(213) 462-6933

888 Seventh Avenue
New York, NY 10106
(212) 977-5680

1217 Sixteenth Avenue South
Nashville, TN 37212
(615) 327-2753

ALLIGATOR RECORDS
6249 North Magnolia Avenue
Chicago, IL 60660
(312) 973-7736

THE AMERICAN RECORDING COMPANY
2323 Corinth Avenue
Los Angeles, CA 90064
(213) 479-8522

APPLAUSE RECORDS
258 South Beverly Drive
Beverly Hills, CA 90212
(213) 274-9301

ARISTA RECORDS
6 West Fifty-Seventh Street
New York, NY 10019
(212) 489-7400

1888 Century Park East
Suite 1510
Los Angeles, CA 90067
(213) 553-1777

ARMAGEDDON RECORDS LIMITED
432 Moreland Avenue
Atlanta, GA 30307
(404) 525-1679

ATLANTIC RECORDING CORPORATION
75 Rockefeller Plaza
New York, NY 10019
(212) 484-6000

9229 Sunset Boulevard
Los Angeles, CA 90069
(213) 278-9230

AUDIOFIDELITY ENTERPRISES, INC.
221 West Fifty-Seventh Street
New York, NY 10019
(212) 757-7111

B

BANG RECORDS
2107 Faulkner Road, NE
Atlanta, GA 30324
(404) 329-9535

BEARSVILLE RECORDS, INC.
3300 Warner Boulevard
Burbank, CA 91505
(213) 846-9090

P.O. Box 135, Wittenberg Road
Bearsville, NY 12409
(914) 679-7303

BLIND PIG RECORDS
208 South First Street
Ann Arbor, MI 48103
(313) 428-7216

3409 Santa Clara
El Cerrito, CA 94530
(415) 526-0373

1713 North Austin
Chicago, IL 60639
(312) 745-0760

BLUE SKY RECORDS, INC.
745 Fifth Avenue, Suite 1803
New York, NY 10022
(212) 751-3400

THE BOARDWALK ENTERTAINMENT COMPANY
9884 Santa Monica Boulevard
Beverly Hills, CA 90212
(213) 550-6363

200 West Fifty-Eighth Street
New York, NY 10019
(212) 765-5103

BUDDAH RECORDS, INC.
1790 Broadway
New York, NY 10019
(212) 582-6900

BUTTERMILK RECORDS
1310 Tulane
Houston, TX 77008
(713) 864-0705

C

CBS RECORDS
51 West Fifty-Second Street
New York, NY 10019
(212) 975-4321

1801 Century Park West
Los Angeles, CA 90067
(213) 556-4700

49 Music Square West
Nashville, TN 37203
(615) 259-4321

CADENCE JAZZ RECORDS
Cadence Building
Redwood, NY 13679
(315) 287-2852

CAPITOL RECORDS, INC.
1750 North Vine Street

Hollywood, CA 90028
(213) 462-6252

1370 Avenue of The Americas
New York, NY 10019
(212) 757-7470

29 Music Square East
Nashville, TN 37203
(615) 244-7770

CAPRICORN RECORDS, INC.
561 Cotton Avenue
Macon, GA 31201
(912) 745-8511

CASABLANCA RECORDS
8255 Sunset Boulevard
Los Angeles, CA 90046
(213) 650-8300

CELESTIAL RECORDS
1560 North LaBrea
Los Angeles, CA 90028
(213) 467-7644

CHARTA RECORDS
44 Music Square East
Nashville, TN 37203
(615) 255-2175

CHRYSALIS RECORDS
9255 Sunset Boulevard
Los Angeles, CA 90069
(213) 550-0171

115 East Fifty-Seventh Street
New York, NY 10022
(212) 935-8750

COLUMBIA SPECIAL PRODUCTIONS
51 West Fifty-Second Street
New York, NY 10019
(212) 975-4126

COMPOSERS RECORDINGS, INC.
170 West Seventy-Fourth Street
New York, NY 10023
(212) 873-1250

CONCORD JAZZ, INC.
P.O. Box 845
Concord, CA 94522
(415) 682-6770

CONTEMPORARY RECORDS, INC.
P.O. Box 2628
Los Angeles, CA 90028
(213) 466-1633

CREAM RECORDS, INC.
8025 Melrose Avenue
Los Angeles, CA 90046
(213) 655-0944

1320 South Lauderdale
Memphis, TN 38106
(901) 775-3790

CRYSTAL CLEAR RECORDS, INC.
225 Kearny Street
San Francisco, CA 94108
(415) 398-3100

D

DJM RECORDS
119 West Fifty-Seventh Street
New York, NY 10019
(212) 581-3420

DANI RECORDS
P.O. Box 315
Cleveland, OH 44127
(216) 429-1559

DARVA RECORDS
8914 Georgian Drive
Austin, TX 78753
(512) 836-3201

DIRECT DISK LABS
16 Music Circle South
Nashville, TN 37203
(615) 256-1680

DISCWASHER, INC.
1407 North Providence Road
Columbia, MO 65201
(314) 449-0941

DISNEYLAND/VISTA RECORDS
350 South Buena Vista Street
Burbank, CA 91521
(213) 840-1000

E

EMI-AMERICA/LIBERTY RECORDS
6920 Sunset Boulevard
Los Angeles, CA 90028
(213) 461-9141

1370 Avenue of The Americas
New York, NY 10019
(212) 757-7470

29 Music Square East
Nashville, TN 37203
(615) 244-9596

THE EAST ALLEGHENY RECORDS GROUP
335 Hidenwood Drive
Newport News, VA 23606
(804) 595-9000

6104 Cahuenga Boulevard
North Hollywood, CA 90039
(213) 762-1001

8815 Connecticut Avenue
Chevy Chase, MD 20015
(301) 657-0100

ELEKTRA/ASYLUM/NONESUCH RECORDS
962 North LaCienega
Los Angeles, CA 90069
(213) 655-8280

665 Fifth Avenue
New York, NY 10022
(212) 355-7610

1216 Seventeenth Avenue South
Nashville, TN 37212
(615) 320-7525

EXCELSIOR RECORDS
7500 Excelsior Boulevard
Minneapolis, MN 55426
(612) 932-7869

7100 Tujunga
North Hollywood, CA 91605
(213) 764-5050

P.O. Box 323
Nashville, TN 37221
(615) 646-0049

F

FANTASY/PRESTIGE/MILESTONE/STAX
Tenth & Parker Streets
Berkeley, CA 94710
(415) 549-2500

FISH-HEAD RECORDS
P.O. Box 399
Bay City, MI 48707
(517) 893-8321

FLYING FISH RECORDS
1304 West Schubert
Chicago, IL 60614
(312) 528-5455

FOLKWAYS RECORDS
43 West Sixty-First Street
New York, NY 10023
(212) 586-7260

G

GNP-CRESCENDO RECORDS
8400 Sunset Boulevard
Los Angeles, CA 90069
(213) 656-2614

GEFFEN RECORDS
9126 Sunset Boulevard
Los Angeles, CA 90069
(213) 278-9010

GEMCOM, INC.
5488 Griffin Road
Fort Lauderdale, FL 33314
Cable: GILMADCO

2769 West Pico Boulevard
Los Angeles, Ca 90006
(213) 734-3650

P.O. Box 5087, FDR Station
New York, NY 10022
(212) 688-2818

GHOST RECORDS
1905 Pesos Place
Kalamazoo, MI 49008
(616) 375-2641

GLOLITE RECORDS
827 Thomas St.
Memphis, TN 38107
(901) 525-0540

GRAMAVISION, INC.
P.O. Box, 2772, Grand Central Station
New York, NY 10163
(212) 674-1562

GREAT SOUTHERN RECORD COMPANY, INC.
P.O. Box 13977
New Orleans, LA 70185
(504) 482-4211

GUSTO RECORDS, INC.
1900 Elm Hill Pike
Nashville, TN 37210
(615) 889-8000

H

HAPPY JAZZ RECORDS
P.O. Box 66
San Antonio, TX 78291

522 River Walk
San Antonio, TX 78205

HARTSONG CORPORATION
5006 Vineland Avenue
North Hollywood, CA 91601
(213) 766-5281

HEADFIRST RECORDS, INC.
9000 Sunset Boulevard, Suite 611
Los Angeles, CA 90069
(213) 550-1010

HICKORY RECORDS, INC.
2510 Franklin Road
Nashville, TN 37204
(615) 385-3031

HULA RECORDS, INC.
2290 Alahao Place, Building C
Honolulu, HI 96819
(808) 847-4608

I

IMPROVISING ARTISTS, INC.
26 Jane Street
New York, NY 10014
(212) 243-2018

INTERNATIONAL RECORD SYNDICATE
1416 North LaBrea
Hollywood, CA 90028
(213) 469-2411

ISLAND RECORDS, INC.
444 Madison Avenue
New York, NY 10022
(212) 355-6550

7720 Sunset Boulevard
Los Angeles, CA 90046
(213) 874-7760

J

JAMIE RECORDS
919 North Broad Street
Philadelphia, PA 19123
(215) 232-8383

JAZZ COMPOSER'S ORCHESTRA ASSOCIATION, INC.
500 Broadway
New York, NY 10012
(212) 925-2121

JAZZOLOGY-GHB RECORDS
3008 Wadsworth Mill Place
Decatur, GA 30032
(404) 288-1480

JET RECORDS, INC.
9959 Beverly Grove Drive
Beverly Hills, CA 90210
(213) 553-6801

JUNE APPAL RECORDINGS
Box 743
Whitesburg, KY 41858
(606) 633-9958

K

KALEIDOSCOPE RECORDS
P.O. Box O
El Cerrito, CA 94530
(415) 527-6242

KICKING MULE RECORDS, INC.
P.O. Box 158
Alderpoint, CA 95411
(707) 926-5312

KIRSHNER RECORDS
1370 Avenue of The Americas
New York, NY 10019
(212) 489-0440

L

LA LOUISIANNE RECORDS, INC.
711 Stevenson Street
Lafayette, LA 70501
(318) 234-5577

LAND O'JAZZ RECORDS
P.O. Box 26393
New Orleans, LA 70126
(504) 241-4246

LIBRARY OF CONGRESS MOTION PICTURE, BROADCASTING & RECORDED SOUND DIVISION
Recording Laboratory
Washington, D.C. 20540
(202) 287-5509

LIFESONG RECORDS, INC.
488 Madison Avenue
New York, NY 10022
(212) 752-3033

LITTLE DAVID RECORDINGS, INC.
8033 Sunset Boulevard, Suite 1037
Los Angeles, CA 90046
(213) 876-9602

LUCIFER RECORDS
P.O. Box 263
Hasbrouck Heights, NJ 07604
(201) 288-8935

M

MCA RECORDS, INC.
70 Universal City Plaza
Universal City, CA 91608
(213) 508-4000

10 East Fifty-Third Street
New York, NY 10022
(212) 888-9700

27 Music Square East
Nashville, TN 37203
(615) 244-8944

MSS RECORDS, INC.
P.O. Box 429
Sheffield, AL 35660
(205) 381-9200

MAJEGA RECORDS
240 East Radcliffe Drive
Claremont, CA 91711
(714) 624-0677

MESSENGER RECORDS
421 South Main Street
Memphis, TN 38103

P.O. Box 25066
Nashville, TN 37202
(615) 885-0475

MILL CITY RECORDS
P.O. Box 3759
Minneapolis, MN 55403
(612) 452-2105

MIRROR RECORDS, INC.
645 Titus Avenue
Rochester, NY 14617
(716) 544-3500

MODERN RECORDS
10 East Forty-Ninth Street
New York, NY 10017
(212) 355-3905

MONITOR RECORDS
156 Fifth Avenue
New York, NY 10010
(212) 989-2323

MONMOUTH/EVERGREEN RECORDS
1697 Broadway, Suite 1201
New York, NY 10019
(212) 757-5105

MONUMENT RECORDS
21 Music Square East
Nashville, TN 37203
(615) 244-6565

MOONLIGHT RECORDS
P.O. Box 184
Chapel Hill, NC 27514
(919) 967-6666

THE MOSS MUSIC GROUP, INC.
48 West Thirty-Eighth Street
New York, NY 10018
(212) 944-9560

MOTOWN RECORDS
6255 Sunset Boulevard
Los Angeles, CA 90028
(213) 468-3500

MUSE RECORDS
160 West Seventy-First Street

New York, NY 10023
(212) 873-2020

MYSTIC RECORDS
6277 Selma Avenue
Los Angeles, CA 90028
(213) 464-9667

N

NASHBORO RECORD COMPANY
1011 Woodland Street
Nashville, TN 37206
(615) 227-5081

NEMPEROR RECORDS, INC.
888 Seventh Avenue
New York, NY 10019
(212) 541-6210

NEOSTAT MUSIC COMPANY
425 Bryn Mawr
Birmingham, MI 48009
(313) 538-4444

NESSA RECORDS
5404 North Kimball Avenue
Chicago, IL 60625
(312) 588-1204

NIRVANA RECORDS
1145 Green Street
Manville, NJ 08835
(201) 725-4366

O

ORIGINAL SOUND RECORDS
7120 Sunset Boulevard
Los Angeles, CA 90046
(213) 851-2500

ORION MASTER RECORDINGS, INC.
P.O. Box 4087
5840 Busch Drive
Malibu, CA 90265
(213) 457-3370

OVATION RECORDS
1249 Waukegan Road
Glenview, IL 60025
(312) 729-7300

803 Eighteenth Avenue
Nashville, TN 37203
(615) 327-4871

P

PA ENTERPRISES, INC.
John Hancock Center, Suite 5404
Chicago, IL 60611
(312) 337-5643

PM RECORDS, INC.
20 Martha Street
Woodcliff Lake, NJ 07675
(201) 391-2486

PABLO RECORDS, INC.
451 North Canon Drive
Beverly Hills, Ca 90210
(213) 274-9831

PACIFIC ARTS CORPORATION
P.O. Box 22770
Carmel, CA 93922
(408) 624-4704

PANINI RECORDS
P.O. Box 15808
Honolulu, HI 96815
(808) 947-4985

PARADISE RECORDS, INC.
4720 Magnolia Boulevard
Burbank, CA 91505
(213) 846-9090

PASSPORT RECORDS, INC.
3619 Kennedy Road
South Plainfield, NJ 07080
(201) 753-6100

PETERS INTERNATIONAL, INC.
619 West Fifty-Fourth Street
New York, NY 10019
(212) 246-2400

PHILADELPHIA INTERNATIONAL RECORDS
309 South Broad Street
Philadelphia, PA 19107
(215) 985-0900

PHILLY JAZZ
P.O. Box 8167
Philadelphia, PA 19101

P.O. Box 232
West Hurley, NY 12491
(914) 338-7640

PHILO RECORDS, INC.
The Barn
North Ferrisburg, VT 05473
(802) 425-2111

PHOENIX JAZZ RECORDS, INC.
P.O. Box 3
Kingston, NJ 08528

PICKWICK RECORDS
7500 Excelsior Boulevard
Minneapolis, MN 55426
(612) 932-7869

PLANET RECORDS
9130 Sunset Boulevard
Los Angeles, CA 90069
(213) 275-4710

PLATINUM RECORDS (MUSIC FACTORY)
P.O. Box 4173
Miami, FL 33141
(305) 757-0900

POLYDOR RECORDS, INC.
810 Seventh Avenue
New York, NY 10019
(212) 399-7075

6255 Sunset Boulevard
Los Angeles, CA 90028
(213) 466-9574

POLYGRAM CLASSICS
810 Seventh Avenue
New York, NY 10019
(212) 399-7000

POLYGRAM CORPORATION
450 Park Avenue
New York, NY 10022
(212) 888-9800

Q

QWEST RECORDS
7250 Beverly Boulevard, Suite 207
Los Angeles, CA 90036
(213) 934-4711

R

RCA RECORDS
1133 Avenue of The Americas
New York, NY 10036
(212) 598-5900

6363 Sunset Boulevard
Los Angeles, CA 90028
(213) 468-4000

30 Music Square West
Nashville, TN 37203
(615) 244-9880

RMS TRIAD PRODUCTIONS
30125 John Road
Madison Heights, MI 48071
(313) 585-8885

RSO RECORDS
8335 Sunset Boulevard
Los Angeles, CA 90069
(213) 650-1234

1775 Broadway
New York, NY 10019
(212) 975-0700

RECORD COMPANY OF THE SOUTH
5220 Essen Lane
Baton Rouge, LA 70808
(504) 766-3233

REGENCY RECORDS, INC.
1116 North Cory Avenue
Los Angeles, CA 90069
(213) 278-5131

REQUEST RECORDS
5937 Ravenswood Road
Fort Lauderdale, FL 33312
(305) 966-0680

REUBEN RECORDS
8537 Sunset Boulevard, No. 2
Los Angeles, CA 90069
(213) 657-8852

RHYTHMS PRODUCTIONS
P.O. Box 34485
Los Angeles, CA 90034
(213) 836-4678

RIVA RECORDS, INC.
232 East Sixty-First Street
New York, NY 10021
(212) 750-9494

ROLLING STONES RECORDS
75 Rockefeller Plaza
New York, NY 10019
(212) 484-6411

ROUNDER RECORDS CORPORATION
186 Willow Avenue
Somerville, MA 02144
(617) 354-0700

S

SALSOUL RECORDS
401 Fifth Avenue
New York, NY 10016
(212) 889-7340

SANDCASTLE RECORDS
157 West Fifty-Seventh Street
New York, NY 10019
(212) 582-6135

4045½ Radford Avenue
Studio City, CA 91604
(213) 985-7933

337 Rue Chartres
New Orleans, LA 70130
(504) 561-0531

SCOTTI BROTHERS RECORDS
2114 Pico Boulevard
Santa Monica, CA 90404
(213) 450-3193

SESAME STREET RECORDS
1 Lincoln Plaza
New York, NY 10023
(212) 874-2700

SIERRA/BRIAR RECORDS
P.O. Box 5853
Pasadena, CA 91107
(213) 355-0181

SIRE RECORDS
3 East Fifty-Fourth Street
New York, NY 10022
(212) 832-0950

3300 Warner Boulevard
Burbank, CA 91510
(213) 846-9090

SIVATT MUSIC COMPANY, INC.
P.O. Box 7172
Greenville, SC 29610
(803) 269-5529

SKYLITE-SING, INC.
1008 Seventeenth Avenue South
Nashville, TN 37212
(615) 327-4557

SLASH RECORDS
7381 Beverly Boulevard
Los Angeles, CA 90036
(213) 937-4660

SMITHSONIAN INSTITUTION PERFORMING ARTS DIVISION
Washington, D.C. 20560
(202) 381-6525

SOLAR RECORDS
9044 Melrose Avenue, Suite 200
Los Angeles, CA 90069
(213) 859-1717

SOUL CITY RECORDS
10609 Budlong
Los Angeles, Ca 90044
(213) 777-9393

PHIL SPECTOR INTERNATIONAL
P.O. Box 69529
Los Angeles, CA 90069
(213) 846-9900

STYLETONE RECORDS
254 East Twenty-Ninth Street
Suite 7
Los Angeles, CA 90011
(213) 746-2923

SWEETSONG RECORDING
P.O. Box 2041
Parkersburg, WV 26101
(304) 485-0525

SYMPOSIUM RECORDS
204 Fifth Avenue
Minneapolis, MN 55414
(612) 331-5750

T

TK RECORDS
495 SE Tenth Court
Hialeah, FL 33010
(305) 888-1685

65 East Fifty-Fifth Street
New York, NY 10022
(212) 752-0160

TABU RECORDS
9911 West Pico Boulevard
Los Angeles, CA 90035
(213) 277-1097

TAKOMA RECORDS & STUDIOS
9255 Sunset Boulevard
Los Angeles, CA 90069
(213) 550-0171

TEROCK RECORDS
P.O. Box 4740
Nashville, TN 37216
(615) 361-5356

20TH CENTURY FOX RECORDS
8544 Sunset Boulevard
Los Angeles, CA 90069
(213) 657-8210

U

UNICORN RECORDS
8615 Santa Monica Boulevard
Los Angeles, CA 90069
(213) 652-2070

UNLIMITED GOLD RECORDS
12403 Ventura Court
Studio City, CA 91604
(213) 760-1665

V

VANGUARD RECORDING SOCIETY
71 West Twenty-Third Street
New York, NY 10010
(212) 255-7732

VARESE SARABANDE RECORDS, INC.
13006 Saticoy Street
North Hollywood, CA 91605
(213) 764-1172

VEE JAY INTERNATIONAL MUSIC
131 East Magnolia Boulevard
Burbank, CA 91502
(213) 849-2469

W

WATT WORKS, INC.
Willow, NY 12495
(914) 688-5373

WEA INTERNATIONAL, INC.
75 Rockefeller Plaza
New York, NY 10019
(212) 484-7100

WARNER BROTHERS RECORDS
3300 Warner Boulevard
Burbank, CA 91505
(213) 846-9090

3 East Fifty-Fourth Street
New York, NY 10022
(212) 832-0600

1706 Grand Avenue
Nashville, TN 37212
(615) 256-4282

WHITE ROCK RECORDS, INC.
401 Wintermantle Avenue
Scranton, PA 18505
(717) 343-6718

WINDHAM HILL RECORDS
247 High Street
Palo Alto, CA 94301
(415) 329-0647

WORD RECORDS
4800 West Waco Drive
Waco, TX 76703
(817) 772-7650

X

XANADU RECORDS LIMITED
3242 Irwin Avenue
Kingsbridge, NY 10463
(212) 549-3655

Y

YAZOO RECORDS, INC.
245 Waverly Place
New York, NY 10014
(212) 255-3698

Independent Record Producers

U.S. independent record producers are listed alphabetically.

A

ADS AUDIO VISUAL PRODUCTIONS
115 Hillwood Avenue
Falls Church, VA 22046
(202) 536-9000

6464 Sunset Boulevard
Los Angeles, CA 90028
(213) 465-3672

A/S PRODUCTIONS
441 La Salle Street
Chicago, IL 60610
(312) 644-2044

AVI RECORD PRODUCTIONS
7060 Hollywood Boulevard, Suite 1212
Hollywood, CA 90028
(213) 462-7151

AIR TRANS RECORDS, INC.
P.O. Box 28835
Memphis, TN 38128
(901) 386-7360

AKRON SOUND PRODUCTIONS
P.O. Box F-161
Akron, OH 44308
(216) 688-9113

ALJEAN RECORDS
7 Colonial Avenue
Myerstown, PA 17067
(717) 866-5067

ALL EARS PRODUCTIONS
7033 Sunset Boulevard, Suite 309
Hollywood, CA 90028
(213) 465-3990

ALL-MARTIN PRODUCTIONS, INC.
9701 Taylorsville Road
Louisville, KY 40299
(502) 267-9658

AMALISA PRODUCTIONS
P.O. Box 4559
Long Island City, NY 11104
(212) 361-2582

AMBIENTE MUSIC PRODUCTIONS, INC.
Box 91120
Worldway Postal Center
Los Angeles, CA 90056
(213) 641-0178

AMERICAN CREATIVE ENTERTAINMENT, LTD.
1616 Pacific Avenue, Suite 818
Atlantic City, NJ 08401
(609) 347-0484

ANATOM MUSIC CORPORATION, INC.
203 West Sixth Avenue
Cherry Hill, NJ 08002
(609) 662-0096

ANDREWS COMMUNICATIONS COMPANY
3410 Avenue R
Lubbock, TX 79412
(806) 744-5590

FREDRIC W. ANSIS
2029 Century Park East
Los Angeles, CA 90067
(213) 553-6666

APON RECORD COMPANY, INC.
44-16 Broadway
Box 3082 Steinway Station
Long Island City, NY 11103
(212) 721-5599

MIKE APPEL PRODUCTIONS
330 East Thirty-Ninth Street, Suite H
New York, NY 10016
(212) 867-7775

APPLEBEE MUSIC, INC.
114 El Hemmorro
Carmel Valley, CA 93924
(408) 659-3666

APPLEWOOD STUDIOS
680 Indiana Street
Golden, CO 80401
(303) 279-2500

APPROPRIATE PRODUCTIONS
474 Atchison Street
Pasadena, CA 91104
(213) 463-8400

ARGON PRODUCTIONS, INC.
P.O. Box 325
Englewood, NJ 07631
(201) 567-7538

ARGONAUT MUSIC
P.O. Box 32044
San Jose, CA 95152
(408) 258-6000

ARGUS RECORD PRODUCTIONS
P.O. Box 58
Glendora, NJ 08029
(609) 939-0034

ARISTON PRODUCTIONS
2047 Deborah Drive
Atlanta, GA 30345
(404) 325-9916

PETER ASHER
644 North Doheny Drive
Los Angeles, CA 90069
(213) 273-9433

ASTRAL PRODUCTIONS, INC.
First National Bank Towers, Box 4527
Topeka, KS 66604
(913) 233-9716

AUDIGRAM, INC.
3501 Belmont Boulevard
Nashville, TN 37215
(615) 383-8318

AURA PRODUCTIONS
7911 Willoughby Avenue
Los Angeles, CA 90046
(213) 656-9373

AUSPEX RECORDS
12188 Laurel Terrace Drive
Studio City, CA 91604
(213) 877-1078

AUTUMN PRODUCTIONS, INC.
3810 Cavalier Street
Garland, TX 75045
(214) 494-3494

AZURE RECORDS
1450 Terrell Street
Beaumont, TX 77701
(713) 832-0748

B

BAS ENTERPRISES
5925 Kirby Drive, Suite 226
Houston, TX 77005
(713) 522-2713

BC ENTERPRISES OF MEMPHIS, INC.
726 East McLemore Street
Memphis, TN 38106
(901) 947-2553

B-C RECORDING STUDIO
8244 Fairview Road
Elkins Park, PA 19117
(215) 635-6441

B-H PRODUCTIONS, INC.
P.O. Box 49259
Los Angeles, CA 90049
(213) 652-7239

BAKER, HARRIS & YOUNG
225 South Fifteenth Street,
Suites, 817-819
Philadelphia, PA 19102
(215) 546-4683

RAY BAKER PRODUCTIONS, INC.
1609 Hawkins Street
Nashville, TN 37203
(615) 329-1323

BAND BOX RECORDING COMPANY
P.O. Box 15477
Lakewood, CO 80215
(303) 232-4387

RUE BARCLAY ENTERPRISES
7436 Genesta Avenue
Van Nuys, CA 91406
(213) 342-2636

STEVE BARRI
Care of Warner Brothers Records, Inc.
3300 Warner Boulevard
Burbank, CA 91510
(213) 846-9090

JEFF BARRY ENTERPRISES, INC.
9100 Sunset Boulevard, Suite 200
Los Angeles, CA 90069
(213) 550-8280

BASIC RECORDS
1309 Celesta Way
Sellersburg, IN 47172
(812) 246-2959

ABDUL BASIT MUSIC, INC.
152 Roseville Avenue, Suite 4-C
Newark, NJ 07107
(201) 675-6995

BEAUTIFUL MUSIC UNLIMITED, LTD.
545 Fifth Avenue, Suite 1205
New York, NY 10017
(212) 582-8800

GARY BECK PRODUCTIONS
P.O. Box 6390
Corpus Christi, TX 78411
(512) 854-7376

BEE/ALEXANDER PRODUCTIONS, INC.
1100 Glendon, Suite 2129
Los Angeles, CA 90024
(213) 208-7871

BEE HIVE JAZZ RECORDS
1130 Colfax Street
Evanston, IL 60201
(312) 328-5593

BEE JAY PRODUCTIONS
5000 Eggleston Avenue
Orlando, FL 32810
(305) 293-1781

THOM BELL PRODUCTIONS
117 South Main Street, Suite 200
Seattle, WA 98104
(206) 682-5278

BENDER PRODUCTIONS
1320 West Columbia Street
Chicago, IL 60626
(312) 764-8945

ART BENION PRODUCTIONS
1560 North LaBrea
Los Angeles, CA 90022
(213) 467-7644

BENT OAK MUSIC
246 Oakborough Drive
O'Fallon, MO 63661
(314) 625-3488

THE BERKLEY MUSIC GROUP
108 Berkley Drive
Madison, TN 37115
(615) 868-3407

HAL BERNARD ENTERPRISES, INC.
2181 Victory Parkway
Cincinnati, OH 45206
(513) 861-1500

JACK BIELAN PRODUCTIONS
6381 Hollywood Boulevard, Suite 307
Hollywood, CA 90028
(213) 465-3530

BIG SHOT PRODUCTIONS, INC.
161-08 Forty-Sixth Avenue
Flushing, NY 11358
(212) 353-4672

BIL-MAR PRODUCTIONS
8455 Beverly Boulevard, Suite 308
Los Angeles, CA 90048
(213) 653-7250

BIRC RECORDS
601 East Blacklidge Drive
Tucson, AZ 85705
(602) 882-9016

BIRD PRODUCTIONS
1946 North Hudson Avenue
Chicago, IL 60614
(312) 787-6060

MICHAEL R. BIRZON
Main Street
Bailey, NC 27807
(919) 235-4933

BLACK DIAMOND MUSIC
Box 28800
Philadelphia, PA 19151
(215) 477-1148

BLUE CHEK MUSIC, INC.
Saw Mill River Road
Ardsley, NY 10502
(914) 592-3479

BLUE DIAMOND COMPANY
Box 102C, RD 1
Chubbic Road
Canonsburg, PA 15317
(412) 746-2540

BLUE ISLAND INDUSTRIES
1446 North Martel, Unit 3
Los Angeles, CA 90046
(213) 851-3161

BLUE LION PRODUCTIONS
1311 Candlelight Street
Dallas, TX 75116
(214) 298-9576

JACK P. BLUESTEIN
P.O. Box 630175
Miami, FL 33163
(305) 472-7757

ISAAC BOLDEN PRODUCTIONS, INC.
5130 Cameron Boulevard
New Orleans, LA 70122
(504) 282-5460

BOOMERANG PRODUCTIONS, INC.
Care of Grubman & Indursky
65 East Fifty-Fifth Street
New York, NY 10022
(212) 888-6600

ALAN BOTTO
1 Palmer Square
Princeton, NJ 08540
(609) 921-8676

BOTTOM PRODUCTIONS
1247 Lincoln Boulevard

Santa Monica, CA 90401
(213) 393-0346

BOUQUET-ORCHID ENTERPRISES
P.O. Box 18284
Shreveport, LA 71138
(318) 686-7362

BOBBY BOYD PRODUCTIONS
2609 NW Thirty-Sixth Street
Oklahoma City, OK 73112
(405) 942-0462

PATRICK BOYLE & ASSOCIATES
7033 Sunset Boulevard, Suite 309
Los Angeles, CA 90028
(213) 982-0604

OWEN BRADLEY PRODUCTIONS
25 Music Square East
Nashville, TN 37203
(615) 244-1060

BRIANS & FOUTS MUSIC PRODUCTIONS
P.O. Box 775
Tyler, TX 75710
(214) 592-1010

BRIGHTSIDE, INC.
4860 Quail Run
Old Hickory, TN 37138
(615) 758-9166

BRISTOL PRODUCTIONS
134 West Twenty-Ninth Street, Suite 208
New York, NY 10019
(212) 736-4255

BROADWAY PRODUCTIONS, INC.
1307 Broadway, Box 551
Sheffield, AL 35660
(205) 381-1833

BROOKER PRODUCTIONS
2015 North Edgemont Street
Los Angeles, CA 90027
(213) 660-8575

BROOKSIDE MUSIC GROUP
159 West Fifty-Third Street
New York, NY 10019
(212) 541-7761

BROTHER LOVE PRODUCTIONS
P.O. Box 852
Beverly Hills, CA 90213
(213) 980-9271

THE BROVSKY STEWART GROUP, INC.
1209 Baylor Street
Austin, TX 78703
(512) 474-6952

RON BROWN MANAGEMENT
319 Butler Street
Pittsburgh, PA 15223
(412) 781-7740

BENNIE BROWN PRODUCTIONS
3011 Woodway Lane, Box 5702
Columbia, SC 29206
(803) 788-5734

STEVE BUCKINGHAM
3140 East Shadow Lawn
Atlanta, GA 30305
(404) 231-4666

BUCKSKIN PRODUCTIONS, INC.
7800 Woodman Avenue, Suite 19A
Panorama City, CA 91402
(213) 786-3324

BUDDY BUIE PRODUCTIONS, INC.
3297 Northcrest Road, Suite 203
Doraville, GA 30340
(404) 491-0950

BULLDOG PRODUCTIONS, INC.
P.O. Box 763
Madison, WI 53701
(608) 256-0354

BULLDOG RECORDS
50 East Forty-Second Street, Suite 401
New York, NY 10017
(212) 687-2299

C

CHARLES CALELLO PRODUCTIONS, LTD.
P.O. Box 2127
Beverly Hills, CA 90213
(213) 275-8248

CAM PRODUCTIONS
489 Fifth Avenue
New York, NY 10019
(212) 682-8400

CAN SCOR PRODUCTIONS
663 Fifth Avenue
New York, NY 10022
(212) 757-3638

CAN'T STOP PRODUCTIONS, INC.
65 East Fifty-Fifth Street
New York, NY 10022
(212) 751-6177

CAPTAIN CRYSTAL RECORDS
P.O. Box 223
Sky Forest, CA 92385
(714) 337-2802

DAVIS CARL PRODUCTIONS
8 East Chestnut Street
Chicago, IL 60611
(312) 664-7548

CARMEN PRODUCTIONS, INC.
15456 Cabrito Road
Van Nuys, CA 91406
(213) 873-7370

PETE CARR PRODUCTIONS, INC.
809 Whipperwill Drive
Port Orange, Fl 32019
(904) 761-9685

CASHWEST PRODUCTIONS, INC.
488 Madison Avenue
New York, NY 10022
(212) 752-3033

BUZZ CASON PRODUCTIONS, INC.
2804 Azalea Place
Nashville, TN 37204
(615) 383-8682

CASTALIA/DISTANT SHORES PUBLISHING & PRODUCTION COMPANY
30 Christopher Street, Suite 5H
New York, NY 10014
(212) 242-7543

CASTLE PRODUCTIONS
P.O. Box 7574
Tulsa, OK 74105
(918) 299-1223

CHALICE PRODUCTIONS, INC.
326 North LaCienaga Boulevard
Los Angeles, CA 90048
(213) 658-7002

THE CHUCK CHELLMAN COMPANY
Chellman Building
1201 Sixteenth Avenue South
Nashville, TN 37212
(615) 320-7287

CHICAGO KID PRODUCTIONS
2228 Observatory Avenue
Los Angeles, CA 90067
(213) 666-0494

CHROME PRODUCTIONS
2040 Davies Way
Los Angeles, CA 90046
(213) 650-5046

CHU YEKO MUSICAL FOUNDATION
P.O. Box 1314
Englewood Cliffs, NY 07632
(201) 567-5524

LOU CICCHETTI
211 Birchwood Avenue
Upper Nyack, NY 10960
(914) 358-0861

ALEX CIMA
P.O. Box 1594
Hollywood, CA 90028
(213) 662-8588

CLAY PIGEON PRODUCTIONS
P.O. Box 20346
Chicago, IL 60620
(312) 778-8760

CLEAR GOSPEL RECORDS
RR 1, Box 224
Sewell, NJ 08080
(609) 728-3880

CLOCK RECORDS
6277 Selma Avenue
Hollywood, CA 90028
(213) 464-9667

COMMODORES ENTERTAINMENT PUBLISHING CORPORATION
39 West Fifty-Fifth Street,
Penthouse South

New York, NY 10019
(212) 246-0385

CON BRIO PRODUCTIONS/ CONCORDE PRODUCTIONS
P.O. Box 196
Nashville, TN 37202
(615) 244-1964

CONTEMPORARY ARTIST ENTERPRISES, INC.
8817 Rangely Avenue
Los Angeles, CA 90048
(213) 273-5687

CORY PRODUCTIONS
164 South Kingsley Drive
Los Angeles, CA 90004
(213) 383-8026

FRED COSTELLO STUDIOS
2198 Monroe Avenue, Suite A
Rochester, NY 14618
(716) 461-4940

COUNTERPART CREATIVE STUDIOS
3744 Applegate Avenue
Cincinnati, OH 45211
(513) 661-8810

COUNTRY STAR PRODUCTIONS
439 Wiley Avenue
Franklin, PA 16323
(814) 432-4633

COUSINS MUSIC
211 Birchwood Avenue
Upper Nyack, NY 10960
(914) 358-0861

COVENANT RECORDINGS, INC.
1345 Major Street
Salt Lake City, UT 84126
(801) 487-1096

COYOTE PRODUCTIONS, INC.
14002 Palawan Way
Marina Del Ray, CA 90291
(213) 823-0171

DAVID CRAWFORD PRODUCTIONS
P.O. Box 54021
Los Angeles, CA 90054
(213) 782-5410

CRESCENDO MANAGEMENT, INC.
5333 Mission Center Road, Suite 305
San Diego, CA 92109
(714) 274-2877

CRESCENT ENTERPRISES
P.O. Box 135
Vashon, WA 98070
(206) 463-9025

THE CHRISTOPHER COMPANY
573 Ford Street
Lincoln Park, MI 48146
(313) 928-7390

THE EDDIE CROOK COMPANY
P.O. Box 213
Hendersonville, TN 37075
(615) 822-1360

CROSS-OVER ENTERPRISES, INC.
880 NE Seventy-First Street
Miami, FL 33138
(305) 759-1405

CROW PRODUCTIONS
60 Westwood Drive
Westbury, NY 11590
(516) 997-8499

JERRY CRUTCHFIELD
1106 Seventeenth Avenue South
Nashville, TN 37212
(615) 327-4622

CUMMINGS PRODUCTIONS
14045 South Main Street, Suite 303
Houston, TX 77035
(713) 645-5391

MIKE CURB PRODUCTIONS
3300 Warner Boulevard
Burbank, CA 91510
(213) 846-9090

CURTIS PRODUCTIONS
1530 Tern Court
Ventura, CA 93003
(805) 644-3454

MICHAEL CUSCUNA
350 East Seventy-Eighth Street
New York, NY 10021
(212) 737-0680

D

D.J. RECORD SERVICE
2200 Fremont, Department R
Bakersfield, CA 93304
(805) 832-6633

DALLAS STAR RECORDS
6247 Melody Lane, Suite 1521
Dallas, TX 75231
(214) 750-8936

DONALD DAVIS
15855 Wyoming Avenue
Detroit, MI 48238
(313) 861-2363

DEE-BEE RECORDING SERVICE
704 Ninth Avenue South
Myrtle Beach, SC 29577
(803) 448-8091

DEE PRODUCTIONS OF PHILADELPHIA
23 Darby Lane
Cherry Hill, NJ 08002
(609) 779-9111

LOU DE LISE PRODUCTIONS
2712 Carrell Lane
Willow Grove, PA 19090
(215) 672-3636

AL DE LORY PRODUCTIONS
23391 Park Sorrento
Calabasas, CA 91302
(213) 348-5951

DONALD L. DELUCIA
15041 Wabash Avenue
South Holland, IL 60473
(312) 339-0307

RICHARD DELVY ENTERPRISES, INC.
8127 Elrita Drive
Los Angeles, CA 90046
(213) 650-4761

DE MARCO DIRECTIONS
23 Darby Lane
Cherry Hill, NJ 08002
(215) 473-3111

ALDOUS DEMIAN PUBLISHING, LTD.
Box 1348, Radio City Station
New York, NY 10101
(212) 375-2639

DE SANTO ENTERPRISES
P.O. Box 4796
Nashville, TN 37216
(615) 859-0355

DESTINY PRODUCTIONS, LTD.
P.O. Box 2389
Los Angeles, CA 90028
(213) 276-2063

DESTITUTE PRODUCTIONS
P.O. Box 33
Marion, OR 97359
(503) 769-3327

DIAMOND JIM PRODUCTIONS
5929 Hillview Park Avenue
Van Nuys, CA 91401
(213) 988-4969

STEVE DIGGS PRODUCTIONS
22 Music Square West
Nashville, TN 37203
(615) 259-4024

DIX-ANN PRODUCTIONS
692 Lee Place
Azusa, CA 91702
(213) 334-2473

DOC RON PRODUCTIONS
717 Washington Avenue
Miami Beach, FL 33139
(305) 538-3513

DOCTOR SOUND
3191 Adams Avenue
San Diego, CA 92116
(714) 563-0164

JOHN DOELP ASSOCIATES
1 Astor Place, Suite 7S
New York, NY 10003
(212) 674-3939

FRANK DOLCI
245 East Twenty-Fourth Street

New York, NY 10010
(212) 686-4616

DOLCRAVE MUSIC COMPANY
1054 Fifty-Ninth Street
Oakland, CA 94608
(415) 652-4760

DOORKNOB RECORDS
2125 Eighth Avenue South
Nashville, TN 37204
(615) 383-6540

COLONEL BUSTER DOSS PRESENTS
P.O. Box 312
Estill Springs, TN 37330
(615) 649-2158

DOUBLE M PRODUCTIONS
1776 Broadway
New York, NY 10019
(212) 245-1100

MIKE DOUGLAS & ASSOCIATES
Drawer 12406
St. Petersburg, FL 33733
(813) 327-5525

TOM DOWD
Care of Criteria Recording
1755 NE 149th Street
Miami, FL 33181
(305) 947-5611

DRAGON INTERNATIONAL PRODUCTIONS
P.O. Box 8263
Haledon, NJ 07508
(201) 942-6810

DRAGON RECORDINGS, INC.
872 Morris Park Avenue
New York, NY 10462
(212) 792-2198

BARRY DRAKE ENTERPRISES
Red Kill Road
Fleischmanns, NY 12430
(914) 254-4565

PETE DRAKE PRODUCTIONS, INC.
809 Eighteenth Avenue South
Nashville, TN 37203
(615) 327-3211

DUANE MUSIC, INC.
382 Clarence Avenue
Sunnyvale, CA 94086
(408) 739-6133

DUNMORE PRODUCTIONS, LTD.
40 West Fifty-Fifth Street
New York, NY 10019
(212) 765-3750

DUPUY PRODUCTIONS
10960 Ventura Boulevard, Suite 200
Studio City, CA 91604
(213) 980-6412

STEVE DWORKIN PRODUCTIONS
60-23 Marathon Parkway
Little Neck, NY 11362
(212) 423-1113

E

EARTH PRODUCTIONS, LTD.
109 West Hubbard Street
Chicago, IL 60610
(312) 329-0616

EASTERN PACIFIC SOUNDS, INC.
11012 Ventura Boulevard, Studio G
Studio City, CA 91604
(213) 760-7900

EASTEX MUSIC
8537 Sunset Boulevard
Los Angeles, CA 90069
(213) 657-8852

EBB-TIDE PRODUCTIONS
P.O. Box 2544
Baton Rouge, LA 70821
(504) 924-6865

EBTIDE MUSIC/ YOUNG COUNTRY MUSIC
P.O. Box 5412
Buena Park, CA 90602
(213) 864-6302

ECHO RECORDS
824 Eighty-Third Street
Miami Beach, FL 33141
(305) 865-8960

GARY EDWARDS MUSIC, INC.
8700 West Judge Perez Drive
Chalmette, LA 70043
(504) 279-1120

DON ELLIOT PRODUCTIONS
15 Bridge Road
Weston, CT 06883
(203) 226-4200

EN POINTE PRODUCTIONS
P.O. Box 1451
Beverly Hills, CA 90213
(805) 497-1584

THE ENTERTAINMENT COMPANY
40 West Fifty-Seventh Street
New York, NY 10019
(212) 256-2600

ENTERTAINMENT SHOWCASE, INC.
4606 Clawson Road
Austin, TX 78745
(512) 444-5489

ESQUIRE INTERNATIONAL
Box 6032, Station B
Miami, FL 33123
(305) 547-1424

THE ESTATE
343 Amenia Road
Sharon, CT 06069
(203) 364-0254

FRANK EVANS PRODUCTIONS
P.O. Box 6025
Newport News, VA 23606
(804) 595-9000

TODD EVANS PRODUCTIONS
230 South Coronado, Suite 1
Los Angeles, CA 90057
(213) 385-5616

EXCLUSIVE SOUND PRODUCTIONS
P.O. Box 481
Easton, PA 18042
(215) 253-7467

EXECUTIVE MUSIC PUBLISHERS INTERNATIONAL
20 F. Robert Pitt Drive
Monsey, NY 10952
(914) 425-2244

F

FAME PRODUCTION COMPANY, INC.
603 East Avalon Avenue
Muscle Shoals, AL 35660
(205) 381-0801

FANFARE STUDIOS
110 East Main Street
El Cajon, CA 92020
(714) 447-2555

FANTA PROFESSIONAL SERVICES
1811 Division Street
Nashville, TN 37203
(615) 327-1731

FAR OUT PRODUCTIONS, INC.
7417 Sunset Boulevard
Los Angeles, Ca 90046
(213) 874-1300

FAT ALBERT PRODUCTIONS
10626 NE Eleventh Avenue
Miami Shores, FL 33138
(305) 893-7813

MAYNARD FERGUSON MUSIC
P.O. Box 716
Ojai, CA 93023
(805) 646-8156

FERN PRODUCTIONS, LTD.
6255 Sunset Boulevard, Suite 1903
Hollywood, CA 90028
(213) 466-3261

FIFTY-FIFTY PRODUCTIONS, INC.
11 East Twenty-Sixth Street
New York, NY 10010
(212) 686-7010

FIGMA SOUND PRODUCTION
3031 Senic Highway South
Snellville, GA 30278
(404) 972-0603

FIRST AMERICAN RECORDS, INC.
73 Marion Street
Seattle, WA 98104
(206) 625-9992

FIVE STAR PRODUCTIONS
1100 Sixteenth Avenue South
Nashville, TN 37212
(615) 244-1264

MIKE FLICKER PRODUCTIONS
P.O. Box 827
Seahurst, WA 98062
(206) 246-0383

LARRY FONTINE ENTERPRISES
16027 Sunburst Street
Sepulveda, CA 91343
(213) 892-0044

FOX-GIMBEL PRODUCTIONS, INC.
280 South Beverly Drive
Beverly Hills, CA 90212
(213) 274-6965

FOUNTAIN RECORD PRODUCTIONS, INC.
1321 South Michigan Avenue
Chicago, IL 60605
(312) 939-5042

ED FREEMAN PRODUCTIONS
8439 Ridpath Drive
Los Angeles, CA 90046
(213) 656-1310

FREQUENCY PRODUCTIONS
2705 Fair Oaks Avenue
Hatboro, PA 19040
(215) 443-0935

FULL CIRCLE PRODUCTIONS, INC.
80 East San Francisco Street
Santa Fe, NM 87501
(505) 982-2900

FUTURA PRODUCTIONS
Box 48, City Island
New York, NY 10464
(212) 885-2380

FUTURE 1 PRODUCTIONS
8924 East Calle Norlo
Tucson, AZ 85710
(602) 885-5931

FYDAQ PRODUCTIONS
240 East Radcliffe Drive
Claremont, CA 91711
(714) 624-0677

G

GK PRODUCTIONS, INC.
P.O. Box 1407
Nashua, NH 03061
(603) 429-0798

MILT GABLER
Care of Commodore Recording Company
3 Kensington Oval
New Rochelle, NY 10805
(914) 235-1229

GALAXIE III STUDIOS
118 Fifth Street
Taylorsville, NC 28681
(704) 632-4735

GARAGE MUSIC PRODUCTIONS
297 East Reed Street, Suite 3
San Jose, CA 95112
(408) 289-1897

GARRETT MUSIC ENTERPRISES, INC.
6255 Sunset Boulevard, Suite 1019
Los Angeles, CA 90028
(213) 467-2181

MARTIN GARY PRODUCTIONS
Box 104, Route 2
Hanover, VA 23069
(804) 288-7288

GEE PRODUCTIONS
8 Cherry Hill Court
Reisterstown, MD 21136
(301) 883-3816

GEE-JAY PRODUCTIONS
2039 Antione Street
Houston, TX 77055
(713) 683-7171

GENERAL MUSIC, INC.
3007 East Eight Mile Road
Warren, MI 48091
(313) 756-8890

PAT GLEESON PRODUCTIONS
3470 Nineteenth Street
San Francisco, CA 94110
(415) 864-1965

DWIGHT M. GLODELL
21 Sumner Park
Rochester, NY 14607
(716) 244-1525

GLOLITE PRODUCTIONS
827 Thomas Street
Memphis, TN 38107
(901) 525-0540

GOLD BAND RECORDING STUDIO
313 Church Street
Lake Charles, LA 70601
(318) 439-8839

GOLD FUTURE PRODUCTIONS
231 Midway
St. Louis, MO 63122
(314) 966-3278

GOLLENDER PRODUCTIONS
12 Marshall Street
Irvington, NJ 07111
(201) 373-6050

GORDO ENTERPRISES
255 North New Hampshire
Los Angeles, CA 90004
(213) 384-9586

ARTHUR GORSON PRODUCTIONS
56 Irving Place
New York, NY 10003
(212) 777-7864

GOSPEL EXPRESS
1899 South Third Street
Memphis, TN 38101
(901) 774-5689

GOSPEL RECORDS, INC.
Box 90, Rugby Station
Brooklyn, NY 11203
(212) 773-5910

GRAMEX, INC.
749 Peachtree Street
Atlanta, GA 30308
(404) 874-4451

GRAPEFRUIT PRODUCTIONS, INC.
P.O. Box 121017
Nashville, TN 37212
(615) 383-7412

GRATE DAIN PRODUCTIONS
P.O. Box 24570
Nashville, TN 37202
(615) 832-6630

MILES GRAYSON PRODUCTIONS
1159 South La Jolla Avenue
Los Angeles, CA 90035
(213) 938-3531

GREAT LAKES PRODUCTIONS, INC.
15855 Wyoming Avenue
Detroit, MI 48238
(313) 861-2363

GREAT METROPOLITAN GRAMAPHONE
240 West Fifty-Fifth Street
New York, NY 10019
(212) 247-3690

GREAT NORTHWEST MUSIC
73 Marion Street
Seattle, WA 98104
(206) 622-0470

FORREST GREEN STUDIOS
5004 West Francis Road
Clio, MI 48420
(313) 686-0189

GREEN MENU MUSIC FACTORY, INC.
50 West Fifty-Seventh Street
New York, NY 10019
(212) 489-0859

GRP RECORDS
330 West Fifty-Eighth Street
New York, NY 10019
(212) 245-7033

GST MUSIC PRODUCTIONS
17 Ponca Trail
St. Louis, MO. 63122
(314) 821-2741

GEORGE GUESS PRODUCTIONS
1223 South Twenty-Sixth Street
Philadelphia, PA 19143
(215) 477-7122

E.J. GURREN MUSIC
3929 Kentucky Drive
Los Angeles, CA 90068
(213) 980-7501

H

JAMES R. HALL III
7901 South La Salle Street
Chicago, IL 60620
(312) 224-0396

JIM HALL/GIDGET STARR PRODUCTIONS
5 Aldom Circle
West Caldwell, NY 07006
(201) 226-0035

HALLWAYS TO FAME PRODUCTIONS
P.O. Box 18918
Los Angeles, CA 90018
(213) 935-7277

HALPERN SOUNDS
1775 Old Country Road, Suite 9
Belmont, CA 94002
(415) 592-4900

AL HAM PRODUCTIONS, INC.
90 Morningside Drive
New York, NY 10027
(212) 866-1234

HAM-SEM RECORDS, INC.
541 South Spring Street
Los Angeles, CA 90013
(213) 627-0557

R.L. HAMMEL ASSOCIATES
Box 418-C, Route 4
Alexandria, IN 46001
(317) 642-7030

HAMSOUND PRODUCTIONS
996 Cumberland Road NE
Atlanta, GA 30306
(404) 872-4435

HAPPY DAY PRODUCTIONS
800 North Ridgeland Avenue
Oak Park, IL 60302
(312) 848-3322

HARD HAT PRODUCTIONS
519 North Halifax Avenue
Daytona Beach, FL 32018
(904) 252-0381

HARD BOILED RECORDS
484 Lake Park Avenue, Suite 6
Oakland, CA 94610
(415) 482-4854

HATTON & ASSOCIATES, INC.
P.O. Box 4157
Winter Park, FL 32793
(305) 678-0002

HAVEN RECORDS, INC.
9220 Sunset Boulevard
Los Angeles, CA 90069
(213) 278-8970

HEAVY SOUND PRODUCTIONS
P.O. Box 2875
Washington, DC 20013
(202) 396-3009

WALTER HEEBNER PRODUCTIONS
P.O. Box 1278
North Hollywood, CA 91604
(213) 766-4693

JEFF HEST PRODUCTIONS, LTD.
750 Kappock Street
Bronx, NY 10463
(212) 543-7030

HETZER THEATRICAL PRODUCTIONS
408 West Sixteenth Street
Huntington, WV 25704
(304) 429-5553

HI-HO PRODUCTIONS
P.O. Box 8135
Chicago, IL 60680
(312) 787-5612

JOHN HILL MUSIC, INC.
116 East Thirty-Seventh Street
New York, NY 10016
(212) 683-2448

HIPPOPOTAMUS PRODUCTIONS
7460 Melrose Avenue
Los Angeles, CA 90046
(213) 655-2996

RON HITCHCOCK PRODUCTIONS
1929 Rome Drive
Los Angeles, CA 90065
(213) 223-9993

HIT MACHINE MUSIC COMPANY
P.O. Box 20692
San Diego, CA 92120
(714) 277-3141

THE HOLMES LINE OF RECORDS, INC.
712 Fifth Avenue
New York, NY 10019
(212) 765-3850

HOLY SPIRIT PRODUCTIONS
27335 Penn Street
Inkster, MI 48141
(313) 562-8975

HOME SWEET HOME PRODUCTIONS
2020 Sunnyside Drive
Brentwood, TN 37207
(615) 383-8567

HOMETOWN PRODUCTIONS, INC.
280 South Beverly Drive, Suite 402
Beverly Hills, CA 90212
(213) 656-8490

HOPSACK & SILK PRODUCTIONS, INC.
332 West Seventy-First Street
New York, NY 10023
(212) 873-2179

PAUL HORNSBY
297 Bass Road
Macon, GA 31210

HORUS MUSIC COMPANY
228 Haight Street
San Francisco, CA 94102
(415) 431-8074

HOTSHOT PRODUCTIONS
P.O. Box 307
Eastham, MA 02642
(212) 582-8800

HUDDLESTON'S RECORDING STUDIO
11819 Lippitt Avenue
Dallas, TX 75218
(214) 328-9056

I

IAM PRODUCTIONS
17422 Murphy Avenue
Irvine, CA 92714
(714) 751-2015

IBIS RECORDINGS, INC.
9701 Wilshire Boulevard, Suite 1000
Beverly Hills, CA 90212
(213) 550-8115

ICY CALM PRODUCTIONS
21044 Sherman Way
Canoga Park, CA 91305
(213) 467-4344

INTERNATIONAL RECORDING COMPANY
1649 West Evergreen Street
Chicago, IL 60622
(312) 227-2000

IN ZANE PRODUCTIONS, INC.
1529 Walnut Street
Philadelphia, PA 19102
(215) 568-0500

J

J.K. PRODUCTIONS
1140 Rosalie Street
Philadelphia, PA 19149
(215) 535-4231

JAC PRODUCTIONS
6430 Sunset Boulevard, Suite 912
Hollywood, CA 90028
(213) 469-8234

JAMAKA RECORD COMPANY
3621 Heath Lane
Mesquite, TX 75150
(214) 279-5858

BRUCE JAMES COMPANY
P.O. Box 439
Lyndonville, VT 05851
(802) 626-3317

JESSE JAMES PRODUCTIONS, INC.
P.O. Box 129
Worcester, PA 19490
(215) 424-0800

ALEXANDER JANOULIS
P.O. Box 13584
Atlanta, GA 30324
(404) 876-1073

JED RECORD PRODUCTIONS
39 Music Square East
Nashville, TN 57203
(615) 255-6535

JOE-PORTER PRODUCTIONS
144 South Canon Drive
Beverly Hills, CA 90212
(213) 275-9533

LITTLE RICHIE JOHNSON
913 South Main Street
Belen, NM 87002
(505) 864-7441

PAUL JOHNSON PRODUCTIONS
P.O. Box 552
Woodland Hills, CA 91365
(213) 703-6707

QUINCY JONES PRODUCTIONS
Care of A&M Records
1416 North La Brea Avenue
Hollywood, CA 90028
(213) 469-2411

K

KDR RECORDING & PRODUCTIONS
1063 North Liberty Street
Elgin, IL 60120
(312) 695-2798

KGW PRODUCTIONS, INC.
18945 Livernios Avenue
Detroit, MI 48221
(313) 491-7031

KAHUKU PRODUCTIONS
P.O. Box 48440
Los Angeles, CA 90028
(213) 462-6871

KALIMBA PRODUCTIONS
9615 Brighton Way, Suite 216
Beverly Hills, CA 90210
(213) 274-0683

BOB KARCY PRODUCTIONS
437 West Sixteenth Street
New York, NY 10011
(212) 989-1989

KARLBHY PRODUCTIONS
Care of Criteria Recording
1755 NE 149th Street
Miami, FL 33181
(305) 947-5611

KASENETZ-KATZ PRODUCTIONS
323 East Shore Road
Great Neck, NY 11023
(516) 482-5930

KAT FAMILY PRODUCTIONS
5775 Peachtree Dunwoody Road NE
Suite B-130
Atlanta, GA 30342
(404) 252-5800

RICK KEEFER PRODUCTIONS
P.O. Box 30186
Honolulu, HI 96820

GENE KENNEDY ENTERPRISES
2125 Eighth Avenue South
Nashville, TN 37204
(615) 383-6002

DAVID KERSHENBAUM
Care of A&M Records, Inc.
1416 North La Brea Avenue
Hollywood, CA 90028
(213) 469-2411

E. JIMMY & JACK J. KEY
11 Music Circle South
Nashville, TN 37203
(615) 242-2461

KEYNOTE PRODUCTIONS
P.O. Box 4185
Youngstown, OH 44515
(216) 793-7295

KIDERIAN RECORDING
4926 West Gunnison Street
Chicago, IL 60630
(312) 545-0861

KENNETH KING PRODUCTIONS
850 Seventh Avenue
New York, NY 10019
(212) 247-3188

KING & MOORE PRODUCTIONS, INC.
233 East Ontario Street
Chicago, IL 60611
(312) 944-1125

KING HENRY PRODUCTIONS
1855 Fairview Avenue
Easton, PA 18042
(215) 258-4461

CHARLES KIPPS MUSIC, INC.
1 Lincoln Plaza
New York, NY 10023
(212) 580-0154

KNOWN ARTIST PRODUCTIONS
1219 Kerlin Avenue
Brewton, AL 36426
(205) 867-2228

FREDDIE KOBER PRODUCTIONS
P.O. Box 11967
Houston, TX 77016
(713) 694-2971

GLEN KOLOTKIN PRODUCTIONS
4 Pegs Lane
Huntington, NY 11743
(516) 673-7031

KOMOS PRODUCTIONS, INC.
11935 Laurel Hills Road
Studio City, CA 91604
(213) 762-1144

KRUGER ASSOCIATES
9 Murray Street NE
New York, NY 10007
(212) 227-0700

L

LA TRAX, INC.
8033 Sunset Boulevard, Suite 1010
Los Angeles, CA 90046
(213) 852-1980

GREG LADANYI
1592 Crossroads of the World
Hollywood, CA 90028
(213) 462-6156

LAKCO RECORDINGS
3235 West Fullerton Avenue
Chicago, IL 60647
(213) 772-9444

LAKE COUNTRY MUSIC
P.O. Box 88
Decatur, TX 76234
(817) 627-2128

LA MAS PRODUCTIONS
12202 Union Avenue
Cleveland, OH 44105
(216) 752-3440

LAMBERT & POTTER
9220 Sunset Boulevard
Los Angeles, CA 90069
(213) 278-8970

LA RONDE MUSIC INTERNATIONAL
4014 Murietta Avenue
Sherman Oaks, CA 91423
(213) 981-5331

LAS VEGAS RECORDING
3977 Vegas Valley Drive
Las Vegas, NV 89121
(702) 457-4365

LAST MINUTE PRODUCTIONS
Care of Bette Hisiger
320 East Twenty-Third Street
New York, NY 10010
(212) 254-9338

LAURIE RECORDS, INC.
20 F. Robert Pitt Drive
Monsey, NY 10952
(914) 425-7000

LAVETTE PRODUCTIONS
7400 Osuna NE
Albuquerque, NM 87109
(505) 299-0674

LAZER RECORDS
P.O. Box 77
Center Square, PA 19422
(215) 635-6921

ROOSEVELT LEE
3966 Standish Avenue
Cincinnati, OH 45213
(513) 793-8191

PAUL LEKA PRODUCTIONS
1122 Main Street
Bridgeport, CT 06604
(203) 366-9186

TY LEMLEY MUSIC
430 Pearce Road
Pittsburgh, PA 15234
(412) 341-0991

LEMON SQUARE PRODUCTIONS
P.O. Box 31819
Dallas, TX 75231
(214) 750-0720

LEONARD PRODUCTIONS, INC.
2241 Valwood Parkway
Dallas, TX 75234
(214) 241-0254

ERV LEWIS
Wellman Heights, Box 218
Johnsonville, SC 29555
(803) 386-2600

LIFESINGER PRODUCTIONS
50 Music Square West, Suite 902
Nashville, TN 37203
(615) 329-2278

TOMMY LIPUMA
Care of Warner Brothers Records
3300 Warner Boulevard
Burbank, CA 91510
(213) 846-9090

A LITTLE BIT OF FAITH PRODUCTIONS
10519 South Forest Avenue
Chicago, Il 60628
(312) 848-5935

LITTLE GIANT ENTERPRISES
P.O. Box 205
White Lake, NY 12786
(914) 583-4471

MICK LLOYD PRODUCTIONS
1014 Sixteenth Avenue South
Nashville, TN 37217
(615) 244-1630

BUD LOGAN
Care of Music City Records
821 Nineteenth Avenue South
Nashville, TN 37203
(615) 327-4927

LOVE-ZAGER PRODUCTIONS, INC.
1697 Broadway, Suite 1209
New York, NY 10019
(212) 246-0575

DON LOVING ENTERPRISES
P.O. Box 5698
Cleveland, OH 44101
(216) 631-5868

BILL LOWERY PRODUCTIONS
P.O. Box 49386
Atlanta, GA 30359
(404) 325-0832

DANNY LUCIANO PRODUCTIONS
2655 Philmont Avenue, Suite 206
Huntingdon Valley, PA 19006
(215) 947-7743

HAROLD LUICK & ASSOCIATES
110 Garfield Street, Box B
Carlisle, IA 50047
(515) 989-3679

LUNCHTIME PRODUCTIONS, INC.
64 St. Marks Park
New York, NY 10003
(212) 982-4619

M

MBA PRODUCTIONS
8914 Georgian Drive
Austin, TX 78753
(512) 836-3201

MCI PRODUCTIONS
20 East First Street, Suite 308
Mount Vernon, NY 10550
(914) 699-4003

M-D PRODUCTIONS
209 State Street
Bay City, MI 48706
(517) 893-8321

M.D.M. PRODUCTIONS
115 West Thirty-Fifth Street
Hays, KS 67601
(913) 628-1666

M.F. PRODUCTIONS, INC.
295 Madison Avenue
New York, NY 10017
(212) 686-5326

BROWNIE MACINTOSH MUSICAL ENTERPRISES
P.O. Box 40
Hampton, NH 03842
(603) 659-2361

JOHN MADARA ENTERPRISES, LTD.
3146 Arrowhead Drive
Hollywood, CA 90068
(213) 461-4755

MAD DOG PRODUCTIONS
10 High Terrace
Monteclair, NY 07024
(201) 744-6551

LEE MAGID PRODUCTIONS
P.O. Box 532
Malibu, CA 90265
(213) 858-7282

MAGNUM GOLD PRODUCTIONS
50 Music Square West, Suite 309
Nashville, TN 37203
(615) 254-5074

MAIKIN MUSIC, LTD.
147 West Twenty-Fourth Street
New York, NY 10011
(212) 691-7674

MAINLINE PRODUCTIONS
P.O. Box 902
Provo, UT 84603
(801) 225-4674

MANDALA INTERNATIONAL
112 Maureen Drive
Hendersonville, TN 37075
(615) 824-7144

MANHATTAN MADNESS PRODUCTIONS
186 Fifth Avenue
New York, NY 10010
(212) 242-2887

MAN QUIN PRODUCTIONS
P.O. Box 2388
Toluca Lake, CA 91602
(213) 985-8284

ROBERT MARGOULEFF & ASSOCIATES
2040 Davies Way
Los Angeles, CA 90046
(213) 650-5046

MARIER MUSIC
9 Walnut Road
Glen Ellyn, IL 60137
(312) 469-3940

MARINO & ROSENBERG
1111 Kearny Street
San Francisco, CA 94133
(415) 391-0444

MARLO RECORD COMPANY
Route 1, Box 49
Utica, NY 13502
(315) 724-0895

JOE MARTIN PRODUCTIONS
10245 Collins Avenue
Bal Horbour, FL 33154
(305) 861-6947

MARULLO PRODUCTIONS, INC.
1121 Market Street
Galveston, TX 77550
(713) 762-4590

MASKED ANNOUNCER CORPORATION
166 East Sixty-First Street
New York, NY 10021
(212) 751-6901

MASTER AUDIO, INC.
1227 Spring Street NW
Atlanta, GA 30309
(404) 875-1440

MASTER SOUND PRODUCTIONS, INC.
921 Hampstead Turnpike
Franklin Square, NY 11010
(516) 354-3374

MASTER SOURCE PRODUCTIONS
440 North Mayfield Avenue
Chicago, IL 60644
(312) 921-1446

MASTERVIEW MUSIC PUBLISHING CORPORATION
Ridge Road & Butler Land
Perkasie, PA 18944
(215) 257-9616

DAVE MATHES PRODUCTIONS
P.O. Box 22653
Nashville, TN 37202

CURTIS MAYFIELD
Care of Curtom Records
5915 North Lincoln Avenue
Chicago, IL 60659
(312) 769-4676

MAX PRODUCTIONS
P.O. Box 7386
Beaumont, TX 77706
(713) 866-6726

TIM MCCABE PRODUCTIONS
2460 Spring Lake Drive
Marietta, GA 30062
(404) 973-1170

TOM MCCONNEL PRODUCTIONS
P.O. Box 111291
Nashville, TN 37211
(615) 385-1960

AL MCKAY
19301 Ventura Boulevard, Suite 205
Tarzana, CA 91356
(213) 708-1300

EDD L. MCNEELY PRODUCTIONS
14621 Allen Street
Westminster, CA 92683
(714) 898-7317

MEDIA MASTERS PRODUCTIONS, INC.
3015 Ocean Park Boulevard
Santa Monica, CA 90405
(213) 450-2288

MEDRESS & APPELL PRODUCTIONS, INC.
211 West Fifty-Sixth Street
New York, NY 10019
(212) 581-2413

MELODEE ENTERPRISES, INC.
158 Gatone Drive
Hendersonville, TN 37075
(615) 824-3172

MEMPHIS MANAGEMENT CORPORATION
P.O. Box 17272
Memphis, TN 38117
(901) 685-8533

MERCANTILE PRODUCTIONS
P.O. Box 2271
Palm Springs, CA 92263
(714) 320-4848

MERRY SOUNDS
P.O. Box 313, Kingsbridge Station
Bronx, NY 10463
(212) 543-7770

METROBEAT PRODUCTIONS, INC.
P.O. Box 775
Minneapolis, MN 55440
(612) 636-0841

MIGHTY "T" PRODUCTIONS
441 South Beverly Drive
Beverly Hills, CA 91042
(213) 855-0525

JAY MILLER PRODUCTIONS
413 North Parkerson Avenue
Crowley, LA 70526
(318) 783-1601

MILLER-MARTIN PRODUCTIONS CORPORATION
132 East Forty-Fifth Street, Suite C
New York, NY 10017
(212) 288-8728

BILL MILLER'S PRODUCTIONS
347 Litchfield Avenue
Babylon, NY 11702
(516) 661-9842

MIMOSA PRODUCTIONS
9315 Carmichael Drive
La Mesa, CA 92041
(714) 464-0910

MOBILE RECORDERS, LTD.
P.O. Box 363
Southbury, CT 06488
(203) 264-9176

MOBY DICK RECORDS
573 Castro Street
San Francisco, CA 94114
(415) 861-0476

MONOTONE RECORDS
281 East Kingsbridge Road
Bronx, NY 10458
(212) 582-3240

MONSTER PRODUCTIONS, INC.
1919 Cobden Road
Philadelphia, PA 19118
(215) 887-8371

VINCENT MONTANA JR. PRODUCTIONS
203 West Sixth Avenue
Cherry Hill, NJ 08002
(609) 662-0096

MONTEREY SOUND PRODUCTIONS
121-A Oceanview Boulevard
Pacific Grove, CA 93950
(408) 373-1778

BOB MONTGOMERY PRODUCTIONS
P.O. Box 120967, Acklen Station
Nashville, TN 37212
(615) 383-4667

DOUG MOODY PRODUCTIONS
Mystic Music Center
6277 Selma Avenue
Hollywood, CA 90028
(213) 462-0346

MOOGTOWN PRODUCTIONS
237 West Fifty-Fourth Street
New York, NY 10019
(212) 582-6414

MOONCHILD PRODUCTIONS
13216 Bloomfield Street
Sherman Oaks, CA 91423
(213) 872-1854

BOB MORGAN
16065 Jeanne Lane
Encino, CA 91436
(213) 981-1577

THE MORGAN MUSIC GROUP
P.O. Box 2388
Prescott, AZ 86302
(602) 445-5801

GIORGIO MORODER ENTERPRISES, LTD.
8531 Appian Way
Los Angeles, CA 90046
(213) 650-0030

JOEL W. MOSS PRODUCTIONS
11558 Huston Street
North Hollywood, CA 91602
(213) 766-0690

MOTHER CLEO PRODUCTIONS
P.O. Box 521
Newberry, SC 29108
(803) 276-0639

BOB W. MOTTA
9411 Shore Road
Brooklyn, NY 11209
(212) 745-1487

MOUNTED RECORDINGS, INC.
888 Eighth Avenue
New York, NY 10019
(212) 582-4572

MR. BONES PRODUCTIONS, INC.
P.O. Box 49259
Los Angeles, CA 90049
(213) 652-7239

MTS MUSIC GROUP, INC.
676 North La Salle Street
Chicago, IL 60610
(312) 266-8844

MUSCADINE PRODUCTIONS
297 Bass Road
Macon, GA 31210
(912) 477-2887

MUSIC ENTERPRISES, INC.
5626 Brock Street
Houston, TX 77023
(713) 926-4431

THE MUSIC FACTORY, INC.
567 NW Twenty-Seventh Street
Miami, FL 33127
(305) 576-2600

MUSIC MEN, LTD.

2049 West Broad Street
Richmond, VA 23220
(804) 358-3852

MUSIC RESOURCES INTERNATIONAL
21 West Thirty-Ninth Street
New York, NY 10018
(212) 869-2299

MUSIVERSE
10 Music Circle South
Nashville, TN 37203
(615) 242-5544

N

JOHN NAGY PRODUCTIONS
100 Bellevue Street
Newton, MA 02158
(617) 964-8010

NASHVILLE INTERNATIONAL PRODUCTIONS
20 Music Square West
Nashville, TN 37203
(615) 373-2575

NEON CORNFIELD
5761 Park Plaza
Indianapolis, IN 46220
(317) 849-9230

NEW HORIZON RECORDS
3398 Nathan Way
Las Vegas, NV 89109
(702) 732-2576

NEW WORLD RECORDS
2309 North Thirty-Sixth Street, Suite 11
Milwaukee, WI 53210
(414) 445-4872

THE NEXT BIG THING, INC.
250 West Fifty-Seventh Street, Suite 808
New York, NY 10019
(212) 765-0540

JOSEPH NICOLETTI
P.O. Box 2818
Newport Beach, CA 92663
(714) 497-3758

NIGHTWING PRODUCTIONS
P.O. Box 2
Brea, CA 92621
(714) 529-9558

NISE PRODUCTIONS, INC.
413 Cooper Street
Camden, NJ 08102
(215) 276-0100

JOSH NOLAND PRODUCTIONS
P.O. Box 265
Deefield Beach, FL 33441
(305) 428-2644

ERIC NORBERG PRODUCTIONS
911 SW Broadway, Suite 15
Portland, OR 97201
(503) 227-2989

NORTH AMERICAN LITURGY RESOURCES
10802 North Twenty-Third Avenue
Phoenix, AZ 85029
(602) 864-1980

NOTS PRODUCTIONS
11257 Blix Street
North Hollywood, CA 91602
(213) 508-9865

O

OTL PRODUCTIONS
74 Main Street, Suite 5
Maynard, MA 01754
(617) 897-8459

OAKRIDGE MUSIC RECORDING
2001 Elton Road
Haltom City, TX 76117
(817) 838-8001

OAKTREE PRODUCTIONS
216 Chatsworth Drive
San Fernando, CA 91340
(213) 361-1238

O'BRIEN PRODUCTIONS
234 Fifth Avenue, Suite 8
Redwood City, CA 94063
(415) 367-0298

OLD HAT RECORDS
3442 Nies Street
Fort Worth, TX 76111
(817) 838-8189

OLLIE RECORD PRODUCTIONS
334 Arno Way
Pacific Palisades, CA 90272
(213) 459-5956

ONE TEN PRODUCTIONS
26150 Veva Way
Calabasas, CA 91302
(213) 880-5071

ORION MASTER RECORDINGS, INC.
P.O. Box 4087
5840 Busch Drive
Malibu, CA 90265
(213) 457-3370

OVAL PRODUCTIONS
2429 Cheremoya Avenue
Los Angeles, CA 90068
(213) 464-1933

OZARK OPRY RECORDS
P.O. Box 242
Osage Beach, MO 65065
(314) 348-3383

P

PANDORA PRODUCTIONS, LTD.
2665 South Bayshore Drive, Suite 107
Coconut Grove, FL 33133
(305) 854-0257

PANIOLO PRODUCTIONS
5121 Franklin Street
Los Angeles, CA 90027
(213) 662-7962

PARASOUND, INC.
680 Beach Street
San Francisco, CA 94109
(415) 673-4544

R.N. PARKER & ASSOCIATES
215 Argonne Street
Jefferson, MO 65101
(314) 653-3795

THE PASHA MUSIC ORGANIZATION, INC.
5615 Melrose Avenue
Hollywood, CA 90038
(213) 466-3507

DAVE PATON PRODUCTIONS
9502 Harrell Street
Pico Rivera, CA 90660
(213) 692-1472

PEACEABLE MUSIC
3525 Encinal Canyon Road
Malibu, CA 90265
(213) 457-4405

PEACHY KEEN PRODUCTIONS
3904 Fifty-Fifth Street
Des Moines, IA 50310
(515) 276-8678

PEARL SOUND, LTD.
2705 Provincial Drive
Ann Arbor, MI 48104
(313) 971-2414

DAVE PELL PRODUCTIONS
6362 Hollywood Boulevard, Suite 222
Hollywood, CA 90029
(213) 462-5466

PELLEGRINO PRODUCTIONS
311 Brook Avenue
Bayshore, NY 11706
(516) 665-1003

PENELOPY PRODUCTION SERVICES
54 West Seventy-First Street
New York, NY 11706
(212) 787-5035

PENUMBRA PRODUCTIONS, LTD.
Care of Electric Lady Studios
52 West Eighth Avenue
New York, NY 10011
(212) 677-4700

PERFEC RECORDINGS
1214 S Street SE
Washington, DC 20020
(202) 889-7949

PERISCOPE PRODUCTIONS
129 Bishop Street
Brockton, MA 02402
(617) 588-6348

DON PERRY ENTERPRISES, INC.
8961 Sunset Boulevard, Suite 2A
Los Angeles, CA 90069
(213) 278-8962

PHOENIX PRODUCTIONS
1033 Kingsmill Parkway
Columbus, OH 43229
(614) 846-4494

PIRANHA BROTHERS MUSIC
2162 Broadway
New York, NY 10024
(212) 787-1900

PIROUETTE PRODUCTIONS
P.O. Box 1451
Beverly Hills, CA 90213
(213) 277-8181

PLATINUM SOUND PRODUCTIONS
P.O. Box 480257
West Hollywood, CA 90048
(213) 851-9418

RICHARD PODOLOR PRODUCTIONS, INC.
11386 Ventura Boulevard
Studio City, CA 91604
(213) 985-7558

POGOLOGO PRODUCTIONS, INC.
256 South Robertson Boulevard
Beverly Hills, CA 90211
(213) 476-9157

JOE PORTER PRODUCTIONS
144 South Canon Drive, Suite 2
Beverly Hills, CA 90212
(213) 275-9533

PORTER-WARREN PRODUCTIONS
1410 East Seventy-Second Street
Chicago, IL 60619
(312) 752-2755

POSITIVE ATTITUDE PRODUCTIONS
P.O. Box 6066
Bridgewater, NJ 08807
(201) 356-6066

POSTHORN RECORDINGS
142 West Twenty-Sixth Street
New York, NY 10001
(212) 242-3737

MIKE POST PRODUCTIONS, INC.
4507 Carpenter Avenue
North Hollywood, CA 91607
(213) 985-9510

POTTER PRODUCTIONS, INC.
2213 North Seventy-Fourth Avenue
Elmwood Park, IL 60635
(312) 542-7919

PRE-CAMBRIAN MUSIC COMPANY
P.O. Box 568
San Rafael, CA 94902
(415) 454-5770

THE PRESCRIPTION COMPANY
70 Murray Avenue
Port Washington, NY 10050
(516) 767-1929

PREWITT ROSE PRODUCTIONS
P.O. Box 372
Antioch, TN 37013
(615) 331-2378

LLOYD PRICE GROUP, INC.
39 West Fifty-Fifth Street
New York, NY 10019
(212) 586-3350

PRIME CUT PRODUCTIONS, LTD.
141 West Seventy-Third Street
Suite 10E
New York, NY 10023
(212) 799-5506

PRITCHETT PUBLICATION
38603 Sage Tree Street
Palmdale, CA 93550
(805) 947-4657

PRODIGY PRODUCTIONS, LTD.
323 East Twenty-Third Street
Chicago, IL 60616
(312) 225-2110

PRO-PIANO PRODUCTIONS
3916 Eighteenth Street
San Francisco, CA 94114
(415) 621-1210

PROUD PARENT PRODUCTIONS
442 West Fifty-Seventh Street
New York, NY 10019
(212) 247-4884

PYRAMID'S EYE RECORDING STUDIO
P.O. Box 331
Lookout Mountain, TN 37350
(404) 820-2356

Q

QL MOBILE RECORDINGS, INC.
314 Romano Street
Coral Gables, FL 33134
(305) 446-2477

Q-ONE PRODUCTIONS
P.O. Box 480615
Los Angeles, CA 90048
(213) 658-5577

QUACK PRODUCTIONS, INC.
12 East Twelfth Street
New York, NY 10003
(212) 989-6524

QUADRAPHONIC TALENT, INC.
P.O. Box 630175
Miami, FL 33163
(305) 472-7757

QUINTO RECORDS
P.O. Box 2388
Toluca Lake, CA 91602
(213) 985-8284

R

RBG PRODUCTIONS
7859 Bastille Place
Severn, MD 21144
(301) 552-7761

REF RECORDS
404 Bluegrass Avenue
Madison, TN 37115
(615) 865-6380

RHB PRODUCTIONS
P.O. Box 775
Tyler, TX 75710
(214) 592-1010

CAROL J. RACHOU, SR.
711 Stevenson Street
Lafayette, LA 70501
(318) 234-5577

RADMUS PRODUCTIONS, INC.
164 Onderdonck Avenue
Manhasset, NY 10030
(212) 957-9330

THE RAINBOW COLLECTION, LTD.
101 West Fifty-Seventh Street, Suite 2A
New York, NY 10019
(212) 765-8160

RAINBOW RECORDING STUDIOS
2322 South Sixty-Fourth Avenue
Omaha, NE 68132
(402) 554-0123

RAINBOW ROAD RECORDS
1212 Bell Grimes Lane
Nashville, TN 37207
(615) 865-0653

RAND COMMUNICATIONS, LTD.
15701 Kruhm Road
Burtonsville, MD 20730
(301) 384-4485

RAPP/METZ MANAGEMENT
1650 Broadway
New York, NY 10019
(212) 581-6162

NORMAN RATNER PRODUCTIONS, INC.
265 North Robertson Boulevard
Beverly Hills, CA 90211
(213) 559-3555

REAL TO REEL PRODUCTIONS
P.O. Box 4026
Woodbridge, CT 06401
(203) 735-5883

REALITY PRODUCTIONS
P.O. Box 824
Elizabeth, NJ 07207
(201) 353-3485

RUSS REEDER
7406 Theisswood Road
Spring, TX 77379
(713) 376-3480

REFLECTION SOUND PRODUCTIONS, INC.
1018 Central Avenue
Charlotte, NC 28204
(704) 377-4596

REHTOM PRODUCTIONS
135 Dotson Drive, Suite A-26
Ames, IA 50010
(515) 292-5558

REMARKABLE PRODUCTIONS, INC.
Rustling Lane
Bedford, NY 10506
(914) 234-6332

REVDOC PRODUCTIONS
220 Decibel Road
State College, PA 16801
(814) 238-8509

REYNOLDS PRODUCTIONS, INC.
16 Woodland Drive
Irvine, CA 92714
(714) 559-5125

RHYTHM VALLEY MUSIC
1304 Blewett Street
Graham, TX 76046
(817) 549-1641

RICHEY RECORDS
7121 West Vickery Street, Suite A118
Fort Worth, TX 76116
(817) 731-7375

RICOCHET RECORDS
8 Pasture Lane
Roslyn Heights, NY 11577
(516) 621-4307

RIVERTOWN PRODUCTIONS
P.O. Box 120657
Nashville, TN 37212
(615) 385-2555

ROBEHR ARTISTS
121 West Sixth Street
St. Paul, MN 55102
(612) 291-2927

CHARLIE ROBERTS
428 Peskin Road
West Farms, NY 07727
(201) 938-4351

ROCK GARDEN PRODUCTIONS
26442 Sand Canyon Road
Canyon Country, CA 91351
(805) 251-2559

ROCK HARD PRODUCTIONS
13010 West Thirtieth Drive
Golden, CO 80401
(303) 278-8367

ROCKOKO PRODUCTIONS, INC.
9000 Sunset Boulevard, Suite 704
Los Angeles, CA 90069
(213) 876-7718

ROCK PRODUCTIONS
958 West Edgemont Drive
San Bernardino, CA 92405
(714) 882-6796

ROCK STEADY PRODUCTIONS, INC.
10960 Wilshire Boulevard
Los Angeles, CA 90024
(213) 479-6511

ROMA 88 PRODUCTIONS
609 Eighteenth Street
Union City, NJ 07087
(201) 865-8866

ANGELO ROMAN ENTERPRISES
P.O. Box 3144
Covina, CA 91723
(213) 339-9769

ROSE HILL PRODUCTIONS
3929 New Seneca Turnpike
Marcellus, NY 13108
(315) 673-1117

ROSEMARY MELODY LINE COMPANY
633 Almond Street
Vineland, NY 08360
(609) 696-0943

SY ROSENBERG ORGANIZATION
1201 Sixteenth Avenue South
Nashville, TN 37212
(615) 385-2750

BRIAN ROSS PRODUCTIONS
3884 Franklin Avenue
Los Angeles, CA 90027
(213) 662-3121

ROUGH TRADE, INC.
326 Sixth Street
San Francisco, CA 94103
(415) 621-4164

ROYAL K PRODUCTIONS
6 Melrose Drive
Livingston, NJ 07039
(201) 533-0448

DAVID RUBINSON & FRIENDS, INC.
827 Folsom Street
San Francisco, CA 94107
(415) 777-2930

M.D. RUFFIN PRODUCTIONS
P.O. Box 3501
Flint, MI 48502
(313) 398-6070

RUSTRON MUSIC PRODUCTIONS
35 South Broadway, Suite B-3
Irvington, NY 10533
(914) 946-1689

S

SPQR MUSIC
69 Robinhood Road
Clifton, NJ 07013
(201) 778-6759

STP PRODUCTIONS, INC.
P.O. Box 9628
Atlanta, GA 30319
(404) 349-3848

SAGITTAR RECORDS
1311 Candlelight Avenue
Dallas, TX 75116

SAMARAH PRODUCTIONS, INC.
P.O. Box 2501
Columbia, SC 29202
(803) 754-5554

SANSU ENTERPRISES, INC.
3809 Clematis Avenue
New Orleans, LA 70122
(504) 949-8386

SAPPHIRE RECORD COMPANY
2815 Octavia Street
New Orleans, LA 70115
(504) 866-3478

SARACENO/COLLINS PRODUCTIONS, INC.
15910 Ventura Boulevard
Encino, CA 91436
(213) 990-7361

STEVEN C. SARGEANT
31632 Second Avenue
South Laguna Beach, CA 92677
(714) 499-4409

DON SCHAFER PRODUCTIONS
P.O. Box 57291
Dallas, TX 75207
(214) 339-5891

STEVE SCHARF
Care of Double Header Productions
61 Jane Street
New York, NY 10014
(212) 929-2068

AL SCHMITT PRODUCTIONS
5050 Vanalden Avenue
Tarzana, CA 91356
(213) 996-1771

JASON SCHWARTZ
5934 Buffalo Avenue, Suite 105
Van Nuys, CA 91401
(213) 997-8819

SEA CRUISE PRODUCTIONS
P.O. Box 110830
Nashville, TN 37211
(615) 242-1037

LARRY SEALFON PRODUCTIONS
13310 Collingwood Terrace
Silver Spring, MD 20904
(301) 384-8826

SEASUN EXPERIENCE MUSIC PRODUCTIONS
P.O. Box 1725
Daytona Beach, FL 32015
(904) 255-4891

SECOND SUN PRODUCTIONS
Box 133, Route 2
Vashon Island, WA 98013
(206) 463-2850

SEVEN HILLS RECORDING
905 North Main Street
Evansville, IN 47711
(812) 423-1861

SEVENTH RAY RECORDS
P.O. Box 3771
Hollywood, CA 90028
(213) 467-0611

SHAGGY DOG STUDIOS
Box 766, Route 7
Stockbridge, MA 01262
(413) 298-3737

SHALYNN PRODUCTIONS
P.O. Box 34131
Dallas, TX 75234
(214) 270-2678

DON D. SHEETS PRODUCTIONS
Box 212, Route 3
Nashville, IN 47448
(812) 988-2000

SHEKERE PRODUCTIONS
P.O. Box 2034
Richmond, VA 23260
(804) 355-3586

MICKEY SHERMAN
2108 NW 115th Street
Oklahoma City, OK 73120
(405) 751-8954

SHOWCASE OF STARS
310 Franklin Street
Boston, MA 02110
(617) 396-0751

SHU-QUA-LOK RECORDS/ ACORN RECORDS
233 Penner Drive
Pearl, MS 39208
(601) 939-6616

SILVER BLUE PRODUCTIONS, LTD.
220 Central Park South
New York, NY 10019
(212) 586-3535

LEE SILVER PRODUCTIONS
136 South Swall Drive
Beverly Hills, CA 90211
(213) 657-4895

SIR CHARLES PRODUCTIONS
Care of Sound Seventy
Twenty-Fifth Avenue North, Suite 210
Nashville, TN 37203
(615) 327-1711

SKOKIE RECORDING
5320 West Howard Street
Skokie, IL 60077
(312) 675-4285

SKYHIGH PRODUCTIONS, INC.
8515 Hollywood Boulevard
Los Angeles, CA 90069
(213) 654-3760

SKY'S THE LIMIT PRODUCTIONS
100 Main Street
Reading, MA 01867
(617) 944-0423

SNUGGLEBUSH MUSIC PRODUCTIONS
144 South Beverly Drive, Suite 500
Beverly Hills, CA 90212
(213) 273-3553

DENNY SOMACH PRODUCTIONS
P.O. Box 333
Narberth, PA 19072
(215) 820-9090

SONGCO PRODUCTION COMPANY, INC.
10802 North Twenty-Third Avenue
Phoenix, AZ 85029
(602) 864-1980

SOUND COLUMN
46 East Herbert Avenue
Salt Lake City, UT 84111
(801) 355-5327

SOUNDS OF WINCHESTER
P.O. Box 574
Winchester, VA 22601
(703) 667-9379

SOUTHERN SOUND PRODUCTIONS
100 Labon Street
Tabor City, NC 28463
(919) 653-2546

SPARROW RECORDS, INC.
8025 Deering Avenue
Canoga Park, CA 91304
(213) 703-6599

SPECIAL DELIVERY PROMOTIONS
210 Twenty-Fifth Avenue North
Nashville, TN 37203
(615) 327-1711

SPECTRUM
P.O. Box 757
San Carlos, CA 94070
(425) 593-9554

SPICEWOOD ENTERPRISES, INC.
Box 753, FDR Station
New York, NY 10022
(212) 758-7436

STACHE RECORDS, INC.
4050 Buckingham Road, Suite 208
Los Angeles, CA 90008
(213) 290-2262

STAIRCASE PROMOTION
P.O. Box 211
East Prairie, MO 63845
(314) 649-2211

WADE STALEY PRODUCTIONS
P.O. Box 5712
High Point, NC 27262
(919) 885-0263

STAR FOX PRODUCTIONS
623 Brown's Valley Road
Atlanta, GA 30324
(408) 724-4402

STARGEM RECORD PRODUCTIONS
20 Music Square West, Suite 200
Nashville, TN 37203
(615) 244-1025

STARMAN RECORDS
P.O. Box 20604
Sacramento, CA 95820
(916) 454-4525

STARTOWN ENTERPRISES
1037 East Parkway South
Memphis, TN 38104
(901) 725-7019

STAR WORLD PRODUCTIONS, INC.
1610 North Argyle Avenue, Suite 203
Los Angeles, CA 90028
(213) 464-7751

A. STEWART PRODUCTIONS
9761 Baden Avenue
Chatsworth, CA 91311
(213) 709-8636

STEVE STONE, INC.
6255 Sunset Boulevard, Suite 723
Hollywood, CA 90028
(213) 462-6933

STONEDOG PRODUCTIONS
1819 West Thome Street
Chicago, IL 60660
(312) 869-0175

STONE-HIGH RECORDS, INC.
P.O. Box 2544
Baton Rouge, LA 70821
(504) 924-6865

STOY PRODUCTIONS
279 East Forty-Fourth Street
New York, NY 10017
(212) 986-4994

STREET MUSIC PRODUCTIONS
5307 East Mockingbird Lane, Suite 401
Dallas, TX 75206
(214) 827-0830

STRONGSONG, INC.
250 West Fifty-Seventh Street
Suite 200
New York, NY 10019
(212) 581-7782

STUDIO N PRODUCTIONS
741 Carlisle Way
Sunnyvale, CA 94087
(408) 739-2684

STYLETONE/HOOKS RECORDS
254 East Twenty-Ninth Street, Suite 7

Los Angeles, CA 90011
(213) 746-6499

SUNBURST MUSIC PRODUCTIONS
26949 Chagrin Boulevard, Suite 209
Cleveland, OH 44122
(216) 464-4150

SUN-RAY RECORDS
1662 Wyatt Parkway
Lexington, KY 40505
(606) 254-7474

SUNSET RECORDS, INC.
1577 Redwood Drive
Harvey, LA 70058
(504) 367-8501

THE SUNSHINE MUSIC GROUP
800 South Fourth Street
Philadelphia, PA 19147
(215) 755-7000

SUNTMESTRA PRODUCTIONS
1954 Carmen Avenue
Los Angeles, CA 90028
(213) 466-0400

SURVIVOR PRODUCTIONS
5934 Buffalo Avenue
Van Nuys, CA 91401
(213) 997-8819

SWEETSONG PRODUCTIONS
P.O. Box 2041
Parkersburg, WV 26102
(304) 489-2911

SWEET WHEATS
Drawer W
Manhattan Beach, CA 90266
(213) 379-9069

SWORD RECORDS
P.O. Box 8374
Greenville, SC 24604
(803) 271-1104

T

TNG/EARTHLING, INC.
110 West Eighty-Sixth Street
New York, NY 10024
(212) 799-4181

TRC PRODUCTION GROUP
1330 North Illinois Street
Indianapolis, IN 46202
(317) 638-1491

TAKE HOME TUNES
P.O. Box 1314
Englewood Cliffs, NJ 07632
(201) 567-5524

TALLISBROOKE CORPORATION
420 Lexington Avenue
New York, NY 10017
(212) 986-1355

TANDEM RECORDINGS
13 Moore Street
Bristol, VA 24201
(703) 466-8675

CHIP TAYLOR PRODUCTIONS, LTD.
405 East Fifty-Fourth Street
New York, NY 10022
(212) 489-0470

THIRD STORY RECORDING
3436 Sansom Street
Philadelphia, PA 19104
(215) 386-5998

311 PRODUCTIONS
311 West Fifty-Seventh Street
New York, NY 10019
(212) 765-8200

TIGER RECORDS
P.O. Box 2544
Baton Rouge, LA 70821
(504) 924-6865

RIK TIMORY PRODUCTIONS
622 Route 3A
Cohasset, MA 02025
(617) 383-9494

STEVE TOLIN
7033 Sunset Boulevard, Suite 222
Los Angeles, CA 90028
(213) 464-8300

TREBRON PRODUCTIONS
1802 Grand Avenue
Nashville, TN 37212
(615) 327-4568

TREE PRODUCTIONS
8 Music Square West
Nashville, TN 37203
(615) 327-3162

TREND PRODUCTIONS
P.O. Box 201
Smyrna, GA 30080
(404) 432-2454

TRIBAL JARGON RECORDING
129 Grasmere Street
Newton, MA 02158
(617) 244-6803

TROD NOSSEL ARTISTS
10 George Street
Wallingford, CT 06492
(203) 269-4465

TRYAN PRODUCTIONS
110 Sutter Street
San Francisco, CA 94101
(415) 433-4040

TUMAC MUSIC
2097 Vistadale Court
Tucker, GA 30084
(404) 938-1210

TRAVIS TURK PRODUCTIONS
P.O. Box 17464
Nashville, TN 37212
(615) 367-0144

SCOTT TUTT MUSIC
P.O. Box 121213
Nashville, TN 37212
(615) 329-0856

TWO HEADS PRODUCTIONS
21 Sumner Park
Rochester, NY 14607
(716) 473-0773

HARRISON TYNER INTERNATIONAL, INC.
38 Music Square East, Suite 115
Nashville, TN 37203
(615) 244-4224

U

ULSYRA PRODUCTIONS
1966 Broadway, Suite 45
New York, NY 10023
(212) 874-1200

UNITED AUDIO RECORDING
8535 Fairhaven Avenue
San Antonio, TX 78229
(512) 690-8888

UNITED PRODUCTION CORPORATION OF AMERICA
161 North Mount Prospect Road
Des Plaines, IL 60016
(312) 297-7542

V

VENTURE PRODUCTIONS
121 Meadowbrook Drive
Somerville, NJ 08876
(201) 359-5110

CHARLES VICKERS
171 Pine Haven Drive
Daytona Beach, FL 32014
(904) 252-4849

VIRTUE PRODUCTIONS
1618 North Broad Street
Philadelphia, PA 19121
(215) 763-2825

VOICE BOX RECORDS
3835-B Summer Avenue
Memphis, TN 38122
(901) 458-2371

W

EIRIK WANGBERG
1800 North Argyle Avenue
Los Angeles, CA 90008
(213) 466-3463

WILLIAM F. WAGNER
14343 Addison Street, Suite 218
Sherman Oaks, CA 91423
(213) 501-4161

KENT WASHBURN PRODUCTIONS
10622 Commerce Avenue
Tujunga, CA 91042
(213) 855-0525

WEDNESDAY'S CHILD PRODUCTIONS, INC.
8811 Santa Monica Boulevard
Los Angeles, CA 90069
(213) 657-6751

FRED WEINBERG PRODUCTIONS, INC.
16 Dundee Road
Stamford, CT 06903
(203) 322-5778

WEIRZ WORLD PRODUCTIONS
1414 Summitridge Drive
Beverly Hills, CA 90210
(213) 858-5913

THE WEISMAN PRODUCTION GROUP
449 North Vista Street
Los Angeles, CA 90036
(213) 653-0693

THE WELTY AGENCY
P.O. Box 561
Wooster, OH 44691
(216) 262-0361

WHIPLASH PRODUCTIONS
231 Coler Street
Jackson, MI 49203
(517) 782-4263

RUTH WHITE PRODUCTIONS
Box 34485, Whitney Building
Los Angeles, CA 90034
(213) 836-4678

WHITEWAY PRODUCTIONS, INC.
65 West Fifty-Fifth Street
New York, NY 10019
(212) 757-4317

SHANE WILDER PRODUCTIONS
P.O. Box 3503
Los Angeles, CA 90028
(213) 557-3500

ALEX WILLIAMS ENTERPRISES, INC.
699 McDaniel Street SW
Atlanta, GA 30310
(404) 524-9174

DON WILLIAMS MUSIC GROUP
1888 Century Park East, Suite 1106
Los Angeles, CA 90067
(213) 556-2458

MARTY WILSON PRODUCTIONS, INC.
185 West End Avenue
New York, NY 10023
(212) 580-0255

WIL-TOO MUSIC
2405 Pennington Bend Road
Nashville, TN 37214
(615) 883-2457

WINDY HILL RECORDS
2300 Henderson Mill Road NE
Atlanta, GA 30345
(404) 493-1210

WISHBONE, INC.
P.O. Box 2631
Muscle Shoals, AL 35660
(205) 381-1455

JIMMY WISNER PRODUCTIONS
11 Harrison Court
South Orange, NJ 07079
(201) 762-2504

WITHOUT FAIL PRODUCTIONS
1806 North Normandie Avenue
Los Angeles, CA 90027
(213) 669-1404

WIZARD PRODUCTIONS, INC.
2501 Ocean Drive
Hollywood, FL 33019
(305) 921-6550

WORLDWIDE BIGGIES, INC.
595 West End Avenue, Suite 2C
New York, NY 10024
(212) 799-1438

Y

YEARS AHEAD PRODUCTIONS
P.O. Box 6145
Albany, CA 94706
(415) 526-2450

BARRY YEARWOOD ENTERPRISES
200 West Fifty-First Street
New York, NY 10019
(212) 245-3939

YELLOW BEE PRODUCTIONS, INC.
245 Waverly Place
New York, NY 10014
(212) 255-3698

Z

PAUL ZALESKI
P.O. Box 34032
Bartlett, TN 38134
(901) 377-1439

DAN ZAM PRODUCTIONS
183 Thompson Street
New York, NY 10012
(212) 982-1374

ZEMBU PRODUCTIONS, INC.
Care of Schoenbaum
10 West Sixty-Sixth Street
New York, NY 10023
(212) 580-9159

Music Publishers

U.S. music publishers are listed alphabetically by state. The listings for Canada follow those for the U.S. The symbols *, †, and ‡ indicate affiliation.

- * Member of BMI (Broadcast Music, Inc.)
- † Member of ASCAP (American Society of Composers, Authors and Publishers)
- ‡ Member of SESAC, Inc.

An alphabetical cross-index appears at the end of this section.

ALABAMA

AMERICAN PIE MUSIC*
50 Southmont Dr.
Tuscaloosa, AL 35405
(205) 345-2162
Jim Salem, Pres

BIG HAIR MUSIC*
217 Watts Bar
Sheffield, AL 35660

BROWNLEAF MUSIC CO*
PO Box 7221
Mobile, AL 36607
(205) 342-1177
John N. Blackburn, Pres

CHEAVORIA MUSIC CO.*
1219 Kerlin Ave.
Brewton, AL 36426
(205) 867-2228
Mike Tracy, Mgr

FAME PUBLISHING CO., INC.*
Box 2527
Muscle Shoals, AL 35660
(205) 381-0801
Tommy Brasfield, Gen Mgr

LAW PUBLISHING CO.
305 North Highway 43
Satsuma, AL 36571
(205) 675-4431
Lois Anne Whiting, Pres

MUSCLE SHOALS SOUND PUBLISHING CO., INC.*
Box 915
1000 Alabama Ave.
Sheffield, AL 35660
(205) 381-2060
Jimmy R. Johnson, Pres

ROUND SOUND MUSIC*
1918 Wise Dr.
Dothan, AL 36303
(205) 794-9067
Jerry Wise, Pres

SHERI GLEN PUBLICATIONS INC.*
1316 Alford Ave.
Birmingham, AL 35226
(205) 823-5602
Becky Davis, Pres

SONG TAILORS MUSIC*
PO Box 2631
Muscle Shoals, AL 35660
(205) 381-1455

TIDEWATER MUSIC CO.*
11318 Dellcrest Dr., SE
Huntsville, AL 35803
(205) 881-7976
George Wells, Owner

TOP DRAWER MUSIC*
PO Box 8011
Mobile, AL 36608
(205) 343-3124
M. Brown, Pres

WIDGET PUBLISHING*
PO Box 2446
Muscle Shoals, AL 35660
(205) 381-1300
Ron Ballew, Pres

WOODRICH PUBLISHING CO.*
Box 38
Lexington, AL 35648
(205) 247-3983
Woody Richardson, Pres

ALASKA

UNREGULATED MUSIC*
Box 81485
Fairbanks, AK 99708
(907) 456-3419
Michael States, Pres

ARIZONA

ANCORA PUBLISHING*
2439 S. Dorsey
Tempe, AZ 85282
(602) 966-7764
V. Val Michael, Owner

AUTOGRAPH MUSIC*
601 E. Blacklidge Dr.
Tucson, AZ 85705
(602) 882-9016
Erin Brooks, Mgr

CARDIO MUSIC*
964 W. Grant Rd.
Tucson, AZ 85705
(602) 884-9060
William Cashman, Pres

CHROMEWOOD MUSIC
Box 2388
Prescott, AZ 86302
Gaye Ellen Foreman, Pres, Pub Div

EPOCH UNIVERSAL PUBLICATIONS, INC.*
10802 North 23rd Ave.
Phoenix, AZ 85029
(602) 864-1980
David Serey, Exec VP; Ray Bruno, Pres

E.V. MUSIC PUBLISHING CO.†
4930 N. Calle Bendita

Tucson, AZ 85718
(602) 299-4031
Eve Smith, Pres

GOLDEN GUITAR MUSIC*
Box 40602
Tucson, AZ 85717
Jeff Johnson, Pres

MIGHTY MUSIC*
Box 27160
Phoenix, AZ 85061
(602) 276-7116
Mike Lenaburg, Pres

THE MORGAN MUSIC GROUP
Box 2388
Prescott, AZ 86302
(602) 445-5801
Gaye Ellen Foreman, Pres-Pub

NALR MUSIC PUBLISHING
(North American Liturgy Resources)
10802 N. 23 Ave.
Phoenix, AZ 85023
(602) 864-1980
Ray Bruno, Pres

PANTHEON DESERT PUBLISHING*
6325 N. Invergordon Rd.
Scottsdale, AZ 85253
(602) 948-5883
Brent Burns, Gen Mgr

RENDA MUSIC CO.*
3830 N. 7th St.
Phoenix, AZ 85014
(602) 277-1336
Floyd M. Ramsey, Pres

SOUTHWEST WORDS & MUSIC*
14 E. 2nd St.
Tuscon, AZ 85705
(602) 792-3194
Fred Knipe, Pres

TWIFORD MUSIC*
4640 E. Lewis
Phoenix, AZ 85008
(602) 959-2076
L. John Twiford, Owner

UP WITH PEOPLE†
3103 N. Campbell Ave.
Tucson, AZ 85719
(602) 327-7351
J.B. Belk, Pres

CALIFORNIA

AAO†
7231 Franklin Ave.
Hollywood, CA 90046
(213) 876-3588
Spike Janson, Pres

ACCADIA MUSIC CO.†
9962½ Durant Dr.
Beverly Hills, CA 90212
(213) 277-8383
Mary Herscher, Pres & Gen Mgr

ADDISON STREET†
c/o Sterling Music Co.
8150 Beverly Blvd., Ste. 202
Los Angeles, CA 90048
(213) 651-0471

FRED AHLERT MUSIC CORP†
8150 Beverly Blvd., Ste. 202
Los Angeles, CA 90048
(213) 651-0471
Fred E. Ahlert, Jr., Pres

ALEXIS†
Box 532
Malibu, CA 90265
(213) 858-7282
Lee Magid, Pres

ALFIE RECORDS*
7769 Melrose Ave.
Los Angeles, CA 90046
(213) 653-4818
Al Durand, Pres

ALFIE-SOUND MUSIC PUBLISHING, LOS ANGELES, CA
(*See* Alfie Records)

ALFRED PUBLISHING CO. INC.†
Box 5964
Sherman Oaks, CA 91413
Morton Manus, Pres

ALJONI MUSIC CO.*
Box 18918
Los Angeles, CA 90018
(213) 935-7277
Al Hall, Jr., Owner

ALKATRAZ KORNER MUSIC CO.*
PO Box 3316
San Francisco, CA 94119
Bill Belmont, Mng Dir

ALRUBY MUSIC INC.†
Fryder, Bider & Montgomery
1900 Ave. of the Stars, Ste. 755
Los Angeles, CA 90067

ALSHIRE PUBLISHING CO.
1015 Isabel
Burbank, CA 91505
(213) 849-4671
Al Sherman, Pres

ALTERNATIVES IN AMERICAN MUSIC†
PO Box 6127
Albany, CA 94706
(415) 527-3606
George M. Lely, Gen Mgr

AMERICAN BROADCASTING MUSIC, INC.†
4151 Prospect Ave.
Hollywood, CA 90027
(213) 663-3311
Georgett Studnicka, Dir

AMESTOY MUSIC*
117 N. Las Palmas Ave.
Los Angeles, CA 90004
(213) 938-5482
Albert Marx, Pres

AMIRON MUSIC†
20531 Plummer St.
Chatsworth, CA 91311
(213) 998-0443
A. Sullivan, Gen Mgr

ANY PRODUCTION INC.†
2118 W. 12th St.
Santa Ana, CA 92703
(714) 836-1760
Craig A. Kitchens, Pres

APEX MUSIC PUBLICATIONS*
19146 Twig Lane
Cupertino, CA 95014
(408) 252-1580
E.F. Moss, Pres

A-PLUS MUSIC INC (CALIF)
(*See* Arista Music Publishing Group)

ARDAVAN MUSIC†
PO Box 2512
Hollywood, CA 90028
(213) 462-3745
Ardie Bryant, Pres

ARISTA MUSIC PUBLISHING GROUP†‡
8304 Beverly Blvd.
Los Angeles, CA 90048
(213) 852-0771
Linda Blum, Mgr

ATJACK MUSIC*
4050 Buckingham Rd.
Los Angeles, CA 90008
(213) 290-2262
James Earl Jackson, Pres

ATV MUSIC CORP*
6255 Sunset Blvd.
Hollywood, CA 90028
(213) 462-6933

AUDIO ARTS PUBLISHING†
5617 Melrose Ave.
Los Angeles, CA 90038
(213) 461-3507
Madelon Baker, Pres

BAL & BAL MUSIC PUBLISHING CO.†
Box 369
LaCanada, CA 91011
(213) 790-1242
Adrian Bal, Pres

BARADAT MUSIC*
1384 E. Sequoia Ave.

Tulare, CA 93274
(209) 686-2533

Raymond Baradat, Pres

BARTON MUSIC CORP†
9220 Sunset Blvd.
Los Angeles, CA 90069
(213) 273-3590

Paula Sanicola, Pres

BARUTH MUSIC
8033 Sunset Blvd., Ste. 101
Hollywood, CA 90046
(213) 840-0490

Jain Baruth, Mgr

BEE MOR MUSIC*
1100 Glendon Station 2129
Los Angeles, CA 90024
(213) 208-7871

Morey Alexander, VP

BEECHWOOD MUSIC CORP*
6255 Sunset Blvd.
Hollywood, CA 90028
(213) 469-8371

Lester Sill, Pres

BELMONT MUSIC PUBLISHERS†
PO Box 49961
Los Angeles, Ca 90049
(213) 472-2557

Lawrence A. Schoenber, Pres

QUINT BENEDETTI MUSIC
Box 2388
Toluca Lake, Ca 91602
(213) 985-8284

Quint Benedetti, Pres

BENFEL MUSIC*
10th & Parker Sts.
Berkeley, CA 94710
(415) 549-2500

Paul Zaentz, Mgr

BERDOO MUSIC*
PO Box 8875
Universal City, CA 91608
(213) 985-2539

George Clements, Pres

BESERKLEY RECORDS
2054 University Ave.
Berkeley, CA 94704
(415) 848-6701

Mathew King Kaufman

BEVERLY HILLS MUSIC*
c/o Lawrence Herbst Investment Trust Fund
PO Box 1659
Beverly Hills, CA 90213

Lawrence Herbst, Pres

BICYCLE MUSIC CO.
8756 Holloway Dr.
Los Angeles, CA 90069
(213) 659-6361

David Rosner, Pres

BIG HEART MUSIC*
9454 Wilshire Blvd., Ste. 309
Beverly Hills, CA 90212
(213) 273-7020

Randy Bash, Mng Dir

BIRTHRIGHT MUSIC†
3101 S. Western Ave.
Box 18705
Los Angeles, CA 90018
(213) 731-2460

Byron Spears, Pres

BLACK BULL MUSIC INC.†
c/o Steveland Morris
9000 Sunset Blvd., Ste. 617
Los Angeles, CA 90069

BLACK STALLION COUNTRY PUBLISHING*
Box 2250
Culver City, CA 90230
(213) 674-9280

Kenn Kingsbury, Pres

BLUE BOOK MUSIC*
1225 N. Chester Ave.
Bakersfield, CA 93308
(805) 393-1011

Buck Owens, Owner

BLUE CANYON MUSIC*
563 Loganbury Dr.
San Rafael, CA 94903

Jim Terr, Owner

BLUE ISLAND PUBLISHING
1446 N. Martel, Unit 3
Los Angeles, CA 90046
(213) 851-3161

Bob Gilbert, Pres

BLUE RIVER MUSIC INC.*
1626 N. Vine St.
Hollywood, CA 90028
(213) 463-7661

c/o Harry Bluestone

FRED BOCK MUSIC CO.†
Box 333
Tarzana, CA 91356
(213) 996-6181

Fred Bock, Pres

BOSS TWEED MUSIC*
Box 23
Sun Valley, CA 91352
(213) 982-2174

J. Eric Freedner

BOURNE CO.
6381 Hollywood Blvd.
Los Angeles, CA 90028
(213) 469-5101

TOMMY BOYCE & MELVIN POWERS MUSIC ENTERPRISES†
12015 Sherman Rd.
North Hollywood, CA 91605
(213) 875-1711

Melvin Powers, Pres

BRAINTREE MUSIC*
c/o Segel and Goldman Inc.
9348 Santa Monica Blvd.
Beverly Hills, CA 90210
(213) 278-9200

BRAVE NEW MUSIC*
6253 Hollywood Blvd., Ste. 1116
Hollywood, CA 90028
(213) 466-3534

Daniel Friedman, Pres

BREAD 'N HONEY†
PO Box 3391
Ventura, CA 93006
(805) 644-7618

BROTHER PUBLISHING CO.*
c/o Michael Mesnick
9100 Wilshire Blvd., #460
Beverly Hills, CA 90212

BRUNSWICK MUSIC PUBLISHING CO.*
136 South Swall Dr.
Beverly Hills, CA 90211
(213) 657-4895

Lee Silver, Owner

BUG MUSIC GROUP*
6777 Hollywood Blvd.
Los Angeles, CA 90028
(213) 466-4352

Fred Bourgoise, VP

BUTTERFLY-GONG MUSIC*
c/o Moultrie Accountancy Corp.
PO Box 5270
Beverly Hills, CA 90210

CALWEST SONGS*
c/o Lee Anderson Enterprises
PO Box 4141
North Hollywood, CA 91607
(213) 782-6915

Lee Anderson, Owner

CAMBRIA PUBLISHING†
Box 2163
Rancho Palos Verdes, CA 90274
(213) 541-1114

Lance Bowling, Dir of Pub

CAMILLO-BARKER ENTERPRISES
6430 Sunset Blvd.
Los Angeles, CA 90028
(213) 462-3162

GLEN CAMPBELL ENTERPRISES, LTD.
1900 Ave. of the Stars, Ste. 2530
Los Angeles, CA 90067
(213) 553-8434

CAN YOU HEAR ME MUSIC*
Box 14243
San Francisco, CA 94114
(415) 824-3676
R. Hanrahan

CANOPY MUSIC†
c/o William F. William
1427 7th St.
Santa Monica, CA 90401

CAPTAIN NEMO MUSIC†
11800 Mayfield Ave.
Los Angeles, CA 90049
(213) 820-5061

CAREER MUSIC*
1888 Century Park E.
Los Angeles, CA 90067
(213) 553-1777

CARLIN MUSIC PUBLISHING CO.
PO Box 2289
Oakhurst, CA 93644
(209) 683-7613
Sidney A. Carlin, President

CASCADE MOUNTAIN MUSIC†
18039 S. Crenshaw Blvd., Ste. 300
Torrance, CA 90504
(213) 538-5476
William J. Wickline, Pres

CHALK FARM MUSIC*
9570 Wilshire Blvd.
Beverly Hills, CA 90212
(213) 276-7663
Rich Neigher, Pres

CHAPPELL MUSIC CO.
6255 Sunset Blvd.
Hollywood, CA 90028
(213) 469-5141
Roger Gordon, VP & Gen Mgr

CHICAGO MUSIC PUBLISHING
c/o Greene & Reynolds
1900 Ave. of the Stars
Los Angeles, CA 90067
(213) 553-5434

CHINNICHAP PUBLISHING INC, CA
(*See* Career Music Inc. Los Angeles, CA)

CHINWAH SONGS/BIRTHRIGHT MUSIC‡
3101 S. Western Ave.
Box 18709
Los Angeles, CA 90018
(213) 258-8011
Leroy C. Lovett, Gen Mgr

CHRYSALIS MUSIC GROUP
9255 Sunset Blvd.
Los Angeles, CA 90069
(213) 550-0174
Steve Moir, Mgr

CLARKEE MUSIC*
c/o Mr. A. Kim Guggenheim
Schlesizer & Guggenheim
6255 Sunset Blvd., Ste. 1214
Hollywood, CA 90028

CLEVETOWN MUSIC‡
c/o James Bullard
5505 Zelzah Ave.
Encino, CA 91316
(213) 931-2662

CLOCKUS MUSIC CO.*
Star Rt.
Milford, CA 96121
(916) 253-3689
Ed Marmor, Owner

MARTIN COHEN
6430 Sunset Blvd.
Los Angeles, CA 90028
(213) 463-1151

BRUCE COHN MUSIC
Box 359
Sonoma, CA 95476
(707) 938-4060
Bruce Cohn, Owner

COM MUSIC‡
Attn: Lee Houghnane
c/o Kaufman Eisenberg & Co.
9301 Wilshire Blvd., Ste. 212
Beverly Hills, CA 90210
(213) 550-1580

COMBINE MUSIC CORP
Div. of Monument Record Corp.
1800 N. Highland Ave.
Hollywood, CA 90028
(213) 463-1652
Bill Anthony, Mgr.

CONDUCIVE MUSIC INC.*
PO Box 78645
Los Angeles, CA
(213) 299-8722

CONTEMPORARY MUSIC
Box 2628
Los Angeles, CA 90028
(213) 466-1633
John Koenig, Pres

MARTIN COOPER MUSIC‡
PO Box 3331
Beverly Hills, CA 90212
(213) 275-4508
Marty Cooper, Owner

COUNTRY MOON PUBLISHING‡
463 S. Robertson Blvd.
Beverly Hills, CA 90211
James R. Halper, Pres

COUNTRY ROAD MUSIC*
c/o Gelfand, Rennert & Feldman
1880 Century Park E, #900
Los Angeles, CA 90067
(213) 553-1707

COYOTE PRODUCTIONS INC.‡
306 Bora Bora Way, #309
Marina Del Ray, CA 90291
(213) 823-0171
Leonard Sachs, President

CRABSHAW MUSIC‡
4334 Fran Way
El Sobrante, CA 94803
Elvin Bishop, Pres

CREATIVE CONCEPTS PUBLISHING CORP.
967 E. Ojai Ave.
Ojai, CA 93023
(805) 646-4811
John L. Haag, Pres

CREATIVE CORPS
6607 W. Sunset, Ste. E
Hollywood, CA 90028
(213) 464-3495
Kurt Hunter, Pres

CREATIVE MUSIC GROUP
6430 Sunset Blvd.
Hollywood, CA 90028
(213) 467-1135

CRISTEVAL MUSIC
15015 Ventura Blvd.
Sherman Oaks, CA
(213) 996-1771

CRITERION MUSIC CORP.†
6124 Selma Ave.
Hollywood, CA 90028
(213) 469-2296
Michael H. Goldsen, Pres

THE CRYSTAL JUKEBOX*
c/o CBS Studio Center
4024 Radford Ave.
North Hollywood, CA 91604
(213) 760-5000

V & M CUTLER MUSIC CO.
Box 43
Chatsworth, CA 91311
(213) 886-7746
Max Cutler, Mgr

DAIN & DEJOY*
6363 Sunset Blvd.
Los Angeles, CA 90028
(213) 465-1108
Bud Dain

DAVIKE MUSIC CO.†
Box 8842
Los Angeles, CA 90008
(213) 292-5138
Isaiah Jones, Owner

DAWNBREAKER MUSIC CO.*
Manatt, Phelps, Rothenberg & Tunney
1888 Century Park E.
Los Angeles, CA 90067
(213) 556-5555

DE WALDEN MUSIC INTERNATIONAL, INC.*
6255 Sunset Blvd., #1911
Hollywood, CA 90028
(213) 462-1922
Christian de Walden, Mng Dir

DEERTRACK MUSIC
c/o Mitchell, Silberberg & Knupp
1800 Century Park E.
Los Angeles, CA 90067
(213) 553-5000

DELMORE MUSIC CO.†
PO Box 2324
Menlo Park, CA 94025
(415) 322-2947
Cy Coben, Pres

RICHARD DELVY ENTERPRISES INC.†
8127 Elrita Dr.
Los Angeles, CA 90046
(213) 650-4761
Richard Delvy, Pres

DERRY MUSIC CO.*
601 Montgomery St.
San Francisco, CA 94111
(415) 433-1800
Richard Singer, Mgr

DIAMONDBACK MUSIC*
10 Waterville St.
San Francisco, CA 94124
Joseph Buchwald, Admin

WALT DISNEY MUSIC CO.†
350 S. Buena Vista St.
Burbank, CA 91521
(213) 840-1000
Gary Krisel, VP

DOHENY MUSIC*
8571 Holloway Dr.
Los Angeles, CA 90069
(213) 659-5479
J.W. Alexander, Pres

DOLLY BEE MUSIC*
515 East Racquet Club Rd.
Palm Springs, CA 92262
(714) 327-9216
George R. Brown, Owner

DOORS MUSIC CO.†
Att: Jerry Swartz
9200 Sunset Blvd., Ste 704
Los Angeles, CA 90069
(213) 278-9944

DRIVE-IN MUSIC CO., INC.*
7120 Sunset Blvd.
Hollywood, CA 90046
(213) 851-2500

DRUNK MONEY MUSIC*
22458 Ventura Blvd., Ste. E
Woodland Hills, CA 91364

DUANE MUSIC, INC.*†
382 Clarence Ave.
Sunnyvale, CA 94086
(408) 739-6133
Garrie Thompson, Pres

DUPUY RECORDS/ PRODUCTIONS/PUBLISHING, INC.
10960 Ventura Blvd., Ste. 200
Studio City, CA 91604
(213) 980-6412
Pedro Dupuy, Pres

DUSKSONGS MUSIC*
Div. of Dusk Recording Studios
2217-A The Alameda
Santa Clara, CA 95050
(408) 248-3875

DYNAMO PUBLISHING CO.
Box 6
484 Lake Park Ave.
Oakland, CA 94610
(415) 482-4854
Dan Orth, A & R Dir

EAGLE ROCK MUSIC CO.†
5414 Radford Ave.
North Hollywood, CA 91607
(213) 760-8771
Mort Katz, Pres

EARLY BIRD MUSIC*
Waltner Enterprises
14702 Canterbury
Tustin, CA 92680
(714) 731-2981
Steve Waltner, Owner

EASTEX MUSIC*
8537 Sunset Blvd., #2
Los Angeles, CA 90069
(213) 657-8852
Travis Lehman, Owner

EASY MONEY MUSIC
c/o Gelfand, Rennert & Feldman
Att: Bobbie Green
1880 Century Park E, Ste. #900
Los Angeles, CA 90067
(213) 553-1707

EL CHICANO MUSIC†
20531 Plummer St.
Chatsworth, CA 91311
(213) 998-0443
A. Sullivan, Gen Mgr

ELIZABETH MUSIC PUBLISHING*
515 E. Racquet Club Rd.
Palm Springs, CA 92262
(714) 327-9216
George R. Brown, Owner

ELM PUBLISHING CO.*
PO Box 1100
14621 Allen St.
Westminster, CA 92683
Edd L. McNeely, Pres
(714) 898-7317

Local Branch:
John Robinson Music
6461 Walt St.
Westminster, CA 92683
(714) 893-3637
John E. Robinson, Chief Exec

EMANDELL TUNES‡
10220 Glade Ave.
Chatsworth, CA 91311
(213) 341-2264
Leroy C. Lovett, Jr., Pres

EQUA MUSIC†
1800 Mowry Ave.
Fremont, CA 94538
(415) 794-6637
Warren M. Johnson, Pres

EVANTON MUSIC*
PO Box 2217
Inglewood, CA 90305
(213) 644-8182
Leonard S. Falconer, Pres

EXXTRA FOXX PUBLISHING*
PO Box 5430
Vallejo, CA 94590
(707) 644-0971
Linda and Louis McCall

FAIRCHILD MUSIC PUBLISHING*
13112 Halcourt
Norwalk, CA 90650
(213) 466-5418
Jerry Wood, Owner

FALLEN ANGEL PUBLISHING*
11035 Hayvenhurst, #11
Granada Hills, CA 91344

FAMOUS MUSIC CORP.
6430 Sunset Blvd.
Los Angeles, CA 90028
(213) 461-3091
Julie Chester, Mgr

FARJO MUSIC*
11257 Blix St.
North Hollywood, CA 91602
(213) 508-9865
Vince Ciavarella, Prdctn Mgr; Joe Farrell, Pres

FARO MUSIC PUBLISHING*
255 N. New Hampshire Ave.
Los Angeles, CA 90004
(213) 384-9586
Edward L. Davis, Owner

FATE MUSIC†
1046 Carol Dr.
Los Angeles, CA 90069

FATHER MUSIC GROUP*
7647 Woodrow Wilson Dr.
Hollywood, CA 90046
(213) 462-1922
Barry Richards, Exec VP

F E L PUBLICATIONS LTD.†
Attn: Dennis J. Fitzpatrick
1925 S. Pontius Ave.
Los Angeles, CA 90025
(213) 478-0053

MAYNARD FERGUSON MUSIC PUBLISHING†
Box 716
Ojai, CA 93023
(805) 646-8156
Kim Ferguson

FERMATA INTERNATIONAL MELODIES†
6290 Sunset Blvd., Ste. 916
Hollywood, CA 90028
(213) 462-7473
Enrique Lebendiger, Pres

FIRELIGHT PUBLISHING†
c/o SRS
6772 Hollywood Blvd.
Hollywood, CA 90028
(213) 764-3980
Doug Thiele, Pres

FIRST ARTISTS MUSIC CO.
c/o Management III Music
9744 Wilshire Blvd.
Beverly Hills, CA 90212
(213) 550-7100

CARL FISCHER INC.
1101 South Hope St.
Los Angeles, CA 90015
(213) 749-5227
Morton Baumgart, Mgr

FLEETWOOD MAC MUSIC*
c/o Shapiro & Steinberg
315 South Beverly Dr.
Beverly Hills, CA 90212
(213) 553-1601

FOLKLORE PRODUCTIONS INC.†
1671 Appian Way
Santa Monica, CA 90401
(213) 451-0767
Manuel Greenhill, Pres

FOSTER FREES MUSIC*
c/o Shankman DeBlasio
185 Pier Ave.
Santa Monica, CA 90405

FOUR BUDDIES†
Div of Ham-Sem Records
541 S. Spring St. #8
Los Angeles, CA 90013
(213) 627-0122
William Campbell, Pres

FOUR KNIGHTS MUSIC*
6000 Sunset Blvd.
Hollywood, CA 90028
(213) 461-3484

FOUR STAR INTERNATIONAL INC.
19770 Bahama St.
Northridge, CA 91324
(213) 709-1122
David B. Charnay, Pres

FOURTH HOUSE MUSIC PUBLISHING CO.
1436 S. LaCienega Blvd., Ste 209
Los Angeles, CA 90035
(213) 652-7731
Lim Taylor, Prdctn Chief

SAM FOX PUBLISHING CO. INC.†
73-941 Highway 111, Ste. 11
Palm Desert, CA 92260
(714) 568-4144
Frederick Fox, President

FREE & SHOW MUSIC†
652 Hilary Dr.
Tiburon, CA 94920
(415) 435-5223
Ron Patton, Pres

FUENTE MUSIC CO.*
PO Box 1233
Santa Monica, CA 90406
(213) 822-9022
Bobby Manrique, Owner

FYDAQ MUSIC*
240 E. Radcliffe Dr.
Claremont, CA 91711
(714) 624-0677
Gary Buckley, Pres

AL GALLICO MUSIC CORP
9255 Sunset Blvd., Ste. 507
Los Angeles, CA 90069
Kevin Magowan, Air Asst

GARAGE MUSIC*
297 E. Reed St., Apt. 3
San Jose, CA 95112

GARRETT MUSIC ENTERPRISES
6255 Sunset Blvd., Ste. 1019
Hollywood, CA 90028
(213) 467-2181
Snuff Garrett, Pres

GENTLE WIND PUBLISHING CO.*
1030 48th St.
Sacramento, CA 95819
(916) 451-3400
Charles M. Brandt, Pres

GLENWOOD MUSIC CORP.†
6255 Sunset Blvd., Ste 1201
Hollywood, CA 90028
(213) 469-8371

GLORY ALLELUIA MUSIC*
1711 E. Sobronte Ct.
Yuba City, CA 95991

GOLD HILL MUSIC, INC.†
5032 Lankershim Blvd.
North Hollywood, CA 91601
(213) 766-7142
Stephen Stills, Pres

GOLD HORIZON MUSIC CORP*
c/o Screen-Gems-EMI Music Inc.
PO Box 80699
Los Angeles, CA 90080
(213) 469-8371

GOLDEN WEST MELODIES INC.*
5858 Sunset Blvd.
Hollywood, CA 90028
Gene Autry, Pres

GOLDGRESH MUSIC*
7033 Sunset Blvd., Ste. 309
Los Angeles, CA 90028
David Gresham, Pres

GOOD HIGH MUSIC†
c/o Fred S. Moultrie, CPA
PO Box 5270
Beverly Hills, CA 90210

GOOSEBUMP MUSIC*
Div of The Record Co.
6362 Hollywood Blvd.
Los Angeles, CA 90028
(213) 462-2038

GORDON MUSIC CO. INC.†
12111 Strathern St., Ste. 103
North Hollywood, CA 91605
Jeff Gordon, Pres

GRAJONCA*
c/o Bill Graham Presents
201 11th St.
San Francisco, CA 94103
(415) 864-0815
Bill Graham, Pres

THE GRAND PASHA PUBLISHER*
5615 Melrose Ave.
Hollywood, CA 90038
(213) 466-3507
Larry Marks, Mgr

GRANITE ROCK MUSIC*
PO Box 1206
Studio City, CA 91604
(213) 877-1351
Dan Mark, Pres

GRASSROOTS PROJECTS UNLIMITED*
PO Box 4689
San Francisco, CA 94101
(415) 922-3227
James Heisterkamp, Owner

GREAT HONESTY MUSIC INC.*
Box 547

Larkspur, CA 94939
(415) 924-8778
Erik Jacobsen, Pres

GREAT PYRAMID MUSIC*
10 Waterville St.
San Francisco, CA 94124
(415) 468-4288
Martyn Buchwald, Pres

GREENBAR MUSIC CORP.†
7235 Hollywood Blvd.
Los Angeles, CA 90046
(213) 874-4275
Ben Barton, Pres

GROUP 88 MUSIC†
PO Box 8190
Universal City, CA 91608
(213) 787-3344
Carlos Saenz, Pres

E.J. GURREN MUSIC†
3929 Kentucky Dr.
Los Angeles, CA 90068
(213) 760-3670
Eddie Gurren, Pres

HALL OF FAME MUSIC CO.*
Box 921
Beverly Hills, CA 90213

HAMPSTEAD HEATH MUSIC PUBLISHERS†
7505 Jerez Ct.
Rancho La Costa
Carlsbad, CA 92008
Jay Senter, Pres

HANOVER MUSIC CORP†
PO Box 6296
Beverly Hills, CA 90212
Paul Weston, Pres

HARRISON MUSIC CORP.†
6253 Hollywood Blvd., Ste. 807
Hollywood, CA 90028
(213) 466-3834
Tad Maloney, Mgr

HEAVEN SONGS*
9502 Harrell St.
Pica Rivera, CA 90660
(213) 692-1472
Dave Paton

HIGH-MINDED MOMO PUBLISHING & PRODUCTION*
Empire Ranch
2329 Empire Grade
Santa Cruz, CA 95060
(408) 427-1248
Kai Moore Snyder

HIGHTREE*
c/o Renaissance Management
433 N. Camden Dr.
Beverly Hills, CA 90210
(213) 550-1276

THE HIT MACHINE MUSIC CO.
Sub. Diversified Management Group
Box 20692
San Diego, CA 92120
(714) 277-3141
Marty Kuritz, Pres

HOBBY HORSE MUSIC*
6255 Sunset Blvd.
Los Angeles, CA 90028
(213) 467-2181

HOMEWOOD HOUSE MUSIC*
c/o James Golden
3128 Cavendish Dr.
Los Angeles, CA 90064

JERRY HOOKS SR.
254 E. 29th St.
Los Angeles, CA 90011
(213) 746-6490
Jerry Hooks Sr.

HORTTOR MUSIC CO.*
313 El Tejon Ave.
Oildale
Bakersfield, CA 93308
(805) 399-9028
Robert L. Horttor, Owner

HOUSE OF KNOX*†
41418 50th St. W.
Quartz Hill, CA 93534
(805) 943-4183
Robert B. Knox, Owner

HOUSE OF ROCK MUSIC*
958 W. Edgemont Dr.
San Bernardino, CA 92405
(714) 882-6796
Bill & Myral Bellman, Owners

I.A.M. MUSIC†
17422 Murphy Ave.
Irvine, CA 92719
(714) 751-2015
Paul Freeman, VP; Skip Konte, Pres

ICE NINE PUBLISHING CO. INC†
PO Box 1073
San Rafael, CA 94901
(415) 457-2322
Robert Hunger, Pres

INDIA MUSIC INK
c/o Greene & Reynolds
1900 Ave. of the Stars
Los Angeles, CA 90067
(213) 553-5434

INSTANT REPLAY MUSIC CO.†
Box 353
Marina, CA 93933
Robert Waldrup II, Gen Mgr Pub

INTERMOUNTAIN MUSIC*
PO Box 1067
Hollywood, CA 90028
Reta Chandler, Owner

INVADOR MUSIC CO.*
2974 Parkview Dr.
Thousand Oaks, CA 91362
(805) 497-4738
Don Perry, Pres

IRVING MUSIC*
1336 North LaBrea
Hollywood, CA 90028
(213) 469-2411

ISLAND MUSIC/UFO MUSIC, INC.*
6525 Sunset Blvd.
Hollywood, CA 90028
(213) 469-1285
Lionel Conway, Pres

ALICE M. JACKSON MUSIC†
9000 Sunset Blvd., Ste. 807
West Hollywood, CA 90069
(213) 550-0397
Alice M. Jackson, Pres

JACON MUSIC*
c/o Jack Conrad
2958 N. Beachwood Dr.
Los Angeles, CA 90068
(213) 465-1261

JAMES S. ENTERPRISES
7120-261 Carlson Circle
Canoga Park, CA 91303
James Leach, Pres

JANELL MUSIC PUBLISHING/TIKI ENTERPRISES, INC.*
792 E. Julian St.
San Jose, CA 95112
(408) 286-9840
Gradie O'Neal, Pres

JAY MUSIC†
6654 Allott Ave.
Van Nuys, CA 91401
(213) 873-2699
Johnny Rotella, Pres

J E D O MUSIC†
5062 Calatrana Dr.
Woodland Hills, CA 91364
(213) 703-0083
Jon Devirian, Pres

JOBETE MUSIC CO., INC.†
6255 Sunset Blvd., Ste. 1600
Hollywood, CA 90028
(213) 468-3400
Robert Gordy, Exec VP

JOMARK MUSIC US†
936 N. Sierra Bonita, #5
Los Angeles, CA 90046
Joel Wertman, Pres

JONDORA MUSIC*
10th & Parker Sts.
Berkeley, CA 94710
(415) 549-2500
Paul Zaentz, Mgr

JUGUMBA MUSIC†
c/o Jim Golden
3128 Cavendish Dr.
Los Angeles, CA 90064
Jim Golden, Pres

JUMP TUNES
c/o Jess S. Morgan & Co.
6420 Wilshire Blvd.
Los Angeles, CA 90048
(213) 651-1601

KARLA MUSIC PUBLISHING†
11042 Aqua Vista St.
North Hollywood, CA 91602
James Argiro, Pres

KECA MUSIC INC.†
9440 Santa Monica Blvd., Ste. 704
Beverly Hills, CA 90210
(213) 278-3156
Larry Gordon, Pres

KENGORUS MUSIC†
c/o Perry Potkin & co.
9200 Sunset Blvd.
Los Angeles, CA 90069
(213) 273-6167
Brenda Russell, Bus Mgr

KENTUCKY COLONEL MUSIC*
734 Fairview Ave.
Sierra Madre, CA 91024
John M. Delgatto, Pres

KERISTENE MUSIC, LTD.*
1605 N. Martel, #21
Hollywood, CA 90046
(213) 851-9418
Kenneth H. Smith, Gen Mgr

KICKING MULE PUBLISHING/DESK DRAWER PUBLISHING*
Box 158
Alderpoint, CA 95411
(707) 926-5312
Ed Denson, Pres

KIDADA MUSIC INC.*
c/o A & M Records
1416 North LaBrea Ave.
Hollywood, CA 90028
(213) 469-2411

KINDNESS OF STRANGERS MUSIC*
c/o Zane Lubin
6767 Forest Lawn Dr.
Los Angeles, CA 90068

KINETIC PRODUCTIONS
8055 Selma Ave.
Los Angeles, CA 90046
(213) 654-6744

KIPAHULU MUSIC CO.†
c/o David A. Gates
24344 Rolleny View Dr.
Calabaasas, CA 91302

KIRSHNER/CBS MUSIC PUBLISHING
9000 Sunset Blvd.
Los Angeles, CA 90069
(213) 278-4160

NEIL A. KJOS MUSIC CO.‡
4382 Jutland Dr.
San Diego, CA 92117
(714) 270-9800
Neil A. Kjos, Jr., Pres

KOALA
6253 Hollywood Blvd.
Los Angeles, CA 90028
(213) 467-3203

KOLBER PUBLISHING CO.*
332 W. 14th St.
Upland, CA 91786
(714) 985-0073

KYODO TOKYO INC.
c/o Henry Miller Associates
9454 Wilshire Blvd.
Beverly Hills, CA 90028
(213) 278-9454

LADERA MUSIC PUBLISHING*
Box 91120
Worldway Postal Center
Los Angeles, CA 90009
(213) 641-0178
Philip Sonnichsen, Pres

LADY JANE MUSIC*
PO Box 614
Tahoe City, CA 95730
(916) 583-6587
Hoyt Axton, Pres

JAY LANDERS MUSIC†
9255 Sunset Blvd., Ste. 509
Los Angeles, CA 90069
(213) 550-8819
Jay Landers, Pres

STUART LANIS MUSIC, INC.*
1273½ N. Crescent Hts. Blvd.
Los Angeles, CA 90046
(213) 550-4500
Stuart Lanis, Pres

LARKSPUR MUSIC PUBLISHING*
Box 1001
Soquel, CA 95073
(408) 462-6537
Jon Hutchings, Gen Mgr

LAUGHING BIRD SONGS PUBLISHING CO.
Box 3144
Covina, CA 91723
(213) 339-9769
Angelo Roman, Jr., Pres

LEAR MUSIC INC.†
314 Huntley Dr.
Los Angeles, CA 90048
(213) 652-2222
Jack Rael, Pres

LEN-LON MUSIC CO.*
c/o Sandra R. Newman
1326 N. Flores St.
Los Angeles, CA 90069
(213) 654-4601
Leonard C. Williams, Pres

LEXICON MUSIC INC.†
PO Box 2222
Newbury Park, CA 91320
Ralph Carmichael, Pres

LIDO MUSIC*
c/o Segel & Goldman
9348 Santa Monica Blvd.
Beverly Hills, CA 90210
(213) 278-9200

LION'S GATE FILMS INC.†
1861 S. Bundy Dr.
Los Angeles, CA 90025
(213) 820-7751

LITO MUSIC*
c/o Recorded Treasures Inc.
PO Box 1278
North Hollywood, CA 91604
(213) 766-4693
Walt Heebner

LONE STAR GRASS MUSIC
Box 6546
Burbank, CA 91510
E. Snead/T. Stafford, Owners

LORETTA MUSIC*
1116 N. Cory Ave.
Los Angeles, CA 90069
(213) 278-5131
Lloyd Segal, Pres

LORING MUSIC CO.*
1048 N. Carol Dr.
Los Angeles, CA 90069
(213) 276-7103
Mike Conner, Pres

LUCKY BULL MUSIC
3645 Midvale Ave.
Los Angeles, CA 90034
(213) 204-1954
James & Nancy Bullock, Partners

LUCKYU*
c/o Jess S. Morgan & Co.
6420 Wilshire Blvd.
Los Angeles, CA 90048
(213) 651-1601

LUNATUNES MUSIC*
2400 Fulton St.
San Francisco, CA 94118

LYNNSTORM PUBLISHING CO.†
10787 Wilshire Blvd.
Los Angeles, CA 90024
Irving Mills, Pres

MACARTHUR MUSIC*
PO Box 82

1659 Sweetbrier St.
Palmdale, CA 93550
(805) 947-1232
Glen MacArthur, Pres

MAD EAGLE MUSIC*
Box 8621
Anaheim, CA 92802
(714) 636-1208
Alice Maenza, Pres

MAD LAD MUSIC INC.*
Attn: Sam Trust
ATV Music Corp.
6255 Sunset Blvd., Ste. 723
Hollywood, CA 90028

MADRID MUSIC CO.†
Box 504
4290 Acacia Ave.
Bonita, CA 92002
(714) 421-0865
Virginia Anderson, Pres

MAIN STAVE MUSIC†
PO Box 3763
Hollywood, CA 90028
(213) 894-9487
Jeff Oxman, Pres

MAINSPRING WATCHWORKS MUSIC†
PO Box 40133
San Francisco, CA 94104
(415) 626-4467
H.S. Carr, Gen Mgr

MANAGEMENT III MUSIC*
9744 Wilshire Blvd.
Los Angeles, CA 90212
(213) 550-7100
Sandi Beach, Music Oper Dir

MANDINA MUSIC*
6255 Sunset Blvd., #723
Hollywood, CA 90028
(213) 462-6933
Steve Stone, VP

MANNA MUSIC, INC.†
2111 Kenmere Ave.
Burbank, CA 91504
(213) 843-8100
Hal Spencer, Pres

MANTRA MUSIC*
222 E. Garvey Ave.
Monterey Park, CA 91754
(213) 280-8783
Johnny Thompson, Owner

MANWIN MUSIC*
c/o Chapman Distributing Co.
1212 Albany St.
Los Angeles, CA 90015
(213) 749-9484
Al Chapman, Owner

MARSHALL SONGS MUSIC*
Div. of Echo Park Records
7985 Santa Monica Blvd.
Los Angeles, CA 90046
(213) 413-2188
Marshall Heaney, Pres

MARVIN GARDENS†
9884 Santa Monica Blvd.
Beverly Hills, CA 90212
(213) 550-6363
Neil Bogart, Pres

MARZIQUE MUSIC*
5752 Bowcroft St.
Los Angeles, CA 90016
(213) 295-0058
Harold R. Battiste Jr., Pres

MAY 12TH MUSIC INC.
Div. of Whitfield Records Inc.
8425 Melrose Ave.
Los Angeles, CA 90069
(213) 652-5850

MCA MUSIC
MCA Inc.
70 Universal City Plaza
Universal City, CA 91608
(213) 508-4550

JIMMY MCHUGH MUSIC INC.†
9301 Wilshire Blvd.
Beverly Hills, CA 90210
(213) 271-1967
Lucille Meyers, Pres

MEADOWEE MUSIC*
1727 Roanoke Ave.
Sacramento, CA 95838
(916) 925-4886
Jerry Parker, Owner

MEDBERY MUSIC
2408 Rockefeller Lane #2
Redondo Beach, CA 90278
(213) 376-1113
Michael Sandomeno, Pres

MERCANTILE MUSIC*
Box 2271
Palm Springs, CA 92263
(714) 320-4848
Kent Fox, Pres

MESA LANE MUSIC†
(*See* MizMo Enterprises)

EARL MILES PUBLISHING CO.*
1704 Wagner Heights Rd.
Stockton, CA 95209
Earl Miles, Owner

MILK MONEY MUSIC†
9348 Santa Monica Blvd., #304
Beverly Hills, CA 90210
(213) 278-9200

MILLS & MILLS*
c/o Six Continents Music Pub. Co.
8304 Beverly Blvd.
Los Angeles, CA 90048

MIRSONG MUSIC USA*
PO Box 946
Hollywood, CA 90028
(213) 721-1637
Marko Perko, Pres

MIZMO ENTERPRISES†
2512 Chandler Blvd.
Burbank, CA 91505
(213) 954-9946
Maureen Woods, Pres

MOBY DICK RECORDS†
573 Castro St.
San Francisco, CA 94114
(415) 861-0476
Bill Motley, Pres

MODERN MUSIC PUBLISHING INC.*
5810 S. Normandie Ave.
Los Angeles, CA 90044
(213) 753-5121

MONSTEROUS MUSIC†
5105 Varna Ave.
Sherman Oaks, CA 91423
(213) 467-1135
John Davis, Pres

DOUG MOODY MUSIC
Mystic Music Centre
6277 Selma Ave.
Hollywood, CA 90028
Doug Moody, Pres

JESS H. MORGAN & CO., INC.
6420 Wilshire Blvd.
Los Angeles, CA 90048
(213) 651-1601

MORRIS MUSIC, INC.*
9255 Sunset Blvd., Ste. 319
Hollywood, CA 90069
(213) 550-0171
Alison Witlin, Mgr

MOTHER BERTHA MUSIC INC.*
PO Box 69529
Los Angeles, CA 90069
(213) 846-9900
Phil Spector, Pres

MULTI-MILL†
31203 Ganado Dr.
Rancho Palos Verdes, CA 90274
(213) 541-6710
Dean Chambers, Pres

MUNKA MUSIC*
4920 Marden Lane
La Mesa, CA 92041
(714) 464-0910
Stephen C. LaVere, Pres

MUSIC CONCEPTS INTERNATIONAL
9348 Santa Monica Blvd.

Beverly Hills, CA 90210
(213) 550-6255
Steve Bedell, Pres

MUSIC PUBLISHING CORPORATION/CREAM PUBLISHING GROUP
8025 Melrose Ave.
Los Angeles, CA 90046
(213) 655-0944
Marty Sadler, Mgr

MUSICTONE MUSIC*
PO Box 343
Santa Monica, CA 90406
(213) 394-5110
Irvin A. Brock, Pres

MUSICWAYS INC.*
9033 Wilshire Blvd., Ste. 310A
Beverly Hills, CA 90211
(213) 278-8118
Terri Fricon, Pres

NARWHAL MUSIC*
3612 Coldwater Ave.
Studio City, CA 91604

NASHCAL MUSIC*
3746 Mount Diablo Blvd.
Lafayette, CA 94546
(415) 283-7624
Chris Blake

NEIL MUSIC INC.*
8400 Sunset Blvd., Ste. 4A
Los Angeles, CA 90069
(213) 656-2614
Gene Norman, Pres

NEURON MUSIC†
PO Box 1594
Hollywood, CA 90028
(213) 662-8588

NEW WINE PRODUCTIONS†
PO Box 544
Lomita, CA 90717
(213) 454-1528
G. Nelson Stringer, Pres

NEWORLD MEDIA MUSIC PUBLISHERS†
c/o Gelfand Breslauer Et Al
431 S. Palm Canyon Dr. #104
PO Box 2202
Palm Springs, CA 92263

NEWPORT BEACH MUSIC*
17422 Murphy Ave.
Irving, CA 92714
(714) 751-2015
Paul Freeman, VP Record Prod

JOSEPH NICOLETTI MUSIC CO.†
1550 S. Beverly Dr.
S-6
Los Angeles, CA 90039
Joseph Nicoletti, Pres

NIDA MUSIC PUBLISHING CO.†
4014 Murietta Ave.
Sherman Oaks, CA 91403
(213) 981-5331
Nicholas S. Carras, Pres

NINTH MUSIC*
c/o Lawrence N. Rogers
2323 Curinth Ave.
Los Angeles, CA 90064

NITE-STALK MUSIC†
c/o Wm. A. Cohen, Esq.
6399 Wilshire Blvd. Penthouse
Los Angeles, CA 90048

KENNY NOLAN PUBLISHING CO.†
c/o Peter C. Bennett
9060 Santa Monica Blvd., Ste. 300
Los Angeles, CA 90069
(213) 278-7344
Kenny Nolan, Pres

O'BRIEN PUBLISHING CO.
234 5th Ave.
Redwood City, CA 94063
(415) 367-0298
E.J. O'Brien, Pres

MICHAEL O'CONNOR MUSIC*
Box 1869
Studio City, CA 91604
(213) 762-7551
Michael O'Connor, Pres

OCTAVE HIGHER MUSIC*
46501 Aster Ave., Ste. 222
Sherman Oaks, CA 91403

OLEO MUSIC*
228 S. Helberta
Redondo Beach, CA 90277
(213) 372-9317
Jim Turnage, Owner

O'LYRIC MUSIC†
11833 Laurelwood Dr.
Studio City, CA 91604
(213) 506-5473
Jim O'Loughlin, Pres

OPEN END MUSIC INC.*
7720 Sunset Blvd.
Los Angeles, CA 90046
(213) 851-9115
Bennett H. Glotzer, Pres

ORIGATUNES PUBLISHING CO.*
Box 1143
Bellflower, CA 90706
(213) 866-4146
Mearl Ellison, Owner

OVER THE RAINBOW MUSIC†
6430 Sunset Blvd.
Hollywood, CA 90028
(213) 467-1135

PACIFIC CHALLENGER MUSIC*
2940 E. Miraloma Ave.
Anaheim, CA 92806
(714) 992-6827
C.E. Whittington, Pres

PALE PACHYDERM PUBLISHING*
444 Grove St.
San Francisco, CA 94102
(415) 431-7480
John E. Kennedy, Chmn

PARASOUND INC.
680 Beach St.
San Francisco, CA 94109
(415) 673-4544
Bernard Krause, Pres

PASHA MUSIC ORG.†
5615 Melrose Ave.
Hollywood, CA 90038
(213) 466-3507
Spencer D. Proffer, Pres

PEACEABLE KINGDOM†
3525 Encinal Canyon Rd.
Malibu, CA 90265
(213) 457-4405
C. Randolph Nauert, Pres

PEACEFUL MUSIC CO.*
c/o Warner-Tamerlane Pub. Co.
9200 Sunset Blvd., Ste. 222
Los Angeles, CA 90069

PEACOCK MUSIC*
8544 Sunset Blvd.
Los Angeles, CA 90069

PEER-SOUTHERN ORGANIZATION
6777 Hollywood Blvd.
Hollywood, CA 90028
(213) 469-1667
Roy Kohn, Mgr

PERENNIAL MUSIC*
3099 Diablo View Rd.
Lafayette, CA 94509
(415) 930-7573
Hillel Resner, Gen Mgr

PERREN VIBES†
c/o The Mom & Pops Co. Store
11704 Ventura Blvd.
Studio City, CA 91604
(213) 877-2797

DON PERRY PRODUCTIONS†
2974 Parkview Dr.
Thousands Oaks, CA 91362
(805) 497-4738
Don Perry

PESO MUSIC*
6255 Sunset Blvd.
Los Angeles, CA 90028
(213) 467-2181

PEWTER PAL MUSIC*
PO Box 133
524 Del Oro Dr.

Ojai, CA 93023
Jim Pewter, Pres

PHILIPPOPOLIS MUSIC*
12027 Califa St.
North Hollywood, CA 91607
Milcho Leviev, Pres

PIGFOOT MUSIC†
c/o Weinzveg
536 B. St.
Santa Rosa, CA 95401

PIROOTING MUSIC†
c/o Segel & Goldman
9348 Santa Monica Blvd., #304
Beverly Hills, CA 90210
(213) 278-9200

POIEMA MUSIC PUBLISHING*
506 Cottonwood St.
Woodland, CA 95695

POLISH PRINCE MUSIC†
c/o Kaufman Eisenberg & Co.
9301 Wilshire Blvd., Ste. 212
Beverly Hills, CA 90210
(213) 550-1580

PORPETE MUSIC PUBLISHING CO.*
PO Box 777
Hollywood, CA 90028
(213) 882-1558
Anita Poree, Pres

PRINGLE MUSIC PUBLISHERS*
7021 Hatillo Ave.
Canoga Park, CA 91306
(213) 347-3902

PRITCHETT PUBLICATIONS*
38603 Sage Tree St.
Palmdale, CA 93550
(805) 947-4657
L.R. Pritchett, Pres

PROFESSIONAL MUSIC PRODS. INC.
14731-E Franklin Ave.
Tustin, CA 92680
(714) 838-8421
Leon White, Pres

PROTONE MUSIC†
970 Bel Air Rd.
Los Angeles, CA 90024
(213) 472-5344
Jane Courtland Welton, Dir

PURPLE LADY PUBLISHING*
PO Box 757
Tiburon, CA 94920
(415) 435-0720
Barbara Meislin, Pres

PZAZZ MUSIC*
257 Ashdale Pl.
Los Angeles, CA 90049
(213) 476-2286
Stephen L. Bedell, President

QUACKENBUSH MUSIC LTD.†
c/o Gelfand Rennert & Feldman
1880 Century Park East, #900
Los Angeles, CA 90067
(213) 553-1707

RAC RACOUILLAT MUSIC ENTERPRISES
7934 Mission Center Ct.
San Diego, CA 92108
(714) 296-9641
Robert Racouillat, Pres

RADA DARA MUSIC*
29518 Rainsford Pl.
Malibu, CA 90265

FRED RAPHAEL MUSIC INC.†
319 Via Don Benito
Cathedral City, CA 92234
(714) 328-0170
Hermione Greene, Pres

RARE BLUE MUSIC†
9255 Sunset Blvd.
Los Angeles, CA 90069
(213) 550-0171

BILL RASE PRODUCTIONS INC.*
955 Venture Ct.
Sacramento, CA 95825
(916) 929-9181
Bill Rase, Pres

RAYDIOLA MUSIC*
Box 5270
Beverly Hills, CA 90210
(213) 857-5517
Fred S. Moultrie, Mgr

RED DWARF MUSIC*
13006 Saticoy St.
North Hollywood, CA 91605
(213) 764-1172
Chris Kuchler, Pres

RED RIVER SONGS INC.*
1001 N. Lincoln St.
Burbank, CA 91506
(213) 557-2553
Dorothy L. Bond, Pres

RED TENNIES MUSIC*
816 North LaCienega
Los Angeles, CA 90069
(213) 657-4521
Dale Gonyea, Pres

LEON RENE PUBLICATIONS†
2124 W. 24th St.
Los Angeles, CA 90018
(213) 737-5125

RENO/METZ MUSIC INC.†
8265 Sunset Blvd., Ste. 200
Los Angeles, CA 90046
Bob Reno, Pres

RESPECT MUSIC CO.*
1159 S. LaJolla Ave.
Los Angeles, CA 90035
(213) 938-3531
Miles Grayson, Pres

RHYTHMS PRODUCTIONS†
Whitney Bldg.
Box 34485
Los Angeles, CA 90034
Ruth White, Pres

DON ROBERTSON MUSIC CORP.†
PO Box 4141
Thousand Oaks, CA 91359
(213) 889-0876
Don Robertson, Pres

ROBIN HOOD MUSIC CO.*
5531 Tuxedo Terr.
Hollywood, CA 90028
(213) 465-9758
John Marascalco, Pres

JOHN ROBINSON MUSIC
(*See* Elm Publishing Co., CA)

ROCKET PUBLISHING*
3459 Cahuenga
Los Angeles, CA 90068
(213) 851-9845

ROCKMORE MUSIC*
1733 Carmona Ave.
Los Angeles, CA 90019
(213) 933-6521
Willie H. Rocquemore, Owner

ROGER MUSIC INC.†
17752 Skypark Blvd., Ste. 265
Irvine, CA 92714
Joseph S. Shribman, Pres

ROLLING DICE MUSIC PUBLISHING†
Box 794
Hollywood, CA 90028
(213) 208-2728
Sharon Schwartz-Kugell, Mgr

RONDOR MUSIC INC.
1358 North LaBrea Ave.
Hollywood, CA 90028
(213) 469-2411
Charles B. Kaye, Pres

BRIAN ROSS MUSIC*
7120 Sunset Blvd.
Hollywood, CA 90046
(213) 851-2500
Brian Ross, Pres

ROUGH TRADE, INC.†
326 6th St.
San Francisco, CA 94103
(415) 621-4102
Anne Lehman

ROWCHAR MUSIC†
716 W. 33 St.
San Pedro, CA 90731

(213) 833-1233
John Rowin, Pres

RUBICON MUSIC
8319 Lankershim Blvd.
North Hollywood, CA 91605
(213) 875-1775
Teri Piro, VP

DAVID RUBINSON & FRIENDS, INC.†
827 Folsom St.
San Francisco, CA 94107
(415) 777-2930
David Rubinson, Pres

S & R MUSIC PUBLISHING CO.†
39 Belmont
Rancho Mirage, CA 92270
(714) 346-0075
Scott Seely, Pres

ST. CECILIA MUSIC*
1414 Summitridge Dr.
Beverly Hills, CA 90210
(213) 858-5913
Larry Weir, Pub

SAME OLD MUSIC PUBLISHING*
PO Box 622
Orangevale, CA 95662
(916) 726-4816
John Roberts, Pres

SAN JUAN AVENUE MUSIC*
8909 W. Olympic Blvd.
Beverly Hills, CA 90211
(213) 657-8795

SANGRE PUBLISHING†
9844 Business Park Dr.
Sacramento, CA 95827
(916) 361-3652
Jan Eric Volz, Exec Coord

SASHA SONGS, UNLIMITED & THE GRAND PASHA PUBLISHERS*
Div. of The Pash Music Org., Inc.
5615 Melrose
Hollywood, CA 90038
(213) 466-3507
Spencer D. Proffer, Pres

SATRYCON MUSIC*
PO Box 75692
Los Angeles, CA 90075
(213) 656-0982
David Austin, Owner

DAVID SCHINE & CO. INC.†
626 S. Hudson Ave.
Los Angeles, CA 90005
(213) 937-5000
G. David Schine, Pres

SCHRODER MUSIC CO.†
2027 Parker St.
Berkeley, CA 94704
(415) 843-2365
Nancy Schimmel, Owner

SCOTT MUSIC PUBLICATIONS
PO Box 148
Hollywood, CA 90028
(714) 992-1522
Scott Fredrickson, Pres

SCOTTI BROTHERS MUSIC PUBLISHING†
2114 Pico Blvd.
Santa Monica, CA 90405
(213) 450-3193
Tony Scotti, Pres

SCREEN GEMS-EMI MUSIC INC.*
6255 Sunset Blvd.
Hollywood, CA 90028
(213) 469-8371
Lester Sill, Pres

SEAFOOD MUSIC*
PO Box 42338
San Francisco, CA 94101
(415) 821-7311
Barry Melton, Dir

JOHN SEBASTIAN MUSIC
c/o Mitchell, Silberberg & Knupp
1800 Century Park E.
Los Angeles, CA 90067
(213) 553-5000

SEVENTH RAY PUBLISHING†
Box 3771
Hollywood, CA 90020
(213) 467-0611
Alan Ames, Prod

SHADE TREE MUSIC INC.*
Box 500
Bella Vista, CA 96008
(916) 241-9020

SHAMGA PUBLISHING CO.*
254 E. 29th St., Ste. 7
Los Angeles, CA 90011
(213) 746-6499
Duffy Hooks, III, Pres

CYRIL SHANE MUSIC INC.†
1724 Bowcliff Terr.
Southshore Hills,
Westlake Village, CA 91361
Cyril Shane, Pres

LARRY SHAYNE ENTERPRISES†
6362 Hollywood Blvd. #222
Hollywood, CA 90028
(213) 462-5466

SILK PURSE MUSIC*
5801 Margavido Dr.
Oakland, CA 94618
Michael Cogan, Owner

SILVER FIDDLE MUSIC†
c/o Segel & Goldman
9348 Santa Monica Blvd., #304
Beverly Hills, CA 90210
(213) 278-9200

SILVER NIGHTINGALE MUSIC†
Attn: Jan Bulkin
200 Neptune Ave.
Encinitas, CA 92024

SILVERHILL MUSIC*
PO Box 39439
Los Angeles, CA 90039
(213) 663-8073
Paul F. Wells, Exec. Asst

GEORGE SIMON INC.†
2147 Sunshine Circle
Palm Springs, CA 92262
(714) 327-4464
George Simon, Pres

SIREN SONGS*
c/o Gelfand, Rennert & Feldman
1880 Century Park E., #900
Los Angeles, CA 90067
(213) 553-1707

SIX CONTINENTS MUSIC PUBLISHING*
8304 Beverly Blvd.
Los Angeles, CA 90048

SKINNY ZACH MUSIC†
6430 Sunset Blvd.
Hollywood, CA 90028
(213) 461-2988
Zachary Glickman, Pres

SKYHILL PUBLISHING CO.*
6525 Sunset Blvd.
Hollywood, CA 90028
(213) 469-1285
Denny Cordell, Pres

SKYWAY MUSIC PUBLISHING*
PO Box 133
Hollywood, CA 90028
Everett L. Whenham, Owner

SLASH MUSIC*
7381 Beverly Blvd.
Los Angeles, CA 90036
(213) 937-4660
Robert Biggs, Pres

SLEEPY HOLLOW MUSIC CO.
c/o Magic Touch Music
9134 Sunset Blvd.
Los Angeles, CA 90069
(213) 273-6580

SMALL HILL MUSIC†
c/o Neil Levin & Co.
9595 Wilshire Blvd., #505
Beverly Hills, CA 90212

SNOW MUSIC*
9120 Sunset Blvd.
Los Angeles, CA 90069
(213) 274-8584
Dona Spangler, Prof Rep

SOLID SMOKE SONGS†
PO Box 22372

San Francisco, CA 94122
(415) 731-0500
Mary Arbunich, Contact

SOLO MUSIC INC.†
4708 Van Noord Ave.
Sherman Oak, CA 91403
(213) 762-2219
Paul Mills, Pres

SONG DOCTOR MUSIC*
c/o Dick Glasser
12660 King St.
Studio City, CA 91604

SONG SONGS†
229 San Vicente, Ste. D
Santa Monica, CA 90402
(213) 393-1343
Peter Kaye, Pres

SONGPAINTER MUSIC*
c/o Segel & Goldman, Inc.
9348 Santa Monica Blvd.
Beverly Hills, CA 90210

SONLIFE MUSIC†
Box 552
Woodland Hills, Ca 91365
(213) 703-6707
Paul A. Johnson, Pres

SOPRANO MUSIC CO.
4118 W. 106 St.
Inglewood, CA 90303
(213) 673-3562
Tina L. Thompson, Pres

SOUNDS OF NOLAN MUSIC*
c/o Peter C. Bennett
9060 Santa Monica Blvd.
Los Angeles, CA 90069

SPACEARK ENTS.†
PO Box 1150
Yermo, CA 92398
Trou B. Raglin, Pres

SPARROW/BIRDWING MUSIC
8025 Deering
Canoga Park, CA 91304
(213) 703-6599
Phil Perkins, Dir of Pub

SPINA MUSIC†
2232 Vista Del Mar Pl.
Hollywood, CA 90028
(213) 467-6018
Harold Spina, Pres

TERRY STAFFORD MUSIC*
Box 6546
Burbank, CA 91510
Terry Stafford, Pres

STANYAN MUSIC CO.†
1155 Angelo Dr.
Beverly Hills, CA 90210
(213) 656-7311
Rod McKuen, Pres

STARTIME MUSIC†
Box 643
48 780 Eisenhowever Dr.
LaQuinta, CA 92253
(714) 564-4823
Fred Rice, Pres

STAX RECORD CO.
2600 10th St.
Berkeley, CA 94710
(415) 549-2500
Paul Zaentz

STEAMED CLAM MUSIC*
c/o Mitchell, Silberkey & Knupp
1800 Century Park E
Los Angeles, CA 90067

STEPHEN STILLS MUSIC*
5032 Lankersham Blvd.
North Hollywood, CA 91601
(213) 766-7142

STONE DIAMOND MUSIC CORP*
6255 Sunset Blvd.
Hollywood, CA 90028
(213) 468-3400
Lay Lowy, VP/Gen Mgr

STONEBASS MUSIC CO.*
163 Orizaba Ave.
San Francisco, CA 94132
(415) 334-2247
Walter C. Stone, Pres

STREET SENSE MUSIC†
c/o Mitchell Silberberg Knupp
1800 Century Park E, Ste. 700
Los Angeles, CA 90067
(213) 553-5000

SUFI PIPKIN MUSIC*
PO Box 3991
Hollywood, CA 90028
(213) 276-2063
Linda R. Moxley, Owner

TAKOMA MUSIC
9255 Sunset Blvd.
Los Angeles, CA 90069
(213) 550-0171
Jon Monday, Gen Mgr

TANGLED WEB MUSIC CO.*
7050 Shoup Ave.
No. 22
Canoga Park, CA 91504
(213) 884-4495
Michael Hart, Pres

TANTALIZING TUNES/ATOMIC TUNES*
474 Atchison St.
Pasadena, CA 91104
(213) 463-8400
Ben Brooks, Gen Mgr

TARANTULA MUSIC†
c/o Segal & Goldman
9348 Santa Monica Blvd., #304
Beverly Hills, CA 90210
(213) 278-9200

10 OF DIAMONDS MUSIC
5934 Buffalo Ave.
Van Nuys, CA 91401
(213) 997-8819
Jason Schwartz, Pres

PETER TEVIS MUSIC
PO Box 1102
Burbank, CA 91507
(213) 874-7656
Peter Tevis, Pres

THIRTY FOUR MUSIC†
4329 Colfax Ave.
Studio City, CA 91604
(213) 766-6411
Russell Shaw, President

3 H'S MUSIC
1103 Neff Ave. So.
West Covina, CA 91790
(213) 919-5055
Henry Oakes, Pres

THREESOME MUSIC†
1801 Ave of the Stars
Los Angeles, CA 90067

TIKI ENTS. INC.†
792 E. Julian
San Jose, CA 95112
(408) 286-9840
Gradie O'Neal, Pres

TOOTER SCOOTER MUSIC*
792 E. Julian
San Jose, CA 95112
(408) 286-9840
Jeanne Osborn, Pres

TOULOUSE MUSIC PUBLISHING CO., INC.
Box 96
El Cerrito, CA 94530
(415) 526-3491
James Bronson Jr., Exec VP

TRADITION MUSIC CO.*
PO Box 9195
Berkeley, CA 94709
C. Strachwitz, Pres

TRANSATLANTIC MUSIC*
Box 1998
Beverly Hills, CA 90213
Fred de Rafois, Pres

TRIDEX MUSIC*
PO Box 1646
Burbank, CA 91507
(213) 849-5774
Robert L. Bogle, Owner

TRUE BLUE MUSIC PUBLISHING CO.†
16027 Sunburst St.
Sepulveda, CA 91343
(213) 892-0044
Larry Fotine, Pres

TRUST MUSIC MGMT. INC.
6255 Sunset Blvd.
Los Angeles, CA 90028
(213) 462-6933
Samuel S. Tryst, Pres

TUFF TURKEY TOONS INC.*
c/o Craig Wilson
160555 Ventura Blvd., Ste. 721
Encino, CA 91436
Tony Jacks, Pres

TUMBLEWEED MUSIC
4344 Promenade Way, Ste. 300
Marina del Rey, CA 90291
(213) 823-8311

TUNEWORKS RECORDS
15625 Vandorf Pl.
Encino, CA 91436
(213) 278-8970
Dennis Lambert, Pres

TYMER MUSIC*
PO Box 1669
Carlsbad, CA 92008
(714) 729-8406

ULTIMA THULE MUSIC PUBLISHING CO.*
Box 20604
2351 Fourth Ave.
Sacramento, CA 95820
(916) 454-4525
Almerritt Covington, Pres

ULTIMATE RECORDS MUSIC PUBLISHING
7087 Bark Ln.
San Jose, CA 95129
(408) 996-1868

UNDERWOOD MUSIC*
19273 Berclair Lane
Tarzana, CA 91356

UNIROYCE MUSIC*
c/o Harrison & Hearn
Crocker Plaza, Ste. 600
84 W. Santa Clara St.
San Jose, CA 95113
(408) 298-7565
Charles Privitera, Pres

UNITED ARTISTS MUSIC†
6753 Hollywood Blvd.
Los Angeles, CA 90028
(213) 469-3600
Harold Seider, President

VAAM MUSIC*
3740 Evans St.
Los Angeles, CA 90027
(213) 664-7765
Pete Martin, Pres

VERDE VISTA MUSIC†
2383 Union St., No. 4
San Francisco, CA 94123
(415) 567-6935
S. White, Pres

VETTE MUSIC CO.
6262 Sunset Blvd.
Hollywood, CA 90028
(213) 462-5466

WARNER BROS., MUSIC
9200 Sunset Blvd.
Los Angeles, CA 90069
(213) 273-3323
Mel Bly, Pres

RON WEISER PUBLISHING*
6918 Peach Ave.
Van Nuys, CA 91406
(213) 781-4805
Ron Weiser, Pres

SHANE WILDER MUSIC*
Box 3503
Hollywood, CA 90028
(213) 762-1613
Shane Wilder, Pres

WILL-DU MUSIC PUBLISHERS
833 N. Orange Grove Ave.
Los Angeles, CA 90046
(213) 653-8358
Lou Dulfon, Pres

DOOTSIE WILLIAMS PUBLICATIONS*
121 S. Hope St., Ste. 334
Los Angeles, CA 90012
(213) 628-7768
Dootsie Williams, Pres

DON WILLIAMS MUSIC GROUP
1888 Century Park E.
Los Angeles, CA 90067
(213) 556-2458
Don Williams, Owner

WINDHAM HILL MUSIC*
PO Box 9388
Stanford, CA 94305
(415) 329-0647
William Ackerman, Pres

WOODEN NICKEL MUSIC INC.†
3128 Cavendish Dr., Ste. 820
Los Angeles, CA 90064
James Golden, Pres

WOOLNOUGH MUSIC*
1550 Neptune
Leucadia, CA 92024
(213) 752-6688

YATAHEY MUSIC*
c/o Ray Ruff
PO Box 1746
Hollywood, CA 90028

YBARRA MUSIC†
Box 665
Lemon Grove, CA 92045
(714) 462-6538
Richard Braum, Owner

YUGGOTH MUSIC CO.*
c/o James Golden
3128 Cavendish Dr.
Los Angeles, CA 90064

ZEBRA DISCORDE MUSIC GROUP*
6255 Sunset Blvd., Ste. 1911
Hollywood, CA 90028
Christian De Walden

COLORADO

BREGAR MUSIC†
428 E 11th Ave.
Denver, CO 80203
(303) 839-5789
Edward F. Pierson, Esq.

FERNDOCK MUSIC†
Div of Wormwood Projects
1540 Lehigh St.
Boulder, CO 80303
(303) 499-1108
Michael D. Aisner, Gen Mgr

RED ROCK MUSIC CO.
PO Box 2671
Denver, CO 80201
(303) 572-9099
James C. Scott, Pres

TWELVE TRIBES MUSIC CO., INC.*
PO Box 18785
1106-8 E. 17th Ave.
Denver, CO 80218
(303) 832-3999
Jim Ransom, Pres

CONNECTICUT

BELL HOLDING MUSIC†
Div. Bell Holding Properties Corp.
Att: Pharon Capitol Corp.
25 Woodhaven
Glastonbury, CT 06033

BIG MUSIC*
PO Box 57
10 George St.
Wallingford, CT 06492
(203) 269-4465
Thomas Cavalier, Pres

BREAKTHROUGH QUALITY MUSIC
Bo 354
Curham, CT 06422

(203) 349-9637
Michael Frost, Mgr

DRAGON FLY MUSIC*
219 Meriden Rd.
Waterbury, CT 06705
(203) 754-3674
Ralph Calabrese, Owner

FOLK LEGACY RECORDS INC.*
Sharon Mountain Rd.
Sharon, CT 06069
(203) 364-5661
Lee B. Haggerty, Pres

LAUREN KIM MUSIC†
16 Dundee Rd.
Stamford, CT 06903
(203) 322-5778
Joan R. Weinberg, Pres

MAYFLOWER MUSIC CORP.†
605 Ridgefield Rd.
Wilton, CT 06897
(203) 762-0558
Eckert Rahn, Pres

MENTOR MUSIC INC.*
18 Broadview Dr.
Brookfield, CT 06804
(203) 775-1358
Robert E. Nagel, Pres

WILLIE NELSON MUSIC INC.*
225 Main St.
Danbury, CT 06810

H & G RANDALL INC.
29 Elaine Rd.
Milford, CT 06460
(203) 878-7383
Gerald Randall, Pres

ROHM MUSIC*
10 George St.
Box 57
Wallingford, CT. 06492
(203) 265-0010
Doug Synder, A & R Dlr; Thomas Cavalier, Pres

SOMETHING ELSE MUSIC CO.*
917 Silvermine Rd.
New Canaan, CT 06840
(203) 966-7078
Sture A. Linden, Pres

TAKE HOME TUNES RECORD CO.
PO Box 496
Georgetown, CT 06829
(203) 544-8288
Bruce Yeko, Chief Exec

TANNEN MUSIC INC.*
38 Laurel Ledge Ct.
Stamford, CT 06903
(212) 489-6740
Paul Tannen, Pres

DELAWARE

BETH-ANN MUSIC CO.
615 Baldwin Ln.
Wilmington, DE 19803
(302) 762-2410
Albert G. Teoli, Pres

STRAIGHT FACE MUSIC†
Box 324
Newark, DE 19711
(215) 692-2777

WHITE CLAY PRODUCTIONS, INC.*
1103 Elktan Rd.
Newark, DE 19711
(302) 368-1211
E. Michael Fisher, Pres

DISTRICT OF COLUMBIA

BAND OF ANGELS, INC.*
1420 K St. NW, Ste. 1400
Washington, DC 20005
(202) 347-1420
Yolanda McFarlane, Dir of Pub

DIAMOND IN THE ROUGH MUSIC*
1532 U St. NW
Washington, DC 20009
(202) 635-0464
Rodney Brown, VP A&R

LAST COLONY MUSIC*
Div of Last Colony Presentations Inc.
PO Box 3253
Washington, DC 20010
(202) 667-2995
M. Nicholas Mann Jr., Pres

FLORIDA

CHUCK ANTHONY MUSIC INC.*
111 W. 57th St.
New York, NY 10019
(305) 869-7300
Peter Shukat

AURA LOVE PUBLISHING*
PO Box 553
600 Diane Circle
Casselberry, FL 32707
(305) 331-4453
Terry R. Brooks, Pres

AVILO MUSIC
880 NE 71st St.
Miami, FL 33138
(305) 759-1405
Carlos Oliva, Pres

BEANTOWN PUBLISHING CO.*
910 E. Maxwell St.
Pensacola, FL 32503
(904) 438-2763
Earl Lett, Pres

BELLAMY BROS. MUSIC†
Rt. 2, Box 294
Dade City, FL 33525

BUFFALO BILL MUISC*
2501 S. Ocean Dr.
Hollywood, FL 33022
(305) 921-6550
Robert S. Taran, Pres

BUSCH COUNTRY PUBLISHING
1002 West Busch Blvd.
Tampa, FL 33612
(813) 935-6289
Randall Bethencourt, Owner

CARLSON MUSIC CO.*
4625 NW 44th St.
Fort Lauderdale, FL 33319
(904) 731-4669
Harry Carlson, Owner

CARRHORN MUSIC INC.*
809 Whipporwill Dr.
Port Orange, FL 32019
(904) 761-9685
Pete and Jo Ann Carr, Owners

CLEAR LIGHT INC.
1500 Gateway Dr.
Ft. Lauderdale, FL 33309
(305) 973-4900

COUNTRY SUN PUBLISHING CO.*
401 Magnolia
Auburndale, FL 33823
(813) 967-3088
Leo Gillman, Pres

COWBOY JUNCTION PUBLISHING CO.*
Box 1, Star Rt. 1
Highway 44 West
Lecanto, FL 32661
(904) 746-2394
Boris Pastuch, Pres

CUDE & PICKENS PUBLISHING*
519 N. Halifax Ave.
Daytona Beach, FL 32018
(904) 252-0381
Bobby Lee Cude, A & R Dir

DANA PUBLISHING CO.*
824 83rd St.
Mlami Beach, FL 33141
(305) 865-8960
Walter Dana, President

DOC RON PUBLISHING*
301 NW Second Ave.
Boynton Beach, FL 33135
(305) 732-1145
Dr. Ron Stander, Pres

EARTH AND SKY MUSIC PUBLISHING, INC.*
Box 4157

Winter Park, FL 32793
Ernest Hatton, Pres

FOUNTAIN OF LIFE MUSIC*‡
PO Box 10846
5535 25th St. W
Bradenton, FL 33507
(813) 756-7781

FRIENDLY FINLEY MUSIC*
103 Westview Ave.
PO Box 98
Valparaiso, FL 32580
(904) 678-7211
Finley Duncan, Owner

GIL GILDAY PUBLISHING CO.
Box 600516
North Miami Beach, FL 33160
(305) 945-3738
J. Gilday, Owner

G.J. MUSIC CO.*
Box 4171
Princeton, FL 33030
Morton Glosser, Owner

GRAND ARTISTS MUSIC*
Div of Paul Stevens Assoc. Inc.
1033 Coral Way
Coral Gables, FL
Paul Stevens, Pres

GREAT ALPS PUBLISHING*
17745 NW 19th Ave.
Miami, FL 33056
Aaron L. Broomfield, Pres

HAMMAN PUBLISHING, INC.*
Rt. 1, Box 195A, Dean Rd.
Maitland, FL 32751
(305) 677-0611
Glenn Hamman, Pres

HARRICK MUSIC, INC.*
Box 1780
Hialeah, FL 33011
(305) 888-1685
Sherry Smith, Mgr

JAY JAY PUBLISHING CO.*
35 NE 62nd St.
Miami, FL 33138
W. Jagiello, Owner

EDWIN F. KALMUS & CO. INC.†
13125 NW 47th Ave.
OpaLocka, FL 33054
(305) 681-4683
Lawrence Galison, Owner

KENVAD MUSIC INC.†
PO Box 2331
Orlando, FL 32802
(305) 896-5601
Kenneth W. Davies, Pres

LINDSEYANNE CO INC.*
495 SE 10 Ct.
Hialeah, FL 33010
(305) 888-1685
Steve Alaimo

LISAS THEME MUSIC*
Drawer 12406
St. Petersburg, FL 33733
(813) 327-5525
Mike Douglas, Pres

MOSIE LISTER PUBLICATIONS‡
11306 Corrollwood Dr.
Tampa, FL 33618
(813) 935-2988

MDK MUSIC, LTD.
c/o Paul Kigar
Amcongen, Sao Paulo
APO Miami, FL 34030
(011) 203-6692
Malcolm Forest, Owner

MICHAVIN MUSIC
1260 North F. St.
Pensacola, FL 32501
Vincent L. Smith III, Owner

MUSIC FOR PERCUSSION, INC.*
170 NE 33rd St.
Fort Lauderdale, FL 33334
(305) 563-1844
Bernard Fisher, Gen Mgr

PALAMAR MUSIC PUBLISHERS*
726 Carlson Dr.
Orlando, FL 32804
(305) 644-3853
Will Campbell, Pres

PINE ISLAND MUSIC*
Box 630175
Miami, FL 33163
(305) 472-7757
Jack P. Bluestine, Pres

PLATINUM MUSIC PUBLISHING
567 NW 27 St.
Miami, FL 33127
(305) 576-2600
Bob Archibald, Pres

PLYMOUTH MUSIC CO. INC.‡
170 NE 33rd St.
Fort Lauderdale, FL 33334
(305) 563-1844
Bernard Fisher, Gen Mgr

PRITCHETT PUBLICATIONS
171 Pine Haven
Daytona Beach, FL 32014
(904) 252-4849
Charles Vickers, Gen Mgr

REVOLVER MUSIC†
7901 4th St. North, Ste. 310
St. Petersburg, FL 33702
Charles R. Kimp, Gen Mgr

RUBANK INC.†
16215 NW 15th Ave.
Miami, FL 33169
(305) 625-5323

SAKA MUSIC CO.*
5937 Ravenswood Rd.
Bldg H-11
Fort Lauderdale, FL 33312
(305) 456-0847
Eugene Settler, Pres

SCHABRAF MUSIC*
5000 Eggleston Ave.
Orlando, FL 32810
(305) 293-1781
Eric T. Schabacker, Pres

SEACOAST MUSIC PUBLISHING CO. INC.*
1440 79th St. Causeway, Ste. 301
Miami Beach, FL 33141
(305) 861-2181
Hal Fein, Co-Pres

SHERLYN PUBLISHING CO.
495 SE 10 Ct.
Hialeah, FL 33010
(305) 888-1685

SOLA GRATIA MUSIC
5000 Eggleston Ave.
Orlando, FL 32810
(305) 293-1781
Eric T. Schabacker, Pres

STEADY ARM MUSIC*
Box 13222
Gainesville, FL 32604
(904) 378-8156
Charles V. Steadham, Jr., Gen Mgr

JEB STUART MUSIC CO.*
Box 6032, Station B
Miami, FL 33123
(305) 547-1424
Jeb Stuart, Pres

TREEHOUSE MUSIC†
PO Box 3174
Miami, FL 33013

UPWARD BOUND MUSIC CO.*
12911 SW 82 Terrace
Miami, FL 33138
(305) 279-2523
Samuel Solomon, Jr., Pres

VELVET RECORDS INC.
10128 NW 80 Ave.
Hialeah Gardens, FL 33016
(305) 823-0812

VIC-RAY PUBLISHING
Box 13222
Gainesville, FL 32604
(904) 378-8156
Charles V. Steadham Jr., Gen Mgr

NORM VINCENT PUBLISHING*
PO Box 10553
Jacksonville, FL 32207
Norman F. Vincent, Pres

GEORGIA

AZINDA PUBLICATIONS*
Div of Star Song Records
2460 Spring Lake Dr.
Marietta, GA 30062
(404) 973-1170
Tim McCabe, Pres

DB RECORDS†
PO Box 1773
Decatur, GA 30031
(404) 289-9273
T.M. Brady, Owner

FOCAL POINT MUSIC PUBLISHERS*
920 McArthur Blvd.
Warner Robins, GA 31093
(912) 923-6533
Ray Melton, Owner

FROZEN INCA MUSIC*
450 14th St., Ste. 201
Atlanta, GA 30318
(404) 873-3918
Michael Rothschild, Pres

GENELLE MUSIC CO.*
1304 Fletcher Rd.
Tifton, GA 31794
(912) 382-6257
Gus Statiras, Pres

GREAT AMERICAN PUBLISHING CO.*
c/o Blane Gauss
1332-B Euclid Ave., NE
Atlanta, GA 30307
(404) 688-0799

GUSMAN CO.*
PO Box 9202
1210½ E. Broad St.
Savannah, GA 31402
Waymon A. Jones, Pres

HUSTLERS, INC.*
5722 Kentucky Downs
Macon, GA 31210
(912) 474-2603
Alan Walden, Pres

KAT FAMILY MUSIC PUBLISHING*
5775 Peachtree Dunwood Rd. NE
Atlanta, GA 30342
(404) 252-6600
Joel A. Katz, Pres

SONNY LIMBO MUSIC*
PO Box 9869
Atlanta, GA 30319
(404) 633-4659
Sonny Limbo, Pres

LITTLE THINGS MUSIC*
2300 Henderson Mill Rd. NE #322
Atlanta, GA 30345
(404) 493-1210
Jim Oliver, Publisher

LOW-SAL MUSIC INC.*
3051 Clairmont Rd. NE
Atlanta, GA 30329

LOWERY MUSIC CO., INC.*
3051 Clairmont Rd. NE
Atlanta GA 30329
(404) 325-0832
Bill Lowery, Pres

LYRESONG INC.*
1227 Spring St. NW
Atlanta, GA 30309
(404) 873-6425
Harry Karras, Pres

MIMIC MUSIC*
Box 201
Smyrna, GA 30080
(404) 432-2454
Tom Hodges, Mgr

NO EXIT MUSIC CO. INC.*
535 Cotton Ave.
Macon, GA 31201
(912) 745-8511
Phil Walden, Pres

OAS MUSIC PUBLISHING†
3140 E. Shadowlawn Ave. NE
Atlanta, GA 30305
(404) 231-9888
Keith C. Andrews, Pres

RALPH'S RADIO MUSIC*
Hwy 441-23
Box 127
Demorest, GA 30535
(404) 754-6249

ROCKY'S RAGDOLL PUBLISHING*
Box 13781
205A Television Circle
Savannah, GA 31406
(912) 927-1761
David M. Evans, Pres

SATSONG MUSIC†
Box 720636
Atlanta, GA 30328
(404) 393-4640
Steven Kaye

SEYAH MUSIC*
Master Audio, Inc.
1227 Spring St. NW
Atlanta, GA 30309
(404) 873-6425
Barbara Richardson, Pres

SNOOPY MUSIC*
1975 NE 149th St.
North Miami, FL 33181
(305) 949-5222
Jim Rudd, Exec VP

SNAPFINGER MUSIC*
Box 35158
Decatur, GA 30035
Don Bryant, Owner

STARFOX PUBLISHING*
Box 13584
1957 Kilburn Dr.
Atlanta, GA 30324
(404) 872-6000
Alexander Janoulis, VP

STRAWBERRY PATCH†
PO Box 7417
Marietta, GA 30065
Diane Pfeifer, Pres

THIRD HOUSE MUSIC PUBLISHING*
Ste. 919, Lenox Tower
Atlanta, GA 30326
John Persico

TUMAC MUSIC PUBLISHING†
Rte. 1, Box 143
Senola, GA 30276
(404) 599-6935
Phil McDaniel, Mgr

HAWAII

LEHUA MUSIC CO.†
1365 Colburn St.
Honolulu, HI 96817
(808) 847-0855
C. Robert Clarke, Pres

MELWAY MUSIC INC.†
c/o Music of Polynesia Inc.
1441 Kapiolani Blvd., Ste. 1500
Honolulu, HI 96814
(808) 946-3244

MUSIC PUBLISHERS OF HAWAII*
PO Box 25141
Honolulu, HI 96825
(808) 955-4773/7509
Gil M. Tanaka, Pres

NEW CHILD MUSIC PUBLISHING†
PO Box 524
Kailua-Kona, HI 96740
Jeanne Nakashima, Pres

PANINI MUSIC*
PO Box 15808
Honolulu, HI 96815
(808) 947-4985
Steven O. Siegfried, Pres

PUNALUU MUSIC†
PO Box 30186
Honolulu, HI 96820
(808) 293-1800
Rich Asher Keefer

IDAHO

AMERICAN HERITAGE MUSIC CORP.*
1208 Everett St.
Caldwell, ID 83605
(208) 459-7382
Lloyd J. Wanzer, Gen Mgr

ILLINOIS

AMALGAMATED TULIP CORP.*
Div of Saturn Industries Inc.
PO Box 615
117 W. Rockland Rd.
Libertyville, IL 60048
(312) 362-4060
Perry H. Johnson, Pres

ATHON MUSIC CO.*
26 W. Benton Ave.
Naperville, IL 60540

BILLETDOUX MUSIC PUBLISHING*
One East Scott
Chicago, IL 60610
(312) 266-0040
Clifford Rubin, Pres

BIRD SEED MUSIC*
1946 N. Hudson Ave.
Chicago, IL 60614
(312) 787-6060
Robin McBride, Pres

THE CAMERON ORGANIZATION, INC.
822 Hillgrove Ave.
Western Springs, IL 60525
(312) 246-8222
Scott A. Cameron, Mgr

CARA PUBLICATIONS†
233 E. Wacker Dr., Ste. 3802
Chicago, IL 60601
John Tatgenhorst, Owner

CARLEEN-GAETANA MUSIC†
8 E. Chestnut
Chicago, IL 60611
(312) 943-0305
George R. Davis

CETRA MUSIC*
5828 S. University Ave.
Chicago, IL 60637
(312) 493-9781
Morton A. Kaplan, Pres

C.J. PUBLISHING*
CJ Records & Publishing
5240 N. Sheridan Rd.
Chicago, IL 60640

CLARK MUSIC PUBLISHING
Clark Musical Productions
Box 299
Watseka, IL 60970
(815) 432-4518
Dr. Paul E. Clark, Pres

M.M. COLE PUBLISHING CO.
919 N. Michigan Ave.
Chicago, IL 60611
(312) 787-0804
Shepard Stern, Pres

DENTURE WHISTLE MUSIC*
2 E Oak, Ste. 3005
Chicago, IL 60611
(312) 951-0246
Donn Marier

DON-DEL MUSIC/DON-DE MUSIC*
15041 Wabash Ave.
South Holland, IL 60473
(312) 339-0307
Donald De Lucia, Pres

DRAMATIC PUBLISHING CO.
4150 N. Milwaukee Ave.
Chicago, IL 60641
(312) 545-2062

DROP TOP MUSIC
2615 N. Wilton Ave.
Chicago, IL 60614
(312) 281-3385
Jim & Amy O'Neal, Partners

EYEBALL MUSIC*
PO Box 60234
Chicago, IL 60660
(312) 973-7736
Bruce Iglauer, Pres

FEMA MUSIC PUBLICATIONS†
PO Box 395
8 Bunting Lane
Naperville, IL 60540
(312) 357-0207
Frances Adams, Owner

CARL FISCHER INC.
312 S. Wabash Ave.
Chicago, IL 60604
(312) 427-6652
Gary Sigurdson, Mgr.

H.T. FITZSIMONS CO. INC.‡
357 W. Erie St.
Chicago, IL 60610
(312) 944-1841
Ruth E. FitzSimons, Pres

FLYING FISH MUSIC*
1304 W. Schubert
Chicago, IL 60614
(312) 528-5455
Bruce Kaplan, Pres

MARK FOSTER MUSIC CO.
PO Box 4012
Champaign, IL 61802
(217) 398-2760
Dr. James McKelvy, Pres
Local Branch:
710 S. Goodwin
Urbana, IL 61801
(217) 367-3939
Ira Feldman, Chief Exec

GARAMONI MUSIC PUBLISHING CO.*
676 N. LaSalle St.
Chicago, IL 60610
(312) 236-3632
John Garamoni, Pres

HANNAN-PHILLIPS MUSIC*
1819 W. Thome
Chicago, IL 60202
(312) 869-0175
Stoney Phillips, Pres

HOPE PUBLISHING COMPANY†
380 S. Main Pl.
Carol Stream, IL 60187
(312) 665-3200
George Herbert Shorney, Pres

HOUSE OF HI HO*
PO Box 8135
Chicago, IL 60680
(312) 254-5612
R.C. Hillsman, Exec VP

INSURANCE MUSIC PUBLISHING*
11616 S. Lafayette Ave.
Chicago, IL 60628
(312) 264-2166
Bill Tyson, Pres

INTERPLANETARY MUSIC
7901 S. LaSalle St.
Chicago, IL 60620
(312) 224-0396
James R. Hall III, Pres

JERJOY MUSIC*
Box 3615
Peoria, IL 61604
(309) 673-5755
Jerry Hanlon, Owner

KING AND MOORE MUSIC*
Box 10273
Chicago, IL 60610
(312) 944-1125
Ralph J. Moore, VP Pub; Xavier King Roy III, Pres

NEIL A. KJOS MUSIC CO.
525 Busse Highway
Park Ridge, IL 60068
(312) 825-2166
Neil A. Kjos, Pres

KRISHANE MUSIC CO.†
1445 Elizabeth Ct.
Hoffman Estates, IL 60195
Eddie Mascari

LARDON MUSIC*
Box 200
River Grove, IL 60171
Larry Nestor, Gen Mgr

MARIELLE MUSIC PUBLISHING CO.
Box 11012
Chicago, IL 60611
(312) 266-9616

MARMIK MUSIC, INC.
135 E. Muller Rd.
East Peoria, IL 61611
(309) 699-7204
Martin Mitchell, Pres

MEDIA INTERSTELLAR MUSIC*
Box 20346
Chicago, IL 60620
(312) 778-8760
V. Beleska, Mgr

MIGHTY TWINNS MUSIC*
9134 S. Indiana Ave.
Chicago, IL 60619
(312) 263-5452
Ronald Scott, Pres

NIKEDA MUSIC CO.*
1907 Central
Alton, IL 62002
(618) 465-5619
Howard E. Neal, Pres

NYSSA PUBLISHING
676 N. LaSalle St.
Chicago, IL 60610
(312) 266-8844
Dick Lux, Pres

PAULY IPPOLITO MUSIC
800 N. Ridgeland
Oak Park, IL 60302
(312) 848-3322
Vincent Ippolito, Gen Mgr

PHOENIXONGS†
PO Box 622
1652 Longvalley Dr.
Northbrook, IL 60062
(312) 564-2484
James Durst, Owner

ROWILCO
Box 8135
Chicago, IL 60680
(312) 224-5612
R.C. Hillsman, Mgr

RUMBLIN' SONGS*
PO Box 84
Peopria, IL 61650
(309) 674-5685
Todd Waddell, Contact

SATCHITANANDA PUBLISHING*
Box 2315
Springfield, IL 62705
Dave Hoffman, Gen Mgr

SEMERAK PUBLISHING CO.
4327 Sacramento Ave.
Chicago, IL 60632
(312) 523-3914
R.M. Semerak, Pres

SHELVIEW PUBLICATIONS CO.*
4148 S. King Dr.
Chicago, IL 60653
(312) 624-8060
James W. Shelton Jr., Pres

STONE ROW MUSIC CO.*
2022 Vardon Ln.
Flossmoor, IL 60422
(312) 799-7194
Joanne Swanson, Pres

SWING BEE MUSIC*
1130 Colfax
Evanston, IL 60201
(312) 328-5593
Susan Neumann, Producer

THREE WILLOWS MUSIC*
515 W. 62 St.
Chicago, IL 60621
(312) 987-3081
Frances Wiloughby, Pres

TRIPOLI MUSIC*
Box 25664
Chicago, IL 60625
(312) 883-8667
Ed Kammer; Tom Seymour, Pres

VITAK-ELSNIC CO.
6400A S. Woodward Ave.
Downers Grove, IL 60515
(312) 963-0200
Lawrence Musielak, Pres

WARUS MUSIC*
1410 E. 72nd St.
Chicago, IL 60619
(312) 752-2755
U.S. Warren, Pres

WINNER MUSIC*
c/o International Recording Co.
1649 W. Evergreen
Chicago, IL 60622
(312) 227-2000
Leonard March, Pres

INDIANA

ALEXANDRIA HOUSE INC.
PO Box 300
Alexandria, IN 46001
(317) 724-4438
William J. Gaither, Pres

CANAL PUBLISHING, INC.*
6325 Guilford Ave., #4
Indianapolis, IN 46220
(317) 255-3116
Terry Barnes, VP

HOOSIER HILLS PUBLISHING*
1309 Celesta Way
Sellersburg, IN 47172
(812) 246-2959
Buddy Powell, Owner

PERSONIFIED MUSIC CO.*
Rt. 1
Tennyson, IN 47637
(812) 567-4354
R.E. Willis Sr., Pres

PINPOINT MUSIC PUBLISHING*
c/o Little Nashville Recs.
Box 212 Rt. 3
Box 137
Nashville, IN 47448
(812) 988-2000
Don D. Sheets, Owner

SEVEN HILLS PUBLISHING AND RECORDING CO. INC.*
905 Main St.
Evansville, IN 47711
(812) 423-1861
Ed Krietemeyer, Pres

SLINGSHOT MUSIC
c/o TRC Mid-America Rec'g Center
1330 N. Illinois St.
Indianapolis, IN 46202
(317) 638-1491

STUDIO P/R INC.*†
224 S. Lebanon St.
Box 746
Lebanon, IN 46052
(317) 482-4440
James G. Houston, Pres

WORLD'S FINEST MUSIC*
1109 Brooks Ln.
Indianapolis, IN 46202
(317) 542-7460
Karriem Musheer, Pres

IOWA

AMPHORA MUSIC CORP*
1727 Division St.
Davenport, IA 52804
Frank L. Engle, Pres

C.L. BARNHOUSE CO.‡
110 B. Ave. E
Oskaloosa, IA 52577
(515) 673-8397
C.L. Barnhouse III, Pres

LOVE STREET PUBLISHING*
Box 2501
Des Moines, IA 50315
(515) 285-6564
Art Smart Stenstrom, Pres

HAROLD LUICK & ASSOCIATES MUSIC PUBLISHER*
110 Garfield St.

Box B
Carlisle, IA 50047
(515) 989-3679
Harold L. Luick, Pres

MONROE-AMES MUSIC*
Box 871
2700 Ford St.
Ames, IA 50010
(515) 232-2991
Steve Monroe, Pres

ROYAL FLAIR PUBLISHING*
106 Navajo
Coucil Bluffs, IA 51501
(712) 366-1136

SUGARVINE MUSIC PUBLISHING*
PO Box 3013
Davenport, IA
Gary Unger, Prof Mgr

TIMBERLAND PUBLISHING CO.*
Forest City, IA 50436
(515) 582-2992
Arlo C. Johnson, Pres

KANSAS

ROCKY BELL MUSIC*
Box 3247
Shawnee, KS 66203
(913) 631-6060
Frank Fara, Mgr

WHITE CAT MUSIC†
Box 3247
Shawnee, KS 66203
Frank Fara, Mgr

KENTUCKY

APPALSHOP INC.
306 Madison
Whitesburg, KY 41858
(606) 633-0108
Dee Davis, Pres

FALLS CITY MUSIC
9701 Taylorsville Rd.
Louisville, KY 40299
(502) 267-5466

HOLY SPIRIT MUSIC
PO Box 31
Edmonton, KY 42129
(502) 628-3573
Rev. W. Junior Lawson, Pres

LEMCO MUSIC PUBLISHING CO.*
PO Box 8013
2518 Southview Dr.
Lexington, KY 40503
(606) 277-1184

MOLLIE MUSIC PUBLISHING CO.*
PO Box 3081
Bridge St. Station
Paducah, KY 42001
(502) 898-7206
Mark Collier, Owner

JIMMY PRICE MUSIC PUBLISHING*
1662 Wyatt Parkway
Lexington, KY 40505
(606) 254-7474
James T. Price, Pres

STICKBUDDY MUSIC*
901 18th Ave. S
Nashville, TN 37212

TRUSTY PUBLICATIONS*
Rt. 1, Box 100
Nebo, KY 42441
(502) 249-3194
Elsie Childers, Pres

THE WILLIS MUSIC COMPANY
7380 Industrial Rd.
Florence, KY 41042
(606) 283-2050
Edward R. Cranley, Pres

LOUISIANA

BREAK OF DAWN MUSIC INC.*
PO Box 958
434 Ave. U
Bogalusa, LA 70427
(504) 732-2942
R.S. Evans, Pres

JOHN BERTHELOT & ASSOC.†
PO Box 13977
New Orleans, LA 70185
(504) 482-4211
John Berthelot, Pres

BRIARMEADE MUSIC UNLIMITED
PO Box 1830
Gretna, LA 70053
Ken Keene, Pres

CABRIOLET MUSIC*
Box 7422
Shreveport, LA 71107
Don Logan, Mgr

COUNTRY LEGS MUSIC†
1577 Redwood Dr.
Harvey, LA 70058
(504) 367-8501
George Leger, Pres

DAYS OF OLD PUBLISHING CO*
408 Holy Cross Pl.
Kenner, LA 70062
Traci Borges, Pres

DREW MARK MUSIC INC.*
3500 North Causeway
Metairie, LA 70002
(504) 831-9474
Dale Murray, Pres

FLAT TOWN MUSIC*
PO Drawer 10
434 E. Main
Ville Platte, LA 70586
(318) 363-2139
Floyd Soileau, Pres

FRENCH MARKET MUSIC*
915 Louisa St.
New Orleans, LA 70117
(504) 949-2911
Clive Wilson, Partner

HAYSEED PUBLISHING*
PO Box 1528
Shreveport, LA 71102
(318) 742-7803
David Kent, Pres

HAYSTACK PUBLISHING COMPANY†
Box 1528
Shreveport, LA 71165
(318) 742-7803
David Kent, Pres

JAKE-CARL PUBLICATIONS*
744 North Main St.
Opelousa, LA 70570
(318) 942-7092

JAMIL MUSIC*
413 N. Parkerson Ave.
Crowley, LA 70526
(318) 783-1601

JON MUSIC*
Box 233
329 N. Main St.
Church Point, LA 70525
(318) 684-2176
Lee Lavergne, Owner

LA LOU MUSIC*
711 Stevenson St.
Lafayette, LA 70501
(318) 234-5577
Carol J. Rachou, Sr., Pres

LAYBACK MUSIC INC.*
887 Hedgewood Dr.
Baton Rouge, LA 70815
(504) 766-3233
John Fred, Pres

MARSAINT MUSIC, INC.*
3809 Clematis Ave.
New Orleans, LA 70122
(504) 949-8386
M.E. Sehorn, Gen Mgr

MIDNIGHT GOLD PUBLISHING CO.*
PO Box 287
Berwick, LA 70342

(504) 384-0546
Vincent A. Guzzetta, Jr., Pres

NASETAN PUBLISHING*
Box 1485
Lake Charles, LA 70602
(318) 439-8839
Jody Mallory, Admin

ONE-THREE-NINE MUSIC LTD.†
Box 1528
Shreveport, LA 71165
(318) 742-7803
David Kent, Pres

ORCHID PUBLISHING
Bouquet-Orchid Enterprises
Box 18284
Shreveport, LA 71138
(318) 686-7362
Bill Bohannon, Pres

QUEEN OF HEARTS MUSIC
6105A Youree Dr.
Shreveport, LA 71105
(318) 861-0569
George Clinton, Owner

RCS PUBLISHING CO.†
5220 Essen Ln.
Baton Rouge, LA 70808
(504) 766-3233
John Fred, Gen Mgr

SAPPHIRE MUSIC PUBLISHERS*
2815 Octavia St.
New Orleans, LA 70115
(504) 866-3478
Lou Welsch, Jr., Pres

SCALES OF JUSTICE MUSIC INC.*
PO Box 2609
119½ E. Main St.
Lafayette, LA 70502
(318) 235-3587
J. Michael Fernandez, Pres

SEA CRUISE PRODUCTIONS
Box 1830
Gretna, LA 70053
Ken Keene, Pres

SU-MA PUBLISHING CO., INC.
Box 1125
728 Texas St.
Shreveport, LA 71163
(318) 222-0195
Stanley J. Lewis, Pres

TOUPAT MUSIC PUBLISHING CO. INC.*
402 Shotwell Ave.
Monroe, LA 71202
(318) 322-2537
Toussaint L. McCall, Pres

TUNE-KEL PUBLISHING CO. INC.*
PO Box 50650
New Orleans, LA 70150
(504) 392-1525
Joseph Banashak, Pres

UNIVERSAL STARS MUSIC
Rt. 3
Box 5B
Leesville, LA 71446
Sherree Stephens, Nat'l Rep

MARYLAND

BOULDIN MUSIC PUBLISHING CO.*
PO Box 1375
Baltimore, MD 21203
(301) 327-8236
Ray Donahoe, Pres

CONNECTIONS UNLIMITED INC.†
2817 Parker Ct.
Wheaton, MD 20902
(301) 942-6281
Margaret Cafarelli

JULDANE MUSIC CO.*
8037 13th St.
Silver Springs, MD 20910
(301) 585-2776
Jules M. Damian, Owner

MCCULLY MUSIC*
255 Waysons Ct.
Lothian, MD 20711
(301) 627-5830
Robert M. Johnson, Pres

OLD HOME PLACE MUSIC*
8705 Deanna Dr.
Gaithersburg, MD 20760
(301) 253-5962
Wayne Busbice, Pres

HENRY J. SOMMERS†
PO Box 322
Silver Spring, MD 20907
(301) 946-9039
Henry J. Sommers, Owner

SONE SONGS
10101 Woodlake Dr.
Cockeysville, MD 21030
(301) 628-7357
George Brigman, Gen Mgr

MASSACHUSETTS

BOSTON MUSIC CO.†
116 Boylston St.
Boston, MA 02116
(617) 426-5100
Warren W. Morris, Gen Mgr

BRANDEN PRESS INC.
21 Station St.
Brookline, MA 02146
(617) 734-2045

CRITIQUE MUSIC PUBLISHING CO.*
100 Main St.
Reading, MA 01867
(617) 944-0423
Carl Strube, Pres

DONNA MUSIC PUBLISHING CO.*
Box 113
Woburn, MA 01801
(617) 933-1474
Frank Paul, Gen Mgr

DRAYENIV MUSIC PUBLISHING CO.*
PO Box 934
15 Simpson South Lane
Edgartown, MA 02539
Benjamin L. Hall, Owner

CARL FISCHER INC.
156 Boylston St.
Boston, MA 02116
(617) 426-0740
Warren Patterson, Mgr

HAPPY VALLEY MUSIC*
186 Willow Ave.
Somerville, MA 02144
(617) 354-0700
Ken Irwin

ROBERT KINGS MUSIC CO.*
7 Canton St.
North Easton, MA 02356
Robert D. King, Owner

MARGUN MUSIC INC./GUNMAR MUSIC*
167 Dudley Rd.
Newton Centre, MA 02158
(617) 332-6398
Bruce M. Creditor, Gen Mgr

MUSIC DESIGNERS
241 White Pond Rd.
Hudson, MA 01749
(617) 890-8787
Jeff Gilman, Pres

NEW VALLEY MUSIC PRESS
c/o Smith College Music Dept.
Sage Hall 21
Northampton, MA 01063
(413) 584-2700
Leslie C. Usher, Exec Sec

NEWPORT MUSIC CO.†
1105 Little Bldg.
80 Boylston St.
Boston, MA 02116
(617) 482-7678
Harry Paul, Owner

OLD BOSTON PUBLISHING*
180 Pond St.
Cohasset, MA 02025
(617) 383-9494
Claire Babcock, Writer Relations;
Richard Timory, Pres

PENNY THOUGHTS MUSIC*
259A Beech St.
Belmont, MA 02178
(717) 924-6722
Jim Penny, Pres

PERISCOPE MUSIC.*
129 Bishop St.
Brockton, MA 02402
(617) 588-6348
Edward M. Hurvitz, Pres

PHONETONES
400 Essex St.
Salem, MA 01970
Don Roze, Pres

E.C. SCHIRMER MUSIC CO.†
112 South St.
Boston, MA 02111
(617) 426-3137
Robert MacWilliams, Pres

STANDARD-COLONIAL MUSIC PUBLISHING CO.*
52 Cummings Park
Woburn, MA 01801
(617) 935-7500
Robert D. Levinson, Pres

TOPSAIL MUSIC*
71 Boylston St.
Brookline, MA 02147
(617) 739-2010
Fred Berk, Pres

MICHIGAN

ALPHA-ROBINSON†
19176 Mitchell
Detroit, MI 48234
(313) 893-9370
Juanita Robinson, Pres

ART AUDIO PUBLISHING CO.*
9706 Cameron St.
Detroit, MI 48212
(313) 893-3406
Albert M. Leigh, Pres
Branch:
12080 Moenart St.
Detroit, MI 48212

BRIDGEPORT MUSIC INC.*
c/o Norman R. Kurtz
712 5th Ave.
New York, NY 10019

CHRIS MUSIC PUBLISHING*
133 Arbutus Ave.
Manistique, MI 49865
Reg. B. Christensen, Pres

ERNKEL MUSIC CO.*
Div of Ernest Kelley Inc.
20414 Warrington Dr.
Detroit, MI 48221
Ernest Kelley, Pres

GEAR MUSIC
c/o Punch Andrews
567 Purdy
Birmingham, MI 48009
(313) 642-0910

GOD'S WORLD‡
27335 Penn St.
Inkster, MI 48141
(313) 562-8975
Elder Otis G. Johnson, Pres

GOLDEN DAWN MUSIC*
26177 Kinyon Dr.
Taylor, MI 48180
(313) 292-5281
Peggy La Sarda, Pres

GROOVESVILLE MUSIC*
15855 Wyoming
Detroit, MI 48238
(313) 861-2363
Brian A. Spears, Pub Dir; Will Davis, Dir

INSANITY'S MUSIC
24548 Pierce
Southfield, MI 48075
(313) 559-7630
Bruce Lorfel, Pres

JAYMORE MUSIC*
Box 100
6260 Meyer St.
Brighton, MI 48116
(313) 227-1997
John Morris, Pres

JIBARO MUSIC CO., INC.*
Box 424
Mount Clemens, MI 48043
(313) 791-2678
Jim Roach, Pres

LOOK HEAR MUSIC*
24548 Pierce
Southfield, MI 48075
(313) 559-7630
Bruce Lorfel, Pres

LUCK'S MUSIC LIBRARY INC.
15701 East Warren
Detroit, MI 48224
(313) 881-3532
Paul A. Luck, Pres

LUCKY'S KUM-BA-YA PUBLISHING CO.†
PO Box 6
Brohman, MI 49312
(616) 689-6886
Ross Fulton, Owner

MANFIELD MUSIC*
Holy Spirit Records
27335 Penn St.
Inkster, MI 48141
(313) 862-8220
Elder Otis G. Johnson, Pres

MUZACAN PUBLISHING CO.*
44844 Michigan Ave.
Canton, MI 48188
Bruce Young, Pres

NEOSTAT MUSIC CO.*
425 Bryn Mawr
Birmingham, MI 48009
(313) 647-1662
Harvey M. Yates, Pres

OLENIK RECORDS†
G-10292 N. Dixie Highway
Clio, MI 48420
(313) 686-9644
Nicholas H. Olejnik, Pres

RAY OVERHOLT MUSIC
112 S. 26th St.
Battle Creek, MI 49015
(616) 963-0554
Mildred Overholt, A & R Dir

PATLOW PUBLICATION CO.*
18475 Evergreen
Detroit, MI 48219
M.J. Patlow, Pres

PETOSKEY MUSIC INC.*
3007 E. Eight Mile Rd.
Warren, MI 48091
(313) 756-8890
John Pavlik, Pres

PLATINUM PEN MUSIC PUBLISHING CO.*
18000 Mack Ave.
Grosse Pointe, MI 48224
(313) 882-0566
Gary Praeg, Pres

RMS TRIAD PUBLISHING†
6267 Potomac Circle
West Bloomfield, MI 48033
(313) 661-5167
Bob Szajner, Owner
Branch:
Madison Hts., MI 48071

SINGING RIVER PUBLISHING CO. INC.*
205 Acacia St.
Biloxi, MS 39530
(601) 436-3927
Marion Carpenter, Pres

SINGSPIRATION INC.
1415 Lake Dr. SE
Grand Rapids, MI 49506
(616) 459-6900
Peter Kladder, Pres

SOUND INC. MUSIC
56880 North Ave.
New Haven, MI 48048
(313) 749-5184

STAR DATA MUSIC*
Rt. 1, Box 125

Corinth, MI 38834
(601) 287-4282

Bill Stottlemeyer, Pres

TEEBO PUBLISHING/TEE-WEB MUSIC CO.
12842 Fenkell Ave.
Detroit, MI 48227

Tito Lewis, Pres

ULTRA SOUNDS UNLIMITED PUBLISHING*
1182 E. Russell
Flint, MI 48505
(313) 787-2962

Morris D. Ruffin, Board Chairman

VIPER MUSIC*
c/o Blind Pig Records
208 South 1st St.
Ann Arbor, MI 48103
(313) 428-7216

Jerry Del Giudice, A & R Dir

THE KENNETH GREGORY WILSON PUBLISHING CO.*
18945 Livernios Ave.
Detroit, MI 48221
(313) 862-8221

Kenneth Wilson

MINNESOTA

AUGSBURG PUBLISHING HOUSE‡
426 South Fifth St.
Minneapolis, MN 55415
(612) 330-3300

Albert E. Anderson, CEO

BOSS APPLE TUNES*
1517 W. Lake St.
Minneapolis, MN 55408
(612) 827-6111

Charles F. Campbell, Pres

GRAVY PUBLISHING CO.
Div of Cookhouse Productions
2541 Nicollet Ave. S.
MInneapolis, MN 55404
(612) 872-0646

HAL LEONARD PUBLISHING CORP‡
960 E. Mark St.
Winona, MN 55987
(507) 454-2920

Robert Gilbertson, Operations Mgr

REGUS PUBLISHER*
10 Birchwood Ln.
White Bear Lake, MN 55110
(612) 227-2600

Marion Frances, Mgr.

SANSKRIT PUBLISHING CO.†
411 Kenmar Circle
Minnetonka, MN 55343
(612) 920-9590

Michael J. Johnson

SYMPOSIUM MUSIC PUBLISHING INC.*
204 Fifth Ave. SE
Minneapolis, MN 55414
(612) 331-5750

George Hanson, Prof. Mgr.

TEKTRA PUBLISHING*
711 Broadway
Minneapolis, MN 55411
(612) 521-7631

Dan R. Holmes, Pres

WATERHOUSE MUSIC, INC.*
526 Nicallet Mall
Minneapolis, MN 55402
(612) 332-6575

Gary Marx, Dir of Operations

WRENSONG, INC.*†
215 E. Wentworth Ave.
West St. Paul, MN 55118
(612) 451-8228

Tom Oliver

MISSISSIPPI

GAYLN MUSIC
233 Penner Dr.
Pearl, MS 39208
(601) 939-6616

George W. Allen

MALACO INC.
Box 9287
Jackson, MS 39206
(601) 982-4522

James Griffin, Producer; Tom Couch, Pres

RAINBOW ROAD PUBLISHING†
PO Box 204
Belden, MS 38806
(615) 865-0653

MISSOURI

EARL BARTON MUSIC*
1121 S. Glenstone
Springfield, MO 65804
(417) 869-6379

E.E. Siman, Jr., Pres

MEL BAY PUBLICATIONS INC.
PO Box 66
Pacific, MO 63069
(314) 257-3970

Bill Bay, VP

BLACKHEART MUSIC*
c/o Nighthawk Records
PO Box 15856
St. Louis, MO 63114

Robert Schoenfeld, Pres

BRIDGER MUSIC PUBLISHING CO.*
PO Box 929
Sikeston, MO 63801
(314) 471-5428

ALBERT E. BRUMLEY & SONS
Powell, MO 65730
(417) 435-2225

Bob Brumley, Gen Mgr

CALWEST SONGS/LEE ANDERSON ENTERPRISES
415 N. Main St.
St. Clair, MO 63077
(314) 629-1123

Lee Anderson

CHAPIE MUSIC*
Chapman Record Studios
228 W. 5th St.
Kansas City, MO 64105
(816) 842-6854

Chuck Chapman, Owner

COLUMN ONE MUSIC†
PO Box 4086
Springfield, MO 65804
(417) 881-5015

James M. Martin, Pres

CONCORDIA PUBLISHING HOUSE‡
3558 S. Jefferson Ave.
St. Louis, MO 63118
(314) 664-7000

COUNTRY STREAM MUSIC*
5053 Tholozan Ave.
St. Louis, MO 63109
(314) 481-3916

Tony Mazzola, Pres

E.L.J. RECORD CO.
1344 Waldron
St. Louis, MO 63130
(314) 803-3605

Eddie Johnson, Pres

FRANDORO MUSIC INC.*
8 Heather Dr.
St. Louis, MO 63123
(314) 843-9142

Frank Daniels, Pres

EUGENE GOLD MUSIC*
Div of NMI Prod. Corp.
7008 Monroe
Kansas City, MO 64132

Eugene Gold, Pres

GRADUATION MUSIC INC.†
212 N. Kingshighway
St. Louis, MO 63108
(314) 361-4400
Julian H. Miller II, Pres

HAPPY DAY MUSIC CO.*
Box 602
Kennet, MO 63857
Joe Keene, Pres

IRONSIDE MUSIC†
PO Box 564
Hollister, MO 65672

JOE KEENE MUSIC CO.*
Box 602
Kennett, MO 63857
(314) 888-2995
Joe Keene, Pres

LILLENAS PUBLISHING CO.†
Box 527
Kansas City, MO 64141
(816) 931-1900
Ken Bible, Dir

LINEAGE PUBLISHING CO.*
Box 211
East Prairie, MO 63845
(314) 649-2211
Tommy Loomas, Pres

MAGNAMUSIC-BATON INC.†
10370 Page Industrial Blvd.
St. Louis, MO 63132
(314) 427-5660

MASTERLEASE MUSIC PUBLICATIONS*
Box 234
St. Louis, MO 63166
(314) 296-9526
Bob Box, Pres

MENDE MUSIC PUBLISHING*
PO Box 833
West Plains, MO 65775
J.D. Mendenhall, Pres

MID AMERICA MUSIC
Box 242
Osage Beach, MO 65065
(314) 348-3383
Lee Mace, Gen Mgr

LEE MACES OZARK OPRY MUSIC PUBLISHING†
Box 242
Osage Beach, MO 65065
(314) 348-2702
Lee Mace, Gen Mgr

OZARK RAMBLIN' MUSIC*
430 S. Glenstone, Ste. C
Springfield, MO 65802
(417) 864-4404
Keith O'Neil, Pres

PELIPERUS MUSIC CO.†
4142 Benton Blvd.
Kansas City, MO 64130
(816) 861-0582
Robert Motley, Pres

QUINONES MUSIC CO.*
1344 Waldron St.
St. Louis, MO 63130
(314) 863-3605
Eddie L. Johnson, Pres

TRAGREY MUSIC PUBLISHING*
17 Ponca Trail
St. Louis, MO 63122
(314) 821-2741
Gregory Trampe, Pub

JERRY VAMPLE PUBLISHING CO.*
Box 23152
Kansas City, MO 64141
Jerry Vample, Pres

LUTHER WILSON MUSIC CO.
Box 2664
Kansas City, MO 66110
(913) 621-1676
Luther Wilson, Jr.

NEBRASKA

FLIN-FLON MUSIC*
102 Veteran's Ave.
Mullen, NE 69152
(308) 546-2294
L.E. Walker, Gen Mgr

THOMAS JACKSON PUBLISHING, INC.*
Rainbow Recording Studios
2322 South 64th Ave.
Omaha, NE 68106
(402) 554-0123
Thomas Jackson, Mgr

PRAIRIE WIND MUSIC*
504 Lincoln
Norfolk, NE 68701
(402) 371-7658
Jim Casey, President

NEVADA

DERBY MUSIC‡
Las Vegas Recording Studio
3977 Vegas Valley Dr.
Las Vegas, NV 89121
(702) 457-4365
Hank Castro, Pres

NEW HAMPSHIRE

BRANDY RIVER MUSIC CO.‡
PO Box 413
Durham, NH 03824
(603) 749-2811
Richard R. Shaw/Ronald B. Shaw/VP

JASPAR MUSIC PUBLISHING CO. LTD.*
852 Elm St.
Manchester, NH 03101
(603) 623-9749
James Parks, Managing Dir

NEW JERSEY

ASHLEY DEALERS, INC
263 Veterans Blvd.
Carlstadt, NJ 07072
(201) 935-1113
Al Ashley, Pres

ABDUL BASIT MUSIC, INC.*
152 Roseville Ave.
Ste. 4-C
Newark, NJ 07107
(201) 675-6995
Abdul Basit, Pres

CACTUS MUSIC AND GIDGET PUBLISHING‡
5 Aldom Circle
West Caldwell, NJ 07006
(201) 226-0035
Jim Hall

CAMILLO-BARKER ENTERPRISES‡
121 Meadowbrook Dr.
Sommerville, NJ 08876
(201) 359-5110
Cecile Barker, Co-Pres

CAPANO MUSIC‡
Div of Britone Inc.
237 Chestnut St.
Westville, NJ 08093
(609) 456-4402
Anthony J. Capano, Pres

THE CHU YEKO MUSICAL FOUNDATION*
Box 1314
Englewood Cliffs, NJ 07632
(201) 567-5524
Doris Chu Yeko, Prod

CIANO PUBLISHING*
Box 263
37 Woodside Ave.
Hasbrouck Heights, NJ 07604
(201) 288-8935
Ron Luciano, Pres

DONNA MARIE MUSIC‡
c/o American Creative Entertainment Ltd.
1616 Pacific Ave.
Atlantic City, NJ 08401
(609) 347-0484
Danny Luciano, Pres

DRAGON INTERNATIONAL MUSIC*
Box 8263
Haledon, NJ 07508
(201) 942-6810
Samuel Cummings, Pres

EDEN MUSIC CORP.*
Box 325
Englewood, NJ 07631
(201) 567-7528
Clyde Otis, Pres

EUROPEAN-AMERICAN MUSIC DISTRIBUTORS CORP.†
11 West End Rd.
Totowa, NJ 07512
(201) 256-7100
Ronald Freed, Pres

GLORIA GAYNOR MUSIC†
PO Box 374
Fairview, NJ 07022
Gloria Gaynor

G.G. MUSIC, INC.
Box 374
Fairview, NJ 07022
Linwood Simon, Pres

GOYDISH MUSIC & PUBLISHING CO.*
PO Box 24
Belle Mead, NJ 08502
Bernard L. Goydish, Owner

INSPIRATIONAL SOUNDS INC.†
PO Box 1363
Union, NJ 07083
(21) 376-3955
David Casey, Pres

JERONA MUSIC CORP.†
81 Trinity Pl.
Hackensack, NJ 07601
(201) 488-0550
Joseph M. Boonin, Pres

JLT CHRISTIAN AGAPE MUSIC CO.†
104 8th St.
Salem, NJ 08079
(609) 935-1908
John L. Tussey, Jr., Owner

JONAN MUSIC†
PO Box 279
Elizabeth, NJ 07207
Henel Gottesmann, Office Mgr

KENSINGTON MUSIC SERVICE
Box 471
Tenafly, NJ 07670
(201) 567-4791
Lynne Hartman Richter, Owner

ROB LEE MUSIC
Box 1338
Merchantville, NJ 08109
(609) 665-8934
Bob Francis, VP

LIVE MUSIC PUBLISHING GROUP*
793 Bingham Rd.
Ridgewood, NJ 07450
(201) 447-4700

MIRACLE-JOY PUBLICATIONS
Box 711
Hackensack, NJ 07601
(201) 488-5211
Johnny Miracle, Pres

MORRISON HILL MUSIC†
227 Union St.
Lodi, NJ 07644
(201) 471-2770
Joseph A. Sterner, Mgr

MOUNTAIN GLORY MUSIC*
52 Werah Pl.
Oceanport, NJ 07757
(201) 222-4460
Russell N. Scalzo, Jr., Owner

NEVER ENDING MUSIC
Box 58
Glendora, NJ 08029
(609) 939-0034
Eddie Jay Harris, Pres

NISE PRODUCTIONS INC.
413 Cooper St., Ste. 101
Camden, NJ 08102
(215) 276-0100
Michael Nise, Pres

ONESIMUS MUSIC*
PO Box 235
Pitman, NJ 08701
(609) 881-6743

PACKAGE GOOD MUSIC
1145 Green St.
Manville, NJ 08835
March Zydiack, Pres

PAGANINIANA PUBLICATIONS INC.
PO Box 27
211 W. Sylvania Ave.
Neptune, NJ 07753
(201) 988-8400
Dr. Herbert R. Axelrod, Pres

PAVANNE MUSIC CO.†
36 W. Williams St.
Lincoln Park, NY 07035
Angelo Baldalamenti

PERLA MUSIC
20 Marth St.
Woodcliff Lake, NJ 07675
(201) 391-2486
Gene A. Perla, Pres

POSITIVE PRODUCTIONS
Box 1405
Highland Park, NJ 08904
(201) 463-8845
J. Vincenzo, Pres

RASHONE MUSIC*
455 W. Hanover St.
Trenton, NJ 08618
(609) 989-9202
Eddie Toney, Pres

ROMONA MUSIC†
702 S. 15 St.
Newark, NJ 07013
Gloria Black, Pres

ROOTS MUSIC*
Box 111
Sea Bright, NJ 07760
Robert Bowden, Pres

ROYAL K MUSIC
6 Melrose Dr.
Livingston, NJ 07039
(201) 533-0448
Marc Katz, Pres

FRANK RUSSELL MUSIC†
170 Linwood Ave.
Paterson, NJ 07502
(201) 595-7557
Frank Russell, Pres

SANDMAN MUSIC PUBLISHING CO.†
6 Morris Ave.
Montville, NJ 07045
(201) 334-0863
Sandy Nelson, Prof. Mgr.

SAVGOS MUSIC, INC.
342 Westminster Ave.
Elizabeth, NJ 07208
(201) 351-6800
Fred Mendelsohn, VP; Helen Gottesmann, Office Mgr

SUMMY-BIRCHARD MUSIC
Box CN 27
Princeton, NJ 08540
(609) 896-1411
David K. Sengstack, Pres

TRAJAMES MUSIC CO.*
130 Old Denville Rd.
Boontown Township, NJ 07005
Jimmy Wisner, Pres

NEW MEXICO

ASTRONETTE PUBLISHING CO.*
2037 Alvarado Dr., NE
Albuquerque, NM 87110
(505) 268-8405
A. Medley, Pres

COWBOY KAZOO MUSIC*
5926 El Prado NW
Albuquerque, NM 87107
(505) 345-4835
Jeff Burrows, Pres

ENCHANTMENT MUSIC CO.*
PO Box 998

Mesilla Park
Las Cruces, NM 88047
(505) 524-1889
Emmit H. Brooks, Owner

FULL CYCLE MUSIC PUBLISHING CO.*
80 E. San Francisco St.
Santa Fe, NM 87501
(505) 982-2900
Reno Myerson, Pres

LITTLE RICHIE JOHNSON MUSIC*
913 S. Main St.
PO Box 3
Belen, NM 87002
(505) 864-7441
Little Richie Johnson, Pres

NEW YORK

A DISH-A-TUNES LTD.*
1650 Broadway
New York, NY 10019
(212) 245-9612
Ken Williams, Pres

ABC DUNHILL MUSIC*
c/o Ron Schubart
1926 Broadway, 4th Fl.
New York, NY 10023

ABI/ALEXANDER BROUDE INC.
225 W. 75th St.
New York, NY 10019
(212) 586-1674
Robert J. Bregman, Pres

ABKCO MUSIC, INC.*
1700 Broadway
New York, NY 10019
(212) 399-0300
Allen Klein, Pres

ABP PUBLISHING†
240 Central Park S.
New York, NY 10019
(212) 582-7379
Allen Abdulezer, Pres

AL-BO MUSIC CO.
37 Odell Ave.
Yonkers, NY 10701
(914) 969-5673
Joe Bollon, VP & Gen Mgr

ALDOUS DEMIAN PUBLISHING, LTD.
Radio City Station, Box 1348
New York, NY 10101
(212) 375-2639
(212) 824-7842
Harold Weber, VP

ALLIED ARTISTS MUSIC CO. INC.†
15 Columbus Circle
New York, NY 10023
(212) 541-9200

ALPHA MUSIC INC.*
40 East 49th St.
New York, NY 10017
(212) 753-3234
Michael Nurko, Pres

AMADEUS MUSIC CO.*†
c/o Franklin, Weinrib, Rudell & Vassallo
950 Third Ave.
New York, NY 10022
(212) 222-2225
Earl Rose, Pres

AMALISA, LTD.†
Box 4559
Long Island City, NY 11104
(212) 361-2582
Charles Lucy, Pres

AMERICAN BROADCASTING MUSIC INC.
1330 Ave of the Americas
New York, NY 10019
(212) 887-7777
Ronald Schubert, Dir

AMERICAN COMPOSERS ALLIANCE*
170 West 74th St.
New York, NY 10023
(212) 362-8900
Nicolas Roussakis, Pres

AMERICAN DREAM MUSIC CO.†
c/o Yellow Dog Music Inc.
1618 Broadway
New York, NY 10019
(212) 489-8170

AMERICAN MUSIC CENTER
250 W. 54th St.
New York, NY 10019
(212) 247-3121
Margaret Jory, Exec Dir

ANDUSTIN MUSIC†
Box 669
Woodstock, NY 12498
(914) 679-6069
Harris Goldberg, Pres

ANTISIA MUSIC, INC.†
1650 Broadway, Ste. 1001
New York, NY 10019
(212) 489-7555
Kirk Fancher, Gen Mgr

APON PUBLISHING CO.†
Box 3082
Steinway Station
44-16 Broadway
Long Island City, NY 11103
(212) 721-5599
Andrew M. Poncic, Pres

MIKE APPEL PRODUCTIONS
330 E. 39th St.
New York, NY 10016
(212) 867-7775
Mike Appel, Pres

APRIL-BLACKWOOD MUSIC
(*See* CBS Songs, NY)

AQUATARIUS MUSIC LTD.
1501 Broadway
New York, NY 10036
(212) 221-1940
Arnold H. Goldstein, Pres

ARISTA MUSIC PUBLISHING GROUP
6 West 57th St.
New York, NY 10019
(212) 489-7400
Steve Sussmann, Mgr

ASC PUBLISHING CO. INC.†
168 Water St.
Binghamton, NY 13901
(607) 722-7259
David J. Lebous, Pres

ASILOMAR MUSIC†
43 W. 61st St.
New York, NY 10023
(212) 757-8805
Ron Beigel, VP

ASSOCIATED MUSIC PUBLISHERS INC.*
866 Third Ave.
New York, NY 10022
(212) 935-5100
B. O'Neal, Mgr

ATLANTIC RECORDS MUSIC PUBLISHING
75 Rockefeller Pl.
New York, NY 10019
(212) 484-6000

ATV MUSIC CORP.
888 7th Ave.
New York, NY 10019
(212) 977-580
Marv Goodman, Mgr

AUCOIN MANAGEMENT INC.
645 Madison Ave.
New York, NY 10022
(212) 826-8800
William Aucoin, Pres

AUDIBLE MUSIC PUBLISHING CO.†
1802 Ocean Parkway, Ste. 2A
Brooklyn, NY 11223
(212) 627-8499
Cosmo Ohms, Pres

AULOS MUSIC PUBLISHERS
PO Box 54
Montgomery, NY 12549
(914) 692-6270
Howard M. Feldsher, Pub Dir

BADCO MUSIC INC.†
34 Pheasant Run
Old Westbury, NY 11568
(516) 626-3535
Stevens H. Weiss

M. BARON CO. INC.†
PO Box 149

Oyster Bay, NY 11771
Virginia L. Baron, Pres

BEARCE PUBLISHING CO.†
7635 Telephone Rd.
Leroy, NY 14482
Kenny or Jim Bearce

BEAUTIFUL DAY MUSIC*
15 Glenby Lane
Brookville, NY 11545
(516) 626-9504
Thomas R. Ingegno, Co-Pres

BEECHWOOD MUSIC CORP
1370 Ave of the Americas
New York, NY 10019
(212) 489-6740

BEEZ WEEZ MUSIC*
c/o Jones, Michael & Cherot
888 Seventh Ave.
New York, NY 10019
(212) 757-1100
Ben Adkins, Pres

BELWIN-MILLS PUBLISHING COPR.*
1776 Broadway
New York, NY 10019
(212) 245-1100
Martin Winkler, Pres

Branch:
25 Deshon Dr.
Melville, NY 11747
(516) 293-3400

BENNER PUBLISHERS
1739 Randolph Rd.
Schenectady, NY 12308
(518) 377-5254
Lora Benner, Pres

PHIL BENNETT MUSIC CO.†
1 East 42nd St.
New York, NY 10017
(212) 682-2539

BETTER-HALF MUSIC CO.†
c/o Estate of Jacqueline Hilliard
David's Way
Bedford Hills, NY 10507
Howard E. Guedalia, Executor

BIENSTOCK PUBLISHING CO.*†
1619 Broadway
New York, NY 10019
(212) 489-8170

BIG HURRY MUSIC CO. INC.
(*See* Mietus Copyright Management, New York, NY)

BIG MIKE MUSIC*
Big Mike Productions
408 W. 115th St.
Ste. 2-W
New York, NY 10025
(212) 222-8715
Bill Downs, Mgr

BIG SEVEN MUSIC CORP*
1790 Broadway
New York, NY 10019
(212) 582-4267
Morris Levy, Pres

BIG SKY MUSIC†
PO Box 860
Cooper Station
New York, NY 10276
(212) 473-5900
Naomi Saltzman, Admin

BIOGRAPH RECORDS INC.†
PO Box 109
Canaan, NY 12029
Arnold S. Caplin, Pres

BLACK BULL MUSIC†
(*See* Black Bull Music, Inc., Los Angeles, CA)

BLANCHRIS MUSIC*
160 W. 71st St.
New York, NY 10023
(212) 873-2020
Renee Steele, Off Mgr

BLENDING WELL MUSIC
(*See* Publishers' Licensing Corp., NY)

BLUE UMBRELLA MUSIC PUBLISHING CO.†
3011 Beach 40th St.
Brooklyn, NY 11224
(212) 372-6436
Kadish Millet, Owner

BOCA MUSIC CO.†
6 E. 45th St.
New York, NY 10017

BOOSEY & HAWKES INC.†
24 West 57th St.
New York, NY 10019
(212) 757-3332
W. Stuart Pope, Pres

BOURNE CO.†
1212 Ave of the Americas
New York, NY 10036
(212) 575-1800
Al Atuckman, Off Mgr; Bonnie Bourne, Pres

BOVINA MUSIC INC.†
c/o Mae Attaway
330 W. 56th St.
Apt. 12F
New York, NY 10019

HAROLD BRANCH PUBLISHING INC.
95 Eads St.
West Babylon, NY 11704
(516) 420-8360
Harold Branch, Pres

BRONJO MUSIC PUBLISHING†
1637 Utica Ave.
Brooklyn, NY 11234
(212) 253-4600
David Last, Pres

BROOKLYN COUNTRY MUSIC
Ste. 1705, 150 E. 39th St.
New York, NY 10016
(212) 889-3754
Zhaba Jay, A & R Dir

BROOKSIDE MUSIC CORP.†
159 West 53rd St.
Ste. A
New York, NY 10019
(212) 541-7761
Reid Whitelaw, Pres

BROUDE BROTHERS LTD.†
170 Varick St.
New York, NY 10013
(212) 242-7001
Ronald Broude, Pres

BRUT MUSIC PUBLISHING†
1345 Ave of the Americas
New York, NY 10019
(212) 581-3114
Stan Krell, VP

BUDDAH MUSIC INC.†
1790 Broadway
New York, NY 10019
(212) 582-6900
Art Kass, Pres

BURLINGTON MUSIC CORP
539 W 25th St.
New York, NY 10001
(212) 675-6060

BUSH/LEHRMAN PRODUCTIONS
119 W. 57th St.
New York, NY 10019
Red Lehrman, Mgr

BUTTERMILK SKY ASSOCIATES*
515 Madison Ave.
New York, NY 10022
(212) 759-2275
Murray Deutch, Pres

CALIGULA, INC.†
60 Pearl St.
New York, NY 10004
(212) 483-1939
David Forman, Pres

CAMERICA MUSIC†
489 5th Ave.
New York, NY 10017
(212) 682-8400
Mike Corbett, Mgr; Vittorio Benedetto, Pres

CAMPBELL CONNELLY, INC.†
33 W. Hawthorn Rm. 5
PO Box 359
Valley Stream, NY 11582

CANDUE MUSIC INC.†
19 S. Broadway
White Plains, NY 10601
(914) 682-8069
Ron Carran, Pres

CAN'T STOP MUSIC*
Can't Stop Productions, Inc.
65 E. 55th St.
New York, NY 10022
(212) 751-6177
Maximilian Dahan-Lavelle, Pres

CAPAQUARIUS PUBLISHING & ARTISTS MGT., INC.†
750 Kappock St., Ste. 1015
Riverdale, NY 10463
(212) 549-6318
P. Januari Watts, Pres

ALAN CARTEE MUSIC*
c/o Copyright Service Bureau
221 W. 57th St.
New York, NY 11019

DON CASALE MUSIC, INC.*
377 Plainfield St.
Westbury, NY 11590
(516) 333-7898
Don Casale, Pres

CASTLE HILL PUBLISHING LTD.†
923 5th Ave.
New York, NY 10021
(212) 772-9335
Peter Casperson, Pres

CBS SONGS
1350 Ave of the Americas
New York, NY 10019
(212) 975-4886

CHAPPELL MUSIC CO.†
810 Seventh Ave.
New York, NY 10019
(212) 399-7373
Irwin Z. Robinson, Pres

CHARING CROSS MUSIC, INC.
36 East 61st St.
New York, NY 10021
(212) 751-0590
Ian E. Hoblyn, Gen Mgr

CHAR-LIZ MUSIC INC.
46 W. 11th
New York, NY 10011
(212) 674-1111
Vic Chirumbolo, Gen Mgr

C. CHASE MUSIC PRODUCTIONS†
83 Kneeland Ave.
Binghamton, NY 13905
(607) 797-1190
Dr. Clarence W. Chase, Dir

CHERIO CORP*
c/o Lee V. Eastman
39 W. 54th St.
New York, NY 10019

CHERRY LANE MUSIC PUBLISHING CO., INC.†
110 Midland Ave.
PO Box 430
Port Chester, NY 10573
(914) 937-8601

CHILLYWINDS MUSIC*
c/o Linden & Deutsch
110 E. 59th St.
New York, NY 10022
(212) 758-1100

CHRYSALIS MUSIC CORP
115 E. 57th St.
New York, NY 10022
(212) 935-8754

CLARA MUSIC PUBLISHING CORP.†
157 W. 57th St.
New York, NY 10019
(212) 757-9660

CLARIDGE MUSIC PUBLISHING CO. (NY)
(*See* Mietus Copyright Management, NY)

CLARUS MUSIC LTD.†
340 Bellevue Ave.
Yonkers, NY 10703
(914) 375-0864
Selma Fass, Pres

COMMODORES ENTERTAINMENT PUBLISHING CORP.†
39 W. 55th St.
New York, NY 10019
(212) 246-0385

COMRECO MUSIC INC.†
3 Kensington Oval
New Rochelle, NY 10805
(914) 235-1229
Milt Gabler, Pres

CONTROLLED SHEET MUSIC SERVICE INC.
112 Hudson St.
Copiague, NY 11726
(516) 842-8080
Ronald Ravitz, Pres

COPYRIGHT SERVICE BUREAU LTD.
221 W. 57th St.
New York, NY 10019
(212) 582-5030
Ms. Jeri R. Spencer, VP Admin

COTILLION MUSIC, INC.*
75 Rockefeller Plaza
New York, NY 10019
(212) 484-8208
Lindo Wortman, VP

COUSINS MUSIC*
211 Birchwood Ave.
Upper Nyack, NY 10960
(914) 358-0861
Lou Cicchetti, Pres

CROMA MUSIC CO.†
37 West 57th St.
New York, NY 10019
(212) 759-8730

DAKSEL MUSIC CORP.*
c/o Leber & Krebs, Inc.
65 West 55th St.
New York, NY 10019
(212) 765-2600
David Wilkes, VP

DAVID MUSIC*
1650 Broadway
New York, NY 10019
(212) 247-2159
Morton Wax, Pres

PIETRO DIERO PUBLICATION‡
133 7th Ave. S.
New York, NY 10014
(212) 675-5460
Pietro Deiro, Owner

DELIGHTFUL MUSIC LTD.*
1733 Broadway
New York, NY 10019
(212) 757-6770
Martin Feig, VP

DENTON & HASKINS CORP.†
PO Box 340
Radio City Station
New York, NY 10101
(212) 227-4714
Chelsy V. Young, Pres

DIANA MUSIC CO.†
c/o Sidney Mills
23 W. 73rd St.
New York, NY 10023

DOBRO PUBLISHING CO.
Rt. 1, Box 49
Utica, NY 13502
(315) 724-0895
Floyd Ketchum, Mgr

DOC DICK ENTERPRISES*
16 East Broad St.
Mt. Vernon, NY 10552
(914) 668-4488
Richard Rashbaum, Pres

DOMESTIC MUSIC CO.†
147 Bay 41st ST.
Brooklyn, NY 11214
Constantine Alexiou

DOVER PUBLICATIONS INC.
180 Varick St.
New York, NY 10014
(212) 255-3755
Hayward Cirker, Pres

DY-COR INC.*
792 Columbus Ave.
New York, NY 10025
Harvey Cort, VP

ELVIS MUSIC INC.*
1619 Broadway
New York, NY 10019
(212) 489-8170
Lester Boles

EMKO MUSIC CORP.
Div of Emko Talent Assoc. Corp.
PO Box 176
Monsey, NY 10952
(914) 425-6040

THE EMPIRE PROJECT†
119 West 57th St., Ste. 620
New York, NY 10019
(212) 586-0004
Don Silver, Mgr

ENTERTAINMENT CO. MUSIC GROUP
40 W. 57th St.
New York, NY 10019
(212) 265-2600
Charles Koppelman

EVANSONGS
c/o Prager-Phantom Records
1790 Broadway, Penthouse
New York, NY 10019
(212) 765-8450
E.S. Prager, Pres

EXBROOK PUBLISHING CO.*
c/o Unichappel Music Inc.
810 7th Ave.
New York, NY 10019
(212) 399-7373

EXTRA MONEY MUSIC†
1290 Ave of the Americas[6]
Ste. 264
New York, NY 10019
(212) 399-0090
Lanny Lambert, Pres

FAIRYLAND MUSIC CORP.†
240 W. 55th St.
New York, NY 10019
(12) 246-3000
Jack Benanty, Pres

FAMOUS MUSIC CORP†
c/o Sidney Herman
Div of Gulf & Western
1 Gulf & Western Plaza
New York, NY 10023
(212) 333-3433
Marvin Cane, CEO

FINCHLEY MUSIC CORP.†
c/o Arro Edelstein & Gross
919 Third Ave.
New York, NY 10022
(212) 371-7111

CARL FISCHER INC.†
62 Cooper Square
New York, NY 10003
(212) 777-0900
Walter F. Connor, Pres

FISHER MUSIC CORP.†
1619 Broadway
New York, NY 10019
(212) 586-1504
Dan Fisher, Pres

FORT KNOX MUSIC CO.*
1619 Broadway
New York, NY 10019
(212) 489-8170
Jerry Leiber, Partner

FOUR ACES MUSIC INC.*
PO Box 860
Cooper Station
New York, NY 10003
(212) 473-5900
Naomi Saltzman, Gen Mgr

FOUR MOONS MUSIC PUBLISHING GROUP†
279 East 44th St.
Penthouse E
New York, NY 10017
(212) 288-2446
Norman Dolph, Pres

FOURTH FLOOR MUSIC*
Box 135
Bearsville, NY 12409
(914) 679-7303
Albert Grossman, Pres

FRANK & NANCY MUSIC INC.*
1619 Broadway
New York, NY 10019
(212) 489-8170

FREDOLA MUSIC PUBLISHING CO.*
7-11 E. Genesee St.
Auburn, NY 13021
(315) 253-5380
Frank Mucedola, Owner

FUNKY ACRES MUSIC CO.†
145 W. 55th St.
New York, NY 10019
(212) 245-7179
Warren Baker

GALAXY MUSIC CORP.†
131 West 86th St.
New York, NY 10024
(212) 874-2100
John M. Kernochan, Pres

AL GALLICO MUSIC CORP.*
120 East 56th ST.
New York, NY 10022
(212) 355-5980
Al Gallico, Pres

GATES MUSIC INC.*
1 Marine Midland Plaza
Rochester, NY 14604
(716) 232-2490
Tom Iannaccone

GAUCHO MUSIC*
161 West 54th ST.
New York, NY 10019
(212) 581-5398
Roy Rifkind, Pres

GENERAL MUSIC PUBLISHING CO. INC.†
145 Palisade St.
Dobbs Ferry, NY 10522
(914) 693-9321
Paul Kapp, Pres

GLAD HAMP MUSIC INC.†
1995 Broadway
New York, NY 10023
(212) 787-1222
Lionel Hampton, Pres

GLEN EAGLE PUBLISHING COMPANY*
64 New Hyde Park Rd.
Garden City, NY 11530
P. Noonan

GLORI GOSPEL MUSIC*
246 Richmond Ave.
Staten Island, NY 10302
Steven Herman, Pres

MANNY GOLD MUSIC PUBLISHER†
895 McDonald Ave.
Brooklyn, NY 11218
(212) 435-1910
Manny Gold, Pres

GOOD PRODUCT MUSIC†
539 W. 25th St.
New York, NY 10001
(212) 675-6060
Nicholas Cosmas, Pres

THE GOODMAN GROUP‡
110 E. 59th St.
New York, NY 10022
(212) 751-7300
Eugene Goodman, Gen Mgr

GOPAM ENTERPRISES, INC.*
11 Riverside Dr. #13C-W
New York, NY 10023
(212) 724-6120
Laurie Goldstein, Mng Dir

GOSPEL BIRDS INC.*
c/o Weiss & Meibach
888 Seventh Ave.
New York, NY 10019
(212) 765-4936
Vicki Wickham, Pres

GOSPEL CLEF
Box 90
Rugby Station
Brooklyn, NY 11203
(212) 773-5910
John R. Lockley, Pres

G.Q. MUSIC†
c/o Tony Lopez
1020 Grand Concourse
Bronx, NY 10451

GRAMAVISION MUSIC CO.*
PO Box 2772
Grand Central Station
New York, NY 10163
(212) 674-1562
Jonathan Rose, Pres

GRAPH MUSIC†
49 West 96th St.
New York, NY 10025
(212) 665-0214

GREEN MENU MUSIC CO.†
Div of Green Menu Music Factory Inc.
50 W. 57th St.
New York, NY 10019
(212) 397-3060
Henry Jerome, Pres

GUDI MUSIC*
337 rue de Chartes
New Orleans, LA 70130

HARGAIL MUSIC INC.
51 E. 12th St.
New York, NY 10003
(212) 245-7246
Harold Newman, Pres

HARLEM MUSIC*
c/o Lynn Boehringer
355 Harlem Rd.
West Seneca, NY 14224

HELIOS MUSIC CORPORATION*
221 W. 57th St.
New York, NY 10019
(212) 581-0280
Claus Ogerman, Pres

HOB & NOB MUSIC PUBLISHERS*
158 W. 15th St.
New York, NY 10011
(212) 255-7214
LeRoy De Gregory, Gen Mgr

HOMETOWN MUSIC CO.†
80-08 35th Ave.
Jackson Heights, NY 11372
(212) 651-8213
Sidney Prosen, Pres

HUDSON BAY MUSIC CO.*
1619 Broadway
New York, NY 10019
(212) 489-8170
Freddy Bienstock, Partner

IGUANA MUSIC*
c/o Virgil Jones
52 Riverside Dr.
New York, NY 10025

INFINITY-MUSIC PUBLISHING GROUP
485 Madison Ave.
New York, NY 10022
(212) 888-9711

INTEGRITY MUSIC CORP.†
1050 Fifth Ave., Apt. 14A
New York, NY 10028
(212) 348-6700
Jack Wolf, Pres

INTERNATIONAL MUSIC CO.
545 Fifth Ave.
New York, NY 10017
(212) 687-2205

JACKAROE MUSIC PUBLISHERS
Div of Vanguard Recording Society Inc.
71 W. 23rd St.
New York, NY 10010
(212) 255-7732
Maynard Solomon, Pres

DICK JAMES MUSIC INC.*
230 W. 55th St.
Ste. 17D
New York, NY 10019
Dick James, Pres

TOMMY JAMES MUSIC INC.*
c/o Magna Artists Inc.
595 Madison Ave.
New York, NY 10022
(212) 752-0363

JEMAVA MUSIC*
c/o Dee Anthony
33 E. 70th St.
New York, NY 10021

JEPALANA MUSIC*
723 Seventh Ave.
New York, NY 10019
(212) 245-7640
Nathan Schnapf, Pres

JIMPIRE MUSIC INC.*
110 East 59th St.
New York, NY 10022
(212) 371-4387

JIRU MUSIC, INC.†
201 W. 77th St., Ste. 3-C
New York, NY 10024
(212) 799-0228
Richard Gottehrer, Pres

JOBETE OF NEW YORK
157 W. 57th St.
New York, NY 10019
(212) 581-7420

JOLI MUSIC INC.*
41 Algonquin Rd.
Yonkers, NY 10710
(914) 779-2080
Jim McCarthy, Pres

JOURNEYMAN MUSIC*
135-46 Grand Central Pkway
Kew Gardens, NY 11435
(212) 847-6377
Ernest Petito, Manager

K AND R MUSIC, INC.†
112 E. Main St.
Box 616
Trumansburg, NY 14886
(607) 387-5325
William M. Kelly, Pres

KACK KLICK, INC.*
Mirror Records, Inc.
645 Titus Ave.
Rochester, NY 14617
(716) 544-3500
Armand Schaubroeck, VP

KAMAKAZI MUSIC CORPORATION*
314 W. 71st St.
New York, NY 10023
(212) 595-4330
Miles J. Lourie, Mgr

BOB KARCY MUSIC
437 W. 16th St.
New York, NY 10011
(212) 989-1989
Bob Karcy, Pres

KARJAN MUSIC PUBLISHING CO.‡
Box 205
White Lake, NY 12786
(914) 583-4471
Mickey Barnett, Pres

KATCH NAZAR MUSIC†
c/o Rose Hill Group
3929 New Seneca Turnpike
Marcellus, NY 13108
(315) 673-1117
Vincent Taft, Mgr

KENDOR MUSIC INC.‡
Main & Grove Sts.
Delevan, NY 14042
(716) 492-1254
Lester P. Chappell, Pres

KICK-A-ROCK†
c/o Aucoin Management Corp.
645 Madison Ave.
New York, NY 10022

CHARLES KIPPS MUSIC INC.*
1 Lincoln Plaza
New York, NY 10023
(212) 580-0154
Charles H. Kipps Jr., Pres

KIRSHNER/CBS MUSIC PUBLISHING
1370 Ave of the Americas
New York, NY 10019
(212) 489-0440

KISS SONGS
c/o Aucoin Management
645 Madison Ave.
New York, NY 10022
(212) 826-8800

KOOL KAT MUSIC*
Div of Kool Kat Productions Inc.
60 Carlton Rd.
PO Box 176
Monsey, NY 10952
(914) 425-6040

LARBALL MUSIC*
c/o Arrow, Edelstein & Gross
1370 Ave of the Americas
New York, NY 10019
(212) 586-1451

DAVID LASLEY MUSIC*
c/o Robert J. Epstein Esq.
1780 Broadway, Ste. 1200
New York, NY 10019
(212) 765-5038

LAUGHING WILLOW MUSIC†
c/o Arnold Liebman
159 W. 53rd St.
New York, NY 10019
(212) 765-3620

LAURIE PUBLISHING GROUP†
20-F Robert Pitt Dr.
Monsey, NY 10952
(914) 425-7000
Gene Schwartz, Pres

LEA POCKET SCORES
PO Box 138, Audubon Sta.
New York, NY 10025
(212) 866-4026
Fritz Steinhardt, Pres

LEVINE & BROWN MUSIC*
c/o Arrow, Edelstein & Gross
919 Third Ave.
New York, NY 10022
(212) 371-7111

IRWIN LEVINE MUSIC*
c/o Arrow, Edelstein & Gross
919 Third Ave.
New York, NY 10022
(212) 371-7111

LIDO
c/o Padell, Nadell, Fine, Weinberger & Co.
1775 Broadway
New York, NY 10019

LITTLE OTIS MUSIC*
101 Westchester Ave.
Port Chester, NY 10573
(914) 939-1066
Judy Novy, Gen Mgr; Carmine Riale, Pres

LOENA MUSIC PUBLISHING CO.
239 West 18th St.
New York, NY 10011
(212) 989-7200

LOLLIPOP MUSIC CORP.*
132 East 45th St.
Penthouse C
New York, NY 10017
(212) 557-9109
Eddie Miller, Pres

LONE LAKE SONGS, INC.†
Box 126
93 North Central Ave.
Elmsford, NY 10523
(914) 592-7983
Ron Carpenter, Pres

LORESTA MUSIC†
c/o Jeff Graubert
485 Madison Ave., 17th Flr.
New York, NY 10022
(212) 980-0120

LORIJOY MUSIC, INC.*
39 West 55th St.
New York, NY 10019
(212) 586-3350
Debra Martinez, Gen Mgr

LUCY'S STORE MUSIC*
Box 268
133 Mountaindale Rd.
Yonkers, NY 10710
(914) 779-4684
Guy & Pipp Gillette, Co-Owners

LYRA MUSIC CO.†
133 W. 69th St.
New York, NY 10023
(212) 874-3360
Don Henry, Owner

MACHARMONY MUSIC†
400 W. 43rd St., Ste. 5C
New York, NY 10036
(212) 244-8148
Walter Herman, Dir.; C. Roger Bartlett, Pres

MAD VINCENT MUSIC*
1776 Broadway
New York, New York, 10019

MARIELLE MUSIC PUBLISHING CO.*
Box 842
Radio City Station
New York, NY 10019
(212) 580-9723
Don Seat, Pres

EDWARD B. MARKS MUSIC CORPORATION*
1790 Broadway
New York, NY 10019
(212) 247-7277
Joseph Auslander, Pres

ANDY MARVEL MUSIC*
8 Pasture Lane
Roslyn Hts., NY 11577
(516) 621-4307
Andy Marvel, Pres

JOSEF MARX MUSIC CO.
PO Box 229
Planetarium Sta.
New York, NY 10024
(212) 799-5214
Margaret Gresh, Prod Mgr

MCA MUSIC†
MCA Inc.
445 Park Ave.
New York, NY 10022
(212) 759-7500
Salvatoare T. Chiantia, Pres; Mike Millius

MCGINNIS & MARX MUSIC PUBLISHERS*
Estate of Josef Marx
201 W. 86th St.
New York, NY 10024
Mrs. Josef Marx

MCRON MUSIC CO.†
521 Fifth Ave.
New York, NY 10017
(212) 682-5844
Tsipora Miron, Pres

M-E MUSIC CO.†
1697 Broadway
New York, NY 10019
(212) 757-5105
William H. Borden, Co-Owner

MEDIA CONCEPTS, INC./MCI MUSIC
20 E. 1st St.
Ste. 308
Mt. Vernon, NY 10550
(914) 699-4003
Michael Berman, Mgr.; Frank Rigo, Pres

MEGA-STAR MUSIC†
c/o Norm Walters Assoc.
1290 Ave. of the Americas
New York, NY 10019

METORION MUSIC CORP†
210 Fifth Ave.
New York, NY 10010
(212) 679-9312

MEXICAN MUSIC CENTRE INC.†
345 W. 58th St.
New York, NY 10019
(212) 582-5705
Gerard de La Chapelle, Mng Dir

MIDEB MUSIC†
1501 Broadway
New York, NY 10036
(212) 786-7667
Sam Weiss, Pres

MIETUS COPYRIGHT MANAGEMENT†
527 Madison Ave., Ste. 317
New York, NY 10022
(212) 371-7950

MILLER SONG-KRAFT MUSIC*
347 Litchfield Ave.
Babylon, NY 11702
(516) 661-9842
William H. Miller, Pub

MIND TO SOUND MUSIC PUBLISHING*
Box 229
Planetarium Station
New York, NY 10024
(212) 799-1591
Margaret Gresh

MINUTE BY MINUTE PUBLISHING
c/o Bette Hisiger
320 E. 23rd St.
New York, NY 10010
(212) 254-9338

MJQ MUSIC INC.
200 W. 57th St.
New York, NY 10019
(212) 582-6667
Paul Schwartz, Gen Mgr

M M O MUSIC GROUP INC.‡
423 W. 55th St.
New York, NY 10019
(212) 245-4861
Irving Kratka, Pres

IVAN MOGULL MUSIC CORP.†
625 Madison Ave.
New York, NY 10022
(212) 355-5636
Ivan Mogull, Pres

MONSTER ISLAND MUSIC PUBLISHING†
Padell, Wadell, Fine, Weinberger
1775 Broadway
New York, NY 10019
(212) 957-0900

MORLEY MUSIC CO.†
c/o Eastman & Eastman
39 W. 54th St.
New York, NY 10019
(212) 581-1330
Robert Jones, Prof Dept

EDWIN H. MORRIS & CO.†
39 W. 54th St.
New York, NY 10019
(212) 581-1330
Robert Jones, Mgr

MPL COMMUNICATIONS INC.
c/o Lee Eastman
39 W. 54th St.
New York, NY 10019
(212) 581-1330

M R I MUSIC
Div. of Music Resources Int'l Corp.
21 W. 39th St.
New York, NY 10018
(212) 869-2299

MUSIC COPYRIGHT HOLDING CORPORATION
Box 767
New York, NY 10101
R.O'Brien, Pres

MUSIC FOR UNICEF*
c/o Unichappell Music Inc.
810 Seventh Ave.
32nd Fl
New York, NY 10019

MUSIC MUSIC MUSIC INC.†
157 W. 57th St.
New York, NY 10019
(212) 582-6135
Chet Gierlach, Pres

MUSIC RESOURCES INTERNATIONAL CORP.†
21 W. 39th St.
New York, NY 10018
(212) 869-2299
Andy Hussakowsky, Pres

MUSIC SALES CORP†‡
799 Broadway
New York, NY 10003
Herbert H. Wise, Pres

MUSIC TREASURE PUBLICATIONS
620 Ft. Washington Ave.
New York, NY 10040
D. Garvelmann, Dir

MUSICANZA CORP.‡
2878 Bayview Ave.
Wantagh, NY 11793
(516) 826-2735
Al Rubin, Pres

MUSTEVIC SOUND INC.*
193-18 120th Ave.
St. Albans, NY 11412
(212) 527-1586
Brenda Reid, Pres

NARROW GATE MUSIC INC.†
PO Box 860
Cooper Station
New York, NY 10276
(212) 473-5900
Naomi Saltzman, Gen Mgr

NEPTUNE MUSIC PUBLISHERS*
82 Aldine St.
Rochester, NY 14619
(716) 328-4649
Martha Pitoni, Pres

NEVERLAND MUSIC PUBLISHING CO.
225 E. 57th St.
New York, NY 10022
(212) 888-7711
Earl S. Shuman, Pres

NICK-O-VAL MUSIC†
332 W. 71st St.
New York, NY 10023
(212) 873-2179
Nickolas Ashford, Pres

NOTABLE MUSIC CO. INC.†
161 W. 54th St.
New York, NY 10019
(212) 757-9547
Eric Colodne, Gen Mgr

NOVELLO PUBLICATIONS INC.
145 Palisade St.
Dobbs Ferry, NY 10522
(914) 693-5445

NRP MUSIC GROUP
160 East 56th St.
New York, NY 10022
(212) 233-5949
Fred Bailim, A & R Dir

ONEIDA MUSIC PUBLISHING CO.*
760 Blandina St.
Utica, NY 13501
(315) 735-6187
Stanley Markowski, Pres

OOZLE MUSIC
PO Box 669
Woodstock, NY 12498
(914) 679-6069/2458
Harris Goldberg, Pres

OTHER MUSIC INC.†
c/o Music Management
PO Box 174
Pleasantville, NY 10570
(914) 769-5580

OXFORD UNIVERSITY PRESS INC.†
200 Madison Ave.
New York, NY 10016
(212) 679-7300
Susan Brailove, Music Dept Mgr

O. PAGANI & BRO. INC.
289 Bleecker St.
New York, NY 10014
(212) 242-6744
Theresa Costello, Pres

PARTICIPATION MUSIC INC.†
c/o Zoomba House
1348 Lexington Ave.
New York, NY 10028

JOSEPH PATELSON MUSIC HOUSE†
160 W. 56th St.
New York, NY 10019
(212) 757-5587
Joseph Patelson, Pres

PEER-SOUTHERN ORGANIZATION
1740 Broadway
New York, NY 10019
(212) 265-3910
Monique Peer, Pres

PELTON PUBLISHING CO.*
PO Box 182
Midwood Station
Brooklyn, NY 11230
(212) 339-3536
Jim Pelton, Pres

PERSIMMON PRESS†
131 Prince St.
New York, NY 10012
(212) 477-0544
Emanuel Ghent, Owner

PETCO INTERNATIONAL INC.†
88-20 Corona Ave.
Elmhurst, NY 11373

(212) 699-5258
Robert Petrone, Pres

C.F. PETERS CORP.*
373 Park Ave. S.
New York, NY 10016
(212) 686-4147
Henry Hinrichsen, Pres

GEORGE PINCUS & SONS MUSIC CORP.†
1650 Broadway
New York, NY 10019
(212) 245-0110
George Pincus, Pres

POLKA TOWNE MUSIC*
211 Post Ave.
Westbury, NY 11590
(516) 334-6228
Teresa Zapolska, Pres

POPULAR MUSIC CO.†
49 W. 45th St.
New York, NY 10036
(212) 840-8833
Morton Browne, Pres

PPX PUBLISHERS*
c/o PPX Ent. Inc.
301 W. 54th St.
New York, NY 10019
(212) 247-6010

PRESCRIPTION CO.*
70 Murray Ave.
Port Washington, NY 11050
(516) 767-1929
David F. Gasman, Pres

PRIMA DONNA MUSIC CO.*
c/o Al Gallico Music Corp.
120 E. 56th St., Ste. 620
New York, NY 10022

PROCLAMATION PRODUCTIONS INC.†
Orange Square
Port Jervis, NY 12771
(914) 856-6686

PUBLISHERS' LICENSING CORP.†
488 Madison Ave.
New York, NY 10022
(212) 753-1110
Philip S. Kurnit, Contact

GERALD W. PURCELL ASSOCIATES
964 Second Ave.
New York, NY 10022
(212) 421-2670
Gerald Purcell, Pres

RADMUS PUBLISHING INC.†
c/o Larry Shane Ent.
250 W. 57th St.
New York, NY 10019
(212) 957-9330

RAE-COX & COOKE MUSIC CORP
1697 Broadway
New York, NY 10019
(212) 586-9406
Theodore McRae, Pres

TEDDY RANDAZZO MUSIC INC.*
51 W. 86th St.
New York, NY 10024
(212) 873-1800
Teddy Randazzo, Pres

RAYBIRD MUSIC*
457 W. 57th St.
New York, NY 10019
(212) 245-2299
Ray Passman, Pres

RAZZLE DAZZLE MUSIC INC.*
51 W. 86th St.
New York, NY 10024
(212) 873-1800
Hermi Hanlin, Pres

REN MAUR MUSIC CORP.
663 5th Ave.
New York, NY 10022
(212) 757-3638
Rena L. Feeney, Pres

WILLIAM REZEY MUSIC CO.*
PO Box 1257
Albany, NY 12201
(518) 438-3333

THE RICHMOND ORGANIZATION
10 Columbus Circle
New York, NY 10019
(212) 765-9889

RICK'S MUSIC*
c/o Right Song Music Inc.
810 7th Ave.
New York, NY 10019

RIGHTSONG MUSIC INC.*
c/o Irwin Z. Robinson
810 7th Ave.
New York, NY 10019

RIVA MUSIC, INC.†
c/o Mr. Alvin Gladstone
Schultz & Gladstone
98 Cutter Mill Rd.
Great Neck NY 10021

ROADS OF MUSIC PUBLISHING CORP.†
196-10F 65 Crescent
Fresh Meadows, NY 11365
(212) 454-7467
Niko Anducic, Pres

ROCKFORD MUSIC CO.*
150 W. End Ave., Ste. 6-D
New York, NY 10023
(212) 873-5968
Louis A. Chieli, Mgr

RONCOM MUSIC CO.†
305 Northern Blvd.
Great Neck, NY 11021
(516) 466-5810

ROTHSTEIN MUSIC, LTD.
720 E. 79th St.
Brooklyn, NY 11236
(212) 444-3283
Sharon Rothstein, Pres

ROYAL SPIN MUSIC INC.†
Mietus Copyright Mgmt.
527 Madison Ave., Ste. 317
New York, NY 10022

RSO MUSIC PUBLISHING GROUP*
(The Robert Stigwood Organization)
1775 Broadway
New York, NY 10019
(212) 975-0700
Fredric B. Gershon, Pres

RUSTRON MUSIC PUBLISHERS*
200 Westmoreland Ave.
White Plains, NY 10606
(914) 946-1689
Rusty Gordon, Pres

ST. NICHOLAS MUSIC INC.†
1619 Broadway
New York, NY 10019
(212) 582-0970
Johnny Marks, Pres

SALSOUL MUSIC PUBLISHING CORP.†
401 Fifth Ave.
New York, NY 10016
(212) 889-7340
Joseph Cayre, Pres

SANGA MUSIC INC.*
250 W. 57th St.
Ste. 2017
New York, NY 10019
(212) 586-6553
Harold Leventhal, Pres

G. SCHIRMER INC.†
866 Third Ave.
New York, NY 10022
(212) 935-5100
Edward Murphy, Pres

A. SCHROEDER INTERNATIONAL LTD.
1650 Broadway
New York, NY 10019
(212) 582-8995
Beldeen Fortunato, VP

SCREEM GEMS-EMI MUSIC, INC.
1370 Ave of the Americas
New York, NY 10019
(212) 489-6740

NEIL SEDAKA MUSIC PUBLISHING
315 W. 57th St.
New York, NY 10019
(212) 586-5712

SEESAW MUSIC GROUP†
2067 Broadway

New York, NY 10023
(212) 874-1200
Raoul R. Ronson, Pres

SIDNEY A. SEIDENBERG MUSIC LTD.*
1414 Ave. of the Americas
New York, NY 10019
(212) 421-2021
Sidney A. Seidenberg, Pres

SELLERS MUSIC, INC.*
1350 Ave. of the Americas
New York, NY 10019
(212) 687-4800

SEPTEMBER MUSIC CORP.†
250 W. 57th St.
New York, NY 10019
(212) 581-1338
Stanley Mills, Pres

SHAPIRO BERNSTEIN & CO. INC.†
10 E. 53rd St.
New York, NY 10022
(212) 751-3395
Richard M. Voltter, Exec VP

SHERLYN PUBLISHING CO.*
1790 Broadway
New York, NY 10019
(212) 582-4267
Phil Kahl, VP

SHOTGUN MUSIC CO.*
22 Pine St.
Freeport, NY 11520
(516) 546-8008
Anthony Ferrante, Pres

SHOWPIECE PRODUCTIONS*
PO Box 79
Main Station
Yonkers, NY 10702
(914) 965-0801
Robert B. Schoen, Pres

SILVER BLUE PRODUCTIONS LTD.†
220 Central Park S.
New York, NY 10019
(212) 586-3535
Joel Diamond, Pres

PAUL SIMON*
1619 Broadway, Ste. 500
New York, NY 10019
Ian Hoblyn, Gen Mgr

SOLAR SYSTEMS MUSIC†
441 E. 20th St.
New York, NY 10010
(212) 674-1143
Sheila Davis, Pres

SON-DEANE PUBLISHERS
25 Jenifer Lane
Hartsdale, NY 10530
(914) 693-1590
Howard Deanto, Pres

SONGS FOR TODAY, INC.
50 E. 42nd St.
New York, NY 10017
(212) 687-2299
H. Kruger, Pres

SOPHISTICATE MUSIC INC.*
41 Algonquin Rd.
Yonkers, NY 10710
(914) 779-2080
Josie Nelson Johnson, Pres

SOUTHERN CRESCENT PUBLISHING
320 W. 30th St.
New York, NY 10001
(212) 564-3246
Jonathan Strong, VP

SPECIAL RIDER†
Box 860
New York, NY 10276
Jeff Rosen, Mgr

LARRY SPIER INC.†
401 Fifth Ave.
New York, NY 10016
(212) 686-1777
Larry Spier, Pres

SPIRAL REC. CORP. PUBLISHERS†
c/o Gladys Shelly
875 Fifth Ave.
New York, NY 10021
(212) 737-3304

BRUCE SPRINGSTEEN MUSIC†
c/o Michael Tannen
36 E. 61st St.
New York, NY 10021
(212) 752-2276

STALLMAN RECORDS, INC.*
1697 Broadway
New York, NY 10019
(212) 582-6928
Julio Fernandez, Asst to Pres; Lou Stallman, Pres

SUDDEN RUSH MUSIC INC.*
750 Kappock St.
Riverdale, NY 10463
(212) 884-6014
Alan Korwin, Pres

SUGAR N'SOUL MUSIC, INC.†
109-23 71st Rd.
Forest Hills, NY 11375
(212) 268-8060
Mark Sameth, Mgr

SUMAC MUSIC INC.*
1697 Broadway
Ste. 1209
New York, NY 10019
(212) 246-0575
Susan McCusker, Pres

SUMMIT MUSIC CORP.†
250 W. 57 St.
New York, NY 10019
(212) 957-9330
Margo Reis, Pres

SUN-BEAR CORP.†
1650 Broadway
New York, NY 10019
(212) 765-4495

SWEET SWAMP MUSIC
Red Hill Rd.
Fleischmanns, NY 12430
(914) 254-4565
Barry Drake, Pres

SWING & TEMPO MUSIC PUBLISHING INC.*
1995 Broadway
New York, NY 10023
(212) 787-1222
Bill Titone, VP

TAKYA MUSIC†
265 W. 20 St.
New York, NY 10011
(212) 989-8048
Stuart Scharf, Pres

TEMPI MUSIC CO.
133 W. 87th St.
New York, NY 10024
(212) 799-5557

3 B MUSIC CORP†
1212 Ave of the Americas
New York, NY 10036
(212) 575-1805
Richard Berardi, VP

TOPOGRAPHIC MUSIC INC.†
565 Fifth Ave.
New York, NY 10017
(212) 490-0400
Elliott L. Hoffman, Pres

TRANSACTION MUSIC LTD.
225 E. 57th St.
New York, NY 10022
(212) 838-2590
Mildred Fields, Pres

TRANSCONTINENTAL MUSIC PUBLICATIONS
838 5th Ave.
New York, NY 10021
(212) 249-0100
Judith Tischler, Editor

TRINA JILL MUSIC CORP.†
401 Fifth Ave.
New York, NY 10016
(212) 889-7340
Joseph Cayre, Pres

TRIO MUSIC CO. INC.*
1619 Broadway
New York, NY 10019
(212) 489-8170
Jerry Lieber, Co-Pres

THE TUNE ROOM INC.†
200 W. 57th St.
New York, NY 10019
(212) 265-0741
Jerry Ragovoy, Pres

TWC MUSIC
TWC Entertainment Corp
Box 2021
New York, NY 10001
(212) 691-4565
Walter Balderson, Mgr

UNITED ARTISTS MUSIC
729 7th Ave.
New York, NY 10019
(212) 575-3000
Barry Bergman, VP Creative/Prof Mgr

VADO MUSIC†
2226 McDonald Ave.
Brooklyn, NY 11223
(212) 946-4405
Vincent A. Velardi, Pres

TOMMY VALANDO PUBLISHING GROUP, INC.
1270 Ave. of the Americas
Ste. 2110
New York, NY 10020
(212) 489-9696
Tommy Valando, Pres

THOMAS J. VALENTINO INC.†
151 W. 46th St.
New York, NY 10036
(212) 246-4675
R.J. Valentino, Pres

PAUL VANCE PUBLISHING CO.
159 W. 53rd St.
New York, NY 10019
(212) 581-0030
Paul Vance, Pres

VANGUARD MUSIC CORP.†
1595 Broadway, Rm. 313
New York, NY 10019
(212) 246-1343
Frank Seigfreid, Pres

JERRY VOGEL MUSIC CO. INC.†
58 W. 54th St.
New York, NY 10036
(212) 730-0478
Mabel Cram, Gen Mgr

WARNER BROS. MUSIC*
75 Rockefeller Plaza
New York, NY 10019
(212) 484-8000
Henry Marks, Mgr

WANESSA MUSIC INC.
PO Box 387
443 W. 50th St.
Radio City Station
New York, NY 10019
(212) 582-0543

WARNER-LEVENSON PUBLISHING CO.
9 E. 46th St.
New York, NY 10017
(212) 661-2106

WATT WORKS INC.*
Willow, NY 12495
(914) 688-5373
Michael Mantler, Pres

WEB IV MUSIC INC.*
c/o Grubman & Indursky
65 E. 55th St.
New York, NY 10022
(212) 888-6600

H.B. WEBMAN & CO.
1650 Broadway, Ste. 701
New York, NY 10019
(212) 586-0240
Hal Webman, Owner

WEEZE MUSIC CO. & DOUBLE HEADER PRODUCTIONS*
61 Jane St.
New York, NY 10014
(212) 929-2068
Steve Scharf

WESTERN HEMISPHERE MUSIC CO.*
252 Robby Ln.
New Hyde Park, NY 11040
(516) 627-8861
Harvey Rachlin, Pres

WEYAND MUSIC PUBLISHING†
297 Rehn Rd.
Depew, NY 14043
(716) 684-5323
C.D. Weyand, Owner

WHITE DWARF MUSIC
c/o dba Recs.
875 Ave. of the Americas
Ste. 1001
New York, NY 10001
(212) 279-9321
Alex Alexander, Gen Mgr

WHITE WAY MUSIC CO.†
65 West 55th St.
New York, NY 10019
(212) 245-1958
Eddie White, Pres

WORLD MUSIC INC.†
18 E. 48th St.
New York, NY 10017
(212) 688-6230
Sammy Kaye, Pres

XANADU RECORDS LTD.†
3242 Irwin Ave.
Kingsbridge, Bronx, NY 10463
(212) 549-3655
Don Schlitten, Pres

YELLOW BEE MUSIC*
245 Waverly Pl.
New York, NY 10014
(212) 255-3698
Nick Perls, Pres

ZEUS BOLTS PUBLISHING CO.†
87-79 115th St.
Richmond Hills, NY 11418
Harold D. Sessa, Pres

ZOMBA ENTS. INC.*
330 W. 58th St.
New York, NY 10019
(212) 265-2520
Clive Calder, Pres

NORTH CAROLINA

BAKER-GARRIS PUBLISHING CO.*
107 Spruce Pine
Shopping Center
Spruce Pine, NC 28777
(704) 765-4834
W.W. Garris, Pres

BIVENS MUSIC*
PO Box 1628
Elizabeth City, NC 27909
(919) 232-2703
Ernie Bivens, Pres

BRODT MUSIC CO.†
PO Box 9345
Charlotte, NC 28299
(704) 332-2177
Gladys F. Brodt, Owner

CREEKSIDE MUSIC*
100 Labon St.
Tabor City, NC 28463
(919) 653-2546
Elson H. Stevens, Pres

EXISTENTIAL MUSIC*
Box 176
118 5th St. SW
Taylorsville, NC 28681
(704) 632-4735
Harry Deal, Pres

GREENFIELDS MUSIC*
PO Box 21931
Greensboro, NC 27420
(919) 272-7336

METROLINA PUBLISHING CO. INC.*
2624 Chesterfield Ave.
Charlotte, NC 28205
John Roger Branch, Pres

NELMS MUSIC*
PO Box 12
Rocky Mount, NC 27801
(919) 459-4691
John Nelms, Pres

PEOPLE PLEASER MUSIC*
1018 Central Ave.
Charlotte, NC 28204

(704) 377-4596
Wayne Jernigan, Owner

FREDDIE ROBERTS MUSIC*
Box 99
Rougemont, NC 27572
(919) 477-4077
Freddie Roberts, Mgr

SAFMAR PUBLISHING CO.*
PO Box 978
146 W. Park Ave.
Mooresville, NC 28115
(704) 663-4892
Jack Safrit, Pres

SLEEPY HOLLOW MUSIC CO.†
PO Box 7
Swannanoa, NC 28778
(704) 686-3235
Billy Edd Wheeler, Pres

SOUTHERN MELODY PUBLISHING CO.*
122 W. Woodridge Dr.
Durham, NC 27707
(919)) 489-4349
Barry Poss, Pres

WADE STALEY MUSIC
Box 5712
High Point, NC 27262
(919) 885-0263
W.C. Staley, Pres

STONEY POINT MUSIC*
38 Stoney Point Ln.
Charlotte, NC 28210
(704) 554-8505
Bill Bradford, Contact

SUENO PUBLISHING CO.*
Rt. 2
Troutman, NC 28166
(704) 528-4843
Don E. Moose, Pres

TOMPAUL MUSIC CO.*
628 South St.
Mount Airy, NC 27030
(919) 786-2865
Paul E. Johnson, Owner

CURTIS L. WOODS PUBLISHING CO.*
PO Box 701
North Wilksboro, NC 28659
(919) 667-6662
Curtis L. Woods, Gen Mgr

NORTH DAKOTA

COTTONBLOSSOM MUSIC†
Star Rt. 2
Bismarck, ND 58501
(701) 223-7316
W.R. Townsend

OHIO

ACCURA MUSIC†
Box 887
Athens, OH 45701
(614) 594-3547
Reginald H. Fink, Pres

AL-KRIS MUSIC*
Box 4185
Youngstown, OH 44515
(216) 793-7295
Richard M. Hahn, Mgr

BARUTH PRODUCTIONS INC.†
(Baruth Music Div.)
3628 W. 159th St.
Cleveland, OH 44111
(216) 941-0911

BECKENHOURST PRESS INC.†
PO Box 14273
3841 N. High St.
Columbus, OH 43214
(614) 268-3010
John Ness Beck, Pres

HAL BERNARD ENTERPRISES, INC.
Box 6507
2181 Victory Parkway
Cincinnati, OH 45206
(513) 861-1500
Stan Hertzman, Pres

CANYON PRESS INC.
PO Box 1235
Cincinnati, OH 45201
(513) 852-7850
G.W. Fahrer, Jr., Pres

CARWIN PUBLISHING CO.*
Carwin Country Records
13357 Lorain Ave.
Cleveland, OH 44111
(216) 476-2695
Carl French, Pres

CAYTON PUBLISHING†
PO Box 367
West Main St.
Orwell, OH 44076
(216) 437-8422
P.J. Naples, D.O.

CHANTRY MUSIC PRESS INC.‡
PO Box 1101
32-34 N. Center St.
Springfield, OH 45501
(513) 325-9992
Dr. Frederick M. Otto. Pres

CINCINNATI MUSIC CO.*
906 Main St.
Cincinnati, OH 45202
(513) 241-3447
Michael S. Schwartz, Pres

COUNTERPART MUSIC*
3744 Applegate Ave.
Cincinnati, OH 45211
(513) 661-8810
Howard Lovdal,Pres

DEER CREEK PUBLISHING*
Aulon Rd. NE, Box 7
Rushville, OH 43150

ENGLISH MOUNTAIN PUBLISHING CO.*
332 N. Brinker Ave.
Columbus, OH 43204
(614) 279-5251
Jetta Brown, Script Mgr

ERIC DYNAMIC CO.*
c/o Robert Eric Wilson, Jr.
PO Box 147551
Cincinnati, OH 45214
(513) 281-8645

FINCH PUBLISHING*
2430 Spring Grove Ave.
Cincinnati, OH 45214
(513) 421-0850

GRENOBLE SONGS
Box 222
Groveport, OH 43125
(614) 837-7506
Ed Graham, Gen Mgr

HALNAT MUSIC PUBLISHING CO.†
Box 37156
Cincinnati, OH 45222
(513) 531-7605
Saul Halper, Pres

JEVERT MUSIC*
639 Bulen Ave.
Columbus, OH 43205
(614) 258-7112
Jeffrey V. Smith, Pres

THE LORENZ CORPORATION†
501 E. 3rd. St.
Dayton, OH 45401
(513) 228-6118
Gene McClusky, Music Editor

PARK J. TUNES†
813 Heritage Ln.
Waterville, OH 43566
(419) 878-8387
Michael Drew, Pres

PAUBIL MUSIC PUBLISHING CO.*
3516 Champlain Ave.
Youngstown, OH 44502
(216) 755-7794
Bill Schaffert, Pres

RITE MUSIC*
9745 Lockland Rd.
Cincinnati, OH 45215
(513) 733-5533
Carl J. Burkhardt, Pres

ROBADON MUSIC*
PO Box 2094

Sheffield Lake, OH 44054
(216) 949-2078

Robert W. Sellers, Owner

SOKIT MUSIC*
455 N. Snyder Rd.
Dayton, OH 45427
(513) 854-2797

Al Freeders, Pres

STARSOUND MUSIC*
973-D Chesterdale Dr.
Cincinnati, OH 45246

David Chastain

SUNNYSLOPE MUSIC†
PO Box 6507
2181 Victory Pkwy
Cincinnati, OH 45206
(513) 861-1500

Stanley B. Hertzman, Pres

TERMYA MUSIC PUBLISHING CO.*
909 Keil Rd.
Toledo, OH 43607
(419) 531-2271

Porter Roberts, Pres

TOMLEW PUBLISHING*
12202 Union Ave.
Cleveland, OH 44105
(216) 752-3440

Thomas R. Boddie, Pres

THE WELDEE MUSIC COMPANY*
Box 561
Wooster, OH 44691

Quentin W. Welty, Gen Mgr

XC MUSIC PUBLISHING†
Box 651
Worthington, OH 43085

OKLAHOMA

ALVERA PUBLISHING CO.*
PO Box 9304
Tulsa, OK 74107
(918) 242-3303

Al Clauser, Pres

BIG DIAMOND PUBLISHING*
RR 1 Box 515
Depew, OK 74028

Ken Holiday Garton, Owner

BIG SWING PUBLISHING*
c/o L.D. Allen
3120 S. Robinson
Oklahoma City, OK 73109
(405) 235-3500

CASTLE MUSIC INC.
PO Box 7574
Tulsa, OK 74105
(918) 299-9203

CATALPA PUBLISHING CO.*
2609 NW 36th St.
Oklahoma City, OK 73112
(405) 942-0462

Bobby Boyd, Mgr

COUNTRY CLASSICS MUSIC PUBLISHING CO.*
105 Burk Dr.
Oklahoma City, OK 73115
(405) 677-6448

Sonny Lane, Gen Mgr

LACKEY PUBLISHING CO.*
Box 269
Caddo, OK 74720
(405) 367-2798

Robert F. Lakcey, Pres

NITFOL MUSIC*
PO Box 7723
Tulsa, OK 74105
(918) 747-4118

Dick Loftin, Pres

OKISHER MUSIC*
Box 20814
Oklahoma City, OK 73156
(405) 751-8954

Mickey Sherman, Pres

SPIRIT AND SOUL PUBLISHING CO.†
Box 7574
Tulsa, OK 74105
(918) 299-1223

Ben Ferrell, Pres

WATONGA PUBLISHING CO.
2609 NW 36th St.
Oklahoma City, OK 73112
(405) 942-0462

OREGON

MOON JUNE MUSIC*
5821 SE Powell Blvd.
Portland, OR 97206

Bob Stoutenburg, Pub

SAND ISLAND MUSIC CO.*PO Box 688
Eugene, OR 97440
(503) 686-0779

Kathy L. Waisanen, Pres

RALPH L. SELTZER, INC.†
c/o Music World-Selma
1751 Draper Valley Rd.
Selma, OR 97538
(503) 597-2161

Ralph L. Seltzer, Pres

SOLA SCRIPTURA SONGS*
12235 SW Bull Mountain Rd.
Tigard, OR 97223
(503) 620-5680

PENNSYLVANIA

ACROSS THE MILES MUSIC PUBLISHING CO.*
c/o David J. Steinberg
818 Widener Blvd.
1339 Chestnut St.
Philadelphia, PA 19107
(215) 564-3880

William P. Neale, Pres

AMIGO MUSIC PUBLISHING CO.†
6137 N. Sixth St.
Philadelphia, PA 19120
(215) 548-4038

Ray Karol, Pres

ANDREA MUSIC CO.‡
925 N. Third St.
Philadelphia, PA 19123
(215) 627-2277

ARCADE MUSIC CO.†
Arzee Recording Co.
3010 N. Front St.
Philadelphia, PA 19133
(215) 426-5682

Rex Zario, Pres

BEAGLE PUBLISHING CO.†
PO Box 368
Biglerville, PA 17307

Craig Dayton

BLACK DIAMOND MUSIC PUBLISHING & PRODUCTION CO.
Box 28800
Philadelphia, PA 19151
(215) 477-1148

Allen Gabriel, Pres

CHARTER PUBLICATIONS INC.†
Div of J.W. Pepper & Son
PO Box 850
Valley Forge, PA 19484
(215) 666-0363

CHAUTAUQUA MUSIC PUBLISHING CO.*
1521 Seventh Ave.
Beaver Falls, PA 15010
(412) 846-2225

M. David Breit, Pres

CONYPOL MUSIC, INC.*
2595 Carrell Ln.
Willow Grove, PA 19090
(215) 443-0935

Sal Barbieri, Pres

COUNTRY STAR MUSIC†
439 Wiley Ave.
Franklin, PA 16323
(814) 432-4633

Norman Kelly, Pres

CREATIVE LIGHT MUSIC*
PO Box 2767
Philadelphia, PA 19120
(215) 745-9616

Richard T. Towey, Sr., Exec Dir

CRIMSON DYNASTY†
Crimson Dynasty Record Corp.

Box 271
Cedar & West Ave.
Jenkintown, PA 19046
(215) 757-8022

Stan Peahota, Pres

LOU DELISE PRODUCTIONS*
2001 W. Moyamensing Ave.
Philadelphia, PA 19145
(215) 248-1683

Lou DeLise, Pres

HENRI ELKAN MUSIC INC.
1316 Walnut St.
Philadelphia, PA 19107
(215) 735-1900

S. Van Gobes, Pres

ELLEBIE MUSIC PUBLISHING CO.*
409 Union St.
Farrell, PA 16121
(412) 342-9330

Willie James Ellebie, Pres

FEE BEE MUSIC CO.*
4517 Wainwright Ave.
Pittsburgh, PA 15227
(412) 884-4727

J.M. Averbach, Pres

GOLDEN FLEECE MUSIC PUBLISHING CO.
c/o David J. Steinberg
818 Widener Blvd.
1339 Chestnut St.
Philadelphia, PA 19107
(215) 564-3888

Norman Harris, Pres

GOOSEPIMPLE MUSIC*
7 Colonial Ave.
Myerstown, PA 17067
(717) 866-5067

Al Shade, Mgr

GRAVENHURST MUSIC*
105 Park Lane
Beaver Falls, PA 15010
(412) 843-2431
(412) 847-0111

Jerry Reed, Pres

Branch:
1469 3rd Ave.
New Brighton, PA 15066

JAMES BOY PUBLISHING CO.
Box 128
Worcester, PA 19490
(215) 424-0800

J. James, Pres

JAMIE MUSIC PUBLISHING CO.*
919 N. Broad St.
Philadelphia, PA 19123
(215) 232-8383

Harold B. Lipsius, Pres

JOCHER MUSIC CO.*
Box 102C, RD 1
Chubbic Rod
Canonsburg, PA 15317
(412) 746-2540

Joe Diamond, Pres

K-4 MUSIC†
1405 Locust St., Ste. 1815
Philadelphia, PA 19102
(215) 735-6695

LADD MUSIC CO.*
401 Wintermantle Ave.
Scranton, PA 18505
(717) 343-6718

Phil Ladd, Pres

LAZAR MUSIC*
Box 77
Center Square, PA 19422
(215) 635-6921

A. Gravatt, Pres

LITTLE DOVE PUBLISHING CO.*
1228 Reed St.
Philadelphia, PA 19147

Grace Marchesani, Owner

LITTLE JOE MUSIC CO.
604 Broad St.
Johnstown, PA 15906
(814) 539-8117

Al Page, Owner

MASTERVIEW MUSIC PUBLISHING*
PO Box 52
Ridge Rd. & Butler Ln.
Perkasie, PA 18944
(215) 257-9616

John Wolf, Pres

METRONOME MUSIC PUBLISHING CO. OF PENNSYLVANIA, INC.
Collins & Willard Sts.
Philadelphia, PA 19134
(215) 426-5925

Albert Schwab, Pres

THE MIGHTY THREE MUSIC GROUP*
309 S. Broad St.
Philadelphia, PA 19107
(215) 546-3510

Earl Shelton, Pres

MOM BELL MUSIC PUBLISHING CO.*
c/o David Steinberg, Esq.
818 Widener Bldg.
1339 Chestnut St.
Philadelphia, PA 19107
(215) 564-3880

Tony Bell, Pres

THEODORE PRESSER CO.†
Presser Pl.
Bryn Mawr, PA 19010
(215) 525-3636

Arnold Broido, Pres

RED BARN MUSIC PUBLISHING CO.*
PO Box 84
Strausstown, PA 19559
(215) 488-1782

Patrick Sickafus, Pres

LLOYD ZANE REMICK
1529 Walnut St., 6th Fl.
Philadelphia, PA 19102
(215) 568-0500

Lloyd Zane Remick, Pres

SCRUNGE MUSIC*
8947 Alton St.
Philadelphia, PA 19115
(215) 671-1590

Larry Feldman, Pres

SCULLY MUSIC CO.†
The Sunshine Group
800 South 4th St.
Philadelphia, PA 19147
(215) 755-7000

Michele Quigley, Asst to Pres; Walter B. Kohn, Pres

SHAWNEE PRESS, INC.†
Delaware Water Gap, PA 18327
(717) 476-0550

Lewis M. Kirby, Jr., Dir of Pub; Fred Waring, Pres

SHELTON ASSOCIATES*
2250 Bryn Mawr Ave.
Philadelphia, PA 19131
(215) 477-7122

George Guess, Pres

SOUTHERN CRESCENT PUBLISHING*
121 N. 4th St.
Easton, PA 18042
(215) 258-5990

James H. Kirkhuff, Jr., Pres

SULZER MUSIC*
Dave Wilson Productions
3505 Kensington Ave.
Philadelphia, PA 19134
(215) 744-6111

Dave Wilson, Pres

THIRD STORY MUSIC, INC.†
3436 Sansom St.
Philadelphia, PA 19104
(215) 386-5987

John O. Wicks III, Pres

TWIN TAIL MUSIC*
8809-11 Rising Sun Ave.
Philadelphia, PA 19115
(215) 676-8992

Frank Virtue, Pres

TYMENA MUSIC*
430 Pearce Rd.
Pittsburgh, PA 15234
(412) 341-0991

Ty Lemley, Pres

URSULA MUSIC
Box 300

Mt. Gretna, PA 17064
Joey Welz, Pres

VOKES MUSIC PUBLISHING*
Box 12
New Kensington, PA 15068
(412) 335-2775
Howard Vokes, Pres

VOLKWEIN BROS. INC.
117 Sandusky St.
Pittsburgh, PA 15212
(412) 322-5100
Carl W. Volkwein, Pres

DON WHITE PUBLISHING/D& W MUSIC†
2020 Ridge Ave.
Philadelphia, PA 19121
(215) 765-4889
P. Donald White, Pres

ZANE MUSIC*
1529 Walnut St.
Philadelphia, PA 19102
(215) 568-0500
Lloyd Zane Remick, Pres

REX ZARIO MUSIC*
3010 N. Front St.
Philadelphia, PA 19133
(215) 426-5682
Rex Zario, Pres

RHODE ISLAND

GREEN MOUNTAIN MUSIC CORP.*
806 Oaklawn Ave.
Cranston, RI 02920
(401) 944-9005
Stuart Wiener, Co-Pres

FRANK GUBALA MUSIC*
Hillside Rd.
Cumberland, RI 02864
(401) 333-6097
Frank Gubala

SOUTH CAROLINA

ADONIKAM MUSIC*
Box 8374, Station A
Greenville, SC 29604
(803) 271-1104
Rick Sandidge, Pres

THE HERALD ASSOCIATION, INC.†
Box 218
Wellman Heights
Johnsonville, SC 29555
(303) 386-2600
Erv Lewis, Pres

JEMIAH PUBLISHING*
Box 2501
Columbia, SC 29202
(803) 754-5554
Myron Alford, Pres

ARTHUR KENT MUSIC CO.†
1412 Golfview Dr.
North Myrtle Beach, SC 29582
Arthur Kent, Owner

JACK REDICK MUSIC*
Rt. 1, Box 85
Georgetown, SC 29440
(803) 546-7139
Jack Redick, Owner

SILHOUETTE MUSIC
Box 218
Wellman Heights
Johnsonville, SC 29555
(803) 386-2600
Erv Lewis, Dir

SIVATT MUSIC PUBLISHING*
Box 7172
Greenville, SC 29610
(803) 295-3177
Jesse B. Evatte, Pres

HAROLD THOMAS MUSIC CO.*
203 Culver Ave.
Charleston, SC 29407
(803) 766-2500
Harold Thomas, Pres

WESJAC MUSIC*
Box 743
129 W. Main St.
Lake City, SC 29560
(803) 394-3712
W.R. Bragdton Jr., Gen Mgr

TENNESSEE

ABINGDON PRESS*
201 8th Ave. S.
Nashville, TN 37201
(615) 749-6347
Harold L. Fair, Gen Mgr

ACE MUSIC
(*See* Acuff-Rose Publishing Inc.)

ACOUSTIC MUSIC, INC.*
Box 1546
Nashville, TN 37202
(615) 242-9198
Nancy Dunne, Admin

ACUFF-ROSE PUBLISHING INC.‡
2510 Franklin Rd.
PO Box 40427
Nashville, TN 37204
(615) 385-3031
Wesley H. Rose, Pres

ADVENTURE MUSIC CO.†
1201 16th Ave. S
Nashville, TN 37212
(615) 320-7287
Charles Chellman, Pres

AHAB MUSIC CO. INC.*
1707 Grand Ave.
Nashville, TN 37212
(615) 327-4629
Ray Stevens, Pres

ALAMO VILLAGE MUSIC
2816 Columbine Pl.
Nashville, TN 37204
(615) 292-5236

ALL NIGHT*
c/o Odyssey Productions Inc.
PO Box 12384
Acklen Station
Nashville, TN 37212
(615) 327-9301
C.E. Jackson, Pres

JOE ALLEN MUSIC INC.*
PO Box 120156
Nashville, TN 37212

ALMARIE MUSIC*
c/o Ray Pennington
Rt. 1
New Hope Rd.
Hendersonville, TN 37075

ALMO IRVING MUSIC PUBLISHING
1010 16th Ave. S.
Nashville, TN 37212
(615) 255-0636

AMERICAN COWBOY MUSIC CO.*
14 Music Circle East
Nashville, TN 37203
(615) 256-8812
William G. Hall, Gen Mgr

AMERICUS MUSIC†
PO Box 314
120 Bostring Dr.
Hendersonville, TN 37075
(615) 822-5511
Donald L. Riis, Pres

ANGEL WING MUSIC†
c/o James E. Cason
2804 Azalea Pl.
Nashville, TN 37204

ANNEXTRA MUSIC*
PO Box 40364
Nashville, TN 37204
(615) 327-0845
Ann J. Morton, Pres

ANNIE OVER MUSIC†
Box 2333
Nashville, TN 37202
Bobby Fischer, Gen Mgr

APACHE'S RHYTHM MUSIC PUBLISHER†
PO Box 34032

Memphis, TN 38134
Paul Zaleski, Pres

APRIL-BLACKWOOD MUSIC
(*See* CBS Songs, TN)

ARGONAUT MUSIC*
Box 1800
Nashville, TN 37202
Eric R. Hilding, Pres

ASH VALLEY MUSIC INC.†
1609 Hawkins St.
Nashville, TN 37203
(615) 244-1060
Owne Bradley, Pres

ATLAS PUBLISHING GROUP
Box 50
Goodlettsville, TN 37072
Dick Shuey, Mgr

ATV MUSIC CORP
1217 16th Ave. S.
Nashville, TN 37212
(615) 327-2753
Garry Teifer, VP

AUDIGRAM MUSIC*
PO Box 22635
Nashville, TN 37202

AUNT POLLY'S PUBLISHING CO.*
Box 121657
Nashville, TN 37212
(615) 385-2555
Allen Reynolds, Owner

BABY HUEY MUSIC
234 E. Morton Ave.
Nashville, TN 37211
(615) 834-3481
Mark Stephan Hughes, Mgr

BARAY MUSIC INC.*
49 Music Square E.
Nashville, TN 37203
Ray Baker, Pres & Gen Mgr

BARKAY MUSIC*
1264 Royal Oaks Dr.
Memphis, TN 38116

B.C. ENTERPRISES OF MEMPHIS, INC.
726 E. McLemore Ave.
Memphis, TN 38106
(901) 947-2553
Bob Catron, Pres

BEECHWOOD MUSIC CORP.
1207 16th Ave., S.
Nashville, TN 37212
(615) 320-7700
Charlie Feldman, Gen Mgr

THE JOHN T. BENSON PUBLISHING CO., INC.†‡
365 Great Circle Rd.
Nashville, TN 37228

BEXLEY PUBLISHING CO.*
3333 Scenic Highway
Memphis, TN 38128
(901) 386-8102
Cordell Jackson, Pres

BIG KAHUNA MUSIC
663 Watson St.
Memphis, TN 38111
(901) 454-9760
Phillip Rauls, Pres

BIG SWAN PUBLISHING CO.*
156 Darkes Ln.
Summertown, TN 38483
(615) 964-3571
Paul Mendelstein, Pres

BISIAR MUSIC PUBLISHING*
PO Box 23261
Nashville, TN 37202
(615) 361-7058
Ed Bisiar III, Pres

BLENDINGWELL MUSIC
812 19th Ave. S.
Nashville, TN 37203
(615) 329-9282
Karen Conrad, Mgr

BLUE LAKE MUSIC*
14 Music Circle E.
Nashville, TN 37203

BOJAN MUSIC CORP.*
38 Music Square E.
Nashville, TN 37203
(615) 244-4336
Buddy Lee, Pres

ROGER BOWLING MUSIC*
PO Box 120537
Nashville, TN 37212

BOXER MUSIC*
PO Box 120501
Nashville, TN 37212
(615) 254-9798
Curtis L. Allen, Pres

BRANDWOOD MUSIC, INC.*
Box 24214
Nashville, TN 37202
(615) 292-3593
Ansley R. Fleetwood, Pres

THE BRASS PRESS*
136 8th Ave. N.
Nashville, TN 37203
(615) 254-8969
Stephen L. Glover, Pres

BRIDGER MUSIC PUBLISHING CO.
34 Music Square E.
Nashville, TN 37203

BRIM MUSIC INC.†
Herford Music Division
PO Box 120591
Nashville, TN 37212
(615) 269-4410
Gary S. Musick, Pres

BROADMAN PRESS‡
127 9th Ave. N.
Nashville, TN 37234
(615) 251-2500
Dessel Aderholt, Pres

BRONCO MUSIC‡
Sewanee, TN 37375
Topper Saussy

BROOKS BROTHERS PUBLISHERS*
311 Margo Lane
Nashville, TN 37211
(615) 834-4124
Jake Brooks, Mgr

BUCKHORN MUSIC PUBLISHING CO. INC.*
1007 17th Ave. S.
Nashville, TN 37212
(615) 327-4590
Marijohn Wilkin, Pres

BURIED TREASURE MUSIC†
524 Doral Country Dr.
Nashville, TN 37221

CALVARY RECORDS INC.
142 8th Ave. N.
Nashville, TN 37203
(615) 244-8800
Rex W. Bledsoe, Exec Dir

CARESS ME PUBLISHING CO.
1212 Bellgrimes Ln.
Nashville, TN 37207
(615) 865-0653
Glenn Summers

CARY AND MR. WILSON MUSIC INC.*
PO Box 500
Nashville, TN 37202
(615) 242-5400
Ernest Tubb, Pres

CBS SONGS
31 Music Square W.
Nashville, TN 37203
(615) 329-2374
Charlie Monk, Mgr

CEDARWOOD*
39 Music Square E.
Nashville, TN 37203
(615) 255-6535
J. William Denny, Pres

CHAPPELL MUSIC CO.
11 Music Square S.
Nashville, TN 37203
(615) 244-3382

CHARTBOUND MUSIC PUBLICATIONS, LTD.†

1508 Harlem, Ste. 204
Memphis, TN 38114
Reginald Eskridge, Exec Dir

CHENANIAH MUSIC‡
PO Box 40772
Nashville, TN 37204
Derric Johnson, Pres

CHESTNUT HOUSE MUSIC INC.*
c/o Jerry Chestnut Music Inc.
Nashville, TN 37212
Jerry Chestnut, Pres

CHESTNUT MOUND MUSIC*
Box 213
Hendersonville, TN 37075
(615) 822-1360
Eddie Crook, Owner

CHIP 'N' DALE MUSIC PUBLISHERS, INC.†
2125 8th Ave., S.
Nashville, TN 37204
(615) 363-6002
Gene Kennedy, Pres

CHRISWOOD MUSIC*
1204 16th Ave., S.
Nashville, TN 37212

COAL MINERS MUSIC INC.*
7 Music Circle N.
Nashville, TN 37203
(615) 259-9448
O.V. Lynn, Jr., Pres

COMBINE MUSIC GROUP*
35 Music Square E.
Nashville, TN 37203
(615) 255-0624
Robert J. Beckham, Pres

CON BRIO MUSIC*
PO Box 196
Nashville, TN 37202
(615) 329-1944
Bill Walker, Pres

CONTENTION MUSIC‡
PO Box 834
Nashville, TN 37202
(615) 244-8839
Ted Harris, Pres

COOKHOUSE MUSIC*
Div. of Picalic Inc.
1204 16th Ave. S.
Nashville, TN 37212
(615) 320-0303

COURT OF KINGS MUSIC*
1300 Division St., Ste. 103
Nashville, TN 37203
(615) 244-7116
Billy Deaton, Pres

COVERED BRIDGE MUSIC*
615 Darrett Dr.
Nashville, TN 37211
(615) 833-1457
Bill Wence, Gen Mgr

THE EDDIE CROOK COMPANY
Box 213
Hendersonville, TN 37075
(615) 822-1360

CROWN BLACK MUSIC, NASHVILLE, TN
(*See* John T. Benson Publishing Co., Inc., Nashville, TN)

DEBDAVE MUSIC INC.*
PO Box 140110
Nashville, TN 37214
(615) 320-7227
James Edward Malloy, Pres

DIVERSIFIED MUSIC, INC.
Box 17087
Nashville, TN 37217
(615) 754-9400
Gene Vowell, Mgr

DOOR KNOB MUSIC PUBLISHING, INC.*
2125 8th Ave. S.
Nashville, TN 37204
(615) 383-6002
Gene Kennedy, Pres

E & M PUBLISHING CO.*
2674 Steele
Memphis, TN 38127
(901) 357-0064
Pam Frith, Mus Dir

EN AVANT MUSIC CO.
Box 381585
Memphis, TN 38138
(901) 761-3709
Robert Shindler, Pres

EXCELLOREC MUSIC CO. INC.*
1011 Woodland St.
Nashville, TN 37206
(615) 226-2660

FAMOUS MUSIC CORP.
2 Music Circle S.
Nashville, TN 37203
(615) 242-3531

FIRST LADY SONGS INC.*
6 Music Circle N.
Nashville, TN 37203
(615) 255-3531

BOBBY FISCHER MUSIC†
50 Music Square W., Ste. 902
Nashville, TN 37203
(615) 329-2279

FLAGSHIP MUSIC INC.*
PO Box 23062
Nashville, TN 37202

FORREST HILLS MUSIC, INC.*
1609 Roy Acuff Pl.
Nashville, TN 37203
(615) 244-1060

FORT WAYNE MUSIC†
601 United Artists Towers
50 Music Square W.
Nashville, TN 37203

FREBAR MUSIC CO.*
5514 Kelly Rd.
Brentwood, TN 37027
(615) 373-4086
Fred Kelly, Pres

FRICK MUSIC PUBLISHING CO.*
404 Bluegrass Ave.
Madison, TN 37115
(615) 865-6380
Bob Frick, Pres

FUNKY BUT MUSIC INC.
PO Box 1770
155 Saunders Ferry Rd.
Hendersonville, TN 37075
(615) 824-9439
Kyle Lehning, Pres

AL GALLICO MUSIC CORP
50 Music Square W.
Nashville, TN 37203
(615) 327-2773
Josh Whitmore, Mgr; Dan Darst, Gen Mgr

DON GANT ENTERPRISES
PO Box 121076
1225 16th Ave. S.
Nashville, TN 37212
(615) 329-0490

GINGHAM MUSIC†
1022 16th Ave. S.
Nashville, TN 37212
(615) 255-5711

GLOLITE PUBLISHING CO.*
827 Thomas
Memphis, TN 38107
(901) 525-0540

GRAND PRIX PUBLISHING CO.
2087 Union Ave.
Memphis, TN 38104
(901) 278-4900
Ed Dubay, Partner

GRAWICK MUSIC*
Box 9039
Nashville, TN 37209
(615) 321-3319
James Hendrix, Pres

GREAK BEEK PRODUCTIONS†
2999 Smith Springs Rd.
Nashville, TN 37212
Dair Arther

GREAT LEAWOOD MUSIC, INC.†
Box 1014
1920 Hampton Dr.

Lebanon, TN 38087
(615) 444-3735
Orlene Johnson, Sec/Treas

AL GREEN
3208 Winchester Rd.
Memphis, TN 38118
(901) 794-6220

RAY GRIFF ENTERPRISES
PO Box 23245
1300 Division
Nashville, TN 37202
(615) 242-1816
Ray Griff, Pres

HALLNOTE MUSIC CO.*
PO Box 40209
Nashville, TN 37204
(615) 373-5221
Tom T. Hall, Pres

HARBOT MUSIC‡
2 Music Circle S.
Nashville, TN 37203
Joe Talbot, Owner

HAT BAND MUSIC*
c/o Sound Seventy Ste.
210 25th Ave. N.
Nashville, TN 37203
(615) 327-1711

HEAVY JAMIN' MUSIC†
PO Box 4796
Nashville, TN 37216
(615) 859-0355
Duane T. DeSanto

HIGHBALL MUSIC
PO Box 40484
2803 Azalea Pl.
Nashville, TN 37204
(615) 383-6564
Jack D. Johnson, Pres

HITKIT MUSIC*
PO Box 22325
Nashville, TN 37202
(615) 385-0900
David N. Gib, Pres

HITSBURGH MUSIC CO.*
Box 195
147 Ford Ave.
Gallatin, TN 37066
(615) 452-1479
Harold Gilbert, Pres

HOLLYTREE MUSIC*
4916 Franklin Rd.
Nashville, TN 37220
Sherry Sanders, Pres

HORSE HAIRS MUSIC INC.*
c/o Ted Hacker
PO Box 121017
Nashville, TN 37212

HOUSE OF BRYANT PUBLICATIONS*
PO Box 120608
Nashville, TN 37212
(615) 385-3245
Nona Thomas, Gen Mgr

HOUSE OF CASH INC.*
PO Box 508
Hendersonville, TN 37075
(615) 824-5110
J.R. Cash, Pres

HOUSE OF GOLD MUSIC, INC.*‡
1614 16th Ave. S.
Nashville, TN 37212
(615) 383-4667
Bobby Goldsboro, Pres

JAMES M. HUDGINS PUBLISHING CO.
610 West Due W. Ave.
Madison, TN 37115
(615) 868-1158
James M. Hudgins, Owner

JACK MUSIC INC.*
PO Box 120477
Nashville, TN 37212
(615) 383-0330
Bob Webster, VP

JACKPOT MUSIC*
133 Walton Ferry
Hendersonville, TN 37075
(615) 824-2820
Clyde Beavers, Pres

JACLYN MUSIC*
467 Millwood Dr.
Nashville, TN 37217
(615) 366-6906
Jack Lynch, Pres

DICK JAMES MUSIC, INC.
24 Music Square E.
Nashville, TN 37203
(615) 242-0600
Arthur Braun, Gen Mgr

JEVY MUSIC†
The Jevy Music Co.
1025 Vaughn
Memphis, TN 38122
Evelyn Graves, Pres

JMR ENTERPRISES
1014 16th Ave. S.
Nashville, TN 37212
(615) 244-1630
Roy Sikovich, Pres

JULEP PUBLISHING CO.*
Div of Julep Inc.
PO Box 15551
Nashville, TN 37215
(615) 383-5698

KELLY & LLOYD MUSIC†
1014 16th Ave. S.
Nashville, TN 37212
(615) 244-1630
Mick Lloyd, Pres

GENE KENNEDY ENTERPRISES, INC.
2125 8th Ave. S.
Nashville, TN 37204
(615) 383-6002
Gene Kennedy, Pres

KIM-PAT PUBLISHING‡
Box 654
Hillwood Dr.
Fayetteville, TN 37334
(615) 433-2323

JIMMY KISH MUSIC PUBLISHING CO.*
PO Box 140316
Nashville, TN 37214
(615) 889-6675
Jimmy Kish, Pres

KOBAL MUSIC PUBLISHING CO.*
PO Box 22988
Nashville, TN 37202

LADY JANE MUSIC
PO Box 1077
Hendersonville, TN 37075
(615) 824-9412
John B. Axton, VP; Mae B. Axton, VP

LANCE JAY MUSIC†
Box 62
Shiloh, TN 38376
(901) 689-5141
Carol Morris, VP

CHRISTY LANE MUSIC
LS Record Co.
120 Hickory St.
Madison, TN 37115
(615) 868-7171
Harold Hodges, Pub Dir

LEONARD PRODUCTIONS INC.*
PO Box 222
Gainesville, TX 76240
(817) 466-4076
Joe M. Leonard Jr., Pres

LEON INTERNATIONAL INC.†
1006 17th Ave. S.
Nashville, TN 37212
(615) 327-4565
Kathleen Pynor, Pres

LIZZIE LOU PUBLISHING*
PO Box 647
Hendersonville, TN 37075

LODESTAR MUSIC
2125 8th Ave. S.
Nashville, TN 37204
(615) 383-6002
Gene Kennedy, Pres

LYN-LOU MUSIC INC.*
PO Box 50381
Nashville, TN 37205

MARK THREE MUSIC*
Rte. 1, Box 222
Lyles, TN 37098
Jerry Allison

MARSON INC.*
c/o Jimmie Loden
3833 Cleghorn Ave., Ste. 400
Nashville, TN 37215

MATRIX PUBLISHING CO.†
PO Box 12246
Memphis, TN 38112
(901) 274-7788
Dane & Gala Sullivan

MCA MUSIC
MCA Inc.
1106 17th Ave. S.
Nashville, TN 37212
(615) 327-4622
Jerry Crutchfield

ME MUSIC
158 Gatone Dr.
Hendersonville, TN 37075
(615) 824-3172
Dee Mullins, Gen Mgr

MELLYRIC MUSIC†
PO Box 1077
2325 Oakland Dr., NW
Cleveland, TN 37311
(615) 479-1415
Donald B. Gibson, Pres

MEMPHIS MANAGEMENT CORPORATION
Box 17272
Memphis, TN 38117
(901) 685-8533
Ron Blackwood, Pres

MILL HOUSE MUSIC INC.
c/o Music Mill
1526 Laurel St.
Nashville, TN 37203
(615) 255-0428

MR. MORT MUSIC†
44 Music Square E.
Nashville, TN 37203
(615) 255-2175
Charles Fields, Pres

MONKEY MUSIC, INC.
A Monkey Business Company
Box 21288
Nashville, TN 37221
(615) 646-3335
Robert A. May, Pres

MONKHOUSE MUSIC*
5009 Ashby Dr.
Brentwood, TN 37027
(615) 255-3500
Ann Stuckey, Pres

MONTGOMERY PUBLISHING*
8914 Georgian Dr.
Austin, TX 78753
(512) 836-3201
Shirley A. Montgomery, Gen Mgr

MORNING MUSIC (USA) INC.†
Box 120478
Nashville, TN 37212
Jury Krytiuk, Pres

MULLET MUSIC CORP.*
PO Box 65006
Nashville, TN 37215

MULL-TI HIT MUSIC CO.
50 Music Square W.
Nashville, TN 37203
(615) 329-4487
Frank Mull, Pres

MURFREEZONGES†
1204 16th Ave. S.
Nashville, TN 37212

MUSIC CRAFTSHOP
Box 22325
Nashville, TN 37202
(615) 385-0900

MUSIC PUBLISHING CORP.
815 18th Ave. S.
Nashville, TN 37203
(615) 327-0518
Dave Burgess, Mgr

MUSIC RIVER PUBLISHING CO.*
Meeman Journalism Bldg., Rm 302
Memphis State University
Memphis, TN 38152
(901) 454-2350/2892
Dr. Thomas Carpenter, Pres

NBC MUSIC INC.†
PO Box 392
Brentwood, TN 37027
(615) 793-7085
Linda Adams, Prof Mgr

NEEDAHIT PUBLISHING CO. INC.*
264 Old Hickory Blvd.
Madison, TN 37115
(615) 865-6543
Johnnie R. Wright, Pres

NEWCREATURE MUSIC*
108 Berkley Dr.
Madison, TN 37115
(615) 868-3407
Bill Anderson, Jr., Pres

NEWKEYS MUSIC INC.*
11 Music Cirle, S.
Nashville, TN 37203
(615) 242-2461
Jack J. Key, Pres

NEWWRITERS MUSIC*
20 Music Square W., Ste. 200
Nashville, TN 37203
(615) 244-1025
Chuck Dixon, Nat'l Promo Dir

O.A.S. MUSIC GROUP
805 18th Ave. S.
Nashville, TN 37203
(615) 327-3900
Dane Bryant, Admin

OLD FOX PUBLISHING CO.*
1767 Fort Heary Dr.
Kingsport, TN 37664
(615) 246-8651
Basil J. Palmer, Pres

ONE NOTE BEYOND MUSIC†
819 18th Ave., S.
Nashville, TN 37203
(615) 329-0532
John Weaver, Mgr

ONNYSAY PUBLISHING CO.*
PO Box 9154
Wells Rd. SW
Knoxville, TN 37920
(615) 970-2327
H.S. Watson, Pres

PARAGON/ASSOCIATES INC.†
19 Ave. N. & Hayes
Nashville, TN 37203
(615) 327-2836
Robert R. MacKenzie, Pres

PARTNERSHIP MUSIC*†
1518 Chelsea Ave.
Memphis, TN 38108
(901) 275-2285
Larry Rogers, Gen Mgr

PEER-SOUTHERN ORGANIZATION
7 Music Circle N.
Nashville, TN 37203
(615) 244-6200

BEN PETERS MUSIC*
900 Old Hickory Blvd.
Rte. 6
Brentwood, TN 37027
(615) 373-5530
Ben Peters, Pres

PICK-A-HIT MUSIC*
812-16 19th Ave. S.
Nashville, TN 37203
(615) 327-3553
Dale Morris

PLUM CREEK MUSIC*
803 18th Ave. S.
Nashville, TN 37203

POMMARD*
c/o Dick, K. Withers
Box 53
Nashville, TN 37221
(615) 352-5684

PORTER MUSIC CO.*
811 18 Ave. S.
Nashville, TN 37203
(615) 329-2122
Porter Wagoner, Owner

POWER-PLAY PUBLISHING*
1900 Elm Hill Pike
Nashville, TN 37210
(615) 889-8000
Mark Mathis

JEANNE PRUETT MUSIC INC.*
303 Williamsburg Rd.
Brentwood, TN 37076

RAGGED ISLAND MUSIC*
4307 Sandersville Rd.
Old Hickory, TN 37138
(615) 847-3895
Margaret Lewis, Pres

RAINDANCE MUSIC*
Box 22322
Nashville, TN 37202

RED MAPLE MUSIC PUBLISHING CO.
1100 16th Ave. S.
Nashville, TN 37212
(615) 244-1264
Jolie Blon, A & R Mgr

JERRY REED ENTERPRISES
1107 18th Ave. S.
Nashville, TN 37212
(615) 327-3818

JIM REEVES ENTERPRISES
Drawer 1, 200 Madison St.
Madison, TN 37115
(615) 868-1150
Lee Morgan, Mgr

RE'GENERATION, INC.
Box 40772
Nashville, TN 37204
(615 256-2242
Eric Wyse, Catalog Admin

RICH WAY MUSIC INC.*
1111 17th Ave. S.
Nashville, TN 37212
(615) 327-4722

MARTY ROBBINS ENTERPRISES
713 18th Ave. S.
Nashville, TN 37203
(615) 327-4940

RODEO COWBOY MUSIC INC.*
PO Box 23062
Nashville, TN 37202

ROKBLOK
203 Louis Ave.
Nashville, TN 37203
(615) 329-9988
Steve Gibson, Co-Pres

RONTOM MUSIC CO.†
602 W. Iris Dr.
PO Box 150394
Nashville, TN 37215

RUSTIC RECORDS†
38 Music Square
Nashville, TN 37203
(615) 254-0892
Jack Stillwell, Pres

SABAL†
1520 Demonbreun St.
Nashville, TN 37203

SAWGRASS MUSIC PUBLISHERS*‡
1520 Demonbreun St.
Nashville, TN 37203
(615) 327-4104
Lonnis M. Tillis, Pres

SCOTT-CH & BRANDY†
c/o IBC Music Groups
1302 Division St.
Nashville, TN 37203
(615) 329-0714

SCREEN GEMS-EMI MUSIC INC.
1207 16th Ave. S.
Nashville, TN 37212
(615) 320-7700

SHINDLER MUSIC CO. INC.*
PO Box 381585
Memphis, TN 38138
(901) 685-2321
Robert Shindler, Pres

SHOW BIZ MUSIC GROUP*
1006 Baker Bldg.
Nashville, TN 37203
Reg Dunlap, Pres

SIDE POCKET MUSIC*
c/o Gene Eichelberger
Rte. 2
Countyline Rd.
Fairview, TN 37062

SILVERMINE MUSIC INC.
329 Rockland Rd.
Hendersonville, TN 37075
(615) 824-7273
Duane Allen, Pres
Branch:
1019 17th Ave. S.
Hendersonville, TN 37075
(615) 327-4815

SING ME MUSIC, INC.†‡
501 Chesterfield Ave.
Nashville, TN 37212
(615) 297-0024
Jean S. Zimmerman, Pres

SHELBY SINGLETON MUSIC INC.*
3106 Belmont Blvd.
Nashville, TN 37212
(615) 385-1960
Sidney Singleton, Mgr

SINGLETREE MUSIC CO.‡
815 18th Ave. S.
Nashville, TN 37213
(615) 327-0518
Dave Burgess, Pres

SONG FARM MUSIC*
Box 24561
Nashville, TN 37202
(615) 242-1037
Tom Pallardy, Pres

SONGS FROM THE BOX*
3935-B Summer Ave.
Memphis, TN 38122
(901) 458-2371
Mark Blackwood, Pres

SONGS OF CALVARY*
Calvary Records Inc.
142 8th Ave. N.
Nashville, TN 37203
Rex W. Bledsoe, A & R Dir

SONGS OF THE SOUTHLAND*
Box 120536
Nashville, TN 37212
(615) 320-5151
James J. Petrie, Mng Partner

SOUNDS OF MEMPHIS
904 Rayner
Memphis, TN 38114
(901) 274-9814

SOUNDSTAGE STUDIOS INC.
10 Music Circle S.
Nashville, TN 37203
(615) 256-2676

SOUTHERN WRITERS GROUP USA
Box 40764
2804 Azalea Pl.
Nashville, TN 37204
(615) 383-8682
Buzz Cason, Pres

BEN SPEER MUSIC
Box 40201
54 Music Square W.
Nashville, TN 37204
(615) 329-9999
Ben L. Speer, Pres

STAFREE PUBLISHING CO.*
3114 Radford Rd.
Memphis, TN 38111
(901) 327-8187

STARGEM RECS. INC.
20 Music Square W.
Nashville, TN 37203
(615) 244-1025
Wayne Hodge, Pres

STARGOLD PUBLICATIONS INC.†
PO Box 140542
211 Cumberland Circle
Nashville, TN 37214

(615) 889-2320
Roy G. Edwards, Jr., Pres

RAY STEVENS MUSIC*
1707 Grand Ave.
Nashville, TN 37212

STONEHILL MUSIC CO.*
51 Music Square E.
Nashville, TN 37203
Bill Gatzimos, Pres

STUCKEY PUBLISHING CO.*
50 Music Square W.
Nashville, TN 37203
(615) 327-0222
Ann M. Stuckey, Mgr

SUGARPLUM MUSIC CO.*
1022 16th Ave. S.
Nashville, TN 37212
(615) 255-5711
Joe Allen, Admin Asst; Patsy Bruce, Pres

SULYN PUBLISHING INC.*
PO Box 28835
3538 Arsenal
Memphis, TN 38128
(901) 386-7360
Louis Chiozza, Pres

SURE-FIRE MUSIC CO., INC.
60 Music Square W.
Nashville, TN 37203
(615) 244-1401
Leslie Wilburn, VP

SWEET POLLY MUSIC*
Box 521
Newberry, SC 29108
(803) 276-0639
Polly Davis, Studio Mgr

SWEET SINGER MUSIC
The Mathes Company
Box 22653
Nashville, TN 37202
Dave Mathes, Pres

SWEET SUMMER NIGHT MUSIC†
1224 N. Vine St.
Los Angeles, CA 90038

TAYLOR & WATTS MUSIC, INC.*
1010 17th Ave. S.
Nashville, TN 37212
(615) 327-4656
Carmol Taylor, Pres

JOE TAYLOR MUSIC†
2401 Granny White Pike
Nashville, TN 37204
Joe Taylor, Pres

TEARDROP MUSIC†
PO Box 40001
Trousdale Dr.
Nashville, TN 37204

(615) 385-3726
Ronnie Hayes, Pres

TERRACE MUSIC GROUP†
14 Music Circle E.
Nashville, TN 37203
(615) 327-4871
Robert John Jones, Prof Mgr

TESSALOU MUSIC†
62 Music Square W.
Nashville, TN 37203
(615) 325-4538
Cliff Ayers, Pres

TOMPALLAND MUSIC*
916 19 Ave.
Nashville, TN 37212
(615) 327-0005
June Glaser, Partner

TREBRON MUSIC INC.*
7 Music Circle N.
Nashville, TN 37203
Norbert Putnam, Pres

TREE PUBLISHING CO., INC.*
8 Music Square W.
Nashville, TN 37202
(615) 327-3162
Buddy Killen, Pres

TRIUNE MUSIC, INC.†
PO Box 23088
824 19th Ave. S.
Nashville, TN 37203
(615) 329-1429
Buryl Red, Pres

TROLL MUSIC*
2300 21st Ave. S.
Nashville, TN 37212
(615 385-2750
Seymour Rosenberg

TUFF MUSIC CO.*
Rte. 8, Box 66-A
Lebanon, TN 37087

TUNINGFORK PUBLISHING CORP.*
1302 Division St.
Nashville, TN 37203
(615) 242-0392

SCOTT TUTT MUSIC
Box 121213
Nashville, TN 37212
(615) 329-0856
Susan Marshall, Mgr; R. Scott Tutt, Pres

TWITTY BIRD MUSIC PUBLISHING CO.†
PO Box 1273
Nashville, TN 32703
Harrianne Condra

TYNER MUSIC†
38 Music Square E.
Nashville, TN 37203
(615) 244-4224
Harrison Tyner, Pres

UNITED ARTISTS MUSIC
1013 16th Ave. S.
Nashville, TN 37212
(615) 327-4594
Buzz Arledge, Mgr

VECTOR MUSIC*
1107 18th Ave. S.
Nashville, TN 37212
(615) 327-4161
Harry M. Warner, Mgr

VELVET APPLE MUSIC*
4301 Hillsboro Rd.
Ste. 224
Nashville, TN 37215
(615) 327-2338
Dolly Parton, Owner

WARNER BROS. MUSIC
44 Music Square W.
Nashville, TN 37203
(615) 254-8777
Tim Wipperman, Gen Mgr

WEE-B MUSIC†
1300 Division
Nashville, TN 37203
(615) 245-7543
Cal Everhart, Pres

WINDOW MUSIC PUBLISHING CO., INC.*
809 18th Ave. S.
Nashville, TN 37203
(615) 327-3211
Pete Drake, Pres

CURTIS WOOD MUSIC†
PO Box 312
Nashville, TN 37202
(615) 876-1729
Curtis Wood, Pres

WORD RECORD & MUSIC GROUP
2300 21st. Ave. S.
Nashville, TN 37212
(615) 383-8964

WORLD WIDE MUSIC INC.
1300 Division St.
Nashville, TN 37203
(615) 256-7543
Calvin H. Everhart, Pres

WORM WOOD PUBLISHING CO.*
1108 Cinderella St.
Madison, TN 37115

WRITERS NIGHT MUSIC†
PO Box 22635
Madison, TN 37202
(615) 383-8318
Audie Ashworth

TEXAS

ABNAK MUSIC ENTERPRISES INC.
825 Olive at Ross
Dallas, TX 75201
(214) 742-6111

ADAMS-ETHRIDGE PUBLISHING*
Box 434
Galveston, TX 77550
(713) 763-8344
Leon Ethridge, Mgr

ANDRADE PUBLISHING COMPANY*
Drawer 520
Stafford, TX 77477
(713) 723-3918
Daniel Andrade, Mgr

ANODE MUSIC
Box 11967
Houston, TX 77016
(713) 694-2971
Freddie Kober, Pres

B.A.S. MUSIC PUBLISHING†
5925 Kirby Dr.
Houston, TX 77005
(713) 522-2713
Shelton Bissell, Pres

BIG STATE MUSIC*
Texas Sound Inc.
1311 Candlelight Ave.
Dallas, TX 75116
Paul Ketter, Pres

BOXCAR MUSIC PUBLISHING CO.*
6316 Porterway
Houston, TX 77084
(713) 859-0332
Peter Breaz, Pres

BRANCH INTERNATIONAL MUSIC*
Box 31819
Dallas, TX 75231
(214) 690-8875
Pat McKool, Owner

BROWN MOON MUSIC†
Box 19274
Houston, TX 77024
(713) 661-2498
Rusty Holster, Pres

BUCKBOARD MUSIC*
1909 Hood Circle
Carrollton, TX 75006
(214) 242-1762
Larry Fargo, Pres

BUENA VISTA PUBLISHING CO.*
PO Box 28553
Dallas, TX 75228
(214) 270-4887
B.L. Bollman, Owner

CATCHUP MUSIC*
PO Box 9830
3507 W. Vickery
Fort Worth, TX 76107
(817) 737-9911
J.P. Kinzey, Pres

CHERIE MUSIC CO.*
3621 Heath Ln.
Mesquite, TX 75149
(214) 279-5858
Jimmy Fields

CHORISTERS GUILD
2834 W. Kingsley Rd.
Garland, TX 75041
(214) 271-1521
John T. Burke, Exec Dir

COCHISE PUBLISHING CO.*
PO Box 1415
Athens, TX 75751
(214) 675-5192

COLLBECK PUBLISHING CO.*
4817 Karchner
Corpus Christi, TX 78415
(512) 854-7376
Gary Beck, Pres

CONNELL PUBLISHING
130 Pilgrim Dr.
San Antonio, TX 78213
(512) 344-5033
Jerry Connell, Owner

CRAZY CAJUN MUSIC, INC.*
5626 Brock St.
Houston, TX 77023
(713) 926-4431
Huey F. Meaux

DAWN TREADER MUSIC‡
2223 Strawberry Ave.
Pasadena, TX 77502
(713) 472-5563
Darrell A. Harris, Pres

EARTHBOUND PUBLISHING CO.*
8428 Kate St.
Dallas, TX 75225
(214) 368-1305
Sam Lobello III, Pres

EARTHSCREAM MUSIC PUBLISHING CO.*
2036 Pasket, Ste. A
Houston, TX 77018
(713) 688-8067
Jeff Johnson

DON EDGAR MUSIC*
2312 Jasper
Forth Worth, TX 76106
(817) 626-3448
Don and Darrell Edgar

EDMARK PRODUCTIONS*
20802 Cedar Lane
Tomball, TX 77375
(713) 351-1807
Edmond A. Evey, Pres

FELICITY MUSIC INC.
2006 Sharon Lane
Austin, TX 78703
(512) 472-1004
Craig D. Hills, Pres

FIFTY ONE PUBLISHING CO.*
29803 Oakview
Magnolia, TX 77355
Stephen F. King, Pres

CHARLIE FITCH MUSIC CO.*
311 E. Davis
Luling, TX 78648
(512) 875-3350
Charlie Fitch, Pres & Gen Mgr

CLINTON H. FORSMAN PUBLISHING CO.*
210 E. Main
Robstown, TX 78380
(512) 387-1615
Clinton H. Forsman, Pres

FREE FLOW PRODUCTIONS†
1209 Baylor
Austin, TX 78703
Michael Brovsky

DON GILBERT MUSIC*
1450 Terrell
Beaumont, TX 77701
(713) 832-0748
Don Gilbert, Pres

GLAD MUSIC CO.*
3409 Brinkman
Houston, TX 77018
(713) 861-3630
H.W. Daily, Pres

GOLD STREET, INC.*
Box 124
Kirbyville, TX 75956
(713) 423-2234
James L. Gibson, Pres

GOSPEL SENDERS MUSIC PUBLISHING CO.*
Box 55943
Houston, TX 77055
(713) 686-1749
Gary R. Smith, Pres

GRASS MOUNTAIN PUBLISHING
7121 W. Vickery Blvd.
Fort Worth, TX 76116
(817) 731-7375
Slim Richey, Owner

GREEN DOOR MUSIC*
1616 Park Pl. Ave.
Fort Worth, TX 76110
(817) 923-1111
Marvin Moore, Gen Mgr

JOHN HALL MUSIC‡
PO Box 13344
Fort Worth, TX 76118
(817) 281-6605

JOHN HARVEY PUBLISHING CO.*
Box 245
Encinal, TX 78019
John Harvey, Pres

HORNSBY MUSIC CO.*
PO Box 13661
Houston, TX 77019
Ezzard Topps

HOUSE OF DIAMONDS MUSIC
Box 449
Cleburne, TX 76031
(817) 641-3029
Jim Diamond; Jan Diamond, Owners

INTERNATIONAL DOORWAY MUSIC†
3410 Ave. R
Lubbock, TX 79412
(806) 744-5590
Bud Andrews, Pres

LAKE COUNTRY MUSIC*
Box 88
Decatur, TX 76234
(817) 627-2128
Danny Wood, Pres

LE BILL MUSIC INC.*
PO Box 11152
Fort Worth, TX 76110
(817) 738-8843
Major Bill Smith, Pres

MARFRE MUSIC PUBLISHING CO.*
6118 S. Padre Island Dr.
Corpus Christi, TX 78412

MARULLO MUSIC PUBLISHERS*
1121 Market St.
Galveston, TX 77550
(713) 762-4590
A.W. Marullo, Pres

METROPOLITAN MUSIC CO.*
4225 University Blvd.
Houston, TX 77005
(713) 668-3279
J.R. Lee, Mgr

TIFFANIE MIKO MUSIC*
9646 Rylie Rd.
Dallas, TX 75217
(214) 286-1711
David A. Coffey, Owner

MONTROY MUSIC CO.*
7210 Roos
Houston, TX 77074
(713) 774-0075
Dr. John D. Montroy, Pres

MUSEDCO PUBLISHING CO.*
Box 5916
Richardson, TX 75080
(214) 783-9925
Dick A. Shuff

MUSIC WEST OF THE PECOS*
PO Box 8545
3012 N. Main St.
Houston, TX 77009
(713) 225-0450
Jay Collier, Pres

MYSTERY MUSIC INC.*
2520 Cedar Elm Ln.
Plano, TX 75075
(214) 867-6656
Pink L. Murphy, VP

OAKRIDGE MUSIC RECORDING SERVING*
2001 Elton Rd.
Haltom City, TX 76117
(817) 838-8001
Homer Lee Sewell, Pres

MARY FRANCES ODLE RECORDING & PUBLISHING CO.*
Box 4335
Pasadena, TX 77502
(713) 477-9432
Mary Frances Odle, Pres

PANTEGO SOUND*
2310 Rapier Blvd.
Pantego, TX 76013
(817) 461-8481
Charles Stewart, Pres

POCKET-MONEY MUSIC*
PO Box 29342
Dallas, TX 75229
(214) 243-2933
Terry Rose, Pres

JANIE PRICE MUSIC†
PO Box 30384
Dallas, TX 75230
(214) 750-9993
Janie Price, Pres

PROPHECY PUBLISHING, INC.†
Box 4945
Austin, TX 78765
(512) 452-9412
T. White, Pres

PUBLICARE MUSIC, LTD.†
Nashville Sound, Inc.
9717 Jensen
Houston, TX 77093
(713) 695-3648
Jim D. Johnson, Pres

QUIXOTIC MUSIC CORP.†
c/o Eddie Reeves
3807 Lewis Lane
Amarillo, TX 79109

RAMMS MUSIC*
821 N 23, PO Box 1689
McAllen, TX 78501
(512) 687-7121
A. Ramirez, Jr., Pres

CHARLES RICH MUSIC INC.*
8229 Rockcreek Pkwy.
Cordova, TX 38018
(901) 382-2100

RIDGE RUNNER PUBLISHING†
7121 W. Vickery, A118
Fort Worth, TX 76116
(817) 731-7375
D.M. Richey

ROYAL T MUSIC
3442 Nies
Fort Worth, TX 76111
(817) 834-3879
J.M. Taylor, Pres

SEA THREE MUSIC*
1310 Tulane
Houston, TX 77008
(713) 864-0705
Charles Bickley

SEVENTH NOTE MUSIC*
Box 400843
Dallas, TX 75240
(214) 690-8165
Michael Stanglin, Pres

SILICON MUSIC PUBLISHING CO.*
22 Tulane St.
Garland, TX 75043
Gene Summers, Pres

SIRLOIN MUSIC PUBLISHING CO.*
14045 South Main
Houston, TX 77035
(713) 641-0793
Robert L. Cummings, Pres

SONGLINE MUSIC*
1909 Clemson Dr.
Richardson, TX 75081
(214) 235-4635
Eddie Fargason

SORO PUBLISHING
1322 Inwood Rd.
Dallas, TX 75247
(214) 638-7712
Bob Cline, Pres

SOUTHERN MUSIC CO.
PO Box 329
1100 Broadway
San Antonio, TX 78292
(512) 226-8167
Arthur Gurwitz, Pres

STABLE MUSIC CO.*
6503 Wolfcreek Pass
Austin, TX 78749
(512) 288-3370
Rex T. Sherry, Owner

STONEWAY PUBLISHING CO.*
2817 Laura Koppe
Houston, TX 77093
(713) 697-7867
Roy M. Stone, Pres

SUNNYBROOK MUSIC CO.*
2200 Sunnybrook
Tyler, TX 75701
(214) 592-7677

SUNSHINE COUNTRY ENTERPRISES, INC.
Box 31351
Dallas, TX 75231
(214) 690-8875
Bart Barton, Pres

SWEET TOOTH MUSIC PUBLISHING*
2716 Springlake Ct.
Irving, TX 75060
(214) 259-4032
Kenny Wayne Halger, Gen Mgr

TEXAS RED SONGS*
Rte. 1, Box 621
Azie, TX 76020

TIFFANIE MIKO MUSIC*
9646 Rylie Rd.
Dallas, TX 75217
(214) 286-8785
D.A. Coffey, Mgr

FLOYD TILLMAN MUSIC CO.*
400 San Jacinto St.
Houston, TX 77002
(713) 225-6654
Byron Benton, Pres

BOBE WES MUSIC*
Box 28609
Dallas, TX 75228
(214) 681-0345
Bobe Wes, Pres

WOODGLEN PUBLICATIONS*
PO Box 35855
Houston, TX 77035
(713) 499-5943
Dan Mechura Sr., Owner

WORD MUSIC
Div of Word, Inc.
Box 1790
Waco, TX 76796
(817) 772-7650
Bill Wolaver, Music Editor

WORKIN' COUNTRY MUSIC*
10031 Monroe Dr.
#310
Dallas, TX 75229
Ralph Hollis, Pres

UTAH

BLANDING PUBLISHING CO.*
PO Box 162
Provo, UT 84601
(801) 224-1775
Stan Bronson, Pres

COVENANT PUBLISHING, INC.
Box 26817
1345 Major St.
Salt Lake City, UT 84126
(801) 487-1096
Don Fulton, Communications Officer

RONARTE PUBLICATIONS†
46 E. Herbert Ave.
Salt Lake City, UT 84111
(801) 355-5327
Ron W. Simpson, Pres

SCARLET STALLION MUSIC*
Box 902
Provo, UT 84601
(801) 225-4674

THE SOUND COLUMN COMPANIES
46 E. Herbert Ave.
Salt Lake City, UT 84111
(801) 355-5327
Erica Erekson, Mgr

VERMONT

BYGOSH MUSIC CORP†
RD 1
Brookfield, VT 05036
(802) 276-3393
Bobby Gosh, Pres

THE PLEIADES MUSIC GROUP*
The Barn
North Ferrisburg, VT 05473
(802) 425-2111
William H. Schubart, Pres

VIRGINIA

ABLE MUSIC, INC.*
Box 387
Oakwood, VA 24631
(703) 935-6170
T. Arrington, VP

BLUE MACE MUSIC*
PO Box 62263
2716 Sandy Valley Rd.
Virginia Beach, VA 23462
(804) 340-3366
Alex Spencer, Pres

CHAR BARB MUSIC*
Rte. 1, Box 120F
Swoope, VA 24479
(703) 885-3309
Barbara Flowers, Pres

DOOMS MUSIC PUBLISHING CO.*
Box 2072
Waynesboro, VA 22980
(703) 942-0106
John Major, Margie Major, Owners

FAIRYSTONE PUBLISHING CO.*
PO Box 594
Rocky Mountain, VA 24151
(703) 483-0689
W. Rod Shively, Pres

FESTIVE MUSIC
15394 Warwick Blvd.
Newport News, VA 23602
(804) 877-6877
W.H. Smith, Pres

HOT GOLD MUSIC PUBLISHING CO.
Box 25654
Richmond, VA 23260
(804) 225-7810
Joseph J. Carter, Jr., Pres

IFFIN MUSIC PUBLISHING CO.*
216 Applewood Ln.
Virginia Beach, VA 23452

MAIDEN MUSIC*
PO Box 691
Petersbury, VA 23803

JIM MCCOY MUSIC/ALEAR MUSIC*
Box 574
Winchester, VA 22601
(703) 667-9379
Jim McCoy, Owner

MIDSTREAM MUSIC PUBLISHERS*
Box 225A
Mountain Falls Rt.
Winchester, VA 22601
(703) 877-1820
Max Mandel, Pres

PENNY PINCHER PUBLISHING, INC.
Box 387
Oakwood, VA 24631
(703) 935-6170
R.J. Fuller, Pres

PERPETUAL MUSIC*
744 W. 28th St.
Norfolk, VA 23508
(804) 623-5710
Lucille Seals, Pres

POWHATAN MUSIC PUBLISHING*
Box 993
Salem, VA 24153
(703) 387-0208
Jack Mullins, Pres

ROCK MASTERS INC.*
317 Granby St.
Norfolk, VA 23510
(804) 625-3470
Frank Guida, Pres

SHEKERE MUSIC*
218 Rosewood Ave.
Richmond, VA 23220

(804) 355-3586
Plunky Nkabinde, Pres

SHORT PUMPS ASSOCIATES*
PO Box 11292
1901*E N. Hamilton St.
Richmond, VA 23230
(804) 355-4117
Dennis Huber

SUMMER DUCK PUBLISHING CORP.*
1216 Granby St.
Norfolk, VA 23510
(804) 625-0534
D.H. Burlage, Pres

WILSING MUSIC PUBLICATIONS*
Box 100-N, RFD 3
Stuart, VA 24171
(703) 694-6128
John F. Williams, Pres

WYNWOOD MUSIC CO., INC.*
Box 101
Broad Run, VA 22014
(703) 754-7353
Peter V. Kuykendall, Pres

WASHINGTON

ALIMA MUSIC PUBLISHING*
9937 Rainier Ave. S.
Seattle, WA 98118
(206) 447-1696
Paul Speer, Pres

BAINBRIDGE MUSIC CO.*
73 Marion St.
Seattle, WA 98104
(206) 625-9992
Bill Angle, Dir of Pub

CALWEST SONGS/LEE ANDERSON ENTERPRISES
1509 Broadway
Bellingham, WA 78225
(206) 676-9961
Bob Wood, Gen Mgr

FERRY BOAT MUSIC†
Rte. 2, Box 133
Burton, WA 98013
(206) 463-2850
Robert Koch, Mgr

FOURTH CORNER MUSIC§
2140 St. Clair St.
Bellingham, WA 98225
(206) 733-3807
Renie Peterson, Catalog Promo

FUNKY ACRES MUSIC CO.†
Rte. 2, Box 133
Burton Vashon Island, WA 98103
(206) 463-2850
Robert Krinsky

GJP PRODUCTIONS INC.‡
3210 Conrad Johnson Rd.
Summer, WA 98390
(509) 525-0913
Gilbert J. Praeger, Pres

HEARTSTONE MUSIC PUBLISHING CO.*
2140 St. Clair St.
Bellingham, WA 98225
(206) 733-3807
Renie Peterson, Mgr

JERDEN MUSIC CO.†
73 Marion St.
Seattle, WA 98104
Gerald B. Dennon, Pres

KAYE-SMITH PRODUCTIONS†
PO Box 3010
Bellevue, WA 98009
Lester M. Smith, CEO

KNOW MUSIC†
PO Box 66558
Seattle, WA 98166
Nancy Wilson, Pres

OAK SPRINGS MUSIC*
Rte. 5, Box 382
Yakima, WA 98903
(509) 966-1193
Hiram White, Pres

RAVEN MUSIC*
4107 Woodland Park N.
Seattle, WA 98103
(206) 632-0887
Ron Ellis, Pres

RIPCORD MUSIC
PO Box 2098
Vancouver, WA 98668
(206) 695-2112
Blaine H. Allen, Owner

STARWEST MUSIC*
1048 14 St.
PO Box 21
Longview, WA 98632
(206) 423-9085

MIKE WING MUSIC PUBLISHING*
PO Box 171
Bellevue, WA 98009
(206) 828-3642
Mike Wing, Owner

WEST VIRGINIA

BO GAL MUSIC*
Box 6687
Wheeling, WV 26003
(614) 758-5812
Bob Gallion, Pres

BROAD RIVER PUBLISHING CO.*
Dyer Rd.
Cowen, WV 26202
(304) 226-3424
Gladys Spearman, Music Ed

FOLKSTONE MUSIC PUBLISHING CO.*
Box 638
Franklin, WV 26807
(304) 358-2504
I. Lynn Beckman, Pres

WISCONSIN

ADULT MUSIC*
c/o Ken Adamany
315 W. Gorham St.
Madison, WI 53703

APPLE-GLASS MUSIC*
Box 8604
Madison, WI 53708
(608) 251-2000
Daniel W. Miller, Pres

CASTALIA MUSIC*
Box 11516
3339 N. Cramer
Milwaukee, WI 53211
Jim Spencer, Pres

CHICOREL MUSIC CORP. INC.†
4447 N. Oakland Ave.
Milwaukee, WI 53211
(414) 964-4888
Ralph Chicorel

HILARIA MUSIC INC.†
315 W. Gorham St.
Madison, WI 53703
(608) 251-2644
Ken Adamany, Pres

JENNIEJOHN MUSIC*
4123 N. 44th St.
Milwaukee, WI 53216
(414) 873-4287
Ken Wright, Pres

JENSON PUBLICATIONS INC.*†
2880 S. 171st St.
New Berlin, WI 53151
(414) 784-4620
Art Jenson, Pres

JERO LTD PUBLISHING*
2309 N. 36th St.
Milwaukee, WI 53210
(414) 445-4872
Marvell Love, Pres

HAL LEONARD PUBLISHING CORP.
8112 W. Bluemound Rd.
Milwaukee, WI 53213
(414) 774-3630
Keith Mardak, Exec VP

MINNIEPAUL MUSIC PUBLISHING CO.*
PO Box 228

New Richmond, WI 54017
David Anthony, Pres

MONTELLO MUSIC*
5709 Hempstead Rd.
Madison, WI 53711
(608) 271-5924
Jon W. Whirry, Pres

MOUNTAIN RAILROAD MUSIC
3602 Atwood Ave.
Madison, WI 53714
(608) 241-2001
Stephen Powers, Pres

NU-TRAVEL PUBLISHING CO.
10015 W. 8 Mile Rd.
Franksville, WI 53126
(414) 835-4622
Tommy O'Day

SCHAUM PUBLICATIONS INC.
2018 E. North Ave.
Milwaukee, WI 53202
(414) 276-9984
John W. Schaum, Pres

SIGHT & SOUND INT'L INC.
PO Box 27
3200 S. 166 St.
New Berlin, WI 53151
(414) 784-5850

PUERTO RICO

PEER-SOUTHERN ORG.
Edificio Banco Ponce
1250 Ponce de Leon Ave.
Santurce, PR 00908
(809) 725-2380
Paquito Fonfrias, Gen Mgr

CANADA

ALTERNATIVE DIRECTION MUSIC PUBLISHERS
Box 3278
Station D
Ottawa, ON K1P 6H8
(613) 820-6066
David Stein, Pres

APRIL-BLACKWOOD MUSIC CANADA, LTD.
1121 Leslie St.
Don Mill, ON L1U 2V8
(416) 447-3311
Sandra Carruthers, Copyright Admin

ATTIC PUBLISHING GROUP
98 Queen St. E.
Ste. 3
Toronto, ON M5C 1S6
(416) 862-0352
Al Mair, Pres

ATV MUSIC PUBLISHING OF CANADA LIMITED
180 Bloor St. W
Ste. 1400
Toronto, ON M5S 2V6
(416) 967-3375
Val Azzoli, Mgr

BEE SHARP PUBLISHING
Box 400, Station R
Toronto, ON M4G 4C3
(416) 421-3601
Jeff Smith, VP

CORE MUSIC PUBLISHING
c/o Oak Manor, Box 1000
Oak Ridges, ON L0G 1P0
(416) 773-4371
Ray Daniels, Pres

DALSTAR PUBLISHING
7812 5th St. SW
Calgary, AB T2V 1B9
(403) 253-6892
Dave Stark, Mgr

DANBORO PUBLISHING CO.
Box 299
Vancouver, BC V6B 3V7
(604) 688-1820
John Rodney, Pres

HUGH DIXON MUSIC, INC.
292 Lorraine Dr.
Montreal/Baie d'Urfe, PQ H9X 2R1
(514) 457-5959
Hugh D. Dixon, Pres

DO SOL PUBLISHING
Box 2262
Dorval, PQ H9S 5J4
(514) 631-9384
Robert Salagan, Mgr

EDITEURS ASSOCIES
2364 Sherbrooke St. E
Montreal, PQ H2K 1E6
(514) 526-2831
Andree Badeaux-Gosselin, Mgr

EDITIONS NAHEJ (PROCAN)
5514 Isabella
Montreal, PQ H3X 1R6
(514) 487-0859
Jehan V. Valiquet, Pres

FOR MY LADY MUSIC
Box 1317
New Liskeard, ON P0J 1P0

GAMELON MUSIC
Box 525, Station P
Toronto, ON M5S 2T1
Michael Kleniec, Mgr

HALBEN MUSIC PUBLISHING CO.
4824 Cote des Neiges Rd., Ste. 38
Montreal, PQ H3V 1G4
(514) 739-4774
Ben Kaye, Mgr

HAVE A HEART MUSIC*
Heart Records & Tapes of Canada Ltd.
Box 3713, Station B
Calgary, AB T2M 4M4
(403) 230-3545
Ron Mahonin, Pres

HELPING HAND MUSIC
9229 58th Ave.
Edmonton, AB T6E 0B7
(403) 436-0665
R. Harlan Smith, Dir A & R

IRVING/ALMO MUSIC OF CANADA, LTD.
939 Warden Ave.
Toronto, ON
(416) 752-7191
Brian Chater, Admin

JAY-ME MUSIC
Box 8343
Dundas, ON L9H 6M1
James Taylor, Mgr

KITCHEN TABLE MUSIC
Box 861
Edmonton, AB T5J 2L8
(403) 477-6844
Holger Petersen, Mng Dir

LAPELLE MUSIC PUBLISHING
1310 Centre St. S.
Calgary, AB T2G 2E2
(403) 269-7270
Bruce Thompson

MAINROADS PUBLISHING
100 Huntley St.
Toronto, ON M4Y 2L1
(416) 961-8001
Bruce W. Stacey, Mgr

MANHOLE MUSIC
11602 75th Ave.
Edmonton, AB
(403) 436-3096
Frank Pillet

MASTER'S COLLECTION PUBLISHING & T.M.C. PUBLISHING
Box 189, Station W
Toronto, ON M6M 4Z2
(416) 746-1991
Paul J. Young, Pres

BRIAN MILLAN MUSIC CORP.†
3475 St. Urbain St., Ste. 1212
Montreal, PQ H2X 2N4
Brian Millan, Pres

MINNALOUSHE MUSIC
Box 1175
Victoris, BC V8W 2T6
(604) 736-1161
J. Gothe, Pres

MONTREAL ROSE PUBLISHING LTD.
201 Perry
Morin Heights, PQ J0R 1H0
(514) 226-2419

Y. Brandeis, Mng Dir

MORNING MUSIC, LTD.
1343 Matheson Blvd. E
Mississauga, ON L4W 1R1

Mark Altman, Gen Mgr

NOTEWORTHY PUBLISHING CO.
6979 Curragh Ave.
Burnaby, BC V5J 4V6
(604) 438-8266

Paul Yardshuk, Mgr

ON THE WING MUSIC PUBLISHING CO.
12024 Riverside Dr. E
Windsor, ON N8P 1A9
(519) 735-7769

Jim Thomson II, Pres

PEER-SOUTHERN ORGANIZATION
180 Bloor St. W
Toronto, ON N56 2V6

Matthew Heft, Mngng Dir

QUALITY MUSIC PUBLISHING, LTD.
380 Birchmount Rd.
Scarborough, ON M1K 1M7
(416) 698-5511

Madine Langlois, Gen Mgr

SUNBURY/DUNBAR MUSIC CANADA, LTD.
2245 Markham Rd.
Scarborough, ON M1B 2W3

Jack Feeney, Pres

T.P. MUSIC PUBLISHING
North Country Faire Recording Co.
314 Clemow Ave.
Ottawa, ON K1S 2B8
(613) 234-6992

T. Peter Hern, Pres

Music Publishers Index

A

B

C

D

E

F

G

K

L

M

N

O

P

Q

R

S

T

General Index